PRINCIPLES OF FINANCIAL AND MANAGERIAL ACCOUNTING

CARL S. WARREN, CPA, PhD
Professor of Accounting
University of Georgia, Athens

PHILIP E. FESS, CPA, PhD
Professor of Accountancy
University of Illinois, Champaign-Urbana

A20

Published by

SOUTH-WESTERN PUBLISHING CO.

CINCINNATI   WEST CHICAGO, IL   DALLAS   PELHAM MANOR, NY   LIVERMORE, CA

COVER PHOTO: © Thomas Leighton

PREFACE

PRINCIPLES OF FINANCIAL AND MANAGERIAL ACCOUNTING is a conceptually oriented text that presents basic financial and managerial accounting principles in a logical, concise, and clear manner. The text provides a foundation that allows instructors to elaborate on issues and thereby increase the students' understanding of financial and managerial accounting.

HIGHLIGHTS OF COVERAGE

Financial accounting topics comprise the first half of the text and managerial accounting topics the remaining half. The text is especially designed to serve those colleges and universities that cover an equal amount of financial accounting and managerial accounting in an introductory course.

Financial Accounting

A brief summary of the content of Chapters 1-14 is as follows:

○ Chapter 1 presents basic financial accounting concepts and principles, including the rules of debit and credit, the use of accounts, the preparation of a trial balance, and the preparation of financial statements for a corporate form of organization.
○ Chapter 2 reinforces the principles and concepts introduced in Chapter 1 by discussing basic financial principles and concepts in the context of merchandising enterprises.
○ Chapters 3 and 4 complete the accounting cycle by discussing the adjusting process, including the adjustments necessary for merchandise inventory.
○ Chapters 5-9 begin with a brief discussion of the basic concepts of accounting systems design. Financial accounting principles for cash, receivables and temporary investments, inventories, plant and intangible assets, and payroll and other current liabilities are then discussed in depth in balance sheet order.
○ Chapters 10 and 11 discuss alternative forms of business organization in depth. These alternative forms include sole proprietorships, partnerships, and corporations.
○ Chapter 12 discusses long-term liabilities and investments in bonds. Present value concepts are integrated throughout this chapter.
○ Chapter 13 discusses principles and concepts involving long-term investments in stocks, consolidations, and accounting for international opera-

tions. Accounting for international operations is increasing in importance as more and more businesses of all sizes engage in foreign transactions.

o Chapter 14 emphasizes the principles and conceptual logic of the statement of changes in financial position. An appendix is provided for those instructors who wish to use a work sheet for preparing the statement of changes in financial position.

Managerial Accounting

A brief summary of the content of Chapters 15-28 is as follows:

o Chapter 15 eases the transition from financial accounting to managerial accounting by discussing and contrasting the nature of managerial accounting with financial accounting. Included in this discussion is a description of the basic principles underlying the preparation of managerial accounting reports. Chapter 15 concludes with a description and illustration of an accounting system for a manufacturing enterprise using a job order cost system.

o Chapter 16 describes and illustrates the accounting system for a manufacturing operation using a process cost system.

o Chapters 17 and 18 present the concepts of budgeting and standard cost systems, with extensive illustrations. A brief discussion of the effects of budgeting on human behavior and the computerization of budgeting procedures is also presented.

o Chapters 19-23 focus on concepts and principles useful to management in decision making, including presentations of absorption costing, variable costing, cost-volume-profit analysis, differential analysis, product pricing, capital investment analysis, and income taxes and their impact on management decisions.

o Chapters 24 and 25 describe the concepts and principles underlying responsibility accounting for cost, profit, and investment centers. Transfer pricing is also discussed in Chapter 25.

o Chapters 26 and 27 discuss quantitative techniques that are especially useful to management in controlling inventory, estimating costs, and coping with uncertainty. The presentation emphasizes concepts and principles rather than computations.

o Chapter 28 describes basic financial analyses useful to management in planning and controlling operations. A brief discussion of price-level changes is also included.

Appendixes

Five appendixes are included at the end of the text. Appendix A is a glossary of technical terms and common business and accounting expressions. Appendix B discusses and illustrates special journals and subsidiary ledgers. Appendix C presents a work sheet that can be used in the preparation of the statement of changes in financial position. Appendix D discusses general accounting systems for manufacturing operations. Appendix E discusses annual reports and contains the financial statements of a privately-held manufacturing company (Carter Manufacturing Company) and a publicly-held company (The Coca-Cola Company).

MAJOR FEATURES

PRINCIPLES OF FINANCIAL AND MANAGERIAL ACCOUNTING is student oriented. It is clearly written and readable, with graphics and many other significant features used to highlight important concepts and to improve understanding.

Enrichment Material

Each major part of the text begins with one or two excerpts from books or from articles that have appeared in well-known periodicals, such as the *Journal of Accountancy* and *Forbes*. These excerpts are designed to stir the students' interest and enrich their learning experience by providing real data and/or discussing the problems that real companies face relevant to the topics that are discussed in the forthcoming parts of the text.

Chapter Objectives

Each chapter begins with chapter objectives, which serve as guides for study and learning.

Self-Examination Questions

Self-examination questions for each chapter are provided, so that students can assess the degree to which they understand the material presented. After studying the chapter, the students can answer these questions and compare their answers with the correct ones that appear at the end of the chapter. An explanation of both the correct and incorrect answers for each question is provided in order to increase students' understanding and to further enhance the learning process.

Discussion Questions, Exercises, and Problems

The discussion questions, exercises, and problems presented at the end of each chapter have been carefully written to emphasize chapter concepts and principles. The variety and volume of these materials provide a wide choice of subject matter and a broad range of difficulty. A set of alternate problems that are similar to others in the chapter is also included at the end of each chapter.

Mini-Cases

Each chapter includes a mini-case that is designed to stimulate students' interest by presenting situations with which students may easily identify. Each case puts the student in a decision-making role and requires some analysis beyond chapter illustrations.

Check Figures

Check figures are presented at the end of the textbook for student use in solving end-of-chapter problems. Agreement with the check figures is an indication that a significant portion of the solution is basically correct.

SUPPLEMENTARY MATERIALS

A wide variety of teaching aids and learning aids are available for use by instructors and students.

Available to Instructors

Solutions Manual. This manual contains solutions to all the end-of-chapter materials, including the discussion questions, exercises, problems, and mini-cases.

Instructor's Manual. This manual contains a summary of the chapter objectives, terminology, and concepts. In a section organized according to chapter objectives, a basis for developing class lectures and assigning home-work is provided. In addition, exercise and problem descriptions, estimated time requirements for the problems, suggestions for use of the appendixes and other supplementary items, and copies of the teaching transparencies are also included.

Keys to Practice Sets. The solutions to the two practice sets that are available for use with the textbook are contained in this booklet.

Transparencies. Transparencies of solutions to the exercises and problems, both regular end-of-chapter problems and alternate problems, are available.

Teaching Transparencies. Teaching transparencies are designed to aid the instructor's focus on key principles and concepts discussed in various parts of the text.

Test Bank. A collection of examination problems, multiple-choice questions, and true or false questions for each chapter, accompanied by solutions, is available. The Test Bank is designed to save time in preparing and grading periodic and final examinations. Individual items may also be selected for use as short quizzes. The number of questions and problems is sufficient to provide variety from year to year and from class section to class section.

Computerized Test Bank. South-Western Automated Testing (Micro-SWAT) is available. The test bank and MicroSWAT program are supplied on diskettes.

The Administrator. A software management package is available to adopters. This package is specifically designed for use in maintaining a grade book, creating an interactive testing and/or study guide file, and generating tests.

Available to Students

Template Diskettes. Microcomputer templates compatible with the Apple IIe and the IBM PC are available for working selected end-of-chapter problems. These templates require student access to VISICALC or LOTUS 1-2-3.

Working Papers. Appropriate printed forms on which to work end-of-chapter problems and mini-cases are available in two bound volumes. The first volume is for use with Chapters 1-14, and the second volume is for use with Chapters 15-28.

Study Guide. This publication is designed to assist in comprehending the principles and concepts presented in the text. The Study Guide includes a summary of each chapter as well as brief questions and problems. Solutions to these questions and problems are presented at the back of the Study Guide.

Practice Sets. Two practice sets are available in manual and computerized versions. The first set is a corporation set that is designed to be used with the financial chapters of the text. The second set is a budgeting set that is designed to be used with the managerial chapters of the text. Both sets are decision oriented, with a minimal emphasis on forms and procedures.

ACKNOWLEDGMENTS

Throughout the textbook, relevant professional statements of the Financial Accounting Standards Board and other authoritative publications are discussed, quoted, paraphrased, or footnoted. The authors acknowledge their indebtedness to the American Accounting Association, the American Institute of Certified Public Accountants, the Financial Accounting Standards Board, and the National Association of Accountants for permission to use materials from their publications.

The authors acknowledge with gratitude the helpful suggestions received from the following faculty, who extensively reviewed the manuscript in its preliminary stages of development: Wayne Bremser, Villanova University; Chee Chow, San Diego State University; Raymond Green, Texas Tech University; J. Edward Ketz, Pennsylvania State University; Michael Maher, University of Michigan; James Pattillo, Indiana University at South Bend; Robert Sanborn, University of Virginia; and Mikel G. Tiller, Indiana University.

ABOUT THE AUTHORS

Professor Carl S. Warren is the Arthur Andersen & Co. Alumni Professor of Accounting at the J. M. Tull School of Accounting at the University of Georgia, Athens. Professor Warren received his PhD from Michigan State University in 1973 and has taught accounting at the University of Iowa, Michigan State University, the University of Chicago, and the University of Georgia. He has received teaching awards from three different student organizations at the University of Georgia.

Professor Warren is a CPA and has served in various committee capacities for the American Institute of CPAs, the Georgia Society of CPAs, and the American Accounting Association. He is also a member of the Financial Executives Institute. Professor Warren is past director of the Center for Auditing Research at the University of Georgia and has served on editorial boards of the American Accounting Association, including a term as editor for *Auditing: A Journal of Practice and Theory.* He has written four textbooks and more than forty articles in such journals as the *Journal of Accountancy,* the *Accounting Review,* the *Journal of Accounting Research,* the *CPA Journal, Corporate Accounting, Cost and Management,* and *Managerial Planning.*

Professor Warren resides in Athens, Georgia, with his wife and two children. His hobbies include golf and fishing.

Professor Philip E. Fess is the Arthur Andersen & Co. Alumni Professor of Accountancy at the University of Illinois, Champaign-Urbana. Professor Fess received his PhD from the University of Illinois and has been involved in textbook writing for over twenty years. In addition to having more than 30 years of teaching experience, he has won numerous teaching awards, including the University of Illinois, College of Commerce Alumni Association Excellence in Teaching Award.

Professor Fess is a CPA and a member of the American Institute of CPAs and the Illinois Society of CPAs. He has served many professional associations in a variety of ways, including a term as a member of the Auditing Standards Board, editorial advisor to the *Journal of Accountancy,* and chairperson of the American Accounting Association Committee on CPA Examinations. Professor Fess has written more than 100 books and articles, which have appeared in such journals as the *Journal of Accountancy,* the *Accounting Review,* the *CPA Journal,* and *Management Accounting.* He has also served as an expert witness before the U.S. Tax Court.

Professor Fess resides in Champaign, Illinois, with his wife. He has two daughters who are employed in public accounting, and a daughter who attends the University of Illinois. Professor Fess' primary hobby is tennis, and he has represented the United States in international tennis competition.

NOTE TO STUDENTS

This text was written with the objective of preparing you for your future professional career. Accounting is a stimulating, rewarding field of study. To be effective, professionals in all areas of business, such as finance, production, marketing, personnel, and general management, must have a good understanding of accounting.

As you begin your study of accounting, you may find the following suggestions helpful:

○ Read each chapter objective carefully before you begin studying a chapter.
○ Take a few minutes and scan the chapter to get a flavor of the material before you begin a detailed reading of the chapter.
○ As you read each chapter, you may wish to underline points that you feel are especially important.
○ After reading each chapter, answer the self-examination questions to help you test your understanding of the chapter material.
○ Work all assigned homework. In many cases, the homework is related to specific chapter illustrations, and you may find it helpful to review the relevant chapter sections before you begin a homework assignment.
○ Take notes during class lectures and discussions and pay careful attention to topics covered by your instructor. Do not hesitate to ask questions in those areas where you lack understanding.
○ In reviewing for examinations, keep in mind those topics that your instructor has emphasized, and review your class notes and the text.
○ If you feel you need additional aid, you may find the Study Guide that accompanies this textbook helpful. The Study Guide can be ordered from South-Western Publishing Co. by your college or university bookstore.

CONTENTS IN BRIEF

CONTENTS

PART 1

Fundamentals of Financial Accounting

The Importance of Accounting to Business

Business couldn't work without accounting. Double-entry bookkeeping, conceived centuries ago by a forgotten Catholic priest, probably had much more to do with the blossoming of business than any other single innovation.

SOURCE   Richard Cornuelle, *De-Managing America: The Final Revolution* (New York: Random House, 1975), p. 101.

The demand for accounting services is expanding faster than the supply. It is a demand partially created by laws and regulations in a society that seems to feel it can cure all human ills simply by passing laws and regulations—happiness through red tape. Every year fewer and fewer Americans are even trying to do their own income taxes. Every year additional requirements are laid on business for record keeping and disclosure.

SOURCE   Adapted from "The U.S.' Newest Glamour Job," *Forbes*, September 1, 1977, pp. 32-36.

A study of U.S. corporations revealed that finance and accounting was the most common background of chief executive officers. Interviews with corporate executives produced the following comments:

"Today, it's vital that the chief executive officer know the corporation and that he have an understanding of accounting."

"...my training in accounting and auditing practice has been extremely valuable to me throughout."

"A knowledge of accounting carries with it an understanding of the establishment and the maintenance of sound financial controls—an area which is absolutely essential to a chief executive officer."

"I try to have my entire staff understand the financial function and how to use financial data."

SOURCE   Adapted from John R. Linden, "Rising Corporate Stars: The Accountant as Chief Executive Officer," *Journal of Accountancy*, September, 1978, pp. 64-71.

CHAPTER 1

Concepts and Principles of Accounting

CHAPTER OBJECTIVES

Describe the nature of contemporary accounting and its role in society.

Describe the profession of accounting.

Identify and illustrate the basic financial accounting concepts and principles and their application to specific business situations.

Describe and illustrate the preparation of the basic financial statements for a corporation.

Accounting,[1] which is often called "the language of business," has been defined broadly as:

> ...the process of identifying, measuring, and communicating economic information to permit informed judgments and decisions by users of the information.[2]

This definition implies that accountants must have a broad knowledge of the socioeconomic environment in order to identify and develop relevant information. Sound decisions, based on reliable information, are essential for the efficient distribution and use of the nation's scarce resources. Accounting, therefore, plays an essential role in our economic and social system.

USERS OF ACCOUNTING INFORMATION

Various individuals and institutions use the economic data that are gathered and communicated by the accounting system for assistance in making decisions regarding future actions. For example, investors in a business enterprise need information on the financial condition and results of operations of the enterprise in order to assess the profitability and riskiness of their investments in the enterprise. Bankers and suppliers need information with

---

[1]A glossary of terms appears in Appendix A. The terms included in the glossary are printed in color the first time they appear in the text.

[2]*A Statement of Basic Accounting Theory* (Evanston, Illinois: American Accounting Association, 1966), p. 1.

which to appraise the financial soundness of a business organization and to assess the risks involved in making loans and granting credit. Government agencies are concerned with the financial activities of business organizations for purposes of taxation and regulation. Employees and their union representatives are vitally interested in the stability and the profitability of the organization that hires them.

The individuals most dependent upon and most involved with the end products of accounting are those charged with the responsibility for directing the operations of enterprises. They are often referred to collectively as "management." Managers rely upon accounting information to assist them in evaluating current operations and in planning future operations.

Although the information for one category of users may differ markedly from that needed by other users, the accounting system satisfies the needs of each user group by recording essential information and periodically summarizing this information in financial reports. This process of providing information to users is illustrated in the following diagram. First, user groups are identified and their information needs determined. These needs determine which economic data are gathered and processed by the accounting system. Finally, the accounting system generates reports that communicate essential information to users.

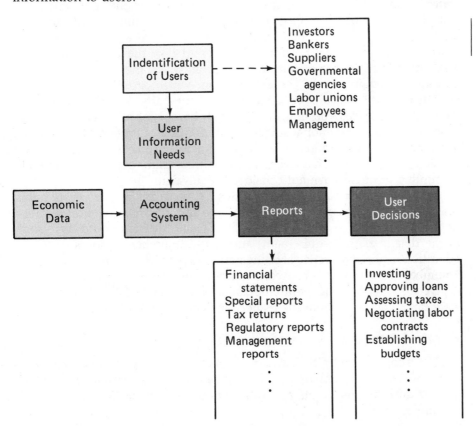

ACCOUNTING AS A
PROVIDER OF
INFORMATION
TO USERS

PROFESSION OF ACCOUNTANCY

Accountancy is a profession with stature comparable to that of law or medicine. Accountants who provide accounting services on a fee basis, and staff accountants employed by them, are said to be engaged in **public accounting**. Accountants employed by a particular business firm or nonprofit organization, perhaps as chief accountant, controller, or financial vice-president, are said to be engaged in **private accounting**.

Both public and private accounting have long been recognized as excellent training for top managerial responsibilities. Many executive positions in government and in industry are held by men and women with education and experience in accounting.

Public Accounting

In public accounting, an accountant may practice as an individual or as a member of a public accounting firm. Public accountants who have met a state's education, experience, and examination requirements may become **certified public accountants**, commonly called **CPAs**.

The qualifications required for the CPA certificate differ among the various states. A specified level of education is required, often the completion of a collegiate course of study in accounting. All states require that a candidate pass a standardized examination administered twice a year, in May and November. Many states permit candidates to take the examination upon graduation from college or during the term in which they will complete the educational requirements. The examination, which occupies one afternoon and two all-day sessions, is divided into four parts: Accounting Theory, Accounting Practice, Auditing, and Business Law. Some states also require an examination in an additional subject, such as Rules of Professional Conduct. Most states do not permit successful candidates to practice as independent CPAs until they have had from one to three years' experience in public accounting or in employment considered equivalent.

In recent years a majority of the states have enacted laws requiring public practitioners to participate in a program of continuing professional education or forfeit their right to continue in public practice. The states differ as to some of the details of the requirement, such as the number of hours of formal education required for renewal of the permit to practice. The rules adopted by a number of State Boards of Accountancy require 40 hours per year.

Details regarding the requirements for practice as a CPA in any particular state can be obtained from the respective State Board of Accountancy.

Private Accounting

The scope of activities and responsibilities of private accountants varies widely. They are frequently referred to as managerial accountants. Various governmental units and other nonprofit organizations also employ accountants.

The **National Association of Accountants (NAA)**, the largest organization of managerial accountants in the world, established the Institute of Certified Management Accountants (ICMA) and a program to recognize managerial accountants as professional accountants. The specific objectives of the program, which is administered by the ICMA and which leads to the **Certificate in Management Accounting (CMA)**, are stated as follows:

1. To establish managerial accounting as a recognized profession by identifying the role of the managerial accountant and the underlying body of knowledge, and by outlining a course of study by which such knowledge can be acquired.
2. To foster higher educational standards in the field of managerial accounting.
3. To establish an objective measure of an individual's knowledge and competence in the field of managerial accounting.

The requirements for the CMA designation include the baccalaureate degree or equivalent, two years of experience in managerial accounting, and successful completion of a 2½-day examination. The examination is divided into five parts: Economics and Business Finance; Organization and Behavior (including ethics); Public Reports, Standards, and Taxes; Periodic Reporting for Internal and External Purposes; and Decision Analysis (including Modeling and Information Systems). Participation in a program of continuing professional education is also required for renewal of the certificate.

The Institute of Internal Auditors administers a program for internal auditors–accountants who review the accounting and operating procedures and policies prescribed by their firms. Accountants qualifying under this program are entitled to use the designation Certified Internal Auditor (CIA).

FINANCIAL AND MANAGERIAL ACCOUNTING

As a result of rapid technological advances and accelerated economic growth, a number of specialized fields in accounting have evolved. The two most important accounting fields, financial and managerial accounting, are briefly described in the following paragraphs.

Financial accounting is concerned with the measuring and recording of transactions for a business enterprise or other economic unit and the periodic preparation of various reports from such records. The reports, which may be for general purposes or for a special purpose, provide useful information for managers, owners, creditors, governmental agencies, and the general public. Of particular importance to financial accountants are the principles of accounting, termed **generally accepted accounting principles**. These principles were developed because of the demand by "Outsiders," such as stockholders and creditors, for accurate financial information for use in judging the performance of management. Corporate enterprises must use these principles in preparing their annual reports on profitability and financial status for their stockholders and the investing public. Comparability of financial reports is essential if the nation's resources are to be divided among business organizations in a socially desirable manner.

Managerial accounting employs both historical and estimated data, which management uses in conducting daily operations and in planning future operations. For example, in directing day-to-day operations, management relies upon accounting to provide information concerning the amount owed to each creditor, the amount owed by each customer, and the date each amount is due. The treasurer uses these data and other data in the management of cash. Accounting data may be used by top management in determining the selling price of a new product. Production managers, by comparing past performances with planned objectives, can take steps to accelerate favorable trends and reduce those trends that are unfavorable.

As indicated in the following diagram, managerial accounting overlaps financial accounting to the extent that management uses the financial statements or reports in directing current operations and planning future operations. However, managerial accounting extends beyond financial accounting by providing additional information and reports for management's use. In providing this additional information, the managerial accountant is *not* governed by generally accepted accounting principles. Since these data are used only by management, the accountant provides the data in the format that is most useful for management. The principle of "usefulness," then, is dominant in guiding the accountant in preparing management reports.

FINANCIAL AND
MANAGERIAL
ACCOUNTING

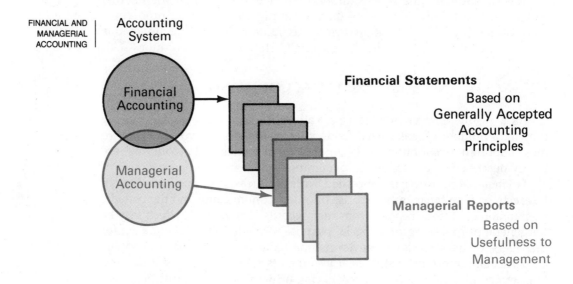

The first fourteen chapters of this text focus on financial accounting and the concepts and principles underlying the preparation of financial statements. Managerial accounting and the concepts and principles underlying the preparation of managerial accounting reports are discussed in Chapters 15-28.

DEVELOPMENT OF FINANCIAL ACCOUNTING CONCEPTS AND PRINCIPLES

The historical development of the practice of accounting has been closely related to the economic development of the country. In the earlier stages of the American economy, a business enterprise was very often managed by its owner, and the accounting records and reports were used mainly by the owner-manager in conducting the business. Bankers and other lenders often relied on their personal relationship with the owner rather than on financial statements as the basis for making loans for business purposes. If a large amount was owed to a bank or supplier, the creditor often participated in management decisions.

As business organizations grew in size and complexity, "management" and "outsiders" became more clearly differentiated. Outsiders demanded accurate financial information. In addition, as the size and complexity of the business unit increased, the accounting problems involved in the issuance of financial statements became more and more complex. With these developments came an awareness of the need for a framework of concepts and generally accepted accounting principles to serve as guidelines for the preparation of the basic financial statements.

The word "principle" as used in the context of generally accepted accounting principles does not have the same authoritativeness as universal principles or natural laws relating to the study of astronomy, physics, or other physical sciences. Accounting principles have been developed by individuals to help make accounting data more useful in an ever-changing society. They represent guides for the achievement of the desired results, based on reason, observation, and experimentation. The selection of the best method from among many alternatives has come about gradually, and in some areas a clear consensus is still lacking. These principles are continually reexamined and revised to keep pace with the increasing complexity of business operations. General acceptance among the members of the accounting profession is the criterion for determining an accounting principle.

Responsibility for the development of accounting principles has rested primarily on practicing accountants and accounting educators, working both independently and under the sponsorship of various accounting organizations. These principles are also influenced by business practices and customs, ideas and beliefs of the users of the financial statements, governmental agencies, stock exchanges, and other business groups.

Accounting Organizations

Among the oldest and most influential organizations of accountants are the American Institute of Certified Public Accountants (AICPA) and the

American Accounting Association (AAA). Each organization publishes a monthly or quarterly periodical and, from time to time, issues other publications in the form of research studies, technical opinions, and monographs. There are also other national accounting organizations as well as many state societies and local chapters of the national and state organizations. These groups provide forums for the exchange of ideas and discussion of accounting principles.

Financial Accounting Standards Board

The **Financial Accounting Standards Board (FASB)**, which was organized in 1973, is presently the dominant body in the development of accounting principles. It is composed of seven members, four of whom must be CPAs drawn from public practice. They serve full time, receive a salary, and must resign from the firm or institution with which they have been affiliated. The FASB is assisted by an Advisory Council of approximately twenty members, whose major responsibilities include recommendations as to priorities and agenda, and the review of FASB plans, activities, and statements proposed for issuance. The FASB employs full-time research and administrative staffs as well as task forces to study specific matters from time to time.

As problems in financial reporting are identified, the FASB conducts extensive research to identify the principal issues involved and the possible solutions. Generally, after issuing discussion memoranda and preliminary proposals and evaluating comments from interested parties, the Board issues *Statements of Financial Accounting Standards,* which become part of generally accepted accounting principles. To explain, clarify, or elaborate on existing pronouncements, the Board also issues *Interpretations,* which have the same authority as the standards.

The Board is presently developing a broad conceptual framework for financial accounting. This project is an attempt to develop a "constitution" that can be used to evaluate current standards and can serve as the basis for future standards. The results of this project are being published as *Statements of Financial Accounting Concepts.*

Governmental and Other Influential Organizations

Various governmental agencies have been influential in the development of accounting principles. The **Securities and Exchange Commission (SEC),** established by an act of Congress in 1934, issues regulations that must be observed in the preparation of financial statements and other reports filed with the Commission. The **Internal Revenue Service (IRS)** issues regulations that govern the determination of income for purposes of federal income taxation.

Other influential organizations include the Financial Executives Institute (FEI), the National Association of Accountants (NAA), the Institute of Internal Auditors, the Financial Analysts Federation (investors and investment advisors), and the Securities Industry Associates (investment bankers). These organizations influence the development of accounting principles by commenting on proposed pronouncements and by encouraging and sponsoring accounting research.

FINANCIAL ACCOUNTING CONCEPTS AND PRINCIPLES

The remainder of this chapter is devoted to the underlying assumptions, concepts, and principles of the greatest importance and widest applicability. Attention will also be directed toward applications of financial accounting concepts and principles to specific situations.

Business Entity Concept

The **business entity concept** is based on the applicability of accounting to individual economic units in society. These individual economic units include all business enterprises organized for profit; numerous governmental units, such as states, cities, and school districts; other nonprofit units, such as charities, churches, hospitals, and social clubs; and individual persons and family units. The basic economic data for a unit must be measured, recorded, analyzed, summarized, and periodically reported. Thus, accounting applies to each separate economic unit.

It is possible to combine the data for similar economic units to obtain an overall view. For example, accounting data accumulated by each of the airline companies may be assembled and summarized to provide financial information about the entire industry. Similarly, reports on gross national product (GNP) are developed from the accounting records or reports of many separate economic units.

This textbook is concerned primarily with the accounting concepts and principles applicable to profit-making businesses. Such businesses are customarily organized as sole proprietorships, partnerships, or corporations. A **sole proprietorship** is owned by one individual. A **partnership** is owned by two or more individuals in accordance with a contractual arrangement. A **corporation**, organized in accordance with state or federal statutes, is a separate legal entity in which ownership is divided into shares of stock.

Business Transactions

A **business transaction** is the occurrence of an economic event or a condition that must be recorded. For example, the payment of a monthly telephone bill of $68, the purchase of $1,750 of merchandise on credit, and the acquisition of land and a building for $210,000 are illustrative of a variety of business transactions.

The first two transactions are relatively simple: the payment of a $68 telephone bill is the exchange of money for a service, and the credit purchase is a promise to pay within a short time in exchange for goods. The purchase of a building and the land on which it is situated is usually a more complex transaction. The total price agreed upon must be allocated between the land and the building, and the agreement usually provides for spreading the payment of a large part of the price over a period of years and for the payment of interest on the unpaid balance.

A particular business transaction may lead to an event or a condition that results in another transaction. For example, the purchase of merchandise on credit will be followed by payment to the creditor, which is another transaction. Each time a portion of the merchandise is sold, another transaction occurs. Similarly, partial payments for the land and the building are additional transactions, as are periodic payments of interest on the debt. Each of these events must be recorded.

Unit of Measurement

All business transactions are recorded in terms of money. Other pertinent information of a nonfinancial nature may also be recorded, such as the the terms of purchase and sale contracts, and the purpose, amount, and term of insurance policies. But it is only through the record of dollar amounts that the diverse transactions and activities of a business may be measured, reported, and periodically compared. Money is both the common factor of all business transactions and the only feasible unit of measurement that can be used to achieve uniform financial data.

As a unit of measurement, the dollar differs from such quantitative standards as the kilogram, liter, or meter, which have not changed for centuries. The instability of the purchasing power of the dollar is well known, and the disruptive effect of the declining value of the dollar is acknowledged by accountants. In the past, however, this declining value generally was not given recognition in the financial statements.

The use of a monetary unit that is assumed to be stable insures objectivity. In spite of the inflationary trend in the United States, historical-dollar financial statements are considered to be better than statements based on movements of the general price level. Many accountants recommend that businesses use supplemental statements to indicate the effect of changing prices. However, only large companies are required to present selected supplemental information that reflects changing prices.[3] This subject will be discussed in more detail in Chapter 28.

---

[3]*Statement of Financial Accounting Standards*, No. 33, "Financial Reporting and Changing Prices" (Stamford: Financial Accounting Standards Board, 1979) and *Statement of Financial Accounting Standards*, No. 82, "Financial Reporting and Changing Prices: Elimination of Certain Disclosures" (Stamford: Financial Accounting Standards Board, 1984).

The Cost Principle

Properties and services purchased by a business are recorded in accordance with the **cost principle**, which requires that the monetary record be in terms of *cost*. For example, if a building is purchased at a cost of $150,000, that is the amount used in the purchaser's accounting record. The seller may have been asking $170,000 for the building up to the time of sale; the buyer may have initially offered $130,000 for it; the building may have been assessed at $125,000 for property tax purposes and insured for $135,000; and the buyer may have received an offer of $175,000 for the building the day after it was acquired. These latter amounts have no effect on the accounting records because they do not originate from an exchange transaction. The transaction price, or cost, of $150,000 determines the monetary amount at which the building is recorded.

Continuing the illustration, the $175,000 offer received by the buyer is an indication that it was a bargain purchase at $150,000. To record the building at $175,000, however, would give recognition to an illusory or unrealized profit. If the purchaser should accept the offer and sell the building for $175,000, a profit of $25,000 would be realized, and the new owner would record the building at its $175,000 cost.

The determination of costs incurred and revenues earned is fundamental to accounting. In transactions between buyer and seller, both attempt to get the best price. Only the amount agreed upon is objective enough for accounting purposes. If the monetary amounts at which properties were recorded were constantly revised upward and downward on the basis of mere offers, appraisals, and opinions, accounting reports would soon become unstable and unreliable, and therefore their usefulness would be limited.

ASSETS, LIABILITIES, AND OWNER'S EQUITY

The properties owned by a business entity are referred to as **assets** and the rights or claims to the assets are referred to as **equities**. If the assets owned by a business amount to $100,000, the equities in the assets must also amount to $100,000. The relationship between the two may be stated in the form of an equation, as follows:

$$\text{Assets} = \text{Equities}$$

Equities may be subdivided into two principal types: the rights of creditors and the rights of owners. The rights of creditors represent *debts* of the business and are called **liabilities**. The rights of the owner or owners are called **owner's equity** or **capital**. Expansion of the equation to give recognition to the two basic types of equities yields the following, which is known as the **accounting equation**:

$$\text{Assets} = \text{Liabilities} + \text{Owner's Equity}$$

It is customary to place "Liabilities" before "Owner's Equity" in the accounting equation because creditors have preferential rights to the assets. The residual claim of the owner or owners is sometimes given greater emphasis by transposing liabilities to the other side of the equation, yielding:

$$\text{Assets} - \text{Liabilities} = \text{Owner's Equity}$$

TRANSACTIONS AND THE ACCOUNTING EQUATION

All business transactions, from the simplest to the most complex, can be stated in terms of the resulting change in the three basic elements of the accounting equation. In all cases, the recording of the effects of transactions on the elements of the accounting equation must be such that the equality of the equation is maintained. For example, if a business organizes as a corporation by selling shares of ownership interests, generally referred to as **capital stock**, for $50,000, the asset cash will increase by **$50,000** and the owner's equity will increase by **$50,000**. The effect of this transaction on the accounting equation is as follows:

$$
\left. \begin{array}{c} \underline{\text{Assets}} \\[4pt] \text{Cash} \\ +\$50,000 \end{array} \right\} = \left\{ \begin{array}{c} \underline{\text{Liabilities} + \text{Owner's Equity}} \\[4pt] \text{Capital Stock} \\ +\$50,000 \end{array} \right.
$$

The transactions completed by an enterprise during a specific period may number into the thousands and may cause increases and decreases in many different asset, liability, and owner's equity items. To provide timely reports on the effects of these transactions, accountants must record them in a systematic manner. Although the effects of transactions can be recorded in terms of the accounting equation, as illustrated, such a format is not practical as a design for actual accounting systems. On a day-to-day basis, separate records are maintained for each major asset, liability, and owner's equity item of a business entity. For example, a single record must be used only for recording increases and decreases in cash.

The type of record traditionally used for the purpose of recording individual transactions is called an **account**. A group of related accounts that comprise a complete unit, such as all of the accounts of a specific business enterprise, is called a **ledger**. These individual accounts are summarized at periodic intervals, and the information thus obtained is presented in financial statements.

NATURE OF AN ACCOUNT

The simplest form of an account has three parts: (1) a title, which is the name of the item recorded in the account; (2) a space for recording increases in the amount of the item, in terms of money; and (3) a space for recording decreases in the amount of the item, also in monetary terms. This form of an account, illustrated below, is known as a **T account** because of its similarity to the letter T.

	Title	
Left side		Right side
debit		*credit*

| T-ACCOUNT

The left side of the account is called the **debit** side and the right side is called the **credit** side.[4] Amounts entered on the left side of an account, regardless of the account title, are called **debits** to the account, and the account is said to be **debited**. Amounts entered on the right side of an account are called **credits**, and the account is said to be **credited**.

In the following illustration, receipts of cash during a period of time have been listed vertically on the debit side of the cash account. The cash payments for the same period have been listed in similar fashion on the credit side of the account. A memorandum total of the cash receipts for the period to date, $109,500 in the illustration, may be inserted below the last debit at any time the information is desired. This figure should be identified in such a way that it is not mistaken for an additional debit. The total of the cash payments, $68,500 in the illustration, may be inserted on the credit side in a similar manner. Subtraction of the smaller sum from the larger, $109,500 − $68,500, yields the amount of cash on hand, $41,000, which is called the **balance of the account**. This amount is inserted on the debit side of the account, next to the total of the debits, thus identifying the balance of the account as a debit balance. If financial statements were to be prepared at this time, the amount of cash reported thereon would be $41,000.

	Cash	
	50,000	8,500
	30,500	14,000
	29,000	7,000
41,000	*109,500*	29,000
		10,000
		68,500

RECORDING TRANSACTIONS IN ACCOUNTS

To illustrate the manner of recording transactions, assume that Ingram Corporation is to be organized on January 1, 1986. Each transaction or group

---

[4]Often abbreviated as *Dr.* for "debit" and *Cr.* for "credit," derived from the Latin *debere* and *credere*.

of similar transactions that occurs during January, the first month of operations, is described. The recording of the transaction in the accounts is then
illustrated.

Transaction (a)

Ingram Corporation sells $60,000 of capital stock.

As illustrated previously, assets can be reported on the left side of
the accounting equation. Consistent with this presentation, transactions
increasing assets are entered on the left side of asset accounts as debits, and
decreases are entered on the right side as credits. This pattern was followed
in recording the debits and credits in the cash account illustrated on page 13.
Since liabilities and owner's equity can be reported on the right side of the
accounting equation, the procedure for entering increases and decreases is
reversed. Therefore, increases in liabilities and owner's equity are entered on
the right side of those accounts as credits and decreases are entered on the left
side as debits. Thus, the effect of Ingram Corporation's first transaction on the
accounts in the ledger can be described as a $60,000 debit (increase) to Cash
and a $60,000 credit (increase) to Capital Stock. The equation is maintained by
the equality of the debit and credit.

Transaction information is initially entered in a record called a **journal**. The
process of recording a transaction in the journal is called **journalizing**, and the
form of presentation is called a **journal entry**. In the journal, the transaction
information is recorded by listing the title of the account and the amount to
be debited, followed by a similar listing, below and to the right of the debit,
of the title of the account and the amount to be credited. For transaction (a),
the journal entry is as follows:

(a) Cash.. 60,000
        Capital Stock................................   60,000

The data in the journal entry are transferred to the appropriate accounts
by a process known as **posting**. The posting process for transaction (a) is
illustrated as follows:

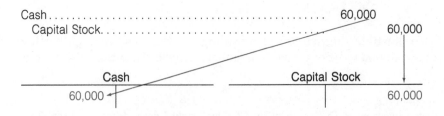

After recording the transaction through the use of a journal entry and posting it to the accounts, the accounting equation and the accounts would appear as follows:

Assets	=	Liabilities +	Owner's Equity
Cash			**Capital Stock**
(a) 60,000			(a) 60,000

Note that the amount of cash, which is reported on the left side of the accounting equation under Assets, is posted to the left (debit) side of Cash. The owner's equity in the enterprise, which is reported on the right side of the accounting equation, is posted to the right (credit) side of Capital Stock.

Transaction (b)

During the month, Ingram Corporation purchases $12,000 of supplies from various suppliers, agreeing to pay in the near future.

This type of transaction is called a purchase *on account,* and the liability created is termed an **account payable**. Liabilities of various types are commonly described as **payables**. Consumable goods purchased, such as supplies, are considered to be **prepaid expenses,** or assets. In actual practice, each purchase would be recorded as it occurred, and a separate record would be kept for each creditor.

The effect of this transaction on the accounts in the ledger can be described as a $12,000 debit (increase) to Supplies and a $12,000 credit (increase) to Accounts Payable. Transaction (b) is recorded in the journal by the following entry:

(b) Supplies..	12,000	
Accounts Payable		12,000

After posting journal entry (b), the accounting equation and the accounts would appear as follows:

Assets	=	Liabilities	+	Owner's Equity
Cash		**Accounts Payable**		**Capital Stock**
(a) 60,000		(b) 12,000		(a) 60,000
Supplies				
(b) 12,000				

Transaction (c)

During the month, Ingram Corporation pays $8,000 to the creditors on account.

The effect of this transaction is to decrease both the assets and the liabilities of the enterprise. The effect on the accounts in the ledger can be described as an $8,000 credit (decrease) to Cash and an $8,000 debit (decrease) to Accounts Payable. Transaction (c) is recorded in the journal by the following entry:

(c) Accounts Payable 8,000
       Cash..   8,000

After posting journal entry (c), the accounting equation and the accounts would appear as follows:

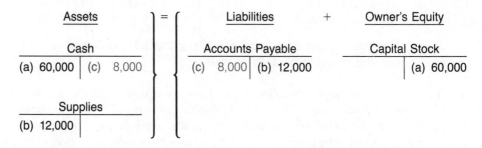

Before continuing with the illustration, the general rules for recording transactions in the asset, liability, and owner's equity accounts are summarized. As illustrated in the recording of transactions (a), (b), and (c), the left side of asset accounts is used for recording increases and the right side is used for recording decreases.

It was also illustrated that the right side of liability and owner's equity accounts is used to record increases. It naturally follows that the left side of such accounts is used to record decreases. The left side of all accounts, whether asset, liability, or owner's equity, is the debit side and the right side is the credit side. Consequently, a debit may be either an increase or a decrease, depending on the nature of the account affected. A credit may likewise be either an increase or a decrease, depending on the nature of the account. The rules of debit and credit for asset, liability, and owner's equity accounts may therefore be stated as follows:

RULES OF DEBIT AND CREDIT— ASSET, LIABILITY, AND OWNER'S EQUITY ACCOUNTS	*Debit* may signify:	*Credit* may signify:
	Increase in asset accounts	Decrease in asset accounts
	Decrease in liability accounts	Increase in liability accounts
	Decrease in owner's equity accounts	Increase in owner's equity accounts

The general rules of debit and credit for asset, liability, and owner's equity accounts may also be stated in relationship to the accounting equation, as in the following diagram:

ASSETS				LIABILITIES		+	OWNER'S EQUITY		GENERAL RULES OF DEBIT AND CREDIT—THE ACCOUNTING EQUATION
Asset Accounts				Liability Accounts			Owner's Equity Accounts		
Debit for increases	Credit for decreases			Debit for decreases	Credit for increases		Debit for decreases	Credit for increases	

Every business transaction affects a minimum of two accounts. Regardless of the complexity of a transaction or the number of accounts affected, the sum of the debits is always equal to the sum of the credits. This equality of debit and credit for each transaction is inherent in the equation A = L + OE. It is also because of this duality that the system is known as **double-entry accounting.**

The manner of recording additional types of transactions is described in the remainder of the illustration for Ingram Corporation.

Transaction (d)

During the first month of operations, Ingram Corporation earned fees of $62,000, receiving the amount in cash.

The principal objective of a business enterprise is to increase owner's equity through earnings. For Ingram Corporation, this objective means that the cash and other assets acquired through the rendering of services must be greater than the cost of the supplies used, the wages of employees, the rent, and all the other expenses of operating the business.

In general, the amount charged to customers for goods or services sold to them is called **revenue**. Other terms may be used for certain kinds of revenue, such as *sales* for the sale of merchandise, *fares earned* for an enterprise that provides transportation services, *rent earned* for the use of real estate or other property, and *fees earned* for charges by a professional, such as an accountant or physician, to clients.

The rules of debit and credit for revenue accounts are based upon the relationship of revenue transactions to owner's equity. Revenues increase the owner's equity in the business enterprise. Just as increases in owner's equity are recorded as credits, increases in revenues during an accounting period are recorded as credits.

The effect of transaction (d) on the accounts in the ledger can be described as a $62,000 debit (increase) to Cash and a $62,000 credit (increase) to Fees Earned. Transaction (d) is recorded in the journal by the following entry:

| (d) | Cash | 62,000 | |
| | Fees Earned | | 62,000 |

After posting journal entry (d), the accounting equation and the accounts would appear as follows:

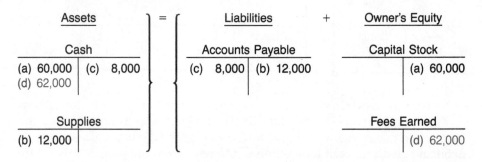

Instead of requiring the payment of cash at the time goods or services are sold, a business may make sales *on account,* allowing the customer to pay later. In such cases the firm acquires an **account receivable,** which is a claim against the customer. An account receivable is as much an asset as cash, and the revenue is realized in exactly the same manner as if cash had been immediately received. At a later date, when the money is collected, there is only an exchange of one asset for another, with cash increasing and accounts receivable decreasing.

Transaction (e)

Various business expenses incurred and paid during the month were as follows: wages, $25,000; rent, $10,000; utilities, $6,000; miscellaneous, $2,500.

In a broad sense, the amount of assets consumed or services used in the process of earning revenue is called **expense.** Expenses would include supplies used, wages of employees, and other assets and services used in operating the business.

The rules of debit and credit for expense accounts are based upon the relationship of expense transactions to owner's equity. Expenses decrease the owner's equity in the business enterprise. Just as decreases in owner's equity are recorded as debits, increases in expenses during an accounting period are recorded as debits.

The effect of transaction (e) on the accounts in the ledger can be described as a $25,000 debit (increase) to Wages Expense, a $10,000 debit (increase) to Rent Expense, a $6,000 debit (increase) to Utilities Expense, a $2,500 debit (increase) to Miscellaneous Expense, and a $43,500 credit (decrease) to Cash. Transaction (e) is recorded in the journal by the following entry:

(e)	Wages Expense	25,000	
	Rent Expense	10,000	
	Utilities Expense	6,000	
	Miscellaneous Expense	2,500	
	Cash		43,500

Entry (e) is called a **compound journal entry** because it is composed of two or more debits or two or more credits. In all compound entries, the total debits must equal the total credits. After posting journal entry (e), the accounting equation and the accounts would appear as follows:

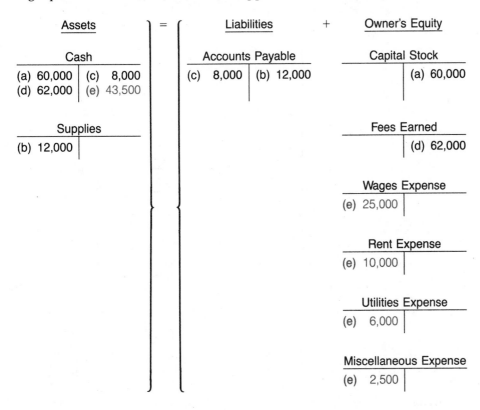

Transaction (f)

At the end of the month, it is determined that the cost of the supplies on hand is $4,500. The remainder of the supplies purchased in transaction (b), $7,500 ($12,000 − $4,500), were used in the operations of the business.

The effect of transaction (f) on the accounts in the ledger can be described as a $7,500 debit (increase) to Supplies Expense and a $7,500 credit (decrease) to Supplies. Transaction (f) is recorded in the journal by the following entry:

(f) Supplies Expense 7,500
          Supplies...................................... 7,500

After posting journal entry (f), the accounting equation and the accounts would appear as follows:

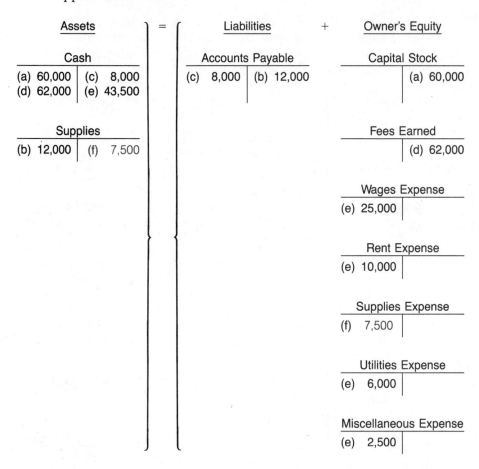

Assets	=	Liabilities	+	Owner's Equity

Cash

(a) 60,000	(c) 8,000
(d) 62,000	(e) 43,500

Supplies

(b) 12,000	(f) 7,500

Accounts Payable

(c) 8,000	(b) 12,000

Capital Stock

	(a) 60,000

Fees Earned

	(d) 62,000

Wages Expense

(e) 25,000	

Rent Expense

(e) 10,000	

Supplies Expense

(f) 7,500	

Utilities Expense

(e) 6,000	

Miscellaneous Expense

(e) 2,500	

Based upon transactions (d), (e), and (f), the rules of debit and credit as applied to revenue and expense accounts may be stated as follows:

RULES OF DEBIT AND CREDIT— REVENUE AND EXPENSE ACCOUNTS

Debit may signify:	*Credit* may signify:
Increase in expense accounts	Decrease in expense accounts
Decrease in revenue accounts	Increase in revenue accounts

In summary, the general rules of debit and credit for asset, liability, owner's equity, revenue, and expense accounts may be stated in relationship to the accounting equation, as shown in the following diagram:

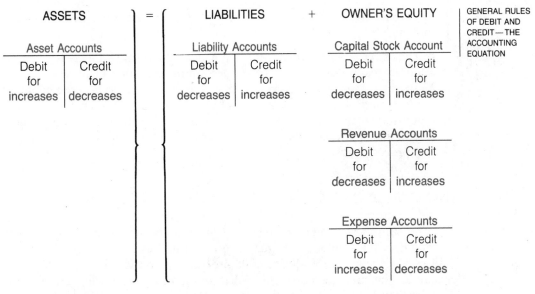

GENERAL RULES OF DEBIT AND CREDIT—THE ACCOUNTING EQUATION

Summary of Transactions

The business transactions of Ingram Corporation are summarized by the accounting equation and accounts as follows. The transactions are identified by letter, and the balance of each account at the end of the month is shown.

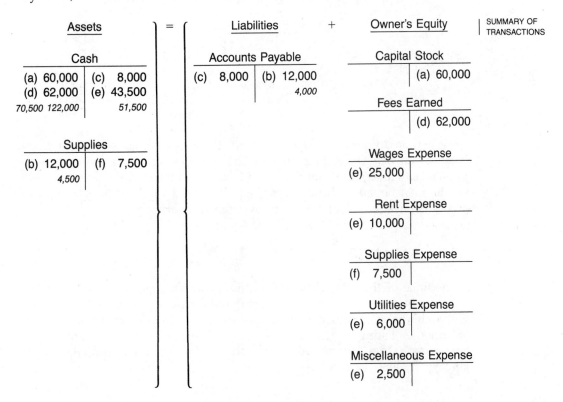

SUMMARY OF TRANSACTIONS

The following observations, which apply to all types of businesses, should be noted:

1. The effect of every transaction can be stated in terms of increases and/or decreases in one or more of the accounting equation elements.
2. The increases and decreases in the elements of the accounting equation are recorded initially in a journal entry as debits and credits. In each journal entry, the sum of the debits must equal the sum of the credits.
3. The debits and credits in a journal entry are transferred to accounts by a process known as posting.

NORMAL BALANCES OF ACCOUNTS

The sum of the increases recorded in an account is usually equal to or greater than the sum of the decreases recorded in the account. For this reason, the normal balances of all accounts are positive rather than negative. For example, the total debits (increases) in an asset account will ordinarily be greater than the total credits (decreases). Thus, asset accounts normally have debit balances.

The rules of debit and credit and the normal balances of the various types of accounts are summarized as follows:

NORMAL ACCOUNT BALANCES	Type of Account	Increase	Decrease	Normal Balance
	Asset	Debit	Credit	Debit
	Liability	Credit	Debit	Credit
	Owner's Equity			
	Capital Stock	Credit	Debit	Credit
	Revenue	Credit	Debit	Credit
	Expense	Debit	Credit	Debit

When an account that normally has a debit balance actually has a credit balance, or vice versa, it is an indication of an accounting error or of an unusual situation. For example, a credit balance in the supplies account could result only from an accounting error. On the other hand, a debit balance in an accounts payable account could result from an overpayment.

TRIAL BALANCE

Because of the way in which business transactions are recorded in the accounts by following the rules of debit and credit, the total of the accounts with debit balances must always equal the total of the accounts with credit balances. A listing of the account balances which verifies this equality is known as a **trial balance.** The trial balance for Ingram Corporation as of January 31, 1986, is as follows:

Ingram Corporation
Trial Balance
January 31, 1986

Cash	70,500	
Supplies	4,500	
Accounts Payable		4,000
Capital Stock		60,000
Fees Earned		62,000
Wages Expense	25,000	
Rent Expense	10,000	
Supplies Expense	7,500	
Utilities Expense	6,000	
Miscellaneous Expense	2,500	
	126,000	126,000

If the two totals of the trial balance are not equal, an error has occurred. Chapter 2 discusses the types of errors that could occur and how errors may be discovered.

FINANCIAL STATEMENTS

The principal financial statements of a corporation are the income statement, the retained earnings statement, and the balance sheet. The nature of the data presented in each statement, in general terms, is as follows:

Income statement
   A summary of the revenue and the expenses of a business entity for a specific period of time, such as a month or a year.
Retained earnings statement
   A summary of the changes in the earnings retained in the business entity for a specific period of time, such as a month or a year.
Balance sheet
   A list of the assets, liabilities, and owner's equity of a business entity on a specific date, usually at the close of the last day of a month or a year.

The basic features of these three statements and their interrelationships are described and illustrated in the following paragraphs. The data for the statements were taken from the summary of transactions and the trial balance of Ingram Corporation previously presented.

An additional statement, referred to as the **statement of changes in financial position,** is also useful in appraising changes in the financial position of a business enterprise and is an essential part of financial reports to owners and creditors.[5] The preparation and interpretation of this statement will be

[5]*Opinions of the Accounting Principles Board, No. 19,* "Reporting Changes in Financial Position" (New York: American Institute of Certified Public Accountants, 1971), par. 7.

considered in a later chapter, after various basic concepts and principles have been explained and illustrated.

All financial statements should be identified by the name of the business, the title of the statement, and the date or period of time. The data presented in the balance sheet are for a specific date. The data presented in the income statement, the retained earnings statement, and the statement of changes in financial position are for a period of time.

Income Statement

The excess of the revenue over the expenses incurred in earning the revenue is called **net income** or **net profit.** If the expenses of the enterprise exceed the revenue, the excess is a **net loss.** It is ordinarily impossible to determine the exact amount of expense incurred in connection with each revenue transaction. Therefore, it is satisfactory to determine the net income or the net loss for a stated period of time, such as a month or a year, rather than for each revenue transaction or group of transactions.

The revenue earned and the expenses incurred during the month by Ingram Corporation were recorded in the revenue and expense accounts. The balances of these accounts provide the basis for **matching** the revenues earned during the month and the expenses incurred in earning these revenues to determine the amount of net income or net loss. The details of this matching for Ingram Corporation, together with the net income in the amount of $11,000, are reported in the following income statement:

INCOME STATEMENT

Ingram Corporation
Income Statement
For Month Ended January 31, 1986

Fees earned		$62,000
Operating expenses:		
Wages expense	$25,000	
Rent expense	10,000	
Supplies expense	7,500	
Utilities expense	6,000	
Miscellaneous expense	2,500	
Total operating expenses		51,000
Net income		$11,000

The order in which the operating expenses are presented in the income statement varies among businesses. One of the arrangements commonly followed is to list them in the order of size, beginning with the larger items. Miscellaneous expense is usually shown as the last item, regardless of the amount.

Retained Earnings Statement

It is customary for corporations to distinguish between (1) the investment of the owners, who are called **stockholders**, and (2) the retained earnings, or net income retained in the business. Because changes in the amounts invested by stockholders occur infrequently, the primary focus for analyzing changes in the owner's equity of a corporation is the retained earnings statement. If there have been significant changes in capital stock during a period, such data should be reported in a separate additional statement. The details of minor changes in capital stock need not be reported.

The retained earnings statement for Ingram Corporation for the month of January is as follows:

Ingram Corporation
Retained Earnings Statement
For Month Ended January 31, 1986

Net income for the month	$11,000
Retained earnings, January 31, 1986	$11,000

RETAINED
EARNINGS
STATEMENT

Since January was Ingram Corporation's first month of operations, the January 31, 1986 retained earnings equals the month's net income of $11,000. Changes in Ingram Corporation's retained earnings in future months may result from (1) the additional net income (or net loss) and (2) the distribution of earnings, called **dividends**, to stockholders. To illustrate, assume that Ingram Corporation earned net income of $35,000 and paid dividends of $15,000 during February. The retained earnings statement for Ingram Corporation for February would appear as follows:

Ingram Corporation
Retained Earnings Statement
For Month Ended February 28, 1986

Retained earnings, February 1, 1986		$11,000
Net income for the month	$35,000	
Less dividends	15,000	
Increase in retained earnings		20,000
Retained earnings, February 28, 1986		$31,000

In the retained earnings statement for Ingram Corporation, the distribution of dividends decreases retained earnings. Since decreases in owner's equity accounts are recorded as debits, the distribution of dividends could be recorded initially as a debit to the retained earnings account. Alternatively, the distribution of dividends could be recorded initially as a debit to the dividends account. Throughout this text, this latter alternative will be used for recording dividends, because the balance of the dividends account is a convenient summary of the total dividends declared during the period. Thus, the distribution of $15,000 of dividends in February by Ingram Corporation is recorded as a debit (increase) to Dividends and a credit (decrease) to Cash, as shown in the following journal entry:

Dividends.	15,000	
Cash		15,000

Balance Sheet

The balance sheet for Ingram Corporation is as follows:

BALANCE SHEET |

Ingram Corporation Balance Sheet January 31, 1986		
Assets		
Cash		$70,500
Supplies		4,500
Total assets		$75,000
Liabilities		
Accounts payable.		$ 4,000
Stockholders' Equity		
Capital stock	$60,000	
Retained earnings	11,000	
Total stockholders' equity		71,000
Total liabilities and stockholders' equity.		$75,000

It is customary to begin the asset section with cash. This item is followed by receivables, supplies, and other assets that will be converted into cash or used up in the near future. It is also customary on corporation balance sheets to refer to the owner's equity as **stockholders' equity.** For Ingram Corporation, the January 31, 1986 stockholders' equity consists of $60,000 of capital stock and retained earnings of $11,000. The retained earnings amount of $11,000 is taken from the retained earnings statement.

The form of balance sheet illustrated for Ingram Corporation, with liability and owner's equity sections presented below the asset section, is called the **report form.** Another arrangement in common use lists the assets on the left and the liabilities and owner's equity on the right. Because of its similarity to the T account, it is referred to as the **account form of balance sheet.**

Preparation of Financial Statements

In preparing the financial statements of a business enterprise, the income statement is usually prepared first because the net income for the period is needed in order to prepare the retained earnings statement. The retained earnings statement is prepared next because the ending balance of retained earnings for the period is needed for the preparation of the balance sheet. Then the balance sheet is prepared, and finally, as will be discussed in a later chapter, the statement of changes in financial position is prepared. For Ingram Corporation, the following diagram illustrates the relationship between the financial statements.

RELATIONSHIP BETWEEN FINANCIAL STATEMENTS

Ingram Corporation
Income Statement
For Month Ended January 31, 1986

Fees earned		$62,000
Operating expenses:		
Wages expense	$25,000	
Rent expense	10,000	
Supplies expense	7,500	
Utilities expense	6,000	
Miscellaneous expense	2,500	
Total operating expenses		51,000
Net income		$11,000

Ingram Corporation
Retained Earnings Statement
For Month Ended January 31, 1986

Net income for the month	$11,000
Retained earnings, January 31, 1986	$11,000

Ingram Corporation
Balance Sheet
January 31, 1986

Assets		
Cash		$70,500
Supplies		4,500
Total assets		$75,000
Liabilities		
Accounts payable		$ 4,000
Stockholders' Equity		
Capital stock	$60,000	
Retained earnings	11,000	
Total stockholders' equity		71,000
Total liabilities and stockholders' equity		$75,000

ADDITIONAL CONCEPTS AND PRINCIPLES

The remainder of this chapter is devoted to some additional financial accounting concepts and principles. These concepts and principles require an understanding of the process of recording transactions and preparing financial statements, as discussed previously.

Revenue Recognition and the Matching Concept

The determination of the periodic net income (or net loss) is a two-step process. First, revenues are recognized during the period. Second, the assets consumed in generating the revenues must be matched against the revenues in order to determine the net income or the net loss.

Revenues are recognized and recorded in the accounts according to various criteria. Generally, revenues for the rendering of services are recognized after the service has been rendered to the customer. Revenues for the sale of merchandise are generally recognized after the ownership of the goods has passed to the buyer. Depending upon the terms of shipment, ownership may pass upon shipment of the merchandise or when the goods are delivered to their final destination. Shipping terms are discussed in Chapter 2.

The assets consumed in generating revenue during a period must be recognized as expenses. In this way, the expenses are properly matched against the revenues generated. Some assets are treated as expenses at the time of purchase because they will expire by the end of the period. For example, when monthly rent is paid at the beginning of the month, the asset purchased (the right to use property for a month) will be wholly expired at the end of the month. For this reason, the rental payment is usually debited directly to an expense account. The allocation (matching) to proper periods of the costs of assets consumed is an important consideration, which will be further discussed in later chapters.

Adequate Disclosure

Financial statements and their accompanying footnotes or other explanatory materials should contain all of the pertinent data believed essential to the reader's understanding of the enterprise's financial status. Criteria for standards of disclosure often must be based on value judgments rather than on objective facts.

The use of headings and subheadings and the merging of items in significant categories in the financial statements illustrated in the preceding paragraphs are examples of the application of the concept of adequate disclosure. Additional examples will be presented in many of the remaining chapters after more complex accounting matters have been presented.

Consistency

A number of accepted alternative principles affecting the determination of income statement and balance sheet amounts will be presented in later chapters. Recognizing that different methods may be used under varying circumstances, some guide or standard is needed to assure that the periodic financial statements of an enterprise can be compared. It is common practice to compare an enterprise's current income statement and balance sheet with the statements of the preceding year.

The amount and the direction of change in net income and financial position from period to period is very important to readers and may greatly influence their decisions. Therefore, interested persons should be able to assume that successive financial statements of an enterprise are based consistently on the same generally accepted accounting principles. If the principles are not applied consistently, the trends indicated could be the result of changes in the principles used rather than the result of changes in business conditions or managerial effectiveness.

The concept of **consistency** does not completely prohibit changes in the accounting principles used. Changes are permissible when it is believed that the use of a different principle will more fairly state net income and financial position. In such cases, the reason for the change and its effect on income should be disclosed in the financial statements of the period in which the change in principle is made.

Materiality

In following generally accepted accounting principles, the accountant must consider the relative importance of any event, accounting procedure, or change in procedure that affects items on the financial statements. Absolute accuracy in accounting and full disclosure in reporting are not ends in themselves, and there is no need to exceed the limits of practicality. The determination of what is significant and what is not requires the exercise of judgment. Precise criteria cannot be formulated.

To determine **materiality**, the size of an item and its nature must be considered in relationship to the size and the nature of other items. The erroneous identification of a $10,000 expense on an income statement exhibiting total expenses of $10,000,000 would probably be immaterial. In this situation, the size of the error would not necessitate a correction. If the total expenses were $20,000, however, the error would certainly be material and the income statement should be corrected.

Custom and practicality also influence criteria of materiality. Corporate financial statements seldom report the cents amounts or even the hundreds of dollars. A common practice is to round to the nearest thousand. For large corporations, there is an increasing tendency to report financial data in terms of millions, carrying figures to one decimal. For example, an amount stated in millions as $907.4 may be read as nine hundred seven million, four hundred thousand.[6]

---

[6]Examples are presented in Appendix E.

Going Concern

Generally, a business is not organized with the expectation of operating for only a certain period of time. In most cases, it is not possible to determine in advance the length of life of an enterprise, and so an assumption must be made. The nature of the assumption will affect the manner of recording some of the business transactions, which in turn will affect the data reported in the financial statements.

It is customary to assume that a business entity has a reasonable expectation of continuing in business at a profit for an indefinite period of time. This **going concern concept** provides much of the justification for recording the purchase of a building at the price paid and subsequently recognizing a portion of this purchase price as the cost of using the building. The current value of the building is not reported in the basic financial statements because there is no immediate expectation of selling it. If the firm continues to use the building, the fluctuation in market value causes no gain or loss, nor does it increase or decrease the usefulness of the building. Thus, if the going concern assumption is a valid concept, the investment in the building will serve the purpose for which it was made.

When there is conclusive evidence that a business entity has a limited life, the accounting procedures should be appropriate to the expected terminal date of the entity. Changes in the application of normal accounting procedures may be needed for business organizations in receivership or bankruptcy, for example. In such cases, the financial statements should clearly disclose the limited life of the enterprise and should be prepared from the "quitting concern" or liquidation point of view, rather than from a "going concern" point of view.

Self-Examination Questions (Answers at end of chapter.)

1. A profit-making business that is a separate legal entity and in which ownership is divided into shares of stock is known as a:
   A. sole proprietorship
   B. single proprietorship
   C. partnership
   D. corporation

2. The properties owned by a business enterprise are called:
   A. assets
   B. liabilities
   C. capital
   D. owner's equity

3. A debit may signify:
   A. an increase in an asset account
   B. a decrease in an asset account
   C. an increase in a liability account
   D. an increase in an owner's equity account

4. The type of account with a normal credit balance is:
   A. an asset
   B. a dividend
   C. a revenue
   D. an expense

5. A list of assets, liabilities, and owner's equity of a business entity as of a specific date is:

A. a balance sheet

B. an income statement

C. a statement of changes in financial position

D. a retained earnings statement

1–1. Define accounting.

1–2. Name some of the categories of individuals and institutions who use accounting information.

1–3. Distinguish between public accounting and private accounting.

1–4. Accounting principles are broad guides to accounting practice. (a) How do these principles differ from the principles relating to the physical sciences? (b) Of what significance is acceptability in the development of accounting principles? (c) Why must accounting principles be continually reexamined and revised?

1–5. Since 1973, what body has been dominant in the development of accounting principles?

1–6. What are the three principal forms of profit-making business organizations?

1–7. (a) Land with an assessed value of $71,000 for property tax purposes is acquired by a business enterprise for $132,000. At what amount should the land be recorded by the purchaser?

(b) Five years later, the plot of land in (a) has an assessed value of $105,000 and the business enterprise receives an offer of $196,000 for it. Should the monetary amount assigned to the land in the business records now be increased and, if so, by what amount?

(c) Assuming that the land was sold for $200,000, (1) how much would owner's equity increase, and (2) at what amount would the purchaser record the land?

1–8. Conventional financial statements do not give recognition to the instability of the purchasing power of the dollar. How can the effect of the fluctuating dollar on business operations be presented to the users of the financial statements?

1–9. (a) If the assets owned by a business enterprise total $300,000, what is the amount of the equities of the enterprise? (b) What are the two principal types of equities?

1–10. (a) An enterprise has assets of $80,000 and liabilities of $25,000. What is the amount of its owner's equity?

(b) An enterprise has assets of $120,000 and owner's equity of $68,000. What is the total amount of its liabilities?

(c) A corporation has assets of $270,000, liabilities of $90,000, and capital stock of $100,000. What is the amount of its retained earnings?

(d) An enterprise has liabilities of $40,000 and owner's equity of $110,000. What is the total amount of its assets?

1–11. Describe how the following business transactions affect the three elements of the accounting equation.

(a) Issued capital stock for cash.

(b) Purchased supplies on account.

(c) Paid for utilities used in the business.

(d) Received cash for services performed.

Discussion
Questions

1–12. (a) A vacant lot acquired for $50,000, on which there is a balance owed of $25,000, is sold for $71,000 in cash. What is the effect of the sale on the total amount of the seller's (1) assets, (2) liabilities, and (3) owner's equity?

(b) After receiving the $71,000 cash in (a), the seller pays the $25,000 owed. What is the effect of the payment on the total amount of the seller's (1) assets, (2) liabilities, and (3) owner's equity?

1–13. Differentiate between an account and a ledger.

1–14. What is the name of the accounting record in which transaction data are initially entered?

1–15. Define posting.

1–16. Do the terms *debit* and *credit* signify increase or decrease, or may they signify either? Explain.

1–17. Indicate whether each of the following is recorded by a debit or by a credit: (a) decrease in an asset account, (b) decrease in a liability account, (c) increase in an owner's equity account.

1–18. What is the effect (increase or decrease) of debits to expense accounts (a) in terms of owner's equity, (b) in terms of expense?

1–19. Operations of an enterprise for a particular month are summarized as follows:
Sales: on account, $42,000; for cash, $12,000
Expenses incurred: on account, $26,000; for cash, $11,000
What was the amount of the enterprise's (a) revenue, (b) expenses, and (c) net income?

1–20. If the expenses of an enterprise exceed the revenue for a particular month, what is this excess of expenses over revenue called?

1–21. Give the title of a corporation's three major financial statements illustrated in this chapter, and briefly describe the nature of the information provided by each.

1–22. What particular item of financial or operating data of a service enterprise, organized as a corporation, appears on (a) both the income statement and the retained earnings statement, and (b) both the balance sheet and the retained earnings statement?

1–23. If total assets have increased by $19,000 during a specific period of time and owner's equity has decreased by $10,000 during the same period, what was the amount and direction (increase or decrease) of the period's change in total liabilities?

1–24. For accounting purposes, what is the nature of the assumption as to the length of life of an enterpise?

Exercises

1–25. The following selected transactions were completed by Castell Delivery Service during November:

(1) Received cash from the issuance of capital stock, $20,000.
(2) Paid advertising expense, $520.
(3) Purchased supplies of gas and oil for cash, $780.
(4) Received cash from cash customers, $1,500.
(5) Charged customers for delivery services on account, $2,100.
(6) Paid creditors on account, $470.
(7) Paid rent for November, $1,000.

Concepts and Principles of Accounting

(8) Received cash from customers on account, $1,810.
(9) Purchased supplies of gas and oil on account, $900.
(10) Determined by taking an inventory that $650 of supplies of gas and oil had been used during the month.

Indicate the effect of each transaction on the accounting equation by listing the numbers identifying the transactions, (1) through (10), in a vertical column, and inserting at the right of each number the appropriate letter from the following list:

(a) Increase in one asset, decrease in another asset.
(b) Increase in an asset, increase in a liability.
(c) Increase in an asset, increase in owner's equity.
(d) Decrease in an asset, decrease in a liability.
(e) Decrease in an asset, decrease in owner's equity.

1–26. Foreman Corporation, engaged in a service business, completed the following selected transactions during the period:

(1) Issued additional capital stock, receiving cash.
(2) Purchased supplies on account.
(3) Returned defective supplies purchased on account and not yet paid for.
(4) Received cash as a refund from the erroneous overpayment of an expense.
(5) Charged customers for services sold on account.
(6) Paid utilities expense.
(7) Paid a creditor on account.
(8) Received cash on account from charge customers.
(9) Paid cash dividends to stockholders.
(10) Determined the amount of supplies used during the month.

Using a tabular form with four column headings entitled Transaction, Assets, Liabilities, and Owner's Equity, respectively, indicate the effect of each transaction. Use + for increase and − for decrease.

1–27. One item is omitted in each of the following summaries of balance sheet and income statement data for four different corporations, A, B, C, and D.

	A	B	C	D
Beginning of the year:				
Assets..........................	$100,000	$60,000	$27,000	(d)
Liabilities	40,000	20,000	6,000	$12,600
End of year:				
Assets..........................	140,000	75,000	34,000	68,000
Liabilities	50,000	10,000	12,000	37,000
During the year:				
Additional issuance				
of capital stock	(a)	5,000	12,000	30,000
Dividends......................	12,000	8,000	(c)	21,000
Revenue.......................	80,000	(b)	42,100	92,000
Expenses......................	65,000	30,000	43,600	84,000

Determine the amounts of the missing items, identifying them by letter. (Suggestion: First determine the amount of increase or decrease in owner's equity during the year.)

1–28. Banister Corporation has the following accounts in its ledger: Cash; Accounts Receivable; Supplies; Accounts Payable; Capital Stock; Retained Earnings; Dividends; Fees Earned; Rent Expense; Advertising Expense; Utilities Expense.

Banister completed the following transactions during January of the current year:
(a) Paid rent for the month, $700.
(b) Paid cash for supplies, $68.
(c) Paid advertising expense, $100.
(d) Received cash from customers on account, $3,810.
(e) Paid cash dividends, $1,000.
(f) Purchased supplies on account, $100.
(g) Paid creditor on account, $55.
(h) Paid telephone bill for the month, $89.
(i) Fees earned and billed to customers for the month, $4,160.
(j) Paid electricity bill for the month, $220.

Record the transactions in a journal.

1–29. Eight transactions are recorded in the following T accounts:

Cash		Equipment		Dividends	
(1) 8,000	(2) 1,500	(2) 10,000		(8) 2,000	
(7) 18,100	(3) 150				
	(4) 1,100				
	(5) 4,800				
	(8) 2,000				

Accounts Receivable		Accounts Payable		Service Revenue	
(6) 22,500	(7) 18,100	(5) 4,800	(2) 8,500		(6) 22,500

Supplies		Capital Stock		Operating Expenses	
(3) 150			(1) 8,000	(4) 1,100	

Indicate for each debit and each credit: (a) the type of account affected (asset, liability, owner's equity, dividend, revenue, or expense) and (b) whether the account was increased (+) or decreased (−). Answers should be presented in the following form (transaction (1) is given as an example):

Transaction	Account Debited Type	Effect	Account Credited Type	Effect
(1)	asset	+	owner's equity	+

1–30. The accounts (all normal balances) in the ledger of Braves Realty Inc. as of June 30, the *end* of the current year, are in alphabetical order as follows. The balance of the cash account has been intentionally omitted.

Accounts Payable	$ 8,910
Accounts Receivable	12,600
Buildings	225,000
Capital Stock	300,000
Cash	X

Dividends	$ 20,000
Equipment	197,280
Fees Earned	280,000
Land	160,000
Miscellaneous Expense.	2,500
Note Payable.	25,000
Prepaid Insurance.	2,400
Retained Earnings	215,000
Salary Expense.	180,000
Supplies	4,500
Supplies Expense.	3,120
Utilities Expense.	11,600

(a) Prepare a trial balance, listing the accounts in the following order: assets, liabilities, owner's equity, revenues, and expenses. Insert the missing figure for cash.

(b) Prepare an income statement for Braves Realty Inc. for the current year ended June 30, 19--.

(c) Prepare a retained earnings statement for Braves Realty Inc. for the current year ended June 30, 19--. The amount of retained earnings in the trial balance represents the balance on July 1, the *beginning* of the current year.

(d) Prepare a balance sheet for Braves Realty Inc. as of June 30, 19--.

Problems

1–31. On August 1 of the current year, C. W. Collins established a corporation under the name of Collins Realty Inc. Collins Realty Inc. completed the following transactions during the month:

(a) Issued capital stock for $50,000.

(b) Paid rent on office and equipment for the month, $12,000.

(c) Purchased supplies (stationery, stamps, pencils, ink, etc.) on account, $3,400.

(d) Paid creditor on account, $2,500.

(e) Earned sales commissions, receiving cash, $48,500.

(f) Paid dividends, $10,000.

(g) Paid automobile expenses (including rental charge) for month, $2,800, and miscellaneous expenses, $1,750.

(h) Paid office salaries, $6,000.

(i) Determined that the cost of supplies used was $650.

Instructions:

(1) Prepare a ledger of T accounts for the following accounts: Cash, Supplies, Accounts Payable, Capital Stock, Dividends, Sales Commissions, Rent Expense, Office Salaries Expense, Automobile Expense, Supplies Expense, Miscellaneous Expense.

(2) Prepare journal entries for transactions (a) through (i).

(3) Post the journal to the ledger, and determine the balances after all posting is complete.

(4) Prepare a trial balance as of August 31, 19--.

(5) Determine the following:

  (a) Amount of total revenue recorded in the ledger.

  (b) Amount of total expenses recorded in the ledger.

  (c) Amount of net income for August.

1–32. Following are the amounts of O'Neal Corporation's assets and liabilities at May 31, the *end* of the current year, and its revenue and expenses for the year ended on that date, listed in alphabetical order. O'Neal Corporation had capital stock of $50,000 and retained earnings of $87,390 on June 1, the *beginning* of the current year. During the current year, the corporation paid cash dividends of $25,000.

Accounts payable	$ 48,320
Accounts receivable	68,840
Advertising expense	14,600
Cash	40,150
Insurance expense	12,000
Land	150,000
Miscellaneous expense	3,140
Notes payable	22,000
Prepaid insurance	2,000
Rent expense	43,100
Salaries payable	18,600
Salary expense	186,000
Sales	378,500
Supplies	3,280
Supplies expense	11,700
Taxes expense	16,900
Utilities expense	28,100

Instructions:

(1) Prepare an income statement for the current year ending May 31, exercising care to include each item of expense listed.
(2) Prepare a retained earnings statement for the current year ending May 31.
(3) Prepare a balance sheet as of May 31 of the current year. There was no change in the amount of capital stock during the year.

1–33. Dupree Dry Cleaners Inc. is a corporation operated by F. A. Dupree. Currently, a building and equipment are being rented pending completion of construction of new facilities. The actual work of dry cleaning is done by another company at wholesale rates. The assets, liabilities, and owner's equity of the business on September 1 of the current year are as follows: Cash, $4,800; Accounts Receivable, $10,400; Supplies, $450; Land, $10,000; Accounts Payable, $6,750; Capital Stock, $10,000; Retained Earnings, $8,900. Business transactions during September are summarized as follows:

(a) Received cash from cash customers for dry cleaning sales, $5,150.
(b) Purchased supplies on account, $120.
(c) Paid rent for the month, $600.
(d) Paid creditors on account, $1,260.
(e) Charged customers for dry cleaning sales on account, $3,520.
(f) Received monthly invoice for dry cleaning expense for September (to be paid on October 10), $4,800.
(g) Paid dividends of $950.
(h) Reimbursed a customer $80 for a garment lost by the cleaning company, which agreed to deduct the amount from the invoice received in transaction (f).
(i) Paid the following: wages expense, $1,100; truck expense, $380; utilities expense, $360; miscellaneous expense, $130.

(j) Received cash from customers on account, $4,100.

(k) Determined the cost of supplies used during the month, $170.

Instructions:

(1) Prepare a ledger of T accounts for Dupree Dry Cleaners Inc., using the following account titles: Cash, Accounts Receivable, Supplies, Land, Accounts Payable, Capital Stock, Retained Earnings, Dividends, Dry Cleaning Sales, Dry Cleaning Expense, Wages Expense, Rent Expense, Truck Expense, Utilities Expense, Supplies Expense, Miscellaneous Expense.

(2) Record the normal balances in the T accounts by writing "Bal." and entering the appropriate amount on the debit or credit side of the account.

(3) Prepare journal entries for transactions (a) through (k).

(4) Post the journal to the ledger, and determine the balances after all posting is complete.

(5) Prepare a trial balance as of September 30, 19--.

(6) Prepare an income statement and retained earnings statement for September.

(7) Prepare a balance sheet as of September 30, 19--.

1-34. The following business transactions were completed by Whipple Theatre Corporation during July of the current year:

(a) Received and deposited in a bank account $60,000 cash for capital stock.

(b) Purchased the Clinton Drive-In Theatre for $100,000, allocated as follows: land, $58,000; buildings, $23,600; equipment, $18,400. Paid $35,000 in cash and gave a note payable for the remainder.

(c) Entered into a contract for the operation of the refreshment stand concession at a rental of 20% of the concessionaire's sales, with a guaranteed minimum of $600 a month, payable in advance. Received cash of $600 as the advance payment for the month of July.

(d) Paid premiums for property and casualty insurance policies, $2,750.

(e) Purchased supplies, $420, and equipment, $3,180, on account.

(f) Paid for July billboard and newspaper advertising, $150.

(g) Cash received from admissions for the week, $2,130.

(h) Paid miscellaneous expense, $265.

(i) Paid semimonthly wages, $1,160.

(j) Cash received from admissions for the week, $1,980.

(k) Paid miscellaneous expenses, $310.

(l) Returned portion of supplies purchased in transaction (e) to the supplier, receiving full credit for the cost, $90.

(m) Paid cash to creditors on account, $1,755.

(n) Cash received from admissions for the week, $2,420.

(o) Purchased supplies for cash, $85.

(p) Paid for advertising leaflets for special promotion during last week in July, $240.

(q) Recorded invoice of $3,500 for rental of film for July. Payment is due on August 15.

(r) Paid electricity and water bills, $920.

(s) Paid semimonthly wages, $950.

(t) Cash received from admissions for remainder of the month, $2,870.

(u) Recorded additional amount owed by the concessionaire for the month of July; sales for the month totaled $4,350. Rental charges in excess of the advance payment of $600 are not due and payable until August 5.

Instructions:

(1) Prepare a ledger of T accounts for Whipple Theatre Corporation, using the following account titles: Cash, Accounts Receivable, Prepaid Insurance, Supplies, Land, Buildings, Equipment, Accounts Payable, Note Payable, Capital Stock, Admissions Income, Concession Income, Wages Expense, Film Rental Expense, Advertising Expense, Electricity and Water Expense, Miscellaneous Expense.

(2) Prepare journal entries for transactions (a) through (u).

(3) Post the journal to the ledger, and determine the balances after all posting is complete.

(4) Prepare a trial balance as of July 31, 19--.

(5) Determine the following:

(a) Amount of total revenue recorded in the ledger.

(b) Amount of total expenses recorded in the ledger.

(c) Amount of the net income for July, assuming that additional unrecorded expenses (including supplies used, insurance expired, etc.) totaled $758.

(d) The understatement or overstatement of net income for July that would have resulted from the failure to record the invoice for film rental until it was paid in August. (see transaction q).

(e) The understatement or overstatement of liabilities as of July 31 that would have resulted from the failure to record the invoice for film rental in July (see transaction q).

1-35. Seawell Realty Inc. acts as an agent in buying, selling, renting, and managing real estate. The account balances at the end of July of the current year are as follows:

Cash	46,240	
Accounts Receivable	23,600	
Prepaid Insurance	240	
Office Supplies	830	
Land	0	
Accounts Payable		4,250
Notes Payable		0
Capital Stock		20,000
Retained Earnings		19,606
Dividends	2,000	
Fees Earned		305,600
Salary and Commission Expense	244,480	
Rent Expense	12,000	
Advertising Expense	10,300	
Automobile Expense	8,450	
Miscellaneous Expense	1,316	
	349,456	349,456

The following business transactions were completed by Seawell Realty Inc. during August of the current year:

(a) Paid rent on office for month, $1,000.

(b) Purchased office supplies on account, $250.

(c) Received cash from clients on account, $16,280.

(d) Paid insurance premiums, $1,400.

(e) Paid salaries and commissions, $12,870.

(f) Purchased land for a future building site for $20,500, paying $5,500 in cash and giving a note payable for the remainder.

(g) Recorded revenue earned and billed to clients during first half of month, $14,160.

(h) Paid creditors on account, $2,420.

(i) Returned a portion of the supplies purchased on August 3, receiving full credit for their cost, $80.

(j) Received cash from clients on account, $10,190.

(k) Paid advertising expense, $820.

(l) Discovered an error in computing a commission; received cash from the salesperson for the overpayment, $350.

(m) Paid automobile expenses (including rental charges), $630.

(n) Paid miscellaneous expenses, $216.

(o) Recorded revenue earned and billed to clients during second half of month, $16,300.

(p) Paid salaries and commissions, $19,840.

(q) Paid dividend, $2,000.

Instructions:

(1) Prepare a ledger of T accounts for Seawell Realty Inc., using the account titles in the trial balance as of July 31. Record the balances in the accounts by writing "Bal." and entering the appropriate amount on the debit or credit side of the account.

(2) Prepare journal entries for transactions (a) through (q) completed during August.

(3) Post the journal to the ledger, and determine the balances after all posting is complete.

(4) Prepare a trial balance of the ledger as of August 31.

1–36. On March 1 of the current year, Express Delivery Inc. was organized as a corporation. The summarized transactions of the business for its first two months of operations, ending on April 30, are as follows:

(a) Received cash from stockholders for capital stock............		$50,000
(b) Purchased a portion of a delivery service that had been operating as a partnership in accordance with the following details:		
Assets acquired by the corporation:		
Accounts receivable	$12,400	
Truck supplies	3,810	
Office supplies.............................	960	$17,170
Liabilities assumed by the corporation:		
Accounts payable		8,670
Payment to be made as follows:		
Cash..	$ 2,500	
Notes payable, representing a liability to be paid in three equal installments of $2,000...............	6,000	$ 8,500
(c) Purchased truck supplies on account		$ 1,615
(d) Paid creditors on account		5,280
(e) Purchased office supplies for cash		120
(f) Paid insurance premiums in advance.............		600
(g) Received cash from customers on account.........		8,690

(h) Paid advertising expense.........................	$ 1,100
(i) Paid first of the three notes payable	2,000
(j) Charged delivery service sales to customers on account	30,550
(k) Paid rent expense on office and trucks.............	3,025
(l) Paid utilities expense	840
(m) Paid miscellaneous expenses......................	1,475
(n) Paid wages expense...............................	16,600
(o) Paid taxes expense...............................	220
(p) Truck supplies used	2,680
(q) Office supplies used	340
(r) Insurance premiums that expired and became an expense..	200
(s) Purchased land as future building site, paying $8,000 cash and giving a note payable due in 5 years for the balance of $20,000.............................	28,000
(t) Paid cash dividends to stockholders	750

Instructions:

(1) Prepare a ledger of T accounts for Express Delivery Inc., using the following account titles: Cash, Accounts Receivable, Truck Supplies, Office Supplies, Prepaid Insurance, Land, Notes Payable, Accounts Payable, Capital Stock, Dividends, Delivery Service Sales, Wages Expense, Rent Expense, Truck Supplies Expense, Advertising Expense, Utilities Expense, Office Supplies Expense, Taxes Expense, Insurance Expense, Miscellaneous Expense.

(2) Prepare journal entries for transactions (a) through (t) completed during March and April.

(3) Post the journal to the ledger, and determine the balances after all posting is complete.

(4) Prepare a trial balance of the ledger as of April 30.

(5) Prepare the following: (a) income statement for two months, (b) retained earnings statement for two months, and (c) balance sheet as of April 30.

Alternate Problems

1–32A. Following are the amounts of Tucker Corporation's assets and liabilities at October 31, the *end* of the current year, and its revenue and expenses for the year ended on that date, listed in alphabetical order. Tucker Corporation had capital stock of $20,000 and retained earnings of $15,755 on November 1, the *beginning* of the current year. During the current year, the corporation paid cash dividends of $5,000.

Accounts payable...........................	$ 6,175
Accounts receivable.........................	12,840
Advertising expense	1,750
Cash.......................................	8,175
Insurance expense..........................	720
Land.......................................	36,000
Miscellaneous expense......................	580
Notes payable..............................	3,000
Prepaid insurance	120

Rent expense	$14,400
Salaries payable.	2,430
Salary expense.	38,960
Sales.	84,160
Supplies	865
Supplies expense.	2,910
Taxes expense	2,800
Utilities expense	6,400

Instructions:
1. (1) Prepare an income statement for the current year ending October 31, exercising care to include each item of expense listed.
2. (2) Prepare a retained earnings statement for the current year ending October 31.
3. (3) Prepare a balance sheet as of October 31 of the current year. There was no change in the amount of capital stock during the year.

1–33A. Dupree Dry Cleaners Inc. is a corporation operated by F. A. Dupree. Currently, a building and equipment are being rented pending completion of construction of new facilities. The actual work of dry cleaning is done by another company at wholesale rates. The assets, liabilities, and owner's equity of the business on May 1 of the current year are as follows: Cash, $5,400; Accounts Receivable, $3,700; Supplies, $410; Land, $9,500; Accounts Payable, $2,380; Capital Stock, $10,000; Retained Earnings, $6,630. Business transactions during May are summarized as follows:

(a) Paid rent for the month, $850.
(b) Charged customers for dry cleaning sales on account, $5,646.
(c) Paid creditors on account, $1,680.
(d) Purchased supplies on account, $254.
(e) Received cash from cash customers for dry cleaning sales, $2,894.
(f) Received cash from customers on account, $2,750.
(g) Paid dividends of $760.
(h) Received monthly invoice for dry cleaning expense for May (to be paid on June 10), $3,416.
(i) Paid the following: wages expense, $675; truck expense, $310; utilities expense, $260; miscellaneous expense, $89.
(j) Reimbursed a customer $50 for a garment lost by the cleaning company, which agreed to deduct the amount from the invoice received in transaction (h).
(k) Determined the cost of supplies used during the month, $328.

Instructions:
1. (1) Prepare a ledger of T accounts for Dupree Dry Cleaners Inc., using the following account titles: Cash, Accounts Receivable, Supplies, Land, Accounts Payable, Capital Stock, Retained Earnings, Dividends, Dry Cleaning Sales, Dry Cleaning Expense, Rent Expense, Wages Expense, Supplies Expense, Truck Expense, Utilities Expense, Miscellaneous Expense.
2. (2) Record the normal balances in the T accounts by writing "Bal." and entering the appropriate amount on the debit or credit side of the account.
3. (3) Prepare journal entries for transactions (a) through (k).
4. (4) Post the journal to the ledger, and determine the balances after all posting is complete.
5. (5) Prepare a trial balance as of May 31, 19--.
6. (6) Prepare an income statement and retained earnings statement for May.
7. (7) Prepare a balance sheet as of May 31, 19--.

1–34A. The following business transactions were completed by Southern Theatre Corporation during April of the current year:

(a) Deposited in a bank account $80,000 cash received for capital stock.

(b) Purchased the King Drive-In Theatre for $125,000, allocated as follows: land, $75,000; buildings, $36,000; equipment, $14,000. Paid $70,000 in cash and gave a note payable for the remainder.

(c) Entered into a contract for the operation of the refreshment stand concession at a rental of 25% of the concessionaire's sales, with a guaranteed minimum of $500 a month, payable in advance. Received cash of $500 as the advance payment for the month of April.

(d) Paid for advertising leaflets for April, $120.

(e) Paid premiums for property and casualty insurance policies, $3,200.

(f) Purchased supplies, $864, and equipment, $2,960, on account.

(g) Paid for April billboard and newspaper advertising, $1,280.

(h) Cash received from admissions for the week, $4,120.

(i) Paid miscellaneous expense, $179.

(j) Paid semimonthly wages, $1,540.

(k) Cash received from admissions for the week, $3,810.

(l) Paid miscellaneous expenses, $258.

(m) Returned portion of supplies purchased in transaction (f) to the supplier, receiving full credit for the cost, $160.

(n) Paid cash to creditors on account, $2,350.

(o) Cash received from admissions for the week, $3,980.

(p) Purchased supplies for cash, $282.

(q) Recorded invoice of $4,800 for rental of film for April. Payment is due on May 5.

(r) Paid electricity and water bills, $574.

(s) Paid semimonthly wages, $1,410.

(t) Cash received from admissions for remainder of the month, $4,450.

(u) Recorded additional amount owed by the concessionaire for the month of April; sales for the month totaled $5,280. Rental charges in excess of the advance payment of $500 are not due and payable until May 12.

Instructions:

(1) Prepare a ledger of T accounts for Southern Theatre Corporation, using the following account titles: Cash, Accounts Receivable, Prepaid Insurance, Supplies, Land, Buildings, Equipment, Accounts Payable, Note Payable, Capital Stock, Admissions Income, Concession Income, Wages Expense, Film Rental Expense, Advertising Expense, Electricity and Water Expense, Miscellaneous Expense.

(2) Prepare journal entries for transactions (a) through (u).

(3) Post the journal to the ledger, and determine the balances after all posting is complete.

(4) Prepare a trial balance as of April 30, 19--.

(5) Determine the following:

(a) Amount of total revenue recorded in the ledger.

(b) Amount of total expenses recorded in the ledger.

(c) Amount of net income for April, assuming that additional unrecorded expenses (including supplies used, insurance expired, etc.) totaled $2,280.

(d) The understatement or overstatement of net income for April that would have resulted from the failure to record the invoice for film rental until it was paid in May (see transaction q).

(e) The understatement or overstatement of liabilities as of April 30 that would have resulted from the failure to record the invoice for film rental in April (see transaction q).

Mini-Case

1–37. Victoria Getz, a sophomore in college, has been seeking ways to earn extra spending money. As an active sports enthusiast, Victoria plays tennis regularly at the Georgetown Golf and Tennis Club, where her father has a family membership. The president of the club recently approached Victoria with the proposal that Victoria manage the club's tennis courts on weekends. Victoria's primary duty would be to supervise the operation of the club's two indoor and six outdoor courts, including court reservations. In return for her services, the club agreed to pay Victoria $50 per weekend, plus Victoria could keep whatever she earned from lessons and the fees from the use of the ball machine. The club and Victoria agreed to a one-month trial, after which both would consider an arrangement for the remaining three years of Victoria's college career. On this basis, Victoria organized Tennis Services Unlimited as a sole proprietorship. During September, Victoria managed the tennis courts and entered into the following transactions:

(a) Opened a business bank account by depositing $350.

(b) Paid $80 for tennis supplies (practice tennis balls, etc.).

(c) Paid $110 for the rental of video tape equipment to be used in offering lessons during September.

(d) Arranged for the rental of a ball machine during September for $40. Paid $20 in advance, with the remaining $20 due October 1.

(e) Received $375 for lessons given during September.

(f) Paid $45 for salaries of part-time employees who answered the telephone and took reservations while Victoria was giving lessons.

(g) Received $60 in fees from the use of the ball machine during September.

(h) Paid $35 for miscellaneous expenses.

(i) Received $200 from the club for managing the tennis courts during September.

(j) Supplies on hand at the end of the month total $55.

(k) Victoria withdrew $300 for personal use on September 30.

As a friend and accounting student, Victoria has asked you to aid her in assessing the venture.

Instructions:

(1) To assist Victoria with her record keeping, prepare a ledger of T accounts that would be appropriate. Note: Small business enterprises such as Tennis Services Unlimited are often organized as sole proprietorships. The accounting for sole proprietorships is similar to that for a corporation, except that the owner's equity accounts differ. Specifically, instead of the account Capital Stock, a capital account entitled Victoria Getz, Capital is used to record investments in the business. In addition, instead of a dividends account, withdrawals from the business enterprise are debited to Victorial Getz, Drawing.

(2) Prepare journal entries for transactions (a) through (k).
(3) Post the journal to the ledger, and determine the balances after all posting is complete.
(4) Prepare a trial balance as of September 30, 19--.
(5) Prepare an income statement for September.
(6) (a) Assume that Victoria Getz could earn $3.50 per hour working 16 hours per weekend for a fast food restaurant. Evaluate which of the two alternatives, the fast food restaurant or Tennis Services Unlimited, would provide Victoria with the most income per month.
　　(b) Discuss any other factors that you believe Victoria should consider before discussing a long-term arrangement with Georgetown Golf and Tennis Club.

Answers to Self-Examination Questions

1. **D** A corporation, organized in accordance with state or federal statutes, is a separate legal entity in which ownership is divided into shares of stock (answer D). A sole proprietorship, sometimes referred to as a single proprietorship (answers A and B), is a business enterprise owned by one individual. A partnership (answer C) is a business enterprise owned by two or more individuals.

2. **A** The properties owned by a business enterprise are referred to as assets (answer A). The debts of the business are called liabilities (answer B), and the equity of the owners is called capital or owner's equity (answers C and D).

3. **A** A debit may signify an increase in asset accounts (answer A) or a decrease in liability and owner's equity accounts. A credit may signify a decrease in asset accounts (answer B) or an increase in liability and owner's equity accounts (answers C and D).

4. **C** Liability, capital stock, and revenue (answer C) accounts have normal credit balances. Asset (answer A), dividend (answer B), and expense (answer D) accounts have normal debit balances.

5. **A** The balance sheet is a listing of the assets, liabilities, and owner's equity of a business entity at a specific date (answer A). The income statement (answer B) is a summary of the revenue and expenses of a business entity for a specific period of time. The statement of changes in financial position (answer C) summarizes the changes in the financial position of a business entity. The retained earnings statement (answer D) summarizes the changes in retained earnings for a corporation during a specific period of time.

CHAPTER 2

Accounting for Merchandise Transactions

CHAPTER OBJECTIVES

Describe accounting for purchases and sales transactions.

Describe the major classifications of accounts.

Describe and illustrate accounting for the transactions of a merchandising enterprise.

Describe the procedures for discovering errors in accounts.

The recording of business transactions for a service enterprise was described and illustrated in Chapter 1. This chapter describes the recording of transactions for an enterprise that sells merchandise, and describes the classification of accounts, the standard account form, and the general journal. In Chapters 3 and 4, a merchandising enterprise's summarizing and reporting procedures at year end, including the preparation of financial statements, are discussed.

PURCHASING AND SELLING PROCEDURES

Merchandising enterprises acquire merchandise for resale to customers. These purchases and the sales of merchandise are the transactions that differ from those of enterprises that render services. Although these transactions result in differences in accounting for merchandising enterprises and service enterprises, the flow of accounting data, as described in Chapter 1, is the same. This flow, from the time a transaction occurs to its recording in the ledger, may be diagrammed as follows:

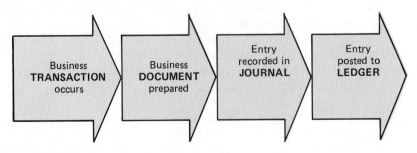

The initial record of each transaction, or a group of similar transactions, is evidenced by a business document such as a sales ticket, a check stub, or a cash register tape. On the basis of the evidence provided by the business documents, the transactions are entered in chronological order in a journal. The amounts of the debits and the credits in the journal are then transferred or posted to the accounts in the ledger.

The common procedures for recording purchasing and selling transactions are discussed in the following paragraphs. These procedures may vary from business to business, however. For example, purchases and sales may be made for cash or on credit (on account), and many different arrangements may be made for making payments on account. In addition, policies for the return of merchandise and for the payment of transportation costs may be different.

ACCOUNTING FOR PURCHASES

Purchases of merchandise are usually identified in the ledger as *Purchases*. A more exact account title, such as "Purchases of Merchandise," could be used, but the briefer title is customarily used. Thus, a merchandising enterprise can accumulate in the purchases account the cost of all merchandise purchased for resale during the accounting period.

When purchases are made for cash, the transaction may be recorded in the journal as follows:

Purchases	510	
Cash		510

Most purchases of merchandise are made on account and may be recorded as follows:

Purchases	925	
Accounts Payable		925

Purchases Discounts

The arrangements agreed upon by the purchaser and the seller as to when payments for merchandise are to be made are called the **credit terms**. If payment is required immediately upon delivery, the terms are said to be "cash" or "net cash." Otherwise, the purchaser is allowed a certain amount of time, known as the **credit period,** in which to pay.

It is usual for the credit period to begin with the date of the sale as shown by the date of the **invoice** or **bill.** If payment is due within a stated number of days after the date of the invoice, for example 30 days, the terms are said to be "net 30 days,"[1] which may be written as "n/30." If payment is due by

---

[1]The word "net" in this context does not have the usual meaning of a remainder after all relevant deductions have been subtracted, as in "net income," for example.

the end of the month in which the sale was made, it may be expressed as "n/eom."

As a means of encouraging payment before the end of the credit period, a discount may be offered for the early payment of cash. Thus the expression "2/10, n/30" means that, although the credit period is 30 days, the purchaser may deduct 2% of the amount of the invoice if payment is made within 10 days of the invoice date. This deduction is known as a **cash discount.**

From the purchaser's standpoint, it is important to take advantage of all available discounts, even though it may be necessary to borrow the money to make the payment. To illustrate, assume that the following invoice for $1,500 is received by ROC Corporation:

| INVOICE

Wallace Electronics Supply
3800 MISSION STREET
SAN FRANCISCO, CA 94110-1732

FOR CUSTOMER'S USE ONLY

Calculations Checked	Price Approved
W. M. L.	
Material Received	
_10-13_ 19 _86_ *A. S.* Rec. Cl.	
Date Signature Title	
Audited	Final Approval
L. R. A.	

Customer's Order No. & Date 412 Oct. 9, 1986

Refer to Invoice No. 106-8

Invoice Date Oct. 11, 1986

Vendor's Nos.

SOLD ROC Corporation
TO   1200 San Vicente Blvd.
     Los Angeles, CA 90019-2350

Date Shipped Oct. 11, 1986 From San Francisco   Prepaid or Collect?

How Shipped and Route Western Trucking Co.   F.O.B. Los Angeles   Prepaid

Terms 2/10, n/30   Made in U. S. A.

QUANTITY	DESCRIPTION	UNIT PRICE	AMOUNT
20	392E Transformers	75.00	1,500.00

The invoice, with terms of 2/10, n/30, is to be paid within the discount period with money borrowed for the remaining 20 days of the credit period. If an annual interest rate of 12% is assumed, the net savings to the purchaser is $20.20, determined as follows:

Discount of 2% on $1,500	$30.00
Interest for 20 days, at rate of 12%, on $1,470 ($1,500 − $30)....	9.80
Savings effected by borrowing	$20.20

Discounts taken by the purchaser for early payment of an invoice are called **purchases discounts.** They are recorded by crediting the purchases discount account and are shown on the income statement as a deduction from the amount initially recorded as Purchases. Thus, the purchases discount account is sometimes referred to as a *contra* (or offsetting) account to Purchases.

To illustrate the recording of purchases discounts, the receipt of the purchase invoice presented on page 47 and its payment at the end of the discount period may be recorded as follows:

Oct. 11	Purchases	1,500	
	Accounts Payable		1,500
Oct. 21	Accounts Payable	1,500	
	Cash		1,470
	Purchases Discount		30

Purchases Returns and Allowances

When merchandise is returned or a price adjustment is requested, the purchaser usually communicates with the seller in writing. The details may be stated in a letter or the purchaser (debtor) may use a **debit memorandum** form. This form, illustrated as follows, is a convenient medium for informing the seller (creditor) of the amount the purchaser proposes to debit to the account payable account. It also states the reasons for the return or request for a price reduction.

DEBIT MEMORANDUM

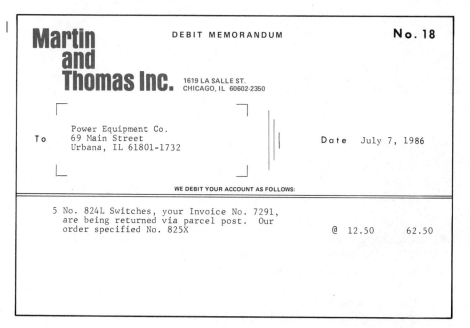

The debtor may use a copy of the debit memorandum as the basis for an entry or may wait for confirmation from the creditor, which is usually in the form of a **credit memorandum.** In either event, Accounts Payable must be debited and Purchases must be credited. To illustrate, the entry by Martin and

Thomas Inc. to record the return of the merchandise identified in the debit memo on page 48 would be as follows:

July 7	Accounts Payable	62.50	
	Purchases		62.50

Most businesses credit the purchases account for merchandise returned and allowances granted, as illustrated in the preceding entry, because the benefits are not worth the costs of keeping a separate record of purchases returns and allowances. This procedure will be used in this text. In contrast, most businesses use a separate purchases discount account, for accumulating the discounts taken, because the failure to take advantage of all available discounts is a serious oversight. If a business prefers to maintain a separate record of the amount of purchases returned and allowances granted, then a separate purchases returns and allowances account, rather than the purchases account, is credited for all returns and allowances. If this alternative is used, the purchases returns and allowances account would be a contra (offsetting) account to Purchases, and the balance would be deducted from the amount reported as Purchases on the income statement.

When a purchaser returns merchandise or has been granted an allowance prior to the payment of the invoice, the amount of the debit memorandum is deducted from the invoice amount before the purchases discount is computed. For example, assume that the details related to the amount payable to Power Equipment Co., for which the debit memo illustrated above was issued, are as follows:

Invoice No. 7291 dated July 1 (terms 2/10, n/30)	$2,045.00
Debit Memo No. 18 dated July 7	62.50
Balance of account	$1,982.50
Discount (2% of $1,982.50)	39.65
Cash payment, July 11	$1,942.85

The cash payment could be recorded by Martin and Thomas Inc. as follows:

July 11	Accounts Payable	1,982.50	
	Cash		1,942.85
	Purchases Discount		39.65

ACCOUNTING FOR SALES

Merchandise sales are usually identified in the ledger as *Sales*, or *Sales of Merchandise*. Sales are recorded in the accounting records based upon the **realization principle.** Under this principle, sales are generally recorded when the title to the merchandise passes to the buyer. The passing of title usually occurs when the merchandise has been delivered to the buyer or when the merchandise has been placed in the custody of a shipping agent, such as a freight company. Usually at that time, rather than when a sales order is received, the buyer incurs a specific obligation to pay for the merchandise.

A business may sell merchandise for cash. These sales are generally "rung up" on a cash register and totaled at the end of the day. Such sales may be recorded as follows:

Cash	1,872.50	
Sales		1,872.50

Sales to customers who use bank credit cards (such as MasterCard and VISA) are generally treated as cash sales. The credit card invoices representing these sales are deposited by the seller directly into the bank, along with the currency and checks received from customers. Periodically, the bank charges a service fee for handling these credit card sales. The service fee should be debited to an expense account.

A business may also sell merchandise on account. Such sales result in a debit to Accounts Receivable and a credit to Sales, as illustrated in the following entry:

Accounts Receivable	510	
Sales		510

Sales made by the use of nonbank credit cards (such as American Express) generally must be reported periodically to the card company before cash is received. Therefore, such sales create a receivable with the card company. Before the card company remits cash, it normally deducts a service fee. To illustrate, assume that nonbank credit card sales of $1,000 are made and reported to the card company on January 20. On January 27, the company deducts a service fee of $50 and remits $950. The transactions may be recorded as follows:

Jan. 20	Accounts Receivable	1,000	
	Sales		1,000
Jan. 27	Cash	950	
	Credit Card Collection Expense	50	
	Accounts Receivable		1,000

Sales Discounts

The seller refers to the discounts taken by the purchaser for early payment of an invoice as **sales discounts.** Most businesses maintain a separate record of sales discounts by debiting the sales discount account. The sales discount account is a contra (offsetting) account to Sales and is shown on the income statement as a deduction from the amount initially recorded as Sales.

To illustrate the recording of sales discounts, assume that the seller receives cash within the discount period from a previously recorded credit sale of $500, with terms of 2/10, n/30. This transaction would be recorded as follows:

June 10	Cash.	490	
	Sales Discount	10	
	Accounts Receivable		500

Sales Returns and Allowances

Merchandise sold may be returned by the customer (**sales return**) or, because of defects or for other reasons, the customer may be allowed a reduction from the original price at which the goods were sold (**sales allowance**). If the return or allowance is for a sale on account, the seller usually gives the customer a **credit memorandum**. This memorandum shows the amount for which the customer is to be credited and the reason therefor. A typical credit memorandum is illustrated as follows:

```
        CREDIT MEMORANDUM              No. 32

   Baker
     Manufacturing
       Company    1277 SIXTH AVENUE
                  LOS ANGELES, CA 90019-2350


                                Date   October 13, 1986
   CREDIT     Berry Company
     TO       7608 Melton Avenue
              Los Angeles, CA 90025-3942



              WE CREDIT YOUR ACCOUNT AS FOLLOWS:


    1 Model 393 F Transformer returned         225.00
```

The effect of a sales return or allowance is a reduction in sales revenue and a reduction in cash or accounts receivable. If the sales account is debited, however, the balance of the account at the end of the period will represent net sales, and the volume of returns and allowances will not be disclosed. Because of the loss in revenue resulting from allowances, and the various expenses (transportation, unpacking, repairing, reselling, etc.) related to returns, it is advisable that management know the amount of such transactions. Such a policy will allow management to determine the causes of returns and allowances, should they become excessive, and to take corrective action. It is therefore preferable to maintain a separate record of the amount of sales returns and allowances by debiting a contra (offsetting) account to Sales, entitled Sales Returns and Allowances. If the original sale is on account, the remainder of the transaction is recorded as a credit to Accounts Receivable. To illustrate, the following entry would be made by Baker Manufacturing Company to record the credit memo presented on page 51:

Oct. 13	Sales Returns and Allowances	225	
	Accounts Receivable		225

If a cash refund is made because of merchandise returned or for an allowance, Sales Returns and Allowances is debited and Cash is credited.

TRANSPORTATION COSTS

The terms of the agreement between buyer and seller include a provision concerning which party is to bear the cost of delivering the merchandise to the buyer. If the purchaser is to absorb the cost, the terms are stated **FOB (free on board) shipping point;** if the seller is to assume the cost of transportation, the terms are said to be **FOB (free on board) destination.**

Costs to Purchaser

When merchandise is purchased on FOB shipping point terms, the transportation costs paid by the purchaser should be debited to Purchases and credited to Cash. Some enterprises maintain an account titled "Freight In" or "Transportation In" for accumulating all separately charged delivery costs on merchandise purchased. The balance of this account is then added to the balance of Purchases to determine the total cost of acquiring the merchandise.

In some cases, the seller may prepay the transportation costs and add them to the invoice, even though the agreement states that the purchaser bear such costs (terms FOB shipping point). If the seller prepays the transportation charges, the purchaser will include the costs in the debit to Purchases and the credit to Accounts Payable. To illustrate, assume that on June 10 the Durban Co. purchases merchandise from Bell Corp. on account, $900, terms FOB shipping point, 2/10, n/30, with prepaid transportation costs of $50 added to the invoice. The entry by Durban Co. would be as follows:

June 10	Purchases	950	
	Accounts Payable		950

When the terms provide for a discount for early payment, the discount is based on the amount of the sale rather than on the invoice total. To illustrate, if Durban Co. pays the amount due on the purchase of June 10 within 10 days, the amount of the discount and the amount of the payment may be determined as follows:

Invoice from Bell Corp., including prepaid transportation of $50		$950
Amount subject to discount	$900	
Rate of discount	2%	
Amount of purchases discount		18
Amount of payment		$932

Durban Co. may record the payment as follows:

June 20	Accounts Payable	950	
	Cash		932
	Purchases Discount		18

Costs to Seller

When the agreement states that the seller is to bear the delivery costs (FOB destination), the amount paid by the seller for delivery are debited to "Delivery Expense," "Transportation Out," or a similarly titled account. The total delivery cost incurred during a period is reported on the seller's income statement.

SALES TAXES

Almost all states and many other taxing units levy a tax on sales of merchandise. The liability for the sales tax is ordinarily incurred at the time the sale is made, regardless of the terms of the sale. The seller normally collects the sales tax from the purchaser, who should include any sales tax paid to the seller as an addition to the cost of the merchandise purchased. Periodically, the seller remits the amount of the sales tax to the taxing unit.

CLASSIFICATION OF ACCOUNTS

Before the recording of a series of transactions for a merchandising enterprise is illustrated, the classifications and accounts characteristically used are described in the following paragraphs. Accounts in the ledger are customarily classified according to a common characteristic: assets, liabilities, owner's equity, revenue, and expenses. In addition, there may be subgroupings within these major categories.

Assets

Any physical object or right that has a money value is an asset. Assets are customarily divided into groups for presentation on the balance sheet. The two groups used most often — current assets and plant assets — are discussed in the following paragraphs. Additional groups, such as investments and intangible assets, are discussed in later chapters.

Current assets. Cash and other assets that a business may reasonably expect to be sold, used up, or realized in cash through the normal operations of the business, usually within a year, are called current assets. Current assets are generally listed on the balance sheet in the order of liquidity. Cash is therefore listed first, followed by marketable securities, accounts receivable, notes receivable, merchandise inventory, supplies, and other prepaid expenses in the order in which they will be converted to cash or consumed.

Cash is any medium of exchange that a bank will accept at face value. It includes bank deposits, currency, checks, bank drafts, and money orders. Notes receivable are claims against debtors evidenced by a written promise to pay a certain sum in money at a definite time to the order of a specified person or to bearer. Accounts receivable are also claims against debtors, but are less formal than notes. Merchandise inventory is unsold merchandise that is held for resale to customers. Prepaid expenses include supplies on hand and advance payments of expenses such as insurance and property taxes.

Plant assets. Tangible assets used in the business that are of a permanent or relatively fixed nature are called plant assets or **fixed assets.** Plant assets include equipment, machinery, buildings, and land. With the exception of land, these assets gradually lose their usefulness with the passage of time. They are said to **depreciate**. The concept of depreciation is discussed in more detail in Chapter 3.

Liabilities

Liabilities are debts owed to outsiders (creditors) and are frequently described on the balance sheet by titles that include the word "payable." The two categories occurring most frequently are (1) current liabilities and (2) long-term liabilities.

Current liabilities. Liabilities that will be due within a short time (usually one year or less) and that are to be paid out of current assets are called current liabilities. The most common liabilities in this group are notes payable and accounts payable, which are exactly like their receivable counterparts except that the debtor-creditor relationship is reversed. Other current liability accounts commonly found in the ledger are Salaries Payable, Interest Payable, and Taxes Payable.

Long-term liabilities. Liabilities that will not be due for a comparatively long time (usually more than one year) are called long-term liabilities or **fixed**

liabilities. As they come within the one-year range and are to be paid, these liabilities become current. If the obligation is to be renewed rather than paid at maturity, however, it would continue to be classified as long-term. When a long-term debt is to be paid over a number of years, the installments due within one year from a balance sheet date are classified as a current liability. When a note is accompanied by security in the form of a mortgage, the obligation may be referred to as *mortgage note payable* or *mortgage payable.*

Owner's Equity

Owner's equity is the term applied to the equity of the owner or owners in the business. It is a residual claim against the assets of the business after the total liabilities are deducted. Other commonly used terms for owner's equity are **stockholders' equity,** *shareholders' equity, shareholders' investment,* and **net worth** (or *capital* in referring to a sole proprietorship or partnership).

Revenue

Revenue is the gross increase in owner's equity attributable to business activities. It results from the sale of merchandise, the performance of services for a customer or a client, the rental of property, the lending of money, and other business and professional activities entered into for the purpose of earning income. Revenue from sales of merchandise is often identified merely as sales.

Expense

Costs that have been consumed in the process of producing revenue are **expired costs** or **expenses**. The number of expense categories and individual expense accounts maintained in the ledger varies with the nature and the size of an enterprise. A large business with authority and responsibility spread among many employees may use an elaborate classification and hundreds of accounts as an aid in controlling expenses.

For merchandise enterprises, the cost of merchandise purchased for resale is identified as purchases. The merchandise purchased is an asset until it is sold. At the time of sale, the cost of the merchandise purchased becomes an expense and is identified as **cost of merchandise sold.** The recording of the cost of merchandise sold and its presentation on the income statement is discussed and illustrated in Chapters 3 and 4.

CHART OF ACCOUNTS — MERCHANDISING ENTERPRISE

The number of accounts maintained by a specific enterprise is affected by the nature of its operations, its volume of business, and the extent to which details are needed for taxing authorities, managerial decisions, credit purposes, etc. For example, one enterprise may have separate accounts for executive salaries, office salaries, and sales salaries, while another may find it satisfactory to record all types of salaries in a single salary expense account.

Insofar as possible, the order of the accounts in the ledger should agree with the order of the items in the balance sheet and the income statement. The accounts are numbered to permit indexing and also for use as posting references.

Although accounts in the ledger may be numbered consecutively as in the pages of a book, a flexible system of indexing is preferable. In the following **chart of accounts** for Taylor Inc., each account number has two digits. The first digit indicates the major division of the ledger in which the account is placed. Accounts beginning with 1 represent assets; 2, liabilities; 3, owner's equity; 4, revenue; and 5, expenses. The second digit indicates the position of the account within its division. A numbering system of this type has the advantage of permitting the later insertion of new accounts in their proper sequence without disturbing the other account numbers. For a large enterprise with a number of departments or branches, it is not unusual for each account number to have four or more digits.

CHART OF
ACCOUNTS FOR
TAYLOR INC.

Balance Sheet Accounts	Income Statement Accounts
1. Assets	4. Revenue
11 Cash	41 Sales
12 Accounts Receivable	42 Sales Returns and Allowances
13 Merchandise Inventory	43 Sales Discount
14 Store Supplies	
15 Prepaid Rent	5. Expenses
18 Store Equipment	51 Purchases
19 Accumulated Depreciation	52 Purchases Discount
	53 Advertising Expense
2. Liabilities	54 Salary Expense
21 Accounts Payable	55 Rent Expense
22 Salaries Payable	56 Depreciation Expense
	57 Utilities Expense
3. Owner's Equity	59 Miscellaneous Expense
31 Capital Stock	
32 Retained Earnings	
33 Dividends	
34 Income Summary	

LEDGER ACCOUNTS

Accounts in the simple T form were used for illustrative purposes in Chapter 1. A more formal form is the **standard account form,** which includes balance columns. The primary advantage of the standard account form is that the account balance is readily available, as shown in the following illustration:

ACCOUNT *Cash*   ACCOUNT NO. *11*   STANDARD ACCOUNT FORM

DATE		ITEM	POST. REF.	DEBIT	CREDIT	BALANCE DEBIT	BALANCE CREDIT
1986 May	1	Balance	✔			5 2 4 5 00	
	1		17	1 8 2 2 25		7 0 6 7 25	
	1		17		3 5 0 00	6 7 1 7 25	
	1		17		9 9 5 50	5 7 2 1 75	
	3		17	9 6 0 40		6 6 8 2 15	
	3		17		1 9 2 00	6 4 9 0 15	
	3		17		1 8 8 2 25	4 6 0 7 90	

GENERAL JOURNAL AND POSTING

The basic features of a journal entry and posting were illustrated in Chapter 1 when the use of accounts and debit and credit were introduced. The **general journal** is the formalized device used for recording journal entries in chronological order, illustrated as follows:

JOURNAL   PAGE *17*   GENERAL JOURNAL

	DATE		DESCRIPTION	POST. REF.	DEBIT	CREDIT	
1	1986 May	1	Cash		1 8 2 2 25		1
2			Sales			1 8 2 2 25	2
3			Cash sales for the day.				3
4							4
5		1	Advertising Expense		3 5 0 00		5
6			Cash			3 5 0 00	6
7			Advertisements in Lima News.				7
8							8
9		1	Store Supplies		1 7 5 00		9
10			Accounts Payable			1 7 5 00	10
11			On account from Crom Co.				11
12							12
13							13

Note that brief explanations have been written below each journal entry. Many accountants prefer to omit explanations when the nature of the entry is obvious.

The posting of a debit or credit general journal entry to a standard ledger account is performed in the following manner:

1. Record the date and the amount of the entry in the account.
2. Insert the number of the journal page in the Posting Reference column of the account.
3. Insert the ledger account number in the Posting Reference column of the journal.

These procedures are illustrated as follows by the posting of a debit to the cash account. The posting of a credit uses the same sequence of procedures.

DIAGRAM OF THE
POSTING OF A DEBIT

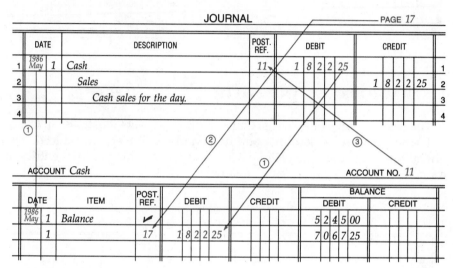

ILLUSTRATIVE PROBLEM

To illustrate the procedures discussed in the preceding sections, assume that Taylor Inc. is organized as a corporation on June 1, 1986, to sell merchandise. The transactions for Taylor Inc.'s first month of operations are described below, followed by the appropriate journal entry. To reduce repetition, some of the transactions are stated as a summary. For example, sales for cash are ordinarily recorded on a daily basis, but in this illustration, summary totals are given only at the middle and end of the month.

June 1.   Taylor Inc. was organized by issuing shares of capital stock for $80,000 in cash.

	JOURNAL			PAGE 1	
DATE	DESCRIPTION	POST. REF.	DEBIT	CREDIT	
1986 June 1	Cash	11	80 0 0 0 00		1
	Capital Stock	31		80 0 0 0 00	2

June 2. Paid $3,600 on a lease rental contract, the payment representing two months' rent of store space in a local shopping mall. The asset acquired in exchange for the cash payment is the use of the property for two months. Thus, an asset entitled Prepaid Rent is debited for $3,600.

3						3
4	2	Prepaid Rent	15	3 6 0 0 00		4
5		Cash	11		3 6 0 0 00	5

June 3. Purchased store equipment on account from Roswell Equipment Suppliers for $15,000, terms n/60. The terms of the purchase indicate that the full amount of the liability is due at the end of 60 days.

6						6
7	3	Store Equipment	18	15 0 0 0 00		7
8		Accounts Payable	21		15 0 0 0 00	8

June 5. Purchased $30,000 of merchandise on account from Owen Clothing, terms 2/10, n/30. The terms of the purchase indicate that a 2% discount is available if the amount is paid within 10 days, but that the full amount is due, in any case, at the end of 30 days.

9						9
10	5	Purchases	51	30 0 0 0 00		10
11		Accounts Payable	21		30 0 0 0 00	11

June 8. Paid $600 for a newspaper advertisement.

12						12
13	8	Advertising Expense	53	6 0 0 00		13
14		Cash	11		6 0 0 00	14

June 10. Purchased $3,000 of store supplies, paying one half in cash and agreeing to pay the remainder in 30 days.

15							15
16	10	Store Supplies	14	3 0 0 0 00			16
17		Cash	11		1 5 0 0 00		17
18		Accounts Payable	21		1 5 0 0 00		18

June 14. Paid salesperson $600 for two weeks' salary.

19							19
20	14	Salary Expense	54	6 0 0 00			20
21		Cash	11		6 0 0 00		21

June 15. Received $8,000 from cash sales for the first half of June.

22							22
23	15	Cash	11	8 0 0 0 00			23
24		Sales	41		8 0 0 0 00		24

June 15. Paid Owen Clothing for purchases of June 5 on account, less discount of $600 ($30,000 × 2%).

25							25
26	15	Accounts Payable	21	30 0 0 0 00			26
27		Cash	11		29 4 0 0 00		27
28		Purchases Discount	52		6 0 0 00		28

June 15. Sales on account totaled $12,500 for the first half of June. All sales are made with terms 1/10, n/30.

29							29
30	15	Accounts Receivable	12	12 5 0 0 00			30
31		Sales	41		12 5 0 0 00		31

June 19.   Received merchandise returned on account, $4,000.

32							32
33	19	Sales Returns and Allowances	42	4 0 0 0 00			33
34		Accounts Receivable	12		4 0 0 0 00		34

June 22.   Purchased merchandise from Norcross Clothiers, $15,000, terms FOB shipping point, 2/15, n/30, with prepaid transportation charges of $750 added to the invoice. The prepaid transportation charges of $750 must be added to the cost of the merchandise purchased and the accounts payable, since the merchandise was shipped FOB shipping point. The transportation charges are not eligible for the 2% discount.

35							35
36	22	Purchases	51	15 7 5 0 00			36
37		Accounts Payable	21		15 7 5 0 00		37

June 25.   Received $6,930 cash from customers on account, after discounts of $70 had been deducted.

38							38
39	25	Cash	11	6 9 3 0 00			39
40		Sales Discount	43	7 0 00			40
41		Accounts Receivable	12		7 0 0 0 00		41

June 28. Paid $1,400 for electricity and telephone charges for the month.

				DEBIT	CREDIT	
42						42
43	28	Utilities Expense	57	1 4 0 0 00		43
44		Cash	11		1 4 0 0 00	44

June 30. Paid $380 for postage and other miscellaneous expenses for the month.

	DATE		DESCRIPTION	POST. REF.	DEBIT	CREDIT	
	1986 June	30	Miscellaneous Expense	59	3 8 0 00		1
2			Cash	11		3 8 0 00	2

Centered title: JOURNAL PAGE 2

June 30. Paid salesperson $600 for two weeks' salary.

				DEBIT	CREDIT	
3						3
4	30	Salary Expense	54	6 0 0 00		4
5		Cash	11		6 0 0 00	5

June 30. Received $11,000 from cash sales for the second half of June.

				DEBIT	CREDIT	
6						6
7	30	Cash	11	11 0 0 0 00		7
8		Sales	41		11 0 0 0 00	8

June 30. Sales on account totaled $14,000 for the second half of June. All sales are made with terms 1/10, n/30.

				DEBIT	CREDIT	
9						9
10	30	Accounts Receivable	12	14 0 0 0 00		10
11		Sales	41		14 0 0 0 00	11

After all entries for the month have been posted, the ledger will appear as shown on pages 63-66. In practice, each account would appear on a separate page in the ledger. Tracing each entry from the journal to the accounts in the ledger will give a clear understanding of the posting process.

The accounts are numbered in accordance with the chart shown on page 56. However, some of the accounts listed in the chart are not shown in the illustrative ledger. The additional accounts will be used later when the work of the accounting period is completed.

ACCOUNT *Cash* ACCOUNT NO. *11*

DATE	ITEM	POST. REF.	DEBIT	CREDIT	BALANCE DEBIT	BALANCE CREDIT
1986 June 1		1	80 000 00		80 000 00	
2		1		3 600 00	76 400 00	
8		1		600 00	75 800 00	
10		1		1 500 00	74 300 00	
14		1		600 00	73 700 00	
15		1	8 000 00		81 700 00	
15		1		29 400 00	52 300 00	
25		1	6 930 00		59 230 00	
28		1		1 400 00	57 830 00	
30		2		380 00	57 450 00	
30		2		600 00	56 850 00	
30		2	11 000 00		67 850 00	

ACCOUNT *Accounts Receivable* ACCOUNT NO. *12*

DATE	ITEM	POST. REF.	DEBIT	CREDIT	BALANCE DEBIT	BALANCE CREDIT
15		1	12 500 00		12 500 00	
19		1		4 000 00	8 500 00	
25		1		7 000 00	1 500 00	
30		2	14 000 00		15 500 00	

ACCOUNT *Store Supplies* ACCOUNT NO. *14*

DATE	ITEM	POST. REF.	DEBIT	CREDIT	BALANCE DEBIT	BALANCE CREDIT
10		1	3 000 00		3 000 00	

ACCOUNT *Prepaid Rent*   ACCOUNT NO. *15*

DATE	ITEM	POST. REF.	DEBIT	CREDIT	BALANCE DEBIT	BALANCE CREDIT
1986 June 2		1	3 600 00		3 600 00	

ACCOUNT *Store Equipment*   ACCOUNT NO. *18*

DATE	ITEM	POST. REF.	DEBIT	CREDIT	BALANCE DEBIT	BALANCE CREDIT
1986 June 3		1	15 000 00		15 000 00	

ACCOUNT *Accounts Payable*   ACCOUNT NO. *21*

DATE	ITEM	POST. REF.	DEBIT	CREDIT	BALANCE DEBIT	BALANCE CREDIT
1986 June 3		1		15 000 00		15 000 00
5		1		30 000 00		45 000 00
10		1		1 500 00		46 500 00
15		1	30 000 00			16 500 00
22		1		15 750 00		32 250 00

ACCOUNT *Capital Stock*   ACCOUNT NO. *31*

DATE	ITEM	POST. REF.	DEBIT	CREDIT	BALANCE DEBIT	BALANCE CREDIT
1986 June 1		1		80 000 00		80 000 00

ACCOUNT *Sales*   ACCOUNT NO. *41*

DATE	ITEM	POST. REF.	DEBIT	CREDIT	BALANCE DEBIT	BALANCE CREDIT
1986 June 15		1		8 000 00		8 000 00
15		1		12 500 00		20 500 00
30		2		11 000 00		31 500 00
30		2		14 000 00		45 500 00

ACCOUNT *Sales Returns and Allowances*   ACCOUNT NO. 42

DATE		ITEM	POST. REF.	DEBIT	CREDIT	BALANCE	
						DEBIT	CREDIT
1986 June	19		1	4 000 00		4 000 00	

ACCOUNT *Sales Discount*   ACCOUNT NO. 43

DATE		ITEM	POST. REF.	DEBIT	CREDIT	BALANCE	
						DEBIT	CREDIT
1986 June	25		1	7 0 00		7 0 00	

ACCOUNT *Purchases*   ACCOUNT NO. 51

DATE		ITEM	POST. REF.	DEBIT	CREDIT	BALANCE	
						DEBIT	CREDIT
1986 June	5		1	30 000 00		30 000 00	
	22		1	15 750 00		45 750 00	

ACCOUNT *Purchases Discount*   ACCOUNT NO. 52

DATE		ITEM	POST. REF.	DEBIT	CREDIT	BALANCE	
						DEBIT	CREDIT
1986 June	15		1		6 00 00		6 00 00

ACCOUNT *Advertising Expense*   ACCOUNT NO. 53

DATE		ITEM	POST. REF.	DEBIT	CREDIT	BALANCE	
						DEBIT	CREDIT
1986 June	8		1	6 00 00		6 00 00	

ACCOUNT *Salary Expense*   ACCOUNT NO. 54

DATE		ITEM	POST. REF.	DEBIT	CREDIT	BALANCE	
						DEBIT	CREDIT
1986 June	14		1	6 00 00		6 00 00	
	30		2	6 00 00		1 2 00 00	

ACCOUNT *Utilities Expense*   ACCOUNT NO. *57*

DATE	ITEM	POST. REF.	DEBIT	CREDIT	BALANCE DEBIT	BALANCE CREDIT
1986 June 28		1	1 4 0 0 00		1 4 0 0 00	

ACCOUNT *Miscellaneous Expense*   ACCOUNT NO. *59*

DATE	ITEM	POST. REF.	DEBIT	CREDIT	BALANCE DEBIT	BALANCE CREDIT
1986 June 30		2	3 8 0 00		3 8 0 00	

As discussed in Chapter 1, the equality of debits and credits in the ledger should be verified at the end of each accounting period, if not more often, through preparing a **trial balance**, which is illustrated as follows:

	Taylor Inc. Trial Balance June 30, 1986	
Cash	67 8 5 0 00	
Accounts Receivable	15 5 0 0 00	
Store Supplies	3 0 0 0 00	
Prepaid Rent	3 6 0 0 00	
Store Equipment	15 0 0 0 00	
Accounts Payable		32 2 5 0 00
Capital Stock		80 0 0 0 00
Sales		45 5 0 0 00
Sales Returns and Allowances	4 0 0 0 00	
Sales Discount	7 0 00	
Purchases	45 7 5 0 00	
Purchases Discount		6 0 0 00
Advertising Expense	6 0 0 00	
Salary Expense	1 2 0 0 00	
Utilities Expense	1 4 0 0 00	
Miscellaneous Expense	3 8 0 00	
	158 3 5 0 00	158 3 5 0 00

DISCOVERY OF ERRORS

The existence of errors in the accounts may be determined in various ways: (1) by audit procedures, (2) by chance discovery, or (3) by preparing a trial balance. If the debit and the credit totals of the trial balance are not in agreement, the exact amount of the difference between the totals should be determined before proceeding to search for the error.

The trial balance does not provide complete proof of the accuracy of the ledger. It indicates only that the *debits* and the *credits* are *equal*. This proof is of value, however, because errors frequently affect the equality of debits and credits. If the two totals of a trial balance are not equal, it is probably due to one or more of the following types of errors:

1. Error in preparing the trial balance, such as:
   a. One of the columns of the trial balance was incorrectly added.
   b. The amount of an account balance was incorrectly recorded on the trial balance.
   c. A debit balance was recorded on the trial balance as a credit, or vice versa, or a balance was omitted entirely.
2. Error in determining the account balances, such as:
   a. A balance was incorrectly computed.
   b. A balance was entered in the wrong balance column.
3. Error in recording a transaction in the ledger, such as:
   a. An erroneous amount was posted to the account.
   b. A debit entry was posted as a credit, or vice versa.
   c. A debit or a credit posting was omitted.

Among the types of errors that will not cause an inequality in the trial balance totals are the following:

1. Failure to record a transaction or to post a transaction.
2. Recording the same erroneous amount for both the debit and the credit parts of a transaction.
3. Recording the same transaction more than once.
4. Posting a part of a transaction correctly as a debit or credit but to the wrong account.

The amount of the difference between the two totals of a trial balance sometimes gives a clue as to the nature of the error or where it occurred. For example, a difference of 10, 100, or 1,000 between two totals is frequently the result of an error in addition. A difference between totals can also be due to the omission of a debit or a credit posting or, if it is divisible evenly by 2, to the posting of a debit as a credit, or vice versa. For example, if the debit and the credit totals of a trial balance are $20,640 and $20,236 respectively, the difference of $404 may indicate that a credit posting of that amount was omitted or that a credit of $202 was erroneously posted as a debit.

Two other common types of errors are known as **transpositions** and **slides**. A transposition is the erroneous rearrangement of digits, such as writing $542 as $452 or $524. In a slide, the entire number is erroneously moved one or more spaces to the right or the left, such as writing $542.00 as $54.20 or $5,420.00. If an error of either type has occurred and there are no other errors, the discrepancy between the two trial balance totals will be evenly divisible by 9.

A preliminary examination along the lines suggested by the preceding paragraphs will frequently disclose the error. If it does not, the general procedure is to retrace the various steps in the accounting process, beginning with the last step and working back to the original entries in the journal. While there are no rigid rules for discovering errors, the errors that have caused the trial balance totals to be unequal will ordinarily be discovered before all of the procedures outlined in the following suggested plan have been completed:

1. Verify the accuracy of the trial balance totals by re-adding the columns.
2. Compare the listings in the trial balance with the balances shown in the ledger, making certain that no accounts have been omitted.
3. Recompute the balance of each account in the ledger.
4. Trace the postings in the ledger back to the journal, placing a small check mark by the item in the ledger and also in the journal. If the error is not found, examine each account to see if there is an entry without a check mark. Do the same with the entries in the journal.
5. Verify the equality of the debits and the credits in the journal.

It is readily apparent that care should be exercised both in recording transactions in the journal and in posting to the accounts. The desirability of accuracy in determining account balances and reporting them on the trial balance is equally obvious.

Self-Examination Questions
(Answers at end of chapter.)

1. If merchandise sold on account is returned, the purchaser may inform the seller of the details by issuing a:
   A. debit memorandum
   B. credit memorandum
   C. invoice
   D. bill

2. If merchandise is sold on account to a customer for $1,000, terms FOB shipping point, 1/10, n/30 and the seller prepays $50 in transportation costs, the amount of the discount for early payment would be:
   A. $0
   B. $5.00
   C. $10.00
   D. $10.50

3. Merchandise is sold on account to a customer for $1,000, terms FOB destination, 1/10, n/30. If the seller pays $50 in transportation costs and the customer returns $100 of the merchandise prior to payment, what is the amount of the discount for early payment?
   A. $0
   B. $9.00
   C. $10.00
   D. $10.50

4. The current asset category would include:
   A. cash
   B. accounts receivable
   C. merchandise inventory
   D. all of the above

5. The plant asset category would include:
   A. merchandise inventory
   B. accounts payable
   C. equipment
   D. all of the above

2–1. Rearrange the following in proper sequence: (a) entry recorded in journal, (b) business document prepared, (c) entry posted to ledger, (d) business transaction occurs.

2–2. What makes the activities in accounting for merchandising enterprises different from those of service enterprises?

2–3. What account in the ledger of a merchandising enterprise is used to identify the purchase of merchandise?

2–4. What is the meaning of (a) 1/10, n/30; (b) n/30; (c) n/eom?

2–5. What is the term applied to discounts for early payment by (a) the purchaser, (b) the seller?

2–6. The debits and credits from three related transactions are presented in the following T accounts. (a) Describe each transaction. (b) What is the rate of the discount and on what amount was it computed?

Discussion
Questions

Cash			Accounts Payable			
	(3)	8,415	(2)	500	(1)	9,000
			(3)	8,500		

Purchases			Purchases Discount		
(1)	9,000	(2)	500	(3)	85

2–7. After the amount due on a sale of $1,000, terms 1/10, n/30, is received from a customer within the discount period, the seller consents to the return of the entire shipment. (a) What is the amount of the refund owed to the customer? (b) What accounts should be debited and credited to record the return and the refund?

2–8. When merchandise is returned or a price adjustment is requested, what forms are issued by (a) the purchaser in communicating with the seller and (b) the seller in communicating with the purchaser?

2–9. What accounts are debited and credited to record sales to customers who use (a) bank credit cards and (b) nonbank credit cards?

2–10. In what account are discounts taken for early payment of an invoice recorded by (a) the seller and (b) the purchaser?

2–11. Who bears the transportation costs when the terms of sale are (a) FOB shipping point, (b) FOB destination?

2–12. A retailer is considering the purchase of 5 units of a specific commodity from either of two suppliers. Their offers are as follows:

A: $100 a unit, total of $500, 1/10, n/30, no charge for transportation.

B: $90 a unit, total of $450, 2/10, n/30, plus transportation costs of $65.

Which of the two offers, A or B, yields the lower price?

2–13. Merchandise is sold on account to a customer for $5,000, terms FOB shipping point, 1/10, n/30, the seller paying the transportation costs of $100. Determine the following: (a) amount of the sale, (b) amount debited to Accounts Receivable, (c) amount of the discount for early payment, (d) amount of the remittance due within the discount period.

2–14. A sale of merchandise on account for $500 is subject to a 5% sales tax. (a) Should the sales tax be recorded at the time of sale or when payment is received? (b) What is the amount of the sale? (c) What is the amount debited to Accounts Receivable? (d) What is the title of the account to which the $25 is credited?

2–15. Describe the nature of the assets that compose the following categories: (a) current assets, (b) plant assets.

2–16. As of the time a balance sheet is being prepared, a business enterprise owes a mortgage note payable of $60,000, the terms of which provide for monthly payments of $1,200. How should the liability be classified on the balance sheet?

2–17. Bruce Evans Company adheres to a policy of depositing all cash receipts in a bank account and making all payments by check. The cash account as of March 31 has a credit balance of $400 and there is no undeposited cash on hand. (a) Assuming that there were no errors in journalizing or posting, what is the explanation of this unusual balance? (b) Is the $400 credit balance in the cash account an asset, a liability, owner's equity, a revenue, or an expense?

2–18. Describe the three procedures required to post the credit portion of the following journal entry. (Sales is account No. 41.)

		JOURNAL			PAGE 18
19--					
May	20	Accounts Receivable	12	1,150	
		Sales			1,150

2–19. (a) Describe the trial balance. (b) What proof is provided by a trial balance?

2–20. When a trial balance is prepared, an account balance of $28,500 is listed as $25,800, and an account balance of $6,400 is listed as $640. Identify the transposition and the slide.

2–21. When a purchase of supplies of $278 for cash was recorded, both the debit and the credit were journalized and posted as $287. (a) Would this error cause the trial balance to be out of balance? (b) Would the answer be the same if the $278 entry had been journalized correctly, the debit to Supplies had been posted correctly, but the credit to Cash had been posted as $287?

2–22. Indicate which of the following errors, each considered individually, would cause the trial balance totals to be unequal:

(a) A payment of $12,000 for equipment purchased was posted as a debit of $21,000 to Equipment and a credit of $12,000 to Cash.

(b) A dividend of $1,200 was journalized and posted as a debit of $120 to Salary Expense and a credit of $120 to Cash.

(c) A fee of $600 earned and due from a client was not debited to Accounts Receivable or credited to a revenue account because the cash had not been received.

(d) A receipt of $275 from an account receivable was journalized and posted as a debit of $275 to Cash and a credit of $275 to Sales.

(e) A payment of $950 to a creditor was posted as a credit of $950 to Accounts Payable and a credit of $950 to Cash.

2-23. Determine the amount to be paid in full settlement of each of the following invoices, assuming that credit for returns and allowances was received prior to payment and that all invoices were paid within the discount period.

Exercises

	Purchase Invoice		Terms	Returns and Allowances
	Merchandise	**Transportation**		
(a)	$2,500	—	FOB shipping point, 1/10, n/30	—
(b)	5,000	$80	FOB shipping point, 2/10, n/30	$400
(c)	1,000	—	FOB destination, n/30	100
(d)	1,750	—	FOB destination, 2/10, n/30	50
(e)	2,400	50	FOB shipping point, 1/10, n/30	200

2-24. Hume Co. purchases merchandise from a supplier on account, $3,000, terms FOB shipping point, 2/10, n/30. The supplier adds transportation charges of $40 to the invoice. Hume Co. returns some of the merchandise, receiving a credit memorandum for $200, and then pays the amount due within the discount period. Present Hume Co.'s entries to record (a) the purchase, (b) the merchandise return, and (c) the payment. (Hume Co. records merchandise purchases returns and allowances in the purchases account.)

2-25. Present entries for the following related transactions:

June 10. Sold merchandise to a customer for $5,000, terms FOB shipping point, 1/10, n/30.

10. Paid the transportation charges of $70, debiting the amount to Accounts Receivable.

15. Issued a credit memorandum for $200 to the customer for merchandise returned.

20. Received a check for the amount due from the sale.

2-26. Evans Corp. sells merchandise to Park Co. on account, list price $3,500, FOB shipping point, 2/10, n/30. Evans Corp. pays the transportation charges of $100 as an accommodation and adds it to the invoice. Evans Corp. issues a credit memorandum for $150 for merchandise returned and subsequently receives the amount due within the discount period. Present Evans Corp.'s entries to record (a) the sale and the transportation costs, (b) the credit memorandum, and (c) the receipt of the check for the amount due.

2-27. Present entries for the following related transactions of F. Barker and Son. Record merchandise purchases returns and allowances in the purchases account.

(a) Purchased $2,000 of merchandise from Carr Co. on account, terms 2/10, n/30.

(b) Paid the amount owed on the invoice within the discount period.

(c) Discovered that some of the merchandise was defective and returned items with an invoice price of $500, receiving credit.

(d) Purchased an additional $300 of fabrics from Carr Co. on account, terms 2/10, n/30.

(e) Received a check for the balance owed from the return in (c), after deducting for the purchase in (d).

2–28. Norman Services Co. is a newly organized enterprise. The list of asset, liability, owner's equity, revenue, and expense accounts to be opened in the general ledger is as follows:

Miscellaneous Expense	Accounts Receivable
Retained Earnings	Salary Expense
Sales	Equipment
Accumulated Depreciation	Cash
Rent Expense	Salaries Payable
Supplies	Supplies Expense
Prepaid Rent	Merchandise Inventory
Capital Stock	Accounts Payable
	Depreciation Expense

List the accounts in the order in which they should appear in the ledger of Norman Services Co. and assign account numbers. Each account number is to have two digits: the first digit is to indicate the major classification ("1" for assets, etc.) and the second digit is to identify the specific account within each major classification ("11" for Cash, etc.).

2–29. The following preliminary trial balance of Hudson Company Inc. does not balance. When the ledger and other records are reviewed, you discover the following: (1) the debits and credits in the cash account total $68,600 and $52,140 respectively; (2) a receipt of $600 from a customer on account was not posted to the accounts receivable account; (3) a payment of $1,100 to a creditor on account was not posted to the accounts payable account; (4) the balance of the equipment account is $41,200; (5) each account had a normal balance. Prepare a corrected trial balance.

Hudson Company
Trial Balance
August 31, 19--

Cash.........................	68,600	
Accounts Receivable	14,900	
Prepaid Insurance...............		300
Equipment......................	42,100	
Accounts Payable		8,300
Salaries Payable................	900	
Capital Stock...................		30,000
Retained Earnings..............		21,100
Dividends......................		4,000
Service Revenue		26,900
Salary Expense.................	8,400	
Advertising Expense............	1,200	
Miscellaneous Expense		240
	136,100	90,840

2–30. The following errors occurred in posting from a two-column journal:

(1) A credit of $120 to Accounts Payable was posted as a debit.
(2) An entry debiting Advertising Expense and crediting Cash for $250 was not posted.
(3) A debit of $1,500 to Equipment was posted twice.
(4) A debit of $200 to Cash was posted as $2,000.
(5) A debit of $180 to Supplies was posted as $810.
(6) A debit of $350 to Accounts Receivable was not posted.
(7) A credit of $400 to Sales was posted to Cash.

Considering each case individually (i.e., assuming that no other errors had occurred), indicate: (a) by "yes" or "no" whether the trial balance would be out of balance; (b) if answer to (a) is "yes," the amount by which the trial balance totals would differ and (c) the column of the trial balance that would have the larger total. Answers should be presented in the following form (error (1) is given as an example):

Error	(a) Out of Balance	(b) Difference	(c) Larger Total
(1)	yes	$240	debit

2–31. The following selected transactions were completed during May between Maxwell Company and Thaxton Inc.:

May 2. Maxwell Company sold merchandise on account to Thaxton Inc., $8,200, terms FOB shipping point, 2/10, n/30. Maxwell Company prepaid transportation costs of $300, which was added to the invoice.

6. Maxwell Company sold merchandise on account to Thaxton Inc., $12,500, terms FOB destination, 1/15, n/eom.

6. Maxwell Company paid transportation costs of $500 for delivery of the merchandise sold to Thaxton Inc. on May 6.

9. Thaxton Inc. returned merchandise purchased on account on May 6 from Maxwell Company, $2,500.

12. Thaxton Inc. paid Maxwell Company on account for purchases of May 2, less discount.

21. Thaxton Inc. paid Maxwell Company on account for purchases of May 6, less return and less discount.

23. Maxwell Company sold merchandise on account to Thaxton Inc., $5,000, terms FOB destination, n/eom.

26. Thaxton Inc. paid transportation charges of $350 on the May 23 purchase from Maxwell Company. Maxwell was not notified of this transaction until May 31.

31. Thaxton Inc. paid Maxwell Company on account for the purchase of May 23, less transportation charges paid on May 26.

Problems

Instructions:

Journalize the transactions for May for (1) Maxwell Company and (2) Thaxton Inc.

2–32. The following were selected from among the transactions completed by Miller Co. during June of the current year:

June 2. Purchased merchandise on account from Eastwood Co., $5,500, terms FOB destination, 2/10, n/30.
    3. Purchased office supplies for cash, $475.
    6. Purchased merchandise on account from Plymouth Co., $2,200, terms FOB shipping point, 1/10, n/30, with prepaid transportation costs of $70 added to the invoice.
    7. Returned merchandise purchased on June 2 from Eastwood Co., $500.
  10. Sold merchandise for cash, $3,625.
  11. Paid Eastwood Co. on account for purchases of June 2, less returns of June 7 and discount.
  15. Sold merchandise on nonbank credit cards and reported accounts to the card company, $1,950.
  15. Paid Plymouth Co., on account for purchases of June 6, less discount.
  19. Sold merchandise on account to Joan Downs Co., $900, terms 1/10, n/30.
  20. Sold merchandise on account to Bowen and Son, $1,500, terms 1/10, n/30.
  23. Received cash from card company for nonbank credit card sales of June 15, less $117 service fee.
  28. Received cash on account from sale of June 19 to Joan Downs Co., less discount.
  29. Purchased merchandise for cash, $600.
  30. Received merchandise returned by Bowen and Son from sale of June 20, $1,500.

Instructions:

Journalize the transactions.

2–33. The account balances at January 1 of the current year for Spur Inc. are as follows:

11	Cash	$18,575
12	Accounts Receivable	26,900
13	Merchandise Inventory	40,100
14	Prepaid Insurance	1,250
15	Store Supplies	900
21	Accounts Payable	12,500
31	Capital Stock	50,000
32	Retained Earnings	25,225
33	Dividends	—
41	Sales	—
42	Sales Returns and Allowances	—
43	Sales Discount	—
51	Purchases	—
52	Purchases Discount	—
53	Sales Salaries Expense	—
54	Advertising Expense	—
55	Store Supplies Expense	—
56	Miscellaneous Selling Expense	—
57	Office Salaries Expense	—
58	Rent Expense	—

59 Insurance Expense . . . .   —
60 Miscellaneous General Expense . . . .   —

The following transactions were completed during January of the current year:

Jan. 2. Paid rent for month, $3,000.
      3. Purchased merchandise on account, $9,900.
      4. Received $9,405 cash from customers on account after discounts of $95 were deducted.
      5. Paid creditors $12,250 on account after discounts of $250 had been deducted.
      6. Sold merchandise for cash, $7,500.
      9. Purchased merchandise on account, $11,600.
    10. Sold merchandise on account, $14,200.
    11. Returned merchandise purchased on account on January 9, $600.
    13. Received merchandise returned on account, $500.
    16. Paid sales salaries of $2,100 and office salaries of $1,400.
    18. Paid creditors $10,780 on account after discounts of $220 had been deducted.
    19. Received $14,058 cash from customers on account after discounts of $142 had been deducted.
    20. Sold merchandise for cash, $4,100.
    23. Sold merchandise on account, $11,750.
    27. Refunded $100 cash on sales made for cash.
    29. Paid advertising expense, $1,250.
    30. Sold merchandise for cash, $3,900.
    30. Purchased merchandise on account, $8,800.
    31. Paid sales salaries of $1,970 and office salaries of $1,400.
    31. Paid creditors $9,900 on account, no discount.
    31. Received $16,900 cash from customers on account, no discount.

Instructions:
(1) Open a ledger of standard accounts for the accounts listed. Record the balances in the appropriate balance column as of January 1, write "Balance" in the item section, and place a check mark (✔) in the posting reference column.
(2) Record the transactions for January in a journal.
(3) Post to the ledger, extending the month-end balances to the appropriate balance columns after all posting is completed.
(4) Prepare a trial balance of the ledger as of January 31.

2–34. The following records of Wiley TV Service Inc. are presented in the working papers:

    Journal containing entries for the period October 1–31.
    Ledger to which the October entries have been posted.
    Preliminary trial balance as of October 31, which does not balance.

    Locate the errors, supply the information requested, and prepare a corrected trial balance, proceeding in accordance with the following detailed instructions. The balances recorded in the accounts as of October 1 and the entries in the journal are correctly stated. If it is necessary to correct any posted amounts in the ledger, a line should be drawn through the erroneous figure and the correct amount inserted above. Corrections or notations may be inserted on the preliminary trial balance in any manner desired. It is

(If the working papers correlating with the textbook are not used, omit Problem 2-34.)

not necessary to complete all of the instructions if equal trial balance totals can be obtained earlier. However, the requirements of instructions (8) and (9) should be completed in any event.

Instructions:

(1) Verify the totals of the preliminary trial balance, inserting the correct amounts in the schedule provided in the working papers.
(2) Compute the difference between the trial balance totals.
(3) Determine whether the difference obtained in (2) is evenly divisible by 9.
(4) If the difference obtained in (2) is an even number, determine half the amount.
(5) Compare the listings in the trial balance with the balances appearing in the ledger.
(6) Verify the accuracy of the balances of each account in the ledger.
(7) Trace the postings in the ledger back to the journal, using small check marks to identify items traced. (Correct any amounts in the ledger that may be necessitated by errors in posting.)
(8) Journalize as of October 31 the purchase of an adjacent piece of land at a cost of $11,000, for which a note payable was given. The transaction had occurred on October 31 but was inadvertently omitted from the journal. Post to the ledger. (Revise any amounts necessitated by posting this entry.)
(9) Prepare a new trial balance.

2–35. The following trial balance for Church Carpet Inc., as of September 30 of the current year, does not balance because of a number of errors:

Cash	3,752	
Accounts Receivable	5,683	
Merchandise Inventory.............	25,000	
Supplies	1,457	
Prepaid Insurance.................	100	
Equipment	14,600	
Notes Payable....................		13,000
Accounts Payable.................		2,960
Capital Stock....................		20,000
Retained Earnings		15,042
Dividends	3,500	
Sales..........................		38,200
Wages Expense	21,400	
Rent Expense	4,500	
Advertising Expense..............	200	
Gas, Electricity, and Water Expense..	900	
	81,092	89,202

(a) The balance of cash was overstated by $1,000.
(b) A cash receipt of $210 was posted as a debit to Cash of $120.
(c) A debit of $2,000 for a dividend was posted as a credit to the retained earnings account.
(d) The balance of $1,200 in Advertising Expense was entered as $200 in the trial balance.
(e) A debit of $450 to Accounts Receivable was not posted.

(f) A return of $310 of defective supplies was erroneously posted as a $130 credit to Supplies.

(g) The balance of Notes Payable was overstated by $3,000.

(h) An insurance policy acquired at a cost of $200 was posted as a credit to Prepaid Insurance.

(i) Miscellaneous Expense, with a balance of $1,060, was omitted from the trial balance.

(j) A credit of $710 in Accounts Payable was overlooked when determining the balance of the account.

Instructions:

Prepare a corrected trial balance as of September 30 of the current year.

2–31A. The following selected transactions were completed during October between Oconee Enterprises and Blair Inc.:

Alternate Problems

Oct. 3. Oconee Enterprises sold merchandise on account to Blair Inc., $12,300, terms FOB shipping point, 1/10, n/30. Oconee Enterprises prepaid transportation costs of $450, which was added to the invoice.

5. Oconee Enterprises sold merchandise on account to Blair Inc., $18,000, terms FOB destination, 2/15, n/eom.

5. Oconee Enterprises paid transportation costs of $800 for delivery of the merchandise sold to Blair Inc. on October 5.

8. Blair Inc. returned merchandise purchased on account on October 5 from Oconee Enterprises, $4,000.

13. Blair Inc. paid Oconee Enterprises on account for purchases of October 3, less discount.

20. Blair Inc. paid Oconee Enterprises on account for purchases of October 5, less return and less discount.

24. Oconee Enterprises sold merchandise on account to Blair Inc., $8,000, terms FOB destination, n/eom.

27. Blair Inc. paid transportation charges of $400 on the October 24 purchase from Oconee Enterprises. Oconee was not notified of this transaction until October 31.

31. Blair Inc. paid Oconee Enterprises on account for the purchase of October 24, less transportation charges paid on October 27.

Instructions:

Journalize the transactions for October for (1) Oconee Enterprises and (2) Blair Inc.

2–32A. The following were selected from among the transactions completed by Perez Company during July of the current year:

July 1. Purchased merchandise for cash, $3,500.

3. Purchased merchandise on account from Wei Co., $7,500, terms FOB destination, 1/10, n/30.

5. Returned merchandise purchased on July 3 from Wei Co., $1,500.

6. Sold merchandise on account to J. W. Valdez Co., $4,000, terms 2/10, n/30.

9. Purchased office supplies for cash, $170.

12. Purchased merchandise on account from A. C. Simon, Inc., $3,500, terms FOB shipping point, 1/10, n/30, with prepaid transportation costs of $65 added to the invoice.
12. Paid Wei Co. on account for purchases of July 3, less returns of July 5 and discount.
15. Received cash on account from sale of July 6 to J. W. Valdez Co., less discount.
17. Sold merchandise on nonbank credit cards and reported accounts to the card company, $1,625.
20. Sold merchandise on account to Alice Block and Co., $1,400, terms 2/10, n/30.
21. Paid A. C. Simon, Inc. on account for purchases of July 12, less discount.
24. Received cash from card company for nonbank credit card sales of July 17, less $96 service fee.
26. Sold merchandise for cash, $2,150.
28. Received merchandise returned by Alice Block and Co. from sale of July 20, $175.

Instructions:

Journalize the transactions.

(If the working papers correlating with the textbook are not used, omit Problem 2-34A.)

2–34A. The following records of Wiley TV Service Inc. are presented in the working papers:

Journal containing entries for the period October 1–31.
Ledger to which the October entries have been posted.
Preliminary trial balance as of October 31, which does not balance.

Locate the errors, supply the information requested, and prepare a corrected trial balance, proceeding in accordance with the following detailed instructions. The balances recorded in the accounts as of October 1 and the entries in the journal are correctly stated. If it is necessary to correct any posted amounts in the ledger, a line should be drawn through the erroneous figure and the correct amount inserted above. Corrections or notations may be inserted on the preliminary trial balance in any manner desired. It is not necessary to complete all of the instructions if equal trial balance totals can be obtained earlier. However, the requirements of instructions (8) and (9) should be completed in any event.

Instructions:

(1) Verify the totals of the preliminary trial balance, inserting the correct amounts in the schedule provided in the working papers.
(2) Compute the difference between the trial balance totals.
(3) Determine whether the difference obtained in (2) is evenly divisible by 9.
(4) If the difference obtained in (2) is an even number, determine half the amount.
(5) Compare the listings in the trial balance with the balances appearing in the ledger.
(6) Verify the accuracy of the balances of each account in the ledger.
(7) Trace the postings in the ledger back to the journal, using small check marks to identify items traced. (Correct any amounts in the ledger that may be necessitated by errors in posting.)
(8) Journalize as of October 31 the payment of $112 for gas and electricity. The bill had been paid on October 31 but was inadvertently omitted from the journal. Post to the ledger. (Revise any amounts necessitated by posting this entry.)
(9) Prepare a new trial balance.

2-35A. The following trial balance for Winder Inc., as of March 31 of the current year, does not balance because of a number of errors:

Cash.............................	1,260	
Accounts Receivable...............	13,920	
Merchandise Inventory	30,000	
Supplies.........................	1,012	
Prepaid Insurance	50	
Equipment	9,950	
Notes Payable.....................		3,600
Accounts Payable..................		2,252
Capital Stock.....................		30,000
Retained Earnings		18,760
Dividends........................	2,250	
Sales............................		24,650
Wages Expense...................	13,800	
Rent Expense.....................	1,500	
Advertising Expense	138	
Gas, Electricity, and Water Expense ..	980	
	74,860	79,262

(a) The balance of cash was understated by $650.
(b) A cash receipt of $810 was posted as a debit to Cash of $180.
(c) A debit of $250 to Accounts Receivable was not posted.
(d) A return of $123 of defective supplies was erroneously posted as a $231 credit to Supplies.
(e) An insurance policy acquired at a cost of $400 was posted as a credit to Prepaid Insurance.
(f) The balance of Notes Payable was understated by $1,200.
(g) A credit of $58 in Accounts Payable was overlooked when the balance of the account was determined.
(h) A debit of $750 for a dividend was posted as a credit to the retained earnings account.
(i) The balance of $1,380 in Advertising Expense was entered as $138 in the trial balance.
(j) Miscellaneous Expense, with a balance of $480, was omitted from the trial balance.

Instructions:

Prepare a corrected trial balance as of March 31 of the current year.

2-36. Your mother, who owns and operates Classic Store Inc., recently asked your advice on which of three suppliers to use for the purchase of a specific commodity. The offers of the suppliers are as follows:

Mini-Case

Supplier X: $85 per unit; n/eom; FOB shipping point
Supplier Y: $90 per unit; 4/10, n/30; FOB shipping point
Supplier Z: $88 per unit; 2/10, n/30; FOB destination

The average transportation charges from each supplier to Classic Store Inc.'s warehouse are as follows:

Supplier X: $2.00 per unit
Supplier Y: 1.20
Supplier Z: 1.50

Instructions:

(1) Determine the net cost per unit for each supplier, assuming that all available discounts are taken.

(2) Based upon net cost per unit, which supplier would you recommend to Classic Store Inc.?

(3) What additional considerations other than net cost per unit might influence the selection of a supplier?

(4) Assuming that Supplier Z is chosen, what is the maximum interest rate at which Classic Store Inc. would be willing to borrow funds in order to pay Supplier Z's invoices within the discount period?

Answers to Self-Examination Questions

1. **A** A debit memorandum (answer A) is issued by the purchaser to indicate the amount the purchaser proposes to debit to the accounts payable account. A credit memorandum (answer B) is issued by the seller to indicate the amount the seller proposes to credit to the accounts receivable account. An invoice (answer C) or a bill (answer D) is issued by the seller to indicate the amount and terms of a sale.

2. **C** The amount of discount for early payment is $10 (answer C), or 1% of $1,000. Although the $50 of transportation costs paid by the seller are debited to the customer's account, the customer is not entitled to a discount on that amount.

3. **B** The customer is entitled to a discount of $9 (answer B) for early payment. This amount is 1% of $900, which is the sales price of $1,000 less the return of $100. The $50 of transportation costs is an expense of the seller.

4. **D** The current asset category includes cash and other assets that may reasonably be expected to be realized in cash or sold or consumed usually within a year or less and therefore would include cash (answer A), accounts receivable (answer B), and merchandise inventory (answer C).

5. **C** Tangible assets that are used in the business and that are of a permanent or relatively fixed nature, such as equipment (answer C) are called plant assets. Merchandise inventory (answer A) is a current asset, and accounts payable (answer B) is a current liability.

CHAPTER 3

The Matching Concept and the Adjusting Process

CHAPTER OBJECTIVES

Discuss the matching concept as it relates to the cash basis and the accrual basis of accounting.

Describe and illustrate the need for adjusting the accounting records to comply with the matching concept.

Describe the nature of the adjusting process.

Describe and illustrate the preparation of adjusting entries related to:
> *plant assets*
> *prepaid expenses*
> *unearned revenues*
> *accrued assets*
> *accrued liabilities*
> *merchandise inventory*

As was demonstrated in the preceding chapters, transactions are recorded during an accounting period as they occur. At the end of the period, the ledger accounts must be brought up-to-date (adjusted) to assure that revenues and expenses are properly matched (matching concept), so that the financial statements will fairly present the results of operations for the period and the financial condition at the end of the period. In addition to further discussing the matching concept, which was discussed briefly in Chapter 1, this chapter discusses and illustrates the use of the adjusting process to achieve the proper matching of revenues and expenses. In Chapter 4, the preparation of the financial statements will be addressed.

FISCAL YEAR

The maximum length of an accounting period is usually one year, which includes a complete cycle of the seasons and of business activities. Income and property taxes are also based on yearly periods and thus require that annual determinations be made.

The annual accounting period adopted by an enterprise is known as its **fiscal year**. Fiscal years ordinarily begin with the first day of the particular month selected and end on the last day of the twelfth month hence. The period most commonly adopted is the calendar year, but other periods are not unusual, particularly for incorporated businesses.

A period ending when a business's activities have reached the lowest point in its annual operating cycle is termed the **natural business year**.

The long-term financial history of a business enterprise may be shown by a succession of balance sheets, prepared every year. The history of operations for the intervening periods is presented in a series of income statements. If the life of a business enterprise is represented by a line moving from left to right, a series of balance sheets and income statements may be diagrammed as follows:

THE LIFE OF A BUSINESS

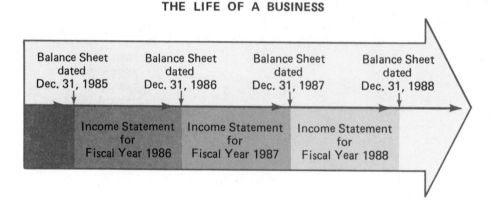

MATCHING CONCEPT

Revenues and expenses may be reported on the income statement by (1) the **cash basis** or (2) the **accrual basis** of accounting. When the cash basis is used, revenues are recognized in the period in which cash is received, and expenses are recognized in the period in which cash is paid. For example, sales would be recorded only when cash is received from customers, and salaries expense would be recorded only when cash is paid to employees. The net income (or net loss) is the difference between the cash receipts (revenues) and the cash disbursements (expenses). Small service enterprises and practicing professionals that have few receivables and payables may use the cash basis. For most businesses, however, the cash basis does not measure revenues and expenses accurately enough to be considered an acceptable method.

Generally accepted accounting principles require the use of the accrual basis of accounting. Therefore, most enterprises use this basis, under which revenues are recognized in the period earned and expenses are recognized in the period incurred in the process of generating revenues, as discussed in Chapter 1. For example, sales would be recognized when the merchandise is sold to customers and not when the cash is received from those customers. Supplies expense would be recognized when the supplies are used and not when the supplies are purchased.

The accrual basis of accounting requires the use of an adjusting process at the end of the accounting period in order to match revenues and expenses for the period properly. The common characteristics of the adjusting process are discussed in the remainder of the chapter.

NATURE OF THE ADJUSTING PROCESS

The entries required at the end of an accounting period to bring the accounts up to date and to assure the proper matching of revenues and expenses are called **adjusting entries.** In a broad sense, they may be called corrections to the ledger. But bringing the ledger up to date at the end of a period is part of the accounting procedure; it is not caused by errors. The term "adjusting entries" is therefore more appropriate than the term "correcting entries."

The following ledger accounts require adjustment: plant assets, prepaid expenses, unearned revenues, accrued assets, accrued liabilities, and merchandise inventory. The entries that adjust these accounts affect both the balance sheet and the income statement. To illustrate, assume that the effect of the credit portion of a particular adjusting entry is to increase a liability account (balance sheet). It follows that the effect of the debit portion of the entry will be either (1) to increase an expense account (income statement) or (2) to decrease a revenue account (income statement). In no case will an adjustment affect only an asset and a liability (both balance sheet) or only an expense and a revenue (both income statement).

PLANT ASSETS

As time passes, many plant assets, such as buildings, lose their capacity to provide useful services. This decrease in usefulness is a business expense called **depreciation.** The factors involved in computing depreciation are discussed in a later chapter.

The adjusting entry to record depreciation must recognize the expense as well as the decrease in the plant assets. However, for reasons to be described in a later chapter, it is not practical to reduce plant asset accounts by the amount estimated as depreciation. In addition, it is common practice to show on the balance sheet both the original cost of plant assets and the amount of depreciation accumulated since their acquisition. Accordingly, the costs of plant assets are recorded as debits to the appropriate asset accounts, and the decreases in usefulness are recorded as credits to the related **accumulated depreciation accounts.** The latter are called **contra accounts** because they are offset against the plant asset accounts. The unexpired or remaining cost of a plant asset is the debit balance in the plant asset account minus the credit balance in the related accumulated depreciation account.

Typical titles for plant asset accounts and their related contra asset accounts are as follows:

Plant Asset	Contra Asset
Land	*None—land does not usually depreciate*
Buildings	Accumulated Depreciation—Buildings
Equipment	Accumulated Depreciation—Equipment

The ledger could show more detail by having a separate account for each of a number of buildings. Equipment may also be subdivided according to function, such as Delivery Equipment, Store Equipment, and Office Equipment, with a related accumulated depreciation account for each plant asset account.

To illustrate an adjusting entry to record depreciation, assume that a building was purchased on January 2, 1986. If the estimated amount of depreciation for 1986 is $2,250, the adjusting entry to record the $2,250 decrease in the asset and the corresponding increase in the expense is as follows:

Adjusting Entry

Dec. 31	Depreciation Expense—Buildings............	2,250	
	Accumulated Depreciation—Buildings......		2,250

After the entry has been posted, the accounts affected appear as follows:

ADJUSTMENT FOR
DEPRECIATION

ACCOUNT BUILDINGS   ACCOUNT NO. 131

Date		Item	Debit	Credit	Balance Debit	Balance Credit
1986 Jan.	2		90,000.00		90,000.00	

ACCOUNT DEPRECIATION EXPENSE—BUILDINGS   ACCOUNT NO. 522

Date		Item	Debit	Credit	Balance Debit	Balance Credit
1986 Dec.	31	Adjusting	2,250.00		2,250.00	

ACCOUNT ACCUMULATED DEPRECIATION—BUILDINGS   ACCOUNT NO. 132

Date		Item	Debit	Credit	Balance Debit	Balance Credit
1986 Dec.	31	Adjusting		2,250.00		2,250.00

The difference between the balance of a plant asset account and its related accumulated depreciation account is called the **book value** of the asset, which may be presented on the balance sheet in the following manner:

Plant assets:
Buildings $90,000
       Less accumulated depreciation 2,250 $87,750

A plant asset's book value represents the undepreciated original cost of the asset. This book value would generally differ from the asset's current market value.

PREPAID EXPENSES

Prepaid expenses are the costs of goods and services that have been purchased but not used at the end of the accounting period. The portion of the asset that has been used during the period has become an expense. Since the remainder will not become an expense until some time in the near future, it will be listed as a current asset on the balance sheet. Prepaid expenses include such items as prepaid insurance, prepaid rent, prepaid advertising, prepaid interest, and various kinds of supplies.

At the time an expense is prepaid, it may be debited either to an asset account or to an expense account. The two alternative systems are explained and illustrated in the paragraphs that follow. In any particular situation, either alternative may be elected. The only difference between the systems is in the procedure used. Their effect on the financial statements is the same.

Prepaid Expenses Recorded Initially as Assets

Insurance premiums or other services or supplies that are used may be debited to asset accounts when purchased, even though all or a part of them is expected to be consumed during the accounting period. The amount actually used is then determined at the end of the period and the accounts adjusted accordingly.

To illustrate, assume that the prepaid insurance account has a balance of $2,034 at the end of the year. This amount represents the total of premiums on policies purchased during the year. Assume further that $906 of insurance premiums has expired during the year. The adjusting entry to record the $906 decrease of the asset and the corresponding increase in expense is as follows:

Adjusting Entry
Dec. 31   Insurance Expense 906
               Prepaid Insurance 906

After this entry has been posted, the two accounts affected appear as follows:

ACCOUNT INSURANCE EXPENSE   ACCOUNT NO. 716

Date		Item	Debit	Credit	Balance	
					Debit	Credit
1986 Dec.	31	Adjusting	906		906	

ACCOUNT PREPAID INSURANCE   ACCOUNT NO. 118

Date		Item	Debit	Credit	Balance	
					Debit	Credit
1986 Jan.	1		1,250		1,250	
Mar.	18		225		1,475	
Aug.	26		379		1,854	
Nov.	11		180		2,034	
Dec.	31	Adjusting		906	1,128	

After the $906 of expired insurance is transferred to the expense account, the balance of $1,128 in Prepaid Insurance represents the cost of premiums on various policies that apply to future periods. The $906 expense appears on the income statement for the period and the $1,128 asset appears on the balance sheet as of the end of the period as a current asset.

Prepaid Expenses Recorded Initially as Expenses

Instead of being debited to an asset account, prepaid expenses may be debited to an expense account at the time of the expenditure, even though all or a part of the prepayment is expected to be unused at the end of the accounting period. The amount actually unused is then determined at the end of the period and the accounts are adjusted accordingly.

To illustrate this alternative system, assume that the insurance expense account has a balance of $2,034 at the end of the year. This amount represents the total premiums on policies purchased during the year. Assume further that $1,128 of the insurance premiums applies to future periods. The adjusting entry to record the $1,128 decrease of the expense and the corresponding increase in the asset is as follows:

Adjusting Entry

Dec. 31   Prepaid Insurance......................   1,128
                Insurance Expense   1,128

After this entry has been posted, the two accounts affected appear as follows:

ACCOUNT PREPAID INSURANCE				ACCOUNT NO. 118		ADJUSTMENT FOR PREPAID EXPENSE RECORDED AS EXPENSE
Date	Item	Debit	Credit	Balance		
				Debit	Credit	
1986 Dec. 31	Adjusting	1,128		1,128		

ACCOUNT INSURANCE EXPENSE				ACCOUNT NO. 716	
Date	Item	Debit	Credit	Balance	
				Debit	Credit
1986 Jan. 1		1,250		1,250	
Mar. 18		225		1,475	
Aug. 26		379		1,854	
Nov. 11		180		2,034	
Dec. 31	Adjusting		1,128	906	

After the $1,128 of unexpired insurance is transferred to the asset account, the balance of $906 in Insurance Expense represents the cost of premiums on various policies that has expired during the year. The $1,128 asset appears on the balance sheet at the end of the period and the $906 expense appears on the income statement for the period.

Comparison of the Two Systems

Either of the two systems of recording prepaid expenses may be used for all of the prepaid expenses of an enterprise, or one system may be used for some kinds of prepaid expenses and the other system for other kinds. Initial debits to the asset account seem to be logical for prepayments of insurance, which are usually for periods of from one to three years. On the other hand, interest charges on notes payable are usually for short periods. Some charges may be recorded when a note is issued; other charges may be recorded when a note is paid; and few, if any, of the debits for interest may require adjustment at the end of the period. It therefore seems logical to record all interest charges initially by debiting the expense account rather than the asset account.[1]

As was noted earlier, the amounts reported as expenses in the income statement and as assets on the balance sheet will not be affected by the system used. To avoid confusion, the system adopted by an enterprise for each kind of prepaid expense should be followed consistently from year to year.

UNEARNED REVENUES

Revenue received during a particular period may be only partly earned by the end of the period. Items of revenue that are received in advance represent a liability that may be termed **unearned revenue.** The portion of the liability

---

[1]Notes payable and related interest charges are discussed in more detail in Chapter 9.

that is discharged during the period through delivery of goods or services has been earned; the remainder will be earned in the future. For example, magazine publishers usually receive advance payment for subscriptions covering periods ranging from a few months to a number of years. At the end of an accounting period, that portion of the receipts which is related to future periods has not been earned and should, therefore, appear in the balance sheet as a liability.

Other examples of unearned revenue are rent received in advance on property owned, premiums received in advance by an insurance company, tuition received in advance by a school, an annual retainer fee received in advance by an attorney, and amounts received in advance by an advertising firm for advertising services to be rendered in the future.

By accepting advance payment for a good or service, a business commits itself to furnish the good or the service at some future time. At the end of the accounting period, if some portion of the good or the service has been furnished, part of the revenue has been earned. The earned portion appears in the income statement. The unearned portion represents a liability of the business to furnish the good or the service in a future period and is reported in the balance sheet as a liability. As in the case of prepaid expenses, two systems of accounting are explained and illustrated.

Unearned Revenues Recorded Initially as Liabilities

When revenue is received in advance, it may be credited to a liability account. To illustrate, assume that on October 1 a business rents a portion of its building for a period of one year, receiving $7,200 in payment for the entire term of the lease. Assume also that the transaction was originally recorded by a debit to Cash and a credit to the liability account Unearned Rent. On December 31, the end of the fiscal year, one fourth of the amount has been earned and three fourths of the amount remains a liability. The entry to record the revenue and reduce the liability appears as follows:

Adjusting Entry

Dec. 31	Unearned Rent............................		1,800	
	Rent Income			1,800

After this entry has been posted, the unearned rent account and the rent income account appear as follows:

ACCOUNT UNEARNED RENT   **ACCOUNT NO.** 218

ADJUSTMENT FOR
UNEARNED REVENUE
RECORDED AS LIABILITY

Date		Item	Debit	Credit	Balance	
					Debit	Credit
1986						
Oct.	1			7,200		7,200
Dec.	31	Adjusting	1,800			5,400

ACCOUNT RENT INCOME   ACCOUNT NO. 812

Date		Item	Debit	Credit	Balance Debit	Balance Credit
1986 Dec.	31	Adjusting		1,800		1,800

After the amount earned, $1,800, is transferred to Rent Income, the balance of $5,400 remaining in Unearned Rent is a liability to render a service in the future. It appears as a current liability in the balance sheet because the service is to be rendered within the next accounting period. Rent Income is reported in the income statement.

Unearned Revenues Recorded Initially as Revenues

Instead of being credited to a liability account, unearned revenue may be credited to a revenue account as the cash is received. To illustrate this alternative, assume the same facts as in the preceding illustration, except that the transaction was originally recorded on October 1 by a debit to Cash and a credit to Rent Income. On December 31, the end of the fiscal year, three fourths of the balance in Rent Income is still unearned and the remaining one fourth has been earned. The entry to record the transfer to the liability account appears as follows:

Adjusting Entry

Dec. 31   Rent Income   5,400
            Unearned Rent   5,400

After this entry has been posted, the unearned rent account and the rent income account appear as follows:

ACCOUNT UNEARNED RENT   ACCOUNT NO. 218   ADJUSTMENT FOR UNEARNED REVENUE RECORDED AS REVENUE

Date		Item	Debit	Credit	Balance Debit	Balance Credit
1986 Dec.	31	Adjusting		5,400		5,400

ACCOUNT RENT INCOME   ACCOUNT NO. 812

Date		Item	Debit	Credit	Balance Debit	Balance Credit
1986 Oct.	1			7,200		7,200
Dec.	31	Adjusting	5,400			1,800

The unearned rent of $5,400 is listed in the current liability section of the balance sheet, and the rent income of $1,800 is reported in the income statement.

Comparison of the Two Systems

Either of the two systems of recording unearned revenues may be used for all revenues received in advance, or the first system may be used for advance receipts of some kinds of revenue and the second system for other kinds. The results obtained are the same under both systems, but to avoid confusion the system used should be followed consistently from year to year.

ACCRUED ASSETS

Some revenues are earned from day to day during an accounting period but are commonly recorded only as cash is received. An example is interest on notes receivable that is earned daily but is usually recorded only when the interest is received. The amounts of any such accrued but unrecorded revenues at the end of the fiscal period are both an asset and a revenue. The amount of the accrued revenue must be recorded by debiting an asset account and crediting a revenue account. Because of the dual nature of such accruals, they are called **accrued assets** or **accrued revenues.**

To illustrate the adjusting entry for an accrued asset, assume that on December 31, the end of the fiscal year, the fees earned account has a credit balance of $50,500. Assume further that on the same date unbilled services have been performed for a client for $8,050. The entry to record this increase in the amount due from clients and the additional revenue earned is as follows:

Adjusting Entry

Dec. 31   Fees Receivable.   8,050
            Fees Earned   8,050

After this entry has been posted, the fees receivable account and the fees earned account appear as follows:

ADJUSTMENT FOR
ACCRUED ASSET

ACCOUNT FEES RECEIVABLE   ACCOUNT NO. 114

Date		Item	Debit	Credit	Balance	
					Debit	Credit
1986 Dec.	31	Adjusting	8,050		8,050	

ACCOUNT FEES EARNED   ACCOUNT NO. 401

Date		Item	Debit	Credit	Balance	
					Debit	Credit
1986						
Dec.	12			4,750		50,500
	31	Adjusting		8,050		58,550

The accrued fees of $8,050 recorded in Fees Receivable will appear in the balance sheet of December 31 as a current asset. The credit balance of $58,550 in Fees Earned will appear in the income statement for the year ended December 31.

The treatment of accrued fees illustrates the method of handling accrued assets in general. If there are other accrued assets at the end of a fiscal period, separate accounts may be set up. Each of these accounts will be similar to the account with fees receivable. When such items are numerous, a single account entitled Accrued Receivables or Accrued Assets may be used. All accrued assets may then be recorded as debits to this account.

ACCRUED LIABILITIES

Some expenses accrue from day to day but are usually recorded only when they are paid. Examples are salaries paid to employees and interest paid on notes payable. The amounts of such accrued but unpaid items at the end of the fiscal period are both an expense and a liability. It is for this reason that such accruals are called **accrued liabilities** or **accrued expenses**.

To illustrate the adjusting entry for an accrued liability, assume that on December 31, the end of the fiscal year, the salary expense account has a debit balance of $72,800. During the year, salaries have been paid each Friday for the five-day week then ended. For this particular fiscal year, December 31 falls on Wednesday. The records of the business show that the salary accrued for these last three days of the year amounts to $940. The entry to record the additional expense and the liability is as follows:

Adjusting Entry

Dec. 31	Salary Expense..........................	940	
	Salaries Payable........................		940

After the adjusting entry has been posted to the two accounts, they appear as follows:

ACCOUNT SALARIES PAYABLE   ACCOUNT NO. 214

Date		Item	Debit	Credit	Balance	
					Debit	Credit
1986 Dec.	31	Adjusting		940		940

ADJUSTMENT FOR ACCRUED LIABILITY

ACCOUNT SALARIES EXPENSE   ACCOUNT NO. 611

Date		Item	Debit	Credit	Balance	
					Debit	Credit
1986						
Dec.	26		1,425		72,800	
	31	Adjusting	940		73,740	

The accrued salaries of $940 recorded in Salaries Payable will appear in the balance sheet of December 31 as a current liability. The balance of $73,740 now recorded in Salary Expense will appear in the income statement for the year ended December 31.

The discussion of the treatment of accrued salary expense illustrates the method of handling accrued liabilities in general. If, in addition to accrued salaries, there are other accrued liabilities at the end of a fiscal period, separate liability accounts may be set up for each type. When there are many accrued liability items, however, a single account entitled Accrued Payables or Accrued Liabilities may be used. All accrued liabilities may then be recorded as credits to this account instead of to separate accounts.

MERCHANDISE INVENTORY

There are two main systems for accounting for merchandise held for sale: **periodic** and **perpetual**. Most merchandising enterprises use the periodic system. In this system, the revenues from sales are recorded when sales are made, but no attempt is made on the sales date to record the cost of the merchandise sold. It is only by a detailed listing of the merchandise on hand (called a physical inventory) at the end of the accounting period that a determination is made of (1) the cost of the merchandise sold during the period and (2) the cost of the inventory on hand at the end of the period. The periodic method is used in illustrations in this chapter.

Under the perpetual system, both the sales amount and the cost of merchandise sold amount are recorded when each item of merchandise is sold. In this manner, the accounting records continuously (perpetually) disclose the inventory on hand. The perpetual system is discussed in later chapters.

For merchandising enterprises using the periodic system, the cost of merchandise sold and the beginning and ending inventories are reported in the income statement in the following manner:

Cost of merchandise sold:
Merchandise inventory, January 1, 1986	$ 35,000	
Purchases	360,500	
Merchandise available for sale	$395,500	
Less merchandise inventory, December 31, 1986	37,500	
Cost of merchandise sold		$358,000

The best method of making the above data readily available is to maintain a separate account entitled Merchandise Inventory. Throughout an accounting period, this account shows the inventory at the beginning of the period. Purchases of merchandise during the period, including costs for transportation and sales taxes, are then debited to an account entitled Purchases. As explained in Chapter 2, returns and allowances are usually recorded directly in the purchases account, and cash discounts are recorded in a purchases discount account.

At the end of the period, it is necessary to adjust the merchandise inventory account. This adjustment is accomplished by two entries that remove from Merchandise Inventory the amount representing the inventory at the beginning of the period and replace this amount with the inventory at the end of the period. The first entry transfers the beginning inventory to Income Summary, an account that is used during the adjusting process as well as the closing process, which is discussed in Chapter 4. Since this beginning inventory is part of the cost of merchandise sold, it is debited to Income Summary. It is also a subtraction from the asset account, Merchandise Inventory, and hence is credited to that account. The first adjusting entry is as follows:

Adjusting Entry

Dec. 31	Income Summary.........................	35,000	
	Merchandise Inventory		35,000

The second adjusting entry debits the cost of the merchandise inventory at the end of the period to the asset account, Merchandise Inventory. The credit portion of the entry effects a deduction of the unsold merchandise from the total cost of the merchandise available for sale during the period. In terms of the illustration of the partial income statement above, the credit portion of the second entry accomplishes the subtraction of $37,500 from $395,500 to yield the $358,000 cost of merchandise sold. The second adjusting entry is as follows:

Adjusting Entry

Dec. 31	Merchandise Inventory	37,500	
	Income Summary.........................		37,500

The effect of the two inventory adjustments is indicated by the following accounts, Merchandise Inventory and Income Summary:

ACCOUNT MERCHANDISE INVENTORY   ACCOUNT NO. 114

Date		Item	Debit	Credit	Balance	
					Debit	Credit
1985 Dec.	31	Adjusting	35,000.00		35,000.00	
1986 Dec.	31	Adjusting		35,000.00	—	—
	31	Adjusting	37,500.00		37,500.00	

ACCOUNT INCOME SUMMARY   ACCOUNT NO. 313

Date		Item	Debit	Credit	Balance	
					Debit	Credit
1986 Dec.	31	Mer. inv., Jan. 1	35,000.00		35,000.00	
	31	Mer. inv., Dec. 31		37,500.00		2,500.00

In the accounts, the inventory of $35,000 at the end of 1985 (beginning of 1986) has been transferred to Income Summary as a part of the cost of merchandise available for sale. It is replaced by a debit of $37,500, the merchandise inventory at the end of 1986. The credit of $37,500 to Income Summary represents a deduction from the cost of merchandise available for sale. The credit balance of $2,500 in the income summary account represents the net effect of the merchandise inventory adjustments on the cost of merchandise sold for the period. As will be illustrated in Chapter 4, the balance of the purchases account, $360,500, will also be transferred to Income Summary. The sum of the $360,500 debit from the purchases account and the $2,500 credit balance from the merchandise inventory adjustments ($360,500 − $2,500) equals $358,000, the cost of merchandise sold.

Self-Examination Questions (Answers at end of chapter.)

1. If the effect of the debit portion of a specific adjusting entry is to increase an asset account, the effect of the credit portion of the entry would be to:
   A. decrease an asset account
   B. increase a liability account
   C. decrease a liability account
   D. decrease an expense account

2. If the estimated amount of depreciation on equipment for a period is $2,000, the adjusting entry to record depreciation would be:
   A. debit Depreciation Expense, $2,000; credit Equipment, $2,000
   B. debit Equipment, $2,000; credit Depreciation Expense, $2,000
   C. debit Depreciation Expense, $2,000; credit Accumulated Depreciation, $2,000
   D. debit Accumulated Depreciation, $2,000; credit Depreciation Expense, $2,000

3. Purchases of office supplies during the year were $2,910, and inventory at the end of the year was $595. If office supplies are initially recorded as an expense, the adjusting entry at the end of the year would be:
   A. Dr. Office Supplies, $595; Cr. Office Supplies Expense, $595
   B. Dr. Office Supplies, $2,315; Cr. Office Supplies Expense, $2,315
   C. Dr. Office Supplies Expense, $595; Cr. Office Supplies, $595
   D. Dr. Office Supplies Expense, $2,315; Cr. Office Supplies, $2,315

4. Prepaid expenses are listed on the balance sheet under:
   A. current assets
   B. plant assets
   C. current liabilities
   D. long-term liabilities

5. The balance in Unearned Rent at the end of a period represents:
   A. an asset
   B. a liability
   C. a revenue
   D. an expense

3–1. Why are adjusting entries needed at the end of an accounting period?

3–2. If the effect of the debit portion of an adjusting entry is to increase the balance of an asset account, which of the following statements describes the effect of the credit portion of the entry: (a) increases the balance of a liability account? (b) increases the balance of a revenue account? (c) decreases the balance of a capital account?

3–3. Does every adjusting entry have an effect on the determination of the amount of net income for a period? Explain.

3–4. (a) Explain the purpose of the two accounts, Depreciation Expense and Accumulated Depreciation. (b) What is the normal balance of each account? (c) Is it usual for the balances of the two accounts to be equal in amount? (d) In what financial statements, if any, will each account appear?

3–5. What term is applied to the difference between the balance in a plant asset account and its related accumulated depreciation account?

3–6. A purchase of office supplies can be debited to one of two types of accounts. Name the two types of accounts that can be debited.

3–7. From time to time during the fiscal year, an enterprise makes an advance payment of premiums on three-year and one-year property insurance policies. Which of the following types of accounts will be affected by the related adjusting entry at the end of the fiscal year: (1) asset, (2) liability, (3) revenue, (4) expense?

3–8. (a) Will a business enterprise that occasionally places advertisements in the local newspaper, for which it makes advance payments, always have prepaid advertising at the end of each fiscal year? Explain.
   (b) Will a business enterprise almost always have prepaid property and casualty insurance at the end of each fiscal year? Explain.
   (c) Would it be logical to record prepayments of the type referred to in (a) as expenses and prepayments of the type referred to in (b) as assets? Discuss.

3–9. At the end of March, the first month of the fiscal year, the usual adjusting entry transferring supplies used to an expense account is inadvertently omitted. Which items will be incorrectly stated, because of the error, on (a) the income statement for March and (b) the balance sheet as of March 31? Also indicate whether the items in error will be overstated or understated.

3–10. On January 3, an enterprise receives $24,000 from a tenant as rent for the current calendar year. The fiscal year of the enterprise is from September 1 to August 31. (a) Which of the following types of accounts will be affected by the adjusting entry as of August 31: (1) asset, (2) liability, (3) revenue, (4) expense? (b) How much of the $24,000 rent should be reported as revenue for the current fiscal year ending August 31?

3–11. On June 30, the end of its fiscal year, an enterprise owed salaries of $3,100 for an incomplete payroll period. Which of the following types of accounts will be affected by the related adjusting entry: (1) asset, (2) liability, (3) revenue, (4) expense?

3–12. Accrued salaries of $3,860 owed to employees for August 29, 30, and 31 are not taken into consideration in preparing the financial statements for the fiscal year ended August 31. Which items will be erroneously stated, because of the error, on (a) the income statement for the year and (b) the balance sheet as of August 31? Also indicate whether the items in error will be overstated or understated.

3–13. Assume that the error in 3-12 was not corrected and that the $3,860 of accrued salaries was included in the first salary payment in September. Which items will be erroneously stated, because of failure to correct the initial error, on (a) the income statement for the month of September and (b) the balance sheet as of September 30?

3–14. Where would (a) accrued expenses and (b) accrued revenues, both due within a year, appear on the balance sheet?

3–15. Classify the following items as (a) prepaid expense, (b) unearned revenue, (c) accrued expense, or (d) accrued revenue.
    (1) Receipts from sales of meal tickets by a restaurant.
    (2) Property taxes paid in advance.
    (3) A two-year premium paid on a fire insurance policy.
    (4) Life insurance premiums received by an insurance company.
    (5) Utilities owed but not yet paid.
    (6) Fees earned but not yet received.
    (7) Supplies on hand.
    (8) Tuition collected in advance by a university.
    (9) Storage fees earned but not yet received.
    (10) Taxes owed but payable in the following period.
    (11) Salary owed but not yet due.
    (12) Fees received but not yet earned.

3–16. Each of the following debits and credits represents one half of an adjusting entry. Name the title of the account that would be used for the remaining half of the entry.
    (a) Fees Earned is debited.
    (b) Office Supplies Expense is debited.
    (c) Unearned Subscriptions is credited.
    (d) Salary Expense is debited.
    (e) Property Tax Payable is credited.
    (f) Prepaid Insurance is credited.
    (g) Unearned Rent is debited.

3–17. Which type of system for accounting for merchandise held for sale continuously discloses the amount of inventory on hand?

3–18. The merchandise inventory account contains a debit of $65,000 and a credit of $60,000, representing adjustments made at the end of the current year. Which of the amounts represents the amount of inventory (a) at the beginning of the year and (b) at the end of the year?

3–19. What term is applied to the annual accounting period adopted by a business enterprise?

Exercises

3–20. On December 31, a business enterprise estimates depreciation on equipment used during the first year of operations to be $1,360. (a) Journalize the adjusting entry required as of December 31. (b) If the adjusting entry in (a) were omitted, which items would be erroneously stated on (1) the income statement for the year, and (2) the balance sheet as of December 31?

3–21. The balance in the prepaid insurance account before adjustment at the end of the year is $2,780. Journalize the adjusting entry required under each of the following alternatives: (a) the amount of insurance expired during the year is $1,730; (b) the amount of unexpired insurance applicable to future periods is $1,730.

3–22. The store supplies purchased during the year total $2,450, and the inventory at the end of the year is $530.

    (a) Set up T accounts for Store Supplies and Store Supplies Expense, and record the following directly in the accounts, employing the system of initially recording store supplies as an asset (identify each entry by number): (1) purchases for the period; (2) adjusting entry at the end of the period.

    (b) Set up T accounts for Store Supplies and Store Supplies Expense, and record the following directly in the accounts, employing the system of initially recording store supplies as an expense (identify each entry by number): (1) purchases for the period; (2) adjusting entry at the end of the period.

3–23. The advertising revenues received during the year total $280,500, and the unearned advertising revenue at the end of the year is $30,800.

    (a) Set up T accounts for Unearned Advertising Revenue and Advertising Revenue and record the following directly in the accounts, employing the system of initially recording advertising fees as a liability (identify each entry by number): (1) revenues received during the period; (2) adjusting entry at the end of the period.

    (b) Set up T accounts for Unearned Advertising Revenue and Advertising Revenue and record the following directly in the accounts, employing the system of initially recording advertising fees as a revenue (identify each entry by number): (1) revenues received during the period; (2) adjusting entry at the end of the period.

3–24. In their first year of operations, Southern Publishing Co. received $290,000 from advertising contracts and $625,000 from magazine subscriptions, crediting the two amounts to Advertising Revenue and Circulation Revenue respectively. At the end of the year, the unearned advertising revenue amounts to $32,000 and the unearned circulation revenue amounts to $197,000. (a) If no adjustments are made at the end of the year, will revenue for the year be overstated or understated, and by what amount? (b) Present the adjusting entries that should be made at the end of the year.

3–25. A business enterprise pays weekly salaries of $8,500 on Friday for a five-day week ending on that day. Journalize the necessary adjusting entry at the end of the fiscal period, assuming that the fiscal period ends (a) on Monday, (b) on Wednesday.

3–26. On March 1 of the current year, a business enterprise pays $2,400 to the city for taxes (license fees) for the coming year. The same enterprise is also required to pay an annual tax (on property) at the end of the year. The estimated amount of the current year's accrued property tax for March is $550. (a) Journalize the two adjusting entries required to bring the accounts affected by the two taxes up to date as of March 31. (b) What is the amount of tax expense for the month of March?

3–27. Merchandise inventory was $88,500 on January 1, 1986, and $87,200 on December 31, 1986. Present the two entries on December 31, 1986, to adjust the merchandise inventory account.

Problems

3–28. The trial balance of Herman Company at July 31, 1986, the end of the current fiscal year, and the data needed to determine year-end adjustments are as follows:

Herman Company
Trial Balance
July 31, 1986

Cash	5,180	
Merchandise Inventory........................	15,500	
Supplies	3,850	
Prepaid Insurance............................	1,200	
Equipment	87,600	
Accumulated Depreciation		43,200
Accounts Payable............................		1,620
Capital Stock................................		25,000
Retained Earnings		19,930
Sales..		112,400
Purchases	49,250	
Wages Expense	17,900	
Rent Expense	14,000	
Utilities Expense.............................	7,260	
Miscellaneous Expense.......................	410	
	202,150	202,150

Adjustment data:
    (a) Merchandise inventory at July 31............................$14,750
    (b) Supplies on hand at July 31 940
    (c) Insurance premiums expired during the year 800
    (d) Depreciation on equipment during the year................... 5,220
    (e) Wages accrued but not paid at July 31...................... 850

Instructions:
    Prepare journal entries to adjust the accounts at July 31, 1986.

3–29. The information presented below was obtained from a review of the ledger (before adjustments) and other records of Chin Company at the end of the current fiscal year ended December 31:
    (a) As office supplies have been purchased during the year, they have been debited to Office Supplies Expense, which has a balance of $995 at December 31. The inventory of supplies at that date totals $280.
    (b) On December 31, Rent Expense has a debit balance of $26,000, which includes rent of $2,000 for January of the following year, paid on December 31 of the preceding year.
    (c) Sales commissions are uniformly 1% of net sales and are paid the tenth of the month following the sales. Net sales for the month ended December 31 were $90,500. Only commissions paid have been recorded during the year.
    (d) Prepaid Advertising has a debit balance of $7,800 at December 31, which represents the advance payment on March 1 of a yearly contract for a uniform amount of space in 52 consecutive issues of a weekly publication. As of December 31, advertisements had appeared in 44 issues.

(e) Unearned Rent has a credit balance of $14,700, composed of the following: (1) January 1 balance of $2,700, representing rent prepaid for three months, January through March, and (2) a credit of $12,000, representing advance payment of rent for twelve months at $1,000 a month, beginning with April.

(f) Management Fees Earned has a credit balance of $130,750 at December 31. The unbilled fees at December 31 total $7,150.

(g) As advance premiums have been paid on insurance policies during the year, they have been debited to Prepaid Insurance, which has a balance of $1,248 at December 31. Details of premium expirations are as follows:

Policy No.	Premium Cost per Month	Period In Effect During Year
3172	$30	Jan. 1–March 31
D701	25	April 1–Dec. 31
5154	42	Jan. 1–Dec. 31
744B	18	Jan. 1–May 31
649C	22	June 1–Dec. 31

Instructions:

(1) Determine the amount of each adjustment, identifying all principal figures used in the computations.

(2) Journalize the adjusting entries as of December 31 of the current fiscal year, identifying each entry by letter.

3–30. The accounts listed below appear in the ledger of Knight Company at December 31, the end of the current fiscal year. None of the year-end adjustments have been recorded.

112	Fees Receivable.......	—	313	Income Summary.....	—
113	Merchandise Inventory..	$11,200	411	Fees Earned	$62,250
114	Supplies..............	675	511	Salary Expense	41,700
115	Prepaid Insurance......	3,725	513	Advertising Expense ..	10,340
116	Prepaid Advertising	—	514	Insurance Expense ...	—
213	Salaries Payable.......	—	515	Supplies Expense	—
215	Unearned Rent	—	611	Rent Income	9,100

The following information relating to adjustments at December 31 is obtained from physical inventories, supplementary records, and other sources:

(a) Unbilled fees at December 31, $7,750.

(b) Supplies on hand at December 31, $190.

(c) The insurance record indicates that $2,100 of insurance has expired during the year.

(d) Of a prepayment of $1,000 for advertising space in a local newspaper, 75% has been used and the remainder will be used in the following year.

(e) Salaries accrued at December 31, $1,140.

(f) Rent collected in advance that will not be earned until the following year, $700.

(g) Merchandise inventory at December 31, $12,125.

Instructions:

(1) Open the accounts listed and record the balances in the appropriate balance columns, as of December 31.

(2) Journalize the adjusting entries and post to the appropriate accounts after each entry, extending the balances. Identify the postings by writing "Adjusting" in the item columns.

3–31. Selected accounts from the ledger of Byrne Co. at the end of the fiscal year are as follows. The account balances are shown before and after adjustment.

	Unadjusted Balance	Adjusted Balance
Fees Receivable	—	$ 3,250
Merchandise Inventory	$21,125	26,000
Supplies	2,125	675
Prepaid Insurance	5,600	2,450
Wages Payable	—	2,970
Utilities Payable	—	475
Unearned Rent	—	600
Income Summary (credit)	—	4,875
Fees Earned	91,000	94,250
Wages Expense	60,050	63,020
Utilities Expense	4,950	5,425
Insurance Expense	—	3,150
Supplies Expense	—	1,450
Rent Income	7,800	7,200

Instructions:

Journalize the adjusting entries that were posted to the ledger at the end of the fiscal year.

3–32. Transactions related to advertising and rent are presented below. Accounts are adjusted at December 31, the end of the fiscal year.

Advertising

Apr. 1. Payment of $7,200 (allocable at $600 a month for 12 months beginning April 1).

Rent

May 1. Receipt of $9,600 (allocable at $800 a month for 12 months beginning May 1).

July 1. Receipt of $19,200 (allocable at $1,600 a month for 12 months beginning July 1).

Instructions:

(1) Open accounts for Prepaid Advertising, Advertising Expense, Unearned Rent, and Rent Income. Using the system of initially recording prepaid expense as an asset and unearned revenue as a liability, record the following directly in the accounts: (a) transactions of April 1, May 1, and July 1; (b) adjusting entries at December 31. Identify each entry in the item section of the accounts as transaction or adjusting, and extend the balance after each entry.

(2) Open a duplicate set of accounts and follow the remaining instructions in Instruction (1), except to employ the system of initially recording prepaid expense as an expense and unearned revenue as revenue.

(3) Determine the amounts that would appear in the balance sheet at December 31 as asset and liability respectively, and in the income statement for the year as expense and revenue respectively, according to the system employed in Instruction (1) and the system employed in Instruction (2). Present your answers in the following form:

System	Asset	Expense	Liability	Revenue
Instruction (1)	$	$	$	$
Instruction (2)				

3–33. As of December 31, the end of the current fiscal year, the accountant for Saunders Company prepared a trial balance, journalized and posted the adjusting entries, and prepared an adjusted trial balance. The two trial balances as of December 31, one before adjustments and the other after adjustments, are as follows:

Saunders Company
Trial Balance
December 31, 19--

	Unadjusted		Adjusted	
Cash.	11,200		11,200	
Merchandise Inventory	32,000		29,750	
Accounts Receivable.	17,500		17,500	
Supplies.	8,450		3,240	
Prepaid Rent.	7,200		1,200	
Prepaid Insurance	1,800		650	
Land	40,000		40,000	
Buildings	96,000		96,000	
Accumulated Depreciation — Buildings		62,400		67,200
Trucks.	82,000		82,000	
Accumulated Depreciation — Trucks		22,800		26,900
Accounts Payable.		7,120		7,340
Salaries Payable.		—		1,450
Taxes Payable		—		920
Capital Stock.		100,000		100,000
Retained Earnings		30,430		30,430
Dividends.	20,500		20,500	
Income Summary.			2,250	
Sales.		311,180		311,180
Purchases	145,000		145,000	
Salary Expense	67,200		68,650	
Rent Expense.	—		6,000	
Supplies Expense	—		5,210	
Depreciation Expense — Buildings	—		4,800	
Depreciation Expense — Trucks	—		4,100	
Utilities Expense.	3,700		3,920	
Taxes Expense.	600		1,520	
Insurance Expense	—		1,150	
Miscellaneous Expense	780		780	
	533,930	533,930	545,420	545,420

Instructions:

Present the ten journal entries that were required to adjust the accounts at December 31. Only the merchandise inventory and income summary accounts were affected by more than one adjusting entry.

Alternate Problems

3–28A. The trial balance of Dillow Company at October 31, 1986, the end of the current fiscal year, and the data needed to determine year-end adjustments are as follows:

Dillow Company
Trial Balance
October 31, 1986

Cash	12,650	
Merchandise Inventory	29,200	
Supplies	6,410	
Prepaid Insurance	2,800	
Equipment	92,100	
Accumulated Depreciation		25,200
Accounts Payable		4,900
Capital Stock		50,000
Retained Earnings		20,510
Sales		224,750
Purchases	97,500	
Wages Expense	42,300	
Rent Expense	28,500	
Utilities Expense	11,200	
Miscellaneous Expense	2,700	
	325,360	325,360

Adjustment data:

(a) Merchandise inventory at October 31 .... $26,950
(b) Supplies on hand at October 31 3,100
(c) Insurance premiums expired during the year 2,000
(d) Depreciation on equipment during the year 4,600
(e) Wages accrued but not paid at October 31 1,750

Instructions:

Prepare journal entries to adjust the accounts at October 31, 1986.

3–29A. The information presented below was obtained from a review of the ledger (before adjustments) and other records of Koo Company at the end of the current fiscal year ended December 31:

(a) Prepaid Advertising has a debit balance of $6,500 at December 31, which represents the advance payment on June 1 of a yearly contract for a uniform amount of space in 52 consecutive issues of a weekly publication. As of December 31, advertisements had appeared in 30 issues.

(b) Unearned Rent has a credit balance of $14,100, composed of the following: (1) January 1 balance of $2,700, representing rent prepaid for three months, January through March, and (2) a credit of $11,400, representing advance payment of rent for twelve months at $950 a month, beginning with April.

(c) Management Fees Earned has a credit balance of $125,800 at December 31. The unbilled fees at December 31 total $9,550.

(d) As office supplies have been purchased during the year, they have been debited to Office Supplies Expense, which has a balance of $930 at December 31. The inventory of supplies at that date totals $345.

(e) On December 31, Rent Expense has a debit balance of $19,500, which includes rent of $1,500 for January of the following year, paid on December 31 of the preceding year.

(f) Sales commissions are uniformly 2% of net sales and are paid the tenth of the month following the sales. Net sales for December were $70,000. Only commissions paid have been recorded during the year.

(g) As advance premiums have been paid on insurance policies during the year, they have been debited to Prepaid Insurance, which has a balance of $1,236 at December 31. Details of premium expirations are as follows:

Policy No.	Premium Cost per Month	Period In Effect During Year
B115	$25	Jan. 1–June 30
210A	27	July 1–Dec. 31
917Y	12	Jan. 1–Dec. 31
881C	30	Jan. 1–Apr. 30
419X	29	May 1–Dec. 31

Instructions:

(1) Determine the amount of each adjustment, identifying all principal figures used in the computations.

(2) Journalize the adjusting entries as of December 31 of the current fiscal year, identifying each entry by letter.

3–30A. The accounts listed below appear in the ledger of Hunter Company at June 30, the end of the current fiscal year. None of the year-end adjustments have been recorded:

112	Fees Receivable.......	—	313	Income Summary.........	—
113	Merchandise Inventory .	$30,500	411	Fees Earned	$188,800
114	Supplies	1,950	511	Salary Expense...........	115,750
115	Prepaid Insurance	4,800	513	Advertising Expense	25,500
116	Prepaid Advertising	—	514	Insurance Expense........	—
213	Salaries Payable.......	—	515	Supplies Expense.........	—
215	Unearned Rent	—	611	Rent Income	19,500

The following information relating to adjustments at June 30 is obtained from physical inventories, supplementary records, and other sources.

(a) Of a prepayment of $7,500 for newspaper advertising, 70% has been used and the remainder will be used in the following year.
(b) Rent collected in advance that will not be earned until the following year, $1,500.
(c) Salaries accrued at June 30, $2,975.
(d) Unbilled fees at June 30, $8,500.
(e) The insurance record indicates that $1,600 of insurance relates to future years.
(f) Supplies on hand at June 30, $675.
(g) Merchandise inventory at June 30, $31,950.

Instructions:

(1) Open the accounts listed and record the balances in the appropriate balance columns, as of June 30.
(2) Journalize the adjusting entries and post to the appropriate accounts after each entry, extending the balances. Identify the postings by writing "Adjusting" in the item columns.

3–31A. Selected accounts from the ledger of Linens and Things at the end of the fiscal year are as follows. The account balances are shown before and after adjustment.

	Unadjusted Balance	Adjusted Balance
Fees Receivable.	—	$ 11,250
Merchandise Inventory	$ 43,250	40,750
Supplies.	2,325	975
Prepaid Insurance	5,900	2,650
Wages Payable.	—	3,090
Advertising Payable.	—	3,750
Unearned Rent.	—	500
Income Summary (debit)	—	2,500
Fees Earned	187,000	198,250
Wages Expense.	79,100	82,190
Insurance Expense	—	3,250
Advertising Expense	20,250	24,000
Supplies Expense	—	1,350
Rent Income	6,500	6,000

Instructions:

Journalize the adjusting entries that were posted to the ledger at the end of the fiscal year.

3–33A. As of April 30, 1986, the end of the current fiscal year, the accountant for Aaron Company prepared a trial balance, journalized and posted the adjusting entries, and prepared an adjusted trial balance. The two trial balances as of April 30, one before adjustments and the other after adjustments, are as follows:

Aaron Company
Trial Balance
April 30, 1986

	Unadjusted		Adjusted	
Cash.....................................	6,138		6,138	
Accounts Receivable......................	12,200		12,200	
Merchandise Inventory	20,600		21,900	
Supplies.................................	7,526		1,430	
Prepaid Rent.............................	14,400		1,200	
Prepaid Insurance	1,180		262	
Equipment...............................	69,750		69,750	
Accumulated Depreciation—Equipment....		20,632		23,422
Automobiles..............................	36,500		36,500	
Accumulated Depreciation—Automobiles ..		18,250		21,900
Accounts Payable.........................		4,310		4,500
Salaries Payable..........................		—		3,480
Taxes Payable		—		1,200
Capital Stock.............................		50,000		50,000
Retained Earnings		24,500		24,500
Dividends................................	18,000		18,000	
Income Summary.........................	—	—		1,300
Sales....................................		410,600		410,600
Purchases	225,000		225,000	
Salary Expense	112,300		115,780	
Rent Expense............................	—		13,200	
Supplies Expense	—		6,096	
Depreciation Expense—Equipment........	—		2,790	
Depreciation Expense—Automobiles	—		3,650	
Utilities Expense..........................	2,130		2,320	
Taxes Expense...........................	858		2,058	
Insurance Expense	—		918	
Miscellaneous Expense	1,710		1,710	
	528,292	528,292	540,902	540,902

Instructions:

Present the ten journal entries that were required to adjust the accounts at April 30. Only the merchandise inventory and income summary accounts were affected by more than one adjusting entry.

Mini-Case

3–34. Assume that you recently accepted a position with First National Bank as an assistant loan officer. As one of your first duties, you have been assigned the responsibility of evaluating a loan request for $50,000 from Stillwell Pest Control, a small local corporation. In support of the loan application, Alice Stillwell, principal stockholder, submitted the following "Statement of Accounts" (trial balance) for the first year of operations ended October 31, 1986:

Stillwell Pest Control
Statement of Accounts
October 31, 1986

Cash..	3,850	
Billings Due from Others	7,400	
Supplies (chemicals, etc.)	16,550	
Trucks	22,300	
Equipment....................................	15,730	
Amounts Owed to Others		3,420
Capital Stock		40,000
Service Revenue.............................		86,750
Wages Expense..............................	56,200	
Utilities Expense	4,210	
Rent Expense................................	1,800	
Insurance Expense...........................	1,400	
Other Expenses..............................	730	
	130,170	130,170

Instructions:

(1) Explain to Alice Stillwell why a set of financial statements (income statement, retained earnings statement, and balance sheet) would be useful to you in evaluating the loan request.

(2) In discussing the "Statement of Accounts" with Alice Stillwell, you discovered that the accounts had not been adjusted at October 31. Through analysis of the "Statement of Accounts", indicate possible adjusting entries that might be necessary before an accurate set of financial statements could be prepared.

(3) Assuming that an accurate set of financial statements will be submitted by Alice Stillwell in a few days, what other considerations or information would you require before making a decision on the loan request?

Answers
to Self-
Examination
Questions

1. D Every adjusting entry affects both a balance sheet account and an income statement account. Therefore, if the debit portion of an adjusting entry increases an asset (balance sheet) account, the credit portion of the entry must affect an income statement account, as would be the case for a decrease in an expense account (answer D).

2. C Since increases in expense accounts (such as depreciation expense) are recorded by debits and it is customary to record the decreases in usefulness of plant assets as credits to accumulated depreciation accounts, answer C is the correct entry.

3. A Under the system of initially recording office supplies as an expense, the office supplies expense account would have a balance of $2,910 before adjustment, representing the cost of office supplies purchased during the year. The accounts are therefore adjusted by debiting Office Supplies and crediting Office Supplies Expense for $595 (answer A). The adjustment transfers $595, representing the unconsumed supplies on hand at the end of the year, to the asset account.

4. A Prepaid expenses are listed on the balance sheet among the current assets (answer A).

5. B Unearned revenues are revenues received in advance that will be earned in the future. They represent a liability (answer B) of the business to furnish the service in a future period.

CHAPTER 4

Periodic Reporting

CHAPTER OBJECTIVES

Describe and illustrate the summarizing and reporting procedures for merchandising enterprises at the end of the accounting period.

Describe and illustrate the preparation of financial statements for merchandising enterprises.

Describe and illustrate procedures for preparing the accounting records of a merchandising enterprise for use in accumulating data for the following accounting period.

The sequence of the principal accounting procedures followed during an accounting period is frequently called the **accounting cycle**. The accounting cycle begins with the analysis and journalizing of transactions. These two phases in the accounting cycle were discussed in Chapters 1 and 2.

At the end of each accounting period, or accounting cycle, the operating data for the period must be summarized, adjusted, and reported in the financial statements for the use of managers, owners, creditors, various governmental agencies, and other interested persons. The ledger, which contains the basic data for the reports, must then be prepared to receive entries for transactions that will occur in the following period.

The sequence of the end-of-period procedures, which are discussed and illustrated in this chapter, may be outlined as follows:

1. Prepare a trial balance of the ledger on a work sheet form.
2. Review the accounts and gather the data required for the adjustments.
3. Insert the adjustments and complete the work sheet.
4. Prepare financial statements from the data in the work sheet.
5. Journalize the adjusting entries and post to the ledger.
6. Journalize the closing entries and post to the ledger.
7. Prepare a post-closing trial balance of the ledger.
8. Journalize the reversing entries required to facilitate the recording of transactions in the following period and post to the ledger.

WORK SHEET FOR FINANCIAL STATEMENTS

The most significant output of the end-of-period procedures is the financial statements. To assist the accountant in accumulating data for the statements, a **work sheet** is often used. The work sheet provides a convenient means of accumulating essential data, verifying arithmetical accuracy, and arranging data in a logical form.

The work sheet for Kimco Inc. is presented on pages 110-111. It has an account title column and eight money columns arranged in four pairs of debit and credit columns. The main headings for the four sets of money columns are:

1. Trial Balance
2. Adjustments
3. Income Statement
4. Balance Sheet

Trial Balance Columns

The trial balance data for Kimco Inc. appear on the work sheet on pages 110-111. All of the accounts, with their balances, are listed in the order in which they appear in the ledger.

Adjustments Columns

Both the debit and the credit parts of an adjustment should be inserted on the appropriate lines before going on to another adjustment. Cross-referencing the related debit and credit of each adjustment by letters is useful to anyone who may have occasion to review the work sheet. It is also helpful later when the adjusting entries are recorded in the journal. The sequence of adjustments is not important, except that there is a time and accuracy advantage in following the order in which the adjustment data are assembled.

The data needed for adjusting the accounts of Kimco Inc. are summarized as follows:

Merchandise inventory as of December 31, 1986		$62,150
Inventories of supplies as of December 31, 1986:		
Store supplies		960
Office supplies....................................		480
Insurance expired during 1986 on:		
Merchandise and store equipment	$2,080	
Office equipment and building......................	830	2,910
Depreciation during 1986 on:		
Building		4,500
Office equipment..................................		1,490
Store equipment		3,100
Salaries accrued on December 31, 1986:		
Sales salaries....................................	$ 780	
Office salaries	372	1,152

WORK
SHEET

Kimco
Work
For Year Ended

ACCOUNT TITLE	TRIAL BALANCE	
	DEBIT	CREDIT
Cash	23,590	
Notes Receivable	10,000	
Accounts Receivable	20,880	
Merchandise Inventory	59,700	
Store Supplies	2,970	
Office Supplies	1,090	
Prepaid Insurance	4,560	
Land	20,000	
Building	140,000	
Accumulated Depreciation—Building		29,400
Office Equipment	15,570	
Accumulated Depreciation—Office Equipment		7,230
Store Equipment	27,100	
Accumulated Depreciation—Store Equipment		12,600
Accounts Payable		22,420
Salaries Payable		
Mortgage Note Payable		25,000
Capital Stock		100,000
Retained Earnings		59,888
Dividends	18,000	
Income Summary		
Sales		732,163
Sales Returns and Allowances	6,140	
Sales Discount	5,822	
Purchases	530,280	
Purchases Discount		2,525
Sales Salaries Expense	59,264	
Advertising Expense	10,460	
Depreciation Expense—Store Equipment		
Insurance Expense—Selling		
Store Supplies Expense		
Miscellaneous Selling Expense	630	
Office Salaries Expense	20,660	
Heating and Lighting Expense	8,100	
Taxes Expense	6,810	
Depreciation Expense—Building		
Depreciation Expense—Office Equipment		
Insurance Expense—General		
Office Supplies Expense		
Miscellaneous General Expense	760	
Interest Income		3,600
Interest Expense	2,440	
	994,826	994,826
Net Income		

Explanations of the adjusting entries in the work sheet are as follows:

(a), (b) Merchandise inventory. The $59,700 balance of merchandise inventory appearing in the trial balance represents the amount of the inventory at the end of the preceding year (beginning of the current year). It is a part of the merchandise available for sale during the year and, as discussed in Chapter 3, is transferred to Income Summary, where it will be

Inc.
Sheet
December 31, 1986

ADJUSTMENTS		INCOME STATEMENT		BALANCE SHEET	
DEBIT	CREDIT	DEBIT	CREDIT	DEBIT	CREDIT
				23,590	
				10,000	
				20,880	
(b) 62,150	(a) 59,700			62,150	
	(c) 2,010			960	
	(d) 610			480	
	(e) 2,910			1,650	
				20,000	
				140,000	
	(f) 4,500				33,900
				15,570	
	(g) 1,490				8,720
				27,100	
	(h) 3,100				15,700
					22,420
	(i) 1,152				1,152
					25,000
					100,000
					59,888
				18,000	
(a) 59,700	(b) 62,150	59,700	62,150		
			732,163		
		6,140			
		5,822			
		530,280			
			2,525		
(i) 780		60,044			
		10,460			
(h) 3,100		3,100			
(e) 2,080		2,080			
(c) 2,010		2,010			
		630			
(i) 372		21,032			
		8,100			
		6,810			
(f) 4,500		4,500			
(g) 1,490		1,490			
(e) 830		830			
(d) 610		610			
		760			
			3,600		
		2,440			
137,622	137,622	726,838	800,438	340,380	266,780
		73,600			73,600
		800,438	800,438	340,380	340,380

combined with the net cost of merchandise purchased during the year [entry (a)].

The merchandise on hand at the end of the current year, as determined by a physical inventory, is an asset and must be debited to the asset account, Merchandise Inventory. It must also be deducted from the cost of merchandise available for sale (beginning inventory plus purchases less purchases discounts) to yield the cost of the merchandise sold. These objectives are accomplished by debiting Merchandise Inventory and crediting Income Summary for $62,150 [entry (b)].

(c), (d) **Supplies.** The $2,970 balance of the store supplies account in the trial balance is the combined cost of store supplies on hand at the beginning of the year and the cost of store supplies purchased during the year. The physical inventory at the end of the year indicates store supplies on hand totaling $960. The excess of $2,970 over the inventory of $960 is $2,010, which is the cost of the store supplies used during the period. The accounts are adjusted by debiting Store Supplies Expense and crediting Store Supplies for $2,010 [entry (c)]. The adjustment for office supplies used is determined in the same manner [entry (d)].

(e) **Prepaid insurance.** The adjustment for insurance expired is similar to the adjustment for supplies consumed. The balance in Prepaid Insurance is the amount prepaid at the beginning of the year plus the additional premium costs incurred during the year. Analysis of the various insurance policies reveals that a total of $2,910 in premiums has expired, of which $2,080 is related to merchandise and store equipment and $830 is related to office equipment and building. Insurance Expense—Selling is debited for $2,080, Insurance Expense—General is debited for $830, and Prepaid Insurance is credited for $2,910.

(f), (g), (h) **Depreciation of plant assets.** The expired cost of a plant asset is debited to a depreciation expense account and credited to an accumulated depreciation account. A separate account for the current period's expense and for the accumulation of prior periods is maintained for each plant asset account. Thus, the adjustment for $4,500 depreciation of the building is recorded by a debit to Depreciation Expense—Building and a credit to Accumulated Depreciation—Building for $4,500 [entry (f)]. The adjustments for depreciation of the office equipment and the store equipment are recorded in a similar manner [entries (g) and (h)].

(i) **Salaries payable.** The liability for the salaries earned by employees but not yet paid is recorded by a credit of $1,152 to Salaries Payable and debits of $780 and $372 to Sales Salaries Expense and Office Salaries Expense respectively.

Income Statement and Balance Sheet Columns

The data in the trial balance columns are combined with the adjustments data and extended to one of the remaining four columns. The amounts of assets, liabilities, and stockholders' equity (including dividends) are extended to the balance sheet columns, and the revenues and expenses are extended to the income statement columns. This procedure must be applied to the balance of each account listed.

In the illustrative work sheet, the first account listed is Cash and the balance appearing in the trial balance is $23,590. Since there are no adjustments to Cash, the trial balance amount should be extended to the appropriate column. Cash is an asset, it is listed on the balance sheet, and it has a debit balance. Accordingly, the $23,590 amount is extended to the debit column of the balance sheet section. The balance of Accounts Receivable is extended in similar fashion. Store Supplies has an initial debit balance of $2,970 and a credit adjustment (decrease) of $2,010. The amount to be extended is the remaining debit balance of $960. The same procedure is continued until all account balances, with or without adjustment as the case may be, have been extended to the appropriate columns. The balances of the retained earnings and dividends accounts are extended to the balance sheet section, because this work sheet does not provide for separate retained earnings statement columns.

An exception to the usual practice of extending only the account balances should be noted. Both the debit and credit amounts for Income Summary are extended to the Income Statement columns. Since both the amount of the debit adjustment (beginning inventory of $59,700) and the amount of the credit adjustment (ending inventory of $62,150) may be reported on the income statement, there is no need to determine the difference between the two amounts.

After all of the balances have been extended, each of the four columns is totaled. The net income or the net loss for the period is the amount of the difference between the totals of the two income statement columns. If the credit column total is greater than the debit column total, the excess is the net income. For the work sheet presented on page 111, the computation of net income is as follows:

Total of credit column	$800,438
Total of debit column	726,838
Net income	$ 73,600

Revenue and expense accounts, which are in reality subdivisions of stockholders' equity, are temporary in nature. They are used during the accounting period to facilitate the accumulation of detailed operating data. After they have served their purpose, the net balance will be transferred to the retained earnings account in the ledger. This transfer is accomplished on the work sheet by entries in the income statement debit column and the balance sheet credit column, as illustrated on page 111. If there had been a net loss instead of a net income, the amount would have been entered in the income statement credit column and the balance sheet debit column.

After the final total is made on the work sheet, each of the four statement columns is totaled to verify the arithmetic accuracy of the amount of net income or net loss transferred from the income statement to the balance sheet. The totals of the two income statement columns must be equal, as must the totals of the two balance sheet columns. The work sheet may be expanded by the addition of a pair of columns solely for retained earnings statement data. However, because of the very few items involved, this variation is not illustrated. If there are a great many adjustments, it may be advisable to insert a section entitled Adjusted Trial Balance between the adjustments section and the income statement section. The arithmetic of combining the data may then be verified before extending balances to the statement sections.

PREPARATION OF FINANCIAL STATEMENTS

The income statement, the retained earnings statement, and the balance sheet are prepared from the account titles and the data in the statement sections of the work sheet.

Many variations are possible in the general format of the principal financial statements, in the terminology used, and in the extent to which details are presented. The forms most frequently used are described and illustrated in the sections that follow.[1]

Income Statement

There are two widely used forms for the income statement, **multiple-step** and **single-step**. An income statement in the multiple-step form is presented on page 115. The single-step form is illustrated on page 117.

Multiple-Step Form

The multiple-step income statement is so called because of its many sections, subsections, and intermediate balances. In practice, there is considerable variation in the amount of detail presented in these sections. For example, instead of reporting separately gross sales and the related returns, allowances, and discounts, the statement may begin with net sales. Similarly, the supporting data for the determination of the cost of merchandise sold may be omitted from the statement.

The various sections of a conventional multiple-step income statement for a mercantile enterprise are discussed briefly in the paragraphs that follow.

Revenue from sales. The total of all charges to customers for merchandise sold, both for cash and on account, is reported in this section. Sales returns and allowances and sales discounts are deducted from the gross amount to yield net sales.

Cost of merchandise sold. The cost of merchandise sold section is one of the most important parts of the income statement, since the cost of merchandise sold is often the largest deduction from sales. The determination of this important figure for a merchandising enterprise was explained and illustrated in Chapter 3. Other descriptive terms frequently used are **cost of goods sold** and **cost of sales**.

---

[1]Examples of some of the forms described are also presented in Appendix E.

Kimco Inc.
Income Statement
For Year Ended December 31, 1986

Revenue from sales:			
Sales		$732,163	
Less: Sales returns and allowances	$ 6,140		
Sales discount	5,822	11,962	
Net sales			$720,201
Cost of merchandise sold:			
Merchandise inventory, January 1, 1986		$ 59,700	
Purchases	$530,280		
Less purchases discount	2,525		
Net purchases		527,755	
Merchandise available for sale		$587,455	
Less merchandise inventory,			
December 31, 1986		62,150	
Cost of merchandise sold			525,305
Gross profit			$194,896
Operating expenses:			
Selling expenses:			
Sales salaries expense	$ 60,044		
Advertising expense	10,460		
Depreciation expense—store equipment	3,100		
Insurance expense—selling	2,080		
Store supplies expense	2,010		
Miscellaneous selling expense	630		
Total selling expenses		$ 78,324	
General expenses:			
Office salaries expense	$ 21,032		
Heating and lighting expense	8,100		
Taxes expense	6,810		
Depreciation expense—building	4,500		
Depreciation expense—office equipment	1,490		
Insurance expense–general	830		
Office supplies expense	610		
Miscellaneous general expense	760		
Total general expenses		44,132	
Total operating expenses			122,456
Income from operations			$ 72,440
Other income:			
Interest income		$ 3,600	
Other expense:			
Interest expense		2,440	1,160
Net income[2]			$ 73,600

---

[2]This amount is further reduced by corporation income tax. The discussion of income taxes levied on corporate entities is reserved for later chapters.

The first item presented in the section is the merchandise inventory at the beginning of the accounting period. To this figure is added the purchases (less purchases discount) to determine the total cost of the merchandise available for sale during the period. The deduction of the unsold merchandise at the end of the period (ending inventory) yields the cost of the merchandise sold during the period.

Gross profit. The excess of the net revenue from sales over the cost of merchandise sold is called **gross profit, gross profit on sales,** or **gross margin.** It is called *gross* because operating expenses must be deducted from it.

Operating expenses. The operating expenses of a business may be grouped under any desired number of headings and subheadings. In a retail business of the kind that has been used for illustrative purposes, it is usually satisfactory to subdivide operating expenses into two categories, selling and general.

Expenses that are incurred directly and entirely in connection with the sale of merchandise are classified as **selling expenses.** They include such expenses as salaries of the sales force, store supplies used, depreciation of store equipment, and advertising.

Expenses incurred in the general operations of the business are classified as **general expenses** or **administrative expenses.** Examples of these expenses are office salaries, depreciation of office equipment, and office supplies used. Expenses that are partly connected with selling and partly connected with the general operations of the business may be divided between the two categories. In a small business, however, mixed expenses such as rent, insurance, and taxes are commonly reported as general expenses.

Expenses of relatively small amounts that cannot be identified with the principal accounts are usually accumulated in accounts entitled Miscellaneous Selling Expense and Miscellaneous General Expense.

Income from operations. The excess of gross profit over total operating expenses is called **income from operations,** or **operating income.** The amount of the income from operations and its relationship to capital investment and to net sales are important factors in judging the efficiency of management and the degree of profitability of an enterprise. If operating expenses are greater than the gross profit, the excess is called **loss from operations.**

Other income. Revenue from sources other than the principal activity of a business is classified as **other income,** or **nonoperating income.** In a merchandising business this category often includes income from interest, rent, dividends, and gains resulting from the sale of plant assets.

Other expense. Expenses that cannot be associated definitely with operations are identified as **other expense,** or **nonoperating expense.** Interest expense that results from financing activities and losses incurred in the disposal of plant assets are examples of items that are reported in this section.

The two categories of nonoperating items are offset against each other on the income statement. If the total of other income exceeds the total of other expense, the difference is added to income from operations. If the reverse is true, the difference is subtracted from income from operations.

Net income. The final figure on the income statement is labeled **net income** (or **net loss**). It is the net increase in stockholders' equity resulting from profit-making activities. (As noted on page 115, the reporting of corporation income tax is discussed later.)

Single-Step Form

The single-step form of income statement derives its name from the fact that the total of all expenses is deducted from the total of all revenues. A single-step statement is illustrated as follows for Kimco Inc. The illustration has been condensed to focus attention on its principal features.

Kimco Inc.
Income Statement
For Year Ended December 31, 1986

Revenues:		
Net sales		$720,201
Interest income		3,600
Total revenues		$723,801
Expenses:		
Cost of merchandise sold	$525,305	
Selling expenses	78,324	
General expenses	44,132	
Interest expense	2,440	
Total expenses		650,201
Net income		$ 73,600

The single-step form has the advantage of being simple and emphasizing total revenues and total expenses as the factors that determine net income. An objection to the single-step form is that such relationships as gross profit to sales and income from operations to sales are not as readily determinable as they are when the multiple-step form is used.

Balance Sheet

The traditional arrangement of assets on the left-hand side of the statement, with the liabilities and stockholders' equity on the right-hand side, is referred to as the **account form**. If the entire statement is limited to a single page, it is customary to present the three sections in a downward sequence, with the total of the assets section equaling the combined totals of the other two sections. The latter form, called the **report form**, is illustrated in the following balance sheet for Kimco Inc.

REPORT FORM
OF BALANCE SHEET

Kimco Inc.
Balance Sheet
December 31, 1986

Assets

Current assets:			
Cash		$ 23,590	
Notes receivable		10,000	
Accounts receivable		20,880	
Merchandise inventory		62,150	
Store supplies		960	
Office supplies		480	
Prepaid insurance		1,650	
Total current assets			$119,710
Plant assets:			
Land		$ 20,000	
Building	$140,000		
Less accumulated depreciation	33,900	106,100	
Office equipment	$ 15,570		
Less accumulated depreciation	8,720	6,850	
Store equipment	$ 27,100		
Less accumulated depreciation	15,700	11,400	
Total plant assets			144,350
Total assets			$264,060

Liabilities

Current liabilities:		
Accounts payable	$ 22,420	
Mortgage note payable (current portion)	5,000	
Salaries payable	1,152	
Total current liabilities		$ 28,572
Long-term liabilities:		
Mortgage note payable (final payment, 1990)		20,000
Total liabilities		$ 48,572

Stockholders' Equity

Capital stock	$100,000	
Retained earnings	115,488	
Total stockholders' equity		215,488
Total liabilities and stockholders' equity		$264,060

Retained Earnings Statement

The retained earnings statement summarizes the changes which have occurred in the retained earnings account during the fiscal period. It serves as a connecting link between the income statement and the balance sheet. The retained earnings statement for Kimco Inc. is illustrated as follows:

Kimco Inc. Retained Earnings Statement For Year Ended December 31, 1986		
Retained earnings, January 1, 1986		$ 59,888
Net income for the year	$73,600	
Less dividends	18,000	
Increase in retained earnings		55,600
Retained earnings, December 31, 1986		$115,488

It is not unusual to add the analysis of retained earnings at the bottom of the income statement to form a **combined income and retained earnings statement**. The income statement portion of the combined statement may be shown either in multiple-step form or in a single-step form, as in the following illustration:

Kimco Inc. Income and Retained Earnings Statement For Year Ended December 31, 1986		
Revenues:		
Net sales		$720,201
Interest income		3,600
		$723,801
Expenses:		
Cost of merchandise sold	$525,305	
Selling expenses	78,324	
General expenses	44,132	
Interest expense	2,440	
Total expenses		650,201
Net income		$ 73,600
Retained earnings, January 1, 1986		59,888
		$133,488
Deduct dividends		18,000
Retained earnings, December 31, 1986		$115,488

The combined statement form emphasizes net income as the connecting link between the income statement and the retained earnings portion of stockholders' equity and thus helps the reader's understanding. A criticism of the combined statement is that the net income figure is buried in the body of the statement.

ADJUSTING ENTRIES

At the end of the accounting period, the adjusting entries appearing in the work sheet are recorded in the journal and posted to the ledger. This procedure brings the ledger into agreement with the data reported on the financial statements. The adjusting entries are dated as of the last day of the period, even though they are usually recorded at a later date. Each entry may be supported by an explanation, but a suitable caption above the first adjusting entry is sufficient. The adjusting entries for Kimco Inc. are as follows:

ADJUSTING ENTRIES

	DATE		DESCRIPTION	POST. REF.	DEBIT	CREDIT	
1			Adjusting Entries				1
2	1986 Dec.	31	Income Summary	313	59 7 0 0 00		2
3			Merchandise Inventory	114		59 7 0 0 00	3
4							4
5		31	Merchandise Inventory	114	62 1 5 0 00		5
6			Income Summary	313		62 1 5 0 00	6
7							7
8		31	Store Supplies Expense	615	2 0 1 0 00		8
9			Store Supplies	115		2 0 1 0 00	9
10							10
11		31	Office Supplies Expense	717	6 1 0 00		11
12			Office Supplies	116		6 1 0 00	12
13							13
14		31	Insurance Expense — Selling	614	2 0 8 0 00		14
15			Insurance Expense — General	716	8 3 0 00		15
16			Prepaid Insurance	117		2 9 1 0 00	16
17							17
18		31	Depreciation Expense — Building	714	4 5 0 0 00		18
19			Accumulated Depreciation — Building	126		4 5 0 0 00	19
20							20
21		31	Depreciation Expense — Office Equipment	715	1 4 9 0 00		21
22			Accumulated Depr. — Office Equip.	124		1 4 9 0 00	22

23							23
24	31	Depreciation Expense—Store Equipment	613	3 1 0 0 00			24
25		Accumulated Depr.—Store Equip.	122		3 1 0 0 00		25
26							26
27	31	Sales Salaries Expense	611	7 8 0 00			27
28		Office Salaries Expense	711	3 7 2 00			28
29		Salaries Payable	213		1 1 5 2 00		29
30							30
31							31

CLOSING ENTRIES

As was discussed in Chapter 1, the revenue, expense, and dividends accounts are used in classifying and summarizing changes in stockholders' equity during the accounting period. At the end of the period, the net effect of the balances in these accounts must be recorded in the retained earnings account. The balances must also be removed from the revenue, expense, and dividends accounts, so that they will be ready for use in accumulating data for the following accounting period. Both of these goals are accomplished by a series of entries called **closing entries.**

The account titled **Income Summary,** which was used in Chapter 3 for the merchandise inventory adjustment, is used for summarizing the data in the revenue and expense accounts. Thus, Income Summary is used only at the end of the accounting period during the adjusting and closing process.

Four entries are required to close the revenue, expense, and dividend accounts of a corporation at the end of the period. They may be described as follows:

1. The first entry closes all income statement accounts with *credit* balances by transferring the total to the *credit* side of Income Summary.
2. The second entry closes all income statement accounts with *debit* balances by transferring the total to the *debit* side of Income Summary.
3. The third entry closes Income Summary by transferring its balance, the net income or the net loss for the year, to Retained Earnings.
4. The fourth entry closes Dividends by transferring its balance to Retained Earnings.

The closing entries are recorded in the journal immediately following the adjusting entries. The closing entries for Kimco Inc. are shown on page 122.

After the closing entries have been recorded and posted, the revenue, expense, and dividend accounts have zero balances. The only accounts with balances are the asset, contra asset, liability, and stockholders' equity accounts. The balances of these accounts in the ledger will correspond exactly with the amounts appearing on the balance sheet on page 118.

CLOSING
ENTRIES

	DATE		DESCRIPTION	POST. REF.	DEBIT	CREDIT	
1			Closing Entries				1
2	1986 Dec.	31	Sales	411	732 1 6 3 00		2
3			Purchases Discount	512	2 5 2 5 00		3
4			Interest Income	812	3 6 0 0 00		4
5			Income Summary	313		738 2 8 8 00	5
6							6
7		31	Income Summary	313	667 1 3 8 00		7
8			Sales Returns and Allowances	412		6 1 4 0 00	8
9			Sales Discount	413		5 8 2 2 00	9
10			Purchases	511		530 2 8 0 00	10
11			Sales Salaries Expense	611		60 0 4 4 00	11
12			Advertising Expense	612		10 4 6 0 00	12
13			Depreciation Expense—Store Equip.	613		3 1 0 0 00	13
14			Insurance Expense—Selling	614		2 0 8 0 00	14
15			Store Supplies Expense	615		2 0 1 0 00	15
16			Miscellaneous Selling Expense	619		6 3 0 00	16
17			Office Salaries Expense	711		21 0 3 2 00	17
18			Heating and Lighting Expense	712		8 1 0 0 00	18
19			Taxes Expense	713		6 8 1 0 00	19
20			Depreciation Expense—Building	714		4 5 0 0 00	20
21			Depreciation Expense—Office Equip.	715		1 4 9 0 00	21
22			Insurance Expense—General	716		8 3 0 00	22
23			Office Supplies Expense	717		6 1 0 00	23
24			Miscellaneous General Expense	719		7 6 0 00	24
25			Interest Expense	911		2 4 4 0 00	25
26							26
27		31	Income Summary	313	73 6 0 0 00		27
28			Retained Earnings	311		73 6 0 0 00	28
29							29
30		31	Retained Earnings	311	18 0 0 0 00		30
31			Dividends	312		18 0 0 0 00	31
32							32

POST-CLOSING TRIAL BALANCE

After the adjusting and closing entries have been recorded in the journal and posted, it is advisable to take another trial balance to verify the debit-credit equality of the ledger at the beginning of the following year. This post-closing trial balance may consist of two adding machine listings, one for the debit balances and the other for the credit balances, or its details may be shown in a more formal fashion as follows:

Kimco Inc.
Post-Closing Trial Balance
December 31, 1986

Cash	23,590	
Notes Receivable	10,000	
Accounts Receivable	20,880	
Merchandise Inventory	62,150	
Store Supplies	960	
Office Supplies	480	
Prepaid Insurance	1,650	
Land	20,000	
Building	140,000	
Accumulated Depreciation — Building		33,900
Office Equipment	15,570	
Accumulated Depreciation — Office Equipment		8,720
Store Equipment	27,100	
Accumulated Depreciation — Store Equipment		15,700
Accounts Payable		22,420
Salaries Payable		1,152
Mortgage Note Payable		25,000
Capital Stock		100,000
Retained Earnings		115,488
	322,380	322,380

REVERSING ENTRIES

Some of the adjusting entries recorded at the end of a fiscal year have an important effect on otherwise routine transactions that occur in the following year. A typical example is the adjusting entry for accrued salaries owed to employees at the end of the year. The wage or salary expense of an enterprise and the accompanying liability to employees actually accumulates or accrues day by day, or even hour by hour, during any part of the fiscal year. Nevertheless, the practice of recording the expense only at the time of payment is more efficient. When salaries are paid weekly, an entry debiting Salary Expense and crediting Cash will be recorded 52 or 53 times during the year. If there has been an adjusting entry for accrued salaries at the end of the year, however, the first payment of salaries in the following year will include this year-end accrual. In the absence of some special provision, it will be necessary to debit Salaries Payable for the amount owed for the earlier year and Salary Expense for the portion of the payroll that represents expense for the later year.

To illustrate, assume the following facts for an enterprise that pays salaries weekly and ends its fiscal year on December 31:

1. Salaries are paid on Friday for the five-day week ending on Friday.
2. The balance in Salary Expense as of Friday, December 27, is $62,500.
3. Salaries accrued for Monday and Tuesday, December 30 and 31, total $500.
4. Salaries paid on Friday, January 3, of the following year total $1,250.

The foregoing data may be diagrammed as follows:

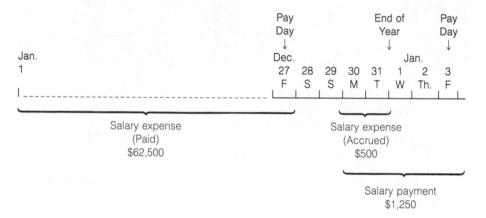

The adjusting entry to record the accrued salary expense and salaries payable for Monday and Tuesday, December 30 and 31, is as follows:

Dec. 31	Salary Expense	500	
	Salaries Payable		500

After the adjusting entry is posted, Salary Expense has a debit balance of $63,000 ($62,500 + $500) and Salaries Payable has a credit balance of $500. After the closing entries are posted, Salary Expense has a zero balance and is ready for entries of the following year, but Salaries Payable continues to have a credit balance of $500. As matters now stand, it would be necessary to record the $1,250 payroll on January 3 as a debit of $500 to Salaries Payable and a debit of $750 to Salary Expense. This means that the employee who records payroll entries must not only record this particular payroll in a different manner from all other weekly payrolls for the year, but must also refer to the adjusting entries in the journal or the ledger to determine the amount of the $1,250 payment to be debited to each of the two accounts.

The need to refer to earlier entries and to divide the debit between two accounts can be avoided by an optional procedure of recording a **reversing entry** as of the first day of the following fiscal period. As the term implies, such an entry is the exact reverse of the adjusting entry to which it relates. The amounts and the accounts are the same; the debits and credits are merely reversed.

Continuing with the illustration, the reversing entry for the accrued salaries is as follows:

Jan. 1	Salaries Payable	500	
	Salary Expense		500

The effect of the reversing entry is to transfer the $500 liability from Salaries Payable to the credit side of Salary Expense. The real nature of the $500 balance is unchanged; it remains a liability. When the payroll is paid on January 3, Salary Expense will be debited and Cash will be credited for $1,250, the entire amount of the weekly salaries. After the entry is posted, Salary Expense will have a debit balance of $750, which is the amount of expense incurred for January 1–3. The sequence of entries, including adjusting, closing, and reversing entries, may be traced in the following accounts:

ACCOUNT SALARY EXPENSE   ACCOUNT NO. 611

ADJUSTMENT AND REVERSAL FOR ACCRUED SALARIES

Date		Item	Debit	Credit	Balance Debit	Balance Credit
1986						
Jan.	5		1,240		1,240	
Dec.	6		1,300		58,440	
	13		1,450		59,890	
	20		1,260		61,150	
	27		1,350		62,500	
	31	Adjusting	500		63,000	
	31	Closing		63,000	—	—
1987						
Jan.	1	Reversing		500		500
	3		1,250		750	

ACCOUNT SALARIES PAYABLE   ACCOUNT NO. 213

Date		Item	Debit	Credit	Balance Debit	Balance Credit
1986						
Dec.	31	Adjusting		500		500
1987						
Jan.	1	Reversing	500		—	—

Reversing entries can be used with the adjustments for all accrued liabilities and accrued assets. They are also appropriate with the adjustments for prepaid expenses recorded initially as expenses and unearned revenues recorded initially as revenues.

The year-end procedures for Kimco Inc. are completed by journalizing and posting the reversing entry for accrued salaries. The entry is as follows:

REVERSING ENTRY

	DATE		DESCRIPTION	POST. REF.	DEBIT	CREDIT	
			JOURNAL			PAGE 29	
			Reversing Entry				
32	1987 Jan.	1	Salaries Payable	213	1 1 5 2 00		32
33			Sales Salaries Expense	611		7 8 0 00	33
34			Office Salaries Expense	711		3 7 2 00	34
35							35
36							36
37							37
38							38

After the reversing entry is posted, Salaries Payable has a zero balance and the liabilities for sales and office salaries appear as credits in the respective expense accounts. The entire amount of the first payroll in January will be debited to the salary expense accounts and the balances of the accounts will then automatically represent the expense of the new period.

INTERIM STATEMENTS

The preceding illustration for Kimco Inc. was based on an accounting period of one year. In practice, most business enterprises also prepare financial statements at various intervals during the fiscal year, such as monthly, quarterly, or semiannually. Statements issued for periods covering less than a fiscal year are called interim statements.

The work sheet discussed in this chapter is especially useful in accumulating data for interim statements. In such a case, the work sheet provides the data for the statements. However, because the data are for an interim period, the adjustments listed on the work sheet are not entered into the accounts. In this way, the statements can be prepared on an up-to-date basis without affecting the ledger. Likewise, no closing entries would be prepared for the temporary accounts reported in the interim statements.

Self-Examination Questions
(Answers at end of chapter.)

1. The amount for merchandise inventory that appears in the trial balance columns of the work sheet represents:
   A. inventory at the beginning of the current period
   B. inventory at the end of the current period
   C. cost of merchandise sold during the current period
   D. none of the above

2. The income statement in which the total of all expenses is deducted from the total of all revenues is termed:

A. multiple-step form   C. account form
B. single-step form   D. report form

3. At the end of the fiscal year, the adjusting entry for accrued salaries was inadvertently omitted. The effect of the error (assuming that it is not corrected) would be to:

A. understate expenses for the year
B. overstate net income for the year
C. understate liabilities at the end of the year
D. all of the above

4. Which of the following accounts would be closed to the income summary account at the end of a period?

A. Sales   C. Both Sales and Salary Expense
B. Salary Expense   D. Neither Sales nor Salary Expense

5. The post-closing trial balance would include which of the following accounts?

A. Cash   C. Salary Expense
B. Sales   D. All of the above

4–1. Is the work sheet a substitute for the financial statements? Discuss.

Discussion Questions

4–2. In the Balance Sheet columns of the work sheet for Scott Company for the current year, the Credit column total is $19,450 greater than the Debit column total. Would the income statement report a net income or a net loss? Explain.

4–3. In the following questions, identify the items designated by X:

(a) Sales − (X + X) = Net sales.
(b) Purchases − X = Net purchases.
(c) Merchandise inventory (beginning) + X = Merchandise available for sale.
(d) Merchandise available for sale − X = Cost of merchandise sold.
(e) Net sales − cost of merchandise sold = X.

4–4. The account Merchandise Inventory is listed at $98,500 on the trial balance as of January 31, the end of the first month in the fiscal year. Which one of the following phrases describes the item correctly?

(a) Inventory of merchandise at January 1, beginning of the month.
(b) Purchases of merchandise during January.
(c) Merchandise available for sale during January.
(d) Inventory of merchandise at January 31, end of the month.
(e) Cost of merchandise sold during January.

4–5. The following data appear in a work sheet as of December 31, the end of the fiscal year:

	Adjustments		Income Statement	
	Dr.	Cr.	Dr.	Cr.
Income Summary	(a) 95,000	(b) 85,000	95,000	85,000

(a) To what account was the $95,000 credited in adjustment (a)?
(b) To what account was the $85,000 debited in adjustment (b)?
(c) What was the amount of the merchandise inventory at January 1, the beginning of the fiscal year?
(d) What amount will be listed for merchandise inventory on the balance sheet at December 31, the end of the fiscal year?
(e) If the totals of the Income Statement columns of the work sheet are $910,000 debit and $980,000 credit, what is the amount of the net income for the year?
(f) Would the amount determined to be net income be affected by extending only the net amount of $10,000 ($95,000 − $85,000) into the Income Statement debit column?

4–6. For the fiscal year, net sales were $975,000 and net purchases were $650,000. Merchandise inventory at the beginning of the year was $75,000 and at the end of the year it was $80,000. Determine the following amounts:
(a) Merchandise available for sale.
(b) Cost of merchandise sold.
(c) Gross profit.
(d) Merchandise inventory listed on the balance sheet as of the end of the year.

4–7. Differentiate between the multiple-step and the single-step forms of the income statement.

4–8. The following expenses were incurred by a merchandising enterprise during the year. In which expense section of the income statement should each be reported: (a) selling, (b) general, or (c) other?
(1) Depreciation expense on store equipment.
(2) Interest expense on notes payable.
(3) Salary of salespersons.
(4) Insurance expense on office equipment.
(5) Heating and lighting expense.
(6) Salary of general manager.
(7) Advertising expense.
(8) Office supplies used.

4–9. What major advantages and disadvantages does the single-step form of income statement have in comparison to the multiple-step statement?

4–10. Differentiate between the account form and the report form of balance sheet.

4–11. (a) What two financial statements are frequently combined and presented as a single statement? (b) What is the major criticism directed at the combined statement?

4–12. Why are closing entries required at the end of an accounting period?

4–13. To what account is the income summary account closed for a corporation?

4–14. To what account in the ledger of a corporation is the account "Dividends" periodically closed?

4–15. From the following list, identify the accounts that should be closed to Income Summary at the end of the fiscal year: (a) Accounts Payable, (b) Advertising Expense, (c) Capital Stock, (d) Cash, (e) Depreciation Expense, (f) Miscellaneous Expense, (g) Office Equipment, (h) Prepaid Insurance, (i) Retained Earnings, (j) Sales, (k) Supplies, (l) Wages Payable.

4–16. (a) What is the effect of closing the revenue, expense, and dividends accounts of a corporation at the end of a fiscal year? (b) After the closing entries have been posted, what type of accounts remain with balances?

4–17. Which of the following accounts in the ledger of a corporation will ordinarily appear in the post-closing trial balance? (a) Accounts Receivable, (b) Accumulated Depreciation, (c) Capital Stock, (d) Cash, (e) Depreciation Expense, (f) Dividends, (g) Equipment, (h) Retained Earnings, (i) Sales, (j) Supplies, (k) Wages Expense, (l) Wages Payable.

4–18. Before adjustment at December 31, the end of the fiscal year, the salary expense account has a debit balance of $462,000. The amount of salary accrued (owed but not paid) on the same date is $9,750. Indicate the necessary (a) adjusting entry, (b) closing entry, and (c) reversing entry.

4–19. As of May 1, the first day of the fiscal year, Salary Expense has a credit balance of $5,000. On May 3, the first payday of the year, salaries of $12,500 are paid. (a) What is the salary expense for May 1–3: $5,000, $7,500, $12,500, or $17,500? (b) What entry should be made to record the payment on May 3?

4–20. What term is applied to financial statements issued for periods covering less than a fiscal year?

4–21. After all revenue and expense accounts have been closed at the end of the fiscal year, Income Summary has a debit of $312,600 and a credit of $296,500. As of the same date, Retained Earnings has a credit balance of $60,240 and Dividends has a debit balance of $18,300. (a) Journalize the entries required to complete the closing of the accounts. (b) State the amount of Retained Earnings at the end of the period.

Exercises

4–22. Two or more items are omitted in each of the following tabulations of income statement data. Determine the amounts of the missing items, identifying them by letter.

Sales	Sales Returns	Net Sales	Beginning Inventory	Net Purchases	Ending Inventory	Cost of Merchandise Sold	Gross Profit
$98,000	$5,000	(a)	$45,000	$80,000	(b)	$70,000	(c)
72,000	(d)	$70,000	19,000	45,000	$20,000	(e)	(f)
89,000	(g)	89,000	(h)	65,000	37,000	(i)	$28,000
65,000	2,000	63,000	22,000	43,000	(j)	(k)	20,000

4-23. On the basis of the following data, journalize (a) the adjusting entries at December 31, the end of the current fiscal year, and (b) the reversing entry on January 1, the first day of the following year.

(1) The prepaid insurance account before adjustment on December 31 has a balance of $6,750. An analysis of the policies indicates that $4,850 of premiums has expired during the year.

(2) Store supplies account balance before adjusting, $990; store supplies physical inventory, December 31, $220.

(3) Merchandise inventory: January 1 (beginning), $88,500; December 31 (ending), $87,200.

(4) Sales salaries are uniformly $12,000 for a five-day workweek, ending on Friday. The last payday of the year was Friday, December 27.

4-24. Portions of the salary expense account of an enterprise are presented below. (a) Indicate the nature of the entry (payment, adjusting, closing, reversing) from which each numbered posting was made. (b) Present the complete journal entry from which each numbered posting was made.

ACCOUNT Salary Expense   ACCOUNT NO. 52

Date		Item	Post. Ref.	Dr.	Cr.	Balance Dr.	Cr.
19--							
Jan.	8		39	3,200		3,200	

Date		Item	Post. Ref.	Dr.	Cr.	Balance Dr.	Cr.
Dec.	26	(1)	44	3,350		85,800	
	31	(2)	44	1,350		87,150	
	31	(3)	45		87,150	—	—
19--							
Jan.	1	(4)	45		1,350		1,350
	9	(5)	46	3,400		2,050	

4-25. Salary Expense has a balance of $722,150 as of June 26.

(a) Present entries for the following:

June 30. Recorded accrued salaries, $6,050.

    30. Closed the salaries expense account.

July 1. Recorded a reversing entry for accrued salaries.

    3. Recorded salaries paid, $15,700.

(b) Answer the following questions:

(1) What is the balance of the salary expense account on July 1?

(2) Is the balance of the salary expense account on July 1 an asset, a liability, a revenue, or an expense?

(3) What is the balance of the salary expense account on July 3?

(4) Of the $15,700 salary payment on July 3, how much is expense in July?

(5) If there had been no reversing entry on July 1, how should the debit for the salary payment of July 3 have been recorded?

4-26. Selected account titles and related amounts appearing in the Income Statement and Balance Sheet columns of the work sheet of the Levis Company for December 31 are listed in alphabetical order as follows:

Building	$220,000	Purchases	$735,000
Capital Stock	250,000	Purchases Discount	14,000
Cash	81,500	Retained Earnings	192,500
Dividends	50,000	Salaries Payable	3,100
General Expenses	72,500	Sales	998,000
Interest Expense	5,700	Sales Discount	8,600
Merchandise Inventory (1/1)	170,450	Sales Returns and Allowances	9,200
Merchandise Inventory (12/31)	192,950	Selling Expenses	102,500
Office Supplies	7,100	Store Supplies	6,000

All selling expenses have been recorded in the account entitled "Selling Expenses," and all general expenses have been recorded in the account entitled "General Expenses."
  (a) Prepare a multiple-step income statement for the year.
  (b) Determine the amount of retained earnings to be reported in the balance sheet at the end of the year.
  (c) Journalize the entries to adjust the merchandise inventory.
  (d) Journalize the closing entries.

4–27. Summary operating data for the Martha Ross Company during the current year ending December 31 are as follows: cost of merchandise sold, $605,000; general expenses, $98,000; interest expense, $22,000; rent income, $40,000; net sales, $950,000; and selling expenses, $142,500. Prepare a single-step income statement.

4–28. From the data presented in Exercise 4-27 and assuming that the balance of Retained Earnings was $155,500 on January 1 and that $100,000 of dividends were paid during the year, prepare a combined income and retained earnings statement. (Use the single-step form for the income statement portion of the statement.)

4–29. The following data for C. Wells and Co. were selected from the ledger after adjustment at December 31, the end of the current fiscal year:

Problems

Accounts payable	$ 42,300
Accounts receivable	134,250
Accumulated depreciation–office equipment	34,000
Accumulated depreciation–store equipment	62,700
Capital stock	200,000
Cash	87,550
Cost of merchandise sold	605,500
Dividends	80,000
Dividends payable	20,000
General expenses	89,650
Interest expense	15,200
Merchandise inventory	172,500
Mortgage note payable (due in 1991)	75,000
Office equipment	60,200
Prepaid insurance	8,700
Rent income	12,900
Retained earnings	112,800
Salaries payable	8,100

Sales	$942,700
Selling expenses	111,250
Store equipment	145,700

Instructions:

   (1) Prepare a combined income and retained earnings statement, using the single-step form for the income statement.

   (2) Prepare a balance sheet in report form.

4–30. The accounts in the ledger of Whitmore Company, with the unadjusted balances on June 30, the end of the current fiscal year, are as follows:

Cash	$ 43,750	Purchases	$610,050
Accounts Receivable	96,150	Sales Salaries Expense	77,400
Merchandise Inventory	145,250	Advertising Expense	24,800
Prepaid Insurance	12,690	Depreciation Expense—	
Store Supplies	8,250	Store Equipment	—
Store Equipment	89,500	Store Supplies Expense	—
Accum. Depreciation—Store		Misc. Selling Expense	4,400
Equipment	25,300	Office Salaries Expense	39,845
Accounts Payable	44,740	Rent Expense	40,000
Salaries Payable	—	Heating and Lighting Exp. ...	16,100
Capital Stock	180,000	Taxes Expense	8,500
Retained Earnings	81,445	Insurance Expense	—
Dividends	60,000	Misc. General Expense	3,600
Income Summary	—	Gain on Disposal of Equip. ..	3,800
Sales	945,000		

The data needed for year-end adjustments on June 30 are as follows:

Merchandise inventory on June 30	$150,500
Insurance expired during the year	6,400
Store supplies inventory on June 30	2,150
Depreciation for the current year	19,200
Accrued salaries on June 30:	
Sales salaries $2,800	
Office salaries 1,300	4,100

Instructions:

   (1) Prepare a work sheet for the fiscal year ended June 30, listing all of the accounts in the order given.

   (2) Prepare a multiple-step income statement.

   (3) Prepare a retained earnings statement.

   (4) Prepare a report form balance sheet.

   (5) Compute the following:

      (a) Percent of gross profit to sales.

      (b) Percent of income from operations to sales.

4–31. The accounts and their balances in the ledger of Abrams Company on December 31 of the current year are as follows:

Cash	$ 30,750
Accounts Receivable	71,500
Merchandise Inventory	92,750
Prepaid Insurance	7,910
Store Supplies	1,525
Office Supplies	1,065
Store Equipment	70,500
Accum. Depreciation–Store Equipment	23,350
Office Equipment	22,750
Accum. Depreciation–Office Equipment	10,000
Accounts Payable	42,115
Salaries Payable	—
Mortgage Note Payable (due 1993)	80,000
Capital Stock	50,000
Retained Earnings	48,500
Dividends	36,000
Income Summary	—
Sales	622,250
Sales Returns and Allowances	3,250
Purchases	410,300
Purchases Discount	2,150
Sales Salaries Expense	56,850
Advertising Expense	17,150
Rent Expense–Selling	16,000
Depreciation Expense–Store Equipment	—
Insurance Expense–Selling	—
Store Supplies Expense	—
Misc. Selling Expense	1,190
Office Salaries Expense	29,450
Rent Expense–General	8,000
Depreciation Expense–Office Equipment	—
Insurance Expense–General	—
Office Supplies Expense	—
Miscellaneous General Expense	1,225
Gain on Disposal of Plant Assets	9,400
Interest Expense	9,600

The data for year-end adjustments on December 31 are as follows:

Merchandise inventory on December 31		$89,200
Insurance expired during the year:		
Allocable as selling expense	$2,200	
Allocable as general expense	810	3,010
Inventory of supplies on December 31:		
Store supplies		775
Office supplies		415
Depreciation for the year:		
Store equipment		6,750
Office equipment		2,500
Salaries payable on December 31:		
Sales salaries	$2,100	
Office salaries	1,050	3,150

Instructions:

(1) Prepare a work sheet for the current year ended December 31, listing all accounts in the order given.
(2) Prepare a multiple-step income statement.
(3) Prepare a retained earnings statement.
(4) Prepare a report form balance sheet.
(5) Journalize the adjusting entries.
(6) Journalize the closing entries.
(7) Journalize the reversing entries as of January 1.

4-32. A portion of the work sheet of Frank Betts Company for the current fiscal year ended June 30 is presented as follows:

Account Title	Income Statement		Balance Sheet	
	Debit	Credit	Debit	Credit
Cash...........................			41,750	
Accounts Receivable			140,650	
Merchandise Inventory			161,100	
Prepaid Rent			6,000	
Prepaid Insurance			11,950	
Supplies.................................			2,150	
Store Equipment			58,500	
Accumulated Depr.—Store Equipment ..				22,200
Office Equipment			30,400	
Accumulated Depr.—Office Equipment .				10,150
Accounts Payable				62,500
Sales Salaries Payable...............				3,000
Mortgage Note Payable				100,000
Capital Stock.........................				150,000
Retained Earnings				62,350
Dividends			40,000	
Income Summary	172,750	161,100		
Sales		827,050		
Sales Returns and Allowances	8,120			
Purchases	512,410			
Purchases Discount		4,250		
Sales Salaries Expense	72,500			
Delivery Expense.....................	21,200			
Depreciation Expense—Store Equipment .	8,900			
Supplies Expense	1,250			
Miscellaneous Selling Expense.........	1,200			
Office Salaries Expense	40,500			
Rent Expense........................	36,000			
Heating and Lighting Expense	8,950			
Insurance Expense	7,750			
Depreciation Expense—Office Equipment.	3,750			
Miscellaneous General Expense	1,320			
Interest Expense	13,500			
	910,100	992,400	492,500	410,200

Instructions:

(1) From the partial work sheet, determine the eight entries that appeared in the adjustments columns and present them in general journal form. The only accounts affected by more than one adjusting entry were Merchandise Inventory and Income Summary. The balance in Prepaid Rent before adjustment was $42,000, representing a prepayment for 14 months' rent at $3,000 a month.

(2) Determine the following:
   (a) Amount of net income for the year.
   (b) Amount of the retained earnings at the end of the year.

4–33. Autoset Lanes Inc. prepares interim statements at the end of each month and closes its accounts annually as of December 31. The trial balance at September 30 of the current year, the adjustment data needed at September 30, and the interim income statement for the eight months ended August 31 of the current year are as follows:

Autoset Lanes Inc.
Trial Balance
September 30, 19--

Cash	8,040	
Prepaid Insurance	1,200	
Supplies	1,060	
Land	30,000	
Building	86,500	
Accumulated Depreciation — Building		21,625
Equipment	61,250	
Accumulated Depreciation — Equipment		25,300
Accounts Payable		3,170
Capital Stock		50,000
Retained Earnings		56,245
Dividends	6,500	
Bowling Revenue		80,600
Salaries and Wages Expense	31,150	
Advertising Expense	4,500	
Utilities Expense	4,380	
Repairs Expense	1,320	
Miscellaneous Expense	1,040	
	236,940	236,940

Adjustment data at September 30:

(a) Insurance expired for the period January 1–September 30	$ 900
(b) Inventory of supplies on September 30	140
(c) Depreciation of building for the period January 1–September 30	1,620
(d) Depreciation of equipment for the period January 1–September 30	5,150
(e) Accrued salaries and wages on September 30	1,950

Autoset Lanes Inc.
Income Statement
For Eight Months Ended August 31, 19--

Bowling revenue		$68,500
Operating expenses:		
Salaries and wages expense	$28,690	
Depreciation expense — equipment	4,400	
Advertising expense.	3,755	
Utilities expense	3,702	
Depreciation expense — building	1,440	
Repairs expense.	1,148	
Supplies expense	760	
Insurance expense.	750	
Miscellaneous expense	827	
Total operating expenses		45,472
Net income.		$23,028

Instructions:

(1) Prepare a work sheet for the nine months ended September 30.
(2) Prepare a single-step interim income statement for the nine months ended September 30.
(3) Prepare an interim retained earnings statement for the nine months ended September 30.
(4) Prepare an interim balance sheet as of September 30.
(5) On the basis of the income statement for the nine-month period and the income statement for the eight-month period, prepare a single-step income statement for the month of September.
(6) Compute the percent of net income to revenue for:
  (a) The eight-month period ended August 31.
  (b) The nine-month period ended September 30.
  (c) The month of September.
(7) Compute the percent of net income for the nine-month period ended September 30 to total stockholders' equity as of the beginning of the fiscal year. The capital stock account remained unchanged during the nine-month period.

(If the working papers correlating with the textbook are not used, omit Problem 4-34.)

4–34. John Cox Company prepares interim financial statements at the end of each month and closes its accounts annually on December 31. Its income statement for the two-month period, January and February of the current year, is presented in the working papers. In addition, the trial balance of the ledger as of one month later is presented on a work sheet in the working papers. Data needed for adjusting entries at March 31, the end of the three-month period, are as follows:

(a) Estimated merchandise inventory at March 31, $247,500.
(b) Insurance expired during the three-month period:
   Allocable as selling expense, $360.
   Allocable as general expense, $150.
(c) Estimated inventory of store supplies at March 31, $435.

(d) Depreciation for the three-month period:
   Store equipment, $1,800.
   Office equipment, $600.

(e) Salaries accrued at March 31:
   Sales salaries, $1,650.
   Office salaries, $250.

(f) Unearned rent income at March 31, $305.

Instructions:

(1) Complete the work sheet for the three-month period ended March 31 of the current year.

(2) Prepare a multiple-step income statement for the three-month period, using the last three-column group of the nine-column form in the working papers.

(3) Prepare a multiple-step income statement for the month of March, using the middle three-column group of the nine-column form in the working papers.

(4) Prepare a retained earnings statement for the three-month period.

(5) Prepare a report form balance sheet as of March 31.

4–29A. The following data for C. C. Romano Co. were selected from the ledger after adjustment at June 30, the end of the current fiscal year:

Alternate Problems

Account payable	$ 45,800
Accounts receivable	88,750
Accumulated depreciation—office equipment	20,500
Accumulated depreciation—store equipment	60,700
Capital stock	200,000
Cash	30,150
Cost of merchandise sold	572,360
Dividends	40,000
Dividends payable	10,000
General expenses	72,500
Interest expense	18,750
Merchandise inventory	310,200
Mortgage note payable (due in 1991)	100,000
Office equipment	72,750
Prepaid insurance	3,500
Rent income	12,650

Retained earnings	$197,630
Salaries payable	3,750
Sales	827,150
Selling expenses	113,720
Store equipment	155,500

Instructions:

(1) Prepare a combined income and retained earnings statement, using the single-step form for the income statement.
(2) Prepare a balance sheet in report form.

4–30A. The accounts in the ledger of Snyder Company, with the unadjusted balances on December 31, the end of the current year, are as follows:

Cash	$ 22,200	Purchases	$642,450
Accounts Receivable	66,700	Sales Salaries Expense	103,550
Merchandise Inventory	151,850	Advertising Expense	29,150
Prepaid Insurance	3,100	Depreciation Expense—	
Store Supplies	2,650	Store Equipment	—
Store Equipment	207,750	Store Supplies Expense	—
Accum. Depreciation—		Misc. Selling Expense	2,010
Store Equipment	105,800	Office Salaries Expense	65,350
Accounts Payable	39,950	Rent Expense	30,000
Salaries Payable	—	Heating and Lighting Exp.	21,100
Capital Stock	100,000	Taxes Expense	9,800
Retained Earnings	150,600	Insurance Expense	—
Dividends	20,000	Misc. General Expense	3,050
Income Summary	—	Loss on Disposal of	
Sales	985,600	Equipment	1,240

The data needed for year-end adjustments on December 31 are as follows:

Merchandise inventory on December 31		$125,800
Insurance expired during the year		1,950
Store supplies inventory on December 31		700
Depreciation for the current year		11,700
Accrued salaries on December 31:		
Sales salaries	$2,200	
Office salaries	1,550	3,750

Instructions:

(1) Prepare a work sheet for the year ended December 31, listing all of the accounts in the order given.
(2) Prepare a multiple-step income statement.
(3) Prepare a retained earnings statement.
(4) Prepare a report form balance sheet.
(5) Compute the following:
  (a) Percent of gross profit to sales.
  (b) Percent of income from operations to sales.

4–32A. A portion of the work sheet of Benton Supply Co. for the current fiscal year ended May 31 is presented as follows:

Account Title	Income Statement		Balance Sheet	
	Debit	Credit	Debit	Credit
Cash.....................................			48,250	
Accounts Receivable....................			102,100	
Merchandise Inventory			277,600	
Prepaid Rent...........................			2,000	
Prepaid Insurance			1,950	
Supplies...............................			1,150	
Store Equipment........................			126,900	
Accumulated Depr.—Store Equipment				42,500
Office Equipment			37,600	
Accumulated Depr.—Office Equipment....				29,150
Accounts Payable.......................				97,200
Sales Salaries Payable				3,750
Mortgage Note Payable..................				200,000
Capital Stock..........................				150,000
Retained Earnings				62,500
Dividends..............................			36,000	
Income Summary........................	295,100	277,600		
Sales..................................		850,000		
Sales Returns and Allowances	17,010			
Purchases	514,755			
Purchases Discount.....................		4,910		
Sales Salaries Expense	102,500			
Delivery Expense.......................	13,650			
Depreciation Expense—Store Equipment .	7,500			
Supplies Expense	795			
Miscellaneous Selling Expense...........	3,100			
Office Salaries Expense	55,000			
Rent Expense..........................	24,000			
Heating and Lighting Expense............	19,950			
Insurance Expense	4,950			
Depreciation Expense—Office Equipment.	3,800			
Miscellaneous General Expense..........	1,950			
Interest Expense	20,000			
	1,084,060	1,132,510	633,550	585,100

Instructions:

(1) From the partial work sheet, determine the eight entries that appeared in the adjustments columns and present them in general journal form. The only accounts affected by more than one adjusting entry were Merchandise Inventory and Income Summary. The balance in Prepaid Rent before adjustment was $26,000, representing 13 months' rent at $2,000 per month.

(2) Determine the following:

    (a) Amount of net income for the year.

    (b) Amount of the retained earnings at the end of the year.

(If the working papers correlating with the textbook are not used, omit Problem 4-34A.)

4–34A. John Cox Company prepares interim financial statements at the end of each month and closes its accounts annually on December 31. Its income statement for the two-month period, January and February of the current year, is presented in the working papers. In addition, the trial balance of the ledger as of one month later is presented on a work sheet in the working papers. Data needed for adjusting entries at March 31, the end of the three-month period, are as follows:

(a) Estimated inventory of store supplies at March 31, $435.

(b) Salaries accrued at March 31:
Sales salaries, $1,750.
Office salaries, $350.

(c) Depreciation for the three-month period:
Store equipment, $1,800.
Office equipment, $600.

(d) Insurance expired during the three-month period:
Allocable as selling expense, $360.
Allocable as general expense, $150

(e) Estimated merchandise inventory at March 31, $246,100.

(f) Unearned rent income at March 31, $305.

Instructions:

(1) Complete the work sheet for the three-month period ended March 31 of the current year.

(2) Prepare a multiple-step income statement for the three-month period, using the last three-column group of the nine-column form in the working papers.

(3) Prepare a multiple-step income statement for the month of March, using the middle three-column group of the nine-column form in the working papers.

(4) Prepare a retained earnings statement for the three-month period.

(5) Prepare a report form balance sheet as of March 31.

Mini-Case

4–35. Your brother operates Tapes Unlimited Inc., a video tape distributorship that is in its second year of operation. Recently, Ruby Hobbs, the firm's accountant, resigned to enter nursing school. Before leaving, she completed the work sheet for the year ended July 31, 1986, and recorded the necessary adjusting entries. From this work sheet, your brother prepared the following financial statements:

Tapes Unlimited Inc.
Income Statement
For Year Ended July 31, 1986

Sales		$652,000
Less cost of merchandise sold:		
Purchases	$386,000	
Net decrease in merchandise inventory	8,500	394,500
Gross profit...................................		$257,500
Operating expenses:		
Salaries expense	$126,100	
Heat and lighting expense	12,900	
Insurance expense	6,750	
Depreciation expense—building	4,800	
Depreciation expense—office equipment	2,100	
Depreciation expense—store equipment	3,600	
Supplies expense	7,400	
Miscellaneous expense	2,700	
Delivery expense	23,600	189,950
		$ 67,550
Selling expenses:		
Advertising expense		13,040
Income from operations		$ 54,510
Other income:		
Purchases discount	$ 3,300	
Interest income	1,500	4,800
		$ 59,310
Other expenses:		
Sales returns	$ 3,800	
Dividends	10,000	
Interest expense	12,000	
Taxes expense	6,450	32,250
Net income.................................		$ 27,060

Tapes Unlimited Inc.
Retained Earnings Statement
For Year Ended July 31, 1986

Retained earnings, August 1, 1985	$13,202
Net income for the year.....................................	27,060
Retained earnings, July 31, 1986..........................	$40,262

Tapes Unlimited Inc.
Balance Sheet
July 31, 1986

Assets

Cash	$ 25,312
Merchandise inventory	103,900
Supplies	4,350
Prepaid insurance	2,800
Accounts receivable	42,600
Store equipment	18,000
Office equipment	10,500
Building	96,000
Land	25,000
Notes receivable	10,000
Total assets	$338,462

Liabilities and Stockholders' Equity

Accumulated depreciation—store equipment	$ 7,200
Accumulated depreciation—office equipment	4,200
Accumulated depreciation—building	9,600
Accounts payable	23,000
Salaries payable	4,200
Mortgage note payable— First Federal Savings Bank (due 1995)	80,000
Capital stock	170,000
Retained earnings	40,262
Total liabilities and stockholders' equity	$338,462

As part of the existing loan agreement with First Federal Savings Bank, Tapes Unlimited Inc. must submit financial statements annually to the bank. In reviewing your brother's statements and supporting records before he submits the statements to the bank, you discover the following information:

Merchandise inventory:
August 1, 1985 .... $112,400
July 31, 1986 103,900

Supplies inventory at July 31, 1986:
Store supplies .... $ 2,610
Office supplies 1,740

Salaries expense:
Sales salaries .... $ 90,440
Office salaries 35,660

Insurance expense:
Selling $4,200
General 2,550

Supplies expense:
Store supplies $4,440
Office supplies 2,960

Miscellaneous expense:
Selling $1,620
General 1,080

Instructions:

(1) Revise your brother's statements as necessary to conform to proper form for a multiple-step income statement, a retained earnings statement, and a report form balance sheet .

(2) Prepare a projected single-step income statement based upon the following data:

Your brother is considering a proposal to increase net income by offering sales discounts of 2/15, n/30, and by shipping all merchandise FOB shipping point. Currently, no sales discount is allowed and merchandise is shipped FOB destination. It is estimated that these credit terms will increase gross sales by 10% and that 75% of all customers will take the discount by paying within the discount period. The remaining 25% will pay within 30 days, which is the current experience for all sales. The ratio of cost of merchandise sold to *gross* sales is 60% and is not expected to change under the proposed plan. Sales returns and allowances are expected to increase proportionately with increased gross sales. All selling and general expenses are expected to remain unchanged, except for store supplies, miscellaneous selling, office supplies, and miscellaneous general expenses, which are expected to increase proportionately with increased gross sales. The other income and other expense items will remain unchanged. The shipment of all merchandise FOB shipping point will eliminate all delivery expenses.

(3) (a) Based upon the projected income statement in (2), would you recommend the implementation of the proposed changes?

  (b) Describe any possible concerns you may have related to the proposed changes described in (2).

1. A The amount of merchandise inventory appearing in the trial balance columns of the work sheet represents the inventory at the beginning of the period (answer A). This amount and the amount of the merchandise inventory at the end of the period (answer B) are included on the work sheet as inventory adjustments. These two adjustments and the net cost of merchandise purchased provide the data to determine the cost of merchandise sold (answer C).

2. B The single-step form of income statement (answer B) is so named because the total of all expenses is deducted from the total of all revenues. The multiple-step form (answer A) includes numerous sections and subsections with several intermediate balances before arriving at net income. The account form (answer C) and the report form (answer D) are two common forms of the balance sheet.

Answers to Self-Examination Questions

3. D The omission of the adjustment for accrued salaries at the end of the year understates expenses (answer A) and consequently overstates net income (answer B) for the year. The liability for salaries payable is also omitted and results in understating liabilities at the end of the year (answer C).

4. C Since all revenue and expense accounts are closed at the end of the period, both Sales (revenue) and Salary Expense (expense) would be closed to Income Summary (answer C).

5. A Since the post-closing trial balance includes only balance sheet accounts (all of the revenue and expense accounts have been previously closed), Cash (answer A) would appear on the trial balance. Both Sales (answer B) and Salary Expense (answer C) are temporary accounts that are closed prior to the preparation of the post-closing trial balance.

PART 2

Financial Accounting Systems

Accounting Systems, Profit Measurement, and Management

A Greek restaurant owner in Canada had his own system of accounting. He kept his accounts payable in a cigar box on the left-hand side of his cash register, his daily cash returns on the cash register, and his receipts for paid bills in another cigar box on the right.

When his youngest son graduated as an accountant, he was appalled by his father's primitive methods. "I don't know how you can run a business that way," he said. "How do you know what your profits are?"

"Well, son," the father replied, "when I got off the boat from Greece, I had nothing but the pants I was wearing. Today, your brother is a doctor. You are an accountant. Your sister is a speech therapist. Your mother and I have a nice car, and city house, a country home. We have a good business, and everything is paid for..."

"So, you add all that together, subtract the pants, and there's your profit!"

SOURCE Anonymous

In 1950, Congress passed the Budget and Accounting Procedures Act, which required the comptroller general to prescribe accounting principles for federal executive agencies to follow in designing their accounting systems. However, the full and satisfactory implementation of this Act was a slow process and, in the interim, serious deficiencies were noted.

In a speech before a group of government accountants, the comptroller general cited examples of some of the problems that resulted from failing to use a good accounting system. The Department of the Army, for instance, experienced a breakdown in the control over its procurements in the late 1970s, resulting in excess obligations totaling about $225 million. Some top officials were reprimanded, and more than 28,000 staff days were used in unraveling the accounting records. In 1975, the Social Security Administration estimated that it had made nearly a billion dollars in erroneous Supplemental Security income payments. In commenting on this case, the comptroller general indicated that "if more effort had been devoted to better accounting systems, these errors might have been lessened."

The comptroller general noted that those agencies which devote the time and effort required to design and implement a good accounting system, in accordance with prescribed principles, generally have less problems and are able to manage their operations more efficiently and economically. In addition, agency management is provided with better accounting data on which to base decisions, control funds and property, and make full disclosure of financial results.

SOURCE Adapted from "A Good Accounting System—A Key to Good Management," *Journal of Accountancy*, February, 1978, pp. 66-69.

CHAPTER 5

Accounting Systems and Cash

CHAPTER OBJECTIVES

Describe the qualities of a properly designed accounting system.

Describe and illustrate the principles of internal control for directing operations.

Describe and illustrate the application of internal control principles in controlling cash.

Describe and illustrate accounting for cash.

The way in which management is given the information for use in conducting the affairs of the business and in reporting to owners, creditors, and other interested parties is called the **accounting system.** In a general sense, an accounting system includes the entire network of communications used by a business organization to provide needed information. Indeed, there are frequent references to accounting systems as the "total informational system" of an enterprise.

In this chapter, the qualities of a properly designed accounting system and the principles of internal control for directing operations are discussed. The chapter also presents the application of these internal control principles to the design of an effective system for controlling cash and accounting for cash transactions.

PRINCIPLES OF ACCOUNTING SYSTEMS

The entire amount of data needed by an enterprise is called its **data base.** Depending upon the enterprise, the variety and amount of data included in the data base, and the uses made of the data, various accounting systems — manual and computerized — may be used.

In preceding chapters, manual accounting systems were illustrated because they are the easiest systems to understand. If the data base is relatively small, the manual system illustrated may serve a business reasonably well. As an enterprise becomes larger and more complex, the manual system can be modified in order to make the system more efficient and to better meet the needs of the enterprise. For example, as the number of sales on account increases, including in the ledger with all of the other accounts an account for each customer may result in a ledger that is unwieldy. In such a case, the individual customers' accounts could be placed in a separate ledger called a **subsidiary ledger.** This subsidiary ledger would be represented in the principal ledger (now called the **general ledger**) by a summarizing account called a **controlling account.** The balance in the accounts receivable controlling account in the general ledger would agree with the total of the balances of all of the customers' accounts in the subsidiary ledger.[1]

The concept of the subsidiary ledger can be extended to any group of individual accounts with a common characteristic, when it is desirable to reduce the number of accounts in the principal ledger. For example, a subsidiary ledger for creditors' accounts payable could be used, with Accounts Payable serving as the controlling account in the general ledger.

When the data base for an enterprise becomes too large and complex for the manual system to handle efficiently, the manual accounting system may be replaced by a computerized system. Regardless of whether the accounting system for a particular enterprise uses manual or computerized procedures to process its transactions, however, there are basic principles of accounting systems that are applicable in all cases. These principles are discussed in the following paragraphs.

Cost-Effectiveness Balance

An accounting system must be tailored to meet the specific needs of each business. Since costs must be incurred in meeting these needs, one of the major considerations in developing an accounting system is cost effectiveness. For example, although the reports produced by an accounting system are a

---

[1]Another means by which the manual system can be modified in order to reduce costs and more efficiently process accounting data is to use special journals, in which selected kinds of transactions are recorded. The basic features of special journals and a more detailed discussion of subsidiary ledgers are presented in Appendix B.

valuable end product of the system, the value of the reports produced should be at least equal to the cost of producing them. No matter how detailed or informational a report may be, it should not be produced if it costs more than the benefits received by those who use it.

Flexibility to Meet Future Needs

A characteristic of the modern business environment is change. Each business must adapt to the constantly changing environment in which it operates. Whether the changes are the result of new government regulations, changes in accounting principles, organizational changes necessary to meet practices of competing businesses, changes in data processing technology, or other factors, the accounting system must be flexible enough to meet the changing demands made of it. For example, when granting credit to customers became a common practice, it was necessary for many businesses to maintain accounts receivable, accounts payable, and related statistical and other useful information. Regulatory agencies, such as the Securities and Exchange Commission, often require a continually changing variety of reports that require changes in the accounting system.

Adequate Internal Controls

An accounting system must provide the information needed by management in reporting to owners, creditors, and other interested parties and in conducting the affairs of the business. In addition, the system should aid management in controlling operations. The detailed procedures used by management to control operations are called internal controls. The broad principles of internal control are discussed later in the chapter.

Effective Reporting

Users of the information provided by the accounting system rely on various reports for relevant information presented in an understandable manner. When these reports are prepared, the requirements and knowledge of the user should be recognized. For example, management may need detailed reports for controlling operations on a weekly or even daily basis, and regulatory agencies often require uniform data and establish certain deadlines for the submission of certain reports.

Adaptation to Organizational Structure

Only by effectively using and adapting to the human resources of a business can the accounting system meet information needs at the lowest cost. Since no two businesses are structured alike, the accounting system must be tailored to the organizational structure of each business. The lines of authority and responsibility will affect the information of each business. In addition, an effective system needs the approval and support of all levels of management.

ACCOUNTING SYSTEM INSTALLATION AND REVISION

Before designing and installing an accounting system for an enterprise, the designer must have a complete knowledge of the business' operations. At the time that a business is organized, however, there are likely to be many unknown factors that will affect such areas of the system as the types and design of the forms needed, the number and titles of the accounts required, and the exact procedures to be used. It is also quite common for a firm to expand its already successful operations into new areas not originally thought about, to increase its volume of transactions, to use additional personnel, and in other ways to "outgrow" its accounting system.

Many large business enterprises maintain an almost continuous review of their accounting system and may constantly be involved in changing some part of it. The job of changing an accounting system, either in its entirety or only in part, is made up of three phases: (1) analysis, (2) design, and (3) implementation.

Systems Analysis

The goal of **systems analysis** is to determine information needs, the sources of such information, and the deficiencies in procedures and data processing methods presently used. The analysis usually begins with a review of organizational structure and job descriptions of the personnel affected. This is followed by a study of the forms, records, procedures, processing methods, and reports used by the enterprise. A detailed description of the system used by the enterprise, including specific instructions to personnel and minute details of procedures, is of great value to the systems analyst in the fact-finding review. Such a compilation is usually referred to as the firm's *Systems Manual*.

In addition to looking at the shortcomings of the present system, the analyst should determine management's plans for changes in operations (volume, products, territories, etc.) in the foreseeable future.

Systems Design

Accounting systems are changed as a result of the kind of analysis described above. The design of the new system may involve only minor changes from the existing system, such as revision of a particular form and the related procedures and processing methods, or it may be a complete revision of the entire system. Systems designers must have a general knowledge of the qualities of different kinds of data processing equipment, and the ability to evaluate alternatives. Although successful systems design depends to a large extent upon the creativity, imagination, and general capabilities of the designer, observance of the broad principles previously discussed is necessary.

Systems Implementation

The final phase of the creation or revision of an accounting system is to carry out, or implement, the proposals. New or revised forms, records, procedures, and equipment must be installed, and any that are no longer useful must be withdrawn. All personnel responsible for operating the system must be carefully trained and closely supervised until satisfactory efficiency is achieved.

For a large organization, a major revision such as a change from manual processing to electronic processing is usually done gradually over an extended period rather than all at once. With such a procedure, there is less likelihood that the flow of useful data will be seriously slowed down during the critical phase of implementation. Weaknesses and conflicting or unnecessary elements in the design may also become apparent during the implementation phase. They are more easily seen and corrected when changes in a system are adopted gradually, and possible chaos is thereby avoided.

INTERNAL CONTROLS

Internal controls are classified as (1) administrative controls and (2) accounting controls. **Internal administrative controls** consist of procedures and records that aid management in achieving business goals. For example, with records of defective work by production employees, management can evaluate personnel performance and thus control the quality of the product manufactured. **Internal accounting controls** consist of procedures and records that are mainly concerned with the reliability of financial records and reports and with the safeguarding of assets. For example, procedures established to make sure that all transactions are recorded according to generally accepted accounting principles help assure reliable financial records. A way of safeguarding assets is to limit access to assets to authorized personnel.

Details of a system of internal control will vary according to the size and type of business enterprise. In a small business where it is possible for the owner-manager to personally supervise the employees and to direct the affairs of the business, few controls are necessary. As the number of employees and the complexities of an enterprise increase, it becomes more difficult for management to maintain control over all phases of operations. As a firm grows, management needs to delegate authority and to place more reliance on the accounting system in controlling operations.

Several broad principles of internal control are discussed in the following paragraphs. Many of these principles should be considered by all businesses, large and small.

Competent Personnel and Rotation of Duties

Successful operation of an accounting system requires people who are able to perform the duties to which they are assigned. Hence it is necessary that all accounting employees be adequately trained and supervised to perform their jobs. It is also advisable to rotate clerical personnel periodically from job to job. In addition to broadening their understanding of the system, the knowledge that others may in the future perform their jobs tends to discourage deviations from prescribed procedures. Occasional rotation is also helpful in disclosing any irregularities that may have occurred. For these same reasons all employees should be required to take annual vacations, with their jobs assigned to others during their absence.

Assignment of Responsibility

If employees are to work efficiently, their responsibilities must be clearly defined. There should be no overlapping or undefined areas of responsibility. For example, if a certain cash register is to be used by two or more salesclerks, each one should be assigned a separate cash drawer and register key. Thus, daily proof of the handling of cash can be obtained for each clerk.

Separation of Responsibility for Related Operations

To decrease the possibility of inefficiency, errors, and fraud, responsibility for a sequence of related operations should be divided among two or more persons. For example, no one individual should be authorized to order merchandise, verify the receipt of the goods, and pay the supplier. To do so would invite such abuses as placing orders with a supplier on the basis of friendship rather than on price, quality, and other objective factors; indifferent and routine verification of the quantity and quality of goods received; conversion of goods to the personal use of the employee; carelessness in verifying and the accuracy of invoices; and payment of false invoices. When the responsibility for purchasing, receiving, and paying are divided among three persons or departments, the possibilities of such abuses are minimized.

The "checks and balances" provided by distributing responsibility among various departments requires no duplication of effort. The work of each department, as evidenced by the business documents that it prepares, must "fit" with those prepared by the other departments.

Separation of Operations and Accounting

Responsibility for maintaining the accounting records should be separated from the responsibility for engaging in business transactions and for the custody of the firm's assets. By so doing, the accounting records serve as an independent check on the business operations. For example, the employees entrusted with handling cash receipts from customers should not have access to the journal or ledger. Separation of the two functions reduces the possibilities of errors and embezzlement.

Proofs and Security Measures

Proofs and security measures should be used to safeguard business assets and assure reliable accounting data. This principle applies to many different techniques and procedures, such as the use of a bank account and other safekeeping measures for cash and other valuable documents. Cash registers are widely used in making the initial record of cash sales. The conditioning of the public to observe the amount recorded as the sale or to accept a printed receipt from the salesclerk increases the machine's effectiveness as a part of internal control.

The use of fidelity insurance is also an aid to internal control. It insures against losses caused by fraud on the part of employees who are entrusted with company assets and serves as a psychological deterrent to the misuse of assets.

Independent Review

To determine whether the other internal control principles are being effectively applied, the system should be periodically reviewed and evaluated by internal auditors. These auditors must be independent of the employees responsible for operations. The auditors should report any weaknesses and recommend changes to correct them. For example, a review of cash disbursements may disclose that invoices were not paid within the discount period, even though enough cash was available.

CONTROL OVER CASH

Because of the high value of money in relation to its mass, and its easy transferability, cash is the asset most likely to be diverted and used improperly by employees. In addition, many transactions either directly or indirectly affect its receipt or payment. It is therefore necessary that cash be effectively safeguarded by special controls.

The Bank Account as a Tool for Controlling Cash

One of the major devices for maintaining control over cash is the bank account. To get the most benefit from a bank account, all cash received must be deposited in the bank and all payments must be made by checks drawn on the bank or from special cash funds. When such a system is strictly followed, there is a double record of cash, one maintained by the business and the other by the bank.

The forms used by the depositor in connection with a bank account are a signature card, deposit ticket, check, and a record of checks drawn.

Signature Card

At the time an account is opened, an identifying number is assigned to the account and the bank requires that a **signature card** be signed by each person authorized to sign checks drawn on the account. The card is used by the bank to determine the authenticity of the signature on checks presented to it for payment.

Deposit Ticket

The details of a deposit are listed by the depositor on a printed form supplied by the bank. **Deposit tickets** may be prepared in duplicate, in which case the copy is stamped or initialed by the bank's teller and given to the depositor as a receipt. The receipt of a deposit may be indicated by means other than a duplicate deposit ticket, but all methods give the depositor written proof of the date and the total amount of the deposit.

Check

A **check** is a written instrument signed by the depositor, ordering the bank to pay a certain sum of money to the order of a designated person. There are three parties to a check: the **drawer**, the one who signs the check; the **drawee**, the bank on which the check is drawn; and the **payee**, the one to whose order the check is drawn. When checks are issued to pay bills, they are recorded as credits to Cash on the day issued, even though they are not presented to the drawer's bank until some later time. When checks are received from customers, they are recorded as debits to Cash, on the assumption that the customer has enough money on deposit.

Check forms may be obtained in many styles. The name and the address of the depositor are often printed on each check, and the checks are usually numbered in sequence to facilitate the depositor's internal control. Most banks use automatic sorting and posting equipment and provide check forms on which the bank's identification number and the depositor's account number are printed along the lower margin in magnetic ink. When the check is presented for payment, the amount for which it is drawn is inserted next to the account number, also in magnetic ink.

Record of Checks Drawn

A memorandum record of the basic details of a check should be prepared at the time the check is written. The record may be a stub from which the check is detached or it may be a small booklet designed to be kept with the check forms. Each type of record also provides spaces for recording deposits and the current bank balance.

Business firms may prepare a copy of each check drawn and then use it as a basis for recording the transaction. Checks issued to a creditor on account are usually accompanied by a notification of the specific invoice that is being paid. The purpose of such notification, sometimes called a **remittance advice,** is to make sure that proper credit is recorded in the accounts of the creditor. Mistakes are less likely to happen and the possible need for exchanges of correspondence is reduced. The invoice number or other descriptive data may be inserted in spaces provided on the face or on the back of the check, or on an attachment to the check as in the following illustration:

CHECK AND
REMITTANCE ADVICE

MONROE COMPANY					363
813 Greenwood Street	Detroit, MI 48206-4070	April 12	19 86		9-42 / 720

Pay to the Order of _Hammond Office Products Inc._ $ 921.20

Nine hundred twenty-one 20/100-- Dollars

A NB AMERICAN NATIONAL BANK OF DETROIT
DETROIT, MI 48201-2500   (313)933-8547   MEMBER FDIC

K. R. Simms   Treasurer
Earl M. Hartman   Vice President

⑈072000423⑈ 1627042 363

DETACH THIS PORTION BEFORE CASHING

DATE	DESCRIPTION	GROSS AMOUNT	DEDUCTIONS	NET AMOUNT
4/12/86	Invoice No. 529482	940.00	18.80	921.20

MONROE COMPANY

Before depositing the check at the bank, the payee removes the part of the check containing the remittance information. The removed part may then be used by the payee as written proof of the details of the cash receipt.

Bank Statement

Although there are some differences in procedure, banks usually maintain an original and a copy of all checking accounts. When this is done, the original becomes the statement of account that is mailed to the depositor, usually once each month. Like any account with a customer or a creditor, the bank statement shows the beginning balance, debits (deductions by the bank) and credits (additions by the bank), and the balance at the end of the period. The depositor's checks received by the bank during the period may accompany the bank statement, arranged in the order of payment. The paid or canceled checks are perforated or stamped "Paid," together with the date of payment.

Debit or credit memorandums describing other entries in the depositor's account may also be enclosed with the statement. For example, the bank may have debited the depositor's account for service charges or for deposited checks returned because of insufficient funds. It may have credited the account for receipts from notes receivable left for collection or for loans to the depositor. A typical bank statement is illustrated as follows:

```
A                                        PAGE    1
NB                MEMBER FDIC
                              ACCOUNT NUMBER   1627042
AMERICAN NATIONAL BANK
OF DETROIT                    FROM   6/30/86      TO      7/31/86
DETROIT, MI 48201-2500 (313)933-8547   BALANCE           4,218.60
                              22  DEPOSITS       13,749.75
                              52  WITHDRAWALS    15,013.57

MONROE COMPANY                 2  OTHER DEBITS
813 GREENWOOD STREET              AND CREDITS          405.00CR
DETROIT, MI 48206-4070
                                 NEW BALANCE          3,359.78
```

```
*--CHECKS AND OTHER DEBITS---*---DEPOSITS--*--DATE--*--BALANCE--*


   819.40    122.54                    585.75    07/01    3,862.41
   369.50    732.26      20.15         421.53    07/02    3,162.03
   600.00    190.70      52.50         781.30    07/03    3,100.13
    25.93    160.00                    662.50    07/05    3,576.70
    36.80    181.02                    503.18    07/07    3,862.06


    32.26    535.09                    932.00    07/29    3,389.40
    21.10    126.20                    705.21    07/30    3,947.31
                        SC 3.00    MS  408.00    07/30    4,352.31
    26.12  1,615.13                    648.72    07/31    3,359.78


   EC--ERROR CORRECTION           OD--OVERDRAFT
   MS--MISCELLANEOUS              PS--PAYMENT STOPPED
   NSF--NOT SUFFICIENT FUNDS      SC--SERVICE CHARGE

   ***                    ***                        ***

   THE RECONCILEMENT OF THIS STATEMENT WITH YOUR RECORDS IS ESSENTIAL.
        ANY ERROR OR EXCEPTION SHOULD BE REPORTED IMMEDIATELY.
```

Bank Reconciliation

When all cash receipts are deposited in the bank and all payments are made by check, the cash account is often called Cash in Bank. This account in the depositor's ledger is the reciprocal of the account with the depositor in the bank's ledger. Cash in Bank in the depositor's ledger is an asset with a debit balance, and the account with the depositor in the bank's ledger is a liability with a credit balance.

It might seem that the two balances should be equal, but they are not likely to be equal on any specific date because of either or both of the following: (1) delay by either party in recording transactions, and (2) errors by either party in recording transactions. Ordinarily, there is a time lag of one day or more between the date a check is written and the date that it is presented to the bank for payment. If the depositor mails deposits to the bank or uses the night depository, a time lag between the date of the deposit and the date that it is recorded by the bank is also probable. Conversely, the bank may debit or credit the depositor's account for transactions about which the depositor will not be informed until later. Examples are service or collection fees charged by the bank and the proceeds of notes receivable sent to the bank for collection.

To determine the reasons for any difference and to correct any errors that may have been made by the bank or the depositor, the depositor's own records should be reconciled with the bank statement. The **bank reconciliation** is divided into two major sections: one section begins with the balance according to the bank statement and ends with the adjusted balance; the other section begins with the balance according to the depositor's records and also ends with the adjusted balance. The two amounts designated as the adjusted balance must be equal. The form and the content of the bank reconciliation are outlined as follows:

FORMAT FOR BANK
RECONCILIATION

Bank balance according to bank statement...............		$xxx
Add: Additions by depositor not on bank statement........	$xx	
Bank errors.....................................	xx	xx
		$xxx
Deduct: Deductions by depositor not on bank statement ...	$xx	
Bank errors....................................	xx	xx
Adjusted balance		$xxx
Bank balance according to depositor's records		$xxx
Add: Additions by bank not recorded by depositor	$xx	
Depositor errors.................................	xx	xx
		$xxx
Deduct: Deductions by bank not recorded by depositor....	$xx	
Depositor errors...............................	xx	xx
Adjusted balance		$xxx

The following procedures are used in finding the reconciling items and determining the adjusted balance of Cash in Bank:

1. Individual deposits listed on the bank statement are compared with unrecorded deposits appearing in the preceding reconciliation and with deposit receipts or other records of deposits. Deposits not recorded by the bank are added to the balance according to the bank statement.

2. Paid checks are compared with outstanding checks appearing on the preceding reconciliation and with the record of checks written. Checks issued that have not been paid by the bank are outstanding and are deducted from the balance according to the bank statement.

3. Bank credit memorandums, representing additions made by the bank, are traced to the records of cash receipts. Credit memorandums that have not been recorded are added to the balance according to the depositor's records.

4. Bank debit memorandums, representing deductions made by the bank, are traced to the records of cash payments. Debit memorandums that have not been recorded are deducted from the balance according to the depositor's records.

5. Errors discovered during the process of making the foregoing comparisons are listed separately on the reconciliation. For example, if the amount for which a check was drawn had been recorded erroneously by the depositor, the amount of the error should be added to or deducted from the balance according to the depositor's records. Similarly, errors by the bank should be added to or deducted from the balance according to the bank statement.

Illustration of Bank Reconciliation

The bank statement for Monroe Company, reproduced on page 155, indicates a balance of $3,359.78 as of July 31. The balance in Cash in Bank in Monroe Company's ledger as of the same date is $2,234.99. Use of the procedures outlined above reveals the following reconciling items:

1. Deposit of July 31 not recorded on bank statement. . . . . $ 816.20
2. Checks outstanding: No. 812, $1,061.00; No. 878, $435.39; No. 883, $48.60 . . . . 1,544.99
3. Note from Wilson Co. plus interest of $8 collected by bank (credit memorandum), not recorded by Monroe Company . . 408.00
4. Bank service charges (debit memorandum) not recorded by Monroe Company 3.00
5. Check No. 879 for $732.26 to Taylor Co. on account, recorded by Monroe Company as $723.26 . . . . 9.00

The bank reconciliation based on the bank statement and the reconciling items is as follows:

BANK
RECONCILIATION

Monroe Company
Bank Reconciliation
July 31, 1986

Balance per bank statement		$3,359.78
Add deposit of July 31, not recorded by bank.		816.20
		$4,175.98
Deduct: Outstanding checks		
No. 812.	$1,061.00	
No. 878.	435.39	
No. 883.	48.60	1,544.99
Adjusted balance		**$2,630.99**
Balance per depositor's records.		$2,234.99
Add note and interest collected by bank		408.00
		$2,642.99
Deduct: Bank service charges	$3.00	
Error in recording Check No. 879.	9.00	12.00
Adjusted balance		**$2,630.99**

Entries Based on Bank Reconciliation

Bank memorandums not recorded by the depositor and depositor's errors shown by the bank reconciliation require that entries be made in the accounts. The entries for Monroe Company, based on the bank reconciliation on page 157, are as follows. The data needed for these entries are provided by the section of the bank reconciliation that begins with the balance per depositor's records.

July 31	Cash in Bank........................	408	
	Notes Receivable....................		400
	Interest Income.....................		8
	Note collected by bank.		
31	Miscellaneous General Expense.........	3	
	Accounts Payable....................	9	
	Cash in Bank.......................		12
	Bank service charges and error in recording Check No. 879.		

After the foregoing entries are posted, the cash in bank account will have a debit balance of $2,630.99, which agrees with the adjusted balance shown on the bank reconciliation. This is the amount of cash available for use as of July 31 and the amount that would be reported on the balance sheet on that date.

Importance of Bank Reconciliation

The bank reconciliation is an important part of the system of internal control because it is a means of comparing recorded cash, per the accounting records, with the amount of cash reported by the bank. It thus provides for finding and correcting errors and irregularities. Greater internal control is achieved when the bank reconciliation is prepared by an employee who does not take part in or record cash transactions with the bank. Without a proper separation of these duties, cash is more likely to be embezzled. For example, an employee who takes part in all of these duties could prepare an unauthorized check, omit it from the accounts, and cash it. Then to account for the canceled check when returned by the bank, the employee could understate the amount of the outstanding checks on future bank reconciliations by the amount of the embezzlement.

INTERNAL CONTROL OF CASH RECEIPTS

Department stores and other retail businesses ordinarily receive cash from two main sources: (1) over the counter from cash customers and (2) by mail from charge customers making payments on account. At the end of the business day, each salesclerk counts the cash in the assigned cash drawer and records the amount on a memorandum form. An employee from the cashier's department removes the cash register tapes on which total receipts were recorded for each cash drawer, counts the cash, and compares the total with the memorandum and the tape, noting any differences. The cash is then taken to the cashier's office and the tapes and memorandum forms are forwarded to the accounting department, where they become the basis for journal entries.

The employees who open incoming mail compare the amount of cash received with the amount shown on the accompanying remittance advice to be certain that the two amounts agree. If there is no separate remittance advice, an employee prepares one on a form designed for such use. All cash received, usually in the form of checks and money orders, is sent to the cashier's department, where it is combined with the receipts from cash sales and a deposit ticket is prepared. The remittance advices are delivered to the accounting department, where they become the basis for journal entries.

The duplicate deposit tickets or other bank receipt forms obtained by the cashier are sent to the controller or other financial officer, who compares the total amount with that reported by the accounting department as the total debit to Cash in Bank for the period.

Cash Short and Over

The amount of cash actually received during a day often does not agree with the record of cash receipts. Whenever there is a difference between the record and the actual cash and no error can be found in the record, it must be assumed that the mistake occurred in making change. The cash shortage or overage is recorded in an account entitled Cash Short and Over. For example, if the actual cash received from cash sales is less than the amount indicated by the cash register tally, the entry to record the receipts would include a debit to Cash Short and Over. An example for one day's receipts follows:

Cash in Bank	4,577.60	
Cash Short and Over	3.16	
Sales		4,580.76

If there is a debit balance in the cash short and over account at the end of the fiscal period, it is an expense and may be included in "Miscellaneous general expense" on the income statement. If there is a credit balance, it is revenue and may be listed in the "Other income" section. If the balance becomes larger than may be accounted for by minor errors in making change, the management should take corrective measures.

Cash Change Funds

Retail stores and other businesses that receive cash directly from customers must maintain a fund of currency and coins in order to make change. The fund may be established by drawing a check for the required amount, debiting the account Cash on Hand and crediting Cash in Bank. No additional charges or credits to the cash on hand account are necessary unless the amount of the fund is to be increased or decreased. At the end of each business day, the total amount of cash received during the day is deposited and the original amount of the change fund is retained. The desired composition of the fund is maintained by exchanging bills or coins for those of other denominations at the bank.

INTERNAL CONTROL OF CASH PAYMENTS

It is common practice for business enterprises to require that every payment of cash be evidenced by a check signed by a designated official. As an additional control, some firms require two signatures on all checks or only on checks which are larger than a certain amount. It is also common to use a check protector, which produces amounts on the check that are not easily removed or changed.

When the owner of a business has personal knowledge of all goods and services purchased, the owner may sign checks, with the assurance that the creditors have followed the terms of their contracts and that the exact amount of the obligation is being paid. Disbursing officials are seldom able to have such a complete knowledge of affairs, however. In enterprises of even moderate size, the responsibility for issuing purchase orders, inspecting goods received, and verifying contractual and arithmetical details of invoices is divided among the employees of several departments. It is desirable, therefore, to coordinate these related activities and to link them with the final issuance of checks to creditors. One of the best systems used for this purpose is the voucher system.

The Voucher System

A **voucher system** is made up of records, methods, and procedures used in proving and recording liabilities and in paying and recording cash payments. A voucher system uses (1) vouchers, (2) a file for unpaid vouchers, and (3) a file for paid vouchers. As in all areas of accounting systems and internal controls, many differences in detail are possible. The discussion that follows refers to a medium-size merchandising enterprise with separate departments for purchasing, receiving, accounting, and disbursing.

Vouchers

The term **voucher** is widely used in accounting. In a general sense, it means any document that serves as proof of authority to pay cash, such as an invoice approved for payment, or as evidence that cash has been paid, such as a canceled check. The term has a narrower meaning when applied to the voucher system: a voucher is a special form on which is recorded relevant data about a liability and the details of its payment.

An important characteristic of the voucher system is the requirement that a voucher be prepared for each expenditure. In fact, a check may not be issued except in payment of a properly authorized voucher. Vouchers may be paid immediately after they are prepared or at a later date, depending upon the circumstances and the credit terms.

A voucher form is illustrated below. The face of the voucher provides space for the name and address of the creditor, the date and number of the voucher, and basic details of the invoice or other supporting document, such as the vendor's invoice number and the amount and terms of the invoice. One half of the back of the voucher is devoted to the account distribution and the other half to summaries of the voucher and the details of payment. Spaces are also provided for the signature or initials of certain employees.

VOUCHER

Vouchers are customarily prepared by the accounting department on the basis of an invoice or a memorandum that serves as proof of an expenditure. This is usually done only after the following comparisons and verifications have been completed and noted on the invoice:

1. Comparison of the invoice with a copy of the purchase order to verify quantities, prices, and terms.
2. Comparison of the invoice with the receiving report to verify receipt of the items billed.
3. Verification of the arithmetical accuracy of the invoice.

After all data except details of payment have been inserted, the invoice or other supporting evidence is attached to the face of the voucher, which is then folded with the account distribution and summaries on the outside. The voucher is then given to the designated official or officials for final approval.

Unpaid Voucher File

After approval by the designated official, each voucher is recorded in a journal. It is then filed in an unpaid voucher file, where it remains until it is paid. The amount due on each voucher represents the credit balance of an account payable.

All voucher systems include some way to assure payment within the discount period or on the last day of the credit period. A simple but effective method is to file each voucher in the unpaid voucher file according to the earliest date that consideration should be given to its payment. The file may be made up of a group of folders, numbered from 1 to 31, the numbers representing days of a month. Such a system brings to the attention of the disbursing official the vouchers that are to be paid on each day. It also provides management with a convenient means of forecasting the amount of cash needed to meet maturing obligations.

When a voucher is to be paid, it is removed from the unpaid voucher file and a check is issued in payment. The date, the number, and the amount of the check are listed on the back of the voucher for use in recording the payment. Paid vouchers and the supporting documents are often run through a canceling machine to prevent accidental or intentional reuse.

An exception to the general rule that vouchers be prepared for all expenditures may be made for bank charges shown by debit memorandums or notations on the bank statement. For example, such items as bank service charges, safe-deposit box rentals, and returned NSF (Not Sufficient Funds) checks from customers may be charged to the depositor's account without either a formal voucher or a check. For large expenditures, such as the repayment of a bank loan, a supporting voucher may be prepared, if desired, even though a check is not written. The paid note may then be attached to the voucher as evidence of the obligation. All bank debit memorandums are the equivalent of checks as evidence of payment.

Paid Voucher File

The payment of a voucher is recorded in a journal in the usual manner. After payment, vouchers are usually filed in numerical order in a paid voucher file. They are then readily available for examination by employees or independent auditors needing information about a certain expenditure. Eventually the paid vouchers are destroyed according to the firm's policies concerning the retention of records.

Voucher System and Management

The voucher system not only provides effective accounting controls but also aids management in discharging other responsibilities. For example, the voucher system gives greater assurance that all payments are in liquidation of valid liabilities. In addition, current information is always available for use in determining future cash requirements. This in turn enables management to make the best use of cash resources. Invoices on which cash discounts are allowed can be paid within the discount period and other invoices can be paid on the final day of the credit period, thus reducing costs and maintaining a favorable credit standing. Seasonal borrowing for working capital purposes can also be planned more accurately, with a consequent saving in interest costs.

Purchases Discounts

In earlier chapters, purchases of merchandise were recorded at the invoice price, and cash discounts taken were credited to the purchases discount account at the time of payment. There are two opposing views on how such discounts should be reported in the income statement.

The most widely accepted view, which has been followed in this textbook, is that purchases discounts should be reported as a deduction from purchases. For example, the cost of merchandise with an invoice price of $1,000, subject to terms of 2/10, n/30, is recorded initially at $1,000. If payment is made within the discount period, the discount of $20 reduces the cost to $980. If the invoice is not paid within the discount period, the cost of the merchandise remains $1,000. This treatment of purchases discounts may be attacked on the grounds that the date of payment should not affect the cost of a commodity. The additional payment required beyond the discount period adds nothing to the value of the commodities purchased.

The second view reports discounts taken as "other income." In terms of the example above, the cost of the merchandise is considered to be $1,000 regardless of the time of payment. If payment is made within the discount period, revenue of $20 is considered to be realized. The objection to this procedure lies in the recognition of revenue from the act of purchasing and paying for a commodity. Theoretically, an enterprise might make no sales of merchandise during an accounting period and yet might report as revenue the amount of cash discounts taken.

A major disadvantage of recording purchases at the invoice price and recognizing purchases discounts at the time of payment is that this method does not measure the cost of failing to take discounts. Well-managed enterprises maintain enough cash to pay within the discount period all invoices subject to a discount, and view the failure to take a discount as an inefficiency. To measure the cost of this inefficiency, purchases invoices may be recorded at the net amount, assuming that all discounts will be taken. Any discounts not taken are then recorded in an expense account called Discounts Lost. This method measures the cost of failure to take cash discounts and gives management an opportunity to take remedial action. Again assuming the same data, the invoice for $1,000 would be recorded as a debit to Purchases of $980 and a credit to Accounts Payable for the same amount. If the invoice is not paid until after the discount period has passed, the entry would be as follows:

Accounts Payable	980	
Discounts Lost	20	
Cash in Bank		1,000

When this method is used with the voucher system, all vouchers are prepared and recorded at the net amount. Any discount lost is noted on the related voucher and recorded in the journal when the voucher is paid.

Another advantage of this treatment of purchases discounts is that all merchandise purchased is recorded initially at the net price and hence no later adjustments to cost are necessary. An objection, however, is that the amount reported as accounts payable in the balance sheet may be less than the amount needed to discharge the liability.

Petty Cash

In most businesses there is a frequent need for the payment of relatively small amounts, such as for postage due, for transportation charges, or for the purchase of urgently needed supplies at a nearby retail store. Payment by check in such cases would result in delay, annoyance, and excessive expense of maintaining the records. Yet because these small payments may occur frequently and therefore amount to a considerable total sum, it is desirable to retain close control over such payments. This may be done by maintaining a special cash fund called petty cash.

In establishing a petty cash fund, the first step is to estimate the amount of cash needed for disbursements of relatively small amounts during a certain period such as a week or a month. If the voucher system is used, a voucher is then prepared for this amount and it is recorded as a debit to Petty Cash and a credit to Accounts Payable. The check drawn to pay the voucher is recorded as a debit to Accounts Payable and a credit to Cash in Bank.

The money obtained from cashing the check is placed in the custody of a specific employee who is authorized to disburse the fund according to restrictions as to maximum amount and purpose. Each time a disbursement is made from the fund, the employee records the essential details on a receipt form, obtains the signature of the payee as proof of the payment, and initials the completed form.

When the amount of money in the petty cash fund is reduced to the predetermined minimum amount, the fund is replenished. If the voucher system is used, the accounts debited on the replenishing voucher are those indicated by a summary of expenditures. The voucher is then recorded as a debit to the various expense and asset accounts and a credit to Accounts Payable. The check in payment of the voucher is recorded in the usual manner.

After the petty cash fund has been replenished, the fund will be restored to its original amount. It should be noted that the only entry in the petty cash account will be the initial debit, unless at some later time the standard amount of the fund is increased or decreased.

Because disbursements are not recorded in the accounts until the fund is replenished, petty cash funds and other special funds that operate in a like manner should always be replenished at the end of an accounting period. The amount of money actually in the fund will then agree with the balance in the related fund account, and the expenses and the assets for which payment has been made will be recorded in the proper period.

Other Cash Funds

Cash funds may also be established to meet other special needs of a business. For example, money advanced for travel expenses may be accounted for in the same manner as petty cash. An amount is advanced for travel as needed; then periodically after receipt of expense reports, the expenses are recorded and the fund is replenished. A similar procedure may be used to provide a working fund for a sales office located in another city. The amount of the fund may be deposited in a local bank and the sales representative may be authorized to draw checks for payment of rent, salaries, and other operating expenses. Each month, the representative sends the invoices, bank statement, paid checks, bank reconciliation, and other business documents to the home office. The data are audited, the expenditures are recorded, and a reimbursing check is returned for deposit in the local bank.

CASH TRANSACTIONS AND ELECTRONIC FUNDS TRANSFER

Currently most cash payments are made by check or currency and most cash receipts are in the form of currency or check. The broad principles discussed in earlier sections provide the basis for developing an effective system to control such cash transactions. However, the development of electronic funds transfer (EFT) may eventually change the form in which many cash transactions are executed and could affect the processing and controlling of cash transactions.

EFT can be defined as a payment system that uses computerized electronic impulses rather than paper (money, checks, etc.) to effect a cash transaction. For example, a business may pay its employees by means of EFT. Under such a system, employees who want their payroll checks deposited directly in a checking account sign an authorization form. For each pay period, the business' computer transfers the relevant payroll data to the bank, which automatically debits the business' account for the entire payroll and credits the checking account of each employee. Similar cash payments might be made for other preauthorized payments. The federal government currently processes several million social security checks through EFT.

EFT is also beginning to play a role in retail sales. Through a point-of-sale (POS) system, a customer pays for goods at the time of purchase by presenting a plastic card. The card is used to activate a terminal in the store and thereby effect an immediate transfer from the customer's checking account to the retailer's account at the bank.

Studies have indicated that EFT systems may reduce the cost of processing certain cash transactions and contribute to better control over cash receipts and cash payments. Offsetting these potential advantages are problems of protecting the privacy of information stored in computers, and difficulties in documenting purchase and sale transactions. In any event, developments with EFT systems are likely to be followed very closely by most businesses over the next few years.

1. The detailed procedures adopted by management to control operations are collectively termed:
   A. internal controls
   B. internal accounting controls
   C. internal administrative controls
   D. none of the above

2. In preparing a bank reconciliation, the amount of checks outstanding would be:
   A. added to the bank balance according to the bank statement
   B. deducted from the bank balance according to the bank statement
   C. added to the cash balance according to the depositor's records
   D. deducted from the cash balance according to the depositor's records

3. Journal entries based on the bank reconciliation are required for:
   A. additions to the cash balance according to the depositor's records
   B. deductions from the cash balance according to the depositor's records
   C. both A and B
   D. neither A nor B

4. A voucher system is used, all vouchers for purchases are recorded at the net amount, and a purchase is made for $500 under terms 1/10, n/30.
   A. Purchases would be debited for $495 to record the purchase.
   B. Discounts Lost would be debited for $5 if the voucher is not paid within the discount period.
   C. If the voucher is not paid until after the discount period has expired, the discount lost would be reported as an expense on the income statement.
   D. All of the above

5. A petty cash fund is:
   A. used to pay relatively small amounts
   B. established by estimating the amount of cash needed for disbursements of relatively small amounts during a specified period
   C. reimbursed when the amount of money in the fund is reduced to a predetermined minimum amount
   D. all of the above

Discussion Questions

5–1. The owner of a small successful gift shop uses only two of ten reports provided by its accounting system to analyze monthly sales. What principle of accounting systems is violated by this situation?

5–2. What is the objective of "systems analysis"?

5–3. How do internal administrative controls and internal accounting controls differ?

5–4. How does a policy of rotating clerical employees from job to job aid in strengthening internal control?

5–5. Why should the responsibility for a sequence of related operations be divided among different persons?

5–6. The ticket seller at a movie theater doubles as ticket taker for a few minutes each day while the ticket taker is on a "break." Which principle of internal control is violated in this situation?

5–7. Why should the responsibility for maintaining the accounting records be separated from the responsibility for operations?

5–8. How does a periodic review by internal auditors strengthen the system of internal control?

5–9. Why is cash the asset that often warrants the most attention in the design of an effective internal control system?

5–10. What name is often given to the notification attached to a check that indicates the specific invoice that is being paid?

5–11. When checks are received, they are recorded as debits to Cash, the assumption being that the drawer has sufficient funds on deposit. What entry should be made if a check received from a customer and deposited is returned by the bank for lack of sufficient funds (NSF)?

5–12. What is the purpose of preparing a bank reconciliation?

5–13. Identify each of the following reconciling items as: (a) an addition to the balance per bank statement, (b) a deduction from the balance per bank statement, (c) an addition to the balance per depositor's records, or (d) a deduction from the balance per depositor's records. (None of the transactions reported by bank debit and credit memorandums have been recorded by the depositor.)
(1) Deposit in transit, $670.20.
(2) Note collected by bank, $1,010.
(3) Outstanding checks, $879.50.
(4) Check for $20 charged by bank as $200.
(5) Bank service charge, $17.20.
(6) Check of a customer returned by bank to depositor because of insufficient funds, $47.
(7) Check drawn by depositor for $67 but recorded by depositor as $76.

5–14. Which of the reconciling items listed in Question 5-13 necessitate an entry in the depositor's accounts?

5–15. The procedures employed by Hardy's for over-the-counter receipts are as follows: At the close of each day's business, the salesclerks count the cash in their respective cash drawers, after which they determine the amount recorded by the register and prepare the memorandum cash form, noting any discrepancies. An employee from the cashier's office counts the cash, compares the total with the memorandum, and takes the cash to the cashier's office. (a) Indicate the weak link in internal control. (b) How can the weakness be corrected?

5–16. The mailroom employees of Baker Co. send all remittances and remittance advices to the cashier. The cashier deposits the cash in the bank and forwards the remittance advices and duplicate deposit slips to the accounting department. (a) Indicate the weak link in internal control in the handling of cash receipts. (b) How can the weakness be corrected?

5–17. The combined cash count of all cash registers at the close of business is $2.10 more than the cash sales indicated by the cash register tapes. (a) In what account is the cash overage recorded? (b) Are cash overages debited or credited to this account?

5–18. The bookkeeper pays all obligations by prenumbered checks. What are the strengths and weaknesses in the internal control over cash disbursements in this situation?

5–19. What is meant by the term "voucher" as applied to the voucher system?

5–20. Before a voucher for the purchase of merchandise is approved for payment, three documents should be compared to verify the accuracy of the liability. Name these three documents.

5–21. Marvin Maxwell, controller of Carlson Company, approves all vouchers before they are submitted to the treasurer for payment. What procedure can Maxwell add to the system to assure that the documents accompanying the vouchers and supporting the expenditures are not "reused" to improperly support future vouchers?

5–22. In what order are vouchers ordinarily filed (a) in the unpaid voucher file, and (b) in the paid voucher file? Give reasons for answers.

5–23. What are two possibilities for reporting "purchases discounts" on the income statement?

5–24. Merchandise with an invoice price of $10,000 is purchased subject to terms of 1/10, n/30. Determine the cost of the merchandise according to each of the following systems:

  (a) Discounts taken are treated as deductions from the invoice price.
    (1) The invoice is paid within the discount period.
    (2) The invoice is paid after the discount period has expired.
  (b) Discounts taken are treated as other income.
    (1) The invoice is paid within the discount period.
    (2) The invoice is paid after the discount period has expired.
  (c) Discounts allowable are treated as deductions from the invoice price regardless of when payment is made.
    (1) The invoice is paid within the discount period.
    (2) The invoice is paid after the discount period has expired.

5–25. What account or accounts are debited when recording the voucher (a) establishing a petty cash fund and (b) replenishing a petty cash fund?

5–26. The petty cash account has a debit balance of $500. At the end of the accounting period, there is $93 in the petty cash fund along with petty cash receipts totaling $407. Should the fund be replenished as of the last day of the period? Discuss.

5–27. What is meant by electronic funds transfer?

Exercises

5–28. The following data are accumulated for use in reconciling the bank account of C. D. Roberts Co. for May:

  (a) Balance per bank statement at May 31, $6,912.15.
  (b) Balance per depositor's records at May 31, $6,371.70.
  (c) Deposit in transit not recorded by bank, $525.50.
  (d) Checks outstanding, $1,059.20.
  (e) Bank debit memorandum for service charges, $11.25.
  (f) A check for $135 in payment of a voucher was erroneously recorded by C. D. Roberts Co. as $153.

Prepare a bank reconciliation.

5–29. Using the data presented in Exercise 5-28, prepare the entry or entries that should be made by the depositor.

5–30. Accompanying a bank statement for Wilson Inc. is a credit memorandum for $1,230, representing the principal ($1,200) and interest ($30) on a note that had been collected by the bank. The depositor had been notified by the bank at the time of the collection but had made no entries. In general journal form, present the entry that should be made by the depositor.

5–31. Record the following selected transactions. All invoices are recorded at invoice price.

Oct.   1. Recorded Voucher No. 471 for $5,000, payable to LaMarr Co., for merchandise purchased on terms 1/10, n/30.

        9. Recorded Voucher No. 485 for $2,400, payable to Blair Inc., for merchandise purchased on terms 2/10, n/30.

     19. Issued Check No. 464 in payment of Voucher No. 485.

     24. Recorded Voucher No. 490 for $184.37 to replenish the petty cash fund for the following disbursements: store supplies, $60.12; office supplies, $49.95; miscellaneous general expense, $39.60; miscellaneous selling expense, $34.70.

     25. Issued Check No. 474 in payment of Voucher No. 490.

     30. Issued Check No. 479 in payment of Voucher No. 471.

5–32. Record the following related transactions, assuming that invoices for commodities purchased are recorded at their net price after deducting the allowable discount:

May   5. Voucher 610 is prepared for merchandise purchased from Lee Co., $2,000, terms 1/10, n/30

     15. Voucher No. 621 is prepared for merchandise purchased from Miller Co., $4,500, terms 2/10, n/30.

     25. Check No. 590 is issued, payable to Miller Co., in payment of Voucher No. 621.

June   3. Check No. 599 is issued, payable to Lee Co., in payment of Voucher No. 610.

5–33. Prepare the entries to record the following:

  (a) Voucher No. 91 is prepared to establish a petty cash fund of $250.

  (b) Check No. 80 is issued in payment of Voucher No. 91.

  (c) The amount of cash in the petty cash fund is now $24.45. Voucher No. 120 is prepared to replenish the fund, based on the following summary of petty cash receipts: office supplies, $77.75; miscellaneous selling expense, $66.50; miscellaneous general expense, $80.85.

  (d) Check No. 110 is issued by the disbursing officer in payment of Voucher No. 120. The check is cashed and the money is placed in the fund.

5–34. Record the following transactions:

  (a) Voucher No. 112 is prepared to establish a change fund of $200.

  (b) Check No. 101 is issued in payment of Voucher No. 112.

  (c) Cash sales for the day, according to the cash register tapes, were $942.40, and cash on hand is $1,145.10. A bank deposit ticket was prepared for $945.10.

5–35. D. Hogan Corp. is a medium-size merchandising enterprise. When its current income statement was reviewed, it was noted that the amount of purchases discount was disproportionately small in comparison with earlier periods. Further investigation revealed that in spite of a sufficient bank balance, a significant amount of available cash discounts had been lost because of failure to make timely payments. In addition, it was discovered that several purchases invoices had been paid twice.

Outline procedures for the payment of vendor's invoices so that the possibilities of losing available cash discounts and of paying an invoice a second time will be minimized.

Problems

5–36. The cash in bank account for Martin Co. at July 31 of the current year indicated a balance of $12,192.50. The bank statement indicated a balance of $19,955.65 on July 31. Comparison of the bank statement, the canceled checks, and the accompanying memorandums with the records revealed the following reconciling items:

    (a) A deposit of $4,015.20, representing receipts of July 31, had been made too late to appear on the bank statement.

    (b) Checks outstanding totaled $9,090.75.

    (c) The bank had collected for Martin Co. $3,045 on a note left for collection. The face of the note was $3,000.

    (d) A check drawn for $470 had been erroneously charged by the bank as $740.

    (e) A check for $72.50 returned with the statement had been recorded by Martin Co. as $7.25. The check was for the payment of an obligation to Shaw Equipment Company for the purchase of office equipment on account.

    (f) Bank service charges for July amounted to $22.15.

Instructions:

    (1) Prepare a bank reconciliation.

    (2) Journalize the necessary entries. The accounts have not been closed.

5–37. The cash in bank account for Del Rey Co. at April 1 of the current year indicated a balance of $9,992.50. Cash deposited and checks written during April totaled $20,500.40 and $18,850.47, respectively. The bank statement indicated a balance of $14,519.55 on April 30. Comparison of the bank statement, the canceled checks, and the accompanying memorandums with the records revealed the following reconciling items:

    (a) Checks outstanding totaled $4,291.37.

    (b) A deposit of $2,592.80, representing receipts of April 30, had been made too late to appear on the bank statement.

    (c) A check for $100 had been erroneously charged by the bank as $10.

    (d) A check for $57.45 returned with the statement had been recorded by Del Rey Co. as $75.45. The check was for the payment of an obligation to Brandon Office Supply Co. for the purchase of office supplies on account.

    (e) The bank had collected for Del Rey Co. $1,080 on a note left for collection. The face of the note was $1,000.

    (f) Bank service charges for April amounted to $9.45.

Instructions:

    (1) Prepare a bank reconciliation as of April 30.

    (2) Journalize the necessary entries. The accounts have not been closed.

5–38. Record the following selected transactions. Assume the use of a voucher system, with all invoices recorded at their net price.

Sept. 1. Recorded Voucher No. 240 for $2,100, payable to Philips Supply Co., for office equipment purchased on terms n/30.

4. Recorded Voucher No. 242 for $500, payable to A. Adair Co., for merchandise purchased on terms 1/10, n/30.

7. Recorded Voucher No. 248 for $1,400, payable to Kennedy Inc., for merchandise purchased on terms 1/10, n/30.

17. Issued Check No. 364 in payment of Voucher No. 248.

22. Recorded Voucher No. 260 for $209.84 to replenish the petty cash fund for the following disbursements: store supplies, $72.88; office supplies, $59.95; miscellaneous general expense, $42.45; miscellaneous selling expense, $34.56.

23. Issued Check No. 370 in payment of Voucher No. 260.

24. Issued Check No. 377 in payment of Voucher No. 242.

30. Issued Check No. 389 in payment of Voucher No. 240.

5–39. Anderson Company has just adopted the policy of depositing all cash receipts in the bank and of making all payments by check in conjunction with the voucher system. The following transactions were selected from those completed in May of the current year:

May 1. Recorded Voucher No. 1 to establish a petty cash fund of $150 and a change fund of $750.

1. Issued Check No. 729 in payment of Voucher No. 1.

2. Recorded Voucher No. 3 to establish an advance to salespersons fund of $1,000.

2. Issued Check No. 731 in payment of Voucher No. 3.

15. The cash sales for the day, according to the cash register tapes, totaled $2,917.20. The combined count of all cash on hand (including the change fund) totaled $3,668.70.

20. Recorded Voucher No. 29 to reimburse the petty cash fund for the following disbursements, each evidenced by a petty cash receipt:

May 3. Store supplies, $8.50.

6. Express charges on merchandise purchased, $12.50.

7. Office supplies, $15.75.

9. Office supplies, $9.20.

11. Postage stamps, $20 (Office Supplies).

12. Repair to adding machine, $22.50 (Misc. General Expense).

14. Postage due on special delivery letter, $1.05 (Misc. General Expense).

15. Repair to typewriter, $26.85 (Misc. General Expense).

16. Express charges on merchandise purchased, $5.75.

19. Telegram charges, $3.75 (Misc. Selling Expense).

20. Issued Check No. 760 in payment of Voucher No. 29.

26. The cash sales for the day, according to the cash register tapes, totaled $2,605.50. The count of all cash on hand totaled $3,351.10.

31. Recorded Voucher No. 60 to replenish the advances to salespersons fund for the following expenditures for travel: Frank Bowen, $212.40; Linda James, $301.50; Martha Potter, $297.10.

31. Issued Check No. 773 in payment of Voucher No. 60.

Instructions: Record the transactions.

5–40. Ferris Company employs the voucher system in controlling expenditures and disbursements. All cash receipts are deposited in a night depository after banking hours each Wednesday and Friday. The data required to reconcile the bank statements as of July 31 have been abstracted from various documents and records and are reproduced as follows:

Ferris Company Records

CASH IN BANK ACCOUNT BALANCE AS OF JULY 1 . . . . $11,917.15

CASH RECEIPTS FOR MONTH OF JULY 6,772.60

DUPLICATE DEPOSIT TICKETS:
Date and amount of each deposit in July:

Date	Amount	Date	Amount	Date	Amount
July 2	$760.10	July 12	$589.10	July 23	$792.10
5	819.75	16	797.60	26	601.50
9	784.14	19	701.26	30	927.05

CHECKS WRITTEN:
Number and amount of each check issued in July:

Check No.	Amount	Check No.	Amount	Check No.	Amount
414	$ 68.70	421	$202.75	428	$ 291.34
415	620.55	422	VOID	429	179.22
416	319.10	423	VOID	430	882.20
417	627.13	424	918.01	431	982.16
418	103.80	425	558.63	432	62.40
419	220.10	426	530.03	433	675.48
420	238.87	427	338.73	434	97.90

Total amount of checks issued in July $7,917.10

BANK RECONCILIATION FOR PRECEDING MONTH:

Ferris Company
Bank Reconciliation
June 30, 19--

Balance per bank statement		$11,899.29
Add deposit of June 30, not recorded by bank		725.10
		$12,624.39
Deduct outstanding checks:		
No. 379	$217.60	
407	172.50	
412	97.97	
413	219.17	707.24
Adjusted balance		$11,917.15
Balance per depositor's records		$11,927.65
Deduct service charges		10.50
Adjusted balance		$11,917.15

Bank Statement Items

JULY BANK STATEMENT:

Balance as of July 1...	$11,899.29
Deposits and other credits	9,145.65
Checks and other debits......................................	(8,172.45)
Balance as of July 31..	$12,872.49

Date and amount of each deposit in July:

Date	Amount	Date	Amount	Date	Amount
July 1	$725.10	July 11	$784.14	July 21	$701.26
3	760.10	13	589.10	24	792.10
6	819.75	17	797.60	28	601.50

CHECKS ACCOMPANYING JULY BANK STATEMENT:

Number and amount of each check, rearranged in numerical sequence:

Check No.	Amount	Check No.	Amount	Check No.	Amount
379	$217.60	418	$103.80	426	$530.03
412	97.97	419	220.10	427	338.73
413	219.17	420	238.87	429	179.22
414	68.70	421	212.75	430	882.20
415	620.55	424	918.01	431	982.16
416	319.10	425	558.63	432	62.40
417	627.13			433	675.48

BANK MEMORANDUMS ACCOMPANYING JULY BANK STATEMENT:

Date, description, and amount of each memorandum:

Date	Description	Amount
July 7	Bank credit memo for note collected:	
	Principal...	$2,500.00
	Interest...	75.00
20	Bank debit memo for check returned because of insufficient	
	funds..	90.10
31	Bank debit memo for service charges	9.75

Instructions:

(1) Prepare a bank reconciliation as of July 31. If errors in recording deposits or checks are discovered, assume that the errors were made by the company. Assume that all deposits are from cash sales. All checks are in payment of vouchers.

(2) Journalize the necessary entries. The accounts have not been closed.

(3) What is the amount of cash in bank that should appear on the balance sheet as of July 31?

5–36A. The cash in bank account for R. C. Graziano Co. at April 30 of the current year indicated a balance of $7,424.95. The bank statement indicated a balance of $11,740.50 on April 30. Comparison of the bank statement, the canceled checks, and the accompanying memorandums with the records revealed the following reconciling items:

(a) Checks outstanding totaled $4,840.75.

(b) A deposit of $2,672.10, representing receipts of April 30, had been made too late to appear on the bank statement.

(c) The bank had collected for R. C. Graziano Co. $2,050 on a note left for collection. The face of the note was $2,000.

(d) A check for $24.50 returned with the statement had been recorded by R. C. Graziano Co. as $42.50. The check was for the payment of an obligation to Rey Office Supply Co. for the purchase of office supplies on account.

(e) A check drawn for $100 had been erroneously charged by the bank as $10.

(f) Bank service charges for April amounted to $11.10.

Instructions:

(1) Prepare a bank reconciliation.

(2) Journalize the necessary entries. The accounts have not been closed.

5–37A. The cash in bank account for Graham Co. at July 1 of the current year indicated a balance of $11,221.70. Cash deposited and checks written during July totaled $20,650.75 and $21,770.25, respectively. The bank statement indicated a balance of $18,243.30 on July 31. Comparison of the bank statement, the canceled checks, and the accompanying memorandums with the records revealed the following reconciling items:

(a) A deposit of $3,248.21, representing receipts of July 31, had been made too late to appear on the bank statement.

(b) Checks outstanding totaled $9,103.84.

(c) The bank had collected for Graham Co. $2,650 on a note left for collection. The face of the note was $2,500.

(d) A check drawn for $360 had been erroneously charged by the bank as $630.

(e) A check for $84.20 returned with the statement had been recorded by Graham Co. as $8.42. The check was for the payment of an obligation to Carmine Equipment Company for the purchase of office equipment on account.

(f) Bank service charges for July amounted to $18.75.

Instructions:

(1) Prepare a bank reconciliation as of July 31.

(2) Journalize the necessary entries. The accounts have not been closed.

5–40A. M. C. Levin Co. employs the voucher system in controlling expenditures and disbursements. All cash receipts are deposited in a night depository after banking hours each Wednesday and Friday. The data required to reconcile the bank statement as of June 30 have been abstracted from various documents and records and are reproduced as follows:

<u>M. C. Levin Co. Records</u>

CASH IN BANK ACCOUNT BALANCE AS OF JUNE 1 . . . . $7,016.50

CASH RECEIPTS FOR MONTH OF JUNE 7,812.50

DUPLICATE DEPOSIT TICKETS:

Date and amount of each deposit in June:

Date	Amount	Date	Amount	Date	Amount
June 1	$978.36	June 10	$791.71	June 22	$999.90
3	849.40	15	957.85	24	876.71
8	901.50	17	946.47	29	510.60

CHECKS WRITTEN:

Number and amount of each check issued in June:

Check No.	Amount	Check No.	Amount	Check No.	Amount
615	$401.70	622	$490.90	629	$ 97.75
616	232.45	623	Void	630	249.75
617	401.90	624	640.13	631	113.95
618	604.84	625	376.77	632	907.95
619	506.88	626	299.37	633	359.60
620	117.25	627	537.01	634	601.50
621	298.66	628	380.95	635	486.39

Total amount of checks issued in June $8,105.70

BANK RECONCILIATION FOR PRECEDING MONTH:

M. C. Levin Co.
Bank Reconciliation
May 31, 19--

Balance per bank statement.		$7,019.57
Add deposit of May 31, not recorded by bank		690.25
		$7,709.82
Deduct outstanding checks:		
No. 606	$112.15	
611	219.22	
613	301.40	
614	60.55	693.32
Adjusted balance		$7,016.50
Balance per depositor's records.		$7,026.00
Deduct service charges.		9.50
Adjusted balance		$7,016.50

Bank Statement Items

JUNE BANK STATEMENT:

Balance as of June 1.	$7,019.57
Deposits and other credits	8,516.15
Checks and other debits.	(7,638.55)
Balance as of June 30.	$7,897.17

Date and amount of each deposit in June:

Date	Amount	Date	Amount	Date	Amount
June 1	$690.25	June 9	$910.50	June 18	$946.47
2	978.36	11	791.71	23	999.90
4	849.40	16	957.85	30	876.71

CHECKS ACCOMPANYING JUNE BANK STATEMENT:
Number and amount of each check, rearranged in numerical sequence:

Check No.	Amount	Check No.	Amount	Check No.	Amount
606	$112.15	619	$506.88	626	$299.37
613	301.40	620	117.25	627	537.01
614	60.55	621	298.66	628	380.95
615	401.70	622	490.90	630	249.75
616	232.45	624	640.13	631	113.95
617	401.90	625	376.77	632	907.95
618	604.84			635	486.39

BANK MEMORANDUMS ACCOMPANYING JUNE BANK STATEMENT:
Date, description, and amount of each memorandum:

Date	Description	Amount
June 15	Bank credit memo for note collected:	
	Principal...	$500.00
	Interest...	15.00
20	Bank debit memo for check returned because of insufficient funds...	103.50
30	Bank debit memo for service charges........................	14.10

Instructions:

(1) Prepare a bank reconciliation as of June 30. If errors in recording deposits or checks are discovered, assume that the errors were made by the company. Assume that all deposits are from cash sales. All checks are in payment of vouchers.

(2) Journalize the necessary entries. The accounts have not been closed.

(3) What is the amount of cash in bank that should appear on the balance sheet as of June 30?

Mini-Case

5–41. The records of Valdez Company indicate a November 30 cash in bank balance of $18,901.62, which includes undeposited receipts for November 28, 29, and 30. The cash balance on the bank statement as of November 30 is $16,344.41. This balance includes a note of $1,200 plus $30 of interest collected by the bank but not recorded by Valdez Company. Checks outstanding on November 30 were as follows: No. 62,

$116.25; No. 183, $150.00; No. 284, $253.25; No. 1621, $190.71; No. 1623, $206.80; and No. 1632, $145.28.

On November 1, the Valdez Company cashier submitted his resignation, effective at the end of the month. Before leaving on November 30, the cashier prepared the following bank reconciliation:

Balance per books, November 30		$18,901.62
Add outstanding checks:		
1621	$190.71	
1623	206.80	
1632	145.28	442.79
		$19,344.41
Less undeposited receipts		3,000.00
Balance per bank, November 30		$16,344.41
Deduct unrecorded note with interest		1,230.00
True cash, November 30		$15,114.41

Adding Machine Tape of Outstanding Checks

0·	*
190·71	+
206·80	+
145·28	+
442·79	*

Subsequently, the owner of Valdez Company discovered that the cashier had stolen all undeposited receipts on hand on November 30 in excess of $3,000. The owner, a close family friend, has asked your help in determining the amount that the former cashier has stolen.

Instructions:

(1) Determine the amount the cashier stole from Valdez Company. Show your computations in good form.

(2) How did the cashier attempt to conceal the theft?

(3) (a) Identify two major weaknesses in Valdez Company's internal accounting controls, which allowed the cashier to steal the undeposited cash receipts.
(b) Recommend improvements in Valdez Company's internal accounting controls, so that similar types of thefts of undeposited cash receipts could be prevented. (AICPA adapted)

Answers to Self-Examination Questions

1. **A** The detailed procedures adopted by management to control operations are collectively termed internal controls (answer A). Internal controls are classified as administrative controls (answer C) and accounting controls (answer B). Internal administrative controls consist of procedures and records that assist management in achieving business objectives. Internal accounting controls consist of procedures and records that are primarily concerned with the reliability of financial records and reports and with the safeguarding of assets.

2. **B** On any specific date, the cash in bank account in a depositor's ledger may not agree with the reciprocal account in the bank's ledger because of delays by either party in recording transactions, and/or errors made by either party in recording transactions. The purpose of a bank reconciliation, therefore, is to determine the reasons for any discrepancies between the two account balances. All errors should then be corrected by the depositor or the bank as appropriate. In arriving at the adjusted (correct) balance according to the bank statement, outstanding checks must be deducted (answer B) to adjust for checks that have been written by the depositor but that have not yet been presented to the bank for payment.

3. **C** All reconciling items that are added to and deducted from the "balance per depositor's records" on the bank reconciliation (answer C) require that journal entries be made by the depositor to correct errors made in recording transactions or to bring the cash account up to date for delays in recording transactions.

4. **D** A major advantage of recording purchases at the net amount (answer A) is that the cost of failing to take discounts is recorded in the accounts (answer B) and then reported as an expense on the income statement (answer C).

5. **D** To avoid the delay, annoyance, and expense that is associated with paying all obligations by check, relatively small amounts (answer A) are paid from a petty cash fund. The fund is established by estimating the amount of cash needed to pay these small amounts during a specified period (answer B) and it is then reimbursed when the amount of money in the fund is reduced to a predetermined minimum amount (answer C).

CHAPTER 6

Receivables and Temporary Investments

CHAPTER OBJECTIVES

Describe and illustrate accounting for receivables.

Describe and illustrate accounting for uncollectible receivables.

Describe and illustrate accounting for temporary investments.

For many businesses, the revenue from sales on a credit basis is the largest factor influencing the amount of net income. As credit is granted, businesses must account for the resulting receivables, which may represent a substantial portion of the total current assets. As the receivables are collected, the cash realized is accounted for in the manner discussed in Chapter 5. If the amount of cash on hand exceeds immediate cash requirements, the excess cash might be invested in securities until needed. These securities are accounted for as temporary investments.

CLASSIFICATION OF RECEIVABLES

The term **receivables** includes all money claims against people, organizations, or other debtors. Receivables are acquired by a business enterprise in various kinds of transactions, the most common being the sale of merchandise or services on a credit basis.

Credit may be granted on open account or on the basis of a formal instrument of credit such as a promissory note. Promissory notes are usually used for credit periods of more than sixty days, as in sales of equipment on the installment plan, and for transactions of relatively large dollar amounts. Promissory notes may also be used in settlement of an open account and in borrowing or lending money.

A **promissory note**, frequently referred to simply as a **note,** is a written promise to pay a sum certain in money on demand or at a definite time. As in the case of a check, it must be payable to the order of a certain person or firm, or to bearer. It must also be signed by the person or firm that makes the promise. The one to whose order the note is payable is called the **payee,** and the one making the promise is called the **maker.** The enterprise owning a note refers to it as a **note receivable** and records it as an asset at its face amount.

A note that provides for the payment of interest for the period between the issuance date and the due date is called an **interest-bearing note.** If a note makes no provision for interest, it is said to be **non-interest-bearing.**

The amount that is due at the maturity or due date is called the **maturity value.** The maturity value of a non-interest-bearing note is the face amount. The maturity value of an interest-bearing note is the sum of the face amount and the interest.

From the point of view of the creditor, a claim evidenced by a note has some advantages over a claim in the form of an account receivable. By signing a note, the debtor acknowledges the debt and agrees to pay it according to the terms given. The note is therefore a stronger legal claim if there is court action. It is also more liquid than an open account because the holder can usually transfer it more readily to a bank or other financial agency in exchange for cash.

Accounts and notes receivable originating from sales transactions are sometimes called **trade receivables.** In the absence of other descriptive words or phrases, accounts and notes receivable may be assumed to have originated from sales in the usual course of the business.

Other receivables include interest receivable, loans to officers or employees, and loans to affiliated companies. To facilitate their classification and presentation on the balance sheet, a general ledger account should be maintained for each type of receivable, with proper subsidiary ledgers.

All receivables that are expected to be realized in cash within a year are presented in the current assets section of the balance sheet. Those that are not currently collectible, such as long-term loans, should be listed under the caption "Investments" below the current assets section.

DETERMINING INTEREST

Interest rates are usually stated in terms of a period of a year, regardless of the actual period of time involved. Thus the interest on $2,000 for a year at 12% would be $240 (12% of $2,000); the interest on $2,000 for one fourth of a year at 12% would be $60 (¼ of $240).

Notes covering a period of time longer than a year ordinarily provide that the interest be paid semiannually, quarterly, or at some other stated interval. The time involved in commercial credit transactions is usually less than a year, and the interest provided for by a note is payable at the time the note is paid. In computing interest for a period of less than a year, agencies of the federal government use the actual number of days in the year. For example, 90 days is considered to be 90/365 of a year. The usual commercial practice is to use 360 as the denominator of the fraction; thus 90 days is considered to be 90/360 of a year.

The basic formula for computing interest is as follows:

$$\text{Principal} \times \text{Rate} \times \text{Time} = \text{Interest}$$

To illustrate the use of the formula, assume that a note for $1,500 is payable in 20 days with interest at 12%. The interest would be $10, computed as follows:

$$\$1,500 \times \frac{12}{100} \times \frac{20}{360} = \$10 \text{ interest}$$

One of the commonly used shortcut methods of computing interest is called the 60-day, 6% method. The 6% annual rate is converted to the effective rate of 1% for a 60-day period (60/360 of 6%). Accordingly, the interest on any amount for 60 days at 6% is determined by moving the decimal point in the principal two places to the left. For example, the interest on $1,500 at 6% for 60 days is $15. The amount obtained by moving the decimal point must be adjusted (1) for interest rates greater or less than 6% and (2) for periods of time greater or less than 60 days. For example, the interest on $1,500 at 6% for 90 days is $22.50 (90/60 of $15). The interest on $1,500 at 12% for 60 days is $30 (12/6 of $15).

Comprehensive interest tables are available and are commonly used by financial institutions and other enterprises that require frequent interest calculations. Nevertheless, students of business should know the mechanics of interest computations well enough to use them with complete accuracy and to recognize major errors in interest amounts that come to their attention.

When the term of a note is stated in months instead of in days, each month may be considered as being 1/12 of a year, or, alternatively, the actual number of days in the term may be counted. For example, the interest on a 3-month note dated June 1 could be computed on the basis of 3/12 of a year or on the basis of 92/360 of a year. It is the usual commercial practice to use the first method, while banks usually charge interest for the exact number of days. For the sake of simplicity, the usual commercial practice will be assumed in all cases.

DETERMINING DUE DATE

The period of time between the issuance date and the maturity date of a short-term note may be stated in either days or months. When the term of a note is stated in days, the due date is the specified number of days after its issuance. To illustrate, the due date of a 90-day note dated March 16 may be determined as follows:

Term of the note		90
March (days)	31	
Date of note	16	15
Number of days remaining		75
April (days)		30
		45
May (days)		31
Due date, June		14

When the term of a note is stated as a certain number of months after the issuance date, the due date is determined by counting the number of months from the issuance date. Thus, a 3-month note dated June 5 would be due on September 5. In those cases in which there is no date in the month of maturity that corresponds to the issuance date, the due date becomes the last day of the month. For example, a 2-month note dated July 31 would be due on September 30.

NOTES RECEIVABLE AND INTEREST INCOME

The typical retail enterprise makes most of its sales for cash or on account. If the account of a customer becomes delinquent, the creditor may insist that the account be converted into a note. In this way, the debtor is given more time, and if the creditor needs more funds, the note may be endorsed and transferred to a bank or other financial agency. Notes may also be received by retail firms that sell merchandise on long-term credit. For example, a dealer in household appliances may require a down payment at the time of sale and accept a note or a series of notes for the remainder. Such arrangements usually provide for monthly payments. Wholesale firms and manufacturers are likely to receive notes more often than retailers, although here, too, much depends upon the kind of product and the length of the credit period.

When a note is received from a customer to apply on account, the facts are recorded by debiting the notes receivable account and crediting the accounts receivable controlling account and the account of the customer from whom the note is received. If the note is interest-bearing, interest must also be recorded as appropriate.

To illustrate, assume that the account of W. A. Bunn Co., which has a debit balance of $6,000, is past due. A 30-day, 12% note for that amount, dated December 21, 1986, is accepted in settlement of the account. The entry to record the transaction is as follows:

Dec. 21	Notes Receivable	6,000	
	Accounts Receivable — W. A. Bunn Co. . .		6,000
	Received a 30-day, 12% note dated		
	December 21, 1986.		

On December 31, 1986, the end of the fiscal year, an adjusting entry would be recorded for the accrual of the interest from December 21 to December 31. The entry to record the accrued revenue of $20 ($6,000 × 12/100 × 10/360) is as follows:

Adjusting Entry

Dec.	31	Interest Receivable	20	
		Interest Income.		20

Interest receivable is reported on the balance sheet at December 31, 1986, as a current asset. The interest income account is closed at December 31 and the amount is reported in the Other Income section of the income statement for the year ended December 31, 1986.

When the amount due on the note is collected in 1987, part of the interest received will effect a reduction of the interest that was receivable at December 31, 1986, and the remainder will represent revenue for 1987. To avoid the possibility of failing to recognize this division and to avoid the inconvenience of analyzing the receipt of interest in 1987, a reversing entry is made after the accounts are closed. The effect of the entry, which is illustrated as follows, is to transfer the debit balance in the interest receivable account to the debit side of the interest income account.

Reversing Entry

Jan.	1	Interest Income.	20	
		Interest Receivable		20

At the time the note matures and payment is received, the entire amount of the interest received is credited to Interest Income, as illustrated by the following entry:

Jan. 20	Cash.	6,060	
	Notes Receivable		6,000
	Interest Income		60

After the foregoing entries are posted, the interest income account will appear as follows:

ACCOUNT INTEREST INCOME   ACCOUNT NO. 811

Date		Item	Debit	Credit	Balance Debit	Balance Credit
1986						
Dec.	12			120		946
	31	Adjusting		20		966
	31	Closing	966		—	—
1987						
Jan.	1	Reversing	20		20	
	20			60		40

The adjusting and reversing process divided the $60 of interest received on January 20, 1987, into two parts for accounting purposes: (1) **$20** representing the interest income for 1986 (recorded by the adjusting entry) and (2) **$40** representing the interest income for 1987 (the balance in the interest income account at January 20, 1987).

Discounting Notes Receivable

Instead of being retained by the holder until maturity, notes receivable may be transferred to a bank by endorsement. The **discount** (interest) charged is computed on the maturity value of the note for the period of time the bank must hold the note, namely the time that will pass between the date of the transfer and the due date of the note. The amount of the **proceeds** paid to the endorser is the excess of the maturity value over the discount.

To illustrate, assume that a 90-day, 12% note receivable for $1,800, dated November 8, is discounted at the payee's bank on December 3 at the rate of 14%. The data used in determining the effect of the transaction are as follows:

Face value of note dated Nov. 8	$1,800.00
Interest on note—90 days at 12%	54.00
Maturity value of note due Feb. 6	$1,854.00
Discount period—Dec. 3 to Feb. 6 .... 65 days	
Discount on maturity value—65 days at 14%	46.87
Proceeds	$1,807.13

The same information is presented graphically in the following flow diagram. In reading the data, follow the direction of the arrows.

DIAGRAM OF DISCOUNTING A NOTE RECEIVABLE

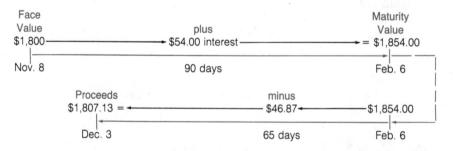

The excess of the proceeds from discounting the note, $1,807.13, over its face value, $1,800, is recorded as interest income. The entry for the transaction is as follows:

Dec.	3	Cash	1,807.13	
		Notes Receivable		1,800.00
		Interest Income		7.13

It should be observed that the proceeds from discounting a note receivable may be less than the face value. When this happens, the excess of the face value over the proceeds is recorded as interest expense. The amount and direction of the difference between the interest rate and the discount rate will affect the result, as will the relationship between the full term of the note and the length of the discount period.

Without a statement limiting responsibility, the endorser of a note is committed to paying the note if the maker should default. Such potential obligations that will become actual liabilities only if certain events occur in the future are called **contingent liabilities**. Thus, the endorser of a note that has been discounted has a contingent liability that is in effect until the due date. If the maker pays the promised amount at maturity, the contingent liability is removed without any action on the part of the endorser. If, on the other hand, the maker defaults and the endorser is notified according to legal requirements, the liability becomes an actual one.

Significant contingent liabilities should be disclosed on the balance sheet or in an accompanying note. Disclosure requirements for contingent liabilities are discussed and illustrated in Chapter 9.

Dishonored Notes Receivable

If the maker of a note fails to pay the debt on the due date, the note is said to be **dishonored**. A dishonored note receivable is no longer negotiable, and for that reason the holder usually transfers the claim, including any interest due, to the accounts receivable account. For example, if the $6,000, 30-day, 12% note received and recorded on December 21 (page 182) had been dishonored at maturity, the entry to charge the note, including the interest, back to the customer's account would have been as follows:

Jan. 20	Accounts Receivable — W. A. Bunn Co.	6,060	
	Notes Receivable.		6,000
	Interest Income.		60
	Dishonored note and interest.		

If there had been some assurance that the maker would pay the note within a relatively short time, action would have been delayed until the matter was resolved. However, for future guidance in extending credit, it may be desirable that the customer's account in the subsidiary ledger disclose the dishonor of the note.

When a discounted note receivable is dishonored, the holder usually notifies the endorser of such fact and asks for payment. If the request for payment and notification of dishonor are timely, the endorser is legally obligated to pay the amount due on the note. The entire amount paid to the holder by the endorser, including the interest, should be debited to the account receivable of the maker. To illustrate, assume that the $1,800, 90-day, 12% note discounted on December 3 (page 184) is dishonored at maturity by the maker, Pryor & Co. The entry to record the payment by the endorser would be as follows:

Feb.	6	Accounts Receivable — Pryor & Co.........	1,854	
		Cash..................................		1,854

In some cases, the holder of a dishonored note gives the endorser a notarized statement of the facts of the dishonor. The fee for this statement, known as a **protest fee,** is charged to the endorser, who in turn charges it to the maker of the note. If there had been a protest fee of $6 in connection with the dishonor and the payment recorded above, the debit to the maker's account and the credit to Cash would have been $1,860.

UNCOLLECTIBLE RECEIVABLES

When merchandise or services are sold without the immediate receipt of cash, a part of the claims against customers usually proves to be uncollectible. This is usually the case, regardless of the care used in granting credit and the effectiveness of the collection procedures used. The operating expense incurred because of the failure to collect receivables is called an expense or a loss from **uncollectible accounts, doubtful accounts,** or **bad debts.**[1]

There is no single general rule for determining when an account or a note becomes uncollectible. The fact that a debtor fails to pay an account according to a sales contract or dishonors a note on the due date does not necessarily mean that the account will be uncollectible. Bankruptcy of the debtor is one of the most positive indications of partial or complete worthlessness of a receivable. Other evidence includes closing of the debtor's business, disappearance of the debtor, failure of repeated attempts to collect, and the barring of collection by the statute of limitations.

There are two methods of accounting for receivables that are believed to be uncollectible. The allowance method, which is sometimes called the **reserve method,** provides in advance for uncollectible receivables. The other procedure, called the direct write-off method or **direct charge-off method,** recognizes the expense only when certain accounts are judged to be worthless.

ALLOWANCE METHOD OF ACCOUNTING FOR UNCOLLECTIBLES

Most large business enterprises provide currently for the amount of their trade receivables estimated to become uncollectible in the future. The advance

---

[1]If both notes and accounts are involved, both may be included in the title, as in "uncollectible notes and accounts expense," or the general term "uncollectible receivables expense" may be substituted. Because of its wide usage and simplicity, "uncollectible accounts expense" will be used in this book.

provision for future uncollectibility is made by an adjusting entry at the end of the fiscal period. As with all periodic adjustments, the entry serves two purposes. In this instance, it provides for (1) the reduction of the value of the receivables to the amount of cash expected to be realized from them in the future and (2) the allocation to the current period of the expected expense resulting from such reduction.

Assumed data for a new business firm will be used to explain and illustrate the allowance method. The enterprise began business in August and chose to use the calendar year as its fiscal year. The accounts receivable account, illustrated as follows, has a balance of $105,000 at the end of the period.

ACCOUNT ACCOUNTS RECEIVABLE   ACCOUNT NO. 114

Date		Item	Debit	Credit	Balance	
					Debit	Credit
19--						
Aug.	31		20,000		20,000	
Sept.	30		25,000		45,000	
	30			15,000	30,000	
Oct.	31		40,000		70,000	
	31			25,000	45,000	
Nov.	30		38,000		83,000	
	30			23,000	60,000	
Dec.	31		75,000		135,000	
	31			30,000	105,000	

Among the individual customers accounts making up the $105,000 balance in Accounts Receivable are a number of balances which are a varying number of days past due. No specific accounts are believed to be wholly uncollectible at this time, but it seems likely that some will be collected only in part and that others are likely to become entirely worthless. Based on a careful study, it is estimated that a total of $3,000 will eventually prove to be uncollectible. The amount expected to be realized from the accounts receivable is, therefore, $105,000 − $3,000, or $102,000, and the $3,000 reduction in value is the uncollectible accounts expense for the period.

The $3,000 reduction in accounts receivable cannot yet be identified with specific customers accounts in the subsidiary ledger and should therefore not be credited to the controlling account in the general ledger. The customary practice is to use a contra asset account entitled Allowance for Doubtful Accounts. The adjusting entry to record the expense and the reduction in the asset is as follows:

Adjusting Entry

Dec. 31   Uncollectible Accounts Expense   3,000
              Allowance for Doubtful Accounts   3,000

The two accounts to which the above entry is posted are illustrated as follows:

ACCOUNT UNCOLLECTIBLE ACCOUNTS EXPENSE   ACCOUNT NO. 717

| Date | | Item | Debit | Credit | Balance | |
					Debit	Credit
19-- Dec.	31	Adjusting	3,000		3,000	

ACCOUNT ALLOWANCE FOR DOUBTFUL ACCOUNTS   ACCOUNT NO. 115

| Date | | Item | Debit | Credit | Balance | |
					Debit	Credit
19-- Dec.	31	Adjusting		3,000		3,000

The debit balance of $105,000 in Accounts Receivable is the amount of the total claims against customers on open account, and the credit balance of $3,000 in Allowance for Doubtful Accounts is the amount to be deducted from Accounts Receivable to determine the **expected realizable value.** The $3,000 reduction in the asset was transferred to Uncollectible Accounts Expense, which will in turn be closed to Income Summary.

Uncollectible accounts expense is generally reported on the income statement as a general expense, because the credit-granting and collection duties are the responsibilities of departments within the general administrative framework. The accounts receivable may be listed on the balance sheet at the net amount of $102,000, with a notation in parentheses showing the amount of the allowance, or the details may be presented as shown on the following partial balance sheet. When the allowance account includes provision for doubtful notes as well as accounts, it should be deducted from the total of Notes Receivable and Accounts Receivable.

ACCOUNTS
RECEIVABLE ON
BALANCE SHEET

Richards Company
Balance Sheet
December 31, 19--

Assets

Current assets:
Cash . . . . $ 21,600
Accounts receivable $105,000
   Less allowance for doubtful accounts   3,000   102,000

Write-Offs to the Allowance Account

When an account is believed to be uncollectible, it is written off against the allowance account as in the following entry:

Jan. 21   Allowance for Doubtful Accounts   110
         Accounts Receivable— John Parker   110
        To write off the uncollectible account.

During the year, as more accounts or portions of accounts are determined to be uncollectible, they are written off against Allowance for Doubtful Accounts in the same manner. Instructions for write-offs should originate with the credit manager or other designated official. The authorizations, which should always be written, serve as objective evidence in support of the accounting entry.

Naturally enough, the total amount written off against the allowance account during the period will rarely be equal to the amount in the account at the beginning of the period. The allowance account will have a credit balance at the end of the period if the write-offs during the period amount to less than the beginning balance. It will have a debit balance if the write-offs exceed the beginning balance. After the year-end adjusting entry is recorded, the allowance account will have a credit balance.

An account receivable that has been written off against the allowance account may later be collected. In such cases the account should be reinstated by an entry that is the exact reverse of the write-off entry. For example, assume that the account of $110 written off in the preceding journal entry is later collected. The entry to reinstate the account would be as follows:

```
June 10   Accounts Receivable—John Parker........      110
              Allowance for Doubtful Accounts..........              110
              To reinstate account written off earlier in
              the year.
```

The cash received in payment would be recorded in the usual manner as a receipt on account. Although it is possible to combine the reinstatement and the receipt of cash into a single debit and credit, the entries in the customer's account, with a proper notation, provide useful credit information.

Estimating Uncollectibles

The estimate of uncollectibles at the end of the fiscal period is based on past experience and forecasts of future business activity. When the trend of general sales volume is upward and there is relatively full employment, the amount of the expense should usually be less than when the trend is in the opposite direction. The estimate is customarily based on either (1) the amount of sales for the entire fiscal period or (2) the amount and the age of the receivable accounts at the end of the fiscal period.

Estimate Based on Sales

Accounts receivable are acquired as a result of sales on account. The amount of such sales during the year may therefore be used to determine the probable amount of the accounts that will be uncollectible. For example, if it is known from past experience that about 1% of charge sales will be uncollectible and the charge sales for a certain year amount to $300,000, the adjusting entry for uncollectible accounts at the end of the year would be as follows:

Adjusting Entry

Dec. 31   Uncollectible Accounts Expense   3,000

Allowance for Doubtful Accounts   3,000

Instead of charge sales, total sales (including those made for cash) may be used in developing the percentage. Total sales is obtainable from the ledger without the analysis that may be needed to determine charge sales. If the ratio of sales on account to cash sales does not change very much from year to year, the results obtained will be equally satisfactory. If in the above example the balance of the sales account at the end of the year is assumed to be $400,000, the application of ¾ of 1% to that amount would also yield an estimate of $3,000.

If it becomes apparent over a period of time that the amount of write-offs is always greater or less than the amount provided by the adjusting entry, the percentage applied to sales data should be changed accordingly. A newly established business enterprise, having no record of credit experience, may obtain data on the probable amount of the expense from trade association journals and other publications containing information on credit and collections.

The estimate-based-on-sales method of determining the uncollectible accounts expense is widely used. It is simple and it provides the best basis for charging uncollectible accounts expense to the period in which the related sales were made.

Estimate Based on Analysis of Receivables

The process of analyzing the receivable accounts is sometimes called **aging the receivables**. The base point for determining age is the due date of the account. The number and breadth of the time intervals used will vary according to the credit terms granted to customers. A portion of a typical analysis is as follows:

ANALYSIS OF ACCOUNTS RECEIVABLE

CUSTOMER	BALANCE	NOT DUE	DAYS PAST DUE					
			1–30	31–60	61–90	91–180	181–365	over 365
Ashby & Co.	$ 150			$ 150				
B. T. Barr	610					$ 350	$260	
Brock Co.	470	$ 470						
J. Zimmer Co.	160							160
Total	$86,300	$75,000	$4,000	$3,100	$1,900	$1,200	$800	$300

The analysis is completed by adding the columns to determine the total amount of receivables in each age group. A sliding scale of percentages, based on experience, is next applied to obtain the estimated amount of uncollectibles in each group. The manner in which the data may be presented is illustrated as follows:

Age Interval	Balance	Estimated Uncollectible Accounts		
		Percent	Amount	ESTIMATE OF UNCOLLECTIBLE ACCOUNTS
Not due.....................	$75,000	2%	$1,500	
1–30 days past due..........	4,000	5	200	
31–60 days past due	3,100	10	310	
61–90 days past due	1,900	20	380	
91–180 days past due	1,200	30	360	
181–365 days past due	800	50	400	
Over 365 days past due......	300	80	240	
Total.....................	$86,300		$3,390	

The estimate of uncollectible accounts, $3,390 in the example above, is the amount to be deducted from accounts receivable to yield their expected realizable value. It is thus the amount of the desired balance of the allowance account after adjustment. The excess of this figure over the balance of the allowance account before adjustment is the amount of the current provision to be made for uncollectible accounts expense.

To continue the illustration, assume that the allowance account has a credit balance of $510 before adjustment. The amount to be added to this balance is therefore $3,390 − $510, or $2,880, and the adjusting entry is as follows:

Adjusting Entry

Dec. 31	Uncollectible Accounts Expense	2,880	
	Allowance for Doubtful Accounts..........		2,880

After the adjusting entry is posted, the balance in the allowance account will be $3,390, which is the desired amount. If there had been a debit balance of $300 in the allowance account before the year-end adjustment, the amount of the adjustment would have been $3,390 (the desired balance) + $300 (the negative balance), or $3,690.

Estimation of uncollectible accounts expense based on an analysis of receivables is less common than estimations based on sales volume. It is sometimes preferred because it gives a more accurate estimate of the current realizable value of the receivables.

DIRECT WRITE-OFF METHOD OF ACCOUNTING FOR UNCOLLECTIBLES

The use of the allowance method, as illustrated in the preceding paragraphs, results in the uncollectible accounts expense being reported in the period in which the sales are made. This matching of expenses with related revenue is the preferred method of accounting for uncollectible receivables. However, there are situations in which it is impossible to estimate the uncollectibles at the end of the period with reasonable accuracy. Also, if an enterprise sells most of its goods or services on a cash basis, the amount of its expense from uncollectible accounts is usually small in relation to its revenue. The amount of its receivables at any time is also likely to represent a relatively small part of its total current assets. In such cases, it is satisfactory to delay recognition of uncollectibility until the period in which certain accounts are believed to be worthless and are actually written off as an expense. Accordingly, an allowance account or an adjusting entry is not needed at the end of the period. The entry to write off an account when it is believed to be uncollectible is as follows:

May 10   Uncollectible Accounts Expense   42
          Accounts Receivable—D. L. Ross   42
          To write off uncollectible account.

If an account that has been written off is collected later, the account should be reinstated. If the recovery is in the same fiscal year as the write-off, the earlier entry should be reversed to reinstate the account. To illustrate, assume that the account written off in the May 10 entry above is collected in November of the same fiscal year. The entry to reinstate the account would be as follows:

Nov. 21   Accounts Receivable   42
          Uncollectible Accounts Expense   42
          To reinstate account written off earlier in
          the year.

The receipt of cash in payment of the reinstated amount would be recorded in the usual manner.

When an account that has been written off is collected in a later fiscal year, it may be reinstated by an entry like that just illustrated. An alternative is to credit some other appropriately titled account, such as Recovery of Uncollectible Accounts Written Off. The credit balance in such an account at the end of the year may then be reported on the income statement as a deduction from Uncollectible Accounts Expense, or the net expense only may be reported. Such amounts are likely to be small compared to net income.

RECEIVABLES FROM INSTALLMENT SALES

In some businesses, especially in the retail field, it is common to make sales on the installment plan. In the typical installment sale, the purchaser makes a down payment and agrees to pay the remainder in specified amounts at stated intervals over a period of time. The seller may retain technical title to the goods or may take other means to make repossession easier in the event that the purchaser defaults on the payments. Despite such provisions, installment sales should ordinarily be treated in the same manner as any other sale on account, in which case the revenue is considered to be realized at the point of sale.[2]

In some exceptional cases, the circumstances are such that the collection of receivables is not reasonably assured. In these cases, another method of determining revenue may be used.[3] The alternative is to consider each receipt of cash to be revenue and to be composed of partial amounts of (1) the cost of merchandise sold and (2) gross profit on the sale. This method may be used for federal income tax purposes by dealers who regularly sell personal property on the installment plan.

As a basis for illustration, assume that in the first year of operations of a dealer in household appliances, installment sales totaled $300,000 and the cost of the merchandise sold amounted to $180,000. Assume also that collections of the installment accounts receivable were spread over three years as follows: 1st year, $140,000; 2d year, $100,000; 3d year, $60,000. According to the point of sale method, all of the revenue would be recognized in the first year and the gross profit realized in that year would be determined as follows:

Installment sales........................	$300,000	POINT OF SALE METHOD
Cost of the merchandise sold	180,000	
Gross profit	$120,000	

The alternative to the point of sale method, the installment method, allocates gross profit according to the amount of receivables collected in each year, based on the percent of gross profit to sales. The rate of gross profit to sales is determined as follows:

$$\frac{\text{Gross Profit}}{\text{Installment Sales}} = \frac{\$120,000}{\$300,000} = 40\%$$

The amounts reported as gross profit for each of the three years, based on collections of installment accounts receivable, are as follows:

1st year collections: $140,000 × 40%..............	$ 56,000	INSTALLMENT METHOD
2d year collections: $100,000 × 40%...............	40,000	
3d year collections: $ 60,000 × 40%..............	24,000	
Total $300,000.....................	$120,000	

Under the installment method, the adjusting and closing process for sales and cost of merchandise sold would be modified so that the amount of gross

---

[2]*Opinions of the Accounting Principles Board*, No. 10, "Omnibus Opinion—1966" (New York: American Institute of Certified Public Accountants, 1966), par. 12.

[3]*Ibid.*

profit for a year is recorded in a deferred gross profit account and reported in a "deferred credits" section of the balance sheet, following long-term liabilities. The amount of gross profit to be reported, as the cash is collected, is then transferred from the deferred gross profit account to a gross profit on installment sales account.

TEMPORARY INVESTMENTS

A business may have a large amount of cash on hand that is not needed immediately, but this cash may be needed later in operating the business, possibly within the coming year. Rather than allow this excess cash to lie idle until it is actually needed, the business may put all or a part of it in income-yielding investments. These investments may be in certificates of deposit, money market funds, or similar instruments. In many cases, the idle cash is invested in securities that can be sold quickly when cash is needed. Such securities are known as **temporary investments** or **marketable securities**. Although they may be retained as an investment for a number of years, they continue to be classified as temporary, provided that: (1) the securities are readily marketable and thus can be sold for cash at any time and (2) management intends to sell them at such time as the enterprise needs more cash for normal operations.

Temporary investments in securities include stocks and bonds. Stocks are equity securities issued by corporations, and bonds are debt securities issued by corporations and various government agencies. Stocks and bonds held as temporary investments are classified on the balance sheet as current assets. They may be listed after "Cash," or they may be combined with cash and described as "Cash and marketable securities."

A temporary investment in a portfolio of debt securities is usually carried at cost. However, the **carrying amount** (also called **basis**) of a temporary investment in a portfolio of equity securities is the lower of its total cost or market price, determined at the date of the balance sheet.[4] Note that in the following illustration, the carrying amount is based on the comparison between the *total* cost and the *total* market price of the portfolio, rather than the lower of cost or market price of *each item*.

Temporary Investment Portfolio	Cost	Market	Unrealized Gain (Loss)
Equity security A...........	$150,000	$100,000	$(50,000)
Equity security B..........	200,000	200,000	—
Equity security C	180,000	210,000	30,000
Equity security D	160,000	150,000	(10,000)
Total..................	$690,000	$660,000	$(30,000)

[4]*Statement of Financial Accounting Standards*, No. 12, "Accounting for Certain Marketable Securities" (Stamford: Financial Accounting Standards Board, 1975), par. 8.

The marketable equity securities would be reported in the current assets section of the balance sheet at a cost of $690,000 less an allowance for decline to market price of $30,000 to yield a carrying amount of $660,000. The unrealized loss of $30,000 is included in the determination of net income and reported as a separate item on the income statement. If the market value of the portfolio later rises, the unrealized loss is reversed and included in net income, but only to the extent that it does not exceed the original cost. In such cases, the increase is reported separately in the other income section of the income statement and the amount reported on the balance sheet is likewise adjusted.[5]

Some accountants believe that marketable equity securities should be valued at their current market prices, regardless of whether these prices are above or below cost. They argue for current market prices because (1) the securities are readily marketable, (2) the current market prices can be objectively and simply determined, and (3) current market prices are more useful as an indication of the amount of cash that can be made available for normal operations. Although the merits of the valuation of marketable equity securities at current market prices continues to be debated within the profession, the lower of cost or market price method is the current generally accepted method of valuation. To date, only certain industries, such as securities brokers and mutual fund dealers, are permitted to report their marketable equity securities at current market prices.

TEMPORARY INVESTMENTS AND RECEIVABLES IN THE BALANCE SHEET

Temporary investments (marketable securities) and all receivables that are expected to be realized in cash within a year are presented in the current assets section of the balance sheet. It is customary to list the assets in the order of liquidity, that is, in the order in which they can be converted to cash in normal operations. An illustration of the presentation of receivables and temporary investments is shown in the following partial balance sheet.

Pilar Enterprises Inc.
Balance Sheet
December 31, 19--

TEMPORARY INVESTMENTS AND RECEIVABLES IN BALANCE SHEET

Current assets:		
Cash		$119,500
Marketable equity securities........................	$690,000	
Less allowance for decline to market.............	30,000	660,000
Notes receivable....................................		250,000
Accounts receivable	$445,000	
Less allowance for doubtful accounts	15,000	430,000
Interest receivable		14,500

[5]*Ibid.*, par. 11.

Self-
Examination
Questions
(Answers
at end of
chapter.)

1. What is the maturity value of a 90-day, 12% note for $10,000?
A. $8,800
B. $10,000
C. $10,300
D. $11,200

2. On June 16, an enterprise discounts a 60-day, 10% note receivable for $15,000, dated June 1, at the rate of 12%. The proceeds are:
A. $15,000.00
B. $15,021.25
C. $15,250.00
D. $15,478.75

3. At the end of the fiscal year before the accounts are adjusted, Accounts Receivable has a balance of $200,000 and Allowance for Doubtful Accounts has a credit balance of $2,500. If the estimate of uncollectible accounts determined by aging the receivables is $8,500, the current provision to be made for uncollectible accounts expense would be:
A. $2,500
B. $6,000
C. $8,500
D. $200,000

4. At the end of the fiscal year, Accounts Receivable has a balance of $100,000 and Allowance for Doubtful Accounts has a balance of $7,000. The expected realizable value of the accounts receivable is:
A. $7,000
B. $93,000
C. $100,000
D. $107,000

5. Under what caption would an investment in stock that is held as a temporary investment be reported in the balance sheet?
A. Current assets
B. Plant assets
C. Investments
D. None of the above

Discussion Questions

6-1. What are the advantages, to the creditor, of a note receivable in comparison to an account receivable?

6-2. In what section should a five-year note receivable from the president of Wilcox Corporation be listed on the corporation's balance sheet?

6-3. Baker Corporation issued a promissory note to Stevens Company. (a) Name the payee. (b) What is the title of the account employed by Stevens Company in recording the note?

6-4. If a note provides for payment of principal of $1,000 and interest at the rate of 14%, will the interest amount to $140? Explain.

6-5. The following questions refer to a 60-day, 12% note for $10,000, dated July 10: (a) What is the face value of the note? (b) What is the amount of interest payable at maturity? (c) What is the maturity value of the note? (d) What is the due date of the note?

6–6. At the end of the fiscal year, an enterprise holds a 60-day note receivable accepted from a customer fifteen days earlier. (a) Will the interest on the note as of the end of the year represent a deferral or an accrual? (b) Which of the following types of accounts will be affected by the related adjusting entry at the end of the fiscal year: (1) asset, (2) liability, (3) revenue, (4) expense? (c) If the note is held until maturity, what fraction of the total interest should be allocated to the year in which the note is collected?

6–7. The payee of a 60-day, 12% note for $1,000, dated April 10, endorses it to a bank on April 30. The bank discounts the note at 14%, paying the endorser $1,004.13. Identify or determine the following, as they relate to the note: (a) face value, (b) maturity value, (c) due date, (d) number of days in the discount period, (e) proceeds, (f) interest income or expense recorded by payee, (g) amount payable to the bank if the maker should default.

6–8. A discounted note receivable is dishonored by the maker and the endorser pays the bank the face of the note, $5,000, the interest, $50, and a protest fee of $8. What entry should be made in the accounts of the endorser to record the payment?

6–9. During the year, notes receivable of $350,000 were discounted to a bank by an enterprise. By the end of the year, $290,000 of these notes have matured. What is the amount of the endorser's contingent liability for notes receivable discounted at the end of the year?

6–10. The series of six transactions recorded in the following T accounts were related to a sale to a customer on account and receipt of the amount owed. Briefly describe each transaction.

Cash		Notes Receivable		Accounts Receivable	
(4) 1,882	(5) 1,938	(3) 1,900	(4) 1,900	(1) 2,000	(2) 100
(6) 1,950				(5) 1,938	(3) 1,900
					(6) 1,938

Sales		Interest Income		Interest Expense	
(2) 100	(1) 2,000		(6) 12	(4) 18	

6–11. Which of the two methods of accounting for uncollectible accounts provides for the recognition of the expense at the earlier date?

6–12. What kind of an account (asset, liability, etc.) is Allowance for Doubtful Accounts, and is its normal balance a debit or a credit?

6–13. Give the adjusting entry to increase Allowance for Doubtful Accounts by $11,150.

6–14. After the accounts are adjusted and closed at the end of the fiscal year, Accounts Receivable has a balance of $197,400 and Allowance for Doubtful Accounts has a balance of $6,100.
(a) What is the expected realizable value of the accounts receivable?
(b) If an account receivable of $1,000 is written off against the allowance account, what will be the expected realizable value of the accounts receivable after the write-off, assuming that no other changes in either account have occurred in the meantime?

6–15. A firm has consistently adjusted its allowance account at the end of the fiscal year by adding a fixed percent of the period's net sales on account. After six years, the balance in Allowance for Doubtful Accounts has become disproportionately large in relationship to the balance in Accounts Receivable. Give two possible explanations.

6–16. The $750 balance of an account owed by a customer is considered to be uncollectible and is to be written off. Give the entry to record the write-off in the general ledger, (a) assuming that the allowance method is used and (b) assuming that the direct write-off method is used.

6–17. Which of the two methods of estimating uncollectibles, when advance provision for uncollectible receivables is made, provides for the most accurate estimate of the current realizable value of the receivables?

6–18. During the current year, merchandise costing $60,000 was sold on the installment plan for $100,000. The down payments and installment payments received during the current year total $50,000. What is the amount of gross profit considered to be realized in the current year, applying (a) the point-of-sale principle of revenue recognition and (b) the installment method of accounting?

6–19. Under what caption should securities held as a temporary investment be reported on the balance sheet?

6–20. A corporation has two equity securities which it holds as a temporary investment. If they have a total cost of $125,000 and a fair market value of $120,000, at what amount should these securities be reported in the current assets section of the corporation's balance sheet?

Exercises

6–21. Determine the interest on the following notes:

Face Amount	Number of Days	Interest Rate
(a) $7,500	60	12%
(b) 3,000	60	14%
(c) 2,000	75	12%
(d) 4,000	75	15%
(e) 7,200	50	10%

6–22. Dixon Company issues a 60-day, 12% note for $4,500, dated April 20, to Thomas Corporation on account.
   (a) Determine the due date of the note.
   (b) Determine the amount of interest to be paid on the note at maturity.
   (c) Present entries to record the following:
     (1) Receipt of the note by the payee.
     (2) Receipt by payee of payment of the note at maturity.

6–23. (a) Present entries for the following:
   May 31. Received from Cox Co., on account, a $5,000, 90-day, 12% note dated May 31.

June 30. Recorded an adjusting entry for accrued interest on the note of May 31.

30. Closed the interest income account. The only entry in this account originated from the above adjustment.

July 1. Recorded a reversing entry for accrued interest.

Aug. 29. Received $5,150 from Cox Co. for the note due today.

(b) What is the balance in interest income after the entry of August 29?

(c) How many days' interest on $5,000 at 12% does the amount reported in (b) represent?

6–24. Baxter & Son holds a 90-day, 14% note for $5,000, dated June 20, that was received from a customer on account. On July 20, the note is discounted at the Ogden National Bank at the rate of 16%.

(a) Determine the maturity value of the note.

(b) Determine the number of days in the discount period.

(c) Determine the amount of the discount.

(d) Determine the amount of the proceeds.

(e) Present the entry to record the discounting of the note on July 20.

6–25. Record the following transactions in the accounts of C. Reed and Daughter.

May 1. Received a $6,000, 60-day, 14% note dated May 1 from Shaul Corp. on account.

31. Discounted the note at Royal National Bank; discount rate, 15%.

June 30. The note is dishonored; paid the bank the amount due on the note plus a protest fee of $7.

July 30. Received the amount due on the dishonored note plus interest for 30 days at 14% on the total amount debited to Shaul Corp. on June 30.

6–26. At the end of the current year, the accounts receivable account has a debit balance of $75,000 and net sales for the year total $800,000. Determine the amount of the adjusting entry to record the provision for doubtful accounts under each of the following assumptions:

(a) The allowance account before adjustment has a credit balance of $700.

(1) Uncollectible accounts expense is estimated at ½ of 1% of net sales.

(2) Analysis of the individual customers' accounts indicates doubtful accounts of $5,250.

(b) The allowance account before adjustment has a debit balance of $300.

(1) Uncollectible accounts expense is estimated at ¾ of 1% of net sales.

(2) Analysis of the individual customers' accounts indicates doubtful accounts of $5,250.

6–27. Carlson Company makes all sales on the installment plan. Data related to merchandise sold during the current fiscal year are as follows:

Sales.	$950,000
Cash received on the $950,000 of installment contracts	300,000
Merchandise inventory, beginning of year.	112,500
Merchandise inventory, end of year	117,500
Purchases	670,000

Determine the amount of gross profit that would be recognized for the current fiscal year according to (a) the point of sale method and (b) the installment method.

6–28. As of December 31 of the first year of operations, DCA Corporation has the following portfolio of temporary equity securities:

	Cost	Market
Security A	$15,500	$17,750
Security B	8,000	6,200
Security C	22,750	19,500
Security D	85,800	87,000

Describe how the portfolio of temporary equity securities would be reported on the balance sheet and income statement of DCA Corporation.

Problems

6–29. The following were selected from among the transactions completed by D. L. Parton Co. during the current year:

Jan. 9. Sold merchandise on account to Haggart Co., $5,000.

19. Accepted a 30-day, 12% note for $5,000 from Haggart Co. on account.

Feb. 18. Received from Haggart Co. the amount due on the note of January 19.

May 1. Sold merchandise on account to C. D. Chow Inc., for $2,000.

10. Loaned $3,000 cash to John Johnson, receiving a 30-day, 14% note.

11. Received from C. D. Chow Inc. the amount due on the invoice of May 1, less 2% discount.

June 9. Received the interest due from John Johnson and a new 60-day, 14% note as a renewal of the loan. (Record both the debit and the credit to the notes receivable account.)

Aug. 8. Received from John Johnson the amount due on his note.

Sept. 16. Sold merchandise on account to West and Son, $6,000.

Oct. 11. Received from West and Son a 60-day, 12% note for $6,000.

Nov. 10. Discounted the note from West and Son at the Palmer National Bank at 10%.

Dec. 10. Received notice from Palmer National Bank that West and Son had dishonored its note. Paid the bank the maturity value of the note.

20. Received from West and Son the amount owed on the dishonored note, plus interest for 10 days at 10% computed on the maturity value of the note.

Instructions:

Record the transactions in a journal.

6–30. During the last three months of the current fiscal year, Denton Co. received the following notes. Notes (1), (2), (3), and (4) were discounted on the dates and at the rates indicated.

Date	Face Amount	Term	Interest Rate	Date Discounted	Discount Rate
(1) July 7	$ 9,000	60 days	12%	July 27	10%
(2) July 20	8,000	60 days	12%	July 30	15%
(3) Aug. 4	3,000	90 days	10%	Sep. 3	12%
(4) Aug. 19	7,200	60 days	11%	Sep. 28	12%
(5) Dec. 11	4,500	30 days	14%	—	—
(6) Dec. 16	12,000	60 days	13%	—	—

Instructions:

(1) Determine for each note (a) the due date and (b) the amount of interest due at maturity, identifying each note by number.

(2) Determine for each of the first four notes (a) the maturity value, (b) the discount period, (c) the discount, (d) the proceeds, and (e) the interest income or interest expense, identifying each note by number.

(3) Present the entries to record the discounting of notes (2) and (3) at a bank.

(4) Assuming that notes (5) and (6) are held until maturity, determine for each the amount of interest earned (a) in the current fiscal year and (b) in the following fiscal year.

6–31. Mahan Co. closes its accounts annually as of December 31, the end of the fiscal year. The following data relate to notes receivable and interest from November 1 through February 14 of the following year. (All notes are dated as of the day they are received.)

Nov. 1. Received a $2,000, 12%, 60-day note on account.
     11. Received a $9,000, 14%, 90-day note on account.
Dec. 16. Received a $12,000, 11%, 60-day note on account.
     21. Received a $3,000, 12%, 30-day note on account.
     31. Received $2,040 on note of November 1.
     31. Recorded an adjusting entry for the interest accrued on the notes dated November 11, December 16, and December 21. There are no other notes receivable on this date.
Jan. 1. Recorded a reversing entry for the accrued interest.
     11. Received a $3,500, 12%, 30-day note on account.
     20. Received $3,030 on note of December 21.
Feb. 9. Received $9,315 on note of November 11.
     10. Received $3,535 on note of January 11.
     14. Received $12,220 on note of December 16.

Instructions:

(1) Open accounts for Interest Receivable (Account No. 116) and Interest Income (Account No. 611), and record a credit balance of $1,150 in the latter account as of November 1 of the current year.

(2) Present entries to record the transactions and other data, posting to the two accounts after each entry affecting them.

(3) If the reversing entry had not been recorded as of January 1, indicate how each interest receipt in January and February should be allocated. Submit the data in the following form:

Note (Face Amount)	Total Interest Received	Cr. Interest Receivable	Cr. Interest Income
$ 9,000	$	$	$
12,000			
3,000			
3,500			
Total	$	$	$

(4) Do the February 14 balances of Interest Receivable and Interest Income obtained by the use of the reversing entry technique correspond to the balances that would have been obtained by analyzing each receipt?

6–32. The following transactions, adjusting entries, and closing entries are related to uncollectible accounts. All were completed during the current fiscal year ended December 31.

Feb. 12. Reinstated the account of Charles Ling that had been written off in the preceding year and received $700 cash in full payment.

Apr. 20. Wrote off the $3,125 balance owed by Fuller Co., which has no assets.

July 30. Received 30% of the $6,000 balance owed by L. Born Corp., a bankrupt, and wrote off the remainder as uncollectible.

Nov. 25. Reinstated the account of Lawrence Cox that had been written off two years earlier and received $510 cash in full payment.

Dec. 20. Wrote off the following accounts as uncollectible (compound entry): Colbert and Collins, $375; J. C. Davis Co., $3,700; John Gordon, $390; H. A. Powell Corp., $5,150.

31. Based on an analysis of the $217,550 of accounts receivable, it was estimated that $14,700 will be uncollectible. Recorded the adjusting entry.

31. Recorded the entry to close the appropriate account to Income Summary.

Instructions:

(1) Open the following selected accounts, recording the credit balance indicated as of January 1 of the current fiscal year:

115 Allowance for Doubtful Accounts $17,300

313 Income Summary . . . . ——

718 Uncollectible Accounts Expense. ——

(2) Record the transactions and the adjusting and closing entries described above. After each entry, post to the three selected accounts affected and extend the new balances.

(3) Determine the expected realizable value of the accounts receivable as of December 31.

(4) Assuming that, instead of basing the provision for uncollectible accounts on an analysis of receivables, the adjusting entry on December 31 had been based on an estimated loss of ½ of 1% of the net sales of $2,700,000 for the year, determine the following:

(a) Uncollectible accounts expense for the year.

(b) Balance in the allowance account after the adjustment of December 31.

(c) Expected realizable value of the accounts receivable as of December 31.

6–33. Oakwood Sales Inc. has just completed its fourth year of operations. The direct write-off method of recording uncollectible accounts expense has been employed during the entire period. Because of substantial increases in sales volume and amount of uncollectible accounts, the firm is considering the possibility of changing to the allowance method. Information is requested as to the effect that an annual provision of ½ of 1% of sales would have had on the amount of uncollectible accounts expense reported for each of the past four years. It is also considered desirable to know what the balance of Allowance for Doubtful Accounts would have been at the end of each year. The following data have been obtained from the accounts:

Year	Sales	Uncollectible Accounts Written Off	Year of Origin of Accounts Receivable Written off as Uncollectible			
			1st	2d	3d	4th
1st	$500,000	$ 500	$ 500			
2d	650,000	2,150	1,500	$ 650		
3d	800,000	3,200	200	2,400	$ 600	
4th	950,000	4,150		600	2,600	$950

Instructions:

(1) Assemble the desired data, using the following columnar captions:

Year	Uncollectible Accounts Expense			Balance of Allowance Account, End of Year
	Expense Actually Reported	Expense Based on Estimate	Increase in Amount of Expense	

(2) Does the estimate of ½ of 1% of sales appear to be reasonably close to the actual experience with uncollectible accounts originating during the first two years?

6–34. Horowitz Co. makes all sales on the installment basis and recognizes revenue at the point of sale. Condensed income statements and the amounts collected from customers for each of the first three years of operations are as follows:

	First Year	Second Year	Third Year
Sales.....................................	$319,000	$340,000	$382,000
Cost of merchandise sold................	216,920	227,800	248,300
Gross profit	$102,080	$112,200	$133,700
Operating expenses	40,000	47,500	62,500
Net income	$ 62,080	$ 64,700	$ 71,200
Collected from sales of first year	$ 97,000	$126,000	$ 96,000
Collected from sales of second year		97,500	140,000
Collected from sales of third year.........			95,500

Instructions:

Determine the amount of net income that would have been reported in each year if the installment method of recognizing revenue had been employed, ignoring the possible effects of uncollectible accounts on the computation. Present figures in good order.

6–35. Video Sales employs the installment method of recognizing gross profit for sales made on the installment plan. Details of a particular installment sale, amounts collected from the purchaser, and the repossession of the item sold are as follows:

First year:

Sold for $1,200 a color television set having a cost of $960 and received a down payment of $200.

Second year:

Received twelve monthly payments of $40 each.

Third year:

The purchaser defaulted on the monthly payments, the set was repossessed, and the remaining 13 installments were canceled. The set was estimated to be worth $450.

Instructions:

(1) Determine the gross profit to be recognized in the first year.
(2) Determine the gross profit to be recognized in the second year.
(3) Determine the gain or loss to be recognized from the repossession of the set.

Alternate Problems

6–29A. The following were selected from among the transactions completed by Michael Levin and Co. during the current year:

Jan. 15. Loaned $6,000 cash to Frank Reilly, receiving a 90-day, 12% note.
Mar. 1. Sold merchandise on account to A-1 Supply, $3,000.
     11. Received from A-1 Supply the amount due on the invoice of March 1, less 1% discount.
     12. Sold merchandise on account to Caldwell Co., $4,000.
Apr. 11. Accepted a 30-day, 15% note for $4,000 from Caldwell Co. on account.
     15. Received the interest due from Frank Reilly and a new 90-day, 14% note as a renewal of the loan. (Record both the debit and the credit to the notes receivable account.)
May 11. Received from Caldwell Co. the amount due on the note of April 11.
July 12. Sold merchandise on account to Swartz and Sons, $10,000.
     14. Received from Frank Reilly the amount due on his note of April 15.
Aug. 11. Received from Swartz and Sons a 60-day, 12% note for $10,000.
Sept. 10. Discounted the note from Swartz and Sons at the Commercial National Bank at 14%.
Oct. 13. Received notice from the Commercial National Bank that Swartz and Sons had dishonored its note. Paid the bank the maturity value of the note.
Nov. 9. Received from Swartz and Sons the amount owed on the dishonored note, plus interest for 30 days at 12% computed on the maturity value of the note.

Instructions:

Record the transactions in a journal.

6-30A. During the last three months of the current fiscal year, Bailey Co. received the following notes. Notes (1), (2), (3), and (4) were discounted on the dates and at the rates indicated.

Date	Face Amount	Term	Interest Rate	Date Discounted	Discount Rate
(1) Oct. 2	$4,800	60 days	14%	Oct. 22	12%
(2) Oct. 6	7,500	30 days	12%	Oct. 21	14%
(3) Oct. 28	3,100	90 days	14%	Dec. 27	15%
(4) Nov. 3	4,000	60 days	12%	Nov. 13	16%
(5) Dec. 16	6,000	60 days	11%	—	—
(6) Dec. 21	8,700	30 days	12%	—	—

Instructions:
   (1) Determine for each note (a) the due date and (b) the amount of interest due at maturity, identifying each note by number.
   (2) Determine for each of the first four notes (a) the maturity value, (b) the discount period, (c) the discount, (d) the proceeds, and (e) the interest income or interest expense, identifying each note by number.
   (3) Present the entries to record the discounting of notes (2) and (4) at a bank.
   (4) Assuming that notes (5) and (6) are held until maturity, determine for each the amount of interest earned (a) in the current fiscal year and (b) in the following fiscal year.

6-31A. B. Olin Co. closes its accounts annually as of December 31, the end of the fiscal year. The following data relate to notes receivable and interest from November 1 through February 29 of the following year. (All notes are dated as of the day they are received.)

Nov. 1. Received a $4,500, 12%, 60-day note on account.
Dec. 1. Received a $10,000, 15%, 90-day note on account.
     16. Received a $12,000, 13%, 60-day note on account.
     21. Received a $6,000, 12%, 30-day note on account.
     31. Received $4,590 on note of November 1.
     31. Recorded an adjusting entry for the interest accrued on the notes dated December 1, December 16, and December 21. There are no other notes receivable on this date.
Jan. 1. Recorded a reversing entry for the accrued interest.
     20. Received $6,060 on note of December 21.
     21. Received a $3,500, 12%, 30-day note on account.
Feb. 14. Received $12,260 on note of December 16.
     20. Received $3,535 on note of January 21.
     29. Received $10,375 on note of December 1.

Instructions:
   (1) Open accounts for Interest Receivable (Account No. 116) and Interest Income (Account No. 611), and record a credit balance of $1,410 in the latter account as of November 1 of the current year.
   (2) Present entries to record the transactions and other data, posting to the two accounts after each entry affecting them.
   (3) If the reversing entry had not been recorded as of January 1, indicate how each interest receipt in January and February should be allocated. Submit the data in the following form:

Note (Face Amount)	Total Interest Received	Cr. Interest Receivable	Cr. Interest Income
$ 6,000	$	$	$
12,000			
3,500			
10,000			
Total	$	$	$

(4) Do the February 29 balances of Interest Receivable and Interest Income obtained by use of the reversing entry technique correspond to the balances that would have been obtained by analyzing each receipt?

6–32A. The following transactions, adjusting entries, and closing entries are related to uncollectible accounts. All were completed during the current fiscal year ended December 31.

Mar. 10. Received 40% of the $10,000 balance owed by Porter Co., a bankrupt, and wrote off the remainder as uncollectible.

Apr. 18. Reinstated the account of Virginia Babb that had been written off three years earlier and received $725 cash in full payment.

June 15. Wrote off the $2,900 balance owed by Vance Corp., which has no assets.

Sept. 5. Reinstated the account of Suburban Cleaners that had been written off in the preceding year and received $925 cash in full payment.

Dec. 30. Wrote off the following accounts as uncollectible (compound entry): Baker and Dodds, $1,120; Flowers Inc., $2,975; McMann Distributors, $7,100; J. J. Stevens, $420.

31. Based on an analysis of the $420,000 of accounts receivable, it was estimated that $22,700 will be uncollectible. Recorded the adjusting entry.

31. Recorded the entry to close the appropriate account to Income Summary.

Instructions:

(1) Open the following selected accounts, recording the credit balance indicated as of January 1 of the current fiscal year:

115 Allowance for Doubtful Accounts $19,500
313 Income Summary................................... —
718 Uncollectible Accounts Expense..................... —

(2) Record the transactions and the adjusting and closing entries described above. After each entry, post to the three selected accounts affected and extend the new balances.

(3) Determine the expected realizable value of the accounts receivable as of December 31.

(4) Assuming that, instead of basing the provision for uncollectible accounts on an analysis of receivables, the adjusting entry on December 31 had been based on an estimated loss of ½ of 1% of the net sales of $4,700,000 for the year, determine the following:

(a) Uncollectible accounts expense for the year.

(b) Balance in the allowance account after the adjustment of December 31.

(c) Expected realizable value of the accounts receivable as of December 31.

6–34A. J. A. Horn Inc. makes all sales on the installment basis and recognizes revenue at the point of sale. Condensed income statements and the amounts collected from customers for each of the first three years of operations are as follows:

	First Year	Second Year	Third Year
Sales.	$300,000	$340,000	$400,000
Cost of merchandise sold.	195,000	224,400	256,000
Gross profit	$105,000	$115,600	$144,000
Operating expenses.	57,500	68,500	87,500
Net income	$ 47,500	$ 47,100	$ 56,500
Collected from sales of first year	$ 75,000	$125,000	$100,000
Collected from sales of second year		110,000	180,000
Collected from sales of third year.			105,000

Instructions:

Determine the amount of net income that would have been reported in each year if the installment method of recognizing revenue had been employed, ignoring the possible effects of uncollectible accounts on the computation. Present figures in good order.

Mini-Case

6–36. For several years, Weberg Furniture's sales have been on a "cash only" basis. On January 1, 1983, however, Weberg began offering credit to selected customers on terms of n/30. The adjusting entry to estimate uncollectible receivables at the end of each year has been based on sales and has been uniformly 1% of credit sales, which is the rate reported as the average for the retail furniture industry. Credit sales and the year-end credit balances in Allowance for Doubtful Accounts for the past four years are as follows:

Year	Credit Sales	Allowance for Doubtful Accounts
1983	$400,000	$2,100
1984	415,000	3,750
1985	395,000	5,100
1986	420,000	6,600

Richard Weberg, president of Weberg Furniture, is concerned that the method of accounting for uncollectible receivables and for the write-off of uncollectible accounts are unsatisfactory. He has asked your advice in the analysis of past operations in this area and recommendations for change.

Instructions:

(1) Determine the amount of (a) the addition to Allowance for Doubtful Accounts and (b) the accounts written off for each of the four years.

(2) Advise Weberg as to whether the estimate of 1% of credit sales appears reasonable.

(3) Assume that after discussing item (2) with Weberg, he asked you what action might be taken to determine what the balance of Allowance for Doubtful Accounts should be at December 31, 1986, and possible changes, if any, you might recommend in accounting for uncollectible receivables. How would you respond?

Answers to Self-Examination Questions

1. C Maturity value is the amount that is due at the maturity or due date. The maturity value of $10,300 (answer C) is determined as follows:

Face amount of note $10,000
Plus interest ($10,000 × 12/100 × 90/360) 300
Maturity value of note................................ $10,300

2. B The proceeds of $15,021.25 (answer B) is determined as follows:

Face value of note dated June 1.................... $15,000.00
Interest on note — 60 days at 10% 250.00
Maturity value of note due July 31 .... $15,250.00
Discount period — June 16–July 31 .... 45 days
Discount on maturity value — 45 days at 12% 228.75
Proceeds $15,021.25

3. B The estimate of uncollectible accounts, $8,500, is the amount of the desired balance of Allowance for Doubtful Accounts *after adjustment.* The amount of the current provision to be made for uncollectible accounts expense is thus $6,000 (answer B), which is the amount that must be added to the Allowance for Doubtful Accounts credit balance of $2,500 so that the account will have the desired balance of $8,500.

4. B The amount expected to be realized from accounts receivable is the balance of Accounts Receivable, $100,000, less the balance of Allowance for Doubtful Accounts, $7,000, or $93,000 (answer B).

5. A Securities held as temporary investments are classified on the balance sheet as current assets (answer A).

CHAPTER 7

Inventories

CHAPTER OBJECTIVES

Describe and illustrate the importance of inventory in the operations and the accounting for trading and manufacturing enterprises.

Identify and illustrate the two principal inventory systems.

Identify and illustrate the procedures for the determination of the actual quantity in inventory and the most common methods of determining the cost of this inventory.

Identify and illustrate the proper presentation of inventory in the financial statements.

Describe and illustrate methods of estimating the cost of inventory.

The term **inventories** is used to designate (1) merchandise held for sale in the normal course of business, and (2) materials in the process of production or held for such use. This chapter discusses the determination of the inventory of merchandise purchased for resale, commonly called merchandise inventory. Inventories of raw materials and partially processed materials of a manufacturing enterprise will be considered in a later chapter.

IMPORTANCE OF INVENTORIES

Merchandise, being continually purchased and sold, is one of the most active elements in the operation of wholesale and retail businesses. The sale of merchandise provides the principal source of revenue for such enterprises. When the net income is determined, the cost of merchandise sold is the largest deduction from sales. In fact, it is usually larger than all other deductions combined. In addition, a substantial part of a merchandising firm's resources is invested in inventory. It is frequently the largest of the current assets of such a firm.

Inventory determination plays an important role in matching expired costs with revenues of the period. As was explained and illustrated in Chapter 3, the total cost of merchandise available for sale during a period of time must be divided into two parts at the end of the period. The cost of the merchandise determined to be in the inventory will appear on the balance sheet as a current asset. The other element, which is the cost of the merchandise sold, will be reported on the income statement as a deduction from net sales to yield gross profit. An error in the determination of the inventory figure at the end of the period will cause an equal misstatement of gross profit and net income, and the amount reported for both assets and owner's equity in the balance sheet will be incorrect by the same amount. The effects of understatements and overstatements of merchandise inventory at the end of the period are demonstrated in the following three sets of condensed income statements and balance sheets. The first set of statements is based on a correct inventory of $20,000; the second set, on an incorrect inventory of $12,000; and the third set, on an incorrect inventory of $27,000.

Income Statement for the Year — Balance Sheet at End of Year

1. Inventory at end of period correctly stated at $20,000.

Net sales	$200,000	Merchandise inventory	$ 20,000
Cost of merchandise sold	120,000	Other assets	80,000
Gross profit	$ 80,000	Total	$100,000
Expenses	55,000		
		Liabilities	$ 30,000
Net income	$ 25,000	Owner's equity	70,000
		Total	$100,000

2. Inventory at end of period incorrectly stated at $12,000; **(understated by $8,000).**

Net sales	$200,000	Merchandise inventory	$ 12,000
Cost of merchandise sold	128,000	Other assets	80,000
Gross profit	$ 72,000	Total	$ 92,000
Expenses	55,000		
		Liabilities	$ 30,000
Net income	$ 17,000	Owner's equity	62,000
		Total	$ 92,000

3. Inventory at end of period incorrectly stated at $27,000; **(overstated by $7,000).**

Net sales	$200,000	Merchandise inventory	$ 27,000
Cost of merchandise sold	113,000	Other assets	80,000
Gross profit	$ 87,000	Total	$107,000
Expenses	55,000		
		Liabilities	$ 30,000
Net income	$ 32,000	Owner's equity	77,000
		Total	$107,000

Note that in the illustration the total cost of merchandise available for sale was constant at $140,000. It was the way in which the cost was allocated that varied. The variations in allocating the $140,000 of merchandise cost are summarized as follows:

	Merchandise Available		
	Total	Inventory	Sold
1. Inventory correctly stated	$140,000	$20,000	$120,000
2. Inventory understated by $8,000............	140,000	12,000	128,000
3. Inventory overstated by $7,000	140,000	27,000	113,000

The effect of the wrong allocations on net income, assets, and owner's equity may also be summarized. Comparison of the amounts reported in financial statements 2 and 3 with the comparable amounts reported in financial statement 1 yields the following:

	Net Income	Assets	Owner's Equity
2. Ending inventory understated $8,000	Understated $8,000	Understated $8,000	Understated $8,000
3. Ending inventory overstated $7,000	Overstated $7,000	Overstated $7,000	Overstated $7,000

The inventory at the end of one period becomes the inventory for the beginning of the following period. Thus, if the inventory is incorrectly stated at the end of the period, the net income of that period will be misstated and so will the net income for the following period. The amount of the two misstatements will be equal and in opposite directions. Therefore, the effect on net income of an incorrectly stated inventory, if not corrected, is limited to the period of the error and the following period. At the end of this following period, assuming no additional errors, both assets and owner's equity will be correctly stated.

Elements of the foregoing analyses are closely related to the different inventory systems and methods. A thorough understanding of the effect of inventories on the determination of net income will be helpful when these systems and methods are presented later in this chapter.

INVENTORY SYSTEMS

As discussed in Chapter 3, there are two principal systems of inventory accounting, periodic and perpetual. When the periodic system is used, only the revenue from sales is recorded each time a sale is made. No entry is made at the time of the sale to record the cost of the merchandise that has been sold. Consequently, a physical inventory must be taken in order to determine the cost of the inventory at the end of an accounting period. Ordinarily, it is possible to take a complete physical inventory only at the end of the fiscal year. In the earlier chapters dealing with purchases and sales of merchandise, the use of the periodic system was assumed.

In contrast to the periodic system, the perpetual inventory system uses accounting records that continuously disclose the amount of the inventory. A separate account for each type of merchandise is maintained in a subsidiary ledger. Increases in inventory items are recorded as debits to the proper accounts, and decreases are recorded as credits. The balances of the accounts are called the **book inventories** of the items on hand. Regardless of the care with which the perpetual inventory records are maintained, their accuracy must be tested by taking a physical inventory of each type of commodity at least once a year. The records are then compared with the actual quantities on hand and any differences are corrected.

The periodic inventory system is often used by retail enterprises that sell many kinds of low unit cost merchandise, such as groceries, hardware, and drugs. The expense of maintaining perpetual inventory records may be prohibitive in such cases. In recent years, however, the application of electronic data processing equipment to such businesses has reduced this expense considerably. Firms selling a relatively small number of high unit cost items, such as office equipment, automobiles, or fur garments, are more likely to use the perpetual system.

Although much of the discussion that follows applies to both systems, the use of the periodic inventory system will be assumed. Later in the chapter, principles and procedures related only to the perpetual inventory system will be presented.

DETERMINING ACTUAL QUANTITIES IN THE INVENTORY

The first stage in the process of "taking" an inventory is to determine the quantity of each kind of merchandise owned by the enterprise. When the periodic system is used, the counting, weighing, and measuring should be done at the end of the accounting period. To accomplish this, the inventory crew may work during the night, or business operations may be stopped until the count is finished.

The details of the specific procedures for determining quantities and assembling the data differ among companies. A common practice is to use teams made up of two persons. One person counts, weighs, or otherwise determines quantity, and the other lists the description and the quantity on inventory sheets. The quantity indicated for high-cost items is verified by a third person at some time during the inventory-taking period. It is also advisable for the third person to verify other items selected at random from the inventory sheets.

All of the merchandise owned by the business on the inventory date, and only such merchandise, should be included in the inventory. It may be necessary to examine purchase and sales invoices of the last few days of the accounting period and the first few days of the following period to determine who has legal title to merchandise in transit on the inventory date. When goods are purchased or sold **FOB shipping point**, title usually passes to the buyer when the goods are shipped. When the terms are **FOB destination**, title usually does not pass to the buyer until the goods are delivered. To illustrate, assume that merchandise purchased FOB shipping point is shipped by the seller on the last day of the buyer's fiscal period. The merchandise does not arrive until the following period and hence is not available for "counting" by the inventory crew. However, such merchandise should be included in the buyer's inventory because title has passed. It is also evident that a debit to Purchases and a credit to Accounts Payable should be recorded by the buyer as of the end of the period, rather than recording it as a transaction of the following period.

Another example, although less common, will further show the importance of closely examining transactions involving shipments of merchandise. Manufacturers sometimes ship merchandise on a consignment basis to retailers who act as the manufacturer's agent when selling the merchandise. The manufacturer retains title until the goods are sold. Obviously, such unsold merchandise is a part of the manufacturer's (consignor's) inventory, even though the manufacturer does not have physical possession. It is just as obvious that the consigned merchandise should not be included in the retailer's (consignee's) inventory.

DETERMINING THE COST OF INVENTORY

The cost of merchandise inventory is made up of the purchase price and all expenditures incurred in acquiring such merchandise, including transportation, customs duties, and insurance against losses in transit. The purchase price can be readily determined, as may some of the other costs. Those that are difficult to associate with specific inventory items may be prorated on some equitable basis. Minor costs that are difficult to allocate may be left out entirely from inventory cost and treated as operating expenses of the period.

If purchases discounts are treated as a deduction from purchases on the income statement, they should also be deducted from the purchase price of items in the inventory. If it is not possible to determine the exact amount of discount applicable to each inventory item, a pro rata amount of the total discount for the period may be deducted instead. For example, if net purchases and purchases discount for the period amount to $200,000 and $3,000 respectively, the discount represents 1½% of net purchases. If the inventory cost, before considering the cash discount, is $30,000, the amount may be reduced by 1½% or $450, to yield an inventory cost of $29,550.

One of the most significant problems in determining inventory cost comes about when identical units of a certain commodity have been acquired at different unit cost prices during the period. When such is the case, it is necessary to determine the unit prices of the items still on hand. This problem and its relationship to the determination of net income and inventory cost are indicated by the illustration that follows.

Assume that during the fiscal year three identical units of Commodity X, one of which was in the inventory at the beginning of the year, were available for sale to customers. Details as to the dates of purchase and the costs per unit are as follows:

Commodity X	Units	Cost
Jan. 1 Inventory	1	$ 9
Mar. 4 Purchase....................	1	13
May 9 Purchase....................	1	14
Total........................	3	$36
Average cost per unit		$12

During the period, two units of Commodity X were sold, leaving one unit in the inventory at the end of the period. Information is not available as to which two of the three units were sold and which unit remains. Therefore, it becomes necessary to use an arbitrary assumption as to the *flow of costs* of merchandise through the enterprise. The three most common assumptions of determining the cost of the merchandise sold are as follows:

1. Cost flow is in the order in which the expenditures were made.
2. Cost flow is in the reverse order in which the expenditures were made.
3. Cost flow is an average of the expenditures.

Details of the cost of the two units of Commodity X assumed to be sold and the cost of the one unit remaining, determined in accordance with each of these assumptions, are as follows:

	Commodity X Costs		
	Units Available	Units Sold	Unit Remaining
1. In order of expenditures	$36	− ($ 9 + $13) =	$14
2. In reverse order of expenditures............	36	− (14 + 13) =	9
3. In accordance with average expenditures	36	− (12 + 12) =	12

In actual practice, it may be possible to identify units with specific expenditures if both the variety of merchandise carried in stock and the volume of sales are relatively small. Ordinarily, however, **specific identification** procedures are too time consuming to justify their use. It is customary, therefore, to use one of the three generally accepted costing methods, each of which is also acceptable in determining income subject to the federal income tax.

First-In, First-Out Method

The **first-in, first-out (fifo)** method of costing inventory is based on the assumption that costs should be charged against revenue in the order in which they were incurred. Hence the inventory remaining is assumed to be made up of the most recent costs. The illustration of the application of this method is based on the following data for a particular commodity:

Jan. 1 Inventory..............	200 units at $ 9............	$ 1,800
Mar. 10 Purchase..............	300 units at 10............	3,000
Sept. 21 Purchase..............	400 units at 11............	4,400
Nov. 18 Purchase..............	100 units at 12............	1,200
Available for sale during year .. 1,000	....	$10,400

The physical count on December 31 shows that 300 units of the particular commodity are on hand. In accordance with the assumption that the inventory is composed of the most recent costs, the cost of the 300 units is determined as follows:

Most recent costs, Nov. 18	100 units at $12.	$ 1,200
Next most recent costs, Sept. 21 . .	200 units at 11.	2,200
Inventory, Dec. 31	300	$ 3,400

Deduction of the inventory of **$3,400** from the $10,400 of merchandise available for sale yields **$7,000** as the cost of merchandise sold, which represents the earliest costs incurred for this commodity.

In most businesses, there is a tendency to dispose of goods in the order of their acquisition. This would be particularly true of perishable merchandise and goods in which style or model changes are frequent. Thus, the fifo method is generally in harmony with the physical movement of merchandise in an enterprise. To the extent that this is the case, the fifo method approximates the results that would be obtained by specific identification of costs.

Last-In, First-Out Method

The **last-in, first-out (lifo)** method is based on the assumption that the most recent costs incurred should be charged against revenue. Hence the inventory remaining is assumed to be composed of the earliest costs. Based on the illustrative data presented in the preceding section, the cost of the inventory is determined in the following manner:

Earliest costs, Jan. 1.	200 units at $ 9.	$ 1,800
Next earliest costs, Mar. 10	100 units at 10.	1,000
Inventory, Dec. 31	300	$ 2,800

Deduction of the inventory of **$2,800** from the $10,400 of merchandise available for sale yields **$7,600** as the cost of merchandise sold, which represents the most recent costs incurred for this particular commodity.

The use of the lifo method was originally confined to the relatively rare situations in which the units sold were taken from the most recently acquired stock. Its use has greatly increased during the past few decades, and it is now often used even when it is not like the physical flow of goods.

Average Cost Method

The **average cost method,** sometimes called the **weighted average method,** is based on the assumption that costs should be charged against revenue according to the weighted average unit costs of the goods sold. The same weighted average unit costs are used in determining the cost of the merchandise remaining in the inventory. The weighted average unit cost is determined by dividing the total cost of the identical units of each commodity available for sale during the period by the related number of units of that commodity. Assuming the same cost data as in the preceding illustrations, the average cost of the 1,000 units and the cost of the inventory are determined as follows:

Average unit cost............... $10,400 ÷ 1,000 = $10.40
Inventory, Dec. 31 ....300 units at $10.40............ $3,120

Deduction of the inventory of **$3,120** from the $10,400 of merchandise available for sale yields **$7,280** as the cost of merchandise sold, which represents the average of the costs incurred for this commodity.

For businesses in which various purchases of identical units of a commodity are mingled, the average method has some relationship to the physical flow of goods.

Comparison of Inventory Costing Methods

Each of the three alternative methods of costing inventories under the periodic system is based on a different assumption as to the flow of costs. If the cost of goods and the prices at which they were sold remained stable, all three methods would yield the same results. Prices do change, however, and as a consequence the three methods will usually yield different amounts for both (1) the inventory at the end of the period and (2) the cost of the merchandise sold and net income reported for the period. The examples presented in the preceding sections illustrated the effect of rising prices. They may be summarized as follows:

	First-In, First-Out	Average Cost	Last-In, First-Out
Merchandise available for sale	$10,400	$10,400	$10,400
Merchandise inventory, December 31	3,400	3,120	2,800
Cost of merchandise sold....................	$ 7,000	$ 7,280	$ 7,600

The method that yields the lowest figure for the cost of merchandise sold will yield the highest figure for gross profit and net income reported on the income statement. It will also yield the highest figure for inventory reported on the balance sheet. On the other hand, the method that yields the highest figure for the cost of merchandise sold will yield the lowest figure for gross profit and net income and the lowest figure for inventory.

During a period of inflation or rising prices, the use of the first-in, first-out method will result in a greater amount of net income than the other two methods. The reason is that the costs of the units sold is assumed to be in the order in which they were incurred, and the earlier unit costs were lower than the more recent unit costs. Much of the benefit of the larger amounts of gross profit is lost, however, as the inventory is continually replenished at ever higher prices. During the 1970's, when the rate of inflation increased to "double-digit" percentages, the resulting increases in net income were frequently referred to as "inventory profits" or "illusory profits" by the financial press.

In a period of deflation or declining prices the effect described above is reversed, and the fifo method yields the lowest amount of net income. The major criticism of the first-in, first-out method is this tendency to maximize the effect of inflationary and deflationary trends on amounts reported as net income. However, the dollar amount reported as merchandise inventory on the balance sheet will usually be about the same as its current replacement cost.

During a period of rising prices, the use of the last-in, first-out method will result in a lesser amount of net income than the other two methods. The reason is that the cost of the most recently acquired commodities most nearly approximates their cost of replacement. Thus, it can be argued that the use of the lifo method more nearly matches current costs with current revenues. There is also the practical advantage of a saving in income taxes. The effect of the use of different inventory methods on income taxes is discussed in more detail in Chapter 23.

In a period of deflation or falling price levels, the effect described above is reversed and the lifo method yields the highest amount of net income. The major justification for lifo is this tendency to minimize the effect of price trends on reported net income and, therefore, to exert a stabilizing influence on the economy. A criticism of the use of lifo is that the dollar amount reported for merchandise inventory on the balance sheet may be quite far removed from current replacement cost. However, in such situations it is customary to indicate the approximate replacement cost (i.e., as though fifo had been used) in a note accompanying published financial statements.

The average cost method of inventory costing is, in a sense, a compromise between fifo and lifo. The effect of price trends is averaged, both in the determination of net income and the determination of inventory cost. For any given series of acquisitions, the average cost will be the same, regardless of the direction of price trends. For example, a complete reversal of the sequence of unit costs presented in the illustration on page 214 would not affect the reported net income or the inventory cost. The time required to assemble the data is likely to be greater for the average cost method than for the other two methods. The additional expense incurred could be large if there are many purchases of a wide variety of merchandise items.

The foregoing comparisons show the importance attached to the selection of the inventory costing method. It is not unusual for manufacturing enterprises to apply one method to a particular class of inventory, such as merchandise ready for sale, and a different method to another class, such as raw materials purchased. The method(s) used may be changed for a valid reason. The effect of any change in method and the reason for the change should be fully disclosed in the financial statements for the fiscal period in which the change occurred.

Throughout the discussion of inventory costing methods, it has been assumed that the goods on hand were salable at normal sales prices. Because of imperfections, shop wear, style changes or other causes, there may be items that are not salable except at prices below cost. Such merchandise should be valued at estimated selling price less any direct cost of disposition, such as sales commission.

VALUATION AT THE LOWER OF COST OR MARKET

A frequently used alternative to valuing inventory at cost is to compare cost with market price and use the lower of the two. It should be noted that regardless of the method used, it is first necessary to determine the cost of the inventory. "Market," as used in the phrase **lower of cost or market** or **cost or market, whichever is lower,** is interpreted to mean the cost to replace the merchandise on the inventory date. To the extent practicable, the market or replacement price should be based on quantities typically purchased from the usual source of supply. In the discussion that follows, the salability of the merchandise at normal sales prices will be assumed. The valuation of articles that have to be sold at a price below their cost would be determined by the method described in the preceding paragraph.

If the replacement price of an item in the inventory is lower than its cost, the use of the lower of cost or market method provides two advantages: (1) the gross profit (and net income) are reduced for the period in which the decline occurred and (2) an approximately normal gross profit is realized during the period in which the item is sold. To illustrate, assume that merchandise with a unit cost of $70 has sold at $100 during the period, yielding a gross profit of $30 a unit, or 30% of sales. Assume also that at the end of the year, there is a single unit of the commodity in the inventory and that its replacement price has declined to $63. Under such circumstances it would be reasonable to expect that the selling price would also decline, if indeed it had not already done so. Assuming a reduction in selling price to $90, the gross profit based on replacement cost of $63 would be $27, which is also 30% of the selling price. Accordingly, valuation of the unit in the inventory at $63 reduces gross profit of the past period by $7 and permits a normal gross profit of $27 to be realized on its sale in the following period. If the unit had been valued at its original cost of $70, the gross profit determined for the past year would have been $7 greater, and the gross profit attributable to the sale of the item in the following period would have been $7 less.

It would be possible to apply the lower of cost or market basis (1) to each item in the inventory, (2) to major classes or categories, or (3) to the inventory as a whole. The first procedure is the one usually followed in practice. To illustrate the application of the lower of cost or market to individual items, assume that there are 400 identical units of Commodity A in the inventory, each acquired at a unit cost of $10.25. If at the inventory date the commodity would cost $10.50 to replace, the cost price of $10.25 would be multiplied by 400 to determine the inventory value. On the other hand, if the commodity could be replaced at $9.50 a unit, the replacement price of $9.50 would be used for valuation purposes. The following tabulation illustrates one of the forms that may be followed in assembling inventory data.

Description	Quantity	Unit Cost Price	Unit Market Price	Total Cost	Lower of C or M	DETERMINATION OF INVENTORY AT LOWER OF COST OR MARKET
Commodity A	400	$10.25	$ 9.50	$ 4,100	$ 3,800	
Commodity B	120	22.50	24.10	2,700	2,700	
Commodity C	600	8.00	7.75	4,800	4,650	
Commodity D	280	14.00	14.00	3,920	3,920	
Total				$15,520	$15,070	

Although it is not essential to accumulate the data for total cost, as in the illustration, it permits the measurement of the reduction in inventory because of a decline in market prices. When the amount of the market decline is known ($15,520 − $15,070, or $450), it may be reported as a separate item on the income statement. Otherwise, the market decline will be included in the amount reported as the cost of merchandise sold and will reduce gross profit by a corresponding amount. In any event, the amount reported as net income will not be affected. It will be the same, regardless of whether the amount of the market decline is determined and separately stated.

As with the method elected for the determination of inventory cost (first-in, first-out; last-in, first-out; or average cost), the method elected for inventory valuation (cost, or lower of cost or market) must be followed consistently from year to year.

PERPETUAL INVENTORY SYSTEM

The use of a perpetual inventory system for merchandise provides the most effective means of control over this important asset. Although it is possible to maintain a perpetual inventory in memorandum records only or to limit the data to quantities, a complete set of records integrated with the general ledger is preferable. The basic feature of the system is the recording of all merchandise increases and decreases in a manner somewhat similar to the recording of increases and decreases in cash. Just as receipts of cash are debited to Cash, so are purchases of merchandise debited to Merchandise Inventory. Similarly, sales or other reductions of merchandise are recorded in a manner like that used for reductions in Cash, that is, by credits to Merchandise Inventory. Thus, just as the balance of the cash account shows the amount of cash presumed to be on hand, so the balance of the merchandise inventory account represents the amount of merchandise presumed to be on hand.

Inventory Ledger

Unlike cash, merchandise is a mixed mass of goods. Details of the cost of each type of merchandise purchased and sold, together with such related transactions as returns and allowances, could be maintained in a subsidiary ledger, called an **inventory ledger**, which would include a separate account for each type. Thus, an enterprise that stocks five hundred kinds of merchandise could have five hundred separate accounts in its inventory ledger. In the following illustration of the flow of costs through a subsidiary account, there is a beginning inventory, three purchases, and six sales of the particular commodity during the year. The number of units on hand after each transaction, together with total cost and unit prices, appears in the inventory section of the account.

PERPETUAL INVENTORY ACCOUNT

COMMODITY			127B				
	PURCHASED		SOLD		INVENTORY		
DATE	QUANTITY	TOTAL COST	QUANTITY	TOTAL COST	QUANTITY	TOTAL COST	UNIT PRICE
JAN. 1					10	200	20
FEB. 4			7	140	3	60	20
MAR. 10	8	168			3	60	20
					8	168	21
APR. 22			4	81	7	147	21
MAY 18			2	42	5	105	21
AUG. 30	10	220			5	105	21
					10	220	22
OCT. 7			4	84	1	21	21
					10	220	22
NOV. 11			8	175	3	66	22
DEC. 13	10	230			3	66	22
					10	230	23
18			3	66	10	230	23

With a perpetual system, as in a periodic system of inventory determination, it is necessary to determine the specific cost of each item sold or to use a cost flow assumption. In the foregoing illustration, the first-in, first-out method of cost flow was assumed. Note that after the 7 units of the commodity were sold on February 4, there was a remaining inventory of 3 units at $20 each. The 8 units purchased on March 10 were acquired at a unit cost of $21, instead of $20, and hence could not be combined with the 3 units. The inventory after the March 10 purchase is therefore reported on two lines, 3 units at $20 each and 8 units at $21 each. Next, it should be noted that the $81 cost of the 4 units sold on April 22 is composed of the remaining 3 units at $20 each and 1 unit at $21. At this point, 7 units remain in inventory at a cost of $21 per unit. The remainder of the illustration is explained in a similar manner.

When the last-in, first-out method of cost flow is strictly applied to a perpetual inventory system, the unit cost prices assigned to the ending inventory will not necessarily be those associated with the earliest unit costs of the period. This situation will occur if at any time during a period the number of units of a commodity sold exceeds the number previously purchased during the same period. If this should happen, the excess quantity sold is priced at the cost of the beginning inventory, even though the excess number of units sold is restored later during the period by additional purchases. The effect of such a situation is to depart from the underlying purpose of the lifo costing system, which is to deduct current costs from current sales revenues.

To illustrate the foregoing situation, assume that the beginning inventory includes 100 units of a particular commodity priced at $50 a unit. During the year 70 units are sold, reducing the inventory to 30 units at $50 a unit. Later, near the end of the fiscal year, the inventory is restored to its original number by the purchase of 70 units at $58 a unit. The ending inventory of the commodity would be composed of 30 units at $50 a unit and 70 units at $58 a unit, for a total of $5,560. If the periodic system of inventory determination had been used, the last-in, first-out inventory would have been 100 units at $50 a unit, or $5,000.

One method of avoiding pricing problems of this nature is to maintain the perpetual inventory accounts throughout the period in terms of quantities only, inserting cost data at the end of the period. Another variation in procedure is to record costs in the perpetual inventory accounts in the usual manner in order to provide data needed for interim statements. At the end of the fiscal year, the necessary adjustments to apply the earliest costs to the ending inventory are then made.

The average cost method of cost flow can be applied to the perpetual system, though in a modified form. Instead of determining an average cost price for each type of commodity at the end of a period, an average unit price is computed each time a purchase is made. The unit price is then used to determine the cost of the items sold until another purchase is made. This averaging technique is called a **moving average**.

In earlier chapters, sales of merchandise were recorded by debits to the cash or accounts receivable account and credits to the sales account. The cost of the merchandise sold was not determined for each sale. It was determined only periodically by means of a physical inventory. In contrast to the periodic system, the perpetual system provides the cost data related to each sale. The cost data would be recorded by a debit to Cost of Merchandise Sold and a credit to Merchandise Inventory. To illustrate accounting under the perpetual inventory system, assume that the cost of the merchandise sold is $140,000 and that the sales amount (on account) is $210,000. The effect on the general ledger accounts is indicated by the following entries:

Cost of Merchandise Sold	140,000	
Merchandise Inventory		140,000
Accounts Receivable	210,000	
Sales		210,000

The control feature is the most important advantage of the perpetual system. The inventory of each type of merchandise is always readily available in the subsidiary ledger. A physical count of any type of merchandise can be made at any time and compared with the balance of the subsidiary account to determine the existence and seriousness of any shortages. When a shortage is discovered, an entry is made debiting Inventory Shortages and crediting Merchandise Inventory for the cost. If the balance of the inventory shortages account at the end of a fiscal period is relatively small, it may be included in miscellaneous general expense on the income statement. Otherwise it may be separately reported in the general expense section.

In addition to the usefulness of the perpetual inventory system in the preparation of interim statements, the subsidiary ledger can be an aid in maintaining inventory quantities at an optimum level. Frequent comparisons of balances with predetermined maximum and minimum levels facilitate both (1) the timely reordering of merchandise to avoid the loss of sales and (2) the avoidance of excess inventory.

Automated Perpetual Inventory Records

A perpetual inventory system may be maintained using manually kept records. However, such a system is often too costly and time consuming for enterprises with a large number of inventory items and/or with many purchase and sales transactions. In such cases, because of the mass of data to be processed, the frequently recurring and routine nature of the processing, and the importance of speed and accuracy, the record keeping is often automated. An automated system may use electronic equipment that operates with little human intervention.

One use of electronic equipment in maintaining perpetual inventory records for department and variety stores is described in the following outline:

1. The quantity of inventory for each commodity, along with its color, unit size or other descriptive data, and any other information desired, is stored within the computer.
2. Each time a commodity is purchased or returned by a customer, the data are recorded and processed by the computer, so that the inventory records in the storage unit are updated.
3. Each time a commodity is sold, a sales clerk runs an electronic wand or similar device over the price tag attached to the merchandise. The electronic wand "reads" the magnetic code on the price tag and causes the inventory records in the storage unit to be updated.
4. Data from a physical inventory count are periodically entered into the computer. These data are compared with the current balances and a listing of the overages and shortages is printed. The appropriate commodity balances are adjusted to the quantities determined by the physical count.

By entering additional data, the system described can be extended to aid in maintaining inventory quantities at optimum levels. For example, data on the most economical quantity to be purchased in a single order and the minimum quantity to be maintained for each commodity can be entered into the computer. The equipment is then programmed to compare these data with data on actual inventory and to start the purchasing activity by preparing purchase orders.

The system described above can also be extended to aid in processing the related accounting transactions. For example, the electronic cash register is often used in conjuction with the electronic wand. As cash sales are rung up on the register, the sales data can be accumulated and used for the appropriate accounting entries. These entries would include a debit to Cash and a credit to Sales as well as a debit to Cost of Merchandise Sold and a credit to Merchandise Inventory.

PRESENTATION OF MERCHANDISE INVENTORY ON THE BALANCE SHEET

Merchandise inventory is usually presented on the balance sheet immediately following receivables. Both the method of determining the cost of the inventory (lifo, fifo, or average) and the method of valuing the inventory (cost, or lower of cost or market) should be shown. Both are important to the reader. The details may be disclosed by a parenthetical notation or a footnote. The use of a parenthetical notation is illustrated by the following partial balance sheet:

MERCHANDISE
INVENTORY ON
BALANCE SHEET

Afro-Arts Company		
Balance Sheet		
December 31, 1986		
Assets		
Current assets:		
Cash		$ 19,400
Accounts receivable	$80,000	
Less allowance for doubtful accounts	3,000	77,000
Merchandise inventory—at lower of cost (first-in, first-out method) or market		216,300

It is not unusual for large enterprises with diversified activities to use different costing methods for different segments of their inventories. The following note from the balance sheet of a merchandising chain is illustrative: "Merchandise inventories in stores are stated at the lower of cost (first-in, first-out method) or market. Merchandise in warehouses is stated at cost."

ESTIMATING INVENTORY COST

In practice, an inventory figure may be needed in order to prepare an income statement when it is impractical or impossible to take a physical inventory or to maintain perpetual inventory records. For example, taking a physical inventory each month may be too costly, even though monthly income statements are desired. Taking a physical inventory may be impossible when a catastrophe, such as a fire, has destroyed the inventory. In such cases, the inventory cost might be estimated for use in preparing an income statement. Two commonly used methods of estimating inventory cost are (1) the retail method and (2) the gross profit method.

Retail Method of Inventory Costing

The **retail inventory method** of inventory costing is widely used by retail businesses, particularly department stores. It is based on the relationship of the cost of merchandise available for sale to the retail price of the same merchandise. The retail prices of all merchandise acquired are accumulated in supplementary records, and the inventory at retail is determined by deducting sales for the period from the retail price of the goods that were available for sale during the period. The inventory at retail is then converted to cost on the basis of the ratio of cost to selling (retail) price for the merchandise available for sale. Determination of inventory by the retail method is illustrated as follows:

DETERMINATION OF INVENTORY BY RETAIL METHOD

	Cost	Retail
Merchandise inventory, January 1	$19,400	$ 36,000
Purchases in January (net)	42,600	64,000
Merchandise available for sale	$62,000	$100,000
Ratio of cost to retail price: $\dfrac{\$62,000}{\$100,000} = 62\%$		
Sales for January (net)		70,000
Merchandise inventory, January 31, at retail		$ 30,000
Merchandise inventory, January 31, at estimated cost ($30,000 × 62%)		$ 18,600

There is an inherent assumption in the retail method of inventory costing that the composition or "mix" of the commodities in the ending inventory, in terms of percent of cost to selling price, is comparable to the entire stock of merchandise available for sale. In the illustration, for example, it is unlikely that the retail price of every item was composed of exactly 62% cost and 38% gross profit. It is assumed, however, that the weighted average of the cost percentages of the merchandise in the inventory ($30,000) is the same as in the merchandise available for sale ($100,000). When the inventory is made up of different classes of merchandise with very different gross profit rates, the cost percentages and the inventory should be developed separately for each class.

One of the major advantages of the retail method is that it provides inventory figures for use in preparing interim statements. Department stores and similar merchandisers usually determine gross profit and operating income each month but take a physical inventory only once a year. In addition to facilitating frequent income determinations, a comparison of the computed inventory total with the physical inventory total, both at retail prices, will show the extent of inventory shortages and the consequent need for corrective measures.

The retail method can also be used in conjunction with the periodic system when a physical inventory is taken at the end of the year. In such cases, the items counted are recorded on the inventory sheets at their selling prices instead of their cost prices. The physical inventory at selling price is then converted to cost by applying the ratio of cost to selling (retail) price for the merchandise available for sale. To illustrate, assume that the data presented in the example on page 224 are for an entire fiscal year rather than for the first month of the year only. If the physical inventory taken on December 31 totaled $29,000, priced at retail, it would be this amount rather than the $30,000 that would be converted to cost. Accordingly, the inventory at cost would be $17,980 ($29,000 × 62%) instead of $18,600 ($30,000 × 62%). The $17,980 is generally accepted for use on the year-end financial statements and for income tax purposes.

Gross Profit Method of Estimating Inventories

The **gross profit method** uses an estimate of the gross profit realized during the period to estimate the inventory at the end of the period. By using the rate of gross profit, the dollar amount of sales for a period can be divided into its two components: (1) gross profit and (2) cost of merchandise sold. The latter may then be deducted from the cost of merchandise available for sale to yield the estimated inventory of merchandise on hand.

To illustrate this method, assume that the inventory on January 1 is $57,000, that net purchases during the month amount to $180,000, that net sales during the month amount to $250,000, and finally that gross profit is *estimated* to be 30% of net sales. The inventory on January 31 may be estimated as follows:

Merchandise inventory, January 1		$ 57,000
Purchases in January (net)		180,000
Merchandise available for sale		$237,000
Sales in January (net)	$250,000	
Less estimated gross profit ($250,000 × 30%)	75,000	
Estimated cost of merchandise sold		175,000
Estimated merchandise inventory, January 31		$ 62,000

ESTIMATE OF INVENTORY BY GROSS PROFIT METHOD

The estimate of the rate of gross profit is ordinarily based on the actual rate for the preceding year, adjusted for any changes made in the cost and sales prices during the current period. Inventories estimated in this manner are useful in preparing interim statements. The method may also be used in establishing an estimate of the cost of merchandise destroyed by fire or other disaster.

INVENTORIES OF MANUFACTURING ENTERPRISES

In the preceding discussion, the principles and procedures for inventory were presented in the context of a trading enterprise. These same principles and procedures, with some modification, also apply to inventories of a manufacturing enterprise. Although attention is directed to these basic principles and procedures in the following paragraphs, it should be noted that they are discussed in more detail in the managerial accounting chapters of this text.

Manufacturing businesses maintain three inventory accounts instead of a single merchandise inventory account. Separate accounts are maintained for (1) goods in the state in which they are to be sold, (2) goods in the process of manufacture, and (3) goods in the state in which they were acquired. These inventories are called respectively **finished goods, work in process**, and **materials**. The balances in the inventory accounts may be presented in the balance sheet in the following manner:

Inventories:
Finished goods.................................. $300,000
Work in process................................ 55,000
Materials 123,000 $478,000

The finished goods inventory and work in process inventory are composed of three separate categories of manufacturing costs: direct materials, direct labor, and factory overhead. **Direct materials** represent the delivered cost of the materials that enter directly into the finished product. **Direct labor** represents the wages of the factory workers who change the materials into a finished product. **Factory overhead** includes all of the remaining costs of operating the factory, such as wages for factory supervision, supplies used in the factory but not entering directly into the finished product, and taxes, insurance, depreciation, and maintenance related to factory plant and equipment.

LONG-TERM CONSTRUCTION CONTRACTS

Enterprises engaged in large construction projects may devote several years to the completion of a particular contract or project. In such cases, the costs incurred in construction may be accumulated in a work in process account, called Construction in Progress, until the project is completed. After the project is completed and accepted by the customer, the full revenue and the related net income are recognized. To illustrate, assume that a contractor engages in a project that will require three years to complete, for a contract price of $50,000,000. If the total costs accumulated during construction total $44,000,000, the revenue of $50,000,000 and the net income of $6,000,000 would be reported in the third year.

Whenever the total cost of a long-term contract and the extent of the project's progress can be reasonably estimated, it is preferable to consider the revenue as being realized over the entire life of the contract.[1] The amount of revenue to be recognized in any particular period is then determined on the basis of the estimated percentage of the contract that has been completed during the period. The estimated percentage of completion can be developed by comparing the incurred costs with the most recent estimates of total costs or by estimates by engineers, architects, or other qualified personnel of the progress of the work performed. To continue with the illustration, assume that by the end of the first fiscal year the contract is estimated to be one-fourth completed and the costs incurred during the year were $11,200,000. According to the **percentage-of-completion method**, the revenue to be recognized and the income for the year would be determined as follows:

Revenue ($50,000,000 × 25%)	$12,500,000
Costs incurred	11,200,000
Income (Year 1)	$ 1,300,000

The costs actually incurred during the year plus the income recognized would be accumulated in the construction in progress account. The income of $1,300,000 would be recorded in an income account. In this manner, the income is recognized over the life of the contract.

The use of the percentage-of-completion method, which is discussed in more detail in Chapter 23, involves some subjectivity, and hence possible error, in the determination of the amount of reported revenue. In spite of estimates, however, the financial statements may be more informative and useful than they would be if none of the revenue were recognized until completion of the contract. The method used should be noted on the financial statements.

---

1. If the merchandise inventory at the end of the year is overstated by $7,500, the error will cause an:
   A. overstatement of cost of merchandise sold for the year by $7,500
   B. understatement of gross profit for the year by $7,500
   C. overstatement of net income for the year by $7,500
   D. understatement of net income for the year by $7,500

Self-Examination Questions (Answers at end of chapter.)

---

[1] *Accounting Research and Terminology Bulletins—Final Edition,* "No. 45, Long-term Construction-type Contracts" (New York: American Institute of Certified Public Accountants, 1961), par. 15.

2. The inventory system employing accounting records that continuously disclose the amount of inventory is called:

A. periodic   C. physical

B. perpetual   D. retail

3. The inventory costing method that is based on the assumption that costs should be charged against revenue in the order in which they were incurred is:

A. fifo   C. average cost

B. lifo   D. perpetual inventory

4. The following units of a particular commodity were available for sale during the period:

Beginning inventory .... 40 units at $20

First purchase .... 50 units at $21

Second purchase .... 50 units at $22

Third purchase .... 50 units at $23

What is the unit cost of the 35 units on hand at the end of the period as determined under the periodic system by the fifo costing method?

A. $20   C. $22

B. $21   D. $23

5. If merchandise inventory is being valued at cost and the price level is steadily rising, the method of costing that will yield the largest net income is:

A. lifo   C. average

B. fifo   D. periodic

Discussion Questions

7-1. The merchandise inventory at the end of the year was inadvertently understated by $10,000. (a) Did the error cause an overstatement or an understatement of the net income for the year? (b) Which items on the balance sheet at the end of the year were overstated or understated as a result of the error?

7-2. The $10,000 inventory error in Question 7-1 was not discovered and the inventory at the end of the following year was correctly stated. (a) Will the earlier error cause an overstatement or understatement of the net income for the following year? (b) Which items on the balance sheet at the end of the following year will be overstated or understated as a result of the error in the earlier year?

7-3. (a) Differentiate between the periodic system and the perpetual system of inventory determination. (b) Which system is more costly to maintain?

7-4. What is the meaning of the following terms: (a) physical inventory; (b) book inventory?

7-5. In which of the following types of businesses would a perpetual inventory system be practicable: (a) retail furrier, (b) wholesale office equipment distributor, (c) retail drug store, (d) grocery supermarket, (e) retail hardware store?

7-6. When does title to merchandise pass from the seller to the buyer if the terms of shipment are (a) FOB shipping point; (b) FOB destination?

7–7. Which of the three methods of inventory costing, fifo, lifo, or average cost, is based on the assumption that costs should be charged against revenue in the order in which they were incurred?

7–8. Do the terms *fifo* and *lifo* refer to techniques employed in determining quantities of the various classes of merchandise on hand? Explain.

7–9. Does the term *last-in* in the lifo method mean that the items in the inventory are assumed to be the most recent (last) acquisitions? Explain.

7–10. Under which method of cost flow are (a) the earliest costs assigned to inventory; (b) the most recent costs assigned to inventory; (c) average costs assigned to inventory?

7–11. The following units of a particular commodity were available for sale during the year:

Beginning inventory....................	8 units at $125
First purchase........................	10 units at $130
Second purchase.....................	10 units at $135

The firm uses the periodic system and there are 7 units of the commodity on hand at the end of the year. (a) What is their unit cost according to fifo? (b) What is their unit cost according to lifo? (c) Is the average unit cost $130?

7–12. If merchandise inventory is being valued at cost and the price level is steadily falling, which of the three methods of costing, fifo, lifo, or average cost, will yield (a) the highest inventory cost, (b) the lowest inventory cost, (c) the largest net income, (d) the smallest net income?

7–13. Which of the three methods of inventory costing, fifo, lifo, or average cost, will in general yield an inventory cost most nearly approximating current replacement cost?

7–14. An enterprise using "cost" as its method of inventory valuation proposes to value at $900 a group of items having a total cost of $1,400. On what basis could this reduction in value be justified?

7–15. In the phrase *lower of cost or market,* what is meant by market?

7–16. The cost of a particular inventory item is $75, the current replacement cost is $70, and the selling price is $110. At what amount should the item be included in the inventory according to the lower of cost or market basis?

7–17. An enterprise using a perpetual inventory system sells merchandise to a customer on account for $995; the cost of merchandise was $715. (a) What are the effects of the transaction on general ledger accounts? (b) What is the amount and direction of the net change in the amount of assets and capital resulting from the transaction?

7–18. What are the three most important advantages of the perpetual inventory system over the periodic system?

7–19. What are the two principal advantages of using the retail method of estimating inventory cost?

7–20. Under which, if any, of the following systems or methods of inventory determination is a periodic physical inventory unnecessary: (a) periodic inventory system, (b) perpetual inventory system, (c) retail inventory method, (d) gross profit method?

7–21. What uses can be made of the estimate of the cost of inventory determined by the gross profit method?

7–22. Name the three inventory accounts for a manufacturing business and describe what each balance represents at the end of an accounting period.

7–23. Name and describe the three categories of manufacturing costs included in the cost of finished goods and the cost of work in process.

7–24. What are the advantages and disadvantages of using the percentage-of-completion method for reporting income on long-term construction projects?

Exercises

7–25. The beginning inventory and the purchases of Commodity X3C during the year were as follows:

Jan. 1 Inventory .... 10 units at $135
Mar. 17 Purchase .... 20 units at $141
July 2 Purchase .... 20 units at $145
Oct. 30 Purchase .... 15 units at $144

There are 18 units of the commodity in the physical inventory at December 31 (the periodic system is used). Determine the inventory cost and the cost of merchandise sold by three methods, presenting your answers in the following form:

	Cost	
Inventory Method	**Merchandise Inventory**	**Merchandise Sold**
(1) First-in, first-out	$	$
(2) Last-in, first-out		
(3) Average cost		

7–26. On the basis of the following data, determine the value of the inventory at the lower of cost or market. Assemble the data in the form illustrated on page 219, in order that the inventory reduction attributable to price declines may be ascertained.

Commodity	Inventory Quantity	Unit Cost	Unit Market
B19	20	$270	$260
H30	32	65	67
N11	10	195	200
S92	45	80	77
V47	8	495	480

7–27. Beginning inventory, purchases, and sales data for Commodity 92-D are as follows. The enterprise maintains a perpetual inventory system, costing by the first-in, first-out method. Determine the cost of the merchandise sold in each sale and the inventory balance after each sale, presenting the data in the form illustrated on page 220.

July	1.	Inventory.	24 units at $30
	5.	Sold.	10 units
	13.	Purchased	15 units at $31
	19.	Sold.	18 units
	22.	Sold.	5 units
	30.	Purchased	15 units at $32

7–28. Beginning inventory, purchases, and sales data for Commodity 276D for May are as follows:

Inventory, May 1.	20 units at $30
Sales, May 7.	6 units
15.	12 units
25.	5 units
Purchases, May 4	10 units at $31
22	13 units at $33

(a) Assuming that the perpetual inventory system is used, costing by the lifo method, determine the cost of the inventory balance at May 31.

(b) Assuming that the periodic inventory system is used, costing by the lifo method, determine the cost of the 20 units in the physical inventory at May 31.

(c) Determine the amount of the difference between the inventory cost in (a) and (b), and explain the reason for the difference.

7–29. On the basis of the following data, estimate the cost of the merchandise inventory at July 31 by the retail method:

		Cost	Retail
July 1	Merchandise inventory.	$214,100	$319,500
July 1–31	Purchases (net).	181,870	271,500
July 1–31	Sales (net)		259,000

7–30. The merchandise inventory of Casler Company was destroyed by fire on May 17. The following data were obtained from the accounting records:

Jan. 1	Merchandise inventory	$194,500
Jan. 1–May 17	Purchases (net)	208,000
	Sales (net).	310,000
	Estimated gross profit rate	35%

Estimate the cost of the merchandise destroyed.

7–31. During the current year, Davis Construction Company obtained a contract to build an apartment building. The total contract price was $10,000,000 and the estimated construction costs were $8,500,000. During the current year, the project was estimated to be 40% completed and the costs incurred totaled $3,500,000. Under the percentage-of-completion method of recognizing revenue, what amount of (a) revenue, (b) cost, and (c) income should be recognized from the contract for the current year?

Problems

7–32. Good Vibes employs the periodic inventory system. Details regarding the inventory of television sets at July 1, purchases invoices during year, and the inventory count at June 30 are summarized as follows:

Model	Inventory, July 1	Purchases Invoices			Inventory Count, June 30
		1st	2d	3d	
A29	6 at $150	4 at $150	7 at $155	8 at $155	5
G12	5 at 173	10 at 175	10 at 177	8 at 182	8
J47	4 at 700	2 at 725	2 at 725	2 at 750	2
M59	3 at 520	4 at 531	2 at 549	3 at 542	4
P30	9 at 213	7 at 215	6 at 222	6 at 225	8
T99	6 at 305	3 at 310	3 at 316	4 at 321	5
W71	————	2 at 440	2 at 460	————	1

Instructions:

(1) Determine the cost of the inventory on June 30 by the first-in, first-out method. Present data in columnar form, using the following columnar headings. If the inventory of a particular model is composed of an entire lot plus a portion of another lot acquired at a different unit price, use a separate line for each lot.

Model	Quantity	Unit Cost	Total Cost

(2) Determine the cost of the inventory on June 30 by the last-in, first-out method, following the procedures indicated in instruction (1).

(3) Determine the cost of the inventory on June 30 by the average cost method, using the columnar headings indicated in instruction (1).

7–33. The beginning inventory of Commodity P741 and data on purchases and sales for a three-month period are as follows:

April	1.	Inventory	7 units at $180	$1,260
	6.	Purchase.................	10 units at 182	1,820
	13.	Sale	10 units at 245	2,450
	24.	Sale	3 units at 245	735
May	4.	Purchase.................	12 units at 183	2,196
	6.	Sale	6 units at 250	1,500
	19.	Sale	5 units at 250	1,250
	25.	Purchase.................	15 units at 184	2,760
June	5.	Sale	6 units at 250	1,500
	12.	Sale	7 units at 250	1,750
	19.	Purchase.................	10 units at 185	1,850
	30.	Sale	9 units at 250	2,250

Instructions:

(1) Record the inventory, purchases, and cost of merchandise sold data in a perpetual inventory record similar to the one illustrated on page 220, using the first-in, first-out method.

(2) Determine the total sales and the total cost of Commodity P741 sold for the period and indicate their effect on the general ledger, using two journal entries. Assume that all sales were on account.

(3) Determine the gross profit from sales of Commodity P741 for the period.

(4) Determine the cost of the inventory at June 30, assuming that the periodic system of inventory had been employed and that the inventory cost had been determined by the last-in, first-out method.

7-34. Data on the physical inventory of Rodrig Corporation as of June 30, the end of the current fiscal year, are presented in the working papers. The quantity of each commodity on hand has been determined and recorded on the inventory sheet. Unit market prices have also been determined as of June 30 and recorded on the sheet. The inventory is to be determined at cost and also at the lower of cost or market, using the first-in, first-out method. Quantity and cost data from the last purchases invoice of the year and the next-to-the-last purchases invoice are summarized as follows:

(If the working papers correlating with the text-book are not used, omit Problem 7-34.)

	Last Purchases Invoice		Next-to-the-Last Purchases Invoice	
Description	Quantity Purchased	Unit Cost	Quantity Purchased	Unit Cost
B16	40	$ 45	35	$ 44
72C	15	120	15	125
GH4	25	90	25	92
6X1	100	25	100	27
23P	6	310	8	320
85J	300	10	200	10
D22	8	400	5	410
EF9	500	6	500	7
Z91	70	17	50	16
39A	5	250	4	260
14P	25	305	25	310
KC2	75	14	100	13
T11	8	48	10	47
L19	150	8	100	9
92Y	50	15	40	16
A72	40	29	50	28
S29	55	28	50	28
G88	8	210	7	215

Instructions:

Record the appropriate unit costs on the inventory sheet and complete the pricing of the inventory. When there are two different unit costs applicable to a commodity, proceed as follows:

(1) Draw a line through the quantity and insert the quantity and unit cost of the last purchase.

(2) On the following line, insert the quantity and unit cost of the next-to-the-last purchase. The first item on the inventory sheet has been completed as an example.

7-35. Selected data on merchandise inventory, purchases, and sales for Lane Co. and W. Jones Supply Co. are as follows:

Lane Co.

	Cost	Retail
Merchandise inventory, March 1	$277,100	$432,950
Transactions during March:		
Purchases...........................	121,600 } 188,300	
Purchases discount...................	1,100 }	
Sales		202,100
Sales returns and allowances		2,600

W. Jones Supply Co.

Merchandise inventory, July 1	$417,700
Transactions during July and August:	
Purchases...........................	360,500
Purchases discount...................	3,600
Sales	510,250
Sales returns and allowances	5,250
Estimated gross profit rate	35%

Instructions:

(1) Determine the estimated cost of the merchandise inventory of Lane Co. on March 31 by the retail method, presenting details of the computations.
(2) Estimate the cost of the merchandise inventory of W. Jones Supply Co. on August 31 by the gross profit method, presenting details of the computations.

7-36. The following preliminary income statement of Theis Enterprises Inc. was prepared before the accounts were adjusted or closed at the end of the fiscal year. The company uses the periodic inventory system.

Theis Enterprises Inc.
Income Statement
For Year Ended June 30, 19--

Sales (net)...		$817,450
Cost of merchandise sold:		
Merchandise inventory, July 1, 19--	$201,400	
Purchases (net)	511,100	
Merchandise available for sale	$712,500	
Less merchandise inventory, June 30, 19--	220,000	
Cost of merchandise sold......................		492,500
Gross profit		$324,950
Operating expenses.................................		231,850
Net income		$ 93,100

The following errors in the ledger and on the inventory sheets were discovered by the independent CPA retained to conduct the annual audit:

(a) A number of errors were discovered in pricing inventory items, in extending amounts, and in footing inventory sheets. The net effect of the errors, exclusive of those described below, was to increase by $2,500 the amount stated as the ending inventory on the income statement.

(b) A sales order for $5,000, dated June 30, had been recorded as a sale on that date, but title did not pass to the purchaser until shipment was made on July 3. The merchandise, which had cost $3,025, was excluded from the June 30 inventory.

(c) A sales invoice for $1,250, dated June 30, had not been recorded. The merchandise was shipped on June 30, FOB shipping point, and its cost, $750, was excluded from the June 30 inventory.

(d) An item of store equipment, received on June 29, was erroneously included in the June 30 merchandise inventory at its cost of $6,425. The invoice had been recorded correctly.

(e) A purchases invoice for merchandise of $750, dated June 29, had been received and correctly recorded, but the merchandise was not received until July 2 and had not been included in the June 30 inventory. Title had passed to Theis Enterprises Inc. on June 29.

(f) A purchases invoice for merchandise of $3,400, dated June 30, was not received until July 2 and had not been recorded by June 30. However, the merchandise, to which title had passed, had arrived and had been included in the June 30 inventory.

Instructions:

(1) Journalize the entries necessary to correct the general ledger accounts as of June 30, inserting the identifying letters in the date column. All purchases and sales were made on account.

(2) Determine the correct inventory for June 30, beginning your analysis with the $220,000 shown on the preliminary income statement. Assemble the corrections in two groupings, "Additions" and "Deductions," allowing six lines for each group. Identify each correction by the appropriate letter.

(3) Prepare a revised income statement.

7–37. Parkhill Sales Inc. is a distributor of imported mopeds. Its unadjusted trial balance as of the end of the current fiscal year is as follows:

Cash.	19,700	
Accounts Receivable.	30,600	
Allowance for Doubtful Accounts		675
Merchandise Inventory	41,100	
Equipment.	56,000	
Accumulated Depreciation—Equipment.		12,250
Accounts Payable		16,750
Capital Stock.		50,000
Retained Earnings.		17,500
Dividends.	6,000	
Sales.		301,600
Purchases.	189,900	
Operating Expenses (control account).	55,575	
Rent Income.		1,200
Interest Expense	1,100	
	399,975	399,975

Data needed for adjustments at December 31:
- (a) Merchandise inventory at December 31, at lower of cost (first-in, first-out method) or market, $45,800.
- (b) Uncollectible accounts expense for current year is estimated at $1,325.
- (c) Depreciation on equipment for current year, $2,250.
- (d) Accrued wages on December 31, $750.

Instructions:
- (1) Journalize the necessary adjusting entries.
- (2) Prepare (a) an income statement, (b) a retained earnings statement, and (c) a balance sheet.

Alternate Problems

7–32A. A & W Associates employs the periodic inventory system. Details regarding the inventory of television sets at January 1, purchases invoices during the year, and the inventory count at December 31 are summarized as follows:

| Model | Inventory, Jan. 1 | Purchases Invoices | | | Inventory Count, Dec. 31 |
		1st	2d	3d	
72B	3 at $119	2 at $125	4 at $130	5 at $133	6
11D	6 at 77	5 at 82	8 at 89	8 at 99	10
19X	4 at 108	4 at 110	5 at 118	6 at 130	4
32C	8 at 88	4 at 79	3 at 85	6 at 92	8
97A	1 at 250	1 at 260	2 at 271	2 at 275	2
42L	6 at 175	2 at 200	2 at 210	5 at 220	7
66P	—	4 at 150	4 at 200	2 at 205	7

Instructions:
- (1) Determine the cost of the inventory on December 31 by the first-in, first-out method. Present data in columnar form, using the following columnar headings. If the inventory of a particular model is composed of an entire lot plus a portion of another lot acquired at a different unit price, use a separate line for each lot.

Model	Quantity	Unit Cost	Total Cost

- (2) Determine the cost of the inventory on December 31 by the last-in, first-out method, following the procedures indicated in instruction (1).
- (3) Determine the cost of the inventory on December 31 by the average cost method, using the columnar headings indicated in instruction (1).

7–33A. The beginning inventory of soybeans at the Champaign Farmer's Co-Op and data on purchases and sales for a three-month harvest period are as follows:

June	1. Inventory	30,000 bushels at $6.90	$207,000
	15. Purchase	70,000 bushels at 7.10	497,000
	20. Sale	35,000 bushels at 7.50	262,500
	30. Sale	20,000 bushels at 7.45	149,000

July	8. Sale	10,000 bushels at	7.40	74,000
	16. Purchase	40,000 bushels at	6.75	270,000
	17. Sale	35,000 bushels at	7.35	257,250
	28. Sale	15,000 bushels at	7.30	109,500
Aug.	10. Purchase	60,000 bushels at	6.60	396,000
	15. Sale	50,000 bushels at	7.20	360,000
	18. Purchase	50,000 bushels at	6.50	325,000
	30. Sale	40,000 bushels at	7.00	280,000

Instructions:

(1) Record the inventory, purchases, and cost of merchandise sold data in a perpetual inventory record similar to the one illustrated on page 220, using the first-in, first-out method.

(2) Determine the total sales and the total cost of soybeans sold for the period and indicate their effect on the general ledger, using two journal entries. Assume that all sales were on account.

(3) Determine the gross profit from sales of soybeans for the period.

(4) Determine the cost of the inventory at August 31, assuming that the periodic system of inventory had been employed and that the inventory cost had been determined by the last-in, first-out method.

7-34A. Data on the physical inventory of Bargh Corporation as of June 30, the end of the current fiscal year, are presented in the working papers. The quantity of each commodity on hand has been determined and recorded on the inventory sheet. Unit market prices have also been determined as of June 30 and recorded on the sheet. The inventory is to be determined at cost and also at the lower of cost or market, using the first-in, first-out method. Quantity and cost data from the last purchases invoice of the year and the next-to-the-last purchases invoice are summarized as follows:

(If the working papers correlating with the textbook are not used, omit Problem 7-34A.)

	Last Purchases Invoice		Next-to-the-Last Purchases Invoice	
Description	Quantity Purchased	Unit Cost	Quantity Purchased	Unit Cost
B16	40	$ 45	50	$ 44
72C	15	130	10	128
GH4	20	90	25	92
6X1	100	22	50	23
23P	4	305	6	310
85J	300	10	100	10
D22	10	380	5	385
EF9	500	6	500	6
Z91	80	17	50	18
39A	5	250	4	260
14P	30	315	2	320
KC2	70	15	50	15
T11	7	48	5	49
L19	150	8	50	9
92Y	60	16	40	17
A72	50	29	25	28
S29	75	26	60	25
G88	8	210	7	215

Instructions:

Record the appropriate unit costs on the inventory sheet and complete the pricing of the inventory. When there are two different unit costs applicable to a commodity, proceed as follows:

(1) Draw a line through the quantity and insert the quantity and unit cost of the last purchase.

(2) On the following line, insert the quantity and unit cost of the next-to-the-last purchase. The first item on the inventory sheet has been completed as an example.

7–35A. Selected data on merchandise inventory, purchases, and sales for Hendricks Co. and Fiore Co. are as follows:

Hendricks Co.

	Cost	Retail
Merchandise inventory, June 1	$216,500	$310,000
Transactions during June:		
Purchases	305,700 ⎫	
Purchases discount	2,450 ⎭	432,500
Sales		450,000
Sales returns and allowances		5,000

Fiore Co.

Merchandise inventory, November 1		$606,150
Transactions during November and December:		
Purchases		384,900
Purchases discount		4,900
Sales		635,500
Sales returns and allowances		4,500
Estimated gross profit rate		40%

Instructions:

(1) Determine the estimated cost of the merchandise inventory of Hendricks Co. on June 30 by the retail method, presenting details of the computations.

(2) Estimate the cost of the merchandise inventory of Fiore Co. on December 31 by the gross profit method, presenting details of the computations.

Mini-Case

7–38. Eubanks Company began operations in 1986 by selling a single product. Data on sales and purchases for the year were as follows:

Sales

April,	1,000 units	September,	1,500 units
May,	1,400 units	October,	1,350 units
June,	1,450 units	November,	1,400 units
July,	1,300 units	December,	1,350 units
August,	1,250 units		

Sales totaled $240,000.

Purchases

Date	Units Purchased	Unit Cost	Total Cost
April 10	3,000	$11.00	$ 33,000
May 10	3,000	12.50	37,500
June 8	3,000	14.00	42,000
July 12	3,000	14.20	42,600
September 10	1,000	15.10	15,100
October 12	1,000	15.50	15,500
November 9	600	16.00	9,600
December 11	600	16.50	9,900
	15,200		$205,200

On January 2, 1987, the president of the company, Tony Eubanks, asked for your advice on costing the 3,200-unit physical inventory that was taken on December 31, 1986. Also, since the firm plans to expand its product line, he asked your advice on the use of a perpetual inventory system in the future.

Instructions:

(1) Determine the cost of the December 31, 1986 inventory by the periodic method, using the (a) first-in, first-out method, (b) last-in, first-out method, and (c) average cost method.

(2) Determine the gross profit for the year under each of the three methods in (1).

(3) (a) In your opinion, which of the three inventory costing methods best reflects the results of operations for 1986? Why?

(b) In your opinion, which of the three inventory costing methods best reflects the replacement cost of the inventory on the balance sheet as of December 31, 1986? Why?

(c) Which inventory costing method would you choose to use for income tax purposes?

(4) Discuss the advantages and disadvantages of using a perpetual inventory system. From the data presented in this case, is there any indication of the adequacy of inventory levels during the year?

1. C The overstatement of inventory by $7,500 at the end of a period will cause the cost of merchandise sold for the period to be understated by $7,500, the gross profit for the period to be overstated by $7,500, and the net income for the period to be overstated by $7,500 (answer C).

2. B The perpetual system (answer B) continuously discloses the amount of inventory. The periodic inventory system (answer A) relies upon a detailed listing of the merchandise on hand, called a physical inventory (answer C), to determine the cost of inventory at the end of a period. The retail inventory method (answer D) is based on the relationship of the cost of merchandise available for sale to the retail price of the same merchandise.

Answers to Self-Examination Questions

3. A The fifo method (answer A) is based on the assumption that costs are charged against revenue in the order in which they were incurred. The lifo method (answer B) charges the most recent costs incurred against revenue, and the average cost method (answer C) charges a weighted average of unit costs of commodities sold against revenue. The perpetual inventory system (answer D) is a system that continuously discloses the amount of inventory.

4. D The fifo method of costing is based on the assumption that costs should be charged against revenue in the order in which they were incurred (first-in, first-out). Thus the most recent costs are assigned to inventory. The 35 units would be assigned a unit cost of $23 (answer D).

5. B When the price level is steadily rising, the earlier unit costs are lower than recent unit costs. Under the fifo method (answer B), these earlier costs are matched against revenue to yield the largest possible net income. The periodic inventory system (answer D) is a system and not a method of costing.

CHAPTER 8

Plant Assets and Intangible Assets

CHAPTER OBJECTIVES

Describe the characteristics of plant assets and illustrate the accounting for the acquisition of plant assets.

Describe and illustrate the accounting for depreciation, asset disposals, and depletion.

Describe and illustrate the reporting of plant assets and depreciation expense in the financial statements.

Describe and illustrate the accounting for and reporting of intangible assets.

"Long-lived" is a general term that may be applied to assets of a relatively fixed or permanent nature owned by a business enterprise. Such assets that are tangible in nature, used in the operations of the business, and not held for sale in the ordinary course of the business are classified on the balance sheet as **plant assets** or **fixed assets.** Other descriptive titles frequently used are **property, plant, and equipment,** used either alone or in various combinations. The properties most frequently included in plant assets may be described in more specific terms as equipment, furniture, tools, machinery, buildings, and land. Although there is no standard criterion as to the minimum length of life necessary for classification as plant assets, they must be capable of repeated use and are ordinarily expected to last more than a year. However, the asset need not actually be used continuously or even often. Items of standby equipment held for use in the event of a breakdown of regular equipment or for use only during peak periods of activity are included in plant assets.

Assets acquired for resale in the normal course of business cannot be characterized as plant assets, regardless of their durability or the length of time they are held. For example, undeveloped land or other real estate acquired as a speculation should be listed on the balance sheet in the asset section entitled "Investments."

INITIAL COSTS OF PLANT ASSETS

The initial cost of a plant asset includes all expenditures *necessary* to get it in place and ready for use. Sales tax, transportation charges, insurance on the asset while in transit, special foundations, and installation costs should be added to the purchase price of the related plant asset. Similarly, when a secondhand asset is purchased, the initial costs of getting it ready for use, such as expenditures for new parts, repairs, and painting, are debited to the asset account. On the other hand, costs associated with the acquisition of a plant asset should be excluded from the asset account if they do not increase the asset's usefulness. Expenditures resulting from carelessness or errors in installing the asset, from vandalism, or from other unusual occurrences do not increase the usefulness of the asset and should be allocated to the period as an expense.

The cost of constructing a building includes the fees paid to architects and engineers for plans and supervision, insurance incurred during construction, and all other needed expenditures related to the project. Generally, interest incurred during the construction period on money borrowed to finance construction should also be treated as part of the cost of the building.[1]

The cost of land includes not only the negotiated price but also broker's commissions, title fees, surveying fees, and other expenditures connected with securing title. If delinquent real estate taxes are assumed by the buyer, they also are chargeable to the land account. If unwanted buildings are located on land acquired for a plant site, the cost of their razing or removal, less any salvage recovered, is properly chargeable to the land account. The cost of leveling or otherwise permanently changing the contour is also an additional cost of the land.

Other expenditures related to the land may be charged to Land, Buildings, or Land Improvements, depending upon the circumstances. If the property owner bears the initial cost of paving the public street bordering the land, either by direct payment or by special tax assessment, the paving may be considered to be as permanent as the land. On the other hand, the cost of constructing walkways to and around the building may be added to the building account if the walkways are expected to last as long as the building. Expenditures for improvements that are neither as permanent as the land nor directly associated with the building may be set apart in a land improvements account and depreciated according to their different life spans. Some of the

---

[1]*Statement of Financial Accounting Standards, No. 34,* "Capitalization of Interest Cost" (Stamford: Financial Accounting Standards Board, 1979), par. 6.

more usual items of this nature are trees and shrubs, fences, outdoor lighting systems, and paved parking areas.

NATURE OF DEPRECIATION

As time passes, all plant assets with the exception of land lose their capacity to yield services.[2] Accordingly, the cost of such assets should be transferred to the related expense accounts in an orderly manner during their expected useful life. This periodic cost expiration is called **depreciation.**

Factors contributing to a decline in usefulness may be divided into two categories, *physical* depreciation, which includes wear from use and deterioration from the action of the elements, and *functional* depreciation, which includes inadequacy and obsolescence. A plant asset becomes inadequate if its capacity is not sufficient to meet the demands of increased production. A plant asset is obsolete if the commodity that it produces is no longer in demand or if a newer machine can produce a commodity of better quality or at a great reduction in cost. The continued growth of technological progress during this century has made obsolescence an increasingly important part of depreciation. Although the several factors comprising depreciation can be defined, it is not feasible to identify them when recording depreciation expense.

The meaning of the term "depreciation" as used in accounting is often misunderstood because the same term is also commonly used in business to mean a decline in the market value of an asset. The amount of unexpired cost of plant assets reported in the balance sheet is not likely to agree with the amount that could be realized from their sale. Plant assets are held for use in the enterprise rather than for sale. It is assumed that the enterprise will continue forever as a going concern. Consequently, the decision to dispose of a plant asset is based mainly on its usefulness to the enterprise.

Another common misunderstanding is that depreciation accounting automatically provides the cash needed to replace plant assets as they wear out. The cash account is neither increased nor decreased by the periodic entries that transfer the cost of plant assets to depreciation expense accounts. The misconception probably occurs because depreciation expense, unlike most expenses, does not require an equivalent outlay of cash in the period in which the expense is recorded.

RECORDING DEPRECIATION

Depreciation may be recorded by an entry at the end of each month, or the adjustment may be delayed until the end of the year. The part of the entry that records the decrease in the plant asset is credited to a contra asset account

---

[2]Land is here assumed to be used only as a site. Consideration will be given later in the chapter to land acquired for its mineral deposits or other natural resources.

entitled Accumulated Depreciation or Allowance for Depreciation. The use of a contra asset account permits the original cost to remain unchanged in the plant asset account. This facilitates the computation of periodic depreciation, the listing of both cost and accumulated depreciation on the balance sheet, and the reporting required for property tax and income tax purposes.

An exception to the general procedure of recording depreciation monthly or annually is often made when a plant asset is sold, traded in, or scrapped. As discussed and illustrated later in the chapter, the disposal is recorded by removing from the accounts both the cost of the asset and its related accumulated depreciation as of the date of the disposal. Hence, it is advisable to record the additional depreciation on the item for the current period before recording the transaction disposing of the asset. A further advantage of recording the depreciation at the time of the disposal of the asset is that no additional attention need be given the transaction when the amount of the periodic depreciation adjustment is later determined.

DETERMINING DEPRECIATION

Factors to be considered in computing the periodic depreciation of a plant asset are its initial cost, its recoverable cost at the time it is retired from service, and the length of life of the asset. It is clear that neither of these latter two factors can be accurately determined until the asset is retired. They must be estimated at the time the asset is placed in service.

The estimated recoverable cost of a depreciable asset as of the time of its removal from service is called **residual, scrap, salvage,** or **trade-in value.** The excess of cost over the estimated residual value is the amount that is to be recorded as depreciation expense during the asset's life. When residual value is expected to be very small in comparison with the cost of the asset, it may be ignored in computing depreciation.

There are no hard-and-fast rules for estimating either the period of usefulness of an asset or its residual value at the end of such period. These two related factors may be greatly affected by management policies. The estimates of a company that provides its sales representatives with a new automobile every year will differ from those of a firm that keeps its cars for three years. Such variables as climate, frequency of use, maintenance, and minimum standards of efficiency will also affect the estimates.

Life estimates for depreciable assets are available in various trade association and other publications. For federal income tax purposes, the Internal Revenue Service has also established guidelines for life estimates. These guidelines may be useful in determining depreciation for financial reporting purposes.

In addition to the many factors that may influence the life estimate of an asset, there is a wide range in the degree of exactness used in the computation. A calendar month is ordinarily the smallest unit of time used. When this period of time is used, all assets placed in service or retired from service during the first half of a month are treated as if the event had occurred on the first day of that month. Similarly, all plant asset additions and reductions during the second half of a month are considered to have occurred on the first day of the next month. In the absence of any statement to the contrary, this practice will be assumed throughout this chapter.

It is not necessary that an enterprise use a single method of computing depreciation for all classes of its depreciable assets. The methods used in the accounts and financial statements may also differ from the methods used in determining income taxes and property taxes. The four methods used most often, straight-line, units-of-production, declining-balance, and sum-of-the-years-digits, are described and illustrated.

Straight-Line Method

The **straight-line method** of determining depreciation provides for equal periodic charges to expense over the estimated life of the asset. To illustrate this method, assume that the cost of a depreciable asset is $16,000, its estimated residual value is $1,000, and its estimated life is 5 years. The annual depreciation is computed as follows:

$$\frac{\$16{,}000 \text{ cost} - \$1{,}000 \text{ estimated residual value}}{5 \text{ years estimated life}} = \$3{,}000 \text{ annual depreciation}$$

STRAIGHT-LINE
METHOD OF
DEPRECIATION

The annual depreciation of $3,000 would be prorated for the first and the last partial years of use. Assuming a fiscal year ending on December 31 and first use of the asset on October 15, the depreciation for that fiscal year would be $750 (3 months). If usage had begun on October 16, the depreciation for the year would be $500 (2 months).

When the residual value of a plant asset represents a small part of its cost, it is often ignored. In such cases, the annual straight-line depreciation is determined on the basis of cost and the estimated life of the asset is converted to a percentage rate. The conversion to an annual percentage rate is accomplished by dividing 100 by the number of years of life. Thus a life of 50 years is equivalent to a 2% depreciation rate, 20 years is equivalent to a 5% rate, 8 years is equivalent to a 12½% rate, and so on.

The straight-line method is widely used. In addition to its simplicity, it provides a reasonable allocation of costs to periodic revenue when usage is relatively the same from period to period.

Units-of-Production Method

The **units-of-production method** yields a depreciation charge that varies with the amount of asset usage. To apply this method, the length of life of the asset is expressed in terms of productive capacity, such as hours, miles, or number of operations. Depreciation is first computed for the appropriate unit of production, and the depreciation for each accounting period is then determined by multiplying the unit depreciation by the number of units used during the period. To illustrate, assume that a machine with a cost of $16,000 and estimated residual value of $1,000 is expected to have an estimated life of 10,000 hours. The depreciation for a unit of one hour is computed as follows:

UNITS-OF-
PRODUCTION
METHOD OF
DEPRECIATION

$$\frac{\$16,000 \text{ cost } - \$1,000 \text{ estimated residual value}}{10,000 \text{ estimated hours}} = \$1.50 \text{ hourly depreciation}$$

Assuming that the machine was in operation for 2,200 hours during a particular year, the depreciation for that year would be $1.50 × 2,200, or $3,300.

When the amount of usage of a plant asset changes from year to year, the units-of-production method is more logical than the straight-line method. It may yield fairer allocations of cost against periodic revenue.

Declining-Balance Method

The **declining-balance method** yields a declining periodic depreciation charge over the estimated life of the asset. The most common technique is to double the straight-line depreciation rate, computed without regard to residual value, and apply the resulting rate to the cost of the asset less its accumulated depreciation. For an asset with an estimated life of five years, the rate would be double the straight-line rate of 20%, or 40%. The double rate is then applied to the cost of the asset for the first year of its use and thereafter to the declining book value (cost minus accumulated depreciation). The method is illustrated in the following table:

DECLINING-BALANCE
METHOD OF
DEPRECIATION

Year	Cost	Accumulated Depreciation at Beginning of Year	Book Value at Beginning of Year	Rate	Depreciation for Year	Book Value at End of Year
1	$16,000	——	$16,000.00	40%	$6,400.00	$9,600.00
2	16,000	$ 6,400.00	9,600.00	40%	3,840.00	5,760.00
3	16,000	10,240.00	5,760.00	40%	2,304.00	3,456.00
4	16,000	12,544.00	3,456.00	40%	1,382.40	2,073.60
5	16,000	13,926.40	2,073.60	40%	829.44	1,244.16

Note that estimated residual value is not considered in determining the depreciation rate. It is also ignored in computing periodic depreciation, except that the asset should not be depreciated below the estimated residual value. In the above example, it was assumed that the estimated residual value at the end of the fifth year approximates the book value of $1,244.16. If the residual value had been estimated at $1,500, the depreciation for the fifth year would have been $573.60 ($2,073.60 − $1,500) instead of $829.44.

There was an implicit assumption in the above illustration that the first use of the asset coincided with the beginning of the fiscal year. This would usually not occur in actual practice, however, and would require a slight change in the computation for the first partial year of use. If the asset in the example had been placed in service at the end of the third month of the fiscal year, only the pro rata portion of the first full year's depreciation, $9/12 \times (40\% \times \$16,000)$, or $4,800, would be allocated to the first fiscal year. The method of computing the depreciation for the following years would not be affected. Thus, the depreciation for the second fiscal year would be $40\% \times (\$16,000 - \$4,800)$, or $4,480.

Sum-of-the-Years-Digits Method

The **sum-of-the-years-digits method** yields results like those obtained by use of the declining-balance method. The periodic charge for depreciation declines steadily over the estimated life of the asset because a successively smaller fraction is applied each year to the original cost of the asset less the estimated residual value. The denominator of the fraction, which remains the same, is the sum of the digits representing the years of life. The numerator of the fraction, which changes each year, is the number of remaining years of life. For an asset with an estimated life of 5 years, the denominator is $5 + 4 + 3 + 2 + 1$, or 15.[3] For the first year, the numerator is 5, for the second year 4, and so on. The method is illustrated by the following depreciation schedule for an asset with an assumed cost of $16,000, residual value of $1,000, and life of 5 years:

Year	Cost Less Residual Value	Rate	Depreciation for Year	Accumulated Depreciation at End of Year	Book Value at End of Year	
1	$15,000	5/15	$5,000	$ 5,000	$11,000	SUM-OF-THE-YEARS-DIGITS METHOD OF DEPRECIATION
2	15,000	4/15	4,000	9,000	7,000	
3	15,000	3/15	3,000	12,000	4,000	
4	15,000	2/15	2,000	14,000	2,000	
5	15,000	1/15	1,000	15,000	1,000	

When the first use of the asset does not coincide with the beginning of a fiscal year, it is necessary to allocate each full year's depreciation between the two fiscal years benefited. Assuming that the asset in the example was placed in service after three months of the fiscal year had elapsed, the depreciation for that fiscal year would be $9/12 \times (5/15 \times \$15,000)$, or $3,750. The depreciation for the second year would be $4,250, computed as follows:

$3/12 \times (5/15 \times \$15,000)$ $1,250
$9/12 \times (4/15 \times \$15,000)$ 3,000
Total, second fiscal year $4,250

---

[3]The denominator can also be determined from the following formula, where S = sum of the digits and N = number of years of estimated life:

$$S = N\left(\frac{N + 1}{2}\right)$$

Comparison of Depreciation Methods

The straight-line method provides for uniform periodic charges to depreciation expense over the life of the asset. The units-of-production method provides for periodic charges to depreciation expense that may vary considerably, depending upon the amount of usage of the asset.

Both the declining-balance and the sum-of-the-years-digits methods provide for a higher depreciation charge in the first year of use of the asset and a gradually declining periodic charge thereafter. For this reason they are frequently referred to as **accelerated depreciation methods.** These methods are most appropriate for situations in which the decline in productivity or earning power of the asset is proportionately greater in the early years of its use than in later years. Further justification for their use is based on the tendency of repairs to increase with the age of an asset. The reduced amounts of depreciation in later years are therefore offset to some extent by increased maintenance expenses.

The periodic depreciation charges for the straight-line method and the accelerated methods are compared in the following chart. This chart is based on an asset cost of $16,000, an estimated life of 5 years, and an estimated residual value of $1,000.

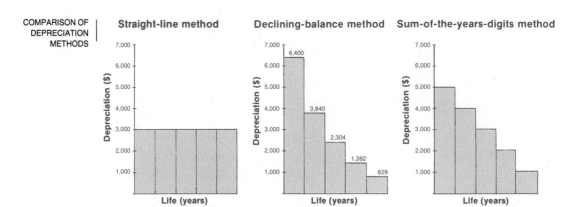

COMPARISON OF DEPRECIATION METHODS

DEPRECIATION FOR FEDERAL INCOME TAX

Each of the four depreciation methods described in the paragraphs above can be used to determine the amount of depreciation for federal income tax purposes for plant assets acquired prior to 1981. The accelerated depreciation methods especially are widely used. Acceleration of the "write-off" of the asset reduces the income tax liability in the earlier years and thus increases the amount of cash available in those years to pay for the asset or for other purposes.

For plant assets acquired after 1980, the straight-line method may be used to determine depreciation deductions for federal income tax purposes. Alternatively, the **Accelerated Cost Recovery System (ACRS)** may be used to provide deductions that approximate the depreciation calculated by the 150-percent declining-balance method.

The Accelerated Cost Recovery System, which is discussed in more detail in Chapters 22 and 23, permits the use of asset lives that are often much shorter than the actual useful life. Generally, ACRS provides for three classes of useful life for most business property — 3-year, 5-year, and 19-year classes. The 3-year class includes automobiles, light-duty trucks, and some special tools. Most machinery and equipment is included in the 5-year class, while buildings are in the 19-year class. The Internal Revenue Service has prepared tables that indicate the annual percentages to be used in determining depreciation for each class. In using these rates, salvage value is ignored and a full year's percentage is allowed for the year of acquisition. The following schedule illustrates the table that provides the ACRS depreciation rates for the 3-year and 5-year classes:

Year	3-Year Class Assets	5-Year Class Assets
1	25%	15%
2	38	22
3	37	21
4		21
5		21
	100%	100%

ACRS DEPRECIATION RATE SCHEDULE

REVISION OF PERIODIC DEPRECIATION

Earlier in this chapter, it was noted that two of the factors that must be considered in computing the periodic depreciation of a plant asset — its recoverable cost at the time it is retired from service and its length of life — must be estimated at the time the asset is placed in service. Minor errors resulting from the use of these estimates are normal and tend to be recurring.[4] When such errors occur, the revised estimates are used to determine the amount of the remaining undepreciated asset cost to be charged as an expense in future periods.

To illustrate, assume that a plant asset purchased for $130,000 and originally estimated to have a life of 30 years and residual value of $10,000 has been depreciated for 10 years by the straight-line method. At the end of ten years, its book value (undepreciated cost) would be $90,000, determined as follows:

[4]The correction of material or large errors made in computing depreciation is discussed in Chapter 11.

Asset cost	$130,000
Less accumulated depreciation	
($4,000 per year × 10 years)	40,000
Book value (undepreciated cost), end of tenth year	$ 90,000

If during the eleventh year it is estimated that the remaining useful life is 25 years (instead of 20) and that the residual value is $5,000 (instead of $10,000), the depreciation expense for each of the remaining 25 years would be **$3,400,** determined as follows:

Book value (undepreciated cost), end of tenth year	$90,000
Less revised estimated residual value	5,000
Revised remaining depreciation	$85,000
Revised annual depreciation expense	
($85,000 ÷ 25)	$ 3,400

Note that the correction of minor errors in the estimates used in the determination of depreciation does not correct the amounts of depreciation expense recorded in earlier years. The use of estimates, and the resulting likelihood of minor errors in such estimates, is inherent in the accounting process. Therefore when such errors do occur, the amounts recorded for depreciation expense in the past are not corrected; only future depreciation expense amounts are affected.

CAPITAL AND REVENUE EXPENDITURES

In addition to the initial cost of acquiring a plant asset, other costs related to its efficiency or capacity may be incurred during its service life. It is often difficult to recognize the difference between expenditures that add to the utility of the asset for more than one accounting period and those that benefit only the period in which they are incurred. Costs that add to the utility for more than one period are chargeable to an asset account or to a related accumulated depreciation account and are called capital expenditures. Expenditures that benefit only the current period are chargeable to expense accounts and are called revenue expenditures.

Expenditures for an addition to a plant asset are clearly capital expenditures. For example, the cost of installing an air conditioning unit in an automobile or of adding a wing to a building should be debited to the respective asset accounts. It is equally clear that expenditures for maintenance and repairs of a recurring nature should be classified as revenue expenditures. Thus, the cost of replacing spark plugs in an automobile or of repainting a building should be debited to proper expense accounts. In less obvious situations, several criteria may be considered in classifying the expenditures.

Expenditures that increase operating efficiency or capacity for the remaining useful life of an asset should be capitalized; that is, they should be treated as capital expenditures. For example, if the power unit attached to a machine is replaced by one of greater capacity, the cost and the accumulated depreciation related to the old motor should be removed from the accounts and the cost of the new one added to the asset account.

Expenditures that increase the useful life of an asset beyond the original estimate are also capital expenditures. They should be debited to the appropriate accumulated depreciation account, however, rather than to the asset account. To illustrate, assume that a machine with an estimated life of ten years is substantially rebuilt at the end of its seventh year of use, and that the extraordinary repairs are expected to extend the life of the machine an additional three years beyond the original estimate. In such circumstances the expenditures may be said to restore or "make good" a portion of the depreciation accumulated in prior years, and it is therefore appropriate that they be debited to the accumulated depreciation account.

When the cost of improvements or extraordinary repairs is great or when there is a material change in estimated life, the periodic depreciation allocable to future periods should be redetermined on the basis of the new book value of the asset and the new estimate of the remaining useful life.

Small expenditures are usually treated as repair expense even though they may have the characteristics of capital expenditures. The saving in time and clerical expenses justifies the sacrifice of the small degree of accuracy. Some businesses establish a minimum amount required to classify an item as a capital expenditure.

DISPOSAL OF PLANT ASSETS

Plant assets that are no longer useful may be discarded, sold, or applied toward the purchase of other plant assets. The details of the entry to record a disposal will vary, but in all cases it is necessary to remove the book value of the asset from the accounts. This is done by debiting the proper accumulated depreciation account for the total depreciation to the date of disposal and crediting the asset account for the cost of the asset.

A plant asset should not be removed from the accounts only because it has been depreciated for the full period of its estimated life. If the asset is still useful to the enterprise, the cost and accumulated depreciation should remain in the ledger. Otherwise the accounts would contain no evidence of the continued existence of such plant assets and the control function of the ledger would be impaired. In addition, the cost and the accumulated depreciation data on such assets are often needed in reporting for property tax and income tax purposes.

Discarding Plant Assets

When plant assets are no longer useful to the business and have no market value, they are discarded. If the asset has been fully depreciated, no loss is realized. To illustrate, assume that an item of equipment acquired at a cost of

$6,000 became fully depreciated at December 31, the end of the preceding fiscal year, and is now to be discarded as worthless. The entry to record the disposal is as follows:

```
Mar. 24   Accumulated Depreciation — Equipment . . . . .   6,000
              Equipment . . . . . . . . . . . . . . . . . . . . . . . . . . . . .          6,000
                  To write off equipment discarded.
```

If the accumulated depreciation applicable to the $6,000 of discarded equipment had been less than $6,000, there would have been a loss on its disposal. Furthermore, it would have been necessary to record depreciation for the three months of use in the current period before recording the disposal. To illustrate these differences, assume that annual depreciation on the equipment is computed at 10% of cost and that the accumulated depreciation balance is $4,750 after the annual adjusting entry at the end of the preceding year. The entry to record depreciation of $150 for the three months of the current period is as follows:

```
Mar. 24   Depreciation Expense — Equipment . . . . . . . . .   150
              Accumulated Depreciation — Equipment . . .          150
                  To record current depreciation on equip-
                  ment discarded.
```

The equipment is then removed from the accounts and the loss is recorded by the following entry:

```
Mar. 24   Accumulated Depreciation — Equipment . . . . .   4,900
          Loss on Disposal of Plant Assets . . . . . . . . . . .   1,100
              Equipment . . . . . . . . . . . . . . . . . . . . . . . . . . . . .          6,000
                  To write off equipment discarded.
```

Ordinary losses and gains on the disposal of plant assets are nonoperating items and may be reported in the Other Expense and Other Income sections, respectively, of the income statement.

Sale of Plant Assets

The entry to record the sale of a plant asset is like the entries illustrated in the preceding section, except that the cash or other asset received must also be recorded. If the selling price is more than the book value of the asset, the transaction results in a gain; if the selling price is less than the book value, there is a loss. To illustrate some possibilities, assume that equipment acquired at a cost of $10,000 and depreciated at the annual rate of 10% of cost is sold for cash on October 12 of the eighth year of its use. The accumulated depreciation in the account as of the preceding December 31 is $7,000. The entry to record the depreciation for the nine months of the current year is as follows:

```
Oct. 12   Depreciation Expense—Equipment .........        750
              Accumulated Depreciation—Equipment ...              750
                 To record current depreciation on equip-
                 ment sold.
```

After the current depreciation is recorded, the book value of the asset is $2,250. The entries to record the sale under three different assumptions as to selling price are as follows:

```
              Sold at book value, for $2,250. No gain or loss.
Oct. 12   Cash.......................................      2,250
              Accumulated Depreciation—Equipment ........  7,750
                 Equipment...............................             10,000

              Sold below book value, for $1,000. Loss of $1,250.
Oct. 12   Cash.......................................      1,000
              Accumulated Depreciation—Equipment ........  7,750
              Loss on Disposal of Plant Assets..............  1,250
                 Equipment...............................             10,000

              Sold above book value, for $3,000. Gain of $750.
Oct. 12   Cash.......................................      3,000
              Accumulated Depreciation—Equipment ........  7,750
                 Equipment...............................             10,000
                 Gain on Disposal of Plant Assets............             750
```

Exchange of Plant Assets

Old equipment is often traded in for new equipment having a similar use. The trade-in allowance is deducted from the price of the new equipment, and the balance owed **(boot)** is paid according to the credit terms. The trade-in allowance given by the seller is often greater or less than the book value of the old equipment traded in. In the past, it was acceptable for financial reporting purposes to recognize the difference between the trade-in allowance and the book value as a gain or a loss. For example, a trade-in allowance of $1,500 on equipment with a book value of $1,000 would have yielded a recognized gain of $500. Such treatment is no longer acceptable for financial reporting purposes on the ground that revenue occurs from the production and sale of items produced by plant assets and not from the exchange of similar plant assets.[5] However, if the trade-in allowance is less than the book value of the old equipment, the loss is recognized immediately.

---

[5]*Opinions of the Accounting Principles Board*, No. 29, "Accounting for Nonmonetary Transactions" (New York: American Institute of Certified Public Accountants, 1973), pars. 16, 21(b), and 22.

Nonrecognition of Gain

The acceptable method of accounting for an exchange in which the trade-in allowance exceeds the book value of the old plant asset requires that the cost of the new asset be determined by adding the amount of boot given to the book value of the old asset. To illustrate, assume an exchange based on the following data:

Equipment traded in (old):

Cost of old equipment	$4,000
Accumulated depreciation at date of exchange	3,200
Book value at June 19, date of exchange	$ 800

Similar equipment acquired (new):

Price of new equipment	$5,000
Trade-in allowance on old equipment	1,100
Boot given (cash)	$3,900

The cost basis of the new equipment is $4,700, which is determined by adding the boot given (**$3,900**) to the book value of the old equipment (**$800**). The compound entry to record the exchange and the payment of cash is as follows:

June 19 Accumulated Depreciation—Equipment	3,200	
Equipment	4,700	
Equipment		4,000
Cash		3,900

It should be noted that the nonrecognition of the $300 gain ($1,100 trade-in allowance minus $800 book value) at the time of the exchange is really a postponement. The periodic depreciation expense is based on a cost of $4,700 rather than on the quoted price of $5,000. The unrecognized gain of $300 at the time of the exchange will be matched by a reduction of $300 in the total amount of depreciation taken during the life of the equipment.

Recognition of Loss

To illustrate the accounting for a loss on the exchange of one plant asset for another which is similar in use, assume an exchange based on the following data:

Equipment traded in (old):

Cost of old equipment	$ 7,000
Accumulated depreciation at date of exchange	4,600
Book value at September 7, date of exchange	$ 2,400

Similar equipment acquired (new):

Price of new equipment...........................	$10,000
Trade-in allowance on old equipment................	**2,000**
Boot given (cash)	$ 8,000

The amount of the loss to be recognized on the exchange is the excess of the book value of the equipment traded in ($2,400) over the trade-in allowance ($2,000), or $400. The entry to record the exchange is as follows:

Sept. 7	Accumulated Depreciation—Equipment	4,600	
	Equipment....................................	10,000	
	Loss on Disposal of Plant Assets..............	400	
	Equipment.................................		7,000
	Cash......................................		8,000

Federal Income Tax Requirements

The Internal Revenue Code (IRC) requires that neither gains nor losses be recognized for income tax purposes if (1) the asset acquired by the taxpayer is similar in use to the asset given in exchange and (2) any boot involved is given (rather than received) by the taxpayer. Thus, the treatment of a nonrecognized gain corresponds to the acceptable method prescribed for financial reporting purposes, the boot given being added to the book value of the old equipment. In the first illustration, the cost basis for federal income tax purposes corresponds to the amount recorded as the cost of the new equipment, namely $4,700.

The cost basis of the new equipment in the second illustration, for federal income tax purposes, is determined in a like manner. The boot given ($8,000) is added to the book value of the old equipment ($2,400), yielding a cost basis of $10,400. The unrecognized loss of $400 at the time of the exchange will be matched by an increase of $400 in the total amount of depreciation allowed for income tax purposes during the life of the asset.

SUBSIDIARY LEDGERS FOR PLANT ASSETS

When depreciation is to be computed individually on a large number of assets making up a functional group, it is advisable to maintain a subsidiary ledger. To illustrate, assume that an enterprise owns about 200 items of office equipment with a total cost of about $100,000. Unless the business is newly organized, the equipment would have been acquired over a number of years. The individual cost, estimated residual value, and estimated life would be different in any case, and the makeup of the group will continually change because of acquisitions and disposals.

There are many variations in the form of subsidiary records for depreciable assets. Multicolumn analysis sheets may be used, or a separate ledger account may be maintained for each asset. The form should be designed to provide spaces for recording the acquisition and the disposal of the asset, the depreciation charged each period, the accumulated depreciation to date, and any other pertinent data desired. Following is an example of a subsidiary ledger account for a plant asset:

PLANT ASSET RECORD

ACCOUNT NO.: 123-215   GENERAL LEDGER ACCOUNT: OFFICE EQUIPMENT
ITEM: SF 490 COPIER
SERIAL NO.: AT 47-3926
FROM WHOM PURCHASED: HAMILTON OFFICE MACHINES CO. INC.
ESTIMATED LIFE: 10 YEARS   ESTIMATED RESIDUAL VALUE: $500   DEPRECIATION PER YEAR: $240

DATE	ASSET DEBIT	CREDIT	BALANCE	ACCUMULATED DEPRECIATION DEBIT	CREDIT	BALANCE	BOOK VALUE
04/08/86	2,900		2,900				2,900
12/31/86					180	180	2,720
12/31/87					240	420	2,480

AN ACCOUNT IN THE OFFICE EQUIPMENT LEDGER

The number assigned to the account illustrated is made up of the number of the office equipment account in the general ledger (123) followed by the number assigned to the specific item of office equipment purchased (215). An identification tag or plaque with the corresponding account number is attached to the asset. Depreciation for the year in which the asset was acquired, computed for nine months on a straight-line basis, is $180; for the following year it is $240. These amounts, together with the corresponding amounts from all other accounts in the subsidiary ledger, provide the figures for the respective year-end adjusting entries debiting the depreciation expense account and crediting the accumulated depreciation account.

The sum of the asset balances and the sum of the accumulated depreciation balances in all of the accounts should be compared periodically with the balances of their respective controlling accounts in the general ledger. When a certain asset is disposed of, the asset section of the subsidiary account is credited and the accumulated depreciation section is debited. This reduces the balances of both sections to zero. The account is then removed from the ledger and filed for possible future reference.

Subsidiary ledgers for plant assets are useful to the accounting department in (1) determining the periodic depreciation expense, (2) recording the disposal of individual items, (3) preparing tax returns, and (4) preparing insurance claims in the event of insured losses. The forms may also be expanded to provide spaces for accumulating data on the operating efficiency of the asset. Such information as number of breakdowns, length of time out of service, and cost of repairs is useful in comparing similar equipment produced by different manufacturers. When new equipment is to be purchased, the data are useful to management in deciding upon size, model, and other specifications and the best source of supply.

Regardless of whether subsidiary equipment ledgers are maintained, plant assets should be inspected periodically in order to determine their state of repair and whether or not they are still in use.

COMPOSITE-RATE DEPRECIATION METHOD

In the preceding illustrations, depreciation has been computed on each individual plant asset and, unless otherwise stated, this procedure will be assumed in the problem materials at the end of the chapter. Another procedure, called the **composite-rate depreciation method,** is to determine depreciation for entire groups of assets by use of a single rate. The basis for grouping may be similarity in life estimates or other common traits, or it may be broadened to include all assets within a functional class, such as office equipment or factory equipment.

When depreciation is computed on the basis of a composite group of assets of differing life spans, a rate based on averages must be developed. This may be done by (1) computing the annual depreciation for each asset, (2) determining the total annual depreciation, and (3) dividing the sum thus determined by the total cost of the assets. The procedure is illustrated as follows:

Asset No.	Cost	Estimated Residual Value	Estimated Life	Annual Depreciation	
101	$ 20,000	$4,000	10 years	$ 1,600	COMPOSITE-RATE METHOD OF DEPRECIATION
102	15,600	1,500	15 years	940	
147	41,000	1,000	8 years	5,000	
Total	$473,400			$49,707	

$$\frac{\$49,707 \text{ annual depreciation}}{\$473,400 \text{ cost}} = 10.5\% \text{ composite rate}$$

Although new assets of differing life spans and residual values will be added to the group and old assets will be retired, the "mix" is assumed to remain relatively unchanged. Accordingly, a depreciation rate based on averages (10.5% in the illustration) also remains unchanged for an indefinite time in the future.

When a composite rate is used, it may be applied against total asset cost on a monthly basis, or some reasonable assumption may be made regarding the timing of increases and decreases in the group. A common practice is to assume that all additions and retirements have occurred uniformly throughout the year. The composite rate is then applied to the average of the beginning and the ending balances of the account. Another acceptable averaging technique is to assume that all additions and retirements during the first half of the year occurred as of the first day of that year, and that all additions and retirements during the second half of the year occurred on the first day of the following year.

When assets within the composite group are retired, no gain or loss should be recognized. Instead, the asset account is credited for the cost of the asset and the accumulated depreciation account is debited for the excess of cost over the amount realized from the disposal. Any deficiency in the amount of depreciation recorded on the shorter-lived assets is presumed to be balanced by excessive depreciation on the longer-lived assets.

Regardless of whether depreciation is computed for each individual unit or for composite groups, the periodic depreciation charge is based on estimates. The effect of obsolescence and inadequacy on the life of plant assets is particularly difficult to forecast. Any system that provides for the allocation of depreciation in a systematic and rational manner fulfills the requirements of good accounting.

DEPRECIATION OF PLANT ASSETS OF LOW UNIT COST

Subsidiary ledgers are not usually maintained for classes of plant assets that are made up of individual items of low unit cost. Hand tools and other portable equipment of small size and value are typical examples. Because of hard usage, breakage, and pilferage, such assets may be relatively short-lived and require constant replacement. In such cases, the usual depreciation methods are not practical. One common method of determining cost expiration is to take a periodic inventory of the items on hand, estimate their fair value based on original cost, and transfer the remaining amount from the asset account to an appropriately titled account, such as Tools Expense. Other categories to which the same method is often applied are dies, molds, patterns, and spare parts.

ACQUISITION OF PLANT ASSETS THROUGH LEASING

Instead of owning plant assets, a business may use lease agreements for acquiring the use of plant assets. In such a contractual agreement, a lease conveys the right to use an asset for a stated period of time. The two parties to a lease contract are the **lessor** and the **lessee**. The lessor is the party who legally owns the asset and who conveys the rights to use the asset to the lessee. Typical lease transactions include the leasing of automobiles, computers, airplanes, and communication satellites.

In agreeing to a lease, the lessee incurs an obligation to make periodic rent payments for the lease term. In accounting for lease obligations, all leases are classified by the lessee as either capital leases or operating leases. **Capital leases** are defined as leases which include one or more of the following provisions: (1) the lease transfers ownership of the leased asset to the lessee at the end of the lease term; (2) the lease contains an option for a bargain purchase of the leased asset by the lessee; (3) the lease term extends over most of the economic life of the leased asset; or (4) the lease requires rental payments which approximate the fair market value of the leased asset. Leases which do not meet the preceding criteria for a capital lease are classified as **operating leases.**

A capital lease is accounted for as if the lessee has, in fact, purchased the asset. Accordingly, when a lease is executed, the lessee would debit an asset account for the fair market value of the leased asset and would credit a long-term lease liability account. The complex accounting procedures applicable to capital leases are discussed in detail in more advanced accounting texts.

In accounting for operating leases, rent expense is recognized as the leased asset is used. Neither future lease obligations nor the future rights to use the leased asset are recognized in the accounts. However, the lessee must disclose future lease commitments in footnotes to the financial statements.

DEPLETION

The periodic allocation of the cost of metal ores and other minerals removed from the earth is called **depletion.** The amount of the periodic cost allocation is based on the relationship of the cost to the estimated size of the mineral deposit and on the quantity extracted during the particular period. To illustrate, assume that the cost of certain mineral rights is $400,000 and that the deposit is estimated at 1,000,000 tons of ore of uniform grade. The depletion rate would be $400,000 ÷ 1,000,000, or $.40 a ton. If 90,000 tons are mined during the year, the depletion, amounting to $36,000, would be recorded by the following entry:

Adjusting Entry

Dec. 31	Depletion Expense.	36,000	
	Accumulated Depletion		36,000

The accumulated depletion account is a contra asset account and is presented in the balance sheet as a deduction from the cost of the mineral deposit.

In determining income subject to the federal income tax, the IRC permits, with certain limitations, a depletion deduction equal to a specified percent of gross income from the extractive operations. Thus, for income tax purposes, it is possible for total depletion deductions to be more than the cost of the property. Detailed examination of the tax law and regulations regarding "percentage depletion" is beyond the scope of this discussion, however.

INTANGIBLE ASSETS

Long-lived assets that are useful in the operations of an enterprise, not held for sale, and without physical qualities are usually classified as **intangible assets.** The basic principles of accounting for intangible assets are like those described earlier for plant assets. The major concerns are the determination of the initial costs and the recognition of periodic cost expiration, called **amortization,** due to the passage of time or a decline in usefulness. Intangible assets often include patents, copyrights, and goodwill.

Patents

Manufacturers may acquire exclusive rights to produce and sell goods with one or more unique features. Such rights are evidenced by **patents,** which are issued to inventors by the federal government. They continue in effect for 17 years. An enterprise may obtain patents on new products developed in its own research laboratories or it may purchase patent rights from others. The initial cost of a purchased patent should be debited to an asset account and then written off, or amortized, over the years of its expected usefulness. This period of time may be less than the remaining legal life of the patent, and the expectations are also subject to change in the future.

To illustrate, assume that at the beginning of its fiscal year an enterprise acquires for $100,000 a patent granted six years earlier. Although the patent will not expire for another eleven years, it is expected to be of value for only five years. A separate contra asset account is normally not credited for the write-off or amortization of patents. In most situations, the credit is recorded directly in the patents account. This practice is common for all intangible assets. The entry to amortize the patent at the end of the fiscal year is as follows:

Adjusting Entry

Dec. 31	Amortization Expense—Patents	20,000	
	Patents		20,000

Continuing the illustration, assume that after two years of use it appears that the patent will have no value at the end of an additional two years. The cost to be amortized in the third year would be the balance of the asset account, $60,000, divided by the remaining two years, or $30,000. The straight-line method of amortization should be used unless it can be shown that another method is more appropriate.[6]

An enterprise that develops patentable products in its own research laboratories often incurs substantial costs for the experimental work involved. In theory, some accountants believe that such costs, normally referred to as **research and development costs,** should be treated as an asset in the same manner as patent rights purchased from others. However, business enterprises are generally required to treat expenditures for research and development as current operating expenses.[7] The reason for this requirement is that there is a high degree of uncertainty about their future benefits, and therefore expensing these costs as incurred seems most appropriate. In addition, from a practical standpoint, a reasonably fair cost figure for each patent is difficult

[6]*Opinions of the Accounting Principles Board, No. 17,* "Intangible Assets" (New York: American Institute of Certified Public Accountants, 1970), par. 30.
[7]*Statement of Financial Accounting Standards, No. 2,* "Accounting for Research and Development Costs" (Stamford: Financial Accounting Standards Board, 1974), par. 12.

to establish because a number of research projects may be in process at the same time or work on some projects may extend over a number of years. As a result, a specific relationship between research and development costs and future revenue seldom can be established.

Whether patent rights are purchased from others or result from the efforts of its own research laboratories, an enterprise often incurs substantial legal fees related to the patents. For example, legal fees may be incurred in establishing the legal validity of the patents. Such fees should be debited to an asset account and then amortized over the years of the usefulness of the patents.

Copyrights

The exclusive right to publish and sell a literary, artistic, or musical composition is obtained by a **copyright.** Copyrights are issued by the federal government and extend for 50 years beyond the author's death. The costs assigned to a copyright include all costs of creating the work plus the cost of obtaining the copyright. A copyright that is purchased from another should be recorded at the price paid for it. Because of the uncertainty regarding the useful life of a copyright, it is usually amortized over a relatively short period of time.

Goodwill

In the sense that it is used in business, **goodwill** is an intangible asset that attaches to a business as a result of such favorable factors as location, product superiority, reputation, and managerial skill. Its existence is evidenced by the ability of the business to earn a rate of return on the investment that is in excess of the normal rate for other firms in the same line of business.

Accountants are in general agreement that goodwill should be recognized in the accounts only if it can be objectively determined by an event or transaction, such as the purchase or sale of a business. Accountants also agree that the value of goodwill eventually disappears and that the recorded costs should be amortized over the years during which the goodwill is expected to be of value. This period should not, however, exceed 40 years.[8]

REPORTING DEPRECIATION EXPENSE, PLANT ASSETS, AND INTANGIBLE ASSETS IN THE FINANCIAL STATEMENTS

The amount of depreciation expense of a period should be set forth separately in the income statement or disclosed in some other manner. A general description of the method or methods used in computing depreciation should also accompany the financial statements.[9]

---

[8]*Opinions of the Accounting Principles Board, No. 17,* "Intangible Assets," *op. cit.*, par. 29.

[9]*Opinions of the Accounting Principles Board, No. 22,* "Disclosure of Accounting Policies" (New York: American Institute of Certified Public Accountants, 1972), par. 13.

The balance of each major class of depreciable assets should be disclosed in the financial statements or in notes thereto, together with the related accumulated depreciation, either by major class or in total.[10] When there are too many classes of plant assets to permit such a detailed listing in the balance sheet, a single figure may be presented, supported by a separate schedule.

Intangible assets are usually presented in the balance sheet in a separate section immediately following plant assets. The balance of each major class of intangible assets should be disclosed at an amount net of amortization taken to date.

An illustration of the presentation of plant assets and intangible assets is shown in the following partial balance sheet:

PLANT ASSETS AND
INTANGIBLE ASSETS
IN THE
BALANCE SHEET

Clinton Door Inc.
Balance Sheet
December 31, 19--

Assets

	Cost	Accumulated Depreciation	Book Value	
Total current assets				$462,500
Plant assets:				
Land	$ 30,000	———	$ 30,000	
Buildings.	110,000	$ 26,000	84,000	
Factory equipment	650,000	192,000	458,000	
Office equipment	120,000	13,000	107,000	
Total plant assets	$910,000	$231,000		679,000
Intangible assets:				
Patents			$ 75,000	
Goodwill			50,000	
Total intangible assets				125,000

REPLACEMENT COST OF PLANT ASSETS

In preceding illustrations, plant assets were recorded at the cost actually incurred in acquiring them (historical cost), and depreciation was based on this cost. This principle is generally accepted for financial reporting purposes. The basic financial statements, therefore, do not indicate the effect of changes in price levels on plant assets and depreciation. In periods of inflation, which have been common in the past, many accountants have questioned the usefulness of financial statements that ignore the effects of inflation on operations.

---

[10]*Opinions of the Accounting Principles Board*, No. 12, "Omnibus Opinion—1967" (New York: American Institute of Certified Public Accountants, 1967), par. 5.

To indicate the nature of the problem, assume that plant assets acquired by an enterprise ten years ago for $1,000,000 are now to be replaced with similar assets which, at present price levels, will cost $2,000,000. Assume further that during the ten-year period the plant assets had been fully depreciated and that the net income of the enterprise had amounted to $5,000,000. Although the initial outlay of $1,000,000 for the plant assets was recovered through depreciation charges, the amount represents only one half of the cost of replacing the assets. Instead of considering the current value of the new assets to have doubled compared to a decade earlier, the dollars recovered can be said to have declined to one half of their earlier value. From either point of view, the firm has suffered a loss in purchasing power, which is the same as a loss of capital. In addition, $1,000,000 of the net income reported during the period might be said to be illusory, since it must be used to replace the assets.

The use of historical cost in accounting for plant assets insures objectivity. Therefore, in spite of inflationary trends, historical-cost financial statements are considered to be better than statements based on movements in the price level. Many accountants, however, recommend that businesses provide supplemental information that indicates the replacement cost, or current cost, of plant assets and the depreciation based on such cost. This supplemental information would match current costs for depreciation against current revenues and would therefore give a net income figure that would be useful in evaluating operating results. For example, a net income figure that has been determined after considering plant asset depreciation based on replacement cost would be especially useful in evaluating the amount of net income that should be made available for dividends.

There are many obstacles to the use of replacement costs for accounting for plant assets. For many businesses, such as a steel company with its many buildings and special machinery and equipment, it would be difficult to determine replacement costs with reasonable accuracy. In addition, if replacement costs were used, the process of estimating costs would have to be repeated each year, which would further increase the subjectivity of the accounting method. For reasons such as these, the use of replacement costs in accounting for plant assets has been generally restricted to experimental situations involving supplementary data.

Currently, the Financial Accounting Standards Board is undertaking an experiment for approximately 1,300 of the largest U.S. companies.[11] These companies are required to report, as supplemental information, the estimated current cost to replace plant assets, including the determination of depreciation on this basis. The results of this experiment and others like it may lead to a change in accounting for plant assets. For the present, the use of historical costs is required in financial reporting for plant assets and depreciation.

---

[11]*Statement of Financial Accounting Standards, No. 82,* "Financial Reporting and Changing Prices: Elimination of Certain Disclosures" (Stamford, Financial Accounting Standards Board, 1984).

Self-
Examination
Questions
(Answers
at end of
chapter.)

1. Which of the following expenditures incurred in connection with the acquisition of machinery is a proper charge to the asset account?
   A. Transportation charges   C. Both A and B
   B. Installation costs   D. Neither A nor B

2. What is the amount of depreciation, using the sum-of-the-years-digits method, for the first year of use for equipment costing $9,500 with an estimated residual value of $500 and an estimated life of 3 years?
   A. $4,500.00   C. $3,000.00
   B. $3,166.67   D. None of the above

3. An example of an accelerated depreciation method is:
   A. straight-line   C. units of production
   B. sum-of-the-years-digits   D. none of the above

4. A plant asset priced at $100,000 is acquired by trading in a similar asset that has a book value of $25,000. Assuming that the trade-in allowance is $30,000 and that $70,000 cash is paid for the new asset, what is the cost basis for the new asset for financial reporting purposes?
   A. $100,000   C. $30,000
   B. $70,000   D. None of the above

5. Which of the following is an example of an intangible asset?
   A. Patents   C. Copyrights
   B. Goodwill   D. All of the above

Discussion Questions

8–1. Which of the following qualities of an asset are characteristic of *plant assets?*
(a) Capable of repeated use in operations of the business.
(b) Held for sale in normal course of business.
(c) Tangible.
(d) Intangible.
(e) Long-lived.
(f) Used continuously in operations of the business.

8–2. Blum Office Supply Co. has a fleet of automobiles and trucks for use by salespersons and for delivery of office supplies and equipment. Parkhill Auto Sales Inc. has automobiles and trucks for sale. Under what caption would the automobiles and trucks be reported on the balance sheet of (a) Blum Office Supply Co., (b) Parkhill Auto Sales Inc.?

8–3. John Ryan & Co. acquired an adjacent vacant lot as a speculation. The lot will hopefully be sold in the future at a gain. Where should such real estate be listed in the balance sheet?

8–4. Indicate which of the following expenditures incurred in connection with the acquisition of a printing press should be charged to the asset account: (a) insurance while in transit, (b) freight charges, (c) sales tax on purchase price, (d) fee paid to factory representative for assembling and adjusting, (e) cost of special foundation, (f) new parts to replace those damaged in unloading.

8–5. Which of the following expenditures incurred in connection with the purchase of a secondhand printing press should be debited to the asset account: (a) new parts to replace those worn out, (b) freight charges, (c) installation costs, (d) repair of vandalism damages occurring during installation?

8–6. To increase its parking area, Lincolnshire Shopping Center acquired adjoining land for $90,000 and a building located on the land for $50,000. The net cost of razing the building and leveling the land was $10,000, after amounts received from sale of salvaged building materials were deducted. What accounts should be debited for (a) the $90,000, (b) the $50,000, (c) the $10,000?

8–7. (a) Does the recognition of depreciation in the accounts provide a special cash fund for the replacement of plant assets? (b) Describe the nature of depreciation as the term is used in accounting.

8–8. Is it necessary for an enterprise to use the same method of computing depreciation for (a) all classes of its depreciable assets, (b) the financial statements and in determining income taxes?

8–9. Convert each of the following life estimates to a straight-line depreciation rate, stated as a percent, assuming that residual value of the plant asset is to be ignored: (a) 4 years, (b) 5 years, (c) 10 years, (d) 20 years, (e) 25 years, (f) 40 years, (g) 50 years.

8–10. A plant asset with a cost of $95,000 has an estimated residual value of $5,000 and an estimated life of 5 years. What is the amount of the annual depreciation, computed by the straight-line method?

8–11. A plant asset with a cost of $45,000 has an estimated residual value of $5,000 and an estimated productive capacity of 400,000 units. What is the amount of annual depreciation, computed by the units-of-production method, for a year in which production is (a) 40,000 units, (b) 60,000 units?

8–12. The declining-balance method, at double the straight-line rate, is to be used for an asset with a cost of $25,000, estimated residual value of $1,000, and estimated life of 10 years. What is the depreciation for the first fiscal year, assuming that the asset was placed in service at the beginning of the year?

8–13. An asset with a cost of $20,750, an estimated residual value of $750, and an estimated life of 4 years is to be depreciated by the sum-of-the-years-digits method. (a) What is the denominator of the depreciation fraction? (b) What is the amount of depreciation for the first full year of use? (c) What is the amount of depreciation for the second full year of use?

8–14. (a) Name the two accelerated depreciation methods described in this chapter. (b) Why are the accelerated depreciation methods used frequently for income tax purposes?

8–15. A plant asset with a cost of $125,000 has an estimated residual value of $5,000, an estimated life of 40 years, and is depreciated by the straight-line method. (a) What is the amount of the annual depreciation? (b) What is the book value at the end of the twentieth year of use? (c) If at the start of the twenty-first year it is estimated that the remaining life is 25 years and that the residual value is $5,000, what is the depreciation expense for each of the remaining 25 years?

8–16. (a) Differentiate between capital expenditures and revenue expenditures. (b) Why are some items that have the characteristics of capital expenditures not capitalized?

8–17. Immediately after a used truck is acquired, a new motor is installed and the tires are replaced at a total cost of $2,500. Is this a capital expenditure or a revenue expenditure?

8–18. For a number of subsidiary plant ledger accounts of an enterprise, the balance in accumulated depreciation is exactly equal to the cost of the asset. (a) Is it permissible to record additional depreciation on the assets if they are still in use? (b) When should an entry be made to remove the cost and accumulated depreciation from the accounts?

8–19. In what sections of the income statement are gains and losses from the disposal of plant assets presented?

8–20. A plant asset priced at $60,000 is acquired by trading in a similar asset and paying cash for the remainder. (a) Assuming the trade-in allowance to be $25,000, what is the amount of "boot" given? (b) Assuming the book value of the asset traded in to be $20,000, what is the cost basis of the new asset for financial reporting purposes? (c) What is the cost basis of the new asset for the computation of depreciation for federal income tax purposes?

8–21. Assume the same facts as in Question 8-20, except that the book value of the asset traded in is $30,000. (a) What is the cost basis of the new asset for financial reporting purposes? (b) What is the cost basis of the new asset for the computation of depreciation for federal income tax purposes?

8–22. The cost of a composite group of equipment is $500,000 and the annual depreciation, computed on the individual items, totals $55,000. (a) What is the composite straight-line depreciation rate? (b) What would the rate be if the total depreciation amounted to $45,000 instead of $55,000?

8–23. What is the term applied to the periodic charge for (a) ore removed from a mine, and (b) the write-off of the cost of an intangible asset?

8–24. (a) Over what period of time should the cost of a patent acquired by purchase be amortized? (b) In general, what is the required treatment for research and development costs?

8–25. Are the amounts at which plant assets are reported in the balance sheet their approximate market values as of the balance sheet date? Discuss.

8–26. Is the use of replacement cost generally accepted for accounting for plant assets and depreciation?

Exercises

8–27. A plant asset acquired on January 3 at a cost of $165,000 has an estimated life of 10 years. Assuming that it will have no residual value, determine the depreciation for each of the first two years (a) by the straight-line method, (b) by the declining-balance method, using twice the straight-line rate, and (c) by the sum-of-the-years-digits method.

8–28. A diesel-powered generator with a cost of $150,000 and estimated salvage value of $10,000 is expected to have a useful operating life of 70,000 hours. During January, the generator was operated 720 hours. Determine the depreciation for the month.

8–29. Balances in Trucks and Accumulated Depreciation—Trucks at the end of the year, prior to adjustment, are $63,800 and $28,970 respectively. Details of the subsidiary ledger are as follows:

Truck No.	Cost	Estimated Residual Value	Estimated Useful Life in Miles	Accumulated Depreciation at Beginning of Year	Miles Operated During Year
1	$24,400	$4,400	200,000	$ 8,500	20,000
2	10,900	2,600	100,000	1,660	25,000
3	19,500	3,000	150,000	11,110	30,000
4	9,000	1,000	100,000	7,700	6,000

(a) Determine the depreciation rates per mile and the amount to be credited to the accumulated depreciation section of each of the subsidiary accounts for the current year.
(b) Present the journal entry to record depreciation for the year.

8–30. An item of equipment acquired at the beginning of the fiscal year at a cost of $38,000 has an estimated trade-in value of $2,000 and an estimated useful life of 8 years. Determine the following: (a) the amount of annual depreciation by the straight-line method, (b) the amount of depreciation for the second year computed by the declining-balance method (at twice the straight-line rate), (c) the amount of depreciation for the second year computed by the sum-of-the-years-digits method.

8–31. A piece of office equipment acquired at a cost of $15,900 has an estimated residual value of $900 and an estimated life of 5 years. It was placed in service on October 1 of the current fiscal year, which ends on December 31. Determine the depreciation for the current fiscal year and for the following fiscal year (a) by the declining-balance method, at twice the straight-line rate, and (b) by the sum-of-the-years-digits method.

8–32. An item of equipment acquired on January 3, 1984, at a cost of $27,500 has an estimated residual value of $2,500 and an estimated life of 10 years. Depreciation has been recorded for each of the first three years ending December 31, 1986, by the straight-line method. Determine the amount of depreciation for the current year ending December 31, 1987, if the revised estimated residual value is $3,800 and the estimated remaining useful life (including the current year) is 9 years.

8–33. A number of major structural repairs completed at the beginning of the current fiscal year at a cost of $80,000 are expected to extend the life of a building ten years beyond the original estimate. The original cost of the building was $750,000 and it has been depreciated by the straight-line method for 25 years. Residual value is expected to be negligible and has been ignored. The balance of the related accumulated depreciation account after the depreciation adjustment at the end of the preceding year is $375,000. (a) What has the amount of annual depreciation been in past years? (b) To what account should the $80,000 be debited? (c) What is the book value of the building after the repairs have been recorded? (d) What is the amount of depreciation for the current year, using the straight-line method (assume that the repairs were completed at the very beginning of the year)?

8–34. On September 1, Martin Co. acquired a new computer with a list price of $92,500, receiving a trade-in allowance of $12,500 on an old computer of a similar type, paying cash of $20,000, and giving a series of five notes payable for the remainder. The following information about the old computer is obtained from the account in the office equipment ledger: cost $55,000; accumulated depreciation on December 31, the end of the preceding fiscal year, $32,500; annual depreciation, $7,500. Present entries to record: (a) current depreciation on the old computer to date of trade-in; (b) the transaction on September 1 for financial reporting purposes.

8–35. On the first day of the fiscal year, a delivery truck with a list price of $25,000 was acquired in an exchange for an old delivery truck and $21,400 cash. The old truck has a book value of $2,500 at the date of the exchange. The new truck is to be depreciated over 5 years by the straight-line method, assuming a trade-in value of $2,900. Determine the following: (a) annual depreciation for financial reporting purposes, (b) annual depreciation for income tax purposes, (c) annual depreciation for financial reporting purposes, assuming that the book value of the old delivery truck was $5,500, (d) annual depreciation for income tax purposes, assuming the same facts as indicated in (c).

8–36. Details of a plant asset account for the fiscal year ended December 31 are as follows. A composite depreciation rate of 12% is applied annually to the account.

Office Equipment			
Jan. 1 Balance	560,400	Apr. 9	8,900
Feb. 10	25,000	Oct. 5	3,800
May 2	6,500	Dec. 17	11,300
Sep. 11	11,900		
Nov. 3	19,800		

Determine the depreciation for the year according to each of the following assumptions: (a) that all additions and retirements have occurred uniformly throughout the year and (b) that additions and retirements during the first half of the year occurred on the first day of that year and those during the second half occurred on the first day of the succeeding year.

8–37. On July 1 of the current fiscal year ending December 31, McLevin Co. acquired a patent for $50,000 and mineral rights for $100,000. The patent, which expires in 15 years, is expected to have value for 5 years. The mineral deposit is estimated at 500,000 tons of ore of uniform grade. Present entries to record the following for the current year: (a) amortization of the patent, (b) depletion, assuming that 70,000 tons were mined during the year.

8–38. For each of the following unrelated transactions, (a) determine the amount of the amortization or depletion expense for the current year, and (b) present the adjusting entries required to record each expense.
    (1) Governmental and legal costs of $13,300 were incurred at midyear in obtaining a patent with an estimated economic life of 7 years. Amortization is to be for one-half year.
    (2) Goodwill in the amount of $120,000 was purchased on January 5, the first month of the fiscal year. It is decided to amortize over the maximum period allowable.
    (3) Timber rights on a tract of land were purchased for $60,000. The stand of timber is estimated at 600,000 board feet. During the current year, 50,000 feet of timber were cut.

8–39. The following expenditures and receipts are related to land, land improvements, and buildings acquired for use in a business enterprise. The receipts are identified by an asterisk.

(a) Cost of real estate acquired as a plant site: Land........................... $150,000
                                             Building....................... 50,000
(b) Finder's fee paid to real estate agency..................................... 12,000
(c) Fee paid to attorney for title search....................................... 750
(d) Delinquent real estate taxes on property, assumed by purchaser.............. 18,500
(e) Cost of razing and removing the building.................................. 9,000
(f) Proceeds from sale of salvage materials from old building 1,500*
(g) Cost of land fill and grading 7,500
(h) Architect's and engineer's fees for plans and supervision.................... 70,000
(i) Premium on 1-year insurance policy during construction 9,000
(j) Cost of paving parking lot to be used by customers 15,250
(k) Cost of trees and shrubbery planted...................................... 7,000
(l) Special assessment paid to city for extension of water main to the property.... 2,000
(m) Cost of repairing windstorm damage during construction.................... 3,500
(n) Cost of repairing vandalism damage during construction 800
(o) Proceeds from insurance company for windstorm and vandalism damage...... 3,300*
(p) Interest incurred on building loan during construction 60,000
(q) Money borrowed to pay building contractor................................ 1,000,000*
(r) Paid to building contractor for new building............................... 1,150,000
(s) Refund of premium on insurance policy (i) canceled after 10 months 750*

Instructions:

    Assign each expenditure and receipt (indicate receipts by an asterisk) to Land (permanently capitalized), Land Improvements (limited life), Building, or Other Accounts. Identify each item by letter and list the amounts in columnar form, as follows:

Item	Land	Land Improvements	Building	Other Accounts
	$	$	$	$

8–40. An item of new equipment, acquired at a cost of $160,000 at the beginning of a fiscal year, has an estimated life of 4 years and an estimated trade-in value of $10,000. The manager requested information (details given in Instruction 1) regarding the effect of alternative methods on the amount of depreciation expense each year. Upon the basis of the data presented to the manager, the declining-balance method was elected.

    In the first week of the fourth year, the equipment was traded in for similar equipment priced at $250,000. The trade-in allowance on the old equipment was $25,000, cash of $25,000 was paid, and a note payable was issued for the balance.

Instructions:

    (1) Determine the annual depreciation for each of the estimated 4 years of use, the accumulated depreciation at the end of each year, and the book value of the equipment at the end of each year by (a) the straight-line method, (b) the declining-balance method (at twice the straight-line rate), and (c) the sum-of-the-years-digits method. The following columnar headings are suggested for each schedule:

Year	Depreciation Expense	Accumulated Depreciation, End of Year	Book Value, End of Year

(2) For financial reporting purposes, determine the cost basis of the new equipment acquired in the exchange.

(3) Present the entry to record the exchange.

(4) What is the cost basis of the new equipment for purposes of computing the amount of depreciation allowable for income tax purposes?

(5) For financial reporting purposes, determine the cost basis of the new equipment acquired in the exchange, assuming that the trade-in allowance was $10,000 instead of $25,000.

(6) Present the entry to record the exchange, assuming the data presented in Instruction (5).

(7) What is the cost basis of the new equipment for purposes of computing the amount of depreciation allowable for income tax purposes, assuming the data presented in Instruction (5)?

(If the working papers correlating with the textbook are not used, omit Problem 8-41.)

8–41. Lakeland Press Co. maintains a subsidiary equipment ledger for the printing equipment and accumulated depreciation accounts in the general ledger. A small portion of the subsidiary ledger, the two controlling accounts, and a journal are presented in the working papers. The company computes depreciation on each individual item of equipment. Transactions and adjusting entries affecting the printing equipment are described as follows:

1984

June 29. Purchased a power binder (Model 20, Serial No. 70010) from Dunn Manufacturing Co. on account for $72,000. The estimated life of the asset is 12 years, it is expected to have no residual value, and the straight-line method of depreciation is to be used. (This is the only transaction of the year that directly affected the printing equipment account.)

Dec. 31. Recorded depreciation for the year in subsidiary accounts 125–40 to 125–42, and inserted the new balances. (An assistant recorded the depreciation and the new balances in accounts 125–1 to 125–39.)

31. Journalized and posted the annual adjusting entry for depreciation on printing equipment. The depreciation for the year, recorded in subsidiary accounts 125–1 to 125–39, totaled $51,200, to which was added the depreciation entered in accounts 125–40 to 125–42.

1985

Oct. 2. Purchased a Model A7 rotary press from Titus Press Inc., priced at $60,000, giving the Model C8 flatbed press (Account No. 125–41) in exchange plus $20,000 cash and a series of ten $2,500 notes payable, maturing at 6-month intervals. The estimated life of the new press is 10 years and it is expected to have a residual value of $8,500. (Recorded depreciation to date in 1985 on item traded in.)

Instructions:

(1) Journalize the transaction of June 29. Post to Printing Equipment in the general ledger and to Account No. 125–42 in the subsidiary ledger.

(2) Journalize the adjusting entry on December 31 and post to Accumulated Depreciation—Printing Equipment in the general ledger.

(3) Journalize the entries required by the purchase of printing equipment on October 2. Post to Printing Equipment and to Accumulated Depreciation—Printing Equipment in the general ledger and to Account Nos. 125–41 and 125–43 in the subsidiary ledger.

(4) If the rotary press purchased on October 2 had been depreciated by the declining-balance method at twice the straight-line rate, determine the depreciation on this press for the fiscal years ending (a) December 31, 1985 and (b) December 31, 1986.

8–42. The following transactions, adjusting entries, and closing entries were completed by Weberg Furniture Co. during 3 fiscal years ending on June 30. All are related to the use of delivery equipment. The declining-balance method (twice the straight-line rate) of depreciation is used.

1984–1985 Fiscal Year

July   2. Purchased a used delivery truck for $10,000, paying cash.

      3. Paid $800 to replace the automatic transmission and install new brakes on the truck. (Debit Delivery Equipment.)

Aug. 21. Paid garage $199 for changing the oil, replacing the oil filter, and tuning the engine on the delivery truck.

June 30. Recorded depreciation on the truck for the fiscal year. The estimated life of the truck is 8 years, with a trade-in value of $2,000.

     30. Closed the appropriate accounts to the income summary account.

1985–1986 Fiscal Year

Oct.   8. Paid garage $175 to tune the engine and make other minor repairs on the truck.

     30. Traded in the used truck for a new truck priced at $21,575, receiving a trade-in allowance of $8,000 and paying the balance in cash. (Record depreciation to date in 1985.)

June 30. Recorded depreciation on the truck. It has an estimated trade-in value of $2,500 and an estimated life of 10 years.

     30. Closed the appropriate accounts to the income summary account.

1986–1987 Fiscal Year

Apr. 2. Purchased a new truck for $24,000, paying cash.

     3. Sold the truck purchased October 30, 1985, for $16,000. (Record depreciation for the year.)

June 30. Recorded depreciation on the remaining truck. It has an estimated trade-in value of $3,250 and an estimated life of 8 years.

     30. Closed the appropriate accounts to the income summary account.

Instructions:

(1) Open the following accounts in the ledger:

    122 Delivery Equipment

    123 Accumulated Depreciation—Delivery Equipment

    616 Depreciation Expense—Delivery Equipment

    617 Truck Repair Expense

    812 Gain on Disposal of Plant Assets

(2) Record the transactions and the adjusting and closing entries. Post to the accounts and extend the balances after each posting.

8–43. The following recording errors occurred and were discovered during the current year:

(a) The sale of an electric typewriter for $375 was recorded by a $375 credit to Office Equipment. The original cost of the machine was $1,050 and the related balance in Accumulated Depreciation at the beginning of the current year was $625. Depreciation of $100 accrued during the current year, prior to the sale, had not been recorded.

(b) The $450 cost of repairing factory equipment damaged in the process of installation was charged to Factory Equipment.

(c) Office equipment with a book value of $8,950 was traded in for similar equipment with a list price of $50,000. The trade-in allowance on the old equipment was $15,000, and a note payable was given for the balance. A gain on disposal of plant assets of $6,050 was recorded.

(d) Property taxes of $4,000 were paid on real estate acquired during the year and were debited to Property Tax Expense. Of this amount, $2,800 was for taxes that were delinquent at the time the property was acquired.

(e) The $925 cost of a major motor overhaul expected to prolong the life of a truck one year beyond the original estimate was debited to Delivery Expense. The truck was acquired new three years earlier.

(f) A $190 charge for incoming transportation on an item of factory equipment was debited to Purchases.

(g) The $9,900 cost of repainting the interior of a building was debited to Building. The building had been owned and occupied for ten years.

(h) The cost of a razed building, $40,000, was charged to Loss on Disposal of Plant Assets. The building and the land on which it was located had been acquired at a total cost of $110,000 ($70,000 debited to Land, $40,000 debited to Building) as a parking area for the adjacent plant.

(i) The fee of $5,400 paid to the wrecking contractor to raze the building in (h) was debited to Miscellaneous Expense.

Instructions: Journalize the entries necessary to correct the errors during the current year. Identify each entry by letter.

8–44. The trial balance of Nunn Corporation at the end of the current fiscal year, before adjustments, is shown at the top of page 273.

Data needed for year-end adjustments:

(a) Merchandise inventory at December 31, $139,900.

(b) Insurance and other prepaid operating expenses expired during the year, $7,100.

(c) Estimated uncollectible accounts at December 31, $5,250.

(d) Depreciation is computed at composite rates on the average of the beginning and the ending balances of the plant asset accounts. The beginning balances and rates are as follows:

Office equipment, $23,900; 10%   Delivery equipment, $42,650; 20%
Store equipment, $38,500; 8%   Buildings, $190,000; 2%

(e) Amortization of patents computed for the year, $2,000.

(f) Accrued liabilities at the end of the year, $2,800, of which $220 is for interest on the notes and $2,580 is for wages and other operating expenses.

Cash	19,750	
Accounts Receivable	40,700	
Allowance for Doubtful Accounts		750
Merchandise Inventory	144,500	
Prepaid Expense	14,900	
Land	40,000	
Buildings	190,000	
Accumulated Depreciation—Buildings		61,000
Office Equipment	25,100	
Accumulated Depreciation—Office Equipment		6,900
Store Equipment	41,500	
Accumulated Depreciation—Store Equipment		20,860
Delivery Equipment	47,350	
Accumulated Depreciation—Delivery Equipment		21,750
Patents	16,000	
Accounts Payable		30,250
Notes Payable (short-term)		15,000
Capital Stock		200,000
Retained Earnings		127,020
Dividends	45,000	
Sales (net)		989,000
Purchases (net)	711,700	
Operating Expenses (control account)	135,170	
Interest Expense	860	
	1,472,530	1,472,530

Instructions:

(1) Prepare a multiple-step income statement for the current year.

(2) Prepare a balance sheet, presenting the plant assets in the manner illustrated in this chapter.

8–39A. The following expenditures and receipts are related to land, land improvements, and buildings acquired for use in a business enterprise. The receipts are identified by an asterisk.

Alternate Problems

(a) Cost of real estate acquired as a plant site: Land	$100,000
Building	40,000
(b) Delinquent real estate taxes on property assumed by purchaser	7,500
(c) Cost of razing and removing the building	4,650
(d) Fee paid to attorney for title search	950
(e) Cost of land fill and grading	5,500
(f) Architect's and engineer's fees for plans and supervision	50,000
(g) Premium on 1-year insurance policy during construction	4,800
(h) Paid to building contractor for new building	675,000
(i) Cost of repairing windstorm damage during construction	1,500
(j) Cost of paving parking lot to be used by customers	9,750
(k) Cost of trees and shrubbery planted	12,000
(l) Special assessment paid to city for extension of water main to the property	1,200
(m) Cost of repairing vandalism damage during construction	500

(n) Interest incurred on building loan during construction .... $ 22,000
(o) Cost of floodlights installed on parking lot..................................... 6,000
(p) Proceeds from sale of salvage materials from old building.................... 1,100*
(q) Money borrowed to pay building contractor 600,000*
(r) Proceeds from insurance company for windstorm damage.................... 1,000*
(s) Refund of premium on insurance policy (g) canceled after 11 months.......... 300*

Instructions:

Assign each expenditure and receipt (indicate receipts by an asterisk) to Land (permanently capitalized), Land Improvements (limited life), Building, or Other Accounts. Identify each item by letter and list the amounts in columnar form, as follows:

Item	Land	Land Improvements	Building	Other Accounts
	$	$	$	$

8-40A. An item of new equipment, acquired at a cost of $80,000 at the beginning of a fiscal year, has an estimated life of 5 years and an estimated trade-in value of $5,000. The manager requested information (details given in Instruction 1) regarding the effect of alternative methods on the amount of depreciation expense each year. Upon the basis of the data presented to the manager, the declining-balance method was elected.

In the first week of the fifth year, the equipment was traded in for similar equipment priced at $140,000. The trade-in allowance on the old equipment was $15,000, cash of $25,000 was paid, and a note payable was issued for the balance.

Instructions:

(1) Determine the annual depreciation (round to nearest dollar) for each of the estimated 5 years of use, the accumulated depreciation at the end of each year, and the book value of the equipment at the end of each year by (a) the straight-line method, (b) the sum-of-the-years-digits method, and (c) the declining balance method (at twice the straight-line rate). The following columnar headings are suggested for each schedule:

Year	Depreciation Expense	Accumulated Depreciation, End of Year	Book Value, End of Year

(2) For financial reporting purposes, determine the cost basis of the new equipment acquired in the exchange.
(3) Present the entry to record the exchange.
(4) What is the cost basis of the new equipment for purposes of computing the amount of depreciation allowable for income tax purposes?
(5) For financial reporting purposes, determine the cost basis of the new equipment acquired in the exchange, assuming that the trade-in allowance was $10,000 instead of $15,000.
(6) Present the entry to record the exchange, assuming the data presented in Instruction (5).
(7) What is the cost basis of the new equipment for purposes of computing the amount of depreciation allowable for income tax purposes, assuming the data presented in Instruction (5)?

8–41A. Nessinger Press Inc. maintains a subsidiary equipment ledger for the printing equipment and accumulated depreciation accounts in the general ledger. A small portion of the subsidiary ledger, the two controlling accounts, and a journal are presented in the working papers. The company computes depreciation on each individual item of equipment. Transaction and adjusting entries affecting the printing equipment are described as follows:

(If the working papers correlating with the textbook are not used, omit Problem 8-41A.)

1984

Sept. 3. Purchased a power binder (Model 17, Serial No. P73) from Wise Manufacturing Co. on account for $30,000. The estimated life of the asset is 10 years, it is expected to have no residual value, and the straight-line method of depreciation is to be used. (This is the only transaction of the year that directly affected the printing equipment account.)

Dec. 31. Recorded depreciation for the year in subsidiary accounts 125-40 to 125-42, and inserted the new balances. (An assistant recorded the depreciation and the new balances in accounts 125-1 to 125-39.)

     31. Journalized and posted the annual adjusting entry for depreciation on printing equipment. The depreciation for the year, recorded in subsidiary accounts 125-1 to 125-39, totaled $48,200, to which was added the depreciation entered in accounts 125-40 to 125-42.

1985

Mar. 30. Purchased a Model B3 rotary press from Carson Press, Inc., priced at $50,000, giving the Model C8 flatbed press (Account No. 125-41) in exchange plus $6,000 cash and a series of eight $3,000 notes payable, maturing at 6-month intervals. The estimated life of the new press is 10 years and it is expected to have a residual value of $5,000. (Recorded depreciation to date in 1985 on item traded in.)

Instructions:

(1) Journalize the transaction of September 3. Post to Printing Equipment in the general ledger and to Account No. 125-42 in the subsidiary ledger.

(2) Journalize the adjusting entry required on December 31 and post to Accumulated Depreciation—Printing Equipment in the general ledger.

(3) Journalize the entries required by the purchase of printing equipment on March 30. Post to Printing Equipment and to Accumulated Depreciation—Printing Equipment in the general ledger and to Account Nos. 125-41 and 125-43 in the subsidiary ledger.

(4) If the rotary press purchased on March 30 had been depreciated by the declining-balance method at twice the straight-line rate, determine the depreciation on this press for the fiscal years ending (a) December 31, 1985 and (b) December 31, 1986.

8–42A. The following transactions, adjusting entries, and closing entries were completed by Jane Barr Furniture Co. during a 3-year period. All are related to the use of delivery equipment. The declining-balance method (twice the straight-line rate) of depreciation is used.

1984

Jan. 2. Purchased a used delivery truck for $7,200, paying cash.

     5. Paid $800 for major repairs to the truck.

July 20. Paid garage $210 for miscellaneous repairs to the truck.

1984

Dec. 31. Recorded depreciation on the truck for the fiscal year. The estimated life of the truck is 4 years, with a trade-in value of $1,200.

31. Closed the appropriate accounts to the income summary account.

1985

July 3. Traded in the used truck for a new truck priced at $15,000, receiving a trade-in allowance of $3,500 and paying the balance in cash. (Record depreciation to date in 1985.)

Dec. 21. Paid garage $250 for miscellaneous repairs to the truck.

31. Recorded depreciation on the truck. It has an estimated trade-in value of $2,000 and an estimated life of 5 years.

31. Closed the appropriate accounts to the income summary account.

1986

Oct. 1. Purchased a new truck for $16,200, paying cash.

2. Sold the truck purchased in 1985 for $9,000. (Record depreciation to date in 1986.)

Dec. 31. Recorded depreciation on the remaining truck. It has an estimated trade-in value of $2,200 and an estimated life of 6 years.

31. Closed the appropriate accounts to the income summary account.

Instructions:

(1) Open the following accounts in the ledger:
122 Delivery Equipment
123 Accumulated Depreciation—Delivery Equipment
616 Depreciation Expense—Delivery Equipment
617 Truck Repair Expense
812 Gain on Disposal of Plant Assets

(2) Record the transactions and the adjusting and closing entries. Post to the accounts and extend the balances after each posting.

Mini-Case

8–45. Joan Palmer, president of J.P. Company, is considering the purchase of machinery for $150,000. The machinery has a useful life of 5 years and no residual value. In the past, all plant assets have been leased. Palmer is considering depreciating the machinery by (1) the straight-line method or (2) the sum-of-the-years-digits method, and has asked your advice as to which method to use.

Instructions:

(1) Compute depreciation for each of the five years of useful life by (a) the straight-line method and (b) the sum-of-the-years-digits method.

(2) Assuming that income before depreciation and income tax is estimated to be uniformly $110,000 per year, that the depreciation method selected will be used for both financial reporting and income tax purposes, and that the income tax rate is 30%, compute the net income for each of the five years of useful life if (a) the straight-line method is used and (b) the sum-of-the-years-digits method is used.

(3) What factors would you present for Palmer's consideration in the selection of a depreciation method?

1. C All expenditures necessary to get a plant asset (such as machinery) in place and ready for use are proper charges to the asset account. In the case of machinery acquired, the transportation costs (answer A) and the installation costs (answer B) are both (answer C) proper charges to the machinery account.

2. A The periodic charge for depreciation under the sum-of-the-years-digits method is determined by multiplying a fraction by the original cost of the asset after the estimated residual value has been subtracted. The denominator of the fraction, which remains constant, is the sum of the digits representing the years of life, or 6 (3 + 2 + 1), in the question. The numerator of the fraction, which changes each year, is the number of years of remaining life, or 3 for the first year, 2 for the second year, and 1 for the third year in the question. The $4,500 (answer A) of depreciation for the first year is determined as follows:

$$\frac{\text{Years of Life Remaining}}{\text{Sum of Digits for Years of Life}} \times \text{Cost} - \text{Estimated Residual Value}$$

$$\frac{3}{3+2+1} \times (\$9,500 - \$500)$$

$$= \tfrac{1}{2} \times \$9,000 = \$4,500$$

3. B Depreciation methods that provide for a higher depreciation charge in the first year of the use of an asset and a gradually declining periodic charge thereafter are referred to as accelerated depreciation methods. Examples of such methods are the sum-of-the-years-digits (answer B) and the declining balance methods.

4. D The acceptable method of accounting for an exchange of similar assets in which the trade-in allowance ($30,000) exceeds the book value of the old asset ($25,000) requires that the cost of the new asset be determined by adding the amount of boot given ($70,000) to the book value of the old asset ($25,000), which totals $95,000.

5. D Long-lived assets that are useful in operations, not held for sale, and without physical qualities are referred to as intangible assets. Patents, goodwill, and copyrights are examples of intangible assets (answer D.)

CHAPTER 9

Payroll and Other Current Liabilities

CHAPTER OBJECTIVES

Describe and illustrate accounting for payrolls, including liabilities arising from employee earnings, deductions from earnings, and employer's payroll taxes.

Describe and illustrate accounting for pensions and notes payable.

Describe and illustrate accounting for contingent liabilities.

Payables are the opposite of receivables. They are debts owed by an enterprise to its creditors. Money claims against a firm may originate in many ways, such as purchases of merchandise or services on a credit basis, loans from banks, purchases of equipment, and purchases of marketable securities. At any particular moment, a business may also owe its employees for wages or salaries accrued, banks or other creditors for interest accrued on notes, and governmental agencies for taxes.

In addition to known liabilities of a definite or reasonably approximate amount, there may be potential obligations that will materialize only if certain events take place in the future. Such uncertain liabilities are termed **contingent liabilities.**

Some types of current liabilities, such as accounts payable, have been discussed in earlier chapters. Additional types of current liabilities, including liabilities arising from payrolls, pensions, and notes payable, are discussed in this chapter. Contingent liabilities are also discussed. Long-term liabilities are presented in Chapter 12.

PAYROLL

The term **payroll** is often used to refer to the total amount paid to employees for a certain period. Payroll expenditures are usually significant for several reasons. First, employees are sensitive to payroll errors or irregularities, and maintaining good employee morale requires that the payroll be paid on a timely, accurate basis. Second, payroll expenditures are subject to various federal and state regulations. Finally, the amount of these payroll expenditures and related payroll taxes has a significant effect on the net income of most business enterprises. Although the degree of importance of such expenses varies widely, it is not unusual for a business to expend nearly a third of its sales revenue for payroll and payroll-related expenses. These expenses and their related liabilities are discussed in the following sections.

LIABILITY FOR PAYROLL

The term **salary** is usually applied to payment for managerial, administrative, or similar services. The rate of salary is ordinarily expressed in terms of a month or a year. Remuneration for manual labor, both skilled and unskilled, is commonly called **wages** and is stated on an hourly, weekly, or piecework basis. In practice, the terms salary and wages are often used interchangeably.

The basic salary or wage of an employee may be supplemented by commissions, bonuses, profit sharing, or cost-of-living adjustments. The form in which remuneration is paid generally has no effect on the manner in which it is treated by either the employer or the employee. Although payment is usually in terms of cash, it may take such forms as securities, notes, lodging, or other property or services.

Salary and wage rates are determined, in general, by agreement between the employer and the employees. Enterprises engaged in interstate commerce must also follow the requirements of the Fair Labor Standards Act. Employers covered by this legislation, which is commonly called the Federal Wage and Hour Law, are required to pay a minimum rate of 1½ times the regular rate for all hours worked in excess of 40 hours per week. Exemptions from the requirements are provided for executive, administrative, and certain supervisory positions. Premium rates for overtime or for working at night or other less desirable times are fairly common, even when not required by law, and the premium rates may be as much as twice the base rate.

Determination of Employee Earnings

To illustrate the computation of the earnings of an employee, it is assumed that Thomas C. Johnson is employed at the rate of $19 per hour for the first 40 hours in the weekly pay period and at $28.50 ($19 + $9.50) per hour for any additional hours. His time card shows that he worked 43 hours during the week ended December 27. His earnings for that week are computed as follows:

Earnings at base rate (40 × $19)................	$760.00
Earnings at overtime rate (3 × $28.50)..........	85.50
Total earnings.................................	$845.50

The foregoing computations can be stated in generalized arithmetic formulas or **algorithms.** If the hours worked during the week are less than or equal to (≤) 40, the formula may be expressed by the following equation, where E represents total earnings, H represents hours worked, and R represents hourly rate:

$$E = H \times R$$

This equation cannot be used to determine the earnings of an employee who has worked more than (>) 40 hours during the week, because the overtime rate differs from the basic rate. The expansion of the equation to include the additional factor of overtime yields the following:

$$E = 40\,R + 1.5\,R\,(H - 40)$$

The two equations can be expressed as shown in the following algorithm:

If	Then
$H \leq 40$	$E = H \times R$
$H > 40$	$E = 40R + 1.5R(H - 40)$

After the value of H and R are known for each employee at the end of a payroll period, the earnings of each employee can be computed accurately and speedily. Application of the standardized procedure of the algorithm to mechanized or electronic processing equipment makes it possible to process a payroll routinely, regardless of its size.

Determination of Profit-Sharing Bonuses

Many enterprises pay their employees an annual bonus in addition to their regular salary or wage. The amount of the bonus is often based on the productivity of the employees, as measured by the net income of the enterprise. Such profit-sharing bonuses are treated in the same manner as wages and salaries.

The method used in determining the amount of a profit-sharing bonus is usually stated in the agreement between the employer and the employees. When the amount of the bonus is measured by a certain percentage of income, there are four basic formulas for the computation. The percentage may be applied (1) to income before deducting the bonus and income taxes, (2) to income after deducting the bonus but before deducting income taxes, (3) to income before deducting the bonus but after deducting income taxes, or (4) to net income after deducting both the bonus and income taxes.

Determination of a 10% bonus according to each of the four methods is illustrated as follows, based on the assumption that the employer's income before deducting the bonus and income taxes amounts to $150,000, and that income taxes are levied at the rate of 40% of income. Bonus and income taxes are abbreviated as B and T respectively.

(1) Bonus based on income before deducting bonus and taxes.
$$B = .10\ (\$150{,}000)$$
$$\text{Bonus} = \$15{,}000$$

(2) Bonus based on income after deducting bonus but before deducting taxes.
$$B = .10\ (\$150{,}000 - B)$$

Simplifying:	$B = \$15{,}000 - .10B$
Transposing:	$1.10B = \$15{,}000$
	$\text{Bonus} = \$13{,}636.36$

(3) Bonus based on income before deducting bonus but after deducting taxes.

B equation: $B = .10 (\$150,000 - T)$
T equation: $T = .40 (\$150,000 - B)$

Substituting for T in the B equation and solving for B:

$B = .10 [\$150,000 - .40 (\$150,000 - B)]$

Simplifying: $B = .10 (\$150,000 - \$60,000 + .40B)$
Simplifying: $B = \$15,000 - \$6,000 + .04B$
Transposing: $.96B = \$9,000$
$\text{Bonus} = \$9,375$

(4) Bonus based on net income after deducting bonus and taxes.

B equation: $B = .10 (\$150,000 - B - T)$
T equation: $T = .40 (\$150,000 - B)$

Substituting for T in the B equation and solving for B:

$B = .10 [\$150,000 - B - .40 (\$150,000 - B)]$

Simplifying: $B = .10 (\$150,000 - B - \$60,000 + .40B)$
Simplifying: $B = \$15,000 - .10B - \$6,000 + .04B$
Transposing: $1.06B = \$9,000$
$\text{Bonus} = \$8,490.57$

With the amount of the bonus possibilities ranging from the high of $15,000 to the low of $8,490.57, the importance of strictly following the agreement is evident. If the bonus is to be shared by all of the employees, the agreement must also provide for the manner by which the bonus is divided among them. A common method is to express the bonus as a percentage of total earnings for the year. For example, if the bonus were computed to be $15,000 and employee earnings before the bonus had been $100,000, the bonus for each of the employees could be stated as 15% of their earnings.

DEDUCTIONS FROM EMPLOYEE EARNINGS

The total earnings of an employee for a payroll period are often called the **gross pay.** From this amount is subtracted one or more **deductions** to arrive at the **net pay,** which is the amount the employer must pay the employee. The deductions for federal taxes are of the widest applicability and usually the largest in amount. Deductions may also be needed for state or local income taxes and for contributions to state unemployment compensation programs. Other deductions may be made for contributions to pension plans and for items authorized by individual employees.

FICA Tax

Most employers are required by the Federal Insurance Contributions Act (FICA) to withhold a portion of the earnings of each of their employees. The amount of **FICA tax** withheld is the employees' contribution to the combined federal programs for old-age and disability benefits, insurance benefits to survivors, and health insurance for the aged (medicare). With very few exceptions, employers are required to withhold from each employee a tax at a specified rate on earnings up to a specified amount paid in the calendar year. Although both the schedule of future tax rates and the maximum amount subject to tax are revised often by Congress, such changes have no effect on the basic outline of the payroll system.[1] For purposes of illustration, a rate of 7% on maximum annual earnings of $40,000, or a maximum annual tax of $2,800, will be assumed.

Federal Income Tax

Except for certain types of employment, all employers must withhold a portion of the earnings of their employees for payment of the employees' liability for federal income tax. The amount that must be withheld from each employee differs according to the amount of gross pay, marital status, and the estimated deductions and exemptions claimed when filing the annual income tax return.

Other Deductions

Deductions from gross earnings for payment of taxes are compulsory. Neither the employer nor the employee has any choice in the matter. In addition, however, there may be other deductions authorized by individual employees or by the union representing them. For example, an employee may authorize deductions for the purchase of United States savings bonds, for contributions to a United Fund or other charitable organization, for payment of premiums on various types of employee insurance, or for the purchase of a retirement annuity. The union contract may also require the deduction of union dues or other deductions for group benefits.

COMPUTATION OF EMPLOYEE NET PAY

Gross earnings for a payroll period less the payroll deductions yields the amount to be paid to the employee, which is often called the **net pay** or **take-home pay**. To illustrate, the following summary of a week's gross earnings and deductions for an employee, Thomas C. Johnson, shows that the amount to be paid Johnson is $609.30:

Gross earnings for the week...........		$845.50
Deductions:		
FICA tax...........................	$ 24.50	
Federal income tax	186.70	
U.S. savings bonds.................	20.00	
United Fund	5.00	
Total deductions..................		236.20
Net pay		$609.30

---

[1]Current tax rates may be located in Internal Revenue Service publications and in standard tax reporting services.

Payroll and Other Current Liabilities

As has been indicated, there is a ceiling on the annual earnings subject to the FICA tax, and consequently the amount of the annual tax is also limited. Therefore, when the amount of FICA tax to withhold from an employee is determined for a payroll period, it is necessary to refer to one of the following cumulative amounts:

1. Employee gross earnings for the year prior to the current payroll period, or
2. Employee tax withheld for the year prior to the current payroll period.

To continue with the Johnson illustration, reference to his earnings record shows cumulative earnings of $39,650 prior to the current week's earnings of $845.50. The amount of the current week's earnings subject to FICA tax is therefore the maximum of $40,000 − $39,650, or $350, and the FICA tax to be withheld is 7% of $350, or $24.50. Alternatively, the determination could be based on the amount of FICA tax withheld from Johnson prior to the current payroll period. This amount, according to the employee record, is $2,775.50 and the amount to be withheld is the maximum of $2,800 − $2,775.50, or $24.50.

There is no ceiling on the amount of earnings subject to withholding for income taxes and hence no need to consider the cumulative earnings. The amount of federal income tax withheld would be determined by reference to official withholding tax tables issued by the Internal Revenue Service. For purposes of this illustration, the amount of federal income tax withheld was assumed to be $186.70. The deductions for the purchase of bonds and for the charitable contribution were in accordance with Johnson's authorizations.

As in the determination of gross earnings when overtime rates are a factor, the computation of some deductions can be generalized in the form of algorithms. The algorithm for the determination of the FICA tax deduction, based on the maximum deduction approach, is as follows, where E represents current period's earnings, F represents current period's FICA deduction, and f represents cumulative FICA deductions prior to the current period:

If	Then
$f + (.07E) \leq \$2,800$	$F = .07E$
$f + (.07E) > \$2,800$	$F = \$2,800 - f$

An alternative generalization of the method of determining FICA deductions, based on the maximum taxable earnings approach, is illustrated by the following decision diagram. The additional symbol "e" represents cumulative earnings prior to the current period.

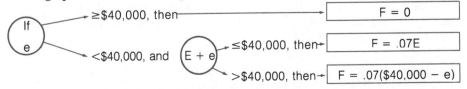

The elements of the decision diagram are examples of standardized instructions that can be applied to computations involving many variables. They are used in many situations as an aid to routine processing of repetitive data, regardless of whether the processing is performed manually or electronically.

LIABILITY FOR EMPLOYER'S PAYROLL TAXES

Thus far the discussion of taxes has been limited to those levied against employees and withheld by employers. Most employers are subject to federal and state taxes based on the amount of remuneration earned by their employees. Such taxes are an operating expense of the business and may amount to a relatively large sum.

FICA Tax

Employers are required to contribute to the Federal Insurance Contributions Act program for each employee. The tax rate and the maximum amount of employee remuneration entering into an employer's tax base are the same as those applicable to employees, which for purposes of illustration are assumed to be 7% and $40,000 respectively.

Federal Unemployment Compensation Tax

Unemployment insurance provides temporary relief to those who become unemployed as a result of economic forces beyond their control. Types of employment subject to the unemployment insurance program are similar to those covered by the FICA tax. The tax of .8% is levied on employers only, rather than on both employers and employees. It is applicable only to the first $7,000 of the remuneration of each covered employee during a calendar year. As with the FICA tax, the rate and the maximum amount subject to federal unemployment compensation tax are revised often by Congress. The funds collected by the federal government are not paid out as benefits to the unemployed, but are allocated among the states for use in administering state programs.

State Unemployment Compensation Tax

The amounts paid as benefits to unemployed persons are obtained, for the most part, by taxes levied upon employers only. A very few states also require employee contributions. The rates of tax and the tax base vary, and in most states, employers who provide steady employment for their employees are awarded reduced rates. The employment experience and the status of each employer's tax account are reviewed annually, and the merit ratings and tax rates are revised accordingly.[2]

---

[2]As of January 1, 1985, the maximum state rate recognized by the federal unemployment system was 5.4% of the first $7,000 of each employee's earnings during a calendar year.

ACCOUNTING SYSTEMS FOR PAYROLL AND PAYROLL TAXES

Accounting systems for payroll and payroll taxes are concerned with the records and reports associated with the employer-employee relationship. It is important that the accounting system provide safeguards to insure that payments are in accord with management's general plans and its specific authorizations.

All employees of a firm expect and are entitled to receive their remuneration at regular intervals following the close of each payroll period. Regardless of the number of employees and the difficulties in computing the amounts to be paid, the payroll system must be designed to process the necessary data quickly and assure payment of the correct amount to each employee. The system must also provide adequate safeguards against payments to fictitious persons and other misappropriations of funds.

Various federal, state, and local laws require that employers accumulate certain specified data in their payroll records, not only for each payroll period but also for each employee. Periodic reports of such data must be submitted to the appropriate governmental agencies and remittances made for amounts withheld from employees and for taxes levied on the employer. The records must be retained for specified periods of time and be available for inspection by those responsible for enforcement of the laws. In addition, payroll data may be useful in negotiations with labor unions, in settling employee grievances, and in determining rights to vacations, sick leaves, and retirement pensions.

Although complex organizational structures may necessitate the use of detailed subsystems, the major parts common to most payroll systems are the payroll register, payroll checks, and employee's earnings record. Each of these major payroll components is illustrated and discussed in the following sections. Although the illustrations are relatively simple, many modifications might be introduced in actual practice.

Payroll Register

The multicolumn form used in assembling and summarizing the data needed at the end of each payroll period is called the **payroll register**. Its design varies according to the number and classes of employees, the extent to which automation is used, and the type of equipment used. A form suitable for a small number of employees is illustrated at the top of pages 286 and 287.

The nature of most of the data appearing in the illustrative payroll register is evident from the columnar headings. The number of hours worked and the earnings and deduction data are inserted in the appropriate columns. The sum of the deductions applicable to an employee is then deducted from the total earnings to yield the amount to be paid. Recording the check numbers in the payroll register as the checks are written eliminates the need to maintain other detailed records of the payments.

PAYROLL
REGISTER

PAYROLL FOR WEEK ENDING

NAME	TOTAL HOURS	EARNINGS			TAXABLE EARNINGS	
		REGULAR	OVERTIME	TOTAL	UNEMPLOY-MENT COMP.	FICA
ARKIN, JOAN E.	40	500.00		500.00	500.00	500.00
DAWSON, LOREN A.	44	392.00	58.80	450.80		450.80
GREEN, MINDY M.		840.00		840.00		
JOHNSON, THOMAS C.	43	760.00	85.50	845.50		350.00
WYATT, WILLIAM R.	40	480.00		480.00		480.00
ZACHS, ANNA H.		525.00		525.00	150.00	525.00
TOTAL		13,328.70	574.00	13,902.70	2,710.00	11,354.70

The two columns under the general heading of Taxable Earnings are used in accumulating data needed to compute the employer's payroll taxes. The last two columns of the payroll register are used to accumulate the total wages or salaries to be charged to the expense accounts. This process is usually termed **payroll distribution.** If there is an extensive account classification of labor expense, the charges may be analyzed on a separate payroll distribution sheet.

The format of the illustrative payroll register aids the determination of arithmetic accuracy before checks are issued to employees and before the summary amounts are formally recorded. Specifically, all columnar totals except those in the Taxable Earnings columns should be cross-verified. The miscellaneous deductions must also be summarized by account classification. The following tabulation illustrates the method of cross-verification. The amounts could be listed on an adding machine, taking the figures directly from the payroll register.

Earnings:
    Regular $13,328.70
    Overtime 574.00
      Total $13,902.70
Deductions:
    FICA tax .... $ 794.83
    Federal income tax 3,332.18
    U.S. savings bonds 680.00
    United Fund 470.00
    Accounts receivable 50.00
      Total 5,327.01
Paid—net amount .... $ 8,575.69

DECEMBER 27, 19--

		DEDUCTIONS				PAID		ACCOUNTS DEBITED	
FICA TAX	FEDERAL INCOME TAX	U.S. SAVINGS BONDS	MISCEL- LANEOUS		TOTAL	NET AMOUNT	CHECK NO.	SALES SALARIES EXPENSE	OFFICE SALARIES EXPENSE
35.00	74.10	20.00	UF	10.00	139.10	360.90	6857	500.00	
31.56	62.60		AR	50.00	144.16	306.64	6858		450.80
	186.30	25.00	UF	10.00	221.30	618.70	6859	840.00	
24.50	186.70	20.00	UF	5.00	236.20	609.30	6860	845.50	
33.60	69.20	10.00			112.80	367.20	6880	480.00	
36.75	71.36	5.00	UF	2.00	115.11	409.89	6881		525.00
794.83	3,332.18	680.00	UF AR	470.00 50.00	5,327.01	8,575.69		11,122.16	2,780.54

MISCELLANEOUS DEDUCTIONS: AR—ACCOUNTS RECEIVABLE   UF—UNITED FUND

Accounts debited:
Sales Salaries Expense $11,122.16
Office Salaries Expense 2,780.54
Total (as above) $13,902.70

Recording Employees' Earnings

The payroll register may be used as a supporting record for a compound journal entry that records the payroll data. The entry based on the payroll register illustrated is as follows:

Dec. 27	Sales Salaries Expense	11,122.16	
	Office Salaries Expense	2,780.54	
	FICA Tax Payable.		794.83
	Employees Income Tax Payable		3,332.18
	Bond Deductions Payable		680.00
	United Fund Deductions Payable.		470.00
	Accounts Receivable—Loren A. Dawson . .		50.00
	Salaries Payable.		8,575.69
	Payroll for week ended December 27.		

The total expense incurred for the services of employees is recorded by the debits to the salary expense accounts. Amounts withheld from employees' earnings have no effect on the debits to these accounts. Five of the credits in the entry represent increases in specific liability accounts and one represents a decrease in the accounts receivable account.

Recording and Paying Payroll Taxes

Each time the payroll register is prepared, the amounts of all employees' current earnings entering the tax base are listed in the respective taxable earnings columns. As explained earlier, the cumulative amounts of each employee's earnings just prior to the current period are available in the employee's earnings record.

According to the payroll register illustrated for the week ended December 27, the amount of remuneration subject to FICA tax was $11,354.70 and the amount subject to state and federal unemployment compensation taxes was $2,710. Multiplication by the applicable tax rates yields the following amounts:

FICA tax.	$794.83
State unemployment compensation tax (5.4% × $2,710).	146.34
Federal unemployment compensation tax (.8% × $2,710).	21.68
Total payroll taxes expense	$962.85

The journal entry to record the payroll tax expense for the week and the liability for the taxes accrued is as follows:

Dec. 27	Payroll Taxes Expense	962.85	
	FICA Tax Payable.		794.83
	State Unemployment Tax Payable		146.34
	Federal Unemployment Tax Payable		21.68
	Payroll taxes for week ended		
	December 27.		

Payment of the liability for each of the taxes is recorded in the same manner as the payment of other liabilities. Employers are required to compute and report all payroll taxes on the calendar year basis, regardless of the fiscal year they may use for financial reporting and income tax purposes. Details of the federal income tax and FICA tax withheld from employees are combined with the employer's FICA tax on a single return accompanied by the amount of tax due. Payments are required on a weekly, semimonthly, monthly, or quarterly basis, depending on the amount of the combined taxes. Unemployment compensation tax returns and payments are required by the federal government on an annual basis. Earlier payments are required when the tax exceeds a certain minimum. Unemployment compensation tax returns and payments are required by most states on a basis similar to that required by the federal government.

All payroll taxes levied against employers become liabilities at the time the related remuneration is *paid* to employees, rather than at the time the liability to the employees is incurred. Observance of this requirement may cause a problem of expense allocation between fiscal periods. To illustrate, assume that an enterprise using the calendar year as its fiscal year pays its employees on Friday for a weekly payroll period ending the preceding Wednesday, the two-day lag between Wednesday and Friday being needed to process the payroll. Regardless of the day of the week on which the year ends, there will be some accrued wages. If it ends on a Thursday, the accrual will cover a full week plus an extra day. Logically, the unpaid wages and the related payroll taxes should both be charged to the period that benefited from the services performed by the employees. On the other hand, there is legally no liability for the payroll taxes until the wages are paid in January, when a new cycle of earnings subject to tax is begun. The distortion of net income that would result from failure to accrue the payroll taxes might well be insignificant. The practice adopted should be followed consistently.

Payroll Checks

One of the principal outputs of most payroll systems is a series of **payroll checks** at the end of each pay period. The data needed for this purpose are provided by the payroll register, each line of which applies to an individual employee. It is possible to prepare the checks solely by reference to the Net Amount column of the register. However, the customary practice is to provide each employee with a statement of the details of the computation. The statement may be entirely separate from the check or it may be in the form of a detachable stub attached to the check.

When employees are paid by checks drawn on the regular bank account and the voucher system is used, it is necessary to prepare a voucher for the net amount to be paid the employees. The voucher is then recorded as a debit to Salaries Payable and a credit to Accounts Payable, and payment is recorded in the usual manner. If the voucher system is not used, the payment would be recorded by a debit to Salaries Payable and a credit to Cash.

It should be understood that the journal entry derived from the payroll register, such as the compound entry illustrated on page 287, would precede the entries just described. It should also be noted that the entire amount paid may be recorded as a single item, regardless of the number of employees. There is no need to record each check separately because all of the details are available in the payroll register for future reference.

Most employers with a large number of employees use a special bank account and payroll checks designed specifically for the purpose. After the data for the payroll period have been recorded and summarized in the payroll register, a single check for the total amount to be paid is drawn on the firm's regular bank account and deposited in a special account. The individual payroll checks are then drawn against the special payroll account, and the numbers of the payroll checks are inserted in the payroll register.

The use of special payroll checks relieves the treasurer or other executives of the task of signing a large number of regular checks each payday. The responsibility for signing payroll checks may be given to the paymaster, or mechanical means of signing the checks may be used. Another advantage of this system is that reconciling the regular bank statement is simplified. The paid payroll checks are returned by the bank separately from regular checks and are accompanied by a statement of the special bank account. Any balance shown on the bank's statement will correspond to the sum of the payroll checks outstanding because the amount of each deposit is exactly the same as the total amount of checks drawn. The recording procedures are the same as when checks on the regular bank account are used.

Currency is sometimes used as the medium of payment when the payroll is paid each week or when the business location or the time of payment is such that banking or check-cashing facilities are not readily available to employees. In such cases, a single check, payable to Payroll, is drawn for the entire amount to be paid. The check is then cashed at the bank and the money is inserted in individual pay envelopes. Each employee should be required to sign a receipt which serves as evidence of payment. The procedures for recording the payment correspond to those outlined for payroll checks.

Employee's Earnings Record

The necessity of having the cumulative amount of each employee's earnings readily available at the end of each payroll period was discussed earlier. Without such information or the related data on the cumulative amount of FICA tax previously withheld, there would be no means of determining the appropriate amount to withhold from current earnings. It is essential, therefore, that detailed records be maintained for each employee.

A portion of the **employee's earnings record** is illustrated below and on page 291. The relationship between this record and the payroll register can be seen by tracing the amounts entered on Johnson's earnings record for December 27 back to its source, which is the fourth line of the payroll register illustrated on pages 286 and 287.

EMPLOYEE'S EARNINGS RECORD

THOMAS C. JOHNSON
4990 COLUMBUS AVENUE
STATESVILLE, IOWA 52732-6142
PHONE: 555-3148

MARRIED

NUMBER OF WITHHOLDING ALLOWANCES: 4

PAY RATE: $760.00 PER WEEK

OCCUPATION: SALESPERSON

EQUIVALENT HOURLY RATE: $19

LINE NO.	PERIOD ENDED	TOTAL HOURS	EARNINGS REGULAR	EARNINGS OVERTIME	EARNINGS TOTAL	CUMULATIVE TOTAL
39	SEPT. 27	41	760.00	28.50	788.50	30,330.50
THIRD QUARTER			9,880.00	256.50	10,136.50	
40	OCT. 4	40	760.00		760.00	31,090.50
46	NOV. 15	41	760.00	28.50	788.50	35,679.00
47	NOV. 22	40	760.00		760.00	36,439.00
48	NOV. 29	42	760.00	57.00	817.00	37,256.00
49	DEC. 6	40	760.00		760.00	38,016.00
50	DEC. 13	40	760.00		760.00	38,776.00
51	DEC. 20	44	760.00	114.00	874.00	39,650.00
52	DEC. 27	43	760.00	85.50	845.50	40,495.50
FOURTH QUARTER			9,880.00	285.00	10,165.00	
YEARLY TOTAL			39,520.00	975.50	40,495.50	

In addition to spaces for recording data for each payroll period and the cumulative total of earnings, there are spaces for quarterly totals and the yearly total. These totals are used in various reports for tax, insurance, and other purposes. Copies of one such annual report, known as Form W-2, Wage and Tax Statement, must be given to each employee as well as to the Social Security Administration. The source of the amounts inserted in the following statement was the employee's earnings record.

1 Control number 44012	For Paperwork Reduction Act Notice, see back of Copy D. OMB No. 1545-0008	For Official Use Only		WAGE AND TAX STATEMENT

2 Employer's name, address, and ZIP code	3 Employer's identification number 61-843652	4 Employer's State number

Langford Supply Co.
560 Hudson Avenue
Cedar Rapids, Iowa 52731-6148

5 Stat. em-ployee	De-ceased	Legal rep.	942 emp.	Sub-total	Void
☐	☐	☐	☐	☐	☐

6 Allocated tips	7 Advance EIC payment

8 Employee's social security number 381-48-9120	9 Federal income tax withheld $8,942.06	10 Wages, tips, other compensation $40,495.50	11 Social security tax withheld $2,800.00

12 Employee's name (first, middle, last)	13 Social security wages $40,000.00	14 Social security tips

	16 *

Thomas C. Johnson
4990 Columbus Avenue
Statesville, Iowa 52732-6142

17 State income tax	18 State wages, tips, etc.	19 Name of State
20 Local income tax	21 Local wages, tips, etc.	22 Name of locality

15 Employee's address and ZIP code

Form **W-2 Wage and Tax Statement** 19-- Copy A For Social Security Administration
* See Instructions for Forms W-2 and W-2P

Department of the Treasury
Internal Revenue Service

SOC. SEC. NO.: 381-48-9120   EMPLOYEE NO.: 814

DATE EMPLOYED: FEBRUARY 15, 1974

DATE OF BIRTH: OCTOBER 4, 1952

DATE EMPLOYMENT TERMINATED:

	DEDUCTIONS				PAID		
FICA TAX	FEDERAL INCOME TAX	U.S. BONDS	OTHER	TOTAL	NET AMOUNT	CHECK NO.	LINE NO.
55.20	174.11	20.00		249.31	539.19	6175	39
709.56	2,238.30	260.00	AR 40.00	3,247.86	6,888.64		
53.20	167.82	20.00	UF 5.00	246.02	513.98	6225	40
55.20	174.11	20.00		249.31	539.19	6530	46
53.20	167.82	20.00		241.02	518.98	6582	47
57.19	180.41	20.00		257.60	559.40	6640	48
53.20	167.82	20.00	UF 5.00	246.02	513.98	6688	49
53.20	167.82	20.00		241.02	518.98	6743	50
61.18	192.99	20.00		274.17	599.83	6801	51
24.50	186.70	20.00	UF 5.00	236.20	609.30	6860	52
711.55	2,244.60	260.00	UF 15.00	3,231.15	6,933.85		
2,800.00	8,942.06	1,040.00	AR 40.00	12,882.06	27,613.44		
			UF 60.00				

PAYROLL SYSTEM DIAGRAM

The flow of data within segments of an accounting system may be shown by diagrams such as the one illustrated below. It depicts the interrelationships of the principal parts of the payroll system described in this chapter. The requirement of constant updating of the employee's earnings record is indicated by the dotted line.

FLOW DIAGRAM OF A
PAYROLL SYSTEM

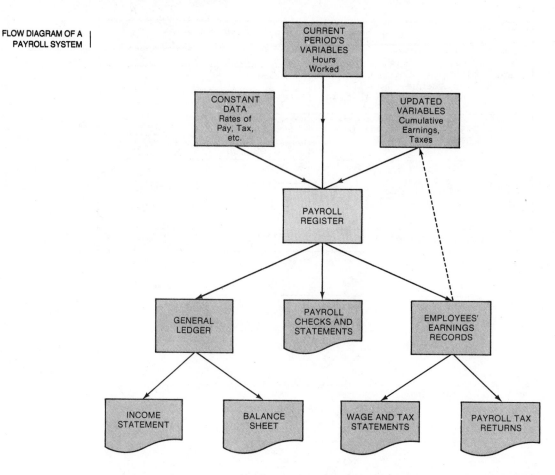

Attention thus far has been directed to the end product or *output* of a payroll system, namely the payroll register, the checks payable to individual employees, the earnings records for each employee, and reports for tax and other purposes. The basic data entering the payroll system are sometimes called the *input* of the system. Input data that remain relatively unchanged and do not need to be reintroduced into the system for each payroll period are characterized as *constants*. Those that differ from period to period are termed *variables*.

Constants include such data for each employee as name and social security number, marital status, number of income tax withholding allowances claimed, rate of pay, functional category (office, sales, etc.), and department where employed. The FICA tax rate, maximum earnings subject to tax, and various tax tables are also constants which apply to all employees. The variable data for each employee include the number of hours or days worked during each payroll period, days of sick leave with pay, vacation credits, and cumulative amounts of earnings and taxes withheld. If salespersons are employed on a commission basis, the amount of their sales would also vary from period to period. The forms used in initially recording both the constant and the variable data vary widely according to the complexities of the payroll system and the processing methods used.

INTERNAL CONTROLS FOR PAYROLL SYSTEMS

The large amount of data and the computations necessary to process the payroll are evident. As the number of employees and the mass of data increase, the number of individuals needed to manage and process payroll data likewise increases. Such characteristics, together with the relative magnitude of labor costs, indicate the need for controls that will assure the reliability of the data and minimize the opportunity for misuse of funds.

The expenditure and cash disbursement controls discussed in Chapter 5 are applicable to payrolls. Thus, the use of the voucher system and the requirement that all payments be supported by vouchers are desirable. The addition or deletion of names on the payroll should be supported by written authorizations from the personnel department. It is also essential that employees' attendance records be controlled in such a manner as to prevent errors and abuses. Perhaps the most basic and widely used records are "In and Out" cards, whereby employees indicate, often by "punching" a time clock, their time of arrival and departure. Employee identification cards or badges may also be used in this connection to assure that all salaries and wages paid are paid to the proper individuals.

EMPLOYEE STOCK OPTIONS

Stock options are rights given by a corporation to its employees to purchase shares of the corporation's stock at a stated price. Employee stock options generally involve an element of salary expense when the employees have the right to purchase the corporation's stock at a price below market value. In such a case, the expense is the difference between the market price of the stock and the amount the employees are required to pay for it. The amount of the expense is debited to an appropriate expense account and credited to an owner's equity account. The details of accounting for employee stock options are discussed in more advanced accounting texts.

LIABILITY FOR PENSIONS

Many companies have established retirement pension plans for their employees. In recent years, such plans have increased rapidly in number, variety, and complexity. Although the details of the plans vary from employer to employer, pension benefits are usually based on factors such as employee age, years of service, and salary level. In 1974, Congress enacted the Employee Retirement Income Security Act (ERISA), which established guidelines for safeguarding employee benefits.

Pension plans may be classified as contributory or noncontributory, funded or unfunded, and qualified or unqualified. A **contributory plan** requires the employer to withhold a portion of each employee's earnings as a contribution to the plan. The employer then makes a contribution according to the provisions of the plan. A **noncontributory plan** requires the employer to bear the entire cost. A **funded plan** requires the employer to set aside funds to meet future pension benefits by making payments to an independent funding agency. The funding agency is responsible for managing the assets of the pension fund and for disbursing the pension benefits to employees. For many pension plans, insurance companies serve as the funding agency. An **unfunded plan** is managed entirely by the employer instead of by an independent agency. A **qualified plan** is designed to comply with federal income tax requirements which allow the employer to deduct pension contributions for tax purposes and which exempt pension fund income from tax. Most pension plans are qualified.

The accounting for pension plans can be complex due to the uncertainties of projecting future pension obligations. Future pension obligations depend upon such factors as employee life expectancies, expected employee compensation levels, and investment income on pension contributions. Pension funding requirements are estimated by individuals known as actuaries, who use sophisticated mathematical and statistical models.

The employer's contribution to a pension plan for normal pension cost associated with pension benefits earned by employees in a given year is debited to an operating expense account, Pension Expense. The credit is to Cash if the pension cost is fully funded. If the pension cost is partially funded, any unfunded amount is credited to Pension Contribution Payable. To illustrate, assume that the pension plan of Flossmoor Industries requires an annual pension cost of $25,000, and Flossmoor Industries pays $15,000 to the fund trustee, Equity Insurance Company. The entry to record the transaction is as follows:

Pension Expense	25,000	
Cash		15,000
Pension Contribution Payable		10,000

Depending upon when the pension liability is to be paid, the $10,000 will be classified on the balance sheet as either a long-term or a current liability.

An entity's financial statements should fully disclose the nature of its pension plans and pension obligations. The financial statement disclosures should include the pension cost for the year and a description of the pension plan, including the employee groups covered, the entity's accounting and funding policies, and any pension changes affecting comparability among years.[3]

When an employer first adopts or changes a pension plan, special considerations must be given as to whether the employer will grant employees credit for prior years service. If a company does grant credit to employees for past service, a past service cost obligation must be recognized. The funding of past service cost is normally provided for over a number of years, thus creating a long-term past service pension cost liability.

NOTES PAYABLE AND INTEREST EXPENSE

Notes may be issued to creditors in temporary satisfaction of an account payable created earlier, or they may be issued at the time merchandise or other assets are purchased. To illustrate the former, assume that an enterprise, which owes F. B. Murray Co. $1,000 on an overdue account, issues a 90-day, 12% note for $1,000, dated December 1, 1986, in settlement of the account. The entry to record the transaction is as follows:

```
Dec.  1   Accounts Payable—F. B. Murray Co. . . . . . . . .   1,000
              Notes Payable . . . . . . . . . . . . . . . . . . . . . . . .           1,000
              Issued a 90-day, 12% note on account.
```

On December 31, 1986, the end of the fiscal year, an adjusting entry would be recorded for the accrual of the interest from December 1 to December 31. The entry to record the accrued expense of $10 ($1,000 × 12/100 × 30/360) is as follows:

Adjusting Entry

```
Dec. 31   Interest Expense . . . . . . . . . . . . . . . . . . . . . . . .   10
              Interest Payable . . . . . . . . . . . . . . . . . . . . . . . .           10
```

Interest payable is reported on the balance sheet at December 31, 1986, as a current liability. The interest expense account is closed at December 31, and the amount is reported in the Other Expense section of the income statement for the year ended December 31, 1986.

When the amount due on the note is paid in 1987, part of the interest paid will effect a reduction of the interest that was payable at December 31, 1986, and the remainder will represent expense for 1987. To avoid the possibility of failing to recognize this division and to avoid the inconvenience of analyzing

---

[3]*Statement of Financial Accounting Standards*, No. 36, "Disclosure of Pension Information" (Stamford: Financial Accounting Standards Board, 1980), par. 7.

the payment of interest in 1987, a reversing entry is made after the accounts are closed. The effect of the entry, illustrated as follows, is to transfer the credit balance in the interest payable account to the credit side of the interest expense account.

Reversing Entry

Jan. 1	Interest Payable........................	10	
	Interest Expense		10

At the time the note matures and payment is made, the entire amount of the interest payment is debited to Interest Expense, as illustrated by the following entry:

Mar. 1	Notes Payable.........................	1,000	
	Interest Expense	30	
	Cash.................................		1,030

After the foregoing entries are posted, the interest expense account will appear as follows:

ACCOUNT INTEREST EXPENSE   ACCOUNT NO. 911

Date		Item	Debit	Credit	Balance	
					Debit	Credit
1986						
Nov.	10		250		890	
Dec.	31	Adjusting	10		900	
	31	Closing		900	———	———
1987						
Jan.	1	Reversing		10		10
Mar.	1		30		20	

The adjusting and reversing process divided the $30 of interest paid on March 1, 1987, into two parts for accounting purposes: (1) $10 representing the interest expense for 1986 (recorded by the adjusting entry) and (2) $20 representing the interest expense for 1987 (the balance in the interest expense account at March 1, 1987).

There are many variations in interest and repayment terms when money is borrowed from banks. The most direct procedure is for the borrower to issue an interest-bearing note for the amount of the loan. For example, assume that on September 19 a firm borrows $4,000 from the First National Bank, with the loan evidenced by the firm's 90-day, 15% note. The effect of this transaction is as follows:

Sept. 19	Cash.....................................	4,000	
	Notes Payable		4,000

On the due date of the note, ninety days later, the borrower owes $4,000, the face amount of the note, and interest of $150. The accounts affected by the payment are as follows:

Dec. 18	Notes Payable	4,000	
	Interest Expense	150	
	Cash.		4,150

A variant of the bank loan transaction just illustrated is to issue a non-interest-bearing note for the amount that is to be paid at maturity. When this plan is followed, the interest is deducted from the maturity value of the note and the borrower receives the remainder. The deduction of interest from a future value is termed **discounting.** The rate used in computing the interest may be termed the **discount rate,** the deduction may be called the **discount,** and the net amount available to the borrower is called the **proceeds.**

To illustrate the discounting of a note payable, assume that on August 10 an enterprise issued to a bank a $4,000, 90-day, non-interest-bearing note and that the bank discount rate is 15%. The amount of the discount is $150 and the proceeds $3,850. The debits and credit required to record the transaction follow:

Aug. 10	Cash.	3,850	
	Interest Expense	150	
	Notes Payable		4,000

The note payable is recorded at its face value, which is also its maturity value, and the interest expense is recorded at the time the note is issued. When the note is paid, the entry is as follows:

Nov. 8	Notes Payable	4,000	
	Cash.		4,000

CONTINGENT LIABILITIES

If it is likely that a liability will materialize and if the amount of the liability can be reasonably estimated, it should be recorded in the accounts as a "liability."[4] On the other hand, if it is not possible to determine whether a liability will materialize or it is not possible to reasonably estimate the amount of a liability, it is deemed to be "contingent." Contingent liabilities arise from discounting notes receivable, litigation, guarantees of products,

[4]*Statement of Financial Accounting Standards, No. 5,* "Accounting for Contingencies" (Stamford: Financial Accounting Standards Board, 1975), pars. 8, 10, 12.

possible tax assessments, or other causes. Contingent liabilities are normally disclosed in the notes to the financial statements. An example of a note is as follows:

Due to 1985 weather conditions which caused a peanut crop shortage, the Company was required to allocate available peanuts to customers with whom, in accordance with customary practice, it had entered into firm sales contracts. In accepting or otherwise responding to the allocation arrangements, which generally represented a significant reduction from the contracted quantities, a number of customers indicated that they reserve all their rights to challenge the fairness and reasonableness and other aspects of the allocation program. The Company's management maintains that it is not liable by virtue of the conditions of the 1985 crop and that it allocated its available peanut supply as provided by law. At present, one suit is pending and while no estimate can be made as to the likelihood of other customers challenging the allocations or likelihood of an unfavorable outcome if challenges are made, the Company's management is of the opinion that no material liability will result.

Self-Examination Questions
(Answers at end of chapter.)

1. An employee's rate of pay is $20 per hour, with time and a half for all hours worked in excess of 40 during a week. The following data are available:

Hours worked during current week.................................. 45
Cumulative earnings for year prior to current week.................. $39,500
FICA rate, on maximum of $40,000 of annual earnings.............. 7%
Federal income tax withheld....................................... $ 212

Based on these data, the amount of the employee's net pay for the current week is:
A. $500   C. $800
B. $703   D. $950

2. Which of the following taxes are employers required to withhold from employees?
A. Federal income tax
B. Federal unemployment compensation tax
C. State unemployment compensation tax
D. All of the above

3. With limitations on the maximum earnings subject to the tax, employers incur operating costs for which of the following payroll taxes?
A. FICA tax
B. Federal unemployment compensation tax
C. State unemployment compensation tax
D. All of the above

4. The unpaid balance of a mortgage note payable is $50,000 at the end of the current fiscal year. If the terms of the note provide for monthly principal payments of $1,000, how should the liability for the principal be presented on the balance sheet?
A. $50,000 current liability
B. $50,000 long-term liability
C. $12,000 current liability; $38,000 long-term liability
D. $12,000 long-term liability; $38,000 current liability

5. An enterprise issued a $5,000, 60-day non-interest-bearing note to the bank, and the bank discounts the note at 12%. The proceeds are:
A. $4,400   C. $5,000
B. $4,900   D. $5,100

Discussion Questions

9–1. If an employee is granted a profit-sharing bonus, is the amount of the bonus (a) part of the employee's earnings and (b) deductible as an expense of the enterprise in determining the federal income tax?

9–2. The general manager of a business enterprise is entitled to an annual profit-sharing bonus of 5%. For the current year, income before bonus and income taxes is $200,000 and income taxes are estimated at 40% of income before income taxes. Determine the amount of the bonus, assuming that the bonus is based on net income after deducting both bonus and income taxes.

9–3. What is (a) gross pay? (b) net or take-home pay?

9–4. (a) Identify the federal taxes that most employers are required to withhold from employees. (b) Give the titles of the accounts to which the amounts withheld are credited.

9–5. For each of the following payroll-related taxes, indicate whether there is a ceiling on the annual earnings subject to the tax: (a) FICA tax, (b) federal income tax, (c) federal unemployment compensation tax?

9–6. Identify the payroll taxes levied against employers.

9–7. Prior to the last weekly payroll period of the calendar year, the cumulative earnings of employees E and F are $39,800 and $40,200 respectively. Their earnings for the last completed payroll period of the year are $800 each, which will be paid in January. If the amount of earnings subject to FICA tax is $40,000 and the tax rate is 7%, (a) what will be the employer's FICA tax on the two salary amounts of $800 each; (b) what is the employer's total FICA tax expense for employees E and F for the calendar year just ended?

9–8. Do payroll taxes levied against employers become liabilities at the time the liabilities for wages are incurred or at the time the wages are paid?

9–9. Indicate the principal functions served by the employee's earnings record.

9–10. Explain how a payroll system that is properly designed and operated tends to give assurance (a) that wages paid are based upon hours actually worked, and (b) that payroll checks are not issued to fictitious employees.

9–11. An employer pays the employees in currency and the pay envelopes are prepared by an employee rather than by the bank. (a) Why would it be advisable to obtain from the bank the exact amount of money needed for a payroll? (b) How could the exact number of each bill and coin denomination needed be determined efficiently in advance?

9–12. A company uses a weekly payroll period and a special bank account for payroll. (a) When should deposits be made in the account? (b) How is the amount of the deposit determined? (c) Is it necessary to have in the general ledger an account entitled "Cash — Special Payroll Account"? Explain. (d) The bank statement for the payroll bank account for the month ended August 31 indicates a bank balance of $3,478.30. Assuming that the bank has made no errors, what does this amount represent?

9–13. What is an employee stock option?

9–14. Differentiate between a contributory and a noncontributory pension plan.

9–15. Identify several factors which influence the future pension obligation of an enterprise.

9–16. How does past service cost arise in a new or revised pension plan?

9–17. The unpaid balance of a mortgage note payable is $200,000 at the end of the current fiscal year. The terms of the note provide for quarterly principal payments of $10,000. How should the liability for the principal be presented on the balance sheet as of this date?

9–18. A business enterprise issued a 60-day, 12% note for $10,000 to a creditor on account. Give the entries to record (a) the issuance of the note and (b) the payment of the note at maturity, including interest of $200.

9–19. In borrowing money from a bank, an enterprise issued a $10,000, 60-day, non-interest-bearing note, which the bank discounted at 15%. Are the proceeds $10,000? Explain.

9–20. A business firm is contesting a suit for damages of a substantial amount, brought by a customer for an alleged faulty product. Is this a contingent liability for the defendant? If so, should it be disclosed in financial statements issued during the period of litigation? Discuss.

Exercises

9–21. Develop an algorithm, in the form illustrated in this chapter, to compute the amount of each employee's weekly earnings subject to state unemployment compensation tax. Assume that the tax is 4.2% on the first $7,000 of each employee's earnings during the year and that the following symbols are to be used:

  e — Cumulative earnings subject to state unemployment compensation tax prior to current week
  E — Current week's earnings
  S — Amount of current week's earnings subject to state unemployment compensation tax

9-22. The general manager of a business enterprise is entitled to an annual profit-sharing bonus of 4%. For the current year, income before bonus and income taxes is $320,000 and income taxes are estimated at 40% of income before income taxes. Determine the amount of the bonus, assuming that (a) the bonus is based on income before deductions for bonus and income taxes and (b) the bonus is based on income after deduction for both bonus and income taxes.

9-23. In the following summary of data for a payroll period, some amounts have been intentionally omitted:

Earnings:

(1) At regular rate	——	(7) Union Dues	——
(2) At overtime rate. . . .	$2,590.60	(8) Total deductions	$ 9,854.80
(3) Total earnings.	——	(9) Net amount paid. . . .	36,948.70

Deductions:

Accounts debited:

(4) FICA tax	2,697.50	(10) Factory Wages	33,740.60
(5) Income tax withheld	5,801.70	(11) Sales Salaries	——
(6) Medical insurance. .	469.00	(12) Office Salaries	3,045.00

(a) Determine the totals omitted in lines (1), (3), (7), and (11). (b) Present the journal entry to record the payroll. (c) Present the entry to record the voucher for the payroll. (d) Present the entry to record the payment of the payroll. (e) From the data given in this exercise and your answer to part (a), would you conclude that this payroll was paid sometime during the first few weeks of the calendar year? Explain.

9-24. According to a summary of the payroll of Garcia Publishing Co., the amount of earnings for the four weekly payrolls paid in December of the current year was $480,000, of which $40,000 was not subject to FICA tax and $466,000 was not subject to state and federal unemployment taxes. (a) Determine the employer's payroll taxes expense for the month, using the following rates: FICA, 7%; state unemployment, 4.8%; federal unemployment, .8%. (b) Present the journal entry to record the accrual of payroll taxes for the month of December.

9-25. Bryant Corporation maintains a funded pension plan for its employees. The plan requires quarterly installments to be paid to the funding agent, Crawford Insurance Company, by the fifteenth of the month following the end of each quarter. If for the quarter ending December 31 the normal pension cost is $28,000, prepare entries to record (a) the accrued pension liability on December 31 and (b) the payment to the funding agent on January 15.

9-26. Bingham Co. issues a 120-day, non-interest-bearing note for $80,000 to Republic Bank and Trust Co., and the bank discounts the note at 15%. (a) Present the maker's entries to record (1) issuance of the note and (2) payment of the note at maturity. (b) Present the payee's entries to record (1) receipt of the note and (2) receipt of payment of the note at maturity.

9-27. In negotiating a 90-day loan, an enterprise has the option of either (1) issuing a $150,000, non-interest-bearing note that will be discounted at the rate of 16%, or (2) issuing a $150,000 note that bears interest at the rate of 16% and that will be accepted at face value.
    (a) Determine the amount of the interest expense for each option.
    (b) Determine the amount of the proceeds for each option.
    (c) Indicate the option that is more favorable to the borrower.

9–28. On October 1, Village West purchased land for $250,000 and a building for $600,000, paying $170,000 cash and issuing a 14% note for the balance, secured by a mortgage on the property. The terms of the note provide for seventeen semiannual payments of $40,000 on the principal plus the interest accrued from the date of the preceding payment. Present the entry to record (a) the transaction on October 1, (b) the adjusting entry on December 31 for accrued interest, (c) the reversing entry on January 1, (d) the payment of the first installment on March 31, and (e) the payment of the second installment the following September 30.

Problems

9–29. The president of Schwartz Products is entitled to an annual profit-sharing bonus of 5%. For the current year, income before bonus and income taxes is $206,000 and income taxes are estimated at 40% of income before income taxes.

Instructions:

(1) Determine the amount of bonus, assuming that:
   (a) The bonus is based on income before deductions for bonus and income taxes.
   (b) The bonus is based on income after deduction for bonus but before deduction for income taxes.
   (c) The bonus is based on income after deduction for income taxes but before deduction for bonus.
   (d) The bonus is based on income after deduction for both bonus and income taxes.
(2) (a) Which bonus plan would the president prefer? (b) Would this plan always be the president's choice, regardless of Schwartz Products' income level?

9–30. The following information relative to the payroll for the week ended December 30 was obtained from the records of C. H. Beal Inc.:

Salaries:

Sales salaries	$85,800
Warehouse salaries	18,480
Office salaries	9,220
	$113,500

Deductions:

Income tax withheld	$17,150
U.S. savings bonds	1,200
Group insurance	950
FICA tax withheld totals the same amount as the employer's tax.	

Tax rates assumed:
FICA, 7%
State unemployment (employer only), 4.2%
Federal unemployment, .8%

Instructions:

    (1) Assuming that the payroll for the last week of the year is to be paid on December 31, present the following entries:

        (a) December 30, to record the payroll. Of the total payroll for the last week of the year, $84,500 is subject to FICA tax and $6,000 is subject to unemployment compensation taxes.

        (b) December 30, to record the employer's payroll taxes on the payroll to be paid on December 31.

    (2) Assuming that the payroll for the last week of the year is to be paid on January 3 of the following fiscal year, present the following entries:

        (a) December 31, to record the payroll.

        (b) January 3, to record the employer's payroll taxes on the payroll to be paid on January 3.

9–31. The following accounts, with the balances indicated, appear in the ledger of Monico Company on December 1 of the current year:

212 Salaries Payable	————
213 FICA Tax Payable	$ 14,160
214 Employees Federal Income Tax Payable	37,600
215 Employees State Income Tax Payable	11,240
216 State Unemployment Tax Payable	1,460
217 Federal Unemployment Tax Payable	306
218 Bond Deductions Payable	640
219 Medical Insurance Payable	3,280
611 Sales Salaries Expense	531,300
711 Officers Salaries Expense	261,800
712 Office Salaries Expense	68,810
719 Payroll Taxes Expense	82,340

The following transactions relating to payroll, payroll deductions, and payroll taxes occurred during December:

Dec. 3. Prepared Voucher No. 415 for $640 to purchase United States savings bonds for employees.

      4. Issued Check No. 621 in payment of Voucher No. 415.

    11. Prepared a journal entry to record the biweekly payroll. A summary of the payroll record follows:

        Deductions: FICA tax, $2,410; federal income tax withheld, $6,640; state income tax withheld, $1,920; bond deductions, $315; medical insurance deductions, $480.

      Salary distribution: sales, $25,400; officers, $12,900; office, $3,200.

      Net amount: $29,735.

    11. Prepared Voucher No. 418 for the net amount of the biweekly payroll.

    11. Issued Check No. 627 in payment of Voucher No. 418.

    14. Prepared Voucher No. 423 for $51,760 for the amount of employees' federal income tax and FICA tax due on December 15.

    14. Issued Check No. 633 in payment of Voucher No. 423.

    18. Prepared Voucher No. 429 for $3,280 for the semiannual premium on the group medical insurance policy.

    21. Issued Check No. 639 in payment of Voucher No. 429.

    26. Prepared a journal entry to record the biweekly payroll. A summary of the payroll record follows:

Deductions: FICA tax, $2,133; federal income tax withheld, $6,342; state income tax withheld, $1,845; bond deductions, $315.
Salary distribution: sales, $23,540; officers, $12,900; office, $3,200.
Net amount: $29,005.

Dec. 26. Prepared Voucher No. 444 for the net amount of the biweekly payroll.

28. Issued Check No. 671 in payment of Voucher No. 444.

30. Prepared Voucher No. 461 for $630 to purchase United States savings bonds for employees.

30. Issued Check No. 680 in payment of Voucher No. 461.

30. Prepared Voucher No. 462 for $11,240 for employees' state income tax due on December 31.

30. Issued Check No. 681 in payment of Voucher No. 462.

31. Prepared a journal entry to record the employer's payroll taxes on earnings paid in December. Taxable earnings for the two payrolls, according to the payroll records, are as follows: subject to FICA tax, $64,900; subject to unemployment compensation tax, $8,500. Assume the following tax rates: FICA, 7%; state unemployment, 3.8%; federal unemployment, .8%.

Instructions:

(1) Record the transactions in a journal.

(2) Journalize the adjusting entry on December 31 to record salaries for the incomplete payroll period. Salaries accrued are as follows: sales salaries, $8,740; officers salaries, $5,160; office salaries, $1,280. The payroll taxes are immaterial and are not accrued.

9–32. Carey Company began business on January 2 of last year. Salaries were paid to employees on the last day of each month, and both FICA tax and federal income tax were withheld in the required amounts. All required payroll tax reports were filed and the correct amount of payroll taxes was remitted by the company for the calendar year. Before the Wage and Tax Statements (Form W-2) could be prepared for distribution to employees and filing with the Social Security Administration, the employees' earnings records were inadvertently destroyed.

None of the employees resigned or were discharged during the year, and there were no changes in salary rates. The FICA tax was withheld at the rate of 7% on the first $40,000 of salary. Data on dates of employment, salary rates, and employees' income taxes withheld, which are summarized as follows, were obtained from personnel records and payroll records.

Employee	Date First Employed	Monthly Salary	Monthly Income Tax Withheld
Altman	Mar. 16	$2,800	$ 471.20
Bayer	Nov. 1	2,500	394.25
Gibbons	Jan. 2	4,200	895.60
Klein	July 16	3,400	636.50
Maxwell	Jan. 2	5,400	1,374.10
Rodgers	May 1	3,600	652.30
Tang	Feb. 16	4,000	864.10

Instructions:

(1) Determine the amounts to be reported on each employee's Wage and Tax Statement (Form W-2) for the year, arranging the data in the following form:

Employee	Gross Earnings	Federal Income Tax Withheld	Earnings Subject to FICA Tax	FICA Tax Withheld

(2) Determine the following employer payroll taxes for the year: (a) FICA; (b) state unemployment compensation at 4.6% on first $7,000; (c) federal unemployment compensation at .8% on first $7,000; (d) total.

(3) In a manner similar to the illustrations in this chapter, develop four algorithms to describe the computations required to determine the four amounts in part (1), using the following symbols:

n = Number of payroll periods
g = Monthly gross earnings
f = Monthly federal income tax withheld
G = Total gross earnings
F = Total federal income tax withheld
T = Total earnings subject to FICA tax
S = Total FICA tax withheld

9–33. The following items were selected from among the transactions completed by Califano Co. during the current year:

Feb. 10. Purchased merchandise on account from Tudor Co., $5,200.

Mar. 10. Purchased merchandise on account from Patrick Co., $4,800.

12. Issued a 30 day, 12% note for $5,200 to Tudor Co., on account.

20. Paid Patrick Co. for the invoice of March 10, less 2% discount.

Apr. 11. Paid Tudor Co. the amount owed on the note of March 12.

June 15. Borrowed $8,000 from Merchants National Bank, issuing a 90-day, 13% note for that amount.

25. Issued a 120-day, non-interest-bearing note for $20,000 to Dubuque State Bank. The bank discounted the note at the rate of 15%.

Sept. 13. Paid Merchants National Bank the interest due on the note of June 15 and renewed the loan by issuing a new 30-day, 15% note for $8,000. (Record both the debit and credit to the notes payable account.)

Oct. 13. Paid Merchants National Bank the amount due on the note of September 13.

23. Paid Dubuque State Bank the amount due on the note of June 25.

Dec. 1. Purchased office equipment from Weaver Equipment Co. for $31,250, paying $7,250 and issuing a series of ten 14% notes for $2,400 each, coming due at 30-day intervals.

31. Paid the amount due Weaver Equipment Co. on the first note in the series issued on December 1.

Instructions:

(1) Record the transactions.

(2) Determine the total amount of interest accrued as of December 31 on the nine notes owed to Weaver Equipment Co.

(3) Record the adjusting entry for the accrued interest at December 31 and the reversing entry on January 1.

(4) Assume that a single note for $24,000 had been issued on December 1 instead of the series of ten notes, and that its terms required principal payments of $2,400 each 30 days, with interest at 14% on the principal balance before applying the $2,400 payment. Determine the amount that would have been due and payable on December 31.

Alternate Problems

9–29A. The president of Minish Products is entitled to an annual profit-sharing bonus of 4%. For the current year, income before bonus and income taxes is $480,000 and income taxes are estimated at 40% of income before income taxes.

Instructions:

(1) Determine the amount of bonus, assuming that:
  (a) The bonus is based on income before deductions for bonus and income taxes.
  (b) The bonus is based on income after deduction for bonus but before deduction for income taxes.
  (c) The bonus is based on income after deduction for income taxes but before deduction for bonus.
  (d) The bonus is based on income after deduction for both bonus and income taxes.

(2) (a) Which bonus plan would the president prefer? (b) Would this plan always be the president's choice, regardless of Minish Products' income level?

9–30A. The following information relative to the payroll for the week ended December 30 was obtained from the records of E. Thurmond Inc.:

Salaries:		Deductions:	
Sales salaries.........	$109,200	Income tax withheld..........	$23,850
Warehouse salaries....	16,280	U. S. savings bonds..........	2,400
Office salaries.........	7,020	Group insurance............	1,800
	$132,500	FICA tax withheld totals the same amount as the employer's tax.	

Tax rates assumed:
  FICA, 7%
  State unemployment (employer only), 3.8%
  Federal unemployment, .8%

Instructions:

(1) Assuming that the payroll for the last week of the year is to be paid on December 31, present the following entries:
  (a) December 30, to record the payroll. Of the total payroll for the last week of the year, $92,800 is subject to FICA tax and $10,000 is subject to unemployment compensation taxes.
  (b) December 30, to record the employer's payroll taxes on the payroll to be paid on December 31.

(2) Assuming that the payroll for the last week of the year is to be paid on January 4 of the following year, present the following entries:
  (a) December 30, to record the payroll.
  (b) January 4, to record the employer's payroll taxes on the payroll to be paid on January 4.

9–32A. Jaffe Company began business on March 1 of last year. Salaries were paid to employees on the last day of each month, and both FICA tax and federal income tax were withheld in the required amounts. All required payroll tax reports were filed and the correct amount of payroll taxes was remitted by the company for the calendar year. Before the Wage and Tax Statements (Form W-2) could be prepared for distribution to employees and filing with the Social Security Administration, the employees' earnings records were inadvertently destroyed.

None of the employees resigned or were discharged during the year, and there were no changes in salary rates. The FICA tax was withheld at the rate of 7% on the first $40,000 of salary. Data on dates of employment, salary rates, and employees' income taxes withheld, which are summarized as follows, were obtained from personnel records and payroll records.

Employee	Date First Employed	Monthly Salary	Monthly Income Tax Withheld
Choi	June 2	$3,500	$ 637.25
Gramm	Mar. 15	4,200	854.50
Kaufman	Dec. 1	3,800	748.15
Marlin	Mar. 1	5,800	1,492.75
Rodriguez	Oct. 16	3,600	652.30
Sherman	Apr. 15	2,800	461.10
Wylie	Mar. 1	5,200	1,261.40

Instructions:

(1) Determine the amounts to be reported on each employee's Wage and Tax Statement (Form W-2) for the year, arranging the data in the following form:

Employee	Gross Earnings	Federal Income Tax Withheld	Earnings Subject to FICA Tax	FICA Tax Withheld

(2) Determine the following employer payroll taxes for the year: (a) FICA; (b) state unemployment compensation at 3.8% on first $7,000; (c) federal unemployment compensation at .8% on first $7,000; (d) total.

(3) In a manner similar to the illustrations in this chapter, develop four algorithms to describe the computations required to determine the four amounts in part (1), using the following symbols:

n = Number of payroll periods
g = Monthly gross earnings
f = Monthly federal income tax withheld
G = Total gross earnings
F = Total federal income tax withheld
T = Total earnings subject to FICA tax
S = Total FICA tax withheld

9–33A. The following items were selected from among the transactions completed by Valentine Co. during the current year:

Mar. 2. Purchased merchandise on account from J. W. Stokes Co., $3,600.

8. Purchased merchandise on account from York Co., $7,000.

12. Paid J. W. Stokes Co. for the invoice of March 2, less 3% discount.

Apr. 1. Issued a 60-day, 12% note for $7,000 to York Co. on account.

May 22. Issued a 120-day, non-interest-bearing note for $30,000 to Garden City Bank. The bank discounted the note at the rate of 14%.

31. Paid York Co. the amount owed on the note of April 1.

Aug. 5. Borrowed $7,500 from First Financial Corporation, issuing a 60-day, 14% note for that amount.

Sept. 19. Paid Garden City Bank the amount due on the note of May 22.

Oct. 4. Paid First Financial Corporation the interest due on the note of August 5 and renewed the loan by issuing a new 30-day, 16% note for $7,500. (Record both the debit and the credit to the notes payable account.)

Nov. 3. Paid First Financial Corporation the amount due on the note of October 4.

15. Purchased office equipment from Powell Equipment Brokers Inc. for $24,000, paying $3,000 and issuing a series of seven 12% notes for $3,000 each, coming due at 30-day intervals.

Dec. 15. Paid the amount due Powell Equipment Brokers Inc. on the first note in the series issued on November 15.

Instructions:

(1) Record the transactions.

(2) Determine the total amount of interest accrued as of December 31 on the six notes owed to Powell Equipment Brokers Inc.

(3) Record the adjusting journal entry for the accrued interest at December 31 and the reversing entry on January 1.

(4) Assume that a single note for $21,000 had been issued on November 15 instead of the series of seven notes, and that its terms required principal payments of $3,000 each 30 days, with interest at 12% on the principal balance before applying the $3,000 payment. Determine the amount that would have been due and payable on December 15.

Mini-Case

9–34. Your father recently retired as president of the family-owned business, Keane Inc. A new president was recruited by an executive search firm under an employment contract calling for an annual base salary of $50,000 plus a bonus of 15% of income after deducting the bonus but before deducting income taxes.

In 1986, the first full year under the new president, Keane Inc. reported income of $805,000 before deducting the bonus and income taxes. On January 2, 1987, the new president was fired, and he demanded immediate payment of a $120,750 bonus for 1986.

Your father was concerned about the accounting practices used during 1986 and has asked you to help him in reviewing the accounting records before the bonus is paid. Upon investigation, you have discovered the following facts:

(a) The payroll for December 26–31, 1986, was not accrued at the end of the year. The salaries for the six-day period and the applicable payroll tax rates are as follows:

Sales salaries	$4,800
Warehouse salaries	3,200
Office salaries	2,000
FICA tax	7%
State unemployment tax (employer only)	3.2%
Federal unemployment tax	.8%

The payroll was paid on January 10, 1987, for the period December 26, 1986, through January 8, 1987.

(b) The semiannual pension cost of $20,000 was not accrued for the last half of 1986. The pension cost was paid to First Equity Insurance Company on January 10, 1987, and was recorded by a debit to Pension Expense and a credit to Cash for $20,000.

(c) On December 1, 1986, Keane Inc. purchased a one-year insurance policy for $2,400, debiting the cost to Prepaid Insurance. No adjusting entry was made for insurance expired at December 31, 1986.

(d) Keane Inc. leases a storeroom in a local shopping mall, which requires a monthly rental of $2,000, payable the first of each month, plus 2% of net sales of the storeroom, payable by the 10th of the following month. The net sales for December were $600,000. The lease payment of 2% of storeroom sales was not accrued on December 31, 1986. On January 10, 1987, the lease payment of $12,000 was made and was recorded as a debit to Rent Expense and a credit to Cash.

Instructions:

(1) Based on reported 1986 income of $805,000 before deducting the bonus and income taxes, was the president's calculation of the $120,750 bonus correct? Explain.

(2) What accounting errors were made in 1986 which would affect the amount of the president's bonus?

(3) Based on the employment contract and your answer to (2), what is the correct amount of the president's bonus for 1986, rounded to the nearest dollar?

(4) How much did the president's demand for a $120,750 bonus exceed the correct amount of the bonus under the employment contract?

(5) Late in 1987, Keane Inc. paid the president the amount of the bonus computed in (3), after which the president sued Keane Inc. for breach of contract. The suit requested compensatory and punitive damages of $500,000. How should the lawsuit be reported on the 1987 financial statements?

(6) Describe the major advantage and disadvantage of using profit-sharing bonuses in employment contracts.

1. **B** The amount of net pay of $703 (answer B) is determined as follows:

Gross pay:		
40 hours at $20	$800	
5 hours at $30	150	$950
Deductions:		
Federal income tax withheld	$212	
FICA ($500 × .07)	35	247
Net pay		$703

2. A Employers are required to withhold a portion of the earnings of their employees for payment of federal income taxes (answer A). Generally, federal (answer B) and state (answer C) unemployment compensation taxes are levied against the employer only and thus are not deducted from employee earnings.

3. D The employer incurs operating costs for FICA tax (answer A), federal unemployment compensation tax (answer B), and state unemployment compensation tax (answer C). These costs add significantly to the total labor costs for most businesses.

4. C Liabilities due within a year should be presented as current liabilities and those with a more distant future date should be presented as long-term liabilities on the balance sheet. Therefore the 12 monthly payments of $1,000 each, for a total of $12,000, represent a current liability and the remaining $38,000 is a long-term liability (answer C).

5. B The net amount available to a borrower from discounting a note payable is termed the proceeds. The proceeds of $4,900 (answer B) is determined as follows:

Face amount of note	$5,000
Less discount ($5,000 × 12/100 × 60/360)	100
Proceeds	$4,900

PART 3

Accounting for Equity Rights

Profit-Making Business Organizations

Of the three types of business organizations, the sole proprietorship is the most common and the corporation is the most dominant in terms of dollars of business activity. These characteristics of types of business organizations are indicated by the following charts:

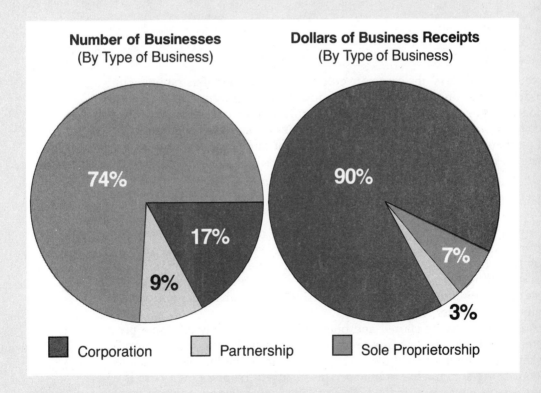

Number of Businesses
(By Type of Business)

74%

17%

9%

Dollars of Business Receipts
(By Type of Business)

90%

7%

3%

■ Corporation   □ Partnership   ■ Sole Proprietorship

SOURCE   U.S. Bureau of the Census, *Statistical Abstract of the United States: 1985*, 105th edition (Washington, DC, 1984), p. 516.

CHAPTER 10

Forms of Business Organization

CHAPTER OBJECTIVES

Describe and illustrate the accounting for sole proprietorships and partnerships.

Describe and illustrate the accounting for corporate capital.

Describe and illustrate the computation of equity per share of stock.

In preceding chapters, the corporate enterprise was used in illustrations. The transactions affecting the stockholders' equity of these enterprises focused on basic accounting concepts and principles. In this chapter, consideration will be given to the two other types of business organizations — sole proprietorships and partnerships. In addition, the accounting for more complex transactions affecting stockholders' equity will be discussed.

CHARACTERISTICS OF SOLE PROPRIETORSHIPS

A sole proprietorship is a business enterprise owned by one individual. Approximately 80% of all business enterprises (sole proprietorships, partnerships, and corporations) in the United States are sole proprietorships. However, sole proprietorships account for only 8% of all business revenues. These statistics indicate that sole proprietorships, although numerous, consist mostly of small enterprises.

A business may be started and operated relatively easily as a sole proprietorship. There are few legal restrictions to establishing a sole proprietorship, and the individual owner can usually make all business decisions without being accountable to others. This ability to be one's own boss is a major reason why many individuals organize their business enterprises as sole proprietorships.

A sole proprietorship is a separate entity for accounting purposes, and when the owner dies or retires, the sole proprietorship ceases to exist. For federal income tax purposes, however, the sole proprietorship is not treated as a separate taxable entity. The income (or loss) is allocated to the owner and is included on the owner's personal tax return.

A primary disadvantage of a sole proprietorship may be the difficulty in raising funds. Investment in the business is limited to the amounts that the owner can provide from personal resources, plus any additional amounts that can be raised through borrowing. The owner is also personally liable for any debts of the business. Thus, if the business becomes insolvent, creditors have rights to the personal assets of the owner, regardless of the amount of the owner's investment in the enterprise.

ACCOUNTING FOR SOLE PROPRIETORSHIPS

Since the sole proprietorship is a separate business entity for accounting purposes, the transactions of the sole proprietorship must be kept separate from the personal financial affairs of the owner. Only in this way can the financial condition and the results of operations of the sole proprietorship be accurately measured and reported.

The day-to-day accounting entries for a sole proprietorship are much the same as for a corporation. The primary differences in accounting for a sole proprietorship include the use of an owner's **capital account,** rather than a capital stock account, to record investments in the enterprise. In addition, this capital account, rather than a retained earnings account, is used to record changes in owner's equity from net income or net loss. Finally, instead of a dividends account, distributions to the owner are recorded in the owner's **drawing account.** At the end of the period, the drawing account is closed to the owner's capital account, and a statement of owner's equity is prepared. The statement of owner's equity thus summarizes changes in owner's equity that have occurred during a specific period of time.

CHARACTERISTICS OF PARTNERSHIPS

The Uniform Partnership Act, which has been adopted by more than ninety percent of the states, defines a partnership as "an association of two or more persons to carry on as co-owners a business for profit." The partnership form of business organization is widely used for comparatively small businesses that wish to take advantage of the combined capital, managerial talent, and experience of two or more persons. In many cases, the alternative to securing the amount of investment needed or the various skills needed to operate a business is to adopt the corporate form of organization. The typical corporate form of organization is sometimes not available, however, to certain professions because of restrictions in state laws or in professional codes of ethics. Hence, a group of physicians, attorneys, or certified public accountants who wish to band together to practice a profession often organize as a partnership. Medical and legal partnerships made up of 20 or more partners are not unusual, and the number of partners in some CPA firms exceeds 1,000.

Partnerships have several characteristics that have accounting implications. These characteristics are described in the following paragraphs.

A partnership has a **limited life.** Dissolution of a partnership occurs whenever a partner ceases to be a member of the firm for any reason, including withdrawal, bankruptcy, incapacity, or death. Similarly, admission of a new partner dissolves the old partnership. In case of dissolution, a new partnership must be formed if the operations of the business are to be continued without interruption. This is the usual situation with professional partnerships. Their composition may change often as new partners are admitted and others are retired.

Another characteristic of a partnership is **unlimited liability.** Each partner is individually liable to creditors for debts incurred by the partnership. Thus, if a partnership becomes insolvent, the partners must contribute sufficient personal assets to settle the debts of the partnership.

Partners have **co-ownership of partnership property.** The property invested in a partnership by a partner becomes the property of all the partners jointly. Upon dissolution of the partnership and distribution of its assets, the partners' claims against the assets are measured by the amount of the balances in their capital accounts.

A significant right of partners is **participation in income** of the partnership. Net income and net loss are distributed among the partners according to their agreement. In the absence of any agreement, all partners share equally. If the agreement specifies profit distribution but is silent as to losses, the losses are shared in the same manner as profits.

A partnership is created by a voluntary contract containing all the elements essential to any other enforceable contract. It is not necessary that this contract be in writing, nor even that its terms be specifically expressed. However, good business practice dictates that the contract should be in writing and should clearly express the intentions of the partners. The contract, known as the **articles of partnership** or **partnership agreement,** should contain provisions regarding such matters as the amount of investment to be made, limitations on withdrawals of funds, the manner in which net income and net loss are to be divided, and the admission and withdrawal of partners.

ACCOUNTING FOR PARTNERSHIPS

Most of the day-to-day accounting for a partnership is the same as the accounting for a sole proprietorship and a corporation. It is in the areas of the formation, income distribution, dissolution, and liquidation of partnerships that transactions peculiar to partnerships arise.

Recording Investments

A separate entry is made for the investment of each partner in a partnership. The various assets contributed by a partner are debited to the proper asset accounts. If liabilities are assumed by the partnership, the appropriate liability accounts are credited. The partner's capital account is credited for the net amount.

To illustrate the entry to record an initial investment, assume that Robert A. Stevens and Earl S. Foster, who are sole owners of competing hardware stores, agree to combine their businesses in a partnership. Each is to contribute certain amounts of cash and other business assets. It is also agreed that the partnership is to assume the liabilities of the separate businesses. The entry to record the assets contributed and the liabilities transferred by Robert A. Stevens is as follows:

Apr.	1	Cash	7,200	
		Accounts Receivable	16,300	
		Merchandise Inventory	28,700	
		Store Equipment	5,400	
		Office Equipment	1,500	
		Allowance for Doubtful Accounts		1,500
		Accounts Payable		2,600
		Robert A. Stevens, Capital		55,000

The monetary amounts at which the noncash assets are stated are those agreed upon by the partners. In arriving at an appropriate amount for such assets, consideration should be given to their market values at the time the partnership is formed. The values agreed upon represent the acquisition cost to the accounting entity created by the formation of the partnership. These amounts may differ from the balances appearing in the accounts of the separate businesses before the partnership was organized.

Division of Net Income or Net Loss

As in the case of a sole proprietorship, the net income of a partnership may be said to include a return for the services of the owners, for the capital invested, and for economic or pure profit. Partners are not legally employees of the partnership, nor are their capital contributions a loan. If each of two partners is to contribute equal services and amounts of capital, an equal sharing in partnership net income would be equitable. But if one partner is to contribute a larger portion of capital than the other, provision for unequal capital contributions should be given recognition in the agreement for dividing net income. Or, if the services of one partner are much more valuable to the partnership than those of the other, provision for unequal service contributions should be given recognition in their agreement.

To illustrate the division of net income and the accounting for this division, assume that Stone and Mills (1) are allowed monthly salaries of $2,500 and $2,000 respectively; (2) are allowed interest at 12% on capital balances at January 1 of the current fiscal year, which amounted to $80,000 and $60,000 respectively; and (3) divide the remainder of net income equally. A report of the division of net income may be presented as a separate statement accompanying the balance sheet and the income statement, or it may be added at the bottom of the income statement. If the latter procedure is adopted, the lower part of the income statement would appear as follows:

Net income			$75,000
Division of net income:	J. L. Stone	C. R. Mills	Total
Salary allowance	$30,000	$24,000	$54,000
Interest allowance	9,600	7,200	16,800
Remaining income	2,100	2,100	4,200
Net income	$41,700	$33,300	$75,000

The division of net income is recorded as a closing entry, regardless of whether the partners actually withdraw any amounts from the partnership. The entry for the division of net income is as follows:

Dec. 31	Income Summary	75,000	
	J. L. Stone, Capital		41,700
	C. R. Mills, Capital		33,300

If Stone and Mills had withdrawn any amounts, the withdrawals would have accumulated as debits in the drawing accounts during the year. At the end of the year, the debit balances in their drawing accounts would be transferred to their respective capital accounts.

In the above illustration, the net income exceeded the sum of the allowances for salary and interest. If the net income is less than the total of the special allowances, the "remaining balance" will be a negative figure that must be divided among the partners as though it were a net loss. The effect of this situation may be illustrated by assuming the same salary and interest allowances as in the preceding illustration, but changing the amount of net income to $50,000. The salary and interest allowances to Stone total $39,600 and the comparable figure for Mills is $31,200. The sum of these amounts, $70,800, exceeds the net income of $50,000 by $20,800. It is therefore necessary to deduct $10,400 (½ of $20,800) from each partner's share to arrive at the net income, as follows:

Net income			$50,000
Division of net income:	J. L. Stone	C. R. Mills	Total
Salary allowance	$30,000	$24,000	$54,000
Interest allowance	9,600	7,200	16,800
Total	$39,600	$31,200	$70,800
Excess of allowances over income	10,400	10,400	20,800
Net income	$29,200	$20,800	$50,000

In closing Income Summary at the end of the year, $29,200 would be credited to J. L. Stone, Capital, and $20,800 would be credited to C. R. Mills, Capital.

Partnership Dissolution

One of the basic characteristics of the partnership form of organization is its limited life. Any change in the personnel of the membership results in the dissolution of the partnership. Thus, admission of a new partner dissolves the old firm. Similarly, death, bankruptcy, or withdrawal of a partner causes dissolution.

Dissolution of the partnership is not necessarily followed by the winding up of the affairs of the business. For example, a partnership composed of two partners may admit an additional partner. Or if one of three partners in a business withdraws, the remaining two partners may continue to operate the business.

Admission of a Partner

An additional person may be admitted to a partnership through either of two procedures:

1. Purchase of an interest from one or more of the current partners.
2. Contribution of assets to the partnership.

When the first procedure is followed, the capital interest of the incoming partner is obtained from current partners, and neither the total assets nor the total capital of the business is affected. When the second procedure is followed, both the total assets and the total capital of the business are increased.

Admission by Purchase of an Interest

When an additional person is admitted to a firm by purchasing an interest from one or more of the partners, the purchase price is paid directly to the selling partners. Payment is for partnership equity owned by the partners as individuals, and hence the cash or other consideration paid is not recorded in the accounts of the partnership. The only entry needed is the transfer of the proper amounts of capital from the capital accounts of the selling partners to the capital account established for the incoming partner.

As an example, assume that partners Tom Andrews and George Bell have capital balances of $50,000 each. On June 1, each sells one fifth of his respective capital interest to Joe Canter for $10,000 in cash. The only entry required in the partnership accounts is as follows:

June 1	Tom Andrews, Capital....................	10,000	
	George Bell, Capital	10,000	
	Joe Canter, Capital		20,000

The effect of the transaction on the partnership accounts is presented in the following diagram:

Partnership Accounts

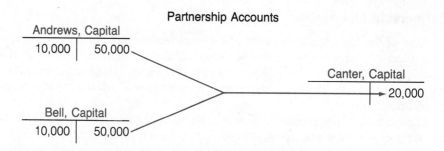

The foregoing entry is made regardless of the amount paid by Canter for the one-fifth interest. If the firm had been earning a high rate of return on the investment and Canter had been very eager to obtain the one-fifth interest, he might have paid considerably more than $20,000. Had other circumstances prevailed, he might have acquired the one-fifth interest for considerably less than $20,000. In either event, the entry to transfer the capital interests would not be affected.

After the admission of Canter, the total capital of the firm is $100,000, in which he has a one-fifth interest, or $20,000. It does not necessarily follow that he will be entitled to a similar share of the partnership net income. Division of net income or net loss will be in accordance with the new partnership agreement.

Admission by Contribution of Assets

Instead of buying an interest from the current partners, the incoming partner may contribute assets to the partnership. In this case, both the assets and the capital of the firm are increased. To illustrate, assume that Donald Lewis and Gerald Morton are partners with capital accounts of $35,000 and $25,000 respectively. On June 1, Sharon Nelson invests $20,000 cash in the business, for which she is to receive an ownership equity of $20,000. The entry to record this transaction is:

```
June  1  Cash....................................  20,000
              Sharon Nelson, Capital .................          20,000
```

The major difference between the circumstances of the admission of Nelson above and of Canter in the preceding example may be observed by comparing the following diagram with the one at the top of this page:

Partnership Accounts

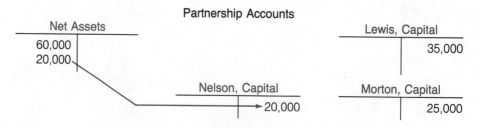

With the admission of Nelson, the total capital of the new partnership becomes $80,000, of which she has a one-fourth interest, or $20,000. The extent of her participation in partnership net income will be governed by the articles of partnership.

Withdrawal of a Partner

When a partner retires or for some other reason wishes to withdraw from the firm, one or more of the remaining partners may purchase the withdrawing partner's interest and the business may be continued without apparent interruption. In such cases, settlement for the purchase and sale is made between the partners as individuals. The only entry required by the partnership is a debit to the capital account of the partner withdrawing and a credit to the capital account of the partner or partners acquiring the interest.

If the settlement with the withdrawing partner is made by the partnership, the effect is to reduce the assets and the capital of the firm. To determine the ownership equity of the withdrawing partner, the asset accounts should be adjusted to current market prices. The net amount of the adjustments should be allocated among the capital accounts of the partners according to the income-sharing ratio. In the event that the cash or the other available assets are insufficient to make complete payment at the time of withdrawal, a liability account should be credited for the balance owed to the withdrawing partner.

Death of a Partner

The death of a partner dissolves the partnership. In the absence of any contrary agreement, the accounts should be closed as of the date of death, and the net income for the fractional part of the year should be transferred to the capital accounts. It is not unusual, however, for the partnership agreement to stipulate that the accounts remain open to the end of the fiscal year or until the affairs are wound up, if that should occur earlier. The net income of the entire period is then allocated, as provided by the agreement, to the respective periods occurring before and after dissolution.

The balance in the capital account of the deceased partner is then transferred to a liability account with the deceased's estate. The surviving partner or partners may continue the business or the affairs may be wound up. If the former course is followed, the procedures for settling with the estate will conform to those outlined earlier for the withdrawal of a partner from the business.

Liquidation of a Partnership

When a partnership goes out of business, it usually sells most of the assets. As cash is realized, it is applied first to the payment of the claims of creditors. After all liabilities have been paid, the remaining cash is distributed to the partners, based on their ownership equities as indicated by their capital accounts.

If the assets are sold piecemeal, the liquidation process may extend over a considerable period of time. This creates no special problem, however, if the distribution of cash to the partners is delayed until all of the assets have been sold.

As a basis for illustration, assume that Farley, Greene, and Hill decide to liquidate their partnership. Their income-sharing ratio is 5:3:2. After discontinuing the ordinary business operations and closing the accounts, the following summary of the general ledger is prepared:

Cash	$11,000	
Noncash Assets	64,000	
Liabilities		$ 9,000
Jane Farley, Capital		22,000
Brad Greene, Capital		22,000
Alice Hill, Capital		22,000
Total	$75,000	$75,000

For the sake of brevity, it will be assumed that all noncash assets are disposed of in a single transaction and that all liabilities are paid at one time. In addition, Noncash Assets and Liabilities will be used as account titles in place of the various asset, contra asset, and liability accounts that in actual practice would be affected by the transactions.

Farley, Greene, and Hill sell all noncash assets for $72,000, realizing a gain of $8,000 ($72,000 − $64,000). The gain is divided among the capital accounts in the income-sharing ratio of 5:3:2, the liabilities are paid, and the remaining cash is distributed to the partners according to the balances in their capital accounts. A tabular summary of the transactions follows:

						Capital	
					J. Farley	B. Greene	A. Hill
	Cash +	Noncash Assets =	Liabilities +	50% +	30% +	20%
Balances before realization	$11,000	$64,000	$ 9,000	$22,000	$22,000	$22,000
Sale of assets and division of gain	+72,000	−64,000		+ 4,000	+ 2,400	+ 1,600
Balances after realization	$83,000		$ 9,000	$26,000	$24,400	$23,600
Payment of liabilities	− 9,000		− 9,000			
Balances	$74,000			$26,000	$24,400	$23,600
Distribution of cash to partners	−74,000			−26,000	−24,400	−23,600

As shown in the foregoing illustration, the distribution of the cash among the partners is determined by reference to the balances of their respective capital accounts after the gain on realization has been allocated. Under no circumstances should the income-sharing ratio be used as a basis for distributing the cash.

If the sale of assets were to result in a loss, the loss would be divided among the partners' capital accounts in the income-sharing ratio. The cash would then be applied first to the payment of the claims of creditors and the remainder would be distributed to the partners according to the balances in their respective capital accounts.

CHARACTERISTICS OF A CORPORATION

In the Dartmouth College case in 1819, Chief Justice Marshall stated: "A corporation is an artificial being, invisible, intangible, and existing only in contemplation of the law." The concept underlying this definition has become the foundation for the prevailing legal doctrine that a corporation is an artificial person, created by law and having a distinct existence separate and apart from the natural persons who are responsible for its creation and operation. Almost all large business enterprises in the United States are organized as corporations.

As a legal entity, the corporation has certain characteristics that make it different from other types of business organizations. The most important characteristics with accounting implications are described briefly in the following paragraphs.

A corporation has a **separate legal existence.** It may acquire, own, and dispose of property in its corporate name. It may also incur liabilities and enter into other types of contracts according to the provisions of its **charter** (also called **articles of incorporation**).

The ownership of a corporation, of which there may be several categories or classes, is divided into **transferable units** known as **shares of stock.** Each share of stock of a certain class has the same rights and privileges as every other share of the same class. The **stockholders** (also called **shareholders**) may buy and sell shares without interfering with the activities of the corporation. The millions of transactions that occur daily on stock exchanges are independent transactions between buyers and sellers. Thus, in contrast to the partnership, the existence of the corporation is not affected by changes in ownership.

The stockholders of a corporation have **limited liability.** A corporation is responsible for its own acts and obligations, and therefore its creditors usually may not look beyond the assets of the corporation for satisfaction of their claims. Thus, the financial loss that a stockholder may suffer is limited to the amount invested. The phenomenal growth of the corporate form of business would not have been possible without this limited liability feature.

The stockholders, who are, in fact, the owners of the corporation, exercise control over the management of corporate affairs indirectly by electing a **board of directors.** It is the responsibility of the board of directors to meet from time to time to determine the corporate policies and to select the officers who manage the corporation. The following chart shows the **organizational structure** of a corporation:

ORGANIZATIONAL
STRUCTURE OF A
CORPORATE
ENTERPRISE

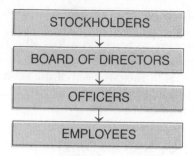

As a separate entity, a corporation is subject to **additional taxes.** It must pay a charter fee to the state at the time of its organization and annual taxes thereafter. If the corporation does business in states other than the one in which it is incorporated, it may also be required to pay annual taxes to such states. The earnings of a corporation may also be subject to a state income tax.

The earnings of a corporation are subject to the federal income tax. When the remaining earnings are distributed to stockholders as dividends, they are again taxed as income to the individuals receiving them. Under certain conditions specified in the Internal Revenue Code, a corporation with a few stockholders may elect to be treated in a manner similar to a partnership for income tax purposes. A corporation electing this optional treatment does not pay federal income taxes. Instead, its stockholders include their distributive shares of corporate income in their own taxable income, regardless of whether the income is distributed to them.

Being a creature of the state and being owned by stockholders who have limited liability, a corporation has less freedom of action than a sole proprietorship and a partnership. There may be **government regulations** in such matters as ownership of real estate, retention of earnings, and purchase of its own stock.

CORPORATE CAPITAL

The owners' equity in a corporation is commonly called **capital, stockholders' equity, shareholders' equity,** or **shareholders' investment.** The two main sources of corporate capital are (1) **paid-in capital,** or investments contributed by the stockholders, and (2) **retained earnings,** or net income retained in the business. As shown in the following illustration, the stockholders' equity section of corporation balance sheets is divided into subsections based on these sources of capital.

Stockholders' Equity

Paid-in capital:	
Common stock	$330,000
Retained earnings	80,000
Total stockholders' equity	$410,000

The capital acquired from the stockholders is recorded in accounts maintained for each class of stock. If there is only one class of stock, the account is entitled Common Stock or Capital Stock.

The retained earnings amount results from transferring the balance in the income summary account to a retained earnings account at the end of a fiscal year. The dividends account, to which distributions of earnings to stockholders have been debited, is also closed to Retained Earnings. If the occurrence of net losses results in a debit balance in Retained Earnings, it is termed a **deficit.** In the stockholders' equity section of the balance sheet, a deficit is deducted from paid-in capital to determine total stockholders' equity.

There are a number of acceptable variants of the term "retained earnings," among which are *earnings retained for use in the business, earnings reinvested in the business, earnings employed in the business,* and *accumulated earnings.* For many years, the term applied to retained earnings was *earned surplus.* However, the use of this term in published financial statements has generally been discontinued.[1] Because of its connotation as an excess, or something left over, "surplus" was sometimes erroneously interpreted by readers of financial statements to mean "cash available for dividends."

CHARACTERISTICS OF STOCK

The general term applied to the shares of ownership of a corporation is **capital stock.** The number of shares that a corporation is *authorized* to issue is set forth in its charter. The term *issued* is applied to the shares issued to the stockholders. A corporation may, under circumstances discussed later in the chapter, reacquire some of the stock that it has issued. The stock remaining in the hands of the stockholders is then referred to as the **stock outstanding.**

The shares of capital stock are often assigned an arbitrary monetary figure, known as **par.** The par amount is printed on the **stock certificate,** which is the evidence of ownership issued to the stockholder. Stock may also be issued without par, in which case it is called **no-par** stock. Many states provide that the board of directors must assign a **stated value** to no-par stock, which makes it similar to par stock.

Because of the limited liability feature, the creditors of a corporation have no claim against the personal assets of stockholders. However, the law requires that some specific minimum contribution by the stockholders be retained by the corporation for the protection of its creditors. This amount, called **legal capital,** varies among the states but usually includes the par or stated value of the shares of capital stock issued.

---

[1]*Accounting Research and Terminology Bulletins — Final Edition,* "Accounting Terminology Bulletins, No. 1, Review and Résumé" (New York: American Institute of Certified Public Accountants, 1961), par. 65–69.

Classes of Stock

The major basic rights that accompany ownership of a share of stock are (1) the right to vote, (2) the right to share in distributions of earnings, (3) the right to maintain the same fractional interest in the corporation by purchasing a proportionate number of shares of any additional issuances of stock (preemptive right),[2] and (4) the right to share in assets upon liquidation.

If a corporation issues only **common stock**, each share has equal rights. In order to appeal to a broader investment market, a corporation may provide for one or more classes of stock with various preferential rights. The preference usually relates to the right to share in distributions of earnings. Such stock is called **preferred stock**.

The board of directors has the sole authority to distribute earnings to the stockholders. When such action is taken, the directors are said to *declare a dividend*. A corporation cannot guarantee that its operations will be profitable and hence it cannot guarantee dividends to its stockholders. Furthermore, the directors have wide discretionary powers in determining the extent to which earnings should be retained by the corporation to provide for expansion, to offset possible future losses, or to provide for other contingencies.

A corporation with both preferred stock and common stock may declare dividends on the common only after it meets the requirements of the stated dividend on the preferred (which may be stated in monetary terms or as a percent of par). To illustrate, assume that a corporation has 1,000 shares of $10 preferred stock (that is, the preferred has a prior claim to an annual $10 per share dividend) and 4,000 shares of common stock outstanding. Assume also that in the first three years of operations, net income was $30,000, $55,000, and $100,000 respectively. The directors authorize the retention of a portion of each year's earnings and the distribution of the remainder. Details of the dividend distribution are presented in the following tabulation:

	First Year	Second Year	Third Year
Net income	$30,000	$55,000	$100,000
Amount retained	10,000	20,000	40,000
Amount distributed	$20,000	$35,000	$ 60,000
Preferred dividend (1,000 shares)	10,000	10,000	10,000
Common dividend (4,000 shares)	$10,000	$25,000	$ 50,000
Dividends per share:			
Preferred	$10.00	$10.00	$10.00
Common	$ 2.50	$ 6.25	$12.50

---

[2]In recent years the stockholders of a significant number of corporations have, by formal action, given up their preemptive rights.

Participating and Nonparticipating Preferred Stock

In the foregoing illustration, the holders of preferred stock received an annual dividend of $10 per share, in contrast to the common stockholders, whose annual per share dividends were $2.50, $6.25, and $12.50 respectively. It is apparent from the example that holders of preferred stock have relatively greater assurance than common stockholders of receiving dividends regularly. On the other hand, holders of common stock have the possibility of receiving larger dividends than preferred stockholders. The preferred stockholders' preferential right to dividends is usually limited to a certain amount, which was assumed to be the case in the preceding example. Such stock is said to be **nonparticipating.**

Preferred stock which provides for the possibility of dividends in excess of a certain amount is said to be **participating.** Preferred shares may participate with common shares to varying degrees, and the contract must be examined to determine the extent of this participation. To illustrate, assume that the contract covering the preferred stock of the corporation in the preceding illustration provides that if the total dividends to be distributed exceed the regular preferred dividend and a comparable dividend on common, the preferred shall share in the excess ratably on a share-for-share basis with the common. According to such terms, the $60,000 dividend distribution in the third year would be allocated as follows:

	Preferred Dividend	Common Dividend	Total Dividends
Regular dividend to preferred (1,000 × $10)	$10,000		$10,000
Comparable dividend to common (4,000 × $10)	—	$40,000	40,000
Remainder to 5,000 shares ratably ($2 per share)	2,000	8,000	10,000
Total	$12,000	$48,000	$60,000
Dividends per share	$12	$12	

Cumulative and Noncumulative Preferred Stock

As was indicated in the preceding section, most preferred stock is nonparticipating. Provision is usually made, however, to assure the continuation of the preferential dividend right if at any time the directors *pass* (do not declare) the usual dividend. This is accomplished by providing that dividends may not be paid on the common stock if any preferred dividends are in arrears. Such preferred stock is said to be **cumulative.** To illustrate, assume that a corporation has outstanding 5,000 shares of cumulative preferred 9% stock of $100 par and that dividends have been passed for the preceding two years. In the current year, no dividend may be declared on the common stock unless the directors first declare preferred dividends of $90,000 for the past two years and $45,000 for the current year. Preferred stock not having this cumulative right is called **noncumulative.**

Other Preferential Rights

Thus far the discussion of preferential rights of preferred stock has related to dividend distributions. Preferred stock may also be given a preference in its claim to assets upon liquidation of the corporation. If the assets remaining after payment of creditors are not sufficient to return the capital contributions of both classes of stock, payment would first be made to the preferred stockholders and any balance remaining would go to the common stockholders. Another difference between preferred and common stock is that the former may have no voting rights. A corporation may also have more than one class of preferred stock, with differences as to the amount of dividends, priority of claims upon liquidation, and voting rights. In any particular case, the rights of a class of stock may be determined by reference to the charter, the stock certificate, or some other abstract of the agreement.

ISSUING STOCK AT PAR

The entries to record the investment of capital in a corporation are like those of other types of business organizations, in that cash and other assets received are debited and any liabilities assumed are credited. The credit to capital differs, however, in that there are accounts for each class of stock. To illustrate, assume that a corporation, with an authorization of 10,000 shares of preferred stock of $100 par and 100,000 shares of common stock of $20 par, issues one half of each authorization at par for cash. The entry to record the stockholders' investment and the receipt of the cash is as follows:

Cash	1,500,000	
Preferred Stock		500,000
Common Stock		1,000,000

The capital stock accounts (Preferred Stock, Common Stock) are controlling accounts. It is necessary to maintain records of each stockholder's name, address, and number of shares held in order to issue dividend checks, proxy forms, and financial reports. Individual stockholders accounts are kept in a subsidiary ledger known as the **stockholders ledger.**

ISSUING STOCK AT A PREMIUM OR DISCOUNT

Par stock is often issued by a corporation at a price other than par. When it is issued for more than par, the excess of the contract price over par is termed a **premium.** When it is issued at a price that is below par, the difference is called a **discount.** Thus, if stock with a par of $50 is issued at $60, the amount of the premium is $10. If the same stock is issued at $45, the amount of the discount is $5.

Theoretically, there is no reason for a newly organized corporation to issue stock at a price other than par. The par designation is merely a part of the plan of dividing capital into a number of units of ownership. Hence, a group of persons investing their funds in a new corporation might all be expected to pay par for the shares. The fortunes of an enterprise do not remain the same, however, even when it is still in the process of organizing. The changing prospects for its future success may affect the price per share at which the incorporators can secure other investors.

A need for additional capital may arise long after a corporation has become established. Losses during the early period may have depleted working capital or the operations may have been successful enough to warrant a substantial expansion of plant and equipment. If the funds are to be obtained by the issuance of additional stock, it is apparent that the current price at which the original stock is selling in the market will affect the price that can be obtained for the new shares.

Generally speaking, the price at which stock can be sold by a corporation is influenced by (1) the financial condition, the earnings record, and the dividend record of the corporation, (2) its potential earning power, (3) the availability of money for investment purposes, and (4) general business and economic conditions and prospects.

Premium on Stock

When capital stock is issued at a premium, cash or other assets are debited for the amount received. The stock account is then credited for the par amount, and a premium account, sometimes called Paid-In Capital in Excess of Par, is credited for the amount of the premium. For example, if Caldwell Company issues 2,000 shares of $50 par preferred stock for cash at $55, the entry to record the transaction would be as follows:

Cash	110,000	
Preferred Stock		100,000
Premium on Preferred Stock		10,000

The premium of $10,000 is a part of the investment of the stockholders and is therefore a part of paid-in capital. It is distinguished from the capital stock account because usually it is not a part of legal capital and in many states may be used as a basis for dividends to stockholders. However, if the premium is returned to stockholders as a dividend at a later date, it should be emphasized that the dividend is a return of paid-in capital rather than a distribution of earnings.

Discount on Stock

Some states do not permit the issuance of stock at a discount. In others, it may be done only under certain conditions. When stock is issued at less than its par, it is considered to be fully paid as between the corporation and the stockholder. In some states, however, the stockholders are contingently liable to creditors for the amount of the discount. If the corporation is liquidated and there are not enough assets to pay creditors in full, the stockholders may be assessed for an additional contribution up to the amount of the discount on their stock.

When capital stock is issued at a discount, cash or other assets are debited for the amount received, and a discount account is debited for the amount of the discount. The capital stock account is then credited for the par amount. For example, if Caldwell Company issues 20,000 shares of $25 par common stock for cash at $23, the entry to record the transaction would be as follows:

Cash	460,000	
Discount on Common Stock	40,000	
Common Stock		500,000

The discount of $40,000 is a contra paid-in capital account and must be offset against Common Stock to arrive at the amount actually invested by the holders of common stock. The discount is not an asset, nor should it be amortized against revenue as though it were an expense.

Premiums and Discounts on the Balance Sheet

The manner in which premiums and discounts may be presented in the stockholders' equity section of the balance sheet is illustrated as follows, based on the two illustrative entries for Caldwell Company:

Stockholders' Equity

Paid-in capital:			
Preferred 10% stock, cumulative, $50 par (2,000 shares authorized and issued)	$100,000		
Premium on preferred stock	10,000	$110,000	
Common stock, $25 par (50,000 shares authorized, 20,000 shares issued)	$500,000		
Less discount on common stock	40,000	460,000	
Total paid-in capital		$570,000	
Retained earnings		175,000	
Total stockholders' equity			$745,000

The following stockholders' equity section illustrates the reporting of a deficit and some differences in terminology from that in the foregoing example:

Shareholders' Equity

Paid-in capital:

Preferred $3 stock, cumulative, $25 par (10,000 shares authorized and issued)	$ 250,000	
Excess of issuance price over par.	20,000	$ 270,000
Common stock, $10 par (200,000 shares authorized, 100,000 shares issued)	$1,000,000	
Less excess of par over issuance price	100,000	900,000
Total paid in by stockholders.		$1,170,000
Less deficit		75,000
Total shareholders' equity.		$1,095,000

ISSUING STOCK FOR ASSETS OTHER THAN CASH

When capital stock is issued in exchange for assets other than cash, such as land, buildings, and equipment, the assets acquired should be recorded at their fair market price or at the fair market price of the stock issued, whichever is more objectively determinable. The determination of the values to be assigned to the assets is the responsibility of the board of directors.

As a basis for illustration, assume that a corporation acquired land for which the fair market price is not determinable. In exchange, the corporation issued 10,000 shares of its $10 par common stock with a current market price of $12 per share. The transaction could be recorded as follows:

Dec. 5	Land	120,000	
	Common Stock.		100,000
	Premium on Common Stock		20,000

ISSUING NO-PAR STOCK

In the early days of rapid industrial expansion and increasing use of the corporate form of business organization, it was customary to assign a par of $100 to shares of stock. It is not surprising that unsophisticated investors, mistakenly considering "par value" to be the equivalent of "value," were often induced to invest in mining and other highly speculative enterprises by the simple means of offering $100 par stock at "bargain" prices. Another misleading practice was the use of par in assigning highly inflated values to assets acquired in exchange for stock. For example, stock with a total par of $1,000,000 might be issued in exchange for patents, mineral rights, or other properties with a conservatively estimated value of $50,000. The assets would be recorded at the full par of $1,000,000, whereas in reality the stock had been issued at a discount of $950,000. Balance sheets that were "window-dressed" in this manner were obviously deceptive.

To combat such abuses and also to eliminate the troublesome discount liability of stockholders, stock without par was conceived. The issuance of stock without par was first permitted by New York in 1912. Its use is now authorized in nearly all of the states.

Over the years, questionable practices in the issuance of securities have been virtually eliminated. Today federal and state laws and rules imposed by organized stock exchanges and governmental agencies such as the Securities and Exchange Commission combine to protect the investor from misrepresentations that were common in earlier days.

In most states, both preferred and common stock may be issued without a par designation. However, preferred stock is usually assigned a par. When no-par stock is issued, the entire proceeds may be credited to the capital stock account, even though the issuance price varies from time to time. For example, if at the time of organization a corporation issues no-par common stock at $40 a share and at a later date issues additional shares at $36, the entries would be:

1. *Original issuance of 10,000 shares of no-par common at $40:*
   Cash 400,000
       Common Stock   400,000

2. *Subsequent issuance of 1,000 shares of no-par common at $36:*
   Cash 36,000
       Common Stock   36,000

The laws of some states require that the entire proceeds from the issuance of no-par stock be regarded as legal capital. The preceding entries conform to this principle, which also conforms to the original concept of no-par stock. In other states, no-par stock may be assigned a stated value per share, and the excess of the proceeds over the stated value may be credited to Paid-In Capital in Excess of Stated Value. Assuming that in the previous example the stated value is $25 and the board of directors wishes to credit the common stock for stated value, the transactions would be recorded as follows:

1. *Original issuance of 10,000 shares of no-par common, stated value $25, at $40:*
   Cash 400,000
       Common Stock   250,000
       Paid-In Capital in Excess of Stated Value   150,000

2. *Subsequent issuance of 1,000 shares of no-par common, stated value $25, at $36:*
   Cash 36,000
       Common Stock   25,000
       Paid-In Capital in Excess of Stated Value   11,000

It is readily apparent that the accounting for no-par stock with a stated value may follow the same pattern as the accounting for par stock.

TREASURY STOCK

Although there are some legal restrictions on the practice, a corporation may purchase shares of its own outstanding stock from stockholders. It may also accept shares of its own stock in payment of a debt owed by a stockholder, which in essence is much the same as acquisition by purchase. There are various reasons why a corporation may buy its own stock. For example, it may be to provide shares for resale to employees, for reissuance to employees as a bonus or according to stock purchase agreements, or to support the market price of the stock.

The term **treasury stock** may be applied only to the issuing corporation's stock that (1) has been issued as fully paid, (2) has later been reacquired by the corporation, and (3) has not been canceled or reissued. In the past, corporations would occasionally list treasury stock on the balance sheet as an asset. The justification for such treatment was that the stock could be reissued and was thus like an investment in the stock of another corporation. The same argument, though indefensible, might well be extended to authorized but unissued stock.

Today, it is generally agreed among accountants that treasury stock should not be reported as an asset. A corporation cannot own a part of itself. Treasury stock has no voting rights, it does not have the preemptive right to participate in additional issuances of stock, nor does it generally participate in cash dividends. When a corporation purchases its own stock, it is returning capital to the stockholders from whom the purchase was made.

There are several methods of accounting for the purchase and the resale of treasury stock. A commonly used method is the **cost basis.** When the stock is purchased by the corporation, the account Treasury Stock is debited for the price paid for it. The par and the price at which the stock was originally issued are ignored. When the stock is resold, Treasury Stock is credited at the price paid for it, and the difference between the price paid and the selling price is debited or credited to an account entitled Paid-In Capital from Sale of Treasury Stock.

As a basis for illustrating the cost method, assume that the paid-in capital of a corporation is composed of common stock issued at a premium, detailed as follows:

Common stock, $25 par (20,000 shares authorized and issued)..... $500,000
Premium on common stock 150,000

The assumed transactions involving treasury stock and the required entries are as follows:

1. *Purchased 1,000 shares of treasury stock at $45.*

Treasury Stock	45,000	
Cash		45,000

2. *Sold 200 shares of treasury stock at $55.*

Cash	11,000	
Treasury Stock		9,000
Paid-In Capital from Sale of Treasury Stock.............		2,000

3. *Sold 200 shares of treasury stock at $40.*

Cash	8,000	
Paid-In Capital from Sale of Treasury Stock	1,000	
Treasury Stock		9,000

The additional capital obtained through the sale of treasury stock is reported in the paid-in capital section of the balance sheet, and the cost of the treasury stock held by the corporation is deducted from the total of the capital accounts. After the foregoing transactions are completed, the stockholders' equity section of the balance sheet would appear as follows:

Stockholders' Equity

Paid-in capital:		
Common stock, $25 par (20,000 shares authorized and issued)	$500,000	
Premium on common stock	150,000	$650,000
From sale of treasury stock		1,000
Total paid-in capital		$651,000
Retained earnings		130,000
Total		$781,000
Deduct treasury stock (600 shares at cost)		27,000
Total stockholders' equity		$754,000

The stockholders' equity section of the balance sheet indicates that 20,000 shares of stock were issued, of which 600 are held as treasury stock. The number of shares outstanding is therefore 19,400. If cash dividends are declared at this time, the declaration would apply to 19,400 shares of stock. Similarly, 19,400 shares could be voted at a stockholders' meeting.

If sales of treasury stock result in a net decrease in paid-in capital, the decrease may be reported on the balance sheet as a reduction of paid-in capital or it may be debited to the retained earnings account.

EQUITY PER SHARE

The amount appearing on the balance sheet as total stockholders' equity can be stated in terms of the **equity per share.** Another term sometimes used in referring to the equity allocable to a single share of stock is **book value per share.** The latter term is not only less accurate but its use of "value" may also be interpreted by nonaccountants to mean "market value" or "actual worth."

When there is only one class of stock, the equity per share is determined by dividing total stockholders' equity by the number of shares outstanding. For a corporation with both preferred and common stock, it is necessary first to allocate the total equity between the two classes. In making the allocation, consideration must be given to the liquidation rights of the preferred stock, including any participating and cumulative dividend features. After the total is allocated to the two classes, the equity per share of each class may then be determined by dividing the respective amounts by the related number of shares outstanding.

To illustrate, assume that as of the end of the current fiscal year, a corporation has both preferred and common shares outstanding, that there are no preferred dividends in arrears, and that the preferred stock is entitled to receive $105 upon liquidation. The amounts of the stockholders' equity accounts of the corporation and the computation of the equity per share are as follows:

Stockholders' Equity

Preferred $9 stock, cumulative, $100 par (1,000 shares outstanding)	$100,000
Premium on preferred stock	2,000
Common stock, $10 par (50,000 shares outstanding)	500,000
Premium on common stock	50,000
Retained earnings	253,000
Total equity	$905,000

Allocation of Total Equity to Preferred and Common Stock

Total equity	$905,000
Allocated to preferred stock:	
Liquidation price	105,000
Allocated to common stock	$800,000

Equity Per Share

Preferred stock: $105,000 ÷ 1,000 shares = $105 per share
Common stock: $800,000 ÷ 50,000 shares = $ 16 per share

If it is assumed that the preferred stock is entitled to dividends in arrears in the event of liquidation, and that there is an arrearage of two years, the computations for the foregoing illustration would be as follows:

Allocation of Total Equity to Preferred and Common Stock

Total equity		$905,000
Allocated to preferred stock:		
Liquidation price	$105,000	
Dividends in arrears	18,000	123,000
Allocated to common stock		$782,000

Equity Per Share

Preferred stock: $123,000 ÷ 1,000 shares = $123.00 per share
Common stock: $782,000 ÷ 50,000 shares = $ 15.64 per share

Equity per share, particularly of common stock, is often stated in corporation reports to stockholders and quoted in the financial press. It is one of the many factors affecting the **market price,** that is, the price at which a share is bought and sold at a particular moment. However, it should be noted that earning capacity, dividend rates, and prospects for the future usually affect the market price of listed stocks to a much greater extent than does equity per share. So-called "glamour" stocks may at times sell at more than ten times the amount of the equity per share. On the other hand, stock in corporations that have suffered severe declines in earnings or whose future prospects appear to be unfavorable may sell at prices which are much less than the equity per share.

ORGANIZATION COSTS

Expenditures incurred in organizing a corporation, such as legal fees, taxes and fees paid to the state, and promotional costs, are charged to an intangible asset account entitled Organization Costs. Although such costs have no realizable value upon liquidation, they are as essential as plant and equipment, for without the expenditures the corporation could not have been created. If the life of a corporation is limited to a definite period of time, the organization costs should be amortized over the period by annual charges to an expense account. However, at the time of incorporation the length of life of most corporations is indeterminate.

There are two possible extreme viewpoints on the proper accounting for organization costs and other intangibles of indeterminate life. One extreme would consider the cost of intangibles as a permanent asset until there was convincing evidence of loss in value. The other extreme would consider the cost of intangibles as an expense in the period in which the cost is incurred. The practical solution to the problem is expressed in the following quotation:

> .... Allocating the cost of goodwill or other intangible assets with an indeterminate life over time is necessary because the value almost inevitably becomes zero at some future date. Since the date at which the value becomes zero is indeterminate, the end of the useful life must necessarily be set arbitrarily at some point or within some range of time for accounting purposes.[3]

The Internal Revenue Code permits the amortization of organization costs ratably over a period of not less than sixty months beginning with the month the corporation commences business. Since the amount of such costs is relatively small in relation to total assets and the effect on net income is ordinarily not significant, amortization of organization costs over sixty months is generally accepted in accounting practice.

---

[3]*Opinions of the Accounting Principles Board, No. 17,* "Intangible Assets" (New York: American Institute of Certified Public Accountants, 1970), par. 23.

Self-
Examination
Questions
(Answers
at end of
chapter.)

1. X and Y invest $100,000 and $50,000 respectively in a partnership and agree to a division of net income that provides for an allowance of interest at 10% on original investments, salary allowances of $12,000 and $24,000, with the remainder divided equally. What would be X's share of a periodic net income of $45,000?
   A. $22,500   C. $19,000
   B. $22,000   D. $10,000

2. If a corporation has outstanding 1,000 shares of $9 cumulative preferred stock of $100 par and dividends have been passed for the preceding three years, what is the amount of preferred dividends that must be declared in the current year before a dividend can be declared on common stock?
   A. $9,000   C. $36,000
   B. $27,000   D. None of the above

3. The stockholders' equity section of the balance sheet may include:
   A. Discount on Common Stock   C. Premium on Preferred Stock
   B. Common Stock   D. all of the above

4. If a corporation reacquires its own stock, the stock is listed on the balance sheet in the:
   A. current assets section   C. stockholders' equity section
   B. long-term liabilities section D. none of the above

5. A corporation's balance sheet includes 10,000 outstanding shares of $8 cumulative preferred stock of $100 par; 100,000 outstanding shares of $20 par common stock; premium on common stock of $100,000; and retained earnings of $540,000. If preferred dividends are three years in arrears and the preferred stock is entitled to dividends in arrears plus $110 per share in the event of liquidation, what is the equity per common share?
   A. $20.00   C. $25.40
   B. $23.00   D. None of the above

10–1. What form of business organization is used most frequently in the United States?

10–2. What is the primary disadvantage of organizing a business enterprise as a sole proprietorship?

10–3. What are the primary differences in accounting for a sole proprietorship and a corporation?

10–4. At the end of the accounting period for a sole proprietorship, the owner's drawing account is closed to what account?

10–5. Gains and Howell are partners, sharing gains and losses equally. At the time they decide to terminate their partnership, their capital balances are $45,000 and $55,000 respectively. After all noncash assets are sold and all liabilities are paid, there is a cash balance of $80,000. (a) What is the amount of gain or loss on realization? (b) How should the gain or loss be divided between Gains and Howell? (c) How should the cash be divided between Gains and Howell?

10–6. The retained earnings account of a corporation at the beginning of the year had a credit balance of $25,000. The only other entry in the account during the year was a debit of $40,000 transferred from the income summary account at the end of the year. (a) What is the term applied to the $40,000 debit? (b) What is the balance in retained earnings at the end of the year? (c) What is the term applied to the balance determined in (b)?

10–7. The charter of a corporation provides for the issuance of a maximum of 100,000 shares of common stock. The corporation issued 75,000 shares of common stock and two years later it reacquired 5,000 shares. After the reacquisition what is the number of shares of stock (a) authorized, (b) issued, and (c) outstanding?

10–8. (a) Differentiate between common stock and preferred stock. (b) Describe briefly (1) participating preferred stock and (2) cumulative preferred stock.

10–9. Assume that a corporation has had outstanding 20,000 shares of $10 cumulative preferred stock of $100 par and dividends were passed for the preceding four years. What amount of total dividends must be paid to the preferred stockholders before the common stockholders are entitled to any dividends in the current year?

10–10. When a corporation issued stock at a premium, does the premium constitute income? Explain.

10–11. The stockholders' equity section of a corporation balance sheet is composed of the following items:

Preferred 8% stock................	$600,000		
Discount on preferred stock........	50,000	$550,000	
Common stock	$900,000		
Premium on common stock	90,000	990,000	$1,540,000
Retained earnings		280,000	$1,820,000

Determine the following amounts: (a) paid-in capital attributable to preferred stock, (b) paid-in capital attributable to common stock, (c) earnings retained for use in the business, and (d) total stockholders' equity.

10–12. Land is acquired by a corporation for 2,500 shares of its $50 par, $5 preferred stock which is currently selling for $60 on a national stock exchange. (a) At what value should the land be recorded? (b) What accounts and amounts should be credited to record the transaction?

10–13. (a) In what respect does treasury stock differ from unissued stock? (b) For what reasons might a company purchase treasury stock? (c) How should treasury stock be presented on the balance sheet?

10–14. A corporation reacquires 1,000 shares of its own $10 par common stock for $19,000, recording it at cost. (a) What effect does this transaction have on revenue or expense of the period? (b) What effect does it have on stockholders' equity?

10–15. The treasury stock in Question 14 is resold for $25,000. (a) What is the effect on the corporation's revenue of the period? (b) What is the effect on stockholders' equity?

10–16. A corporation that had issued 50,000 shares of $20 par common stock subsequently reacquired 10,000 shares, which it now holds as treasury stock. If the board of directors declares a cash dividend of $2 per share, what will be the total amount of the dividend?

10–17. Assume that a corporation at the end of the current period has 20,000 shares of preferred stock and 100,000 shares of common stock outstanding, that there are no preferred dividends in arrears, and that the preferred stock is entitled to receive $110 per share upon liquidation. If total stockholders' equity is $4,000,000, determine the following amounts: (a) equity per share of preferred stock, and (b) equity per share of common stock.

10–18. Common stock has a par of $20 per share, the current equity per share is $49.50, and the market price per share is $83. Suggest reasons for the comparatively high market price in relation to par and to equity per share.

10–19. (a) What type of expenditure is charged to the organization costs account? (b) Give examples of such expenditures. (c) In what section of the balance sheet is the balance of Organization Costs listed?

10–20. Identify each of the following accounts as asset, liability, stockholders' equity, revenue, or expense, and indicate the normal balance of each:
(1) Paid-In Capital from Sale of Treasury Stock
(2) Preferred Stock
(3) Common Stock
(4) Discount on Preferred Stock
(5) Retained Earnings
(6) Treasury Stock
(7) Organization Costs
(8) Premium on Common Stock

Exercises

10–21. Alice Cahn and Mary Denver form a partnership, investing $50,000 and $75,000 respectively. Determine their participation in the year's net income of $70,000, under each of the following assumptions: (a) no agreement concerning division of income; (b) divided in the ratio of original capital investments; (c) interest at the rate of 12% allowed on original investments and the remainder divided in the ratio of 3:2; (d) salary allowances of $25,000 and $20,000 and the balance divided equally; (e) allowance of interest at the rate of 12% on original investments, salary allowances of $25,000 and $20,000 respectively, and the remainder divided equally.

10–22. The capital accounts of Bob Edwards and Jose Ferrara have balances of $82,500 and $65,000 respectively on January 1, the beginning of the current fiscal year. On May 31, Ferrara invested an additional $10,000. During the year, Edwards and Ferrara withdrew $25,000 and $28,000 respectively, and net income for the year was $70,000. The articles of partnership make no reference to the division of net income. (a) Present the journal entries to close (1) the income summary account and (2) the drawing accounts. (b) Prepare a statement of owner's equity for the current year.

10–23. C. D. Mann and P. E. Nehi, with capital balances of $42,500 and $37,500 respectively, decide to liquidate their partnership. After selling the noncash assets and paying the liabilities, there is $60,000 of cash remaining. If the partners share income and losses equally, how should the cash be distributed?

10–24. CMS Inc. has stock outstanding as follows: 5,000 shares of $10 cumulative, nonparticipating preferred stock of $100 par, and 100,000 shares of $20 par common. During its first five years of operations, the following amounts were distributed as dividends: first year, none; second year, $80,000; third year, $130,000; fourth year, $145,000; fifth year, $200,000. Determine the dividends per share on each class of stock for each of the five years.

10–25. R and M Company has outstanding stock composed of 2,500 shares of 9%, $100 par, participating preferred stock and 10,000 shares of no-par common stock. The preferred stock is entitled to participate equally with the common, share for share, in any dividend distributions which exceed the regular preferred dividend and a $2 per share common dividend. The directors declare dividends of $60,000 for the current year. Determine the amount of the dividend per share on (a) the preferred stock and (b) the common stock.

10–26. C. D. Menes Company was organized on January 5 of the current year, with an authorization of 5,000 shares of $4 cumulative preferred stock, $50 par, and 50,000 shares of $10 par common stock.
    (a) Record the following selected transactions completed during the first year of operations:

Jan.	5.	Sold 10,000 shares of common stock at par for cash.
	5.	Issued 750 shares of common stock to an attorney in payment of legal fees for organizing the corporation.
March 10.		Issued 10,000 shares of common stock in exchange for land, buildings, and equipment with fair market prices of $20,000, $75,000, and $25,000 respectively.
Nov.	30.	Sold 2,500 shares of preferred stock at $46 for cash.

    (b) Prepare the stockholders' equity section of the balance sheet as of December 31, the end of the current year. The net income for the year amounted to $30,000.

10–27. The capital accounts of Chow Products are as follows: Preferred 9% Stock, $50 par, $500,000; Common Stock, $20 par, $3,000,000; Premium on Common Stock, $300,000; Premium on Preferred Stock, $40,000; Retained Earnings, $1,155,000. (a) Determine the equity per share of each class of stock, assuming that the preferred stock is entitled to receive $60 upon liquidation. (b) Determine the equity per share of each class of stock, assuming that the preferred stock is to receive $60 plus the dividends in arrears in the event of liquidation, and that only the dividends for the current year are in arrears.

10–28. The following items were listed in the stockholders' equity section of the balance sheet of May 31: Common stock, $10 par (60,000 shares outstanding), $600,000; Premium on common stock, $100,000; Retained earnings, $140,000. On June 1, the corporation purchased 2,000 shares of its stock for $51,200. (a) Determine the equity per share of stock on May 31. (b) Present the entry to record the purchase of the stock on June 1. (c) Determine the equity per share on June 1.

10–29. The following items were listed in the stockholders' equity section of the balance sheet on April 30: Preferred stock, $50 par, $250,000; Common stock, $10 par, $500,000; Premium on common stock, $100,000; Deficit, $175,000. On May 1, the board of directors voted to dissolve the corporation immediately. A short time later, after all noncash assets were sold and liabilities were paid, cash of $475,000 remained for distribution to stockholders. (a) Assuming that preferred stock is entitled to preference in liquidation to the extent of 110% of par, determine the equity per share on April 30 of (1) preferred stock and (2) common stock. (b) Determine the amount of the $475,000 that will be distributed for each share of (1) preferred stock and (2) common stock. (c) Explain the reason for the difference between the common stock equity per share on April 30 and the amount of the cash distribution per common share.

Problems

10–30. Noah and Oaks have decided to form a partnership. They have agreed that Noah is to invest $120,000 and that Oaks is to invest $80,000. Noah is to devote one-half time to the business and Oaks is to devote full time. The following plans for the division of income are being considered:

  (a) Equal division.
  (b) In the ratio of original investments.
  (c) In the ratio of time devoted to the business.
  (d) Interest of 10% on original investments and the remainder equally.
  (e) Interest of 12% on original investments, salaries of $15,000 to Noah and $30,000 to Oaks, and the remainder equally.
  (f) Plan (e), except that Oaks is also to be allowed a bonus equal to 20% of the amount by which net income exceeds the salary allowances.

Instructions:

For each plan, determine the division of the net income under each of the following assumptions: net income of $60,000 and net income of $150,000. Present the data in tabular form, using the following columnar headings:

Plan	$60,000		$150,000	
	Noah	Oaks	Noah	Oaks

10–31. Landmark Corp. was organized by Gass, Snow, and Thom. The charter authorized 10,000 shares of common stock with a par of $50. The following transactions affecting stockholders' equity were completed during the first year of operations:

- (a) Issued 1,000 shares of stock at par to Gass for cash.
- (b) Issued 100 shares of stock at par to Snow for promotional services rendered in connection with the organization of the corporation, and issued 900 shares of stock at par to Snow for cash.
- (c) Purchased land and a building from Thom. The building is encumbered by a 12%, 18-year mortgage of $65,000, and there is accrued interest of $1,300 on the mortgage note at the time of the purchase. It is agreed that the land is to be priced at $30,000 and the building at $115,000, and that Thom's equity will be exchanged for stock at par. The corporation agreed to assume responsibility for paying the mortgage note and the accrued interest.
- (d) Issued 2,000 shares of stock at $60 to various investors for cash.
- (e) Purchased equipment for $80,000. The seller accepted a 6-month, 14% note for $30,000 and 1,000 shares of stock in exchange for the equipment.

Instructions:

- (1) Prepare entries to record the transactions presented above.
- (2) Prepare the stockholders' equity section of the balance sheet as of the end of the first year of operations. Net income for the year amounted to $82,000 and dividends of $5 per share were declared and paid during the year.

10–32. The annual dividends declared by C. G. Steinberg Company during a six-year period are presented in the following table:

Year	Total Dividends	Preferred Dividends		Common Dividends	
		Total	Per Share	Total	Per Share
1981	$ 5,000				
1982	30,000				
1983	40,000				
1984	82,000				
1985	112,000				
1986	21,000				

During the entire period, the outstanding stock of the company was composed of 2,000 shares of cumulative, participating, 10% preferred stock, $100 par, and 10,000 shares of common stock, $100 par. The preferred stock contract provides that the preferred stock shall participate in distributions of additional dividends after allowance of a $5 dividend per share on the common stock, the additional dividends to be prorated among common and preferred shares on the basis of the total par of the stock oustanding.

Instructions:

- (1) Determine the total dividends and the per share dividends declared on each class of stock for each of the six years, using the headings presented above. There were no dividends in arrears on January 1, 1981.
- (2) Determine the average annual dividend per share for each class of stock for the six-year period.
- (3) Assuming that the preferred stock was sold at par and the common stock was sold at $55 at the beginning of the six-year period, determine the percentage

return on initial shareholders' investment, based on the average annual dividend per share (a) for preferred stock and (b) for common stock.

10–33. Selected data from the balance sheets of six corporations, identified by letter, are as follows:

A. Common stock, $20 par.................................... $ 600,000
   Premium on common stock................................   120,000
   Deficit..   75,000

B. Preferred 10% stock, $25 par.............................. $ 500,000
   Common stock, $20 par.................................... 1,200,000
   Premium on common stock................................   130,000
   Retained earnings...   410,000

   Preferred stock has prior claim to assets on liquidation to the extent of par.

C. Preferred 9% stock, $100 par............................. $ 800,000
   Premium on preferred stock................................   50,000
   Common stock, no par, 15,000 shares outstanding.............. 1,200,000
   Deficit..   237,500

   Preferred stock has prior claim to assets on liquidation to the extent of par.

D. Preferred 11% stock, $50 par.............................. $2,500,000
   Premium on preferred stock................................   275,000
   Common stock, $25 par.................................... 3,750,000
   Deficit.. 1,240,000

   Preferred stock has prior claim to assets on liquidation to the extent of 110% of par.

E. Preferred $7 stock, $100 par $1,200,000
   Common stock, $50 par.................................... 3,100,000
   Premium on common stock................................   200,000
   Retained earnings...   104,000

   Dividends on preferred stock are in arrears for 2 years, including the dividend passed during the current year. Preferred stock is entitled to par plus unpaid cumulative dividends upon liquidation to the extent of retained earnings.

F. Preferred $2 stock, $25 par $1,000,000
   Discount on preferred stock................................   80,000
   Common stock, $10 par.................................... 3,000,000
   Deficit..   130,000

   Dividends on preferred stock are in arrears for 3 years, including the dividend passed during the current year. Preferred stock is entitled to par plus unpaid cumulative dividends upon liquidation, regardless of the availability of retained earnings.

Instructions:

Determine for each corporation the equity per share of each class of stock, presenting the total stockholders' equity allocated to each class and the number of shares outstanding.

10–34. The following accounts and their balances appear in the ledger of C. F. Cammack Co. on June 1 of the current year:

Preferred $5 Stock, par $50 (10,000 shares authorized,
9,000 shares issued)...................................... $450,000
Premium on Preferred Stock............................... 19,000
Common Stock, par $10 (100,000 shares authorized, 75,000
shares issued) 750,000
Premium on Common Stock 120,000
Retained Earnings... 190,000

At the annual stockholders' meeting on June 3, the board of directors presented a plan for modernizing and expanding plant operations at a cost of approximately $475,000. The plan provided (a) that the corporation borrow $250,000, (b) that 1,000 shares of the unissued preferred stock be issued through an underwriter, and (c) that a building, valued at $135,000, and the land on which it is located, valued at $35,000, be acquired in accordance with preliminary negotiations by the issuance of 10,000 shares of common stock. The plan was approved by the stockholders and accomplished by the following transactions:

June 12. Issued 10,000 shares of common stock in exchange for land and building in accordance with the plan.

24. Issued 1,000 shares of preferred stock, receiving $55 per share in cash from the underwriter.

30. Borrowed $250,000 from American National Bank, giving a 13% mortgage note.

Instructions:

Assuming for the purpose of the problem that no other transactions occurred during June:

(1) Prepare the entries to record the foregoing transactions.
(2) Prepare the stockholders' equity section of the balance sheet as of June 30.

Alternate Problems

10–30A. Virginia Fox and June Gove have decided to form a partnership. They have agreed that Fox is to invest $60,000 and that Gove is to invest $90,000. Fox is to devote full time to the business and Gove is to devote one-half time. The following plans for the division of income are being considered:

(a) Equal division.
(b) In the ratio of original investments.
(c) In the ratio of time devoted to the business.
(d) Interest of 12% on original investments and the remainder in the ratio of 3 : 2.
(e) Interest of 12% on original investments, salaries of $30,000 to Fox and $15,000 to Gove, and the remainder equally.
(f) Plan (e), except that Fox is also to be allowed a bonus equal to 20% of the amount by which net income exceeds the salary allowances.

Instructions:

For each plan, determine the division of the net income under each of the following assumptions: net income of $75,000 and net income of $51,000. Present the data in tabular form, using the following columnar headings:

Plan	$75,000		$51,000	
	Fox	Gove	Fox	Gove

10–32A. The annual dividends declared by Valentine Company during a six-year period are presented in the following table:

Year	Total Dividends	Preferred Dividends		Common Dividends	
		Total	Per Share	Total	Per Share
1981	$ 79,000				
1982	127,000				
1983	10,000				
1984	5,000				
1985	6,000				
1986	43,000				

During the entire period, the outstanding stock of the company was composed of 1,000 shares of cumulative, participating, $9 preferred stock, $100 par, and 20,000 shares of common stock, $10 par. The preferred stock contract provides that the preferred stock shall participate in distributions of additional dividends after allowance of a $2 dividend per share on the common stock, the additional dividends to be prorated among common and preferred shares on the basis of the total par of the stock outstanding.

Instructions:

(1) Determine the total dividends and the per share dividends declared on each class of stock for each of the six years, using the headings presented above. There were no dividends in arrears on January 1, 1981.
(2) Determine the average annual dividend per share for each class of stock for the six-year period.
(3) Assuming that the preferred stock was sold at par and common stock was sold at $15 at the beginning of the six-year period, determine the percentage return on initial shareholders' investment, based on the average annual dividend per share (a) for preferred stock and (b) for common stock.

10–33A. Selected data from the balance sheets of six corporations, identified by letter, are as follows:

A. Common stock, no par, 100,000 shares outstanding $1,050,000
   Deficit..   130,000

B. Preferred 12% stock, $50 par .... $ 500,000
   Premium on preferred stock................................   25,000
   Common stock, $5 par   2,000,000
   Discount on common stock   190,000
   Deficit...   235,000
   Preferred stock has prior claim to assets on liquidation to the extent of par.

C. Preferred 9% stock, $25 par $1,250,000
Common stock, $10 par 1,000,000
Premium on common stock 50,000
Retained earnings 450,000

Preferred stock has prior claim to assets on liquidation to the extent of par.

D. Preferred 10% stock, $100 par .... $ 750,000
Premium on preferred stock............................. 90,000
Common stock, $25 par 2,500,000
Deficit... 65,000

Preferred stock has prior claim to assets on liquidation to the extent of 110% of par.

E. Preferred $11 stock, $100 par .... $ 800,000
Common stock, $5 par 1,250,000
Premium on common stock 200,000
Retained earnings 104,000

Dividends on preferred stock are in arrears for 2 years, including the dividend passed during the current year. Preferred stock is entitled to par plus unpaid cumulative dividends upon liquidation to the extent of retained earnings.

F. Preferred $2 stock, $25 par............................. $ 500,000
Discount on preferred stock............................. 40,000
Common stock, $10 par 1,500,000
Deficit... 65,000

Dividends on preferred stock are in arrears for 3 years, including the dividend passed during the current year. Preferred stock is entitled to par plus unpaid cumulative dividends upon liquidation, regardless of the availability of retained earnings.

Instructions:

Determine for each corporation the equity per share of each class of stock, presenting the total stockholders' equity allocated to each class and the number of shares outstanding.

Mini-Case

10–35. Pompano Cooperative Electric Corporation needs $1,500,000 to finance a major plant expansion. To raise the $1,500,000, the chairman of the board of directors suggested that the cooperative first offer common stock for sale at a price equal to the January 1, 1987 equity per share of common stock. The chairman indicated that by setting the price in this way, the value of the current common stockholders' interest in the cooperative would be preserved. Any additional funds that might be needed after this offer expired could be obtained from the issuance of preferred stock.

Since no preferred stock is authorized, the board is considering characteristics of the stock, such as the dividend rate and the cumulative and participating features. So as not to jeopardize common stockholder dividends, the board of directors tentatively approved a dividend rate of 3% for the preferred stock. The board agreed to delay any final action on other aspects of the financing plan until the legal counsel can be contacted to determine the procedures necessary to seek authorization of the preferred stock.

As of January 1, 1987, the stockholders' equity is as follows:

Paid-in capital:
Common stock, $100 par (50,000 shares
   authorized, 25,000 shares issued)........... $2,500,000
Premium on common stock...................   300,000

   Total paid-in capital....................... $2,800,000
Retained earnings............................   1,150,000
Total stockholders' equity...................... $3,950,000

Instructions:

(1) Determine the equity per share of common stock on January 1, 1987.
(2) During the board meeting, the chairman asked your opinion of the suggestion for determining the selling price of the common stock. How would you respond?
(3) What characteristics might you suggest the board consider in designing the preferred stock? Comment on the low preferred stock dividend rate tentatively approved by the board.

---

1. C X's share of the $45,000 of net income is $19,000 (answer C), determined as follows:

	X	Y	Total
Interest allowance.....................................	$10,000	$ 5,000	$15,000
Salary allowance.......................................	12,000	24,000	36,000
Total...	$22,000	$29,000	$51,000
Excess of allowances over income	3,000	3,000	6,000
Net income distribution	$19,000	$26,000	$45,000

2. C If a corporation has cumulative preferred stock outstanding, dividends that have been passed for prior years plus the dividend for the current year must be paid before dividends may be declared on common stock. In this case, dividends of $27,000 ($9,000 × 3) have been passed for the preceding three years and the current year's dividends are $9,000, making a total of $36,000 (answer C) that must be paid to preferred stockholders before dividends can be declared on common stock.

3. **D** The stockholders' equity section of corporate balance sheets is divided into two principal subsections: (1) investments contributed by the stockholders and (2) net income retained in the business. Included as part of the investments by stockholders is the excess of par over issued price of stock, such as discount on common stock (answer A); the par of common stock (answer B); and the excess of issued price of stock over par, such as premium on preferred stock (answer C).

4. **C** Reacquired stock, known as treasury stock, should be listed in the stockholders' equity section (answer C) of the balance sheet. The price paid for the treasury stock is deducted from the total of all of the capital accounts.

5. **B** The total stockholders' equity is determined as follows:

Preferred stock	$1,000,000
Common stock	2,000,000
Premium on common stock	100,000
Retained earnings	540,000
Total equity	$3,640,000

The amount allocated to common stock is determined as follows:

Total equity		$3,640,000
Allocated to preferred stock:		
Liquidation price	$1,100,000	
Dividends in arrears	240,000	1,340,000
Allocated to common stock		$2,300,000

The equity per common share is determined as follows:

$2,300,000 ÷ 100,000 shares = $23 per share

CHAPTER 11

Corporations: Stockholders' Equity, Earnings, and Dividends

CHAPTER OBJECTIVES

Identify and illustrate alternative terminology used in preparing the stockholders' equity section of the balance sheet.

Describe and illustrate the accounting for corporate income taxes.

Describe and illustrate the accounting for unusual items in the financial statements.

Describe and illustrate the computation of earnings per share.

Describe and illustrate the accounting for appropriations of retained earnings and for dividends and the preparation of a retained earnings statement.

As has been indicated, the stockholders' equity section of the balance sheet is divided into two major subdivisions, "paid-in capital" and "retained earnings." Although in practice there is wide variation in the amount of detail presented and the descriptive captions used, sources of significant amounts of capital should be properly disclosed.

The emphasis on disclosure and clarity of expression by the accounting profession has been relatively recent. In earlier days, it was not unusual to present only the amount of the par of the preferred and common stock outstanding and a balancing amount described simply as "Surplus." Readers of the balance sheet could only assume that par represented the amount paid in by stockholders and that surplus represented retained earnings. Although it was possible for a "surplus" of $1,000,000, for example, to be composed solely of retained earnings, it could represent paid-in capital from premiums on stock issued or even an excess of $1,200,000 of such premiums over an accumulated deficit of $200,000 of retained earnings.

PAID-IN CAPITAL

As illustrated in Chapter 10, the main credits to paid-in capital accounts result from the issuance of stock. If par stock is issued at a price above or below par, the difference is recorded in a separate premium or discount account. It is also common to use two accounts in recording the issuance of no-par stock, one for the stated value and the other for the excess over stated value. Another account for paid-in capital discussed in the preceding chapter was Paid-In Capital from Sale of Treasury Stock.

Paid-in capital may also originate from donated real estate and redemptions of a corporation's own stock. Civic organizations sometimes give land or land and buildings to a corporate enterprise as an inducement to locate in the community. In such cases, the assets are recorded in the corporate accounts at fair market value, with a credit to Donated Capital. Preferred stock contracts may give to the issuing corporation the right to redeem the stock at varying redemption prices at varying future dates. If the redemption price paid to the stockholder is greater than the original issuance price, the excess is considered to be a distribution of retained earnings. On the other hand, if the amount paid is less than the amount originally received by the corporation, the difference is a retention of capital and should be credited to Paid-In Capital from Preferred Stock Redemption or a similarly titled account.

As with other sections of the balance sheet, there are many variations in terminology and arrangement of the paid-in capital section. Some of these variations are illustrated by the following three examples. The details of each class of stock, including related stock premium or discount, are commonly listed first, followed by the other paid-in capital accounts. Instead of describing the source of each amount in excess of par or stated value, a common practice is to combine all such accounts into a single amount. It is then listed below the capital stock accounts and described as "Additional paid-in capital," "Capital in excess of par (or stated value) of shares," or by a similarly descriptive phrase.

Stockholders' Equity

Paid-in capital:
Common stock, $20 par (50,000 shares authorized, 45,000 shares issued) $900,000
Premium on common stock. 132,000 $1,032,000

From stock redemption.   60,000
From sale of treasury stock   25,000
    Total paid-in capital. $1,117,000

Capital

Paid-in capital:
Common stock, $20 par (50,000 shares authorized, 45,000 shares issued) . . . . $ 900,000
Excess of issuance price over par. $132,000
From redemption of common stock.   60,000
From transactions in own stock   25,000   217,000
    Total paid-in capital. $1,117,000

Shareholders' Investment

Contributed capital:

Common stock, $20 par (50,000 shares au-
thorized, 45,000 shares issued) . . . . $ 900,000

Additional paid-in capital.   217,000

    Total contributed capital. $1,117,000

Significant changes in paid-in capital during the period should also be disclosed. The details of these changes may be presented either in a separate paid-in capital statement or in notes to other financial statements.

CORPORATE EARNINGS AND INCOME TAXES

The determination of the net income or net loss of a corporation is comparable, in most respects, to that of other forms of business organization. Unlike sole proprietorships and partnerships, however, corporations are distinct legal entities. In general, they are subject to the federal income tax and, in many cases, to income taxes levied by states or other political subdivisions. Although the discussion that follows is limited to the income tax levied by the federal government, the basic concepts apply also to state and local income taxes.

For several years, most corporations have been required to estimate the amount of their federal income tax expense for the year and to make advance payments, usually in four installments. To illustrate, assume that a calendar-year corporation estimates its income tax expense for the year to be $84,000. The required entry for each of the four payments of $21,000 (¼ of $84,000) would be as follows:

Income Tax.   21,000

    Cash.   21,000

At year end, the actual taxable income and the actual tax are determined. If an additional amount is owed, this liability must be recorded. Continuing with the above illustration, assume that the corporation's actual tax, based on actual taxable income, is $86,000 instead of $84,000. The following entry would be required in order to include the income tax expense in the fiscal year in which the related income was earned:

Dec. 31   Income Tax.   2,000

        Income Tax Payable   2,000

If the amount of the advance payments exceeds the tax liability based on actual income, the amount of the overpayment would be debited to a receivable account and credited to Income Tax.

Income tax returns and related records and documents are subject to review by the taxing authority, usually for a period of three years after the return is filed. Consequently, the determination made by the taxpayer is provisional rather than final. In recognition of the possibility of an assessment for a tax deficiency, the liability for income taxes is sometimes described in the current liability section of the balance sheet as "Estimated income tax payable."

Because of its substantial size in relationship to net income, income tax is often reported on the income statement as a special deduction, as follows:

Palmer Corporation	
Income Statement	
For Year Ended December 31, 19--	
Sales	$980,000
Income before income tax	$200,000
Income tax	82,500
Net income	$117,500

INCOME TAX ALLOCATION

The taxable income of a corporation, determined according to the tax laws, is often very different from the amount of income (before income tax) determined from the accounts and reported in the income statement. Differences between the two may be classified as "permanent differences" and "timing differences."[1]

Permanent Differences

The tax laws provide for special treatment of certain revenue and expense items. This results in permanent differences between the amount of income tax actually owed and the amount that would be owed if the tax were based on income before income tax. These items may be described as follows:

1. Revenue from a specified source is excludable from taxable income, or an expense for a specified purpose is not deductible in determining taxable income. Example: Interest income on tax-exempt municipal bonds.

---

[1]*Opinions of the Accounting Principles Board*, No. 11, "Accounting for Income Taxes" (New York: American Institute of Certified Public Accountants, 1967), par. 13.

2. A deduction is allowed in determining taxable income, but there is no actual expenditure and hence no expense. Example: The excess of the allowable deduction for percentage depletion of natural resources over depletion expense based on cost.

Permanent differences cause no problem for financial reporting. The amount of income tax determined in accordance with the tax laws is the amount reported on the income statement.

Timing Differences

The treatment of certain items results in differences between income before income tax and taxable income, because the items are recognized in one period for income statement purposes and in another period for tax purposes. These timing differences reverse or turn around in later years. The cases in which such differences occur are described as follows:

1. The method used in determining the amount of a specified revenue or expense for income tax purposes differs from the method used in determining net income for reporting purposes. Example: The installment method of determining revenue is used in determining taxable income and the point-of-sale method is used for reporting purposes.
2. The manner prescribed for the treatment of a specified revenue or expense in determining taxable income is contrary to generally accepted accounting principles and hence not acceptable in determining net income for reporting purposes. Example: Revenue received in advance that is to be earned in future years must be included in taxable income in the year received, which is contrary to the basic accounting principle that such revenue be allocated to the years benefited.

Timing differences require special treatment in the accounts. To illustrate the effect of timing differences and their related effect on the amount of income tax reported in corporate financial statements, assume that a corporation that sells its product on the installment basis recognizes the revenue at the time of sale, and maintains its accounts accordingly. At the end of the first year of operations, the income before income tax according to the ledger is $300,000. Realizing the advantage of reducing current income tax, the corporation elects the installment method of determining revenue and cost of merchandise sold, which yields taxable income of only $100,000. Assuming an income tax rate of 45%, the income tax on $300,000 of income would amount to $135,000. The income tax actually due for the year would be only $45,000 (45% of $100,000). The $90,000 difference between the two amounts is due to the timing difference in recognizing revenue. It represents a deferment of $90,000 of income tax to future years. As the installment accounts receivable are collected in later years, the additional $200,000 of income will be included in taxable income and the $90,000 deferment will become a tax liability of those years. The situation may be summarized as follows:

Income before income tax according to ledger	$300,000	
Income tax based on $300,000 at 45%		$135,000
Taxable income according to tax return	$100,000	
Income tax based on $100,000 at 45%		45,000
Income tax deferred to future years		$ 90,000

If the $90,000 of deferred income tax were not recognized in the accounts, the income statement for the first year of operations would report net income as follows:

Income before income tax	$300,000
Income tax	45,000
Net income	$255,000

Failure to allocate the additional income tax of $90,000 to the year in which the revenue is earned may be viewed as an overstatement of net income and an understatement of liabilities of $90,000. To ignore this additional expense of $90,000 and the accompanying deferred liability of $90,000 would be considered by most accountants to be incorrect and unacceptable. It is considered better to allocate the income tax to the period in which the related income is earned. According to this view, the income tax reported on the financial statements will be the total tax expected to result from the net income of the year, regardless of when the tax will become an actual liability.[2] Applying this latter viewpoint to the illustrative data yields the following results, stated in terms of a journal entry:

Income Tax	135,000	
Income Tax Payable		45,000
Deferred Income Tax Payable		90,000

Continuing with the illustration, the $90,000 in Deferred Income Tax Payable will be transferred to Income Tax Payable as the remaining $200,000 of income becomes taxable in later years. If, for example, $120,000 of untaxed income of the first year of the corporation's operations becomes taxable in the second year, the effect would be as follows, stated as a journal entry:

Deferred Income Tax Payable	54,000	
Income Tax Payable		54,000

If installment sales are made in later years, there will be more differences between taxable and reported income, and an accompanying deferment of tax liability. This will also cause a fluctuation in the balance in the deferred income tax payable account.

---

[2]*Ibid.*, par. 29.

In the illustration, the amount in Deferred Income Tax Payable at the end of a year will be reported as a liability. The amount due within one year will be classified as a current liability, and the remainder will be classified as a long-term liability or reported in a Deferred Credits section following the Long-Term Liabilities section.

REPORTING UNUSUAL ITEMS IN THE FINANCIAL STATEMENTS

In recent years, professional accounting organizations have devoted much time to the development of guidelines for reporting unusual items relating to the determination of net income. These items may be divided into four relatively well-defined categories, as follows:

1. Adjustments or corrections of net income of prior fiscal periods.
2. Segregation of the results of discontinued operations from the results of continuing operations.
3. Recognition of extraordinary items of gain or loss.
4. Change from one generally accepted principle to another.

Before examining the guidelines that are presently in effect, a brief summary of earlier viewpoints may be in order. For several years, there were two conflicting theories about the proper function of the income statement: (1) to report the *current operating performance* and (2) to be *all-inclusive*. According to the first theory, only the effects of the ordinary, normal, and recurring operations were to be reported in the income statement. It was considered better to report nonrecurring items of significant amount in the retained earnings statement. By so doing, it was argued that readers of the income statement would not draw incorrect conclusions about the "normal operating performance" of an enterprise.

On the other hand, the all-inclusive point of view was exactly the opposite of the current operating performance viewpoint. It required that all revenue and expense items recorded in the current period be reported in the income statement, with significant amounts of a nonrecurring nature properly identified. If nonrecurring items were "buried" in the retained earnings statement, they were likely to be overlooked and the total amount of the periodic net income reported over the entire life of an enterprise could not be determined from its income statements. The all-inclusive viewpoint has prevailed, and most professional accountants agree that it is preferable. The generally accepted guidelines on the subject are discussed briefly in the subsections that follow.

Prior Period Adjustments

Minor accounting errors often result from the use of estimates that are inherent in the accounting process. For example, relatively small errors in amounts provided for income taxes of one or more periods are not unusual. Similarly, annual provisions for the uncollectibility of receivables seldom agree with the amounts of the accounts actually written off. Such errors are normal and tend to be recurring. The effect of these errors should be included with the amounts for the current period.

Errors may also result from mathematical mistakes, mistakes in the application of accounting principles, or oversight or misuse of facts that existed at the time transactions were recorded. The treatment of these errors depends on when they are discovered. The procedure recommended for correcting errors that are discovered in the same period in which they occurred and that have been posted to the ledger is summarized as follows: (1) set forth the entire entry in which the error occurred by the use of memorandum T accounts or a journal entry; (2) set forth the entry that should have been made, using a second set of T accounts or a journal entry; and (3) formulate the debits and credits needed to bring the erroneous entry into agreement with the correct entry. This procedure is entirely a matter of technique, and no question of principle is involved. After the correction has been made, the account balances are the same as they would have been in the absence of error, and the information given in the income statement and the balance sheet is unaffected.

The effect of material errors that are not discovered within the same fiscal period in which they occurred should not be included in the determination of net income for the current period.[3] Such errors relating to a prior period or periods should be reported as an adjustment of the retained earnings balance at the beginning of the period in which the correction is made. If financial statements are presented only for the current period, the effect of the adjustment on the net income of the preceding period should also be disclosed. If income statements for prior periods are presented in the current annual report, as is preferable, the effect of the adjustment on each statement should be disclosed.

Corrections of this type of error are usually called **prior period adjustments.** For example, the correction of a material error in computing depreciation expense for a prior period would be a prior period adjustment. In addition, a change from an unacceptable accounting principle to an acceptable accounting principle is considered to be a correction of an error and should be treated as a prior period adjustment. An example of such a situation would be the correction resulting from changing from the cash basis to the accrual basis of accounting for a business enterprise that buys and sells merchandise.

Adjustments applicable to prior periods that meet the criteria for a prior period adjustment are rare in modern financial accounting. Annual audits by independent public accountants, combined with the internal control features of accounting systems, lessen the chances of errors justifying such treatment.

Discontinued Operations

A gain or loss resulting from the disposal of a segment of a business should be identified on the income statement as **discontinued operations.** The term

---

[3]*Statement of Financial Accounting Standards, No. 16,* "Prior Period Adjustments" (Stamford: Financial Accounting Standards Board, 1977), par. 11.

discontinued refers to "the operations of a segment of a business . . . that has been sold, abandoned, spun off, or otherwise disposed of or . . . is the subject of a formal plan for disposal."[4] The term "segment of a business" refers to a part of an enterprise whose activities represent a major line of business, such as a division or department or a certain class of customer.[5] For example, if an enterprise owning newspapers, television stations, and radio stations were to sell its radio stations, the results of the sale would be reported as a gain or loss on discontinued operations.

When an enterprise discontinues a segment of its operations and identifies the gain or loss therefrom, the results of "continuing operations" should also be identified in the income statement. The net income or loss from continuing operations is presented first, beginning with sales and followed by the enterprise's customary analysis of its costs and expenses. In addition to the data on discontinued operations presented in the body of the statement, such details as the identity of the segment disposed of, the disposal date, a description of the assets and liabilities involved, and the manner of disposal should be disclosed in a note to the financial statements.[6]

Extraordinary Items

Extraordinary gains and losses result from "events and transactions that are distinguished by their unusual nature *and* by the infrequency of their occurrence."[7] Such gains and losses, other than those from the disposal of a segment of a business, should be identified in the income statement as **extraordinary items.** To be so classified, an event or transaction must meet both of the following criteria:

1. *Unusual nature*—the underlying event or transaction should possess a high degree of abnormality and be of a type clearly unrelated to, or only incidentally related to, the ordinary and typical activities of the entity, taking into account the environment in which the entity operates.
2. *Infrequency of occurrence*—the underlying event or transaction should be of a type that would not reasonably be expected to recur in the foreseeable future, taking into account the environment in which the entity operates.[8]

Transactions that meet both of the above criteria are rare. For example, gains and losses on the disposal of plant assets do not qualify as extraordinary items because (1) they are not unusual and (2) they recur from time to time in the ordinary course of business activities. Similarly, gains and losses incurred on the sale of investments are usual and recurring for most enterprises. However, if a company had owned only one investment during its entire existence, a gain or loss on its sale might qualify as an extraordinary item, provided there was no intention of acquiring other investments in the foreseeable future.

---

[4]*Opinions of the Accounting Principles Board, No. 30,* "Reporting the Results of Operations" (New York: American Institute of Certified Public Accountants, 1973), par. 8.

[5]*Ibid.,* par. 13.

[6]*Ibid.,* par. 18.

[7]*Ibid.,* par. 20.

[8]*Ibid.*

The more usual extraordinary items result from major casualties, such as floods, earthquakes, and other rare catastrophes not expected to recur. In addition, gains or losses that result when land or buildings are condemned for public use are considered extraordinary.

Changes in Accounting Principles

A change in accounting principle "results from adoption of a generally accepted accounting principle different from the one used previously for reporting purposes."[9] The concept of consistency and its relationship to changes in accounting methods were discussed in Chapter 1. A change from one generally accepted accounting principle or method to another generally accepted principle or method should be disclosed in the financial statements of the period in which the change is made. In addition to describing the nature of the change, the justification for the change should be stated and the effect of the change on net income should be disclosed.

The generally accepted procedures for disclosing the effect on net income of a change in principle are as follows: (1) report the cumulative effect of the change on net income of prior periods as a special item on the income statement, and (2) report the effect of the change on net income of the current period. If the financial statements for prior periods are presented in conjunction with the current statements, the effect of the change in accounting principle should also be applied retroactively to the published statements of the prior periods and reported either on their face or in accompanying notes.

The amount of the cumulative effect on net income of prior periods should be reported in a special section of the income statement located immediately prior to the net income. If an extraordinary item or items are reported on the statement, the amount related to the change in principle should follow the extraordinary items.

The procedures should be modified for a change from the lifo assumption for inventory costing to another method or for a change in the method of accounting for long-term construction contracts. For these changes in principle, the cumulative effect on prior years' income is not reported as a special item on the income statement. Instead, the newly adopted principle should be applied retroactively to the income statements of the prior periods and the effect on income disclosed, either on the face of the statements or in accompanying notes. Financial statements of subsequent periods need not repeat the disclosures.[10]

Allocation of Related Income Tax

The amount reported as a prior period adjustment, a discontinued operation, an extraordinary item, or the cumulative effect of a change in accounting principle should be net of the related income tax. The amount of income tax

---

[9]*Opinions of the Accounting Principles Board*, No. 20, "Accounting Changes" (New York: American Institute of Certified Public Accountants, 1971), par. 7.

[10]*Ibid.*, pars. 27 and 28.

allocable to each item may be disclosed on the face of the appropriate financial statement or by an accompanying note.

Presentation of Unusual Items in the Income Statement

The manner in which discontinued operations, extraordinary items, and the cumulative effect of a change in accounting principle may be presented in the income statement is illustrated as follows. Many variations in terminology and format are possible.

CAP Corporation Income Statement For the Year Ended August 31, 19--	
Net sales	$9,600,950
Income from continuing operations before income tax	$1,310,000
Income tax	620,000
Income from continuing operations	$ 690,000
Loss on discontinued operations (Note A)	100,000
Income before extraordinary item and cumulative effect of a change in accounting principle	$ 590,000
Extraordinary item: Gain on condemnation of land, net of applicable income tax of $65,000.	150,000
Cumulative effect on prior years of changing to a different depreciation method (Note B)	92,000
Net income	$ 832,000

Note A. On July 1 of the current year, the entire electrical products division of the corporation was sold at a loss of $100,000, net of applicable income tax of $50,000. The net sales of the division for the current year were $2,900,000. The assets sold were composed of inventories, equipment, and plant totaling $2,100,000, and the liabilities assumed by the purchaser amounted to $600,000.

Note B. Depreciation of property, plant, and equipment has been computed by the straight-line method at all manufacturing facilities in 19--. Prior to 19--, depreciation of equipment for one of the divisions had been computed on the double-declining balance method. In 19--, the straight-line method was adopted for this division in order to achieve uniformity and to more appropriately match the remaining depreciation charges with the estimated economic utility of such assets. Pursuant to APB Opinion 20, this change in depreciation has been applied retroactively to prior years. The effect of the change was to increase income before extraordinary items for 19-- by approximately $30,000. The adjustment of $92,000 (after reduction for income tax of $88,000) to apply retroactively the new method is also included in income for 19--.

EARNINGS PER COMMON SHARE

Data on earnings per share of common stock are reported on the income statements of public corporations.[11] The data are also often reported in the financial press and by various statistical services. Sometimes called the "bottom line of the income statement," earnings per share is often the item of greatest interest contained in corporate annual reports.

The effect of nonrecurring additions to or deductions from income of a period should be considered in computing earnings per share. Otherwise, a single per share amount based on net income would be misleading. To illustrate this point, assume that the corporation whose partial income statement appears above reported net income of $700,000 for the preceding year, with no extraordinary or other special items. Assume also that its capital stock was composed of 200,000 common shares outstanding during the entire two-year period. If the earnings per share of $3.50 ($700,000 ÷ 200,000) for the preceding year were compared with the earnings per share of $4.16 ($832,000 ÷ 200,000) for the current year, it would appear that operations had greatly improved. The per share amount for the current year comparable to $3.50 is in reality $3.45 ($690,000 ÷ 200,000), which indicates a slight downward trend in normal operations.

Data on earnings per share should be presented in conjunction with the income statement. If there are nonrecurring items on the statement, the per share amounts should be presented for (1) income from continuing operations, (2) income before extraordinary items and cumulative effect of a change in accounting principle, (3) cumulative effect of a change in accounting principle, (4) net income.[12] Presentation of per share amounts is optional for gain or loss on discontinued operations and for extraordinary items. The per share data may be shown in parentheses or added at the bottom of the statement, as in the illustration shown at the top of page 359.

In computing the earnings per share of common stock, all factors that affect the number of shares outstanding must be considered. If there is an issue of preferred stock or bonds with the privilege of converting to common stock, two different amounts of per share earnings should ordinarily be reported. One amount is computed without regard to the conversion privilege and is referred to as "Earnings per common share—assuming no dilution" or "Primary earnings per share." The other computation is based on the assumption that the convertible preferred stock or bonds are converted to common stock, and the amount is referred to as "Earnings per common share—

---

[11]Nonpublic corporations are exempt from this requirement, according to *Statement of Financial Accounting Standards, No. 21*, "Suspension of the Reporting of Earnings per Share and Segment Information by Nonpublic Enterprises" (Stamford: Financial Accounting Standards Board, 1978).

[12]*Opinions of the Accounting Principles Board, No. 15*, "Earnings per Share" (New York: American Institute of Certified Public Accountants, 1969) as amended by *Opinions of the Accounting Principles Board, No. 20* and *Opinions of the Accounting Principles Board, No. 30*.

CAP Corporation
Income Statement
For the Year Ended August 31, 19--

Income from continuing operations $690,000

Net income.. $832,000

Earnings per common share:
Income from continuing operations $3.45
Loss on discontinued operations .... .50

Income before extraordinary item and cumulative effect of a change
in accounting principle $2.95
Extraordinary item... .75
Cumulative effect on prior years of changing to a different depreciation method .... .46

Net income... $4.16

assuming full dilution" or "Fully diluted earnings per share."[13] These and other complexities of capital structure are discussed in advanced accounting texts.

APPROPRIATION OF RETAINED EARNINGS

The amount of a corporation's retained earnings available for distribution to its shareholders may be limited by action of the board of directors. The amount restricted, which is called an appropriation or a reserve, remains a part of retained earnings and should be so classified in the financial statements. An appropriation can be effected by transferring the desired amount from Retained Earnings to a special account designating its purpose, such as Appropriation for Plant Expansion.

Appropriations may be initiated by the directors, or they may be required by law or contract. Some states require that a corporation retain earnings equal to the amount paid for treasury stock. For example, if a corporation with accumulated earnings of $200,000 purchases shares of its own issued stock for $50,000, the corporation would not be permitted to pay more than $150,000 in dividends. The restriction is equal to the $50,000 paid for the treasury stock

[13]*Opinions of the Accounting Principles Board*, No. 15, "Earnings per Share" (New York: American Institute of Certified Public Accountants, 1969), par. 16.

and assures that legal capital will not be impaired by a declaration of dividends. The entry to record the appropriation would be:

```
Apr. 24   Retained Earnings.........................   50,000
              Appropriation for Treasury Stock..........          50,000
```

When a part or all of an appropriation is no longer needed, the amount should be transferred back to the retained earnings account. Thus, if the corporation in the above illustration sells the treasury stock, the appropriation would be eliminated by the following entry:

```
Nov. 10   Appropriation for Treasury Stock............   50,000
              Retained Earnings.......................          50,000
```

When a corporation borrows a large amount through issuance of bonds or long-term notes, the agreement may provide for restrictions on dividends until the debt is paid. The contract may stipulate that retained earnings equal to the amount borrowed be restricted during the entire period of the loan, or it may require that the restriction be built up by annual appropriations. For example, assume that a corporation borrows $700,000 on ten-year bonds. If equal annual appropriations were to be made over the life of the bonds, there would be a series of ten entries, each in the amount of $70,000, debiting Retained Earnings and crediting an appropriation account entitled Appropriation for Bonded Indebtedness. Even if the bond agreement did not require the restriction on retained earnings, the directors might decide to establish the appropriation. In that case, it would be a *discretionary* rather than a *contractual* appropriation. The entries would be the same in either case.

It must be clearly understood that the appropriation account is not directly related to any certain group of asset accounts. Its existence does not imply that there is an equivalent amount of cash or other assets set aside in a special fund. The appropriation serves the purpose of restricting dividends, but it does not assure that the cash that might otherwise be distributed as dividends will not be invested in additional inventories or other assets, or used to reduce liabilities.

Appropriations of retained earnings may be accompanied by a segregation of cash or marketable securities, in which case the appropriation is said to be **funded**. Accumulation of such funds is discussed in Chapter 12.

There are other purposes for which the directors may consider appropriations desirable. A company may earmark earnings for specific contingencies, such as inventory price declines or an adverse decision on a pending law suit. Some companies with properties in many locations may assume their own risk of losses from fire, windstorm, and other casualties rather than obtain protection from insurance companies. In such cases, the appropriation account would be entitled Appropriation for Self-Insurance. Such an appropriation is likely to be permanent, although its amount may vary as the total value of properties and the extent of fire protection change. If a loss occurs, it should be debited to a special loss account rather than to the appropriation account. It is definitely a loss of the particular period and should be reported in the income statement.

The details of retained earnings may be presented in the balance sheet in the following manner. The item designated "Unappropriated" is the balance of the retained earnings account.

Retained earnings:		
Appropriated:		
For plant expansion..........................	$ 250,000	
Unappropriated	1,800,000	
Total retained earnings.......................		$2,050,000

Restrictions on retained earnings do not need to be formalized in the ledger. However, following legal requirements and contractual restrictions is necessary, and the nature and the amount of all restrictions should always be disclosed in the balance sheet. For example, the appropriations data appearing in the foregoing illustration could be presented in a note accompanying the balance sheet. Such an alternative might also be used as a means of simplifying or condensing the balance sheet, even though appropriation accounts are maintained in the ledger. The alternative balance sheet presentation, including the note, might appear as follows:

Retained earnings (see note) $2,050,000

Note: Retained earnings in the amount of $250,000 are appropriated for expansion of plant facilities; the remaining $1,800,000 is unrestricted.

NATURE OF DIVIDENDS

A dividend is a distribution by a corporation to its shareholders. It is usually on a pro rata basis for all shares of a certain class. In most cases, dividends represent distributions from retained earnings. In many states, dividends may be declared from the excess of paid-in capital over par or stated value, but such dividends are unusual. The term **liquidating dividend** is applied to a distribution from paid-in capital when a corporation permanently reduces its operations or winds up its affairs completely. The discussion that follows deals with dividends based on accumulated earnings.

Dividends may be paid in cash, in stock of the company, in scrip, or in other property. The two most common types of dividends are **cash dividends** and **stock dividends** (stock of the company issuing the dividend).

Usually there are three prerequisites to paying a cash dividend: (1) sufficient unappropriated retained earnings, (2) sufficient cash, and (3) formal action by the board of directors. A large amount of accumulated earnings does not always mean that a corporation is able to pay dividends. There must also be enough cash in excess of routine requirements. The amount of retained earnings, which represents net income retained in the business, is not directly related to cash. The cash provided by the net income may have been used to purchase assets, to reduce liabilities, or for other purposes. The directors are not required by law to declare dividends, even when both retained earnings and cash appear to be sufficient. When a dividend has been declared, however, it becomes a liability of the corporation.

Corporations with a wide distribution of stock usually try to maintain a stable dividend record. They may retain a large part of earnings in good years in order to be able to continue dividend payments in lean years. Dividends may be paid once a year or on a semiannual or quarterly basis. The tendency is to pay quarterly dividends on both common and preferred stock. In particularly good years, the directors may declare an "extra" dividend on common stock. It may be paid at one of the usual dividend dates or at some other date. The designation "extra" indicates that the board of directors does not anticipate an increase in the amount of the "regular" dividend.

Notice of a dividend declaration is usually reported in financial publications and newspapers. The notice identifies three different dates related to a declaration: (1) the date of declaration, (2) the date of record, and (3) the date of payment. The first is the date the directors take formal action declaring the dividend, the second is the date as of which ownership of shares is to be determined, and the third is the date payment is to be made. For example, a notice might read: On October 11, the board of directors declared a quarterly cash dividend to stockholders of record as of the close of business on October 21, payable on November 15.

The liability for a dividend is recorded on the declaration date, when the formal action is taken by the directors. No entry is required on the date of record, which merely fixes the date for determining the identity of the stockholders entitled to receive the dividend. The period of time between the record date and the payment date is provided to permit completion of postings to the stockholders ledger and preparation of the dividend checks. The liability of the corporation is paid by the mailing of the checks.

Dividends on cumulative preferred stock do not become a liability of the corporation until formal action is taken by the board of directors. However, dividends in arrears at a balance sheet date should be disclosed by a footnote, a parenthetical notation, or a segregation of retained earnings similar to the following:

Retained earnings:		
Required to meet dividends in arrears on preferred		
stock..	$30,000	
Remainder, unrestricted............................	16,000	
Total retained earnings............................		$46,000

Cash Dividends

Dividends payable in cash are by far the most usual form of dividend. Dividends on common stock are usually stated in terms of dollars and cents rather than as a percentage of par. Dividends on preferred stock may be stated either in monetary terms or as a percentage of par. For example, the annual dividend rate on a particular $100 par preferred stock may be stated as either $10 or 10%.

Assuming a sufficient balance in retained earnings, including estimated net income of the current year, the directors usually consider the following factors in determining whether to declare a dividend:

1. The company's working capital position.
2. Resources needed for planned expansion or replacement of facilities.
3. Maturity dates of large liabilities.
4. Future business prospects of the company and forecasts for the industry and the economy generally.

To illustrate the entries required in the declaration and the payment of cash dividends, assume that on December 1 the board of directors declares the regular quarterly dividend of $2.50 on the 5,000 shares of $100 par, 10% preferred stock outstanding (total dividend of $12,500), and a quarterly dividend of 30¢ on the 100,000 shares of $10 par common stock outstanding (total dividend of $30,000). Both dividends are to stockholders of record on December 10, and checks are to be issued to stockholders on January 2. The entry to record the declaration of the dividends is as follows:

Dec. 1	Cash Dividends	42,500	
	Cash Dividends Payable		42,500

The balance in Cash Dividends would be transferred to Retained Earnings as a part of the closing process and Cash Dividends Payable would be listed on the balance sheet as a current liability. Payment of the liability on January 2 would be recorded in the usual manner as a debit of $42,500 to Cash Dividends Payable and a credit to Cash.

Stock Dividends

A pro rata distribution of shares of stock to stockholders, accompanied by a transfer of retained earnings to paid-in capital accounts, is called a **stock dividend**. Such distributions are usually in common stock and are issued to holders of common stock. It is possible to issue common stock to preferred stockholders or vice versa, but such stock dividends are too unusual to warrant their consideration here.

Stock dividends are quite unlike cash dividends, in that there is no distribution of cash or other corporate assets to the stockholders. They are ordinarily issued by corporations that "plow back" (retain) earnings for use in acquiring new facilities or for expanding their operations.

The effect of a stock dividend on the capital structure of the issuing corporation is to transfer accumulated earnings to paid-in capital. The statutes of most states require that an amount equivalent to the par or stated value of a stock dividend be transferred from the retained earnings account to the common stock account. Compliance with this minimum requirement is considered by accountants to be satisfactory for a nonpublic corporation, whose stockholders are presumed to have enough knowledge of the corporation's affairs to recognize the true import of the dividend. However, many investors in the stock of public corporations are often less knowledgeable. An analysis of this latter situation, and the widely accepted viewpoint of professional accountants, has been expressed as follows:

> ... many recipients of stock dividends look upon them as distributions of corporate earnings and usually in an amount equivalent to the fair value of the additional shares received. Furthermore, it is to be presumed that such views of recipients are materially strengthened in those instances, which are by far the most numerous, where the issuances are so small in comparison with the shares previously outstanding that they do not have any apparent effect upon the share market price and, consequently, the market value of the shares previously held remains substantially unchanged. The committee therefore believes that where these circumstances exist the corporation should in the public interest account for the transaction by transferring from earned surplus to the category of permanent capitalization ... an amount equal to the fair value of the additional shares issued. Unless this is done, the amount of earnings which the shareholder may believe to have been distributed to him will be left, except to the extent otherwise dictated by legal requirements, in earned surplus subject to possible further similar stock issuances or cash distributions.[14]

To illustrate the issuance of a stock dividend according to the procedure recommended above, assume the following balances in the stockholders' equity accounts of a corporation as of December 15:

Common Stock, $20 par (2,000,000 shares issued)...... $40,000,000
Premium on Common Stock......................... 9,000,000
Retained Earnings 26,600,000

On December 15, the board of directors declares a 5% stock dividend (100,000 shares, $20 par), to be issued on January 10. Assuming that the average of the high and low market prices on the declaration date is $31 a share, the entry to record the declaration would be as follows:

Dec. 15   Stock Dividends........................... 3,100,000
                Stock Dividends Distributable............   2,000,000
                Premium on Common Stock   1,100,000

The $3,100,000 debit to Stock Dividends would be transferred to Retained Earnings as a part of the closing process. The issuance of the stock certificates would be recorded on January 10 as follows:

---

[14]*Accounting Research and Terminology Bulletins — Final Edition*, "No. 43, Restatement and Revision of Accounting Research Bulletins" (New York: American Institute of Certified Public Accountants, 1961), Ch. 7, Sec. B, par. 10.

Jan. 10	Stock Dividends Distributable...............	2,000,000	
	Common Stock.........................		2,000,000

The effect of the stock dividend is to transfer $3,100,000 from the retained earnings account to paid-in capital accounts and to increase by 100,000 the number of shares outstanding. There is no change in the assets, liabilities, or total stockholders' equity of the corporation. If financial statements are prepared between the date of declaration and the date of issuance, the stock dividends distributable account should be listed in the paid-in capital section of the balance sheet.

The issuance of the additional shares does not affect the total amount of a stockholder's equity and proportionate interest in the corporation. The effect of the stock dividend on the accounts of a corporation and on the equity of a stockholder owning 1,000 shares is demonstrated by the following tabulation:

The Corporation	Before Stock Dividend	After Stock Dividend
Common stock	$40,000,000	$42,000,000
Premium on common stock	9,000,000	10,100,000
Retained earnings	26,600,000	23,500,000
Total stockholders' equity	$75,600,000	$75,600,000
Number of shares outstanding	2,000,000	2,100,000
Equity per share......................	$37.80	$36.00
A Stockholder		
Number of shares owned	1,000	1,050
Total equity	$37,800	$37,800
Portion of corporation owned.............	.05%	.05%

STOCK SPLITS

Corporations sometimes reduce the par or stated value of their common stock and issue a proportionate number of additional shares. Such a procedure is called a **stock split** or **stock split-up.** For example, a corporation with 10,000 shares of $10 par stock outstanding may reduce the par to $5 and increase the number of shares to 20,000. A stockholder who owned 100 shares before the split would own 200 shares after the split. There are no changes in the balances of any of the corporation's accounts, hence no entry is required. The primary purpose of a stock split is to reduce the market price per share and encourage more investors to enter the market for the company's shares.

DIVIDENDS AND STOCK SPLITS FOR TREASURY STOCK

Cash or property dividends are not paid on treasury stock. To do so would place the corporation in the position of earning income through dealing with itself, an obvious fiction. Accordingly, the total amount of a cash (or property) dividend should be based on the number of shares outstanding at the record date.

When a corporation holding treasury stock declares a stock dividend, the number of shares to be issued may be based on either (1) the number of shares outstanding or (2) the number of shares issued. In practice, the number of shares held as treasury stock represents a small percent of the number of shares issued. Also, the rate of dividend is usually small, so that the difference between the end results of both methods is usually not significant.

There is no legal, theoretical, or practical reason for excluding treasury stock when computing the number of shares to be issued in a stock split. The reduction in par or stated value would apply to all shares of the class, including the unissued, issued, and treasury shares.

RETAINED EARNINGS STATEMENT

The retained earnings statement illustrated in Chapter 4 reported only the changes in the account balance due to earnings and dividends for the period. When there are accounts for appropriations, it is customary to divide the statement into two major sections: (1) appropriated and (2) unappropriated. The first section is composed of an analysis of all appropriation accounts, beginning with the opening balance, listing the additions or the deductions during the period, and ending with the closing balance. The second section is composed of an analysis of the retained earnings account and is similar in form to the first section. The final figure on the statement is the total retained earnings as of the last day of the period. This form of the statement is illustrated as follows:

Shaw Corporation Retained Earnings Statement For Year Ended December 31, 19--			
Appropriated:			
Appropriation for plant expansion, January 1, 19--.........		$ 180,000	
Additional appropriation (see below)...................		100,000	
Retained earnings appropriated, December 31, 19--.......			$ 280,000
Unappropriated:			
Balance, January 1, 19--..............................	$1,414,500		
Net income for the year..............................	580,000	$1,994,500	
Cash dividends declared	$ 125,000		
Transfer to appropriation for plant expansion (see above)..	100,000	225,000	
Retained earnings unappropriated, December 31, 19--.....			1,769,500
Total retained earnings, December 31, 19--			$2,049,500

RETAINED EARNINGS STATEMENT

There are many possible variations in the form of the retained earnings statement. It may also be added to the income statement to form a combined statement of income and retained earnings, which is illustrated in Chapter 4.

Self-Examination Questions (Answers at end of chapter.)

1. Paid-in capital for a corporation may originate from which of the following sources?
   A. Real estate donated to the corporation
   B. Redemption of the corporation's own stock
   C. Sale of the corporation's treasury stock
   D. All of the above

2. During its first year of operations, a corporation elected to use the straight-line method of depreciation for financial reporting purposes and the sum-of-the-years-digits method in determining taxable income. If the income tax rate is 45% and the amount of depreciation expense is $60,000 under the straight-line method and $100,000 under the sum-of-the-years-digits method, what is the amount of income tax deferred to future years?
   A. $18,000   C. $45,000
   B. $27,000   D. None of the above

3. An item treated as a prior period adjustment should be reported in the financial statements as:
   A. an extraordinary item
   B. an other expense item
   C. an adjustment of the beginning balance of retained earnings
   D. none of the above

4. A material gain resulting from the condemnation of land for public use would be reported on the income statement as:
   A. an extraordinary item   C. an item of revenue from sales
   B. an other income item   D. none of the above

5. An appropriation for plant expansion would be reported on the balance sheet in:
   A. the plant assets section   C. the stockholders' equity section
   B. the long-term liabilities section D. none of the above

Discussion Questions

11–1. Name the titles of the two principal subdivisions of the stockholders' equity section of a corporate balance sheet.

11–2. If a corporation is given land as an inducement to locate in a particular community, (a) how should the amount of the debit to the land account be determined, and (b) what is the title of the account that should be credited for the same amount?

11–3. A corporation has paid $250,000 of federal income tax during the year on the basis of its estimated income. What entry should be recorded as of the end of the year if it determines that (a) it owes an additional $25,000? (b) it overpaid its tax by $15,000?

11-4. The income before income tax reported on the income statement for the year is $400,000. Because of timing differences in accounting and tax methods, the taxable income for the same year is $250,000. Assuming an income tax rate of 50%, state (a) the amount of income tax to be deducted from the $400,000 on the income statement, (b) the amount of the actual income tax that should be paid for the year, and (c) the amount of the deferred income tax liability.

11-5. Indicate how prior period adjustments would be reported on the financial statements presented only for the current period.

11-6. Indicate where the following should be reported in the financial statements, assuming that financial statements are presented only for the current year:
   (a) Uninsured loss on building due to flood damage. This was the first time such a loss had been incurred since the firm was organized in 1880.
   (b) Loss on disposal of equipment considered to be obsolete.

11-7. Classify each of the following revenue and expense items as either (a) normally recurring or (b) extraordinary. Assume that the amount of each item is material.
   (1) Interest expense on notes payable
   (2) Uninsured flood loss (Flood insurance is unavailable because of periodic flooding in the area.)
   (3) Uncollectible accounts expense
   (4) Salaries of corporate officers
   (5) Loss on sale of plant assets

11-8. During the current year, five acres of land which cost $50,000 were condemned for construction of an interstate highway. Assuming that an award of $90,000 in cash was received and that the applicable income tax on this transaction is 25%, how would this information be presented in the income statement?

11-9. A corporation reports earnings per share of $4.25 for the most recent year and $4.75 for the preceding year. The $4.25 includes $.75 per share loss from a rare earthquake. (a) Should the composition of the $4.25 be disclosed in the financial report? (b) What is the amount for the most recent year that is comparable to the $4.75 earnings per share of the preceding year? (c) On the basis of the limited information presented, would you conclude that operations had improved or retrogressed?

11-10. Appropriations of retained earnings may be (a) required by law, (b) required by contract, or (c) made at the discretion of the board of directors. Give an illustration of each type of appropriation.

11-11. A credit balance in Retained Earnings does not represent cash. Explain.

11-12. The board of directors votes to appropriate $50,000 of retained earnings for plant expansion. What is the effect of their action on (a) cash, (b) total retained earnings, and (c) retained earnings available for dividends?

11-13. What are the three prerequisites to the declaration and the payment of a cash dividend?

11-14. The dates in connection with the declaration of a cash dividend are May 10, May 24, and June 14. Identify each date.

11-15. A corporation with both cumulative preferred stock and common stock outstanding has a substantial credit balance in the retained earnings account at the beginning of the current fiscal year. Although net income for the current year is sufficient to pay the preferred dividend of $40,000 each quarter and a common dividend of $70,000 each quarter, the board of directors declares dividends only on the preferred stock. Suggest possible reasons for passing the dividends on the common stock.

11–16. State the effect of the following actions on a corporation's assets, liabilities, and stockholders' equity: (a) declaration of a stock dividend; (b) issuance of stock certificates for the stock dividend declared in (a); (c) authorization and issuance of stock certificates in a stock split; (d) declaration of cash dividend; (e) payment of the cash dividend declared in (d).

11–17. An owner of 100 shares of Reed Company common stock receives a stock dividend of 4 shares. (a) What is the effect of the stock dividend on the equity per share of the stock? (b) How does the total equity of 104 shares compare with the total equity of 100 shares before the stock dividend?

11–18. A corporation with 10,000 shares of no-par common stock issued, of which 500 shares are held as treasury stock, declares a cash dividend of $1 a share. What is the total amount of the dividend?

11–19. If a corporation with 50,000 shares of common stock outstanding has a 4-for-1 stock split (3 additional shares for each share issued), what will be the number of shares outstanding after the split?

11–20. If the common stock in Question 11–19 had a market price of $200 per share before the stock split, what would be an approximate market price per share after the split?

11–21. Present entries to record the following selected transactions of Albin Corporation: Exercises

    Apr. 15. Paid the first installment of the estimated income tax for the current fiscal year ending December 31, $140,000. No entry had been made to record the liability.

    June 15. Paid the second installment of $140,000. (Same note as above.)

    Dec. 31. Recorded the additional income tax liability for the year just ended and the deferred income tax liability, based on the two transactions above and the following data:

Income tax rate..	45%
Income before income tax	$1,400,000
Taxable income according to tax return..................	1,250,000
Third installment paid on September 15	140,000
Fourth installment paid on December 15.................	140,000

11–22. Prior to adjusting and closing the accounts at December 31, the end of the current fiscal year, the accountant discovered the following errors which occurred during the year. Present the entry to correct each error.

    (a) The declaration of a cash dividend of $15,000 had been recorded as a debit to Interest Expense and a credit to Interest Payable. Payment of the dividend had been recorded as a debit to Interest Payable and a credit to Cash.

    (b) A purchase of $950 of office equipment on account was debited to Office Supplies and credited to Accounts Payable.

    (c) Delivery equipment that had cost $17,500 and on which $16,500 of depreciation had accumulated at the time of sale was sold for $2,000. The transaction was recorded by a debit to Cash and a credit to Sales for $2,000.

    (d) In recording a purchase of office equipment on December 10, for which a note payable was given, Accounts Payable was credited for $9,500.

11–23. On the basis of the following data for the current fiscal year ended June 30, prepare an income statement for Fagan Company, including an analysis of earnings per share in the form illustrated in this chapter. There were 100,000 shares of $10 par common stock outstanding throughout the year.

Cost of merchandise sold...	$640,000
Cumulative effect on prior years of changing to a different depreciation method..	74,500
Gain on condemnation of land (extraordinary item)	94,500
General expenses	48,600
Income tax applicable to change in depreciation method	22,500
Income tax applicable to gain on condemnation of land	28,500
Income tax reduction applicable to loss from discontinued operations	18,750
Income tax applicable to ordinary income..............................	96,300
Loss on discontinued operations.......................................	61,750
Sales...	995,000
Selling expenses	82,100

11–24. A corporation purchased for cash 2,000 shares of its own $50 par common stock at $75 a share. In the following year, it sold 1,000 of the treasury shares at $88 a share for cash. (a) Present the entries (1) to record the purchase (treasury stock is recorded at cost) and (2) to provide for the appropriation of retained earnings. (b) Present the entries (1) to record the sale of the stock and (2) to reduce the appropriation.

11–25. The dates in connection with a cash dividend of $50,000 on a corporation's common stock are June 30, July 20, and August 5. Present the entries required on each date.

11–26. The balance sheet of Easso Company indicates common stock (100,000 shares authorized), $10 par, $800,000; premium on common stock, $125,000; and retained earnings, $335,000. The board of directors declares a 5% stock dividend when the market price of the stock is $25 a share. (a) Present entries to record (1) the declaration of the dividend, capitalizing an amount equal to market value, and (2) the issuance of the stock certificates. (b) Determine the equity per share (1) before the stock dividend and (2) after the stock dividend. (c) Frank Rossi owned 100 shares of the common stock before the stock dividend was declared. Determine the total equity of his holdings (1) before the stock dividend and (2) after the stock dividend.

11–27. The board of directors of the Gorski Corporation authorized the reduction of par of its common shares from $100 to $20, increasing the number of outstanding shares to 500,000. The market price of the stock immediately before the stock split is $220 a share. (a) Determine the number of outstanding shares prior to the stock split. (b) Present the entry required to record the stock split. (c) At approximately what price would a share of stock be expected to sell immediately after the stock split?

11–28. Janof Corporation reports the following results of transactions affecting net income and retained earnings for its first fiscal year of operations ending on December 31:

Income before income tax	$135,000
Income tax...................................	42,500
Cash dividends declared	30,000
Appropriation for contingencies...............	25,000

Prepare a retained earnings statement for the fiscal year ended December 31.

11–29. Differences in accounting methods between those applied to its accounts and financial reports and those used in determining taxable income yielded the following amounts for the first four years of a corporation's operations:

	First Year	Second Year	Third Year	Fourth Year
Income before income tax	$320,000	$355,000	$451,000	$488,000
Taxable income	295,000	335,000	404,000	438,000

The income tax rate for each of the four years was 45% of taxable income and each year's taxes were promptly paid.

Instructions:

(1) Determine for each year the amounts described in the following columnar captions, presenting the information in the form indicated:

Year	Income Tax Deducted on Income Statement	Income Tax Payments for the Year	Deferred Income Tax Payable	
			Year's Addition (Deduction)	Year-End Balance

(2) Total the first three amount columns.

11–30. Selected transactions completed by Tidwell Corporation during the current fiscal year are as follows:

Jan. 22. Purchased 2,000 shares of the corporation's own common stock at $31, recording the stock at cost. (Prior to the purchase, there were 50,000 shares of $20 par common stock outstanding.)

Feb. 10. Discovered that a receipt of $725 cash on account from R. Carter had been posted in error to the account of R. Carson. The transaction was recorded correctly in the cash receipts journal.

Apr. 10. Declared a semiannual dividend of $1.50 on 5,000 shares of preferred stock and a 25¢ dividend on common stock to stockholders of record on April 30, payable on July 10.

July 10. Paid the cash dividends.

Aug. 22. Sold 800 shares of treasury stock at $35, receiving cash.

Oct. 3. Declared semiannual dividends of $1.50 on the preferred stock and 40¢ on the common stock. In addition, a 5% common stock dividend was declared on the common stock outstanding, to be capitalized at the fair market value of the common stock, which is estimated at $30.

Nov. 16. Paid the cash dividends and issued the certificates for the common stock dividend.

Dec. 8. Recorded $96,250 additional federal income tax allocable to net income for the year. Of this amount, $67,500 is a current liability and $28,750 is deferred.

30. The board of directors authorized the appropriation necessitated by the holding of treasury stock.

Instructions:

Record the transactions.

11–31. The retained earnings accounts of Smid Corporation for the current fiscal year ended December 31 are as follows:

ACCOUNT **APPROPRIATION FOR PLANT EXPANSION**   ACCOUNT NO. **3201**

Date		Item	Debit	Credit	Balance Debit	Balance Credit
19--						
Jan.	1	Balance				200,000
Dec.	31	Retained earnings		50,000		250,000

ACCOUNT **APPROPRIATION FOR BONDED INDEBTEDNESS**   ACCOUNT NO. **3202**

Date		Item	Debit	Credit	Balance Debit	Balance Credit
19--						
Jan.	1	Balance				525,000
Dec.	31	Retained earnings	125,000			400,000

ACCOUNT **RETAINED EARNINGS**   ACCOUNT NO. **3301**

Date		Item	Debit	Credit	Balance Debit	Balance Credit
19--						
Jan.	1	Balance				749,000
Dec.	31	Income summary		165,000		914,000
	31	Appropriation for plant expansion	50,000			864,000
	31	Appropriation for bonded indebtedness		125,000		989,000
	31	Cash dividends	75,000			914,000
	31	Stock dividends	100,000			814,000

ACCOUNT **CASH DIVIDENDS**   ACCOUNT NO. **3302**

Date		Item	Debit	Credit	Balance Debit	Balance Credit
19--						
Nov.	21		75,000		75,000	
Dec.	31	Retained earnings		75,000	——	——

ACCOUNT **STOCK DIVIDENDS**   ACCOUNT NO. **3303**

Date		Item	Debit	Credit	Balance Debit	Balance Credit
19--						
Dec.	10		100,000		100,000	
Dec.	31	Retained earnings		100,000	——	——

Instructions:

Prepare a retained earnings statement for the fiscal year ended December 31.

11–32. The following data were selected from the records of M. C. Yates Inc. for the current fiscal year ended December 31:

Merchandise inventory (January 1)	$115,000
Merchandise inventory (December 31)	138,000
Office salaries expense	40,000
Depreciation expense—store equipment	8,850
Sales	928,500
Sales salaries expense	40,000
Sales commissions expense	52,100
Advertising expense	25,750
Purchases	582,500
Rent expense	21,000
Delivery expense	17,420
Store supplies expense	7,230
Office supplies expense	1,220
Insurance expense	9,000
Depreciation expense—office equipment	4,120
Miscellaneous selling expense	8,750
Miscellaneous general expense	4,560
Interest expense	24,000
Loss from disposal of a segment of the business	35,750
Gain on condemnation of land	13,000
Income tax:	
Net of amounts allocable to discontinued operations and extraordinary item	26,600
Reduction applicable to loss from disposal of a segment of the business	7,150
Applicable to gain on condemnation of land	2,600

Instructions:

Prepare a multiple-step income statement, concluding with a section for earnings per share in the form illustrated in this chapter. There were 20,000 shares of common stock (no preferred) outstanding throughout the year. Assume that the gain on condemnation of land is an extraordinary item.

11–33. The stockholders' equity accounts of Anderson Enterprises Inc., with balances on January 1 of the current fiscal year, are as follows:

Common Stock, stated value $25 (75,000 shares authorized, 40,000 shares issued)	$1,000,000
Paid-In Capital in Excess of Stated Value	125,000
Appropriation for Contingencies	50,000
Appropriation for Treasury Stock	110,000
Retained Earnings	575,500
Treasury Stock (4,000 shares, at cost)	110,000

The following selected transactions occurred during the year:

Jan. 30. Received land with an estimated fair market value of $50,000 from the city as a donation.

Feb. 1. Paid cash dividends of $1 per share on the common stock. The dividend had been properly recorded when declared on December 20 of the preceding fiscal year for $36,000.

Mar. 19. Sold all of the treasury stock for $125,000 cash.

Apr. 29. Issued 2,000 shares of common stock for $56,000 cash.

June 14. Declared a 4% stock dividend on common stock, to be capitalized at the market price of the stock, which is $30 a share.

Aug. 18. Issued the certificates for the dividend declared on June 14.

Nov. 10. Purchased 1,000 shares of treasury stock for $36,000.

Dec. 21. The board of directors authorized an increase of the appropriation for contingencies by $10,000.

21. Declared a $1.20 per share dividend on common stock.

21. Decreased the appropriation for treasury stock to $36,000.

31. Closed the credit balance of the income summary account, $219,250.

31. Closed the two dividends accounts to Retained Earnings.

Instructions:

(1) Open T accounts for the stockholders' equity accounts listed and enter the balances as of January 1. Also open T accounts for the following: Paid-In Capital from Sale of Treasury Stock; Donated Capital; Stock Dividends Distributable; Stock Dividends; Cash Dividends.

(2) Prepare entries to record the selected transactions and post to the eleven selected accounts.

(3) Prepare the stockholders' equity section of the balance sheet as of December 31 of the current fiscal year.

11–34. The stockholders' equity section of the balance sheet of DTK Co. as of January 1 is as follows:

Stockholders' Equity

Paid-in capital:

Common stock, $10 par (100,000 shares authorized, 50,000 shares issued)	$500,000	
Premium on common stock	150,000	
Total paid-in capital		$ 650,000

Retained earnings:

Appropriated for bonded indebtedness	$175,000	
Unappropriated	330,000	
Total retained earnings		505,000
Total		$1,155,000
Deduct treasury stock (5,000 shares at cost)		65,000
Total stockholders' equity		$1,090,000

The following selected transactions occurred during the fiscal year:

Jan. 7. Issued 20,000 shares of stock in exchange for land and buildings with an estimated fair market value of $75,000 and $380,000 respectively. The property was encumbered by a mortgage of $175,000 and the company agreed to assume the responsibility for paying the mortgage note.

Mar. 15. Sold all of the treasury stock for $75,000.

June 25. Declared a cash dividend of $1.50 per share to stockholders of record on July 15, payable on July 30.

July 30. Paid the cash dividend declared on June 25.

Oct. 9. Received additional land valued at $35,000. The land was donated for a plant site by the Urbana Industrial Development Council.

Corporations: Stockholders' Equity, Earnings, and Dividends

Nov. 1. Issued 2,000 shares of stock to officers as a salary bonus. Market price of the stock is $15 a share. (Debit Officers Salaries Expense.)

Dec. 1. Declared a 4% stock dividend on the stock outstanding to stockholders of record on December 20 to be issued on January 15. The stock dividend is to be capitalized at the market price of $15 a share.

30. Increased the appropriation for bonded indebtedness by $25,000.

31. After closing all revenue and expense accounts, Income Summary has a credit balance of $180,000. Closed the account.

31. Closed the two dividends accounts to Retained Earnings.

Instructions:

(1) Open T accounts for the accounts appearing in the stockholders' equity section of the balance sheet and enter the balances as of January 1. Also open T accounts for the following: Paid-In Capital from Sale of Treasury Stock; Donated Capital; Cash Dividends; Stock Dividends; Stock Dividends Distributable.

(2) Prepare entries to record the transactions and post to the ten selected accounts.

(3) Prepare the stockholders' equity section of the balance sheet as of December 31, the end of the fiscal year.

(4) Prepare a retained earnings statement for the fiscal year ended December 31.

11–35. W. C. Hunt Company is in need of additional cash to expand operations. To raise the needed funds, the company is applying to the Miami County Bank for a loan. For this purpose, the bank requests that the financial statements be audited. To assist the auditor, W. C. Hunt Company's accountant prepared the following financial statements related to the current year:

W. C. Hunt Company
Income Statement
For Year Ended December 31, 19--

Revenues:		
Net sales	$668,150	
Gain on expropriation of land	33,000	
Total revenues		$701,150
Expenses:		
Cost of merchandise sold	$400,890	
Salary expense	59,500	
Loss on discontinued operations	31,350	
Depreciation expense—buildings	29,100	
Utilities expense	18,150	
Insurance expense	11,950	
Depreciation expense—equipment	6,200	
Amortization expense—patents	3,500	
Uncollectible accounts expense	2,925	
Miscellaneous general expense	5,875	
Income tax	36,000	
Dividends	16,500	
Total expenses		621,940
Net income		$ 79,210

W. C. Hunt Company
Balance Sheet
December 31, 19--

Current assets:
Cash .... $ 52,500
Accounts receivable......................... 67,660
Merchandise inventory....................... 81,000
Supplies 7,050 $208,210

Plant assets:
Land .... $ 85,000
Buildings.................................... 217,500
Equipment 77,500
Patents 31,500 411,500

Total assets $619,710

Current liabilities:
Accounts payable .... $ 35,700
Salaries payable .... 2,950 $ 38,650

Deferred charges:
Accumulated depreciation—buildings .... $ 77,000
Accumulated depreciation—equipment................ 22,500
Allowance for doubtful accounts 2,850 102,350

Stockholders' equity:
Common stock (25,000 shares authorized, $20 par)..... $235,000
Premium on common stock 25,000
Retained earnings.................................. 139,500
Net income....................................... 79,210 478,710

Total liabilities and stockholders' equity $619,710

In the course of the audit, the auditor examined the common stock and retained earnings accounts, which appeared as follows:

ACCOUNT COMMON STOCK ($20 Par)   ACCOUNT NO. 6400

Date		Item	Debit	Credit	Balance	
					Debit	Credit
19--						
Jan.	1	Balance—10,000 shares				200,000
	2	Issued 1,000 shares for				
		patents		35,000		235,000

ACCOUNT RETAINED EARNINGS   ACCOUNT NO. 6500

Date		Item	Debit	Credit	Balance	
					Debit	Credit
19--						
Jan.	1	Balance				82,000
	30	Error correction	7,500			74,500
June	1	Donation of land		40,000		114,500
Dec.	28	Appropriation for land				
		acquisition		25,000		139,500

A closer examination of the transactions in these and other accounts revealed the following details:

(a) The patent acquired on January 2 by an issuance of 1,000 shares of common stock had a fair market value of $35,000 and an estimated useful life of 10 years.

(b) A computational error was made in the calculation of a prior year's dividend. The corrected amount of the dividend was paid on January 30 and charged to the retained earnings account.

(c) On June 1, W. C. Hunt Company received a donation of a piece of land. The land account was debited for $40,000, the fair market value of the land at that date.

(d) In anticipation of further land acquisition, the board of directors on December 28 authorized a $25,000 appropriation of retained earnings that resulted in a debit to Land and a credit to Retained Earnings.

(e) After three years of using the straight-line method of depreciation for the buildings, the company changed to the sum-of-the-years-digits depreciation method. The following entry recorded this change:

Depreciation Expense — Buildings.	17,600	
Accumulated Depreciation — Buildings		17,600

(f) The income tax expense of $36,000 is the estimated tax paid during the year. The expense based on the corrected net income was determined to be $38,210, allocated as follows:

(1) Income from continuing operations.	$44,590
(2) Loss from discontinued operations	12,540
(3) Gain on expropriation of land.	13,200
(4) Cumulative effect of change in depreciation method	7,040

The tax owed at December 31 of $2,210 has not been recorded.

(g) A $2 cash dividend declared on December 28 and payable on February 9 of the next fiscal year was not recorded. The $16,500 of dividends expense represents the mid-year cash dividend paid on July 30 of the current year.

Instructions:

(1) Prepare the necessary correcting entries for the items discovered by the independent auditor. Assume that the accounts have not been closed for the current fiscal year.

(2) Prepare a multiple-step income statement for the current fiscal year, including the appropriate earnings per share disclosure.

(3) Prepare the retained earnings statement for the current fiscal year.

(4) Prepare a balance sheet as of the end of the current fiscal year.

11-29A. Differences in accounting methods between those applied to its accounts and financial reports and those used in determining taxable income yielded the following amounts for the first four years of a corporation's operations:

Alternate Problems

	First Year	Second Year	Third Year	Fourth Year
Income before income tax.......	$390,000	$350,000	$460,000	$440,000
Taxable income................	340,000	320,000	470,000	460,000

The income tax rate for each of the four years was 45% of taxable income and each year's taxes were promptly paid.

Instructions:

(1) Determine for each year the amounts described in the following columnar captions, presenting the information in the form indicated:

Year	Income Tax Deducted on Income Statement	Income Tax Payments for the Year	Deferred Income Tax Payable	
			Year's Addition (Deduction)	Year End Balance

(2) Total the first three amount columns.

11–30A. Selected transactions completed by the Golan Corporation during the current fiscal year are as follows:

Jan. 30. Declared a semiannual dividend of $4 on the 10,000 shares of preferred stock and a 50¢ dividend on the 40,000 shares of $10 par common stock to stockholders of record on February 14, payable on March 1.

Mar. 1. Paid the cash dividends.

Apr. 9. Purchased 5,000 shares of the corporation's own common stock at $21, recording the stock at cost.

May 15. Discovered that a receipt of $950 cash on account from J. M. Jones Co. had been posted in error to the account of J. Jones. The transaction was recorded correctly in the cash receipts journal.

June 23. Sold 1,000 shares of treasury stock at $24, receiving cash.

July 30. Declared semiannual dividends of $4 on the preferred stock and 50¢ on the common stock. In addition, a 4% common stock dividend was declared on the common stock outstanding, to be capitalized at the fair market value of the common stock, which is estimated at $25.

Sep. 10. Paid the cash dividends and issued the certificates for the common stock dividend.

Nov. 8. Discovered that an invoice of $825 for utilities expense for the month of October was debited to Office Supplies.

Dec. 31. Recorded $97,500 additional federal income tax allocable to net income for the year. Of this amount, $73,000 is a current liability and $24,500 is deferred.

31. The board of directors authorized the appropriation necessitated by the holding of treasury stock.

Instructions:

Record the transactions.

11–31A. The retained earnings accounts of SMID Corporation for the current fiscal year ended December 31 are as follows:

ACCOUNT **APPROPRIATION FOR PLANT EXPANSION**   ACCOUNT NO. **3201**

Date		Item	Debit	Credit	Balance Debit	Balance Credit
19--						
Jan.	1	Balance				300,000
Dec.	31	Retained earnings	50,000			250,000

ACCOUNT **APPROPRIATION FOR BONDED INDEBTEDNESS**   ACCOUNT NO. **3202**

Date		Item	Debit	Credit	Balance Debit	Balance Credit
19--						
Jan.	1	Balance				450,000
Dec.	31	Retained earnings		75,000		525,000

ACCOUNT **RETAINED EARNINGS**   ACCOUNT NO. **3301**

Date		Item	Debit	Credit	Balance Debit	Balance Credit
19--						
Jan.	1	Balance				675,000
Dec.	31	Income summary		270,000		945,000
	31	Appropriation for plant expansion		50,000		995,000
	31	Appropriation for bonded indebtedness	75,000			920,000
	31	Cash dividends	100,000			820,000
	31	Stock dividends	150,000			670,000

ACCOUNT **CASH DIVIDENDS**   ACCOUNT NO. **3302**

Date		Item	Debit	Credit	Balance Debit	Balance Credit
19--						
Feb.	10		50,000		50,000	
Aug.	12		50,000		100,000	
Dec.	31	Retained earnings		100,000	—	—

ACCOUNT **STOCK DIVIDENDS**   ACCOUNT NO. **3303**

Date		Item	Debit	Credit	Balance Debit	Balance Credit
19--						
Aug.	12		150,000		150,000	
Dec.	31	Retained earnings		150,000	—	—

Instructions:

Prepare a retained earnings statement for the fiscal year ended December 31.

11–32A. The following data were selected from the records of M. C. Yates, Inc. for the current fiscal year ended December 31:

Advertising expense	$ 22,100
Delivery expense	9,750
Depreciation expense—office equipment.	3,750
Depreciation expense—store equipment	9,900
Gain on condemnation of land	50,000
Income tax:	
Net of amounts allocable to discontinued operations and extraordinary item	49,500
Reduction applicable to loss from disposal of a segment of a business	5,200
Applicable to gain on condemnation of land	15,000
Insurance expense	7,800
Interest expense	18,000
Loss from disposal of a segment of the business	17,200
Merchandise inventory (January 1)	112,500
Merchandise inventory (December 31)	108,800
Miscellaneous general expense	3,050
Miscellaneous selling expense	3,600
Office salaries expense	44,000
Office supplies expense	1,950
Purchases	582,600
Rent expense	30,400
Sales	995,000
Sales commissions expense	45,700
Sales salaries expense	55,500
Store supplies expense	2,700

Instructions:

Prepare a multiple-step income statement, concluding with a section for earnings per share in the form illustrated in this chapter. There were 20,000 shares of common stock (no preferred) outstanding throughout the year. Assume that the condemnation of land is an extraordinary item.

11–33A. The stockholders' equity accounts of Santos Enterprises, Inc., with balances on January 1 of the current fiscal year, are as follows:

Common Stock, stated value $20 (50,000 shares authorized, 35,000 shares issued)	$700,000
Paid-In Capital in Excess of Stated Value	105,000
Appropriation for Contingencies	100,000
Appropriation for Treasury Stock	37,500
Retained Earnings	505,500
Treasury Stock (1,500 shares, at cost)	37,500

The following selected transactions occurred during the year:

Jan. 21. Paid cash dividends of $1 per share on the common stock. The dividend had been properly recorded when declared on December 19 of the preceding fiscal year.

Mar. 15. Sold all of the treasury stock for $45,000 cash.

Apr. 9. Issued 5,000 shares of common stock for $130,000 cash.

May 11. Received land with an estimated fair market value of $50,000 from the Gibson City Council as a donation.

June 20. Declared a 5% stock dividend on common stock, to be capitalized at the market price of the stock, which is $30 a share.

July 27. Issued the certificates for the dividend declared on June 20.

Aug. 8. Purchased 2,500 shares of treasury stock for $65,000.

Dec. 20. Declared a $1 per share dividend on common stock.

20. The board of directors authorized the increase of the appropriation for contingencies by $25,000.

20. Increased the appropriation for treasury stock to $65,000.

31. Closed the credit balance of the income summary account, $163,000.

31. Closed the two dividends accounts to Retained Earnings.

Instructions:

(1) Open T accounts for the stockholders' equity accounts listed and enter the balances as of January 1. Also open T accounts for the following: Paid-In Capital from Sale of Treasury Stock; Donated Capital; Stock Dividends Distributable; Stock Dividends; Cash Dividends.

(2) Prepare entries to record the selected transactions and post to the eleven selected accounts.

(3) Prepare the stockholders' equity section of the balance sheet as of December 31 of the current fiscal year.

11-36. Gambino Co. has paid quarterly cash dividends since 1980. These dividends have steadily increased from $.25 per share to the latest dividend declaration of $.60 per share. The board of directors would like to continue this trend and are hesitant to suspend or decrease the amount of quarterly dividends. Unfortunately, sales of Gambino Co. dropped sharply in the fourth quarter of 1986 due to worsening economic conditions and increased competition. As a result, the board is uncertain as to whether it should declare a dividend for the last quarter of 1986.

Mini-Case

On December 1, 1986, Gambino borrowed $500,000 from First City Bank to use in modernizing its retail stores and to expand its product line in reaction to its competition. The terms of the 10-year, 10% loan require Gambino Co. to:

(a) Pay monthly the total interest due,

(b) Pay $50,000 of the principal each December 1, beginning in 1987,

(c) Maintain a current ratio (current assets ÷ current liabilities) of 2:1,

(d) Appropriate $500,000 of retained earnings until the loan is fully paid, and

(e) Maintain a minimum balance of $20,000 (called a compensating balance) in its First City Bank account.

On December 31, 1986, 30% of the $500,000 loan had been disbursed in modernization of the retail stores and in expansion of the product line, and the remainder is temporarily invested in U.S. Treasury notes. Gambino Co.'s balance sheet as of December 31, 1986, is shown on page 382.

Gambino Co.
Balance Sheet
December 31, 1986

Assets

Current assets:

Cash............................		$ 30,000
Marketable securities, at cost (market price, $359,500).................		350,000
Accounts receivable	$ 89,500	
Less allowance for doubtful accounts	12,400	77,100
Merchandise inventory		135,500
Prepaid expenses		3,400
Total current assets...............		$ 596,000

Plant assets:

Land...............................		$170,000
Buildings	$960,000	
Less accumulated depreciation	213,500	746,500
Equipment.........................	$436,000	
Less accumulated depreciation	114,500	321,500
Total plant assets.................		1,238,000
Total assets............................		$1,834,000

Liabilities

Current liabilities:

Accounts payable	$ 66,800	
Notes payable (First City Bank)	50,000	
Salaries payable	3,200	
Total current liabilities.............		$120,000

Long-term liabilities:

Notes payable (First City Bank)		450,000
Total liabilities........................		$ 570,000

Stockholders' Equity

Paid-in capital:

Common stock, $30 par (40,000 shares authorized, 15,000 shares issued)...	$450,000	
Premium on common stock...........	22,500	
Total paid-in capital...............		$472,500

Retained earnings:

Appropriated for provision of First City Bank loan	$500,000	
Unappropriated	291,500	
Total retained earnings.............		$791,500
Total stockholders' equity		1,264,000
Total liabilities and stockholders' equity ..		$1,834,000

The board of directors is scheduled to meet January 8, 1987, to discuss the results of operations for 1986 and to consider the declaration of dividends for the fourth quarter of 1986. The chairman of the board has asked your advice on the declaration of dividends.

Instructions:

(1) What factors should the board consider in deciding whether to declare a cash dividend?

(2) The board is considering the declaration of a stock dividend instead of a cash dividend. Discuss the issuance of a stock dividend from the point of view of (a) a stockholder and (b) the board of directors.

1. D Paid-in capital is one of the two major subdivisions of the stockholders' equity of a corporation. It may result from many sources, including the receipt of donated real estate (answer A), the redemption of a corporation's own stock (answer B), and the sale of a corporation's treasury stock (answer C).

2. A The amount of income tax deferred to future years is $18,000 (answer A), determined as follows:

Depreciation expense, sum-of-the-years-digits method	$100,000
Depreciation expense, straight-line method	60,000
Excess expense in determination of taxable income	$ 40,000
Income tax rate	× 45%
Income tax deferred to future years	$ 18,000

3. C The correction of a material error related to a prior period should be excluded from the determination of net income of the current period and reported as an adjustment of the balance of retained earnings at the beginning of the period (answer C).

4. A Events and transactions that are distinguished by their unusual nature and by the infrequency of their occurrence, such as a gain on condemnation of land for public use, are reported in the income statement as extraordinary items (answer A).

5. C An appropriation for plant expansion is a portion of total retained earnings and would be reported in the stockholders' equity section of the balance sheet (answer C).

CHAPTER 12

Long-Term Liabilities and Investments in Bonds

CHAPTER OBJECTIVES

Describe and illustrate the impact of borrowing on a long-term basis as a means of financing corporations.

Describe the characteristics of bonds.

Describe and illustrate the accounting for bonds payable.

Describe and illustrate the accounting for long-term investments in bonds.

The acquisition of cash and other assets by a corporation through the issuance of its stock has been discussed in earlier chapters. Expansion of corporate enterprises through the retention of earnings, in some instances accompanied by the issuance of stock dividends, has also been explored. In addition to these two methods of obtaining relatively permanent funds, corporations may also borrow money on a long-term basis by issuing notes or **bonds,** which are a form of interest-bearing note. Long-term notes may be issued to relatively few lending agencies or to a single investor such as an insurance company. Bonds are usually sold to underwriters (dealers and brokers in securities), who in turn sell them to investors. Although the discussion that follows will be limited to bonds, the accounting principles involved apply equally to long-term notes.

When funds are borrowed through the issuance of bonds, there is a definite commitment to pay interest and to repay the principal at a stated future date. Bondholders are creditors of the issuing corporation and their claims for interest and for repayment of principal rank ahead of the claims of stockholders.

FINANCING CORPORATIONS

Many factors influence the incorporators or the board of directors in deciding upon the best means of obtaining funds. The subject will be limited here to a brief illustration of the effect of different financing methods on the income of a corporation and the common stockholders. To illustrate, assume that three different plans for financing a $4,000,000 corporation are under consideration by its organizers, and that in each case the securities will be issued at their par or face amount. The incorporators estimate that the enterprise will earn $800,000 annually, before deducting interest on the bonds and income tax estimated at 50% of income. The following tabulation indicates the amount of earnings that would be available to common stockholders under each of the three plans:

	Plan 1	Plan 2	Plan 3
12% bonds	—	—	$2,000,000
9% preferred stock, $50 par	—	$2,000,000	1,000,000
Common stock, $10 par	$4,000,000	2,000,000	1,000,000
Total	$4,000,000	$4,000,000	$4,000,000
Earnings before interest and income tax	$ 800,000	$ 800,000	$ 800,000
Deduct interest on bonds	—	—	240,000
Income before income tax	$ 800,000	$ 800,000	$ 560,000
Deduct income tax	400,000	400,000	280,000
Net income	$ 400,000	$ 400,000	$ 280,000
Dividends on preferred stock	—	180,000	90,000
Available for dividends on common stock	$ 400,000	$ 220,000	$ 190,000
Shares of common stock outstanding	400,000	200,000	100,000
Earnings per share on common stock	$1.00	$1.10	$1.90

If Plan 1 is adopted and the entire financing is from the issuance of common stock, the earnings per share on the common stock would be $1 per share. Under Plan 2, the effect of using 9% preferred stock for half of the capitalization would result in $1.10 earnings per common share. The issuance of 12% bonds in Plan 3, with the remaining capitalization split between preferred and common stock, would yield a return of $1.90 per share on common stock.

Under the assumed conditions, Plan 3 would obviously be the most attractive for common stockholders. If the anticipated earnings should increase beyond $800,000, the spread between the earnings per share to common stockholders under Plan 1 and Plan 3 would become even greater. But if successively smaller amounts of earnings are assumed, the attractiveness of Plan 2 and Plan 3 decreases. This is illustrated by the following tabulation, in which earnings, before interest and income tax are deducted, are assumed to be $440,000 instead of $800,000:

	Plan 1	Plan 2	Plan 3
12% bonds	—	—	$2,000,000
9% preferred stock, $50 par	—	$2,000,000	1,000,000
Common stock, $10 par	$4,000,000	2,000,000	1,000,000
Total	$4,000,000	$4,000,000	$4,000,000
Earnings before interest and income tax	$ 440,000	$ 440,000	$ 440,000
Deduct interest on bonds.................	—	—	240,000
Income before income tax	$ 440,000	$ 440,000	$ 200,000
Deduct income tax	220,000	220,000	100,000
Net income	$ 220,000	$ 220,000	$ 100,000
Dividends on preferred stock	—	180,000	90,000
Available for dividends on common stock ...	$ 220,000	$ 40,000	$ 10,000
Shares of common stock outstanding	400,000	200,000	100,000
Earnings per share on common stock	$.55	$.20	$.10

The preceding analysis focused attention on the effect of the different plans on earnings per share of common stock. There are other factors that must be considered when different methods of financing are evaluated. The issuance of bonds represents a fixed annual interest charge that, in contrast to dividends, is not subject to corporate control. Provision must also be made for the eventual repayment of the principal amount of the bonds, in contrast to the absence of any such obligation to stockholders. On the other hand, a decision to finance entirely by an issuance of common stock would require substantial investment by a single stockholder or small group of stockholders who desire to control the corporation.

CHARACTERISTICS OF BONDS

When a corporation issues bonds, it executes a contract with the bondholders known as a **bond indenture** or **trust indenture.** The entire issue is divided into a number of individual bonds, which may be of varying denominations. Usually the principal of each bond, also called the **face value,** is $1,000 or a multiple thereof. The interest on bonds may be payable at annual, semiannual, or quarterly intervals. Most bonds provide for payment on a semiannual basis.

Registered bonds may be transferred from one owner to another only by endorsement on the bond certificate, and the issuing corporation must maintain a record of the name and the address of each bondholder. Interest payments are made by check to the owner of record. Title to **bearer bonds,** which are also called **coupon bonds,** is transferred merely by delivery and the issuing corporation does not know the identity of the bondholders. Interest coupons for the entire term, in the form of checks or drafts payable to bearer, are attached to the bond certificate. At each interest date, the holder detaches the appropriate coupon and presents it to a bank for payment.

When all bonds of an issue mature at the same time, they are called term bonds. If the maturities are spread over several dates, they are called serial bonds. For example, one tenth of an issue of $1,000,000, or $100,000, may mature eleven years from the issuance date, another $100,000 may mature twelve years from the issuance date, and so on until the final $100,000 matures at the end of the twentieth year.

Bonds that may be exchanged for other securities under certain conditions are called **convertible bonds.** If the issuing corporation reserves the right to redeem the bonds before maturity, they are referred to as **callable bonds.**

A **secured bond** is one that gives the bondholder a claim on specific assets in case the issuing corporation fails to meet its obligations on the bonds. The properties mortgaged or pledged may be specific buildings and equipment, the entire plant, or stocks and bonds of other companies owned by the debtor corporation. Bonds issued on the basis of the general credit of the corporation are called **debenture bonds.**

PRESENT VALUE CONCEPTS

The concept of present value plays an important role in many accounting analyses and business decisions. For example, accounting analyses based on the present value concept are useful for evaluating proposals for long-term investments in plant and equipment. Such analyses will be discussed in a later chapter. In this chapter, the concept of present value will be discussed in the context of the role that it plays in determining the selling price of bonds.

The concept of present value is that an amount of cash to be received at some date in the future is not the equivalent of the same amount of cash held at an earlier date. In other words, a sum of cash to be received in the future is not as valuable as the same sum on hand today, because cash on hand today can be invested to earn income. For example, $100 on hand today would be more valuable than $100 to be received a year from today. In this case, if the $100 cash on hand today can be invested to earn 10% per year, the $100 will accumulate to $110 ($100 plus $10 earnings) by one year from today. The $100 on hand today can be referred to as the present value amount that is equivalent to $110 to be received a year from today.

PRESENT VALUE CONCEPTS FOR BONDS PAYABLE

When a corporation issues bonds, it usually incurs two distinct obligations: (1) to pay the face amount of the bonds at a specified maturity date, and (2) to pay periodic interest at a specified percentage of the face amount. The price that a buyer is willing to pay for these future benefits is the sum of (1) the *present value* of the face amount of the bonds at the maturity date and (2) the *present value* of the periodic interest payments.

Present Value of $1

The present value of the face amount of bonds at the maturity date is the value today of the promise to pay the face amount at some future date. To illustrate, assume that $1,000 is to be paid in one year and that the rate of earnings is 12%. The present value amount is $892.86 ($1,000 ÷ 1.12). If the $1,000 is to be paid one year later (two years in all), with the earnings compounded at the end of the first year, the present value amount would be $797.20 ($892.86 ÷ 1.12).

Instead of determining the present value of a future cash sum by a series of divisions in the manner just illustrated, it is customary to use a table of present values to find the present value of $1 for the appropriate number of periods, and to multiply that present value factor by the amount of the future cash sum. A partial table of the present value of $1 appears as follows:[1]

Periods	5%	5½%	6%	6½%	7%	10%	11%	12%	13%	14%
1	0.9524	0.9479	0.9434	0.9390	0.9346	0.9091	0.9009	0.8929	0.8850	0.8772
2	0.9070	0.8985	0.8900	0.8817	0.8734	0.8264	0.8116	0.7972	0.7831	0.7695
3	0.8638	0.8516	0.8396	0.8278	0.8163	0.7513	0.7312	0.7118	0.6931	0.6750
4	0.8227	0.8072	0.7921	0.7773	0.7629	0.6830	0.6587	0.6355	0.6133	0.5921
5	0.7835	0.7651	0.7473	0.7299	0.7130	0.6209	0.5935	0.5674	0.5428	0.5194
6	0.7462	0.7252	0.7050	0.6853	0.6663	0.5645	0.5346	0.5066	0.4803	0.4556
7	0.7107	0.6874	0.6651	0.6435	0.6228	0.5132	0.4817	0.4523	0.4251	0.3996
8	0.6768	0.6516	0.6274	0.6042	0.5820	0.4665	0.4339	0.4039	0.3762	0.3506
9	0.6446	0.6176	0.5919	0.5674	0.5439	0.4241	0.3909	0.3606	0.3329	0.3075
10	0.6139	0.5854	0.5584	0.5327	0.5083	0.3855	0.3522	0.3220	0.2946	0.2697
11	0.5847	0.5549	0.5268	0.5002	0.4751	0.3505	0.3173	0.2875	0.2607	0.2366
12	0.5568	0.5260	0.4970	0.4697	0.4440	0.3186	0.2858	0.2567	0.2307	0.2076
13	0.5303	0.4986	0.4688	0.4410	0.4150	0.2897	0.2575	0.2292	0.2042	0.1821
14	0.5051	0.4726	0.4423	0.4141	0.3878	0.2633	0.2320	0.2046	0.1807	0.1597
15	0.4810	0.4479	0.4173	0.3888	0.3624	0.2394	0.2090	0.1827	0.1599	0.1401
16	0.4581	0.4246	0.3936	0.3651	0.3387	0.2176	0.1883	0.1631	0.1415	0.1229
17	0.4363	0.4024	0.3714	0.3428	0.3166	0.1978	0.1696	0.1456	0.1252	0.1078
18	0.4155	0.3815	0.3503	0.3219	0.2959	0.1799	0.1528	0.1300	0.1108	0.0946
19	0.3957	0.3616	0.3305	0.3022	0.2765	0.1635	0.1377	0.1161	0.0981	0.0829
20	0.3769	0.3427	0.3118	0.2838	0.2584	0.1486	0.1240	0.1037	0.0868	0.0728

PRESENT VALUE OF $1 AT COMPOUND INTEREST

---

[1]The tables illustrated are limited to 20 periods for a small number of interest rates, and the amounts are carried to only four decimal places. Books of tables are available with as many as 360 periods, 45 interest rates (including many fractional rates), and amounts carried to eight decimal places.

Long-Term Liabilities and Investments in Bonds

For the previous example, the table indicates that the present value of $1 to be received two years hence, with earnings at the rate of 12% a year, is .7972. Multiplying $1,000 by .7972 yields $797.20, which is the same amount that was determined previously by two successive divisions. In using the table, it should be noted that the "periods" column represents the number of compounding periods, while the "percentage" columns represent the compound interest rate per period. For example, 12% for two years compounded annually, as in the preceding illustration, is 12% for two periods; 12% for two years compounded semiannually would be 6% (12% per year ÷ 2 semiannual periods) for four periods (2 years × 2 semiannual periods); and 12% for three years compounded semiannually would be 6% (12% ÷ 2) for six periods (3 years × 2 semiannual periods).

Present Value of Annuity of $1

The present value of the periodic interest payments on bonds is the value today of the promise to pay a fixed amount of interest at the end of each of a number of periods. Such a series of fixed payments at fixed intervals is called an **annuity**.

The following partial table of the present value of an annuity of $1 at compound interest indicates the value now (present value) of $1 to be received at the end of *each* period at various compound rates of interest. For example, the present value of $1,000 to be received at the end of each of the next 5 periods at 10% compound interest per period is $3,790.80 (3.7908 × $1,000).

Periods	5%	5½%	6%	6½%	7%	10%	11%	12%	13%	14%
1	0.9524	0.9479	0.9434	0.9390	0.9346	0.9091	0.9009	0.8929	0.8850	0.8772
2	1.8594	1.8463	1.8334	1.8206	1.8080	1.7355	1.7125	1.6901	1.6681	1.6467
3	2.7232	2.6979	2.6730	2.6485	2.6243	2.4869	2.4437	2.4018	2.3612	2.3216
4	3.5460	3.5052	3.4651	3.4258	3.3872	3.1699	3.1024	3.0373	2.9745	2.9137
5	4.3295	4.2703	4.2124	4.1557	4.1002	3.7908	3.6959	3.6048	3.5172	3.4331
6	5.0757	4.9955	4.9173	4.8410	4.7665	4.3553	4.2305	4.1114	3.9976	3.8887
7	5.7864	5.6830	5.5824	5.4845	5.3893	4.8684	4.7122	4.5638	4.4226	4.2883
8	6.4632	6.3346	6.2098	6.0888	5.9713	5.3349	5.1461	4.9676	4.7988	4.6389
9	7.1078	6.9522	6.8017	6.6561	6.5152	5.7590	5.5370	5.3283	5.1317	4.9464
10	7.7217	7.5376	7.3601	7.1888	7.0236	6.1446	5.8892	5.6502	5.4262	5.2161
11	8.3064	8.0925	7.8869	7.6890	7.4987	6.4951	6.2065	5.9377	5.6869	5.4527
12	8.8633	8.6185	8.3838	8.1587	7.9427	6.8137	6.4924	6.1944	5.9176	5.6603
13	9.3936	9.1171	8.8527	8.5997	8.3577	7.1034	6.7499	6.4235	6.1218	5.8424
14	9.8986	9.5896	9.2950	9.0138	8.7455	7.3667	6.9819	6.6282	6.3025	6.0021
15	10.3797	10.0376	9.7123	9.4027	9.1079	7.6061	7.1909	6.8109	6.4624	6.1422
16	10.8378	10.4622	10.1059	9.7678	9.4467	7.8237	7.3792	6.9740	6.6039	6.2651
17	11.2741	10.8646	10.4773	10.1106	9.7632	8.0216	7.5488	7.1196	6.7291	6.3729
18	11.6896	11.2461	10.8276	10.4325	10.0591	8.2014	7.7016	7.2497	6.8399	6.4674
19	12.0853	11.6077	11.1581	10.7347	10.3356	8.3649	7.8393	7.3658	6.9380	6.5504
20	12.4622	11.9504	11.4699	11.0185	10.5940	8.5136	7.9633	7.4694	7.0248	6.6231

PRESENT VALUE OF ANNUITY OF $1 AT COMPOUND INTEREST

ACCOUNTING FOR BONDS PAYABLE

The interest rate specified in the bond indenture is called the contract or **coupon rate,** which may differ from the rate prevailing in the market at the time the bonds are issued. If the **market** or effective rate is higher than the contract rate, the bonds will sell at a discount, or less than their face amount. This discount results because buyers are unwilling to pay the face amount for bonds whose contract rate is lower than the prevailing market rate. The discount, therefore, represents the amount necessary to make up for the difference in the market and the contract interest rates. Conversely, if the market rate is lower than the contract rate, the bonds will sell at a premium, or more than their face amount. In this case, buyers are willing to pay more than the face amount for bonds whose contract rate is higher than the market rate.

Bonds Issued at Face Amount

To illustrate an issuance of bonds, assume that on January 1 a corporation issues for cash $100,000 of 12%, five-year bonds, with interest of $6,000 payable semiannually. The market rate of interest at the time the bonds are issued is 12%. Since the contract rate and the market rate of interest are the same, the bonds will sell at their face amount. This amount, calculated as follows, is the sum of (1) the present value of the face amount of $100,000 to be repaid in 5 years and (2) the present value of 10 semiannual interest payments of $6,000 each:[2]

Present value of face amount of $100,000 due in 5 years, at 12% compounded semiannually: $100,000 × .5584 (present value of $1 for 10 periods at 6%)	$ 55,840
Present value of 10 semiannual interest payments of $6,000, at 12% compounded semiannually: $6,000 × 7.3601 (present value of annuity of $1 for 10 periods at 6%)	44,160
Total present value of bonds	$100,000

The basic data for computing the two present values totaling $100,000 were obtained from the two present value tables presented on pages 388 and 389. The first of the two amounts, $55,840, is the present value of the $100,000 that is to be repaid in 5 years. The $55,840 is determined by locating the present value of $1 for 10 periods (5 years of semiannual payments) at 6% semiannually (12% annual rate) in the present value of $1 table and multiplying by

---

[2]Because the present value tables are rounded to four decimal places, minor rounding errors may appear in the illustrations.

$100,000. If the bond indenture provided that no interest would be paid during the entire 5-year period, the bonds would be worth only $55,840 at the time of their issuance. To express the concept of present value from a different viewpoint, if $55,840 were invested today, with interest at 12% compounded semiannually, the sum accumulated at the end of 10 semiannual periods would be $100,000.

The second of the two amounts, $44,160, is the present value of the series of ten $6,000 payments. The $44,160 is determined by locating the present value of an annuity of $1 for 10 periods (5 years of semiannual payments) at 6% semiannually (12% annual rate) in the present value of an annuity of $1 table and multiplying by $6,000. The present value of $44,160 can also be viewed as the amount of a current deposit earning 12% that would yield ten semiannual withdrawals of $6,000, with the original deposit being reduced to zero by the tenth withdrawal.

The entry to record the issuance of the $100,000 bonds at their face amount is as follows:

| Jan. 1 | Cash..................................... | 100,000 | |
| | Bonds Payable.......................... | | 100,000 |

At six-month intervals following the issuance of the 12% bonds, the interest payment of $6,000 is recorded in the usual manner by a debit to Interest Expense and a credit to Cash. At the maturity date, the payment of the principal sum of $100,000 would be recorded by a debit to Bonds Payable and a credit to Cash.

Bonds Issued at a Discount

If the market rate of interest is 13% and the contract rate is 12%, the bonds will sell at a discount. The present value of the five-year, $100,000 bonds with a market rate of 13% may be calculated as follows:

Present value of $100,000 due in 5 years, at 13% compounded semiannually:
$100,000 × .5327 (present value of $1 for 10 periods at 6½%) $53,270
Present value of 10 semiannual interest payments of $6,000, at 13% compounded semiannually: $6,000 × 7.1888 (present value of an annuity of $1 for 10 periods at 6½%)....................................... 43,133
Total present value of bonds $96,403

The two present values that make up the total are both somewhat less than the comparable amounts in the first illustration, where the contract rate and the market rate were exactly the same. The reason for the lesser present value is that the value now of a future amount becomes less and less as the interest rate rises. In other words, the sum that would have to be invested today to equal a fixed future amount becomes less and less as the interest rate earned on the investment rises.

In the following entry to record the issuance of the 12% bonds, the bond liability is recorded at the face amount, and the discount is recorded in a separate contra account:

```
Jan.  1   Cash....................................    96,403
          Discount on Bonds Payable ...............     3,597
              Bonds Payable.........................              100,000
```

The $3,597 discount may be viewed as the amount that is needed to compensate the investor for accepting a contract rate of interest that is below the prevailing market rate. From another view, the $3,597 represents the additional amount that must be returned by the issuer at maturity; that is, the issuer received $96,403 at the sale date but must return $100,000 at the maturity date. The $3,597 discount must therefore be amortized as additional interest expense over the five-year life of the bonds. There are two widely used methods of allocating bond discount to the various periods: (1) **straight-line** and (2) **interest.** Although the interest method is the recommended method, the straight-line method is acceptable if the results obtained by its use do not materially differ from the results that would be obtained by the use of the interest method.[3]

Amortization of Discount by the Straight-Line Method

The straight-line method is the simpler of the two methods and provides for amortization in equal periodic amounts. Application of this method to the illustration would yield amortization of 1/10 of $3,597, or $359.70, each half year. The amount of the interest expense on the bonds would remain constant for each half year at $6,000 plus $359.70, or $6,359.70. The entry to record the first interest payment and the amortization of the related amount of discount is as follows:

```
July  1   Interest Expense .........................  6,359.70
          Discount on Bonds Payable ..............               359.70
          Cash....................................             6,000.00
```

Amortization of Discount by the Interest Method

In contrast to the straight-line method, which provides for a constant *amount* of interest expense, the interest method provides for a constant *rate* of

[3]*Opinions of the Accounting Principles Board, No. 21,* "Interest on Receivables and Payables" (New York: American Institute of Certified Public Accountants, 1971), par. 14.

Long-Term Liabilities and Investments in Bonds

interest on the **carrying amount** (also called **book value**) of the bonds at the beginning of each period. The interest rate used in the computation is the market rate as of the date the bonds were issued, and the carrying amount of the bonds is their face amount minus the unamortized discount. The difference between the interest expense computed in this manner and the amount of the periodic interest payment is the amount of discount to be amortized for the period. Application of this method to the illustration yields the following data:

AMORTIZATION OF DISCOUNT ON BONDS PAYABLE

Interest Payment	A Interest Paid (6% of Face Amount)	B Interest Expense (6½% of Bond Carrying Amount)	C Discount Amortization (B–A)	D Unamortized Discount (D–C)	E Bond Carrying Amount ($100,000–D)
				$3,597	$ 96,403
1	$6,000	$6,266(6½% of $96,403)	$266	3,331	96,669
2	6,000	6,284(6½% of $96,669)	284	3,047	96,953
3	6,000	6,302(6½% of $96,953)	302	2,745	97,255
4	6,000	6,322(6½% of $97,255)	322	2,423	97,577
5	6,000	6,343(6½% of $97,577)	343	2,080	97,920
6	6,000	6,365(6½% of $97,920)	365	1,715	98,285
7	6,000	6,389(6½% of $98,285)	389	1,326	98,674
8	6,000	6,415(6½% of $98,674)	415	911	99,089
9	6,000	6,441(6½% of $99,089)	441	470	99,530
10	6,000	6,470(6½% of $99,530)	470	—	100,000

The following important details should be observed:

1. The interest paid (column A) remains constant at 6% of $100,000, the face amount of the bonds.
2. The interest expense (column B) is computed at 6½% of the bond carrying amount at the beginning of each period, yielding a gradually increasing amount.
3. The excess of the interest expense over the interest payment of $6,000 is the amount of discount to be amortized (column C).
4. The unamortized discount (column D) decreases from the initial balance, $3,597, to a zero balance at the maturity date of the bonds.
5. The carrying amount (column E) increases from $96,403, the amount received for the bonds, to $100,000 at maturity.

The entry to record the first interest payment and the amortization of the related amount of discount is as follows:

July	1	Interest Expense	6,266	
		Discount on Bonds Payable		266
		Cash		6,000

As an alternative to recording the amortization each time the interest is paid, it may be recorded only at the end of the year. When this procedure is used, each interest payment is recorded as a debit to Interest Expense and a credit to Cash. In terms of the illustration, the entry to amortize the discount at the end of the first year would be as follows:

```
Dec. 31  Interest Expense .........................    550
              Discount on Bonds Payable .............             550
```

The amount of the discount amortized, $550, is made up of the first two semiannual amortization amounts ($266 + $284) from the preceding table.

Bonds Issued at a Premium

If the market rate of interest is 11% and the contract rate is 12%, the bonds will sell at a premium. The present value of the five-year, $100,000 bonds, with a market rate of 11%, may be calculated as follows:

```
Present value of $100,000 due in 5 years, at 11% compounded semiannu-
    ally: $100,000 × .5854 (present value of $1 for 10 periods at 5½%)....   $ 58,540
Present value of 10 semiannual interest payments of $6,000, at 11% com-
    pounded semiannually: $6,000 × 7.5376 (present value of an annuity of
    $1 for 10 periods at 5½%).......................................          45,226
Total present value of bonds .......................................         $103,766
```

The entry to record the issuance of the bonds is as follows:

```
Jan. 1  Cash......................................  103,766
              Bonds Payable...........................           100,000
              Premium on Bonds Payable ................             3,766
```

Procedures for amortization of the premium and determination of the periodic interest expense are basically the same as those used for bonds issued at a discount.

Amortization of Premium by the Straight-Line Method

Application of the straight-line method to the illustration would yield amortization of 1/10 of $3,766, or $376.60 each half year. Just as bond discount can be viewed as additional interest expense, bond premium can be viewed as a reduction in the amount of interest expense. The entry to record the first interest payment and the amortization of the related amount of premium is as follows:

```
July 1  Interest Expense ...........................  5,623.40
              Premium on Bonds Payable ..................    376.60
              Cash.......................................            6,000.00
```

Amortization of Premium by the Interest Method

Application of the interest method of amortization yields the following data:

Interest Payment	A Interest Paid (6% of Face Amount)	B Interest Expense (5½% of Bond Carrying Amount)	C Premium Amortization (A–B)	D Unamortized Premium (D–C)	E Bond Carrying Amount ($100,000 + D)
				$3,766	$103,766
1	$6,000	$5,707(5½% of $103,766)	$293	3,473	103,473
2	6,000	$5,691(5½% of $103,473)	309	3,164	103,164
3	6,000	$5,674(5½% of $103,164)	326	2,838	102,838
4	6,000	$5,657(5½% of $102,838)	343	2,495	102,495
5	6,000	$5,638(5½% of $102,495)	362	2,133	102,133
6	6,000	$5,618(5½% of $102,133)	382	1,751	101,751
7	6,000	$5,597(5½% of $101,751)	403	1,348	101,348
8	6,000	$5,575(5½% of $101,348)	425	923	100,923
9	6,000	$5,551(5½% of $100,923)	449	474	100,474
10	6,000	$5,526(5½% of $100,474)	474	—	100,000

The following important details should be observed:

1. The interest paid (column A) remains constant at 6% of $100,000, the face amount of the bonds.
2. The interest expense (column B) is computed at 5½% of the bond carrying amount at the beginning of each period, yielding a gradually decreasing amount.
3. The excess of the periodic interest payment of $6,000 over the interest expense is the amount of premium to be amortized (column C).
4. The unamortized premium (column D) decreases from the initial balance, $3,766, to a zero balance at the maturity date of the bonds.
5. The carrying amount (column E) decreases from $103,766, the amount received for the bonds, to $100,000 at maturity.

The entry to record the first interest payment and the amortization of the related amount of premium is as follows:

```
July  1  Interest Expense ............................    5,707
            Premium on Bonds Payable ...................      293
               Cash.......................................              6,000
```

BOND SINKING FUND

The bond indenture may provide that funds for the payment of bonds at maturity be accumulated over the life of the issue. The amounts set aside are kept separate from other assets in a special fund called a **sinking fund.** Cash deposited in the fund is usually invested in income-producing securities. The periodic deposits plus the earnings on the investments should approximately equal the face amount of the bonds at maturity. Control over the fund may be exercised by the corporation or by a trustee, which is usually a financial corporation.

When cash is transferred to the sinking fund, an account called Sinking Fund Cash is debited and Cash is credited. The purchase of investments is recorded by a debit to Sinking Fund Investments and a credit to Sinking Fund Cash. As interest or dividends are received, the cash is debited to Sinking Fund Cash and Sinking Fund Income is credited.

To illustrate the accounting for a bond sinking fund, assume that a corporation issues $100,000 of 10-year bonds dated January 1, with the provision that equal annual deposits be made in the bond sinking fund at the end of each of the 10 years. The fund is expected to be invested in securities that will yield approximately 14% per year. Reference to the appropriate mathematical table indicates that annual deposits of $5,171 are sufficient to provide a fund of approximately $100,000 at the end of 10 years. A few of the typical transactions and the related entries affecting the sinking fund during the 10-year period are illustrated as follows:

Deposit of cash in the fund

A deposit is made at the end of each of the 10 years.

Entry: Sinking Fund Cash........................... 5,171
     Cash 5,171

Purchase of investments

The time of purchase and the amount invested at any one time vary, depending upon market conditions and the unit price of securities purchased. The entry summarizes the securities purchased with the first deposit.

Entry: Sinking Fund Investments.................... 5,000
     Sinking Fund Cash......................... 5,000

Receipt of income from investments

Interest and dividends are received at different times during the year. The amount earned per year increases as the fund increases. The entry summarizes the receipt of income for the year on the securities purchased with the first deposit.

Entry: Sinking Fund Cash........................... 700
     Sinking Fund Income....................... 700

Sale of investments

Investments may be sold from time to time and the proceeds reinvested. Prior to maturity, all investments are converted into cash. The entry records the sale of all securities at the end of the tenth year.

Entry: Sinking Fund Cash.......................... 85,100
           Sinking Fund Investments..................   82,480
           Gain on Sale of Investments...............   2,620

Payments of bonds

The cash available in the fund at the end of the tenth year is assumed to be composed of the following:

Proceeds from sale of investments (above)	$ 85,100
Income earned during tenth year	11,520
Last annual deposit	5,171
Total	$101,791

The entry records the payment of the bonds and the transfer of the remaining sinking fund cash to the cash account.

Entry: Bonds Payable 100,000
        Cash   1,791
           Sinking Fund Cash.......................   101,791

In the illustration, the amount of the fund exceeded the amount of the liability by $1,791. This excess was transferred to the regular cash account. If the fund had been less than the amount of the liability, $99,500 for example, the regular cash account would have been drawn upon for the $500 deficiency.

Sinking fund income represents earnings of the corporation and is reported in the income statement as "Other income." The cash and the securities making up the sinking fund are classified in the balance sheet as "Investments," which usually appears immediately below the current assets section.

APPROPRIATION FOR BONDED INDEBTEDNESS

The restriction of dividends during the life of a bond issue is another means of increasing the assurance that the obligation will be paid at maturity. Assuming that the corporation in the preceding example is required by the bond indenture to appropriate $10,000 of retained earnings each year for the 10-year life of the bonds, the following entry would be made annually:

Dec. 31   Retained Earnings........................ 10,000
              Appropriation for Bonded Indebtedness....   10,000

As was indicated in Chapter 11, an appropriation has no direct relationship to a sinking fund. Each is independent of the other. When there is both a fund and an appropriation for the same purpose, the appropriation may be said to be **funded**.

BOND REDEMPTION

Callable bonds are redeemable by the issuing corporation within the period of time and at the price stated in the bond indenture. Usually the call price is above the face value. If the market rate of interest declines after the issuance of the bonds, the corporation may sell new bonds at a lower interest rate and use the funds to redeem the original issue. The reduction of future interest expense is always an incentive to bond redemption. A corporation may also redeem all or a portion of its bonds before maturity by purchasing them on the open market.

When a corporation redeems bonds at a price below their carrying amount, the corporation realizes a gain. If the price is in excess of the carrying amount, a loss is incurred. To illustrate redemption, assume that on June 30 a corporation has a bond issue of $100,000 outstanding, on which there is an unamortized premium of $4,000. The corporation has the option of calling the bonds for $105,000, which it exercises on this date. The entry to record the redemption is:

June 30	Bonds Payable	100,000	
	Premium on Bonds Payable	4,000	
	Loss on Redemption of Bonds	1,000	
	Cash		105,000

If the bonds were not callable, the corporation might purchase a portion on the open market. Assuming that the corporation purchases one fourth ($25,000) of the bonds for $24,000 on June 30, the entry to record the redemption would be as follows:

June 30	Bonds Payable	25,000	
	Premium on Bonds Payable	1,000	
	Cash		24,000
	Gain on Redemption of Bonds		2,000

Note that only the portion of the premium relating to the bonds redeemed is written off. The excess of the carrying amount of the bonds purchased, $26,000, over the cash paid, $24,000, is recognized as a gain.

BALANCE SHEET PRESENTATION OF BONDS PAYABLE

Bonds payable are usually reported on the balance sheet as long-term liabilities. If there are two or more bond issues, separate accounts should be maintained and the details of each should be reported on the balance sheet or in a supporting schedule or note. When the balance sheet date is within one year of the bond maturity date, the bonds should be transferred to the current liability classification if they are to be paid out of current assets. If they are to be paid with funds that have been set aside or if they are to be replaced with another bond issue, they should remain in the noncurrent category and their anticipated liquidation disclosed in an explanatory note.

The balance in a discount account should be reported in the balance sheet as a deduction from the related bonds payable. Conversely, the balance in a premium account should be reported as an addition to the related bonds payable. Either in the financial statements or in accompanying notes, the description of the bonds (terms, security, due date, etc.) should also include the effective interest rate and the maturities and sinking fund requirements for each of the next five years.[4]

INVESTMENTS IN BONDS

The issuance of bonds and related transactions were discussed in the preceding paragraphs from the standpoint of the issuing corporation. Whenever a corporation records a transaction between itself and the owners of its bonds, there is a reciprocal entry in the accounts of the investor.

In the following discussion, attention will be given to the principles underlying the accounting for investments in **debt securities** (bonds and notes) that are identified as long-term investments. **Long-term investments** are investments that are not intended as a ready source of cash in the normal operations of the business. These long-term investments are listed in the balance sheet under the caption "Investments," which usually follows the current assets. By contrast, temporary investments, which were discussed in Chapter 6, are available to meet the needs for additional cash for normal operations and are classified as current assets.

A business may make long-term investments simply because it has cash that is not needed in its normal operations. As discussed previously, cash and securities in bond sinking funds are considered long-term investments, since they are accumulated for the purpose of paying the bond liability. A corporation may also purchase bonds as a means of establishing or maintaining business relations with the issuing company.

Investments in corporate bonds may be purchased directly from the issuing corporation or from other investors. The services of a broker are usually employed in buying and selling bonds listed on the organized exchanges. The record of transactions on bond exchanges is reported daily in the financial pages of newspapers. This record usually includes data on the bond interest rate, maturity date, volume of sales, and the high, low, and closing prices for each corporation's bonds traded during the day. Prices for bonds are quoted as a percentage of the face amount. Thus, the price of a $1,000 bond quoted at 104½ would be $1,045.

---

[4]*Statement of Financial Accounting Standards*, No. 47, "Disclosure of Long-Term Obligations" (Stamford: Financial Accounting Standards Board, 1981), par. 10.

ACCOUNTING FOR INVESTMENTS IN BONDS

A long-term investment in debt securities is customarily carried at cost. The cost of bonds purchased includes the amount paid to the seller plus other costs related to the purchase, such as the broker's commission. When bonds are purchased between interest dates, the purchaser pays the seller the interest accrued from the last interest payment date to the date of purchase. The amount of the interest paid should be debited to Interest Income, since it is an offset against the amount that will be received at the next interest date. To illustrate, assume that a $1,000 bond is purchased at 102 plus a brokerage fee of $5.30 and accrued interest of $10.20. The transaction is recorded by the following entry. Note that the cost of the bond is recorded in a single account, i.e., the face amount of the bond and the premium paid are not recorded in separate accounts.

```
Apr.  2  Investment in Lewis Co. Bonds.................  1,025.30
         Interest Income.............................       10.20
             Cash.......................................              1,035.50
```

As discussed previously, the price investors pay for bonds may be much greater or less than the face amount or the original issuance price. When bonds held as long-term investments are purchased at a price other than the face amount, the discount or premium should be amortized over the remaining life of the bonds. The amortization of discount increases the amount of the investment account and interest income. The amortization of premium decreases the amount of the investment account and interest income. The procedures for determining the amount of amortization each period correspond to those described and illustrated on pages 392 to 394.

Interest received on bond investments is recorded by a debit to Cash and a credit to Interest Income. At the end of a fiscal year, the interest accrued should be recorded by a debit to Interest Receivable and a credit to Interest Income. The adjusting entry should be reversed after the accounts are closed, so that all receipts of bond interest during the following year may be recorded without referring to the adjustment data.

As a basis for illustrating the transactions associated with long-term investments in bonds, assume that $50,000 of 8% bonds of Nowell Corporation, due in 8¾ years, are purchased on July 1 to yield approximately 11%. The purchase price is $41,706 plus interest of $1,000 accrued from April 1, the date of the last semiannual interest payment. Entries in the accounts of the purchaser at the time of purchase and for the remainder of the fiscal year, ending December 31, are as follows:

July 1 Payment for investment in bonds and accrued interest

```
Cost of $50,000 of Nowell Corp. bonds .......................  $41,706
Interest accrued on $50,000 at 8%, April 1–July 1 (3 months) ...    1,000
Total ...............................................  $42,706
```

Entry: Investment in Nowell Corp. Bonds 41,706
      Interest Income 1,000
          Cash 42,706

October 1 Receipt of semiannual interest

Interest on $50,000 at 8%, April 1–October 1 (6 months), $2,000

Entry: Cash 2,000
      Interest Income 2,000

December 31 Adjusting entries

Interest accrued on $50,000 at 8%, October 1–December 31 (3 months), $1,000

Entry: Interest Receivable 1,000
      Interest Income 1,000

Discount to be amortized by interest method, July 1–December 31 (6 months):

Interest income (5½% of bond carrying amount of $41,706).	$2,294
Less interest received (4% of face amount of $50,000)	2,000
Amount to be amortized	$ 294

Entry: Investment in Nowell Corp. Bonds 294
      Interest income 294

The entries in the interest income account in the above illustration may be summarized as follows:

July	1 Paid accrued interest—3 months	$(1,000)
Oct.	1 Received interest payment—6 months	2,000
Dec. 31	Recorded accrued interest—3 months	1,000
31	Recorded amortization of discount—6 months	294
	Interest earned—6 months	$ 2,294

SALE OF INVESTMENTS IN BONDS

When bonds held as long-term investments are sold, the seller will receive the sales price (less commissions and other selling costs) plus the interest accrued since the last payment date. Before recording the proceeds, the seller should record the appropriate amount of the amortization of discount or premium for the current period. Then, in recording the proceeds, any gain or loss incurred on the sale can be recognized. To illustrate the recording of a sale of bonds held as a long-term investment, assume that the Nowell Corporation bonds of the preceding example are sold for $47,350 plus accrued interest on June 30, seven years after their purchase. The carrying amount of the bonds (cost plus amortized discount) as of January 1 of the year of sale is $47,080. The entries to record the amortization of discount for the current year and the sale of the bonds are as follows:

June 30 Amortization of discount for current year

Discount to be amortized by the interest method, January 1–June 30, $589

Entry:	Investment in Nowell Corp. Bonds	589	
	Interest Income		589

June 30 Receipt of interest and sale of bonds

Interest accrued on $50,000 at 8%, April 1–June 30 (3 months), $1,000

Carrying amount of bonds on January 1 of current year	$47,080
Discount amortized in current year	589
Carrying amount of bonds on June 30	$47,669
Proceeds of sale	47,350
Loss on sale	$ 319

Entry:	Cash	48,350	
	Loss on Sale of Investments	319	
	Interest Income		1,000
	Investment in Nowell Corp. Bonds		47,669

Self-
Examination
Questions
(Answers
at end of
chapter.)

1. If a corporation plans to issue $1,000,000 of 12% bonds at a time when the market rate for similar bonds is 10%, the bonds can be expected to sell:
A. at their face amount   C. at a discount
B. at a premium   D. at a price below their face amount

2. If the bonds payable account has a balance of $500,000 and the discount on bonds payable account has a balance of $40,000, what is the carrying amount of the bonds?
A. $460,000   C. $540,000
B. $500,000   D. None of the above

3. The cash and the securities comprising the sinking fund established for the payment of bonds at maturity are classified on the balance sheet as:
A. current assets   C. long-term liabilities
B. investments   D. none of the above

4. If a firm purchases $100,000 of bonds of X Company at 101 plus accrued interest of $2,000 and pays broker's commissions of $50, the amount debited to Investment in X Company Bonds would be:
   A. $100,000
   B. $101,050
   C. $103,000
   D. none of the above

5. The balance in the discount on bonds payable account would be reported in the balance sheet in the:
   A. current assets section
   B. current liabilities section
   C. long-term liabilities section
   D. none of the above

12–1. When underwriters are used by the corporation issuing bonds, what function do the underwriters perform?

12–2. How are interest payments made to holders of (a) bearer or coupon bonds and (b) registered bonds?

12–3. Explain the meaning of each of the following terms as they relate to a bond issue: (a) secured, (b) convertible, (c) callable, and (d) debenture.

12–4. Describe the two distinct obligations incurred by a corporation when issuing bonds.

12–5. A corporation issues $1,000,000 of 10% coupon bonds to yield interest at the rate of 12½%. (a) Was the amount of cash received from the sale of the bonds greater than $1,000,000 or less than $1,000,000? (b) Identify the following terms related to the bond issue: (1) face amount, (2) market or effective rate of interest, (3) contract or coupon rate of interest, and (4) maturity amount.

12–6. If bonds issued by a corporation are sold at a premium, is the market rate of interest greater or less than the coupon rate?

12–7. What is the present value of $5,000 due in 6 months, if the market rate of interest is 11%?

12–8. If the bonds payable account has a balance of $750,000 and the discount on bonds payable account has a balance of $37,420, what is the carrying amount of the bonds?

12–9. The following data are related to a $200,000, 12% bond issue for a selected semiannual interest period:

Bond carrying amount at beginning of period	$212,400
Interest paid at end of period	12,000
Interest expense allocable to the period	11,380

(a) Were the bonds issued at a discount or at a premium? (b) What is the balance of the discount or premium account at the beginning of the period? (c) How much amortization of discount or premium is allocable to the period?

12–10. A corporation issues 12%, 25-year debenture bonds, with a face amount of $5,000,000, for 102½ at the beginning of the current year. Assuming that the premium is to be amortized on a straight-line basis, what is the total amount of interest expense for the current year?

12–11. Indicate the title of (a) the account to be debited and (b) the account to be credited in the entry at year end for amortization of (1) discount on bonds payable and (2) premium on bonds payable.

12–12. When the premium on bonds payable is amortized by the interest method, does the interest expense increase or decrease over the amortization period?

12–13. What is the purpose of a bond sinking fund?

12–14. If the amount accumulated in a sinking fund account exceeds the amount of liability at the redemption date, to what account is the excess transferred?

12–15. How are cash and securities comprising a sinking fund classified on the balance sheet?

12–16. Bonds Payable has a balance of $300,000 and Premium on Bonds Payable has a balance of $11,400. If the issuing corporation redeems the bonds at 106, what is the amount of gain or loss on redemption?

12–17. Indicate how the following accounts should be reported in the balance sheet: (a) Premium on Bonds Payable, and (b) Discount on Bonds Payable.

12–18. The quoted price of James Corp. bonds on October 1 is 108½. On the same day the interest accrued is 4% of the face amount. (a) Does the quoted price include accrued interest? (b) If $20,000 face amount of James Corp. bonds is purchased on October 1 at the quoted price, what is the cost of the bonds, exclusive of commission?

12–19. An investor sells $18,000 of bonds of M Corp., carried at $18,450, for $17,900 plus accrued interest of $300. The broker remits the balance due after deducting a commission of $80. Indicate the debits and credits required to record the transaction.

Exercises

12–20. Two companies are financed as follows:

	Cohen Co.	Epps Inc.
Bonds payable, 10% (issued at face value)	$ 500,000	$1,000,000
Preferred 9% stock (nonparticipating)	500,000	1,000,000
Common stock, $10 par	2,000,000	1,000,000

Income tax is estimated at 50% of income. Determine for each company the earnings per share of common stock, assuming the income before bond interest and income tax for each company to be (a) $300,000, (b) $500,000, and (c) $800,000.

12–21. E. C. Sheets Company issued $1,000,000 of 15-year, 13½% callable bonds on March 1, 1984, with interest payable on March 1 and September 1. The fiscal year of the company is the calendar year. Present entries for the following selected transactions:

1984
Mar. 1 Issued the bonds for cash at their face amount.
Sept. 1 Paid the interest.
Dec. 31 Recorded accrued interest for four months.
     31 Closed the interest expense account.
1985
Jan. 1 Reversed the adjusting entry for accrued interest.
Mar. 1 Paid the interest.
1989
Nov. 1 Called the bond issue at 103, the rate provided in the bond indenture. (Omit entry for payment of interest.)

12–22. On the first day of its fiscal year, Lea Corporation issued $3,000,000 of 10-year, 10% bonds, interest payable semiannually, at an effective interest rate of 12%, receiving cash of $2,655,885.

(a) Present the entries to record the following:
   (1) Sale of the bonds.
   (2) First semiannual interest payment. (Amortization of discount is to be recorded annually.)
   (3) Second semiannual interest payment.
   (4) Amortization of discount at the end of the first year, using the straight-line method. Round to the nearest dollar.
(b) Determine the amount of the bond interest expense for the first year.

12–23. On the first day of its fiscal year, Morrison Co. issued $5,000,000 of 10-year, 12% bonds at an effective interest rate of 10%, with interest payable semiannually. Compute the following, presenting figures used in your computations and rounding to the nearest dollar:

(a) The amount of cash proceeds from the sale of the bonds. (Use the tables of present values appearing in this chapter.)
(b) The amount of premium to be amortized for the first semiannual interest payment period, using the interest method.
(c) The amount of premium to be amortized for the second semiannual interest payment period, using the interest method.
(d) The amount of the bond interest expense for the first year.

12–24. Davis Corporation issued $900,000 of 30-year bonds on the first day of the fiscal year. The bond indenture provides that a sinking fund be accumulated by 30 annual deposits of $20,000, beginning at the end of the first year.

Present the entries to record the following selected transactions related to the bond issue:

(a) The required amount is deposited in the sinking fund.
(b) Investments in securities from the first sinking fund deposit total $18,600.
(c) The sinking fund earned $2,790 during the year following the first deposit (summarizing entry).
(d) The bonds are paid at maturity and excess cash of $6,280 in the fund is transferred to the cash account.

12–25. On August 1 of the current fiscal year, Webster Company purchased $200,000 of 10-year, 10% bonds as a long-term investment directly from the issuing company for $177,059. The effective rate of interest is 12% and the interest is payable semi-annually. Compute the following for Webster Company, presenting figures used in your computations:

(a) The amount of discount to be amortized for the first semiannual interest payment period, using the straight-line method.

(b) The amount of discount to be amortized for the first semiannual interest payment period, using the interest method.

12–26. Present entries to record the following selected transactions of Sampson Corporation:

(a) Purchased for cash $150,000 of Dohr Co. 10% bonds at 98 plus accrued interest of $3,750.

(b) Received first semiannual interest.

(c) Amortized $200 discount on the bond investment at the end of the first year.

(d) Sold the bonds at 96 plus accrued interest of $1,875. The bonds were carried at $148,000 at the time of the sale.

Problems

12–27. The following transactions were completed by Turner Industries Inc., whose fiscal year is the calendar year:

1984

Mar. 31. Issued $4,000,000 of 10-year, 10% callable bonds dated March 31, 1984, receiving cash of $3,760,880. Interest is payable semiannually on September 30 and March 31.

Sept. 30. Paid the semiannual interest on the bonds.

Dec. 31. Recorded the adjusting entry for interest payable.

31. Recorded amortization of $10,461 discount on the bonds, using the interest method.

31. Closed the interest expense account.

1985

Jan. 1. Reversed the adjusting entry for interest payable.

Mar. 31. Paid the semiannual interest on the bonds.

Sept. 30. Paid the semiannual interest on the bonds.

Dec. 31. Recorded the adjusting entry for interest payable.

31. Recorded amortization of $15,256 discount on the bonds, using the interest method.

31. Closed the interest expense account.

1992

Mar. 31. Recorded the redemption of the bonds, which were called at 101½. The balance in the bond discount account is $70,369 after the payment of interest and amortization of discount have been recorded. (Record the redemption only.)

Instructions:

(1) Record the foregoing transactions.

(2) Indicate the amount of the interest expense in (a) 1984 and (b) 1985.

(3) Determine the effective interest rate (divide the interest expense for 1984 by the

bond carrying amount at time of issuance) and express as an annual rate.
(4) Determine the carrying amount of the bonds as of December 31, 1985.

12–28. On March 1, 1986, Redding Corporation issued $5,000,000 of 10-year, 12% bonds at an effective interest rate of 11%. Interest on the bonds is payable semiannually on March 1 and September 1. The fiscal year of the company is the calendar year.

Instructions:

(1) Present the entry to record the amount of the cash proceeds from the sale of the bonds. Use the tables of present values appearing in this chapter to compute the cash proceeds, rounding to the nearest dollar.
(2) Present the entries to record the following:
   (a) The first semiannual interest payment on September 1, 1986.
   (b) The amortization of the bond premium on September 1, 1986, using the interest method.
   (c) The adjusting entry for accrued interest payable on December 31, 1986.
   (d) The amortization of the bond premium on December 31, 1986, using the interest method.
(3) Present the entries for Instruction (2), parts (b) and (d), using the straight-line method of amortization.
(4) Determine the total interest expense for 1986 under (a) the interest method of premium amortization and (b) the straight-line method of premium amortization. (c) Will the annual interest expense using the interest method of premium amortization always be greater than the annual interest expense using the straight-line method of premium amortization?

12–29. During 1986 and 1987, Plain Company completed the following transactions relating to its $1,000,000 issue of 20-year, 12% bonds dated February 1, 1986. Interest is payable on February 1 and August 1. The corporation's fiscal year is the calendar year.

1986
Feb.   1. Sold the bond issue for $1,080,400 cash.
Aug.   1. Paid the semiannual interest on the bonds.
Dec. 31. Recorded the adjusting entry for interest payable.
      31. Recorded amortization of $3,685 of bond premium, using the straight-line method.
      31. Deposited $30,000 cash in a bond sinking fund.
      31. Appropriated $50,000 of retained earnings for bonded indebtedness.
      31. Closed the interest expense account.
1987
Jan.   1. Reversed the adjustment for interest payable.
      20. Purchased various securities with sinking fund cash, cost $26,700.
Feb.   1. Paid the semiannual interest on the bonds.
Aug.   1. Paid the semiannual interest on the bonds.
Dec. 31. Recorded the receipt of $4,025 of income on sinking fund securities, depositing the cash in the sinking fund.
      31. Recorded the adjusting entry for interest payable.
      31. Recorded amortization of $4,020 of bond premium, using the straight-line method.
      31. Deposited $35,000 cash in the sinking fund.
      31. Appropriated $50,000 of retained earnings for bonded indebtedness.
      31. Closed the interest expense account.

Instructions:

   (1) Record the foregoing transactions.
   (2) Prepare a columnar table, using the following headings, and list the information
       for each of the two years.

					Account Balances at End of Year			
						Sinking Fund		
	Bond Interest Expense	Sinking Fund Income	Bonds	Premium				Appropriation for Bonded
Year	for Year	for Year	Payable	on Bonds	Cash	Investments		Indebtedness

12–30. The following transactions relate to the issuance of $600,000 of 10-year, 8%
bonds dated January 1, 1977, and the accumulations in a fund to redeem the bonds at
maturity. Interest on the bonds is payable on June 30 and December 31.

1977

Jan.   3. Sold the bond issue at 100.

June 30. Paid semiannual interest on bonds.

Dec. 31. Paid semiannual interest on bonds and deposited $36,000 in a bond
          sinking fund.

1978

Mar. 20. Purchased $32,100 of investments with bond sinking fund cash.

June 30. Paid semiannual interest on bonds.

Oct. 20. Received $2,560 of income on investments.

Dec. 31. Paid semiannual interest on bonds.

(Assume that all intervening transactions have been recorded properly.)

1987

Jan.   4. All investments in the bond sinking fund were sold for $589,800. The
          sinking fund investments had a book carrying value of $587,200.

      12. The cash available in the sinking fund at this date was $598,550. The
          bonds were paid from the sinking fund cash and the regular cash
          account.

Instructions:

Record the foregoing transactions.

12–31. The following transactions relate to certain securities acquired as a long-term
investment by Brace Company, whose fiscal year ends on December 31:

1984

Apr.   1. Purchased $100,000 of Damen Company 15-year, 12% coupon bonds
          dated April 1, 1984, directly from the issuing company for $102,400.

Oct.   1. Deposited the coupons for semiannual interest on Damen Company
          bonds.

Dec. 31. Recorded the adjustment for interest receivable on the Damen Company
          bonds.

      31. Recorded the amortization of premium of $120 on the Damen Company
          bonds, using the straight-line method.

(Assume that all intervening transactions and adjustments have been recorded
properly, and that the number of bonds owned have not changed from December 31,
1984, to December 31, 1989.)

1990

Jan.   1. Reversed the adjustment of December 31, 1989, for interest receivable on the Damen Company bonds.

Apr.   1. Deposited coupons for semiannual interest on the Damen Company bonds.

July   1. Sold one half of the Damen Company bonds at 103, plus accrued interest. The broker deducted $540 for commission, etc., remitting the balance. Before the sale was recorded, $40 of premium on one half of the bonds was amortized, reducing the carrying amount of those bonds to $50,700.

Oct.   1. Deposited coupons for semiannual interest on the Damen Company bonds.

Dec. 31. Recorded the adjustment for interest receivable on the Damen Company bonds.

     31. Recorded the amortization of premium of $80 on the Damen Company bonds, using the straight-line method.

Instructions:

(1) Record the foregoing transactions.

(2) Determine the amount of interest earned on the bonds in 1984.

(3) Determine the amount of interest earned on the bonds in 1990.

12–27A. The following transactions were completed by Evans Co., whose fiscal year is the calendar year:

Alternate
Problems

1984

Oct.   1. Issued $5,000,000 of 10-year, 12% callable bonds dated October 1, 1984, for cash of $5,623,160. Interest is payable semiannually on October 1 and April 1.

Dec. 31. Recorded the adjusting entry for interest payable.

     31. Recorded amortization of $9,421 premium on the bonds, using the interest method.

     31. Closed the interest expense account.

1985

Jan.   1. Reversed the adjusting entry for interest payable.

Apr.   1. Paid the semiannual interest on the bonds.

Oct.   1. Paid the semiannual interest on the bonds.

Dec. 31. Recorded the adjusting entry for interest payable.

     31. Recorded amortization of $39,592 premium on the bonds, using the interest method.

     31. Closed the interest expense account.

1991

Oct.   1. Recorded the redemption of the bonds, which were called at 104. The balance in the bond premium account is $253,882 after the payment of interest and amortization of premium have been recorded. (Record the redemption only.)

Instructions:

    (1) Record the foregoing transactions.

    (2) Indicate the amount of the interest expense in (a) 1984 and (b) 1985.

    (3) Determine the effective interest rate (divide the interest expense for 1984 by the bond carrying amount at time of issuance) and express as an annual rate.

    (4) Determine the carrying amount of the bonds as of December 31, 1985.

12–28A. On October 1, 1986, Meltzer Corporation issued $4,000,000 of 10-year, 10% bonds at an effective interest rate of 11%. Interest on the bonds is payable semiannually on April 1 and October 1. The fiscal year of the company is the calendar year.

Instructions:

    (1) Present the entry to record the amount of the cash proceeds from the sale of the bonds. Use the tables of present values appearing in this chapter to compute the cash proceeds, rounding to the nearest dollar.

    (2) Present the entries to record the following:

        (a) The adjusting entry for the accrued interest payable on December 31, 1986.

        (b) The amortization of the bond discount on December 31, 1986, using the interest method.

        (c) The reversing entry on January 1, 1987, for the interest payable.

        (d) The first semiannual interest payment on April 1, 1987.

        (e) The amortization of the bond discount on April 1, 1987, using the interest method.

        (f) The amortization of the bond discount on October 1, 1987, using the interest method.

    (3) Present the entries for Instruction (2), parts (b) and (f), using the straight-line method of discount amortization.

    (4) Determine the total interest expense for 1986 for (a) the interest method of discount amortization and (b) the straight-line method of discount amortization. (c) Will the annual interest expense using the interest method of discount amortization always be less than the annual interest expense using the straight-line method of discount amortization?

12–29A. During 1986 and 1987, Mitchum Company completed the following transactions relating to its $3,000,000 issue of 30-year, 11% bonds dated September 1, 1986. Interest is payable on March 1 and September 1. The corporation's fiscal year is the calendar year.

1986

Sept. 1. Sold the bond issue for $2,798,400 cash.

Dec. 31. Recorded the adjusting entry for interest payable.

      31. Recorded amortization of $2,240 of bond discount, using the straight-line method.

      31. Deposited $60,000 cash in a bond sinking fund.

      31. Appropriated $100,000 of retained earnings for bonded indebtedness.

      31. Closed the interest expense account.

1987

Jan. 1. Reversed the adjustment for interest payable.

Feb. 20. Purchased various securities with sinking fund cash, cost $55,600.

Mar. 1. Paid the semiannual interest on the bonds.

Sept. 1. Paid the semiannual interest on the bonds.

Nov. 30. Recorded the receipt of $6,670 of income on sinking fund securities, depositing the cash in the sinking fund.

Dec. 31. Recorded the adjusting entry for interest payable.

　　　31. Recorded amortization of $6,720 of bond discount, using the straight-line method.

　　　31. Deposited $65,000 cash in the sinking fund.

　　　31. Appropriated $100,000 of retained earnings for bonded indebtedness.

　　　31. Closed the interest expense account.

Instructions:

(1) Record the foregoing transactions.

(2) Prepare a columnar table, using the following headings, and list the information for each of the two years.

			Account Balances at End of Year				
					Sinking Fund		
Year	Bond Interest Expense for Year	Sinking Fund Income for Year	Bonds Payable	Discount on Bonds	Cash	Investments	Appropriation For Bonded Indebtedness

12–31A. The following transactions relate to certain securities acquired by Hardigree Company, whose fiscal year ends on December 31:

1984

Aug. 1. Purchased $400,000 of Moody Company 20-year, 9% coupon bonds dated August 1, 1984, directly from the issuing company for $388,000.

Dec. 31. Recorded the adjustment for interest receivable on the Moody Company bonds.

　　　31. Recorded the amortization of discount of $250 on the Moody Company bonds, using the straight-line method.

(Assume that all intervening transactions and adjustments have been recorded properly, and that the number of bonds owned have not changed from December 31, 1984, to December 31, 1988.)

1989

Jan. 1. Reversed the adjustment of December 31, 1988, for interest receivable on the Moody Company bonds.

Feb. 1. Deposited the coupons for semiannual interest on the Moody Company bonds.

May 1. Sold one half of the Moody Company bonds at 98 plus accrued interest. The broker deducted $1,240 for commission, etc., remitting the balance. Before the sale was recorded, $100 of discount on one half of the bonds was amortized, increasing the carrying amount of those bonds to $195,425.

Aug. 1. Deposited coupons for semiannual interest on the Moody Company bonds.

Dec. 31. Recorded the adjustment for interest receivable on the Moody Company bonds.

　　　31. Recorded the amortization of discount of $300 on the Moody Company bonds.

Instructions:

(1) Record the foregoing transactions.

(2) Determine the amount of interest earned on the bonds in 1984.

(3) Determine the amount of interest earned on the bonds in 1989.

Mini-Case

12–32. You hold a 20% common stock interest in the family-owned business, a soft drink bottling distributorship. Your father, who is the manager, has proposed an expansion of plant facilities at an expected cost of $1,000,000. Two alternative plans have been suggested as methods of financing the expansion. Each plan is briefly described as follows:

Plan 1. Issue an additional 10,000 shares of $10 par common stock at $20 per share and $800,000 of 20-year, 15% bonds at face amount.

Plan 2. Issue $1,000,000 of 20-year, 15% bonds at face amount.

The condensed balance sheet of the corporation at the end of the most recent fiscal year is as follows:

Highpoint Bottling of Shelby
Balance Sheet
December 31, 19--

Assets		Liabilities and Stockholders' Equity	
Current assets	$1,600,000	Current liabilities	$1,800,000
Plant assets	6,400,000	Common stock, $10 par	300,000
		Premium on common stock	150,000
		Retained earnings	5,750,000
		Total liabilities and	
Total assets	$8,000,000	stockholders' equity	$8,000,000

Net income has remained relatively constant over the past several years. The expansion program is expected to increase yearly income before bond interest and income tax from $800,000 to $1,080,000. Assume an income tax rate of 50%.

Your father has asked you, as the company treasurer, to prepare an analysis of each financing plan.

Instructions:

(1) Prepare a tabulation indicating the expected earnings per share on the common stock under each plan.

(2) List factors other than earnings per share that should be considered in evaluating the two plans.

(3) Which plan offers the greater benefit to the present stockholders? Give reasons for your opinion.

Answers to Self-Examination Questions

1. B Since the contract rate on the bonds is higher than the prevailing market rate, a rational investor would be willing to pay more than the face amount, or a premium (answer B), for the bonds. If the contract rate and the market rate were equal, the bonds could be expected to sell at their face amount (answer A). Likewise, if the market rate is higher than the contract rate, the bonds would sell at a price below their face amount (answer D) or at a discount (answer C).

2. **A** The bond carrying amount, sometimes called the book value, is the face amount plus unamortized premium or less unamortized discount. For this question, the carrying amount is $500,000 less $40,000, or $460,000 (answer A).

3. **B** Although the sinking fund may consist of cash as well as securities, the fund is listed on the balance sheet as an investment (answer B) because it is to be used to pay the long-term liability at maturity.

4. **B** The amount debited to the investment account is the cost of the bonds, which includes the amount paid to the seller for the bonds (101% × $100,000) plus broker's commissions ($50), or $101,050 (answer B). The $2,000 of accrued interest that is paid to the seller should be debited to Interest Income, since it is an offset against the amount that will be received as interest at the next interest date.

5. **C** The balance of Discount on Bonds Payable is reported as a deduction from Bonds Payable in the long-term liabilities section (answer C) of the balance sheet. Likewise, a balance in a premium on bonds payable account would be reported as an addition to Bonds Payable in the long-term liabilities section of the balance sheet.

CHAPTER 13

Investments in Stocks, Consolidated Statements, and International Operations

CHAPTER OBJECTIVES

Describe and illustrate the accounting for long-term investments in stocks.

Describe alternative methods of combining businesses.

Describe and illustrate the accounting for parent-subsidiary affiliations and the preparation of consolidated financial statements.

Describe and illustrate the accounting for international operations.

In the preceding chapter, the principles of accounting for long-term investments in bonds were discussed. In this chapter, the principles of accounting for long-term investments in stocks will be presented. Accounting for the combining of the operations of two corporations and the expansion of operations into international markets will also be discussed.

INVESTMENTS IN STOCKS

A business may make long-term investments in equity securities (preferred and common shares), simply because it has cash that it does not need for normal operations. A corporation may also purchase stocks as a means of establishing or maintaining business relations with the issuing company. In some cases, a corporation may acquire all or a large part of the voting stock of another corporation in order to control its activities. Similarly, a corporation may organize a new corporation for the purpose of marketing a new product or for some other business reason, receiving stock in exchange for the assets transferred to the new corporation.

Investments in stocks may be purchased directly from the issuing corporation or from other investors. Both preferred and common stocks may be *listed* on an organized stock exchange, or they may be *unlisted*, in which case they are said to be bought and sold *over the counter*. The services of a broker are usually used in buying and selling both listed and unlisted securities.

The record of transactions on the stock exchanges is reported daily in the financial press. This record usually includes, for each stock traded, the high and low price for the past year, the current annual dividend, the volume of sales for the day, and the high, low, and closing price for the day. Prices for stocks are quoted in terms of fractional dollars, with ⅛ of a dollar being the usual minimum fraction, although some low-priced stocks are sold in lower fractions of a dollar, such as ⅟₁₆ or ⅟₃₂. Thus, a price of 40⅜ per share means $40.375; a price of 40½ means $40.50.

In the following discussion, attention will be given to the principles underlying the accounting for investments in stocks that are not intended as a ready source of cash in the normal operations of the business. Such investments are identified as long-term investments and are reported in the balance sheet under the caption "Investments." The principles underlying the accounting for investments in stocks that are classified as temporary investments were discussed in Chapter 6.

ACCOUNTING FOR LONG-TERM INVESTMENTS IN STOCK

There are two methods of accounting for long-term investments in stock: (1) the **cost method** and (2) the **equity method**. The method used depends upon whether the investor owns enough of the voting stock of the investee (company whose stock is owned by the investor) to have a significant influence over its operating and financing policies. If the investor does not have a significant influence, the cost method (with the lower of cost or market rule) must be used. If the investor can exercise a significant influence in a long-term investment situation, the equity method must be used. Evidence of such influence includes, but is not limited to, representation on the board of directors, material intercompany transactions, and interchange of managerial personnel. Guidelines to be applied in making the election are as follows:

> In order to achieve a reasonable degree of uniformity in application, the Board concludes that an investment (direct or indirect) of 20% or more of the voting stock of an investee should lead to a presumption that in the absence of evidence to the contrary an investor has the ability to exercise significant influence over an investee. Conversely, an investment of less than 20% of the voting stock of an investee should lead to a presumption that an investor does not have the ability to exercise significant influence unless such ability can be demonstrated.[1]

---

[1] *Opinions of the Accounting Principles Board, No. 18*, "The Equity Method of Accounting for Investments in Common Stock" (New York: American Institute of Certified Public Accountants, 1971), par. 17.

Cost Method

The cost of stocks purchased includes not only the amount paid to the seller but also other costs related to the purchase, such as broker's commission and postage charges for delivery. When stocks are purchased between dividend dates, there is no separate charge for the pro rata amount of the dividend. Dividends do not accrue from day to day, since they become an obligation of the issuing corporation only when they are declared by the board of directors. The prices of stocks may be affected by the anticipated dividend as the usual declaration date approaches, but this anticipated dividend is only one of many factors that influence stock prices.

The total cost of stocks purchased should be debited to an investment account. To illustrate, assume that 100 shares of Howe Co. common stock are purchased at 55 plus a brokerage fee of $42. The entry to record the transaction is as follows:

```
May  7  Investment in Howe Co. Stock...............    5,542
             Cash....................................            5,542
```

When the cost method is used, cash dividends declared on capital stock held as an investment may be recorded as a debit to Dividends Receivable and a credit to Dividend Income. The receivable account is then credited when the cash is received. A common alternative is to delay recognition of the receivable and the income until the dividend income becomes taxable, which occurs when the cash is received.

A dividend in the form of additional shares of stock is usually not income, and therefore no entry is needed beyond a notation as to the additional number of shares acquired. The receipt of a stock dividend does, however, affect the carrying amount of each share of stock. Thus, if a 5-share common stock dividend is received on 100 shares of common stock with a current carrying amount of $4,200 ($42 per share), the unit carrying amount of the 105 shares becomes $4,200 ÷ 105, or $40 per share.

Long-term investments in stocks of a company over which the investor does not exercise significant influence are subject to the lower of cost or market rule. In applying the rule, the carrying amount of a long-term investment in a portfolio of equity securities is the lower of the *total* cost or *total* market price of the portfolio at the date of the balance sheet. Any market value changes that are recognized are not included in net income, but are reported as a separate item in the stockholders' equity section of the balance sheet.[2] If the decline in market value below cost as of the balance sheet date of an individual security

---

[2]*Statement of Financial Accounting Standards, No. 12*, "Accounting for Certain Marketable Securities" (Stamford: Financial Accounting Standards Board, 1975), par. 11.

is other than temporary, the cost basis of the individual security is written down and the amount of the write-down is accounted for as a realized loss. After the write-down, the carrying amount of the individual security cannot be changed for subsequent recoveries in market value.[3]

Equity Method

When the equity method of accounting is used, a stock purchase is recorded at cost as under the cost method. The features that distinguish the equity method from the cost method relate to the net income and cash dividends of the investee and are summarized as follows:

1. The investor records its share of the periodic net income of the investee as an increase in the investment account and as revenue of the period. Conversely, the investor's share of the investee's periodic loss is recorded as a decrease in the investment and a loss of the period.
2. The investor records its share of cash or property dividends on the stock as a decrease in the investment account and an increase in the appropriate asset accounts.

To illustrate the foregoing, assume that as of the beginning of the fiscal years of Otto Corporation and Parker Corporation, Otto acquires 40% of the common (voting) stock of Parker for $350,000 in cash, that Parker reports net income of $105,000 for the year, and that Parker declared and paid $45,000 in cash dividends during the year. Entries in the accounts of the investor to record these transactions are as follows:

1. *Record purchase of 40% of Parker Corp. common stock for $350,000 cash.*

   Entry: Investment in Parker Corp. Stock. 350,000
            Cash. 350,000

2. *Record 40% of Parker Corp. net income of $105,000.*

   Entry: Investment in Parker Corp. Stock. 42,000
            Income of Parker Corp. 42,000

3. *Record 40% of cash dividends of $45,000 paid by Parker Corp.*

   Entry: Cash. 18,000
            Investment in Parker Corp. Stock. 18,000

---

[3]*Ibid.*, par. 21.

The combined effect of recording 40% of Parker Corporation's income and the dividends received was to increase Cash by $18,000, Investment in Parker Corp. Stock by $24,000, and Income of Parker Corp. by $42,000.

SALE OF LONG-TERM INVESTMENTS IN STOCKS

When shares of stock held as a long-term investment are sold, the investment account is credited for the carrying amount of the shares sold and the cash or appropriate receivable account is debited for the proceeds (sales price less commission and other selling costs). Any difference between the proceeds and the carrying amount is recorded as a gain or loss on the sale. To illustrate, assume that an investment in Drey Corporation stock has a carrying amount of $15,700. If the proceeds from the sale of the stock are $17,500, the entry to record the transaction is as follows:

June 22 Cash.....................................	17,500	
Investment in Drey Corp. Stock.............		15,700
Gain on Sale of Investments...............		1,800

BUSINESS COMBINATIONS

The history of business organization in the United States has been characterized by continuous growth in the size of business entities and the combining of separate enterprises to form even larger operating units. The trend toward combining individual businesses engaged either in similar types of activity or in totally different kinds of pursuits has been influenced by such objectives as efficiencies of large-scale production, broadening of markets and sales volume, reduction of competition, diversification of product lines, and savings in income taxes.

METHODS OF COMBINING BUSINESSES

Combinations may be effected (1) through a joining of two or more corporations to form a single unit by either merger or consolidation or (2) through common control of two or more corporations by means of stock ownership that results in a parent-subsidiary affiliation. These methods of combining separate corporations into larger operating units are complex. Therefore, the discussion that follows is intended to be introductory, with major emphasis on the financial statements of business combinations.

Mergers and Consolidations

When one corporation acquires the properties of another corporation and the latter then dissolves, the joining of the two enterprises is called a **merger.**

Usually, all of the assets of the acquired company, as well as its liabilities, are taken over by the acquiring company, which continues its operations as a single unit. Payment may be in the form of cash, obligations, or capital stock of the acquiring corporation, or there may be a combination of several kinds of consideration. In any event, the consideration received by the dissolving corporation is distributed to its stockholders in final liquidation.

When two or more corporations transfer their assets and liabilities to a corporation which has been created for purposes of the takeover, the combination is called a consolidation. The new corporation usually issues its own securities in exchange for the properties acquired, and the original corporations are dissolved.

There are many legal, financial, managerial, and accounting problems associated with mergers and consolidations. Perhaps the most important matter is the determination of the class and amount of securities to be issued to the owners of the dissolving corporations. In resolving this problem, several factors are considered, including the relative value of the net assets contributed, the relative earning capacities, and the market price of the securities of the respective companies. Bargaining between the parties to the combination may also affect the final outcome.

Parent and Subsidiary Corporations

A common means of achieving a business combination is by one corporation owning a controlling share of the outstanding voting stock of one or more other corporations. When this method is used, none of the participants dissolves. All continue as separate legal entities. The corporation owning all or a majority of the voting stock of another corporation is known as the parent company. The corporation that is controlled is known as the subsidiary company. Two or more corporations closely related through stock ownership are sometimes called affiliated or **associated** companies.

The relationship of a parent and a subsidiary may be accomplished by "purchase" or by a "pooling of interests." When a corporation acquires a controlling share of the voting common stock of another corporation in exchange for cash, other assets, issuance of notes or other debt obligations, or by a combination of these, the transaction is treated as a purchase. It is accounted for by the purchase method. When this method of effecting a parent-subsidiary affiliation is used, the stockholders of the acquired company transfer their stock to the parent corporation.

Alternatively, when two corporations become affiliated by means of an exchange of voting common stock of one corporation (the parent) for substantially all of the voting common stock of the other corporation (the subsidiary), the transaction is termed a pooling of interests. It is accounted for by the pooling of interests method. When this method of effecting a parent-subsidiary affiliation is used, the former stockholders of the subsidiary become stockholders of the parent company.

The accounting implications of the two affiliation methods are very different. The method first described is a "sale-purchase" transaction in contrast to the second method, in which there is a "joining of ownership interests" in the two companies.

ACCOUNTING FOR PARENT-SUBSIDIARY AFFILIATIONS

Although the corporations that make up a parent-subsidiary affiliation may operate as a single economic unit, they continue to maintain separate accounting records and prepare their own periodic financial reports. The parent corporation uses the equity method of accounting for its investment in the stock of a subsidiary.

After the parent-subsidiary relationship has been established, the investment account of the parent is periodically increased by its share of the subsidiary's net income and decreased by its share of dividends received from the subsidiary. At the end of each fiscal year, the parent reports the investment account balance on its own balance sheet as a long-term investment, and its current share of the subsidiary's net income on its own income statement as a separate item.

In addition to the interrelationship through stock ownership, there are usually other intercorporate transactions which have an effect on the financial statements of both the parent and the subsidiary. For example, either may own bonds or other evidences of indebtedness issued by the other and either may purchase or sell goods or services to the other.

Because of the central managerial control factor and the intertwining of relationships, it is usually desirable to present the results of operations and the financial position of a parent company and its subsidiaries as if the group were a single company with one or more branches or divisions. Such statements are likely to be more meaningful to stockholders of the parent company than separate statements for each corporation. However, separate statements are preferable for a subsidiary whose operations are totally different from those of the parent (as when the parent is engaged in manufacturing and the subsidiary is a bank, insurance company, or finance company) or because control over the subsidiary's assets and operations is uncertain (as in a subsidiary that is located outside the United States and that is subject to foreign government controls).

The financial statements resulting from the combining of parent and subsidiary statements are generally called consolidated statements. Specifically, such statements may be identified by the addition of "and subsidiary(ies)" to the name of the parent corporation or by modification of the title of the respective statement, as in *consolidated balance sheet* or *consolidated income statement*.[4]

---

[4]Examples of consolidated statements are presented in Appendix E.

BASIC PRINCIPLES OF CONSOLIDATION OF FINANCIAL STATEMENTS

When the data on the financial statements of the parent corporation and its subsidiaries are combined to form the consolidated statements, special attention should be given to the ties of relationship between the separate corporations. These ties are represented by the intercompany items appearing in their respective ledgers and statements. These intercompany items, called **reciprocals**, must be eliminated from the statements that are to be consolidated. For example, a note representing a loan by a parent corporation to its subsidiary would appear as a note receivable in the parent's balance sheet and a note payable in the subsidiary's balance sheet. When the two balance sheets are combined, the note receivable and the note payable would be eliminated because the consolidated balance sheet is prepared as if the parent and subsidiary were one operating unit. After the proper eliminations are made, the remaining items on the financial statements of the subsidiary are combined with the like items on the financial statements of the parent.

The intercompany accounts of a parent and its subsidiaries may not be entirely reciprocal in amount. Differences may be caused by the manner in which the parent-subsidiary relationship was created, by the extent of the parent's ownership of the subsidiary, or by the nature of their subsequent intercompany transactions. Such factors must be considered when the financial statements of affiliated corporations are consolidated.

To direct attention to the basic concepts of consolidation, most of the data appearing in financial statements will be omitted from many of the illustrations in the following paragraphs. The term "net assets" will be used as a substitute for the specific assets and liabilities that appear in the balance sheet. Explanations will also be simplified by using the term "book equity" in referring to the monetary amount of the stockholders' equity of the subsidiary acquired by the parent. The illustrative companies will be identified as Parent and Subsidiary.

Consolidated Balance Sheet at Date of Acquisition — Purchase Method

When a parent-subsidiary affiliation is effected as a purchase, the parent corporation is deemed to have purchased all or a major part of the subsidiary corporation's net assets. Accordingly, the assets of the subsidiary should be reported on the consolidated balance sheet at their cost to the parent, as measured by the amount of the consideration given in acquiring the stock. In the subsidiary's ledger, the reciprocal of the investment account at the date of acquisition is the composite of all of the subsidiary's stockholders' equity accounts. Any difference between the cost to the parent and the amounts reported on the subsidiary's balance sheet must be given recognition on the consolidated balance sheet.

Income from an investment in assets does not accrue to an investor until after the assets have been purchased. Therefore, subsidiary company earnings accumulated prior to the date of the parent-subsidiary purchase affiliation must be excluded from the consolidated balance sheet and the income statement. Only those earnings of the subsidiary realized subsequent to the affiliation are includable in the consolidated statements.

Wholly Owned Subsidiary Acquired at a Cost Equal to Book Equity

Assume that Parent creates Subsidiary, transferring to it $120,000 of assets and $20,000 of liabilities, and taking in exchange 10,000 shares of $10 par common stock of Subsidiary. The effect of the transaction on Parent's ledger is to replace the various assets and liabilities (net assets of $100,000) with a single account: Investment in Subsidiary, $100,000. The effect on the balance sheet of Parent, together with the balance sheet of Subsidiary prepared immediately after the transaction, is as follows:

	Assets	Stockholders' Equity
Parent:		
Investment in Subsidiary, 10,000 shares.........	$100,000	
Subsidiary:		
Net assets...................................	$100,000	
Common stock, 10,000 shares, $10 par..........		$100,000

When the balance sheets of the two corporations are consolidated, the reciprocal accounts Investment in Subsidiary and Common Stock are offset against each other, or *eliminated*. The individual assets (Cash, Equipment, etc.) and the individual liabilities (Accounts Payable, etc.) making up the $100,000 of net assets on the balance sheet of Subsidiary are then added to the corresponding items on the balance sheet of Parent. The consolidated balance sheet is completed by listing Parent's paid-in capital accounts and retained earnings.

Wholly Owned Subsidiary Acquired at a Cost Above Book Equity

Instead of creating a new subsidiary, a corporation may acquire an already established corporation by purchasing its stock. In such cases, the subsidiary stock's total cost to the parent usually differs from the book equity of such stock. To illustrate, assume that Parent acquires for $180,000 all of the outstanding stock of Subsidiary, a going concern, from Subsidiary's stockholders. Assume further that the stockholders' equity of Subsidiary is made up of common stock of $100,000 (10,000 shares, $10 par) and $50,000 of retained earnings. Parent records the investment at its cost of $180,000, regardless of the amount of the book equity of Subsidiary. It should also be noted that the $180,000 paid to Subsidiary's stockholders has no effect on the assets, liabilities, or stockholders' equity of Subsidiary. The situation immediately after the transaction may be presented as follows:

	Assets	Stockholders' Equity
Parent:		
Investment in Subsidiary, 10,000 shares.........	$180,000	
Subsidiary:		
Net assets....................................	$150,000	
Common stock, 10,000 shares, $10 par.........		$100,000
Retained earnings.............................		50,000

It is readily apparent that the reciprocal items on the separate balance sheets differ by $30,000. If the reciprocals were eliminated, as in the preceding illustration, and were replaced solely by Subsidiary's net assets of $150,000, the consolidated balance sheet would be out of balance.

The treatment of the $30,000 difference depends upon the reason that Parent paid more than book equity for Subsidiary's stock. If the amount paid above book equity is due to an excess of fair market value over book value of Subsidiary's assets, the values of the appropriate assets should be revised upward by $30,000. For example, if land that Subsidiary had acquired several years previously at a cost of $50,000 (book value) has a current fair market value of $80,000, the book amount should be increased from $50,000 to $80,000 when the asset is reported on the consolidated balance sheet. If Parent paid more for Subsidiary's stock because Subsidiary has prospects for high future earnings, the $30,000 should be reported on the consolidated balance sheet under a description such as "Goodwill" or "Excess of cost of business acquired over related net assets." When the additional amount is due to both an excess of fair market value over book value of assets and high future earnings prospects, the excess of cost over book equity should be allocated accordingly.[5]

Wholly Owned Subsidiary Acquired at a Cost Below Book Equity

All of the stock of a corporation may be acquired from its stockholders at a cost that is less than book equity. To illustrate, assume that the stock in Subsidiary is acquired for $130,000 and that the composition of the stockholders' equity of Subsidiary is the same as in the preceding illustration. Parent records the investment at its cost of $130,000. The situation immediately after the transaction is as follows:

---

[5]*Opinions of the Accounting Principles Board, No. 16*, "Business Combinations" (New York: American Institute of Certified Public Accountants, 1970), par. 87.

	Assets	Stockholders' Equity
Parent:		
Investment in Subsidiary, 10,000 shares.........	$130,000	
Subsidiary:		
Net assets...................................	$150,000	
Common stock, 10,000 shares, $10 par..........		$100,000
Retained earnings		50,000

Elimination of the reciprocal accounts and reporting the $150,000 of net assets of Subsidiary on the consolidated balance sheet creates an imbalance of $20,000. The possible reasons for the apparent "bargain" purchase and the treatment of the "imbalance" are generally the reverse of those given in explaining acquisition at a price higher than book equity. The complexities that might arise in some instances are discussed in advanced texts.

Partially Owned Subsidiary Acquired at a Cost Above or Below Book Equity

When one corporation seeks to gain control over another by purchase of its stock, it is not necessary and often not possible to acquire all of the stock. To illustrate this situation, assume that Parent acquires, at a total cost of $190,000, 80% of the stock of Subsidiary, whose book equity is composed of common stock of $100,000 (10,000 shares, $10 par) and $80,000 of retained earnings. The relevant data immediately after the acquisition of the stock are as follows:

	Assets	Stockholders' Equity
Parent:		
Investment in Subsidiary, 8,000 shares..........	$190,000	
Subsidiary:		
Net assets...................................	$180,000	
Common stock, 10,000 shares, $10 par..........		$100,000
Retained earnings		80,000

The explanation of the $10,000 imbalance in the reciprocal items in this illustration is more complex than in the preceding illustrations. Two factors are involved: (1) the amount paid for the stock is greater than 80% of Subsidiary's book equity and (2) only 80% of Subsidiary's stock was purchased. Since Parent acquired 8,000 shares or 80% of the outstanding shares of Subsidiary, only 80% of the stockholders' equity accounts of Subsidiary can be eliminated. The remaining 20% of the stock is owned by outsiders, who are called collectively the minority interest. The eliminations from the partially reciprocal accounts and the amounts to be reported on the consolidated balance sheet, including the minority interest, are determined as follows:

Parent:
Investment in Subsidiary. $190,000
   Eliminate 80% of Subsidiary stock . . . . $ 80,000
   Eliminate 80% of Subsidiary retained earnings   64,000
Excess of cost over book equity of Subsidiary
   interest $46,000

Subsidiary:
Common stock $100,000
   Eliminate 80% of Subsidiary stock   80,000
   Remainder $20,000
Retained earnings . . . . $ 80,000
   Eliminate 80% of Subsidiary retained earnings   64,000
   Remainder   16,000
Minority interest. $36,000

The excess cost of $46,000 is reported on the consolidated balance sheet as goodwill or the valuation placed on other assets is increased by $46,000, according to the principles explained earlier. The minority interest of $36,000, which is the amount of Subsidiary's book equity allocable to outsiders, is reported on the consolidated balance sheet, usually preceding the stockholders' equity accounts of Parent.[6]

Consolidated Balance Sheet Subsequent to Acquisition— Purchase Method

Subsequent to acquisition of a subsidiary, a parent company's investment account is increased periodically for its share of the subsidiary's earnings and decreased for the related dividends received. Correspondingly, the retained earnings account of the subsidiary will be increased periodically by the amount of its net income and reduced by dividend distributions. Because of these periodic changes in the balances of the reciprocal accounts, the eliminations required in preparing a consolidated balance sheet will change each year.

To illustrate consolidation of balance sheets subsequent to acquisition, assume that Subsidiary in the preceding illustration earned net income of $50,000 and paid dividends of $20,000 during the year subsequent to Parent's acquisition of 80% of its stock. The net effect of the year's transactions on Subsidiary were as follows:

	Net Assets	Common Stock	Retained Earnings
Subsidiary:			
Date of acquisition.	$180,000	$100,000	$ 80,000
Add net income	50,000		50,000
Deduct dividends	(20,000)		(20,000)
Date subsequent to acquisition	$210,000	$100,000	$110,000

---

[6] *Accounting Trends and Techniques—1985* indicates that minority interest is reported in the long-term liabilities section by most of the companies surveyed.

Parent's entries to record its 80% share of subsidiary's net income and dividends are as follows:

Parent:

Investment in Subsidiary	40,000	
Income of Subsidiary		40,000
Cash	16,000	
Investment in Subsidiary		16,000

The net effect of the foregoing entries on Parent's investment account is to increase the balance by $24,000, as follows:

Parent:

Investment in Subsidiary, 8,000 shares:		
Date of acquisition		$190,000
Add 80% of Subsidiary's net income	$40,000	
Deduct 80% of Subsidiary's dividends	(16,000)	24,000
Date subsequent to acquisition		$214,000

Continuing the illustration, the eliminations from the partially reciprocal accounts and the amounts to be reported on the consolidated balance sheet are determined as follows:

Parent:

Investment in Subsidiary	$214,000	
Eliminate 80% of Subsidiary stock	$ 80,000◄	
Eliminate 80% of Subsidiary retained earnings	88,000◄	
Excess of cost over book equity of Subsidiary interest		$46,000

Subsidiary:

Common stock	$100,000	
Eliminate 80% of Subsidiary stock	80,000◄	
Remainder		$20,000
Retained earnings	$110,000	
Eliminate 80% of Subsidiary retained earnings	88,000◄	
Remainder		22,000
Minority interest		$42,000

A comparison of the data with the analysis as of the date of acquisition shows the following:

1. Minority interest increased $6,000 (from $36,000 to $42,000), which is equivalent to 20% of the $30,000 net increase ($50,000 of net income less $20,000 of dividends) in Subsidiary's retained earnings.
2. Excess of cost over book equity of the subsidiary interest remained unchanged at $46,000.

To avoid additional complexities, it was assumed that the $46,000 excess at the date of acquisition was not due to goodwill or to assets subject to depreciation or amortization.[7]

Work Sheet for Consolidated Balance Sheet — Purchase Method

The preceding discussion focused on the basic concepts associated with the process of preparing consolidated balance sheets. If the consolidation process becomes quite complex or if the amount of data to be processed is substantial, all of the relevant data for the consolidated statements may be assembled on work sheets. Although a work sheet is not essential, it is used in the following illustration to show an alternate method of accumulating all relevant data for the consolidated balance sheet. Whether or not a work sheet is used, the basic concepts and the consolidated balance sheet would not be affected.

To illustrate the use of the work sheet, assume that (as was the case in the illustration in the preceding section) Parent had purchased 80% of Subsidiary stock for $190,000. For the year since the acquisition, Parent had debited the investment account for its share of Subsidiary earnings and had credited the investment account for its share of dividends declared by Subsidiary. Balance sheet data for Parent and Subsidiary as of December 31 of the year subsequent to acquisition appear as follows. Although these data include amounts for land, other assets, and liabilities, the net assets and stockholders' equity for Subsidiary are the same as in the preceding illustration.

	Parent	Subsidiary
Investment in Subsidiary	$214,000	
Land	100,000	$ 60,000
Other assets	400,000	200,000
	$714,000	$260,000
Liabilities	$164,000	$ 50,000
Common stock:		
Parent	300,000	
Subsidiary		100,000
Retained earnings:		
Parent	250,000	
Subsidiary		110,000
	$714,000	$260,000

---

[7]Any portion of the excess of cost over book equity assigned to goodwill must be amortized according to *Opinions of the Accounting Principles Board, No. 17,* "Intangible Assets." Similarly, any excess of cost over book equity assigned to plant assets of limited life must be gradually reduced by depreciation. The application of such amortization and depreciation techniques to consolidated statements goes beyond the scope of the discussion here.

The account balances at December 31 and the eliminations from the reciprocal accounts would be entered on the work sheet. The amounts would be determined for the consolidated balance sheet items as follows (the right margin notations are added as an aid to understanding):

Parent and Subsidiary
Work Sheet for Consolidated Balance Sheet
December 31, 19--

	Parent	Subsidiary	Eliminations		Consolidated Balance Sheet	
			Debit	Credit		
Investment in Subsidiary ..	214,000			168,000	46,000	Excess of cost over book equity
Land..................	100,000	60,000			160,000	
Other Assets............	400,000	200,000			600,000	
	714,000	260,000			806,000	
Liabilities	164,000	50,000			214,000	
Common Stock:						
Parent...............	300,000				300,000	
Subsidiary		100,000	80,000		20,000	minority interest
Retained Earnings:						
Parent...............	250,000				250,000	
Subsidiary		110,000	88,000		22,000	minority interest
	714,000	260,000	168,000	168,000	806,000	

It should be noted that the work sheet is only an aid for accumulating the data for the consolidated balance sheet. It is not the consolidated balance sheet. Also, if there are other intercompany items that must be eliminated from the statements that are to be consolidated, those eliminations would be entered in the eliminations columns of the work sheet. For example, a loan by a parent to its subsidiary on a note would require an elimination of the amount of the note from both notes receivable and notes payable in the work sheet.

When 80% of Subsidiary common stock and Subsidiary retained earnings is eliminated against the Investment in Subsidiary, as indicated in the eliminations columns of the work sheet, (1) the $46,000 excess of cost over book equity of the subsidiary interest can be identified and (2) the minority interest of $42,000 (consisting of $20,000 related to subsidiary common stock and $22,000 related to subsidiary retained earnings) can be identified. The $46,000 excess of cost over book equity is reported on the consolidated balance sheet according to the principles explained earlier.

In the following balance sheet, it is assumed that the $46,000 is due to an excess of fair value over book value of Subsidiary's land. Thus, the amount for land as reported on the consolidated balance sheet would be $206,000, consisting of the parent's amount of $100,000 plus the subsidiary's amount of $106,000 (the $60,000 book amount plus the $46,000 excess of cost over book equity attributable to the land). The minority interest of $42,000 is also reported on the consolidated balance sheet as explained earlier.

Parent and Subsidiary
Consolidated Balance Sheet
December 31, 19--

Assets

Land	$206,000
Other assets	600,000
Total assets	$806,000

Liabilities and Stockholders' Equity

Liabilities...	$214,000
Minority interest in subsidiary.........................	42,000
Common stock	300,000
Retained earnings	250,000
Total liabilities and stockholders' equity.............	$806,000

Consolidated Balance Sheet at Date of Affiliation— Pooling of Interests

When a parent-subsidiary affiliation is effected as a pooling of interests, the ownership of the two companies is joined together in the parent corporation. The parent deems its investment in the subsidiary to be equal to the carrying amount of the subsidiary's net assets. Any difference that may exist between such carrying amount and the fair value of the subsidiary's assets does not affect the amount recorded by the parent as the investment. Consequently, no change is needed in the amounts at which the subsidiary's assets should be stated in the consolidated balance sheet. They are reported as they appear in the subsidiary's separate balance sheet.

The credit to the parent company's stockholders' equity accounts for the stock issued in exchange for the subsidiary company's stock corresponds to the amount debited to the investment account. In addition to the common stock account, the paid-in capital accounts may be affected, as well as the retained earnings account. According to the concept of continuity of ownership interests, earnings accumulated prior to the affiliation should be combined with those of the parent on the consolidated balance sheet. It is as though there had been a single economic unit from the time the enterprises had begun.

To illustrate the procedure for consolidating the balance sheets of two corporations by the pooling of interests method, their respective financial positions immediately prior to the exchange of stock are assumed to be as follows:

	Assets	Stockholders' Equity
Parent:		
Net assets	$230,000	
Common stock, 4,000 shares, $25 par		$100,000
Retained earnings		130,000
Subsidiary:		
Net assets	$150,000	
Common stock, 10,000 shares, $10 par		$100,000
Retained earnings		50,000

Since poolings must involve substantially all (90% or more) of the stock of the subsidiary,[8] the illustration will assume an exchange of 100% of the stock. It is also assumed that the fair market value of the net assets of both companies is greater than the amounts reported above and that there appears to be an element of goodwill in both cases. Based on recent price quotations, it is agreed that for the purpose of the exchange, Parent's common stock is to be valued at $45 a share and Subsidiary's at $18 a share.[9] According to the agreement, the exchange of stock is brought about as follows:

Parent issues 4,000 shares valued at $45 per share..................... $180,000

in exchange for

Subsidiary's 10,000 shares valued at $18 per share $180,000

The excess of the $180,000 value of Parent's stock issued over the $150,000 of net assets of Subsidiary may be ignored and the investment recorded as follows:

Parent:

Investment in Subsidiary	150,000	
Common Stock		100,000
Retained Earnings		50,000

After the foregoing entry has been recorded, the basic balance sheet data of the two companies are as follows:

	Assets	Stockholders' Equity
Parent:		
Investment in Subsidiary, 10,000 shares	**$150,000**	
Other net assets	230,000	
Common stock, 8,000 shares, $25 par		$200,000
Retained earnings		180,000
Subsidiary:		
Net assets	$150,000	
Common stock, 10,000 shares, $10 par		**$100,000**
Retained earnings		**50,000**

---

[8]*Opinions of the Accounting Principles Board, No. 16, op. cit.,* par. 47b.

[9]In practice, it may be necessary to pay cash for fractional shares or for subsidiary shares held by dissenting stockholders.

To consolidate the balance sheets of the two companies, Parent's investment account and Subsidiary's common stock and retained earnings accounts are eliminated. The net assets of the two companies, $230,000 and $150,000, are combined without any changes in valuation, making a total of $380,000. The consolidated stockholders' equity is composed of common stock of $200,000 and retained earnings of $180,000, for a total of $380,000.

Consolidated Balance Sheet Subsequent to Affiliation — Pooling of Interests

The equity method is used by the parent corporation in recording changes in its investment account subsequent to acquisition. Thus, the account is increased by the parent's share of the subsidiary's earnings and decreased by its share of dividends. Continuing the illustration of the preceding section, assume that Subsidiary's net income and dividends paid during the year subsequent to affiliation with Parent are $20,000 and $5,000 respectively. After Parent has recorded Subsidiary's net income and dividends, the Parent's investment in Subsidiary increases by $15,000 and the Subsidiary's net assets and retained earnings increase by $15,000, yielding the following account balances:

	Assets	Stockholders' Equity
Parent:		
Investment in Subsidiary, 10,000 shares..........	$165,000	
Subsidiary:		
Net assets.....................................	$165,000	
Common stock, 10,000 shares, $10 par..........		$100,000
Retained earnings		65,000

When the balance sheets of the affiliated corporations are consolidated, the reciprocal accounts are eliminated and the $165,000 of net assets of Subsidiary are combined with those of Parent.

Work Sheet for Consolidated Balance Sheet — Pooling of Interests

To illustrate the use of the work sheet to assemble the relevant data for the consolidated balance sheet for an affiliation effected as a pooling of interests, assume that (as was the case in the illustration in the preceding section) Parent had exchanged 4,000 shares of its common stock for all of the 10,000 shares of Subsidiary common stock. For the year since the acquisition, Parent had debited the investment account for its share of Subsidiary earnings and had credited the investment account for its share of dividends declared by Subsidiary. Balance sheet data for Parent and Subsidiary as of December 31 of the year subsequent to acquisition appear as follows. As in the purchase illustration, amounts for land, other assets, and liabilities have been added, but the amounts for net assets and stockholders' equity for Subsidiary are the same as in the preceding illustration.

	Parent	Subsidiary
Investment in Subsidiary	$165,000	
Land..	80,000	$ 40,000
Other assets	325,000	175,000
	$570,000	$215,000
Liabilities	$140,000	$ 50,000
Common stock:		
Parent.....................................	200,000	
Subsidiary		100,000
Retained earnings:		
Parent.....................................	230,000	
Subsidiary		65,000
	$570,000	$215,000

The account balances at December 31 and the eliminations from the reciprocal accounts would be entered on the work sheet and the amounts determined for the consolidated balance sheet items as follows:

Parent and Subsidiary
Work Sheet for Consolidated Balance Sheet
December 31, 19--

	Parent	Subsidiary	Eliminations		Consolidated Balance Sheet
			Debit	Credit	
Investment in Subsidiary ...	165,000			165,000	
Land....................	80,000	40,000			120,000
Other Assets.............	325,000	175,000			500,000
	570,000	215,000			620,000
Liabilities	140,000	50,000			190,000
Common Stock:					
Parent.................	200,000				200,000
Subsidiary		100,000	100,000		
Retained Earnings:					
Parent.................	230,000				230,000
Subsidiary		65,000	65,000		
	570,000	215,000	165,000	165,000	620,000

After 100% of Subsidiary common stock and Subsidiary retained earnings is eliminated against the Investment in Subsidiary, as indicated in the eliminations columns of the work sheet, the amounts for the two companies are combined, without any changes in valuation, and are then reported on the consolidated balance sheet.

As previously discussed, the work sheet is only an aid for accumulating the data for the consolidated balance sheet. These data are the basis for the consolidated balance sheet, which is prepared in the normal manner.

Consolidated Income Statement and Other Statements

Consolidation of income statements and other statements of affiliated companies usually presents fewer difficulties than those encountered in balance sheet consolidations. The difference is largely because of the inherent nature of the statements. The balance sheet reports cumulative effects of all transactions from the very beginning of an enterprise to a current date, whereas the income statement, the retained earnings statement, and the statement of changes in financial position report selected transactions only and are for a limited period of time, usually a year.

The principles used in the consolidation of the income statements of a parent and its subsidiaries are the same, regardless of whether the affiliation is deemed to be a purchase or a pooling of interests. When the income statements are consolidated, all amounts resulting from intercompany transactions, such as management fees or interest on loans charged by one affiliate to another, must be eliminated. Any intercompany profit included in inventories must also be eliminated. The remaining amounts of sales, cost of goods sold, operating expenses, and other revenues and expenses reported on the income statements of the affiliated corporations are then combined. The eliminations required in consolidating the retained earnings statement and other statements are based largely on data assembled in consolidating the balance sheet and income statement.

CORPORATION FINANCIAL STATEMENTS

Examples of retained earnings statements and sections of income statements affected by the corporate form of organization have been presented in preceding chapters. A complete balance sheet of a corporation, containing items discussed in this and preceding chapters, is illustrated on pages 434 and 435. Selected statements from the annual reports of a number of corporations are presented in Appendix E.

ACCOUNTING FOR INTERNATIONAL OPERATIONS

In an effort to expand operations, many U. S. companies conduct business in foreign countries. If the operations of these multinational companies involve currencies other than the dollar, special accounting problems may arise (1) in accounting for transactions with the foreign companies and (2) in the preparation of consolidated statements for domestic and foreign companies that are affiliated. The basic principles used in such situations are presented in the following paragraphs. Details and complexities are reserved for advanced texts.

Connor
Consolidated Balance
December

Assets

Current assets:

Cash		$ 255,000
Marketable securities, at cost (market price, $160,000)		152,500
Accounts and notes receivable	$ 722,000	
Less allowance for doubtful receivables	37,000	685,000
Inventories, at lower of cost (first-in, first-out) or market		917,500
Prepaid expenses		70,000
Total current assets		$2,080,000

Investments:

Bond sinking fund		$ 422,500
Investment in bonds of Dalton Company		240,000
Total investments		662,500

Plant assets (depreciated by the straight-line method):

	Cost	Accumulated Depreciation	Book Value
Land	$ 250,000	—	$ 250,000
Buildings	920,000	$ 379,955	540,045
Machinery and equipment	2,764,400	766,200	1,998,200
Total plant assets	$3,934,400	$1,146,155	2,788,245

Intangible assets:

Goodwill		$ 300,000
Organization costs		50,000
Total intangible assets		350,000
Total assets		$5,880,745

Accounting for Transactions with Foreign Companies

If transactions with foreign companies are executed in dollars, no special accounting problems arise. Such transactions would be recorded as illustrated in the text. For example, the sale of merchandise to a Japanese company that is billed in and paid in dollars would be recorded by the U.S. company in the normal manner, using dollar amounts. However, if transactions involve receivables or payables that are to be received or paid in a foreign currency, the U.S. company may incur an exchange gain or loss.

Corporation and Subsidiaries
Sheet
31, 19--

Liabilities

Current liabilities:

Accounts payable	$ 508,810	
Income tax payable	120,500	
Dividends payable	94,000	
Accrued liabilities	81,400	
Total current liabilities		$ 804,710

Long-term liabilities:

Debenture 8% bonds payable, due			
December 31, 19--	$1,000,000		
Less unamortized discount	60,000	$ 940,000	
Minority interest in subsidiaries		115,000	
Total long-term liabilities			1,055,000

Deferred credits:

Deferred income tax payable		95,500
Total liabilities		$1,955,210

Stockholders' Equity

Paid-in capital:

Common stock, $20 par (250,000 shares			
authorized, 100,000 shares issued)	$2,000,000		
Premium on common stock	320,000		
Total paid-in capital		$2,320,000	

Retained earnings:

Appropriated:

For bonded indebtedness	$250,000		
For plant expansion	750,000	$1,000,000	
Unappropriated		605,535	
Total retained earnings		1,605,535	
Total stockholders' equity			3,925,535
Total liabilities and stockholders' equity			$5,880,745

Realized Currency Exchange Gains and Losses

When a U. S. company executes a transaction with a company in a foreign country using a currency other than the dollar, one currency needs to be converted into another to settle the transaction. For example, a U. S. company purchasing merchandise from a British company that requires payment in British pounds must exchange dollars ($) for pounds (£) to settle the transaction. This exchange of one currency into another involves the use of an exchange rate. The exchange rate is the rate at which one unit of currency (the dollar, for example) can be converted into another currency (the British pound, for example). To continue with the illustration, if the U. S. company had purchased merchandise for £1,000 from a British company on June 1, when the exchange rate was $1.40 per British pound, $1,400 would need to be exchanged for £1,000 to make the purchase.[10] Since the U. S. company maintains its accounts in dollars, the transaction would be recorded as follows:

June 1 Purchases	1,400	
Cash		1,400
Payment of Invoice No. 1725 from W. A. Sterling Co., £1,000; exchange rate, $1.40 per British pound.		

Special accounting problems arise when the exchange rate fluctuates between the date of the original transaction (such as a purchase on account) and the settlement of that transaction in cash in the foreign currency (such as the payment of an account payable). In practice, such fluctuations are frequent. To illustrate, assume that on July 10, when the exchange rate was $.004 per yen (Y), a purchase for Y100,000 was made from a Japanese company. Since the U. S. company maintains its accounts in dollars, the entry would be recorded at $400 (Y100,000 × $.004), as follows:

July 10 Purchases	400	
Accounts Payable—M. Suzuki and Son		400
Invoice No. 818, Y100,000; exchange rate, $.004 per yen.		

If on the date of payment, August 9, the exchange rate had increased to $.005 per yen, the Y100,000 account payable must be settled by exchanging $500 (Y100,000 × $.005) for Y100,000. In such a case, the U. S. company incurs an exchange loss of $100, because $500 was needed to settle a $400 debt (account payable). The cash payment would be recorded as follows:

Aug. 9 Accounts Payable—M. Suzuki and Son	400	
Exchange Loss	100	
Cash		500
Cash paid on Invoice No. 818, for Y100,000, or $400, when exchange rate was $.005 per yen.		

All transactions with foreign companies can be analyzed in the manner described above. For example, assume that on May 1, when the exchange rate

[10]Foreign exchange rates are quoted in major financial reporting services. Because the exchange rates are quite volatile, those used in this chapter are assumed rates which do not necessarily reflect current rates.

was $.25 per Swiss franc (F), a sale on account for $1,000 to a Swiss company was billed in Swiss francs. The transaction would be recorded as follows:

```
May  1 Accounts Receivable—D. W. Robinson Co. .....    1,000
          Sales....................................              1,000
             Invoice No. 9772, F4,000; exchange rate,
             $.25 per Swiss franc.
```

If the exchange rate had increased to $.30 per Swiss franc on May 31, the date of receipt of cash, the U.S. company would realize an exchange gain of $200. The gain was realized because the F4,000, which had a value of $1,000 on the date of sale, had increased in value to $1,200 (F4,000 × $.30) on May 31 when payment was received. The receipt of the cash would be recorded as follows:

```
May 31 Cash.......................................    1,200
          Accounts Receivable—D. W. Robinson Co. ...            1,000
          Exchange Gain............................              200
             Cash received on Invoice No. 9772, for
             F4,000, or $1,000, when exchange rate was
             $.30 per Swiss franc.
```

Unrealized Currency Exchange Gains and Losses

In the previous illustrations, the transactions were completed by either the receipt or the payment of cash. Therefore, any exchange gain or loss was realized and, in an accounting sense, was "recognized" at the date of the cash receipt or cash payment. However, if financial statements are prepared between the date of the original transaction (sale or purchase on account, for example) and the date of the cash receipt or cash payment, and the exchange rate has changed since the original transaction, an unrealized gain or loss must be recognized in the statements. To illustrate, assume that a sale on account for $1,000 had been made to a German company on December 20, when the exchange rate was $.50 per deutsche mark (DM), and that the transaction had been recorded as follows:

```
Dec. 20 Accounts Receivable—T. A. Mueller Inc.........    1,000
          Sales....................................              1,000
             Invoice No. 1793, DM2,000; exchange rate,
             $.50 per deutsche mark.
```

If the exchange rate had decreased to $.45 per deutsche mark on December 31, the date of the balance sheet, the $1,000 account receivable would have a value of only $900 (DM2,000 × $.45). This "unrealized" loss would be recorded as follows:

```
Dec. 31 Exchange Loss................................    100
              Accounts Receivable—T. A. Mueller Inc.........          100
              Invoice No. 1793, DM2,000 × $.05 decrease in
              exchange rate.
```

Assuming that DM2,000 are received on January 19 in the following year, when the exchange rate is $.42, the additional decline in the exchange rate from $.45 to $.42 per deutsche mark must be recognized. The cash receipt would be recorded as follows:

```
Jan. 19 Cash..........................................    840
              Exchange Loss ($.03 × DM2,000)................     60
              Accounts Receivable—T. A. Mueller Inc.........          900
              Cash received on Invoice No. 1793, for
              DM2,000, or $900, when exchange rate was
              $.42 per deutsche mark.
```

If the exchange rate had increased between December 31 and January 19, an exchange gain would be recorded on January 19. For example, if the exchange rate had increased from $.45 to $.47 per deutsche mark during this period, Exchange Gain would be credited for $40 ($.02 × DM2,000).

A balance in the exchange loss account at the end of the fiscal period should be reported in the Other Expense section of the income statement. A balance in the exchange gain account should be reported in the Other Income section.

Consolidated Financial Statements with Foreign Subsidiaries

Before the financial statements of domestic and foreign companies are consolidated, the statements for the foreign companies must be converted to U. S. dollars. Asset and liability amounts are normally converted to U. S. dollars by using the exchange rates as of the balance sheet date. Revenues and expenses are normally converted by using the exchange rates that were in effect when those transactions were executed. (For practical purposes, a weighted average rate for the period is generally used.) The adjustments (gains or losses) resulting from the conversion are reported as a separate item in the stockholders' equity section of the balance sheets of the foreign companies.[11]

After the foreign company statements have been converted to U. S. dollars, the financial statements of U. S. and foreign subsidiaries are consolidated in the normal manner as described previously in this chapter.

---

[11]*Statement of Financial Accounting Standards*, No. 52, "Foreign Currency Translation" (Stamford: Financial Accounting Standards Board, 1981).

Self-
Examination
Questions
(Answers
at end of
chapter.)

1. Which of the following are characteristic of a parent-subsidiary relationship known as a pooling of interests?
   A. Parent acquires a controlling share of the voting stock of subsidiary in exchange for cash
   B. Parent acquires a controlling share of the voting stock of subsidiary in exchange for its bonds payable
   C. Parent acquires a controlling share of the voting stock of subsidiary in exchange for its voting common stock
   D. All of the above

2. P Co. purchased the entire outstanding stock of S Co. for $1,000,000 in cash. If at the date of acquisition, S Co.'s stockholders' equity consisted of $750,000 of common stock and $150,000 of retained earnings, what is the amount of the difference between cost and book equity of the subsidiary interest?
   A. Excess of cost over book equity of subsidiary interest, $250,000
   B. Excess of cost over book equity of subsidiary interest, $100,000
   C. Excess of book equity over cost of subsidiary interest, $250,000
   D. None of the above

3. If in Question 2, P Co. had purchased 90% of the outstanding stock of S Co. for $1,000,000, what is the amount of the difference between cost and book equity of subsidiary interest?
   A. Excess of cost over book equity of subsidiary interest, $100,000
   B. Excess of cost over book equity of subsidiary interest, $190,000
   C. Excess of cost over book equity of subsidiary interest, $250,000
   D. None of the above

4. Based on the data in Question 3, what is the amount of the minority interest at the date of acquisition?
   A. $15,000   C. $100,000
   B. $75,000   D. None of the above

5. On July 9, 1986, a sale on account for $10,000 to a Mexican company was billed for 250,000 pesos. The exchange rate was $.04 per peso on July 9 and $.05 per peso on August 8, 1986, when the cash was received on account. Which of the following statements identifies the exchange gain or loss for the fiscal year ended December 31, 1986?
   A. Realized exchange loss, $2,500   C. Unrealized exchange loss, $2,500
   B. Realized exchange gain, $2,500   D. Unrealized exchange gain, $2,500

13-1. What are two methods of accounting for investments in stock?

Discussion
Questions

13-2. When stocks are purchased between dividend dates, does the purchaser pay the seller the dividend accrued since the last dividend payment date? Explain.

13-3. A stockholder owning 500 shares of Sanders Co. common stock, acquired at a total cost of $14,700, receives a common stock dividend of 25 shares. What is the carrying amount per share after the stock dividend?

13–4. What terms are applied to the following: (a) a corporation that is controlled by another corporation through ownership of a controlling interest in its stock; (b) a corporation that owns a controlling interest in the voting stock of another corporation; (c) a group of corporations related through stock ownership?

13–5. What are the two methods by which the relationship of parent-subsidiary may be accomplished?

13–6. P Company purchases for $3,000,000 the entire common stock of S Corporation. What type of accounts on S's balance sheet are reciprocal to the investment account on P's balance sheet?

13–7. Are the eliminations of the reciprocal accounts in consolidating the balance sheets of P and S in Question 13-6 recorded in the respective ledgers of the two companies?

13–8. Palmer Company purchased from stockholders the entire outstanding stock of Sanchez Inc. for a total of $5,000,000 in cash. At the date of acquisition, Sanchez Inc. had $2,000,000 of liabilities and total stockholders' equity of $4,500,000. (a) As of the acquisition date, what was the total amount of the assets of Sanchez Inc.? (b) As of the acquisition date, what was the amount of the net assets of Sanchez Inc.? (c) What is the amount of difference between the investment account and the book equity of the subsidiary interest acquired by Palmer Company?

13–9. What is the possible explanation of the difference determined in Question 13-8(c) and how will it affect the reporting of the difference on the consolidated balance sheet?

13–10. If, in Question 13-8, Palmer Company had paid only $4,200,000 for the stock of Sanchez Inc., what would the difference in part (c) have been?

13–11. Parent Corporation owns 90% of the outstanding common stock of Subsidiary Corporation, which has no preferred stock. (a) What is the term applied to the remaining 10% interest? (b) If the total stockholders' equity of Subsidiary Corporation is $900,000, what is the amount of Subsidiary's book equity allocable to outsiders? (c) Where is the amount determined in (b) reported on the consolidated balance sheet?

13–12. P Corporation owns 80% of the outstanding common stock of S Co., which has no preferred stock. Net income of S Co. was $150,000 for the year and cash dividends declared and paid during the year amounted to $90,000. What entries should be made by P Corporation to record its share of S Co.'s (a) net income and (b) dividends? (c) What is the amount of the net increase in the equity of the minority interest?

13–13. (a) What purpose is served by the work sheet for a consolidated balance sheet? (b) Is the work sheet a substitute for the consolidated balance sheet?

13–14. At the end of the fiscal year, the amount of notes receivable and notes payable reported on the respective balance sheets of a parent and its wholly owned subsidiary are as follows:

	Parent	Subsidiary
Notes Receivable	$275,000	$40,000
Notes Payable	150,000	35,000

If $25,000 of Subsidiary's notes receivable are owed by Parent, determine the amount of notes receivable and notes payable to be reported on the consolidated balance sheet.

13–15. Sales and purchases of merchandise by a parent corporation and its wholly owned subsidiary during the year were as follows:

	Parent	Subsidiary
Sales	$4,000,000	$850,000
Purchases	2,400,000	620,000

If $500,000 of the sales of Parent were made to Subsidiary, determine the amount of sales and purchases to be reported on the consolidated income statement.

13–16. The relationships of parent and subsidiary were established by the following transactions. Identify each affiliation as a "purchase" or a "pooling of interests."

(a) Company P receives 100% of the voting common stock of Company S in exchange for cash and long-term bonds payable.

(b) Company P receives 95% of the voting common stock of Company S in exchange for voting common stock of Company P.

(c) Company P receives 90% of the voting common stock of Company S in exchange for cash.

(d) Company P receives 75% of the voting common stock of Company S in exchange for voting common stock of Company P.

13–17. Which of the following procedures for consolidating the balance sheet of a parent and wholly owned subsidiary are characteristic of acquisition of control by purchase and which are characteristic of a pooling of interests? (a) Retained earnings of subsidiary at date of acquisition are eliminated. (b) Retained earnings of subsidiary at date of acquisition are combined with retained earnings of parent. (c) Assets are not revalued. (d) Goodwill may not be recognized.

13–18. On June 30, Polk Corp. issued 9,000 shares of its $10 par common stock, with a total market value of $300,000, to the stockholders of Sapp Inc., in exchange for all of Sapp's common stock. Polk Corp. records its investment at $250,000. The net assets and stockholders' equities of the two companies just prior to the affiliation are summarized as follows:

	Polk Corp.	Sapp, Inc.
Net assets	$810,000	$250,000
Common stock	$600,000	$150,000
Retained earnings	210,000	100,000
	$810,000	$250,000

(a) At what amounts would the following be reported on the consolidated balance sheet as of June 30, applying the pooling of interests method: (1) Net assets, (2) Retained earnings?

(b) Assume that, instead of issuing shares of stock, Polk Corp. had given $300,000 in cash and long-term notes. At what amounts would the following be reported on the consolidated balance sheet as of June 30: (1) Net assets, (2) Retained earnings?

13–19. Can a U. S. company incur an exchange gain or loss because of fluctuations in the exchange rate if its transactions with foreign countries, involving receivables or payables, are executed in (a) dollars, (b) the foreign currency?

13–20. A U. S. company purchased merchandise for 5,000 francs on account from a French company. If the exchange rate was $.22 per franc on the date of purchase and $.20 per franc on the date of payment of the account, what was the amount of exchange gain or loss realized by the U. S. company?

13–21. What two conditions give rise to unrealized currency exchange gains and losses from sales and purchases on account that are to be settled in the foreign currency?

Exercises

13–22. On July 22, O'Brien Corporation acquired 1,000 shares of the 50,000 shares of Jones Co. common stock at 26¾ plus commission and postage charges of $250. On September 15, a cash dividend of $1.50 per share and an 8% stock dividend were received. On November 25, 200 shares were sold at 25½ less commission and postage charges of $36. Present entries to record (a) purchase of the stock, (b) receipt of the dividends, and (c) sale of the 200 shares.

13–23. At a total cost of $2,500,000, Arnold Corporation acquires 125,000 shares of Micro-Systems Co. common stock as a long-term investment. Arnold Corporation uses the equity method of accounting for long-tem investments in common stock. Micro-Systems Co. has 312,500 shares of common stock outstanding, including the 125,000 shares acquired by Arnold Corporation. Present entries by Arnold Corporation to record the following information:
   (a) Micro-Systems Co. reports net income of $650,000 for the current period.
   (b) A cash dividend of $.40 per common share is paid by Micro-Systems Co. during the current period.

13–24. On the last day of the fiscal year, Palmquist Inc. purchased 80% of the common stock of Stowe Company for $550,000, at which time Stowe Company reported the following on its balance sheet: assets, $940,000; liabilities, $290,000; common stock, $10 par, $500,000; retained earnings, $150,000. In negotiating the stock sale, it was determined that the book carrying amounts of Stowe's recorded assets and equities approximated their current market values.
   (a) Indicate for each of the following the section, title of the item, and amount to be reported on the consolidated balance sheet as of the date of acquisition:
       (1) Difference between cost and book equity of subsidiary interest.
       (2) Minority interest.
   (b) During the following year, Palmquist Inc. realized net income of $725,000, exclusive of the income of the subsidiary, and Stowe Company realized net income of $200,000. In preparing a consolidated income statement, indicate in what amounts the following would be reported:
       (1) Minority interest's share of net income.
       (2) Consolidated net income.

13–25. On December 31 of the current year, Pace Corporation purchased 90% of the stock of Sisco Company. The data reported on their separate balance sheets immediately after the acquisition are as follows:

Assets	Pace Corporation	Sisco Company
Cash..	$ 40,500	$ 19,500
Accounts receivable (net)	62,500	30,000
Inventories	145,000	54,500
Investment in Sisco Company	350,000	—
Equipment (net)................................	400,000	262,500
	$998,000	$366,500

Liabilities and Stockholders' Equity		
Accounts payable	$ 89,000	$ 27,500
Common stock, $10 par.........................	600,000	250,000
Retained earnings..............................	309,000	89,000
	$998,000	$366,500

The fair value of Sisco Company's assets corresponds to their book carrying amounts, except for equipment, which is valued at $300,000 for consolidation purposes. Prepare a consolidated balance sheet as of that date, in report form, omitting captions for current assets, plant assets, etc. (A work sheet need not be used.)

13–26. As of May 31 of the current year, Peak Corporation exchanged 5,000 shares of its $20 par common stock for the 1,000 shares of Saad Company $100 par common stock held by Saad stockholders. The separate balance sheets of the two enterprises, immediately after the exchange of shares, are as follows:

Assets	Peak Corporation	Saad Company
Cash..	$ 41,000	$ 20,500
Accounts receivable (net)	46,500	30,500
Inventories	145,000	57,000
Investment in Saad Company....................	175,000	—
Equipment (net)................................	510,000	92,000
	$917,500	$200,000

Liabilities and Stockholders' Equity		
Accounts payable	$ 77,000	$ 25,000
Common stock.................................	600,000	100,000
Retained earnings.............................	240,500	75,000
	$917,500	$200,000

Prepare a consolidated balance sheet as of May 31, in report form, omitting captions for current assets, plant assets, etc. (A work sheet need not be used.)

13–27. For the current year ended June 30, the results of operations of Payne Corporation and its wholly owned subsidiary, Saxe Enterprises, are as follows:

	Payne Corporation		Saxe Enterprises	
Sales...........................		$990,000		$310,000
Cost of merchandise sold...........	$675,000		$185,000	
Selling expenses..................	155,000		50,000	
General expenses	75,000		30,000	
Interest income...................	(12,000)		———	
Interest expense..................	———	893,000	12,000	277,000
Net income.......................		$ 97,000		$ 33,000

During the year, Payne sold merchandise to Saxe for $45,000. The merchandise was sold by Saxe to nonaffiliated companies for $75,000. Payne's interest income was realized from a long-term loan to Saxe.

(a) Prepare a consolidated income statement for the current year for Payne and its subsidiary. Use the single-step form and disregard income taxes. (A work sheet need not be used.)

(b) If none of the merchandise sold by Payne to Saxe had been sold during the year to nonaffiliated companies, and assuming that Payne's cost of the merchandise had been $31,000, determine the amounts that would have been reported for the following items on the consolidated income statement: (1) sales, (2) cost of merchandise sold, (3) net income.

13–28. Summarized data from the balance sheets of Pagan Company and Schor Inc., as of April 30 of the current year, are as follows:

	Pagan Company	Schor Inc.
Net assets	$700,000	$80,000
Common stock:		
25,000 shares, $20 par............	500,000	
5,000 shares, $10 par.............		50,000
Retained earnings	200,000	30,000

(a) On May 1 of the current year, the two companies combine. Pagan Company issues 2,500 shares of its $20 par common stock, valued at $95,000, to Schor's stockholders in exchange for the 5,000 shares of Schor's $10 par common stock, also valued at $95,000. Assuming that the affiliation is effected as a pooling of interests, what are the amounts that would be reported for net assets, common stock, and retained earnings as of May 1 of the current year?

(b) Assume that Pagan Company had paid cash of $95,000 for Schor Inc. common stock on May 1 of the current year and that the book value of the net assets of Schor Inc. is deemed to reflect fair value. What are the amounts that would be reported for net assets, common stock, and retained earnings as of May 1 of the current year, using the purchase method? How much goodwill will be reported on the combined balance sheet?

13–29. Vance Company makes sales on account to several Mexican companies which it bills in pesos. Record the following selected transactions completed during the current year:

Jan. 12. Sold merchandise on account, 50,000 pesos; exchange rate, $.04 per peso.

Feb. 20. Received cash from sale of January 12, 50,000 pesos; exchange rate, $.05 per peso.

Apr. 30. Sold merchandise on account, 80,000 pesos; exchange rate, $.05 per peso.

July 2. Received cash from sale of April 30, 80,000 pesos; exchange rate, $.04 per peso.

13–30. Tudor Company purchases merchandise from a German company that requires payment in deutsche marks. Record the following selected transactions completed during the current year:

July 1. Purchased merchandise on account, net 30, 3,000 marks; exchange rate, $.51 per mark.

31. Paid invoice of July 1; exchange rate, $.52 per mark.

Aug. 10. Purchased merchandise on account, net 30, 6,000 marks; exchange rate, $.52 per mark.

Sep. 9. Paid invoice of August 10; exchange rate, $.50 per mark.

13–31. The following transactions relate to certain securities acquired by Atlantis Company, whose fiscal year ends on December 31:

Problems

1986

Feb. 10. Purchased 2,000 shares of the 200,000 common shares of Doyle Corporation at 35 plus commission and other costs of $350.

May 15. Received the regular cash dividend of 80¢ a share on Doyle Corporation stock.

Nov. 15. Received the regular cash dividend of 80¢ a share plus an extra dividend of 10¢ a share on Doyle Corporation stock.

(Assume that all intervening transactions have been recorded properly, and that the number of shares of stocks owned have not changed from December 31, 1986, to December 31, 1988.)

1989

May 20. Received the regular cash dividend of 80¢ a share and a 5% stock dividend on the Doyle Corporation stock.

Oct. 8. Sold 750 shares of Doyle Corporation stock at 36. The broker deducted commission and other costs of $640, remitting the balance.

Nov. 18. Received a cash dividend at the new rate of 84¢ a share on the Doyle Corporation stock.

Instructions:

Record the foregoing transactions.

13–32. On June 30 of the current year, Pondy Company purchased 85% of the stock of Stein Company. On the same date, Pondy Company loaned Stein Company $25,000 on a 90-day note. The data reported on their separate balance sheets immediately after the acquisition and loan are as follows:

Assets	Pondy Company	Stein Company
Cash...	$ 39,000	$ 27,500
Accounts receivable (net).........................	49,500	35,000
Notes receivable	40,000	——
Inventories.....................................	168,000	49,000
Investment in Stein Company.....................	260,000	——
Equipment (net)	375,000	215,000
	$931,500	$326,500

Liabilities and Stockholders' Equity		
Accounts payable................................	$137,500	$ 22,500
Notes payable...................................	——	25,000
Common stock, $20 par..........................	500,000	——
Common stock, $10 par..........................	——	200,000
Retained earnings	294,000	79,000
	$931,500	$326,500

The fair value of Stein Company's assets correspond to the book carrying amounts, except for equipment, which is valued at $225,000 for consolidation purposes.

Instructions:

(1) Prepare a work sheet for a consolidated balance sheet as of June 30 of the current year.

(2) Prepare in report form a consolidated balance sheet as of June 30, omitting captions for current assets, plant assets, etc.

13–33. On January 31, Parr Company purchased 80% of the outstanding stock of Stove Company for $400,000. Balance sheet data for the two corporations immediately after the transaction are as follows:

Assets	Parr Co.	Stove Co.
Cash and marketable securities	$ 175,500	$ 23,600
Accounts receivable	246,150	44,150
Allowance for doubtful accounts	(20,100)	(8,050)
Inventories.....................................	490,250	122,100
Investment in Stove Company	400,000	——
Land...	140,000	75,000
Building and equipment	729,300	494,600
Accumulated depreciation	(232,400)	(261,900)
	$1,928,700	$489,500

Liabilities and Stockholders' Equity		
Accounts payable................................	$ 205,750	$ 71,150
Income tax payable..............................	42,000	6,050
Bonds payable (due in 1999)......................	400,000	——
Common stock, $10 par..........................	750,000	——
Common stock, $20 par..........................	——	300,000
Retained earnings	530,950	112,300
	$1,928,700	$489,500

Instructions:

(1) Prepare a work sheet for a consolidated balance sheet as of the date of acquisition.

(2) Prepare in report form a detailed consolidated balance sheet as of the date of acquisition. The fair value of Stove Company's assets are deemed to correspond to the book carrying amounts, except for land, which is to be increased by $50,000.

(3) Assuming that Stove Company earns net income of $90,000 and pays cash dividends of $40,000 during the ensuing fiscal year and that Parr Company records its share of the earnings and dividends, determine the following as of the end of the year:

(a) The net amount added to Parr Company's investment account as a result of Stove Company's earnings and dividends.

(b) The amount of the minority interest.

13–34. Several years ago, Poll Corporation purchased 18,000 of the 20,000 outstanding shares of stock of Sims Company. Since the date of acquisition, Poll Corporation has debited the investment account for its share of the subsidiary's earnings and has credited the account for its share of dividends declared. Balance sheet data for the two corporations as of March 31 of the current year are as follows:

Assets	Poll Corp.	Sims Co.
Cash.	$ 52,500	$ 21,200
Notes receivable	45,000	15,000
Accounts receivable (net).	130,500	49,500
Interest receivable	3,000	600
Dividends receivable	4,500	——
Inventories.	190,000	60,000
Prepaid expenses	5,100	1,700
Investment in Sims Co.	180,180	——
Land	75,000	40,000
Buildings and equipment	411,000	240,000
Accumulated depreciation	(200,000)	(95,400)
	$896,780	$332,600
Liabilities and Stockholders' Equity		
Notes payable.	$ 40,000	$ 50,000
Accounts payable.	89,500	60,500
Income tax payable	30,000	8,900
Dividends payable	15,000	5,000
Interest payable	2,450	3,000
Common stock, $20 par	600,000	——
Common stock, $5 par	——	100,000
Premium on common stock	——	25,000
Retained earnings	119,830	80,200
	$896,780	$332,600

Poll Corporation holds $30,000 of short-term notes of Sims Company, on which there is accrued interest of $3,000. Sims Company owes Poll Corporation $10,000 for a management advisory fee for the year. It has been recorded by both corporations in their respective accounts payable and accounts receivable accounts.

Instructions:

Prepare in report form a detailed consolidated balance sheet as of March 31 of the current year. (A work sheet is not required.) The excess of book equity in Sims Company over the balance of the Poll Corporation's investment account is attributable to overvaluation of Sims Company's land.

13–35. On June 1 of the current year, the Park Company, after several months of negotiations, issued 4,500 shares of its $50 par common stock for all of Shaw Inc.'s outstanding shares of stock. The fair market value of the Park Company shares issued is $75 per share, or a total of $337,500. Shaw Inc. is to be operated as a separate subsidiary. The balance sheets of the two firms on May 31 of the current year are as follows:

Assets	Park Company	Shaw Inc.
Cash..	$ 225,500	$ 18,500
Accounts receivable (net)........................	240,250	36,900
Inventory	410,000	61,450
Land..	120,000	50,000
Plant and equipment (net)	504,250	123,150
	$1,500,000	$290,000

Liabilities and Stockholders' Equity		
Accounts payable..............................	$ 136,000	$ 42,500
Common stock ($50 par)	900,000	150,000
Retained earnings	464,000	97,500
	$1,500,000	$290,000

Instructions:

(1) (a) What entry would be made by Park Company to record the combination as a pooling of interests? (b) Prepare a consolidated balance sheet of Park Company and Shaw Inc. as of June 1 of the current year, assuming that the business combination has been recorded as a pooling of interests. (A work sheet is not required.)

(2) (a) Assume that Park Company paid $150,000 in cash and issued 2,500 shares of common stock with a fair market value of $187,500 for all the common stock of Shaw Inc. What entry would Park Company make to record the combination as a purchase? (b) Prepare a consolidated balance sheet as of June 1 of the current year, assuming that the business combination has been recorded as a purchase, and that the book values of the net assets of Shaw Inc. are deemed to represent fair value. (A work sheet is not required.)

(3) Assume the same situation as in (2), except that the fair value of the land of Shaw Inc. was $75,000. Prepare a consolidated balance sheet as of June 1 of the current year. (A work sheet is not required.)

13–36. On January 1 of the current year, Pici Corporation exchanged 10,000 shares of its $50 par common stock for 30,000 shares (the entire issue) of Stall Company's $10 par common stock. Stall purchased from Pici Corporation $300,000 of its $500,000 issue of bonds payable, at face amount. All of the items for "interest" appearing on the balance sheets and income statements of both corporations are related to the bonds.

During the year, Pici Corporation sold merchandise with a cost of $151,680 to Stall Company for $189,600, all of which was sold by Stall Company before the end of the year.

Pici Corporation has correctly recorded the income and dividends reported for the year by Stall Company. Data for the income statements of both companies for the current year are as follows:

	Pici Corporation	Stall Company
Revenues:		
Sales..	$1,500,000	$400,000
Income of subsidiary.........................	110,000	——
Interest income...............................	——	30,000
	$1,610,000	$430,000
Expenses:		
Cost of merchandise sold.....................	$ 840,000	$205,000
Selling expenses	150,000	42,000
General expenses	125,000	27,000
Interest expense.............................	50,000	——
Income tax...................................	195,000	46,000
	$1,360,000	$320,000
Net income	$ 250,000	$110,000

Data for the balance sheets of both companies as of the end of the current year are as follows:

Assets	Pici Corporation	Stall Company
Cash...	$ 75,000	$ 18,300
Accounts receivable (net)....................	165,000	51,800
Dividends receivable	50,000	——
Interest receivable	——	15,000
Inventories..................................	325,000	126,300
Investment in Stall Co. (30,000 shares)	641,550	——
Investment in Pici Corp. bonds (at face amount)	——	300,000
Plant and equipment.........................	1,350,000	321,950
Accumulated depreciation	(650,000)	(108,350)
	$1,956,550	$725,000

Liabilities and Stockholders' Equity		
Accounts payable............................	$ 75,200	$ 27,750
Income tax payable..........................	20,510	5,700
Dividends payable	30,000	50,000
Interest payable	25,000	——
Bonds payable, 10% (due in 1998)............	500,000	——
Common stock, $50 par......................	1,000,000	——
Common stock, $10 par	——	300,000
Premium on common stock...................	100,000	50,000
Retained earnings	205,840	291,550
	$1,956,550	$725,000

Instructions:

    (1) Determine the amounts to be eliminated from the following items in preparing the consolidated balance sheet as of December 31 of the current year: (a) dividends receivable and dividends payable; (b) interest receivable and interest payable; (c) investment in Stall Co. and stockholders' equity; (d) investment in Pici Corp. bonds and bonds payable.

    (2) Prepare a detailed consolidated balance sheet in report form.

    (3) Determine the amount to be eliminated from the following items in preparing the consolidated income statement for the current year ended December 31: (a) sales and cost of merchandise sold; (b) interest income and interest expense; (c) income of subsidiary and net income.

    (4) Prepare a single-step consolidated income statement, inserting the earnings per share in parentheses on the same line with net income.

    (5) Determine the amount of the reduction in consolidated inventories, net income, and retained earnings if Stall Company's inventory had included $50,000 of the merchandise purchased from Pici Corporation.

13–37. McVoy Company sells merchandise to and purchases merchandise from various Canadian and Mexican companies. These transactions are settled in the foreign currency. The following selected transactions were completed during the current fiscal year:

Jan. 15. Sold merchandise on account to Vega Company, net 30, 200,000 pesos; exchange rate, $.045 per Mexican peso.

Feb. 14. Received cash from Vega Company; exchange rate, $.044 per Mexican peso.

Apr. 1. Purchased merchandise on account from Leafgren Company, net 30, $10,000 Canadian; exchange rate, $.84 per Canadian dollar.

Apr. 30. Issued check for amount owed to Leafgren Company; exchange rate, $.83 per Canadian dollar.

July 31. Sold merchandise on account to Sanchez Company, net 30, 300,000 pesos; exchange rate, $.044 per Mexican peso.

Aug. 30. Received cash from Sanchez Company; exchange rate, $.046 per Mexican peso.

Oct. 10. Purchased merchandise on account from Chevalier Company, net 30, $20,000 Canadian; exchange rate, $.83 per Canadian dollar.

Nov. 9. Issued check for amount owed to Chevalier Company; exchange rate, $.85 per Canadian dollar.

Dec. 10. Sold merchandise on account to Wilson Company, net 30, $30,000 Canadian; exchange rate, $.85 per Canadian dollar.

    11. Purchased merchandise on account from Santos Company, net 30, 250,000 pesos; exchange rate, $.047 per Mexican peso.

    31. Recorded unrealized currency exchange gain and/or loss on transactions of December 10 and 11. Exchange rates on December 31: $.86 per Canadian dollar; $.048 per Mexican peso.

Instructions:

    (1) Record the transactions and adjusting entries for the year.

    (2) Record the payment of the purchase of December 11, on January 10, when the exchange rate was $.046 per Mexican peso, and the receipt of cash from the sale of December 10, on January 13, when the exchange rate was $.87 per Canadian dollar.

13–38. The accounts in the ledger of Weathersby Industries Inc., with the balances on December 31, 1986, the end of the current fiscal year, are as follows:

Cash.	$ 61,800
Accounts Receivable.	137,760
Allowance for Doubtful Accounts	1,000
Merchandise Inventory	140,000
Prepaid Insurance	9,120
Store Supplies	4,120
Bond Sinking Fund	71,800
Store Equipment.	380,000
Accumulated Depreciation—Store Equipment	84,000
Office Equipment	136,000
Accumulated Depreciation—Office Equipment	51,080
Accounts Payable	58,200
Interest Payable	——
First Mortgage 12% Bonds Payable.	160,000
Premium on Bonds Payable	9,800
Common Stock, $10 par.	200,000
Retained Earnings	230,372
Income Summary.	——
Sales.	1,528,000
Purchases	1,129,760
Purchases Discount.	14,480
Sales Salaries and Commissions Expense.	98,000
Advertising Expense	25,200
Depreciation Expense—Store Equipment	——
Store Supplies Expense	——
Miscellaneous Selling Expense.	9,800
Office and Officers Salaries Expense	74,000
Rent Expense.	48,000
Depreciation Expense—Office Equipment.	——
Uncollectible Accounts Expense.	——
Insurance Expense	——
Miscellaneous General Expense.	4,080
Interest Expense	16,000
Sinking Fund Income.	7,548
Rent Income	960

The data needed for year-end adjustments on December 31, 1986, are as follows:

Merchandise inventory on December 31 (at cost, last-in, first-out)	$148,000
Insurance expired during the year	5,440
Store supplies inventory on December 31	1,520
Depreciation (straight-line method) for the current year on:	
Store equipment.	24,800
Office equipment	18,720

Uncollectible accounts expense is estimated at ¾% of sales.

Bonds payable are due on November 1, 1989. Interest on bonds
is payable on May 1 and November 1. Premium to be amortized
on bonds payable, using the straight-line method............ $ 1,680

Instructions:
  (1) Prepare a work sheet for the fiscal year ended December 31.
  (2) Prepare a multiple-step income statement. (Disregard income tax.)
  (3) Prepare a report form balance sheet.

Alternate Problems

13–32A. On May 1 of the current year, Pena Company purchased 90% of the stock of
Shea Company. On the same date, Pena Company loaned Shea Company $50,000 on
a 120-day note. The data reported on their separate balance sheets immediately after the
acquisition and loan are as follows:

Assets	Pena Company	Shea Company
Cash	$ 41,500	$ 22,750
Accounts receivable (net)	48,250	35,000
Notes receivable....................................	50,000	—
Inventories	164,250	52,250
Investment in Shea Company	290,000	—
Equipment (net).....................................	360,000	215,000
	$954,000	$325,000

Liabilities and Stockholders' Equity		
Accounts payable	$175,000	$ 19,500
Notes payable	—	50,000
Common stock, $10 par..............................	500,000	—
Common stock, $20 par	—	200,000
Retained earnings...................................	279,000	55,500
	$954,000	$325,000

The fair value of Shea Company's assets corresponds to the book carrying amounts,
except for equipment, which is valued at $250,000 for consolidation purposes.

Instructions:
  (1) Prepare a work sheet for a consolidated balance sheet as of May 1 of the current
      year.
  (2) Prepare in report form a consolidated balance sheet as of May 1, omitting
      captions for current assets, plant assets, etc.

13–33A. On June 30, Pile Company purchased 80% of the outstanding stock of Salem
Company for $600,000. Balance sheet data for the two corporations immediately after the
transaction are as follows:

Assets	Pile Company	Salem Company
Cash and marketable securities....................	$ 96,700	$ 51,750
Accounts receivable...............................	110,500	98,600
Allowance for doubtful accounts	(9,500)	(2,200)
Inventories......................................	475,000	192,400
Investment in Salem Company	600,000	—
Land	100,000	35,000
Building and equipment...........................	760,000	495,000
Accumulated depreciation..........................	(210,000)	(110,000)
	$1,922,700	$760,550

Liabilities and Stockholders' Equity		
Accounts payable................................	$ 152,500	$ 71,650
Income tax payable	41,500	9,900
Bonds payable (due in 2000)......................	500,000	—
Common stock, $20 par	900,000	—
Common stock, $25 par	—	500,000
Retained earnings................................	328,700	179,000
	$1,922,700	$760,550

Instructions:

(1) Prepare a work sheet for a consolidated balance sheet as of the date of acquisition.

(2) Prepare in report form a detailed consolidated balance sheet as of the date of acquisition. The fair value of Salem Company's assets are deemed to correspond to the book carrying amounts, except for land, which is to be increased by $50,000 for consolidation purposes.

(3) Assuming that Salem Company earns net income of $95,000 and pays cash dividends of $50,000 during the ensuing fiscal year and that Pile Company records its share of the earnings and dividends, determine the following as of the end of the year:

    (a) The net amount added to Pile Company's investment account as a result of Salem Company's earnings and dividends.

    (b) The amount of the minority interest.

13–36A. On January 1 of the current year, Penn Corporation exchanged 10,000 shares of its $20 par common stock for 25,000 shares (the entire issue) of Shay Company's $10 par common stock. Later in the year, Shay purchased from Penn Corporation $125,000 of its $250,000 issue of bonds payable, at face amount. All of the items for "interest" appearing on the balance sheets and income statements of both corporations are related to the bonds.

During the year, Penn Corporation sold merchandise with a cost of $140,000 to Shay Company for $200,000, all of which was sold by Shay Company before the end of the year.

Penn Corporation has correctly recorded the income and dividends reported for the year by Shay Company. Data for the income statements of both companies for the current year are as follows:

	Penn Corporation	Shay Company
Revenues:		
Sales.....	$1,870,000	$615,000
Income of subsidiary	115,000	—
Interest income	—	3,125
	$1,985,000	$618,125
Expenses:		
Cost of merchandise sold	$1,199,600	$320,500
Selling expenses.....	180,000	57,525
General expenses.....	135,000	37,000
Interest expense	12,500	—
Income tax.....	155,100	88,100
	$1,682,200	$503,125
Net income.....	$ 302,800	$115,000

Data for the balance sheets of both companies as of the end of the current year are as follows:

Assets	Penn Corporation	Shay Company
Cash	$ 96,400	$ 37,150
Accounts receivable (net)	128,500	62,800
Dividends receivable	12,500	—
Interest receivable	—	3,125
Inventories	549,250	199,000
Investment in Shay Co. (25,000 shares)	505,800	—
Investment in Penn Corp. bonds (at face amount)	—	125,000
Plant and equipment	917,650	312,000
Accumulated depreciation.....	(210,100)	(164,075)
	$2,000,000	$575,000

Liabilities and Stockholders' Equity		
Accounts payable.....	$ 106,900	$ 48,600
Income tax payable	17,500	8,100
Dividends payable	20,000	12,500
Interest payable.....	6,250	—
Bonds payable, 10% (due in 1997).....	250,000	—
Common stock, $20 par	1,000,000	—
Common stock, $10 par.....	—	250,000
Premium on common stock	40,000	80,000
Retained earnings.....	559,350	175,800
	$2,000,000	$575,000

Instructions:

(1) Determine the amounts to be eliminated from the following items in preparing the consolidated balance sheet as of December 31 of the current year: (a) dividends receivable and dividends payable; (b) interest receivable and interest payable; (c) investment in Shay Co. and stockholders' equity; (d) investment in Penn Corp. bonds and bonds payable.

(2) Prepare a detailed consolidated balance sheet in report form.

(3) Determine the amount to be eliminated from the following items in preparing the consolidated income statement for the current year ended December 31; (a) sales and cost of merchandise sold; (b) interest income and interest expense; (c) income of subsidiary and net income.

(4) Prepare a single-step consolidated income statement, inserting the earnings per share in parentheses on the same line with net income.

(5) Determine the amount of the reduction in consolidated inventories, net income, and retained earnings if Shay Company's inventory had included $50,000 of the merchandise purchased from Penn Corporation.

13–37A. Allen Company sells merchandise to and purchases merchandise from various Canadian and Mexican companies. These transactions are settled in the foreign currency. The following selected transactions were completed during the current fiscal year:

Feb. 1 Purchased merchandise on account from Bianchi Company, net 30, $20,000 Canadian; exchange rate, $.85 per Canadian dollar.

Mar. 2 Issued check for amount owed to Bianchi Company; exchange rate, $.86 per Canadian dollar.

Apr. 15 Sold merchandise on account to Ruiz Company, net 30, 300,000 pesos; exchange rate, $.045 per Mexican peso.

May 15 Received cash from Ruiz Company; exchange rate, $.046 per Mexican peso.

June 10 Purchased merchandise on account from Blume Company, net 30, $30,000 Canadian; exchange rate, $.86 per Canadian dollar.

July 9 Issued check for amount owed to Blume Company; exchange rate, $.85 per Canadian dollar.

Sept. 30 Sold merchandise on account to Mendoza Company, net 30, 200,000 pesos; exchange rate, $.044 per Mexican peso.

Oct. 30 Received cash from Mendoza Company; exchange rate, $.043 per Mexican peso.

Dec. 20 Sold merchandise on account to Adams Company, net 30, $30,000 Canadian; exchange rate, $.85 per Canadian dollar.

21 Purchased merchandise on account from Orta Company, net 30, 250,000 pesos; exchange rate, $.047 per Mexican peso.

31 Recorded unrealized currency exchange gain and/or loss on transactions of December 20 and 21. Exchange rates on December 31: $.84 per Canadian dollar; $.46 per Mexican peso.

Instructions:

(1) Present entries to record the transactions and adjusting entries for the year.

(2) Present entries to record the payment of the purchase of December 21, on January 20, when the exchange rate was $.048 per Mexican peso, and the receipt of cash from the sale of December 20, on January 23, when the exchange rate was $.83 per Canadian dollar.

13–39. Your grandfather recently retired, sold his home in Flint, Michigan, and moved to a retirement community in Naples, Florida. With some of the proceeds from the sale of his home, he is considering investing $75,000 in the stock market.

Mini-Case

In the process of selecting among alternative stock investments, your grandfather collected annual reports from twenty different companies. In reviewing these reports, however, he has become confused and has questions concerning several items which appear in the financial reports. He has asked your help and has written down the following questions for you to answer:

(a) "In reviewing the annual reports, I noticed many references to 'consolidated financial statements.' What are consolidated financial statements?"

(b) "'Excess of cost of business acquired over related net assets' appears on the consolidated balance sheets in several annual reports. What does this mean? Is it an asset (it appears with other assets)?"

(c) "What is minority interest?"

(d) "A footnote to one of the consolidated statements indicated interest and the amount of a loan from one company to another had been eliminated. Is this good accounting? A loan is a loan. How can a company just eliminate a loan that hasn't been paid off?"

(e) "How can financial statements for an American company (in dollars) be combined with a Japanese subsidiary (in yen)?"

Instructions:

(1) Briefly respond to each of your grandfather's questions.

(2) While discussing the items in (1) with your grandfather, he asked your advice on whether he should limit his investments to one stock. What would you advise?

Answers to Self-Examination Questions

1. C When parent acquires a controlling share of the voting stock of subsidiary in exchange for its voting common stock (answer C), the affiliation is termed a "pooling of interests." When parent acquires a controlling share of the voting stock of subsidiary in exchange for cash (answer A), other assets, issuances of debt obligations (answer B), or a combination of the foregoing, it is termed a "purchase."

2. B The excess of cost over book equity of interest in S Co. is $100,000 (answer B), determined as follows:

Investment in S Co. (cost)	$1,000,000
Eliminate 100% of S Co. stock	(750,000)
Eliminate 100% of S Co. retained earnings	(150,000)
Excess of cost over book equity of subsidiary interest	$ 100,000

3. B The excess of cost over book equity of interest in S Co. is $190,000 (answer B), determined as follows:

Investment in S Co. (cost)	$1,000,000
Eliminate 90% of S Co. stock	(675,000)
Eliminate 90% of S Co. retained earnings	(135,000)
Excess of cost over book equity of subsidiary interest	$ 190,000

4. D The 10% of the stock owned by outsiders is referred to as the minority interest. It amounts to $90,000, determined as follows:

10% of common stock	$75,000
10% of retained earnings	15,000
Total minority interest	$90,000

5. B The 250,000 pesos ($10,000 ÷ $.04) representing the billed price, which had a value of $10,000 on July 9, 1986, had increased in value to $12,500 (250,000 pesos × $.05) on August 8, 1986, when payment was received. The gain, which was realized because the transactions were completed by the receipts of cash, was $2,500 (answer B).

PART 4

Reporting Changes in Financial Position

Cash Flow and Survival

Businesses generally do not go broke because they lack assets but because they have inadequate cash flow. A number of now defunct companies have gone bankrupt while rich in assets but lacking the necessary cash flow to survive. Thus handicapped, they could not convert assets into cash quickly enough to avoid economic disaster.

SOURCE From a speech by Harvey Kapnick, chairman of Arthur Andersen & Co., before an American Petroleum Institute Conference, June 11, 1979.

In January 1981, you might have been tempted to buy stock in Boeing. The most recent quarter's earnings per share were $1.72, up from $1.50 the previous year. Indeed, every quarter in 1980 was up from its counterpart in 1979 and profits for the year were up about 18%.

But if you had looked at cash flow figures, you would have seen an entirely different picture: Operational cash flow had sunk sharply into the red for three quarters, from negative $34.6 million in the second quarter down to negative $680.1 million in the fourth.

Paul Pappadio of Gintel & Co.'s Capital Flow Trends was looking at those figures. "The commercial airlines were cutting their expenditures," he reasoned. "Boeing was going heavily into negative cash flow because of two new generations of aircraft. If Boeing wasn't going into negative cash flow, even with business turning bad, its recovery would be better."

So, in spite of the heady earnings, Pappadio advised selling the stock. You know the end of the story. Since the last quarter of 1980 Boeing's stock has fallen from 44⅛ to 19¾, a 55% drop.

SOURCE Adapted from "A Better Yardstick," *Forbes*, September 27, 1982, pp. 66, 69.

CHAPTER 14

Statement of Changes in Financial Position

CHAPTER OBJECTIVES

Describe the usefulness of reporting changes in financial position.

Describe alternative concepts of funds.

Describe and illustrate the preparation of a statement of changes in financial position based upon the working capital concept of funds.

Describe and illustrate the preparation of a statement of changes in financial position based upon the cash concept of funds.

The financial position of an enterprise as of a specified time is reported on its balance sheet. Indications of the changes in financial position that have occurred during the preceding fiscal period can be determined by comparing the individual items on the current balance sheet with the related amounts on the earlier statement. The income statement and retained earnings statement also reveal some of the details of changes in stockholders' equity. However, significant changes in financial position may be overlooked in the process of examining and comparing the statements and still other changes may be completely undisclosed by the statements. For example, if items of equipment or other plant assets were retired and other items acquired during the period, comparison of the balance sheets will disclose only the net amount of change.

The usefulness of a concise statement devoted entirely to changes in financial position has become increasingly apparent during the past several decades. There has been much experimentation and discussion among accountants concerning the scope, format, and terminology to be used, and the inclusion of such statements in financial reports to stockholders has steadily increased. Guidelines for their preparation were issued by the Accounting Principles Board in 1963.[1] Considerable variation in the form and

---

[1]*Opinions of the Accounting Principles Board*, No. 3, "The Statement of Source and Application of Funds" (New York: American Institute of Certified Public Accountants, 1963).

content of the statement was approved and, although not required, its inclusion as a basic statement in annual financial reports was encouraged. Many titles have been used, including *Statement of Source and Application of Funds, Statement of Resources Provided and Applied, and Statement of Changes in Working Capital.* The term often used as a convenience in discussing the statement is **funds statement.** This shorter term will often be used in the discussions that follow.

The 1963 pronouncement of the Accounting Principles Board was followed by a more definitive opinion in 1971. In addition to broadening the scope of the funds statement, the Board directed that it be a basic financial statement for all profit-oriented enterprises and recommended the adoption of the more descriptive title **Statement of Changes in Financial Position.**[2]

CONCEPTS OF FUNDS

In accounting and financial usage, the term **fund** has many meanings. It was first used in this book to mean segregations of cash for a special purpose, as in "change fund" and "petty cash fund." Later it was used to designate the amount of cash and marketable investments segregated in a "sinking fund" for the purpose of liquidating bonds or other long-term obligations at maturity. When used in the plural form, "funds" is often a synonym for cash, as when a drawee bank refuses to honor a check and returns it to the depositor with the notation "not sufficient funds."

The concept used in funds statements has varied somewhat in practice, with resulting variation in the content of the statements. "Funds" can be interpreted broadly to mean "working capital" or, more narrowly, to mean "cash" or "cash and marketable securities." Two statements, one based on working capital and the other on cash, may be prepared for the use of management, but only one statement is usually presented in published financial reports. Although both statements are widely used, the use of the statement based on cash is increasing.

Regardless of which of the concepts is used for a specific funds statement, financial position may also be affected by transactions that do not involve funds. If such transactions have occurred during the period, their effect, if significant, should be reported in the funds statement.[3]

WORKING CAPITAL CONCEPT OF FUNDS

The excess of an enterprise's total current assets over its total current liabilities at the same point in time may be termed its "net current assets"

---

[2]*Opinions of the Accounting Principles Board,* No. 19, "Reporting Changes in Financial Position" (New York: American Institute of Certified Public Accountants, 1971).

[3]*Ibid.,* par. 8.

or **working capital.** To illustrate, assume that a corporate balance sheet lists current assets totaling $560,000 and current liabilities totaling $230,000. The working capital of the corporation at the balance sheet date is $330,000 ($560,000 − $230,000). The following comparative schedule includes the major categories of current assets and current liabilities:

	December 31		Increase
	1987	1986	Decrease*
Current assets:			
Cash	$ 40,000	$ 35,000	$ 5,000
Marketable securities	60,000	40,000	20,000
Receivables (net)	100,000	115,000	15,000*
Inventories	350,000	295,000	55,000
Prepaid expenses	10,000	15,000	5,000*
Total	$560,000	$500,000	$60,000
Current liabilities:			
Notes payable	$ 70,000	$ 50,000	$20,000
Accounts payable	125,000	145,000	20,000*
Income tax payable	10,000	20,000	10,000*
Dividends payable	25,000	25,000	——
Total	$230,000	$240,000	$10,000*
Working capital	$330,000	$260,000	$70,000

The increase or decrease in each item is reported in the third column of the schedule. The increase of $60,000 in total current assets during the year tended to increase working capital. The decrease of $10,000 in total current liabilities also tended to increase working capital. The combined effect was an increase of $70,000 in working capital. Note that working capital is a "net" concept. An increase or decrease in working capital cannot be determined solely by the amount of change in total current assets or solely by the amount of change in total current liabilities.

The amount of most of the items classified as current assets and current liabilities varies from one balance sheet date to another. Many of the items change daily. Inventories are increased by purchases on account, which also increase accounts payable. Accounts payable are reduced by payment, which also reduces cash. As merchandise is sold on account, inventories decrease and accounts receivable increase. In turn, the collections from customers increase cash and reduce accounts receivable. An understanding of this continuous interaction among the various current assets and current liabilities is essential to an understanding of the concept of working capital and analyses related to it. In the illustration, for example, the absence of increase or decrease in the amount of dividends payable between balance sheet dates should not be thought of as an indication that the account balance remained unchanged throughout the year. If dividends were paid quarterly, four separate liabilities would have been created and four would have been liquidated during the period. Also, the amount of working capital is neither increased nor decreased by a transaction (1) that affects only current assets (such as a purchase of marketable securities for cash), (2) that affects only current liabilities (such as issuance of a short-term note to a creditor on account), or (3) that affects only current assets and current liabilities (such as payment of an account payable).

Working Capital Flow

The working capital schedule on the preceding page shows an increase of $70,000 in working capital, which may be significant in evaluating financial position. However, the schedule gives no indication of the source of the increase. It could have resulted from the issuance of common stock, from the sale of treasury stock, from operating income, or from a combination of these and other sources. It is also possible that working capital would have increased by considerably more during the year had it not been for the purchase of plant assets, the retirement of bonded indebtedness, an adverse judgment as defendant in a damage suit, or other occurrences with a similar effect on working capital.

Both the inflow and the outflow of funds are reported in a funds statement. Those flowing into the enterprise, classified as to source, form the first section of the funds statement. Funds flowing out of the enterprise, classified according to the manner of their use or application, are reported in the second section of the statement. Ordinarily, the totals of the two sections are unequal. If the inflow (sources) has exceeded the outflow (applications), the excess is the amount of the increase in working capital. When the reverse situation occurs, the excess of outflow is a measure of the amount by which working capital has decreased. Accordingly, the difference between the total of the sources and the applications sections of the funds statement is identified as an increase or a decrease in working capital. The details of this balancing amount are presented in a subsidiary section of the statement or in a separate schedule.

Some of the data needed in preparing a funds statement can be obtained from comparing items on the current balance sheet with those on the preceding balance sheet. Information regarding net income may be obtained from the current income statement and dividend data are available in the retained earnings statement. However, there may be sources and applications of funds that are not disclosed by these statements. Some of the relevant data can be obtained only from an examination of accounts in the ledger or from journal entries.

Although there are many kinds of transactions that affect funds, consideration will be limited here to the most common sources and applications. As a matter of convenience in the discussion that follows, all asset accounts other than current assets will be referred to as "noncurrent assets" and all liability accounts other than current liabilities will be referred to as "noncurrent liabilities."

Sources of Working Capital

The amount of inflow of working capital from various sources can be determined without reviewing and classifying every transaction that occurred during the period. There is also no need to determine the individual effects of a number of similar transactions; summary figures are sufficient. For purposes of discussion, transactions that provide working capital are classified in terms of their effect on noncurrent accounts, as follows:

1. Transactions that decrease noncurrent assets.
2. Transactions that increase noncurrent liabilities.
3. Transactions that increase stockholders' equity.

Decreases in noncurrent assets. The sale of long-term investments, equipment, buildings, land, patents, or other noncurrent assets for cash or on account provides working capital. However, the reduction in the balance of the noncurrent asset account between the beginning and end of the period is not necessarily the amount of working capital provided by the sale. For example, if a patent carried in the ledger at $30,000 is sold during the year for $70,000, the patents account will decrease by $30,000 but the funds provided by the transaction amounted to $70,000. Similarly, if the long-term investments carried at $120,000 at the beginning of the year are sold for $80,000 cash, the transaction provided funds of $80,000 instead of $120,000.

Increases in noncurrent liabilities. The issuance of bonds or long-term notes is a common source of working capital. For example, if bonds with a face value of $600,000 are sold at 100 for cash, the amount of funds provided by the transaction would be indicated by a $600,000 increase in the bonds payable account. If the bonds were issued at a price above or below 100, it would be necessary to refer to the bond premium or discount account, in addition to the bonds payable account, in order to determine the amount of funds provided by the transaction. For example, if the $600,000 of bonds had been issued at 90 instead of 100, the funds provided would have been $540,000 instead of $600,000.

Increases in stockholders' equity. Often the largest and most frequent source of working capital is profitable operations. Revenues realized from the sale of goods or services are accompanied by increases in working capital. Conversely, many of the expenses incurred are accompanied by decreases in working capital. Since the significant details of revenues and expenses appear in the income statement, they need not be repeated in the funds statement. However, the amount of income from operations reported on the income statement is not necessarily equivalent to the working capital actually provided by operations. Such expenses as depreciation of plant assets and amortization of patents are deducted from revenue but have no effect on current assets or current liabilities. Similarly, the amortization of premium on bonds payable, which decreases interest expense and therefore increases operating income, does not affect current assets or current liabilities. The amount reported on the income statement as income from operations must therefore be adjusted upward or downward to determine the amount of working capital so provided. If gains or losses are reported as "extraordinary" items on the income statement, they should be identified as such on the funds statement.[4]

If capital stock is sold during the period, the amount of working capital provided will not necessarily coincide with the amount of the increase in the capital stock account. Consideration must be given to accompanying debits or credits to other paid-in capital accounts. There also may be entries in stockholders' equity accounts that do not affect working capital, such as a transfer of retained earnings to paid-in capital accounts in the issuance of a stock dividend. Similarly, transfers between the retained earnings account and appropriations accounts have no effect on working capital.

Applications of Working Capital

As in the case of working capital sources, it is convenient to classify applications according to their effects on noncurrent accounts. Transactions affecting the outflow or applications of working capital may be described as follows:

1. Transactions that increase noncurrent assets.
2. Transactions that decrease noncurrent liabilities.
3. Transactions that decrease stockholders' equity.

Increases in noncurrent assets. Working capital may be applied to the purchase of equipment, buildings, land, long-term investments, patents, or other noncurrent assets. However, the amounts of funds used for such purposes is not necessarily indicated by the net increases in the related accounts. For example, if the debits to the equipment account for acquisitions during the year totaled $160,000 and the credits to the same account for retirements amounted to $30,000, the net change in the account would be $130,000. Such facts can be determined only by reviewing the details in the account.

Decreases in noncurrent liabilities. The liquidation of bonds or long-term notes represents an application of working capital. However, the decrease in the balance of the liability account does not necessarily indicate the amount of working capital applied. For example, if callable bonds issued at their face value of $100,000 are redeemed at 105, the funds applied would be $105,000 instead of $100,000.

Decreases in stockholders' equity. Probably the most frequent application of working capital in decreases of stockholders' equity results from the declaration of cash dividends by the board of directors. Funds may also be applied to the redemption of preferred stock or to the purchase of treasury stock. As indicated earlier, the issuance of stock dividends does not affect working capital or financial position.

---

[4]Extraordinary items are discussed on pages 355–356.

Other Changes in Financial Position

According to the broadened concept of the funds statement, significant transactions affecting financial position should be reported even though they do not affect funds.[5] For example, if an enterprise issues bonds or capital stock in exchange for land and buildings, the transaction has no effect on working capital. Nevertheless, because of the significant effect on financial position, both the increase in the plant assets and the increase in long-term liabilities or stockholders' equity should be reported on the statement. A complete catalog of the kinds of non-fund transactions that usually have a significant effect on financial position is beyond the scope of the discussion here. The following are illustrative of the many possibilities: preferred or common stock may be issued in liquidation of long-term debt, common stock may be issued in exchange for convertible preferred stock, long-term investments may be exchanged for machinery and equipment, and land and buildings may be received from a municipality as a gift.

Transactions of the type indicated in the preceding paragraph may be reported on the funds statement as though there were two transactions: (1) a source of funds and (2) an application of funds. The relationship of the source and the application should be disclosed by proper wording in the descriptive captions or by footnote. To illustrate, assume that common stock of $200,000 par is issued in exchange for $200,000 face amount of bonds payable, on which there is no unamortized discount or premium. The issuance of the common stock should be reported in the sources section of the statement somewhat as follows: "Issuance of common stock at par in retirement of bonds payable, $200,000." The other part of the transaction could be described in the applications section as follows: "Retirement of bonds payable by the issuance of common stock at par, $200,000."

Assembling Data for the Funds Statement Based on Working Capital

Much of the information on funds flow is obtained in the process of preparing the balance sheet, the income statement, and the retained earnings statement. When the volume of data is substantial, experienced accountants may first assemble all relevant facts in working papers designed for the purpose. Specialized working papers are not essential, however. Because of their complexity, they tend to obscure the basic concepts of funds analysis for anyone who is not already familiar with the subject. For this reason, special working papers will not be used in the following discussion. Instead, the emphasis will be on the basic analyses.[6]

---

[5]*Opinions of the Accounting Principles Board, No. 19, op. cit.,* par. 8.

[6]The use of a work sheet as an aid in assembling data for the funds statement is presented in Appendix C.

In the illustration that follows, the necessary information will be obtained from (1) a comparative balance sheet and (2) the ledger accounts for noncurrent assets, noncurrent liabilities, and stockholders' equity. As each change in a noncurrent item is discussed, data from the related account(s) will be presented. Descriptive notations have been inserted in the accounts to facilitate the explanations. Otherwise, it would be necessary to refer to supportive journal entries to determine the complete effect of some of the transactions. The comparative balance sheet in simplified form is as follows:

COMPARATIVE
BALANCE SHEET

T. R. Morgan Corporation
Comparative Balance Sheet
December 31, 1987 and 1986

	1987	1986	Increase Decrease*
Assets			
Cash	$ 49,000	$ 26,000	$ 23,000
Trade receivables (net)	74,000	65,000	9,000
Inventories	172,000	180,000	8,000*
Prepaid expenses	4,000	3,000	1,000
Investments (long-term)	——	45,000	45,000*
Land	90,000	40,000	50,000
Building	200,000	200,000	——
Accumulated depreciation—building	(36,000)	(30,000)	(6,000)
Equipment	180,000	142,000	38,000
Accumulated depreciation—equipment	(43,000)	(40,000)	(3,000)
Total assets	$690,000	$631,000	$ 59,000
Liabilities			
Accounts payable (merchandise creditors)	$ 50,000	$ 32,000	$ 18,000
Income tax payable	2,500	4,000	1,500*
Dividends payable	15,000	8,000	7,000
Bonds payable	120,000	245,000	125,000*
Total liabilities	$187,500	$289,000	$101,500*
Stockholders' Equity			
Common stock	$280,000	$230,000	$ 50,000
Retained earnings	222,500	112,000	110,500
Total stockholders' equity	$502,500	$342,000	$160,500
Total liabilities and stockholders' equity	$690,000	$631,000	$ 59,000

Since only the noncurrent accounts reveal sources and applications of funds, it is not necessary to examine the current asset accounts or the current liability accounts. The first of the noncurrent accounts listed on the comparative balance sheet of the T. R. Morgan Corporation is Investments.

Investments

The comparative balance sheet indicates that investments decreased by $45,000. The notation in the following investments account indicates that the investments were sold for $75,000 in cash.

ACCOUNT INVESTMENTS   ACCOUNT NO.

Date		Item	Debit	Credit	Balance Debit	Balance Credit
1987						
Jan.	1	Balance			45,000	
June	8	Sold for $75,000 cash		45,000	——	——

The $30,000 gain on the sale is included in the net income reported on the income statement. It is necessary, of course, to report also the book value of the investments sold, as an additional source of working capital. To report the entire proceeds of $75,000 as a source of working capital would incorrectly include the gain reported in operating income. Accordingly, to avoid a double reporting of the $30,000 gain, the notation is as follows:

> *Source of working capital:*
> Book value of investments sold (excludes $30,000 gain
> reported in net income)............................ $45,000

The proceeds from the sale of investments would appear on the funds statement in two places: (1) book value of investments sold, $45,000, and (2) gain on sale of investments as part of net income, $30,000.

Land

The comparative balance sheet indicates that land increased by $50,000. The notation in the land account, as shown below, indicates that the land was acquired by issuance of common stock at par.

ACCOUNT LAND   ACCOUNT NO.

Date		Item	Debit	Credit	Balance Debit	Balance Credit
1987						
Jan.	1	Balance			40,000	
Dec.	28	Acquired by issuance of common stock at par	50,000		90,000	

Although working capital was not involved in this transaction, the acquisition represents a significant change in financial position, which may be noted as follows:

> *Application of working capital:*
> Purchase of land by issuance of common stock at par... $50,000

Building

According to the comparative balance sheet, there was no change in the $200,000 balance between the beginning and end of the year. Reference to the building account in the ledger confirms the absence of entries during the year and hence the account is not shown here. The credit in the related accumulated depreciation account, shown below, reduced the investment in building, but working capital was not affected.

ACCOUNT ACCUMULATED DEPRECIATION — BUILDING				ACCOUNT NO.	
Date	Item	Debit	Credit	Balance	
				Debit	Credit
1987					
Jan. 1	Balance				30,000
Dec. 31	Depreciation for year		6,000		36,000

Equipment

The comparative balance sheet indicates that the cost of equipment increased $38,000. The equipment account and the accumulated depreciation account illustrated below reveal that the net change of $38,000 was the result of two separate transactions, the discarding of equipment that had cost $9,000 and the purchase of equipment for $47,000. The equipment discarded had been fully depreciated, as indicated by the debit of $9,000 in the accumulated depreciation account, and no salvage was realized from its disposal. Hence, the transaction had no effect on working capital and is not reported on the funds statement.

ACCOUNT EQUIPMENT				ACCOUNT NO.	
Date	Item	Debit	Credit	Balance	
				Debit	Credit
1987					
Jan. 1	Balance			142,000	
May 9	Discarded, no salvage		9,000		
July 7	Purchased for cash	47,000		180,000	

ACCOUNT ACCUMULATED DEPRECIATION — EQUIPMENT				ACCOUNT NO.	
Date	Item	Debit	Credit	Balance	
				Debit	Credit
1987					
Jan. 1	Balance				40,000
May 9	Discarded, no salvage	9,000			
Dec. 31	Depreciation for year		12,000		43,000

The effect on funds of the purchase of equipment for $47,000 was as follows:

Application of working capital:
Purchase of equipment.............................. $47,000

The credit in the accumulated depreciation account had the effect of reducing the investment in equipment by $12,000 but caused no change in working capital. Further attention will be given to depreciation in a later paragraph.

Bonds Payable

The next noncurrent item listed on the balance sheet, bonds payable, decreased $125,000 during the year. Examination of the bonds payable account, which appears below, indicates that $125,000 of the bonds payable were retired by payment of the face amount.

ACCOUNT BONDS PAYABLE   ACCOUNT NO.

Date		Item	Debit	Credit	Balance Debit	Balance Credit
1987 Jan.	1	Balance				245,000
June	30	Retired by payment of cash at face amount	125,000			120,000

This transaction's effect on funds is noted as follows:

Application of working capital:
Retirement of bonds payable......................... $125,000

Common Stock

The increase of $50,000 in the common stock account, as shown below, is identified as stock having been issued in exchange for land valued at $50,000.

ACCOUNT COMMON STOCK   ACCOUNT NO.

Date		Item	Debit	Credit	Balance Debit	Balance Credit
1987 Jan.	1	Balance				230,000
Dec.	28	Issued at par in exchange for land		50,000		280,000

This change in financial position should be reported on the funds statement and may be noted as follows:

Source of working capital:
Issuance of common stock at par for land.............. $50,000

Retained Earnings

According to the comparative balance sheet, there was an increase of $110,500 in retained earnings during the year. The retained earnings account, as shown below, was credited for $140,500 of net income, which included the gain on sale of investments, and was debited for $30,000 of cash dividends.

ACCOUNT RETAINED EARNINGS   ACCOUNT NO.

Date		Item	Debit	Credit	Balance Debit	Balance Credit
1987 Jan.	1	Balance				112,000
Dec.	31	Net income		140,500		
	31	Cash dividends	30,000			222,500

The net income as reported on the income statement must usually be adjusted upward and/or downward to determine the amount of working capital provided by operations. Although most operating expenses either decrease current assets or increase current liabilities, thus affecting working capital, depreciation expense does not do so. The amount of net income understates the amount of working capital provided by operations to the extent that depreciation expense is deducted from revenue. Accordingly, the depreciation expense for the year on the equipment ($12,000) and the building ($6,000), totaling $18,000, must be added back to the $140,500 reported as net income.

The data to be reported as working capital provided by operations is noted as follows:

> *Source of working capital:*
> Operations during the year:
>   Net income............................ $140,500
>   Add deduction not decreasing working
>   capital during the year:
>   Depreciation 18,000 $158,500

Working capital is applied to cash dividends at the time the current liability is incurred, regardless of when the dividends are actually paid. The effect of the declaration of cash dividends of $30,000, recorded as a debit in the retained earnings account, is indicated as follows:

> *Application of working capital:*
> Declaration of cash dividends........................ $30,000

Form of the Funds Statement Based on Working Capital

Although there are many possible variations in the form and the content of the funds statement, the first section is usually devoted to the source of funds, with income from operations presented as the first item.[7] The second section is devoted to the application or use of funds. There may also be a third section in which changes in the amounts of the current assets and the current liabilities are reported.

---

[7]*Opinions of the Accounting Principles Board, No. 19, op. cit.*, par. 10.

The difference between the totals of the sources section and the applications section of the funds statement is identified as the increase or the decrease in working capital. The net change in the amount of working capital reported on the statement should be supported by details of the changes in each of the working capital components.[8] The information may be presented in a third section of the statement, as in the following illustration for T. R. Morgan Corporation, or it may be presented as a separate tabulation accompanying the statement. The data required in either case can be taken from the comparative balance sheet. The two amounts identified as the increase or decrease in working capital ($1,500 increase in the illustration) must agree.

T. R. Morgan Corporation
Statement of Changes in Financial Position
For Year Ended December 31, 1987

Sources of working capital:		
Operations during the year:		
Net income	$140,500	
Add deduction not decreasing working capital during the year:		
Depreciation	18,000	$158,500
Book value of investments sold (excludes $30,000 gain reported in net income)	45,000	
Issuance of common stock at par for land	50,000	$253,500
Applications of working capital:		
Purchase of land by issuance of common stock at par	$ 50,000	
Purchase of equipment	47,000	
Retirement of bonds payable	125,000	
Declaration of cash dividends	30,000	252,000
Increase in working capital		$ 1,500
Changes in components of working capital:		
Increase (decrease) in current assets:		
Cash	$ 23,000	
Trade receivables (net)	9,000	
Inventories	(8,000)	
Prepaid expenses	1,000	$ 25,000
Increase (decrease) in current liabilities:		
Accounts payable	$ 18,000	
Income tax payable	(1,500)	
Dividends payable	7,000	23,500
Increase in working capital		$ 1,500

[8]*Ibid.*, par. 12.

ANALYSIS OF CASH

When the cash concept of funds is used, the analysis is devoted to the movement of cash rather than to the inflow and outflow of working capital.[9] The portion of the statement devoted to operations may report the total revenue that provided cash, followed by deductions for operating costs and expenses requiring the outlay of cash. The usual practice, however, is to begin with net income from operations as was done in the preceding illustration. This basic amount is then adjusted for increases and decreases of all working capital items except cash, using the procedures demonstrated later in the chapter.

There has been much experimentation in the methodology of cash flow analysis and in the form of the related funds statement. The approach that will be used here is patterned after the procedures used in the preceding discussion and illustrations. Although the working capital concept of funds discussed earlier is used more often, particularly in preparing funds statements for reports to stockholders, the cash concept is useful in evaluating financial policies and current cash position. It is especially useful to management in preparing cash budgets.

The format of a funds statement based on the cash concept may be quite similar to the format of a funds statement based on the working capital concept. It is usually divided into two main sections—sources of cash and applications of cash. The difference between the totals of the two sections is the cash increase or decrease for the period. The main parts of the report may be followed by a listing of the cash balance at the beginning of the period, at the end of the period, and the net change. An alternative is to begin the statement with the beginning cash balance, add the total of the sources section, subtract the total of the applications section, and conclude with the cash balance at the end of the period.

Assembling Data for the Funds Statement Based on Cash

The comparative balance sheet of T. R. Morgan Corporation on page 465 and the related accounts presented on the following pages will be used as the basis for illustration.[10] Reference to the earlier analysis discloses that the sale of investments yielded cash and that there were cash outlays for equipment and the retirement of bonds. These transactions may be noted as follows:

Source of cash:
Book value of investments sold (excludes $30,000 gain
    reported in net income). . . . . $ 45,000
Applications of cash:
Purchase of equipment. . . . . $ 47,000
Retirement of bonds payable. 125,000

---

[9]The concept may be expanded to include temporary investments that are readily convertible into cash.

[10]The use of a work sheet as an aid in assembling data for the funds statement is presented in Appendix C.

The earlier analysis also indicated that land was acquired by the issuance of common stock. Although the transaction did not involve cash, it resulted in a significant change in financial position and should be reported on the statement. It is as if the common stock had been issued for cash and the cash received had then been expended for the parcel of land. The following notation indicates the manner in which the transaction is to be reported in the statement:

> *Source of cash:*
> Issuance of common stock at par for land $50,000
> *Application of cash:*
> Purchase of land by issuance of common stock at par . . . $50,000

The amount of cash provided by operations usually differs from the amount of net income. The amount of cash used to pay dividends may also differ from the amount of cash dividends declared. The determination of these amounts is discussed in the paragraphs that follow.

Cash Provided by Operations

The starting point in the analysis of the effect of operations on cash is net income for the period. This amount was reported for T. R. Morgan Corporation on page 468 as $140,500. As in the earlier analysis, depreciation expense of $18,000 must be added to the $140,500 because depreciation expense did not decrease the amount of cash. In addition, it is necessary to recognize the relationship of the accrual method of accounting to the movement of cash. Usually, a part of some of the other costs and expenses reported on the income statement, as well as a part of the revenue earned, is not accompanied by cash outflow or inflow.

There is often a period of time between the accrual of a revenue and the receipt of the related cash. Perhaps the most common example is the sale of merchandise or a service on account, for which payment is received at a later point in time. Hence, the amount reported on the income statement as revenue from sales is not likely to correspond with the amount of the related cash inflow for the same period.

Timing differences between the incurrence of an expense and the related cash outflow must also be considered in determining the amount of cash provided by operations. For example, the amount reported on the income statement as insurance expense is the amount of insurance premiums expired rather than the amount of premiums paid during the period. Similarly, supplies paid for in one year may be used and thus converted to an expense in a later year. Conversely, a portion of some of the expenses incurred near the end of one period, such as wages and taxes, may not require a cash outlay until the following period.

The T. R. Morgan Corporation balance sheet (page 465) provides the following data that identify timing differences affecting the amount of cash inflow and outflow from operations:

Accounts	December 31		Increase Decrease*
	1987	1986	
Trade receivables (net)...........................	$ 74,000	$ 65,000	$ 9,000
Inventories......................................	172,000	180,000	8,000*
Prepaid expenses	4,000	3,000	1,000
Accounts payable (merchandise creditors)..........	50,000	32,000	18,000
Income tax payable..............................	2,500	4,000	1,500*

The effect of timing differences is indicated by the amount and the direction of change in the balances of the asset and liability accounts affected by operations. Decreases in such assets and increases in such liabilities during the period must be added to the amount reported as income from operations. Conversely, increases in such assets and decreases in such liabilities must be deducted from the amount reported as income from operations.

Trade receivables (net) increase. The additions to trade receivables for sales on account during the year were $9,000 more than the deductions for amounts collected from customers on account. The amount reported on the income statement as sales therefore included $9,000 that did not yield cash inflow during the year. Accordingly, $9,000 must be deducted from income to determine the amount of cash provided by operations.

Inventories decrease. The $8,000 decrease in inventories indicates that the merchandise sold exceeded the cost of the merchandise purchased by $8,000. The amount reported on the income statement as a deduction from the revenue therefore included $8,000 that did not require cash outflow during the year. Accordingly, $8,000 must be added to income to determine the amount of cash provided by operations.

Prepaid expenses increase. The outlay of cash for prepaid expenses exceeded by $1,000 the amount deducted as an expense during the year. Hence, $1,000 must be deducted from income to determine the amount of cash provided by operations.

Accounts payable increase. The effect of the increase in the amount owed creditors for goods and services was to include in expired costs and expenses the sum of $18,000 for which there had been no cash outlay during the year. Income was thereby reduced by $18,000, though there was no cash outlay. Hence, $18,000 must be added to income to determine the amount of cash provided by operations.

Income tax payable decrease. The outlay of cash for income taxes exceeded by $1,500 the amount of income tax deducted as an expense during the period. Accordingly, $1,500 must be deducted from income to determine the amount of cash provided by operations.

The foregoing adjustments to income may be summarized as follows in a format suitable for the funds statement:

Source of cash:
Operations during the year:
  Net income $140,500
  Add deductions not decreasing cash during the year:
    Depreciation $18,000
    Decrease in inventories 8,000
    Increase in accounts payable............... 18,000   44,000
                                   $184,500

  Deduct additions not increasing cash during the year:
    Increase in trade receivables .... $ 9,000
    Increase in prepaid expenses............... 1,000
    Decrease in income tax payable 1,500   11,500 $173,000

Cash Applied to Payment of Dividends

According to the retained earnings account of T. R. Morgan Corporation (page 469), cash dividends of $30,000 were declared during the year. In the earlier funds flow analysis, this was noted as the amount of working capital applied to the declaration of cash dividends. However, the amounts reported as dividends payable on T. R. Morgan Corporation's comparative balance sheet (page 465) are $15,000 and $8,000 respectively, revealing a timing difference between declaration and payment.

According to the dividends payable account, shown below, dividend payments during the year totaled $23,000.

ACCOUNT DIVIDENDS PAYABLE   ACCOUNT NO.

Date		Item	Debit	Credit	Balance	
					Debit	Credit
1987						
Jan.	1	Balance				8,000
	10	Cash paid	8,000		—	—
June	20	Dividend declared		15,000		15,000
July	10	Cash paid	15,000		—	—
Dec.	20	Dividend declared		15,000		15,000

The amount of cash applied to dividend payments may be noted as follows:

    Application of cash:
      Cash dividends declared $30,000
      Deduct increase in dividends payable 7,000 $23,000

Form of the Funds Statement Based on Cash

The funds statement based on cash is comparable in form to the funds statement illustrated on page 470. The greatest difference between the two statements is in the section devoted to funds provided by operations.

The following statement is supported by a reconciliation of the change in cash, but a funds statement based on cash may conclude with the amount of increase or decrease in cash.

T. R. Morgan Corporation
Statement of Changes in Financial Position
For Year Ended December 31, 1987

Sources of cash:
  Operations during the year:
    Net income. $140,500
    Add deductions not decreasing cash during
    the year:
      Depreciation $18,000
      Decrease in inventories. 8,000
      Increase in accounts payable 18,000   44,000
                                    $184,500

    Deduct additions not increasing
    cash during the year:
      Increase in trade receivables . . . . $ 9,000
      Increase in prepaid expenses . . . 1,000
      Decrease in income tax payable . . 1,500   11,500 $173,000
  Book value of investments sold (excludes $30,000 gain reported in net income) 45,000
  Issuance of common stock at par for land 50,000 $268,000

Applications of cash:
  Purchase of land by issuance of common stock at par . . $ 50,000
  Purchase of equipment. 47,000
  Retirement of bonds payable. 125,000
  Payment of dividends:
    Cash dividends declared . . . . $ 30,000
    Deduct increase in dividends payable 7,000   23,000 245,000
Increase in cash. . . . . $ 23,000

Change in cash balance:
  Cash balance, December 31, 1987 . . . . $ 49,000
  Cash balance, December 31, 1986 26,000
Increase in cash. . . . . $ 23,000

CASH FLOW FROM OPERATIONS

The term **cash flow** is sometimes encountered in reports to stockholders. It may be mentioned in a company president's letter to stockholders, in operating summaries, or elsewhere in the published financial report. Although there are variations in the method of determination, cash flow is approximately equivalent to income from operations plus depreciation, depletion, and any other expenses that had no effect on working capital during the period. Many terms have been used to describe the amount so determined, including "cash flow from operations," "cash income," "cash earnings," and "cash throw-off."

The amount of cash flow from operations for a period may be useful to internal financial management in considering the possibility of retiring long-term debt, in planning replacement of plant facilities, or in formulating dividend policies. However, when it is presented without reference to the funds statement and its importance stressed in reporting operations to stockholders, it is likely to be misunderstood. The reporting of so-called cash flow per share of stock may be even more misleading, particularly when the amount is larger, which it usually is, than the net income per share. Readers are quite likely to substitute cash flow for net income in appraising the relative success of operations. Guidelines for determining acceptable terminology and practice have been expressed as follows:

> The amount of working capital or cash provided from operations is not a substitute for or an improvement upon properly determined net income as a measure of results of operations and the consequent effect on financial position. Terms referring to "cash" should not be used to describe amounts provided from operations unless all non-cash items have been appropriately adjusted.... The Board strongly recommends that isolated statistics of working capital or cash provided from operations, especially per-share amounts, not be presented in annual reports to shareholders. If any per-share data relating to flow of working capital or cash are presented, they should as a minimum include amounts for inflow from operations, inflow from other sources, and total outflow, and each per-share amount should be clearly identified with the corresponding total amount shown in the Statement.[11]

Self-Examination Questions (Answers at end of chapter.)

1. If an enterprise's total current assets are $225,000 and its total current liabilities are $150,000, its working capital is:
   A. $75,000
   B. $225,000
   C. $375,000
   D. none of the above

2. Which of the following types of transactions would provide working capital?
   A. Transactions that decrease noncurrent assets
   B. Transactions that decrease noncurrent liabilities
   C. Transactions that decrease stockholders' equity
   D. None of the above

---

[11]*Opinions of the Accounting Principles Board, No. 19, op. cit.,* par. 15.

3. Which of the following transactions represents an application of working capital?
   A. Sale of common stock for cash
   B. Issuance of bonds payable for cash
   C. Acquisition of equipment for cash
   D. None of the above

4. The net income reported on the income statement for the year was $55,000 and depreciation on plant assets for the year was $22,000. The balances of the current asset and current liability accounts at the beginning and end of the year are as follows:

	End	Beginning
Cash...	$ 65,000	$ 70,000
Trade receivables	100,000	90,000
Inventories......................................	145,000	150,000
Prepaid expenses	7,500	8,000
Accounts payable (merchandise creditors).............	51,000	58,000

   The total amount reported for working capital provided by operations in the statement of changes in financial position would be:
   A. $33,000   C. $77,000
   B. $55,000   D. none of the above

5. Based on the data presented in Question 4, the total amount reported for the cash provided by operations in the statement of changes in financial position would be:
   A. $33,000   C. $77,000
   B. $55,000   D. none of the above

Discussion
Questions

14–1. What is the shorter term often employed in referring to the statement of changes in financial position?

14–2. What are the principal concepts of the term *funds,* as employed in referring to the statement of changes in financial position?

14–3. (a) What is meant by *working capital*? (b) Name another term, other than "funds," that has the same meaning.

14–4. State the effect of each of the following transactions, considered individually, on working capital:
   (a) Purchased $5,000 of merchandise on account, terms 1/10, n/30.
   (b) Sold, for $900 cash, merchandise that had cost $600.
   (c) Issued 1,000 shares of $100 par preferred stock for $102 a share, receiving cash.
   (d) Received $400 from a customer on account.
   (e) Purchased office equipment for $1,750 on account.
   (f) Issued a $2,000, 30-day non-interest-bearing note to a creditor in temporary settlement of an account payable.
   (g) Borrowed $50,000 cash, issuing a 90-day, 12% note.

14–5. When the total of the applications section exceeds the total of the sources section on a statement of changes in financial position based on working capital, is this excess identified as an increase or as a decrease in working capital?

14–6. What is the effect on working capital of writing off $2,500 of uncollectible accounts against Allowance for Doubtful Accounts?

14–7. A corporation issued $1,000,000 of 20-year bonds for cash at 95. (a) Did the transaction provide funds or apply funds? (b) What was the amount of funds involved? (c) Was working capital affected? (d) Was cash affected?

14–8. Fully depreciated equipment costing $25,000 was discarded. What was the effect of the transaction on working capital if (a) $500 cash is received, (b) there is no salvage value?

14–9. A long-term investment in bonds with a cost of $90,000 was sold for $75,000 cash. (a) What was the gain or loss on the sale? (b) What was the effect of the transaction on working capital? (c) How should the transaction be reported in the funds statement?

14–10. The board of directors declared a cash dividend of $75,000 near the end of the fiscal year, which ends on December 31, payable in January. (a) What was the effect of the declaration on working capital? (b) Did the declaration represent a source or an application of working capital? (c) Did the payment of the dividend in January affect working capital, and if so, how?

14–11. (a) What is the effect on working capital of the declaration and issuance of a stock dividend? (b) Does the stock dividend represent a source or an application of working capital?

14–12. On its income statement for the current year, a company reported a net loss of $75,000 from operations. On its statement of changes in financial position, it reported an increase of $50,000 in working capital from operations. Explain the seeming contradiction between the loss and the increase in working capital.

14–13. What is the effect on working capital of an appropriation of retained earnings for plant expansion?

14–14. A net loss of $75,000 from operations is reported on the income statement. The only revenue or expense item reported that did not affect working capital was depreciation expense of $45,000. Will the change in financial position attributed to operations appear in the funds statement as a source or as an application of working capital, and at what amount?

14–15. Assume that a corporation has net income of $200,000 that included a charge of $5,000 for the amortization of bond discount and depreciation expense of $75,000. What amount should this corporation report on its funds statement for working capital provided by operations?

14–16. A corporation acquired as a long-term investment all of another corporation's capital stock, valued at $10,000,000, by the issuance of $10,000,000 of its own common stock. Where should the transaction be reported on the statement of changes in financial position (a) if the cash concept of funds is employed, and (b) if the working capital concept of funds is employed?

14–17. A retail enterprise, employing the accrual method of accounting, owed merchandise creditors (accounts payable) $275,000 at the beginning of the year and $240,000 at the end of the year. What adjustment for the $35,000 decrease must be made to income from operations in determining the amount of cash provided by operations? Explain.

14–18. If revenue from sales amounted to $975,000 for the year and trade receivables totaled $120,000 and $95,000 at the beginning and end of the year respectively, what was the amount of cash received from customers during the year?

Statement of Changes in Financial Position

14–19. If salaries payable was $75,000 and $65,000 at the beginning and end of the year respectively, should $10,000 be added to or deducted from income to determine the amount of cash provided by operations? Explain.

14–20. The board of directors declared cash dividends totaling $100,000 during the current year. The comparative balance sheet indicates dividends payable of $30,000 at the beginning of the year and $25,000 at the end of the year. What was the amount of cash disbursed to stockholders during the year?

Exercises

14–21. Using the following schedule of current assets and current liabilities, prepare the section of the statement of changes in financial position entitled "Changes in components of working capital."

	End of Year	Beginning of Year
Cash.....................	$ 49,500	$ 45,400
Trade receivables (net)......	55,500	60,000
Inventories................	151,250	147,750
Prepaid expenses	4,700	4,550
Accounts payable..........	55,000	51,500
Dividends payable	15,000	12,500
Salaries payable...........	9,750	11,000

14–22. The net income reported on an income statement for the current year was $79,250. Adjustments required to determine the amount of working capital provided by operations, as well as some other data used for the year-end adjusting entries, are described as follows:

(a) Uncollectible accounts expense, $6,100.
(b) Depreciation expense, $27,500.
(c) Amortization of patents, $4,500.
(d) Interest accrued on notes payable, $1,150.
(e) Income tax payable, $11,500.
(f) Wages accrued but not paid, $3,750.

Prepare the working-capital-provided-by-operations section of the statement of changes in financial position.

14–23. On the basis of the details of the following plant asset account, indicate the items to be reported as a source of working capital and as an application of working capital on the statement of changes in financial position.

ACCOUNT **LAND**   ACCOUNT NO.

Date		Item	Debit	Credit	Balance	
					Debit	Credit
19--						
Jan.	1	Balance			650,000	
Aug.	29	Purchased with long-term mortgage note	200,000			
Dec.	9	Purchased for cash	75,000		925,000	

14–24. On the basis of the following stockholders' equity accounts, indicate the items, exclusive of net income, to be reported as a source of working capital and as an application of working capital on the statement of changes in financial position.

ACCOUNT **COMMON STOCK, $20 PAR**   ACCOUNT NO.

Date		Item	Debit	Credit	Balance Debit	Balance Credit
19--						
Jan.	1	Balance, 40,000 shares				800,000
Feb.	10	5,000 shares issued for cash		100,000		
July	25	1,350 share stock dividend		27,000		927,000

ACCOUNT **PREMIUM ON COMMON STOCK**   ACCOUNT NO.

Date		Item	Debit	Credit	Balance Debit	Balance Credit
19--						
Jan.	1	Balance				140,000
Feb.	10	5,000 shares issued for cash		50,000		
July	25	Stock dividend		13,500		203,500

ACCOUNT **RETAINED EARNINGS**   ACCOUNT NO.

Date		Item	Debit	Credit	Balance Debit	Balance Credit
19--						
Jan.	1	Balance				425,000
July	25	Stock dividend	40,500			
Dec.	31	Cash dividends	91,350			
	31	Net income		165,000		458,150

14–25. An analysis of the general ledger accounts indicated that delivery equipment, which had cost $35,000 and on which accumulated depreciation totaled $29,750 on the date of sale, was sold for $7,000 during the year. Using this information, indicate the items to be reported as a source of working capital and as an application of working capital on the statement of changes in financial position.

14–26. The net income reported on an income statement for the current year was $92,125. Depreciation recorded on equipment and building for the year amounted to $34,500. Balances of the current asset and current liability accounts at the beginning and end of the year are as follows:

	End	Beginning
Cash	$ 69,750	$ 61,250
Trade receivables	80,500	75,000
Inventories	110,000	97,000
Prepaid expenses	6,900	7,400
Accounts payable (merchandise creditors)	69,700	72,700
Salaries payable	7,500	6,250

Prepare the cash-provided-by-operations section of a statement of changes in financial position.

14–27. The following information was taken from the records of C. D. Collins Co.:
  (a) Equipment and land were acquired for cash.
  (b) There were no disposals of equipment during the year.
  (c) The investments were sold for $80,000 cash.
  (d) The common stock was issued for cash.
  (e) There was a $76,750 credit to Retained Earnings for net income.
  (f) There was a $45,000 debit to Retained Earnings for cash dividends declared.

Based on this information and the following comparative balance sheet, prepare a statement of changes in financial position, employing the working capital concept of funds.

	June 30	
	Current Year	Preceding Year
Cash..	$ 64,200	$ 49,900
Trade receivables (net)...........................	91,500	80,000
Inventories.....................................	105,900	90,500
Investments....................................	———	75,000
Land	85,000	———
Equipment.....................................	355,000	275,000
Accumulated depreciation	(149,000)	(119,000)
	$552,600	$451,400
Accounts payable (merchandise creditors)...........	$ 62,450	$ 55,000
Dividends payable	12,000	10,000
Common stock, $20 par.........................	300,000	250,000
Premium on common stock.......................	22,000	12,000
Retained earnings	156,150	124,400
	$552,600	$451,400

14–28. From the data presented in Exercise 14-27, prepare a statement of changes in financial position, employing the cash concept of funds.

Problems

14–29. The comparative balance sheet of Chow Corporation at September 30 of the current year and the preceding year is as follows:

Assets	Current Year	Preceding Year
Cash..	$ 39,600	$ 52,000
Accounts receivable (net)........................	88,750	70,000
Merchandise inventory	149,550	130,750
Prepaid expenses	4,300	2,700
Plant assets	280,500	260,500
Accumulated depreciation—plant assets.............	(170,500)	(187,000)
	$392,200	$328,950

Liabilities and Stockholders' Equity	Current Year	Preceding Year
Accounts payable..................................	$ 68,700	$ 43,200
Mortgage note payable............................	——	75,000
Common stock, $10 par	150,000	100,000
Premium on common stock........................	40,000	25,000
Retained earnings	133,500	85,750
	$392,200	$328,950

Additional data obtained from the income statement and from an examination of the noncurrent asset, noncurrent liability, and stockholders' equity accounts in the ledger are as follows:

(a) Net income, $87,750.

(b) Depreciation reported on the income statement, $29,500.

(c) An addition to the building was constructed at a cost of $66,000, and fully depreciated equipment costing $46,000 was discarded, no salvage being realized.

(d) The mortgage note payable was not due until 1992, but the terms permitted earlier payment without penalty.

(e) 5,000 shares of common stock were issued at $13 for cash.

(f) Cash dividends declared, $40,000.

Instructions:

Prepare a statement of changes in financial position (working capital concept), including a section on changes in components of working capital.

14–30. The comparative balance sheet of Wei Corporation at December 31 of the current year and the preceding year is as follows:

Assets	Current Year	Preceding Year
Cash..	$ 62,750	$ 82,400
Trade receivables (net)..............................	148,200	119,200
Inventories.......................................	216,350	236,100
Prepaid expenses	4,500	3,900
Land..	100,000	100,000
Buildings	633,300	458,300
Accumulated depreciation—buildings...................	(202,500)	(185,000)
Machinery and equipment	250,000	250,000
Accumulated depreciation—machinery and equipment....	(130,600)	(108,400)
Patents...	50,000	62,500
	$1,132,000	$1,019,000

Liabilities and Stockholders' Equity	Current Year	Preceding Year
Accounts payable (merchandise creditors)...............	$ 36,280	$ 51,780
Dividends payable	25,000	40,000
Salaries payable...................................	18,480	12,480
Mortgage note payable, due 1994	100,000	——
Bonds payable	——	80,000
Common stock, $10 par	450,000	400,000
Premium on common stock	80,000	50,000
Retained earnings	422,240	384,740
	$1,132,000	$1,019,000

An examination of the income statement and the accounting records revealed the following additional information applicable to the current year:

(a) Net income, $62,500.

(b) Depreciation expense reported on the income statement: buildings, $17,500; machinery and equipment, $22,200.

(c) Patent amortization reported on the income statement, $12,500.

(d) A mortgage note for $100,000 was issued in connection with the construction of a building costing $175,000; the remainder was paid in cash.

(e) 5,000 shares of common stock were issued at 16 in exchange for the bonds payable.

(f) Cash dividends declared, $25,000.

Instructions:

Prepare a statement of changes in financial position (working capital concept), including a section for changes in components of working capital.

14–31. The comparative balance sheet of Wei Corporation and other data necessary for the analysis of the corporation's funds flow are presented in Problem 14-30.

Instructions:

Prepare a statement of changes in financial position (cash concept), including a summary of the change in cash balance.

14–32. A comparative balance sheet of W. A. Sussman Inc., at December 31 of the current year and the preceding year, and the noncurrent asset accounts, the noncurrent liability accounts, and the stockholders' equity accounts for the current year, are as follows:

Assets	Current Year	Preceding Year
Cash.....................................	$ 77,900	$ 62,100
Trade receivables (net)........................	128,800	109,200
Income tax refund receivable...................	5,000	——
Inventories...................................	184,800	205,000
Prepaid expenses	7,450	8,150
Investments.................................	100,000	200,000
Land..	56,000	100,000
Buildings	550,000	250,000
Accumulated depreciation—buildings...........	(73,100)	(61,500)
Equipment...................................	482,000	392,000
Accumulated depreciation—equipment	(181,620)	(156,420)
	$1,337,230	$1,108,530

Liabilities and Stockholders' Equity		
Accounts payable (merchandise creditors).......	$ 61,400	$ 82,750
Income tax payable...........................	——	9,000
Notes payable................................	355,000	30,000
Discount on long-term notes payable...........	(24,750)	(1,500)
Common stock, $20 par.......................	515,000	500,000
Premium on common stock....................	70,000	60,000
Appropriation for contingencies................	100,000	75,000
Retained earnings	260,580	353,280
	$1,337,230	$1,108,530

ACCOUNT INVESTMENTS ACCOUNT NO.

Date		Item	Debit	Credit	Balance Debit	Balance Credit
19--						
Jan.	1	Balance			200,000	
Feb.	20	Realized $91,000 cash from sale		100,000	100,000	

ACCOUNT LAND ACCOUNT NO.

Date		Item	Debit	Credit	Balance Debit	Balance Credit
19--						
Jan.	1	Balance			100,000	
May	5	Realized $60,000 from sale		44,000	56,000	

ACCOUNT BUILDINGS ACCOUNT NO.

Date		Item	Debit	Credit	Balance Debit	Balance Credit
19--						
Jan.	1	Balance			250,000	
June	30	Acquired with notes payable	300,000		550,000	

ACCOUNT ACCUMULATED DEPRECIATION — BUILDINGS ACCOUNT NO.

Date		Item	Debit	Credit	Balance Debit	Balance Credit
19--						
Jan.	1	Balance				61,500
Dec.	31	Depreciation for year		11,600		73,100

ACCOUNT EQUIPMENT ACCOUNT NO.

Date		Item	Debit	Credit	Balance Debit	Balance Credit
19--						
Jan.	1	Balance			392,000	
Mar.	19	Discarded, no salvage		25,000		
June	2	Purchased for cash	75,000			
Oct.	10	Purchased for cash	40,000		482,000	

ACCOUNT ACCUMULATED DEPRECIATION — EQUIPMENT ACCOUNT NO.

Date		Item	Debit	Credit	Balance Debit	Balance Credit
19--						
Jan.	1	Balance				156,420
Mar.	19	Equipment discarded	25,000			
Dec.	31	Depreciation for year		50,200		181,620

Statement of Changes in Financial Position

ACCOUNT LONG-TERM NOTES PAYABLE   ACCOUNT NO.

Date		Item	Debit	Credit	Balance Debit	Balance Credit
19--						
Jan.	1	Balance				30,000
June	30	Issued 10-year notes		325,000		355,000

ACCOUNT DISCOUNT ON LONG-TERM NOTES PAYABLE   ACCOUNT NO.

Date		Item	Debit	Credit	Balance Debit	Balance Credit
19--						
Jan.	1	Balance			1,500	
June	30	Notes issued	25,000		26,500	
Dec.	31	Amortization—Jan. 1 Bal.		500		
		June 30 Notes		1,250	24,750	

ACCOUNT COMMON STOCK, $20 PAR   ACCOUNT NO.

Date		Item	Debit	Credit	Balance Debit	Balance Credit
19--						
Jan.	1	Balance				500,000
Dec.	1	Stock dividend		15,000		515,000

ACCOUNT PREMIUM ON COMMON STOCK   ACCOUNT NO.

Date		Item	Debit	Credit	Balance Debit	Balance Credit
19--						
Jan.	1	Balance				60,000
Dec.	1	Stock dividend		10,000		70,000

ACCOUNT APPROPRIATION FOR CONTINGENCIES   ACCOUNT NO.

Date		Item	Debit	Credit	Balance Debit	Balance Credit
19--						
Jan.	1	Balance				75,000
Dec.	31	Appropriation		25,000		100,000

ACCOUNT RETAINED EARNINGS   ACCOUNT NO.

Date		Item	Debit	Credit	Balance Debit	Balance Credit
19--						
Jan.	1	Balance				353,280
Dec.	1	Stock dividend	25,000			
	31	Net loss	17,700			
	31	Cash dividends	25,000			
	31	Appropriated	25,000			260,580

Instructions:

Prepare a statement of changes in financial position (working capital concept), including a section for changes in components of working capital.

14–33. The comparative balance sheet of W. A. Sussman Inc. and other data necessary for the analysis of the corporation's funds flow are presented in Problem 14-32.

Instructions:

Prepare a statement of changes in financial position (cash concept), including a summary of the change in cash balance.

14–34. A comparative income statement and a balance sheet of Mills Company are as follows:

Mills Company
Income Statement
For Current Year Ended December 31

Sales...		$990,000
Cost of merchandise sold............................		615,000
Gross profit.......................................		$375,000
Operating expenses (including depreciation of $32,200)...		250,700
Income from operations..............................		$124,300
Other income:		
Gain on sale of land.................................	$ 25,000	
Gain on sale of investments.........................	3,500	
Interest income.....................................	1,100	29,600
		$153,900
Interest expense....................................		18,000
Income before income tax.............................		$135,900
Income tax...		48,100
Net income...		$ 87,800

Mills Company
Comparative Balance Sheet
December 31, Current and Preceding Year

Assets	Current Year	Preceding Year
Cash...	$ 36,600	$ 41,500
Marketable securities................................	32,100	——
Trade receivables (net).............................	110,000	83,000
Inventories.......................................	168,600	147,100
Prepaid expenses...................................	3,750	4,100
Investments.......................................	——	80,000
Land	60,000	50,000
Buildings...	305,000	150,000
Accumulated depreciation—buildings..................	(87,000)	(79,000)
Equipment	402,500	350,000
Accumulated depreciation—equipment.................	(145,300)	(121,100)
	$886,250	$705,600

Liabilities and Stockholders' Equity	Current Year	Preceding Year
Accounts payable (merchandise creditors)	$ 67,250	$ 52,900
Income tax payable	5,000	11,500
Dividends payable	25,000	15,000
Mortgage note payable	150,000	——
Bonds payable	100,000	150,000
Common stock, $10 par	340,000	300,000
Premium on common stock	65,000	55,000
Retained earnings	134,000	121,200
	$886,250	$705,600

The following additional information on funds flow during the year was obtained from an examination of the ledger:
   (a) Marketable securities were purchased for $32,100.
   (b) Investments (long-term) were sold for $83,500.
   (c) Equipment was purchased for $52,500. There were no disposals.
   (d) A building valued at $155,000 and land valued at $45,000 were acquired by a cash payment of $50,000 and issuance of a five-year mortgage note payable for the balance.
   (e) Land which cost $35,000 was sold for $60,000 cash.
   (f) Bonds payable of $50,000 were retired by the payment of their face amount.
   (g) 4,000 shares of common stock were issued for cash at 12½.
   (h) Cash dividends of $75,000 were declared.

Instructions:
   (1) Prepare a statement of changes in financial position (working capital concept), including a section for changes in components of working capital.
   (2) Prepare a statement of changes in financial position (cash concept), including a summary of the change in cash balance.

14–29A. The comparative balance sheet of Meyers Corporation at June 30 of the current year and the preceding year is as follows:

Alternate Problems

Assets	Current Year	Preceding Year
Cash	$ 47,300	$ 45,300
Accounts receivable (net)	59,400	58,500
Merchandise inventory...............................	77,250	91,850
Prepaid expenses....................................	5,600	4,950
Plant assets..	375,000	310,000
Accumulated depreciation—plant assets	(117,500)	(125,000)
	$447,050	$385,600

Liabilities and Stockholders' Equity	Current Year	Preceding Year
Accounts payable	$ 55,250	$ 38,800
Mortgage note payable	—	50,000
Common stock, $25 par	250,000	200,000
Premium on common stock	35,000	25,000
Retained earnings	106,800	71,800
	$447,050	$385,600

Additional data obtained from the income statement and from an examination of the noncurrent asset, noncurrent liability, and stockholders' equity accounts in the ledger are as follows:

(a) Net income, $75,000.

(b) Depreciation reported on the income statement, $27,500.

(c) An addition to the building was constructed at a cost of $100,000, and fully depreciated equipment costing $35,000 was discarded, no salvage being realized.

(d) The mortgage note payable was not due until 1991, but the terms permitted earlier payment without penalty.

(e) 2,000 shares of common stock were issued at 30 for cash.

(f) Cash dividends declared, $40,000.

Instructions:

Prepare a statement of changes in financial position (working capital concept), including a section on changes in components of working capital.

14–30A. The comparative balance sheet of Brown Corporation at December 31 of the current year and the preceding year is as follows:

Assets	Current Year	Preceding Year
Cash	$ 55,100	$ 42,500
Trade receivables (net)	91,350	61,150
Inventories	104,500	109,500
Prepaid expenses	3,600	2,700
Land	50,000	50,000
Buildings	325,000	245,000
Accumulated depreciation—buildings	(120,600)	(110,400)
Machinery and equipment	255,000	255,000
Accumulated depreciation—machinery and equipment	(92,000)	(65,000)
Patents	35,000	40,000
	$706,950	$630,450

Liabilities and Stockholders' Equity		
Accounts payable (merchandise creditors)	$ 61,150	$ 75,000
Dividends payable	15,000	10,000
Salaries payable	6,650	7,550
Mortgage note payable, due 1992	50,000	—
Bonds payable	—	75,000
Common stock, $20 par	300,000	250,000
Premium on common stock	100,000	75,000
Retained earnings	174,150	137,900
	$706,950	$630,450

An examination of the income statement and the accounting records revealed the following additional information applicable to the current year:

(a) Net income, $96,250.

(b) Depreciation expense reported on the income statement: buildings, $10,200; machinery and equipment, $27,000.

(c) Patent amortization reported on the income statement, $5,000.

(d) A mortgage note for $50,000 was issued in connection with the construction of a building costing $80,000; the remainder was paid in cash.

(e) 2,500 shares of common stock were issued at 30 in exchange for the bonds payable.

(f) Cash dividends declared, $60,000.

Instructions:

Prepare a statement of changes in financial position (working capital concept), including a section for changes in components of working capital.

14–31A. The comparative balance sheet of Brown Corporation and other data necessary for the analysis of the corporation's funds flow are presented in Problem 14-30A.

Instructions:

Prepare a statement of changes in financial position (cash concept), including a summary of the change in cash balance.

14–32A. The comparative balance sheet of D. A. Ruiz Inc., at December 31 of the current year and the preceding year, and the noncurrent asset accounts, the noncurrent liability accounts, and the stockholders' equity accounts for the current year, are as follows:

Assets	Current Year	Preceding Year
Cash	$ 58,000	$ 64,500
Trade receivables (net)	103,325	91,725
Inventories	208,100	188,000
Prepaid expenses	6,850	7,100
Investments	—	50,000
Land	65,000	65,000
Buildings	285,000	185,000
Accumulated depreciation—buildings	(76,400)	(69,000)
Equipment	480,500	410,500
Accumulated depreciation—equipment	(143,500)	(129,000)
	$986,875	$863,825

Liabilities and Stockholders' Equity		
Accounts payable (merchandise creditors)	$ 60,075	$ 77,600
Income tax payable	5,500	2,800
Notes payable	105,000	—
Discount on long-term notes payable	(4,625)	—
Common stock, $20 par	624,000	600,000
Premium on common stock	67,000	55,000
Appropriation for contingencies	35,000	25,000
Retained earnings	94,925	103,425
	$986,875	$863,825

ACCOUNT INVESTMENTS   ACCOUNT NO.

Date		Item	Debit	Credit	Balance Debit	Balance Credit
19--						
Jan.	1	Balance			50,000	
June	29	Realized $57,500 cash from sale		50,000	—	—

ACCOUNT LAND   ACCOUNT NO.

Date		Item	Debit	Credit	Balance Debit	Balance Credit
19--						
Jan.	1	Balance			65,000	

ACCOUNT BUILDINGS   ACCOUNT NO.

Date		Item	Debit	Credit	Balance Debit	Balance Credit
19--						
Jan.	1	Balance			185,000	
Apr.	1	Acquired with notes payable	100,000		285,000	

ACCOUNT ACCUMULATED DEPRECIATION — BUILDINGS   ACCOUNT NO.

Date		Item	Debit	Credit	Balance Debit	Balance Credit
19--						
Jan.	1	Balance				69,000
Dec.	31	Depreciation for year		7,400		76,400

ACCOUNT EQUIPMENT   ACCOUNT NO.

Date		Item	Debit	Credit	Balance Debit	Balance Credit
19--						
Jan.	1	Balance			410,500	
Feb.	8	Discarded, no salvage		35,000		
July	2	Purchased for cash	60,000			
Nov.	1	Purchased for cash	45,000		480,500	

ACCOUNT ACCUMULATED DEPRECIATION — EQUIPMENT   ACCOUNT NO.

Date		Item	Debit	Credit	Balance Debit	Balance Credit
19--						
Jan.	1	Balance				129,000
Feb.	8	Equipment discarded	35,000			
Dec.	31	Depreciation for year		49,500		143,500

ACCOUNT LONG-TERM NOTES PAYABLE ACCOUNT NO.

Date		Item	Debit	Credit	Balance	
					Debit	Credit
19--						
Apr.	1	Issued 10-year notes		105,000		105,000

ACCOUNT DISCOUNT ON LONG-TERM NOTES PAYABLE ACCOUNT NO.

Date		Item	Debit	Credit	Balance	
					Debit	Credit
19--						
Apr.	1	Notes issued	5,000		5,000	
Dec.	31	Amortization		375	4,625	

ACCOUNT COMMON STOCK, $20 PAR ACCOUNT NO.

Date		Item	Debit	Credit	Balance	
					Debit	Credit
19--						
Jan.	1	Balance				600,000
July	10	Stock dividend		24,000		624,000

ACCOUNT PREMIUM ON COMMON STOCK ACCOUNT NO.

Date		Item	Debit	Credit	Balance	
					Debit	Credit
19--						
Jan.	1	Balance				55,000
July	10	Stock dividend		12,000		67,000

ACCOUNT APPROPRIATION FOR CONTINGENCIES ACCOUNT NO.

Date		Item	Debit	Credit	Balance	
					Debit	Credit
19--						
Jan.	1	Balance				25,000
Dec.	31	Appropriation		10,000		35,000

ACCOUNT RETAINED EARNINGS ACCOUNT NO.

Date		Item	Debit	Credit	Balance	
					Debit	Credit
19--						
Jan.	1	Balance				103,425
July	10	Stock dividend	36,000			
Dec.	31	Net income		127,500		
	31	Cash dividends	90,000			
	31	Appropriated	10,000			94,925

Instructions:
    Prepare a statement of changes in financial position (working capital concept), including a section for changes in components of working capital.

14-33A. The comparative balance sheet of D. A. Ruiz Inc. and other data necessary for the analysis of the corporation's funds flow are presented in Problem 14-32A.

Instructions:
    Prepare a statement of changes in financial position (cash concept), including a summary of the change in cash balance.

Mini-Case

14-35. Robert Pickett is the president and majority shareholder of Variety Stores Inc., a small retail store chain. Recently, Pickett submitted a loan application for Variety Stores Inc. to Arcadia State Bank for a $100,000, 14%, 10-year loan to finance the purchase of land and buildings in Clinton, where the company plans to open a new store. The bank's loan officer requested a statement of changes in financial position (based on the working capital concept) in addition to the most recent income statement, balance sheet, and retained earnings statement that Pickett had submitted with the loan application.

    As a close family friend, Pickett asked you to prepare a statement of changes in financial position. Using Variety Stores' records, you prepared the following statement:

Variety Stores Inc.
Statement of Changes in Financial Position
For Year Ended December 31, 19--

Sources of working capital:		
Operations during the year:		
Net income	$ 80,000	
Add deduction not decreasing working capital during the year:		
Depreciation	20,000	$100,000
Book value of investments sold (excludes $5,000 gain)		27,000
Issuance of common stock at par for land		50,000 $177,000
Applications of working capital:		
Purchase of land by issuance of common stock at par	$ 50,000	
Purchase of store equipment	25,000	
Declaration of cash dividends	20,000	95,000
Increase in working capital		$ 82,000

Changes in components of working capital:
Increase (decrease) in current assets:

Cash..............................	$ 16,300	
Trade receivables (net)	24,600	
Inventories	53,600	
Prepaid expenses	(2,500)	$ 92,000

Increase (decrease) in current liabilities:

Accounts payable	$ 12,400	
Income tax payable.................	2,600	
Dividends payable.................	(5,000)	10,000
Increase in working capital		$ 82,000

After reviewing the statement, Pickett telephoned you and commented, "Are you sure this statement is right?" Pickett then raised the following questions:

(a) "How can depreciation be a source of working capital?"

(b) "The issuance of common stock for the land is listed both as a source and an application of working capital. This transaction had nothing to do with working capital! Shouldn't the two items related to this transaction be eliminated from both the sources and applications sections?"

(c) "Why did you list only the $27,000 book value of the investments sold, excluding the gain of $5,000, as a source of funds? We actually received cash of $32,000 from the sale. Shouldn't the $32,000 be included as a source of working capital?"

(d) "Why not eliminate the 'changes in components of working capital' section of the statement? Since the amount of increase in working capital is already shown in the upper portion of the statement, this section adds nothing."

(e) "Why does the bank need this statement anyway? They can compute the increase in working capital from the balance sheets for the last two years."

After jotting down Pickett's questions, you assured him that this statement was "right". However, to alleviate Pickett's concern, you arranged a meeting for the following day.

Instructions:

(1) How would you respond to each of Pickett's questions?

(2) Do you think that the statement of changes in financial position enhances Variety Stores' chances of receiving the loan? Discuss.

---

1. A Working capital is the excess of total current assets over total current liabilities; that is, $225,000 less $150,000, or $75,000 (answer A) in the question.

2. A Working capital is provided by transactions that decrease noncurrent assets (answer A), such as the sale of a plant asset for cash. Transactions that decrease noncurrent liabilities (answer B), such as the redemption of long-term liabilities for cash, and transactions that decrease stockholders' equity (answer C), such as the declaration of cash dividends, are applications of working capital.

Answers to Self-Examination Questions

3. C The acquisition of equipment for cash (answer C) decreases cash and working capital and is therefore an application of working capital. The sale of common stock for cash (answer A) and the issuance of bonds payable for cash (answer B) both increase cash and working capital and therefore are sources of working capital.

4. C The operations section of the statement of changes in financial position would report a total of $77,000 (answer C) for the working capital provided by operations, determined as follows:

Operations during the year:

Net income		$55,000
Add deduction not decreasing working capital during the year:		
Depreciation		22,000 $77,000

5. D The operations section of the statement of changes in financial position would report a total of $65,500 for the cash provided by operations, determined as follows:

Operations during the year:

Net income		$55,000
Add deductions not decreasing cash during the year:		
Depreciation	$22,000	
Decrease in inventories	5,000	
Decrease in prepaid expenses	500	27,500
		$82,500
Deduct additions not increasing cash during the year:		
Increase in trade receivables	$10,000	
Decrease in accounts payable	7,000	17,000
		$65,500

PART 5

Fundamentals of Managerial Accounting Systems

The Managerial Accountant—Futurist

The role of the managerial accountant has been compared to the ancient Roman god, Janus, who faces forward as well as backward. The managerial accountant is concerned not only with the financial history and the resulting financial statements of a company, but with providing forward-looking financial information for management's use in planning the future. The effective managerial accountant is one who can tell management where the organization has been and where it is going, and can advise and assist management in taking the steps needed to improve on past results. The effective managerial accountant must help management identify targets of opportunity and potential areas of weakness, so that the organization can maximize the former and minimize the latter.

Opportunities for the managerial accountant to fulfill the role of "futurist" are numerous. For example, the design and implementation of an effective accounting system is one area. To paraphrase Lincoln's comment about his generals in the Civil War, it's too serious a business to be left to the programmers and systems analysts, important though their roles may be. The future-oriented managerial accountant must be an activist, constantly probing for new ideas, new ways of doing things, new solutions to old problems. If something has been done the same way for five years, the chances are good that there is a better way to do it. If it has been done the same way for *ten* years, it is almost a certainty that there is a better way.

Another future-oriented area to which the managerial accountant can contribute is the evaluation of proposed and alternate expenditures on long-term projects. Frequently, the managerial accountant will be called upon to "crunch" the numbers, but more than that should be done. Reasoned judgment should be offered as to the future effect on the organization of alternative decisions that may be available. The managerial accountant is uniquely situated in the company to have probably greater access to more of the facts than does anyone else. Although *all* the facts are not available—no one has all of them— enough are available for the managerial accountant to be reasonably assured that any decision reached is the best possible under the circumstances.

The managerial accountant must learn to feel as comfortable looking into that always cloudy future as in preparing last period's financial statements. Less and less the historian; more and more the futurist.

SOURCE   Adapted from "The Management Accountant—Futurist," *Management Accounting*, September, 1982, pp. 6, 75.

CHAPTER 15

Managerial Accounting and Job Order Cost Systems

CHAPTER OBJECTIVES

Describe the nature of managerial accounting and the characteristics of managerial accounting reports.

Describe the management process and the organization of the managerial accounting function.

Identify and illustrate concepts used in accounting for manufacturing operations.

Describe the basic characteristics of cost accounting systems.

Describe and illustrate a job order cost accounting system.

Managerial accounting has evolved over many centuries in response to the changing needs of management in planning and controlling operations. Perhaps the most significant change began with the Industrial Revolution, which occurred in England from the mid-eighteenth to the mid-nineteenth centuries. The revolution brought a change from the handicraft method of producing marketable goods to the factory system. With the use of machinery to make many identical products came the need to determine and control the cost of a large volume of machine-made products instead of a relatively small number of individually handcrafted products.

As manufacturing enterprises became larger and more complex and as competition among manufacturers increased, the "scientific management concept" evolved. This concept emphasized a systematic approach to the solution of management problems. Paralleling this trend was the development of more sophisticated managerial accounting concepts to supply management with analytical techniques for measuring the efficiency of current operations and in planning for future operations. This trend was accelerated in the twentieth century by the advent of the electronic computer with its capacity for manipulating large masses of data and its ability to determine the potential effect of alternative courses of action.

In this chapter, attention is directed to managerial accounting concepts for manufacturing enterprises. Although the concepts are presented in the context of a manufacturing enterprise, many of them also apply to service and merchandising enterprises.

NATURE OF MANAGERIAL ACCOUNTING

Managerial accounting uses both historical and estimated data in assisting management in daily operations and in planning future operations. It deals with specific problems that confront enterprise managers at various organizational levels. The managerial accountant is frequently concerned with identifying alternative courses of action and then helping to select the best one. For example, the managerial accountant may develop data to assist the company treasurer in preparing plans for future financing. As discussed in Chapter 1, the accountant provides these data in the format that is most useful for management.

CHARACTERISTICS OF MANAGERIAL ACCOUNTING REPORTS

The managerial accountant can be viewed as the observer and reporter of the business's operations. In carrying out this reporting function, the usefulness of the accountant's reports for management depends on the characteristics presented in the following diagram.

CHARACTERISTICS OF
USEFUL MANAGERIAL
ACCOUNTING REPORTS

Relevance

Relevance means that the economic information reported must be pertinent to the specific action being considered by management. In applying this concept, the accountant must be familiar with the operations of the firm and the needs of management in order to select what is important from the masses of data that are available. Especially in this modern age of the information explosion, this selection process can be difficult. To accomplish this task, the accountant must determine the needs of management for the decision at hand, examine the available data, and select only the relevant data for reporting to management. To illustrate, assume that management is considering the replacement of fully depreciated equipment, which cost $100,000, with new equipment costing $150,000. It is the $150,000 that is relevant for an analysis of financing the replacement. The original cost, $100,000, is irrelevant.

In applying the concept of relevance, it is important to recognize that some accounting information may have a high degree of relevance for one use but may have little or no relevance for another use. For example, in the previous illustration, the $100,000 was irrelevant for purposes of evaluating the financing of the replacement equipment. For tax purposes, however, the $100,000 (and its accumulated depreciation) would be relevant for determining the amount of the gain from the sale or trade-in of the old equipment and the amount of the income tax due on any gain.

Timeliness

Timeliness refers to the need for accounting reports to contain the most up-to-date information. In many cases, outdated data can lead to unwise decisions. For example, if prior years' costs are relied upon in setting the selling price of a product, the resulting selling price may not be sufficient to cover the current year's costs and to provide a satisfactory profit.

In some cases, the timeliness concept may require the accountant to prepare reports on a prearranged schedule, such as daily, weekly, or monthly. For example, daily reports of cash receipts and disbursements assist management in effectively managing the use of cash on a day-to-day basis. On the other hand, weekly reports of the cost of products manufactured may be satisfactory to assist management in the control of costs. In other cases, reports are prepared on an irregular basis or only when needed. For example, if management is evaluating a proposed advertising promotion for the month of May, a report of current costs and other current relevant data for this specific proposal would be needed in sufficient time for management to make and implement the decision.

Accuracy

Accuracy refers to the need for the report to be correct within the constraints of the use of the report and the inherent inaccuracies in the measurement process. If the report is not accurate, management's decision may not be prudent. For example, if an inaccurate report on a customer's past payment practices is presented to management, an unwise decision in granting credit may be made.

As previously indicated, the concept of accuracy must be applied within the constraint of the use to be made of the report. In other words, there are occasions when accuracy should be sacrificed for less precise data that are more useful to management. For example, in planning production, estimates (forecasts) of future sales may be more useful than more accurate data from past sales. In addition, it should be noted that there are inherent inaccuracies in accounting data that are based on estimates and approximations. For example, in determining the unit cost of a product manufactured, an estimate of depreciation expense on factory equipment used in the manufacturing process must be made. Without this estimate, the cost of the product would be of limited usefulness in establishing the product selling price.

Clarity

Clarity refers to the need for reports to be clear and understandable in both format and content. Reports that are clear and understandable will enable management to focus on significant factors in planning and controlling operations. For example, for management's use in controlling the costs of manufacturing a product, a report that compares actual costs with expected costs and clearly indicates the differences enables management to give its attention to significant differences and to take any necessary corrective action.

Conciseness

Conciseness refers to the requirement that the report should be brief and to the point. Although the report must be complete and include all relevant information, the inclusion of unnecessary information wastes management's time and makes it more difficult for management to focus on the significant factors related to a decision. For example, reports prepared for the top level of management should usually be broad in scope and present summaries of data rather than small details.

Cost-Benefit Balance

The characteristics of managerial accounting reports provide general guidelines for the preparation of reports to meet the various needs of management. In applying these guidelines, consideration must be given to the specific needs of each manager, and the reports should be tailored to meet these needs. In preparing reports, costs are incurred, and a primary consideration is that the value of the management reports must at least equal the cost of producing them. This overriding cost-benefit evaluation must be considered, no matter how informational a report may be. A report should not be prepared if its cost exceeds the benefits derived by users.

THE MANAGEMENT PROCESS

Managerial accountants supply accounting information to assist management in the basic functions of planning and control. **Planning** is the process of setting goals for the use of an organization's resources and of developing plans to achieve these goals. Accountants provide information to enable management to plan effectively. For example, accountants provide information to assist management in setting product selling prices. In this context, projections indicating the anticipated results of alternate selling prices can be useful to management in deciding among alternatives.

Control is the process of directing operations to achieve the organization's goals and plans. For example, accounting reports comparing the actual costs with the planned costs of producing products provide management with the basis for making decisions to control costs.

A common ingredient of both planning and control is decision making, and accountants provide information useful to management in making decisions. For example, decisions need to be made in selecting from among alternate proposed plans. Decisions also need to be made to keep actual costs within the bounds of proposed costs. The relationship between managerial accounting, the management process, and decision making is shown in the following diagram:

MANAGERIAL
ACCOUNTING AND THE
BASIC FUNCTIONS OF
MANAGEMENT

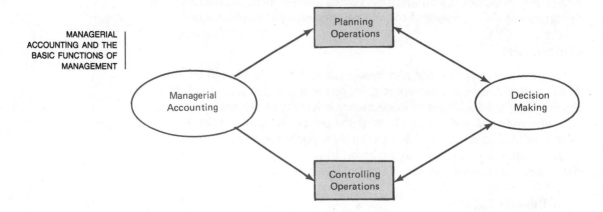

As indicated in the diagram, decisions must be made by management in planning and controlling operations. As the results of these decisions evolve and are reviewed, additional decisions may be necessary to revise plans and modify steps taken to control operations. For example, if accounting information indicates that actual performance is below planned performance, the plans may be revised or the controls modified in an attempt to improve performance. Thus, the interrelationships of the planning and control functions of management may be viewed as an endless loop, with the managerial accountant providing input for the use of management in carrying out both functions.

The accounting system of a particular firm must be responsive to the needs of management for both the planning and control functions. To meet the needs of management, the management accountant applies various concepts of usefulness (discussed in preceding paragraphs) in extracting data from the accounting system for reporting to management.

The accounting system must also be responsive to the needs of those external to the firm. As discussed previously, generally accepted accounting principles guide the accountant in extracting data from the accounting system for external reporting. The relationship of the basic concepts of management to both financial accounting and managerial accounting is summarized in the following diagram:

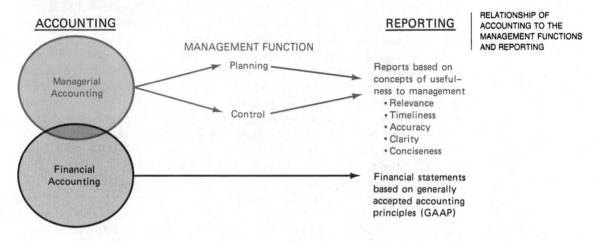

RELATIONSHIP OF ACCOUNTING TO THE MANAGEMENT FUNCTIONS AND REPORTING

ORGANIZATION OF THE MANAGERIAL ACCOUNTING FUNCTION

Business enterprises may be divided into departments or similar units, so that the activities of the business are more manageable. The responsibilities of specific departments can be indicated in an organization chart. The following simplified organization chart is typical for a manufacturing firm.

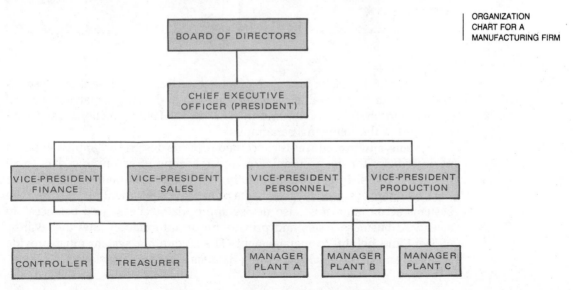

ORGANIZATION CHART FOR A MANUFACTURING FIRM

The individual reporting units can be viewed as having either (1) line or (2) staff responsibilities. A line department is one directly involved in the basic objectives of the organization. In the illustration, the vice-president of production and the managers of plants A, B, and C occupy line positions because they are responsible for an activity that directly contributes to earnings. A staff department is one that provides services and assistance to the operating and other units in the organization. The vice-president of personnel in the illustration occupies a staff position because that person's function is to assist line managers and others in staffing their departments.

In most business organizations, the chief managerial accountant is called the **controller**. The controller, who may report to the vice-president of finance, has a staff relationship with others in the organization, providing advice and assistance to management but assuming no responsibility for the operations of the business. The controller's function might be compared to that of an airplane's navigator. The navigator, with special skills and training, assists the pilot, but the pilot is responsible for flying the airplane. Likewise, the controller, with special accounting training and skills, advises management, but management is responsible for planning and controlling operations.

The controller's staff often consists of several accountants, each of whom is responsible for a specialized accounting function. The following organization chart is typical for an accounting department that reports to the controller:

ORGANIZATION CHART—
CONTROLLER'S
DEPARTMENT

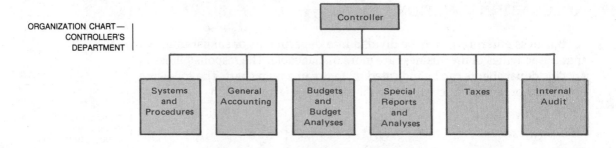

The most important functions of an accounting department are systems and procedures, general accounting, budgets and budget analyses, special reports and analyses, taxes, and internal audit. These functions are briefly described in the following paragraphs.

Systems and procedures is concerned with the design and implementation of procedures for the accumulation and reporting of accounting data to all interested users. In performing this function, the accountant must evaluate the usefulness of various types of data processing equipment for the firm. The systems accountant must also devise appropriate "checks and balances" to safeguard business assets and provide for an information flow that will be efficient and helpful to management. The accounting system must provide financial and managerial accounting data, as discussed previously.

General accounting is primarily concerned with the recording of transactions and the periodic preparation of the basic financial statements. Of particular importance to this area is the gathering of data in conformity with the generally accepted accounting principles for preparing the basic financial statements.

Budgets and budget analyses focuses on the plan for financial operations for future periods and, through records and summaries, focuses on the comparison of actual operations with these plans. This function provides much of the information for planning and controlling operations.

Special reports and analyses is concerned with data that will be useful to management in analyzing current problems and considering alternate courses for future operations. Much of the analysis focuses on providing data related to specific problems that confront management and identifying alternative courses of action related to proposed new projects. Often the accountants who perform this function prepare special reports according to the requirements of regulatory agencies.

Taxes encompasses the preparation of tax returns and the consideration of the tax consequences of proposed business transactions or alternate courses of action. Accountants in this area must be familiar with the tax statutes affecting their business and must also keep up-to-date on administrative regulations and court decisions on tax cases.

Internal audit is a staff of company employees whose principal responsibility is to determine to what extent, if any, the various operating units are deviating from the policies and procedures prescribed by management.

Regardless of the makeup of the controller's department, the main responsibility of the department is to assist managers in carrying out their responsibilities. Since managerial accountants work closely with management, it is not surprising that many managerial accountants are promoted to top management positions.

MANUFACTURING OPERATIONS

Manufacturers employ labor and use machinery to change materials into finished products. In thus changing the form of goods, their activities differ from those of merchandisers. The furniture manufacturer, for example, changes lumber and other materials into furniture. The furniture dealer in turn purchases the finished goods from the manufacturer and sells them without additional processing.

Some functions of manufacturing companies, such as selling, administration, and financing, are like those of merchandising organizations. The accounting procedures for these functions are the same for both types of enterprises.

Accounting procedures for manufacturing businesses must also provide for the accumulation of the accounting data identified with the production processes. Additional ledger accounts are needed and internal controls must be established over the manufacturing operations. Periodic reports to management and other interested parties must include data that will be useful in measuring the efficiency of manufacturing operations and in guiding future operations.

The cost of merchandise acquired for resale to customers is a composite of invoice prices and various additions and deductions to cover such items as delivery charges, allowances, and cash discounts. The merchandise is sold rather than consumed, and the amount sold is called the **cost of merchandise sold**. The cost of manufacturing a product includes not only the cost of tangible materials but also the many costs incurred in changing the materials into a finished product ready for sale. The cost of the manufactured product sold is called the **cost of goods sold**.

Cost of Manufactured Products

As discussed in Chapter 7, manufacturing businesses maintain three inventory accounts: **finished goods, work in process,** and **materials**. The finished goods inventory and work in process inventory are composed of three manufacturing costs: **direct materials** cost, which is the delivered cost of the materials that enter directly into the finished product; **direct labor** cost, which is the wages of the factory workers who change the materials into a finished product; and **factory overhead** cost, which includes all of the remaining costs of operating the factory. The direct materials, direct labor, and factory overhead costs incurred in the process of manufacturing are reported on the balance sheet as work in process inventory until the goods are completed. After the goods are completed, they are reported as finished goods inventory on the balance sheet. The goods that have been sold are reported on the income statement as cost of goods sold. The relationship between the costs incurred in the manufacturing process, inventories, and the cost of goods sold is illustrated in the top portion of the diagram on page 505. The relationship between purchases of merchandise, merchandise inventory, and the cost of merchandise sold is illustrated in the bottom portion of the diagram.

Accounting Systems

Two basic accounting systems are commonly used by manufacturers: general accounting systems and cost accounting systems. A general accounting system is essentially an extension to manufacturing operations of the common system for merchandising enterprises which use periodic inventory procedures.[1] A cost accounting system uses perpetual inventory procedures and provides more detailed information concerning costs of production.

In the remainder of this chapter, the basic concepts of cost accounting systems for manufacturing operations are described, followed by a discussion and illustration of one of the two main types of cost accounting systems. The other main type of cost accounting system is illustrated in Chapter 16.

---

[1]The basic principles of a general accounting system are presented in Appendix D.

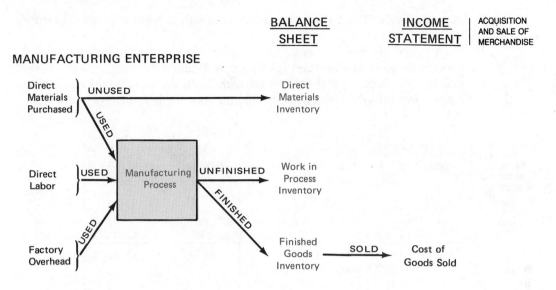

MANUFACTURING ENTERPRISE

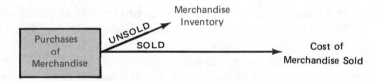

MERCHANDISING ENTERPRISE

COST ACCOUNTING SYSTEM FOR MANUFACTURING OPERATIONS

Through the use of perpetual inventory procedures, a cost accounting system achieves greater accuracy in the determination of costs than is possible with a general accounting system that uses periodic inventory procedures. Cost accounting procedures also permit far more effective control by supplying data on the costs incurred by each factory department and the unit cost of manufacturing each type of product. Such procedures provide not only data useful to management in minimizing costs but also other valuable information about production methods to use, quantities to produce, product lines to promote, and sales prices to charge.

Perpetual Inventory Procedures

Perpetual inventory controlling accounts and subsidiary ledgers are maintained for materials, work in process, and finished goods in cost accounting systems. Each of these accounts is debited for all additions and is credited for all deductions. The balance of each account thus represents the inventory on hand.

All expenditures incidental to manufacturing move through the work in process account, the finished goods account, and eventually into the cost of goods sold account. The flow of costs through the perpetual inventory accounts and into the cost of goods sold account is illustrated as follows:

FLOW OF COSTS
THROUGH
PERPETUAL
INVENTORY
ACCOUNTS

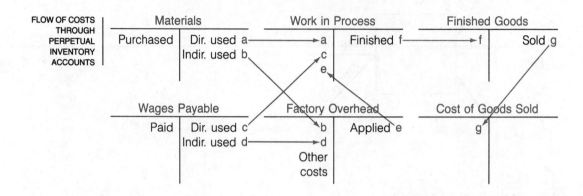

Materials and factory labor used in production are classified as direct and indirect. The materials and the factory labor used directly in the process of manufacturing are debited to Work in Process (**a** and **c** in the diagram). The materials and the factory labor used that do not enter directly into the finished product are debited to Factory Overhead (**b** and **d** in the diagram). Examples of indirect materials are oils and greases, abrasives and polishes, cleaning supplies, gloves, drilling soap, and brushes. Examples of indirect labor are salaries of supervisors, inspectors, material handlers, security guards, and janitors. The proper amount of factory overhead costs are transferred to Work in Process (**e** in the diagram). The costs of the goods finished are transferred from Work in Process to Finished Goods (**f** in the diagram). When the goods are sold, their costs are transferred from Finished Goods to Cost of Goods Sold (**g** in the diagram).

The number of accounts presented in the flowchart was limited in order to simplify the illustration. In practice, manufacturing operations may require many processing departments, each requiring separate work in process and factory overhead accounts.

Types of Cost Accounting Systems

There are two main types of cost systems for manufacturing operations — job order cost and process cost. Each of the two systems is widely used, and a manufacturer may use a job order cost system for some of its products and a process cost system for others.

A **job order cost system** provides for a separate record of the cost of each particular quantity of product that passes through the factory. It is best suited to industries that manufacture goods to fill special orders from customers and to industries that produce different lines of products for stock. It is also appropriate when standard products are manufactured in batches rather than on a continuous basis. In a job order cost system, a summary such as the following would show the cost incurred in completing a job.

Job 565
1,000 Units of Product X200

Direct materials used.	$2,380
Direct labor used	4,400
Factory overhead applied.	3,080
Total cost	$9,860
Unit cost ($9,860 ÷ 1,000).	$ 9.86

Under a **process cost system**, the costs are accumulated for each of the departments or processes within the factory. A process system is best used by manufacturers of like units of product that are not distinguishable from each other during a continuous production process.

JOB ORDER COST SYSTEMS

The basic concepts of job order cost systems are illustrated in this chapter, while process cost systems are discussed in Chapter 16. To simplify the illustration, a nondepartmentalized operation is assumed. In factories with departmentalized operations, costs are accumulated in factory overhead and work in process accounts maintained for each department. The discussion focuses attention on the source documents that serve as the basis for the entries in the job order cost system and to the managerial uses of cost accounting in planning and controlling business operations.

Materials

Procedures used in the procurement and issuance of materials differ considerably among manufacturers and even among departments of a particular manufacturer. The discussion that follows is confined to the basic principles, however, and will disregard relatively minor variations and details.

Some time in advance of the date that production of a certain commodity is to begin, the department responsible for scheduling informs the purchasing department, by means of **purchase requisitions,** of the materials that will be needed. The purchasing department then issues the necessary **purchase orders** to suppliers. After the goods have been received and inspected, the receiving department personnel prepare a receiving report, showing the quantity received and its condition. Quantities, unit costs, and total costs of the goods billed, as reported on the supplier's invoice, are then compared with the purchase order and the receiving report to make sure that the amounts billed agree with the materials ordered and received. After such verifications, the invoice is recorded as a debit to Materials and a credit to Accounts Payable.

The account Materials in the general ledger is a controlling account. A separate account for each type of material is maintained in a subsidiary ledger called the materials ledger. Details as to quantity and cost of materials received are recorded in the materials ledger on the basis of the receiving reports or purchase invoices. A typical form of materials ledger account is illustrated as follows:

MATERIALS LEDGER ACCOUNT

MATERIAL NO. 23   **ORDER POINT** *1,000*

RECEIVED			ISSUED			BALANCE			
REC. REPORT NO.	QUAN- TITY	AMOUNT	MAT. REQ. NO.	QUAN- TITY	AMOUNT	DATE	QUAN- TITY	AMOUNT	UNIT PRICE
						Jan. 1	1,200	600.00	.50
			672	500	250.00	4	700	350.00	.50
196	3,000	1,620.00				8	700	350.00	.50
							3,000	1,620.00	.54
			704	800	404.00	18	2,900	1,566.00	.54

The accounts in the materials ledger may also be used as an aid in maintaining proper inventory quantities of stock items. Frequent comparisons of quantity balances with predetermined order points enable management to avoid costly idle time caused by lack of materials. The subsidiary ledger form may also include columns for recording quantities ordered and dates of the purchase orders.

Materials are transferred from the storeroom to the factory in response to materials requisitions, which may be issued by the manufacturing department concerned or by a central scheduling department. Storeroom personnel record the issuances on the materials requisition by inserting the physical quantity data. Transfer of responsibility for the materials is evidenced by the signature or initials of the storeroom and factory personnel concerned. The requisition is then routed to the materials ledger clerk, who inserts unit prices and amounts. A typical materials requisition is illustrated as follows:

MATERIALS REQUISITION

Job No. 62

Requisition No. 704

Authorized by R. A. Sanders

Date January 18, 19--

Description	Quantity Authorized	Quantity Issued	Unit Price	Amount
Material No. 23	800	700 100	$.50 .54	$350 54
Total issued				$404

Issued by M. K.

Received by J. B.

The completed requisition serves as the basis for posting quantities and dollar data to the materials ledger accounts. In the illustration, the first-in, first-out pricing method was used. A summary of the materials requisitions completed during the month serves as the basis for transferring the cost of materials from the controlling account in the general ledger to the controlling accounts for work in process and factory overhead. The flow of materials into production is illustrated by the following entry:

Work in Process...................................	13,000	
Factory Overhead	840	
Materials		13,840

The perpetual inventory system for materials has three important advantages: (1) it provides for prompt and accurate charging of materials to jobs and factory overhead, (2) it permits the work of inventory-taking to be spread out rather than concentrated at the end of a fiscal period, and (3) it aids in the disclosure of inventory shortages or other irregularities. As physical quantities of the various materials are determined, the actual inventories are compared with the balances of the respective subsidiary ledger accounts. The causes of significant differences between the two should be determined and the responsibility for the differences assigned to specific individuals. Remedial action can then be taken.

Factory Labor

Unlike materials, factory labor is not tangible, nor is it acquired and stored in advance of its use. Hence, there is no perpetual inventory account for labor. The two main objectives in accounting for labor are (1) determination of the correct amount to be paid each employee for each payroll period, and (2) appropriate allocation of labor costs to factory overhead and individual job orders.

The amount of time spent by an employee in the factory is usually recorded on **clock cards**, which are also called **in-and-out cards.** The amount of time spent by each employee and the labor cost incurred for each individual job, or for factory overhead, are recorded on **time tickets.** A typical time ticket form is illustrated as follows:

TIME
TICKET

Time Ticket				
Employee Name Gail Berry			No. 4521	
Employee No. 240			Date January 18, 19--	
Description of work Finishing			Job No. 62	
Time Started	Time Stopped	Hours Worked	Hourly Rate	Cost
10:00	12:00	2	$6.50	$13.00
1:00	2:00	1	6.50	6.50
Total cost				$19.50
Approved by T. D.				

The times reported on an employee's time tickets are compared with the related clock cards as an internal check on the accuracy of payroll disbursements. A summary of the time tickets at the end of each month serves as the basis for recording the direct and indirect labor costs incurred. The flow of labor costs into production is illustrated by the following entry:

Work in Process	10,000	
Factory Overhead	2,200	
Wages Payable		12,200

Factory Overhead

Factory overhead includes all manufacturing costs, except direct materials and direct labor. Examples of factory overhead costs, in addition to indirect materials and indirect labor, are depreciation, electricity, fuel, insurance, and property taxes. It is customary to have a factory overhead controlling account in the general ledger. Details of the various types of cost are accumulated in a subsidiary ledger.

Debits to Factory Overhead come from various sources. For example, the cost of indirect materials is obtained from the summary of the materials requisitions, the cost of indirect labor is obtained from the summary of the time tickets, costs of electricity and water are obtained from invoices, and the cost of depreciation and expired insurance may be recorded as adjustments at the end of the accounting period.

Although factory overhead cannot be specifically identified with particular jobs, it is as much a part of manufacturing costs as direct materials and labor. As the use of machines and automation has increased, factory overhead has represented an ever larger part of total costs. Many items of factory overhead cost are incurred for the entire factory and cannot be directly related to the finished product. The problem is further complicated because some items of factory overhead cost are relatively fixed in amount while others tend to vary according to changes in productivity.

To wait until the end of an accounting period to allocate factory overhead to the various jobs would be quite acceptable from the standpoint of accuracy but highly unsatisfactory in terms of timeliness. If the cost system is to be of maximum usefulness, it is imperative that cost data be available as each job is completed, even though there is a sacrifice in accuracy. It is only through timely reporting that management can make whatever adjustments seem necessary in pricing and manufacturing methods to achieve the best possible combination of revenue and cost on future jobs. Therefore, in order that job costs may be available currently, it is customary to apply factory overhead to production by using a **predetermined factory overhead rate**.

Predetermined Factory Overhead Rate

The factory overhead rate is determined by relating the estimated amount of factory overhead for the forthcoming year to some common activity base, one that will equitably apply the factory overhead costs to the goods manufactured. The common bases include direct labor costs, direct labor hours, and machine hours. For example, if it is estimated that the total factory overhead costs for the year will be $100,000 and that the total direct labor cost will be $125,000, an overhead rate of 80% ($100,000 ÷ $125,000) will be applied to the direct labor cost incurred during the year.

As factory overhead costs are incurred, they are debited to the factory overhead account. The factory overhead costs applied to production are periodically credited to the factory overhead account and debited to the work in process account. The application of factory overhead costs to production (80% of direct labor cost of $10,000) is illustrated by the following entry:

Work in Process.....................................	8,000	
Factory Overhead		8,000

Inevitably, factory overhead costs applied and actual factory overhead costs incurred during a particular period will differ. If the amount applied exceeds the actual costs, the factory overhead account will have a credit balance and the overhead is said to be overapplied or **overabsorbed.** If the amount applied is less than the actual costs, the account will have a debit balance and the overhead is said to be underapplied or **underabsorbed.** Both cases are illustrated in the following account:

ACCOUNT FACTORY OVERHEAD				ACCOUNT NO.	
Date	Item	Debit	Credit	Balance	
				Debit	Credit
May 1	Balance				200
31	Costs incurred	8,320			
31	Cost applied		8,000	120	

Underapplied Balance

Overapplied Balance

Disposition of Factory Overhead Balance

The balance in the factory overhead account is carried forward from month to month until the end of the year. The amount of the balance is reported on interim balance sheets as a deferred item.

The nature of the balance in the factory overhead account (underapplied or overapplied), as well as the amount, will change during the year. If there is a decided trend in either direction and the amount is substantial, the reason should be determined. If the variation is caused by alterations in manufacturing methods or by substantial changes in production goals, it may be advisable to revise the factory overhead rate. The accumulation of a large underapplied balance is more serious than a trend in the opposite direction and may indicate inefficiencies in production methods, excessive expenditures, or a combination of factors.

Despite any corrective actions that may be taken to avoid an underapplication or overapplication of factory overhead, the account will usually have a balance at the end of the fiscal year. Since the balance represents the underapplied or overapplied factory overhead applicable to the operations of the year just ended, it is not proper to report it in the year-end balance sheet as a deferred item.

There are two main alternatives for disposing of the balance of factory overhead at the end of the year: (1) by allocation of the balance among work in process, finished goods, and cost of goods sold accounts on the basis of the total amounts of applied factory overhead included in those accounts at the end of the year, or (2) by transfer of the balance to the cost of goods sold account. Theoretically, only the first alternative is sound because it represents a correction of the estimated overhead rate and brings the accounts into agreement with the costs actually incurred. On the other hand, much time and expense may be required to make the allocation and to revise the unit costs of the work in process and finished goods inventories. Furthermore, in most manufacturing enterprises, a very large part of the total manufacturing costs for the year passes through the work in process and the finished goods accounts into the cost of goods sold account before the end of the year. Therefore, unless the total amount of the underapplied or overapplied balance is great, it is satisfactory to transfer it to Cost of Goods Sold.

Work in Process

Costs incurred for the various jobs are debited to Work in Process. The job costs described in the preceding sections may be summarized as follows:

Direct materials, $13,000 — Work in Process debited and Materials credited; data obtained from summary of materials requisitions.

Direct labor, $10,000 — Work in Process debited and Wages Payable credited; data obtained from summary of time tickets.

Factory overhead, $8,000 — Work in process debited and Factory Overhead credited; data obtained by applying overhead rate to direct labor cost (80% of $10,000).

The work in process account to which these costs were charged is illustrated as follows:

ACCOUNT	WORK IN PROCESS				ACCOUNT NO.	
Date	Item	Debit	Credit	Balance		
				Debit	Credit	
May 1	Balance			3,000	
31	Direct materials	13,000		16,000	
31	Direct labor	10,000		26,000	
31	Factory overhead	8,000		34,000	
31	Jobs completed		31,920	2,080	

The work in process account is a controlling account that contains summary information only. The details concerning the costs incurred on each job order are accumulated in a subsidiary ledger known as the **cost ledger.** Each account in the cost ledger, called a **job cost sheet,** has spaces for recording all direct materials and direct labor chargeable to the job and for the application of factory overhead at the predetermined rate. Postings to the job cost sheets are made from materials requisitions and time tickets or from summaries of these documents.

The four cost sheets in the subsidiary ledger for the work in process account illustrated are summarized as follows:

COST LEDGER

Job 71 (Summary)	
Balance...................	3,000
Direct materials	2,000
Direct labor...............	2,400
Factory overhead	1,920
	9,320

Job 73 (Summary)	
Direct materials	6,000
Direct labor...............	4,000
Factory overhead	3,200
	13,200

Job 72 (Summary)	
Direct materials	4,000
Direct labor...............	3,000
Factory overhead	2,400
	9,400

Job 74 (Summary)	
Direct materials	1,000
Direct labor...............	600
Factory overhead	480
	2,080

The relationship between the work in process controlling account on page 513 and the subsidiary cost ledger may be observed in the following tabulation:

Work in Process (Controlling)		Cost Ledger (Subsidiary)	
Beginning balance..........	$ 3,000 ←→	Beginning balance	
		Job 71	$ 3,000
		Direct materials	
		Job 71	$ 2,000
Direct materials	$13,000 ←→	Job 72	4,000
		Job 73	6,000
		Job 74	1,000
			$13,000
		Direct labor	
		Job 71	$ 2,400
Direct labor...............	$10,000 ←→	Job 72	3,000
		Job 73	4,000
		Job 74	600
			$10,000

Factory overhead..........	$ 8,000 ←→	Factory overhead	
		Job 71..................	$ 1,920
		Job 72..................	2,400
		Job 73..................	3,200
		Job 74..................	480
			$ 8,000

Jobs completed...........	$31,920 ←→	Jobs completed	
		Job 71..................	$ 9,320
		Job 72..................	9,400
		Job 73..................	13,200
			$31,920

Ending balance...........	$ 2,080 ←→	Ending balance	
		Job 74..................	$ 2,080

The data in the cost ledger were presented in summary form for illustrative purposes. A job cost sheet for Job 72, providing for the current accumulation of cost elements entering into the job order and for a summary when the job is completed, is as follows:

JOB COST SHEET

Job No. 72   Date _____ May 7, 19-- _____

Item 5,000 Type C Containers   Date wanted _____ May 23, 19-- _____

For Stock   Date completed _____ May 21, 19-- _____

Direct Materials		Direct Labor				Summary	
Mat. Req. No.	Amount	Time Summary No.	Amount	Time Summary No.	Amount	Item	Amount
834	800.00	2202	83.60	2248	122.50	Direct materials	4,000.00
838	1,000.00	2204	208.40	2250	187.30	Direct labor	3,000.00
841	1,400.00	2205	167.00	2253	155.40	Factory overhead (80% of direct labor cost)	2,400.00
864	800.00	2210	229.00		3,000.00		
	4,000.00	2211	198.30				
		2213	107.20			Total cost	9,400.00
		2216	110.00				
		2222	277.60			No. of units finished	5,000
		2224	217.40			Cost per unit	1.88
		2225	106.30				
		2231	153.20				
		2234	245.20				
		2237	170.00				
		2242	261.60				

When Job 72 was completed, the direct materials costs and the direct labor costs were totaled and entered in the Summary column. Factory overhead was added at the predetermined rate of 80% of the direct labor cost, and the total cost of the job was determined. The total cost of the job, $9,400, divided by the number of units produced, 5,000, yielded a unit cost of $1.88 for the Type C Containers produced.

Upon the completion of Job 72, the job cost sheet was removed from the cost ledger and filed for future reference. At the end of the accounting period, the sum of the total costs on all cost sheets completed during the period is determined and the following entry is made:

```
Finished Goods.....................................    31,920
    Work in Process ..................................            31,920
```

The remaining balance in the work in process account represents the total cost charged to the uncompleted job cost sheets.

Finished Goods and Cost of Goods Sold

The finished goods account is a controlling account. The related subsidiary ledger, which has an account for each kind of commodity produced, is called the **finished goods ledger** or **stock ledger**. Each account in the subsidiary finished goods ledger provides columns for recording the quantity and the cost of goods manufactured, the quantity and the cost of goods shipped, and the quantity, the total cost, and the unit cost of goods on hand. An account in the finished goods ledger is illustrated as follows:

FINISHED GOODS LEDGER ACCOUNT

ITEM: TYPE C CONTAINER

MANUFACTURED			SHIPPED			BALANCE			
JOB ORDER NO.	QUAN-TITY	AMOUNT	SHIP. ORDER NO.	QUAN-TITY	AMOUNT	DATE	QUAN-TITY	AMOUNT	UNIT COST
						May 1	2,000	3,920.00	1.96
			643	2,000	3,920.00	8	—	—	—
72	5,000	9,400.00				21	5,000	9,400.00	1.88
			646	2,000	3,760.00	23	3,000	5,640.00	1.88

Just as there are various methods of pricing materials entering into production, there are various methods of determining the cost of the finished goods sold. In the illustration, the first-in, first-out method is used. The quantities shipped are posted to the finished goods ledger from a copy of the shipping order or other memorandum. The finished goods ledger clerk then records on the copy of the shipping order the unit cost and the total amount of the commodity sold. A summary of the cost data on these shipping orders becomes the basis for the following entry:

Cost of Goods Sold	30,168	
Finished Goods		30,168

If goods are returned by a buyer and are put back in stock, it is necessary to debit Finished Goods and credit Cost of Goods Sold for the cost.

Sales

For each sale of finished goods, it is necessary to maintain a record of both the cost price and the selling price of the goods sold. As previously stated, the cost data may be recorded on the shipping orders. As each sale occurs, the cost of the goods billed is recorded by debiting Cost of Goods Sold and crediting Finished Goods. The selling price of the goods sold is recorded by debiting Accounts Receivable (or Cash) and crediting Sales.

ILLUSTRATION OF JOB ORDER COST ACCOUNTING

To illustrate further the procedures described in the preceding sections, assume that the Spencer Co. uses a job order cost accounting system. The trial balance of the general ledger on January 1, the first day of the fiscal year, is as follows:

Spencer Co.
Trial Balance
January 1, 19--

Cash	85,000	
Accounts Receivable	73,000	
Finished Goods	40,000	
Work in Process	20,000	
Materials	30,000	
Prepaid Expenses	2,000	
Plant Assets	850,000	
Accumulated Depreciation—Plant Assets		473,000
Accounts Payable		70,000
Wages Payable		15,000
Common Stock		500,000
Retained Earnings		42,000
	1,100,000	1,100,000

A summary of the transactions and the adjustments for January, followed in each case by the related journal entry, is presented below and on pages 519 and 520. In practice, the transactions would be recorded daily.

(a) *Materials purchased and prepaid expenses incurred.*

Summary of receiving reports:

Material A	$ 29,000
Material B	17,000
Material C	16,000
Material D	4,000
Total	$ 66,000

Entry:			
Materials		66,000	
Prepaid Expenses		1,000	
Accounts Payable			67,000

(b) *Materials requisitioned for use.*

Summary of requisitions:

By Use

Job 1001	$12,000	
Job 1002	26,000	
Job 1003	22,000	$ 60,000
Factory Overhead		3,000
Total		$ 63,000

By Types

Material A	$27,000	
Material B	18,000	
Material C	15,000	
Material D	3,000	
Total		$ 63,000

Entry:			
Work in Process		60,000	
Factory Overhead		3,000	
Materials			63,000

(c) *Factory labor used.*

Summary of time tickets:

Job 1001................. $ 60,000
Job 1002................. 30,000
Job 1003................ 10,000 $100,000
Factory Overhead.......... 20,000
Total $120,000

Entry: Work in Process 100,000
Factory Overhead 20,000
Wages Payable 120,000

(d) *Other costs incurred.*

Entry: Factory Overhead........................... 56,000
Selling Expenses............................. 25,000
General Expenses........................... 10,000
Accounts Payable.......................... 91,000

(e) *Expiration of prepaid expenses.*

Entry: Factory Overhead........................... 1,000
Selling Expenses........................... 100
General Expenses........................... 100
Prepaid Expenses.......................... 1,200

(f) *Depreciation.*

Entry: Factory Overhead........................... 7,000
Selling Expenses........................... 200
General Expenses........................... 100
Accumulated Depreciation—Plant Assets 7,300

(g) *Application of factory overhead costs to jobs.* The predetermined rate was 90% of direct labor cost.

Summary of factory overhead applied:

Job 1001 (90% of $60,000)........... $ 54,000
Job 1002 (90% of $30,000)........... 27,000
Job 1003 (90% of $10,000).......... 9,000
Total .... $ 90,000

Entry: Work in Process 90,000
Factory Overhead 90,000

(h) Jobs completed.

Summary of completed job cost sheets:

Job 1001	$146,000
Job 1002	83,000
Total	$229,000

Entry:			
Finished Goods		229,000	
Work in Process			229,000

(i) Sales and cost of goods sold.

Summary of sales invoices and shipping orders:

	Sales Price	Cost Price
Product X	$ 19,600	$ 15,000
Product Y	165,100	125,000
Product Z	105,300	80,000
Total	$290,000	$220,000

Entry:			
Accounts Receivable		290,000	
Sales			290,000
Entry: Cost of Goods Sold		220,000	
Finished Goods			220,000

(j) Cash received.

Entry:			
Cash		300,000	
Accounts Receivable			300,000

(k) Cash disbursed.

Entry:			
Accounts Payable		190,000	
Wages Payable		125,000	
Cash			315,000

The flow of costs through the manufacturing accounts, together with summary details of the subsidiary ledgers, is illustrated on page 521. Entries in the accounts are identified by letters to facilitate comparisons with the foregoing summary journal entries.

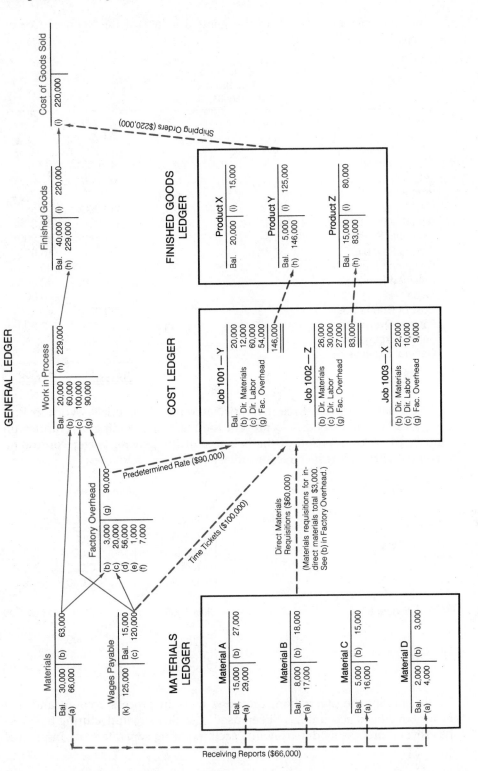

FLOW OF COSTS THROUGH JOB ORDER COST ACCOUNTS

The trial balance taken from the general ledger of the Spencer Co. on January 31 is as follows:

Spencer Co.
Trial Balance
January 31, 19--

Cash	70,000	
Accounts Receivable	63,000	
Finished Goods	49,000	
Work in Process	41,000	
Materials	33,000	
Prepaid Expenses	1,800	
Plant Assets	850,000	
Accumulated Depreciation—Plant Assets		480,300
Accounts Payable		38,000
Wages Payable		10,000
Common Stock		500,000
Retained Earnings		42,000
Sales		290,000
Cost of Goods Sold	220,000	
Factory Overhead		3,000
Selling Expenses	25,300	
General Expenses	10,200	
	1,363,300	1,363,300

The balances of the three inventory accounts—Materials, Work in Process, and Finished Goods—represent the respective ending inventories on January 31. A comparison of the balances of the general ledger controlling accounts with their respective subsidiary ledgers is as follows:

CONTROLLING AND SUBSIDIARY ACCOUNTS COMPARED

Controlling Accounts		*Subsidiary Ledgers*		
Account	Balance	Account	Balance	
		Material A	$17,000	
Materials	$33,000 ⟷	Material B	7,000	
		Material C	6,000	
		Material D	3,000	$33,000
Work in Process	$41,000 ⟷	Job 1003		$41,000
		Product X	$ 5,000	
Finished Goods	$49,000 ⟷	Product Y	26,000	
		Product Z	18,000	$49,000

To simplify the illustration, only one work in process account and one factory overhead account have been used. Usually, a manufacturing business has several processing departments, each requiring separate work in process and factory overhead accounts. In the illustration, one predetermined rate was used in applying the factory overhead to jobs. In a factory with several processing departments, a single factory overhead rate may not provide accurate product costs and effective cost control. A single rate for the entire factory cannot take into consideration such factors as differences among departments in the nature of their operations and in amounts of factory overhead incurred. In such cases, each factory department should have a separate factory overhead rate. For example, in a factory with twenty distinct operating departments, one department might have an overhead rate of 110% of direct labor cost, another a rate of $4 per direct labor hour, and another a rate of $3.50 per machine hour.

The following financial statements are based on the data for Spencer Co. It should be noted that the overapplied factory overhead on January 31 is reported on the balance sheet as a deferred item.

Spencer Co. Income Statement For Month Ended January 31, 19--		
Sales..		$290,000
Cost of goods sold................................		220,000
Gross profit..		$ 70,000
Operating expenses:		
Selling expenses............................	$25,300	
General expenses...........................	10,200	
Total operating expenses...................		35,500
Income from operations		$ 34,500

Spencer Co. Retained Earnings Statement For Month Ended January 31, 19--	
Retained earnings, January 1, 19--	$42,000
Income for the month	34,500
Retained earnings, January 31, 19--	$76,500

Spencer Co.
Balance Sheet
January 31, 19--

Assets

Current assets:			
Cash		$ 70,000	
Accounts receivable		63,000	
Inventories:			
Finished goods	$49,000		
Work in process	41,000		
Materials	33,000	123,000	
Prepaid expenses		1,800	
Total current assets			$257,800
Plant assets:			
Plant assets		$850,000	
Less accumulated depreciation		480,300	369,700
Total assets			$627,500

Liabilities

Current liabilities:			
Accounts payable		$38,000	
Wages payable		10,000	
Total current liabilities		$ 48,000	
Deferred credits:			
Factory overhead		3,000	
Total liabilities			$ 51,000

Stockholders' Equity

Common stock		$500,000	
Retained earnings		76,500	
Total stockholders' equity			576,500
Total liabilities and stockholders' equity			$627,500

Self-Examination Questions
(Answers at end of chapter.)

1. An example of a factory overhead cost is:
   A. gloves for factory workers
   B. salaries for factory plant supervisors
   C. salaries for material handlers
   D. all of the above

2. For which of the following would the job order cost system be appropriate?
   A. Antique furniture repair shop
   B. Rubber manufacturer
   C. Coal manufacturer
   D. All of the above

3. Materials are transferred from the storeroom to the factory in response to:
   A. purchase requisitions
   B. purchase orders
   C. receiving reports
   D. materials requisitions

4. If the factory overhead account has a credit balance, factory overhead is said to be:

A. underapplied

B. overapplied

C. underabsorbed

D. none of the above

5. The details concerning the costs incurred on each job order are accumulated in a subsidiary ledger known as a:

A. cost ledger

B. job cost sheet

C. stock ledger

D. none of the above

15–1. The usefulness of the managerial accountant's reports for management depends upon what five characteristics?

Discussion Questions

15–2. Alexander Company is contemplating the expansion of its operations through the purchase of the assets of Zimmer Lumber Company. Included among the assets of Zimmer Lumber Company is lumber purchased for $275,000 and having a current replacement cost of $310,000. Which cost ($275,000 or $310,000) is relevant for the decision to be made by Alexander Company? Briefly explain the reason for your answer.

15–3. A bank loan officer is evaluating a request for a loan that is to be secured by a mortgage on the borrower's property. The property cost $450,000 twenty years ago and has a current market value of $600,000. Which figure, $450,000 or $600,000, is relevant for the loan officer's use in evaluating the request for the loan? Discuss.

15–4. What is meant by cost-benefit balance as it relates to the preparation of management reports?

15–5. Briefly describe the two basic functions of management.

15–6. (a) Differentiate between a department with line responsibility and a department with staff responsibility. (b) In an organization that has a sales department and a personnel department, among others, which of the two departments has (1) a line responsibility and (2) a staff responsibility?

15–7. (a) What is the role of the controller in a business organization? (b) Does the controller have a line or a staff responsibility?

15–8. What is the principal responsibility of the staff of internal auditors?

15–9. Name the three inventory accounts for a manufacturing business.

15–10. What are the three manufacturing costs included in the finished goods and work in process inventories?

15–11. (a) Name the two principal types of cost accounting systems. (b) Which system provides for a separate record of each particular quantity of product that passes through the factory? (c) Which system accumulates the costs for each department or process within the factory?

15–12. Distinguish between the purchase requisition and the purchase order used in the procurement of materials.

15–13. Briefly discuss how the purchase order, purchase invoice, and receiving report can be used to assist in controlling cash disbursements for materials acquired.

15–14. What document is the source for (a) debiting the accounts in the materials ledger, and (b) crediting the accounts in the materials ledger?

15–15. Briefly discuss how the accounts in the materials ledger can be used as an aid in maintaining appropriate inventory quantities of stock items.

15–16. How does use of the materials requisition help control the issuance of materials for the storeroom?

15–17. Discuss the major advantages of a perpetual inventory system over a periodic system for materials.

15–18. (a) Differentiate between the clock card and the time ticket. (b) Why should the total time reported on an employee's time tickets for a payroll period be compared with the time reported on the employee's clock cards for the same period?

15–19. Discuss how the predetermined factory overhead rate can be used in job order cost accounting to assist management in pricing jobs.

15–20. (a) How is a predetermined factory overhead rate determined? (b) Name three common bases used in determining the rate.

15–21. (a) What is (1) overapplied factory overhead and (2) underapplied factory overhead? (b) If the factory overhead account has a debit balance, was factory overhead underapplied or overapplied? (c) If the factory overhead account has a credit balance at the end of the first month of the fiscal year, where will the amount of this balance be reported on the interim balance sheet?

15–22. At the end of a fiscal year, there was a relatively minor balance in the factory overhead account. What is the simplest satisfactory procedure for the disposition of the balance in the account?

15–23. What name is given to the individual accounts in the cost ledger?

15–24. What document serves as the basis for posting to (a) the direct materials section of the job cost sheet, and (b) the direct labor section of the job cost sheet?

15–25. Describe the source of the data for debiting Work in Process for (a) direct materials, (b) direct labor, and (c) factory overhead.

15–26. What account is the controlling account for (a) the materials ledger, (b) the cost ledger, and (c) the finished goods ledger or stock ledger?

Exercises

15–27. The balance of Material F on February 1 and the receipts and issuances during February are as follows:

Balance, February 1, 120 units at $20.00
Received during February:
    Feb. 8, 300 units at $21.00
    Feb. 15, 240 units at $21.30
    Feb. 22, 180 units at $21.60
Issued during February:
    Feb. 10, 180 units for Job 231
    Feb. 18, 150 units for Job 258
    Feb. 27, 210 units for Job 261

Determine the cost of each of the three issuances under a perpetual system, using (a) the first-in, first-out method and (b) the last-in, first-out method.

15–28. The issuances of materials for the current month are as follows:

Requisition No.	Material	Job No.	Amount
365	W-8	714	$3,640
366	D-2	706	1,876
367	N-06	General factory use	480
368	I-16	720	2,320
369	Q-4	707	3,564

Present the journal entry to record the issuances of materials.

15–29. A summary of the time tickets for the current month follows:

Job No.	Amount	Job No.	Amount
901	$1,120	Indirect labor	$1,280
902	3,020	904	3,120
903	1,850	905	2,310

Present the journal entry to record the factory labor costs.

15–30. Wong Company applies factory overhead to jobs on the basis of machine hours in Department 10 and on the basis of direct labor dollars in Department 11. Estimated factory overhead costs, direct labor costs, and machine hours for the year, and actual factory overhead costs, direct labor costs, and machine hours for August are as follows. Departmental accounts are maintained for work in process and factory overhead.

	Department 10	Department 11
Estimated factory overhead cost for year	$57,600	$153,120
Estimated direct labor costs for year		$264,000
Estimated machine hours for year	12,000 hours	
Actual factory overhead costs for August	$ 6,820	$ 12,820
Actual direct labor costs for August		$ 22,500
Actual machine hours for August	1,350 hours	

(a) Determine the factory overhead rate for Department 10. (b) Determine the factory overhead rate for Department 11. (c) Prepare the journal entry to apply factory overhead to production for August. (d) Determine the balances of the departmental factory overhead accounts as of August 31 and indicate whether the amounts represent overapplied or underapplied factory overhead.

15–31. The following account appears in the ledger after only part of the postings have been completed for April:

Work in Process

Balance, April 1	12,250
Direct Materials	30,820
Direct Labor	48,180
Factory Overhead	26,400

Jobs finished during April are summarized as follows:

Job 602.................	$18,140	Job 611	$29,100
Job 608.................	32,400	Job 618	18,660

(a) Prepare the journal entry to record the jobs completed and (b) determine the cost of the unfinished jobs at April 30.

15–32. Chien Enterprises Inc. began manufacturing operations on October 1. Jobs 101 and 102 were completed during the month, and all costs applicable to them were recorded on the related cost sheets. Jobs 103 and 104 are still in process at the end of the month, and all applicable costs except factory overhead have been recorded on the related cost sheets. In addition to the materials and labor charged directly to the jobs, $1,050 of indirect materials and $1,890 of indirect labor were used during the month. The cost sheets for the four jobs entering production during the month are as follows, in summary form:

Job 101		Job 102	
Direct materials...........	8,750	Direct materials...........	15,680
Direct labor..............	7,000	Direct labor	11,200
Factory overhead	3,500	Factory overhead.........	5,600
Total..................	19,250	Total	32,480

Job 103		Job 104	
Direct materials...........	11,900	Direct materials...........	3,080
Direct labor..............	9,800	Direct labor	4,340
Factory overhead		Factory overhead.........	

Prepare an entry to record each of the following operations for the month (one entry for each operation):
(a) Direct and indirect materials used.
(b) Direct and indirect labor used.
(c) Factory overhead applied (a single overhead rate is used, based on direct labor cost).
(d) Completion of Jobs 101 and 102.

Problems

15–33. Chatham Printing Company uses a job order cost system. The following data summarize the operations related to production for March, the first month of operations:
(a) Materials purchased on account, $69,850.
(b) Materials requisitioned and factory labor used:

	Materials	Factory Labor
Job 101................................	$ 9,900	$5,940
Job 102................................	6,490	4,400
Job 103................................	8,700	3,190
Job 104................................	13,090	8,360
Job 105................................	7,150	4,180
Job 106................................	4,180	1,870
For general factory use	1,490	1,100

(c) Factory overhead costs incurred on account, $13,250.

(d) Depreciation of machinery and equipment, $4,850.

(e) The factory overhead rate is 80% of direct labor cost.

(f) Jobs completed: 101, 102, 104, and 105.

(g) Jobs 101, 102, and 104 were shipped and customers were billed for $30,800, $19,450, and $38,300 respectively.

Instructions:

(1) Prepare entries to record the foregoing summarized operations.

(2) Open T accounts for Work in Process and Finished Goods and post the appropriate entries, using the identifying letters as dates. Insert memorandum account balances as of the end of the month.

(3) Prepare a schedule of unfinished jobs to support the balance in the work in process account.

(4) Prepare a schedule of completed jobs on hand to support the balance in the finished goods account.

15–34. Graco Furniture Company repairs, refinishes, and reupholsters furniture. A job order cost system was installed recently to facilitate (1) the determination of price quotations to prospective customers, (2) the determination of actual costs incurred on each job, and (3) cost reductions.

(If the working papers correlating with the textbook are not used, omit Problem 15-34.)

In response to a prospective customer's request for a price quotation on a job, the estimated cost data are inserted on an unnumbered job cost sheet. If the offer is accepted, a number is assigned to the job and the costs incurred are recorded in the usual manner on the job cost sheet. After the job is completed, reasons for the variances between the estimated and actual costs are noted on the sheet. The data are then available to management in evaluating the efficiency of operations and in preparing quotations on future jobs.

On May 5, an estimate of $510 for reupholstering a couch was given to Jean Ladd. The estimate was based upon the following data:

Estimated direct materials:	
14 meters at $12 per meter................................	$168
Estimated direct labor:	
10 hours at $15 per hour..................................	150
Estimated factory overhead (60% of direct labor cost)	90
Total estimated costs	$408
Markup (25% of production costs)..........................	102
Total estimate...	$510

On May 9, the couch was picked up from the residence of Jean Ladd, 1460 Madison Drive, Clearwater, with a commitment to return it on May 20.

The job was completed on May 18. The related materials requisitions and time tickets are summarized as follows:

Materials Requisition No.	Description	Amount
1215	10 meters at $12	$120
1219	5 meters at $12	60

Time Ticket No.	Description	Amount
3140	4 hours at $15	$ 60
3146	8 hours at $15	120

Instructions:

(1) Complete that portion of the job order cost sheet that would be completed when the estimate is given to the customer.

(2) Assign number 84-5-6 to the job, record the costs incurred, and complete the job order cost sheet. In commenting upon the variances between actual costs and estimated costs, assume that 1 meter of materials was spoiled, the factory overhead rate has been proved to be satisfactory, and an inexperienced employee performed the work.

15–35. The trial balance of Y. M. McInnis Inc., at the beginning of the current fiscal year, is as follows:

Y. M. McInnis Inc.
Trial Balance
October 1, 19--

Cash...	38,610	
Accounts Receivable............................	58,550	
Finished Goods	55,380	
Work in Process...............................	20,300	
Materials	26,840	
Prepaid Expenses	13,240	
Plant Assets	485,200	
Accumulated Depreciation — Plant Assets		274,640
Accounts Payable		19,800
Wages Payable		—
Common Stock.................................		300,000
Retained Earnings.............................		103,680
Sales...		—
Cost of Goods Sold.............................	—	
Factory Overhead	—	
Selling Expenses	—	
General Expenses	—	
	698,120	698,120

Transactions completed during October and adjustments required on October 31 are summarized as follows:

(a) Materials purchased on account		$ 22,900
(b) Materials requisitioned for factory use:		
Direct....................................	$ 21,500	
Indirect	270	21,770
(c) Factory labor costs incurred:		
Direct....................................	$ 10,800	
Indirect	1,520	12,320
(d) Other costs and expenses incurred on account:		
Factory overhead	$ 5,610	
Selling expenses.........................	5,480	
General expenses	4,000	15,090

(e) Cash disbursed:

Accounts payable.........................	$ 41,000	
Wages payable...........................	11,080	$52,080

(f) Depreciation charged:

Factory equipment		3,600
Office equipment.........................		300

(g) Prepaid expenses expired:

Chargeable to factory	$ 540	
Chargeable to selling expenses.............	120	
Chargeable to general expenses............	115	775

(h) Applied factory overhead at a predetermined rate:
   110% of direct labor cost.

(i) Total cost of jobs completed	43,000

(j) Sales, all on account:

Selling price.............................	56,000
Cost price...............................	38,600
(k) Cash received on account	57,000

Instructions:

(1) Open T accounts and record the initial balances indicated in the October 1 trial balance, identifying each as "Bal."
(2) Record the transactions directly in the accounts, using the identifying letters in place of dates.
(3) Prepare an income statement for the month ended October 31, 19--.
(4) Prepare a retained earnings statement for the month ended October 31, 19--.
(5) Prepare a balance sheet as of October 31, 19--.

15–36. The trial balance of the general ledger of Lafayette Corporation as of March 31, the end of the first month of the current fiscal year, is as follows:

Lafayette Corporation
Trial Balance
March 31, 19--

Cash	109,680	
Accounts Receivable	222,360	
Finished Goods...................................	212,760	
Work in Process	73,680	
Materials..	88,560	
Plant Assets.....................................	949,200	
Accumulated Depreciation—Plant Assets..............		423,480
Accounts Payable.................................		159,560
Wages Payable...................................		18,000
Capital Stock....................................		720,000
Retained Earnings		300,780
Sales...		318,480
Cost of Goods Sold	236,160	
Factory Overhead.................................	1,100	
Selling and General Expenses......................	46,800	
	1,940,300	1,940,300

As of the same date, balances in the accounts of selected subsidiary ledgers are as follows:

Finished goods ledger:
   Commodity A, 2,640 units, $23,760; Commodity B, 6,000 units, $132,000; Commodity C, 3,000 units, $57,000.
Cost ledger:
   Job 318, $73,680.
Materials ledger:
   Material X, $48,480; Material Y, $37,920; Material Z, $2,160.

The transactions completed during April are summarized as follows:
(a) Materials were purchased on account as follows:
   Material X $66,000
   Material Y 46,200
   Material Z 1,800
(b) Materials were requisitioned from stores as follows:
   Job 318, Material X, $25,440; Material Y, $20,160 .... $45,600
   Job 319, Material X, $32,400; Material Y, $28,560 60,960
   Job 320, Material X, $16,560; Material Y, $6,720. 23,280
   For general factory use, Material Z 1,920
(c) Time tickets for the month were chargeable as follows:
   Job 318............. $23,520   Job 320 .... $19,680
   Job 319............. 20,160   Indirect labor. 7,200
(d) Factory payroll checks for $77,280 were issued.
(e) Various factory overhead charges of $26,850 were incurred on account.
(f) Depreciation of $10,800 on factory plant and equipment was recorded.
(g) Factory overhead was applied to jobs at 75% of direct labor cost.
(h) Jobs completed during the month were as follows: Job 318 produced 6,720 units of Commodity B; Job 319 produced 4,800 units of Commodity C.
(i) Selling and general expenses of $45,840 were incurred on account.
(j) Payments on account were $171,600.
(k) Total sales on account were $295,080. The goods sold were as follows (use first-in, first-out method): 1,200 units of Commodity A; 6,480 units of Commodity B; 3,600 units of Commodity C.
(l) Cash of $301,200 was received on accounts receivable.

Instructions:
   (1) Open T accounts for the general ledger, the finished goods ledger, the cost ledger, and the materials ledger. Record directly in these accounts the balances as of March 31, identifying them as "Bal." Record the quantities as well as the dollar amounts in the finished goods ledger.
   (2) Prepare entries to record the April transactions. After recording each transaction, post to the T accounts, using the identifying letters as dates. When posting to the finished goods ledger, record quantities as well as dollar amounts.
   (3) Prepare a trial balance.
   (4) Prepare schedules of the account balances in the finished goods ledger, the cost ledger, and the materials ledger.
   (5) Prepare an income statement for the two months ended April 30.

15–37. Following are selected accounts for Fabco Products. For the purposes of this problem, some of the debits and credits have been omitted.

Accounts Receivable

May	1	Balance	59,500	May 31	Collections	127,300
	31	Sales	(A)			

Materials

May	1	Balance	14,350	May 31	Requisitions	(B)
	31	Purchases	21,070			

Work In Process

May	1	Balance	26,250	May 31	Goods finished	(E)
	31	Direct materials	(C)			
	31	Direct labor	28,000			
	31	Factory overhead	(D)			

Finished Goods

May	1	Balance	48,650	May 31	Cost of goods sold	(G)
	31	Goods finished	(F)			

Factory Overhead

May	1	Balance	140	May 31	Applied (75% of direct labor cost)	(H)
	1–31	Costs incurred	22,100			

Cost of Goods Sold

May 31	(I)

Sales

	May 31	(J)

Selected balances at May 31:

Accounts receivable......................	$65,000
Finished goods...........................	30,100
Work in process..........................	22,260
Materials	11,760

Materials requisitions for May included $700 of materials issued for general factory use. All sales are made on account, terms n/30.

Instructions:

(1) Determine the amounts represented by the letters (A) through (J), presenting your computations.

(2) Determine the amount of factory overhead overapplied or underapplied as of May 31.

Alternate
Problems

15–33A. Pendaflex Printing Company uses a job order cost system. The following data summarize production for September, the first month of operations:

(a) Materials purchased on account, $47,850.
(b) Materials requisitioned and factory labor used:

	Materials	Factory Labor
Job 1001	$9,720	$7,630
Job 1002	2,780	1,640
Job 1003	7,100	3,910
Job 1004	3,570	1,580
Job 1005	5,680	2,410
Job 1006	5,150	3,850
For general factory use..............	1,540	2,380

(c) Factory overhead costs incurred on account, $9,390.
(d) Depreciation of machinery and equipment, $4,510.
(e) The factory overhead rate is 60% of direct labor cost.
(f) Jobs completed: 1001, 1002, 1003, and 1004.
(g) Jobs 1001, 1002, and 1004 were shipped and customers were billed for $30,100, $7,300, and $8,500 respectively.

Instructions:

(1) Prepare entries to record the foregoing summarized operations.
(2) Open T accounts for Work in Process and Finished Goods and post the appropriate entries, using the identifying letters as dates. Insert memorandum account balances as of the end of the month.
(3) Prepare a schedule of unfinished jobs to support the balance in the work in process account.
(4) Prepare a schedule of completed jobs on hand to support the balance in the finished goods account.

(If the working papers correlating with the textbook are not used, omit Problem 15-34A).

15–34A. Rubinstein Furniture Company repairs, refinishes, and reupholsters furniture. A job order cost system was installed recently to facilitate (1) the determination of price quotations to prospective customers, (2) the determination of actual costs incurred on each job, and (3) cost reductions.

In response to a prospective customer's request for a price quotation on a job, the estimated cost data are inserted on an unnumbered job cost sheet. If the offer is accepted, a number is assigned to the job and the costs incurred are recorded in the usual manner on the job cost sheet. After the job is completed, reasons for the variances between the estimated and actual costs are noted on the sheet. The data are then available to management in evaluating the efficiency of operations and in preparing quotations on future jobs.

On November 18, an estimate of $742 for reupholstering a chair and couch was given to Chris Joel. The estimate was based upon the following data:

Estimated direct materials:	
20 meters at $16 per meter................................	$320
Estimated direct labor:	
14 hours at $10 per hour.....................................	140
Estimated factory overhead (50% of direct labor cost)	70
Total estimated costs	$530
Markup (40% of production costs)............................	212
Total estimate...	$742

On November 21, the chair and couch were picked up from the residence of Chris Joel, 4810 Beekman Place, Racine, with a commitment to return it on November 30. The job was completed on November 28.

The related materials requisitions and time tickets are summarized as follows:

Materials Requisition No.	Description	Amount
715	6 meters at $16	$ 96
718	10 meters at $16	160
723	6 meters at $16	96

Time Ticket No.	Description	Amount
471	4 hours at $10	$ 40
478	8 hours at $10	80
481	3 hours at $10	30

Instructions:

(1) Complete that portion of the job order cost sheet that would be completed when the estimate is given to the customer.

(2) Assign number 85-11-8 to the job, record the costs incurred, and complete the job order cost sheet. In commenting upon the variances between actual costs and estimated costs, assume that 2 meters of materials were spoiled, the factory overhead rate has been proved to be satisfactory, and an inexperienced employee performed the work.

15–36A. The trial balance of the general ledger of J. J. Koehn Co. as of July 31, the end of the first month of the current fiscal year, is as follows:

J. J. Koehn Co.
Trial Balance
July 31, 19--

Cash	45,700	
Accounts Receivable	92,650	
Finished Goods	88,650	
Work in Process	30,700	
Materials	36,900	
Plant Assets	395,500	
Accumulated Depreciation — Plant Assets		176,450
Accounts Payable		66,485
Wages Payable		7,500
Capital Stock		300,000
Retained Earnings		125,325
Sales		132,700
Cost of Goods Sold	98,400	
Factory Overhead	460	
Selling and General Expenses	19,500	
	808,460	808,460

As of the same date, balances in the accounts of selected subsidiary ledgers are as follows:

Finished goods ledger:
Commodity A, 1,100 units, $9,900; Commodity B, 2,500 units, $55,000; Commodity C, 1,250 units, $23,750.

Cost ledger:
Job 915, $30,700.

Materials ledger:
Material X, $20,200; Material Y, $15,800; Material Z, $900.

The transactions completed during August are summarized as follows:

(a) Materials were purchased on account as follows:
Material X.. $27,500
Material Y.. 19,250
Material Z.. 750

(b) Materials were requisitioned from stores as follows:
Job 915, Material X, $10,600; Material Y, $8,400 .... $19,000
Job 916, Material X, $13,500; Material Y, $11,900 25,400
Job 917, Material X, $6,900; Material Y, $2,800 9,700
For general factory use, Material Z................................. 800

(c) Time tickets for the month were chargeable as follows:
Job 915.................... $9,800   Job 917 .... $8,200
Job 916.................... 8,400   Indirect labor.............. 3,000

(d) Factory payroll checks for $29,700 were issued.

(e) Various factory overhead charges of $4,940 were incurred on account.

(f) Selling and general expenses of $19,100 were incurred on account.

(g) Payments on account were $71,500.

(h) Depreciation of $4,500 on factory plant and equipment was recorded.

(i) Factory overhead was applied to jobs at 50% of direct labor cost.

(j) Jobs completed during the month were as follows: Job 915 produced 2,800 units of Commodity B; Job 916 produced 2,000 units of Commodity C.

(k) Total sales on account were $122,950. The goods sold were as follows (use first-in, first-out method): 500 units of Commodity A; 2,700 units of Commodity B; 1,500 units of Commodity C.

(l) Cash of $125,500 was received on accounts receivable.

Instructions:

(1) Open T accounts for the general ledger, the finished goods ledger, the cost ledger, and the materials ledger. Record directly in these accounts the balances as of July 31, identifying them as "Bal." Record the quantities as well as the dollar amounts in the finished goods ledger.

(2) Prepare entries to record the August transactions. After recording each transaction, post to the T accounts, using the identifying letters as dates. When posting to the finished goods ledger, record quantities as well as dollar amounts.

(3) Prepare a trial balance.

(4) Prepare schedules of the account balances in the finished goods ledger, the cost ledger, and the materials ledger.

(5) Prepare an income statement for the two months ended August 31.

15–37A. Following are selected accounts for Gould Industrial Products. For the purposes of this problem, some of the debits and credits have been omitted.

Accounts Receivable

Aug.	1 Balance	40,800	Aug. 31 Collections	60,175
	31 Sales	(A)		

Materials

Aug.	1 Balance	10,050	Aug. 31 Requisitions	(B)
	31 Purchases	15,190		

Work in Process

Aug.	1 Balance	11,775	Aug. 31 Goods finished	(E)
	31 Direct materials	(C)		
	31 Direct labor	24,000		
	31 Factory overhead	(D)		

Finished Goods

Aug.	1 Balance	5,585	Aug. 31 Cost of goods sold	(G)
	31 Goods finished	(F)		

Factory Overhead

Aug.	1 Balance	200	Aug. 31 Applied (80% of	
	1–31 Costs incurred	18,790	direct labor cost)	(H)

Cost of Goods Sold

Aug.	31	(I)	

Sales

	Aug. 31	(J)

Selected balances at August 31:

Accounts receivable......................	$44,375
Finished goods..........................	11,195
Work in process.........................	14,070
Materials	7,620

Materials requisitions for August included $750 of materials issued for general factory use. All sales are made on account, terms n/30.

Instructions:

(1) Determine the amounts represented by the letters (A) through (J), presenting your computations.

(2) Determine the amount of factory overhead overapplied or underapplied as of August 31.

Mini-Case

15–38. As an assistant cost accountant for Hanratty Industries, you have been assigned to review the activity base for the predetermined factory overhead rate. The president, G. H. Hanratty, has expressed concern that the over- or underapplied overhead has fluctuated excessively over the years.

An analysis of the company's operations and use of the current overhead base (direct materials usage) have narrowed the possible alternative overhead bases to direct labor cost and machine hours. For the past five years, the following data have been gathered:

	1986	1985	1984	1983	1982
Actual overhead......	$ 580,000	$ 540,000	$ 640,000	$ 490,000	$ 450,000
Applied overhead	575,000	565,000	600,000	500,000	440,000
(Over)underapplied overhead........	$ 5,000	$ (25,000)	$ 40,000	$ (10,000)	$ 10,000
Direct labor cost	$1,800,000	$1,400,000	$2,100,000	$1,150,000	$1,050,000
Machine hours.......	363,500	340,000	402,000	302,000	280,000

Instructions:

(1) Calculate a predetermined factory overhead rate for each alternative base, assuming that the rates would have been determined by relating the amount of factory overhead for the past five years to the base.

(2) For each of the past five years, determine the over- or underapplied overhead, based on the two predetermined overhead rates developed in (1).

(3) Which predetermined overhead rate would you recommend? Discuss the basis for your recommendation.

Answers to Self-Examination Questions

1. D Factory overhead includes all manufacturing costs except direct materials and direct labor. Gloves for factory workers (answer A), salaries for factory plant supervisors (answer B), and salaries for material handlers (answer C) are examples of factory overhead items.

2. A Job order cost systems are best suited to businesses manufacturing for special orders from customers, such as would be the case for a repair shop for antique furniture (answer A). A process cost system is best suited for manufacturers of homogeneous units of product, such as rubber (answer B) and coal (answer C).

3. D Materials are transferred from the storeroom to the factory in response to materials requisitions (answer D). Materials needed for production are requested by the department responsible by issuing purchase requisitions (answer A), which serve as the basis for the purchasing department to order the goods by issuing purchase orders (answer B). When the goods are received, the receiving department personnel prepare receiving reports (answer C).

4. B If the amount of factory overhead applied during a particular period exceeds the actual overhead costs, the factory overhead account will have a credit balance and is said to be overapplied (answer B) or overabsorbed. If the amount applied is less than the actual costs, the account will have a debit balance and is said to be underapplied (answer A) or underabsorbed (answer C).

5. A The subsidiary ledger containing the details of each job order is the cost ledger (answer A), while each account in the cost ledger is called a job cost sheet (answer B). The stock ledger (answer C), also called the finished goods ledger, is the subsidiary ledger for the finished goods account and contains an account for each kind of finished product.

CHAPTER 16

Process Cost Systems

CHAPTER OBJECTIVES

Distinguish process cost accounting systems from job order cost accounting systems.

Describe and illustrate a process cost accounting system, including the preparation of a cost of production report.

In many industries, job orders as described in Chapter 15 are not suitable for scheduling production and accumulating the manufacturing costs. Companies manufacturing cement, flour, or paint, for example, do so on a continuous basis. The principal product is a homogeneous mass rather than a collection of distinct units. No useful purpose would be served by maintaining job orders for particular amounts of a product as the material passes through the several stages of production.

PROCESS COST AND JOB ORDER COST SYSTEMS DISTINGUISHED

Many of the methods, procedures, and managerial applications presented in the preceding chapter in the discussion of job order cost systems apply equally to process cost systems. For example, perpetual inventory accounts with subsidiary ledgers for materials, work in process, and finished goods are requisites of both systems. In job order cost accounting, however, the costs of direct materials, direct labor, and factory overhead are charged directly to job orders. In process cost accounting, the costs are charged to processing departments, and the cost of a finished unit is determined by dividing the total cost incurred in each process by the number of units produced. Since all goods produced in a department are identical units, it is not necessary to classify production into job orders.

In factories with departmentalized operations, costs are accumulated in factory overhead and work in process accounts maintained for each department. If there is only one processing department in a factory, the cost accounting procedures are simple. The manufacturing cost elements are charged to the single work in process account, and the unit cost of the finished product is determined by dividing the total cost by the number of units produced.

When the manufacturing procedure requires a sequence of different processes, the output of Process 1 becomes the direct materials of Process 2, the output of Process 2 becomes the direct materials of Process 3, and so on until the finished product emerges. Additional direct materials requisitioned from stores may also be introduced during subsequent processes.

A work in process account for a departmentalized factory is illustrated as follows. In this illustration, the total cost of $96,000 is divided by the output, 10,000 units, to obtain a unit cost of $9.60.

Work in Process — Assembly Department			
Direct materials	32,000	To Sanding Dept., 10,000 units	96,000
Direct labor	40,000	Cost per unit:	
Factory overhead	24,000	$96,000 ÷ 10,000 = $9.60	
	96,000		96,000

SERVICE DEPARTMENTS AND PROCESS COSTS

In a factory with several processes, there may be one or more **service departments** that do not process the materials directly. Examples of service departments are the factory office, the power plant, and the maintenance and repair shop. These departments perform services for the benefit of other production departments. The costs that they incur, therefore, are part of the total manufacturing costs and must be charged to the processing departments.

The services performed by a service department give rise to internal transactions with the processing departments benefited. These internal transactions are recorded periodically in order to charge the factory overhead accounts of the processing departments with their share of the costs incurred by the service departments. The period usually chosen is a month, although a different period of time may be used. To illustrate, assume that the Power Department produced 500 000 kilowatt-hours during the month at a total cost of $30,000, or 6¢ per kilowatt-hour ($30,000 ÷ 500 000). The factory overhead accounts for the departments that used the power are accordingly charged for power at the 6¢ rate. Assuming that during the month the Assembly Department used 200 000 kwh and the Sanding Department used 300 000 kwh, the accounts affected by the interdepartmental transfer of cost would appear as follows:

Power Department			
Fuel	12,000	To Factory Overhead —	
Wages	8,500	Assembly Dept.	12,000
Depreciation	3,000	To Factory Overhead —	
Maintenance	2,500	Sanding Dept.	18,000
Insurance	2,000		
Taxes	1,500		
Miscellaneous	500		
	30,000		30,000

SERVICE DEPARTMENT COSTS CHARGED TO PROCESSING DEPARTMENTS

Factory Overhead — Assembly Dept.		Factory Overhead — Sanding Dept.	
Power	12,000	Power	18,000

Some service departments render services to other service departments. For example, the power department may supply electric current to light the factory office and to operate data processing equipment. At the same time, the factory office provides general supervision for the power department, maintains its payroll records, buys its fuel, and so on. In such cases, the costs of the department rendering the greatest service to other service departments may be distributed first, despite the fact that it receives benefits from other service departments.

PROCESSING COSTS

The accumulated costs transferred from preceding departments and the costs of direct materials and direct labor incurred in each processing department are debited to the related work in process account. Each work in process account is also debited for the factory overhead applied. The costs incurred are summarized periodically, usually at the end of the month. The costs related to the output of each department during the month are then transferred to the next processing department or to Finished Goods, as the case may be. This flow of costs through a work in process account is illustrated as follows:

Work in Process—Sanding Department

10,000 units at $9.60 from Assembly Dept.		96,000	To Polishing Dept., 10,000 units	160,000
Direct labor	36,800		Cost per unit:	
Factory overhead	27,200	64,000	$160,000 ÷ 10,000 = $16	
		160,000		160,000

The three debits in the preceding account may be grouped into two separate categories: (1) direct materials or partially processed materials received from another department, which in this case is composed of 10,000 units received from the Assembly Department, with a total cost of $96,000, and (2) direct labor and factory overhead applied in the Sanding Department, which in this case totaled $64,000. This second group of costs is called the processing cost.

Again referring to the illustration, all of the 10,000 units were completely processed in the Sanding Department and were passed on to the Polishing Department. The $16 unit cost of the product transferred to the Polishing Department is made up of Assembly Department cost of $9.60 ($96,000 ÷ 10,000 units) and processing cost of $6.40 ($64,000 ÷ 10,000 units) incurred in the Sanding Department.

INVENTORIES OF PARTIALLY PROCESSED MATERIALS

In the preceding illustration, all materials entering a process were completely processed at the end of the accounting period. In such a case, the determination of unit costs is quite simple. The total of costs transferred from other departments, direct materials, direct labor, and factory overhead charged to a department, is divided by the number of units completed and passed on to the next department or to finished goods. Often, however, some partially processed materials remain in various stages of production in a department at the end of a period. In this case, the costs in work in process must be allocated between the units that have been completed and transferred to the next process or to finished goods and those that are only partially completed and remain within the department.

To allocate direct materials and transferred costs between the output completed and transferred to the next process and inventory of goods within the department, it is necessary to determine the manner in which materials are placed in production. For some products, all materials must be on hand before any work begins. For other products, materials may be added to production in about the same proportion as processing costs are incurred. In still other situations, materials may enter the process at relatively few points, which may or may not be evenly spaced throughout the process.

To allocate processing costs between the output completed and transferred to the next process and the inventory of goods within the process, it is necessary to determine (1) the number of *equivalent units* of production during the period and (2) the *processing cost per equivalent unit* for the same period. The **equivalent units of production** are the number of units that could have been manufactured from start to finish during the period. To illustrate, assume that there is no inventory of goods in process in a certain processing department at the beginning of the period, that 1,000 units of materials enter the process during the period, and that at the end of the period all of the units are 75% completed. The equivalent production in the processing department for the period would be 750 units (75% of 1,000). Assuming further that the processing costs incurred during the period totaled $15,000, the processing cost per equivalent unit would be $20 ($15,000 ÷ 750).

Usually there is an inventory of partially processed units in the department at the beginning of the period. These units are normally completed during the period and transferred to the next department along with units started and completed in the current period. Other units started in the period are only partially processed and thus make up the ending inventory. To illustrate the computation of equivalent units under such circumstances, the following data are assumed for the Polishing Department:

Inventory within Polishing Department on March 1..... 600 units, ⅓ completed
Completed in Polishing Department and transferred to
    finished goods during March .... 9,800 units, completed
Inventory within Polishing Department on March 31 ... 800 units, ⅖ completed

The equivalent units of production are determined as follows:

To process units in inventory on March 1.......... 600 units × ⅔........	400	DETERMINATION OF EQUIVALENT UNITS OF PRODUCTION
To process units started and completed in March .. 9,800 units − 600 units	9,200	
To process units in inventory on March 31........ 800 units × ⅖........	320	
Equivalent units of production in March...............................	9,920	

The 9,920 equivalent units of production represent the number of units that would have been produced if there had been no inventories within the process either at the beginning or at the end of the period.

Continuing with the illustration, the next step is to allocate the costs incurred in the Polishing Department between the units completed during March and those remaining in process at the end of the month. If materials (including transferred costs) were used and processing costs were incurred uniformly throughout the month, the total costs of the process would be divided by 9,920 units to obtain the unit cost. On the other hand, if all materials were introduced at the beginning of the process, the full materials cost per unit must be assigned to the uncompleted units. The processing costs would then be allocated to the finished and the uncompleted units on the basis of equivalent units of production. Entries in the following account are based on the latter assumption:

ACCOUNT WORK IN PROCESS—POLISHING DEPARTMENT   ACCOUNT NO.

Date		Item	Debit	Credit	Balance	
					Debit	Credit
Mar.	1	Bal., 600 units, ⅓ completed			10,200	
	31	Sanding Dept., 10,000 units at $16	160,000		170,200	
	31	Direct labor	26,640		196,840	
	31	Factory overhead	18,000		214,840	
	31	Goods finished, 9,800 units		200,600		
	31	Bal., 800 units, ⅖ completed			14,240	

The processing costs incurred in the Polishing Department during March total $44,640 ($26,640 + $18,000). The equivalent units of production for March, determined above, is 9,920. The processing cost per equivalent unit is therefore $4.50 ($44,640 ÷ 9,920). Of the $214,840 debited to the Polishing Department, $200,600 was transferred to Finished Goods and $14,240 remained in the account as work in process inventory. The computation of the allocations to finished goods and to inventory is as follows:

ALLOCATION OF DEPARTMENTAL CHARGES TO FINISHED GOODS AND INVENTORY

Goods Finished During March

600 units:	Inventory on March 1, ⅓ completed .... $ 10,200	
	Processing cost in March:	
	600 × ⅔, or 400 units at $4.50 1,800	
	Total	$ 12,000
	(Unit cost: $12,000 ÷ 600 = $20)	
9,200 units:	Materials cost in March, at $16 per unit $147,200	
	Processing cost in March:	
	9,200 at $4.50 per unit 41,400	
	Total	188,600
	(Unit cost: $188,600 ÷ 9,200 = $20.50)	
9,800 units:	Goods finished during March	$200,600

Polishing Department Inventory on March 31

800 units:	Materials cost in March, at $16 per unit............	$ 12,800
	Processing cost in March:	
	800 × ⅖, or 320 at $4.50......................	1,440
800 units:	Polishing Department inventory on March 31.......	$ 14,240

COST OF PRODUCTION REPORT

A report prepared periodically for each processing department sum-marizes (1) the units for which the department is accountable and the dispo-sition of these units and (2) the costs charged to the department and the allocation of these costs. This report, termed the **cost of production report**, may be used as the source of the computation of unit production costs and the allocation of the processing costs in the general ledger to the finished and the uncompleted units. More importantly, the report is used to control costs. Each department head is held responsible for the units entering production and the costs incurred in the department. Any differences in unit product costs from one month to another are studied carefully and the causes of significant differences are determined.

The cost of production report based on the data presented in the preceding section for the Polishing Department is shown on page 546.

JOINT PRODUCTS AND BY-PRODUCTS

In some manufacturing processes, more than one product is produced. In processing cattle, for example, the meat packer produces dressed beef, hides, and other products. In processing logs, the lumber mill produces several grades of lumber in addition to scraps and sawdust. When the output of a manufacturing process consists of two or more different products, the products are either joint products or by-products.

When two or more goods of significant value are produced from a single principal direct material, the products are termed **joint products**. Similarly, the costs incurred in the manufacture of joint products are called **joint costs**. Common examples of joint products are gasoline, naphtha, kerosene, paraf-fin, benzine, and other related goods, all of which come from the processing of crude oil.

If one of the products resulting from a process has little value in relation to the main product or joint products, it is known as a **by-product**. The emergence of a by-product is only incidental to the manufacture of the main product or joint products. By-products may be leftover materials, such as sawdust and scraps of wood in a lumber mill, or they may be separated from the material at the beginning of production, as in the case of cottonseed from raw cotton.

COST OF
PRODUCTION
REPORT

Haworth Manufacturing Company
Cost of Production Report — Polishing Department
For the Month Ended March 31, 19--

Quantities:
  Charged to production:
    In process, March 1................................. 600
    Received from Sanding Department 10,000
    Total units to be accounted for 10,600

  Units accounted for:
    Transferred to finished goods 9,800
    In process, March 31.............................. 800
    Total units accounted for.......................... 10,600

Costs:
  Charged to production:
    In process, March 1.............................. $ 10,200

    March costs:
      Direct materials from Sanding Department ($16 per
        unit)....................................... 160,000

      Processing costs:
        Direct labor .... $ 26,640
        Factory overhead 18,000
        Total processing costs ($4.50 per unit) 44,640
    Total costs to be accounted for.................... $214,840

  Costs allocated as follows:
    Transferred to finished goods:
      600 units at $20 .... $ 12,000
      9,200 units at $20.50.......................... 188,600
      Total cost of finished goods $200,600

    In process, March 31:
      Direct materials (800 units at $16) .... $ 12,800
      Processing costs (800 units × $\frac{2}{5}$ × $4.50) 1,440
      Total cost of inventory in process, March 31 14,240
    Total costs accounted for $214,840

Computations:
  Equivalent units of production:
    To process units in inventory on March 1:
      600 units × $\frac{2}{3}$.................................. 400
    To process units started and completed in March:
      9,800 units − 600 units........................ 9,200
    To process units in inventory on March 31:
      800 units × $\frac{2}{5}$.................................. 320
      Equivalent units of production 9,920

  Unit processing cost:
    $44,640 ÷ 9,920................................... $ 4.50

Accounting for Joint Products

In management decisions concerning the production and sale of joint products, only the relationship of the total revenue to be derived from the entire group to their total production cost is relevant. Nothing is to be gained from an allocation of joint costs to each product because one product cannot be produced without the others. A decision to produce a joint product is in effect a decision to produce all of the products.

Since joint products come from the processing of a common parent material, the assignment of cost to each separate product cannot be based on actual expenditures. It is impossible to determine the amount of cost incurred in the manufacture of each separate product. However, for purposes of inventory valuation, it is necessary to allocate joint costs among the joint products.

One method of allocation commonly used is the **market (sales) value method**. Its main feature is the assignment of costs to the different products according to their relative sales values. To illustrate, assume that 10,000 units of Product X and 50,000 units of Product Y were produced at a total cost of $63,000. The sales values of the two products and the allocation of the joint costs are as follows:

Joint Costs	Joint Product	Units Produced	Sales Value per Unit	Total Sales Value	
$63,000	X	10,000	$3.00	$30,000	ALLOCATION OF JOINT COSTS
	Y	50,000	1.20	60,000	
Total sales value.				$90,000	

Allocation of joint costs:

X: $\frac{30,000}{90,000} \times \$63,000$ $21,000

Y: $\frac{60,000}{90,000} \times \$63,000$ 42,000

Unit cost:
X: $21,000 ÷ 10,000 units. $2.10
Y: $42,000 ÷ 50,000 units. 84

Accounting for By-Products

The amount of manufacturing cost usually assigned to a by-product is the sales value of the by-product reduced by any additional costs necessary to complete and sell it. The amount of cost thus determined is removed from the proper work in process account and transferred to a finished goods inventory account. To illustrate, assume that for a certain period the costs accumulated in Department 4 total $24,400, and that during the same period of time 1,000 units of by-product B, having an estimated value of $200, emerge from the processing in Department 4. Finished Goods—Product B would be debited for $200 and Work in Process—Department 4 would be credited for the same amount, as illustrated in the following accounts:

Work in Process — Department 4		Finished Goods — Product B	
24,400	200 ——————————→ 200		

The accounting for the manufacturing costs remaining in the work in process account and for sale of the by-product would follow the usual procedures.

ILLUSTRATION OF PROCESS COST ACCOUNTING

To illustrate further the basic procedures of the process costing system, assume that Conway Company manufactures Product A. The manufacturing activity begins in Department 1, where all materials enter production. The materials remain in Department 1 for a relatively short time, and there is usually no inventory of work in process in that department at the end of the accounting period. From Department 1, the materials are transferred to Department 2. In Department 2, there are usually inventories at the end of the accounting period. Separate factory overhead accounts are maintained for Departments 1 and 2. Factory overhead is applied at 80% and 50% of direct labor cost for Departments 1 and 2 respectively. There are two service departments, Maintenance and Power.

The trial balance of the general ledger on January 1, the first day of the fiscal year, is as follows:

Conway Company
Trial Balance
January 1, 19--

Cash	39,400	
Accounts Receivable	45,000	
Finished Goods — Product A (1,000 units at $36.50)	36,500	
Work in Process — Department 2 (800 units, ½ completed)	24,600	
Materials	32,000	
Prepaid Expenses	6,150	
Plant Assets	510,000	
Accumulated Depreciation — Plant Assets		295,000
Accounts Payable		51,180
Wages Payable		3,400
Common Stock		250,000
Retained Earnings		94,070
	693,650	693,650

To reduce the illustrative entries to a manageable number and to avoid repetition, the transactions and the adjustments for January are stated as summaries. In practice, the transactions would be recorded from day to day in various journals. The descriptions of the transactions, followed in each case by the entry, are as follows:

(a) Materials purchased and prepaid expenses incurred.

Entry:	Materials..................................	80,500	
	Prepaid Expenses	3,300	
	Accounts Payable		83,800

(b) Materials requisitioned for use.

Entry:	Maintenance Department....................	1,200	
	Power Department........................	6,000	
	Factory Overhead—Department 1	3,720	
	Factory Overhead—Department 2	2,700	
	Work in Process—Department 1	58,500	
	Materials................................		72,120

(c) Factory labor used.

Entry:	Maintenance Department....................	3,600	
	Power Department........................	4,500	
	Factory Overhead—Department 1	2,850	
	Factory Overhead—Department 2	2,100	
	Work in Process—Department 1	24,900	
	Work in Process—Department 2	37,800	
	Wages Payable..........................		75,750

(d) Other costs incurred.

Entry:	Maintenance Department....................	600	
	Power Department........................	900	
	Factory Overhead—Department 1	1,800	
	Factory Overhead—Department 2	1,200	
	Selling Expenses	15,000	
	General Expenses	13,500	
	Accounts Payable		33,000

(e) Expiration of prepaid expenses.

Entry:	Maintenance Department....................	300	
	Power Department........................	750	
	Factory Overhead—Department 1	1,350	
	Factory Overhead—Department 2	1,050	
	Selling Expenses	900	
	General Expenses	600	
	Prepaid Expenses		4,950

(f) Depreciation.

Entry:	Maintenance Department....................	300	
	Power Department........................	1,050	
	Factory Overhead—Department 1	1,800	
	Factory Overhead—Department 2	2,700	
	Selling Expenses	600	
	General Expenses	300	
	Accumulated Depreciation—Plant Assets...		6,750

(g) Distribution of Maintenance Department costs.

Entry: Power Department	300	
Factory Overhead — Department 1	2,700	
Factory Overhead — Department 2	3,000	
Maintenance Department		6,000

(h) Distribution of Power Department costs.

Entry: Factory Overhead — Department 1	5,400	
Factory Overhead — Department 2	8,100	
Power Department		13,500

(i) Application of factory overhead costs to work in process.

The predetermined rates were 80% and 50% of direct labor cost for Departments 1 and 2 respectively. See transaction (c) for the monthly direct labor costs.

Entry: Work in Process — Department 1	19,920	
Work in Process — Department 2	18,900	
Factory Overhead — Department 1		19,920
Factory Overhead — Department 2		18,900

(j) Transfer of production costs from Department 1 to Department 2.

4,100 units were fully processed, and there is no work in process in Department 1 at the beginning or at the end of the month.

Total costs charged to Department 1:	
Direct materials	$ 58,500
Direct labor	24,900
Factory overhead	19,920
Total costs	$103,320

Unit cost of product transferred to Department 2:	
$103,320 ÷ 4,100	$ 25.20

Entry: Work in Process — Department 2	103,320	
Work in Process — Department 1		103,320

(k) Transfer of production costs from Department 2 to Finished Goods.

4,000 units were completed, and the remaining 900 units were ⅔ completed at the end of the month.

Equivalent units of production:	
To process units in inventory on January 1:	
800 × ½	400
To process units started and completed in January:	
4,000 − 800	3,200
To process units in inventory on January 31:	
900 × ⅔	600
Equivalent units of production in January	4,200

Processing costs:

Direct labor (c).............................	$ 37,800
Factory overhead (i).........................	18,900
Total processing costs......................	$ 56,700

Unit processing costs:

$56,700 ÷ 4,200.............................	$ 13.50

Allocation of costs of Department 2:

Units started in December, completed in January:

Inventory on January 1, 800 units ½ completed ..	$ 24,600	
Processing costs in January, 400 at $13.50	5,400	
Total ($30,000 ÷ 800 = $37.50 unit cost)		$ 30,000

Units started and completed in January:

From Department 1, 3,200 units at $25.20	$ 80,640	
Processing costs, 3,200 at $13.50.............	43,200	
Total ($123,840 ÷ 3,200 = $38.70 unit cost) ...		123,840
Total transferred to Product A...............		$153,840

Units started in January, ⅔ completed:

From Department 1, 900 units at $25.20	$ 22,680	
Processing costs, 600 at $13.50	8,100	
Total work in process—Department 2		30,780
Total costs charged to Department 2		$184,620

Entry: Finished Goods—Product A.................	153,840	
Work in Process—Department 2...........		153,840

(l) *Cost of goods sold.*

Product A, 3,800 units:

1,000 units at $36.50	$ 36,500
800 units at $37.50	30,000
2,000 units at $38.70	77,400
Total cost of goods sold.........................	$143,900

Entry: Cost of Goods Sold.........................	143,900	
Finished Goods—Product A...............		143,900

(m) *Sales.*

Entry: Accounts Receivable.......................	210,500	
Sales....................................		210,500

(n) *Cash received.*

Entry: Cash......................................	200,000	
Accounts Receivable....................		200,000

(o) Cash disbursed.

Entry: Accounts Payable   120,000
Wages Payable.   72,500
Cash   192,500

A chart of the flow of costs from the service and processing department accounts into the finished goods accounts and then to the cost of goods sold account is as follows. Entries in the accounts are identified by letters to aid the comparison with the summary journal entries.

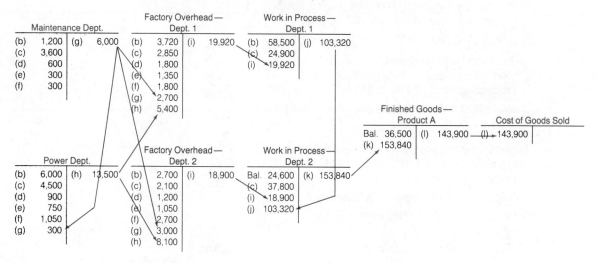

FLOW OF COSTS THROUGH PROCESS COST ACCOUNTS

Cost of Production Reports

The cost of production reports for Departments 1 and 2 are as follows:

Conway Company
Cost of Production Report — Department 1
For the Month Ended January 31, 19--

Quantities:		
Units charged to production and to be accounted for.		4,100
Units accounted for and transferred to Department 2		4,100
Costs:		
Costs charged to production in January:		
Direct materials.		$ 58,500
Direct labor		24,900
Factory overhead		19,920
Total costs to be accounted for.		$103,320
Total costs accounted for and transferred to Department 2 (4,100 units × $25.20).		$103,320

Conway Company
Cost of Production Report—Department 2
For the Month Ended January 31, 19--

Quantities:		
Charged to production:		
In process, January 1		800
Received from Department 1		4,100
Total units to be accounted for		4,900
Units accounted for:		
Transferred to finished goods		4,000
In process, January 31		900
Total units accounted for.		4,900
Costs:		
Charged to production:		
In process, January 1		$ 24,600
January costs:		
Direct materials from Department 1 ($25.20 per		
unit)		103,320
Processing costs:		
Direct labor	$ 37,800	
Factory overhead	18,900	
Total processing costs ($13.50 per unit)		56,700
Total costs to be accounted for.		$184,620
Costs allocated as follows:		
Transferred to finished goods:		
800 units at $37.50.	$ 30,000	
3,200 units at $38.70	123,840	
Total cost of finished goods		$153,840
In process, January 31:		
Direct materials (900 units at $25.20)	$ 22,680	
Processing costs (900 units × 2/3 × $13.50)	8,100	
Total cost of inventory in process, January 31		30,780
Total costs accounted for		$184,620
Computations:		
Equivalent units of production:		
To process units in inventory on January 1:		
800 units × 1/2		400
To process units started and completed in January:		
4,000 units − 800 units.		3,200
To process units in inventory on January 31:		
900 units × 2/3		600
Equivalent units of production		4,200
Unit processing cost:		
$56,700 ÷ 4,200.		$ 13.50

Financial Statements

The financial statements for process cost systems are similar to those for job order cost systems. To illustrate, the trial balance and the condensed financial statements for Conway Company are presented as follows. Note that the net underapplied factory overhead of $1,650 ($1,950 − $300) on January 31 is reported on the balance sheet as a deferred item.

Conway Company
Trial Balance
January 31, 19--

Cash	46,900	
Accounts Receivable	55,500	
Finished Goods — Product A (1,200 units at $38.70)	46,440	
Work in Process — Department 2 (900 units, ⅔ completed)	30,780	
Materials	40,380	
Prepaid Expenses	4,500	
Plant Assets	510,000	
Accumulated Depreciation — Plant Assets		301,750
Accounts Payable		47,980
Wages Payable		6,650
Common Stock		250,000
Retained Earnings		94,070
Sales		210,500
Cost of Goods Sold	143,900	
Factory Overhead — Department 1		300
Factory Overhead — Department 2	1,950	
Selling Expenses	16,500	
General Expenses	14,400	
	911,250	911,250

Conway Company
Income Statement
For Month Ended January 31, 19--

Sales		$210,500
Cost of goods sold		143,900
Gross profit		$ 66,600
Operating expenses:		
Selling expenses	$ 16,500	
General expenses	14,400	
Total operating expenses		30,900
Income from operations		$ 35,700

Conway Company
Retained Earnings Statement
For Month Ended January 31, 19--

Retained earnings, January 1, 19--.............................	$ 94,070
Income for the month...	35,700
Retained earnings, January 31, 19--...........................	$129,770

Conway Company
Balance Sheet
January 31, 19--

Assets

Current assets:			
Cash		$ 46,900	
Accounts receivable		55,500	
Inventories:			
Finished goods....................	$ 46,440		
Work in process	30,780		
Materials.........................	40,380	117,600	
Prepaid expenses....................		4,500	
Total current assets			$224,500
Plant assets:			
Plant assets........................		$510,000	
Less accumulated depreciation		301,750	208,250
Deferred debits:			
Factory overhead underapplied			1,650
Total assets			$434,400

Liabilities

Current liabilities:			
Accounts payable...................		$ 47,980	
Wages payable.....................		6,650	
Total liabilities			$ 54,630

Stockholders' Equity

Common stock		$250,000	
Retained earnings		129,770	
Total stockholders' equity			379,770
Total liabilities and stockholders' equity ..			$434,400

Self-Examination Questions
(Answers at end of chapter.)

1. For which of the following businesses would the process cost system be most appropriate?
   A. Custom furniture manufacturer
   B. Commercial building contractor
   C. Crude oil refinery
   D. None of the above

2. The group of manufacturing costs referred to as *processing costs* includes:
   A. direct materials and direct labor
   B. direct materials and factory overhead
   C. direct labor and factory overhead
   D. none of the above

3. Information relating to production in Department A for May is as follows:

May 1	Balance, 1,000 units, ¾ completed.........................	$22,150
31	Direct materials, 5,000 units.............................	75,000
31	Direct labor..	32,500
31	Factory overhead	16,250

   If 500 units were ¼ completed at May 31 and 5,500 units were completed during May, what was the number of equivalent units of production for May?
   A. 4,500
   B. 4,875
   C. 5,500
   D. None of the above

4. Based on the data presented in Question 3, what is the unit processing cost?
   A. $10
   B. $15
   C. $25
   D. None of the above

5. If one of the products resulting from a process has little value in relation to the principal products, it is known as a:
   A. joint product
   B. by-product
   C. direct material
   D. none of the above

Discussion Questions

16–1. Which type of cost system, process or job order, would be best suited for each of the following: (a) washing machine manufacturer, (b) oil refinery, (c) furniture upholsterer, (d) building contractor, (e) paint manufacturer? Give reasons for your answers.

16–2. In job order cost accounting, the three elements of manufacturing cost are charged directly to job orders. Why is it not necessary to charge manufacturing costs in process cost accounting to job orders?

16–3. (a) How does a service department differ from a processing department? (b) Give two examples of a service department.

16–4. Parnell Company maintains a cafeteria for its employees at a cost of $1,400 per month. On what basis would the company most likely allocate the cost of the cafeteria among the production departments?

16–5. What two groups of manufacturing costs are referred to as processing costs?

16–6. In the manufacture of 5,000 units of a product, direct materials cost incurred was $15,000, direct labor cost incurred was $8,000, and factory overhead applied was $4,000. (a) What is the total processing cost? (b) What is the processing cost per unit? (c) What is the total manufacturing cost? (d) What is the manufacturing cost per unit?

16–7. What is meant by the term "equivalent units"?

16–8. If Department 1 had no work in process at the beginning of the period, 6,000 units were completed during the period, and 2,000 units were 25% completed at the end of the period, what was the number of equivalent units of production for the period?

16–9. The following information concerns production in Department 14 for January. All direct materials are placed in process at the beginning of production. Determine the number of units in work in process inventory at the end of the month.

WORK IN PROCESS—DEPARTMENT 14

Date		Item	Debit	Credit	Balance Debit	Balance Credit
Jan.	1	Bal., 4,000 units, ¾ completed			6,750	
	31	Direct materials, 15,000 units	7,200			
	31	Direct labor	16,800			
	31	Factory overhead	4,400			
	31	Goods finished, 13,500 units		28,110		
	31	Bal.,____ units, ½ completed			7,040	

16–10. For 16–9, determine the equivalent units of production for January.

16–11. What data are summarized in the two principal sections of the cost of production report?

16–12. What is the most important purpose of the cost of production report?

16–13. Distinguish between a joint product and a by-product.

16–14. Department 25 produces two products. How should the costs be allocated (a) if the products are joint products and (b) if one of the products is a by-product?

16–15. Factory employees in Department 1 of Cargile Co. are paid widely varying wage rates. In such circumstances, would direct labor hours or direct labor cost be the more equitable base for applying factory overhead to the production of the department? Explain.

16–16. In a factory with several processing departments, a separate factory overhead rate may be determined for each department. Why is a single factory overhead rate often inadequate in such circumstances?

16–17. Wright & Wright Co. manufactures two products. The entire output of Department 1 is transferred to Department 2. Part of the fully processed goods from Department 2 are sold as Product A and the remainder of the goods are transferred to Department 3 for further processing into Product B. The service department, Factory Office, provides services for each of the processing departments.

Exercises

Prepare a chart of the flow of costs from the service and processing department accounts into the finished goods accounts and then into the cost of goods sold account. The relevant accounts are as follows:

Cost of Goods Sold	Finished Goods — Product A
Factory Office	Finished Goods — Product B
Factory Overhead — Department 1	Work in Process — Department 1
Factory Overhead — Department 2	Work in Process — Department 2
Factory Overhead — Department 3	Work in Process — Department 3

16–18. The Maintenance and Repair Department provides services to processing Departments X, Y, and Z. During June of the current year, the total cost incurred by the Maintenance and Repair Department was $72,000. During June, it was estimated that 36% of the services were provided to Department X, 54% to Department Y, and 10% to Department Z.

Prepare an entry to record the allocation of the Maintenance and Repair Department cost for June to the processing departments.

16–19. Upchurch Company manufactures a single product by a continuous process, involving five production departments. The records indicate that $80,500 of direct materials were issued to and $98,000 of direct labor incurred by Department 1 in the manufacture of the product; the factory overhead rate is 40% of direct labor cost; work in process in the department at the beginning of the period totaled $45,150; and work in process at the end of the period totaled $48,650.

Prepare entries to record (a) the flow of costs into Department 1 during the period for (1) direct materials, (2) direct labor, and (3) factory overhead; (b) the transfer of production costs to Department 2.

16–20. The chief cost accountant for Pratt Electronics estimates total factory overhead cost for Department 10 for the year at $96,000 and total direct labor costs at $128,000. During August, actual direct labor cost totaled $16,000 and factory overhead cost incurred totaled $11,500. (a) What is the predetermined factory overhead rate based on direct labor cost? (b) Prepare the entry to apply factory overhead to production for August. (c) What is the August 31 balance of the account Factory Overhead — Department 10? (d) Does the balance in (c) represent overapplied or underapplied factory overhead?

16–21. The charges to Work in Process — Department 1 for a period, together with information concerning production, are as follows. All direct materials are placed in process at the beginning of production.

Work in Process — Department 1

1,200 units, 80% completed	25,920	To Dept. 2, 4,200 units	102,258
Direct materials, 3,000 at $12	36,000		
Direct labor	25,200		
Factory overhead	15,138		

Determine the following, presenting your computations: (a) equivalent units of production, (b) processing cost per equivalent unit of production, (c) total and unit cost of product started in prior period and completed in the current period, and (d) total and unit cost of product started and completed in the current period.

16–22. Prepare a cost of production report for the Polishing Department of McNair Company for July of the current fiscal year, using the following data:

Inventory, July 1, 5,400 units, 60% completed...................	$131,760
Materials from the Sanding Department, 15,000 units	324,000
Direct labor for July..	52,200
Factory overhead for July....................................	28,980
Goods finished during July (includes units in process, July 1), 16,400 units..	——
Inventory, July 31, 4,000 units, 40% completed................	——

16–23. The charges to Work in Process — Department 6, together with units of product completed during the period, are indicated in the following account:

Work in Process — Department 6

From Department 5	172,700	By-product N, 2,000 units
Direct labor	62,800	Joint product R, 12,800 units
Factory overhead	30,900	Joint product S, 6,000 units

There is no inventory of goods in process at either the beginning or the end of the period. The value of N is $2 a unit; R sells at $15 a unit and S sells at $48 a unit.

Allocate the costs to the three products and determine the unit cost of each, presenting your computations.

16–24. Ferguson Company manufactures Product W. Material C is placed in process in Department 1 where it is ground and partially refined. The output of Department 1 is transferred to Department 2, where Material D is added at the beginning of the process and the refining is completed. On May 1, Ferguson Company had the following inventories:

Finished goods (5,000 units)................................	$121,000
Work in process — Department 1............................	——
Work in process — Department 2 (1,000 units, ¾ completed)	20,100
Materials	27,100

Departmental accounts are maintained for factory overhead and there is one service department, Factory Office. Manufacturing operations for May are summarized as follows:

Problems

(a) Materials purchased on account $48,950
(b) Materials requisitioned for use:
    Material C.. $26,510
    Material D.. 22,000
    Indirect materials—Department 1........................... 1,760
    Indirect materials—Department 2........................... 1,265
(c) Labor used:
    Direct labor—Department 1................................ $55,000
    Direct labor—Department 2................................ 39,250
    Indirect labor—Department 1.............................. 2,090
    Indirect labor—Department 2.............................. 1,980
    Factory Office... 1,870
(d) Miscellaneous costs incurred on account:
    Department 1.. $7,350
    Department 2.. 5,170
    Factory Office... 2,140
(e) Expiration of prepaid expenses:
    Department 1.. $1,045
    Department 2.. 715
    Factory Office... 300
(f) Depreciation charged on plant assets:
    Department 1.. $14,680
    Department 2.. 12,520
    Factory Office... 950
(g) Distribution of Factory Office costs:
    Department 1........................75% of total Factory Office costs
    Department 2........................25% of total Factory Office costs
(h) Application of factory overhead costs:
    Department 1................................55% of direct labor cost
    Department 2................................60% of direct labor cost
(i) Production costs transferred from Department 1 to Department 2:
    8,800 units were fully processed and there was no inventory of work in
    process in Department 1 at May 31.
(j) Production costs transferred from Department 2 to finished goods:
    8,000 units, including the inventory at May 1, were fully processed. 1,800
    units were 1/3 completed at May 31.
(k) Cost of goods sold during May:
    9,500 units (use the first-in, first-out method in crediting the finished goods
    account).

Instructions:

(1) Prepare entries to record the foregoing operations. Identify each entry by letter.
(2) Compute the May 31 work in process inventory for Department 2.

16–25. The data related to production during May of the current year for Department 2 of Ferguson Company are presented in Problem 16-24.

Instructions:

Prepare a cost of production report for Department 2 for May.

16–26. The trial balance of Mathews Inc. at July 31, the end of the first month of the current fiscal year, is as follows:

Mathews Inc.
Trial Balance
July 31, 19--

Cash	78,180	
Marketable Securities	60,000	
Accounts Receivable	210,600	
Finished Goods — Product P1	85,800	
Finished Goods — Product P2	142,200	
Work in Process — Department 1	18,180	
Work in Process — Department 2	31,620	
Work in Process — Department 3	28,800	
Materials	57,000	
Prepaid Expenses	15,000	
Plant Assets	930,220	
Accumulated Depreciation — Plant Assets		491,410
Accounts Payable		119,400
Wages Payable		17,640
Common Stock		600,000
Retained Earnings		378,630
Sales		528,600
Cost of Goods Sold	377,700	
Factory Overhead — Department 1	660	
Factory Overhead — Department 2		270
Factory Overhead — Department 3	750	
Selling Expenses	59,520	
General Expenses	39,720	
	2,135,950	2,135,950

Instructions:

(1) Prepare an income statement.
(2) Prepare a retained earnings statement.
(3) Prepare a balance sheet.

16–27. Townsend Company manufactures Product H by a series of three processes, all materials being introduced in Department 1. From Department 1, the materials pass through Departments 2 and 3, emerging as finished Product H. All inventories are priced at cost by the first-in, first-out method.

The balances in the accounts Work in Process — Department 3 and Finished Goods were as follows on October 1:

Work in Process — Department 3 (3,500 units, ½ completed)	$106,050
Finished Goods (6,000 units at $36.20 a unit)	217,200

The following costs were charged to Work in Process — Department 3 during October:

Direct materials transferred from Department 2: 18,500 units at $24 a unit	$444,000
Direct labor	116,300
Factory overhead	70,000

During October, 17,500 units of H were completed and 18,600 units were sold. Inventories on October 31 were as follows:

Work in Process—Department 3: 4,500 units, 1/3 completed
Finished Goods: 4,900 units

Instructions:

(1) Determine the following, presenting computations in good order:
   (a) Equivalent units of production for Department 3 during October.
   (b) Unit processing cost for Department 3 for October.
   (c) Total and unit cost of Product H started in a prior period and finished in October.
   (d) Total and unit cost of Product H started and finished in October.
   (e) Total cost of goods transferred to finished goods.
   (f) Work in process inventory for Department 3, October 31.
   (g) Cost of goods sold (indicate number of units and unit costs).
   (h) Finished goods inventory, October 31.
(2) Prepare a cost of production report for Department 3 for October.

16–28. Sikes Products manufactures joint products M and N. Materials are placed in production in Department 1, and after processing, are transferred to Department 2, where more materials are added. The finished products emerge from Department 2. There are two service departments: Factory Office, and Maintenance and Repair.

There were no inventories of work in process at the beginning or at the end of December. Finished goods inventories at December 1 were as follows:

Product M, 4,900 units................. $56,350
Product N, 940 units 18,330

Transactions related to manufacturing operations for December are summarized as follows:

(a) Materials purchased on account, $70,000.
(b) Materials requisitioned for use: Department 1, $32,550 ($28,350 entered directly into the products); Department 2, $22,210 ($18,290 entered directly into the products); Maintenance and Repair, $2,660.
(c) Labor costs incurred: Department 1, $23,520 ($21,000 entered directly into the products); Department 2, $25,340 ($22,400 entered directly into the products); Factory Office, $3,850; Maintenance and Repair, $9,170.
(d) Miscellaneous costs and expenses incurred on account: Department 1, $3,570; Department 2, $3,150; Factory Office, $1,400; and Maintenance and Repair, $2,170.
(e) Depreciation charged on plant assets: Department 1, $4,900; Department 2, $3,360; Factory Office, $700; and Maintenance and Repair, $980.
(f) Expiration of various prepaid expenses: Department 1, $280; Department 2, $245; Factory Office, $350; and Maintenance and Repair, $490.
(g) Factory office costs allocated on the basis of hours worked: Department 1, 2,240 hours; Department 2, 2,800 hours; Maintenance and Repair, 560 hours.
(h) Maintenance and repair costs allocated on the basis of services rendered: Department 1, 45%; Department 2, 55%.

(i) Factory overhead applied to production at the predetermined rates: 120% and 115% of direct labor cost for Departments 1 and 2 respectively.

(j) Output of Department 1: 5,460 units.

(k) Output of Department 2: 7,050 units of Product M and 2,820 units of Product N. Unit selling price is $16.80 for Product M and $28 for Product N.

(l) Sales on account: 7,750 units of Product M at $16.80 and 2,660 units of Product N at $28. Credits to the finished goods accounts are to be priced in accordance with the first-in, first-out method.

Instructions:

Present entries to record the transactions, identifying each by letter. Include as an explanation for entry (k) the computations for the allocation of the production costs for Department 2 to the joint products, and as an explanation for entry (l) the number of units and the unit costs for each product sold.

16–29. A process cost system is used to record the costs of manufacturing Product A24C, which requires a series of four processes. The inventory of Work in Process — Department 4 on April 1 and debits to the account during April were as follows:

Balance, 1,600 units, ¼ completed.	$ 6,520
From Department 3, 9,200 units	25,760
Direct labor.	38,500
Factory overhead	9,625

During April, the 1,600 units in process on April 1 were completed, and of the 9,200 units entering the department, all were completed except 2,200 units, which were ¼ completed.

Charges to Work in Process — Department 4 for May were made as follows:

From Department 3, 8,250 units	$23,925
Direct labor.	41,724
Factory overhead	10,431

During May, the units in process at the beginning of the month were completed, and of the 8,250 units entering the department, all were completed except 1,500 units, which were ½ completed.

Instructions:

(1) Set up an account for Work in Process — Department 4. Enter the balance as of April 1 and record the debits and the credits in the account for April. Present computations for the determination of (a) equivalent units of production, (b) unit processing cost, (c) cost of goods finished, differentiating between units started in the prior period and units started and finished in April, and (d) work in process inventory.

(2) Record the transactions for May in the account. Present the computations listed in instruction (1).

(3) Determine the difference in unit cost between the product started and completed in April and the product started and completed in May. Determine also the amount of the difference attributable collectively to operations in Departments 1 through 3 and the amount attributable to operations in Department 4.

16–24A. Rutherford Company manufactures Product G. Material A is placed in process in Department 1, where it is ground and partially refined. The output of Department 1 is transferred to Department 2, where Material B is added at the beginning of the process and the refining is completed. On March 1, Rutherford Company had the following inventories:

Finished goods (4,100 units)	$71,750
Work in process — Department 1	—
Work in process — Department 2 (2,100 units, ⅔ completed)	34,230
Materials	40,980

Departmental accounts are maintained for factory overhead and there is one service department, Factory Office. Manufacturing operations for March are summarized as follows:

(a)	Materials purchased on account	$21,800
(b)	Materials requisitioned for use:	
	Material A	$34,470
	Material B	6,560
	Indirect materials — Department 1	1,440
	Indirect materials — Department 2	360
(c)	Labor used:	
	Direct labor — Department 1	$48,700
	Direct labor — Department 2	20,500
	Indirect labor — Department 1	2,800
	Indirect labor — Department 2	1,280
	Factory Office	2,300
(d)	Depreciation charged on plant assets:	
	Department 1	$19,900
	Department 2	9,600
	Factory Office	1,100
(e)	Miscellaneous costs incurred on account:	
	Department 1	$ 3,690
	Department 2	2,310
	Factory Office	1,200
(f)	Expiration of prepaid expenses:	
	Department 1	$ 2,280
	Department 2	490
	Factory Office	750
(g)	Distribution of Factory Office costs:	
	Department 1	60% of total Factory Office costs
	Department 2	40% of total Factory Office costs
(h)	Application of factory overhead costs:	
	Department 1	70% of direct labor cost
	Department 2	80% of direct labor cost

(i) Production costs transferred from Department 1 to Department 2:
   8,200 units were fully processed and there was no inventory of work in process in Department 1 at March 31.

(j) Production costs transferred from Department 2 to finished goods:
   7,500 units, including the inventory at March 1, were fully processed. There were 2,800 units ¾ completed at March 31.

(k) Cost of goods sold during March:

8,000 units (use the first-in, first-out method in crediting the finished goods account).

Instructions:

(1) Prepare entries in general journal form to record the foregoing operations. Identify each entry by letter.

(2) Compute the March 31 work in process inventory for Department 2.

16-27A. Pugh Company manufactures Product J by a series of four processes, all materials being introduced in Department 1. From Department 1, the materials pass through Departments 2, 3, and 4, emerging as finished Product J. All inventories are priced at cost by the first-in, first-out method.

The balances in the accounts Work in Process — Department 4 and Finished Goods were as follows on March 1:

Work in Process — Department 4 (4,000 units, ¾ completed)	$40,400
Finished Goods (7,200 units at $12.50 a unit)	90,000

The following costs were charged to Work in Process — Department 4 during March:
Direct materials transferred from Department 3: 24,000 units

at $4.80 a unit.	$115,200
Direct labor	127,260
Factory overhead	42,420

During March, 21,600 units of J were completed and 20,800 units were sold. Inventories on March 31 were as follows:

Work in Process — Department 4: 6,400 units, ¼ completed
Finished Goods: 8,000 units

Instructions:

(1) Determine the following, presenting computations in good order:

(a) Equivalent units of production for Department 4 during March.

(b) Unit processing cost for Department 4 for March.

(c) Total and unit cost of Product J started in a prior period and finished in March.

(d) Total and unit cost of Product J started and finished in March.

(e) Total cost of goods transferred to finished goods.

(f) Work in process inventory for Department 4, March 31.

(g) Cost of goods sold (indicate number of units and unit costs).

(h) Finished goods inventory, March 31.

(2) Prepare a cost of production report for Department 4 for March.

16-29A. A process cost system is used to record the costs of manufacturing Product CE5, which requires a series of three processes. The inventory of Work in Process — Department 3 on August 1 and debits to the account during August were as follows:

Balance, 2,400 units, ⅔ completed.	$ 23,280
From Department 2, 10,500 units	18,900
Direct labor.	101,352
Factory overhead	25,338

During August, the 2,400 units in process on August 1 were completed, and of the 10,500 units entering the department, all were completed except 4,000 units, which were ¾ completed.

Charges to Work in Process—Department 3 for September were as follows:

From Department 2, 12,200 units	$ 21,350
Direct labor..	127,000
Factory overhead	31,750

During September, the units in process at the beginning of the month were completed, and of the 12,200 units entering the department, all were completed except 1,500 units, which were ⅔ completed.

Instructions:

(1) Set up an account for Work in Process—Department 3. Enter the balance as of August 1 and record the debits and the credits in the account for August. Present computations for the determination of (a) equivalent units of production, (b) unit processing cost, (c) cost of goods finished, differentiating between units started in the prior period and units started and finished in August, and (d) work in process inventory.

(2) Record the transactions for September in the account. Present the computations listed in instruction (1).

(3) Determine the difference in unit cost between the product started and completed in August and the product started and completed in September. Determine also the amount of the difference attributable collectively to operations in Departments 1 and 2 and the amount attributable to operations in Department 3.

Mini-Case

16–30. Rivera Inc. manufactures product A68 by a series of four processes. All materials are placed in production in the Die Casting Department and, after processing, are transferred to the Tooling, Assembly, and Polishing Departments, emerging as finished product A68.

On April 1, the balance in the account Work in Process—Polishing was $336,600, determined as follows:

Direct materials: 12,000 units	$203,400
Direct labor: 12,000 units, ¾ completed...................	107,550
Factory overhead: 12,000 units, ¾ completed	25,650
Total..	$336,600

The following costs were charged to Work in Process—Polishing during April:

Direct materials transferred from Assembly Department:	
136,000 units	$2,380,000
Direct labor..	1,648,200
Factory overhead......................................	361,800

During April, 138,000 units of A68 were completed and transferred to Finished Goods. On April 30, the inventory in the Polishing Department consisted of 10,000 units, one-half completed.

As a new cost accountant for Rivera Inc., you have just received a phone call from George Herschman, the superintendent of the Polishing Department. He was extremely upset with the cost of production report, which he says does not balance. In addition, he commented:

"I give up! These reports are a waste of time. My department has always been the best department in the plant, so why should I bother with these reports? Just what purpose do they serve?"

The report to which Herschman referred is as follows:

RIVERA INC.
Cost of Production Report — Polishing Department
For Month Ended April 30, 19--

Quantities:
Charged to production:

In process, April 1	9,000
Received from Assembly Department	136,000
Total units to be accounted for	145,000

Units accounted for:

Transferred to finished goods	138,000
In process, April 30	5,000
Total units accounted for	143,000

Costs:
Charged to production:

In process, April 1	$ 336,600

April costs:

Direct materials from Assembly Department ($15.70 per unit)		2,380,000
Processing costs:		
Direct labor	$1,648,200	
Factory overhead	361,800	
Total processing costs ($13.40 per unit)		2,010,000
Total costs to be accounted for		$4,726,600

Costs allocated as follows:

Transferred to finished goods:		
138,000 units at $29.10 ($15.70 + $13.40)		$4,015,800
In process, April 30:		
Materials (5,000 units × $15.70)	$ 78,500	
Processing costs (5,000 units × $13.40)	67,000	
Total cost of inventory in process		145,500
Total costs accounted for		$4,161,300

Computations:
Equivalent units of production:
To process units in inventory on April 1:
12,000 units × ¾ 9,000
To process units started and completed in April 136,000
To process units in inventory on April 30:
10,000 units × ½ 5,000
Equivalent units of production...................... 150,000

Unit processing cost: $2,010,000 ÷ 150,000.............. $ 13.40

Instructions:

(1) Based upon the data for April, prepare a revised cost of production report for the Polishing Department.
(2) Assume that for March, the unit direct materials cost was $16.95 and the unit processing cost was $14.80. Determine the change in the direct materials unit cost and unit processing cost for April.
(3) Based upon (2), what are some possible explanations for the changing unit costs?
(4) Describe how you would explain to Herschman that cost of production reports are useful.

Answers to Self-Examination Questions

1. **C** The process cost system is most appropriate for a business where manufacturing is conducted by continuous operations and involves a series of uniform production processes, such as the processing of crude oil (answer C). The job order cost system is most appropriate for a business where the product is made to customers' specifications, such as custom furniture manufacturing (answer A) and commercial building construction (answer B).

2. **C** The manufacturing costs that are necessary to convert direct materials into finished products are referred to as processing costs. The processing costs include direct labor and factory overhead (answer C).

3. **B** The number of units that could have been produced from start to finish during a period is termed equivalent units. The 4,875 equivalent units (answer B) is determined as follows:

To process units in inventory on May 1: 1,000 units × ¼.............. 250
To process units started and completed in May:
5,500 units − 1,000 units... 4,500
To process units in inventory on May 31: 500 units × ¼.............. 125
Equivalent units of production in May 4,875

4. **A** The processing costs (direct labor and factory overhead) totaling $48,750 are divided by the number of equivalent units (4,875) to determine the unit processing cost of $10 (answer A).

5 **B** The product resulting from a process that has little value in relation to the principal product or joint products is known as a by-product (answer B). When two or more commodities of significant value are produced from a single direct material, the products are termed joint products (answer A). The raw material that enters directly into the finished product is termed direct material (answer C).

PART 6

Planning and Control

The Importance of Planning and Control

In a recent survey, the corporate boards of directors of 600 of the 1,000 largest U.S. corporations emphasized the importance of planning to the success of a business. The results of this survey, which asked the boards to identify the most important issues facing them now and five years from now, are as follows:

Relative Importance of Issues Facing Boards of Directors of Major U.S. Corporations

Issue	Currently Ranking as No. 1 In Importance	Ranking as No. 1 In Importance Five Years from Now
Financial results	50%	37%
Strategic planning	20	44
Day-to-day operations	10	—
Managerial succession	7	17
Mergers/acquisitions	2	—

SOURCE   Adapted from Deloitte Haskins & Sells, "Major Issues Facing Boards of Directors," *DH + S Review*, September 2, 1985, p. 6.

To want to achieve certain year-end results is not enough. Managing means that once you set your business plan and budget for the year, you *must* achieve the sales, the market share, and the earnings to which you committed yourself. If you don't manage to achieve those results, you're not a manager.

A manager must set standards for production, sales, market share, earnings, whatever, and anything short of those standards should be unacceptable to him. Recently I met a man who operates the jewelry concession in a number of department stores. He told me: "I don't think I'm doing my job unless I get 4% of the store's traffic." "How do you know it's 4% you need?" I asked. "I don't," he replied, "it just works out that way." "Why not 5%?" I asked. "No, just 4%," he insisted, explaining that 4% was more than any other counter in the department store got. Without sophisticated controls, this man had set his own standards. He couln't sleep if he did not get that 4%. He would feel guilty if he did not get it. He would work through the night, he would do anything he had to, but he would get that 4%. I don't know precisely what he did to achieve the 4%, and perhaps 5% or even 8% would have been possible, but it makes little difference: he was managing.

SOURCE   Adapted from Harold S. Geneen, "The Case for Managing by the Numbers," *Fortune*, October 1, 1984, pp. 78-81.

CHAPTER 17

Budgeting

CHAPTER OBJECTIVES

Describe the nature and objectives of budgeting and the budget process.

Identify the components of the master budget and illustrate the preparation of a master budget for a manufacturing enterprise.

Describe and illustrate budget performance reports and flexible budgets.

Various uses of accounting data by management have been described in earlier chapters. For example, the role of cost accounting in planning production and controlling costs has been discussed and illustrated. This chapter and Chapter 18 are devoted to budgeting and standard costs, two additional accounting concepts that assist management in planning and controlling the operations of the business.

NATURE OF BUDGETS

A **budget** is a formal written statement of management's plans for the future, expressed in financial terms. A budget charts the course of future action. Thus, it aids management in fulfilling its planning function in the same manner that the architect's blueprints aid the builder and the navigator's flight plan aids the pilot.

A budget, like a blueprint and a flight plan, should contain sound, attainable objectives. If the budget is to contain such objectives, planning must be based on careful study, investigation, and research. Reliance by management on data thus obtained lessens the role of guesses and intuition in managing a business enterprise.

To be effective, managerial planning must be accompanied by control. The control feature of budgeting lies in periodic comparisons of planned objectives and actual performance. Management can then take corrective action in areas where significant differences between the budget and actual performance are reported. The role of accounting is to aid management in the investigation phase of budget preparation, to translate management's plans into financial terms, and to prepare budget performance reports and related analyses.

BUDGET PERIOD

Budgets of operating activities usually include the fiscal year of an enterprise. A year is short enough to make possible fairly dependable estimates of future operations, and yet long enough to make it possible to view the future in a reasonably broad context. However, to achieve effective control, the annual budgets must be subdivided into shorter time periods such as quarters of the year, months, or weeks. It is also necessary to review the budgets from time to time and make any changes that become necessary as a result of unforeseen changes in general business conditions, in the particular industry, or in the individual enterprise.

A frequent variant of fiscal-year budgeting, sometimes called **continuous budgeting**, provides for maintenance of a twelve-month projection into the future. At the end of each time interval used, the twelve-month budget is revised by removing the data for the period just ended and adding the newly estimated budget data for the same period next year.

BUDGETING PROCEDURES

The details of budgeting systems are affected by the type and degree of complexity of a particular company, the amount of its revenues, the relative importance of its various divisions, and many other factors. Budget procedures used by a large manufacturer of automobiles would obviously differ in many ways from a system designed for a small manufacturer of paper products. The differences between a system designed for factory operations of any type and a financial enterprise such as a bank would be even more marked.

The development of budgets for a following fiscal year usually begins several months prior to the end of the current year. The responsibility for their development is ordinarily assigned to a committee made up of the budget director and such high-level executives as the controller, treasurer, production manager, and sales manager. The process is started by requesting estimates of sales, production, and other operating data from the various administrative units concerned. It is important that all levels of management and all departments participate in the preparation and submission of budget estimates. The involvement of all supervisory personnel fosters cooperation both within and among departments and also heightens awareness of each department's importance in the overall processes of the company. All levels of management are thus encouraged to set goals and to control operations in a manner that strengthens the possibilities of achieving the goals.

The process of developing budget estimates differs among enterprises. One method is to require all levels of management to start from zero and estimate sales, production, and other operating data as though operations were being started for the first time. Although this concept, called **zero-base budgeting,** has received wide attention in regard to budgeting for governmental units, it is equally useful to commercial enterprises. Another method of developing estimates is for each level of management to modify last year's budgeted amounts in light of last year's operating results and expected changes for the coming year.

The various estimates received by the budget committee are revised, reviewed, coordinated, cross-referenced, and finally put together to form the **master budget.** The estimates submitted should not be substantially revised by the committee without first giving the originators an opportunity to defend their proposals. After agreement has been reached and the master budget has been adopted by the budget committee, copies of the pertinent sections are distributed to the proper personnel in the chain of accountability. Periodic reports comparing actual results with the budget should likewise be distributed to all supervisory personnel.

As a framework for describing and illustrating budgeting, a small manufacturing enterprise will be assumed. The major parts of its master budget are as follows:

COMPONENTS OF
MASTER BUDGET

Budgeted income statement	Budgeted balance sheet
Sales budget	Capital expenditures budget
Cost of goods sold budget	Cash budget
Production budget	
Direct materials purchases budget	
Direct labor cost budget	
Factory overhead cost budget	
Operating expenses budget	

Sales Budget

The first budget to be prepared is usually the sales budget. An estimate of the dollar volume of sales revenue serves as the foundation upon which the other budgets are based. Sales volume will have a significant effect on all of the factors entering into the determination of operating income.

The sales budget ordinarily indicates (1) the quantity of forecasted sales for each product and (2) the expected unit selling price of each product. These data are often classified by areas and/or sales representatives.

In forecasting the quantity of each product expected to be sold, the starting point is generally past sales volumes. These amounts are revised for various factors expected to affect future sales, such as a backlog of unfilled sales orders, planned advertising and promotion, expected industry and general economic conditions, productive capacity, projected pricing policy, and market research study findings. Statistical analysis can be used in this process to evaluate the effect of these factors on past sales volume. Such analysis can provide a mathematical association between past sales and the several variables expected to affect future sales.

Once the forecast of sales volume is completed, the anticipated sales revenue is then determined by multiplying the volume of forecasted sales by the expected unit sales price, as shown in the following sales budget:

Bowers Company
Sales Budget
For Year Ending December 31, 19--

Product and Area	Unit Sales Volume	Unit Selling Price	Total Sales
Product X:			
Area A	208,000	$ 9.90	$2,059,200
Area B	162,000	9.90	1,603,800
Area C	158,000	9.90	1,564,200
Total	528,000		$5,227,200
Product Y:			
Area A	111,600	$16.50	$1,841,400
Area B	78,800	16.50	1,300,200
Area C	89,600	16.50	1,478,400
Total	280,000		$4,620,000
Total revenue from sales			$9,847,200

Frequent comparisons of actual sales with the budgeted volume, by product, area, and/or sales representative, will show differences between the two. Management is then able to investigate the probable cause of the significant differences and attempt corrective action.

Production Budget

The number of units of each commodity expected to be manufactured to meet budgeted sales and inventory requirements is set forth in the production budget. The budgeted volume of production is based on the sum of (1) the expected sales volume and (2) the desired year-end inventory, less (3) the inventory expected to be available at the beginning of the year. A production budget is illustrated as follows:

Bowers Company
Production Budget
For Year Ending December 31, 19--

	Units	
	Product X	Product Y
Sales...................................	528,000	280,000
Plus desired ending inventory, December 31, 19--........	80,000	60,000
Total.......................................	608,000	340,000
Less estimated beginning inventory, January 1, 19--......	88,000	48,000
Total production.....................................	520,000	292,000

The production needs must be carefully coordinated with the sales budget to assure that production and sales are kept in balance during the period. Ideally, manufacturing operations should be maintained at capacity, and inventories should be neither excessive nor insufficient to fill sales orders.

Direct Materials Purchases Budget

The production needs shown by the production budget, combined with data on direct materials needed, provide the data for the direct materials purchases budget. The quantities of direct materials purchases necessary to meet production needs is based on the sum of (1) the materials expected to be needed to meet production requirements and (2) the desired year-end inventory, less (3) the inventory expected to be available at the beginning of the year. The quantities of direct materials required are then multiplied by the expected unit purchase price to determine the total cost of direct materials purchases.

In the following direct materials purchases budget, materials A and C are required for Product X, and materials A, B, and C are required for Product Y.

Bowers Company
Direct Materials Purchases Budget
For Year Ending December 31, 19--

	Direct Materials		
	A	B	C
Units required for production:			
Product X.....................................	390,000	——	520,000
Product Y.....................................	146,000	292,000	294,200
Plus desired ending inventory, Dec. 31, 19--.........	80,000	40,000	120,000
Total..	616,000	332,000	934,200
Less estimated beginning inventory, Jan. 1, 19--......	103,000	44,000	114,200
Total units to be purchased......................	513,000	288,000	820,000
Unit price......................................	$ .60	$ 1.70	$ 1.00
Total direct materials purchases..................	$307,800	$489,600	$820,000

The timing of the direct materials purchases requires close coordination between the purchasing and production departments so that inventory levels can be maintained within reasonable limits.

Direct Labor Cost Budget

The needs indicated by the production budget provide the starting point for the preparation of the direct labor cost budget. The direct labor hours necessary to meet production needs are multiplied by the estimated hourly rate to yield the total direct labor cost. The manufacturing operations for both Products X and Y are performed in Departments 1 and 2. A direct labor cost budget is illustrated as follows:

DIRECT LABOR
COST BUDGET

Bowers Company
Direct Labor Cost Budget
For Year Ending December 31, 19--

	Department 1	Department 2
Hours required for production:		
Product X	75,000	104,000
Product Y	46,800	116,800
Total	121,800	220,800
Hourly rate	$10	$8
Total direct labor cost	$1,218,000	$1,766,400

The direct labor requirements must be carefully coordinated with available labor time to assure that sufficient labor will be available to meet production needs. Efficient manufacturing operations minimize idle time and labor shortages.

Factory Overhead Cost Budget

The factory overhead costs estimated to be necessary to meet production needs are presented in the factory overhead cost budget. For use as a part of the master budget, the factory overhead cost budget usually presents the total estimated cost for each item of factory overhead. A factory overhead cost budget is illustrated as follows:

FACTORY
OVERHEAD COST
BUDGET

Bowers Company
Factory Overhead Cost Budget
For Year Ending December 31, 19--

Indirect factory wages	$ 732,800
Supervisory salaries	360,000
Power and light	306,000
Depreciation of plant and equipment	288,000
Indirect materials	182,800
Maintenance	140,280
Insurance and property taxes	79,200
Total factory overhead cost	$2,089,080

Supplemental schedules are often prepared to present the factory overhead cost for each individual department. Such schedules enable department supervisors to direct attention to those costs for which each is solely responsible. They also aid the production manager in evaluating performance in each department.

Cost of Goods Sold Budget

The budget for the cost of goods sold is prepared by combining the relevant estimates of quantities and costs in the budget for (1) direct materials purchases, (2) direct labor costs, and (3) factory overhead costs, with the addition of data on estimated inventories. A cost of goods sold budget is illustrated as follows:

COST OF GOODS
SOLD BUDGET

Bowers Company
Cost of Goods Sold Budget
For Year Ending December 31, 19--

Finished goods inventory, January 1, 19--			$1,125,600
Work in process inventory, January 1, 19--		$ 184,400	
Direct materials:			
Direct materials inventory, January 1, 19--.....	$ 250,800		
Direct materials purchases	1,617,400		
Cost of direct materials available for use	$1,868,200		
Less direct materials inventory, Dec. 31, 19-- .	236,000		
Cost of direct materials placed in production.	$1,632,200		
Direct labor	2,984,400		
Factory overhead.............................	2,089,080		
Total manufacturing costs		6,705,680	
Total work in process during period		$6,890,080	
Less work in process inventory, Dec. 31, 19--....		220,000	
Cost of goods manufactured..................			6,670,080
Cost of finished goods available for sale			$7,795,680
Less finished goods inventory, December 31, 19--			1,195,000
Cost of goods sold			$6,600,680

Operating Expenses Budget

Based on past experiences, which are adjusted for future expectations, the estimated selling and general expenses are set forth in the operating expenses budget. For use as part of the master budget, the operating expenses budget ordinarily presents the expenses by nature or type of expenditure, such as sales salaries, rent, insurance, and advertising. An operating expenses budget is illustrated as follows:

Bowers Company
Operating Expenses Budget
For Year Ending December 31, 19--

Selling expenses:		
Sales salaries expense	$595,000	
Advertising expense	360,000	
Travel expense	115,000	
Telephone expense—selling	95,000	
Miscellaneous selling expense	25,000	
Total selling expenses		$1,190,000
General expenses:		
Officers' salaries expense	$360,000	
Office salaries expense	105,000	
Heating and lighting expense	75,000	
Taxes expense	60,000	
Depreciation expense—office equipment	27,000	
Telephone expense—general	18,000	
Insurance expense	17,500	
Office supplies expense	7,500	
Miscellaneous general expense	25,000	
Total general expenses		695,000
Total operating expenses		$1,885,000

Detailed supplemental schedules based on departmental responsibility are often prepared for major items in the operating expenses budget. The advertising expense schedule, for example, should include such details as the advertising media to be used (newspaper, direct mail, television), quantities (column inches, number of pieces, minutes), cost per unit, frequency of use, and sectional totals. A realistic budget is prepared through careful attention to details, and effective control is achieved through assignment of responsibility to departmental supervisors.

Budgeted Income Statement

The budgeted income statement brings together in condensed form the projection of all profit-making phases of operations and enables management to weigh the effects of the individual budgets on the profit plan for the year. If the budgeted net income in relationship to sales or to stockholders' equity is disappointingly low, additional review of all factors involved should be undertaken in an attempt to improve the plans.

A budgeted income statement can usually be prepared from the estimated data presented in the budgets for sales, cost of goods sold, and operating expenses, with the addition of data on other income, other expense, and income tax. A budgeted income statement is illustrated as follows:

Bowers Company
Budgeted Income Statement
For Year Ending December 31, 19--

Revenue from sales....................................		$9,847,200
Cost of goods sold		6,600,680
Gross profit.......................................		$3,246,520
Operating expenses:		
Selling expenses	$1,190,000	
General expenses	695,000	
Total operating expenses............................		1,885,000
Income from operations		$1,361,520
Other income:		
Interest income.....................................	$ 98,000	
Other expense:		
Interest expense....................................	90,000	8,000
Income before income tax..............................		$1,369,520
Income tax..		610,000
Net income		$ 759,520

Capital Expenditures Budget

The **capital expenditures budget** summarizes future plans for acquisition of plant facilities and equipment.[1] Substantial expenditures may be needed to replace machinery and other plant assets as they wear out, become obsolete, or for other reasons fall below minimum standards of efficiency. In addition, an expansion of plant facilities may be planned to keep pace with increasing demand for a company's product or to provide for additions to the product line.

The useful life of many plant assets extends over relatively long periods of time, and the amount of the expenditures for such assets usually changes a great deal from year to year. The customary practice, therefore, is to project the plans for a number of years into the future in preparing the capital expenditures budget. A five-year capital expenditures budget is illustrated as follows:

Bowers Company
Capital Expenditures Budget
For Five Years Ending December 31, 1990

Item	1986	1987	1988	1989	1990
Machinery — Department 1 ...	$400,000			$280,000	$360,000
Machinery — Department 2 ...	180,000	$260,000	$560,000	200,000	
Office equipment		90,000			60,000
Total	$580,000	$350,000	$560,000	$480,000	$420,000

---

[1]The methods of evaluating alternate capital expenditure proposals are discussed in Chapter 22.

The various proposals recognized in the capital expenditures budget must be considered in preparing certain operating budgets. For example, the expected amount of depreciation on new equipment to be acquired in the current year must be taken into consideration when the budgets for factory overhead and operating expenses are prepared. The manner in which the proposed expenditures are to be financed will also affect the cash budget.

Cash Budget

The cash budget presents the expected inflow and outflow of cash for a day, week, month, or longer period. Receipts are classified by source and disbursements by purpose. The expected cash balance at the end of the period is then compared with the amount established as the minimum balance and the difference is the anticipated excess or deficiency for the period.

The minimum cash balance represents a safety buffer for mistakes in cash planning and for emergencies. However, the amount stated as the minimum balance need not remain fixed. It should perhaps be larger during periods of "peak" business activity than during the "slow" season. In addition, for effective cash management, much of the minimum cash balance can often be deposited in interest-bearing accounts.

The interrelationship of the cash budget with other budgets may be seen from the following illustration. Data from the sales budget, the various budgets for manufacturing costs and operating expenses, and the capital expenditures budget affect the cash budget. Consideration must also be given to dividend policies, plans for equity or long-term debt financing, and other projected plans that will affect cash.

Bowers Company
Cash Budget
For Three Months Ending March 31, 19--

CASH
BUDGET

	January	February	March
Estimated cash receipts from:			
Cash sales	$168,000	$185,000	$115,000
Collections of accounts receivable	699,000	712,800	572,000
Other sources (issuance of securities, interest, etc.)	——	——	27,000
Total cash receipts	$867,000	$897,800	$714,000
Estimated cash disbursements for:			
Manufacturing costs	$541,200	$557,000	$536,000
Operating expenses	150,200	151,200	140,800
Capital expenditures	——	144,000	80,000
Other purposes (notes, income tax, etc.)	47,000	20,000	160,000
Total cash disbursements	$738,400	$872,200	$916,800
Cash increase (decrease)	$128,600	$ 25,600	$(202,800)
Cash balance at beginning of month	280,000	408,600	434,200
Cash balance at end of month	$408,600	$434,200	$231,400
Minimum cash balance	300,000	300,000	300,000
Excess (deficiency)	$108,600	$134,200	$ (68,600)

In some cases, it is useful to present supplemental schedules to indicate the details of some of the amounts in the cash budget. For example, the following schedule illustrates the determination of the estimated cash receipts arising from collections of accounts receivable. For the illustration, it is assumed that the accounts receivable balance was $295,800 on January 1, and sales for each of the three months ending March 31 are $840,000, $925,000, and $575,000, respectively. Bowers Company expects to sell 20% of its merchandise for cash. Of the sales on account, 60% are expected to be collected in the month of the sale and the remainder in the following month.

SCHEDULE OF
COLLECTIONS OF
ACCOUNTS
RECEIVABLE

Bowers Company
Schedule of Collections of Accounts Receivable
For Three Months Ending March 31, 19--

	January	February	March
January 1 balance	$295,800		
January sales on account (80% × $840,000):			
Collected in January (60% × $672,000)	403,200		
Collected in February (40% × $672,000)		$268,800	
February sales on account (80% × $925,000):			
Collected in February (60% × $740,000)		444,000	
Collected in March (40% × $740,000)........			$296,000
March sales on account (80% × $575,000):			
Collected in March (60% × $460,000).........			276,000
Totals.....................................	$699,000	$712,800	$572,000

The importance of accurate cash budgeting can scarcely be over-emphasized. An unanticipated lack of cash can result in loss of discounts, unfavorable borrowing terms on loans, and damage to the credit rating. On the other hand, an excess amount of idle cash also shows poor management. When the budget shows periods of excess cash, such funds can be used to reduce loans or purchase investments in readily marketable income-producing securities. Reference to the Bowers Company cash budget shows excess cash during January and February and a deficiency during March.

Budgeted Balance Sheet

The budgeted balance sheet may reveal weaknesses in financial position, such as an abnormally large amount of current liabilities in relation to current assets, or excessive long-term debt in relation to stockholders' equity. If such conditions are indicated, the relevant factors should be given further study, so that the proper corrective action may be taken.

The budgeted balance sheet presents estimated details of financial condition at the end of a budget period, assuming that all budgeted operating and financing plans are fulfilled. A budgeted balance sheet is illustrated as follows:

Bowers Company
Budgeted Balance Sheet
December 31, 19--

Assets

Current assets:
Cash.		$ 360,000	
Accounts receivable.		214,000	
Marketable securities		650,000	
Inventories:			
Finished goods	$1,195,000		
Work in process.	220,000		
Materials	236,000	1,651,000	
Prepaid expenses.		37,500	
Total current assets			$2,912,500

	Cost	Accumulated Depreciation	Book Value	
Plant assets:				
Land.	$ 275,000	——	$ 275,000	
Buildings.	3,100,000	$1,950,000	1,150,000	
Machinery.	950,000	380,000	570,000	
Office equipment.	180,000	75,000	105,000	
Total plant assets	$4,505,000	$2,405,000		2,100,000
Total assets.				$5,012,500

Liabilities

Current liabilities:
Accounts payable.	$ 580,000	
Accrued liabilities	175,000	
Total current liabilities.	$ 755,000	
Long-term liabilities:		
Mortgage note payable	900,000	
Total liabilities.		$1,655,000

Stockholders' Equity

Common stock.	$2,000,000	
Retained earnings.	1,357,500	
Total stockholders' equity		3,357,500
Total liabilities and stockholders' equity.		$5,012,500

BUDGET PERFORMANCE REPORTS

A **budget performance report** comparing actual results with the budgeted figures should be prepared periodically for each budget. This "feedback" enables management to investigate significant differences to determine their cause and to seek means of preventing their recurrence. If corrective action cannot be taken because of changed conditions that have occurred since the budget was prepared, future budget figures should be revised accordingly. A budget performance report is illustrated as follows:

Bowers Company
Budget Performance Report—Factory Overhead Cost, Department 1
For Month Ended June 30, 19--

	Budget	Actual	Over	Under
Indirect factory wages....................	$30,200	$30,400	$200	
Supervisory salaries......................	15,000	15,000		
Power and light..........................	12,800	12,750		$ 50
Depreciation of plant and equipment.......	12,000	12,000		
Indirect materials	7,600	8,250	650	
Maintenance	5,800	5,700		100
Insurance and property taxes	3,300	3,300		
	$86,700	$87,400	$850	$150

The amounts reported in the "Budget" column were obtained from supplemental schedules accompanying the master budget. The amounts in the "Actual" column are the costs actually incurred. The last two columns show the amounts by which actual costs exceeded or were below budgeted figures. As shown in the illustration, there were differences between the actual and budgeted amounts for some of the items of overhead cost. The cause of the significant difference in indirect materials cost should be investigated, and an attempt to find means of corrective action should be made. For example, if the difference in indirect materials cost were found to be caused by a marketwide increase in the price of materials used, a corrective action may not be possible. On the other hand, if the difference resulted from the inefficient use of materials in the production process, it may be possible to eliminate the inefficiency and effect a savings in future indirect materials costs.

FLEXIBLE BUDGETS

In the discussion of budget systems, it has been assumed that the amount of sales and the level of manufacturing activity achieved during a period approximated the goals established in the budgets. When substantial changes in expectations occur during a budget period, the budgets should be revised to give effect to such changes. Otherwise, they will be of questionable value as incentives and instruments for controlling costs and expenses.

The effect of changes in volume of activity can be "built in" to the system by what are termed **flexible budgets.** Particularly useful in estimating and controlling factory overhead costs and operating expenses, a flexible budget is in reality a series of budgets for varying rates of activity. To illustrate, assume that because of extreme variations in demand and other uncontrollable factors, the output of a particular manufacturing enterprise fluctuates widely from month to month. In such circumstances, the total factory overhead costs incurred during periods of high activity are certain to be greater than during periods of low activity. It is equally certain, however, that fluctuations in total factory overhead costs will not be exactly proportionate to the volume of production. For example, if $100,000 of factory overhead costs are usually incurred during a month in which production totals 10,000 units, the factory overhead for a month in which only 5,000 units are produced would unquestionably be more than $50,000.

Items of factory cost and operating expense that tend to remain constant in amount regardless of changes in volume of activity may be said to be **fixed**. Real estate taxes, property insurance, and depreciation expense on buildings are examples of fixed costs. The amounts incurred are substantially independent of the level of operations. Costs and expenses which tend to fluctuate in amount according to changes in volume of activity are called **variable**. Supplies and indirect materials used and sales commissions are examples of variable costs and expenses. The degree of variability is not the same for all variable items; few, if any, vary in exact proportion to sales or production. The terms **semivariable** or **semifixed** are sometimes applied to items that have both fixed and variable characteristics to a significant degree. An example is electric power, for which there is often an initial flat fee and a rate for additional usage. For example, the charge for electricity used might be $700 for the first 10 000 kwh consumed during a month and $.05 per kwh used above 10 000.

Although there are many approaches to the preparation of a flexible budget, the first step is to identify the fixed and variable components of the various factory overhead and operating expenses being budgeted. The costs and expenses can then be presented in variable and fixed categories. For example, in the following flexible budget for factory overhead cost for one department and one product, "electric power" is broken down into its fixed and variable cost components for three different levels of production.

Collins Manufacturing Company Monthly Factory Overhead Cost Budget			
Units of product	8,000	9,000	10,000
Variable cost:			
Indirect factory wages	$ 32,000	$ 36,000	$ 40,000
Electric power	24,000	27,000	30,000
Indirect materials	12,000	13,500	15,000
Total variable cost	$ 68,000	$ 76,500	$ 85,000
Fixed cost:			
Supervisory salaries	$ 40,000	$ 40,000	$ 40,000
Depreciation of plant and equipment	25,000	25,000	25,000
Property taxes	15,000	15,000	15,000
Insurance	12,000	12,000	12,000
Electric power	10,000	10,000	10,000
Total fixed cost	$102,000	$102,000	$102,000
Total factory overhead cost	$170,000	$178,500	$187,000

FLEXIBLE BUDGET
FOR FACTORY
OVERHEAD COST

The fixed portion of electric power is $10,000 for all levels of production. The variable portion is $30,000 for 10,000 units of product, $27,000 ($30,000 × 9,000/10,000) for 9,000 units of product, and $24,000 ($30,000 × 8,000/10,000) for 8,000 units of product.

In practice, the number of production levels and the interval between levels in a flexible budget will vary with the range of production volume. For example, instead of budgeting for 8,000, 9,000, and 10,000 units of product, it might be necessary to provide for levels, at intervals of 500, from 6,000 to 12,000 units. Alternative bases, such as hours of departmental operation or direct labor hours, may also be used in measuring the volume of activity.

In preparing budget performance reports, the actual results would be compared with the flexible budget figures for the level of operations achieved. For example, if Collins Manufacturing Company manufactured 10,000 units during a month, the budget figures reported in the budget performance report would be those appearing in the "10,000 units" column of Collins' flexible budget.

AUTOMATED BUDGETING PROCEDURES

Many firms use computers in the budgeting process. Computers can not only speed up the budgeting process, but they can also reduce the cost of budget preparation when large quantities of data need to be processed. Computers are especially useful in preparing flexible budgets and in continuous budgeting. Budget performance reports can also be prepared on a timely basis by the use of the computer.

By using computerized simulation models, which are mathematical statements of the relationships among various operating activities, management can determine the impact of various operating alternatives on the master budget. For example, if management wishes to evaluate the impact of a proposed change in direct labor wage rates, the computer can quickly provide a revised master budget that reflects the new rates. If management wishes to evaluate a proposal to add a new product line, the computer can quickly update current budgeted data and indicate the effect of the proposal on the master budget.

BUDGETING AND HUMAN BEHAVIOR

The budgeting process sets the overall goals of the business as well as the specific goals for individual units. Significant human behavior problems can develop if these goals are viewed as unrealistic or unachievable by management personnel. In such a case, management may become discouraged as well as uncommitted to the achievement of the goals. As a result, the budget becomes worthless as a tool for planning and controlling operations. On the other hand, goals set within a range that management considers attainable are likely to inspire management's efforts to achieve the goals. Therefore, it is important that all levels of management be involved in establishing the goals which they will be expected to achieve. In such an environment, the budget is a planning tool that will favorably affect human behavior and increase the possibility of achieving the goals.

Human behavior problems can also arise when the budgeted and actual results are compared and reported. These problems can be minimized if budget performance reports are used exclusively to evaluate operating performance and to initiate corrective action when performance can be improved. However, if budget performance reports are also used to evaluate management performance, management may concentrate more on defending its performance than on using the budgeting system to plan and control operations.

There is little doubt that budgets and budget performance reports can have a significant influence on management behavior. Behavioral factors have received increased attention by management accountants and behavioral scientists in recent years, and many behavioral issues are the subject of ongoing research.

---

1. Budgeting of operating activities to provide at all times for maintenance of a twelve-month projection into the future is called:
   A. fixed budgeting
   B. variable budgeting
   C. continuous budgeting
   D. none of the above

2. The budget that summarizes future plans for acquisition of plant facilities and equipment is the:
   A. cash budget
   B. sales budget
   C. capital expenditures budget
   D. none of the above

3. A report comparing actual results with the budget figures is called a:
   A. budget report
   B. budget performance report
   C. flexible budget report
   D. none of the above

4. Costs that tend to remain constant in amount, regardless of variations in volume of activity, are called:
   A. fixed costs
   B. variable costs
   C. semifixed costs
   D. semivariable costs

5. The system that "builds in" the effect of fluctuations in volume of activity into the various budgets is termed:
   A. budget performance reporting
   B. continuous budgeting
   C. flexible budgeting
   D. none of the above

Self-
Examination
Questions
(Answers
at end of
chapter.)

Discussion Questions

17–1. What is a budget?

17–2. (a) Name the two basic functions of management in which accounting is involved. (b) How does a budget aid management in the discharge of these basic functions?

17–3. What is meant by *continuous budgeting*?

17–4. Why should all levels of management and all departments participate in the preparation and submission of budget estimates?

17–5. Which budgetary concept requires all levels of management to start from zero and estimate sales, production, and other operating data as though the operations were being initiated for the first time?

17–6. Why should the production requirements as set forth in the production budget be carefully coordinated with the sales budget?

17–7. Why should the timing of direct materials purchases be closely coordinated with the production budget?

17–8. What is a capital expenditures budget?

17–9. (a) Discuss the purpose of the cash budget. (b) If the cash budget for the first quarter of the fiscal year indicates excess cash at the end of each of the first two months, how might the excess cash be used?

17–10. What is a budget performance report?

17–11. What is a flexible budget?

17–12. Distinguish between (a) fixed costs and (b) variable costs.

17–13. Which of the following costs incurred by a manufacturing enterprise tend to be fixed and which tend to be variable: (a) rent on factory building, (b) cost of raw materials entering into finished product, (c) depreciation on factory building, (d) real estate taxes on factory building, (e) salary of factory superintendent, (f) direct labor, (g) factory supplies?

17–14. What is a semivariable (or semifixed) cost?

17–15. Haas Corporation uses flexible budgets. For each of the following variable operating expenses, indicate whether there has been a saving or an excess of expenses, assuming that actual sales were $400,000.

Expense Item	Actual Amount	Budget Allowance Based on Sales
Factory supplies expense	$ 7,850	2%
Uncollectible accounts expense	17,840	4%

17–16. Briefly discuss the type of human behavior problem that might arise if goals used in developing budgets are unrealistic or unachievable.

Exercises

17–17. Kipling Company manufactures two models of heating pads, HP-1 and HP-2. Based on the following production and sales data for April of the current year, prepare (a) a sales budget and (b) a production budget.

	HP-1	HP-2
Estimated inventory (units), April 1	30,000	13,800
Desired inventory (units), April 30	36,000	12,000
Expected sales volume (units):		
Area 20	21,000	5,400
Area 30	10,800	2,400
Unit sales price	$9.60	$13.20

17–18. James Company was organized on April 1 of the current year. Projected sales for each of the first three months of operations are as follows:

April..................................	$200,000
May..................................	250,000
June	350,000

The company expects to sell 30% of its merchandise for cash. Of sales on account, 40% are expected to be collected in the month of sale, 50% in the month following sale, and the remainder in the following month. Prepare a schedule indicating cash collections of accounts receivable for April, May, and June.

17–19. Burton Company was organized on June 30 of the current year. Projected operating expenses for each of the first three months of operations are as follows:

July..................................	$ 75,000
August	90,000
September............................	111,000

Depreciation, insurance, and property taxes represent $15,000 of estimated monthly operating expenses. Insurance was paid on June 30, and property taxes will be paid in December. Two thirds of the remainder of the operating expenses are expected to be paid in the month in which they are incurred, with the balance to be paid in the following month. Prepare a schedule indicating cash disbursements for operating expenses for July, August, and September.

17–20. Humphreys Company uses flexible budgets. Prepare a flexible operating expenses budget for February of the current year for sales volumes of $400,000, $500,000, and $600,000, based on the following data:

Sales commissions	9% of sales
Advertising expense	$20,000 for $400,000 of sales
	$24,000 for $500,000 of sales
	$28,000 for $600,000 of sales
Miscellaneous selling expense	$2,000 plus 1% of sales
Office salaries expense....................	$18,600
Office supplies expense	1½% of sales
Miscellaneous general expense	$850 plus 1% of sales

17–21. The operating expenses incurred during February of the current year by Humphreys Company were as follows:

Sales commissions.....................	$46,500
Advertising expense....................	22,000
Miscellaneous selling expense..........	7,200

Office salaries expense................	$18,600
Office supplies expense	8,100
Miscellaneous general expense.........	5,600

Assuming that the total sales for February were $500,000, prepare a budget performance report for operating expenses on the basis of the data presented above and in 17–20.

17–22. Arness Company prepared the following factory overhead cost budget for Department F for September of the current year, during which it expected to manufacture 12,000 units:

Variable cost:		
Indirect factory wages..................................	$10,000	
Power and light	8,500	
Indirect materials....................................	3,000	
Total variable cost.................................		$21,500
Fixed cost:		
Supervisory salaries	$ 8,250	
Depreciation of plant and equipment....................	4,100	
Insurance and property taxes..........................	3,250	
Total fixed cost...................................		15,600
Total factory overhead cost.............................		$37,100

Assuming that the estimated costs in September are applicable to October operations, prepare a flexible factory overhead cost budget for October for 11,400, 12,000, and 12,600 units of product.

17–23. During October, Arness Company manufactured 11,400 units, and the factory overhead costs incurred were: indirect factory wages, $9,690; power and light, $8,180; indirect materials, $2,675; supervisory salaries, $8,250; depreciation of plant and equipment, $4,100; and insurance and property taxes, $3,250.

Prepare a budget performance report for October. To be useful for cost control, the budgeted amounts should be based on the data for 11,400 units, as revealed in 17-22.

Problems

17–24. T. I. C. Inc. prepared the following factory overhead cost budget for October of the current year for 9,000 units of product:

T. I. C. Inc.
Factory Overhead Cost Budget
For Month Ending October 31, 19--

Variable cost:		
Indirect factory wages...........................	$14,175	
Indirect materials	10,125	
Power and light.................................	9,000	
Total variable cost		$33,300
Fixed cost:		
Supervisory salaries	$11,500	
Indirect factory wages...........................	4,100	
Depreciation of plant and equipment	3,800	
Insurance.....................................	2,250	
Power and light.................................	2,000	
Property taxes..................................	1,350	
Total fixed cost...............................		25,000
Total factory overhead cost		$58,300

The following factory overhead costs were incurred in producing 8,000 units:

Indirect factory wages..	$16,500
Supervisory salaries	11,500
Power and light	10,600
Indirect materials..	9,450
Depreciation of plant and equipment..........................	3,800
Insurance	2,250
Property taxes	1,350
Total factory overhead cost incurred........................	$55,450

Instructions:
(1) Prepare a flexible factory overhead cost budget for October, indicating capacities of 8,000, 9,000, 10,000, and 11,000 units of product.
(2) Prepare a budget performance report for October.

17-25. The budget director of Feinberg Company requests estimates of sales, production, and other operating data from the various administrative units every month.

Selected information concerning sales and production for March of the current year are summarized as follows:

(a) Estimated sales for March by sales territory:
    East:
        Product P1 .... 10,000 units at $75 per unit
        Product P2 .... 12,000 units at $88 per unit
    Midwest:
        Product P1 .... 8,000 units at $75 per unit
        Product P2 .... 11,500 units at $88 per unit

West:

Product P1 .... 14,000 units at $75 per unit

Product P2 .... 18,000 units at $88 per unit

(b) Estimated inventories at March 1:

Direct materials:

Material E: 10,600 lbs.

Material F: 9,200 lbs.

Material G: 4,800 lbs.

Material H: 11,500 lbs.

Finished products:

Product P1: 4,000 units

Product P2: 7,100 units

(c) Desired inventories at March 31:

Direct materials:

Material E: 12,000 lbs.

Material F: 8,000 lbs.

Material G: 5,000 lbs.

Material H: 10,000 lbs.

Finished products:

Product P1: 5,000 units

Product P2: 6,000 units

(d) Direct materials used in production:

In manufacture of Product P1:

Material E: 3.0 lbs. per unit of product

Material F: 1.6 lbs. per unit of product

Material G: 2.2 lbs. per unit of product

In manufacture of Product P2:

Material E: 1.5 lbs. per unit of product

Material F: 1.0 lbs. per unit of product

Material H: 3.0 lbs. per unit of product

(e) Anticipated purchase price for direct materials:

Material E: $ .45 per lb.

Material F: $1.80 per lb.

Material G: $ .80 per lb.

Material H: $ .75 per lb.

(f) Direct labor requirements:

Product P1:

Department 10: 1.0 hour at $12 per hour

Department 20: 1.5 hours at $15 per hour

Product P2:

Department 10: 2.0 hours at $12 per hour

Department 30: 1.5 hours at $18 per hour

Instructions:

(1) Prepare a sales budget for March.

(2) Prepare a production budget for March.

(3) Prepare a direct materials purchases budget for March.

(4) Prepare a direct labor cost budget for March.

17–26. Trane Company prepared the following sales budget for the current year:

Trane Company
Sales Budget
For Year Ending December 31, 1987

Product and Area	Unit Sales Volume	Unit Selling Price	Total Sales
Product A:			
East	28,000	$22.50	$ 630,000
Central.................................	18,000	22.50	405,000
West.....................................	25,000	22.50	562,500
Total.....................................	71,000		$1,597,500
Product B:			
East	42,000	10.00	$ 420,000
Central.................................	30,000	10.00	300,000
West.....................................	45,000	10.00	450,000
Total.....................................	117,000		$1,170,000
Total revenue from sales....................			$2,767,500

At the end of September, 1987, the following unit sales data were reported for the first nine months of the year:

	Unit Sales	
	Product A	**Product B**
East......................................	23,100	34,650
Central	13,500	20,250
West......................................	21,565	33,750

For the year ending December 31, 1988, unit sales are expected to follow the patterns established during the first nine months of the year ending December 31, 1987. The unit selling price for Product A is not expected to change, and the unit selling price for Product B is expected to be increased to $10.50, effective January 1, 1988.

Instructions:

(1) Compute the increase or decrease of actual *unit* sales for the nine months ended September 30, 1987, over expectations for this nine-month period. Since sales have historically occurred evenly throughout the year, budgeted sales for the first nine months of a year would be 75% of the year's budgeted sales. Comparison of this amount with actual sales will indicate the percentage increase or decrease of actual sales for the nine months over budgeted sales for the nine months. (Round percent changes to the nearest whole percent.) Place your answers in a columnar table with the following format:

	Unit Budgeted Sales		Actual Sales	Increase (Decrease)	
	Year	Nine Months	for Nine Months	Amount	Percent
Product A					
East					
Central					
West					
Product B					
East					
Central					
West					

(2) Assuming that the trend of sales indicated in (1) is to continue in 1988, compute the unit sales volume to be used for preparing the sales budget for the year ending December 31, 1988. Place your answers in a columnar table with the following format:

	1987 Budgeted Units	Percentage Increase (Decrease)	1988 Budgeted Units
Product A			
East			
Central			
West			
Product B			
East			
Central			
West			

(3) Prepare a sales budget for the year ending December 31, 1988.

17–27. The treasurer of Epstein Company instructs you to prepare a monthly cash budget for the next three months. You are presented with the following budget information:

	August	September	October
Sales..............................	$480,000	$450,000	$510,000
Manufacturing costs.................	284,000	230,000	288,000
Operating expenses.................	162,000	150,000	176,000
Capital expenditures	——	200,000	——

The company expects to sell about 30% of its merchandise for cash. Of sales on account, 80% are expected to be collected in full in the month following the sale and the remainder the following month. Depreciation, insurance, and property taxes represent $12,000 of the estimated monthly manufacturing costs and $4,000 of the probable monthly operating expenses. Insurance and property taxes are paid in June and December respectively. Of the remainder of the manufacturing costs and operating expenses, 60% are expected to be paid in the month in which they are incurred and the balance in the following month.

Current assets as of August 1 are composed of cash of $58,500, marketable securities of $50,000, and accounts receivable of $474,500 ($383,500 from July sales and $91,000 from June sales). Current liabilities as of August 1 are composed of an $80,000, 15%, 120-day note payable due September 15, $82,500 of accounts payable incurred in July for manufacturing costs, and accrued liabilities of $48,200 incurred in July for operating expenses.

It is expected that $1,800 in dividends will be received in August. An estimated income tax payment of $26,000 will be made in October. Epstein Company's regular semiannual dividend of $15,000 is expected to be declared in September and paid in October. Management desires to maintain a minimum cash balance of $50,000.

Instructions:

(1) Prepare a monthly cash budget for August, September, and October.

(2) On the basis of the cash budget prepared in (1), what recommendation should be made to the treasurer?

17–28. As a preliminary to requesting budget estimates of sales, costs, and expenses for the fiscal year beginning January 1, 1986, the following tentative trial balance as of December 31 of the preceding year is prepared by the accounting department of Bromley Company:

Cash	58,000	
Accounts Receivable	56,000	
Finished Goods	102,200	
Work in Process	59,200	
Materials	34,800	
Prepaid Expenses	6,800	
Plant and Equipment	540,000	
Accumulated Depreciation—Plant and Equipment		216,000
Accounts Payable		66,000
Notes Payable		40,000
Common Stock, $10 par		100,000
Retained Earnings		435,000
	857,000	857,000

Balances of accounts receivable, prepaid expenses, and accounts payable at the end of the year are expected to differ from the beginning balances by only inconsequential amounts.

For purposes of this problem, assume that federal income tax of $24,000 on 1986 taxable income will be paid during 1986. Regular quarterly cash dividends of $.20 a share are expected to be declared and paid in March, June, September, and December. It is anticipated that plant and equipment will be purchased for $125,000 cash in September.

Factory output and sales for 1986 are expected to total 40,000 units of product, which are to be sold at $18 per unit. The quantities and costs of the inventories (lifo method) at December 31, 1986, are expected to remain unchanged from the balances at the beginning of the year.

Budget estimates of manufacturing costs and operating expenses for the year are summarized as follows:

	Estimated Costs and Expenses	
	Fixed (Total for Year)	**Variable** (Per Unit Sold)
Cost of goods manufactured and sold:		
Direct materials	—	$2.30
Direct labor	—	5.60
Factory overhead:		
Depreciation of plant and equipment	$28,800	—
Other factory overhead	19,200	1.70
Selling expenses:		
Sales salaries and commissions..................	40,000	.90
Advertising.....................................	20,500	—
Miscellaneous selling expense	1,500	.10
General expenses:		
Office and officers salaries.....................	50,000	.40
Supplies..	3,400	.10
Miscellaneous general expense	2,600	.05

Instructions:

(1) Prepare a budgeted income statement for 1986.
(2) Prepare a budgeted balance sheet as of December 31, 1986.

Alternate Problems

17–24A. Alliance Company prepared the following factory overhead cost budget for November of the current year for 21,250 units of product:

Alliance Company
Factory Overhead Cost Budget
For Month Ending November 30, 19--

Variable cost:		
Indirect factory wages.............................	$17,000	
Indirect materials	10,540	
Power and light....................................	7,480	
Total variable cost		$ 35,020
Fixed cost:		
Supervisory salaries	$23,640	
Indirect factory wages............................	8,730	
Depreciation of plant and equipment	16,200	
Insurance..	14,400	
Power and light...................................	7,530	
Property taxes....................................	9,800	
Total fixed cost.................................		80,300
Total factory overhead cost		$115,320

The following factory overhead costs were incurred in producing 18,750 units:

Indirect factory wages	$ 23,230
Supervisory salaries	23,640
Indirect materials	9,275
Power and light	14,680
Depreciation of plant and equipment	16,200
Insurance	14,400
Property taxes	9,800
Total factory overhead cost incurred	$111,225

Instructions:

(1) Prepare a flexible factory overhead cost budget for November, indicating capacities of 18,750, 21,250, 25,000 and 30,000 units of product.

(2) Prepare a budget performance report for November.

17–26A. Trane Company prepared the following sales budget for the current year:

Trane Company
Sales Budget
For Year Ending December 31, 1987

Product and Area	Unit Sales Volume	Unit Selling Price	Total Sales
Product A:			
East	36,000	$10.00	$ 360,000
Central	18,000	10.00	180,000
West	24,000	10.00	240,000
Total	78,000		$ 780,000
Product B:			
East	42,000	$15.00	$ 630,000
Central	30,000	15.00	450,000
West	45,000	15.00	675,000
Total	117,000		$1,755,000
Total revenue from sales			$2,535,000

At the end of September, 1987, the following unit sales data were reported for the first nine months of the year:

	Unit Sales	
	Product A	Product B
East	32,400	28,350
Central	14,850	24,750
West	18,000	33,750

For the year ending December 31, 1988, unit sales are expected to follow the patterns established during the first nine months of the year ending December 31, 1987. The unit selling price for Product A is expected to be increased to $11, effective January 1, 1988, and the unit selling price for Product B is not expected to change.

Instructions:

(1) Compute the increase or decrease of actual *unit* sales for the nine months ended September 30, 1987, over expectations for this nine-month period. Since sales have historically occurred evenly throughout the year, budgeted sales for the first nine months of a year would be 75% of the year's budgeted sales. Comparison of this amount with actual sales will indicate the percentage increase or decrease of actual sales for the nine months over budgeted sales for the nine months. Place your answers in a columnar table with the following format:

| | Unit Budgeted Sales | | Actual Sales | Increase (Decrease) | |
	Year	Nine Months	for Nine Months	Amount	Percent
Product A					
East					
Central					
West					
Product B					
East					
Central					
West					

(2) Assuming that the trend of sales indicated in (1) is to continue in 1988, compute the unit sales volume to be used for preparing the sales budget for the year ending December 31, 1988. Place your answers in a columnar table with the following format:

	1987 Budgeted Units	Percentage Increase (Decrease)	1988 Budgeted Units
Product A			
East			
Central			
West			
Product B			
East			
Central			
West			

(3) Prepare a sales budget for the year ending December 31, 1988.

17–27A. The treasurer of Donovan Company instructs you to prepare a monthly cash budget for the next three months. You are presented with the following budget information:

	May	June	July
Sales..............................	$300,000	$245,000	$350,000
Manufacturing costs..................	195,000	160,000	227,000
Operating expenses..................	45,000	37,000	56,000
Capital expenditures.................	—	100,000	—

The company expects to sell about 20% of its merchandise for cash. Of sales on account, 75% are expected to be collected in full in the month following the sale and the remainder the following month. Depreciation, insurance, and property taxes represent $15,000 of the estimated monthly manufacturing costs and $3,000 of the probable monthly operating expenses. Insurance and property taxes are paid in March and August respectively. Of the remainder of the manufacturing costs and operating expenses, 70% are expected to be paid in the month in which they are incurred and the balance in the following month.

Current assets as of May 1 are composed of cash of $31,000, marketable securities of $20,000, and accounts receivable of $265,000 ($220,000 from April sales and $45,000 from March sales). Current liabilities as of May 1 are composed of a $30,000, 14%, 120-day note payable due June 10, $60,400 of accounts payable incurred in April for manufacturing costs, and accrued liabilities of $14,100 incurred in April for operating expenses.

It is expected that $2,200 in dividends will be received in June. An estimated income tax payment of $12,500 will be made in June. Donovan Company's regular quarterly dividend of $5,000 is expected to be declared in June and paid in July. Management desires to maintain a minimum cash balance of $35,000.

Instructions:
(1) Prepare a monthly cash budget for May, June, and July.
(2) On the basis of the cash budget prepared in (1), what recommendation should be made to the treasurer?

17–29. Your father is president and chief operating officer of Thomas Manufacturing Company and has hired you as a summer intern to assist the controller. The controller has asked you to visit with the production supervisor of the Sanding Department and evaluate the supervisor's concerns with the budgeting process. After this evaluation, you are to meet with the controller to discuss suggestions for improving the budgeting process.

This morning, you met with the supervisor, who expressed dissatisfaction with the budgets and budget performance reports prepared for the factory overhead costs for the Sanding Department. Specifically, June's budget performance report was mentioned as an example. The supervisor indicated that this report is not useful in evaluating the efficiency of the department, because most of the overages for the individual factory overhead items are not caused by inefficiencies, but by variations in the volume of activity between actual and budget. Although you were not provided with a copy of the budget for June, the supervisor indicated that it is standard practice for the plant manager to prepare a budget based on the production of 10,000 units. Actual production varies widely, however, with approximately 11,000 to 12,000 units being produced each month for the past several months. You are provided with the following budget performance report for June of the current year, when actual production was 11,000 units. All of the overages relate to variable costs, and the other costs are fixed.

Mini-Case

Thomas Manufacturing Company
Budget Performance Report—Factory Overhead Cost, Sanding Department
For Month Ended June 30, 19--

	Budget	Actual	Over	Under
Indirect factory wages	$10,000	$10,900	$ 900	
Electric power	8,000	8,950	950	
Supervisory salaries..................	7,500	7,500		
Depreciation of plant assets...........	5,250	5,250		
Indirect materials	5,000	5,400	400	
Insurance and property taxes..........	3,000	3,000		
	$38,750	$41,000	$2,250	

In your discussion, you learned that the department supervisor has little faith in the budgeting process. The supervisor views the budgets as worthless and the budget performance reports as a waste of time, because they require an explanation of the budget overages, which, for the most part, are not departmentally controlled.

Instructions:

Prepare a list of suggestions for improving the budgeting process. Include any reports that you might find useful when you meet with the controller to discuss your suggestions.

Answers to Self-Examination Questions

1. C Continuous budgeting (answer C) is a type of budgeting that continually provides for maintenance of a twelve-month projection into the future.

2. C The capital expenditures budget (answer C) summarizes the plans for the acquisition of plant facilities and equipment for a number of years into the future. The cash budget (answer A) presents the expected inflow and outflow of cash for a budget period, and the sales budget (answer B) presents the expected sales for the budget period.

3. B A budget performance report (answer B) compares actual results with budgeted figures.

4. A Costs that tend to remain constant in amount, regardless of variations in volume of activity, are called fixed costs (answer A). Costs that tend to fluctuate in amount in accordance with variations in volume are called variable costs (answer B). Costs that have both fixed and variable characteristics are called semi-fixed costs (answer C) or semivariable costs (answer D).

5. C Flexible budgeting (answer C) provides a series of budgets for varying rates of activity and thereby builds into the budgeting system the effect of fluctuations in volume of activity. Budget performance reporting (answer A) is a system of reports that compares actual results with budgeted figures. Continuous budgeting (answer B) is a variant of fiscal-year budgeting that provides for continuous twelve-month projections into the future. This is achieved by periodically deleting from the current budget the data for the elapsed period and adding newly estimated budget data for the same period next year.

CHAPTER 18

Standard Cost Systems

CHAPTER OBJECTIVES

Describe the nature of standard costs.

Describe the use of standard costs in planning and controlling operations.

Illustrate the use of variance analysis in controlling operations.

The preceding chapter focused on the use of budgets as an aid to management in planning and controlling the operations of a business. This chapter will focus on standard cost systems and variance analysis, which can also be used by management in planning and controlling operations.

THE NATURE AND OBJECTIVES OF STANDARDS

Standards are used to measure and evaluate performance in many areas of life. For example, colleges and universities set standards for graduation, such as a C average. They may establish a B+ average for graduation with honors. Golfers use par as a standard in evaluating their play on the golf course. In each of these cases, the predetermined standard is used to measure and evaluate an individual's performance. In a like manner, business enterprises may use carefully predetermined standards to evaluate and control operations.

Service, merchandising, and manufacturing enterprises can all use standards. For example, an automobile repair garage may use a *standard* amount of time, as expressed in service manuals, as the basis for computing the labor charges for automobile repairs and measuring the performance of the mechanic. The driver of a truck delivering merchandise may be expected to make a *standard* number of deliveries each day. The widest use of standards is by manufacturing enterprises, which establish standard costs for the three categories of manufacturing costs: direct materials, direct labor, and factory overhead.

Accounting systems that use standards for each element of manufacturing cost entering into the finished product are sometimes called **standard cost systems.** Such systems enable management to determine how much a product should cost (**standard**), how much it does cost (actual), and the causes of any difference (variance) between the two. Standard costs thus serve as a device for measuring efficiency. If the actual costs are compared with the standard costs, unfavorable conditions can be determined and corrective actions taken. Thus, management has a device for controlling costs and motivating employees to become more cost conscious.

Standard costs may be used in either the process cost or the job order cost systems. Both of these systems, as discussed in Chapters 15 and 16, can provide management with timely data on manufacturing costs and may aid in cost control and profit maximization. For more effective control, standard costs should be used for each department or cost center in the factory. It is possible, however, to use standard costs in some departments and actual costs in others.

Setting Standards

The starting point in setting standards is often a review of past operations. In this review, management and the management accountant rely on their knowledge and judgment of past processes and costs to estimate the costs to produce a unit of product. However, standards should not be merely an extension of past costs. Inefficiencies may be reflected in past costs, and these inefficiencies should be considered in determining what the costs should be (standards). In addition, changes in technology, machinery, production methods, and economic conditions must be considered.

The setting of standards is both an art and a science. Although the standard-setting process varies among enterprises, it often requires the joint efforts of accountants, engineers, personnel administrators, and other management personnel. The management accountant plays an important role by expressing the results of judgments and studies in terms of dollars and subsequently reporting how actual results compare with these standards. Engineers contribute to the standard-setting process by studying the requirements of the product and the production process. For example, direct materials requirements can be determined by studying such factors as the materials specifications for the product and the normal spoilage in production. Time and motion studies may be used to determine the length of time required for each of the various manufacturing operations. Engineering studies may also be used to determine standards for some of the elements of factory overhead, such as the amount of power needed to operate machinery.

Types of Standards

Implicit in the use of standards is the concept of an acceptable level of production efficiency. One of the major objectives in selecting this performance level is to motivate workers to expend the efforts necessary to achieve the most efficient operations.

Standards that are too high, that is, standards that are unrealistic, may have a negative impact on performance because workers may become frustrated with their inability to meet the standards and, therefore, may not be motivated to do their best. Such standards represent levels of performance that can be achieved only under perfect operating conditions, such as no idle time, no machine breakdowns, and no materials spoilage. Such standards, often called theoretical standards or **ideal standards**, are not widely used.

Standards that are too low might not motivate employees to perform at their best because the standard level of performance can be reached too easily. As a result, productivity may be lower than that which could be achieved.

Most companies use currently attainable standards (sometimes called **normal standards**), which represent levels of operation that can be attained with reasonable effort. Such currently attainable standards allow for reasonable production problems and errors, such as normal materials spoilage and machinery downtime for maintenance. When reasonable standards are used, employees often become cost conscious and expend their best efforts to achieve the best possible results at the lowest possible cost. Also, if employees are given bonuses for exceeding normal standards, the standards may be even more effective in motivating employees to perform at their best.

VARIANCES FROM STANDARDS

One of the primary purposes of a standard cost system is to facilitate control over costs by comparing actual costs with standard costs. Control is achieved by the action of management in investigating significant deviations of performance from standards and taking corrective action. Differences between the standard costs of a department or product and the actual costs incurred are termed variances. If the actual cost incurred is less than the standard cost, the variance is favorable. If the actual cost exceeds the standard cost, the variance is unfavorable. When actual costs are compared with standard costs, only the "exceptions" or variances are reported to the person responsible for cost control. This reporting by the "principle of exceptions" enables the one responsible for cost control to concentrate on the cause and correction of the variances.

When manufacturing operations are automated, standard cost data can be integrated with the computer that directs operations. Variances can then be detected and reported automatically by the computer system, and adjustments can be made to operations in progress.

The total variance for a certain period is usually made up of several variances, some of which may be favorable and some unfavorable. There may be variances from standards in direct materials costs, in direct labor costs, and in factory overhead costs. Illustrations and analyses of these variances for Ballard Company, a manufacturing enterprise, are presented in the following paragraphs. For illustrative purposes, it is assumed that only one type of direct material is used, that there is a single processing department, and that Product X is the only commodity manufactured by the enterprise. The standard costs for direct materials, direct labor, and factory overhead for a unit of Product X are as follows:

Direct materials:
2 pounds at $1 per pound .... $ 2.00

Direct labor:
.4 hour at $16 per hour 6.40

Factory overhead:
.4 hour at $8.40 per hour.................... 3.36

Total per unit $11.76

Direct Materials Cost Variance

Two major factors enter into the determination of standards for direct materials cost: (1) the quantity (usage) standard and (2) the price standard. If the actual quantity of direct materials used in producing a commodity differs from the standard quantity, there is a **quantity variance.** If the actual unit price of the materials differs from the standard price, there is a **price variance.** To illustrate, assume that the standard direct materials cost of producing 10,000 units of Product X and the direct materials cost actually incurred during June were as follows:

Actual: 20,600 pounds at $1.04 .... $21,424
Standard: 20,000 pounds at $1.00 20,000

The unfavorable variance of $1,424 resulted in part from an excess usage of 600 pounds of direct materials and in part from an excess cost of $.04 per pound. The analysis of the materials cost variance is as follows:

DIRECT MATERIALS
COST VARIANCE

Quantity variance:
Actual quantity .... 20,600 pounds
Standard quantity. .... 20,000 pounds

Variance—unfavorabie.... 600 pounds × standard price, $1........ $ 600

Price variance:
Actual price................ $1.04 per pound
Standard price .... 1.00 per pound

Variance—unfavorable.... $ .04 per pound × actual quantity, 20,600 . 824

Total direct materials cost variance—unfavorable......................... $1,424

Direct Materials Quantity Variance

The direct materials quantity variance is the difference between the actual quantity used and the standard quantity, multiplied by the standard price per unit. If the standard quantity exceeds the actual quantity used, the variance is favorable. If the actual quantity of materials used exceeds the standard quantity, the variance is unfavorable, as shown for Ballard Company in the following illustration:

Direct Materials Quantity Variance $=$ Actual Quantity Used − Standard Quantity $\times$ Standard Price per Unit

Quantity variance = (20,600 pounds − 20,000 pounds) × $1.00 per pound

Quantity variance = 600 pounds × $1.00 per pound

Quantity variance = $600 unfavorable

DIRECT MATERIALS QUANTITY VARIANCE

Direct Materials Price Variance

The direct materials price variance is the difference between the actual price per unit and the standard price per unit, multiplied by the actual quantity used. If the standard price per unit exceeds the actual price per unit, the variance is favorable. If the actual price per unit exceeds the standard price per unit, the variance is unfavorable, as shown for Ballard Company in the following illustration:

Direct Materials Price Variance $=$ Actual Price per Unit − Standard Price $\times$ Actual Quantity Used

Price variance = ($1.04 per pound − $1.00 per pound) × 20,600 pounds

Price variance = $.04 per pound × 20,600 pounds

Price variance = $824 unfavorable

DIRECT MATERIALS PRICE VARIANCE

Reporting Direct Materials Cost Variance

The physical quantity and the dollar amount of the quantity variance should be reported to the factory superintendent and other personnel responsible for production. If excessive amounts of direct materials were used because of the malfunction of equipment or some other failure within the production department, those responsible should correct the situation. However, an unfavorable direct materials quantity variance is not necessarily the result of inefficiency within the production department. If the excess usage of 600 pounds of materials in the example above had been caused by inferior materials, the purchasing department should be held responsible.

The unit price and the total amount of the materials price variance should be reported to the purchasing department, which may or may not be able to control this variance. If materials of the same quality could have been purchased from another supplier at the standard price, the variance was controllable. On the other hand, if the variance resulted from a marketwide price increase, the variance was not subject to control.

Direct Labor Cost Variance

As in the case of direct materials, two major factors enter into the determination of standards for direct labor cost: (1) the time (usage or efficiency) standard, and (2) the rate (price or wage) standard. If the actual direct labor hours spent producing a product differ from the standard hours, there is a time variance. If the wage rate paid differs from the standard rate, there is a rate variance. The standard cost and the actual cost of direct labor in the production of 10,000 units of Product X during June are assumed to be as follows:

Actual: 3,950 hours at $16.40. . . . . $64,780
Standard: 4,000 hours at   16.00.   64,000

The unfavorable direct labor variance of $780 is made up of a favorable time variance and an unfavorable rate variance, determined as follows:

DIRECT LABOR
COST VARIANCE

Time variance:
  Actual time . . . . 3,950 hours
  Standard time . . . . <u>4,000</u> hours

    Variance—favorable. . . .   50 hours × standard rate, $16. . . . . $ 800

Rate variance:
  Actual rate. . . . . $16.40 per hour
  Standard rate . . . .   <u>16.00</u> per hour

    Variance—unfavorable . . $ .40 per hour × actual time, 3,950 hours. . .   <u>1,580</u>

Total direct labor cost variance—unfavorable . . . .   <u>$ 780</u>

Direct Labor Time Variance

The direct labor time variance is the difference between the actual hours worked and the standard hours, multiplied by the standard rate per hour. If the actual hours worked exceed the standard hours, the variance is unfavorable. If the actual hours worked are less than the standard hours, the variance is favorable, as shown for Ballard Company in the following illustration:

DIRECT LABOR
TIME VARIANCE

$$\frac{\text{Direct Labor}}{\text{Time Variance}} = \frac{\text{Actual Hours Worked} -}{\text{Standard Hours}} \times \frac{\text{Standard Rate}}{\text{per Hour}}$$

Time variance = (3,950 hours − 4,000 hours) × $16 per hour
Time variance = −50 hours   × $16 per hour
Time variance = $800 favorable

In the illustration, when the standard hours (4,000) are subtracted from the actual hours worked (3,950), the difference is "−50 hours." The minus sign indicates that the variance of 50 hours, or $800 (50 hours × $16), is favorable.

Direct Labor Rate Variance

The direct labor rate variance is the difference between the actual rate per hour and the standard rate per hour, multiplied by the actual hours worked. If the standard rate per hour exceeds the actual rate per hour, the variance is favorable. If the actual rate per hour exceeds the standard rate per hour, the variance is unfavorable, as shown for Ballard Company in the following illustration:

DIRECT LABOR
RATE VARIANCE

$$\frac{\text{Direct Labor}}{\text{Rate Variance}} = \frac{\text{Actual Rate per Hour} -}{\text{Standard Rate}} \times \frac{\text{Actual Hours}}{\text{Worked}}$$

Rate variance = ($16.40 per hour − $16.00 per hour) × 3,950 hours
Rate variance = $.40 per hour   × 3,950 hours
Rate variance = $1,580 unfavorable

Reporting Direct Labor Cost Variance

The control of direct labor cost is often in the hands of production supervisors. To aid them, daily or weekly reports analyzing the cause of any direct labor variance may be prepared. A comparison of standard direct labor hours and actual direct labor hours will provide the basis for an investigation into the efficiency of direct labor (time variance). A comparison of the rates paid for direct labor with the standard rates highlights the efficiency of the supervisors or the personnel department in selecting the proper grade of direct labor for production (rate variance).

Factory Overhead Cost Variance

Some of the difficulties encountered in allocating factory overhead costs among products manufactured have been considered in Chapter 15. These difficulties stem from the great variety of costs that are included in factory overhead and their nature as indirect costs. For the same reasons, the procedures used in determining standards and variances for factory overhead cost are more complex than those used for direct materials cost and direct labor cost.

A flexible budget is used to establish the standard factory overhead rate and to aid in determining subsequent variations from standard. The standard rate is determined by dividing the standard factory overhead costs by the standard amount of productive activity, generally expressed in direct labor hours, direct labor cost, or machine hours. A flexible budget showing the standard factory overhead rate for a month is as follows:

Ballard Company Factory Overhead Cost Budget For Month Ending June 30, 19--				
Percent of productive capacity............	80%	90%	100%	110%
Direct labor hours	4,000	4,500	5,000	5,500
Budgeted factory overhead:				
Variable cost:				
Indirect factory wages	$12,800	$14,400	$16,000	$17,600
Power and light	5,600	6,300	7,000	7,700
Indirect materials....................	3,200	3,600	4,000	4,400
Maintenance........................	2,400	2,700	3,000	3,300
Total variable cost.................	$24,000	$27,000	$30,000	$33,000
Fixed cost:				
Supervisory salaries	$ 5,500	$ 5,500	$ 5,500	$ 5,500
Depreciation of plant and equipment ...	4,500	4,500	4,500	4,500
Insurance and property taxes..........	2,000	2,000	2,000	2,000
Total fixed cost....................	$12,000	$12,000	$12,000	$12,000
Total factory overhead cost.............	$36,000	$39,000	$42,000	$45,000
Factory overhead rate per direct labor hour ($42,000 ÷ 5,000).... $8.40				

FACTORY OVERHEAD COST BUDGET INDICATING STANDARD FACTORY OVERHEAD RATE

The standard factory overhead cost rate is determined on the basis of the projected factory overhead costs at 100% of productive capacity, where this level of capacity represents the general expectation of business activity under normal operating conditions. In the illustration, the standard factory overhead rate is $8.40 per direct labor hour. This rate can be subdivided into $6 per hour for variable factory overhead ($30,000 ÷ 5,000 hours) and $2.40 per hour for fixed factory overhead ($12,000 ÷ 5,000 hours).

Variances from standard for factory overhead cost result (1) from operating at a level above or below 100% of capacity and (2) from incurring a total amount of factory overhead cost greater or less than the amount budgeted for the level of operations achieved. The first factor results in the **volume variance**, which is a measure of the penalty of operating at less than 100% of productive capacity or the benefit from operating at a level above 100% of productive capacity. The second factor results in the **controllable variance**, which is the difference between the actual amount of factory overhead incurred and the amount of factory overhead budgeted for the level of production achieved during the period. To illustrate, assume that the actual cost and standard cost of factory overhead for Ballard Company's production of 10,000 units of Product X during June were as follows:

Actual:	Variable factory overhead......	$24,600	
	Fixed factory overhead	12,000	$36,600
Standard:	4,000 hours at $8.40		33,600

The unfavorable factory overhead cost variance of $3,000 is made up of a volume variance and a controllable variance, determined as follows:

FACTORY OVERHEAD COST VARIANCE	

Volume variance:

Productive capacity of 100%..........................	5,000 hours	
Standard for amount produced.........................	4,000 hours	
Productive capacity not used	1,000 hours	
Standard fixed factory overhead cost rate..............	× $2.40	
Variance—unfavorable......................................		$2,400

Controllable variance:

Actual factory overhead cost incurred	$36,600	
Budgeted factory overhead for standard product produced..	36,000	
Variance—unfavorable......................................		600
Total factory overhead cost variance—unfavorable		$3,000

Factory Overhead Volume Variance

The factory overhead volume variance is the difference between the productive capacity at 100% and the standard productive capacity, multiplied by the standard fixed factory overhead rate. If the standard capacity for the amount produced exceeds the productive capacity at 100%, the variance is favorable. If the productive capacity at 100% exceeds the standard capacity for the amount produced, the variance is unfavorable, as shown for Ballard Company in the following illustration:

Factory Overhead   Productive Capacity at 100% −   Standard Fixed Factory
Volume Variance   = Standard Capacity for Amount Produced ×   Overhead Rate
Volume variance = (5,000 hours − 4,000 hours)   × $2.40 per hour
Volume variance = 1,000 hours   × $2.40 per hour
Volume variance = $2,400 unfavorable

FACTORY
OVERHEAD
VOLUME
VARIANCE

In the illustration, the unfavorable volume variance of $2,400 can be viewed as the cost of the available but unused productive capacity (1,000 hours). It should also be noted that the variable portion of the factory overhead cost rate was ignored in determining the volume variance. Variable factory overhead costs vary with the level of production. Thus, a curtailment of production should be accompanied by a comparable reduction of such costs. On the other hand, fixed factory overhead costs are not affected by changes in the volume of production. The fixed factory overhead costs represent the costs of providing the capacity for production, and the volume variance measures the amount of the fixed factory overhead cost due to the variance between capacity used and 100% of capacity.

The idle time that resulted in a volume variance may be due to such factors as failure to maintain an even flow of work, machine breakdowns or repairs causing work stoppages, and failure to obtain enough sales orders to keep the factory operating at full capacity. Management should determine the causes of the idle time and should take corrective action. A volume variance caused by failure of supervisors to maintain an even flow of work, for example, can be remedied. Volume variances caused by lack of sales orders may be corrected through increased advertising or other sales effort, or it may be advisable to develop other means of using the excess plant capacity.

Factory Overhead Controllable Variance

The factory overhead controllable variance is the difference between the actual factory overhead and the budgeted factory overhead for the standard amount produced. If the budgeted factory overhead for the standard amount produced exceeds the actual factory overhead, the variance is favorable. If the actual factory overhead exceeds the budgeted factory overhead for the standard amount produced, the variance is unfavorable. For Ballard Company, the standard direct labor hours for the amount produced during June was 4,000 (80% of productive capacity). Therefore, the factory overhead budgeted at this level of production, according to the budget on page 605, was $36,000. When this budgeted factory overhead is compared with the actual factory overhead, as shown in the following illustration for Ballard Company, an unfavorable variance results.

Factory Overhead   =   Actual Factory   −   Budgeted Factory Overhead for
Controllable Variance   Overhead   Standard Amount Produced
Controllable variance = $36,600 $36,000
Controllable variance = $600 unfavorable

FACTORY
OVERHEAD
CONTROLLABLE
VARIANCE

The amount and the direction of the controllable variance show the degree of efficiency in keeping the factory overhead costs within the limits established by the budget. Most of the controllable variance is related to the cost of the variable factory overhead items because generally there is little or no variation in the costs incurred for the fixed factory overhead items. Therefore, responsibility for the control of this variance generally rests with department supervisors.

Reporting Factory Overhead Cost Variance

The best means of presenting standard factory overhead cost variance data is through a factory overhead cost variance report. Such a report, illustrated below, can present both the controllable variance and the volume variance in a format that pinpoints the causes of the variances and aids in placing the responsibility for control.

FACTORY
OVERHEAD COST
VARIANCE REPORT

Ballard Company
Factory Overhead Cost Variance Report
For Month Ended June 30, 19--

Productive capacity for the month . . . .   5,000 hours
Actual production for the month . . . .   4,000 hours

			Variances	
	Budget	Actual	Favorable	Unfavorable
Variable cost:				
Indirect factory wages	$12,800	$13,020		$ 220
Power and light	5,600	5,550	$50	
Indirect materials	3,200	3,630		430
Maintenance	2,400	2,400		
Total variable cost	$24,000	$24,600		
Fixed cost:				
Supervisory salaries	$ 5,500	$ 5,500		
Depreciation of plant and equipment. . .	4,500	4,500		
Insurance and property taxes	2,000	2,000		
Total fixed cost	$12,000	$12,000		
Total factory overhead cost	$36,000	$36,600		
Total controllable variances			$50	$ 650

Net controllable variance — unfavorable . . . . $ 600
Volume variance — unfavorable:
Idle hours at the standard rate for fixed factory overhead —
1,000 × $2.40   2,400
Total factory overhead cost variance — unfavorable $3,000

The variance in many of the individual cost items in factory overhead can be subdivided into quantity and price variances, as were the variances in direct materials and direct labor. For example, the indirect factory wages variance may include both time and rate variances, and the indirect materials variance may be made up of both a quantity variance and a price variance.

The foregoing brief introduction to analysis of factory overhead cost variance suggests the many difficulties that may be encountered in actual practice. The rapid increase of automation in factory operations has been accompanied by increased attention to factory overhead costs. The use of predetermined standards and the analysis of variances from such standards provides management with the best possible means of establishing responsibility and controlling factory overhead costs.

STANDARDS IN THE ACCOUNTS

Although standard costs can be used solely as a statistical device apart from the ledger, it is generally considered preferable to incorporate them in the accounts. One approach, when this plan is used, is to identify the variances in the accounts at the time the manufacturing costs are recorded in the accounts. To illustrate, assume that Marin Corporation purchased, on account, 10,000 pounds of direct materials at $1 per pound, when the standard price was $.95 per pound. The entry to record the purchase and the unfavorable direct materials price variance is as follows:

Materials	9,500	
Direct Materials Price Variance	500	
Accounts Payable		10,000

The materials account is debited for the 10,000 pounds at the standard price of $.95 per pound. The unfavorable direct materials price variance is $500 [($1.00 actual price per pound − $.95 standard price per pound) × 10,000 pounds purchased] and is recorded by a debit to Direct Materials Price Variance. Accounts Payable is credited for the actual amount owed, $10,000 (10,000 pounds at $1 per pound). If the variance had been favorable, Direct Materials Price Variance would have been credited for the amount of the variance.

The accounts affected by the purchase of direct materials would appear as follows:

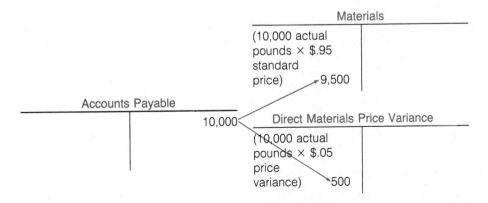

Variances in other manufacturing costs are recorded in a manner similar to the direct materials price variance. For example, if Marin Corporation used 4,900 pounds of direct materials to produce a product with a standard of 5,000 pounds, the entry to record the variance and the materials used would be as follows:

```
Work in Process.....................................    4,750
    Materials.........................................              4,655
    Direct Materials Quantity Variance ...................              95
```

The work in process account is debited for the standard price of the standard amount of direct materials required, $4,750 (5,000 pounds × $.95). Materials is credited for the actual amount of materials used at the standard price, $4,655 (4,900 pounds × $.95). The favorable direct materials quantity variance of $95 [(5,000 standard pounds − 4,900 actual pounds) × $.95 standard price per pound] is credited to Direct Materials Quantity Variance. If the variance had been unfavorable, Direct Materials Quantity Variance would have been debited for the amount of the variance.

The accounts affected by the use of direct materials would appear as follows:

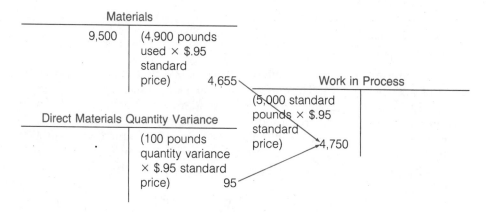

For Marin Corporation, the entries for direct labor, factory overhead, and other variances are recorded in a manner similar to the entries for direct materials. The work in process account is debited for the standard costs of direct labor and factory overhead as well as direct materials. Likewise, the work in process account is credited for the standard cost of the product completed and transferred to the finished goods account.

In a given period, it is possible to have both favorable and unfavorable variances. For example, if a favorable variance has been recorded, such as the direct materials quantity variance for Marin Corporation, and unfavorable direct materials quantity variances occur later in the period, the unfavorable variances would be recorded as debits in the direct materials quantity variance account. Analyses of this account may provide management with insights for controlling direct materials usage.

Another means of incorporating standards in the accounts is to debit the work in process account for the actual cost of direct materials, direct labor, and factory overhead entering into production. The same account is credited for the standard cost of the product completed and transferred to the finished goods account. The balance remaining in the work in process account is then made up of the ending inventory of work in process and the variances of actual cost from standard cost. In the following accounts for Ballard Company, there is assumed to be no ending inventory of work in process:

Work in Process			
Direct materials (actual)	21,424	To finished goods (standard)	117,600
Direct labor (actual)	64,780		
Factory overhead (actual)	36,600		
5,204	122,804		

Finished Goods		
From work in process (standard)	117,600	

The balance in the work in process account is the sum of the variances between the standard and actual costs. In the illustration, the debit balance of $5,204 indicates a net unfavorable variance. If the balance had been a credit, it would have indicated a net favorable variance.

At the end of the fiscal year, the variances from standard are usually transferred to the cost of goods sold account. However, if the variances are significant or if many of the products manufactured are still on hand, the variances should be allocated to the work in process, finished goods, and cost of goods sold accounts. The result of such an allocation is to convert these account balances from standard cost to actual cost.

REPORTING VARIANCES ON THE INCOME STATEMENT

Variances from standard costs are usually not reported to stockholders and others outside of management. If standards are recorded in the accounts, however, it is customary to disclose the variances on income statements prepared for management. An interim monthly income statement prepared for Ballard Company's internal use is illustrated as follows:

612

PART SIX
Planning and Control

VARIANCES FROM STANDARDS IN INCOME STATEMENT

Ballard Company
Income Statement
For Month Ended June 30, 19--

	Favorable	Unfavorable	
Sales			$185,400
Cost of goods sold—at standard			113,500
Gross profit—at standard			$ 71,900
Less variances from standard cost:			
Direct materials quantity		$ 600	
Direct materials price		824	
Direct labor time	$800		
Direct labor rate		1,580	
Factory overhead volume		2,400	
Factory overhead controllable		600	5,204
Gross profit			$ 66,696
Operating expenses:			
Selling expenses		$22,500	
General expenses		19,225	41,725
Income from operations			$ 24,971

REVISION OF STANDARDS

Standard costs should be continuously reviewed, and when they no longer represent the conditions that were present when the standards were set, they should be changed. Standards should not be revised merely because of variances, but because they no longer reflect the conditions that they were intended to measure. For example, the direct labor cost standard would not be revised simply because workers were unable to meet properly determined standards. On the other hand, standards should be revised when prices, product designs, labor rates, manufacturing methods, or other circumstances change to such an extent that the current standards no longer represent a useful measure of performance.

STANDARDS FOR NONMANUFACTURING EXPENSES

The use of standards for nonmanufacturing expenses is not as common as the use of standards for manufacturing costs. This difference in the use of standards is due in part to the fact that nonmanufacturing expenses are, in many cases, not nearly as large as the manufacturing costs. Another major reason is that while many manufacturing operations are repetitive and thus subject to the determination of a per unit cost of output, many nonmanufacturing expenses do not lend themselves to such measurement. In many cases, for example, the costs associated with an assembly line can be measured and related to a uniform product unit. On the other hand, the expenses associated with the work of the office manager are not easily related to any unit of output.

When nonmanufacturing activities are repetitive and generate a somewhat homogeneous product, the concept of standards can be applied. In these cases, the process of estimating and using standards can be similar to that described for a manufactured product. For example, standards can be applied to the work of office personnel who process sales orders, and a standard unit expense for processing a sales order could be determined. The variance between the actual cost of processing a sales order with the standard expense can then be evaluated by management and corrective action taken.

In practice, standards are not widely used for nonmanufacturing expenses. Instead, these expenses are generally controlled by the use of budgets and budget performance reports, as discussed in Chapter 17. However, the use of standards appears to be gaining in acceptance as more attention is being given to the nonmanufacturing expenses by the managerial accountant.

---

1. The actual and standard direct materials costs for producing a specified quantity of product are as follows:

    Actual: 51,000 pounds at $5.05........ $257,550
    Standard: 50,000 pounds at $5.00........ 250,000

    The direct materials price variance is:
    A. $2,500 unfavorable   C. $7,550 unfavorable
    B. $2,550 unfavorable   D. none of the above

2. The actual and standard direct labor costs for producing a specified quantity of product are as follows:

    Actual: 990 hours at $10.90.......... $10,791
    Standard: 1,000 hours at $11.00.......... 11,000

    The direct labor cost time variance is:
    A. $99 favorable   C. $110 favorable
    B. $99 unfavorable   D. $110 unfavorable

3. The actual and standard factory overhead costs for producing a specified quantity of product are as follows:

    Actual: Variable factory overhead $72,500
               Fixed factory overhead....... 40,000 $112,500

    Standard: 19,000 hours at $6
               ($4 variable and $2 fixed).....   114,000

    If 1,000 hours of productive capacity were unused, the factory overhead volume variance would be:
    A. $1,500 favorable   C. $4,000 unfavorable
    B. $2,000 unfavorable   D. none of the above

Self-
Examination
Questions
(Answers
at end of
chapter.)

4. Based on the data in Question 3, the factory overhead controllable variance would be:

A. $3,500 favorable

B. $3,500 unfavorable

C. $1,500 favorable

D. none of the above

5. Variances from standard costs are reported on interim income statements as:

A. selling expenses

B. general expenses

C. other expenses

D. none of the above

Discussion Questions

18–1. What are the basic objectives in the use of standard costs?

18–2. (a) Describe theoretical (ideal) standards and discuss the possible impact of theoretical standards on worker performance. (b) Describe currently attainable (normal) standards and discuss the possible impact of currently attainable standards on worker performance.

18–3. How can standards be used by management to achieve control over costs?

18–4. As the term is used in reference to standard costs, what is a *variance*?

18–5. What is meant by reporting by the "principle of exceptions" as the term is used in reference to cost control?

18–6. (a) What are the two variances between actual cost and standard cost for direct materials? (b) Discuss some possible causes of these variances.

18–7. (a) What are the two variances between actual cost and standard cost for direct labor? (b) Who generally has control over the direct labor cost?

18–8. (a) Describe the two variances between actual costs and standard costs for factory overhead. (b) What is a factory overhead cost variance report?

18–9. If variances are recorded in the accounts at the time the manufacturing costs are incurred, what does a credit balance in Direct Materials Price Variance represent?

18–10. If variances are recorded in the accounts at the time the manufacturing costs are incurred, what does a debit balance in Direct Materials Quantity Variance represent?

18–11. If standards are recorded in the accounts and Work in Process is debited for the actual manufacturing costs and credited for the standard cost of products produced, what does the balance in Work in Process represent?

18–12. Are variances from standard costs usually reported in financial statements issued to stockholders and others outside the firm?

18–13. Assuming that the variances from standards are not significant at the end of the period, to what account are they transferred?

18–14. How often should standards be revised?

18–15. Are standards for nonmanufacturing expenses as widely used as standards for manufacturing costs?

Exercises

18–16. The following data relate to the direct materials cost for the production of 50,000 units of product:

Actual:	101,000 pounds at $2.95	$297,950
Standard:	100,000 pounds at 3.00	300,000

Determine the quantity variance, price variance, and total direct materials cost variance.

18–17. The following data relating to direct materials cost for June of the current year are taken from the records of D. J. Drury Company:

Quantity of direct materials used .... 28 000 kilograms
Unit cost of direct materials.......................... $2 per kilogram
Units of finished product manufactured............... 10,100 units
Standard direct materials per unit of finished product ... 2.5 kilograms
Direct materials quantity variance—unfavorable........ $5,720
Direct materials price variance—favorable $2,240

Determine the standard direct materials cost per unit of finished product, assuming that there was no inventory of work in process at either the beginning or the end of the month. Present your computations.

18–18. The following data relate to direct labor cost for the production of 40,000 units of product:

Actual: 39,500 hours at $15.50 .... $612,250
Standard: 40,000 hours at 15.00 600,000

Determine the time variance, rate variance, and total direct labor cost variance.

18–19. The following data relate to factory overhead cost for the production of 80,000 units of product:

Actual: Variable factory overhead... $177,500
           Fixed factory overhead 150,000 $327,500
Standard: 40,000 hours at $7.50.......   300,000

If productive capacity of 100% was 50,000 hours and the factory overhead costs budgeted at the level of 40,000 standard hours was $330,000, determine the volume variance, controllable variance, and total factory overhead cost variance. The fixed factory overhead rate was $3 per hour.

18–20. Mann Company prepared the following factory overhead cost budget for Department X for September of the current year, when the company expected to operate at 9,600 direct labor hours:

Variable cost:
  Indirect factory wages............................ $10,000
  Power and light 8,800
  Indirect materials................................ 3,000
    Total variable cost............................ $21,800
Fixed cost:
  Supervisory salaries .... $ 8,250
  Depreciation of plant and equipment................. 4,100
  Insurance and property taxes 3,000
    Total fixed cost.................................   15,350
 Total factory overhead cost........................... $37,150

Mann Company has decided to install a standard cost system and has determined that productive capacity is 12,000 direct labor hours. Prepare a flexible budget indicating production levels of 9,600, 10,800, and 12,000 direct labor hours and showing the standard factory overhead rate.

18–21. Black Manufacturing Company incorporates standards in the accounts and identifies variances at the time the manufacturing costs are incurred. Prepare entries to record the following transactions:
  (a) Purchased 500 units of direct material X at $12.25 per unit. The standard price is $12.50 per unit.
  (b) Used 255 units of direct material X in the process of manufacturing 125 units of finished product. Two units of material X are required, at standard, to produce a finished unit.

Problems

18–22. Standard costs and actual costs for direct materials, direct labor, and factory overhead incurred for the manufacture of 3,000 units of product were as follows:

	Standard Costs	Actual Costs
Direct materials.	3,000 pounds at $20	2,900 pounds at $21.50
Direct labor	4,500 hours at $12	4,800 hours at $12.50
Factory overhead	Rates per direct labor hour, based on 100% of capacity of 5,000 labor hours:	
	Variable cost, $4.20	$20,500 variable cost
	Fixed cost, $2.80	$14,000 fixed cost

Instructions:

Determine (a) the quantity variance, price variance, and total direct materials cost variance; (b) the time variance, rate variance, and total direct labor cost variance; and (c) the volume variance, controllable variance, and total factory overhead cost variance.

18–23. Wade Company prepared the following factory overhead cost budget for Department I for June of the current year. The company expected to operate the department at 100% of capacity of 20,000 direct labor hours.

Variable cost:		
Indirect factory wages.	$18,000	
Power and light.	15,300	
Indirect materials	5,400	
Total variable cost		$38,700
Fixed cost:		
Supervisory salaries	$14,850	
Depreciation of plant and equipment.	7,300	
Insurance and property taxes	5,850	
Total fixed cost.		28,000
Total factory overhead cost		$66,700

During June, the department operated at 15,000 direct labor hours, and the factory overhead costs incurred were: indirect factory wages, $13,600; power and light, $11,200; indirect materials, $4,250; supervisory salaries, $14,850; depreciation of plant and equipment, $7,300; and insurance and property taxes, $5,850.

Instructions:

Prepare a standard factory overhead variance report for June. To be useful for cost control, the budgeted amounts should be based on 15,000 direct labor hours.

18-24. Grant Company prepared the following factory overhead cost budget for the Sanding Department for April of the current year:

Grant Company
Factory Overhead Cost Budget — Sanding Department
For Month Ending April 30, 19--

Direct labor hours:		
Productive capacity of 100%		18,000
Hours budgeted.		15,300
Variable cost:		
Indirect factory wages	$20,060	
Indirect materials.	14,280	
Power and light.	5,440	
Total variable cost		$39,780
Fixed cost:		
Supervisory salaries.	$18,300	
Indirect factory wages	12,100	
Depreciation of plant and equipment	8,100	
Insurance	6,800	
Power and light.	5,450	
Property taxes.	3,250	
Total fixed cost		54,000
Total factory overhead cost		$93,780

During April, the Sanding Department was operated for 15,300 direct labor hours and the following factory overhead costs were incurred:

Indirect factory wages	$32,600
Supervisory salaries.	18,300
Indirect materials.	13,950
Power and light.	11,200
Depreciation of plant and equipment	8,100
Insurance	6,800
Property taxes.	3,250
Total factory overhead cost incurred.	$94,200

Instructions:

(1) Prepare a flexible budget for April, indicating capacities of 13,500, 15,300, 18,000, and 21,600 direct labor hours and the determination of a standard factory overhead rate per direct labor hour.

(2) Prepare a standard factory overhead cost variance report for April.

18–25. The following data were taken from the records of Briscoe Company for July of the current year:

Cost of goods sold (at standard).............................	$277,770
Direct materials quantity variance—favorable...................	1,860
Direct materials price variance—favorable	2,550
Direct labor time variance—favorable........................	690
Direct labor rate variance—unfavorable......................	2,535
Factory overhead volume variance—unfavorable	3,000
Factory overhead controllable variance—favorable.............	1,140
General expenses	16,290
Sales...	362,700
Selling expenses	29,970

Instructions:

Prepare an income statement for presentation to management.

18–26. Delwood Inc. maintains perpetual inventory accounts for materials, work in process, and finished goods and uses a standard cost system based on the following data:

	Standard Cost per Unit
Direct materials: 2 kilograms at $3.50 per kg	$ 7
Direct labor: 4 hours at $17.50 per hr	70
Factory overhead: $1.50 per direct labor hour	6
Total	$83

There was no inventory of work in process at the beginning or end of October, the first month of the current fiscal year. The transactions relating to production completed during October are summarized as follows:

(a) Materials purchased on account, $62,480.

(b) Direct materials used, $55,025. This represented 15 500 kilograms at $3.55 per kilogram.

(c) Direct labor paid, $560,700. This represented 31,500 hours at $17.80 per hour. There were no accruals at either the beginning or the end of the period.

(d) Factory overhead incurred during the month was composed of depreciation on plant and equipment, $18,650; indirect labor, $14,300; insurance, $8,000; and miscellaneous factory costs, $9,550. The indirect labor and miscellaneous factory costs were paid during the period, and the insurance represents an expiration of prepaid insurance. Of the total factory overhead of $50,500, fixed costs amounted to $27,200 and variable costs were $23,300.

(e) Goods finished during the period, 8,000 units.

Instructions:

(1) Prepare entries to record the transactions, assuming that the work in process account is debited for actual production costs and credited with standard costs for goods finished.

(2) Prepare a T account for Work in Process and post to the account, using the identifying letters as dates.

(3) Prepare schedules of variances for direct materials cost, direct labor cost, and

factory overhead cost. Productive capacity for the plant is 34,000 direct labor hours.

(4) Total the amount of the standard cost variances and compare this total with the balance of the work in process account.

18–22A. Standard costs and actual costs for direct materials, direct labor, and factory overhead incurred for the manufacture of 1,000 units of product were as follows:

	Standard Costs	Actual Costs
Direct materials..........	1,000 pounds at $75	980 pounds at $75.50
Direct labor	12,500 hours at $9	12,600 hours at $8.95
Factory overhead.......	Rates per direct labor hour, based on 100% of capacity of 15,000 labor hours:	
	Variable cost, $3.50	$44,150 variable cost
	Fixed cost, $1.00	$15,000 fixed cost

Instructions:

Determine (a) the quantity variance, price variance, and total direct materials cost variance; (b) the time variance, rate variance, and total direct labor cost variance; and (c) the volume variance, controllable variance, and total factory overhead cost variance.

18–24A. Barnes Inc. prepared the following factory overhead cost budget for the Painting Department for January of the current year:

Barnes Inc.
Factory Overhead Cost Budget — Painting Department
For Month Ending January 31, 19--

Direct labor hours:		
Productive capacity of 100%		24,000
Hours budgeted......................................		21,600
Variable cost:		
Indirect factory wages	$13,905	
Indirect materials...................................	10,935	
Power and light.....................................	9,720	
Total variable cost...............................		$34,560
Fixed cost:		
Supervisory salaries................................	$12,950	
Indirect factory wages	4,820	
Depreciation of plant and equipment	4,460	
Insurance	2,600	
Power and light.....................................	2,350	
Property taxes......................................	1,620	
Total fixed cost		28,800
Total factory overhead cost...........................		$63,360

During January, the Painting Department was operated for 21,600 direct labor hours and the following factory overhead costs were incurred:

Indirect factory wages	$19,120
Supervisory salaries	12,950
Power and light	13,050
Indirect materials	10,600
Depreciation of plant and equipment	4,460
Insurance	2,600
Property taxes	1,620
Total factory overhead cost incurred	$64,400

Instructions:

(1) Prepare a flexible budget for January, indicating capacities of 19,200, 21,600, 24,000, and 26,400 direct labor hours and the determination of a standard factory overhead rate per direct labor hour.
(2) Prepare a standard factory overhead cost variance report for January.

18–26A. McCloskey Inc. maintains perpetual inventory accounts for materials, work in process, and finished goods and uses a standard cost system based on the following data:

	Standard Cost per Unit
Direct materials: 5 kilograms at $2.80 per kg	$14
Direct labor: 2 hours at $18 per hour	36
Factory overhead: $2.50 per direct labor hour	5
Total	$55

There was no inventory of work in process at the beginning or end of August, the first month of the current fiscal year. The transactions relating to production completed during August are summarized as follows:

(a) Materials purchased on account, $89,600.
(b) Direct materials used, $92,220. This represented 31 800 kilograms at $2.90 per kilogram.
(c) Direct labor paid, $227,500. This represented 13,000 hours at $17.50 per hour. There were no accruals at either the beginning or the end of the period.
(d) Factory overhead incurred during the month was composed of depreciation on plant and equipment, $14,600; indirect labor, $11,750; insurance, $3,000; and miscellaneous factory costs, $5,500. The indirect labor and miscellaneous factory costs were paid during the period, and the insurance represents an expiration of prepaid insurance. Of the total factory overhead of $34,850, fixed costs amounted to $19,600 and variable costs were $15,250.
(e) Goods finished during the period, 6,400 units.

Instructions:

(1) Prepare entries to record the transactions, assuming that the work in process account is debited for actual production costs and credited with standard costs for goods finished.

(2) Prepare a T account for Work in Process and post to the account, using the identifying letters as dates.
(3) Prepare schedules of variances for direct materials cost, direct labor cost, and factory overhead cost. Productive capacity for the plant is 14,000 direct labor hours.
(4) Total the amount of the standard cost variances and compare this total with the balance of the work in process account.

Mini-Case

18–27. Daughtrey Company operates a plant in Mountain View, Missouri, where you have been assigned as the new cost analyst. To familiarize yourself with your new responsibilities, you have gathered the following cost variance data for October. During October, 30,600 units of product were manufactured.

Daughtrey Company
Factory Overhead Cost Variance Report
For Month Ended October 31, 19--

Productive capacity for the month (100%) . . . . 18,000 hours
Standard for amount produced during month . . . . 15,300 hours

			Variances	
	Budget	Actual	Favorable	Unfavorable
Variable cost:				
Indirect factory wages	$ 22,185	$ 22,600		$ 415
Power and light	42,840	42,590	$250	
Indirect materials	7,650	8,000		350
Maintenance	5,355	5,500		145
Total variable cost	$ 78,030	$ 78,690		
Fixed cost:				
Supervisory salaries	$ 32,500	$ 32,500		
Depreciation of plant and equipment . .	8,500	8,500		
Insurance and property taxes	2,200	2,200		
Total fixed cost	$ 43,200	$ 43,200		
Total factory overhead cost	$121,230	$121,890		
Total controllable variances			$250	$ 910
Net controllable variance — unfavorable				$ 660
Volume variance — unfavorable:				
Idle hours at the standard rate for				
fixed factory overhead — 2,700 × $2.40				6,480
Total factory overhead cost variance — unfavorable				$7,140

Direct Materials Cost Variance

Quantity variance:
Actual quantity . . . . 48,300 pounds
Standard quantity . . . . 45,900 pounds

    Variance — unfavorable. . . .   2,400 pounds × standard price, $1.40 . . . . $ 3,360
Price variance:
Actual price . . . . $1.60 per pound
Standard price . . . . 1.40 per pound

    Variance — unfavorable. . . . $ .20 per pound × actual quantity, 48,300 . .   9,660
Total direct materials cost variance — unfavorable $13,020

Direct Labor Cost Variance

Time variance:
Actual time . . . . 15,450 hours
Standard time . . . . 15,300 hours

    Variance — unfavorable. . . .   150 hours × standard rate, $16 . . . . $ 2,400
Rate variance:
Standard rate . . . . $16.00 per hour
Actual rate . . . . 15.60 per hour

    Variance — favorable . . . . . . $ .40 per hour × actual hours, 15,450   6,180
Total direct labor cost variance — favorable . . . . $ 3,780

After your review of the October cost variance data, you arranged a meeting with the factory superintendent to discuss manufacturing operations. During this meeting, the factory superintendent made the following comment:

"Why do you have to compute a factory overhead volume variance? I don't have any control over the level of operations. I can only control costs for the level of production at which I am told to operate. Why not just eliminate the volume variance from the factory overhead cost variance report?"

You next discussed the direct materials variance analyses with the purchasing department manager, who made the following comment:

"The materials price variance is computed incorrectly. The computations should be actual price minus standard price times the standard quantity of materials for the amount produced. By multiplying the difference in the actual and standard price by the actual quantity of materials used, my department is being penalized for the inefficiencies of the production department."

During November, the standard costs were not changed, productive capacity was 18,000 hours, and the following data were taken from the records for the production of 24,000 units of product:

Quantity of direct materials used . . . . 37,900 pounds
Cost of direct materials . . . . $ 1.62 per pound
Quantity of direct labor used . . . . 12,260 hours
Cost of direct labor . . . . $15.70 per hour

Factory overhead costs:

Power and light.	$33,520
Supervisory salaries	32,500
Indirect factory wages.	18,100
Depreciation of plant and equipment.	8,500
Indirect materials	6,940
Maintenance	4,250
Insurance and property taxes	2,200

Instructions:

(1) Prepare a factory overhead cost variance report for November.

(2) Determine (a) the quantity variance, price variance, and total direct materials cost variance, and (b) the time variance, rate variance, and total direct labor cost variance for November.

(3) Based upon the cost variances for October and November, what areas of operations would you investigate and why?

(4) How would you respond to the comments of the factory superintendent?

(5) How would you respond to the comments of the manager of the purchasing department?

1. B The unfavorable direct materials price variance of $2,550 (answer B) is determined as follows:

Actual price	$5.05 per pound
Standard price.	5.00 per pound
Price variance—unfavorable	$ .05 per pound

$.05 × 51,000 actual quantity = $2,550

2. C The favorable direct labor cost time variance of $110 (answer C) is determined as follows:

Actual time	990 hours
Standard time.	1,000 hours
Time variance—favorable.	10 hours

10 hours × $11 standard $110

3. B The unfavorable factory overhead volume variance of $2,000 (answer B) is determined as follows:

Productive capacity not used.	1,000 hours
Standard fixed factory overhead cost rate.	× $2
Factory overhead volume variance—unfavorable.	$2,000

4. A The favorable factory overhead controllable variance of $3,500 (answer A) is determined as follows:

Actual factory overhead cost incurred	$112,500
Budgeted factory overhead for standard product produced [(19,000 hours at $4 variable) + (20,000 hours at $2 fixed)] . . .	116,000
Factory overhead controllable variance—favorable	$ 3,500

5. D Since variances from standard costs represent the differences between the standard cost of manufacturing a product and the actual costs incurred, the variances relate to the product. Therefore, they should be reported on interim income statements as an adjustment to gross profit—at standard.

PART 7

Analyses for Decision Making

Information and Decision Making

People who visit my office at Chrysler are often surprised that I don't have a computer terminal on my desk. Maybe they forget that everything that comes out of a computer, somebody has to put in. The biggest problem facing American business today is that most managers have too much information. It dazzles them, and they don't know what to do with it all.

SOURCE   Lee Iacocca, *Iacocca: An Autobiography* (New York: Bantam Books, 1984), p. 59.

Computer technology has improved the productivity of our factories, our homes, our offices, and our communication networks. But until recently, little has been accomplished in improving productivity where it is needed most — in decision making.

Faced with a flood of facts and figures, the modern manager is like a thirsty man at sea. There is a deluge of information available, yet most of it needs to be filtered to make it appropriate for the decision-making process. And, as our organizations become more information-laden, they become more "decision intensive."

SOURCE   "Thirsty, at Sea," *Journal of Accountancy*, November, 1983, p. 96, from "Putting Relevant Information to Work," *MSA Update*, July-August, 1982.

CHAPTER 19

Profit Reporting for Management Analysis

CHAPTER OBJECTIVES

Describe and illustrate gross profit analysis.

Describe and illustrate absorption and variable costing concepts.

Describe and illustrate managerial uses of variable costing.

The basic accounting systems used by manufacturers to provide accounting information useful to management in planning and controlling operations were described and illustrated in previous chapters. Also presented were budgetary control concepts and standard costs and their use by management. In this chapter, various analyses useful to management in establishing profit goals and developing plans for achieving these goals are presented. Specifically, management's use of gross profit analysis and variable costing is described and illustrated. Gross profit analysis is useful in planning profits because it highlights the effects of changes in sales quantities, unit costs, and unit sales prices on profit. Variable costing is an aid in cost control, product pricing, production planning, and sales analysis.

GROSS PROFIT ANALYSIS

Gross profit is often considered the most significant intermediate figure in the income statement. It is common to determine its percentage relationship to sales and to make comparisons with prior periods. However, the mere knowledge of the percentages and the degree and direction of change from prior periods is insufficient. Management needs information about the causes. The procedure used in developing such information is termed **gross profit analysis**.

Since gross profit is the excess of sales over the cost of goods sold, a change in the amount of gross profit can be caused by (1) an increase or decrease in the amount of sales and (2) an increase or decrease in the amount of cost of goods sold. An increase or decrease in either element may in turn be due to (1) a change in the number of units sold and (2) a change in the unit price. The effect of these two factors on either sales or cost of goods sold may be stated as follows:

1. **Quantity factor.** The effect of a change in the number of units sold, assuming no change in unit price.
2. **Price factor.** The effect of a change in unit price on the number of units sold.

The following data are to be used as the basis for illustrating gross profit analysis. For the sake of simplicity, a single commodity is assumed. The amount of detail entering into the analysis would be greater if a number of different commodities were sold, but the basic principles would not be affected.

	1987	1986	Increase Decrease*
Sales..................................	$900,000	$800,000	$100,000
Cost of goods sold	650,000	570,000	80,000
Gross profit............................	$250,000	$230,000	$ 20,000
Number of units sold....................	125,000	100,000	25,000
Unit sales price	$7.20	$8.00	$.80*
Unit cost price	$5.20	$5.70	$.50*

The following analysis of these data shows that the favorable increase in the number of units sold was partially offset by a decrease in unit selling price. Also, the increase in the cost of goods sold due to increased quantity was partially offset by a decrease in unit cost.

Analysis of Increase in Gross Profit
For Year Ended December 31, 1987

Increase in amount of sales attributed to:			
Quantity factor:			
Increase in number of units sold in 1987 ...	25,000		
Unit sales price in 1986...................	× $8	$200,000	
Price factor:			
Decrease in unit sales price in 1987	$.80		
Number of units sold in 1987..............	×125,000	100,000	
Net increase in amount of sales			$100,000
Increase in amount of cost of goods sold attributed to:			
Quantity factor:			
Increase in number of units sold in 1987 ...	25,000		
Unit cost price in 1986	× $5.70	$142,500	
Price factor:			
Decrease in unit cost price in 1987	$.50		
Number of units sold in 1987..............	×125,000	62,500	
Net increase in amount of cost of goods sold .			80,000
Increase in gross profit			$ 20,000

The data presented in the report may be useful both in evaluating past performance and in planning for the future. The importance of the cost reduction of $.50 a unit is quite clear. If the unit cost had not changed from the preceding year, the net increase in the amount of sales ($100,000) would have been more than offset by the increase in the cost of goods sold ($142,500), causing a decrease of $42,500 in gross profit. The $20,000 increase in gross profit actually was made possible, therefore, by the ability of management to reduce the unit cost of the commodity.

The means by which the $.50 reduction in the unit cost of the commodity was accomplished is also significant. If it was due to the spreading of fixed factory overhead costs over the larger number of units produced, the decision to reduce the sales price in order to achieve a larger volume was probably wise. On the other hand, if the $.50 reduction in unit cost was due to operating efficiencies entirely unrelated to the increased production, the $.80 reduction in the unit sales price was unwise. The accuracy of the conclusion can be demonstrated by comparing actual results with hypothetical results. The hypothetical results are based on (1) a sales volume that did not change from the 1986 level and (2) a unit cost reduction to $5.20 due to operating efficiencies. The following analysis shows the possible loss of an opportunity to have realized an additional gross profit of $30,000 ($280,000 − $250,000).

	Actual		Hypothetical	
Number of units sold	125,000		100,000	
Unit sales price	$7.20		$8.00	
Sales		$900,000		$800,000
Unit cost price	$5.20		$5.20	
Cost of goods sold		650,000		520,000
Gross profit		$250,000		$280,000

If the reduction in unit cost had been achieved by a combination of spreading the fixed factory overhead over more production units and achieving operating efficiencies related to the increased production, the approximate effects of each could be determined by additional analyses. The methods used in gross profit analysis may also be extended, with some changes, to the analysis of changes in selling and general expenses.

ABSORPTION COSTING AND VARIABLE COSTING

In the preceding illustration of gross profit analysis, the importance of the cost of goods sold in determining income was emphasized. In determining the cost of goods sold, two alternate costing concepts can be used. These two costing concepts are absorption costing and variable costing.

The cost of manufactured products consists of direct materials, direct labor, and factory overhead. All such costs become a part of the finished goods inventory and remain there as an asset until the goods are sold. This conventional treatment of manufacturing costs is sometimes called absorption costing because all costs are "absorbed" into finished goods. Although the concept is necessary in determining historical costs and taxable income, another costing concept may be more useful to management in making decisions.

In variable costing, which is also termed **direct costing**, the cost of goods manufactured is composed only of variable costs—those manufacturing costs that increase or decrease as the volume of production rises or falls. These costs are the direct materials, direct labor, and only those factory overhead costs which vary with the rate of production. The remaining factory overhead costs, which are the fixed or nonvariable items, are related to the productive capacity of the manufacturing plant and are not affected by changes in the quantity of product manufactured. Accordingly, the fixed factory overhead does not become a part of the cost of goods manufactured, but is considered an expense of the period.

The distinction between absorption costing and variable costing is illustrated in the following diagram. Note that the difference between the two costing concepts is in the treatment of the fixed manufacturing costs, which consist of the fixed factory overhead costs.

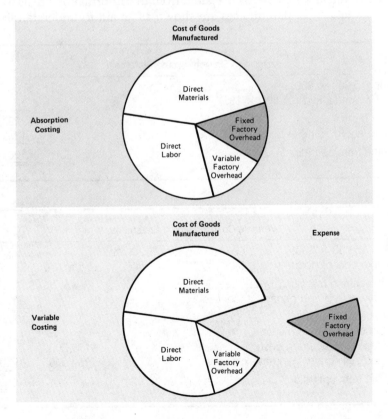

ABSORPTION COSTING COMPARED WITH VARIABLE COSTING

Variable Costing and the Income Statement

The arrangement of data in the variable costing income statement differs considerably from the format of the conventional income statement. Variable costs and expenses are presented separately from fixed costs and expenses, with significant summarizing amounts inserted at intermediate points. As a basis for illustrating the differences between the two forms, assume that 15,000 units were manufactured and sold at a unit price of $50 and the costs and expenses were as follows:

	Total Cost or Expense	Number of Units	Unit Cost
Manufacturing costs:			
Variable	$375,000	15,000	$25
Fixed	150,000	15,000	10
Total	$525,000		$35
Selling and general expenses:			
Variable	$ 75,000		
Fixed	50,000		
Total	$125,000		

The two income statements prepared from this information are as follows. The computations in parentheses are shown as an aid to understanding.

ABSORPTION COSTING INCOME STATEMENT

Absorption Costing Income Statement	
Sales (15,000 × $50)	$750,000
Cost of goods sold (15,000 × $35)	525,000
Gross profit	$225,000
Selling and general expenses ($75,000 + $50,000)	125,000
Income from operations	**$100,000**

VARIABLE COSTING INCOME STATEMENT

Variable Costing Income Statement		
Sales (15,000 × $50)		$750,000
Variable cost of goods sold (15,000 × $25)		375,000
Manufacturing margin		**$375,000**
Variable selling and general expenses		75,000
Contribution margin		**$300,000**
Fixed costs and expenses:		
Fixed manufacturing costs	$150,000	
Fixed selling and general expenses	50,000	200,000
Income from operations		**$100,000**

The absorption costing income statement does not distinguish between variable and fixed costs and expenses. All manufacturing costs are included in the cost of goods sold. The deduction of the cost of goods sold from sales yields the intermediate amount, gross profit. Deduction of selling and general expenses then yields income from operations.

In contrast, the variable costing income statement includes only the variable manufacturing costs in the cost of goods sold. Deduction of the cost of goods sold from sales yields an intermediate amount, termed **manufacturing margin**. Deduction of the variable selling and general expenses yields the **contribution margin,** or **marginal income**. The fixed costs and expenses are then deducted from the contribution margin to yield income from operations.

Units Manufactured Equal Units Sold

In the preceding illustration, 15,000 units were manufactured and sold. Both the absorption and the variable costing income statements reported the same income from operations of $100,000. Assuming no other changes, this equality of income will always be the case when the number of units manufactured and the number of units sold are equal. Only when the number of units manufactured and the number of units sold are not equal, which creates a change in the quantity of finished goods in inventory, will the income from operations differ under the two concepts.

Units Manufactured Exceed Units Sold

For any period in which the number of units manufactured exceeds the number of units sold, the operating income reported under the absorption costing concept will be larger than the operating income reported under the variable costing concept. To illustrate, assume that in the preceding example only 12,000 units of the 15,000 units manufactured were sold. The two income statements that result are as follows. Computations are inserted parenthetically as an aid to understanding.

ABSORPTION
COSTING INCOME
STATEMENT

Absorption Costing Income Statement		
Sales (12,000 × $50)		$600,000
Cost of goods sold:		
Cost of goods manufactured (15,000 × $35)	$525,000	
Less ending inventory (3,000 × $35)	105,000	
Cost of goods sold		420,000
Gross profit		$180,000
Selling and general expenses ($60,000 + $50,000)		110,000
Income from operations		$ 70,000

Variable Costing Income Statement		
Sales (12,000 × $50)		$600,000
Variable cost of goods sold:		
Variable cost of goods manufactured		
(15,000 × $25)	$375,000	
Less ending inventory (3,000 × $25)	75,000	
Variable cost of goods sold		300,000
Manufacturing margin		$300,000
Variable selling and general expenses		60,000
Contribution margin		$240,000
Fixed costs and expenses:		
Fixed manufacturing costs	$150,000	
Fixed selling and general expenses	50,000	200,000
Income from operations		$ 40,000

The $30,000 difference in the amount of income from operations ($70,000 − $40,000) is due to the different treatment of the fixed manufacturing costs. The entire amount of the $150,000 of fixed manufacturing costs is included as an expense of the period in the variable costing statement. The ending inventory in the absorption costing statement includes $30,000 (3,000 × $10) of fixed manufacturing costs. This $30,000, by being included in inventory on hand, is thus excluded from current cost of goods sold and instead is deferred to another period.

Units Manufactured Less Than Units Sold

For any period in which the number of units manufactured is less than the number of units sold, the operating income reported under the absorption costing concept will be less than the operating income reported under the variable costing concept. To illustrate, assume that 5,000 units of inventory were on hand at the beginning of a period, 10,000 units were manufactured during the period, and 15,000 units were sold (10,000 units manufactured during the period plus the 5,000 units on hand at the beginning of the period) at $50 per unit. The manufacturing costs and selling and general expenses are as follows:

	Total Cost or Expense	Number of Units	Unit Cost
Beginning inventory:			
Manufacturing costs:			
Variable	$125,000	5,000	$25
Fixed	50,000	5,000	10
Total	$175,000		$35

	Total Cost or Expense	Number of Units	Unit Cost
Current period:			
Manufacturing costs:			
Variable	$250,000	10,000	$25
Fixed.............................	150,000	10,000	15
Total	$400,000		$40
Selling and general expenses:			
Variable	$ 75,000		
Fixed.............................	50,000		
Total	$125,000		

The two income statements prepared from this information are as follows. Computations are inserted parenthetically as an aid to understanding.

Absorption Costing Income Statement		
Sales (15,000 × $50)		$750,000
Cost of goods sold:		
Beginning inventory (5,000 × $35)	$175,000	
Cost of goods manufactured (10,000 × $40)	400,000	
Cost of goods sold		575,000
Gross profit.......................................		$175,000
Selling and general expenses ($75,000 + $50,000)		125,000
Income from operations		**$ 50,000**

Variable Costing Income Statement		
Sales (15,000 × $50)................................		$750,000
Variable cost of goods sold:		
Beginning inventory (5,000 × $25)	$125,000	
Variable cost of goods manufactured (10,000 × $25).................................	250,000	
Variable cost of goods sold.......................		375,000
Manufacturing margin................................		$375,000
Variable selling and general expenses................		75,000
Contribution margin.................................		$300,000
Fixed costs and expenses:		
Fixed manufacturing costs........................	$150,000	
Fixed selling and general expenses	50,000	200,000
Income from operations		**$100,000**

The $50,000 difference ($100,000 − $50,000) in the amount of income from operations is attributable to the different treatment of the fixed manufacturing costs. The beginning inventory in the absorption costing income statement includes $50,000 (5,000 units × $10) of fixed manufacturing costs incurred in the preceding period. By being included in the beginning inventory, this $50,000 is included in the cost of goods sold for the current period. This $50,000 was included as an expense in a variable costing income statement of a prior period, however. Therefore, none of it is included as an expense in the current period variable costing income statement.

Comparison of Income Reported Under the Two Concepts

The examples presented in the preceding sections illustrated the effects of the absorption costing and variable costing concepts on income from operations when the level of inventory changes during a period. These effects may be summarized as follows:

Units manufactured:

Equal units sold.....................	Absorption costing income equals variable costing income.
Exceed units sold	Absorption costing income is greater than variable costing income.
Less than units sold	Absorption costing income is less than variable costing income.

Income Analysis Under Absorption Costing

As was illustrated in the preceding examples, changes in the quantity of the finished goods inventory, caused by differences in the levels of sales and production, directly affect the amount of income from operations reported under absorption costing. Management should therefore be aware of the possible effects of changing inventory levels on operating income reported under absorption costing in analyzing and evaluating operations. To illustrate, assume that the following two proposed production levels are being evaluated by the management of Brownstein Manufacturing Company:

Proposal 1: 20,000 Units To Be Manufactured

	Total Cost or Expense	Number of Units	Unit Cost
Manufacturing costs:			
Variable	$ 700,000	20,000	$35
Fixed..........................	400,000	20,000	20
Total	$1,100,000		$55
Selling and general expenses:			
Variable	$ 100,000		
Fixed..........................	100,000		
Total	$ 200,000		

Proposal 2: 25,000 Units To Be Manufactured

	Total Cost or Expense	Number of Units	Unit Cost
Manufacturing costs:			
Variable	$ 875,000	25,000	$35
Fixed.............................	400,000	25,000	16
Total	$1,275,000		$51
Selling and general expenses:			
Variable	$ 100,000		
Fixed.............................	100,000		
Total	$ 200,000		

Brownstein Manufacturing Company has no beginning inventory, and sales are estimated to be 20,000 units at $75 per unit, regardless of production levels. If the company manufactures 20,000 units, which is an amount equal to the estimated sales, income from operations under absorption costing would be $200,000. However, the reported income from operations could be increased by $80,000 by manufacturing 25,000 units and adding 5,000 units to the finished goods inventory. The absorption costing income statements illustrating this effect are as follows:

ABSORPTION COSTING INCOME STATEMENTS

Absorption Costing Income Statements	20,000 Units Manufactured	25,000 Units Manufactured
Sales (20,000 units × $75)	$1,500,000	$1,500,000
Cost of goods sold:		
Cost of goods manufactured:		
(20,000 units × $55)........................	$1,100,000	
(25,000 units × $51)........................		$1,275,000
Less ending inventory:		
(5,000 units × $51)		255,000
Cost of goods sold	$1,100,000	$1,020,000
Gross profit......................................	$ 400,000	$ 480,000
Selling and general expenses ($100,000 + $100,000)........................	200,000	200,000
Income from operations	$ 200,000	$ 280,000

The increase in operating income of $80,000 would be caused by the allocation of the fixed manufacturing costs of $400,000 over a greater number of units of production. Specifically, an increase in production from 20,000 units to 25,000 units meant that the fixed manufacturing costs per unit decreased from $20 ($400,000 ÷ 20,000 units) to $16 ($400,000 ÷ 25,000 units). Thus, the cost of goods sold when 25,000 units are manufactured would be $4 per unit less, or $80,000 less in total (20,000 units sold times $4). Since the cost of goods sold is less, operating income is $80,000 more when 25,000 units are manufactured rather than 20,000 units.

Under the variable costing concept, income from operations would have been $200,000, regardless of the amount by which units manufactured exceeded sales, because no fixed manufacturing costs are allocated to the units manufactured. To illustrate, the following variable costing income statements are presented for Brownstein Manufacturing Company for the production of 20,000 units, 25,000 units, and 30,000 units. In each case, the income from operations is $200,000.

VARIABLE COSTING
INCOME
STATEMENTS

Variable Costing Income Statements			
	20,000 Units Manufactured	25,000 Units Manufactured	30,000 Units Manufactured
Sales (20,000 units × $75)	$1,500,000	$1,500,000	$1,500,000
Variable cost of goods sold:			
Variable cost of goods manufactured:			
(20,000 units × $35)............	$ 700,000		
(25,000 units × $35)............		$ 875,000	
(30,000 units × $35)............			$1,050,000
Less ending inventory:			
(0 units × $35).................	0		
(5,000 units × $35)............		175,000	
(10,000 units × $35)...........			350,000
Variable cost of goods sold......	$ 700,000	$ 700,000	$ 700,000
Manufacturing margin..............	$ 800,000	$ 800,000	$ 800,000
Variable selling and general expenses........................	100,000	100,000	100,000
Contribution margin................	$ 700,000	$ 700,000	$ 700,000
Fixed costs and expenses:			
Fixed manufacturing costs.........	$ 400,000	$ 400,000	$ 400,000
Fixed selling and general expenses	100,000	100,000	100,000
Total fixed costs and expenses	$ 500,000	$ 500,000	$ 500,000
Income from operations	$ 200,000	$ 200,000	$ 200,000

As illustrated, if absorption costing is used, management should be careful in analyzing income from operations when large changes in inventory levels occur. Otherwise, increases or decreases in income from operations due to changes in inventory levels could be misinterpreted to be the result of operating efficiencies or inefficiencies.

MANAGEMENT'S USE OF VARIABLE COSTING AND ABSORPTION COSTING

Both variable costing and absorption costing serve useful purposes for management. However, there are limitations to the use of both concepts in certain circumstances. Therefore, management accountants must carefully analyze each situation in evaluating whether variable costing reports or absorption costing reports would be more useful. In many situations, the preparation of reports under both concepts will provide useful insights. Such reports and their advantages and disadvantages are discussed in the following paragraphs.

Cost Control

All costs are controllable by someone within a business enterprise, but they are not all controllable at the same level of management. For example, plant supervisors, as members of operating management, are responsible for controlling the use of direct materials in their departments. They have no control, however, of the amount of insurance coverage or premium costs related to the buildings housing their departments. For a specific level of management, **controllable costs** are costs that it controls directly, and **uncontrollable costs** are costs that another level of management controls. This distinction, as applied to specific levels of management, is useful in fixing the responsibility for incurrence of costs and then for reporting the cost data to those responsible for cost control.

Variable manufacturing costs are controlled at the operating level because the amount of such costs varies with changes in the volume of production. By including only variable manufacturing costs in the cost of the product, variable costing provides a product cost figure that can be controlled by operating management. The fixed factory overhead costs are ordinarily the responsibility of a higher level of management. When the fixed factory overhead costs are reported as a separate item in the variable costing income statement, they are easier to identify and control than when they are spread among units of product as they are under absorption costing.

As is the case with the fixed and variable manufacturing costs, the control of the variable and fixed operating expenses is usually the responsibility of different levels of management. Under variable costing, the variable selling and general expenses are reported in a separate category from the fixed selling and general expenses. Because they are reported in this manner, both types of operating expenses are easier to identify and control than is the case under absorption costing, where they are not reported separately.

Product Pricing

Many factors enter into the determination of the selling price of a product. The cost of making the product is clearly significant. Microeconomic theory deduces, from a set of restrictive assumptions, that income is maximized by expanding output to the volume where the revenue realized by the sale of the final unit (marginal revenue) equals the cost of that unit (marginal cost). Although the degree of exactness assumed in economic theory is rarely attainable, the concepts of marginal revenue and marginal cost are useful in setting selling prices.

In the short run, an enterprise is committed to the existing capacity of its manufacturing facilities. The pricing decision should be based upon making the best use of such capacity. The fixed costs and expenses cannot be avoided, but the variable costs and expenses can be eliminated if the company does not manufacture the product. The selling price of a product, therefore, should at least be equal to the variable costs and expenses of making and selling it. Any price above this minimum selling price contributes an amount toward covering fixed costs and expenses and providing operating income. Variable costing procedures yield data that emphasize these relationships.

In the long run, plant capacity can be increased or decreased. If an enterprise is to continue in business, the selling prices of its products must cover all costs and expenses and provide a reasonable operating income. Hence, in establishing pricing policies for the long run, information provided by absorption costing procedures is needed.

There are no simple solutions to most pricing problems. Consideration must be given to many factors of varying importance. Accounting can contribute by preparing analyses of various pricing plans for both the short run and the long run. Concepts of product pricing are further discussed in Chapter 21.

Production Planning

Production planning also has both short-run and long-run implications. In the short run, production is limited to existing capacity, and operating decisions must be made quickly before opportunities are lost. For example, a company manufacturing products with a seasonal demand may have an opportunity to obtain an off-season order that will not interfere with its production schedule nor reduce the sales of its other products. The relevant factors for such a short-run decision are the revenues and the variable costs and expenses. If the revenues from the special order will provide a contribution margin, the order should be accepted because it will increase the company's operating income. For long-run planning, management must also consider the fixed costs and expenses.

Sales Analysis

The primary objective of the marketing and sales functions is to offer the company's products for sale at prices that will result in an adequate amount of income relative to the total assets employed. To evaluate these functions properly, management needs information concerning the profitability of various types of products and sales mixes, sales territories, and salespersons. Variable costing can make a significant contribution to management decision making in such areas.

Sales Mix Analysis

Sales mix, sometimes referred to as product mix, is generally defined as the relative distribution of sales among the various products manufactured. Some products are more profitable than others, and management should concentrate its sales efforts on those that will provide the maximum total operating income.

Sales mix studies are based on assumptions, such as the ability to sell one product in place of another and the ability to convert production facilities to accommodate the manufacture of one product instead of another. Proposed changes in the sales mix often affect only small segments of a company's total operations. In such cases, changes in sales mix may be possible within the limits of existing capacity, and the presentation of cost and revenue data in the variable costing form is useful in achieving the most profitable sales mix.

Two very important factors that should be determined for each product are (1) the production facilities needed for its manufacture and (2) the amount of contribution margin to be gained from its manufacture. If two or more products require equal use of limited production facilities, then management should concentrate its sales and production efforts on the product or products with the highest contribution margin per unit. The following report, which focuses on product contribution margins, is an example of the type of data needed for an evaluation of sales mix. The enterprise, which manufactures two products and is operating at full capacity, is considering whether to change the emphasis of its advertising and other promotional efforts.

	Product A	Product B
Contribution Margin by Unit of Product **April 15, 19--**		
Sales price	$6.00	$8.50
Variable cost of goods sold	3.50	5.50
Manufacturing margin	$2.50	$3.00
Variable selling and general expenses	1.00	1.00
Contribution margin	$1.50	$2.00

CONTRIBUTION MARGIN STATEMENT—UNIT OF PRODUCT

The statement indicates that Product B yields a greater amount of contribution margin per unit than Product A. Therefore, Product B provides the larger contribution to the recovery of fixed costs and expenses and realization of operating income. If the amount of production facilities used for each product is assumed to be equal, it would be desirable to increase the sales of Product B.

If two or more products require unequal use of production resources, management should concentrate its sales and production efforts on that product or products with the highest contribution margin per unit of resource. For example, assume that in the above illustration, to manufacture Product B requires twice the machine hours required for Product A. Specifically, Product B requires 2 machine hours per unit, while Product A requires only 1 machine hour per unit. Under this assumption, the contribution margin per unit of resource (machine hours) is $1.50 ($1.50 contribution margin ÷ 1 machine hour) for Product A and $1 ($2 contribution margin ÷ 2 machine hours) for Product B. Under such circumstances, a change in sales mix designed to increase sales of Product A would be desirable.

To illustrate, if 2,000 additional units of Product A (requiring 2,000 machine hours) could be sold in place of 1,000 units of Product B (also requiring 2,000 machine hours), the total company contribution margin would increase by $1,000, as follows:

Additional contribution margin from sale of additional 2,000 units of Product A ($1.50 × 2,000 units).......................................	$3,000
Less contribution margin from forgoing production and sale of 1,000 units of Product B ($2 × 1,000 units)..........................	2,000
Increase in total contribution margin	$1,000

Sales Territory Analysis

An income statement presenting the contribution margin by sales territories is often useful to management in appraising past performance and in directing future sales efforts. The following income statement is prepared in such a format, in abbreviated form:

Contribution Margin Statement by Sales Territory
For Month Ended July 31, 19--

	Territory A	Territory B	Total
Sales.................................	$315,000	$502,500	$817,500
Less variable costs and expenses.........	189,000	251,250	440,250
Contribution margin	$126,000	$251,250	$377,250
Less fixed costs and expenses............			242,750
Income from operations			$134,500

In addition to the contribution margin, the **contribution margin ratio** (contribution margin divided by sales) for each territory is useful in evaluating sales territories and directing operations toward more profitable activities. For Territory A, the contribution margin ratio is 40% ($126,000 ÷ $315,000), and for Territory B the ratio is 50% ($251,250 ÷ $502,500). Consequently, more profitability could be achieved by efforts to increase the sales of Territory B relative to Territory A.

Salespersons' Analysis

A report to management for use in evaluating the sales performance of each salesperson could include total sales, gross profit, gross profit percentage, total selling expenses, and contribution to company profit. Such a report is illustrated as follows:

Salespersons' Analysis
For Six Months Ended June 30, 19--

Sales-person	Total Sales	Gross Profit	Gross Profit Percentage	Total Selling Expenses	Contribution to Company Profit
A	$300,000	$120,000	40%	$24,000	$ 96,000
B	250,000	75,000	30	22,500	52,500
C	500,000	125,000	25	35,000	90,000
D	180,000	72,000	40	18,000	54,000
E	460,000	197,800	43	27,600	170,200
F	320,000	112,000	35	22,400	89,600

The preceding report illustrates that the total sales figure is not the only consideration in evaluating a salesperson. For example, although salesperson C has the highest total sales, C's sales are not contributing as much to overall company profits as are the sales of A and E, primarily because C's sales have the lowest gross profit percentage. Of the six salespersons, E is generating the highest dollar contribution to company profit, but E is selling the most profitable mix of products, as measured by a gross profit percentage of 43%.

Other factors should also be considered in evaluating the performance of salespersons. For example, sales growth rates, years of experience, and actual performance compared to budgeted performance may be more important than total sales.

---

1. If sales totaled $800,000 for the current year (80,000 units at $10 each) and $765,000 for the preceding year (85,000 units at $9 each), the effect of the quantity factor on the change in sales is:
   A. a $50,000 increase
   B. a $35,000 decrease
   C. a $45,000 decrease
   D. none of the above

2. The concept that considers the cost of products manufactured to be composed only of those manufacturing costs that vary with the rate of production is known as:
   A. absorption costing
   B. variable costing
   C. replacement cost
   D. none of the above

Self-Examination Questions (Answers at end of chapter.)

3. In an income statement prepared under the variable costing concept, the deduction of the variable cost of goods sold from sales yields an intermediate amount referred to as:
   - A. gross profit
   - B. contribution margin
   - C. manufacturing margin
   - D. none of the above

4. Sales were $750,000, variable cost of goods sold was $400,000, variable selling and general expenses were $90,000, and fixed costs and expenses were $200,000. The contribution margin was:
   - A. $60,000
   - B. $260,000
   - C. $350,000
   - D. none of the above

5. During a year in which the number of units manufactured exceeded the number of units sold, the operating income reported under the absorption costing concept would be:
   - A. larger than the operating income reported under the variable costing concept
   - B. smaller than the operating income reported under the variable costing concept
   - C. the same as the operating income reported under the variable costing concept
   - D. none of the above

Discussion Questions

19–1. Discuss the two factors affecting both sales and cost of goods sold to which a change in gross profit can be attributed.

19–2. The analysis of increase in gross profit for a company includes the effect that an increase in the quantity of goods sold has had on the cost of goods sold. How is this figure determined?

19–3. What types of costs are customarily included in the cost of manufactured products under (a) the *absorption costing* concept and (b) the *variable costing* concept?

19–4. Which type of manufacturing cost (direct materials, direct labor, variable factory overhead, fixed factory overhead) is included in the cost of goods manufactured under the absorption costing concept but is excluded from the cost of goods manufactured under the variable costing concept?

19–5. At the end of the first year of operations, 1,000 units remained in finished goods inventory. The unit manufacturing costs during the year were as follows:

Direct materials	$5.00
Direct labor	3.50
Fixed factory overhead	1.50
Variable factory overhead	1.00

What would be the cost of the finished goods inventory reported on the balance sheet under (a) the absorption costing concept and (b) the variable costing concept?

19–6. Which of the following costs would be included in the cost of a manufactured product according to the variable costing concept? (a) property taxes on factory building, (b) salary of factory supervisor, (c) direct labor, (d) rent on factory building, (e) depreciation on factory equipment, (f) direct materials, and (g) electricity purchased to operate factory equipment.

19-7. In the variable costing income statement, how are the fixed manufacturing costs reported and how are the fixed selling and general expenses reported?

19-8. In the following equations, based on the variable costing income statement, identify the items designated by **X**:
(a) Net sales − **X** = manufacturing margin
(b) Manufacturing margin − **X** = contribution margin
(c) Contribution margin − **X** = income from operations

19-9. If the quantity of ending inventory is smaller than that of beginning inventory, will the amount of income from operations determined by absorption costing be greater than or less than the amount determined by variable costing? Explain.

19-10. Since all costs of operating a business are controllable, what is the significance of the term *uncontrollable cost*?

19-11. Discuss how financial data prepared on the basis of variable costing can assist management in the development of short-run pricing policies.

19-12. What term is used to refer to the relative distribution of sales among the various products manufactured?

19-13. A company, operating at full capacity, manufactures two products, with Product A requiring twice the production facilities as Product B. The contribution margin is $30 per unit for Product A and $12 per unit for Product B. How much would the total contribution margin be increased or decreased for the coming year if the sales of Product A could be increased by 500 units by changing the emphasis of promotional efforts?

Exercises

19-14. From the following data for Gossage Company, prepare an analysis of the decrease in gross profit for the year ended December 31, 1987:

	1987		1986	
Sales..................	40,000 units @ $18	$720,000	48,000 units @ $16.80	$806,400
Cost of goods sold.......	40,000 units @ $12	480,000	48,000 units @ $11.20	537,600
Gross profit.............		$240,000		$268,800

19-15. Borg Company began operations on October 1 and operated at 100% of capacity during the first month. The following data summarize the results for October:

Sales (6,000 units).....................................		$90,000
Production costs (8,000 units):		
Direct materials.....................................	$20,000	
Direct labor	36,000	
Variable factory overhead...........................	6,000	
Fixed factory overhead	10,000	72,000
Selling and general expenses:		
Variable selling and general expenses	$8,400	
Fixed selling and general expenses.................	4,800	13,200

(a) Prepare an income statement in accordance with the absorption costing concept.

(b) Prepare an income statement in accordance with the variable costing concept.

(c) What is the reason for the difference in the amount of operating income reported in (a) and (b)?

19–16. On December 31, the end of the first year of operations, Hart Company manufactured 24,000 units and sold 20,000 units. The following income statement was prepared, based on the variable costing concept:

Hart Company
Income Statement
For Year Ended December 31, 19--

Sales.		$400,000
Variable cost of goods sold:		
Variable cost of goods manufactured.	$240,000	
Less ending inventory.	40,000	
Variable cost of goods sold.		200,000
Manufacturing margin.		$200,000
Variable selling and general expenses.		60,000
Contribution margin.		$140,000
Fixed costs and expenses:		
Fixed manufacturing costs.	$ 72,000	
Fixed selling and general expenses.	28,000	100,000
Income from operations.		$ 40,000

Determine the unit cost of goods manufactured, based on (a) the variable costing concept and (b) the absorption costing concept.

19–17. On January 31, the end of the first month of operations, Pablo Company prepared the following income statement, based on the absorption costing concept:

Pablo Company
Income Statement
For Month Ended January 31, 19--

Sales (1,000 units).		$95,000
Cost of goods sold:		
Cost of goods manufactured.	$84,000	
Less ending inventory (200 units).	14,000	
Cost of goods sold.		70,000
Gross profit.		$25,000
Selling and general expenses.		17,500
Income from operations.		$ 7,500

If the fixed manufacturing costs were $24,000 and the variable selling and general expenses were $4,750, prepare an income statement in accordance with the variable costing concept.

19–18. On July 31, the end of the first month of operations, Stein Company prepared the following income statement, based on the variable costing concept:

Stein Company
Income Statement
For Month Ended July 31, 19--

Sales (10,000 units)................................		$120,000
Variable cost of goods sold:		
Variable cost of goods manufactured...............	$104,000	
Less ending inventory (3,000 units)................	24,000	
Variable cost of goods sold		80,000
Manufacturing margin		$ 40,000
Variable selling and general expenses		7,500
Contribution margin.................................		$ 32,500
Fixed costs and expenses:		
Fixed manufacturing costs........................	$ 19,500	
Fixed selling and general expenses................	10,000	29,500
Income from operations		$ 3,000

Prepare an income statement in accordance with the absorption costing concept.

19–19. Prior to the first month of operations ending June 30, Ryan Company estimated the following operating results:

Sales (500 × $75).....................................	$37,500
Manufacturing costs (500 units):	
Direct materials.....................................	15,000
Direct labor	3,500
Variable factory overhead............................	1,500
Fixed factory overhead..............................	7,500
Fixed selling and general expenses....................	5,000
Variable selling and general expenses	2,500

The company is evaluating a proposal to manufacture 750 units instead of 500 units.

(a) Assuming no change in sales, unit variable manufacturing costs, and total fixed factory overhead and selling and general expenses, prepare an estimated income statement, comparing operating results if 500 and 750 units are manufactured, in the (1) absorption costing format and (2) variable costing format. (b) What is the reason for the difference in income from operations reported for the two levels of production by the absorption costing income statement?

19–20. Carter Company manufactures Products X and Y and is operating at full capacity. To manufacture Product X requires twice the number of machine hours as required for Product Y. Market research indicates that 500 additional units of Product X could be sold. The contribution margin by unit of product is as follows:

	Product X	Product Y
Sales price	$50	$30
Variable cost of goods sold......................	25	15
Manufacturing margin............................	$25	$15
Variable selling and general expenses............	15	9
Contribution margin.............................	$10	$ 6

Prepare a tabulation indicating the increase or decrease in total contribution margin if 500 additional units of Product X are produced and sold.

Problems

19–21. Gibbons Company manufactures only one product. In 1986, the plant operated at full capacity. At a meeting of the board of directors on December 18, 1986, it was decided to raise the price of this product from $32, which had prevailed last year, to $35, effective January 1, 1987. Although the cost price was expected to rise about $1.50 per unit in 1987 because of a direct materials and direct labor wage increase, the increase in selling price was expected to cover this increase and also add to operating income. The comparative income statement for 1986 and 1987 is as follows:

	1987		1986	
Sales....................................		$420,000		$480,000
Cost of goods sold: variable	$150,000		$165,000	
fixed	120,000	270,000	120,000	285,000
Gross profit		$150,000		$195,000
Operating expenses: variable	$ 43,200		$52,500	
fixed	75,000	118,200	75,000	127,500
Operating income.......................		$ 31,800		$ 67,500

Instructions:
(1) Prepare a gross profit analysis report for the year 1987.
(2) At a meeting of the board of directors on March 2, 1988, the president, after reading the gross profit analysis report, made the following comment:
"It looks as if the increase in unit cost price was $3.50 and not the anticipated $1.50. The failure of operating management to keep these costs within the bounds of those in 1986, except for the anticipated $1.50 increase in direct materials and direct labor cost, was a major factor in the decrease in gross profit."
Do you agree with this analysis of the increase in unit cost price? Explain.

19–22. During the first month of operations ended January 31, Dixon Company manufactured 120,000 units, of which 100,000 were sold. Operating data for the month are summarized as follows:

Sales..		$900,000
Manufacturing costs:		
Direct materials................................	$360,000	
Direct labor	240,000	
Variable factory overhead.......................	120,000	
Fixed factory overhead.........................	90,000	810,000
Selling and general expenses:		
Variable	$ 90,000	
Fixed.......................................	60,000	150,000

Instructions:

(1) Prepare an income statement based on the absorption costing concept.

(2) Prepare an income statement based on the variable costing concept.

(3) Explain the reason for the difference in the amount of operating income reported in (1) and (2).

19–23. The demand for Product D, one of numerous products manufactured by UGA Inc., has dropped sharply because of recent competition from a similar product. The company's chemists are currently completing tests of various new formulas, and it is anticipated that the manufacture of a superior product can be started on October 1, one month hence. No changes will be needed in the present production facilities to manufacture the new product because only the mixture of the various materials will be changed.

The controller has been asked by the president of the company for advice on whether to continue production during September or to suspend the manufacture of Product D until October 1. The controller has assembled the following pertinent data:

UGA Inc.
Estimated Income Statement — Product D
For Month Ending August 31, 19--

Sales (50,000 units).........................	$375,000
Cost of goods sold...........................	294,000
Gross profit	$ 81,000
Selling and general expenses.................	95,000
Loss from operations........................	$ 14,000

The estimated production costs and selling and general expenses, based on a production of 50,000 units, are as follows:

Direct materials....................................	$2.30 per unit
Direct labor	1.60 per unit
Variable factory overhead...........................	.70 per unit
Variable selling and general expenses	1.15 per unit
Fixed factory overhead.............................	$64,000 for August
Fixed selling and general expenses..................	$37,500 for August

Sales for September are expected to drop about 40% below those of the preceding month. No significant changes are anticipated in the production costs or operating expenses. No extra costs will be incurred in discontinuing operations in the portion of the plant associated with Product D. The inventory of Product D at the beginning and end of September is expected to be inconsequential.

Instructions:

(1) Prepare an estimated income statement in absorption costing form for September for Product D, assuming that production continues during the month.
(2) Prepare an estimated income statement in variable costing form for September for Product D, assuming that production continues during the month.
(3) State the estimated operating loss arising from the activities associated with Product D for September if production is temporarily suspended.
(4) Prepare a brief statement of the advice the controller should give.

19–24. Chung Company employs seven salespersons to sell and distribute its product throughout the state. Data extracted from reports received from salespersons during the current year ended December 31 are as follows:

Salesperson	Total Sales	Cost of Goods Sold	Total Selling Expenses
A	$400,000	$248,000	$ 94,000
B	350,000	210,000	76,000
C	320,000	185,600	75,000
D	600,000	390,000	145,000
E	450,000	274,500	117,000
F	370,000	218,300	79,000
G	250,000	150,000	52,500

Instructions:

(1) Prepare a report for the year, indicating total sales, gross profit, gross profit percentage, total selling expenses, and contribution to company profit by salesperson.
(2) Which salesperson contributed the highest dollar amount to company profit during the year?
(3) Briefly list factors other than contribution to company profit that should be considered in evaluating the performance of salespersons.

19–25. R. A. Frazier Company manufactures three styles of folding chairs, X, Y, and Z. The income statement has consistently indicated a net loss for Style Z, and management is considering three proposals: (1) continue Style Z, (2) discontinue Style Z and reduce total output accordingly, or (3) discontinue Style Z and conduct an advertising campaign to expand the sales of Style Y so that the entire plant capacity can continue to be used.

If Proposal 2 is selected and Style Z is discontinued and production curtailed, the annual fixed production costs and fixed operating expenses could be reduced by $14,500 and $8,000 respectively. If Proposal 3 is selected, it is anticipated that an additional annual expenditure of $20,000 for advertising Style Y would yield an increase of 35% in its sales volume, and that the increased production of Style Y would utilize the plant facilities released by the discontinuance of Style Z.

The sales, costs, and expenses have been relatively stable over the past few years and they are expected to remain so for the foreseeable future. The income statement for the past year ended December 31 is:

| | Style | | | |
	X	Y	Z	Total
Sales....................................	$400,000	$432,000	$126,000	$958,000
Cost of goods sold:				
Variable costs..........................	$220,000	$246,000	$ 88,200	$554,200
Fixed costs	80,000	84,000	28,000	192,000
Total cost of goods sold...............	$300,000	$330,000	$116,200	$746,200
Gross profit............................	$100,000	$102,000	$ 9,800	$211,800
Less operating expenses:				
Variable expenses.....................	$ 40,000	$ 43,200	$ 12,600	$ 95,800
Fixed expenses	24,000	24,000	10,500	58,500
Total operating expenses..............	$ 64,000	$ 67,200	$ 23,100	$154,300
Income from operations	$ 36,000	$ 34,800	$(13,300)	$ 57,500

Instructions:

(1) Prepare an income statement for the past year in the variable costing format. Use the following headings:

| | Style | | |
X	Y	Z	Total

Data for each style should be reported through contribution margin. The fixed costs and expenses should be deducted from the total contribution margin, as reported in the "total" column, to determine income from operations.

(2) Based on the income statement prepared in (1) and the other data presented above, determine the amount by which total annual operating income would be reduced below its present level if Proposal 2 is accepted.

(3) Prepare an income statement in the variable costing format, indicating the projected annual operating income if Proposal 3 is accepted. Use the following headings:

| | Style | |
X	Y	Total

Data for each style should be reported through contribution margin. The fixed costs and expenses should be deducted from the total contribution margin as reported in the "total" column. For purposes of this problem, the additional expenditure of $20,000 for advertising can be added to the fixed operating expenses.

(4) By how much would total annual income increase above its present level if Proposal 3 is accepted? Explain.

19–21A. Maloney Company manufactures only one product. In 1986, the plant operated at full capacity. At a meeting of the board of directors on December 12, 1986, it was decided to raise the price of this product from $16, which had prevailed for the past few years, to $18, effective January 1, 1987. Although the cost price was expected to rise about $1.20 per unit in 1987 because of a direct materials and direct labor wage increase, the increase in selling price was expected to cover this increase and also add to operating income. The comparative income statement for 1986 and 1987 is as follows:

	1987		1986	
Sales.....................................		$612,000		$640,000
Cost of goods sold: variable	$289,000		$292,000	
fixed.................	136,000	425,000	136,000	428,000
Gross profit		$187,000		$212,000
Operating expenses: variable	$ 71,400		$ 72,000	
fixed................	36,000	107,400	36,000	108,000
Operating income.......................		$ 79,600		$104,000

Instructions:

(1) Prepare a gross profit analysis report for 1987.
(2) At a meeting of the board of directors on February 3, 1988, the president, after reading the gross profit analysis report, made the following comment:

"It looks as if the increase in unit cost price was $1.80 and not the anticipated $1.20. The failure of operating management to keep these costs within the bounds of those in 1986, except for the anticipated $1.20 increase in direct materials and direct labor cost, was a major factor in the decrease in gross profit."

Do you agree with this analysis of the increase in unit cost price? Explain.

19–22A. During the first month of operations ended January 31, Lorenz Company manufactured 24,000 units, of which 20,000 were sold. Operating data for the month are summarized as follows:

Sales		$800,000
Manufacturing costs:		
Direct materials	$320,000	
Direct labor....................................	160,000	
Variable factory overhead	96,000	
Fixed factory overhead..........................	120,000	696,000
Selling and general expenses:		
Variable......................................	$100,000	
Fixed	50,000	150,000

Instructions:

(1) Prepare an income statement based on the absorption costing concept.

(2) Prepare an income statement based on the variable costing concept.

(3) Explain the reason for the difference in the amount of operating income reported in (1) and (2).

19–23A. The demand for Product G, one of numerous products manufactured by Bolton Inc., has dropped sharply because of recent competition from a similar product. The company's chemists are currently completing tests of various new formulas, and it is anticipated that the manufacture of a superior product can be started on May 1, one month hence. No changes will be needed in the present production facilities to manufacture the new product because only the mixture of the various materials will be changed.

The controller has been asked by the president of the company for advice on whether to continue production during April or to suspend the manufacture of Product G until May 1. The controller has assembled the following pertinent data:

Bolton Inc.
Estimated Income Statement — Product G
For Month Ending March 31, 19--

Sales (20,000 units).	$320,000
Cost of goods sold.	280,000
Gross profit	$ 40,000
Selling and general expenses	75,000
Loss from operations.	$ 35,000

The estimated production costs and selling and general expenses, based on a production of 20,000 units, are as follows:

Direct materials.	$3.40 per unit
Direct labor.	6.50 per unit
Variable factory overhead.	.80 per unit
Variable selling and general expenses.	2.20 per unit
Fixed factory overhead	$66,000 for March
Fixed selling and general expenses	$31,000 for March

Sales for April are expected to drop about 30% below those of the preceding month. No significant changes are anticipated in the production costs or operating expenses. No extra costs will be incurred in discontinuing operations in the portion of the plant associated with Product G. The inventory of Product G at the beginning and end of April is expected to be inconsequential.

Instructions:

(1) Prepare an estimated income statement in absorption costing form for April for Product G, assuming that production continues during the month.

(2) Prepare an estimated income statement in variable costing form for April for Product G, assuming that production continues during the month.

(3) State the estimated operating loss arising from the activities associated with Product G for April if production is temporarily suspended.

(4) Prepare a brief statement of the advice the controller should give.

Mini-Case

19–26. Caswell Company is a family-owned business in which you own 20% of the common stock and your brothers and sisters own the remaining shares. The employment contract of Caswell's new president, Ray Hackett, stipulates a base salary of $50,000 per year plus 10% of income from operations in excess of $4,000,000. Caswell uses the absorption costing method of reporting income from operations, which has averaged approximately $4,000,000 for the past several years.

Estimated sales for 1987, Hackett's first year as president of Caswell Company, is estimated at 100,000 units at a selling price of $200 per unit. To maximize the use of Caswell's productive capacity, Hackett has decided to manufacture 120,000 units rather than 100,000 units of estimated sales. The beginning inventory at January 1, 1987, is insignificant in amount, and the manufacturing costs and selling and general expenses for the production of 100,000 and 120,000 units are as follows:

100,000 Units To Be Manufactured

	Total Cost or Expense	Number of Units	Unit Cost
Manufacturing costs:			
Variable	$ 9,000,000	100,000	$ 90
Fixed.........................	3,000,000	100,000	30
Total	$12,000,000		$120
Selling and general expenses:			
Variable	$ 3,000,000		
Fixed.........................	1,000,000		
Total	$ 4,000,000		

120,000 Units To Be Manufactured

	Total Cost or Expense	Number of Units	Unit Cost
Manufacturing costs:			
Variable	$10,800,000	120,000	$ 90
Fixed.........................	3,000,000	120,000	25
Total	$13,800,000		$115
Selling and general expenses:			
Variable	$ 3,000,000		
Fixed.........................	1,000,000		
Total	$ 4,000,000		

Instructions:

(1) Prepare absorption costing income statements for the year ending December 31, 1987, based upon sales of 100,000 units and the manufacture of (a) 100,000 units and (b) 120,000 units.
(2) Explain the difference in the income from operations reported in (1).
(3) Compute Hackett's total salary for 1987, based on sales of 100,000 units and the manufacture of (a) 100,000 units and (b) 120,000 units.

(4) In addition to maximizing the use of Caswell Company's productive capacity, why might Hackett wish to manufacture 120,000 units rather than 100,000 units?

(5) Can you suggest an alternative way in which Hackett's salary could be determined, using a base salary of $50,000 and 10% of income from operations in excess of $4,000,000, so that the salary could not be increased by simply manufacturing more units?

1. **C** A change in sales from one period to another can be attributed to (1) a change in the number of units sold — quantity factor and (2) a change in the unit price — price factor. The $45,000 decrease (answer C) attributed to the quantity factor is determined as follows:

Decrease in number of units sold in current year	5,000
Unit sales price in preceding year	× $9
Quantity factor — decrease	$45,000

The price factor can be determined as follows:

Increase in unit sales price in current year	$1
Number of units sold in current year	×80,000
Price factor — increase	$80,000

The increase of $80,000 attributed to the price factor less the decrease of $45,000 attributed to the quantity factor accounts for the $35,000 increase in total sales for the current year.

2. **B** Under the variable costing concept (answer B), the cost of products manufactured are composed of only those manufacturing costs that increase or decrease as the volume of production rises or falls. These costs include direct materials, direct labor, and variable factory overhead. Under the absorption costing concept (answer A), all manufacturing costs become a part of the cost of the products manufactured. The absorption costing concept is required in the determination of historical cost and taxable income. The variable costing concept is often useful to management in making decisions.

3. **C** In the variable costing income statement, the deduction of the variable cost of goods sold from sales yields the manufacturing margin (answer C). Deduction of the variable selling and general expenses from manufacturing margin yields the contribution margin (answer B).

4. **B** The contribution margin of $260,000 (answer B) is determined by deducting all of the variable costs and expenses ($400,000 + $90,000) from sales ($750,000).

5. **A** In a period in which the number of units manufactured exceeds the number of units sold, the operating income reported under the absorption costing concept is larger than the operating income reported under the variable costing concept (answer A) because fixed manufacturing costs are deferred when the absorption costing concept is used. This deferment has the effect of excluding fixed manufacturing costs from the current cost of goods sold.

CHAPTER 20

Cost-Volume-Profit Analysis

CHAPTER OBJECTIVES

Describe the use of analyses of cost-volume-profit relationships in planning operations.

Describe and illustrate the mathematical approach to cost-volume-profit analysis.

Describe and illustrate the graphic approach to cost-volume-profit analysis.

Describe and illustrate special cost-volume-profit relationships.

In Chapter 19, three forms of profit analysis—gross profit analysis, absorption costing, and variable costing—were discussed. **Cost-volume-profit analysis**, described in this chapter, is the systematic examination of the interrelationships between selling prices, volume of sales and production, costs, expenses, and profits. Cost-volume-profit analysis is another tool for management's use in making decisions affecting the profitability of the business.

COST-VOLUME-PROFIT RELATIONSHIPS

The examination of cost-volume-profit relationships is a complex matter, since these relationships are often affected by forces entirely or partially beyond management's control. For example, the determination of the selling price of a product is often affected by not only the costs of production, but also by uncontrollable factors in the marketplace. On the other hand, the cost of producing the product is affected by such controllable factors as the efficiency of operations and the volume of production.

Accounting can play an important role in cost-volume-profit analysis by providing management with information on the relative profitability of its various products, the probable effects of changes in selling price, and other variables. Such information can help management improve the relationship between these variables. For example, an analysis of sales and cost data can be helpful in determining the level of sales volume necessary for the business to earn a satisfactory profit.

Costs represent one of the most significant factors in cost-volume-profit analysis. For this purpose, all operating costs and expenses must be subdivided into two categories: (1) fixed and (2) variable. In this chapter, the term "cost" is often used as a convenience to represent both "costs" and "expenses."

Variable Costs

Variable costs are costs that change, in total, as the volume of activity changes. For example, assume that Product Q requires $5 of direct materials per unit. The total direct materials cost of manufacturing 10,000 units is $50,000; 20,000 units require direct materials of $100,000; and so on. Note that the unit cost of the direct materials ($5) remains constant with changes in volume. These variable cost relationships are shown in the graphs below:

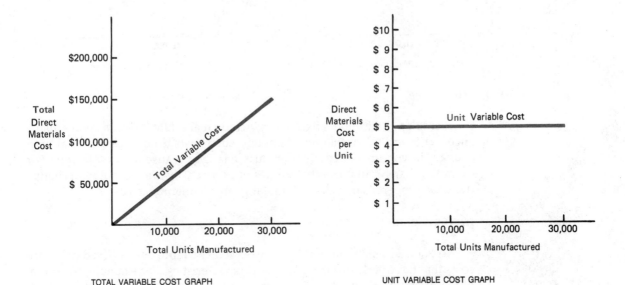

TOTAL VARIABLE COST GRAPH   UNIT VARIABLE COST GRAPH

Direct labor, as well as direct materials, is a variable cost. Similarly, items such as supplies, electricity, indirect materials, and sales commissions are additional examples of variable costs and expenses.

Fixed Costs

Fixed costs remain constant, in total, as the volume of activity changes. For example, straight-line depreciation of $200,000 on factory buildings and equipment will not change, regardless of whether 10,000 units or 20,000 units of product are manufactured. Although fixed costs do not vary in total with changes in volume of activity, the unit cost will change with changes in activity. If volume increases, the unit cost will decrease, and if volume decreases, the unit cost will increase. For example, the unit cost of straight-line depreciation of $200,000 for 10,000 units is $20, and for 20,000 units of product, the unit cost is $10. These fixed cost relationships are shown in the following graphs:

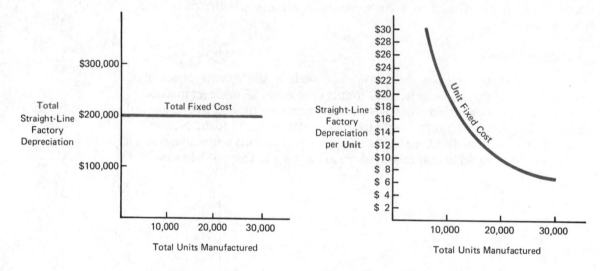

TOTAL FIXED COST GRAPH   UNIT FIXED COST GRAPH

Examples of additional fixed costs include real estate taxes, property insurance, rent, and office salaries. Although such costs do not vary in total with changes in volume of activity, they may change because of other factors. For example, changes in property tax rates or property insurance rates will change the total property tax cost or the total property insurance cost.

Mixed Costs

Mixed costs, sometimes referred to as **semivariable** or **semifixed** costs, are costs that have both variable and fixed characteristics. For example, the rental of manufacturing equipment may require a fixed charge plus a rate for each hour of use above a specified amount. To illustrate, assume that the rental cost for an item of equipment is $15,000, plus $1 per unit of production in excess of 10,000 units to a maximum of 30,000 units. This cost relationship is shown in the following graph:

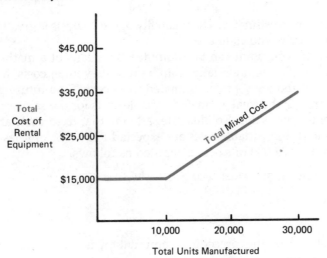

For purposes of analysis, mixed costs can generally be separated into variable and fixed components. In the remainder of this chapter, the variable and fixed components of mixed costs are used in describing and illustrating cost-volume-profit analysis.

MATHEMATICAL APPROACH TO COST-VOLUME-PROFIT ANALYSIS

After the costs and expenses have been classified into fixed and variable components, the effect on profit of these costs and expenses, along with revenues and volume, can be expressed in the form of cost-volume-profit analysis. Although accountants have proposed various approaches for cost-volume-profit analysis, the mathematical approach is one of two common approaches described and illustrated in this chapter.

The mathematical approach to cost-volume-profit analysis generally uses equations (1) to indicate the revenues necessary to achieve the break-even point in operations or (2) to indicate the revenues necessary to achieve a desired or target profit. These two equations and their use by management in profit planning are described and illustrated in the paragraphs that follow.

Break-Even Point

The point in the operations of an enterprise at which revenues and expired costs are exactly equal is called the break-even point. At this level of operations, an enterprise will neither realize an operating income nor incur an operating loss. Break-even analysis can be applied to past periods, but it is most useful when applied to future periods as a guide to business planning, particularly if either an expansion or a curtailment of operations is expected. In such cases, it is concerned with future prospects and future operations and hence relies upon estimates. The reliability of the analysis is greatly influenced by the accuracy of the estimates.

The break-even point can be computed by means of a mathematical formula which indicates the relationship between revenue, costs, and capacity. The data required are (1) total estimated fixed costs for a future period, such as a year, and (2) the total estimated variable costs for the same period, stated as a percent of net sales. To illustrate, assume that fixed costs are estimated at $90,000 and that variable costs are expected to be 60% of sales. The break-even point is $225,000 of sales, computed as follows:

Break-Even Sales (in $) = Fixed Costs (in $) + Variable Costs (as % of Break-Even Sales)
$$S = \$90,000 + 60\%S$$
$$40\%S = \$90,000$$
$$S = \$225,000$$

The validity of the preceding computation is shown in the following income statement:

Sales		$225,000
Expenses:		
Variable costs ($225,000 × 60%)	$135,000	
Fixed costs	90,000	225,000
Operating profit		–0–

The break-even point can be expressed either in terms of total sales dollars, as in the preceding illustration, or in terms of units of sales. For example, in the preceding illustration, if the unit selling price is $25, the break-even point can be expressed as either $225,000 of sales or 9,000 units ($225,000 ÷ $25).

The break-even point can be affected by changes in the fixed costs, unit variable costs, and unit selling price. The effect of each of these factors on the break-even point is briefly described in the following paragraphs.

Effect of Changes in Fixed Costs

Although fixed costs do not change in total with changes in volume of activity, they may change because of other factors, such as changes in property tax rates and salary increases given to factory supervisors. Increases in fixed costs will raise the break-even point. Similarly, decreases in fixed costs will lower the break-even point.

To illustrate, assume that Bishop Co. is evaluating a proposal to budget an additional $100,000 for advertising. Fixed costs (before the additional expenditure of $100,000 is considered) are estimated at $600,000, and variable costs are estimated at 75% of sales. The break-even point (before the additional expenditure is considered) is $2,400,000, computed as follows:

Break-Even Sales (in $) = Fixed Costs (in $) + Variable Costs (as % of Break-Even Sales)
$$S = \$600,000 + 75\%S$$
$$25\%S = \$600,000$$
$$S = \$2,400,000$$

If advertising expense is increased by $100,000, the break-even point is raised to $2,800,000, computed as follows:

Break-Even Sales (in $) = Fixed Costs (in $) + Variable Costs (as % of Break-Even Sales)
$$S = \$700,000 + 75\%S$$
$$25\%S = \$700,000$$
$$S = \$2,800,000$$

The increased fixed cost of $100,000 increases the break-even point by $400,000 of sales, since 75 cents of each sales dollar must cover variable costs. Hence, $4 of additional sales are needed for each $1 increase in fixed costs if the break-even point for Bishop Co. is to remain unchanged.

Effect of Changes in Variable Costs

Although unit variable costs do not change with changes in volume of activity, they may change because of other factors, such as changes in the price of direct materials and salary increases given to factory workers providing direct labor. Increases in unit variable costs will raise the break-even point. Similarly, decreases in unit variable costs will lower the break-even point.

To illustrate, assume that Park Co. is evaluating a proposal to pay an additional 2% sales commission to its sales representatives as an incentive to increase sales. Fixed costs are estimated at $84,000, and variable costs are estimated at 58% of sales (before the additional 2% commission is considered). The break-even point (before the additional commission is considered) is $200,000, computed as follows:

Break-Even Sales (in $) = Fixed Costs (in $) + Variable Costs (as % of Break-Even Sales)
$$S = \$84,000 + 58\%S$$
$$42\%S = \$84,000$$
$$S = \$200,000$$

If the sales commission proposal is adopted, the break-even point is raised to $210,000, computed as follows:

Break-Even Sales (in $) = Fixed Costs (in $) + Variable Costs (as % of Break-Even Sales)
$$S = \$84,000 + 60\%S$$
$$40\%S = \$84,000$$
$$S = \$210,000$$

The additional 2% sales commission (a variable cost) increases the break-even point by $10,000 of sales. If the proposal is adopted, 2% less of each sales dollar is available to cover the fixed costs of $84,000.

Effect of Changing Unit Selling Price

Increases in the unit selling price will lower the break-even point, while decreases in the unit selling price will raise the break-even point. To illustrate the effect of changing the unit selling price, assume that Graham Co. is evaluating a proposal to increase the unit selling price of its product from its current price of $50 to $60 and has accumulated the following relevant data:

	Current	Proposed
Unit selling price.	$50	$60
Unit variable cost	$30	$30
Variable costs (as % of break-even sales):		
$30 unit variable cost ÷ $50 unit selling price.	60%	
$30 unit variable cost ÷ $60 unit selling price.		50%
Total fixed costs	$600,000	$600,000

The break-even point based on the current selling price is $1,500,000, computed as follows:

Break-Even Sales (in $) = Fixed Costs (in $) + Variable Costs (as % of Break-Even Sales)
$$S = \$600,000 + 60\%S$$
$$40\%S = \$600,000$$
$$S = \$1,500,000$$

If the selling price is increased by $10 per unit, the break-even point is decreased to $1,200,000, computed as follows:

Break-Even Sales (in $) = Fixed Costs (in $) + Variable Costs (as % of Break-Even Sales)
$$S = \$600,000 + 50\%S$$
$$50\%S = \$600,000$$
$$S = \$1,200,000$$

The increase in selling price of $10 per unit decreases the break-even point by $300,000 (from $1,500,000 to $1,200,000). In terms of units of sales, the decrease is from 30,000 units ($1,500,000 ÷ $50) to 20,000 units ($1,200,000 ÷ $60).

Desired Profit

At the break-even point, sales and costs are exactly equal. However, business enterprises do not use the break-even point as their goal for future operations. Rather, they seek to achieve the largest possible volume of sales above the break-even point. By modifying the break-even equation, the sales volume required to earn a desired amount of profit may be estimated. For this purpose, a factor for desired profit is added to the standard break-even formula. To illustrate, assume that fixed costs are estimated at $200,000, variable costs are estimated at 60% of sales, and the desired profit is $100,000. The sales volume is $750,000, computed as follows:

Sales (in $) = Fixed Costs (in $) + Variable Costs (as % of Sales) + Desired Profit
$$S = \$200,000 + 60\%S + \$100,000$$
$$40\%S = \$300,000$$
$$S = \$750,000$$

The validity of the preceding computation is shown in the following income statement:

Sales		$750,000
Expenses:		
Variable costs ($750,000 × 60%)	$450,000	
Fixed costs	200,000	650,000
Operating profit		$100,000

GRAPHIC APPROACH TO COST-VOLUME-PROFIT ANALYSIS

Cost-volume-profit analysis can be presented graphically as well as in equation form. Many managers prefer the graphic format because the operating profit or loss for any given level of capacity can be readily determined, without the necessity of solving an equation. The following paragraphs describe two graphic approaches which managers find useful.

Cost-Volume-Profit (Break-Even) Chart

A **cost-volume-profit chart**, sometimes called a break-even chart, is used to assist management in understanding the relationships between costs, sales, and operating profit or loss. To illustrate the cost-volume-profit chart, assume that fixed costs are estimated at $90,000, and variable costs are estimated as 60% of sales. The maximum sales at 100% of capacity is $400,000. The following cost-volume-profit chart is based on the foregoing data:

COST-VOLUME-
PROFIT CHART

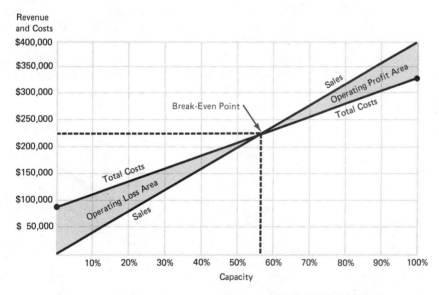

The cost-volume-profit chart is constructed in the following manner:

1. Percentages of capacity of the enterprise are spread along the horizontal axis, and dollar amounts representing operating data are spread along the vertical axis. The outside limits of the chart represent 100% of capacity and the maximum sales potential at that level of capacity.

2. A diagonal line representing sales is drawn from the lower left corner to the upper right corner.
3. A point representing fixed costs is plotted on the vertical axis at the left, and a point representing total costs at maximum capacity is plotted at the right edge of the chart. A diagonal line representing total costs at various percentages of capacity is then drawn connecting these two points.
4. Horizontal and vertical lines are drawn at the point of intersection of the sales and cost lines, which is the break-even point, and the areas representing operating profit and operating loss are identified.

In the illustration, the total costs at maximum capacity are $330,000 (fixed costs of $90,000 plus variable costs of $240,000, which is 60% of $400,000). The dotted line drawn from the point of intersection to the vertical axis identifies the break-even sales amount of $225,000. The dotted line drawn from the point of intersection to the horizontal axis identifies the break-even point in terms of capacity of approximately 56%. Operating profits will be earned when sales levels are to the right of the break-even point (operating profit area), and operating losses will be incurred when sales levels are to the left of the break-even point (operating loss area).

Changes in the unit selling price, total fixed costs, and unit variable costs can also be analyzed using a cost-volume-profit chart. To illustrate, using the preceding example, assume that a proposal to reduce fixed costs by $42,000 is to be evaluated. In this situation, the total fixed costs would be $48,000 ($90,000 − $42,000), and the total costs at maximum capacity would amount to $288,000 ($48,000 of fixed costs plus variable costs of $240,000). The preceding cost-volume-profit chart is revised by plotting the total fixed cost and total cost points and drawing a line between the two points, indicating the proposed total cost line. The following revised chart indicates that the break-even point would decrease to $120,000 of sales (30% of capacity).

REVISED COST-
VOLUME-
PROFIT CHART

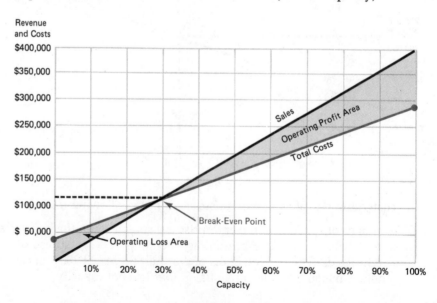

Profit-Volume Chart

Another graphic approach to cost-volume-profit analysis, called the **profit-volume chart**, focuses on profitability rather than on sales revenues and costs, as was the case for the cost-volume-profit chart. On the profit-volume chart, only the difference between total sales revenues and total costs is plotted, which enables management to determine the operating profit (or loss) for various levels of operations.

To illustrate the profit-volume chart, assume that fixed costs are estimated at $50,000, variable costs are estimated at 75% of sales, and the maximum capacity is $500,000 of sales. The maximum operating loss is equal to the fixed costs of $50,000, and the maximum operating profit at 100% of capacity is $75,000, computed as follows:

Sales		$500,000
Expenses:		
Variable costs ($500,000 × 75%)	$375,000	
Fixed costs	50,000	425,000
Operating profit		$ 75,000

The following profit-volume chart is based on the foregoing data:

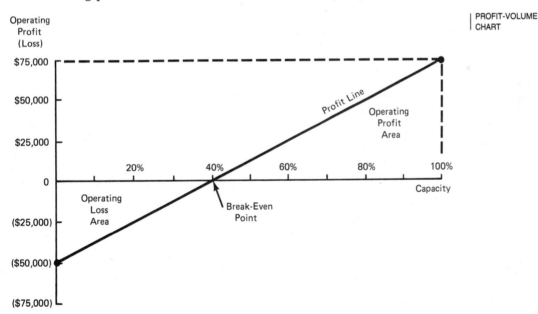

The profit-volume chart is constructed in the following manner:

1. Percentages of capacity of the enterprise are spread along the horizontal axis, and dollar amounts representing operating profits and losses are spread along the vertical axis.

2. A point representing the maximum operating loss is plotted on the vertical axis at the left. This loss is equal to the total fixed costs at 0% of capacity.
3. A point representing the maximum operating profit at 100% of capacity is plotted on the right.
4. A diagonal profit line is drawn connecting the maximum operating loss point with the maximum operating profit point.
5. The profit line intersects the horizontal axis at the break-even point expressed as a percentage of capacity, and the areas representing operating profit and operating loss are identified.

In the illustration, the break-even point is 40% of productive capacity, which can be converted to $200,000 of total sales (maximum capacity of $500,000 × 40%). Operating profit will be earned when sales levels are to the right of the break-even point (operating profit area), and operating losses will be incurred when sales levels are to the left of the break-even point (operating loss area). For example, at 60% of productive capacity, an operating profit of $25,000 will be earned, as indicated in the following profit-volume chart:

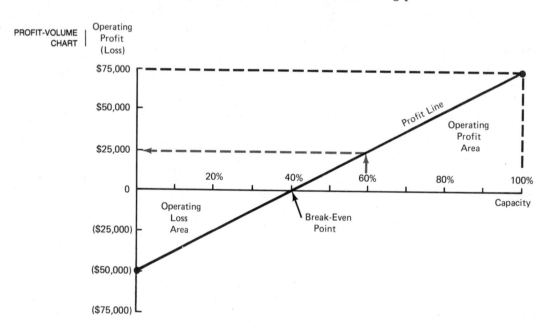

The effect of changes in the unit selling price, total fixed costs, and unit variable costs on profit can be analyzed using a profit-volume chart. To illustrate, using the preceding example, assume that the effect on profit of an increase of $25,000 in fixed costs is to be evaluated. In this case, the total fixed costs would be $75,000 ($50,000 + $25,000), and the maximum operating loss at 0% of capacity would be $75,000. The maximum operating profit at 100% of capacity would be $50,000, computed as follows:

Sales		$500,000
Expenses:		
Variable costs ($500,000 × 75%)	$375,000	
Fixed costs	75,000	450,000
Operating profit		$ 50,000

A revised profit-volume chart is constructed by plotting the maximum operating loss and maximum operating profit points and drawing a line between the two points, indicating the revised profit line. The original and the revised profit-volume charts are as follows:

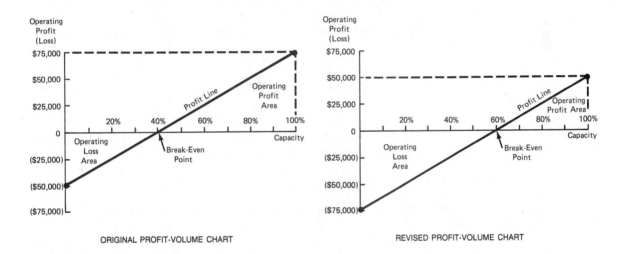

ORIGINAL PROFIT-VOLUME CHART   REVISED PROFIT-VOLUME CHART

The revised profit-volume chart indicates that the break-even point is 60% of capacity, which can be converted to total sales of $300,000 (maximum capacity of $500,000 × 60%). Note that the operating loss area of the chart has increased, while the operating profit area has decreased under the proposed change in fixed costs.

USE OF COMPUTERS IN COST-VOLUME-PROFIT ANALYSIS

In the preceding paragraphs, the use of the mathematical approach to cost-volume-profit analysis and the use of the cost-volume-profit chart and the profit-volume chart for analyzing the effect of changes in selling price, costs, and volume on profits have been demonstrated. Both the mathematical and graphic approaches are becoming increasingly popular and easy to use when managers have access to a computer terminal or a microcomputer. With the wide variety of computer software that is available, managers can vary assumptions regarding selling prices, costs, and volume and can instantaneously analyze the effects of the assumptions on the break-even point and profit.

SALES MIX CONSIDERATIONS

In many businesses, more than one product is sold at varying selling prices. In addition, the products often have different unit variable costs, and each product makes a different contribution to profits. Thus, the total business profit, as well as the break-even point, depends upon the proportions in which the products are sold.

Sales mix is the relative distribution of sales among the various products sold by an enterprise. For example, assume that the sales for Cascade Company during the past year, a typical year for the company, are as follows:

Product	Units Sold	Sales Mix
A	8,000	80%
B	2,000	20
	10,000	100%

The sales mix for products A and B can be expressed as a relative percentage, as shown above, or as the ratio of 80:20.

Sales Mix and the Break-Even Point

The break-even point for an enterprise selling two or more products must be calculated on the basis of a specified sales mix. If the sales mix is assumed to be constant, the break-even point and the sales necessary to achieve desired levels of operating profit can be computed using the standard calculations.

To illustrate the computation of the break-even point for Cascade Company, assume that fixed costs are $200,000. In addition, assume that the unit selling prices, unit variable costs, and sales mix for products A and B are as follows:

Product	Selling Price per Unit	Variable Cost per Unit	Sales Mix
A	$ 90	$70	80%
B	140	95	20

To compute the break-even point when several products are sold, it is useful to think of the individual products as components of one overall enterprise product. For Cascade Company, assume that this overall enterprise product is arbitrarily labeled E. The unit selling price of E can be thought of as equal to the total of the unit selling prices of the individual products A and

B, multiplied by their respective sales mix percentages. Likewise, the unit variable cost of E can be thought of as equal to the total of the unit variable costs of products A and B, multiplied by the sales mix percentages. These computations are as follows:

Unit selling price of E: ($90 × .8) + ($140 × .2) = $100
Unit variable cost of E: ($70 × .8) + ($95 × .2) = $75

The variable costs for enterprise product E are therefore expected to be 75% of sales ($75 ÷ $100). The break-even point can be determined in the normal manner, using the equation, as follows:

Break-Even Sales (in $) = Fixed Costs (in $) + Variable Costs (as % of Break-Even Sales)
S = $200,000 + 75%S
25%S = $200,000
S = $800,000

The break-even point of $800,000 of sales of enterprise product E is equivalent to 8,000 total sales units ($800,000 ÷ $100). Since the sales mix for products A and B is 80% and 20% respectively, the break-even quantity of A is 6,400 (8,000 × 80%) and B is 1,600 (8,000 × 20%) units.

The validity of the preceding analysis can be verified by preparing the following income statement:

Cascade Company
Income Statement
For Year Ended December 31, 19--

	Product A	Product B	Total
Sales:			
6,400 units × $90	$576,000		$576,000
1,600 units × $140		$224,000	224,000
Total sales	$576,000	$224,000	$800,000
Variable costs:			
6,400 units × $70	$448,000		$448,000
1,600 units × $95		$152,000	152,000
Total variable costs	$448,000	$152,000	$600,000
Fixed costs			200,000
Total costs			$800,000
Operating profit			–0–

The effects of changes in the sales mix on the break-even point can be determined by repeating the preceding analysis, assuming a different sales mix.

Sales Mix and Desired Profit

The sales volume needed to earn an amount of profit when an enterprise sells two or more products can be computed using an approach similar to that described in the previous section. For example, the total sales necessary for Cascade Company to earn an operating profit of $40,000, with the original sales mix of 80% and 20% (where fixed costs were $200,000 and variable costs were 75% of sales), can be computed by use of the concept of an overall enterprise product E and solving the following equation:

Sales (in $) = Fixed Costs (in $) + Variable Costs (as a % of Sales) + Desired Profit

$$S = \$200,000 + 75\%S + \$40,000$$
$$25\%S = \$240,000$$
$$S = \$960,000$$

Sales of $960,000 of enterprise product E is equivalent to 9,600 total sales units ($960,000 ÷ $100). Since the sales mix for products A and B is 80% and 20% respectively, the quantity of A to be sold is 7,680 (9,600 × 80%) and B is 1,920 (9,600 × 20%) units. The validity of this approach can be verified by preparing the following income statement:

Cascade Company
Income Statement
For Year Ended December 31, 19--

	Product A	Product B	Total
Sales:			
7,680 units × $90	$691,200		$691,200
1,920 units × $140		$268,800	268,800
Total sales	$691,200	$268,800	$960,000
Variable costs:			
7,680 units × $70	$537,600		$537,600
1,920 units × $95		$182,400	182,400
Total variable costs	$537,600	$182,400	$720,000
Fixed costs			200,000
Total costs			$920,000
Operating profit			$ 40,000

SPECIAL COST-VOLUME-PROFIT RELATIONSHIPS

Additional relationships can be developed from the information presented in both the mathematical and graphic approaches to cost-volume-profit analysis. Two of these relationships that are especially useful to management in decision making are discussed in the following paragraphs.

Margin of Safety

The difference between the current sales revenue and the sales at the break-even point is called the **margin of safety**. It represents the possible decrease in sales revenue that may occur before an operating loss results, and it may be stated either in terms of dollars or as a percentage of sales. For example, if the volume of sales is $250,000 and sales at the break-even point amount to $200,000, the margin of safety is $50,000 or 20%, as shown by the following computation:

$$\text{Margin of Safety} = \frac{\text{Sales} - \text{Sales at Break-Even Point}}{\text{Sales}}$$

$$\text{Margin of Safety} = \frac{\$250,000 - \$200,000}{\$250,000} = 20\%$$

The margin of safety is useful in evaluating past operations and as a guide to business planning. For example, if the margin of safety is low, management should carefully study forecasts of future sales because even a small decline in sales revenue will result in an operating loss.

Contribution Margin Ratio

Another relationship between cost, volume, and profits that is especially useful in business planning because it gives an insight into the profit potential of a firm is the **contribution margin ratio**, sometimes called the **profit-volume ratio.** This ratio indicates the percentage of each sales dollar available to cover the fixed expenses and to provide operating income. For example, if the volume of sales is $250,000 and variable expenses amount to $175,000, the contribution margin ratio is 30%, as shown by the following computation:

$$\text{Contribution Margin Ratio} = \frac{\text{Sales} - \text{Variable Expenses}}{\text{Sales}}$$

$$\text{Contribution Margin Ratio} = \frac{\$250,000 - \$175,000}{\$250,000} = 30\%$$

The contribution margin ratio permits the quick determination of the effect on operating income of an increase or a decrease in sales volume. To illustrate, assume that the management of a firm with a contribution margin ratio of 30% is studying the effect on operating income of adding $25,000 in sales orders. Multiplying the ratio (30%) by the change in sales volume ($25,000) indicates an increase in operating income of $7,500 if the additional orders are obtained. In using the analysis in such a case, factors other than sales volume, such as the amount of fixed expenses, the percentage of variable expenses to sales, and the unit sales price, are assumed to remain constant. If these factors are not constant, the effect of any change in these factors must be considered in applying the analysis.

The contribution margin ratio is also useful in setting business policy. For example, if the contribution margin ratio of a firm is large and production is at a level below 100% capacity, a comparatively large increase in operating income can be expected from an increase in sales volume. On the other hand, a comparatively large decrease in operating income can be expected from a decline in sales volume. A firm in such a position might decide to devote more effort to additional sales promotion because of the large change in operating income that will result from changes in sales volume. On the other hand, a firm with a small contribution margin ratio will probably want to give more attention to reducing costs and expenses before concentrating large efforts on additional sales promotion.

LIMITATIONS OF COST-VOLUME-PROFIT ANALYSIS

The reliability of cost-volume-profit analysis depends upon the validity of several assumptions. One major assumption is that there is no change in inventory quantities during the year; that is, the quantity of units in the beginning inventory equals the quantity of units in the ending inventory. When changes in inventory quantities occur, the computations for cost-volume-profit analysis become more complex.

For cost-volume-profit analysis, a relevant range of activity is assumed, within which all costs can be classified as either fixed or variable. Within the relevant range, which is usually a range of activity within which the company is likely to operate, the unit variable costs and the total fixed costs will not change. For example, within the relevant range of activity, factory supervisory salaries are fixed. For cost-volume-profit analysis, it is assumed that a significant change in activity that would cause these salaries to change, such as adding a night shift that would double production, will not occur.

These assumptions simplify cost-volume-profit relationships, and since substantial variations in the assumptions are often uncommon in practice, cost-volume-profit analysis can be used quite effectively in decision making. Under conditions of substantial variations from the assumptions, the analysis of the cost-volume-profit relationships must be used cautiously.

Self-Examination Questions (Answers at end of chapter.)

1. For cost-volume-profit analysis, costs must be classified as either fixed or variable. Variable costs:
A. change in total as the volume of activity changes
B. do not change in total as the volume of activity changes
C. change on a per unit basis as the volume of activity changes
D. none of the above

2. If variable costs are 40% of sales and fixed costs are $240,000, what is the break-even point?

A. $200,000
B. $240,000

C. $400,000
D. None of the above

3. Based on the data presented in Question 2, how much sales would be required to realize operating profit of $30,000?

A. $400,000
B. $450,000

C. $600,000
D. None of the above

4. If sales are $500,000, variable costs are $200,000, and fixed costs are $240,000, what is the margin of safety?

A. 20%
B. 40%

C. 60%
D. None of the above

5. Based on the data presented in Question 4, what is the contribution margin ratio?

A. 40%
B. 48%

C. 88%
D. None of the above

20-1. How do changes in volume of activity affect total (a) variable costs and (b) fixed costs?

20-2. If total fixed costs are $150,000, what is the unit fixed cost if production is (a) 50,000 units and (b) 60,000 units?

20-3. (a) What are mixed costs? (b) If a leased copying machine costs $200 per month plus 3¢ per copy and 5,000 copies were made during June, what was the total cost for June?

20-4. (a) What is the break-even point? (b) What equation can be used to determine the break-even point?

20-5. If fixed costs are $420,000 and variable costs are 70% of sales, what is the break-even point?

20-6. If sales are $1,000,000, variable costs are $400,000, and fixed costs are $480,000, what is the break-even point?

20-7. If the property tax rates are increased, what effect will this change in fixed costs have on the break-even point?

20-8. If the unit cost of direct materials is decreased, what effect will this change have on the break-even point?

20-9. If fixed costs are $630,000 and variable costs are 70% of sales, what sales are required to realize operating profit of $150,000?

20-10. What is the advantage of presenting cost-volume-profit analysis in the chart form over the equation form?

20-11. Name the following chart and identify the items represented by the letters a through f.

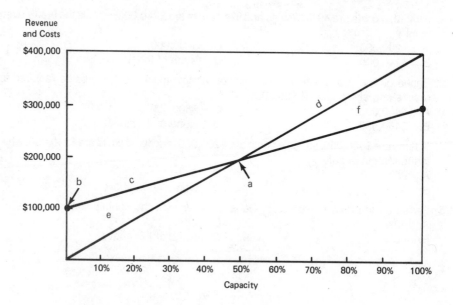

20–12. Name the following chart and identify the items represented by the letters a through f.

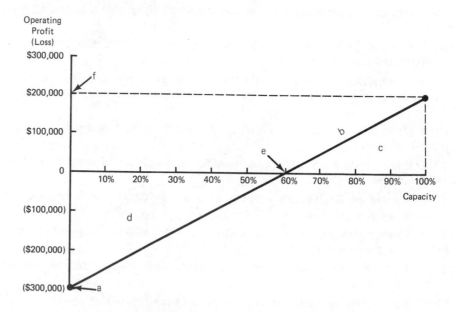

20–13. Both McBride Company and Sherwood Company had the same sales, total costs, and operating profit for the current fiscal year, yet McBride Company had a lower break-even point than Sherwood Company. Explain the reason for this difference in break-even points.

20–14. (a) What is meant by "sales mix"? (b) For conventional break-even analysis, is the sales mix assumed to be constant?

20–15. (a) What is meant by the term "margin of safety"? (b) If sales are $750,000, net income $60,000, and sales at the break-even point $480,000, what is the margin of safety?

20–16. What ratio indicates the percentage of each sales dollar that is available to cover fixed costs and to provide a profit?

20–17. (a) If sales are $350,000 and variable costs are $210,000, what is the contribution margin ratio? (b) What is the contribution margin ratio if variable costs are 55% of sales?

20–18. An examination of the accounting records of Valentine Company disclosed a high contribution margin ratio and production at a level below maximum capacity. Based on this information, suggest a likely means of improving operating profit. Explain.

Exercises

20–19. For the current year ending June 30, Overman Company expects fixed costs and expenses of $360,000 and variable costs and expenses equal to 55% of sales.

(a) Compute the anticipated break-even point.
(b) Compute the sales required to realize operating profit of $90,000.

20–20. For the past year, Vega Company had fixed costs of $600,000 and variable costs equal to 40% of sales. All revenues and costs are expected to remain constant for the coming year, except that property taxes are expected to increase by $30,000 during the year.

(a) Compute the break-even point for the past year.
(b) Compute the anticipated break-even point for the coming year.

20–21. For the current year ending December 31, Rossi Company expects fixed costs of $900,000 and variable costs equal to 50% of sales. For the coming year, a new wage contract will increase variable costs to 55% of sales.

(a) Compute the break-even point for the current year.
(b) Compute the anticipated break-even point for the coming year, assuming that all revenues and costs are to remain constant, with the exception of the costs represented by the new wage contract.

20–22. Currently the unit selling price is $300, unit variable cost is $195, and total fixed costs are $700,000. A proposal is being evaluated to increase the unit selling price to $325.

(a) Compute the current break-even point.
(b) Compute the anticipated break-even point, assuming that the unit selling price is increased and all costs remain constant.

20–23. For the coming year, Rosebud Inc. anticipates fixed costs of $100,000, variable costs equal to 75% of sales, and maximum capacity of $800,000 of sales.

(a) What is the maximum possible operating loss?
(b) Compute the maximum possible operating profit.
(c) Construct a profit-volume chart.
(d) Determine the break-even point as a percentage of capacity by using the profit-volume chart constructed in (c).

20–24. (a) If Pridemore Company, with a break-even point at $600,000 of sales has actual sales of $750,000, what is the margin of safety expressed (1) in dollars and (2) as a percentage of sales? (b) If the margin of safety for Strauss Company was 36%, fixed costs were $180,000, and variable costs were 55% of sales, what was the amount of actual sales?

20–25. (a) If Torino Company budgets sales of $800,000, fixed costs and expenses of $224,000, and variable costs and expenses of $512,000, what is the anticipated contribution margin ratio? (b) If the contribution margin ratio for Underwood Company is 40%, sales were $2,400,000, and fixed costs and expenses were $670,000, what was the operating profit?

20–26. For the past year, Zeller Company had sales of $650,000, a margin of safety of 20%, and a contribution margin ratio of 45%. Compute:

(a) The break-even point.
(b) The variable costs and expenses.
(c) The fixed costs and expenses.
(d) The operating profit.

20–27. For 1986, a company had sales of $2,400,000, fixed costs of $600,000, and a contribution margin ratio of 30%. During 1987, the variable costs were 70% of sales, the fixed costs did not change from the previous year, and the margin of safety was 20%.

(a) What was the operating profit for 1986?
(b) What was the break-even point for 1987?
(c) What was the amount of sales for 1987?
(d) What was the operating profit for 1987?

Problems

20–28. For the coming year, Margo Company anticipates fixed costs of $240,000 and variable costs equal to 60% of sales.

Instructions:

(1) Compute the anticipated break-even point.
(2) Compute the sales required to realize operating profit of $80,000.
(3) Construct a cost-volume-profit chart, assuming sales of $1,000,000 at full capacity.
(4) Determine the probable operating profit if sales total $750,000.

20–29. Elton Company operated at 75% of capacity last year, when sales were $3,000,000. Fixed costs were $1,000,000, and variable costs were 50% of sales. Elton Company is considering a proposal to spend an additional $250,000 on billboard advertising during the current year in an attempt to increase sales and utilize additional capacity.

Instructions:

(1) Construct a cost-volume-profit chart indicating the break-even point for last year.
(2) Using the cost-volume-profit chart prepared in (1), determine (a) the operating profit for last year and (b) the maximum operating profit that could have been realized during the year.

(3) Construct a cost-volume-profit chart indicating the break-even point for the current year, assuming that a noncancelable contract is signed for the additional billboard advertising. No changes are expected in unit selling price or other costs.

(4) Using the cost-volume-profit chart prepared in (3), determine (a) the operating profit if sales total $3,000,000 and (b) the maximum operating profit that could be realized during the year.

20–30. Last year, Nagle Company had sales of $800,000, fixed costs of $200,000, and variable costs of $480,000. Nagle Company is considering a proposal to spend $50,000 to hire a public relations firm, hoping that the company's image can be improved and sales increased. Maximum operating capacity is $1,000,000 of sales.

Instructions:

(1) Construct a profit-volume chart for last year.

(2) Using the profit-volume chart prepared in (1), determine for last year (a) the break-even point, (b) the operating profit, and (c) the maximum operating profit that could have been realized.

(3) Construct a profit-volume chart for the current year, assuming that the additional $50,000 expenditure is made and there is no change in unit selling price or other costs.

(4) Using the profit-volume chart prepared in (3), determine (a) the break-even point, (b) the operating profit if sales total $800,000, and (c) the maximum operating profit that could be realized.

20–31. The expected sales of products X and Y for Baker Company for the current year, which is typical of recent years, are as follows:

Product	Selling Price per Unit	Variable Cost per Unit	Sales Mix
X	$100	$ 80	60%
Y	150	120	40

The estimated fixed costs for the current year are $180,000.

Instructions:

(1) Determine the estimated sales revenues necessary to reach the break-even point for the current year.

(2) Based on the break-even point in (1), determine the unit sales of both X and Y for the current year.

(3) Determine the estimated sales revenues necessary for Baker Company to realize an operating profit of $60,000 for the current year.

(4) Based on the sales revenues determined in (3), determine the unit sales of both X and Y for the current year.

20–32. Blier Company expects to maintain the same inventories at the end of 1987 as at the beginning of the year. The total of all production costs for the year is therefore assumed to be equal to the cost of goods sold. With this in mind, the various department heads were asked to submit estimates of the expenses for their departments during 1987. A summary report of these estimates is as follows:

	Estimated Fixed Expense	Estimated Variable Expense (per unit sold)
Production costs:		
Direct materials	—	$ 7.50
Direct labor	—	5.70
Factory overhead............................	$284,000	1.80
Selling expenses:		
Sales salaries and commissions...............	104,000	.90
Advertising.....................................	63,000	—
Travel..	30,900	—
Miscellaneous selling expense	16,300	.30
General expenses:		
Office and officers' salaries	135,100	—
Supplies.......................................	16,900	.15
Miscellaneous general expense	9,800	.15
	$660,000	$16.50

It is expected that 80,000 units will be sold at a selling price of $27.50 a unit. Capacity output is 100,000 units.

Instructions:

(1) Determine the break-even point (a) in dollars of sales, (b) in units, and (c) in terms of capacity.
(2) Prepare an estimated income statement for 1987.
(3) Construct a break-even chart, indicating the break-even point in dollars of sales.
(4) What is the expected margin of safety?
(5) What is the expected contribution margin ratio?

20–33. Portnoy Company operated at full capacity during 1986. Its income statement for 1986 is as follows:

Sales...		$3,300,000
Cost of goods sold.............................		1,872,000
Gross profit		$1,428,000
Operating expenses:		
Selling expenses	$648,000	
General expenses	180,000	
Total operating expenses.....................		828,000
Operating income..............................		$ 600,000

An analysis of costs and expenses reveals the following division of costs and expenses between fixed and variable:

	Fixed	Variable
Cost of goods sold	25%	75%
Selling expenses.........	20%	80%
General expenses........	68%	32%

Management is considering a plant expansion program that will permit an increase of $700,000 in yearly sales. The expansion will increase fixed costs and expenses by $120,000, but will not affect the relationship between sales and variable costs and expenses.

Instructions:

(1) Determine for present capacity (a) the total fixed costs and expenses and (b) the total variable costs and expenses.
(2) Determine the percentage of total variable costs and expenses to sales.
(3) Compute the break-even point under present conditions.
(4) Compute the break-even point under the proposed program.
(5) Determine the amount of sales that would be necessary under the proposed program to realize the $600,000 of operating income that was earned in 1986.
(6) Determine the maximum operating income possible with the expanded plant.
(7) If the proposal is accepted and sales remain at the 1986 level, what will the operating income be for 1987?
(8) Based upon the data given, would you recommend accepting the proposal? Explain.

20–28A. For the coming year, Wooten Company anticipates fixed costs of $120,000 and variable costs equal to 70% of sales.

Instructions:

(1) Compute the anticipated break-even point.
(2) Compute the sales required to realize operating profit of $60,000.
(3) Construct a cost-volume-profit chart, assuming sales of $1,000,000 at full capacity.
(4) Determine the probable operating profit if sales total $800,000.

20–29A. Rose Company operated at 60% of capacity last year, when sales totaled $3,000,000. Fixed costs were $1,000,000, and variable costs were 60% of sales. Rose Company is considering a proposal to spend an additional $200,000 on billboard advertising during the current year in an attempt to increase sales and utilize additional capacity.

Instructions:

(1) Construct a cost-volume-profit chart indicating the break-even point for last year.
(2) Using the cost-volume-profit chart prepared in (1), determine (a) the operating profit for last year and (b) the maximum operating profit that could have been realized during the year.
(3) Construct a cost-volume-profit chart indicating the break-even point for the current year, assuming that a noncancelable contract is signed for the additional billboard advertising. No changes are expected in unit selling price or other costs.
(4) Using the cost-volume-profit chart prepared in (3), determine (a) the operating profit if sales total $3,000,000 and (b) the maximum operating profit that could be realized during the year.

20–30A. Last year, Perez Company had sales of $800,000, fixed costs of $200,000, and variable costs of $400,000. Perez Company is considering a proposal to spend $50,000 to hire a public relations firm, hoping that the company's image can be improved and sales increased. Maximum operating capacity is $1,000,000 of sales.

Instructions:

(1) Construct a profit-volume chart for last year.
(2) Using the profit-volume chart prepared in (1), determine for last year (a) the break-even point, (b) the operating profit, and (c) the maximum operating profit that could have been realized.
(3) Construct a profit-volume chart for the current year, assuming that the additional $50,000 expenditure is made and there is no change in unit selling price or other costs.
(4) Using the profit-volume chart prepared in (3), determine (a) the break-even point, (b) the operating profit if sales total $800,000, and (c) the maximum operating profit that could be realized.

20–32A. W. F. Epstein Company expects to maintain the same inventories at the end of 1987 as at the beginning of the year. The total of all production costs for the year is therefore assumed to be equal to the cost of goods sold. With this in mind, the various department heads were asked to submit estimates of the expenses for their departments during 1987. A summary report of these estimates is as follows:

	Estimated Fixed Expense	Estimated Variable Expense (per unit sold)
Production costs:		
Direct materials.	—	$ 9.20
Direct labor	—	4.80
Factory overhead	$174,000	2.00
Selling expenses:		
Sales salaries and commissions.	80,400	1.20
Advertising.	21,600	—
Travel	3,600	—
Miscellaneous selling expense	2,400	.48
General expenses:		
Office and officers' salaries	70,500	—
Supplies.	4,500	.24
Miscellaneous general expense	3,000	.08
	$360,000	$18.00

It is expected that 70,000 units will be sold at a selling price of $24 a unit. Capacity output is 75,000 units.

Instructions:

(1) Determine the break-even point (a) in dollars of sales, (b) in units, and (c) in terms of capacity.
(2) Prepare an estimated income statement for 1987.
(3) Construct a break-even chart, indicating the break-even point in dollars of sales.

(4) What is the expected margin of safety?

(5) What is the expected contribution margin ratio?

20-34. Hardman Company manufactures product P, which sold for $20 per unit in 1986. For the past several years, sales and net income have been declining. On sales of $540,000 in 1986, the company operated near the break-even point and used only 60% of its productive capacity. John Hardman, your father-in-law, is considering several proposals to reverse the trend of declining sales and net income, to more fully use production facilities, and to increase profits. One proposal under consideration is to reduce the unit selling price to $19.20.

Your father-in-law has asked you to aid him in assessing the proposal to reduce the sales price by $.80. For this purpose, he provided the following summary of the estimated fixed and variable costs and expenses for 1987, which are unchanged from 1986:

Variable costs and expenses:

Production costs	$8.60 per unit
Selling expenses	2.00 per unit
General expenses	1.40 per unit

Fixed costs and expenses:

Production costs........................	$100,000
Selling expenses	40,000
General expenses	60,000

Instructions:

(1) Determine the break-even point for 1987 in dollars, assuming (a) no change in sales price and (b) the proposed sales price.

(2) How much additional sales are necessary for Hardman Company to break even in 1987 under the proposal?

(3) Determine the net income for 1987, assuming (a) no change in sales price and volume from 1986 and (b) the new sales price and no change in volume from 1986.

(4) Determine the maximum net income for 1987, assuming the proposed sales price.

(5) Briefly list factors that you would discuss with your father-in-law in evaluating the proposal.

1. **A** Variable costs change in total as the volume of activity changes (answer A) or, expressed in another way, the unit variable cost remains constant with changes in volume.

2. **C** The break-even point of $400,000 (answer C) is that point in operations at which revenue and expired costs are exactly equal and is determined as follows:

$$\text{Break-Even Sales (in \$)} = \text{Fixed Costs (in \$)} + \text{Variable Costs (as \% of Sales)}$$

$$S = \$240,000 + 40\%S$$

$$60\%S = \$240,000$$

$$S = \$400,000$$

3. B $450,000 of sales would be required to realize operating profit of $30,000, computed as follows:

$$\frac{\text{Sales}}{\text{(in \$)}} = \frac{\text{Fixed Costs}}{\text{(in \$)}} + \frac{\text{Variable Costs}}{\text{(as \% of Sales)}} + \frac{\text{Desired}}{\text{Profit}}$$

$$S = \$240,000 + 40\%S + \$30,000$$
$$60\%S = \$270,000$$
$$S = \$450,000$$

4. A The margin of safety of 20% (answer A) represents the possible decrease in sales revenue that may occur before an operating loss results and is determined as follows:

$$\text{Margin of Safety} = \frac{\text{Sales} - \text{Sales at Break-Even Point}}{\text{Sales}}$$

$$\text{Margin of Safety} = \frac{\$500,000 - \$400,000}{\$500,000}$$

$$= 20\%$$

The margin of safety can also be expressed in terms of dollars and would amount to $100,000, determined as follows:

Sales	$500,000
Less sales at break-even point	400,000
Margin of safety	$100,000

5. D The contribution margin ratio indicates the percentage of each sales dollar available to cover the fixed expenses and provide operating income and is determined as follows:

$$\text{Contribution Margin Ratio} = \frac{\text{Sales} - \text{Variable Expenses}}{\text{Sales}}$$

$$\text{Contribution Margin Ratio} = \frac{\$500,000 - \$200,000}{\$500,000}$$

$$= 60\%$$

CHAPTER 21

Differential Analysis and Product Pricing

CHAPTER OBJECTIVES

Describe and illustrate differential analysis.

Describe and illustrate a practical approach to product pricing.

Describe and illustrate economic theory underlying product pricing.

A primary objective of accounting is to provide management with analyses and reports that will be useful in resolving current problems and planning for the future. The types of analyses and reports depend on the nature of the decisions to be made. However, all decisions require careful consideration of the consequences of alternative courses of action. This chapter discusses differential analysis, which provides management with data on the differences in total revenues and costs associated with alternative actions.

This chapter also describes and illustrates a practical approach frequently used by managers in setting product prices. In addition, the relationship of economic theory to the more practical approaches to product pricing is briefly discussed.

DIFFERENTIAL ANALYSIS

Planning for future operations is chiefly decision making. For some decisions, revenue and cost information drawn from the general ledger and other basic accounting records is very useful. For example, historical cost data in the absorption costing format are helpful in planning production for the long run. Historical cost data in the variable costing format are useful in planning production for the short run. However, the revenue and cost data needed to evaluate courses of future operations or to choose among competing alternatives are often not available in the basic accounting records.

The relevant revenue and cost data in the analysis of future possibilities are the differences between the alternatives under consideration. The amounts of such differences are called **differentials** and the area of accounting concerned with the effect of alternative courses of action on revenues and costs is called **differential analysis**.

Differential revenue is the amount of increase or decrease in revenue expected from a particular course of action as compared with an alternative. To illustrate, assume that certain equipment is being used to manufacture a product that provides revenue of $150,000. If the equipment could be used to make another product that would provide revenue of $175,000, the differential revenue from the alternative would be $25,000.

Differential cost is the amount of increase or decrease in cost that is expected from a particular course of action as compared with an alternative. For example, if an increase in advertising expenditures from $100,000 to $150,000 is being considered, the differential cost of the action would be $50,000.

Differential analysis can aid management in making decisions on a variety of alternatives, including (1) whether equipment should be leased or sold, (2) whether to discontinue an unprofitable segment, (3) whether to manufacture or purchase a needed part, (4) whether to replace usable plant assets, (5) whether to process further or sell an intermediate product, and (6) whether to accept additional business at a special price. The following discussion relates to the use of differential analysis in analyzing these alternatives.

Lease or Sell

The main advantage of differential analysis is its selection of relevant revenues and costs related to alternative courses of action. Differential analysis reports emphasize the significant factors bearing on the decision, help to clarify the issues and save the time of the reader. To illustrate, assume that an enterprise is considering the disposal of an item of equipment that is no longer needed in the business. Its original cost is $200,000 and accumulated depreciation to date totals $120,000. A tentative offer has been received to lease the machine for a number of years for a total of $160,000, after which the machine would be sold as scrap for a small amount. The repair, insurance, and property tax expenses during the period of the lease are estimated at $35,000. Alternatively, the equipment can be sold through a broker for $100,000 less a 6% commission. The decision to be made is whether the equipment should be leased or sold. The report of the analysis is as follows:

Proposal to Lease or Sell Equipment
June 22, 19--

Differential revenue from alternatives:		
Revenue from lease.................................	$160,000	
Revenue from sale.................................	100,000	
Differential revenue from lease......................		$60,000
Differential cost of alternatives:		
Repair, insurance, and property tax expenses............	$ 35,000	
Commission expense on sale.........................	6,000	
Differential cost of lease............................		29,000
Net advantage of lease alternative......................		$31,000

It should be noted that it was not necessary to consider the $80,000 book value ($200,000 − $120,000) of the equipment. The $80,000 is a **sunk cost;** that is, it is a cost that will not be affected by later decisions. In the illustration, the expenditure to acquire the equipment had already been made, and the choice is now between leasing or selling the equipment. The relevant factors to be considered are the differential revenues and differential costs associated with the lease or sell decision. The undepreciated cost of the equipment is irrelevant. The validity of the foregoing report can be shown by the following conventional analysis:

Lease alternative:			
Revenue from lease.............................		$160,000	
Depreciation expense..........................	$80,000		
Repair, insurance, and property tax expenses.....	35,000	115,000	
Net gain.....................................			$45,000
Sell alternative:			
Sale price		$100,000	
Book value of equipment.......................	$80,000		
Commission expense	6,000	86,000	
Net gain.....................................			14,000
Net advantage of lease alternative..................			$31,000

Discontinuance of an Unprofitable Segment

When a department, branch, territory, or other segment of an enterprise has been operating at a loss, management should consider eliminating the unprofitable segment. It might be natural to assume (sometimes mistakenly) that the total operating income of the enterprise would be increased if the operating loss could be eliminated. Discontinuance of the unprofitable segment will usually eliminate all of the related variable costs and expenses. However, if the segment represents a relatively small part of the enterprise, the fixed costs and expenses (depreciation, insurance, property taxes, etc.)

will not be reduced by its discontinuance. It is entirely possible in this situation for the total operating income of a company to be reduced rather than increased by eliminating an unprofitable segment. As a basis for illustrating this type of situation, the following income statement is presented for the year just ended, which was a normal year. For purposes of the illustration, it is assumed that discontinuance of Product A, on which losses are incurred annually, will have no effect on total fixed costs and expenses.

Condensed Income Statement
For Year Ended August 31, 19--

	Product			
	A	B	C	Total
Sales................................	$100,000	$400,000	$500,000	$1,000,000
Cost of goods sold:				
Variable costs.....................	$ 60,000	$200,000	$220,000	$ 480,000
Fixed costs	20,000	80,000	120,000	220,000
Total cost of goods sold.........	$ 80,000	$280,000	$340,000	$ 700,000
Gross profit.........................	$ 20,000	$120,000	$160,000	$ 300,000
Operating expenses:				
Variable expenses.................	$ 25,000	$ 60,000	$ 95,000	$ 180,000
Fixed expenses	6,000	20,000	25,000	51,000
Total operating expenses........	$ 31,000	$ 80,000	$120,000	$ 231,000
Income (loss) from operations	$ (11,000)	$ 40,000	$ 40,000	$ 69,000

Data on the estimated differential revenue and differential cost related to discontinuing Product A, on which an operating loss of $11,000 was incurred during the past year, may be assembled in a report such as the following. This report emphasizes the significant factors bearing on the decision.

Proposal to Discontinue Product A
September 29, 19--

Differential revenue from annual sales of product:		
Revenue from sales		$100,000
Differential cost of annual sales of product:		
Variable cost of goods sold	$60,000	
Variable operating expenses	25,000	85,000
Annual differential income from sales of Product A........		$ 15,000

Instead of an increase in annual operating income to $80,000 (Product B, $40,000; Product C, $40,000) that might seem to be indicated by the income statement, the discontinuance of Product A would reduce operating income to an estimated $54,000 ($69,000 − $15,000). The validity of this conclusion can be shown by the conventional analysis:

Proposal to Discontinue Product A
September 29, 19--

	Current Operations			Discontinuance of Product A
	Product A	Products B and C	Total	
Sales........................	$100,000	$900,000	$1,000,000	$900,000
Cost of goods sold:				
Variable costs................	$ 60,000	$420,000	$ 480,000	$420,000
Fixed costs	20,000	200,000	220,000	220,000
Total cost of goods sold......	$ 80,000	$620,000	$ 700,000	$640,000
Gross profit....................	$ 20,000	$280,000	$ 300,000	$260,000
Operating expenses:				
Variable expenses.............	$ 25,000	$155,000	$ 180,000	$155,000
Fixed expenses	6,000	45,000	51,000	51,000
Total operating expenses.....	$ 31,000	$200,000	$ 231,000	$206,000
Income (loss) from operations.....	$ (11,000)	$ 80,000	$ 69,000	$ 54,000

For purposes of the illustration, it was assumed that the discontinuance of Product A would not cause any significant reduction in the volume of fixed costs and expenses. If plant capacity made available by discontinuance of a losing operation can be used in some other manner or if plant capacity can be reduced, with a resulting reduction in fixed costs and expenses, additional analysis would be needed.

In decisions involving the elimination of an unprofitable segment, management must also consider such other factors as its effect on employees and customers. If a segment of the business is discontinued, some employees may have to be laid off and others may have to be relocated and retrained. Also important is the possible decline in sales of the more profitable products to customers who were attracted to the firm by the discontinued product.

Make or Buy

The assembly of many parts is often a substantial element in manufacturing operations. Many of the large factory complexes of automobile manufacturers are specifically called assembly plants. Some of the parts of the finished automobile, such as the motor, are produced by the automobile manufacturer, while other parts, such as tires, are often purchased from other manufacturers. Even in manufacturing the motors, such items as spark plugs and nuts and bolts may be acquired from suppliers in their finished state. When parts or components are purchased, management has usually evaluated the question of "make or buy" and has concluded that a savings in cost results from buying the part rather than manufacturing it. However, "make or buy" options are likely to arise anew when a manufacturer has excess productive capacity in the form of unused equipment, space, and labor.

As a basis for illustrating such alternatives, assume that a manufacturer has been purchasing a component, Part X, for $5 a unit. The factory is currently operating at 80% of capacity, and no significant increase in production is anticipated in the near future. The cost of manufacturing Part X, determined by absorption costing methods, is estimated at $1 for direct materials, $2 for direct labor, and $3 for factory overhead (at the predetermined rate of 150% of direct labor cost), or a total of $6. The decision based on a simple comparison of a "make" price of $6 with a "buy" price of $5 is obvious. However, to the extent that unused capacity could be used in manufacturing the part, there would be no increase in the total amount of fixed factory overhead costs. Hence, only the variable factory overhead costs need to be considered. Variable factory overhead costs such as power and maintenance are determined to amount to approximately 65% of the direct labor cost of $2, or $1.30. The cost factors to be considered are summarized in the following report:

<table>
<tr><td rowspan="9">DIFFERENTIAL
ANALYSIS
REPORT—MAKE
OR BUY</td><td colspan="3">Proposal to Manufacture Part X
February 15, 19--</td></tr>
<tr><td>Purchase price of part......................................</td><td></td><td>$5.00</td></tr>
<tr><td>Differential cost to manufacture part:</td><td></td><td></td></tr>
<tr><td>Direct materials.......................................</td><td>$1.00</td><td></td></tr>
<tr><td>Direct labor ....</td><td>2.00</td><td></td></tr>
<tr><td>Variable factory overhead.............................</td><td>1.30</td><td>4.30</td></tr>
<tr><td>Cost reduction from manufacturing Part X..................</td><td></td><td>$ .70</td></tr>
</table>

Other possible effects of a change in policy should also be considered, such as the possibility that a future increase in volume of production would require the use of the currently idle capacity of 20%. The possible effect of the alternatives on employees and on future business relations with the supplier of the part, who may be providing other essential components, are additional factors that might need study.

Equipment Replacement

The usefulness of plant assets may be impaired long before they are considered to be "worn out." Equipment may no longer be ideally adequate for the purpose for which it is used, but on the other hand it may not have reached the point of complete inadequacy. Similarly, the point in time when equipment becomes obsolete may be difficult to determine. Decisions to replace usable plant assets should be based on studies of relevant costs rather than on whims or subjective opinions. The costs to be considered are the alternative future costs of retention as opposed to replacement. The book values of the plant assets being replaced are sunk costs and are irrelevant.

To illustrate some of the factors involved in replacement decisions, assume that an enterprise is considering the disposal of several identical machines having a total book value of $100,000 and an estimated remaining life of five years. The old machines can be sold for $25,000. They can be replaced by a single high-speed machine at a cost of $250,000, with an estimated useful life of five years and no residual value. Analysis of the specifications of the new machine and of accompanying changes in manufacturing methods indicate an estimated annual reduction in variable manufacturing costs from $225,000 to $150,000. No other changes in the manufacturing costs or the operating expenses are expected. The basic data to be considered are summarized in the following report:

Proposal to Replace Equipment
November 28, 19--

Annual variable costs — present equipment..............	$225,000	
Annual variable costs — new equipment.................	150,000	
Annual differential decrease in cost.....................	$ 75,000	
Number of years applicable...........................	× 5	
Total differential decrease in cost......................	$375,000	
Proceeds from sale of present equipment	25,000	$400,000
Cost of new equipment................................		250,000
Net differential decrease in cost, 5-year total............		$150,000
Annual differential decrease in cost — new equipment.....		$ 30,000

DIFFERENTIAL ANALYSIS REPORT— EQUIPMENT REPLACEMENT

Complicating features could be added to the foregoing illustration, such as a disparity between the remaining useful life of the old equipment and the estimated life of the new equipment, or possible improvement in the product due to the new machine, with a resulting increase in selling price or volume of sales. Another factor that should be considered is the importance of alternative uses for the cash outlay needed to obtain the new equipment. The amount of income that would result from the best available alternative to the proposed use of cash or its equivalent is sometimes called **opportunity cost.** If, for example, it is assumed that the cash outlay of $250,000 for the new equipment, less the $25,000 proceeds from the sale of the present equipment, could be used to yield a 10% return, the opportunity cost of the proposal would amount to 10% of $225,000, or $22,500.

The term "opportunity cost" introduces a new concept of "cost." In reality, it is not a cost in any usual sense of the word. Instead, it represents the forgoing of possible income associated with a lost opportunity. Although opportunity cost computations do not appear as a part of historical accounting data, they are unquestionably useful in analyses involving choices between alternative courses of action.

Process or Sell

When a product is manufactured, it progresses through various stages of production. Often, a product can be sold at an intermediate stage of production, or it can be processed further and then sold. In deciding whether to sell a product at an intermediate stage or to process it further, the differential revenues that would be provided and the differential costs that would be incurred from further processing must be considered. Since the costs of producing the intermediate product do not change, regardless of whether the intermediate product is sold or processed further, these costs are not differential costs and are not considered.

To illustrate, assume that an enterprise produces Product Y in batches of 4,000 gallons by processing standard quantities of 4,000 gallons of direct materials, which cost $1.20 per gallon. Product Y can be sold without further processing for $2 per gallon. It is possible for the enterprise to process Product Y further to yield Product Z, which can be sold for $5 per gallon. Product Z will require additional processing costs of $5,760 per batch, and 20% of the gallons of Product Y will evaporate during production. The differential revenues and costs to be considered in deciding whether to process Product Y to produce Product Z are summarized in the following report:

Proposal To Process Product Y Further
October 1, 19--

Differential revenue from further processing per batch:
Revenue from sale of Product Z [(4,000 gallons − 800 gallons evaporation) × $5] ... $16,000
Revenue from sale of Product Y (4,000 gallons × $2) ... 8,000

Differential revenue ... $8,000
Differential cost per batch:
Additional cost of producing Product Z ... 5,760
Net advantage of further processing Product Y per batch ... $2,240

The net advantage of further processing Product Y into Product Z is **$2,240** per batch. Note that the initial cost of producing the intermediate Product Y, $4,800 (4,000 gallons × $1.20), is not considered in deciding whether to process Product Y further. This initial cost will be incurred regardless of whether Product Z is produced.

Acceptance of Business at a Special Price

In determining whether to accept additional business at a special price, management must consider the differential revenue that would be provided and the differential cost that would be incurred. If the company is operating at full capacity, the additional production will increase both fixed and variable production costs. But if the normal production of the company is below full capacity, additional business may be undertaken without increasing fixed production costs. In the latter case, the variable costs will be the differential cost of the additional production. Variable costs are the only costs to be considered in making a decision to accept or reject the order. If the operating expenses are likely to increase, these differentials must also be considered.

To illustrate, assume that the usual monthly production of an enterprise is 10,000 units of a certain commodity. At this level of operation, which is well

Differential Analysis and Product Pricing

below capacity, the manufacturing cost is $20 per unit, composed of variable costs of $12.50 and fixed costs of $7.50. The normal selling price of the product in the domestic market is $30. The manufacturer receives an offer from an exporter for 5,000 units of the product at $18 each. Production can be spread over a three-month period without interfering with normal production or incurring overtime costs. Pricing policies in the domestic market will not be affected. Comparison of a sales price of $18 with the present unit cost of $20 would indicate that this offer should be rejected. However, if attention is limited to the differential cost, which in this case is composed of the variable costs and expenses, the conclusion is quite different. The essentials of the analysis are presented in the following brief report:

Proposal to Sell to Exporter
March 10, 19--

Differential revenue from acceptance of offer:	
Revenue from sale of 5,000 additional units at $18	$90,000
Differential cost of acceptance of offer:	
Variable costs and expenses of 5,000 additional units at $12.50	62,500
Gain from acceptance of offer.	$27,500

DIFFERENTIAL ANALYSIS REPORT—SALE AT REDUCED PRICE

Proposals to sell an increased output in the domestic market at a reduction from the normal price may require additional considerations of a difficult nature. It would clearly be unwise to increase sales volume in one territory by means of a price reduction if sales volume would thereby be jeopardized in other areas. Manufacturers must also exercise care to avoid violations of the Robinson-Patman Act, which prohibits price discrimination within the United States unless the difference in price can be justified by a difference in the cost of serving different customers.

SETTING NORMAL PRODUCT PRICES

Differential analysis, as illustrated, is useful to management in setting product selling prices for special short-run decisions, such as whether to accept business at a price lower than the normal price. In such situations, the short-run price is set high enough to cover all variable costs and expenses plus provide an excess to cover some of the fixed costs and perhaps provide for profit. Such a pricing plan will improve profits in the short run. In the long run, however, the normal selling price must be set high enough to cover all costs and expenses (both fixed and variable) and provide a reasonable amount for profit. Otherwise, the long-run survival of the firm may be jeopardized.

The normal selling price can be viewed as the target selling price which must be achieved in the long run, but which may be deviated from in the short run because of such factors as competition and general market conditions. A practical approach to setting the normal price is the cost-plus approach. Using this approach, managers determine product prices by adding to a "cost" amount a plus, called a **markup**, so that all costs plus a profit are covered in the price.

Three cost concepts commonly used in applying the cost-plus approach are (1) total cost, (2) product cost, and (3) variable cost. Each of these cost concepts is described and illustrated in the following paragraphs.

Total Cost Concept

Using the **total cost concept** of determining the product price, all costs of manufacturing a product plus the selling and general expenses are included in the cost amount to which the markup is added. Since all costs and expenses are included in the cost amount, the dollar amount of the markup equals the desired profit.

The first step in applying the total cost concept is to determine the total cost of manufacturing the product. Under the absorption costing system of accounting for manufacturing operations, the costs of direct materials, direct labor, and factory overhead should be available from the accounting records. The next step is to add the estimated selling and general expenses to the total cost of manufacturing the product. The cost amount per unit is then computed by dividing the total costs and expenses by the total units expected to be produced and sold.

After the cost amount per unit has been determined, the dollar amount of the markup is determined. For this purpose, the markup is expressed as a percentage of cost. This percentage is then multiplied by the cost amount per unit. The dollar amount of the markup is then added to the cost amount per unit to arrive at the selling price.

The markup percentage for the total cost concept is determined by applying the following formula:

$$\text{Markup Percentage} = \frac{\text{Desired Profit}}{\text{Total Costs and Expenses}}$$

The numerator of the markup percentage formula includes only the desired profit, since all costs and expenses will be covered by the cost amount to which the markup will be added. The denominator of the formula includes the total costs and expenses, which are covered by the cost amount.

To illustrate the use of the total cost concept, assume that the costs and expenses for Product N of Moyer Co. are as follows:

Variable costs and expenses:	
Direct materials..................	$ 3.00 per unit
Direct labor	10.00
Factory overhead	1.50
Selling and general expenses	1.50
Total........................	$16.00 per unit
Fixed costs and expenses:	
Factory overhead	$50,000
Selling and general expenses	20,000

Moyer Co. desires a profit equal to a 20% rate of return on assets, $800,000 of assets are devoted to producing Product N, and 100,000 units are expected to be produced and sold. The cost amount for Product N is **$1,670,000**, or **$16.70** per unit, computed as follows:

Variable costs and expenses ($16.00 × 100,000 units)......		$1,600,000
Fixed costs and expenses:		
Factory overhead	$50,000	
Selling and general expenses	20,000	70,000
Total costs and expenses		$1,670,000
Cost amount per unit ($1,670,000 ÷ 100,000 units)		$16.70

The desired profit is $160,000 (20% × $800,000), and the markup percentage for Product N is **9.6%**, computed as follows:

$$\text{Markup Percentage} = \frac{\text{Desired Profit}}{\text{Total Costs and Expenses}}$$

$$\text{Markup Percentage} = \frac{\$160,000}{\$1,670,000}$$

$$\text{Markup Percentage} = 9.6\%$$

Based on the cost amount per unit and the markup percentage for Product N, Moyer Co. would price Product N at **$18.30** per unit, as shown in the following computation:

Cost amount per unit.........	$16.70
Markup ($16.70 × 9.6%)	1.60
Selling price................	$18.30

The ability of the selling price of $18.30 to generate the desired profit of $160,000 is shown in the following condensed income statement for Moyer Co.:

Moyer Co. Income Statement For Year Ended December 31, 19--		
Sales (100,000 units × $18.30)		$1,830,000
Expenses:		
Variable (100,000 units × $16.00)..................	$1,600,000	
Fixed ($50,000 + $20,000)	70,000	1,670,000
Income from operations		$ 160,000

The total cost concept of applying the cost-plus approach to product pricing is frequently used by contractors who sell products to government agencies. In many cases, government contractors are required by law to be reimbursed for their products on a total-cost-plus-profit basis.

Product Cost Concept

Using the **product cost concept** of determining the product price, only the costs of manufacturing the product, termed the product cost, are included in the cost amount to which the markup is added. Selling expenses, general expenses, and profit are covered in the markup. The markup percentage is determined by applying the following formula:

$$\text{Markup Percentage} = \frac{\text{Desired Profit} + \text{Total Selling and General Expenses}}{\text{Total Manufacturing Costs}}$$

The numerator of the markup percentage formula includes the desired profit plus the total selling and general expenses. Selling and general expenses must be covered by the markup, since they are not covered by the cost amount to which the markup will be added. The denominator of the formula includes the costs of direct materials, direct labor, and factory overhead, which are covered by the cost amount.

To illustrate the use of the product cost concept, assume the same data that were used in the preceding illustration. The cost amount for Moyer Co.'s Product N is **$1,500,000**, or **$15** per unit, computed as follows:

Direct materials ($3 × 100,000 units)		$ 300,000
Direct labor ($10 × 100,000 units)		1,000,000
Factory overhead:		
Variable ($1.50 × 100,000 units)	$150,000	
Fixed	50,000	200,000
Total manufacturing costs		$1,500,000
Cost amount per unit ($1,500,000 ÷ 100,000 units)		$15

The desired profit is $160,000 (20% × $800,000), and the total selling and general expenses are $170,000 [(100,000 units × $1.50 per unit) + $20,000]. The markup percentage for Product N is **22%**, computed as follows:

$$\text{Markup Percentage} = \frac{\text{Desired Profit} + \text{Total Selling and General Expenses}}{\text{Total Manufacturing Costs}}$$

$$\text{Markup Percentage} = \frac{\$160,000 + \$170,000}{\$1,500,000}$$

$$\text{Markup Percentage} = \frac{\$330,000}{\$1,500,000}$$

$$\text{Markup Percentage} = 22\%$$

Based on the cost amount per unit and the markup percentage for Product N, Moyer Co. would price Product N at $18.30 per unit, as shown in the following computation:

Cost amount per unit......................	$15.00
Markup ($15 × 22%)......................	3.30
Selling price.............................	$18.30

Variable Cost Concept

Using the **variable cost concept** of determining the product price, only variable costs and expenses are included in the cost amount to which the markup is added. All variable manufacturing costs, as well as variable selling and general expenses, are included in the cost amount. Fixed manufacturing costs, fixed selling and general expenses, and profit are covered in the markup.

The markup percentage for the variable cost concept is determined by applying the following formula:

$$\text{Markup Percentage} = \frac{\text{Desired Profit + Total Fixed Manufacturing Costs +}}{\text{Total Fixed Selling and General Expenses}}{\text{Total Variable Costs and Expenses}}$$

The numerator of the markup percentage formula includes the desired profit plus the total fixed manufacturing costs and the total fixed selling and general expenses. Fixed manufacturing costs and fixed selling and general expenses must be covered by the markup, since they are not covered by the cost amount to which the markup will be added. The denominator of the formula includes the total variable costs and expenses, which are covered by the cost amount.

To illustrate the use of the variable cost concept, assume the same data that were used in the two preceding illustrations. The cost amount for Product N is $1,600,000, or $16.00 per unit, computed as follows:

Variable costs and expenses:	
Direct materials ($3 × 100,000 units)	$ 300,000
Direct labor ($10 × 100,000 units)....................	1,000,000
Factory overhead ($1.50 × 100,000 units).............	150,000
Selling and general expenses ($1.50 × 100,000 units)..	150,000
Total variable costs and expenses	$1,600,000
Cost amount per unit ($1,600,000 ÷ 100,000 units).......	$16.00

The desired profit is $160,000 (20% × $800,000), the total fixed manufacturing costs are $50,000, and the total fixed selling and general expenses are $20,000. The markup percentage for Product N is 14.4%, computed as follows:

$$\text{Markup Percentage} = \frac{\text{Desired Profit} + \text{Total Fixed Manufacturing Costs} + \text{Total Fixed Selling and General Expenses}}{\text{Total Variable Costs and Expenses}}$$

$$\text{Markup Percentage} = \frac{\$160{,}000 + \$50{,}000 + \$20{,}000}{\$1{,}600{,}000}$$

$$\text{Markup Percentage} = \frac{\$230{,}000}{\$1{,}600{,}000}$$

$$\text{Markup Percentage} = 14.4\%$$

Based on the cost amount per unit and the markup percentage for Product N, Moyer Co. would price Product N at **$18.30** per unit, as shown in the following computation:

Cost amount per unit............................	$16.00
Markup ($16.00 × 14.4%)........................	2.30
Selling price....................................	$18.30

The variable cost concept emphasizes the distinction between variable and fixed costs and expenses in product pricing. This distinction is similar to the distinction between absorption and variable costing described in Chapter 19.

Choosing a Cost-Plus Approach Cost Concept

The three cost concepts commonly used in applying the cost-plus approach to product pricing are summarized as follows:

Cost Concept	Covered in Cost Amount	Covered in Markup
Total cost	Total costs and expenses	Desired profit
Product cost	Total manufacturing costs	Desired profit + Total selling and general expenses
Variable cost	Total variable costs and expenses	Desired profit + Total fixed manufacturing costs + Total fixed selling and general expenses

As demonstrated in the Moyer Co. illustration, all three cost concepts will yield the same selling price ($18.30) when the concepts are properly applied. Which of the three cost concepts should be used by management depends on such factors as the cost of gathering the data and the decision needs of management. For example, the data for the product cost concept can be easily gathered by a company using an absorption cost accounting system.

To reduce the costs of gathering data, standard costs rather than actual costs may be used with any of the three cost concepts. However, caution should be exercised by management when using standard costs in applying the cost-plus approach. As discussed in Chapter 18, the standards should be based on normal (attainable) operating levels and not theoretical (ideal) levels of performance. In product pricing, the use of standards based on ideal or maximum capacity operating levels might lead to the establishment of product prices which are too low, since the costs of such factors as normal spoilage or normal periods of idle time would not be covered in the price. As a result, the desired profit would be reduced by these costs and expenses.

ECONOMIC THEORY OF PRODUCT PRICING

As discussed in the preceding paragraphs, the cost-plus approach is frequently used as a general guideline for setting normal product prices. However, other factors may influence the pricing decision. In considering these factors, which include the prices of competing products and the general economic conditions of the marketplace, a knowledge of the economic theory underlying product pricing is useful to the managerial accountant. Although the study of price theory is generally considered a separate discipline in the area of microeconomics, the following paragraphs present an overview of the economic models for explaining pricing behavior.

Maximization of Profits

In microeconomic theory, management's primary objective is assumed to be the maximization of profits. Profits will be maximized at the point at which the difference between total revenues and total costs and expenses is the greatest amount. Consequently, microeconomic theory focuses on the behavior of total revenues as price and sales volume vary and the behavior of total costs and expenses as production varies.

Revenues

Generally, it is not possible to sell an unlimited number of units of product at the same price. At some point, price reductions will be necessary in order to sell more units. Total revenue may increase as the price is reduced, but there comes a point when further price decreases will reduce total revenue. To illustrate, the following revenue schedule shows the effect on revenue when each $1 reduction in the unit selling price increases by 1 unit the number of units sold:

Revenue Schedule

Price	Units Sold	Total Revenue	Marginal Revenue
$11	1	$11	$11
10	2	20	9
9	3	27	7
8	4	32	5
7	5	35	3
6	6	36	1
5	7	35	−1

In the revenue schedule illustrated, a price reduction from $11 to $10 increases total revenue by $9 (from $11 to $20). This increase (or decrease) in total revenue realized from the sale of an additional unit of product is called the **marginal revenue**. With each successive price reduction from $11 to $6, the total revenue increase is less. Finally, a price reduction from $6 to $5 decreases total revenue by $1.

Costs

As production and sales increase, the total cost increases. The amount by which total cost increases, however, varies as more and more production and sales are squeezed from limited facilities. Economists assume that as the total number of units produced and sold increases from a relatively low level, the total cost increases but in decreasing amounts. This assumption is based on efficiencies created by **economies of scale**. Economies of scale generally imply that, for a given amount of facilities, it is more efficient to produce and sell large quantities than small quantities. At some point, however, the total cost will begin to increase by increasing amounts because of inefficiencies created by such factors as employees getting in each other's way and machine breakdowns caused by heavy use. The increase in total cost from producing and selling an additional unit of product is known as **marginal cost**. To illustrate, the following cost schedule shows the effect on cost when one additional unit is produced and sold:

Cost Schedule

Units Produced and Sold	Total Cost	Marginal Cost
1	$ 9	$9
2	17	8
3	24	7
4	30	6
5	37	7
6	45	8
7	54	9

In the cost schedule, the cost of producing 1 unit is $9, and for each additional unit the total cost per unit increases by $8, $7, $6, $7, $8, and $9 respectively. The marginal cost of producing and selling the second unit is $8, which is the difference between the total cost of producing and selling 2 units ($17) and the total cost of 1 unit ($9). As production and sales increase from 1 unit to 4 units, the marginal cost decreases from $9 to $6. After the production and sale of 4 units, however, the marginal cost increases from $6 for the fourth unit to $7 for producing and selling the fifth unit.

Product Price Determination

A price-cost combination that maximizes the total profit of an enterprise can be determined by plotting the marginal revenues and marginal costs on a **price graph**. To illustrate, the marginal revenues and marginal costs for the preceding illustration are plotted on the following graph.

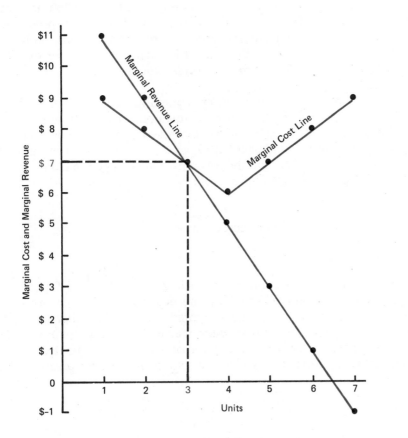

PRICE
GRAPH

A price graph is constructed in the following manner:

1. The horizontal axis is drawn to represent units of production and sales.
2. The vertical axis is drawn to represent dollars for marginal revenues and marginal costs.
3. The marginal revenue for each unit of sales is plotted on the graph by first locating the number of units of sales along the horizontal axis and then proceeding upward until the proper amount of marginal revenue is indicated on the vertical axis.
4. The marginal revenue line is drawn on the price graph by connecting the marginal revenue points.
5. The marginal cost for each unit of production is plotted on the graph by first locating the number of units of production along the horizontal axis

and then proceeding upward until the proper amount of marginal cost is indicated on the vertical axis.

6. The marginal cost line is drawn on the price graph by connecting the marginal cost points.

The point at which the marginal revenue line intersects the marginal cost line on the price graph indicates a level of sales and production at which profits are maximized. In other words, there is no other level of production and sales that will provide a larger amount of profit. For example, at higher levels of production and sales, the change in total cost is greater than the change in total revenue. Therefore, less profit would be achieved by manufacturing and selling more units.

In the illustration, the marginal revenue line intersects the marginal cost line at 3 units of sales and production. At this point, marginal revenue and marginal cost equal $7. To sell 3 units, the revenue schedule on page 695 indicates that the price should be set at $9 per unit. A price of $9 per unit will provide total revenue of $27, and the cost schedule on page 696 indicates that the total cost will be $24. Thus, profit will be $3, as follows:

Total revenue (3 units × $9)........ $27
Total cost (from cost schedule) 24
Profit............................. $ 3

The more theoretical economic approach is not often used for product pricing because the data required by the economic approach are often unavailable. For example, it is difficult to predict the amount that customers will purchase over a range of prices without actually offering the product for sale at those prices. Therefore, since total cost data can be estimated reliably from accounting records, the cost-plus approach to product pricing is frequently used.

Self-Examination Questions
(Answers at end of chapter.)

1. The amount of increase or decrease in cost that is expected from a particular course of action as compared with an alternative is referred to as:
A. differential cost
B. replacement cost
C. sunk cost
D. none of the above

2. Victor Company is considering the disposal of equipment that was originally purchased for $200,000 and has accumulated depreciation to date of $150,000. The same equipment would cost $310,000 to replace. What is the sunk cost?
A. $50,000
B. $150,000
C. $200,000
D. none of the above

3. The amount of income that would result from the best available alternative to a proposed use of cash or its equivalent is referred to as:
A. actual cost
C. opportunity cost
B. historical cost
D. none of the above

4. For which cost concept used in applying the cost-plus approach to product pricing are fixed manufacturing costs, fixed selling and general expenses, and desired profit allowed for in the determination of markup?
A. Total cost
C. Variable cost
B. Product cost
D. None of the above

5. According to microeconomic theory, profits of a business enterprise will be maximized at the point where:
A. marginal revenue equals marginal cost
B. the change in total revenue is greater than the change in total cost
C. the change in total cost is greater than the change in total revenue
D. none of the above

21-1. What term is applied to the type of analysis that emphasizes the difference between the revenues and costs for proposed alternative courses of action?

Discussion Questions

21-2. Explain the meaning of (a) *differential revenue* and (b) *differential cost.*

21-3. Norton Lumber Company incurs a cost of $60 per thousand board feet in processing a certain "rough-cut" lumber which sells for $115 per thousand board feet. An alternative is to produce a "finished-cut" at a total processing cost of $82 per thousand board feet, which can be sold for $150 per thousand board feet. What is the amount of (a) the differential revenue and (b) the differential cost associated with the alternative?

21-4. (a) What is meant by *sunk costs*? (b) A company is contemplating replacing an old piece of machinery which cost $210,000 and has $180,000 accumulated depreciation to date. A new machine costs $300,000. What is the sunk cost in this situation?

21-5. The condensed income statement for Yancey Company for the current year is as follows:

	Product			
	M	**N**	**O**	**Total**
Sales.....................................	$60,000	$380,000	$340,000	$780,000
Less variable costs and expenses	44,400	260,000	233,400	537,800
Contribution margin....................	$15,600	$120,000	$106,600	$242,200
Less fixed costs and expenses..........	20,000	80,000	76,000	176,000
Income (loss) from operations..........	$(4,400)	$ 40,000	$ 30,600	$ 66,200

Management decided to discontinue the manufacture and sale of Product M. Assuming that the discontinuance will have no effect on the total fixed costs and expenses or on the sales of Products N and O, has management made the correct decision? Explain.

21–6. (a) What is meant by *opportunity cost*? (b) Draper Company is currently earning 12% on $100,000 invested in marketable securities. It proposes to use the $100,000 to acquire plant facilities to manufacture a new product that is expected to add $20,000 annually to net income. What is the opportunity cost involved in the decision to manufacture the new product?

21–7. In the long run, the normal selling price must be set high enough to cover what factors?

21–8. What are three cost concepts commonly used in applying the cost-plus approach to product pricing?

21–9. In using the product cost concept of applying the cost-plus approach to product pricing, what factors are included in the markup?

21–10. The variable cost concept used in applying the cost-plus approach to product pricing includes what costs in the cost amount to which the markup is added?

21–11. In determining the markup percentage for the variable cost concept of applying the cost-plus approach, what is included in the denominator?

21–12. Why might the use of ideal standards in applying the cost-plus approach to product pricing lead to setting product prices which are too low?

21–13. Although the cost-plus approach to product pricing may be used by management as a general guideline, what are some examples of other factors that managers should also consider in setting product prices?

21–14. In microeconomic theory, what is assumed to be management's primary objective for a business enterprise?

21–15. Why is it generally not possible to sell an unlimited number of units of product at the same price?

21–16. As the terms are used in microeconomic theory, what is meant by (a) marginal revenue and (b) marginal cost?

21–17. If the total revenue for selling 3 units of Product Y is $20 and the total revenue for selling 4 units is $25, what is the marginal revenue associated with selling the fourth unit?

21–18. What does the concept of economies of scale generally imply?

21–19. For a given amount of facilities, why will the total costs and expenses begin to increase by increasing amounts at some point?

21–20. What point on the price graph indicates a maximum level of profit?

21–21. Why is the more theoretical economic approach to product pricing not used as often as the cost-plus approach?

Exercises

21–22. DeLorenzo Company expects to operate at 80% of productive capacity during July. The total manufacturing costs for July for the production of 12,500 grinders are budgeted as follows:

Direct materials	$ 56,250
Direct labor	156,250
Variable factory overhead	75,000
Fixed factory overhead	31,250
Total manufacturing costs	$318,750

The company has an opportunity to submit a bid for 3,000 grinders to be delivered by July 31 to a governmental agency. If the contract is obtained, it is anticipated that the additional activity will not interfere with normal production during July or increase the selling or general expenses. (a) What is the unit cost below which the DeLorenzo Company should not go in bidding on the government contract? (b) Is a unit cost figure based on absorption costing or one based on variable costing more useful in arriving at a bid on this contract? Explain.

21–23. Farley Company has a plant capacity of 50,000 units and current production is 35,000 units. Monthly fixed costs and expenses are $140,000 and variable costs and expenses are $12.50 per unit. The present selling price is $18 per unit. On February 3, the company received an offer from Wong Yu Company for 5,000 units of the product at $15 each. The Wong Yu Company will market the units in a foreign country under its own brand name. The additional business is not expected to affect the regular selling price or quantity of sales of Farley Company. (a) Prepare a differential analysis report for the proposed sale to Wong Yu Company. (b) Briefly explain the reason why the acceptance of this additional business will increase operating income. (c) What is the minimum price per unit that would produce a contribution margin?

21–24. A condensed income statement by product line for McCaffrey Co. indicated the following for Product X for the past year:

Sales	$160,000
Cost of goods sold	108,000
Gross profit	$ 52,000
Operating expenses	72,000
Loss from operations	$(20,000)

It is estimated that 15% of the cost of goods sold represents fixed factory overhead costs and that 20% of operating expenses is fixed. Since Product X is only one of many products, the fixed costs and expenses will not be materially affected if the product is discontinued. (a) Prepare a differential analysis report, dated January 2 of the current year, for the proposed discontinuance of Product X. (b) Should Product X be retained? Explain.

21–25. Quigley Company has been purchasing carrying cases for its portable typewriters at a delivered cost of $18.75 per unit. The company, which is currently operating below full capacity, charges factory overhead to production at the rate of 60% of direct labor cost. The direct materials and direct labor costs per unit to produce comparable carrying cases are expected to be $5 and $12 respectively. If Quigley Company manufactures the carrying cases, fixed factory overhead costs will not increase and variable factory overhead costs associated with the cases are expected to be 20% of direct labor costs. (a) Prepare a differential analysis report, dated March 6 of the current year, for the make or buy decision. (b) On the basis of the data presented, would it be advisable to make or to continue buying the carrying cases? Explain.

21–26. Rowe Company produces a commodity by applying a machine and direct labor to the direct material. The original cost of the machine is $180,000, the accumulated depreciation is $108,000, its remaining useful life is 8 years, and its salvage value is negligible. On January 18, a proposal was made to replace the present manufacturing procedure with a fully automatic machine that will cost $340,000. The automatic machine has an estimated useful life of 8 years and no significant salvage value. For use in evaluating the proposal, the accountant accumulated the following annual data on present and proposed operations:

	Present Operations	Proposed Operations
Sales....................................	$440,000	$440,000
Direct materials............................	184,800	184,800
Direct labor	79,200	——
Power and maintenance	13,600	31,500
Taxes, insurance, etc.	8,800	12,800
Selling and general expenses	35,200	35,200

(a) Prepare a differential analysis report for the proposal to replace the machine. Include in the analysis both the net differential decrease in costs and expenses anticipated over the 8 years and the annual differential decrease in costs and expenses anticipated. (b) Based only on the data presented, should the proposal be accepted? (c) What are some of the other factors that should be considered before a final decision is made?

21–27. Glasner Company uses the total cost concept of applying the cost-plus approach to product pricing. The costs and expenses of producing and selling 50,000 units of Product M are as follows:

Variable costs and expenses:
Direct materials.......................	$1.60 per unit
Direct labor	3.00
Factory overhead......................	1.00
Selling and general expenses..........	.40
Total	$6.00 per unit

Fixed costs and expenses:
Factory overhead.....................	$70,000
Selling and general expenses..........	30,000

Glasner Company desires a profit equal to a 20% rate of return on invested assets of $450,000. (a) Determine the amount of desired profit from the production and sale of Product M. (b) Determine the total costs and expenses and the cost amount per unit for the production and sale of 50,000 units of Product M. (c) Determine the markup percentage for Product M. (d) Determine the selling price of Product M.

21–28. Based on the data presented in Exercise 21–27, assume that Glasner Company uses the product cost concept of applying the cost-plus approach to product pricing. (a) Determine the total manufacturing costs and the cost amount per unit for the production and sale of 50,000 units of Product M. (b) Determine the markup percentage for Product M. (c) Determine the selling price of Product M.

21–29. Based on data presented in Exercise 21–27, assume that Glasner Company uses the variable cost concept of applying the cost-plus approach to product pricing. (a) Determine the cost amount per unit for the production and sale of 50,000 units of Product M. (b) Determine the markup percentage for Product M. (c) Determine the selling price of Product M. Round to the nearest cent.

21–30. For the following revenue schedule and cost schedule for Product Y, (a) construct a price graph, (b) determine the level of sales and production at which the marginal cost and marginal revenue lines intersect, (c) determine the unit sales price at the level of sales determined in (b), and (d) determine the maximum profit for Product Y at the level of sales determined in (b).

Revenue Schedule

Price	Units Sold	Total Revenue	Marginal Revenue
$9	1	$ 9	$9
8	2	16	7
7	3	21	5
6	4	24	3
5	5	25	1
4	6	24	−1

Cost Schedule

Units Produced and Sold	Total Cost	Marginal Cost
1	$ 6	$6
2	11	5
3	15	4
4	18	3
5	22	4
6	27	5

Problems

21–31. On April 1, Muller Company is considering leasing a building and purchasing the necessary equipment to operate a public warehouse. The project would be financed by selling $500,000 of 10% U.S. Treasury bonds that mature in 15 years. The bonds were purchased at face value and are currently selling at face value. The following data have been assembled:

Cost of equipment...	$500,000
Life of equipment..	15 years
Estimated residual value of equipment..........................	$ 80,000
Yearly costs to operate the warehouse, in addition to depreciation of equipment..	$ 48,500
Yearly expected revenues—first 5 years........................	$120,000
Yearly expected revenues—next 10 years	$150,000

Instructions:

(1) Prepare a differential analysis report presenting the differential revenue and the differential cost associated with the proposed operation of the warehouse for the 15 years as compared with present conditions.

(2) Based on the results disclosed by the differential analysis, should the proposal be accepted?

(3) If the proposal is accepted, what is the total estimated income from operation of the warehouse for the 15 years?

21–32. Packard Company is considering the replacement of a machine that has been used in its factory for three years. Relevant data associated with the operations of the old machine and the new machine, neither of which has any residual value, are as follows:

Old Machine

Cost of machine, 8-year life...	$270,000
Annual depreciation..	33,750
Annual manufacturing costs, exclusive of depreciation	425,000
Related annual operating revenue	280,000
Associated annual revenue	940,000
Estimated selling price of old machine	190,000

New Machine

Cost of machine, 5-year life...	$525,000
Annual depreciation..	105,000
Estimated annual manufacturing costs, exclusive of depreciation..........	325,000

Annual operating expenses and revenue are not expected to be affected by purchase of the new machine.

Instructions:

(1) Prepare a differential analysis report as of January 4 of the current year, comparing operations utilizing the new machine with operations using the present equipment. The analysis should indicate the total differential decrease or increase in costs that would result over the 5-year period if the new machine is acquired.

(2) List other factors that should be considered before a final decision is reached.

21–33. Edens Company is planning a one-month campaign for August to promote sales of one of its two products. A total of $120,000 has been budgeted for advertising, contests, redeemable coupons, and other promotional activities. The following data have been assembled for their possible usefulness in deciding which of the products to select for the campaign:

	Product A	Product B
Unit selling price	$100	$120
Unit production costs:		
Direct materials	$28	$36
Direct labor	20	28
Variable factory overhead	16	16
Fixed factory overhead	12	12
Total unit production costs	$ 76	$ 92
Unit variable operating expenses	10	10
Unit fixed operating expenses	6	6
Total unit costs and expenses	$ 92	$108
Operating income per unit	$ 8	$ 12

No increase in facilities would be necessary to produce and sell the increased output. It is anticipated that 18,000 additional units of Product A or 12,500 additional units of Product B could be sold without changing the unit selling price of either product.

Instructions:

(1) Prepare a differential analysis report as of July 6 of the current year, presenting the additional revenue and additional costs and expenses anticipated from the promotion of Product A and Product B.

(2) The sales manager had tentatively decided to promote Product B, estimating that operating income would be increased by $30,000 ($12 operating income per unit for 12,500 units, less promotion expenses of $120,000). It was also believed that the selection of Product A would increase operating income by only $24,000 ($8 operating income per unit for 18,000 units, less promotion expenses of $120,000). State briefly your reasons for supporting or opposing the tentative decision.

21-34. The management of Kesner Company is considering whether to process further Product H into Product Q. Product Q can be sold for $40 per pound and Product H can be sold without further processing for $6 per pound. Product H is produced in batches of 200 pounds by processing 300 pounds of raw material, which costs $2 per pound. Product Q will require additional processing costs of $5 per pound of Product H, and 4 pounds of Product H will produce 1 pound of Product Q.

Instructions:

(1) Prepare a differential analysis report as of November 15, presenting the differential revenue and differential cost per batch associated with the further processing of Product H to produce Product Q.

(2) Briefly report your recommendations.

21-35. Ingersoll Refining Inc. refines Product C in batches of 80,000 gallons, which it sells for $.28 per gallon. The associated unit costs and expenses are currently as follows:

	Per Gallon
Direct materials	$.144
Direct labor	.040
Variable factory overhead	.020
Fixed factory overhead	.012

	Per Gallon
Sales commissions	$.028
Fixed selling and general expenses.	.008

The company is presently considering a proposal to put Product C through several additional processes to yield Products C and D. Although the company had determined such further processing to be unwise, new processing methods have now been developed. Existing facilities can be used for the additional processing, but since the factory is operating at full 8-hour-day capacity, the processing would have to be performed at night. Additional costs of processing would be $3,200 per batch and there would be an evaporation loss of 15%, with 60% of the processed material evolving as Product C and 25% as Product D. The selling price of Product D is $.80 per gallon. Sales commissions are a uniform percentage based on the sales price.

Instructions:

(1) Prepare a differential analysis report as of March 14, presenting the differential revenue and the differential cost per batch associated with the processing to produce Products C and D, compared with processing to produce Product C only.

(2) Briefly report your recommendations.

21–36. Conklin Company recently began production of a new product, W, which required the investment of $2,000,000 in assets. The costs and expenses of producing and selling 100,000 units of Product W are estimated as follows:

Variable costs and expenses:	
Direct materials	$ 2.40 per unit
Direct labor.	6.50
Factory overhead.	.90
Selling and general expenses.	.20
Total.	$10.00 per unit
Fixed costs and expenses:	
Factory overhead.	$ 60,000
Selling and general expenses.	140,000

Conklin Company is currently considering the establishment of a selling price for Product W. The President of Conklin Company has decided to use the cost-plus approach to product pricing and has indicated that Product W must earn an 18% rate of return on invested assets.

Instructions:

(1) Determine the amount of desired profit from the production and sale of Product W.

(2) Assuming that the total cost concept is used, determine (a) the cost amount per unit, (b) the markup percentage, and (c) the selling price of Product W.

(3) Assuming that the product cost concept is used, determine (a) the cost amount per unit, (b) the markup percentage, and (c) the selling price of Product W.

(4) Assuming that the variable cost concept is used, determine (a) the cost amount per unit, (b) the markup percentage, and (c) the selling price of Product W.

(5) Comment on any additional considerations that could influence the establishment of the selling price for Product W.

21–31A. On November 1, Levy Company is considering leasing a building and purchasing the necessary equipment to operate a public warehouse. The project would be financed by selling $800,000 of 12% U.S. Treasury bonds that mature in 20 years. The bonds were purchased at face value and are currently selling at face value. The following data have been assembled:

Cost of equipment	$800,000
Life of equipment	20 years
Estimated residual value of equipment	$120,000
Yearly costs to operate the warehouse, in addition to depreciation	
of equipment	$ 75,000
Yearly expected revenues—first 10 years	$200,000
Yearly expected revenues—next 5 years	$220,000
Yearly expected revenues—last 5 years	$250,000

Instructions:

(1) Prepare a differential analysis report presenting the differential revenue and the differential cost associated with the proposed operation of the warehouse for the 20 years as compared with present conditions.

(2) Based on the results disclosed by the differential analysis, should the proposal be accepted?

(3) If the proposal is accepted, what is the total estimated income from operation of the warehouse for the 20 years?

21–32A. Fedder Company is considering the replacement of a machine that has been used in its factory for two years. Relevant data associated with the operations of the old machine and the new machine, neither of which has any residual value, are as follows:

Old Machine

Cost of machine, 8-year life.	$224,000
Annual depreciation.	28,000
Annual manufacturing costs, exclusive of depreciation	372,000
Related annual operating expenses.	193,600
Associated annual revenue	600,000
Estimated selling price of old machine	116,000

New Machine

Cost of machine, 6-year life.	$384,000
Annual depreciation.	64,000
Estimated annual manufacturing costs, exclusive of depreciation	300,000

Annual operating expenses and revenue are not expected to be affected by purchase of the new machine.

Instructions:

(1) Prepare a differential analysis report as of January 3 of the current year, comparing operations utilizing the new machine with operations using the present equipment. The analysis should indicate the total differential decrease or increase in costs that would result over the 6-year period if the new machine is acquired.

(2) List other factors that should be considered before a final decision is reached.

21–35A. Ladner Refining Inc. refines Product X in batches of 200,000 gallons, which it sells for $3.20 per gallon. The associated unit costs and expenses are currently as follows:

	Per Gallon
Direct materials.............................	$1.84
Direct labor	.48
Variable factory overhead....................	.18
Fixed factory overhead......................	.12
Sales commissions	.16
Fixed selling and general expenses...........	.08

The company is presently considering a proposal to put Product X through several additional processes to yield Products X and Z. Although the company had determined such further processing to be unwise, new processing methods have now been developed. Existing facilities can be used for the additional processing, but since the factory is operating at full 8-hour-day capacity, the processing would have to be performed at night. Additional costs of processing would be $11,650 per batch and there would be an evaporation loss of 8%, with 70% of the processed material evolving as Product X and 22% as Product Z. The selling price of Product Z is $4.80 per gallon. Sales commissions are a uniform percentage based on the sales price.

Instructions:

(1) Prepare a differential analysis report as of November 12, presenting the differential revenue and the differential cost per batch associated with the processing to produce Products X and Z, compared with processing to produce Product X only.

(2) Briefly report your recommendations.

21–36A. Ahearn Company recently began production of a new product, G, which required the investment of $1,000,000 in assets. The costs and expenses of producing and selling 50,000 units of Product G are as follows:

Variable costs and expenses:	
Direct materials	$ 2.40 per unit
Direct labor.........................	4.80
Factory overhead....................	.80
Selling and general expenses.........	2.00
Total............................	$10.00 per unit

Fixed costs and expenses:	
Factory overhead....................	$70,000
Selling and general expenses.........	30,000

Ahearn Company is currently considering the establishment of a selling price for Product G. The President of Ahearn Company has decided to use the cost-plus approach to product pricing and has indicated that Product G must earn a 12% rate of return on invested assets.

Instructions:

(1) Determine the amount of desired profit from the production and sale of Product G.
(2) Assuming that the total cost concept is used, determine (a) the cost amount per unit, (b) the markup percentage, and (c) the selling price of Product G.
(3) Assuming that the product cost concept is used, determine (a) the cost amount per unit, (b) the markup percentage, and (c) the selling price of Product G. Round to the nearest cent.
(4) Assuming that the variable cost concept is used, determine (a) the cost amount per unit, (b) the markup percentage, and (c) the selling price of Product G.
(5) Comment on any additional considerations that could influence the establishment of the selling price for Product G.

Mini-Case

21–37. Your father operates a family-owned automotive dealership. Recently, the city government has requested bids on the purchase of 20 sedans for use by the city police department. Although the city prefers to purchase from local dealerships, state law requires the acceptance of the lowest bid. The past several contracts for automotive purchases have been granted to dealerships from surrounding communities.

The following data were taken from the dealership records for the normal sale of the automobile for which current bids have been requested:

Retail list price of sedan.	$12,100
Cost allocated to normal sale:	
Dealer cost from manufacturer	8,470
Fixed overhead	1,200
Shipping charges from manufacturer.	500
Preparation charges	100
Sales commission based on selling price.	5%

Your father has asked you to help him in arriving at a "winning" bid price for this contract. In the past, your father has always bid $250 above the total cost (including fixed overhead). No sales commissions will be paid if the bid is accepted, and your father has indicated that the bid price must contribute at least $250 per car to the profits of the dealership.

Instructions:

(1) Do you think that your father has used good bidding procedures for prior contracts? Explain.
(2) What should be the bid price, based upon your father's profit objectives?
(3) Explain why the bid price determined in (2) would not be an acceptable price for normal customers.

Answers to Self-Examination Questions

1. **A** Differential cost (answer A) is the amount of increase or decrease in cost that is expected from a particular course of action compared with an alternative. Replacement cost (answer B) is the cost of replacing an asset at current market prices, and sunk cost (answer C) is a past cost that will not be affected by subsequent decisions.

2. **A** A sunk cost is not affected by later decisions. For Victor Company, the sunk cost is the $50,000 (answer A) book value of the equipment, which is equal to the original cost of $200,000 (answer C) less the accumulated depreciation of $150,000 (answer B).

3. **C** The amount of income that could have been earned from the best available alternative to a proposed use of cash is called opportunity cost (answer C). Actual cost (answer A) or historical cost (answer B) is the cash or equivalent outlay for goods or services actually acquired.

4. **C** Under the variable cost concept of product pricing (answer C), fixed manufacturing costs, fixed general and selling expenses, and desired profit are allowed for in the determination of the markup. Only desired profit is allowed for in the markup under the total cost concept (answer A). Under the product cost concept (answer B), total selling and general expenses, and desired profit are allowed for in the determination of markup.

5. **A** Microeconomic theory indicates that profits of a business enterprise will be maximized at the point where marginal revenue equals marginal cost (answer A). At lower levels of production and sales, the change in total revenue is greater than the change in total cost (answer B); hence, more profit can be achieved by manufacturing and selling more units. At higher levels of production and sales, the change in total cost is greater than the change in total revenue (answer C); hence, less profit will be achieved by manufacturing and selling more units.

CHAPTER 22

Capital Investment Analysis

CHAPTER OBJECTIVES

Describe and illustrate methods used for evaluating capital investment proposals.

Describe and illustrate the capital rationing process.

Describe the basic concepts for planning and controlling capital investment expenditures.

With the accelerated growth of American industry, increasing attention has been given to long-term investment decisions involving property, plant, and equipment. The process by which management plans, evaluates, and controls such investments is called capital investment analysis, or **capital budgeting**. This chapter describes analyses useful for making capital investment decisions, which may involve thousands, millions, or even billions of dollars. Capital investment expenditures normally involve a long-term commitment of funds and thus affect operations for many years. These expenditures must earn a reasonable rate of return, so that the enterprise can meet its obligations to creditors and provide dividends to stockholders. Because capital investment decisions are some of the most important decisions that management makes, the systems and procedures for evaluating, planning, and controlling capital investments must be carefully developed and implemented.

A capital investment program should include a plan for encouraging employees at all levels of an enterprise to submit proposals for capital investments. The plan should provide for communicating to the employees the long-range goals of the enterprise, so that useful proposals are submitted. In addition, the plan may provide for rewarding employees whose proposals are implemented. All reasonable proposals should be given serious consideration, and the effects of the economic implications expected from these proposals should be identified.

The essentials of the most commonly used methods of evaluating capital investment proposals are described in the following sections. The similarities and differences between the methods, as well as the uses of each method, are emphasized. Finally, considerations complicating capital investment analyses, the process of allocating available investment funds among competing proposals (capital rationing), and planning and controlling capital expenditures are briefly discussed.

METHODS OF EVALUATING CAPITAL INVESTMENT PROPOSALS

The methods of evaluating capital investment proposals can be grouped into two general categories that can be referred to as (1) methods that ignore present value and (2) present value methods. The characteristic that distinguishes one category from the other is the way in which the concept of the time value of money is treated. Both the time value of money and the concept of present value are discussed in more detail later in the chapter. Because cash on hand can be invested to earn more cash, while cash to be received in the future cannot, money has a time value. However, the methods that ignore present value do not give consideration to the fact that cash on hand is more valuable than cash to be received in the future. The two methods in this category are (1) the average rate of return method and (2) the cash payback method.

By converting dollars to be received in the future into current dollars, using the concept of present value, the present value methods take into consideration the fact that money has a time value. The two common present value methods used in evaluating capital investment proposals are (1) the discounted cash flow method and (2) the discounted internal rate of return method.

Each of the four methods of analyzing capital investment proposals has both advantages and limitations. Often management will use some combination of the four methods in evaluating the various economic aspects of capital investment proposals.

Methods That Ignore Present Value

The average rate of return and the cash payback methods of evaluating capital investment proposals are simple to use and are especially useful in screening proposals. Management often establishes a minimum standard, and proposals not meeting this minimum standard are dropped from further consideration. When several alternative proposals meet the minimum standard, management will often rank the proposals from the most desirable to the least desirable.

The methods that ignore present value are also useful in evaluating capital investment proposals that have relatively short useful lives. In such situations, management generally focuses its attention on the amount of income to be earned from the investment and the total net cash flows to be received from the investment.

Average Rate of Return Method

The expected average rate of return, sometimes referred to as the accounting rate of return, is a measure of the expected profitability of an investment in plant assets. The amount of income expected to be earned from the investment is stated as an annual average over the number of years the asset is to be used. The amount of the investment may be considered to be the original cost of the plant asset, or recognition may be given to the effect of depreciation on the amount of the investment. According to the latter view, the investment gradually declines from the original cost to the estimated residual value at the end of its useful life. If straight-line depreciation and no residual value are assumed, the average investment would be equal to one half of the original expenditure.

To illustrate, assume that management is considering the purchase of a certain machine at a cost of $500,000. The machine is expected to have a useful life of 4 years, with no residual value, and its use during the 4 years is expected to yield total income of $200,000. The estimated average annual income is therefore $50,000 ($200,000 ÷ 4), and the average investment is $250,000 [($500,000 + $0 residual value) ÷ 2]. Accordingly, the expected average rate of return on the average investment is 20%, computed as follows:

$$\text{Average Rate of Return} = \frac{\text{Estimated Average Annual Income}}{\text{Average Investment}}$$

$$\text{Average Rate of Return} = \frac{\$200,000 \div 4}{(\$500,000 + \$0) \div 2}$$

$$\text{Average Rate of Return} = 20\%$$

The expected average rate of return of 20% should be compared with the rate established by management as the minimum reward for the risks involved in the investment. The attractiveness of the proposed purchase of additional equipment is indicated by the difference between the expected rate and the minimum desired rate.

When several alternative capital investment proposals are being considered, the proposals can be ranked by their average rates of return. The higher the average rate of return, the more desirable the proposal. For example, assume that management is considering the following alternative capital investment proposals and has computed the indicated average rates of return:

	Proposal A	Proposal B
Estimated average annual income.................	$ 30,000	$ 36,000
Average investment..............................	$120,000	$180,000
Average rate of return:		
$30,000 ÷ $120,000............................	25%	
$36,000 ÷ $180,000............................		20%

If only the average rate of return is considered, Proposal A would be preferred over Proposal B, based on its average rate of return of 25%.

The primary advantages of the average rate of return method are its ease of computation and the fact that it emphasizes the amount of income earned over the entire life of the proposal. Its main disadvantages are its lack of consideration of the expected cash flows from the proposal and the timing of these cash flows. These cash flows are important because cash coming from an investment can be reinvested in other income-producing activities. Therefore, the more funds and the sooner the funds become available, the more income that can be generated from their reinvestment.

Cash Payback Method

The expected period of time that will pass between the date of a capital investment and the complete recovery in cash (or equivalent) of the amount invested is called the **cash payback period**. To simplify the analysis, the revenues and the out-of-pocket operating expenses expected to be associated with the operation of the plant assets are assumed to be entirely in the form of cash. The excess of the cash flowing in from revenue over the cash flowing out for expenses is termed **net cash flow**. The time required for the net cash flow to equal the initial outlay for the plant asset is the payback period.

For purposes of illustration, assume that the proposed investment in a plant asset with an 8-year life is $200,000 and that the annual net cash flow is expected to be $40,000. The estimated cash payback period for the investment is 5 years, computed as follows:

$$\frac{\$200,000}{\$40,000} = \text{5-year cash payback period}$$

In the preceding illustration, the annual net cash flows were equal ($40,000 per year). If these annual net cash flows are not equal, the cash payback period is determined by summing the annual net cash flows until the cumulative sum equals the amount of the proposed investment. To illustrate, assume that for a proposed investment, the cumulative net cash flow at the end of the fourth year equals the amount of the investment, $400,000. Therefore, the payback period is 4 years. The annual net cash flows and cumulative net cash flows over the proposal's 6-year life are as follows:

Year	Net Cash Flow	Cumulative Net Cash Flow
1	$ 60,000	$ 60,000
2	80,000	140,000
3	105,000	245,000
4	155,000	400,000
5	140,000	540,000
6	90,000	630,000

The cash payback method is widely used in evaluating proposals for expansion and for investment in new projects. A relatively short payback period is desirable, because the sooner the cash is recovered the sooner it becomes available for reinvestment in other projects. In addition, there is likely to be less possibility of loss from changes in economic conditions, obsolescence, and other unavoidable risks when the commitment is short-term. The cash payback concept is also of interest to bankers and other creditors who may be dependent upon net cash flow for the repayment of claims associated with the initial capital investment. The sooner the cash is recovered, the sooner the debt or other liabilities can be paid. Thus, the cash payback method would be especially useful to managers whose primary concern is liquidity.

One of the primary disadvantages of the cash payback method as a basis for decisions is its failure to take into consideration the expected profitability of a proposal. A project with a very short payback period, coupled with relatively poor profitability, would be less desirable than one with a longer payback period but with satisfactory profitability. Another disadvantage of the cash payback method is that the cash flows occurring after the payback period are ignored. A 5-year project with a 3-year payback period and two additional years of substantial cash flows is more desirable than a 5-year project with a 3-year payback period that has lower cash flows in the last two years.

Present Value Methods

An investment in plant and equipment may be viewed as the acquisition of a series of future net cash flows composed of two elements: (1) recovery of the initial investment and (2) income. The period of time over which these net cash flows will be received may be an important factor in determining the value of an investment.

As discussed in Chapter 12, the concept of present values is that any specified amount of cash to be received at some date in the future is not the equivalent of the same amount of cash held at an earlier date. A sum of cash to be received in the future is not as valuable as the same sum on hand today, because cash on hand today can be invested to earn income. For example, $100 on hand today would be more valuable than $100 to be received a year from today. In other words, if cash can be invested to earn 10% per year, the $100 on hand today will accumulate to $110 ($100 plus $10 earnings) by one year from today. The $100 on hand today can be referred to as the present value amount that is equivalent to $110 to be received a year from today.

Discounted Cash Flow Method

The **discounted cash flow method,** sometimes referred to as the **net present value method,** uses present value concepts to compute the present value of the cash flows expected from a proposal. To illustrate, if the rate of earnings is 12% and the cash to be received in one year is $1,000, the present value amount is $892.86 ($1,000 ÷ 1.12). If the cash is to be received one year later (two years in all), with the earnings compounded at the end of the first year, the present value amount would be $797.20 ($892.86 ÷ 1.12).

Instead of determining the present value of future cash flows by a series of divisions in the manner just illustrated, it is customary to find the present value of 1 from a table of present values and to multiply it by the amount of the future cash flow. Reference to the following partial table indicates that the present value of 1 to be received two years hence, with earnings at the rate of 12% a year, is .797. Multiplication of .797 by $1,000 yields $797, which is the same amount that was determined in the preceding paragraph by two successive divisions. The small difference is due to rounding the present value factors in the table to three decimal places.

	Year	6%	10%	12%	15%	20%
PRESENT VALUE OF 1 AT COMPOUND INTEREST	1	.943	.909	.893	.870	.833
	2	.890	.826	.797	.756	.694
	3	.840	.751	.712	.658	.579
	4	.792	.683	.636	.572	.482
	5	.747	.621	.567	.497	.402
	6	.705	.564	.507	.432	.335
	7	.665	.513	.452	.376	.279
	8	.627	.467	.404	.327	.233
	9	.592	.424	.361	.284	.194
	10	.558	.386	.322	.247	.162

The particular rate of return selected in discounted cash flow analysis is affected by the nature of the business enterprise and its relative profitability, the purpose of the capital investment, the cost of securing funds for the investment, the minimum desired rate of return, and other related factors. If the present value of the net cash flow expected from a proposed investment, at the selected rate, equals or exceeds the amount of the investment, the proposal is desirable. For purposes of illustration, assume a proposal for the acquisition of $200,000 of equipment with an expected useful life of 5 years and a minimum desired rate of return of 10%. The anticipated net cash flow for each of the 5 years and the analysis of the proposal are as follows. The calculation shows that the proposal is expected to recover the investment and provide more than the minimum rate of return.

	Year	Present Value of 1 at 10%	Net Cash Flow	Present Value of Net Cash Flow
DISCOUNTED CASH FLOW ANALYSIS	1	.909	$ 70,000	$ 63,630
	2	.826	60,000	49,560
	3	.751	50,000	37,550
	4	.683	40,000	27,320
	5	.621	40,000	24,840
	Total		$260,000	$202,900

Amount to be invested.................................. 200,000

Excess of present value over amount to be invested .... $ 2,900

When several alternative investment proposals of the same amount are being considered, the one with the largest excess of present value over the amount to be invested is the most desirable. If the alternative proposals involve different amounts of investment, it is useful to prepare a relative ranking of the proposals by using a **present value index**. The present value index for the previous illustration is computed by dividing the total present value of the net cash flow by the amount to be invested, as follows:

$$\text{Present Value Index} = \frac{\text{Total Present Value of Net Cash Flow}}{\text{Amount To Be Invested}}$$

$$\text{Present Value Index} = \frac{\$202,900}{\$200,000}$$

$$\text{Present Value Index} = 1.01$$

To illustrate the ranking of proposals by use of the present value index, assume that the total present values of the net cash flow and the amounts to be invested for three alternative proposals are as follows:

	Proposal A	Proposal B	Proposal C
Total present value of net cash flow.....	$107,000	$86,400	$93,600
Amount to be invested................	100,000	80,000	90,000
Excess of present value over amount to be invested........................	$ 7,000	$ 6,400	$ 3,600

The present value index for each proposal is as follows:

	Present Value Index
Proposal A	1.07 ($107,000 ÷ $100,000)
Proposal B	1.08 ($ 86,400 ÷ $ 80,000)
Proposal C	1.04 ($ 93,600 ÷ $ 90,000)

The present value indexes indicate that although Proposal A has the largest excess of present value over the amount to be invested, it is not as attractive as Proposal B in terms of the amount of present value per dollar invested. It should be noted, however, that Proposal B requires an investment of only $80,000, while Proposal A requires an investment of $100,000. The possible use of the $20,000 if B is selected should be considered before a final decision is made.

The primary advantage of the discounted cash flow method is that it gives consideration to the time value of money. A disadvantage of the method is that the computations are more complex than those for the methods that ignore present value. In addition, this method assumes that the cash received from the proposal during its useful life will be reinvested at the rate of return used to compute the present value of the proposal. Because of changing economic conditions, this assumption may not always be reasonable.

Discounted Internal Rate of Return Method

The discounted internal rate of return method, sometimes called the **internal rate of return** or **time-adjusted rate of return method,** uses present value concepts to compute the rate of return from the net cash flows expected from capital investment proposals. Thus, it is similar to the discounted cash flow method, in that it focuses on the present value of the net cash flows. However, the discounted internal rate of return method starts with the net cash flows and, in a sense, works backwards to determine the discounted rate of return expected from the proposal. The discounted cash flow method requires management to specify a minimum rate of return, which is then used to determine the excess (deficiency) of the present value of the net cash flow over the investment.

To illustrate the use of the discounted internal rate of return method, assume that management is evaluating a proposal to acquire equipment costing $33,530, which is expected to provide annual net cash flows of $10,000 per year for 5 years. If a rate of return of 12% is assumed, the present value of the net cash flows can be computed using the present value of 1 table on page 716, as follows:

Year	Present Value of 1 at 12%	Net Cash Flow	Present Value of Net Cash Flow
1	.893	$10,000	$ 8,930
2	.797	10,000	7,970
3	.712	10,000	7,120
4	.636	10,000	6,360
5	.567	10,000	5,670
Total		$50,000	$36,050

Since the present value of the net cash flow based on a 12% rate of return, $36,050, is greater than the $33,530 to be invested, 12% is obviously not the discounted internal rate of return. The following analysis indicates that 15% is the rate of return that equates the $33,530 cost of the investment with the present value of the net cash flows.

Year	Present Value of 1 at 15%	Net Cash Flow	Present Value of Net Cash Flow
1	.870	$10,000	$ 8,700
2	.756	10,000	7,560
3	.658	10,000	6,580
4	.572	10,000	5,720
5	.497	10,000	4,970
Total		$50,000	$33,530

In the illustration, the discounted internal rate of return was determined by trial and error. A rate of 12% was assumed before the discounted internal rate of return of 15% was identified. Such procedures are tedious and time consuming. When equal annual net cash flows are expected from a proposal, as in the illustration, the computations can be simplified by using a table of the present value of an annuity.[1]

A series of equal cash flows at fixed intervals is termed an **annuity**. The **present value of an annuity** is the sum of the present values of each cash flow. From another point of view, the present value of an annuity is the amount of cash that would be needed today to yield a series of equal cash flows at fixed intervals in the future. For example, reference to the following table of the present value of an annuity of 1 shows that the present value of cash flows at the end of each of five years, with a discounted internal rate of return of 15% per year, is 3.353. Multiplication of $10,000 by 3.353 yields the same amount ($33,530) that was determined in the preceding illustration by five successive multiplications.

Year	6%	10%	12%	15%	20%
1	.943	.909	.893	.870	.833
2	1.833	1.736	1.690	1.626	1.528
3	2.673	2.487	2.402	2.283	2.106
4	3.465	3.170	3.037	2.855	2.589
5	4.212	3.791	3.605	3.353	2.991
6	4.917	4.355	4.111	3.785	3.326
7	5.582	4.868	4.564	4.160	3.605
8	6.210	5.335	4.968	4.487	3.837
9	6.802	5.759	5.328	4.772	4.031
10	7.360	6.145	5.650	5.019	4.192

PRESENT VALUE OF AN ANNUITY OF 1 AT COMPOUND INTEREST

The procedures for using the present value of an annuity of 1 table to determine the discounted internal rate of return are as follows:

1. A present value factor for an annuity of 1 is determined by dividing the amount to be invested by the annual net cash flow, as expressed in the following formula:

$$\text{Present Value Factor for an Annuity of 1} = \frac{\text{Amount To Be Invested}}{\text{Annual Net Cash Flow}}$$

2. The present value factor determined in (1) is located in the present value of an annuity of 1 table by first locating the number of years of expected useful life of the investment in the Year column and then proceeding horizontally across the table until the present value factor determined in (1) is found.
3. The discounted internal rate of return is then identified by the heading of the column in which the present value factor in (2) is located.

---

[1] In the illustration, equal annual net cash flows are assumed, so that attention can be focused on the basic concepts. If the annual net cash flows are not equal, the procedures are more complex, but the basic concepts are not affected. In such cases, computers can be used to perform the computations.

To illustrate the use of the present value of an annuity of 1 table, assume that management is considering a proposal to acquire equipment costing $97,360, which is expected to provide equal annual net cash flows of $20,000 for 7 years. The present value factor for an annuity of 1 is **4.868**, computed as follows:

$$\text{Present Value Factor for an Annuity of 1} = \frac{\text{Amount To Be Invested}}{\text{Annual Net Cash Flow}}$$

$$\text{Present Value Factor for an Annuity of 1} = \frac{\$97,360}{\$20,000}$$

$$\text{Present Value Factor for an Annuity of 1} = 4.868$$

For a period of 7 years, the following table for the present value of an annuity of 1 indicates that the factor **4.868** is associated with a percentage of **10%**. Thus, 10% is the discounted internal rate of return for this proposal.

PRESENT VALUE
OF AN ANNUITY OF
1 AT COMPOUND
INTEREST

Year	6%	10%	12%
1	.943	.909	.893
2	1.833	1.736	1.690
3	2.673	2.487	2.402
4	3.465	3.170	3.037
5	4.212	3.791	3.605
6	4.917	4.355	4.111
7	5.582 →	4.868	4.564
8	6.210	5.335	4.968
9	6.802	5.759	5.328
10	7.360	6.145	5.650

If the minimum acceptable rate of return for similar proposals is 10% or less, then the proposed equipment acquisition should be considered desirable. When several proposals are under consideration, management often ranks the proposals by their discounted internal rates of return, and the proposal with the highest rate is considered the most attractive.

The primary advantage of the discounted internal rate of return method is that the present values of the net cash flows over the entire useful life of the proposal are considered. An additional advantage of the method is that by determining a rate of return for each proposal, all proposals are automatically placed on a common basis for comparison, without the need to compute a present value index as was the case for the discounted cash flow method. The primary disadvantage of the discounted internal rate of return method is that the computations are somewhat more complex than for some of the other methods. In addition, like the discounted cash flow method, this method assumes that the cash received from a proposal during its useful life will be reinvested at the discounted internal rate of return. Because of changing economic conditions, this assumption may not always be reasonable.

FACTORS THAT COMPLICATE CAPITAL INVESTMENT ANALYSIS

In the preceding paragraphs, the basic concepts for four widely used methods of evaluating capital investment proposals were discussed. In practice, additional factors may have an impact on the outcome of a capital investment decision. Some of the most important of these factors, which are described in the following paragraphs, are the federal income tax, the unequal lives of alternative proposals, the leasing alternative, uncertainty, and changes in price levels.

Income Tax

In many cases, the impact of the federal income tax on capital investment decisions can be very significant. Two provisions of the Internal Revenue Code (IRC) which should be considered in capital investment analysis are the investment tax credit and depreciation.[2]

The investment tax credit, which reduces the amount of income tax by the amount of the credit, was enacted in 1962 to encourage businesses to purchase equipment and thereby stimulate the economy. Since its original enactment, the IRC has been changed often in attempts to fine tune the economy. In general, the credit is granted for purchases of certain new or used tangible personal property with a useful life of at least 3 years that is used in the taxpayer's trade or business. The maximum credit is 10% of the cost of property with a life of 5 years or more and 6% for property with a life of three to five years. In determining depreciation, the cost of the asset is generally reduced by one half of the amount of the credit. The basic reduction can be avoided if the taxpayer elects to take a smaller investment credit (8% for property with a life of five years or more, 4% for property with a life of three to five years). Also, the maximum amount of the credit in any year is limited if the potential credit is more than $25,000.

For determining **depreciation**, or the "cost recovery deduction," which is the expensing of the cost of plant assets over their useful lives, the IRC specifies the use of the Accelerated Cost Recovery System (ACRS). ACRS generally provides for three classes for most business property (3-year, 5-year, and 19-year classes) and provides for depreciation that approximates the use of the 150 percent declining-balance method. The 3-year class includes auto-

---

[2]Other income tax considerations relevant for managerial decision making are discussed in Chapter 23.

mobiles and special tools, while most machinery and equipment is included in the 5-year class, and buildings fall into the 19-year class.

ACRS simplifies depreciation accounting by eliminating the need to estimate useful life and salvage value and to decide on a depreciation method. Although a short-run tax saving can usually be realized by using the regular ACRS cost recovery allowance, a taxpayer may elect to use a straight-line deduction based on the property classes prescribed under ACRS. The accelerated write-off of depreciable assets provided by ACRS does not, however, effect a long-run net saving in income tax. The tax reduction of the early years of use is offset by higher taxes as the annual cost recovery allowance diminishes.[3]

To illustrate the potential impact of the investment tax credit and ACRS depreciation on capital investment decisions, assume that Sierra Company is using the discounted cash flow method[4] in evaluating a proposal. The cost of the investment acquired in year 1 is $180,000, with an expected useful life of 3 years, no residual value, and a minimum desired rate of return of 12%. If Sierra Company elects the straight-line method of depreciation, the IRC requires one half of a full year's depreciation to be taken in the first year and one half of a full year's depreciation to be taken in the fourth year. Thus, Sierra Company would deduct the following depreciation amounts during the 3-year life of the asset:

	Depreciation Expense
First year	$30,000 [($180,000 ÷ 3) × 1/2]
Second year	$60,000 ($180,000 ÷ 3)
Third year	$60,000 ($180,000 ÷ 3)
Fourth year	$30,000 [($180,000 ÷ 3) × 1/2]

During the four years in which depreciation expense is deducted, the investment is expected to yield annual operating income, before depreciation and income taxes, of $85,000, $70,000, $70,000, and $30,000, respectively. To simplify the illustration, all revenues and operating expenses except depreciation represent current period cash flows, and no investment credit applies to

---

[3]Taxpayers may also choose to deduct, as a current expense, a limited amount of the cost of plant asset acquisitions that qualify for the investment tax credit. Amounts expended under this provision are not available for computing the investment tax credit or the cost recovery allowance. To simplify the discussions and illustrations in this chapter, it is assumed that this current expense deduction is not applicable to the capital investment analysis being illustrated.

[4]The same general impact of the investment tax credit and depreciation on capital investment decisions would occur, regardless of which of the four capital investment evaluation methods was used. To simplify the discussion in this chapter, only the discounted cash flow method is illustrated.

the acquisition. If the income tax rate is 46%, the annual net aftertax cash flows from acquisition of the asset are as follows:

	Year			
	1	2	3	4
Net cash flow before income taxes....	$85,000	$70,000	$70,000	$30,000
Income tax expense*	25,300	4,600	4,600	0
Net cash flow........................	$59,700	$65,400	$65,400	$30,000

*Income tax expense:				
Operating income before depreciation and income taxes	$85,000	$70,000	$70,000	$30,000
Depreciation expense	30,000	60,000	60,000	30,000
Income before income taxes	$55,000	$10,000	$10,000	0
Income tax rate	46%	46%	46%	46%
Income tax expense...............	$25,300	$ 4,600	$ 4,600	0

Based on the preceding data, using the discounted cash flow method with no investment tax credit, an $8,919 deficiency of the present value over the amount to be invested is computed, as follows:

Year	Present Value of 1 at 12%	Net Cash Flow	Present Value of Net Cash Flow
1	.893	$ 59,700	$ 53,312
2	.797	65,400	52,124
3	.712	65,400	46,565
4	.636	30,000	19,080
Total		$220,500	$171,081
Amount to be invested			180,000
Deficiency of present value over amount to be invested			$ 8,919

Because the discounted cash flow method indicates that there is a deficiency of the present value over the amount to be invested, the decision would be to reject the proposal. However, if the investment tax credit had been available, the present value of the acquisition changes significantly and might lead to a different decision. To illustrate, assume that Sierra Company could take the 6% maximum credit allowable for plant assets with a useful life of 3 years, or $10,800 ($180,000 × 6%). When the maximum investment tax credit is taken, the IRC requires that, for depreciation purposes, the cost of the asset be reduced by one half of the credit. Thus, only $174,600 [$180,000 − (1/2 × $10,800)] of the cost will be available for depreciation purposes. Using the straight-line method, with one half of a full year's depreciation taken in the first and fourth years, the depreciation for Sierra Company will be as follows:

Depreciation Expense

First year..................	$29,100 [($174,600 ÷ 3) × 1/2]
Second year..............	$58,200 ($174,600 ÷ 3)
Third year	$58,200 ($174,600 ÷ 3)
Fourth year...............	$29,100 [($174,600 ÷ 3) × 1/2]

The annual aftertax net cash flows from the acquisition, including the effect of the investment tax credit, are as follows:

	Year			
	1	2	3	4
Net cash flow before income taxes....	$85,000	$70,000	$70,000	$30,000
Income tax expense*	14,914	5,428	5,428	414
Net cash flow......................	$70,086	$64,572	$64,572	$29,586
*Income tax expense:				
Operating income before depreciation and income taxes	$85,000	$70,000	$70,000	$30,000
Depreciation expense	29,100	58,200	58,200	29,100
Income before income taxes	$55,900	$11,800	$11,800	$ 900
Income tax rate	46%	46%	46%	46%
Income tax expense before investment tax credit..................	$25,714	$ 5,428	$ 5,428	$ 414
Investment tax credit	10,800	0	0	0
Income tax expense...............	$14,914	$ 5,428	$ 5,428	$ 414

Based on the preceding data, using the discounted cash flow method, a $1,157 deficiency of the present value over the amount to be invested is computed, as follows:

Year	Present Value of 1 at 12%	Net Cash Flow	Present Value of Net Cash Flow
1	.893	$ 70,086	$ 62,587
2	.797	64,572	51,464
3	.712	64,572	45,975
4	.636	29,586	18,817
Total		$228,816	$178,843

Amount to be invested 180,000

Deficiency of present value over amount to be invested .... $ 1,157

Although the deficiency of the present value over the amount to be invested, $1,157, is less than that computed in the preceding illustration where the investment tax credit was not taken, the decision would still be to reject the proposal. However, if the effects of ACRS depreciation as well as the investment tax credit on income tax expense are considered, the evaluation of the proposal changes even more. To illustrate, assume that Sierra Company can take the maximum investment tax credit of $10,800. The amount available for depreciation will be $174,600 [$180,000 − (1/2 × $10,800)]. Sierra Company is permitted to deduct depreciation over a 3-year period beginning with the year the asset is acquired, using the following ACRS percentages:

	ACRS Percentage Deduction Allowed for Depreciation
First year.....................	25%
Second year..................	38%
Third year	37%

Using ACRS, the depreciation for Sierra Company will be as follows:

	Depreciation Expense
First year.....................	$43,650 ($174,600 × 25%)
Second year..................	$66,348 ($174,600 × 38%)
Third year	$64,602 ($174,600 × 37%)

The annual aftertax net cash flows from the acquisition of the plant asset, including the effect of ACRS depreciation and the investment tax credit, are as follows:

	Year			
	1	2	3	4
Net cash flow before income taxes....	$85,000	$70,000	$70,000	$30,000
Income tax expense*	8,221	1,680	2,483	13,800
Net cash flow.......................	$76,779	$68,320	$67,517	$16,200

*Income tax expense:

Operating income before depreciation and income taxes	$85,000	$70,000	$70,000	$30,000
Depreciation expense	43,650	66,348	64,602	0
Income before income taxes	$41,350	$ 3,652	$ 5,398	$30,000
Income tax rate	46%	46%	46%	46%
Income tax expense before investment tax credit..................	$19,021	$ 1,680	$ 2,483	$13,800
Investment tax credit	10,800	0	0	0
Income tax expense...............	$ 8,221	$ 1,680	$ 2,483	$13,800

Based on the preceding data, using the discounted cash flow method, a $1,390 excess of the present value over the amount to be invested is computed, as follows:

Year	Present Value of 1 at 12%	Net Cash Flow	Present Value of Net Cash Flow
1	.893	$ 76,779	$ 68,564
2	.797	68,320	54,451
3	.712	67,517	48,072
4	.636	16,200	10,303
Total		$228,816	$181,390

Amount to be invested 180,000

Excess of present value over amount to be invested . . . . $ 1,390

The specific dollar effects of tax considerations on the evaluation of capital investment proposals will depend on the deductions and credits allowed by the Internal Revenue Code at the time the capital investment decision is to be made. In this illustration, the discounted cash flow analysis indicates an excess of the present value over the amount to be invested, and the decision would be to invest in the asset.

Unequal Proposal Lives

In the preceding sections, the discussion of the methods of analyzing capital investment proposals was based on the assumption that alternate proposals had the same useful lives. In practice, however, alternate proposals may have unequal lives. In such cases, the proposals must be made comparable. One widely used method is to adjust the lives of projects with the longest lives to a time period that is equal to the life of the project with the shortest life. In this manner, the useful lives of all proposals are made equal. To illustrate, assume that the discounted cash flow method is being used to compare the following two proposals, each of which has an initial investment of $100,000:

Year	Net Cash Flows	
	Proposal X	Proposal Y
1	$30,000	$30,000
2	30,000	30,000
3	25,000	30,000
4	20,000	30,000
5	15,000	30,000
6	15,000	—
7	10,000	—
8	10,000	—

Capital Investment Analysis

If the desired rate of return is 10%, the proposals have an excess of present value over the amount to be invested, as follows:

Proposal X

Year	Present Value of 1 at 10%	Net Cash Flow	Present Value of Net Cash Flow
1	.909	$ 30,000	$ 27,270
2	.826	30,000	24,780
3	.751	25,000	18,775
4	.683	20,000	13,660
5	.621	15,000	9,315
6	.564	15,000	8,460
7	.513	10,000	5,130
8	.467	10,000	4,670
Total		$155,000	$112,060

Amount to be invested   100,000

Excess of present value over amount to be invested. . . . . $ 12,060

Proposal Y

Year	Present Value of 1 at 10%	Net Cash Flow	Present Value of Net Cash Flow
1	.909	$ 30,000	$ 27,270
2	.826	30,000	24,780
3	.751	30,000	22,530
4	.683	30,000	20,490
5	.621	30,000	18,630
Total		$150,000	$113,700

Amount to be invested   100,000

Excess of present value over amount to be invested. . . . . $ 13,700

The two proposals cannot be compared by focusing on the amount of the excess of the present value over the amount to be invested, because Proposal Y has a life of 5 years while Proposal X has a life of 8 years. Proposal X can be adjusted to a 5-year life by assuming that it is to be terminated at the end of 5 years and the asset sold. This assumption requires that the residual value be estimated at the end of 5 years and that this value be considered a cash flow at that date. Both proposals will then cover 5 years, and the results of the discounted cash flow analysis can be used to compare the relative attractiveness of the two proposals. For example, assume that Proposal X has an estimated residual value at the end of year 5 of $40,000. For Proposal X, the excess of the present value over the amount to be invested is **$18,640** for a 5-year life, as follows:

Proposal X			
Year	Present Value of 1 at 10%	Net Cash Flow	Present Value of Net Cash Flow
1	.909	$ 30,000	$ 27,270
2	.826	30,000	24,780
3	.751	25,000	18,775
4	.683	20,000	13,660
5	.621	15,000	9,315
5 (Residual value)	.621	40,000	24,840
Total		$160,000	$118,640
Amount to be invested			100,000
Excess of present value over amount to be invested			$ 18,640

Since the present value over the amount to be invested for Proposal X exceeds that for Proposal Y by **$4,940** ($18,640 − $13,700), Proposal X may be viewed as the more attractive of the two proposals.

Lease Versus Capital Investment

Leasing of plant assets has become common in many industries in recent years. Leasing allows an enterprise to acquire the use of plant assets without the necessity of using large amounts of cash to purchase them. In addition, if management believes that a plant asset has a high degree of risk of becoming obsolete before the end of its useful life, then leasing rather than purchasing the asset may be more attractive. By leasing the asset, management reduces the risk of suffering a loss due to obsolescence. Finally, the Internal Revenue Code provisions which allow the lessor (the owner of the asset) to pass tax deductions and tax credits on to the lessee (the party leasing the asset) have increased the popularity of leasing in recent years. For example, a company that leases for its use a $200,000 plant asset with a life of 8 years for $50,000 per year is permitted to deduct annual lease payments of $50,000 as well as take an investment tax credit of $20,000 ($200,000 × 10%) for the first year of use.

In many cases, before a final decision is made, management should consider the possibility of leasing assets instead of purchasing them. Ordinarily, leasing assets is more costly than purchasing because the lessor must include in the rental price the costs associated with owning the assets as well as a profit. Nevertheless, using the methods of evaluating capital investment proposals, management should consider whether or not the profitability and cash flows from the lease alternative with its risks compares favorably to the profitability and cash flows from the purchase alternative with its risks.

Uncertainty

All capital investment analyses rely on factors that are uncertain; that is, the accuracy of the estimates involved, including estimates of expected revenues, expenses, and cash flows, are uncertain. Although the estimates are subject to varying degrees of risk or uncertainty, the long-term nature of capital investments suggests that many of the estimates are likely to involve considerable uncertainty. Errors in one or more of the estimates could lead to unwise decisions.

Because of the importance of capital investment decisions, management should be aware of the potential impact of uncertainty on their decisions. Some techniques that can be used to assist management in evaluating the effects of uncertainties on capital investment proposals are presented in Chapter 27.

Changes in Price Levels

The past three decades have been characterized by increasing price levels.[5] Such periods are described as periods of **inflation**. In recent years, the rates of inflation have fluctuated widely, making the estimation of future revenues, expenses, and cash flows more difficult. Therefore, management should consider the expected future price levels and their likely effect on the estimates used in capital investment analyses. Fluctuations in the price levels assumed could significantly affect the analyses.

CAPITAL RATIONING

Capital rationing refers to the process by which management allocates available investment funds among competing capital investment proposals. Generally, management will use various combinations of the evaluation methods described in this chapter in developing an effective approach to capital rationing.

In capital rationing, an initial screening of alternative proposals is usually performed by establishing minimum standards for the cash payback and the average rate of return methods. The proposals that survive this initial screening are subjected to the more rigorous discounted cash flow and discounted internal rate of return methods of analysis. The proposals that survive this final screening are evaluated in terms of nonfinancial factors, such as employee morale. For example, the acquisition of new, more efficient equipment which eliminates several jobs could lower employee morale to a level that could decrease overall plant productivity.

The final step in the capital rationing process is a ranking of the proposals and a comparison of proposals with the funds available to determine which proposals will be funded. The unfunded proposals are reconsidered if funds subsequently become available. The following flowchart portrays the capital rationing decision process:

---

[5]The subject of price-level changes is discussed in Chapter 28.

CAPITAL RATIONING
DECISION PROCESS

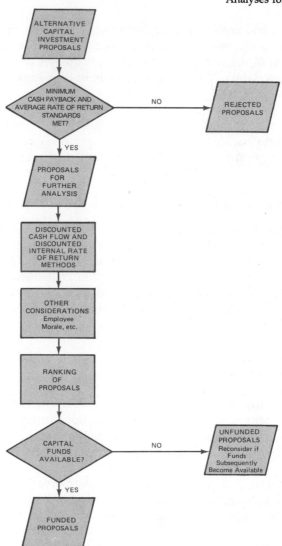

Capital Expenditures Budget

Once capital investment expenditures for a period have been approved, a **capital expenditures budget** should be prepared and procedures should be established for controlling the expenditures. After the assets are placed in service, the actual results of operations should be compared to the initial projected results to determine whether the capital expenditures are meeting management's expectations.

The capital expenditures budget facilitates the planning of operations and the financing of capital expenditures. A capital expenditures budget, which is integrated with the master budget as discussed in Chapter 17, summarizes acquisition decisions for a period typically ranging from one to five years. The following capital expenditures budget was prepared for Sealy Company:

Sealy Company
Capital Expenditures Budget
For Five Years Ending December 31, 1991

Item	1987	1988	1989	1990	1991
Machinery—Department A...	$240,000	—	—	$168,000	$216,000
Machinery—Department B...	108,000	$156,000	$336,000	120,000	—
Delivery equipment..........	—	54,000	—	—	36,000
Total....................	$348,000	$210,000	$336,000	$288,000	$252,000

The capital expenditures budget does not authorize the acquisition of plant assets. Rather, it serves as a planning device to determine the effects of the capital expenditures on operations after management has evaluated the alternative proposals, using the methods described in this chapter. Final authority for capital expenditures must come from the proper level of management. In some corporations, large capital expenditures must be approved by the board of directors.

Control of Capital Expenditures

Once the capital expenditures have been approved, control must be established over the costs of acquiring the assets, including the costs of installation and testing before the assets are placed in service. Throughout this period of acquiring the assets and readying them for use, actual costs should be compared to planned (budgeted) costs. Timely reports should be prepared, so that management can take corrective actions as quickly as possible and thereby minimize cost overruns and operating delays.

After the assets have been placed in service, attention should be focused on comparisons of actual operating expenses with budgeted operating expenses. Such comparisons provide opportunities for management to follow up on successful expenditures or to terminate or otherwise attempt to salvage failing expenditures.

USE OF COMPUTERS IN CAPITAL INVESTMENT ANALYSIS

Some of the computations for the capital investment evaluation methods discussed in this chapter can become rather complex. By use of the computer, the calculations can be performed easily and quickly. The most important use of the computer, however, is in developing various models which indicate the effect of changes in key factors on the results of capital investment proposals. For example, the effect of various potential changes in future price levels on a proposal could be simulated and the results presented to management for its use in decision making.

Self-Examination Questions
(Answers at end of chapter.)

1. Methods of evaluating capital investment proposals that ignore present value include:
   A. average rate of return
   B. cash payback
   C. both A and B
   D. neither A nor B

2. Management is considering a $100,000 investment in a project with a 5-year life and no residual value. If the total income from the project is expected to be $60,000 and recognition is given to the effect of straight-line depreciation on the investment, the average rate of return is:
   A. 12%
   B. 24%
   C. 60%
   D. none of the above

3. As used in the analysis of proposed capital investments, the expected period of time that will elapse between the date of a capital investment and the complete recovery of the amount of cash invested is called:
   A. the average rate of return period
   B. the cash payback period
   C. the discounted cash flow period
   D. none of the above

4. Which method of analyzing capital investment proposals determines the total present value of the cash flows expected from the investment and compares this value with the amount to be invested?
   A. Average rate of return
   B. Cash payback
   C. Discounted cash flow
   D. Discounted internal rate of return

5. The process by which management allocates available investment funds among competing capital investment proposals is referred to as:
   A. capital rationing
   B. capital expenditure budgeting
   C. leasing
   D. none of the above

Discussion Questions

22–1. Which two methods of capital investment analysis ignore present value?

22–2. Which two methods of capital investment analysis can be described as present value methods?

22–3. What is the "time value of money" concept?

22–4. (a) How is the average rate of return computed for capital investment analysis, assuming that consideration is given to the effect of straight-line depreciation on the amount of the investment? (b) If the amount of a 6-year investment is $150,000, the straight-line method of depreciation is used, there is no residual value, and the total income expected from the investment is $135,000, what is the average rate of return?

22–5. What are the principal objections to the use of the average rate of return method in evaluating capital investment proposals?

22–6. (a) As used in analyses of proposed capital investments, what is the cash payback period? (b) Discuss the principal limitations of the cash payback method for evaluating capital investment proposals.

22–7. What is the present value of $5,500 to be received one year from today, assuming an earnings rate of 10%?

22–8. Which method of evaluating capital investment proposals reduces their expected future net cash flows to present values and compares the total present values to the amount of the investment?

22–9. A discounted cash flow analysis used to evaluate a proposed equipment acquisition indicated a $5,000 excess of present value over the amount to be invested. What is the meaning of the $5,000 as it relates to the desirability of the proposal?

22–10. How is the present value index for a proposal determined?

22–11. What are the major disadvantages of the use of the discounted cash flow method of analyzing capital investment proposals?

22–12. What is an annuity?

22–13. What are the major disadvantages of the use of the discounted internal rate of return method of analyzing capital investment proposals?

22–14. What two provisions of the Internal Revenue Code are especially important for consideration in analyzing capital investment proposals?

22–15. What method can be used to place two capital investment proposals with unequal useful lives on a comparable basis?

22–16. What are the major advantages of leasing a plant asset rather than purchasing it?

22–17. What is capital rationing?

22–18. The following data are accumulated by Baxter Company in evaluating two competing capital investment proposals:

Exercises

	Proposal X	Proposal Y
Amount of investment........................	$300,000	$400,000
Useful life....................................	4 years	6 years
Estimated residual value......................	0	0
Estimated total income.......................	$ 90,000	$156,000

Determine the expected average rate of return for each proposal, giving effect to straight-line depreciation on each investment.

22–19. Horten Company is evaluating two capital investment proposals, each requiring an investment of $100,000 and each with a 6-year life and expected total net cash flows of $150,000. Proposal 1 is expected to provide equal annual net cash flows of $25,000, and Proposal 2 is expected to have the following unequal annual net cash flows:

Year 1	$20,000
Year 2	30,000
Year 3	50,000
Year 4	25,000
Year 5	15,000
Year 6	10,000

Determine the cash payback period for both proposals.

22–20. The following data are accumulated by Jackson Company in evaluating the purchase of $100,000 of equipment having a 4-year useful life:

	Net Income	Net Cash Flow
Year 1	$15,000	$40,000
Year 2	15,000	40,000
Year 3	5,000	30,000
Year 4	5,000	30,000

(a) Assuming that the desired rate of return is 15%, determine the excess (deficiency) of present value over the amount to be invested for the proposal. Use the table of the present value of 1 appearing in this chapter. (b) Would management be likely to look with favor on the proposal? Explain.

22–21. Berliner Company has computed the excess of present value over the amount to be invested for capital expenditure proposals G and H, using the discounted cash flow method. Relevant data related to the computation are as follows:

	Proposal G	Proposal H
Total present value of net cash flow	$520,000	$824,000
Amount to be invested	500,000	800,000
Excess of present value over amount to be invested	20,000	24,000

Determine the present value index for each proposal.

22–22. Walsh Company is considering the acquisition of machinery at a cost of $200,000. The machinery has an estimated life of 4 years and no residual value. It is expected to provide yearly income of $30,000 and yearly net cash flows of $80,000. The company's minimum desired rate of return for discounted cash flow analysis is 15%. Compute the following:

(a) The average rate of return, giving effect to straight-line depreciation on the investment.
(b) The cash payback period.
(c) The excess (deficiency) of present value over the amount to be invested, as determined by the discounted cash flow method. Use the table of the present value of 1 appearing in this chapter.

22–23. The discounted internal rate of return method is used by Herr Company in analyzing a capital expenditure proposal that involves an investment of $500,000 and annual net cash flows of $138,700 for each of the 5 years of useful life. (a) Determine a "present value factor for an annuity of 1" which can be used in determining the discounted internal rate of return. (b) Using the factor determined in (a) and the present value of an annuity of 1 table appearing in this chapter, determine the discounted internal rate of return for the proposal.

22–24. Vance and Vance Inc. is evaluating a proposed expenditure of $151,850 on a 4-year project whose estimated net cash flows are $50,000 for each of the four years.

(a) Compute the excess (deficiency) of present value over the amount to be invested, using the discounted cash flow method and an assumed rate of return of

10%. (b) Based on the analysis prepared in (a), is the rate of return (1) more than 10%, (2) 10%, or (3) less than 10%? Explain. (c) Determine the discounted internal rate of return by computing a "present value factor for an annuity of 1" and using the table of the present value of an annuity of 1 presented in the text.

Problems

22–25. The capital investments budget committee is considering two projects. The estimated operating income and net cash flows from each project are as follows:

	Project A		Project B	
Year	Operating Income	Net Cash Flow	Operating Income	Net Cash Flow
1	$12,000	$ 40,000	$10,800	$ 24,000
2	9,000	30,000	10,800	24,000
3	6,000	20,000	7,200	36,000
4	6,000	20,000	3,600	24,000
5	3,000	6,000	3,600	8,000
Total	$36,000	$116,000	$36,000	$116,000

Each project requires an investment of $80,000, with no residual value expected. The committee has selected a rate of 12% for purposes of the discounted cash flow analysis.

Instructions:

(1) Compute the following:
  (a) The average rate of return for each project, giving effect to straight-line depreciation on the investment.
  (b) The excess (deficiency) of present value over the amount to be invested, as determined by the discounted cash flow method for each project. Use the present value of 1 table appearing in this chapter.
(2) Prepare a brief report for the budget committee, advising it on the relative merits of the two projects.

22–26. Jefferson Company is considering two projects. The estimated net cash flows from each project are as follows:

Year	Project P	Project Q
1	$250,000	$ 50,000
2	150,000	150,000
3	100,000	300,000
4	100,000	150,000
5	100,000	50,000
Total	$700,000	$700,000

Each project requires an investment of $500,000, with no residual value expected. A rate of 15% has been selected for the discounted cash flow analysis.

Instructions:

    (1) Compute the following for each project:

        (a) Cash payback period.

        (b) The excess (deficiency) of present value over the amount to be invested, as determined by the discounted cash flow method. Use the present value of 1 table appearing in this chapter.

    (2) Prepare a brief report advising management on the relative merits of each of the two projects.

22–27. Murphy Company wishes to evaluate three capital investment proposals by using the discounted cash flow method. Relevant data related to the proposals are summarized as follows:

	Proposal X	Proposal Y	Proposal Z
Amount to be invested............	$200,000	$200,000	$300,000
Annual net cash flows:			
Year 1........................	90,000	120,000	150,000
Year 2........................	80,000	90,000	140,000
Year 3........................	60,000	60,000	120,000

Instructions:

    (1) Assuming that the desired rate of return is 15%, prepare a discounted cash flow analysis for each proposal. Use the present value of 1 table appearing in this chapter.

    (2) Determine a present value index for each proposal.

    (3) Which proposal offers the largest amount of present value per dollar of investment? Explain.

22–28. Management is considering two capital investment proposals. The estimated net cash flows from each proposal are as follows:

Year	Proposal I	Proposal II
1	$120,000	$40,000
2	120,000	40,000
3	120,000	40,000
4	120,000	40,000

    Proposal I requires an investment of $364,400 while Proposal II requires an investment of $114,200. No residual value is expected from either proposal.

Instructions:

    (1) Compute the following for each proposal:

        (a) The excess (deficiency) of present value over the amount to be invested, as determined by the discounted cash flow method. Use a rate of 10% and the present value of 1 table appearing in this chapter.

        (b) A present value index.

    (2) Determine the discounted internal rate of return for each proposal by (a) computing a "present value factor for an annuity of 1" and (b) using the present value of an annuity of 1 table appearing in this chapter.

    (3) What advantage does the discounted internal rate of return method have over the discounted cash flow method in comparing proposals?

22-29. Using the discounted cash flow method, the accountant for Collins Company prepared the following analysis of a project expected to be undertaken during Year 1:

Year	Present Value of 1 at 15%	Net Cash Flow	Present Value of Net Cash Flow
1	.870	$ 80,000	$ 69,600
2	.756	115,000	86,940
3	.658	130,000	85,540
4	.572	100,000	57,200
Total		$425,000	$299,280

Amount to be invested 300,000

Deficiency of present value over amount to be invested. . $ 720

A review of the analysis and related items disclosed the following:
(a) The straight-line method was used for computing depreciation, with one half of a year's depreciation taken in the first year and the fourth year.
(b) Operating income (and net cash flow) before depreciation and taxes is expected to be $110,000, $130,000, $160,000, and $150,000 for the first through fourth years, respectively.
(c) The income tax rate is 50%.
(d) Although the project qualifies for a 6% investment tax credit, the credit was not considered in the analysis.

Instructions:
(1) Assuming the use of the straight-line depreciation method with a 3-year life, no residual value, and no investment credit, compute the following:
   (a) Amount of depreciation expense for each of the four years covered by the project.
   (b) Income tax expense for each of the four years covered by the project.
   (c) Net cash flow for each of the four years covered by the project. (Note: The net cash flows calculated should agree with those included in the analysis presented in the first paragraph of this problem.)
(2) Compute the following:
   (a) Investment tax credit available for the project.
   (b) Depreciation expense for each of the four years covered by the project, assuming that the investment tax credit is taken and the 3-year-class ACRS depreciation rates appearing in this chapter are used.
   (c) Income tax expense for each of the four years, based on the use of ACRS depreciation and the investment tax credit.
   (d) Net cash flow for each of the four years covered by the project, based on the income tax expense computed in (c).
   (e) The excess (deficiency) of present value over the amount to be invested, based on the net cash flows determined in (d) and as determined by the discounted cash flow method. Use the present value of 1 table appearing in this chapter and round computations to the nearest dollar.
(3) Should the project be accepted? Explain.

22–30. The investment committee of Tyler Company is evaluating two projects. The projects have different useful lives, but each requires an investment of $100,000. The estimated net cash flows from each project are as follows:

| | Net Cash Flows | |
Year	Project Y	Project Z
1	$40,000	$30,000
2	40,000	30,000
3	40,000	30,000
4	40,000	30,000
5	0	30,000
6	0	30,000

The committee has selected a rate of 15% for purposes of discounted cash flow analysis. It also estimates that the residual value at the end of each project's useful life is $0, but at the end of the fourth year, Project Z's residual value would be $60,000.

Instructions:

(1) For each project, compute the excess (deficiency) of present value over the amount to be invested, as determined by the discounted cash flow method. Use the present value of 1 table appearing in this chapter. (Ignore the unequal lives of the projects.)

(2) For each project, compute the excess (deficiency) of present value over the amount to be invested, as determined by the discounted cash flow method, assuming that Project Z is adjusted to a four-year life for purposes of analysis. Use the present value of 1 table appearing in this chapter.

(3) In reporting to the investment committee, what advice would you give on the relative merits of the two projects?

Alternate Problems

22–25A. The capital investments budget committee is considering two projects. The estimated operating income and net cash flows from each project are as follows:

| | Project A | | Project B | |
Year	Operating Income	Net Cash Flow	Operating Income	Net Cash Flow
1	$19,950	$ 60,000	$28,000	$ 75,000
2	13,300	60,000	14,000	75,000
3	13,300	50,000	14,000	50,000
4	13,300	30,000	7,000	20,000
5	10,150	30,000	7,000	10,000
Total	$70,000	$230,000	$70,000	$230,000

Each project requires an investment of $160,000, with no residual value expected. The committee has selected a rate of 15% for purposes of the discounted cash flow analysis.

Instructions:

    (1) Compute the following:

        (a) The average rate of return for each project, giving effect to straight-line depreciation on the investment.

        (b) The excess (deficiency) of present value over the amount to be invested, as determined by the discounted cash flow method for each project. Use the present value of 1 table appearing in this chapter.

    (2) Prepare a brief report for the budget committee, advising it on the relative merits of the two projects.

22-26A. Berra Company is considering two projects. The estimated net cash flows from each project are as follows:

Year	Project X	Project Y
1	$ 25,000	$100,000
2	75,000	100,000
3	150,000	50,000
4	50,000	50,000
5	50,000	50,000
Total	$350,000	$350,000

    Each project requires an investment of $250,000, with no residual value expected. A rate of 12% has been selected for the discounted cash flow analysis.

Instructions:

    (1) Compute the following for each project:

        (a) Cash payback period.

        (b) The excess (deficiency) of present value over the amount to be invested, as determined by the discounted cash flow method. Use the present value of 1 table appearing in this chapter.

    (2) Prepare a brief report advising management on the relative merits of each of the two projects.

22-27A. W. J. Atlantis Company is evaluating three capital investment projects by using the discounted cash flow method. Relevant data related to the projects are summarized as follows:

	Project A	Project B	Project C
Amount to be invested.....	$400,000	$800,000	$400,000
Annual net cash flows:			
Year 1.................	300,000	500,000	100,000
Year 2.................	200,000	400,000	200,000
Year 3.................	100,000	300,000	300,000

Instructions:

    (1) Assuming that the desired rate of return is 20%, prepare a discounted cash flow analysis for each project. Use the present value of 1 table appearing in this chapter.

    (2) Determine a present value index for each project.

    (3) Which project offers the largest amount of present value per dollar of investment? Explain.

22–28A. Management is considering two capital investment projects. The estimated net cash flows from each project are as follows:

Year	Project A	Project B
1	$60,000	$180,000
2	60,000	180,000
3	60,000	180,000
4	60,000	180,000

Project A requires an investment of $171,300, while project B requires an investment of $546,600. No residual value is expected from either project.

Instructions:

(1) Compute the following for each project:
   (a) The excess (deficiency) of present value over the amount to be invested, as determined by the discounted cash flow method. Use a rate of 10% and the present value of 1 table appearing in this chapter.
   (b) A present value index.
(2) Determine the discounted internal rate of return for each project by (a) computing a "present value factor for an annuity of 1" and (b) using the present value of an annuity of 1 table appearing in this chapter.
(3) What advantage does the discounted internal rate of return method have over the discounted cash flow method in comparing projects?

Mini-Case

22–31. Your father is considering an investment of $200,000 in either Project A or Project B. In discussing the two projects with an advisor, it was decided that, for the risk involved, a return of 15% on the cash investment would be required. For this purpose, your father estimated the following economic factors for the projects:

	Project A	Project B
Useful life......................................	4 years	4 years
Residual value	–0–	–0–
Net income:		
Year 1	$40,000	$10,000
2	20,000	20,000
3	10,000	20,000
4	6,000	30,000
Net cash flows:		
Year 1	$90,000	$60,000
2	70,000	70,000
3	60,000	70,000
4	56,000	80,000

Although the average rate of return exceeded 15% on both projects, your father has tentatively decided to invest in Project B because the rate was higher for Project B. Although he doesn't fully understand the importance of cash flow, he has heard others talk about its importance in evaluating investments. In this respect, he noted that the total net cash flow from Project B is $280,000, which exceeds that from Project A by $4,000.

Instructions:

    (1) Determine the average rate of return for both projects.

    (2) How would you explain the importance of net cash flows in the analysis of investment projects? Include a specific example to demonstrate the importance of net cash flows and their timing to these two projects.

1. C Methods of evaluating capital investment proposals that ignore the time value of money are categorized as methods that ignore present value. This category includes the average rate of return method (answer A) and the cash payback method (answer B).

2. B The average rate of return is 24% (answer B), determined by dividing the expected average annual earnings by the average investment, as indicated below:

$$\frac{\$60,000 \div 5}{(\$100,000 + \$0) \div 2} = 24\%$$

3. B Of the three methods of analyzing proposals for capital investments, the cash payback method (answer B) refers to the expected period of time required to recover the amount of cash to be invested. The average rate of return method (answer A) is a measure of the anticipated profitability of a proposal. The discounted cash flow method (answer C) reduces the expected future net cash flows originating from a proposal to their present values.

4. C The discounted cash flow method (answer C) uses the concept of present value to determine the total present value of the cash flows expected from a proposal and compares this value with the amount to be invested. The average rate of return method (answer A) and the cash payback method (answer B) ignore present value. The discounted internal rate of return method (answer D) uses the present value concept to determine the discounted internal rate of return expected from the proposal.

5. A Capital rationing (answer A) is the process by which management allocates available investment funds among competing capital investment proposals. Capital expenditure budgeting (answer B) is the process of summarizing the decisions that have been made for the acquisition of plant assets and preparing a capital expenditures budget to reflect these decisions. Leasing (answer C) is an alternative that management should consider before making a final decision on the acquisition of assets.

CHAPTER 23

Income Taxes and Their Impact on Management Decisions

CHAPTER OBJECTIVES

Describe the federal income tax system and the basic components and computations for determining federal income taxes.

Describe and illustrate the importance of income taxes in management decision making.

The federal government and more than three fourths of the states levy an income tax. In addition, some of the states permit municipalities or other political subdivisions to levy income taxes. For most businesses, the amount of income tax is a significant cost of operations, and it is often one of the most important factors influencing a business decision.

Since the federal income tax regulations are quite complex, many businesses engage professional tax specialists to assist in minimizing taxes and in reviewing the tax effects of major business proposals. Nevertheless, it is important for management and the managerial accountant to be aware of the possible tax consequences of business decisions and to recognize areas in which tax factors may play an important part. If management and the managerial accountant understand the general concepts, the tax specialist can be consulted about the details and the specifics of the tax.

For many reasons, Congress frequently changes the tax laws. For example, the laws may be changed to increase revenues, encourage employment, stimulate economic growth, or help control inflation. Although the current law should be examined before decisions are made, the following discussion should be useful in demonstrating the essential characteristics of the tax system and its effect on business decisions. For demonstration purposes, the explanations and illustrations are brief and relatively free of the many complexities encountered in actual practice.

FEDERAL INCOME TAX SYSTEM

The income tax is not imposed upon business units as such, but upon taxable entities. The principal taxable entities are individuals, corporations, estates, and trusts. Business enterprises organized as sole proprietorships are not taxable entities. The revenues and expenses of such business enterprises are reported in the individual tax returns of the owners. Partnerships are not taxable entities but are required to report in an informational return the details of their revenues, expenses, and allocations to partners. The partners then report on their individual tax returns the amount of net income and other special items allocated to them on the partnership return.

Corporations engaged in business for profit are generally treated as distinct taxable entities. However, it is possible for two or more corporations with common ownership to join in filing a consolidated return. The federal tax laws also permit a nonpublic corporation that conforms to specified requirements to elect to be treated in a manner similar to a partnership. The effect of the election is to tax the shareholders on their distributive shares of the net income instead of taxing the corporation.

INCOME TAX RATES

The federal tax regulations generally provide for a graduated series of tax rates; that is, successively higher rates are applied to successively higher segments of taxable income. Because of this progression of rates, the income tax is sometimes termed a **progressive tax.** This characteristic is illustrated by both the corporate tax rates and the rates for a married couple filing a joint return, as follows:

CORPORATE INCOME TAX RATES

Taxable Income	Tax Rate
$0 − $25,000	15%
Over $25,000 − $50,000	18%
Over $50,000 − $75,000	30%
Over $75,000 − $100,000	40%
Over $100,000	46%

TAX RATE SCHEDULE FOR MARRIED PERSONS FILING JOINTLY

If taxable income is:				The tax is:	
Not over $3,400				−0−	
Over—	But not over—				of the amount over—
$ 3,400	$ 5,500	. . . .		11%	$ 3,400
5,500	7,600	$ 231	+	12%	5,500
7,600	11,900	483	+	14%	7,600
11,900	16,000	1,085	+	16%	11,900
16,000	20,200	1,741	+	18%	16,000
20,200	24,600	2,497	+	22%	20,200
24,600	29,900	3,465	+	25%	24,600
29,900	35,200	4,790	+	28%	29,900
35,200	45,800	6,274	+	33%	35,200
45,800	60,000	9,772	+	38%	45,800
60,000	85,600	15,168	+	42%	60,000
85,600	109,400	25,920	+	45%	85,600
109,400	162,400	36,630	+	49%	109,400
162,400	. . . .	62,600	+	50%	162,400

The highest rate applied to the income of any particular taxpayer is sometimes called the taxpayer's marginal tax rate. For a corporate taxpayer with taxable income of $80,000, the marginal tax rate is 40%. For this corporation, the last dollar of income was taxed at the 40% rate and any additional income, up to $100,000, would be taxed at 40%. Likewise, if a corporation's taxable income exceeds $100,000, the marginal tax rate is 46%.

The use of the marginal tax rate, which is the rate of tax on the increase in income, enables management to consider the impact of income tax on proposed courses of action. For example, a corporation with a marginal tax rate of 46% would gain 54% from any increase in income, after tax. If a proposed course of action is expected to result in incremental income of $100,000 before tax, the income after tax will be $54,000 ($100,000 × 54%).

The same analysis would be applied to the evaluation of the tax effect of a potential expense or loss. For example, if a corporation with a marginal tax rate of 46% is considering the expenditure of $10,000, it would view the aftertax cost as being $5,400 ($10,000 less the tax savings of $4,600).

ILLUSTRATIONS OF IMPACT OF INCOME TAXES ON DECISION MAKING

The importance of income tax on various business decisions has been mentioned in previous chapters. For example, the impact of the income tax on capital investment proposals and equipment replacement proposals has been discussed. The remainder of this chapter is devoted to illustrations of the importance of income tax considerations on management decision making, including various legal means of minimizing federal income tax.

Form of Business Organization

One of the most important considerations in selecting the form of organization to use in operating a business enterprise is the impact of the federal income tax. If a business is a sole proprietorship, income must be reported on the owner's personal income tax return. In a partnership, each individual partner is taxed on the distributive share of the business income in much the same manner as a sole proprietor. If the business is incorporated, the corporation must pay an income tax on its earnings. When the remaining earnings are distributed in the form of dividends, they are taxed to the owners (shareholders).

The double taxation feature of the corporation form might seem to outweigh any possible advantages of using it for a family enterprise or other nonpublic business. This is not necessarily the case, however. For most business enterprises, there are likely to be both advantages and disadvantages in the corporate form. Among the many factors that need to be considered are the following: (1) amount of net income, (2) changes in net income from year to year, (3) disposition of aftertax income (withdrawn from the enterprise or used for expansion), (4) method of financing, (5) number of owners and shares of ownership, and (6) the owners' income from other sources. The type of analysis needed to appraise the relative merits of alternative forms of organization is described in the following paragraphs.

For purposes of illustration, assume that a taxpayer and spouse are engaged in a business partnership and are considering incorporation. The business, in which personal services and capital investment are material income-producing factors, has been yielding income of $77,000 before income tax. The other investments and allowable tax deductions result in a net addition of $16,000 to the income of the taxpayers, making a total taxable income of $93,000 ($77,000 + $16,000). The partners' business withdrawals of $50,000 a year would be treated as salary expense if the enterprise were incorporated. The federal income tax consequences under the partnership and corporate forms of organization are as follows:

Organized as a Partnership

Tax on individuals:		
Business income...	$77,000	
Other items...	16,000	
Taxable income.......................................	$93,000	
Income tax liability:		
On $85,600..	$25,920	
On $7,400 at 45%....................................	3,330	
Total income tax—partnership form......................		$29,250

Organized as a Corporation

Tax on corporation:		
Taxable income ($77,000 − $50,000 salary expense).....	$27,000	
Income tax liability:		
On $25,000 at 15%....................................	$ 3,750	
On $2,000 at 18%....................................	360	$ 4,110
Tax on individuals:		
Salary...	$50,000	
Other items...	16,000	
Taxable income.......................................	$66,000	
Income tax liability:		
On $60,000..	$15,168	
On $6,000 at 42%....................................	2,520	17,688
Total income tax—corporation form......................		$21,798

Comparison of the two tax liabilities indicates an annual tax savings of $7,452 ($29,250 − $21,798) by using the corporate form. However, the possible distribution of the corporation's net income as dividends was not taken into consideration. If the corporation's aftertax income of $22,890 ($27,000 − $4,110) were paid as dividends to the owners, their taxable income would total $88,890 ($66,000 + $22,890) instead of $66,000.[1] This would result in a personal income tax of $31,510.50, computed as follows:

<u>Organized as a Corporation—Aftertax Income Distributed as Dividend</u>

Tax on corporation (as previously computed)......		$ 4,110.00
Tax on individuals:		
Salary.....................................	$50,000.00	
Other items................................	16,000.00	
Dividends	22,890.00	
Taxable income............................	$88,890.00	
Income tax liability:		
On $85,600...............................	$25,920.00	
On $3,290 at 45%........................	1,480.50	27,400.50
Total tax		$31,510.50

If the corporation's aftertax income is distributed as dividends, the total income tax would be $31,510.50, or $2,260.50 more than the total income tax under the partnership form ($31,510.50 − $29,250). In other words, the resulting increase of $9,712.50 ($27,400.50 − $17,688) in the personal income tax would convert the expected $7,452 advantage of the corporate form to a $2,260.50 disadvantage.

Another factor to consider in the analysis is the possibility that earnings accumulated by a corporation may be subject to an accumulated earnings tax. Ordinarily, accumulations up to $250,000 are exempt from this tax. Additional accumulations are subject to the accumulated earnings tax unless it can be proved that they are not in excess of the reasonable needs of the business. The tax rate is 27.5% of the first $100,000 of accumulated taxable income and 38.5% of the excess over $100,000. If additional accumulations are beyond the reasonable needs of the business and the corporation meets certain requirements of the tax laws, the shareholders might then elect partnership treatment and thus avoid the double tax on corporate earnings. Additional information about the intentions of the owners and prospects for the future would be needed to explore additional ramifications of the problem.

Earnings accumulated by the corporation in the foregoing example might at some future time become available to the stockholders through sale of their stock. They would thus be converted into long-term capital gains, which are generally taxable at lower rates than ordinary income. (Capital gains are discussed in a later section.)

The purpose of the above discussion was to indicate that the best form of organization from the standpoint of the federal income tax can be determined only by a detailed analysis of the particular situation. Generalizations are likely to be of little benefit and may even be misleading. The impact of state and local taxes also varies according to the form of business organization, and the

---

[1]For the sake of simplicity, this example is based on the assumption that the dividend exclusion available to individual taxpayers does not apply.

importance of such nontax factors as limited liability and transferability of ownership should be considered.

Choice Between Accounting Principles

There are many cases in which an enterprise may choose from among two or more optional accounting principles in determining the amount of income tax. The particular principle chosen may have a great effect on the amount of income tax, not only in the year in which the choice is made but also in later years. Examples of such cases, described in the following paragraphs, are cash versus accrual methods of accounting, alternate methods of determining cost of inventory, accelerated cost recovery method of determining depreciation, installment method of recognizing sales revenue, and completed-contract method of recognizing income from long-term construction projects.

Accounting Methods

In general, taxpayers have the option of using either the cash method or the accrual method of accounting. Under the cash method, revenues are not considered to be earned until payment is received. Similarly, expenses are recorded only at the time of cash payment. Generally, however, it is not permissible to treat the entire cost of long-lived assets as an expense of the period in which the cash payment is made. Deductions for depreciation on equipment and buildings used for business purposes may be claimed in the same manner as under the accrual basis, regardless of when payment is made. Similarly, when advance payments for insurance premiums or rentals on business property exceed a period of one year, the total cost must be prorated over the life of the contract.

For businesses in which production or trading in merchandise is an important factor, purchases and sales must be accounted for on the accrual basis. Thus, revenues from sales must be reported in the year in which the goods are sold, regardless of when the cash is received. Similarly, the cost of goods purchased or manufactured must be reported in the year in which the liabilities are incurred, regardless of when payment is made. The usual adjustments must also be made for the beginning and ending inventories in order to determine the cost of goods sold and the gross profit.

Business organizations that regularly have taxable incomes so that they have a marginal tax rate at the highest tax rate are unlikely to be greatly affected by their choice of the cash or accrual method of accounting. For example, corporations that regularly have taxable income in excess of $100,000, and thus have a marginal tax rate of 46%, are unlikely to be greatly affected by the choice of accounting method. On the other hand, a small corporation whose taxable income tends to fluctuate above and below $100,000 from year to year may be better able to control the fluctuation if the cash method is used. For example, near the end of a taxable year in which taxable income is likely to exceed $100,000, some of the excess which will be subject to the tax rate of 46% may be shifted to the following year when the marginal rate may be less than 46%. It may be possible to postpone the receipt of gross income by delayed billings for services, or expenses may be increased by payment of outstanding bills before the end of the year. The timing of expenditures and payments for such expenses as redecorating, repairs, and advertising may also be readily subject to control.

Inventory Methods

Basically the tax law permits the enterprise to choose its method of determining the cost of inventory. Two widely used methods are fifo (first-in, first-out) and lifo (last-in, first-out). The more traditional method is fifo, while the more widely used method is lifo. The method chosen may have a significant effect on income and the tax on income in periods of changing price levels.

Under fifo, the first goods purchased during a year are assumed to be the first goods sold. During a period of rising prices, the first goods purchased are the least costly. If the least costly goods are sold, they are charged against revenue, and the most costly goods are included in inventory. Under lifo, however, the last goods purchased during a year are assumed to be the first goods sold. During a period of rising prices, the last goods purchased are the most costly. If the most costly goods are sold, they are charged against revenue, and the least costly goods are included in inventory. Thus, in periods of rising prices, lifo results in a higher cost of goods sold, lower income, and lower taxes than fifo.

To illustrate the effect of fifo and lifo on the cost of goods sold and gross profit (and consequently net income and income taxes) in a period of rising prices, assume the following activity for a year for a firm that sells one product:

Sales, 1,000 units at $200	$200,000
Beginning inventory, 500 units at $150	75,000
Purchases, 1,000 units at $160	160,000
Ending inventory, 500 units	—

The effect of using fifo and lifo on the year's gross profit is as follows:

	Fifo		Lifo	
Sales		$200,000		$200,000
Cost of goods sold:				
Beginning inventory	$ 75,000		$ 75,000	
Purchases	160,000		160,000	
Goods available for sale	$235,000		$235,000	
Ending inventory:				
500 units at $160	80,000			
500 units at $150			75,000	
Cost of goods sold		155,000		160,000
Gross profit		$ 45,000		$ 40,000

Under fifo, the 1,000 units sold include the 500 in beginning inventory at $150, or $75,000, plus 500 of those purchased at $160, or $80,000, for a total of $155,000. Under lifo, the 1,000 units sold would be the 1,000 purchased at $160, or $160,000. Thus, using lifo results in a $5,000 higher cost of goods sold (and lower gross profit). From another view, the $5,000 difference in gross profit can be viewed as the difference in the ending inventory amounts ($80,000 − $75,000).

The income tax effect of using fifo versus lifo during periods of declining prices would be the reverse of that illustrated. During periods of declining prices, gross profit (and net income and income taxes) under lifo would exceed that of fifo.

In times of inflation, which has been the long-term trend in the United States since World War II, the use of lifo not only results in a lower annual income tax, but it also permits the taxpayer to retain more funds, by lowering tax payments, to replace goods sold with higher-priced goods. Clearly, this advantage is one of the most important reasons for lifo's popularity.

Depreciation

In the preceding chapter, the effect of using the Accelerated Cost Recovery System (ACRS) in evaluating capital investment proposals was discussed and illustrated. ACRS can also be used to determine the annual depreciation expense deduction for tax purposes to realize a short-run saving in taxes. The accelerated write-off of depreciable assets provided by ACRS does not, however, effect a long-run net savings in income tax. The accelerated tax deductions provided by the use of ACRS in the early years of an asset's life are offset by lower deductions in the later years.

ACRS provides for depreciation that approximates the use of the 150%-declining-balance method and permits the use of asset lives that are often much shorter than actual useful lives. ACRS generally provides for three classes of useful life for most business property (3-year, 5-year, and 19-year classes). The 3-year class includes automobiles, light-duty trucks, and some special tools. Most machinery and equipment is included in the 5-year class, while buildings fall in the 19-year class. Tables are available that indicate the annual percentages to be used in determining depreciation for each class. In using these percentages, salvage value is ignored, and a full year's percentage is allowed for the year of acquisition. The following schedule indicates the ACRS depreciation rates for the 3-year and 5-year classes:

Year	3-Year-Class Assets	5-Year-Class Assets	
1	25%	15%	ACRS DEPRECIATION RATE SCHEDULE
2	38	22	
3	37	21	
4		21	
5		21	
	100%	100%	

To illustrate the effect of the use of ACRS on income taxes, assume that $90,000 of special tools that qualify as ACRS 3-year-class assets are acquired in the middle of year 1. The tools have a 3-year life for tax purposes and no residual value, and the straight-line method of depreciation is used for book purposes. Although the straight-line method could be elected for tax purposes (in which case only one-half year's depreciation would be available for the year of acquisition and disposal), it is advantageous to use the ACRS rates, as illustrated by the following tabulation:

	Annual Depreciation Deduction			
	Year 1	Year 2	Year 3	Year 4
ACRS depreciation:				
Year 1: $90,000 × 25%..............	$22,500			
Year 2: $90,000 × 38%..............		$34,200		
Year 3: $90,000 × 37%..............			$33,300	
Year 4:				——
Straight-line depreciation:				
Year 1: ($90,000 ÷ 3) × 1/2.........	15,000			
Year 2: $90,000 ÷ 3		30,000		
Year 3: $90,000 ÷ 3			30,000	
Year 4: ($90,000 ÷ 3) × 1/2........				$15,000
Excess (deficiency) of ACRS over straight-line........................	$ 7,500	$ 4,200	$ 3,300	($15,000)

Although the depreciation deduction is the same over the four-year period, $15,000 ($7,500 + $4,200 + $3,300) more depreciation is allowable under ACRS during the first 3 years. During the last year, $15,000 more depreciation would be available under the straight-line method. The ability to delay cash payments for income taxes means that the taxpayer can retain funds longer, and these funds can be invested to earn income, used to reduce debt and thus save on interest costs, or used for some other purpose.

The possibility of adverse changes in tax rates in future years is a factor that must be considered in evaluating the use of ACRS. However, the additional funds made available in the early years of the life of an asset are usually considered to be advantageous enough to justify the use of ACRS for income tax purposes.

Installment Method

Although the point of sale method is used for recognizing income from most sales, the installment method of determining income from merchandise sold on the installment plan is widely used for income tax purposes. To illustrate the savings that may result from the use of the installment method for tax purposes, assume that a company with a marginal tax rate of 46% added a new product line during the year. The installment method may be used to report income from the new line. The data on the first year of sales are as follows (for purposes of illustration, the gross profit for this product is assumed to be taxable income):

Installment sales	$500,000
Cost of installment sales	350,000
Gross profit on installment sales (30% of sales).	$150,000

Collection of installment sales:

First year.	$200,000
Second year.	200,000
Third year	100,000

Using the point of sale method of reporting income, the tax for the first year would be $69,000 ($150,000 gross profit × 46%). Using the installment sales method of reporting income, the tax would still be $69,000, but it would be spread over the three years during which the collections were made, as follows:

	Year 1	Year 2	Year 3	Total Tax
Point of sale method:				
Gross profit.	$150,000	—	—	
Marginal tax rate	× 46%	—	—	
Income tax	$ 69,000	—	—	$69,000
Installment method:				
Gross profit (collections × rate of gross profit):				
$200,000 × 30%.	$ 60,000			
200,000 × 30%.		$60,000		
100,000 × 30%.			$30,000	
Marginal tax rate	× 46%	× 46%	× 46%	
Income tax	$ 27,600	$27,600	$13,800	$69,000

Only $27,600 of tax would be due at the end of the first year if the installment method is used. At the end of the second year, no additional tax would be payable if the point of sale method is used, but $27,600 would be payable if the installment method is used. Likewise, the remaining tax of $13,800 would be payable at the end of the third year if the installment method is used. Although the same amount of tax is payable under both methods, management postpones payment of a portion of the total tax by using the installment method. As explained in preceding sections, cash payments that can be delayed are more valuable than cash payments due currently, since money saved can be invested, or interest on borrowing can be reduced.

Long-Term Construction Contracts

Companies engaged in large construction projects may devote several years to the completion of a particular contract. In such cases, the company can use either the percentage-of-completion method or the completed-contract method for reporting income. Under the **percentage-of-completion method,** income on a contract is recognized over the life of the contract. Under the **completed-contract method,** income is recognized when the project is completed. In either case, the total amount of income for a contract would be the same.

As illustrated in the preceding section, it is advantageous to employ the method that enables the company to postpone the payment of as much of the tax as possible. Therefore, regardless of the method used in preparing the published financial statements, the completed-contract method should be used for reporting income taxes. To illustrate, assume that a taxpayer had a project that took three years to complete, the contract price was $3,000,000, and the construction activities for the three years were as follows:

Year	Costs Incurred	Percent Completed
1	$ 525,000	20%
2	1,075,000	40
3	1,100,000	40

The taxable income reported for each of the three years under the percentage-of-completion and completed-contract methods would be as follows:

	Years			
	1	2	3	Total
Percentage-of-completion method:				
Year 1:				
Revenue (20% × $3,000,000) ..	$600,000			
Costs	525,000			
Year 2:				
Revenue (40% × $3,000,000) ..		$1,200,000		
Costs		1,075,000		
Year 3:				
Revenue (40% × $3,000,000)...			$1,200,000	
Costs			1,100,000	
Taxable income................	$ 75,000	$ 125,000	$ 100,000	$300,000
Completed-contract method:				
Year 3:				
Revenue			$3,000,000	
Costs ($525,000 + $1,075,000 + $1,100,000)................			2,700,000	
Taxable income................			$ 300,000	$300,000

The taxable income from the project over the three years is $300,000. However, none of the income is reported as taxable income until the project is completed under the completed-contract method. A portion of the

$300,000—$75,000, $125,000, and $100,000—would be reported in each of the three years, respectively, using the percentage-of-completion method. As explained in the preceding section, the delay of cash payments means that the company can retain funds longer, and these funds can be invested to earn income or can be used to reduce debt and thus save on interest costs.

Capital Gains and Losses

Gains and losses resulting from individuals selling or exchanging certain types of assets, called **capital assets,** are given special treatment for income tax purposes. Capital assets most commonly owned by taxpayers are stocks and bonds. Under certain conditions, land, buildings, and equipment used in business may also be treated as capital assets.

The gains and losses from the sale or exchange of capital assets are classified as **short-term** or **long-term,** based on the length of time the assets are held (owned). The holding period for short-term gains and losses is six months or less. For long-term gains and losses, the holding period is more than six months.

The aggregate of all short-term gains and losses during a taxable year is called a **net short-term capital gain** (or **loss**) and the aggregate of all long-term gains and losses is similarly identified as a **net long-term capital gain** (or **loss**). The net short-term and net long-term results are then combined to form the **net capital gain** (or **loss**).

For both individuals and corporations, capital gains and losses are accorded special treatment. Although there are some differences in the treatment of capital gains and losses between individuals and corporations, the significance of this special treatment for management decision making is illustrated in the following paragraphs.

Capital Gains

In general, net short-term capital gains are taxed at ordinary rates. Net long-term capital gains are given preferential treatment, with the result that they are often subject to lower rates than those applicable to ordinary income. For a corporation, for example, the maximum tax rate on long-term capital gains is 28%. Thus, for a corporation with a marginal tax rate of 46%, it would be advantageous to convert as much ordinary income as possible to long-term capital gain. To illustrate, assume that a company with a marginal tax rate of 46% is the lessor of a patent (capital asset) which has a zero tax basis. The annual rental income is $100,000, and the total rental income over the patent's remaining life of four years is $400,000. If an offer of $350,000 for the patent is received, it appears that the proposal should be rejected, because the sales price ($350,000) is less than the total income from rentals ($400,000). However, since the gain on the sale of the patent is subject to a maximum tax of 28% and the income from the rental is taxed at 46%, the aftertax income is higher with the sale alternative, shown as follows:

Sale alternative:

Sales price (gain)	$350,000	
Tax, long-term capital gain rate of 28%	98,000	
Net after tax		$252,000

Lease alternative:

Revenue from lease	$400,000	
Tax, marginal rate of 46%	184,000	
Net after tax		216,000
Net advantage of sale alternative		$ 36,000

Although this analysis focuses only on the tax impact of the decision, other factors may also have an effect. One such factor that should be considered is the differential revenue from investing the funds generated by the alternatives.

Capital Losses

Capital losses are deducted from capital gains. If this deduction results in a net capital loss, corporate taxpayers are not permitted to deduct the loss against ordinary income. Corporations may carry back net capital losses to the three preceding years to offset capital gains, and if the total losses are not absorbed, the losses may be carried forward for five years. Thus, if a capital loss is about to expire and therefore be lost as a tax deduction, the corporation should consider selling some capital assets at a gain (to offset the losses) if such assets are available.

Timing of Capital Gains and Losses

The timing of capital gains and losses can usually be controlled because the taxpayer can select the time to sell the capital assets. Delaying a sale by only one day can result in a substantial tax savings. To illustrate, assume that the only sale of a capital asset during the year is the sale of listed stocks that had been held for exactly six months, realizing a gain of $40,000. The gain would be classified as a short-term capital gain and taxed as ordinary income. Assuming that the marginal tax rate is 46%, the tax on the $40,000 gain would be $18,400. Alternatively, if the securities had been held for at least one additional day, the $40,000 gain (assuming no change in selling price) would have qualified as a long-term capital gain, which is subject to a maximum tax of $11,200 (28% of $40,000). Thus, if the sale had occurred at least one day later, there would have been a tax savings of $7,200 ($18,400-$11,200).

When a taxpayer owns various lots of an identical security that were acquired at different dates and at different prices, it may be possible to choose between realizing a gain and realizing a loss, and perhaps to a limited extent to govern the amount realized. For example, a taxpayer who has realized gains from the sale of securities may wish to offset them, in whole or in part, by losses from the sales of other securities. To illustrate, assume that a taxpayer who owns three 100-share lots of common stock in the same corporation, purchased at $40, $48, and $60 a share respectively, plans to sell 100 shares at the current market price of $52. Depending upon which of the three 100-share lots is sold, the taxpayer will realize a gain of $1,200, a gain of $400, or a loss of $800. If the identity of the particular lot sold cannot be determined, the first-in, first-out cost flow assumption must be used. The use of average cost is not permitted.

Use of Corporate Debt

If a corporation is in need of relatively permanent funds, it generally considers borrowing money on a long-term basis or issuing stock. Since interest on debt is a deductible expense in determining taxable income and dividends paid on stock are not, this impact on income tax is one of the important factors to consider in evaluating the two methods of financing. To illustrate, assume that a corporation with a marginal tax rate of 46% is considering issuing (1) $1,000,000 of 10% bonds or (2) $1,000,000 of 10% cumulative preferred stock. If the bonds are issued, the deduction of the yearly $100,000 of interest in determining taxable income results in an annual net borrowing cost of $54,000 ($100,000 less tax savings of 46% of $100,000). If the preferred stock is issued, the dividends are not deductible in determining taxable income and the net annual outlay for this method of financing is $100,000. Thus, issuing bonds instead of preferred stock reduced the annual financing expenditures by $46,000 ($100,000 − $54,000).

Another aspect of evaluating a proposal to use debt instead of stock for financing corporate operations is the impact of the tax on the earnings per share. To illustrate, assume that the corporation is considering the issuance of $1,000,000 of 10% bonds or $1,000,000 of 10% cumulative preferred stock, has 100,000 shares of common stock outstanding, and the income after tax but before interest and preferred dividends is expected to be $400,000 annually. Although there are other factors to consider, the issuance of bonds appears to be more favorable, based on the results of the following calculation of the expected earnings per share on common stock under each possibility:.

	Preferred Stock	Bonds
Income after tax, before interest and preferred dividends..	$400,000	$400,000
Preferred dividends	100,000	
Interest less tax savings [$100,000 − (46% of $100,000)] .		54,000
Remainder—identified with common stock	$300,000	$346,000
Shares of common stock................................	100,000	100,000
Earnings per share on common stock	$3.00	$3.46

Corporate debt can sometimes be used to convert an apparently uneconomical investment into a profitable investment. For example, a corporation with a marginal tax rate of 46% has an opportunity to invest $100,000 in preferred stock yielding 10%. However, it will need to borrow the $100,000 at 15% to make the investment. Although this investment appears to be unattractive, it provides an annual net profit when the effect of income taxes is considered.

When a corporation borrows money, the interest expense is deductible in determining taxable income. The aftertax cost of borrowing is therefore less than the interest expense. Also, when a corporation owns shares of another domestic corporation and receives dividends on the stock, 85% of the dividends received are generally allowed as a special deduction. Thus, only 15% of such dividends are taxable. As shown in the following calculation, the result of a $100,000 investment in preferred stock, financed by debt, is an annual net profit of $1,210:

Dividend income ($100,000 × 10%)		$10,000
Tax on dividend income:		
Dividend	$10,000	
Dividend exclusion	8,500	
Taxable amount	$ 1,500	
Tax rate	× 46%	
Tax		690
Net dividend income after tax		$ 9,310
Interest expense ($100,000 × 15%)		$15,000
Tax savings on interest:		
Interest deduction	$15,000	
Tax rate	× 46%	6,900
Net interest expense after tax		$ 8,100
Net dividend income after tax		$ 9,310
Net interest expense after tax		8,100
Net profit		$ 1,210

Nontaxable Investment Income

Interest on bonds issued by a state or political subdivision is exempt from the federal income tax. Such investments are especially attractive to taxpayers with a high marginal tax rate. To illustrate, the following table compares the income after tax on a $100,000 investment in a 10% industrial bond and a $100,000 investment in a 6% municipal bond for a corporation with a marginal tax rate of 46%.

	Taxable 10% Industrial Bond	Nontaxable 6% Municipal Bond
Income	$10,000	$6,000
Tax (46% of $10,000)	4,600	—
Income after tax	$ 5,400	$6,000

Although the interest rate on the municipal bond (6%) is less than the rate on the industrial bond (10%), the aftertax income is larger from the investment in the municipal bond.

Operating Losses

The net operating loss of a corporation may be used to offset taxable income by being carried back to each of the three preceding years. If the loss is not fully absorbed in those three years, in which case past taxes paid would be refunded, the unused portion may be carried forward to each of the fifteen following years. In addition, this net operating loss carryforward can often be transferred to a successor corporation. Thus, a net operating loss can play an important role in decisions involving the acquisition of one corporation by another. To illustrate, assume that A Corporation with a marginal tax rate of 46%, a profitable past, and a profitable future anticipated is considering the acquisition of Z Company, which has a $1,000,000 operating loss carryforward. Although the operating loss carryforward may be somewhat limited in such cases, one of the factors to be evaluated by A Corporation is the value of the deductibility of the $1,000,000 in computing income tax, should Z Corporation be acquired. For A Corporation, the operating loss carryforward might save $460,000 in future taxes ($1,000,000 $\times$ 46%). As with many aspects of the federal income tax, the rules governing the use of the net operating loss are quite complex and should be consulted before a decision is made.

Investment Tax Credit

As discussed in Chapter 22, the investment tax credit is granted for purchases of certain new or used tangible personal property that has a useful life of at least three years and is used in the taxpayer's trade or business. Since the investment credit is a deduction from the amount of the income tax, it has the effect of lowering the purchase price of the property. Obviously, this lowered price is the relevant cost for evaluating proposed property acquisitions.

The maximum credit is 10% of the cost of property with a life of five years or more and 6% for property with a life of between three and five years. In determining depreciation, the cost of the asset is generally reduced by one half of the amount of the credit. This basic reduction can be avoided if the taxpayer elects to take a smaller investment credit (8% for property with a life of five years or more, 4% for property with a life of between three and five years). Also, the maximum amount of the credit in any year is limited if the potential credit is more than $25,000. Management should therefore consider both the amount of the investment credit and the allowable depreciation in evaluating the best mix of the two in maximizing the return from investments.

Trade Versus Sale of Property

In many cases, especially when ACRS is used for determining depreciation, property that is being replaced has a fair market value that exceeds its book value. If this property is sold, the gain is subject to income tax. On the other hand, if the property is to be replaced with similar property, a trade of the old property for the new property can delay the payment of the tax associated with the gain.

Neither gains nor losses are recognized for income tax purposes when one asset is exchanged for an asset of similar use and cash is paid. Since the trade-in allowance granted by the seller is frequently greater or less than the book value of the asset traded, an unrecognized gain or loss results. To illustrate, assume that old equipment with a book value of $1,000 is to be traded for new equipment with a fair market price of $20,000, and a trade-in allowance of $5,000 is granted for the old equipment. Cash of $15,000 ($20,000 − $5,000) would be paid, and the transaction would result in an unrecognized gain of $4,000 (trade-in allowance of $5,000 less book value of $1,000). The unrecognized gain reduces the basis of the equipment acquired to $16,000 ($20,000 fair market value − $4,000 gain) for tax purposes. The unrecognized gain also decreases the total amount of depreciation allowed for income tax purposes during the life of the equipment. Thus, the same amount of income will be subject to income tax over the life of the property.

From the standpoint of delaying the payment of income tax, it is advantageous to trade property that has a fair market value above book value, rather than sell the old property and purchase the new property. In the previous illustration, if the old equipment is sold for $5,000, a gain of $4,000 would be reported for tax purposes. By trading the equipment, there is no tax on the $4,000 gain at the date of the trade. Instead, the tax will be postponed to future periods, when the depreciation allowed on the new equipment will be reduced by the amount of the gain, or from $20,000 to $16,000.

As in all cases, the amount of the income tax is but one factor to consider in evaluating a proposal. If the equipment in the illustration is sold rather than traded, the amount of tax on the gain, whether the gain is subject to special capital gains treatment, the value of effectively postponing the payment of the tax, the marginal tax rates at the date of the sale or exchange transaction, and the marginal tax rates expected in the future should also be considered.

Contributions of Property Rather Than Cash

Donations to charitable, educational, and other qualifying institutions are generally deductible, up to specified maximum limits, in determining income tax. Donations of property, such as marketable securities, can be more advantageous than donations of cash, if the value of the property has risen since acquisition. The increase in the value of the donated property is not taxed, but the deduction allowed from taxable income is equal to the fair market value of the property. To illustrate, assume that a corporation with a marginal tax rate of 46% wishes to donate $50,000 to a charity, and that it has a capital asset with a cost of $20,000 and a current fair market value of $50,000. If a $50,000 cash gift is given, the net cost to the corporation would be $27,000 ($50,000 donation less tax savings of 46% of $50,000). If the capital asset is sold, an income tax of $8,400 would need to be paid on the gain (classified as long-term), computed as follows:

Sales price.	$50,000
Less cost	20,000
Gain on sale	$30,000
Tax rate for long-term capital gain	× 28%
Tax.	$ 8,400

If the capital asset is sold, only $41,600 ($50,000 − $8,400) is available, after tax, for the contribution. Thus, to make a $50,000 donation, an additional $8,400 would need to be contributed. If the capital asset were donated, the taxpayer would still receive the $50,000 charitable contribution and the charity could sell it for $50,000 without paying an income tax. By donating the property, the taxpayer can save $8,400 without loss of value to the charity.

1. Business enterprises that are treated as taxable entities for federal income tax purposes include:
   A. sole proprietorships   C. corporations
   B. partnerships   D. all of the above

2. The highest tax rate applied to the income of any particular taxpayer is called the:
   A. normal tax rate   C. maximum tax rate
   B. marginal tax rate   D. none of the above

3. In periods of rising prices, the use of lifo (last-in, first-out) instead of fifo (first-in, first-out) for inventory costing results in a:
   A. higher cost of goods sold C. lower income tax
   B. lower net income   D. all of the above

4. A taxpayer may postpone payment of a portion of the income tax by:
   A. using the installment method rather than the point of sale method for reporting sales
   B. using the completed-contract method of reporting income on long-term construction projects rather than the percentage-of-completion method
   C. both A and B
   D. neither A nor B

5. The maximum tax rate on long-term capital gains for a corporation is:
   A. 20%   C. 46%
   B. 28%   D. 50%

Self-Examination Questions (Answers at end of chapter.)

Discussion Questions

23–1. (a) What are the principal taxable entities subject to the federal income tax? (b) How is the income of sole proprietorships and partnerships taxed?

23–2. (a) What is a progressive tax? (b) Is the federal income tax a progressive tax?

23–3. (a) What is meant by the term marginal tax rate? (b) If a corporation has a marginal tax rate of 46%, how much tax would be paid if a proposal were to provide $200,000 of taxable income?

23–4. What is meant by the statement that the income of corporations is subject to double taxation?

23–5. Is it possible that earnings accumulated by a corporation may be subject to an accumulated earnings tax? Explain.

23–6. If the cash method of accounting is used for federal income taxes, is it permissible to deduct payments for the acquisition of long-lived assets as expenses? Explain.

23–7. Which inventory method (lifo or fifo) would result in the lower income tax during a period of rising prices? Explain.

23–8. Is the Accelerated Cost Recovery System (ACRS) for determining depreciation an accelerated method of determining depreciation? Explain.

23–9. For income tax purposes, is it advisable to use the installment method of determining income from merchandise sold on the installment plan? Explain.

23–10. For income tax purposes, is it advantageous to use the percentage-of-completion method for reporting income on long-term construction projects? Explain.

23–11. What criterion distinguishes long-term capital gains or losses from short-term capital gains or losses?

23–12. Are long-term gains from the sale of capital assets taxed at normal tax rates? Discuss.

23–13. If a net capital loss results from deducting capital losses from capital gains, can the net loss be used by a corporation to reduce ordinary income? Discuss.

23–14. During the current year, a taxpayer purchased 100 shares of X stock on January 30 at $40 and 100 shares of X stock on August 1 at $50. If 100 shares are sold on December 10 at $60, what is the amount of the gain on the sale for tax purposes?

23–15. When a corporation owns shares of another domestic corporation and receives dividends on the stock, what percentage of the dividends received is generally taxable?

23–16. A taxpayer with a marginal tax rate of 40% is considering an investment in a 6%, tax-exempt municipal bond. What rate would need to be earned on a taxable bond to yield the same aftertax return as would be earned on the municipal bond investment?

23–17. A corporation has a net operating loss of $100,000 for the current year. How can the loss be used to offset taxable income?

23–18. A taxpayer who has a marginal tax rate of 40% is entitled to an investment tax credit of $25,000. How much will income taxes be reduced by the credit?

23–19. A taxpayer donates an investment in A stock to a charity. If the cost of the stock is $5,000 and its fair market value at the date of the donation is $7,000, what deduction from taxable income is allowed the taxpayer for the donation?

23–20. On April 1 of the current year, Frank Baker began Liquigreen Lawn Service. On December 1, Baker estimated that net income for the current year ending December 31 would be $10,000 by the accrual method, and for the following year it would be $50,000. Liquigreen has no inventory and bills all customers on terms net 30.

    (a) Can Liquigreen Lawn Service use either the cash method or the accrual method for reporting income for tax purposes? Explain.

    (b) Assuming that all of Baker's income is from Liquigreen Lawn Service and the cash method is used, would it be advisable for tax purposes for Baker to consider transferring some net income from the following year to the current year? Explain.

    (c) Determine the maximum amount of income that should be considered for transfer from the following year to the current year. Explain your answer.

    (d) Assuming the use of the cash method, suggest ways in which net income can be transferred from the following year to the current year.

23–21. On January 10 of the current year, Linda Marie Fell opened the Old Fashioned Ice Cream Parlor. During the year, ice cream was purchased at three different prices, as follows:

	Price per Gallon
January 10–May 1	$1.50
May 2–August 20	1.55
August 21–December 31	1.65

    Sales averaged 400 gallons of ice cream per month, and 150 gallons were on hand at December 31.

    (a) Assuming the use of the fifo (first-in, first-out) inventory method, determine the cost of the inventory balance at December 31.

    (b) Assuming the use of the lifo (last-in, first-out) inventory method, determine the cost of the inventory balance at December 31.

    (c) Which inventory method, fifo or lifo, will result in the lower net income, and by how much will the income be lower?

23–22. Cosell Company acquired machinery with a 5-year life and no residual value for $80,000 on July 1, 1985. The machinery qualifies as a 5-year-class asset under ACRS. Determine the excess (or deficiency) of ACRS depreciation over straight-line depreciation for each of the years 1985–1990, applying the ACRS depreciation rate schedule presented in this chapter.

23–23. Fox Corporation, which has never incurred a capital gain or loss, owns 1,000 shares of A Company stock purchased for $100,000 and 500 shares of B Company stock purchased for $250,000. Both stocks qualify as long-term capital assets and can be sold for $300,000 and $50,000, respectively. The Corporation expects to need $250,000 near the end of the current year but foresees no immediate need for additional cash. The long-term capital gains tax rate is 28%, and the Corporation's marginal tax rate is 46%.

    (a) If the A Company stock were sold in the current year, determine the amount of tax that would be owed on the sale.

    (b) If all of the stocks were sold before the end of the current year, determine the amount of tax that would be owed on the sales.

    (c) Discuss why Fox Corporation should consider selling both stocks in the current year, even though only $250,000 is expected to be needed in the current year.

23–24. During the current year, three corporations realized the following income:

	Ordinary Income	Long-Term Capital Gain
Corporation A	$ 10,000	$10,000
Corporation B	20,000	30,000
Corporation C	100,000	50,000

Using the tax rates indicated in the chapter, determine the amount of income tax owed by each corporation.

23–25. A and B are considering the form of organization for their new business. Each will invest $300,000, will devote only part-time to the business, and will receive no salary. Income before tax is expected to be relatively constant at about $150,000 per year. The owners have 50% marginal income tax rates and are expected to make annual withdrawals (or receive dividends) equal to all of the net income (after tax, if applicable) from the business. (a) Determine the amount of cash that will be available to each owner, after taxes, if the business is organized as (1) a partnership (in which income is shared equally among the partners), (2) a corporation. (b) List some of the other factors that should be considered in evaluating the decision.

23–26. Adams Company and Zimmer Company are investigating the acquisition of X Corporation, which has a $25,000 net operating loss carryforward that can be used by both companies. If Adams Company and Zimmer Company have marginal tax rates of 46% and 30% respectively, determine the value of X Corporation's net operating loss carryforward to (a) Adams Company and (b) Zimmer Company.

23–27. Grant Company has 1,000 shares of ICD common stock, which it acquired 10 years ago at $50 per share. The current market price of the stock is $100, Grant Company's marginal tax rate is 46%, and the long-term capital gains maximum tax rate is 28%. (a) Determine the amount of proceeds available to the University of Illinois if (1) the stock is donated to the university and then sold, or (2) the stock is sold by Grant Company, the associated income tax paid, and the proceeds donated to the university. (b) Determine the tax benefits for Grant Company from the deduction of the charitable donation if it (1) donates the stock to the university or (2) sells the stock and donates the aftertax proceeds to the university.

Problems

23–28. Three married individuals, A, B, and C, are engaged in related types of businesses as sole proprietors, but plan to combine their enterprises to form Allen Co. They have discussed the relative merits of the partnership and the corporation forms of organization, exclusive of the effect of the federal income tax. You are engaged to assemble and analyze the relevant data and to determine the immediate income tax consequences to each of them of the two forms of organization. The consolidation is planned to take effect as of January 1, the beginning of the company's fiscal year.

The combined annual net income of the three separate enterprises has typically totaled $150,000. It is anticipated that economies of operation and other advantages of the consolidation will have the immediate effect of increasing annual net income by $30,000, making a total of $180,000 before deducting owners' salaries totaling $90,000.

Each of the owners is to be assigned managerial duties as a partner or, alternatively, be designated an officer of the corporation. In either event, each is to be paid an annual salary, which is to be treated as an operating expense of the enterprise. In addition, they plan to distribute $27,000 of earnings annually, which are to be allocated among them in accordance with their original investments (the income-sharing ratio). It is anticipated that the remaining earnings will be retained for use in expanding operations. The agreed capital investments, salaries, and distributions of earnings are to be as follows:

	A	B	C	Total
Capital investment............	$150,000	$200,000	$150,000	$500,000
Salary........................	27,000	36,000	27,000	90,000
Distribution of earnings	8,100	10,800	8,100	27,000

Dividends are fully taxable, and each owner files a joint return for the calendar year, prepared in accordance with the cash method. For each individual, the estimated taxable income from sources other than Allen Co. is as follows:

A	$23,000
B	9,000
C	24,000

Instructions:

(1) Present the following reports of estimated results of the first year of operations, assuming that Allen Co. is to be organized as a partnership: (a) estimated capital statement of the partners of Allen Co. and (b) statement of estimated federal income tax of A, B, and C, applying the appropriate schedule of tax rates presented in this chapter.

(2) Present the following reports of estimated results of the first year of operations, based on the assumption that Allen Co. is to be organized as a corporation: (a) statement of estimated federal income tax of Allen Co., applying the corporation tax rates presented in this chapter; (b) estimated statement of stockholders' equity of each of the stockholders in Allen Co., allocating each increase and decrease in the manner employed in (1a) above; and (c) estimated federal income tax of A, B, and C, applying the appropriate schedule of tax rates presented in this chapter.

(3) Present a report comparing the estimated federal income tax effects of the two methods of organization on each of the three individuals. For purposes of this report, the income tax on the corporation should be allocated among the individuals as in (2b).

23–29. Nancy Young, DDS, opened her dental office after graduation from dental school in early January of the current year. On December 31, the accounting records indicated the following for the current year to date:

	Total	Cash Received	Cash Paid
Fees earned...............................	$92,000	$79,000	—
Lease of dental office and equipment........	24,000	—	$22,000
Dental assistant salary.....................	18,000	—	16,500
Dental supplies, utilities, etc................	9,000	—	7,400

Instructions:

(1) Determine the amount of net income Young would report from her dental practice for the current year under the (a) cash method and (b) accrual method.
(2) List the advantages of using the cash method rather than the accrual method in accounting for Young's dental practice.
(3) What is the principal advantage of using the accrual method rather than the cash method in accounting for Young's dental practice?

23–30. Acme Limousine Sales sold 25 limousines for $22,500 each during the first year of operations. Data related to purchases during the year are as follows:

	Quantity	Unit Cost
January 3..............	5	$20,000
April 10................	4	20,100
June 30	7	20,250
August 22	10	20,300
November 5	5	20,500

Sales of limousines are the company's only source of income, and operating expenses for the current year are $19,750.

Instructions:

(1) Determine the net income for the current year, using the fifo (first-in, first-out) inventory method.
(2) Determine the net income for the current year, using the lifo (last-in, first-out) inventory method.
(3) Which method of inventory costing, fifo or lifo, would you recommend for tax purposes? Discuss.

23–31. Day Company began construction on three contracts during 1986. The contract prices and construction activities for 1986, 1987, and 1988 were as follows:

Contract	Contract Price	1986 Costs Incurred	1986 Percent Completed	1987 Costs Incurred	1987 Percent Completed	1988 Costs Incurred	1988 Percent Completed
1	$ 5,000,000	$1,780,000	40%	$1,550,000	35%	$1,062,400	25%
2	10,000,000	2,550,000	30	2,625,000	30	2,695,000	30
3	3,600,000	1,495,500	50	1,555,500	50	—	—

Instructions:

(1) Determine the amount of income to be recognized in 1986, 1987, and 1988 by using (a) the percentage-of-completion method and (b) the completed-contract method. Present computations in good order.
(2) Would the total amount of income to be recognized by using the percentage-of-completion method for each contract be the same as the total amount recognized by using the completed-contract method?
(3) What is the principal advantage for tax purposes of using the completed-contract method of recognizing income from long-term contracts?

23–32. The board of directors of Highland Inc. is planning an expansion of plant facilities expected to cost $2,000,000. The board is undecided about the method of financing this expansion and is considering two plans:

Plan 1. Issue 20,000 shares of $100, 8% cumulative preferred stock at par.
Plan 2. Issue $2,000,000 of 20-year, 12% bonds at face amount.

The condensed balance sheet of the corporation at the end of the most recent fiscal year is as follows:

Highland Inc.
Balance Sheet
December 31, 19--

Assets		Liabilities and Capital	
Current assets	$1,400,000	Current liabilities	$1,140,000
Plant assets..........	4,600,000	Common stock, $25 par	2,500,000
		Premium on common	
		stock	1,000,000
		Retained earnings	1,360,000
Total assets..........	$6,000,000	Total liabilities and capital...	$6,000,000

Net income has remained relatively constant over the past several years. As a result of the expansion program, yearly income after tax but before bond interest and related income tax is expected to increase to $450,000.

Instructions:

(1) Prepare a tabulation indicating the net annual outlay (dividends and interest after tax) for financing under each plan. (Use the income tax rates indicated in the chapter.)
(2) Prepare a tabulation indicating the expected earnings per share on common stock under each plan.
(3) List factors other than the net cost of financing and earnings per share that the board should consider in evaluating the two plans.

23–30A. Benny Golf Carts sold 150 electric golf carts for $1,500 each during the first year of operations. Data related to purchases during the year are as follows:

Alternate
Problems

	Quantity	Unit Cost
February 1	25	$1,200
April 20	45	1,225
June 1	50	1,250
August 15	25	1,250
November 1	25	1,280

Sales of electric golf carts are the company's only source of income, and operating expenses for the current year are $15,500.

Instructions:

(1) Determine the net income for the current year, using the lifo method (last-in, first-out) inventory method.
(2) Determine the net income for the current year, using the fifo (first-in, first-out) inventory method.
(3) Which method of inventory costing, lifo or fifo, would you recommend for tax purposes? Discuss.

23–31A. Cosell Company began construction on three contracts during 1986. The contract prices and construction activities for 1986, 1987, and 1988 were as follows:

		1986		1987		1988	
Contract	Contract Price	Costs Incurred	Percent Completed	Costs Incurred	Percent Completed	Costs Incurred	Percent Completed
1	$6,000,000	$2,150,000	40%	$3,250,000	60%	—	—
2	3,000,000	525,000	20	1,075,000	40	$1,100,000	40%
3	3,500,000	305,000	10	985,000	30	1,675,000	50

Instructions:

(1) Determine the amount of income to be recognized from the contracts in 1986, 1987, and 1988 by using (a) the percentage-of-completion method and (b) the completed-contract method. Present computations in good order.
(2) Would the total amount of income to be recognized by using the percentage-of-completion method for each contract be the same as the total amount recognized by using the completed-contract method?
(3) What is the principal advantage for tax purposes of using the completed-contract method of recognizing income from long-term contracts?

23–32A. The board of directors of Mickelsen Inc. is planning an expansion of plant facilities expected to cost $5,000,000. The board is undecided about the method of financing this expansion and is considering two plans:

Plan 1. Issue 50,000 shares of $100, 8% cumulative preferred stock at par.
Plan 2. Issue $5,000,000 of 20-year, 10% bonds at face amount.

The condensed balance sheet of the corporation at the end of the most recent fiscal year is presented as follows:

Mickelsen Inc.
Balance Sheet
December 31, 19--

Assets		Liabilities and Capital	
Current assets	$ 6,000,000	Current liabilities.	$ 3,000,000
Plant assets.	34,000,000	Common stock, $10 par . .	10,000,000
		Premium on common	
		stock	2,000,000
		Retained earnings	25,000,000
Total assets.	$40,000,000	Total liabilities and capital	$40,000,000

Net income has remained relatively constant over the past several years. As a result of the expansion program, yearly income after tax but before bond interest and related income tax is expected to increase to $3,000,000.

Instructions:

(1) Prepare a tabulation indicating the net annual outlay (dividends and interest after tax) for financing under each plan. (Use the income tax rates indicated in the chapter.)

(2) Prepare a tabulation indicating the expected earnings per share on common stock under each plan.

(3) List factors other than the net cost of financing and earnings per share that the board should consider in evaluating the two plans.

Mini-Case

23–33. Your father recently signed a contract for the purchase of a vacation cottage on a nearby mountain lake. A $15,000 down payment is required by December 11, 1987. To raise the $15,000, your father is considering selling 150 of the 200 shares of CBC common stock that he acquired on July 19, 1987, at a total cost of $18,000.

Your father has asked your advice as to whether he should sell the stock or borrow the $15,000 for a maximum of 60 days at the current short-term interest rate of 12%. The stock is currently selling at $101 per share, and brokerage fees are expected to be $150 if the 150 shares are sold.

Instructions:

(1) If your father is in the 50% marginal tax bracket and 60% of long-term capital gains are exempt from taxable income, how much tax would be due if the stock is sold on December 11, 1987?

(2) What would you suggest that your father consider concerning the selling of the stock? Discuss. Assume that any interest paid is deductible in determining taxable income.

Answers to Self-Examination Questions

1. C Corporations are taxable entities (answer C), while individuals practicing as sole proprietors (answer A) and as partners in partnerships (answer B) report their income in their individual tax returns.

2. B The federal income tax is a progressive tax; that is, it provides for a graduated series of tax rates, with successively higher rates being applied to successively higher segments of taxable income. The highest tax rate applied to the income of any particular taxpayer is called the taxpayer's marginal tax rate (answer B).

3. D In periods of rising prices, the use of lifo rather than fifo results in a higher cost of goods sold (answer A), lower net income (answer B), and lower income tax (answer C) because the last goods purchased (which are the most costly) are considered to be the first sold. Thus, since the most costly goods are considered to be sold, the result is a higher cost of goods sold, lower net income, and lower income tax.

4. C By using both the installment method of reporting sales (answer A) and the completed-contract method of reporting income on long-term construction projects (answer B), a taxpayer may postpone the payment of a portion of the income tax. Although the same amount of tax is eventually due in both cases, the delay of cash payments means that the taxpayer can retain cash longer, and this cash can be invested to earn income or to reduce debt and thus save on interest costs.

5. B Net long-term capital gains for both individual and corporate taxpayers are given preferential treatment, with the maximum tax rate for corporations being 28% (answer B).

PART 8

Accounting for Decentralized Operations

Thinking Small

NCR (formerly National Cash Register Co.) is a Dayton-based multinational electronics and computer manufacturing corporation. In 1979, NCR was a troubled company. Examining its problems, management began to wonder whether its very structure was inhibiting its ability to innovate and adapt.

As part of this reevaluation process, NCR commissioned the McKinsey & Co. consulting group to study the attributes of a number of highly successful companies. The researchers looked at such corporations as Sperry, IBM, and Hewlett-Packard, to determine what they had done that might be applied to NCR.

Using this study as background, NCR developed a plan for restructuring itself. Analyzing the path of a product from idea to implementation, it discovered some obvious impediments. The development, production, and marketing of a new product involved three separate divisions. This cumbersome system created opportunities for false starts and misinterpreting the market. It took a long time to get a product through this entire process, and sometimes products got lost in translation.

So NCR proceeded to break up its product-management organization and move the parts to units that would develop, manufacture, and market products. In consulting jargon, this is called shifting from a "functional" to a "divisional" organization, and it has been done many times before in other industries.

These changes transformed NCR Corp. from a highly centralized operation into a series of stand-alone or decentralized units. Today there is no requirement that one unit buy components from another NCR unit if it can find better or cheaper products outside the company. Moreover, based upon the nature of their products, the different divisions make their own decisions about how they want to structure themselves with regard to such activities as marketing.

SOURCE   Adapted from Eugene Linden, "Let a Thousand Flowers Bloom," *Inc.*, April, 1984, pp. 64-76.

CHAPTER 24

Responsibility Accounting for Cost and Profit Centers

CHAPTER OBJECTIVES

Describe the nature of decentralized operations and the special accounting needs of the management of such operations.

Describe and illustrate responsibility accounting for cost centers.

Describe and illustrate responsibility accounting for profit centers.

In a small business, virtually all plans and decisions can be made by one individual. As a business grows or its operations become more diverse, it becomes difficult, if not impossible, for one individual to perform these functions. For example, the responsibility for planning and controlling operations is clear in a one-person real estate agency. If the agency expands by opening an office in a distant city, some of the authority and responsibility for planning and decision making in a given area of operations might be delegated to others. In other words, if centralized operations become unwieldy as a business grows, the need to delegate responsibility for portions of operations arises. This separation of a business into more manageable units is termed decentralization. In a decentralized business, an important function of the managerial accountant is to assist individual managers in evaluating and controlling their areas of responsibility.

A term frequently applied to the process of measuring and reporting operating data by areas of responsibility is responsibility accounting. Some of the concepts useful in responsibility accounting were presented in preceding chapters. For example, in discussing budgetary control of operations, the use of the master budget, budgets for various departments, and budget performance reports in controlling operations by areas of responsibility were discussed. In this chapter, the concept of responsibility accounting as it relates to two types of decentralized operations is described and illustrated. A third type of decentralization is discussed in Chapter 25.

CHARACTERISTICS OF DECENTRALIZED OPERATIONS

A completely centralized business organization is one in which all major planning and operating decisions are made by the top echelon of management. For example, a one-person, owner-manager-operated business is centralized because all plans and decisions are made by one person. In a small owner-manager-operated business, centralization may be desirable, since the owner-manager's close supervision ensures that the business will be operated in conformity with the manager's wishes and desires.

In a decentralized business organization, responsibility for planning and controlling operations is delegated among managers. These managers have the authority to make decisions without first seeking the approval of higher management. The level of decentralization varies significantly, and there is no one best level of decentralization for all businesses. In some companies, for example, plant managers have authority over all plant operations, including plant asset acquisitions and retirements. In other companies, a plant manager may only have authority for scheduling production and for controlling the costs of direct materials, direct labor, and factory overhead. The proper level of decentralization for a company depends on the advantages and disadvantages of decentralization as they apply to a company's specific, unique circumstances.

Advantages of Decentralization

As a business grows, it becomes more difficult for top management to maintain close daily contact with all operations. Hence, a top management that delegates authority in such circumstances has a better chance of sound decisions being made, and the managers closest to the operations may anticipate and react to operating information more quickly. In addition, as a company diversifies into a wide range of products and services, it becomes more difficult for top management to maintain operating expertise in all product lines and services. In such cases, decentralization allows managers to concentrate on acquiring expertise in their areas of responsibility. For example, in a company that maintains diversified operations in oil refining, banking, and the manufacture of office equipment, individual managers could become "expert" in the area of their responsibility.

The delegation of responsibility for day-to-day operations from top management to middle management frees top management to concentrate more on strategic planning. **Strategic planning** is the process of establishing long-term goals for an enterprise and developing plans to achieve these goals. For example, a goal to expand an enterprise's product line into new markets and a plan to finance this expansion through the issuance of long-term debt rather than additional common stock are examples of strategic planning decisions. As the business environment becomes more complex and as companies grow, strategic planning assumes an increasingly important role in the long-run success of a company.

Decentralized decision making provides excellent training for managers, which may be a factor in enabling a company to retain quality managers. Since the art of management can best be acquired through experience, the delegation of responsibility enables managers to acquire and develop managerial expertise early in their careers. Also, the operating personnel may be more creative in suggesting operating improvements, since personnel in a decentralized company tend to identify closely with the operations for which they are responsible.

The delegation of responsibility also serves as a positive reinforcement for managers, in that they may view such delegation as an indication of top management's confidence in their abilities. Thus, manager morale tends to increase because managers feel that they have more control over factors affecting their careers and their performance evaluation.

Disadvantages of Decentralization

The primary disadvantage of decentralized operations is that decisions made by one manager may affect other managers in such a way that the profitability of the entire company may suffer. For example, two managers competing in a common product market may engage in price cutting to win customers. However, the overall company profits are less than the profits that could have been if the price cutting had not occurred.

Other potential disadvantages of decentralized operations may be the duplication of various assets and costs in the operating divisions. For example, each manager of a product line might have a separate sales force and administrative office staff, but centralization of these personnel could save money. Likewise, the costs of gathering and processing operating information in a decentralized operation might be greater than if such information were gathered and processed centrally.

TYPES OF DECENTRALIZED OPERATIONS

Decentralized operations can be classified by the scope of responsibility assigned and the decision making authority given to individual managers. The three common types of decentralized operations are referred to as cost centers, profit centers, and investment centers. Each of these types of decentralized operations is briefly described in the following paragraphs. Responsibility accounting for cost centers and profit centers is then discussed and illustrated in the remainder of this chapter, while responsibility accounting for investment centers is discussed in Chapter 25.

Cost Centers

In a **cost center**, the responsibility for the control of costs incurred and the authority to make decisions that affect these costs is the responsibility of the department or division manager. For example, the marketing manager has responsibility for the costs of the Marketing Department, and the supervisor of the Power Department has responsibility for the costs incurred in providing power. The department manager does not make decisions concerning sales of the cost center's output, nor does the department manager have control over the plant assets available to the cost center.

Cost centers are the most widely used type of decentralization, because the organization and operation of most businesses allow for an easy identification of areas where managers can be assigned responsibility for and authority over costs. Cost centers may vary in size from a small department with a few employees to an entire plant. In addition, cost centers may exist within other cost centers. For example, a manager of a manufacturing plant organized as a cost center may treat individual departments within the plant as separate cost centers, with the department managers reporting directly to the plant manager.

Profit Centers

In a **profit center**, the manager has the responsibility and the authority to make decisions that affect both costs and revenues (and thus profits) for the department or division. For example, a retail department store might decentralize its operations by product line. The manager of each product line would have responsibility for the cost of merchandise and decisions regarding revenues, such as the determination of sales prices. The manager of a profit center does not make decisions concerning the plant assets available to the center. For example, the manager of the Sporting Goods Department does not make the decision to expand the available floor space for that department.

Profit centers are widely used in businesses in which individual departments or divisions sell products or services to those outside the company. A partial organization chart for a department store decentralized by retail departments as profit centers is as follows:

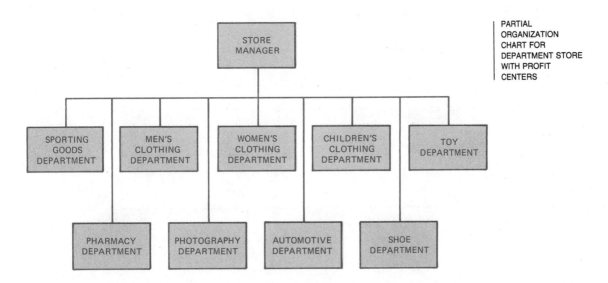

PARTIAL ORGANIZATION CHART FOR DEPARTMENT STORE WITH PROFIT CENTERS

Occasionally, profit centers are established when the center's product or service is consumed entirely within the company. For example, a Repairs and Maintenance Department of a manufacturing plant could be treated as a profit center if its manager were allowed to bill other departments, such as the various production departments, for services rendered. Likewise, the Data Processing Department of a company might bill each of the company's administrative and operating units for computing services.

In a sense, a profit center may be viewed as a business within a business. While the primary concern of a cost center manager is the control of costs, the profit center manager is concerned with both revenues and costs.

Investment Centers

In an investment center, the manager has the responsibility and the authority to make decisions that affect not only costs and revenues, but also the plant assets available to the center. The plant manager sets selling prices of products and establishes controls over costs. In addition, the plant manager could, within general constraints established by top management, expand production facilities through equipment acquisitions and retirements.

The manager of an investment center has more authority and responsibility than the manager of either a cost center or a profit center. The manager of an investment center occupies a position similar to that of a chief operating officer or president of a separate company. As such, an investment center manager is evaluated in much the same way as a manager of a separate company is evaluated.

Investment centers are widely used in highly diversified companies. A partial organization chart for a diversified company with divisions organized as investment centers is as follows:

PARTIAL ORGANIZATION CHART FOR DIVERSIFIED COMPANY WITH INVESTMENT CENTERS

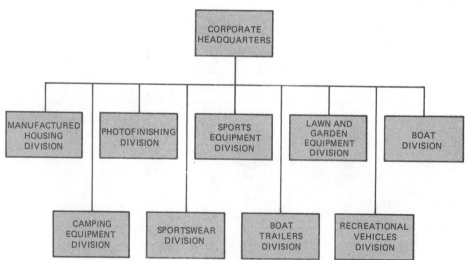

RESPONSIBILITY ACCOUNTING FOR COST CENTERS

Since managers of cost centers have responsibility for and authority to make decisions regarding costs, responsibility accounting for cost centers focuses on costs. The primary accounting tools appropriate for controlling and reporting costs are budgets and standard costs. Since budgets and standard costs were described and illustrated in Chapters 17 and 18, they will not be discussed in detail in this chapter. Instead, responsibility accounting for a cost center which uses budgeting to assist in the control of costs will be illustrated. The basic concepts of responsibility accounting, as illustrated, are equally applicable to cost centers that use standard cost systems to aid in cost control.

For purposes of illustration, assume that the responsibility for the manufacturing operations of an enterprise is as represented in the following organization chart:

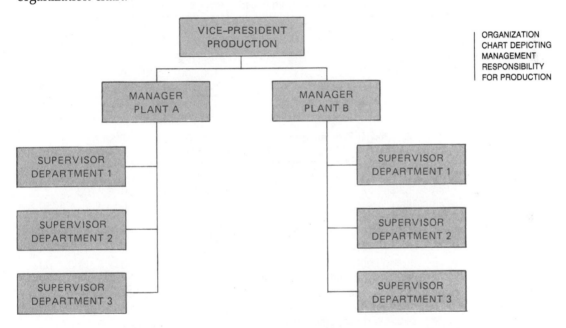

ORGANIZATION CHART DEPICTING MANAGEMENT RESPONSIBILITY FOR PRODUCTION

Also assume that there are three levels of cost centers within the organizational structure. At the operating level, each department is a cost center, with the department supervisors responsible for controlling costs within their departments. At the next level of the organization, each plant is a cost center, with each plant manager responsible for controlling plant administrative costs as well as supervising the control of costs in the plant departments. Finally, at the top level, the office of the vice-president of production is a cost center with responsibility for controlling the administrative costs of the office as well as supervising the control of costs in each plant.

Management reports aid each level of management in carrying out its assigned responsibilities for the control of costs. To illustrate, the following budget performance reports are part of a responsibility accounting system for the enterprise:

Budget Performance Report — Vice-President, Production
For Month Ended October 31, 19--

	Budget	Actual	Over	Under
Administration	$ 19,500	$ 19,700	$ 200	
Plant A	467,475	470,330	2,855	
Plant B	395,225	394,300		$925
	$882,200	$884,330	$3,055	$925

Budget Performance Report — Manager, Plant A
For Month Ended October 31, 19--

	Budget	Actual	Over	Under
Administration	$ 17,500	$ 17,350		$150
Department 1	109,725	111,280	$1,555	
Department 2	190,500	192,600	2,100	
Department 3	149,750	149,100		650
	$467,475	$470,330	$3,655	$800

Budget Performance Report — Supervisor, Department 1-Plant A
For Month Ended October 31, 19--

	Budget	Actual	Over	Under
Direct materials	$ 30,000	$ 31,700	$1,700	
Direct labor	48,000	47,750		$250
Factory overhead:				
Indirect factory wages	10,100	10,250	150	
Supervisory salaries	6,400	6,400		
Power and light	5,750	5,690		60
Depreciation of plant and equipment	4,000	4,000		
Indirect materials	2,500	2,525	25	
Maintenance	2,000	1,990		10
Insurance and property taxes	975	975		
	$109,725	$111,280	$1,875	$320

The amount of detail presented in the budget performance report depends upon the level of management to which the report is directed. The reports prepared for the department supervisors present details of the budgeted and actual manufacturing costs for their departments. Each supervisor can then concentrate on the individual items that resulted in significant variations. In the illustration, the budget performance report for Department 1-Plant A indicates a significant variation between the budget and actual amounts for direct materials. It is clear that supplemental reports providing detailed data on the causes of the variation would aid the supervisor in taking corrective action. One such report, a scrap report, is illustrated as follows. This report indicates the cause of a significant part of the variation.

Direct Materials Scrap Report—Department 1-Plant A
For Month Ended October 31, 19--

Material No.	Units Spoiled	Unit Cost	Dollar Loss	Remarks
A392	50	$3.10	$ 155.00	Machine malfunction
C417	76	.80	60.80	Inexperienced employee
G118	5	1.10	5.50	
J510	120	8.25	990.00	Substandard materials
K277	2	1.50	3.00	
P719	7	2.10	14.70	
V112	22	4.25	93.50	Machine malfunction
			$1,322.50	

SCRAP
REPORT

The scrap report is one example of the type of supplemental report that can be provided to department supervisors. Other examples would include reports on direct labor rate variance, direct labor usage variance, and cost of idle time.

The budget performance reports for the plant managers contain summarized data on the budgeted and actual costs for the departments under their jurisdiction. These reports enable them to identify the department supervisors responsible for significant variances. The report for the vice-president in charge of production summarizes the data by plant so that the persons responsible for plant operations can be held accountable for significant variations from predetermined objectives.

RESPONSIBILITY ACCOUNTING FOR PROFIT CENTERS

Since managers of profit centers have responsibility for and authority to make decisions regarding costs and revenues, responsibility accounting reports for profit centers are normally in the form of income statements. These income statements for individual profit centers report costs and revenues by departments through either gross profit or operating income. Alternatively, profit center income statements may include a breakdown of revenues and expenses by responsibility for their incurrence, and may identify contributions made by each department to overall company profit.

Since profit centers are widely used by merchandising enterprises, such as department stores, a merchandising enterprise is used as the basis for the following discussion and illustration of responsibility accounting for profit centers. Although the degree to which profit centers are used by a merchandising enterprise varies, profit centers are typically established for each major retail department. The enterprise in the illustrations, Garrison Company, has established Departments A and B as profit centers.

Gross Profit by Departments

To compute gross profit by departments, it is necessary to determine by departments each element entering into gross profit. An income statement showing gross profit by departments for Garrison Company appears on the following page. For illustrative purposes, the operating expenses are shown in condensed form. Usually they would be listed in detail.

For a merchandising enterprise, the gross profit is one of the most significant figures in the income statement. Since the sales and the cost of merchandise sold are both controlled by departmental management, the reporting of gross profit by departments is useful in cost analysis and control. In addition, such reports aid management in directing its efforts toward obtaining a mix of sales that will maximize profits. For example, after studying the reports, management may decide to change sales or purchases policies to achieve a higher gross profit for each department. Caution must be exercised in the use of such reports to insure that proposed changes affecting gross profit do not have an adverse effect on net income. A change that increases gross profit could result in an even greater increase in operating expenses and thereby decrease net income.

Operating Income by Departments

Departmental reporting may be extended to operating income. In such cases, each department must be assigned not only the related revenues and the cost of merchandise sold (as in the preceding illustration), but also that part of operating expenses incurred for its benefit. Some of these expenses may be easily identified with the department benefited. For example, if each salesperson is restricted to a certain sales department, the sales salaries may be assigned to the proper departmental salary accounts each time the payroll is prepared. On the other hand, the salaries of company officers, executives, and office personnel are not identifiable with specific sales departments and must therefore be allocated if an equitable and reasonable basis for allocation exists.

When operating expenses are allocated, they should be apportioned to the respective departments as nearly as possible in accordance with the cost of services rendered to them. Determining the amount of an expense chargeable to each department is not always a simple matter. In the first place, it requires the exercise of judgment; and accountants of equal ability may well differ in their opinions as to the proper basis for the apportionment of operating expenses. Second, the cost of collecting data for use in making an apportionment must be kept within reasonable bounds. Consequently, information that is readily available and is substantially reliable may be used instead of more accurate information that would be more costly to collect.

To illustrate the apportionment of operating expenses, assume that Garrison Company extends its departmental reporting through income from operations. The company's operating expenses for the calendar year

Garrison Company
Income Statement
For Year Ended December 31, 19--

	Department A		Department B		Total	
Revenue from sales:						
Sales		$630,000		$270,000		$900,000
Less sales returns and allowances		15,300		7,100		22,400
Net sales		$614,700		$262,900		$877,600
Cost of merchandise sold:						
Merchandise inventory, January 1, 19--		$ 80,150		$ 61,750		$141,900
Purchases	$334,550		$200,350		$534,900	
Less purchases discount	6,200		2,400		8,600	
Merchandise available for sale		$408,500		$259,700		$668,200
Less merchandise inventory, December 31, 19--		85,150		78,950		164,100
Cost of merchandise sold		323,350		180,750		504,100
Gross profit		$291,350		$ 82,150		$373,500
Operating expenses:						
Selling expenses					$113,000	
General expenses					110,200	
Total operating expenses						223,200
Income from operations						$150,300
Other expense:						
Interest expense						2,500
Income before income tax						$147,800
Income tax						64,444
Net income						$ 83,356

INCOME STATEMENT DEPARTMENTALIZED THROUGH GROSS PROFIT

and the methods used in apportioning them are presented in the paragraphs that follow.

Sales Salaries Expense is apportioned to the two departments according to the distributions shown in the payroll records. Of the $84,900 total in the account, $54,000 is chargeable to Department A and $30,900 is chargeable to Department B.

Advertising Expense, covering billboard advertising and newspaper advertising, is apportioned according to the amount of advertising incurred for each department. The billboard advertising totaling $5,000 emphasizes the name and the location of the company. This expense is allocated on the basis of sales, the assumption being that this basis represents a fair allocation of billboard advertising to each department. Analysis of the newspaper space costing $14,000 indicates that 65% of the space was devoted to Department A and 35% to Department B. The computations of the apportionment of the total advertising expense are as follows:

	Total	Department A	Department B
Sales — dollars	$900,000	$630,000	$270,000
Sales — percent	100%	70%	30%
Billboard advertising	$ 5,000	$ 3,500	$ 1,500
Newspaper space — percent . .	100%	65%	35%
Newspaper advertising.	14,000	9,100	4,900
Advertising expense	$19,000	$12,600	$ 6,400

Depreciation Expense — Store Equipment is apportioned according to the average cost of the equipment in each of the two departments. The computations for the apportionment of the depreciation expense are as follows:

	Total	Department A	Department B
Cost of store equipment:			
January 1.	$28,300	$16,400	$11,900
December 31	31,700	19,600	12,100
Total	$60,000	$36,000	$24,000
Average.	$30,000	$18,000	$12,000
Percent.	100%	60%	40%
Depreciation expense	$ 4,400	$ 2,640	$ 1,760

Officers' Salaries Expense and **Office Salaries Expense** are apportioned on the basis of the relative amount of time devoted to each department by the officers and by the office personnel. Obviously, this can be only an approximation. The number of sales transactions may have some bearing on the matter, as may billing and collection procedures and other factors such as promotional campaigns that might vary from period to period. Of the total officers' salaries of $52,000 and office salaries of $17,600, it is estimated that 60%, or $31,200 and $10,560 respectively, is chargeable to Department A and that 40%, or $20,800 and $7,040 respectively, is chargeable to Department B.

Rent Expense and **Heating and Lighting Expense** are usually apportioned on the basis of the floor space devoted to each department. In apportioning rent expense for a multistory building, differences in the value of the various floors and locations may be taken into account. For example, the space near the main entrance of a department store is more valuable than the same amount of floor space located far from the elevator on the sixth floor. For Garrison Company, rent expense is apportioned on the basis of floor space used because there is no significant difference in the value of the floor areas used by each department. In allocating heating and lighting expense, it is assumed that the number of lights, their wattage, and the extent of use are uniform throughout the sales departments. If there are major variations and the total lighting expense is material, further analysis and separate apportionment may be advisable. The rent expense and the heating and lighting expense are apportioned as follows:

	Total	Department A	Department B
Floor space, square feet	160,000	104,000	56,000
Percent	100%	65%	35%
Rent expense	$15,400	$10,010	$ 5,390
Heating and lighting expense	$ 5,100	$ 3,315	$ 1,785

Property Tax Expense and **Insurance Expense** are related primarily to the cost of the merchandise inventory and the store equipment. Although the cost of these assets may differ from their assessed value for tax purposes and their value for insurance purposes, the cost is most readily available and is considered to be satisfactory as a basis for apportioning these expenses. The computations of the apportionment of personal property tax expense and insurance expense are as follows:

	Total	Department A	Department B
Merchandise inventory:			
January 1	$141,900	$ 80,150	$ 61,750
December 31	164,100	85,150	78,950
Total	$306,000	$165,300	$140,700
Average	$153,000	$ 82,650	$ 70,350
Average cost of store equipment (computed previously)	30,000	18,000	12,000
Total	$183,000	$100,650	$ 82,350
Percent	100%	55%	45%
Property tax expense	$ 6,800	$ 3,740	$ 3,060
Insurance expense	$ 3,900	$ 2,145	$ 1,755

Uncollectible Accounts Expense, Miscellaneous Selling Expense, and **Miscellaneous General Expense** are apportioned on the basis of sales. Although the uncollectible accounts expense may be apportioned on the basis of an analysis of accounts receivable written off, it is assumed that the expense is closely related to sales. The miscellaneous selling and general expenses are apportioned on the basis of sales, which are assumed to be a reasonable measure of the benefit to each department. The computation of the apportionment is as follows:

	Total	Department A	Department B
Sales................................	$900,000	$630,000	$270,000
Percent...........................	100%	70%	30%
Uncollectible accounts expense	$ 4,600	$ 3,220	$ 1,380
Miscellaneous selling expense	$ 4,700	$ 3,290	$ 1,410
Miscellaneous general expense	$ 4,800	$ 3,360	$ 1,440

An income statement presenting income from operations by departments for Garrison Company appears on the following page. The amounts for sales and cost of merchandise sold are presented in condensed form. Details could be reported, if desired, in the manner illustrated on page 783.

Departmental Margin

Not all accountants agree as to the merits of the type of responsibility accounting reports for profit centers (departments) discussed in the preceding section. In relying on income statements departmentalized through income from operations, caution should be used, since the use of arbitrary bases in allocating operating expenses is likely to yield incorrect amounts of departmental operating income. In addition, the reporting of operating income by departments may be misleading, since the departments are not independent operating units. The departments are segments of a business enterprise, and no single department of a business can earn an income independently. For these reasons, income statements of segmented businesses may follow a somewhat different format than the one illustrated on the following page. The alternative format emphasizes the contribution of each department to overall company net income and to covering the overall operating expenses incurred on behalf of the business. Income statements prepared in this alternative format are said to follow the **departmental margin** or **contribution margin** approach to responsibility accounting.

Prior to the preparation of an income statement in the departmental margin format, it is necessary to differentiate between operating expenses that are direct and those that are indirect. The two categories may be described in general terms as follows:

Direct expense—Operating expenses directly traceable to or incurred for the sole benefit of a specific department and usually subject to the control of the department manager.

Indirect expense—Operating expenses incurred for the entire enterprise as a unit and hence not subject to the control of individual department managers.

Garrison Company
Income Statement
For Year Ended December 31, 19--

	Department A		Department B		Total	
Net sales		$614,700		$262,900		$877,600
Cost of merchandise sold		323,350		180,750		504,100
Gross profit		$291,350		$ 82,150		$373,500
Operating expenses:						
Selling expenses:						
Sales salaries expense	$ 54,000		$ 30,900		$ 84,900	
Advertising expense	12,600		6,400		19,000	
Depreciation expense—store equipment	2,640		1,760		4,400	
Miscellaneous selling expense	3,290		1,410		4,700	
Total selling expenses		$ 72,530		$ 40,470		$113,000
General expenses:						
Officers' salaries expense	$ 31,200		$ 20,800		$ 52,000	
Office salaries expense	10,560		7,040		17,600	
Rent expense	10,010		5,390		15,400	
Property tax expense	3,740		3,060		6,800	
Heating and lighting expense	3,315		1,785		5,100	
Uncollectible accounts expense	3,220		1,380		4,600	
Insurance expense	2,145		1,755		3,900	
Miscellaneous general expense	3,360		1,440		4,800	
Total general expenses		67,550		42,650		110,200
Total operating expenses		140,080		83,120		223,200
Income (loss) from operations		$151,270		$ (970)		$150,300
Other expense:						
Interest expense						2,500
Income before income tax						$147,800
Income tax						64,444
Net income						$ 83,356

INCOME STATEMENT DEPARTMENTALIZED THROUGH INCOME FROM OPERATIONS

The details of departmental sales and the cost of merchandise sold are presented on the income statement in the usual manner. The direct expenses of each department are then deducted from the related departmental gross profit, yielding balances which are identified as **departmental margin**. The remaining expenses, including the indirect operating expenses, are not departmentalized. They are reported singly below the total departmental margin.

An income statement in the departmental margin format for the Garrison Company is presented on the following page. The basic revenue, cost, and expense data for the period are identical with those reported in the earlier illustration. The expenses identified as "direct" are sales salaries, property tax, uncollectible accounts, insurance, depreciation, and the newspaper advertising portion of advertising. The billboard portion of advertising, which is for the benefit of the business as a whole, as well as officers' and office salaries, and the remaining operating expenses, are identified as "indirect." Although a $970 net loss from operations is reported for Department B on page 783, a departmental margin of $38,395 is reported for the same department on the statement on the following page.

With departmental margin income statements, the manager of each department can be held responsible for operating expenses traceable to the department. A reduction in the direct expenses of a department will have a favorable effect on that department's contribution to the net income of the enterprise.

The departmental margin income statement may also be useful to management in making plans for future operations. For example, this type of analysis can be used when the discontinuance of a certain operation or department is being considered. If a specific department yields a departmental margin, it generally should be retained, even though the allocation of the indirect operating expenses would result in a net loss for that department. This observation is based upon the assumption that the department in question represents a relatively small segment of the enterprise. Its termination, therefore, would not cause any significant reduction in the amount of indirect expenses.

To illustrate the application of the departmental margin approach to long-range planning, assume that a business occupies a rented three-story building. If the enterprise is divided into twenty departments, each occupying about the same amount of space, termination of the least profitable department would probably not cause any reduction in rent or other occupancy expenses. The space vacated would probably be absorbed by the remaining nineteen departments. On the other hand, if the enterprise were divided into three departments, each occupying approximately equal areas, the discontinuance of one could result in vacating an entire floor and significantly reducing occupancy expenses. When the departmental margin analysis is applied to problems of this type, consideration should be given to proposals for the use of the vacated space.

Responsibility Accounting for Cost and Profit Centers

INCOME
STATEMENT
DEPARTMEN-
TALIZED THROUGH
DEPARTMENTAL
MARGIN

Garrison Company
Income Statement
For Year Ended December 31, 19--

	Department A		Department B		Total	
Net sales	....	$614,700	....	$262,900	....	$877,600
Cost of merchandise sold	....	323,350	....	180,750	....	$504,100
Gross profit	....	$291,350	....	$ 82,150	....	$373,500
Direct departmental expenses:						
Sales salaries expense	$54,000	....	$30,900	....	$84,900	....
Advertising expense..	9,100	....	4,900	....	14,000	....
Property tax expense	3,740	....	3,060	....	6,800	....
Uncollectible accounts expense	3,220	....	1,380	....	4,600	....
Depreciation expense—store equipment	2,640	....	1,760	....	4,400	....
Insurance expense ..	2,145	....	1,755	....	3,900	....
Total direct departmental expenses ..	....	74,845	....	43,755	....	118,600
Departmental margin .	....	$216,505	....	$ 38,395	....	$254,900
Indirect expenses:						
Officers' salaries expense	....	....	....	....	$52,000	....
Office salaries expense	....	....	....	....	17,600	....
Rent expense	....	....	....	....	15,400	....
Heating and lighting expense	....	....	....	....	5,100	....
Advertising expense..	....	....	....	....	5,000	....
Miscellaneous selling expense	....	....	....	....	4,700	....
Miscellaneous general expense	....	....	....	....	4,800	....
Total indirect expenses	....	....	....	....	....	104,600
Income from operations	....	....	....	....	....	$150,300
Other expense: Interest expense.....	....	....	....	....	....	2,500
Income before income tax................	....	....	....	....	....	$147,800
Income tax...........	....	....	....	....	....	64,444
Net income	....	....	....	....	....	$ 83,356

To further illustrate the departmental margin approach, assume that an enterprise with six departments has earned $70,000 before income tax during the past year, which is fairly typical of recent operations. Assume also that recent income statements, in which all operating expenses are allocated, indicate that Department F has been incurring losses, the net loss having amounted to $5,000 for the past year. Departmental margin analysis shows that, in spite of the losses, Department F should not be discontinued unless there is enough assurance that a proportionate increase in the gross profit of other departments or a decrease in indirect expenses can be effected. The following analysis, which is considerably condensed, shows a possible reduction of $10,000 in net income (the amount of the departmental margin for Department F) if Department F is discontinued.

DEPARTMENTAL
ANALYSIS—
DISCONTINUANCE
OF UNPROFITABLE
DEPARTMENT

Proposal to Discontinue Department F
January 25, 19--

	Current Operations			Discontinuance of Department F
	Department F	Departments A–E	Total	
Sales........................	$100,000	$900,000	$1,000,000	$900,000
Cost of merchandise sold	70,000	540,000	610,000	540,000
Gross profit..................	$ 30,000	$360,000	$ 390,000	$360,000
Direct departmental expenses ...	20,000	210,000	230,000	210,000
Departmental margin	$ 10,000	$150,000	$ 160,000	$150,000
Indirect expenses			90,000	90,000
Income before income tax......			$ 70,000	$ 60,000

In addition to departmental margin analysis, there are other factors that may need to be considered. For example, there may be problems regarding the displacement of sales personnel. Or customers attracted by the least profitable department may make large purchases in other departments, so that discontinuance of that department may adversely affect the sales of other departments.

The foregoing discussion of departmental income statements has suggested various ways in which income data may be made useful to management in making important policy decisions. Note that the format selected for the presentation of income data to management must be that which will be most useful for evaluating, controlling, and planning departmental operations.

Self-
Examination
Questions
(Answers
at end of
chapter.)

1. When the manager has the responsibility and authority to make decisions that affect costs and revenues, but no responsibility for or authority over assets invested in the department, the department is referred to as:
   A. a cost center
   B. a profit center
   C. an investment center
   D. none of the above

2. Which of the following would be the most appropriate basis for allocating rent expense for use in arriving at operating income by departments?
   A. Departmental sales
   B. Physical space occupied
   C. Cost of inventory
   D. Time devoted to departments

3. The term used to describe the excess of departmental gross profit over direct departmental expenses is:
   A. income from operations
   B. net income
   C. departmental margin
   D. none of the above

4. On an income statement departmentalized through departmental margin, sales commissions expense would be reported as:
   A. a direct expense
   B. an indirect expense
   C. an other expense
   D. none of the above

5. On an income statement departmentalized through departmental margin, office salaries would be reported as:
   A. a direct expense
   B. an indirect expense
   C. an other expense
   D. none of the above

24–1. What is responsibility accounting?

24–2. What is a decentralized business organization?

24–3. Name three common types of responsibility centers for decentralized operations.

24–4. Differentiate between a cost center and a profit center.

24–5. Differentiate between a profit center and an investment center.

24–6. In what major respect would budget performance reports prepared for the use of plant managers of a manufacturing enterprise with cost centers differ from those prepared for the use of the various department supervisors who report to the plant managers?

24–7. The newly appointed manager of the Appliance Department in a department store is studying the income statements presenting gross profit by departments in an attempt to adjust operations to achieve the highest possible gross profit for the department. (a) Suggest ways in which an income statement departmentalized through gross profit can be used in achieving this goal. (b) Suggest reasons why caution must be exercised in using such statements.

24–8. Describe the underlying principle of apportionment of operating expenses to departments for income statements departmentalized through income from operations.

24–9. For each of the following types of expenses, select the allocation basis listed that is most appropriate for use in arriving at operating income by departments.

Expense:	Basis of allocation:
(a) Property tax expense	(1) Cost of inventory and equipment
(b) Sales salaries	(2) Departmental sales
(c) Rent expense	(3) Time devoted to departments
(d) Advertising expense	(4) Physical space occupied

24–10. Describe an appropriate basis for apportioning Officers' Salaries Expense among departments for purposes of the income statement departmentalized through income from operations.

24–11. Differentiate between a direct and an indirect operating expense.

24–12. Indicate whether each of the following operating expenses incurred by a department store is a direct or an indirect expense:

(a) Uncollectible accounts expense	(d) Insurance expense on building
(b) General manager's salary	(e) Sales commissions
(c) Depreciation of store equipment	(f) Heating and lighting expense

24–13. What term is applied to the dollar amount representing the excess of departmental gross profit over direct departmental expenses?

24–14. Recent income statements departmentalized through income from operations report operating losses for Department 19, a relatively minor segment of the business. Management studies indicate that discontinuance of Department 19 would not affect sales of other departments or the volume of indirect expenses. Under what circumstances would the discontinuance of Department 19 result in a decrease of net income of the enterprise?

24–15. A portion of an income statement in condensed form, departmentalized through departmental margin for the year just ended, is as follows:

	Department E
Net sales	$112,300
Cost of merchandise sold	89,840
Gross profit	$ 22,460
Direct expenses	31,500
Departmental margin	$ (9,040)

It is believed that the discontinuance of Department E would not affect the sales of the other departments nor reduce the indirect expenses of the enterprise. Based on this information, what would have been the effect on the income from operations of the enterprise if Department E had been discontinued prior to the year just ended?

Exercises

24–16. The budget for Department A of Plant 2 for the current month ended June 30 is as follows:

Direct materials	$ 95,000
Direct labor	120,000
Power and light	42,500
Supervisory salaries	30,000
Indirect materials	27,500
Indirect factory wages	20,000
Depreciation of plant and equipment	17,750
Maintenance	15,250
Insurance and property taxes	10,000

During June, the costs incurred in Department A of Plant 2 were: direct materials, $95,400; direct labor, $120,600; power and light, $43,000; supervisory salaries, $30,000; indirect materials, $27,200; indirect factory wages, $20,000; depreciation of plant and equipment, $17,750; maintenance, $19,750; insurance and property taxes, $10,000. (a) Prepare a budget performance report for the supervisor of Department A, Plant 2, for the month of June. (b) For what significant variations might the supervisor be expected to request supplemental reports?

24-17. The chief accountant of Emerson Company prepares weekly reports of idleness of direct labor employees. These reports for the plant manager classify the idle time by departments. Idle time data for the week ended March 20 of the current year are as follows:

Department	Standard Hours	Productive Hours
1	4,200	3,990
2	2,800	2,800
3	6,100	5,978
4	1,900	1,786

The hourly direct labor rates are $18.60, $14.00, $16.50, and $15.50 respectively for Departments 1 through 4. The idleness was caused by a machine breakdown in Department 1, a materials shortage in Department 3, and a lack of sales orders in Department 4. Prepare an idle time report, classified by departments, for the week ended March 20. Use the following columnar headings for the report:

	Production			Idle Time		
Dept.	Standard Hours	Actual Hours	Percentage of Standard	Hours	Cost of Idle Time	Remarks

24-18. C. J. Lubin Company occupies a two-story building. The departments and the floor space occupied by each are as follows:

Receiving and Storage	basement	4,000 sq. ft.
Department 1	basement	6,000 sq. ft.
Department 2	first floor	3,200 sq. ft.
Department 3	first floor	8,000 sq. ft.
Department 4	first floor	4,800 sq. ft.
Department 5	second floor	9,800 sq. ft.
Department 6	second floor	4,200 sq. ft.

The building is leased at an annual rental of $80,000, allocated to the floors as follows: basement, 25%; first floor, 40%; second floor, 35%. Determine the amount of rent to be apportioned to each department.

24–19. Mulford Company apportions depreciation expense on equipment on the basis of the average cost of the equipment, and apportions property tax expense on the basis of the combined total of average cost of the equipment and average cost of the merchandise inventories. Depreciation expense on equipment amounted to $110,000 and property tax expense amounted to $26,000 for the year. Determine the apportionment of the depreciation expense and the property tax expense, based on the following data:

Departments	Average Cost	
	Equipment	Inventories
Service:		
R	$ 120,000	
M	60,000	
Sales:		
100	240,000	$160,000
200	420,000	360,000
300	360,000	280,000
Total	$1,200,000	$800,000

24–20. The following data were summarized from the accounting records for Hart Company for the current year ended December 31:

Cost of merchandise sold:
Department 1 .... $208,500
Department 2 296,250

Direct expenses:
Department 1 110,000
Department 2 149,000
Income tax.. 48,000
Indirect expenses.................................. 95,500
Interest Income.................................... 20,000

Net sales:
Department 1 410,500
Department 2 582,750

Prepare an income statement departmentalized through departmental margin.

24–21. A portion of an income statement in condensed form, departmentalized through loss from operations for the year just ended, is as follows:

	Department 5
Net sales	$226,600
Cost of merchandise sold	179,700
Gross profit	$ 46,900
Operating expenses..................	63,000
Loss from operations	$(16,100)

The operating expenses of Dept. 5 include $30,000 for indirect expenses. It is believed that the discontinuance of Department 5 would not affect the sales of the other departments nor reduce the indirect expenses of the enterprise. Based on this information, determine the increase or decrease in income from operations of the enterprise if Department 5 had been discontinued prior to the year just ended.

24–22. The organization chart for manufacturing operations for Carlos Inc. is presented in the working papers. Also presented are the budget performance reports for the three departments in Plant 3 and a partially completed budget performance report prepared for the vice-president in charge of production.

In response to an inquiry into the cause of the direct labor variance in the Plating Shop-Plant 3, the following data were accumulated:

Problems
(If the working papers correlating with the textbook are not used, omit Problem 24–22.)

Job No.	Budgeted Hours	Actual Hours	Hourly Rate
940	110	116	$14.00
942	120	124	14.50
944	80	78	14.00
945	100	112	15.00
950	128	120	15.50
951	90	95	14.80
952	130	130	15.00
958	105	115	14.60

The significant variations from budgeted hours were attributed to machine breakdown on Jobs 940 and 942, to an inexperienced operator on Job 951, and to the fact that Jobs 945 and 958 were of types that were being done for the first time. Experienced operators were assigned to Jobs 944 and 950.

Instructions:
   (1) Prepare a direct labor time variance report for the Plating Shop-Plant 3.
   (2) Prepare a budget performance report for the use of the manager of Plant 3, detailing the relevant data from the three departments in the plant. Assume that the budgeted and actual administration expenses for the plant were $11,340 and $11,520, respectively.
   (3) Complete the budget performance report for the vice-president in charge of production.

24–23. Howington Co. operates two sales departments: Department A for sporting goods and Department B for camping equipment. The following trial balance was prepared at the end of the current fiscal year, after all adjustments, including the adjustments for merchandise inventory, were recorded and posted.

Howington Co.
Trial Balance
November 30, 19--

Cash	48,150	
Accounts Receivable	83,200	
Merchandise Inventory — Department A	55,400	
Merchandise Inventory — Department B	35,300	
Prepaid Insurance	1,875	
Store Supplies	1,700	
Store Equipment	104,100	
Accumulated Depreciation — Store Equipment		27,760
Accounts Payable		71,680
Income Tax Payable		900
Common Stock		100,000
Retained Earnings		127,045
Cash Dividends	20,000	
Income Summary	99,300	90,700
Sales — Department A		338,000
Sales — Department B		182,000
Sales Returns and Allowances — Department A	3,120	
Sales Returns and Allowances — Department B	2,240	
Purchases — Department A	164,500	
Purchases — Department B	114,800	
Sales Salaries Expense	86,000	
Advertising Expense	13,750	
Depreciation Expense — Store Equipment	6,940	
Store Supplies Expense	4,540	
Miscellaneous Selling Expense	3,640	
Office Salaries Expense	44,200	
Rent Expense	14,400	
Heating and Lighting Expense	11,300	
Property Tax Expense	6,400	
Insurance Expense	3,750	
Uncollectible Accounts Expense	3,200	
Miscellaneous General Expense	1,280	
Interest Expense	1,400	
Income Tax	3,600	
	938,085	938,085

Merchandise inventories at the beginning of the year were as follows: Department A, $66,000; Department B, $33,300.

The bases to be used in apportioning expenses, together with other essential inforation, are as follows:

Sales salaries expense — payroll records: Department A, $67,080; Department B, $18,920.

Advertising expense — usage: Department A, $8,250; Department B, $5,500.

Depreciation expense—average cost of equipment. Balances at beginning of year: Department A, $48,600; Department B, $27,300. Balances at end of year: Department A, $59,400; Department B, $44,700.

Store supplies expense—requisitions: Department A, $2,260; Department B, $2,280.

Office salaries expense—Department A, 55%; Department B, 45%.

Rent expense and heating and lighting expense—floor space: Department A, 6,960 sq. ft.; Department B, 5,040 sq. ft.

Property tax expense and insurance expense—average cost of equipment plus average cost of merchandise inventory.

Uncollectible accounts expense, miscellaneous selling expense, and miscellaneous general expense—volume of gross sales.

Instructions:

Prepare an income statement departmentalized through income from operations.

24-24. M. R. Pierson Company is considering discontinuance of one of its twelve departments. If operations in Department 8 are discontinued, it is estimated that the indirect operating expenses and the level of operations in the other departments will not be affected.

Data from the income statement for the past year ended August 31, which is considered to be a typical year, are as follows:

	Department 8		Other Departments	
Sales.		$68,000		$981,000
Cost of merchandise sold.		44,200		588,600
Gross profit		$23,800		$392,400
Operating expenses:				
Direct expenses	$18,400		$208,000	
Indirect expenses.	9,500	27,900	114,000	322,000
Income (loss) before income tax.		$ (4,100)		$ 70,400

Instructions:

(1) Prepare an estimated income statement for the current year ending August 31, assuming the discontinuance of Department 8.

(2) On the basis of the data presented, would it be advisable to retain Department 8?

24-25. Mitchell's Department Store has 18 departments. Those with the least sales volume are Department 16 and Department 17, which were established about a year ago on a trial basis. The board of directors feels that it is now time to consider the retention or the termination of these two departments. The following adjusted trial balance as of May 31, the end of the first month of the current fiscal year, is severely condensed. May is considered to be a typical month. The income tax accrual has no bearing on the decision and is excluded from consideration.

Mitchell's Department Store
Trial Balance
May 31, 19--

Current Assets.	333,200	
Plant Assets.	642,700	
Accumulated Depreciation — Plant Assets.		252,810
Current Liabilities		190,920
Common Stock		100,000
Retained Earnings		291,860
Cash Dividends.	15,000	
Sales — Department 16.		31,900
Sales — Department 17.		24,200
Sales — Other Departments		861,500
Cost of Merchandise Sold — Department 16.	22,330	
Cost of Merchandise Sold — Department 17.	15,730	
Cost of Merchandise Sold — Other Departments	516,900	
Direct Expenses — Department 16	11,450	
Direct Expenses — Department 17	4,820	
Direct Expenses — Other Departments	126,760	
Indirect Expenses.	58,300	
Interest Expense.	6,000	
	1,753,190	1,753,190

Instructions:

(1) Prepare an income statement for May, departmentalized through departmental margin.

(2) State your recommendations concerning the retention of Departments 16 and 17, giving reasons.

24-26. The bases to be used in apportioning expenses, together with other essential data for the Northwest Corporation, are as follows:

Sales salaries and commissions expense — basic salary plus 6% of sales. Basic salaries for Department A, $54,600; Department B, $26,520.

Advertising expense for brochures distributed within each department advertising specific products — usage: Department A, $12,745; Department B, $6,090.

Depreciation expense — average cost of store equipment: Department A, $78,300; Department B, $56,700.

Insurance expense — average cost of store equipment plus average cost of merchandise inventory. Average cost of merchandise inventory was $58,100 for Department A and $26,900 for Department B.

Uncollectible accounts expense — 3/8% of sales. Departmental managers are responsible for the granting of credit on the sales made by their respective departments.

The following data are obtained from the ledger on April 30, the end of the current fiscal year:

Sales—Department A		740,000
Sales—Department B		296,000
Cost of Merchandise Sold—Department A	495,800	
Cost of Merchandise Sold—Department B	192,400	
Sales Salaries and Commissions Expense............	143,280	
Advertising Expense	18,835	
Depreciation Expense—Store Equipment	12,500	
Miscellaneous Selling Expense......................	2,020	
Administrative Salaries Expense.....................	43,850	
Rent Expense......................................	24,000	
Utilities Expense...................................	14,620	
Insurance Expense	6,500	
Uncollectible Accounts Expense.....................	3,885	
Miscellaneous General Expense.....................	710	
Interest Income....................................		4,400
Income Tax.......................................	17,750	

Instructions:

(1) Prepare an income statement departmentalized through departmental margin.
(2) Determine the rate of gross profit for each department.
(3) Determine the rate of departmental margin to sales for each department.

24–22A. The organization chart for manufacturing operations for Carlos Inc. is presented in the working papers. Also presented are the budget performance reports for the three departments in Plant 3 and a partially completed budget performance report prepared for the vice-president in charge of production.

In response to an inquiry into the cause of the direct labor variance in the Plating Shop-Plant 3, the following data were accumulated:

Alternate
Problems
(If the working
papers cor-
relating with
the textbook
are not used,
omit Problem
24–22A.)

Job No.	Budgeted Hours	Actual Hours	Hourly Rate
940	70	75	$16.00
942	120	113	17.00
944	115	119	16.50
945	90	105	18.00
950	80	80	17.20
951	119	128	17.00
952	100	94	15.50
958	65	67	16.50

The significant variations from budgeted hours were attributed to the fact that Job 945 was of a type that was being done for the first time, to machine breakdown on Jobs 940, 944, and 958, and to an inexperienced operator on Job 951. Experienced operators were assigned to Jobs 942 and 952.

Instructions:

(1) Prepare a direct labor time variance report for the Plating Shop-Plant 3.

(2) Prepare a budget performance report for the use of the manager of Plant 3, detailing the relevant data from the three departments in the plant. Assume that the budgeted and actual administration expenses for the plant were $12,400 and $12,210, respectively.

(3) Complete the budget performance report for the vice-president in charge of production.

24–23A. Lawson Appliances operates two sales departments: Department A for small appliances, such as radios and televisions, and Department B for large appliances, such as refrigerators and washing machines. The following trial balance was prepared at the end of the current year, after all adjustments, including the adjustments for merchandise inventory, were recorded and posted.

Lawson Appliances
Trial Balance
July 31, 19--

Cash	29,300	
Accounts Receivable	84,500	
Merchandise Inventory—Department A	20,300	
Merchandise Inventory—Department B	70,500	
Prepaid Insurance	600	
Store Supplies	550	
Store Equipment	92,200	
Accumulated Depreciation—Store Equipment		21,280
Accounts Payable		17,700
Income Tax Payable		5,525
Common Stock		100,000
Retained Earnings		98,491
Cash Dividends	10,000	
Income Summary	89,200	90,800
Sales—Department A		197,080
Sales—Department B		560,920
Sales Returns and Allowances—Department A	2,780	
Sales Returns and Allowances—Department B	6,800	
Purchases—Department A	109,884	
Purchases—Department B	369,232	
Sales Salaries Expense	56,500	
Advertising Expense	14,350	
Depreciation Expense—Store Equipment	6,100	
Store Supplies Expense	2,700	
Miscellaneous Selling Expense	4,450	
Office Salaries Expense	48,000	
Rent Expense	18,000	
Heating and Lighting Expense	16,800	
Property Tax Expense	6,200	
Insurance Expense	2,400	
Uncollectible Accounts Expense	2,200	
Miscellaneous General Expense	3,150	
Interest Expense	3,000	
Income Tax	22,100	
	1,091,796	1,091,796

Merchandise inventories at the beginning of the year were as follows: Department A, $26,400; Department B, $62,800.

The bases to be used in apportioning expenses, together with other essential information, are as follows:

Sales salaries expense—payroll records: Department A, $12,900; Department B, $43,600.

Advertising expense—usage: Department A, $5,600; Department B, $8,750.

Depreciation expense—average cost of equipment. Balances at beginning of year: Department A, $18,600; Department B, $59,200. Balances at end of year: Department A, $22,200; Department B, $70,000.

Store supplies expense—requisitions: Department A, $1,200; Department B, $1,500.

Office salaries expense—Department A, 30%; Department B, 70%.

Rent expense and heating and lighting expense—floor space: Department A, 4,800 sq. ft.; Department B, 7,200 sq. ft.

Property tax expense and insurance expense—average cost of equipment plus average cost of merchandise inventory.

Uncollectible accounts expense, miscellaneous selling expense, and miscellaneous general expense—volume of gross sales.

Instructions:

Prepare an income statement departmentalized through income from operations.

24–24A. R. W. Miller Company is considering discontinuance of one of its twelve departments. If operations in Department L are discontinued, it is estimated that the indirect operating expenses and the level of operations in the other departments will not be affected.

Data from the income statement for the past year ended December 31, which is considered to be a typical year, are as follows:

	Department L		Other Departments	
Sales...........................		$44,000		$765,000
Cost of merchandise sold.........		23,500		420,750
Gross profit.....................		$20,500		$344,250
Operating expenses:				
Direct expenses...............	$16,500		$192,500	
Indirect expenses	9,000	25,500	99,000	291,500
Income (loss) before income tax ...		$ (5,000)		$ 52,750

Instructions:

(1) Prepare an estimated income statement for the current year ending December 31, assuming the discontinuance of Department L.

(2) On the basis of the data presented, would it be advisable to retain Department L?

24–25A. Kearney Fashions has 16 departments. Those with the least sales volume are Department 13 and Department 15, which were established about eighteen months ago on a trial basis. The board of directors believes that it is now time to consider the retention or the termination of these two departments. The following adjusted trial balance as of August 31, the end of the first month of the current fiscal year, is severely condensed. August is considered to be a typical month. The income tax accrual has no bearing on the decision and is excluded from consideration.

Kearney Fashions
Trial Balance
August 31, 19--

Current Assets.	236,200	
Plant Assets.	672,400	
Accumulated Depreciation—Plant Assets.		168,100
Current Liabilities		118,100
Common Stock		200,000
Retained Earnings		403,304
Cash Dividends.	30,000	
Sales—Department 13		32,500
Sales—Department 15		21,400
Sales—Other Departments		948,600
Cost of Merchandise Sold—Department 13.	21,125	
Cost of Merchandise Sold—Department 15.	14,980	
Cost of Merchandise Sold—Other Departments	569,160	
Direct Expenses—Department 13	8,125	
Direct Expenses—Department 15	7,490	
Direct Expenses—Other Departments	227,664	
Indirect Expenses.	94,860	
Interest Expense.	10,000	
	1,892,004	1,892,004

Instructions:

(1) Prepare an income statement for August, departmentalized through departmental margin.

(2) State your recommendations concerning the retention of Departments 13 and 15, giving reasons.

Mini-Case

24-27. Assume that you recently started to work in your family-owned hardware store as an assistant store manager. Your father, the store manager and major stockholder, is considering the elimination of the Garden Supply Department, which has been incurring net losses for several years. Condensed revenue and expense data for the most recent year ended December 31, are presented on the following page. These data are typical of recent years.

Trout Hardware
Income Statement
For Year Ended December 31, 19—

	Garden Supply Department	Other Departments	Total
Net sales	$17,000	$199,200	$216,200
Cost of merchandise sold	12,400	125,000	137,400
Gross profit	$ 4,600	$ 74,200	$ 78,800
Operating expenses:			
Selling expenses:			
Sales commissions expense	$1,360	$15,936	$17,296
Advertising expense	510	6,000	6,510
Depreciation expense—store equipment	400	4,700	5,100
Miscellaneous selling expense	255	2,988	3,243
Total selling expenses	$2,525	$29,624	$32,149
General expenses:			
Administrative salaries expense	$1,730	$15,570	$17,300
Rent expense	568	4,544	5,112
Utilities expense	511	4,090	4,601
Insurance and property tax expense	350	3,340	3,690
Miscellaneous general expense	153	1,793	1,946
Total general expenses	3,312	29,337	32,649
Total operating expenses	5,837	58,961	64,798
Income (loss) from operations	$ (1,237)	$ 15,239	$ 14,002
Other expense:			
Interest expense			1,200
Income before income tax			$ 12,802
Income tax			1,920
Net income			$ 10,882

Bases used in allocating operating expenses among departments are as follows:

Expense	Basis
Sales commissions expense	Actual: 8% of net sales
Advertising expense	Actual: all advertising consists of brochures distributed by the various departments advertising specific products
Depreciation expense	Average cost of store equipment used
Miscellaneous selling expense	Amount of net sales
Administrative salaries expense	Each of the 10 departments apportioned an equal share
Rent expense	Floor space occupied
Utilities expense	Floor space occupied
Insurance and property tax expense	Average cost of equipment used plus average cost of inventory
Miscellaneous general expense	Amount of net sales

Since the Garden Supply Department is under your supervision, your father has asked your opinion as to whether the Garden Supply Department should be eliminated.

Instructions:

Prepare a brief statement of your recommendation to your father, supported by such schedule(s) as you think will be helpful to him in reaching a decision.

Answers to Self-Examination Questions

1. **B** The manager of a profit center (answer B) has responsibility for and authority over costs and revenues. If the manager has responsibility and authority for only costs, the department is referred to as a cost center (answer A). If the responsibility and authority extend to the investment in assets as well as costs and revenues, it is referred to as an investment center (answer C).

2. **B** Operating expenses should be apportioned to the various departments as nearly as possible in accordance with the cost of services rendered to them. For rent expense, generally the most appropriate basis is the floor space devoted to each department (answer B).

3. **C** When the departmental margin approach to income reporting is employed, the direct departmental expenses for each department are deducted from the gross profit for each department to yield departmental margin for each department (answer C). The indirect expenses are deducted from the total departmental margin to yield income from operations (answer A). The final total income is identified as net income (answer B).

4. **A** Operating expenses traceable to or incurred for the sole benefit of a specific department, such as sales commissions expense, are termed direct expenses (answer A) and should be so reported on the income statement departmentalized through departmental margin.

5. **B** Operating expenses incurred for the entire enterprise as a unit and hence not subject to the control of individual department managers, such as office salaries, are termed indirect expenses (answer B) and should be so reported on the income statement departmentalized through departmental margin.

CHAPTER 25

Responsibility Accounting for Investment Centers; Transfer Pricing

CHAPTER OBJECTIVES

Describe and illustrate responsibility accounting for investment centers.

Describe and illustrate transfer pricing for decentralized operations.

Businesses that are separated into two or more manageable units in which divisional managers have authority and responsibility for operations are said to be decentralized. Three types of decentralized operations — cost centers, profit centers, and investment centers — were described in Chapter 24. The role of the managerial accountant in providing useful reports to assist individual managers in evaluating and controlling cost centers and profit centers was also described.

This chapter completes the discussion of decentralized business operations by focusing on responsibility accounting and reporting for investment centers. In addition, the pricing of products or services that are transferred between decentralized segments of a company is discussed.

RESPONSIBILITY ACCOUNTING FOR INVESTMENT CENTERS

Since investment center managers have responsibility for revenues and expenses, operating income is an essential part of investment center reporting. In addition, because the investment center manager also has responsibility for the assets invested in the center, two additional measures of performance are often used. These additional measures are the rate of return on investment and residual income. Each of these measures of investment center performance will be described and illustrated for Harrison Company, a diversified company with three operating divisions, as shown in the following organization chart:

PARTIAL
ORGANIZATION
CHART FOR A
DECENTRALIZED
COMPANY WITH
INVESTMENT
CENTERS

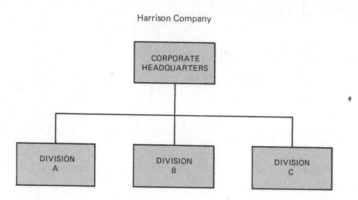

Harrison Company

Operating Income

Because investment centers are evaluated as if they were separate companies, traditional financial statements are normally prepared for each center. For purposes of assessing profitability, operating income is the focal point of analysis. Since the determination of operating income for decentralized operations was described and illustrated in Chapter 24, only condensed divisional income statements will be used for illustrative purposes. The condensed divisional income statements for Harrison Company are as follows:

Harrison Company Divisional Income Statements For Year Ended December 31, 19--			
	Division A	Division B	Division C
Sales..........................	$560,000	$672,000	$750,000
Cost of goods sold	336,000	470,400	562,500
Gross profit....................	$224,000	$201,600	$187,500
Operating expenses	154,000	117,600	112,500
Operating income...............	$ 70,000	$ 84,000	$ 75,000

Based on the amount of divisional operating income, Division B is the most profitable of Harrison Company's divisions, with income from operations of $84,000. Divisions A and C are less profitable, with Division C reporting $5,000 more operating income than Division A.

Although operating income is a useful measure of investment center profitability, it does not reflect the amount of investment in assets committed to each center. For example, if the amount of assets invested in Division B is twice that of the other divisions, then Division B is the least profitable of the divisions in terms of the rate of return on investment. Since investment center managers also control the amount of assets invested in their centers, they should be held accountable for the use of invested assets.

Responsibility Accounting for Investment Centers; Transfer Pricing

Rate of Return on Investment

One of the most widely used measures of divisional performance for investment centers is the **rate of return on investment (ROI)**, or **rate of return on assets.** This rate is computed as follows:

$$\text{Rate of Return on Investment (ROI)} = \frac{\text{Operating Income}}{\text{Invested Assets}}$$

The rate of return on investment is useful because the three factors subject to control by divisional managers (revenues, expenses, and invested assets) are considered in its computation. By measuring profitability relative to the amount of assets invested in each division, the rate of return on investment can be used to compare divisions. The higher the rate of return on investment, the more effectively the division is utilizing its assets in generating income. To illustrate, the rate of return on investment for each division of Harrison Company, based on the book value of invested assets, is as follows:

	Operating Income	Invested Assets	Rate of Return on Investment
Division A	$70,000	$350,000	20%
Division B	84,000	700,000	12%
Division C	75,000	500,000	15%

Although Division B generated the largest operating income, its rate of return on investment (12%) is the lowest. Hence, relative to the assets invested, Division B is the least profitable division. In comparison, the rates of return on investment of Divisions A and C are 20% and 15% respectively. These differences in the rates of return on investment may be analyzed by restating the expression for the rate of return on investment in expanded form, as follows:

$$\text{Rate of Return on Investment (ROI)} = \frac{\text{Operating Income}}{\text{Sales}} \times \frac{\text{Sales}}{\text{Invested Assets}}$$

In the expanded form, the rate of return on investment is the product of two factors: (1) the ratio of operating income to sales, often termed the **profit margin,** and (2) the ratio of sales to invested assets, often termed the **investment turnover.** As shown in the following computation, the use of this expanded expression yields the same rate of return for Division A, 20%, as the previous expression for the rate of return on investment:

$$\text{Rate of Return on Investment (ROI)} = \frac{\text{Operating Income}}{\text{Sales}} \times \frac{\text{Sales}}{\text{Invested Assets}}$$

$$\text{ROI} = \frac{\$70,000}{\$560,000} \times \frac{\$560,000}{\$350,000}$$

$$\text{ROI} = 12.5\% \times 1.6$$

$$\text{ROI} = 20\%$$

The expanded expression for the rate of return on investment is useful in management's evaluation and control of decentralized operations because the profit margin and the investment turnover focus on the underlying operating relationships of each division. The profit margin component focuses on profitability by indicating the rate of profit earned on each sales dollar. When efforts are aimed at increasing a division's profit margin by changing the division's sales mix, for example, the division's rate of return on investment may increase.

The investment turnover component focuses on efficiency in the use of assets and indicates the rate at which sales are being generated for each dollar of invested assets. The more sales per dollar invested, the greater the efficiency in the use of the assets. When efforts are aimed at increasing a division's investment turnover through special sales promotions, for example, the division's rate of return on investment may increase.

The rate of return on investment, using the expanded expression for each division of Harrison Company, is summarized as follows:

	Rate of Return on Investment (ROI) =	Profit Margin	×	Investment Turnover
	ROI =	$\dfrac{\text{Operating Income}}{\text{Sales}}$	×	$\dfrac{\text{Sales}}{\text{Invested Assets}}$
Division A:	ROI =	$\dfrac{\$70,000}{\$560,000}$	×	$\dfrac{\$560,000}{\$350,000}$
	ROI =	12.5%	×	1.6
	ROI =	20%		
Division B:	ROI =	$\dfrac{\$84,000}{\$672,000}$	×	$\dfrac{\$672,000}{\$700,000}$
	ROI =	12.5%	×	.96
	ROI =	12%		
Division C:	ROI =	$\dfrac{\$75,000}{\$750,000}$	×	$\dfrac{\$750,000}{\$500,000}$
	ROI =	10%	×	1.5
	ROI =	15%		

Although Divisions A and B have the same profit margins, Division A's investment turnover is larger than that of Division B (1.6 to .96). Thus, by more efficiently utilizing its invested assets, Division A has a higher rate of return on investment than Division B. Division C has a 10% profit margin and an investment turnover of 1.5, both slightly lower than that of Division A. However, the product of these factors results in a return on investment of 15% for Division C, as compared to 20% for Division A.

To determine possible ways of increasing the rate of return on investment, the profit margin and investment turnover for a division should be analyzed. For example, if Division A is in a highly competitive industry where the profit

Responsibility Accounting for Investment Centers; Transfer Pricing

margin cannot be easily increased, the division manager should concentrate on increasing the investment turnover. To illustrate, assume that sales of Division A could be increased by $56,000 through changes in advertising expenditures. The cost of goods sold is expected to be 60% of sales, and operating expenses will increase to $169,400. If the advertising changes are undertaken, Division A's operating income would increase from $70,000 to $77,000, as shown in the following condensed income statement:

Sales ($560,000 + $56,000)	$616,000
Cost of goods sold ($616,000 × 60%)	369,600
Gross profit	$246,400
Operating expenses	169,400
Operating income	$ 77,000

The rate of return on investment for Division A, using the expanded expression, is recomputed as follows:

$$\text{Rate of Return on Investment (ROI)} = \frac{\text{Operating Income}}{\text{Sales}} \times \frac{\text{Sales}}{\text{Invested Assets}}$$

$$\text{ROI} = \frac{\$77,000}{\$616,000} \times \frac{\$616,000}{\$350,000}$$

$$\text{ROI} = 12.5\% \times 1.76$$

$$\text{ROI} = 22\%$$

Although Division A's profit margin remains the same (12.5%), the division's investment turnover has increased from 1.6 to 1.76, an increase of 10% (.16 ÷ 1.6). The 10% increase in investment turnover has the effect of also increasing the rate of return on investment by 10% (from 20% to 22%).

The major advantage of the use of the rate of return on investment over operating income as a divisional performance measure is that the amount of divisional investment is directly considered. Thus, divisional performances can be compared, even though the sizes of the divisions may vary significantly.

In addition to its use as a performance measure, the rate of return on investment can assist management in other ways. For example, in considering a decision to expand the operations of Harrison Company, management should consider giving priority to Division A because it earns the highest rate of return on investment. If the current rates of return on investment can be maintained in the future, an investment in Division A will return 20 cents (20%) on each dollar invested, while investments in Divisions B and C will return only 12 cents and 15 cents respectively.

A major disadvantage of the rate of return on investment as a performance measure is that it may lead divisional managers to reject new investment proposals, even though the rate of return on these investments exceeds the minimum considered acceptable by the company. For example, a division might have an overall rate of return on investment of 25%, and the company might have an overall rate of return on investment of 15%. If the division accepts a new investment that would earn a 20% rate of return on investment, the overall rate of return for the division would decrease, but the overall rate of return for the company as a whole would increase. Thus, the division manager might reject the proposal, even though its acceptance would be in the best interests of the company.

Residual Income

In the previous illustration for Harrison Company, two measures of evaluating divisional performance were discussed and illustrated. The advantages and disadvantages of both measures were also discussed. An additional measure, residual income, is useful in overcoming some of the disadvantages associated with the operating income and rate of return on investment measures.

Residual income is the excess of divisional operating income over a minimum amount of desired operating income. The minimum amount of desired divisional operating income is set by top management by establishing a minimum rate of return for the invested assets and then multiplying this rate by the amount of divisional assets. To illustrate, assume that the top management of Harrison Company has established 10% as the minimum rate of return on divisional assets. The residual incomes for Divisions A, B, and C are computed as follows:

RESIDUAL INCOME
BY DIVISION

	Division A	Division B	Division C
Divisional operating income	$70,000	$84,000	$75,000
Minimum amount of divisional operating income:			
$350,000 × 10%	35,000		
$700,000 × 10%		70,000	
$500,000 × 10%			50,000
Residual income	$35,000	$14,000	$25,000

The major advantage of residual income as a performance measure is that it not only gives consideration to a minimum rate of return on investment, but also to the total magnitude of the operating income earned by each division. For example, Division A has more residual income than the other divisions of Harrison Company, even though it has the least operating income. Also, Division C earns $11,000 more residual income than Division B, even though Division B generates more operating income than Division C. The reason for this difference is that Division B has $200,000 more assets than Division C. Hence, Division B's operating income is reduced by $20,000 ($200,000 × 10%) more than Division C's operating income in determining residual income.

The preceding paragraphs have described and illustrated three measures — operating income, rate of return on investment, and residual income — which management can use in evaluating and controlling investment center performance. In practice, most companies use some combination of all these measures.

Responsibility Accounting for Investment Centers; Transfer Pricing

TRANSFER PRICING

The use of responsibility accounting and reporting in measuring performance in decentralized companies can be important in motivating managers to achieve common profit goals. However, when decentralized units transfer products or render services to each other, the transfer price—the price to charge for the products or services—becomes an issue. Since transfer prices affect the revenues and expenses of both the receiving unit and the unit providing the product or service, transfer prices affect the performance measures used for evaluating divisional performance.

The objective of transfer pricing is to encourage each divisional manager to transfer goods and services between divisions if overall company income can be increased by doing so. As will be illustrated, however, transfer prices may be misused to the detriment of overall company income.

The following paragraphs describe and illustrate various approaches to establishing transfer prices, the effect of transfer prices on the evaluation of decentralized performance, and their potential impact on overall company income. Three commonly used approaches are (1) the market price approach, (2) the negotiated price approach, and (3) the cost price approach.

Although transfer prices may apply when decentralized units are organized as cost or profit centers, a diversified company (Wilson Company) with two operating divisions (M and N) organized as investment centers will be used for the illustrations in the remainder of this chapter. Condensed income statements for Wilson Company's divisions, with no intracompany transfers and a breakdown of expenses into variable and fixed components, are as follows:

	Division M	Division N	Total
Wilson Company			
Divisional Income Statements			
For Year Ended December 31, 19--			
Sales:			
50,000 units × $20 per unit.........	$1,000,000		$1,000,000
20,000 units × $40 per unit.........		$800,000	800,000
			$1,800,000
Expenses:			
Variable:			
50,000 units × $10 per unit.......	$ 500,000		$ 500,000
20,000 units × $30* per unit.......		$600,000	600,000
Fixed............................	300,000	100,000	400,000
Total expenses...................	$ 800,000	$700,000	$1,500,000
Operating income..................	$ 200,000	$100,000	$ 300,000

*$20 of the $30 per unit represents materials costs, and the remaining $10 per unit represents other expenses incurred within Division N.

Market Price Approach

Under the market price approach, the transfer price is the price at which the product or service transferred could be sold to outside buyers. If an outside market exists for the product or service transferred, then the current market price at which the purchasing division could buy the product or service outside the company would seem to be a reasonable transfer price for intracompany transfers. However, the appropriateness of the market price approach depends on whether the division supplying the product or service is operating at full capacity and can sell all it produces.

To illustrate, assume that materials used by Wilson Company in producing Division N's product are currently purchased from an outside supplier at $20 per unit. The same materials are produced by Division M. If Division M is operating at full capacity of 50,000 units and can sell all it produces to either Division N or to outside buyers, then the use of a transfer price of $20 per unit (the market price) has no effect on the income of Division M or total company income. Division M will earn revenues of $20 per unit on all its production and sales, regardless of who buys its product, and Division N will pay $20 per unit for materials, regardless of whether it purchases the materials from Division M or from an outside supplier. In this situation, the use of the market price as the transfer price is appropriate. The condensed divisional income statements for Wilson Company under such circumstances would be as shown on the previous page.

If unused capacity exists in the supplying division, the use of the market price approach may not lead to the maximization of total company income. To illustrate, assume that Division M has unused capacity of 20,000 units and it can continue to sell only 50,000 units to outside buyers. In this situation, the transfer price should be set to motivate the manager of Division N to purchase from Division M if the variable cost per unit of product of Division M is less than the market price. If the variable costs are less than $20 per unit but the transfer price is set equal to the market price of $20, then the manager of Division N is indifferent as to whether materials are purchased from Division M or from outside suppliers, since the cost per unit to Division N would be the same, $20. However, Division N's purchase of 20,000 units of materials from outside suppliers at a cost of $20 per unit would not maximize overall company income, since this market price per unit is greater than the unit variable expenses of Division M, $10. Hence, the intracompany transfer could save the company the difference between the market price per unit and Division M's unit variable expenses. This savings of $10 per unit would add $200,000 (20,000 units × $10) to overall company income.

Negotiated Price Approach

In the previous illustration, the manager of Division N should be encouraged to purchase from Division M by establishing a transfer price at an amount less than the market price of $20 per unit. Division N's materials cost per unit would thus decrease, and its operating income would increase. In such situations, the negotiated price approach can be used to establish an appropriate transfer price.

The **negotiated price approach** allows the managers of decentralized units to agree (negotiate) among themselves as to the proper transfer price. If agreement cannot be reached among the division managers, the company's top management may have to intervene to set the transfer price. To illustrate, assume that Wilson Company's division managers agree to a transfer price of $15 for Division M's product. By purchasing from Division M, Division N would then report $5 per unit less materials cost. At the same time, Division M would increase its sales to a total of 70,000 units (50,000 units to outside buyers and 20,000 units to Division N). The effect of increasing Division M's sales by $300,000 (20,000 units × $15 per unit) is to increase its income by $100,000 ($300,000 sales − $200,000 variable expenses). The effect of reducing Division N's materials cost by $100,000 (20,000 units × $5 per unit) is to increase its income by $100,000. Therefore, Wilson Company's income is increased by $200,000 ($100,000 reported by Division M and $100,000 reported by Division N), as shown in the following condensed income statements:

Wilson Company
Divisional Income Statements
For Year Ended December 31, 19--

	Division M	Division N	Total
Sales:			
50,000 units × $20 per unit.........	$1,000,000		$1,000,000
20,000 units × $15 per unit.........	300,000		300,000
20,000 units × $40 per unit.........		$800,000	800,000
	$1,300,000	$800,000	$2,100,000
Expenses:			
Variable:			
70,000 units × $10 per unit.......	$ 700,000		$ 700,000
20,000 units × $25* per unit......		$500,000	500,000
Fixed.........................	300,000	100,000	400,000
Total expenses................	$1,000,000	$600,000	$1,600,000
Operating income..............	$ 300,000	$200,000	$ 500,000

*$10 per unit of the $25 is incurred solely within Division N, and $15 per unit represents the transfer price per unit from Division M.

In the Wilson Company illustration, any transfer price less than the market price of $20 but greater than Division M's unit variable expenses of $10 would increase each division's income and would increase overall company income by $200,000. By establishing a range of $20 to $10 for the negotiated transfer price, each division manager will have an incentive to negotiate the intra-company transfer of the materials. For example, a transfer price of $18 would increase Division M's income by $160,000 (from $200,000 to $360,000) and Division N's income by $40,000 (from $100,000 to $140,000). Overall company income would still be increased by $200,000 (from $300,000 to $500,000), as shown in the following condensed income statements:

Wilson Company
Divisional Income Statements
For Year Ended December 31, 19--

	Division M	Division N	Total
Sales:			
50,000 units × $20 per unit.........	$1,000,000		$1,000,000
20,000 units × $18 per unit.........	360,000		360,000
20,000 units × $40 per unit.........		$800,000	800,000
	$1,360,000	$800,000	$2,160,000
Expenses:			
Variable:			
70,000 units × $10 per unit.......	$ 700,000		$ 700,000
20,000 units × $28* per unit......		$560,000	560,000
Fixed.........................	300,000	100,000	400,000
Total expenses.................	$1,000,000	$660,000	$1,660,000
Operating income..................	$ 360,000	$140,000	$ 500,000

*$10 per unit of the $28 is incurred solely within Division N, and $18 per unit represents the transfer price per unit from Division M.

Cost Price Approach

Under the **cost price approach**, cost is used as the basis for setting transfer prices. With this approach, a variety of cost concepts may be used. For example, cost may refer to either total product cost per unit or variable product cost per unit. If total product cost per unit is used, direct materials, direct labor, and factory overhead are included in the transfer price. If variable product cost per unit is used, the fixed factory overhead component of total product cost is excluded from the transfer price.

Either actual costs or standard (budgeted) costs may be used in applying the cost price approach. If actual costs are used, inefficiencies of the producing division are transferred to the purchasing division, and thus there is little incentive for the producing division to control costs carefully. For this reason, most companies use standard costs in the cost price approach, so that differences between actual and standard costs are isolated in the producing divisions for cost control purposes.

When division managers have responsibility for only costs incurred in their divisions, the cost price approach to transfer pricing is frequently used. However, many accountants argue that the cost price approach is inappropriate for decentralized operations organized as profit or investment centers. In profit and investment centers, division managers have responsibility for both revenues and expenses. The use of cost as a transfer price, however, ignores the supplying division manager's responsibility over revenues. When a supplying division's sales are all intracompany transfers, for example, the use of the cost price approach would prevent the supplying division from reporting any operating income. A cost-based transfer price would therefore not motivate the division manager to make intracompany transfers, even though they are in the best interests of the company.

1. Managers of what type of decentralized units have authority and responsibility over revenues, expenses, and invested assets?
   A. Profit center   C. Investment center
   B. Cost center   D. None of the above

2. Division A of Kern Co. has sales of $350,000, cost of goods sold of $200,000, operating expenses of $30,000, and invested assets of $600,000. What is the rate of return on investment for Division A?
   A. 20%   C. 40%
   B. 25%   D. None of the above

3. Which of the following expressions is frequently referred to as the turnover factor in determining the rate of return on investment?
   A. Operating Income ÷ Sales
   B. Operating Income ÷ Invested Assets
   C. Sales ÷ Invested Assets
   D. None of the above

4. Division L of Liddy Co. has a rate of return on investment of 24% and an investment turnover of 1.6. What is the profit margin?
   A. 6%   C. 24%
   B. 15%   D. None of the above

5. Which approach to transfer pricing uses the price at which the product or service transferred could be sold to outside buyers as the transfer price?
   A. Cost price approach   C. Market price approach
   B. Negotiated price approach D. None of the above

Self-
Examination
Questions
(Answers
at end of
chapter.)

Discussion Questions

25–1. What are three ways in which decentralized operations may be organized?

25–2. Name three performance measures useful in evaluating investment centers.

25–3. What is the major shortcoming of using operating income as a performance measure for investment centers?

25–4. Describe how the factors under the control of the investment center manager (revenues, expenses, and invested assets) are considered in the computation of the rate of return on investment?

25–5. Monahan Co. has $200,000 invested in Division N, which earned $54,000 of operating income. What is the rate of return on investment for Division N?

25–6. If Monahan Co. in Question 25–5 had sales of $360,000, what is (a) the profit margin and (b) the investment turnover for Division N?

25–7. What are two ways of expressing the rate of return on investment?

25–8. In evaluating investment centers, what does multiplying the profit margin by the investment turnover equal?

25–9. How could a division of a decentralized company organized as investment centers be considered the least profitable, even though it earned the largest amount of operating income?

25–10. Which component of the rate of return on investment (profit margin factor or investment turnover factor) focuses on efficiency in the use of assets and indicates the rate at which sales are generated for each dollar of invested assets?

25–11. Division F of Platt Co. has a rate of return on investment of 18%. (a) If Division F increases its investment turnover by 10%, what would be the new rate of return on investment? (b) If Division F also increases its profit margin from 12% to 18%, what would be the new rate of return on investment?

25–12. How does the use of the rate of return on investment facilitate comparability of divisions of decentralized companies?

25–13. The rates of return on investment for Gibbon Co.'s three divisions, C, D, and E, are 20%, 24%, and 18%, respectively. In expanding operations, which of Gibbon Co.'s divisions should be given priority? Explain.

25–14. What term is used to describe the excess of divisional operating income over a minimum amount of desired operating income?

25–15. Division Q of Choi Co. reported operating income of $150,000, based on invested assets of $500,000. If the minimum rate of return on divisional investments is 18%, what is the residual income for Division Q?

25–16. What term is used to describe the amount charged for products transferred or services rendered to other decentralized units in a company?

25–17. What is the objective of transfer pricing?

25–18. Name three commonly used approaches to establishing transfer prices.

25–19. What transfer price approach uses the price at which the product or service transferred could be sold to outside buyers as the transfer price?

25–20. When is the negotiated price approach preferred over the market price approach in setting transfer prices?

25–21. If division managers cannot agree among themselves on a transfer price when using the negotiated price approach, how is the transfer price established?

25–22. When using the negotiated price approach to transfer pricing, within what range should the transfer price be established?

Exercises

25–23. One item is omitted from each of the following condensed divisional income statements of Weldon Company:

	Division X	Division Y	Division Z
Sales..................	$500,000	(c)	$560,000
Cost of goods sold.....	(a)	465,000	336,000
Gross profit	$200,000	$155,000	(e)
Operating expenses....	(b)	43,000	64,000
Operating income......	$140,000	(d)	(f)

(a) Determine the amount of the missing items, identifying them by letter. (b) Based on operating income, which division is the most profitable?

25–24. The operating income and the amount of invested assets in each division of Weldon Company are as follows:

	Operating Income	Invested Assets
Division X	$140,000	$700,000
Division Y	112,000	350,000
Division Z	160,000	640,000

(a) Compute the rate of return on investment for each division. (b) Which division is the most profitable per dollar invested?

25–25. Based on the data in Exercise 25-24, assume that management has established a minimum rate of return for invested assets of 10%. (a) Determine the residual income for each division. (b) Based on residual income, which of the divisions is the most profitable?

25–26. One item is omitted from each of the following computations of the rate of return on investment:

Rate of Return on Investment	=	Profit Margin	×	Investment Turnover
(a)		12%		1.25
24%		(b)		1.50
24%		15%		(c)
20%		(d)		2.50
(e)		18%		2.00

Determine the missing items, identifying each by the appropriate letter.

25–27. The condensed income statement for Division K of Streer Company is as follows:

Sales........................	$400,000
Cost of goods sold............	240,000
Gross profit	$160,000
Operating expenses..........	114,000
Operating income............	$ 46,000

The manager of Division K is considering ways to increase the rate of return on investment. (a) Using the expanded expression, determine the profit margin, investment turnover, and rate of return on investment of Division K, assuming that $250,000 of assets have been invested in Division K. (b) If expenses could be reduced by $10,000 without decreasing sales, what would be the impact on the profit margin, investment turnover, and rate of return on investment for Division K?

25–28. One or more items is missing from the following tabulation of rate of return on investment and residual income:

Invested Assets	Operating Income	Rate of Return on Investment	Minimum Rate of Return	Minimum Amount of Operating Income	Residual Income
(a)	(b)	16%	12%	$48,000	$16,000
$600,000	(c)	18%	(d)	(e)	$48,000
$500,000	$110,000	(f)	(g)	$70,000	(h)
$300,000	$ 57,000	19%	15%	(i)	(j)

Determine the missing items, identifying each item by the appropriate letter.

25–29. Materials used by Payne Company in producing Division R's product are currently purchased from outside suppliers at a cost of $40 per unit. However, the same materials are available from Division W. Division W has unused capacity and can produce the materials needed by Division R at a variable cost of $25 per unit. (a) If a transfer price of $32 per unit is established and 50,000 units of material are transferred, with no reduction in Division W's current sales, how much would Payne Company's total operating income increase? (b) How much would operating income of Division R increase? (c) How much would the operating income of Division W increase?

25–30. Based on the Payne Company data in Exercise 25-29, assume that a transfer price of $30 has been established and 50,000 units of materials are transferred, with no reduction in Division W's current sales. (a) How much would Payne Company's total operating income increase? (b) How much would Division R's operating income increase? (c) How much would Division W's operating income increase? (d) If the negotiated price approach is used, what would be the range of acceptable transfer prices?

Problems

25–31. Turnage Company is a diversified company with three operating divisions organized as investment centers. Condensed data taken from the records of the three divisions for the year ended December 31 are as follows:

	Division E	Division F	Division G
Sales...............	$1,200,000	$660,000	$640,000
Cost of goods sold....	900,000	462,000	384,000
Operating expenses...	204,000	118,800	176,000
Invested assets.......	800,000	600,000	400,000

The management of Turnage Company is evaluating each division as a basis for planning a future expansion of operations.

Instructions:

(1) Prepare condensed divisional income statements for Divisions E, F, and G.
(2) Using the expanded expression, compute the profit margin, investment turnover, and rate of return on investment for each division.
(3) If available funds permit the expansion of operations of only one division, which of the divisions would you recommend for expansion, based on (1) and (2)?

25-32. A condensed income statement for Division P of Fairfax Company for the past year is as follows:

Fairfax Company—Division P
Income Statement
For Year Ended December 31, 19--

Sales........................	$1,500,000
Cost of goods sold............	1,050,000
Gross profit	$ 450,000
Operating expenses...........	270,000
Operating income.............	$ 180,000

The president of Fairfax Company is concerned with Division P's low rate of return on invested assets of $1,200,000, and has indicated that the division's rate of return on investment must be increased to at least 18% by the end of the next year if operations are to continue. The division manager is considering the following three proposals:

Proposal 1: Reduce invested assets by discontinuing a product line. This would eliminate sales of $200,000, cost of goods sold of $140,000, and operating expenses of $49,000. Assets of $160,000 would be transferred to other divisions at no gain or loss.

Proposal 2: Purchase new and more efficient machinery and thereby reduce the cost of goods sold by $93,000. Sales would remain unchanged, and the old machinery, which has no remaining book value, would be scrapped at no gain or loss. The new machinery would increase invested assets by $300,000 for the year.

Proposal 3: Transfer equipment with a book value of $200,000 to other divisions at no gain or loss and lease similar equipment. The annual lease payments would exceed the amount of depreciation expense on the old equipment by $6,000. This increase in expense would be included as part of the cost of goods sold. Sales would remain unchanged.

Instructions:

(1) Determine the profit margin, investment turnover, and rate of return on investment for Division P for the past year.
(2) Using the expanded expression, prepare condensed estimated income statements for Division P for each proposal.
(3) Using the expanded expression, determine the profit margin, investment turnover, and rate of return on investment for Division P under each proposal.
(4) Which of the three proposals would meet the required 18% rate of return on investment?
(5) If Division P were in a highly competitive industry where the profit margin and sales could not be increased, how much would invested assets have to be reduced to meet the president's required 18% rate of return on investment?

25-33. Data for Divisions V, W, X, Y, and Z of McGarity Company are as follows:

	Sales	Operating Income	Invested Assets	Rate of Return on Investment	Profit Margin	Investment Turnover
Division V ...	$600,000	(a)	(b)	(c)	15%	1.20
Division W...	(d)	$ 63,000	(e)	(f)	11.2%	1.25
Division X ...	$800,000	$100,000	(g)	(h)	(i)	2.00
Division Y ...	$750,000	(j)	$300,000	24%	(k)	(l)
Division Z ...	(m)	(n)	$425,000	20%	12.5%	(o)

Instructions:

(1) Determine the missing items, identifying each by letters (a) through (o).
(2) Determine the residual income for each division, assuming that the minimum rate of return established by management is 10%.
(3) Which division is the most profitable?

25-34. The vice-president of operations of Parsons Company is evaluating the performance of two divisions organized as investment centers. Division I generates the largest amount of operating income but has the lowest rate of return on investment. Division J has the highest rate of return on investment but generates the smallest operating income. Invested assets and condensed income statement data for the past year for each division are as follows:

	Division I	Division J
Sales.........................	$4,500,000	$4,800,000
Cost of goods sold............	3,075,000	3,120,000
Operating expenses...........	831,000	1,104,000
Invested assets..............	3,600,000	3,200,000

Instructions:

(1) Prepare condensed income statements for the past year for each division.
(2) Using the expanded expression, determine the profit margin, investment turnover, and rate of return on investment for each division.
(3) If management desires a minimum rate of return of 10%, determine the residual income for each division.
(4) Discuss the evaluation of Divisions I and J, using the performance measures determined in (1), (2), and (3).

25–35. Smathers Company is diversified, with two operating divisions, F and G. Condensed divisional income statements, which involve no intracompany transfers and which include a breakdown of expenses into variable and fixed components, are as follows:

Smathers Company
Divisional Income Statements
For Year Ended December 31, 19--

	Division F	Division G	Total
Sales:			
120,000 units × $40 per unit.....	$4,800,000		$4,800,000
40,000 units × $50 per unit......		$2,000,000	2,000,000
			$6,800,000
Expenses:			
Variable:			
120,000 units × $24 per unit...	$2,880,000		$2,880,000
40,000 units × $32* per unit...		$1,280,000	1,280,000
Fixed.........................	920,000	520,000	1,440,000
Total expenses..............	$3,800,000	$1,800,000	$5,600,000
Operating income................	$1,000,000	$ 200,000	$1,200,000

*$28 of the $32 per unit represents materials costs, and the remaining $4 per unit represents other expenses incurred within Division G.

Division F is operating at two thirds of its capacity of 180,000 units. Materials used in producing Division G's product are currently purchased from outside suppliers at a price of $28 per unit. The materials used by Division G are produced by Division F. Except for the possible transfer of materials between divisions, no changes are expected in sales and expenses.

Instructions:

(1) Would the market price of $28 per unit be an appropriate transfer price for Smathers Company? Explain.

(2) If Division G purchases 40,000 units from Division F and a transfer price of $26 per unit is negotiated between the managers of Divisions F and G, how much would the operating income of each division and total company operating income increase?

(3) Prepare condensed divisional income statements for Smathers Company, based on the data in (2).

(4) If a transfer price of $27 per unit had been negotiated, how much would the operating income of each division and total company income have increased?

(5) (a) What is the range of possible negotiated transfer prices that would be acceptable for Smathers Company?

(b) If the division managers of F and G cannot agree on a transfer price, what price would you suggest as the transfer price?

25–36. The vice-president of operations of Vinson Inc. recently resigned, and the president is considering which one of two division managers to promote to the vacated position. Both division managers have been with the company approximately ten years. Operating data for each division for the past three years are as follows:

	1987	1986	1985
Division A:			
Sales.................	$ 770,000	$ 650,000	$ 600,000
Cost of goods sold.....	462,000	390,000	360,000
Gross profit	$ 308,000	$ 260,000	$ 240,000
Operating expenses....	200,200	175,500	163,200
Operating income......	$ 107,800	$ 84,500	$ 76,800
Invested assets........	$ 550,000	$ 500,000	$ 480,000
Total industry sales	$5,500,000	$5,200,000	$5,000,000
Division B:			
Sales.................	$ 966,000	$ 840,000	$ 750,000
Cost of goods sold.....	670,000	588,000	525,000
Gross profit	$ 296,000	$ 252,000	$ 225,000
Operating expenses....	151,100	117,600	105,000
Operating income......	$ 144,900	$ 134,400	$ 120,000
Invested assets........	$ 700,000	$ 600,000	$ 500,000
Total industry sales	$6,440,000	$4,800,000	$3,750,000

Instructions:

(1) For each division for each of the three years, use the expanded expression to determine the profit margin, investment turnover, and rate of return on investment.
(2) Assuming that 15% has been established as a minimum rate of return, determine the residual income for each division for each of the three years.
(3) Determine each division's market share (division sales divided by total industry sales) for each of the three years.
(4) Based on (1), (2), and (3), which division manager would you recommend for promotion to vice-president of operations?
(5) What other factors should be considered in the promotion decision?

Alternate Problems

25–31A. Barrow Company is a diversified company with three operating divisions organized as investment centers. Condensed data taken from the records of the three divisions for the year ended December 31 are as follows:

	Division R	Division S	Division T
Sales	$1,200,000	$750,000	$1,800,000
Cost of goods sold	950,000	600,000	1,300,000
Operating expenses	130,000	60,000	275,000
Invested assets	750,000	500,000	1,500,000

The management of Barrow Company is evaluating each division as a basis for planning a future expansion of operations.

Instructions:

(1) Prepare condensed divisional income statements for Divisions R, S, and T.
(2) Using the expanded expression, compute the profit margin, investment turnover, and rate of return on investment for each division.
(3) If available funds permit the expansion of operations of only one division, which of the divisions would you recommend for expansion, based on (1) and (2)?

25–33A. Data for Divisions P, Q, R, S, and T of Fawcett Company are as follows:

	Sales	Operating Income	Invested Assets	Rate of Return on Investment	Profit Margin	Investment Turnover
Division P ...	(a)	(b)	$400,000	17%	13.6%	(c)
Division Q...	$2,200,000	$176,000	(d)	(e)	(f)	2.75
Division R...	(g)	$135,000	(h)	(i)	15%	1.20
Division S ...	$ 840,000	(j)	$600,000	14%	(k)	(l)
Division T ...	$ 704,000	(m)	(n)	(o)	12.5%	1.28

Instructions:

(1) Determine the missing items, identifying each by letters (a) through (o).
(2) Determine the residual income for each division, assuming that the minimum rate of return established by management is 12%.
(3) Which division is the most profitable?

25–34A. The vice-president of operations of Gustafson Company is evaluating the performance of two divisions organized as investment centers. Division L has the highest rate of return on investment, but generates the smallest amount of operating income. Division M generates the largest operating income, but has the lowest rate of return on investment. Invested assets and condensed income statement data for the past year for each division are as follows:

	Division L	Division M
Sales	$3,125,000	$5,100,000
Cost of goods sold.........	2,500,000	4,000,000
Operating expenses	150,000	590,000
Invested assets	2,500,000	3,000,000

Instructions:

(1) Prepare condensed income statements for the past year for each division.
(2) Using the expanded expression, determine the profit margin, investment turnover, and rate of return on investment for each division.
(3) If management desires a minimum rate of return of 12%, determine the residual income for each division.
(4) Discuss the evaluation of Divisions L and M, using the performance measures determined in (1), (2), and (3).

25–35A. Bradford Company is diversified, with two operating divisions, X and Y. Condensed divisional income statements, which involve no intracompany transfers and which include a breakdown of expenses into variable and fixed components, are as follows:

Bradford Company
Divisional Income Statements
For Year Ended December 31, 19--

	Division X	Division Y	Total
Sales:			
150,000 units × $60 per unit......	$9,000,000		$ 9,000,000
50,000 units × $80 per unit.......		$4,000,000	4,000,000
			$13,000,000
Expenses:			
Variable:			
150,000 units × $30 per unit....	$4,500,000		$ 4,500,000
50,000 units × $50* per unit....		$2,500,000	2,500,000
Fixed.........................	3,000,000	1,000,000	4,000,000
Total expenses...............	$7,500,000	$3,500,000	$11,000,000
Operating income.................	$1,500,000	$ 500,000	$ 2,000,000

*$40 of the $50 per unit represents materials costs, and the remaining $10 per unit represents other expenses incurred within Division Y.

Division X is operating at three fourths of capacity of 200,000 units. Materials used in producing Division Y's product are currently purchased from outside suppliers at a price of $40 per unit. The materials used by Division Y are produced by Division X. Except for the possible transfer of materials between divisions, no changes are expected in sales and expenses.

Instructions:

(1) Would the market price of $40 per unit be an appropriate transfer price for Bradford Company? Explain.

(2) If Division Y purchases 50,000 units from Division X and a transfer price of $35 per unit is negotiated between the managers of Divisions X and Y, how much would the operating income of each division and total company operating income increase?

(3) Prepare condensed divisional income statements for Bradford Company, based on the data in (2).

(4) If a transfer price of $34 per unit is negotiated, how much would the operating income of each division and total company income increase?

(5) (a) What is the range of possible negotiated transfer prices that would be acceptable for Bradford Company?

(b) Assuming that the division managers of X and Y cannot agree on a transfer price, what price would you suggest as the transfer price?

25-37. Your father is the president of Hillsman Company, a privately held, diversified company with five separate divisions organized as investment centers. A condensed income statement for the Sporting Goods Division for the past year is as follows:

Mini-Case

Hillsman Company—Sporting Goods Division
Income Statement
For Year Ended December 31, 19--

Sales..	$32,000,000
Cost of goods sold...............................	19,200,000
Gross profit	$12,800,000
Operating expenses..............................	8,800,000
Operating income...............................	$ 4,000,000

The manager of the Sporting Goods Division was recently presented with the opportunity to add an additional product line, which would require invested assets of $6,000,000. A projected income statement for the new product line is as follows:

New Product Line
Projected Income Statement
For Year Ended December 31, 19--

Sales..	$7,500,000
Cost of goods sold...............................	4,500,000
Gross profit	$3,000,000
Operating expenses..............................	2,040,000
Operating income...............................	$ 960,000

The Sporting Goods Division currently has $20,000,000 in invested assets, and Hillsman Company's overall rate of return on investment, including all divisions, is 14%. Each division manager is evaluated on the basis of divisional rate of return on investment, and a bonus equal to $5,000 for each percentage point by which the division's rate of return on investment exceeds the company average is awarded each year.

Your father is concerned that the manager of the Sporting Goods Division rejected the addition of the new product line, when all the estimates indicated that the product line would be profitable and would increase overall company income. You have been asked to analyze the possible reasons why the Sporting Goods Division manager rejected the new product line.

Instructions:

(1) Determine the rate of return on investment for the Sporting Goods Division for the past year.

(2) Determine the Sporting Goods Division manager's bonus for the past year.

(3) Determine the estimated rate of return on investment for the new product line.

(4) Why might the manager of the Sporting Goods Division decide to reject the new product line?

(5) Can you suggest an alternative performance measure for motivating division managers to accept new investment opportunities that would increase the overall company income and rate of return on investment?

Answers to Self-Examination Questions

1. C Managers of investment centers (answer C) have authority and responsibility for revenues, expenses, and assets. Managers of profit centers (answer A) have authority and responsibility for revenues and expenses. Managers of cost centers (answer B) have authority and responsibility for costs.

2. A The rate of return on investment for Division A is 20% (answer A), computed as follows:

$$\text{Rate of Return on Investment (ROI)} = \frac{\cdot \text{Operating Income}}{\text{Invested Assets}}$$

$$\text{ROI} = \frac{\$350,000 - \$200,000 - \$30,000}{\$600,000}$$

$$\text{ROI} = \frac{\$120,000}{\$600,000}$$

$$\text{ROI} = 20\%$$

3. C Investment turnover is the ratio of sales to invested assets (answer C). The ratio of operating income to sales is the profit margin (answer A). The ratio of operating income to invested assets is the rate of return on investment (answer B).

4. B The profit margin for Division L of Liddy Co. is 15% (answer B), computed as follows:

$$\text{Rate of Return on Investment (ROI)} = \text{Profit Margin} \times \text{Investment Turnover}$$
$$24\% = \text{Profit Margin} \times 1.6$$
$$15\% = \text{Profit Margin}$$

5. C The market price approach (answer C) to transfer pricing uses the price at which the product or service transferred could be sold to outside buyers as the transfer price. The cost price approach (answer A) uses cost as the basis for setting transfer prices. The negotiated price approach (answer B) allows managers of decentralized units to agree (negotiate) among themselves as to the proper transfer price.

PART 9

Quantitative Techniques for Management Use

And The Computer Said...

As competition has become more and more intense in the retail industry, retailers have begun to rely more and more heavily on quantitative techniques and computers to cut expenses, to reduce inventory requirements, and to improve sales. Three examples of the use of quantitative techniques and computers in the retail industry are given in the following paragraphs.

Dylex Ltd., a Toronto operator of apparel stores, uses IBM's Inforem inventory program, which helps restock more than 1,000 stores from Vancouver to Cornerbrook, Newfoundland. "It allows you to keep track of inventory in each store by size and color and the rate at which it is selling, and then forecasts the estimated inventory," explains Chris Schwartz, a vice president of Dylex. "So if a particular store is in a Chinese neighborhood and sells a lot of small sizes, the computer will know that. And when new merchandise arrives, it will automatically allocate small sizes to that store." In addition, such systems help retailers adjust quickly when a product is selling poorly, says Gordon Edelstone, a vice president of Dylex's Tip Top division. "We can identify an item that looks like a dog and mark it down immediately and sell it even before (competitors) recognize the product isn't selling well."

In the next three years, K Mart Corp., with headquarters in Troy, Michigan, expects to spend $300 million to install computerized, laser-scanning registers that will automatically reorder certain merchandise when stock gets low. A similar retailer reduced the time it takes to replenish inventory because purchase orders are electronically transmitted to more than 500 suppliers. In addition, the company figures that average inventory investment has been reduced by about 17% for some products.

New York-based J.C. Penney Co. automatically reorders products accounting for 50% of its $12 billion in annual sales from 281 suppliers, cutting lead time by at least 10 days, says Robert Capone, director of systems and data processing. "There are two ways of getting purchase orders into the Penney system," he explains. "Orders are generated automatically based on reorder points and quantities, and other orders are entered into terminals at Penney stores. The order goes directly into the computer and right to the vendor. It isn't approved in New York."

SOURCE   Adapted from Hank Gilman, "The Technology Edge," *The Wall Street Journal*, September 16, 1985, p. 55C.

CHAPTER 26

Quantitative Techniques: Inventory Control and Cost Estimation

CHAPTER OBJECTIVES

Describe the general use of quantitative techniques by management.

Describe and illustrate the use of quantitative techniques for inventory control.

Describe and illustrate the use of the high-low, scattergraph, and least squares methods in estimating costs.

Describe and illustrate the learning effect in estimating costs.

Previous chapters have discussed many ways in which accounting data can be used by management in planning and controlling business operations, including such analyses as cost-volume-profit analysis, differential analysis, and capital investment analysis. These analyses can be performed using rather simple mathematical relationships, since they usually involve a limited number of objectives and variables. By using quantitative techniques which rely on more sophisticated mathematical relationships and statistical methods, management can consider a larger number of objectives and variables in planning and controlling operations.

The use of quantitative techniques often leads to a clarification of management decision alternatives and their expected effects on the business enterprise. For example, the most economical plan for purchasing materials for a single plant may be easily determined, based on the lowest overall cost per unit of materials. However, the most economical plan for purchasing materials for several plants may not be as easily determined, because transportation costs to the various plant locations may be different, and the amount of purchases from any one supplier may be limited. In this latter case, a quantitative technique known as linear programming may be useful in determining the most economical plan for purchasing materials.

The primary disadvantages of quantitative techniques are their complexity and their reliance on mathematical relationships and statistical methods which may be understood by only the most highly trained experts. When computers are used, however, it is less important to understand these complexities, so that quantitative techniques can be used by all levels of management.

In this chapter and in Chapter 27, several of the most common quantitative techniques are explained, and the practical application of each technique is demonstrated. The quantitative techniques described in this chapter focus on inventory control and the estimation of costs, including the estimation of the fixed and variable cost components. Chapter 27 focuses on quantitative techniques useful for decision making under uncertainty.

INVENTORY CONTROL

For a business enterprise that needs large quantities of inventory to meet sales orders or production requirements, inventory is one of its most important assets. The lack of sufficient inventory can result in lost sales, idle production facilities, production bottlenecks, and additional purchasing costs due to placing special orders or rush orders. On the other hand, excess inventory can result in large storage costs and large spoilage losses, which reduce the profitability of the enterprise. Thus, it is important for a business enterprise to know the ideal quantity to be purchased in a single order and the minimum and maximum quantities to be on hand at any time. Such factors as economies of large-scale buying, storage costs, work interruption due to shortages, and seasonal and cyclical changes in production schedules need to be considered. Two quantitative techniques that are especially useful in inventory control are (1) the economic order quantity formula and (2) linear programming. In addition, the inventory order point and inventory safety stock are also useful in controlling inventory.

Economic Order Quantity

The optimum quantity of inventory to be ordered at one time is termed the **economic order quantity (EOQ)**. Important factors to be considered in determining the optimum quantity are the costs involved in processing an order for the materials and the costs involved in storing the materials.

The annual cost of processing orders for a specified material (cost of placing orders, verifying invoices, processing payments, etc.) increases as the number of orders placed increases. On the other hand, the annual cost of storing the materials (taxes, insurance, occupancy of storage space, etc.) decreases as the number of orders placed increases. The economic order quantity is therefore that quantity that will minimize the combined annual costs of ordering and storing materials.

The combined annual cost incurred in ordering and storing materials can be computed under various assumptions as to the number of orders to be placed during a year. To illustrate, assume the following data for an inventoriable material which is used at the same rate during the year:

Units required during the year 1,200
Ordering cost, per order placed $10.00
Storage cost, per unit 60

If a single order were placed for the entire year's needs, the cost of ordering the 1,200 units would be $10. The average number of units held in inventory during the year would therefore be 600 (1,200 units ÷ 2) and would result in an annual storage cost of $360 (600 units × $.60). The combined order and storage costs for placing only one order during the year would thus be $370 ($10 + $360). If, instead of a single order, two orders were placed during the year, the order cost would be $20 (2 × $10), 600 units would need to be purchased on each order, the average inventory would be 300 units, and the annual storage cost would be $180 (300 units × $.60). Accordingly, the combined order and storage costs for placing two orders during the year would be $200 ($20 + $180). Successive computations will disclose the EOQ when the combined cost reaches its lowest point and starts upward. The following table shows an optimum of 200 units of materials per order, with 6 orders per year, at a combined cost of $120.

| | | | Order and Storage Costs | | |
Number of Orders	Number of Units per Order	Average Units in Inventory	Order Cost	Storage Cost	Combined Cost
1	1,200	600	$10	$360	$370
2	600	300	20	180	200
3	400	200	30	120	150
4	300	150	40	90	130
5	240	120	50	72	122
6	200	100	60	60	120
7	171	86	70	52	122

TABULATION OF ECONOMIC ORDER QUANTITY

The economic order quantity may also be determined by a formula based on differential calculus. The formula and its application to the illustration is as follows:

ECONOMIC ORDER QUANTITY FORMULA

$$EOQ = \sqrt{\frac{2 \times \text{Annual Units Required} \times \text{Cost per Order Placed}}{\text{Storage Cost per Unit}}}$$

$$EOQ = \sqrt{\frac{2 \times 1,200 \times \$10}{\$.60}}$$

$$EOQ = \sqrt{40,000}$$

$$EOQ = 200 \text{ units}$$

Inventory Order Point and Safety Stock

The **inventory order point**, usually expressed in units, is the level to which inventory is allowed to fall before an order for additional inventory is placed. The inventory order point depends on the (1) daily usage of inventory that is expected to be consumed in production or sold, (2) time (in days) that it takes to receive an order for inventory, termed the **lead time**, and (3) **safety stock**, which is the amount of inventory that is available for use when unforeseen circumstances arise, such as delays in receiving ordered inventory as a result of a national truckers' strike. Once the order point is reached, the most economical quantity should be ordered.

The inventory order point is computed by using the following formula:

Inventory Order Point = (Daily Usage × Days of Lead Time) + Safety Stock

To illustrate, assume that Beacon Company, a printing company, estimates daily usage of 3,000 pounds of paper and a lead time of 30 days to receive an order of paper. Beacon Company desires a safety stock of 10,000 pounds. The inventory order point for the paper is 100,000 pounds, computed as follows:

Inventory Order Point = (Daily Usage × Lead Time) + Safety Stock
Inventory Order Point = (3,000 lbs. × 30 days) + 10,000 lbs.
Inventory Order Point = 90,000 lbs. + 10,000 lbs.
Inventory Order Point = 100,000 lbs.

In this illustration, a safety stock of 10,000 pounds of paper was assumed. This level of safety stock should be established by management after considering many factors, such as the uncertainty in the estimates of daily inventory usage and lead time. If management were 100% certain that estimates of the daily usage and lead time were correct, no safety stock would be required. As the uncertainty in these estimates increases, the amount of safety stock normally increases. In addition, the level of safety stock carried by an enterprise will also depend on the costs of carrying inventory and the costs of being out of inventory when materials are needed for production or sales. If the costs of carrying inventory are low and the costs of being out of inventory are high, then relatively large amounts of safety stock would normally be carried by a business enterprise.

Quantitative techniques using statistics and probability theory may be useful to managers in establishing order point and safety stock levels. Such techniques are described in advanced managerial texts.

Linear Programming for Inventory Control

Linear programming is a quantitative method that can provide data for solving a variety of business problems in which management's objective is to minimize costs or maximize profits, subject to several limiting factors. Although a thorough discussion of linear programming is appropriate for more advanced courses, the following simplified illustration demonstrates the way in which linear programming can be applied to determine the most economical purchasing plan. In this situation, management's objective is to minimize the total cost of purchasing materials for several branch locations, subject to the availability of materials from suppliers.

Assume that a manufacturing company purchases Part P for use at both its West Branch and East Branch. Part P is available in limited quantities from two suppliers. The total unit cost price varies considerably for parts acquired from the two suppliers mainly because of differences in transportation charges. The relevant data for the decision regarding the most economical purchase arrangement are summarized in the following diagram:

Supplier X

Units available	75
Unit cost delivered to:	
West Branch	$ 70
East Branch.	$ 90

West Branch

40 units required

Supplier Y

Units available	75
Unit cost delivered to:	
West Branch	$ 80
East Branch.	$120

East Branch

75 units required

It might appear that the most economical course of action would be to purchase (1) the 40 units required by West Branch from Supplier X at $70 a unit, (2) 35 units for East Branch from Supplier X at $90 a unit, and (3) the remaining 40 units required by East Branch from Supplier Y at $120 a unit. If this course of action were followed, the total cost of the parts needed by the two branches would amount to $10,750, as indicated by the following computation:

	Cost of Purchases		
	By West Branch	By East Branch	Total
From Supplier X:			
40 units at $70	$2,800		$ 2,800
35 units at $90		$3,150	3,150
From Supplier Y:			
40 units at $120		4,800	4,800
Total.	$2,800	$7,950	$10,750

Although many different purchasing programs are possible, the most economical course of action would be to purchase (1) the 75 units required by

East Branch from Supplier X at $90 a unit and (2) the 40 units required by West Branch from Supplier Y at $80 a unit. If this plan were used, no units would be purchased at the lowest available unit cost, and the total cost of the parts would be $9,950, calculated as follows:

	Cost of Purchases		
	By West Branch	By East Branch	Total
From Supplier X:			
75 units at $90		$6,750	$6,750
From Supplier Y:			
40 units at $80	$3,200		3,200
Total..................................	$3,200	$6,750	$9,950

Linear programming can be applied to this situation by using either a graphic approach or a mathematical equation approach. This latter approach, called the **simplex method,** uses algebraic equations and is often used more practically with a computer. Because of its complexity and because it is normally covered in advanced managerial accounting texts, the simplex method is not described in this chapter.

To illustrate the graphic approach to linear programming, the preceding facts for the purchase of Part P from Supplier X and Supplier Y by the West Branch and the East Branch will be used. The first step in solving this problem is to place all of the possible purchasing alternatives on a graph. Since the amount purchased from Supplier X will determine the amount purchased from Supplier Y, and vice versa, only a graph showing all possible purchase plans for Supplier X (or Supplier Y) is necessary. The graph for Supplier X, on the following page, is based on the foregoing data.

The linear programming graph is constructed in the following manner:

1. Units for the West Branch are plotted on the horizontal axis, and units for the East Branch are plotted on the vertical axis.
2. A point representing the maximum number of units that could be purchased from Supplier X by the West Branch (75 units) is located on the horizontal axis. A point representing the maximum number of units that could be purchased from Supplier X by the East Branch (75 units) is located on the vertical axis.
3. A diagonal line (labeled Line 1) is drawn connecting the points representing the 75 units on the vertical axis with 75 units on the horizontal axis. This line represents the constraint on the maximum number of units (75) that can be purchased from Supplier X by either branch or both branches.
4. The constraint on the number of units that the West Branch would purchase from Supplier X (40) is indicated by a line (labeled Line 2) which is drawn vertically upward from the point of 40 units on the horizontal axis to intersect Line 1.

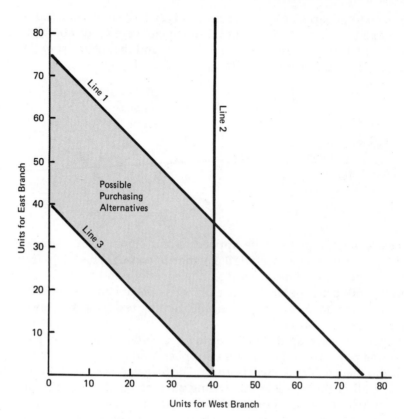

Line 1: Maximum number of units that can be purchased from Supplier X.

Line 2: Maximum number of units that will be purchased by West Branch.

Line 3: Minimum number of units that must be purchased from Supplier X.

5. A line (labeled Line 3) is drawn connecting 40 units on the vertical axis with 40 units on the horizontal axis. This line represents the constraint on minimum purchases from Supplier X (115 units required by the branches less 75 units available from each supplier).
6. The area bounded by the vertical axis and Lines 1, 2, and 3 is shaded. This area represents the set of all possible alternatives for purchases from Supplier X.

To illustrate the interpretation of a linear programming graph, assume that the West Branch purchased no units from Supplier X. The East Branch could then purchase between 40 and 75 units from Supplier X. This purchase alternative is indicated on the following graph between points A and B on the vertical axis. On the other hand, if the West Branch purchased 20 units from Supplier X, the East Branch could purchase between 20 and 55 units from Supplier X. This alternative is indicated on the following graph by the colored dotted line connecting points E and F.

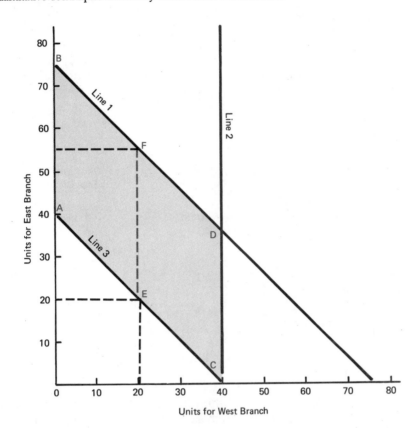

Although any point in the shaded area of the graph is a possible purchasing plan, managers are interested in selecting the most economical plan. According to the mathematical properties of linear programming, an economical purchase plan is located at one of the four points representing the corners of the shaded area of the graph. These corners are labeled A through D on the graph.

Each of the four corners represents the following purchases from Supplier X by the West Branch and the East Branch:

	Purchases by West Branch	Purchases by East Branch
Corner A: From Supplier X	0 units	40 units
Corner B: From Supplier X	0	75
Corner C: From Supplier X	40	0
Corner D: From Supplier X	40	35

Since the amount purchased from Supplier X affects the amount purchased from Supplier Y, the four corners identified above can be rewritten in terms of four separate purchase plans. In other words, if only 40 units are purchased from Supplier X and are shipped to the East Branch (Corner A), then the West Branch must obtain its purchases of 40 units from Supplier Y, and the East Branch must obtain an additional 35 units from Supplier Y to fulfill its total needs of 75 units. The four purchase plans represented by the four corners are as follows:

	Purchases by West Branch	Purchases by East Branch
Plan 1 (Corner A):		
From Supplier X	0 units	40 units
From Supplier Y	40	35
Plan 2 (Corner B):		
From Supplier X	0	75
From Supplier Y	40	0
Plan 3 (Corner C):		
From Supplier X	40	0
From Supplier Y	0	75
Plan 4 (Corner D):		
From Supplier X	40	35
From Supplier Y	0	40

By computing the total cost of the purchases for the West Branch and the East Branch for each of the purchase plans, the most economical purchase plan can be determined. As described earlier and as shown in the following computation, Plan 2 is the most economical of the four purchase plans.

	Cost of Purchases		
	By West Branch	By East Branch	Total
Plan 1:			
From Supplier X:			
40 units at $90.		$3,600	$ 3,600
From Supplier Y:			
40 units at $80.	$3,200		3,200
35 units at $120.		4,200	4,200
Total	$3,200	$7,800	$11,000
Plan 2:			
From Supplier X:			
75 units at $90.		$6,750	$ 6,750
From Supplier Y:			
40 units at $80.	$3,200		3,200
Total	$3,200	$6,750	$ 9,950

	Cost of Purchases		
	By West Branch	By East Branch	Total
Plan 3:			
From Supplier X:			
40 units at $70.........	$2,800		$ 2,800
From Supplier Y:			
75 units at $120........		$9,000	9,000
Total....................	$2,800	$9,000	$11,800
Plan 4:			
From Supplier X:			
40 units at $70.........	$2,800		$ 2,800
35 units at $90.........		$3,150	3,150
From Supplier Y:			
40 units at $120........		4,800	4,800
Total....................	$2,800	$7,950	$10,750

The preceding illustration of the graphic approach to linear programming required the construction of a graph and the consideration of four alternative purchase plans. Although an economical purchasing plan decision could have been determined by trial and error, such an approach can be time-consuming and costly. The trial and error approach could potentially require consideration of a much larger number of possible purchase plans before the most economical plan is found.

QUANTITATIVE TECHNIQUES FOR ESTIMATING COSTS

Although the costs from past operations are known, it is the estimation of future costs that is important for many analyses useful in decision making. In addition, the separation of estimated total costs into fixed and variable cost components is necessary for many analyses. For example, the use of variable costing for cost control, product pricing, production planning, and sales mix analyses requires the separation of costs into variable and fixed components. Break-even analyses and the computations of the contribution margin and the contribution margin ratio also require the separation of total costs into variable and fixed components.

The following paragraphs describe three methods of cost estimation: the high-low method, the scattergraph method, and the least squares method. Each of these methods provides an estimate of total costs and separates total costs into fixed and variable components.

High-Low Method

The **high-low method** is used to estimate the total costs as well as the variable and fixed components by using the highest and lowest total costs revealed by past cost patterns. The production levels associated with past cost patterns are usually measured in terms of units of production. For example, the cost of production during January would be measured relative to the total units produced during January.

To estimate the variable cost per unit and the fixed cost, the following steps are used:

1. a. The difference between the total costs at the highest and lowest levels of production is determined.
   b. The difference between the total units produced at the highest and lowest levels of production is determined.
2. Since only the total variable cost will change as the number of units of production changes, the difference in total costs as determined in (1a) is divided by the difference in units produced as determined in (1b) to determine the variable cost per unit.
3. The total variable cost (variable cost per unit × total units produced) at either the highest or the lowest level of production is determined, and the amount is subtracted from the total cost at that level to determine the fixed cost.

To illustrate, assume that Sutton Company has produced Product A and has incurred the following total costs for various production levels during the past 5 months:

	Units Produced	Total Costs
June	175,000 units	$185,000
July	75,000	80,000
August	200,000	210,000
September	325,000	320,000
October	300,000	270,000

The total units of production and the total costs at the highest and lowest levels of production and the differences are as follows:

	Total Units Produced	Total Costs
Highest level	325,000 units	$320,000
Lowest level	75,000	80,000
Differences	250,000 units	$240,000

Since the total fixed cost does not change with changes in volume of production, the $240,000 difference in the total cost represents the change in the total variable cost. Hence, dividing $240,000 by the change in production of 250,000 units provides an estimate of the variable cost per unit.

In this illustration, the variable cost per unit is **$.96**, as shown in the following computation:

$$\text{Variable Cost per Unit} = \frac{\text{Difference in Total Costs}}{\text{Difference in Production}}$$

$$\text{Variable Cost per Unit} = \frac{\$240,000}{250,000 \text{ units}} = \$.96 \text{ per unit}$$

The fixed costs will be the same at both the highest and the lowest levels of production. Thus, the fixed cost of $8,000 can be estimated by subtracting the estimated total variable cost from the total cost at either the highest or the lowest levels of production, as shown in the following computations:

$$\text{Total Cost} = \text{Variable Cost} + \text{Fixed Cost}$$

Highest level:

$$\$320,000 = (\$.96 \times 325,000) + \text{Fixed Cost}$$
$$\$320,000 = \$312,000 + \text{Fixed Cost}$$
$$\$\ 8,000 = \text{Fixed Cost}$$

Lowest level:

$$\$\ 80,000 = (\$.96 \times 75,000) + \text{Fixed Cost}$$
$$\$\ 80,000 = \$72,000 + \text{Fixed Cost}$$
$$\$\ 8,000 = \text{Fixed Cost}$$

Since the variable and fixed cost components of the total cost have now been identified, the estimated total cost for any level of production can be determined by using the following equation:

$$\text{Total Cost} = \text{Variable Cost} + \text{Fixed Cost}$$
$$\text{Total Cost} = (\$.96 \times \text{Total Units of Production}) + \$8,000$$

For 200,000 units of production, the estimated total cost would be determined as follows:

$$\text{Total Cost} = (\$.96 \times 200,000 \text{ units}) + \$8,000$$
$$\text{Total Cost} = \$200,000$$

Scattergraph Method

The **scattergraph method** of estimating total costs is based on the use of a graph. A distinguishing characteristic of the scattergraph method relative to the high-low method is that the scattergraph method uses total costs at the levels of past production in the analysis, rather than just the highest and lowest levels. Because the scattergraph method uses all the data available, it tends to be more accurate than the high-low method.

The following cost and production data for Sutton Company, which were used in illustrating the high-low method, are used to illustrate the scattergraph method:

	Units Produced	Total Costs
June..............	175,000	$185,000
July..............	75,000	80,000
August...........	200,000	210,000
September	325,000	320,000
October..........	300,000	270,000

The following scattergraph was constructed with these data:

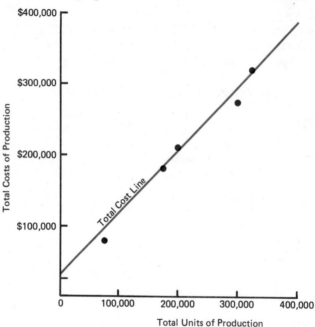

The scattergraph is constructed in the following manner:

1. Levels of total units of production are spread along the horizontal axis. For Sutton Company, it is assumed that a maximum of 400,000 units could be produced.

2. The total costs of production are spread along the vertical axis. For Sutton Company, it is assumed that the total costs of production could not exceed $400,000.

3. The total cost of each past level of production is then plotted on the graph. For example, the total cost of June's 175,000 units of production would be indicated on the graph by a point representing $185,000. The total cost of July's 75,000 units would be indicated by a point representing $80,000.

4. After all the total costs for the past levels of production have been plotted on the graph, a straight line representing the total costs is drawn on the graph. This line is drawn so that the differences between each point and the line are at a minimum in the judgment of the preparer of the graph.

From the following scattergraph for Sutton Company, the estimated total costs for various levels of production and the fixed and variable cost components can be determined. The point at which the total cost line intersects the vertical axis of the scattergraph indicates the estimated fixed cost of production. For Sutton Company, the fixed cost component is approximately $25,000.

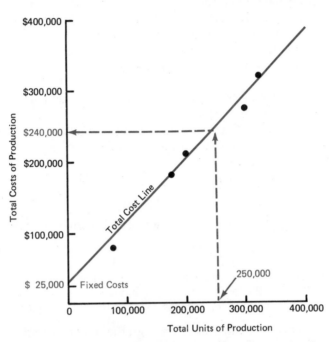

SCATTERGRAPH—
ESTIMATION OF
FIXED COSTS AND
TOTAL COSTS

The estimated total cost for any level of production can be determined by locating the total units of production on the horizontal axis and proceeding vertically upward until the total cost line is intersected, then proceeding horizontally to the left until the vertical axis is intersected. On the scattergraph for Sutton Company, the estimated total cost for 250,000 units of production is determined to be approximately $240,000.

The total variable cost for any level of production is the difference between the estimated total cost and the estimated fixed cost. For Sutton Company, the estimated total variable cost for 250,000 units of production is $215,000 ($240,000 − $25,000). The estimated variable cost per unit is $.86 (215,000 ÷ 250,000 units).

The estimated total fixed cost of $25,000 and the variable cost of $.86 per unit are represented in the following general formula for estimated total cost:

Total Cost = Variable Cost + Fixed Cost
Total Cost = ($.86 × Total Units of Production) + $25,000

For 200,000 units of production, the estimated total cost would be determined as follows:

Total Cost = ($.86 × 200,000 units) + $25,000
Total Cost = $197,000

Least Squares Method

While the scattergraph method requires the judgmental drawing of a total cost line through the plotted total cost points, the **least squares method** uses statistics to determine the total cost line. Thus, the resulting estimated total cost line is based on more objective statistical criteria.

The least squares method fits a straight line through the plotted total cost, according to the following general formula:

Total Cost = (Variable Cost per Unit × Total Units of Production) + Fixed Cost

The variable cost per unit component of the formula is estimated statistically, using the following computational formula:

$$\text{Variable Cost per Unit} = \frac{n(\Sigma P_i C_i) - (\Sigma P_i)(\Sigma C_i)}{n(\Sigma P_i^2) - (\Sigma P_i)^2}$$

The symbols in the preceding formula are explained as follows:

n is the number of total cost observations
Σ is the sum of the numbers
P_i is an observed level of production, in units, at period i
C_i is an observation of total cost, in dollars, at period i
P_i^2 is the square of the value P_i, likewise, $(\Sigma P_i)^2$ is the square of the value (ΣP_i)

The formula can be easily solved through the use of a computational table with columns for P_i, C_i, P_i^2, and $P_i C_i$. To illustrate, the following computational table for the estimation of the variable cost per unit for Sutton Company is prepared, based on the cost and production data that were used in the preceding illustrations. To simplify the computations, the thousands have been deleted from both the cost and production data.

Total Units Produced (P_i)	Total Costs (C_i)	P_i^2	$P_i C_i$
175	$ 185	30,625	$ 32,375
75	80	5,625	6,000
200	210	40,000	42,000
325	320	105,625	104,000
300	270	90,000	81,000
1,075	$1,065	271,875	$265,375
↑	↑	↑	↑
ΣP_i	ΣC_i	ΣP_i^2	$\Sigma P_i C_i$

Using the values from the table, the computational formula yields the following results:

$$\text{Variable Cost per Unit} = \frac{n(\Sigma P_i C_i) - (\Sigma P_i)(\Sigma C_i)}{n(\Sigma P_i^2) - (\Sigma P_i)^2}$$

$$\text{Variable Cost per Unit} = \frac{5(\$265,375) - (1,075)(\$1,065)}{5(271,875) - (1,075)^2}$$

$$\text{Variable Cost per Unit} = \frac{\$1,326,875 - \$1,144,875}{1,359,375 - 1,155,625}$$

$$\text{Variable Cost per Unit} = \frac{\$182,000}{203,750} = \$.89 \text{ per unit}$$

The fixed cost component of total cost is estimated statistically, using the following computational formula:

$$\text{Fixed Cost} = \overline{C} - (\text{Variable Cost per Unit} \times \overline{P})$$

The symbols are explained as follows:

$\overline{C}$ is the average of the monthly total costs
$\overline{P}$ is the average of the monthly units of production

For Sutton Company, the average total cost is $213,000 ($1,065,000 ÷ 5), and the average units of production is 215,000 units (1,075,000 units ÷ 5). When these values are substituted into the formula, the fixed cost is computed as follows:

$$\text{Fixed Cost} = \$213,000 - (\$.89 \times 215,000 \text{ units})$$
$$\text{Fixed Cost} = \$213,000 - \$191,350$$
$$\text{Fixed Cost} = \$21,650$$

The estimated total fixed cost of $21,650 and the variable cost of $.89 per unit are represented in the following general formula for estimated total cost:

$$\text{Total Cost} = \text{Variable Cost} + \text{Fixed Cost}$$
$$\text{Total Cost} = (\$.89 \times \text{Total Units of Production}) + \$21,650$$

For 200,000 units of production, the estimated total cost would be determined as follows:

$$\text{Total Cost} = (\$.89 \times 200,000 \text{ units}) + \$21,650$$
$$\text{Total Cost} = \$199,650$$

Comparison of Cost Estimation Methods

Each of the three methods described provided different estimates of fixed and variable costs, summarized as follows:

	Variable Cost per Unit	Total Fixed Costs
High-low method	$.96	$ 8,000
Scattergraph method	.86	25,000
Least squares method	.89	21,650

The cost estimation method that should be used in any given situation depends on such considerations as the cost of gathering data for the estimates and the importance of the accuracy of the estimates. Although the high-low method is the easiest and the least costly to apply, it is also normally the least accurate. The least squares method is generally more accurate, but it is more complex and more costly to use.

In this illustration, the high-low method differs significantly in its estimates of variable and fixed costs, $.96 and $8,000, compared to the variable and fixed cost estimates of the scattergraph and least squares method, $.86 and $25,000, and $.89 and $21,650, respectively. These differences result because the high-low method uses only two cost and production observations to estimate costs for all levels of production. If these two observations are not representative of the normal cost and production patterns for all levels of production, then inaccurate variable and fixed cost estimates may be obtained. To illustrate, if the July production and total cost data for Sutton Company are eliminated because they are seasonal and not typical of normal operations, then the high-low method yields representative estimates which are comparable to the estimates provided by the scattergraph and least squares methods, as shown in the following computations. In these computations, the fixed cost is estimated at the highest level of production.

	Total Units Produced	Total Costs
Highest level	325,000 units	$320,000
Lowest level (excluding July data)	175,000	185,000
Differences..........................	150,000 units	$135,000

$$\text{Variable Cost per Unit} = \frac{\text{Difference in Total Cost}}{\text{Difference in Production}}$$

$$\text{Variable Cost per Unit} = \frac{\$135,000}{150,000 \text{ units}} = \$.90 \text{ per unit}$$

Total Cost = Variable Cost + Fixed Cost
$320,000 = ($.90 × 325,000 units) + Fixed Cost
$320,000 = $292,500 + Fixed Cost
$27,500 = Fixed Cost

Care should also be exercised in using the scattergraph and least squares methods. The scattergraph method depends on the judgment of the individual who draws the total cost line through the points on the graph. Different individuals could fit different lines and thereby arrive at different estimates of the total cost. The least squares method is more objective, but it is difficult to use without a computer. Additional complications of the least squares method are described in more advanced texts.

Regardless of which cost estimation method is used, the estimated total cost should be compared periodically with actual costs. Large differences between estimated total costs and actual costs might indicate that the way in which total costs are estimated should be revised. For example, a change in the manufacturing process will likely require the gathering of total cost and production data related to the new process and the estimation of a new total cost formula, using one of the three methods discussed in this section.

THE LEARNING EFFECT IN ESTIMATING COSTS

Labor costs and thus total costs are affected by how efficiently and effectively employees perform their tasks. In a manufacturing environment, costs will be affected by how rapidly new employees learn their jobs and by how rapidly experienced employees learn new job assignments. For example, as production for a new product begins or as a new manufacturing process is implemented, workers usually increase their efficiency as more units are produced and as they become more experienced. This **learning effect** is known as the **learning curve phenomenon**. When learning occurs, it can have a significant impact on costs and should be considered in estimating costs.

To illustrate, assume that Barker Company manufactures yachts and has added a new yacht to its product line. Past experience indicates that every time a new line of yachts is added, the total time to manufacture each yacht declines by 10% as each of the next 5 yachts is produced. Thus, the second yacht requires 90% of the total time to manufacture the first yacht, the third yacht requires 90% of the time of the second yacht, and so on. However, past experience also indicates that after the sixth yacht is produced, further reductions in time are insignificant.

For Barker Company, it is estimated that the first yacht will require 500 direct labor hours at $20 per hour, and that 10 yachts are scheduled for initial production. The following table illustrates the learning effect on the total direct labor cost per yacht:

Yacht	Total Direct Labor Hours per Yacht	Direct Labor Cost per Hour	Total Direct Labor Cost per Yacht
1	500	$20	$10,000
2	450	20	9,000
3	405	20	8,100
4	365	20	7,300
5	329	20	6,580
6	296	20	5,920
7	296	20	5,920
8	296	20	5,920
9	296	20	5,920
10	296	20	5,920

In this table, the total direct labor hours per yacht declined by 10% each time an additional yacht was produced, from a high of 500 hours to a low of

296 hours. The total direct labor cost per yacht declined from a high of $10,000 to a low of $5,920. After the sixth yacht was produced, the employees had learned enough from their experience in building the first 6 yachts that no additional reductions in time could be achieved.

The learning effect for Barker Company in terms of total direct labor hours per yacht is shown in the following graph:

GRAPH OF
LEARNING EFFECT

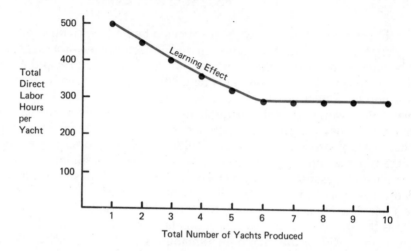

The learning effect does not occur for all production processes, nor does it affect all production processes in the same way. In the preceding illustration of Barker Company, for example, instead of a 10% learning effect each time an additional yacht was produced, the learning effect could have been 10% for the first 3 yachts and 5% for the following 3 yachts. Generally, the more labor that is used in the production process, the greater the opportunity for the learning effect to occur. As production processes become more automated, less opportunity for learning exists.

The learning effect is important to managers, since it directly affects cost estimation. Estimated costs affect the development of such reports and analyses as budgets, standard costs, and cost-volume-profit analyses.

Self-
Examination
Questions
(Answers
at end
of chapter.)

1. A quantitative technique that can be used in solving a variety of business problems in which management's objective is to minimize costs or maximize profits, subject to several limiting factors, is:
   A. economic order quantity
   B. linear programming
   C. least squares method
   D. high-low method

2. In determining the economic order quantity, which, if any, of the following factors are important to consider?
   A. Storage cost per unit
   B. Annual units required
   C. Cost per order placed
   D. All of the above

3. The point at which the total cost line intersects the vertical axis of the scattergraph indicates:
   A. total variable cost
   B. total fixed cost
   C. variable cost per unit
   D. none of the above

4. Which of the following methods of cost estimation uses statistical formulas to determine the total cost and the variable and fixed cost components?
   A. High-low method
   B. Linear programming method
   C. Least squares method
   D. Scattergraph method

5. Which of the following methods is normally considered the least accurate method of estimating total costs and fixed and variable cost components?
   A. High-low method
   B. Scattergraph method
   C. Least squares method
   D. Linear programming

Discussion Questions

26–1. Distinguish quantitative techniques from analyses such as cost-volume-profit analysis and differential analysis.

26–2. What are the primary disadvantages of quantitative techniques?

26–3. For a business enterprise that needs large quantities of inventories to meet sales orders or production requirements, what can result from insufficient inventory?

26–4. What term is used to describe the optimum quantity of inventory to be ordered at one time?

26–5. Assuming that Product N is used at the same rate throughout the year, 500 units are required during the year, the cost per order placed is $12, and the storage cost per unit is $4.80, what is the ecomomic order quantity for Product N?

26–6. What quantitative technique is often useful in determining the most economical plan for purchasing materials for several locations?

26–7. The inventory order point depends on what factors?

26–8. Assuming that Dooley Co. estimates daily usage of 500 pounds of material A, the lead time to receive an order of material A is 20 days, and a safety stock of 2,000 pounds is desired, what is the inventory order point?

26–9. If everything else remains the same, as the cost of carrying inventory increases, would the level of safety stock normally carried by a company increase or decrease?

26–10. What are three methods of cost estimation that are useful to the managerial accountant?

26–11. In applying the high-low method of cost estimation, how is the total fixed cost estimated?

26–12. If the variable cost per unit is $1.50 and the total fixed cost is $50,000, what is the estimated total cost for the production of 30,000 units?

26–13. Describe how the total cost line is drawn on a scattergraph.

26–14. How is the scattergraph method used to determine the estimated total cost for any level of production?

26–15. Assuming that the least squares method of cost estimation is used to estimate a variable cost per unit of $2.40, the average of the observed total costs is $200,000, and the average of the observed levels of production is 50,000 units, what is the least squares estimate of the total fixed cost?

26–16. What might be indicated by large differences between estimated total costs and actual costs?

26–17. As production for a new product begins or as a new manufacturing process is implemented, workers usually increase their efficiency as they produce more units and acquire more experience. What is this phenomenon called?

26–18. Why is the learning effect important to managers?

Exercises

26–19. Fernandez Company estimates that 1,680 units of material F will be required during the coming year. Past experience indicates that the storage costs are $.80 per unit and the cost to place an order is $42. Determine the economic order quantity to be purchased.

26–20. Glaser Company purchases Part Q for use at both its Beloit and Racine branches. Part Q is available in limited quantities from two suppliers. The relevant data for determining an economical purchase plan are as follows:

Units required:
    Beloit Branch...................... 100 units
    Racine Branch..................... 200 units

Supplier M:
    Total units available............... 200 units
    Unit cost delivered to:
        Beloit Branch.................... $40 per unit
        Racine Branch................... $60 per unit

Supplier N:
    Total units available............... 200 units
    Unit cost delivered to:
        Beloit Branch.................... $50 per unit
        Racine Branch................... $75 per unit

The following linear programming graph for units purchased from Supplier M has been constructed, based on the above data:

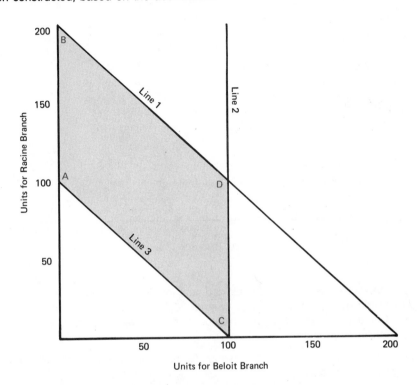

Units for Beloit Branch

(a) For each of the four corners identified on the above graph by letters A through D, determine the purchases from Supplier M for the Beloit and Racine Branches. Use the same format as shown on page 831.

(b) For each of the four corners in (a), indicate the units purchased from both Suppliers M and N for the Beloit and Racine Branches. Use the same format as shown on page 832 and identify Plan 1 with Corner A, Plan 2 with Corner B, Plan 3 with Corner C, and Plan 4 with Corner D.

(c) Determine the most economical purchase plan by computing the total cost of each purchase plan determined in (b).

26-21. Auerbach Company has decided to use the high-low method to estimate the total cost and the fixed and variable cost components of the total cost. The data for the highest and lowest levels of production are as follows:

	Total Units Produced	Total Costs
Highest level	170,000	$150,000
Lowest level.	80,000	96,000

(a) Determine the variable cost per unit and the fixed cost for Auerbach Company.
(b) Based on (a), estimate the total cost for 120,000 units of production.

26–22. A cost accountant for Grimly Company has prepared the following scattergraph as a basis for cost estimation:

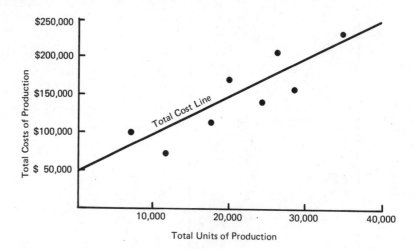

(a) Determine the estimated total fixed cost for Grimly Company.
(b) Determine the estimated total cost for 30,000 units of production.
(c) Compute the estimated variable cost per unit, based on the total cost of producing 30,000 units.

26–23. The assistant controller for Emerson Company prepared the following table for use in estimating costs:

Total Units Produced (P_i)	Total Costs (C_i)	P_i^2	P_iC_i
120	$100	14,400	$12,000
150	145	22,500	21,750
170	180	28,900	30,600
90	90	8,100	8,100
70	80	4,900	5,600
60	65	3,600	3,900
660	$660	82,400	$81,950

The thousands have been deleted from the table. Thus, 120 units in the table represents 120,000 units of production and $100 represents $100,000.

(a) Determine the estimated variable cost per unit, using the table and the least squares formula. Round to the nearest cent.
(b) Determine the estimated fixed cost, using the preceding data and the least squares formula.
(c) Based on (a) and (b), estimate the total cost for 100,000 units of production.

26–24. Eggers Sails Inc. manufactures sailboats and has added a new model of sailboat to its product line. Past experience indicates that every time a new model of sailboat is added, the total time to manufacture each sailboat declines by 5% as each of the next six sailboats are produced. After the seventh sailboat, no further reduction in time is possible. It is estimated that the first sailboat will require 400 direct labor hours at a cost of $15 per hour.

(a) Complete the following table for the manufacture of the first ten sailboats. Round to the nearest direct labor hour.

Sailboat	Total Direct Labor Hours per Sailboat	Direct Labor Cost per Hour	Total Direct Labor Cost per Sailboat
1	400	$15	$6,000

(b) Graph the learning effect for Eggers Sails Inc. in terms of total direct labor hours per sailboat.

26-25. Lehman Company has recently decided to implement a policy designed to control inventory better. Based on past experience, the following data have been gathered for materials, which are used at a uniform rate throughout the year:

Units required during the year 3,600
Ordering cost, per order placed $30.00
Storage cost, per unit..................... .15

Instructions:

(1) Complete the following table for "number of orders" of 1 through 6.

Number of Orders	Number of Units per Order	Average Units in Inventory	Order and Storage Costs		
			Order Cost	Storage Cost	Combined Cost
1	3,600	1,800	$30	$270.00	$300.00

(2) Determine the economic order quantity, based on the table completed in (1).
(3) Determine the economic order quantity, using the formula.

26-26. Based on the data presented in Problem 26-25, assume that Lehman Company is considering the purchase of new automated storage equipment to facilitate access to materials and to increase storage capacity. In addition, the manager of the purchasing department has requested authorization to purchase five microcomputers to expedite the processing of purchase orders.

Instructions:

(1) Assuming that the new storage equipment will increase the storage cost from $.15 to $.60 per unit, determine the economic order quantity for Lehman Company, using the formula.
(2) Assuming that the new storage equipment is not purchased and the acquisition of the microcomputer equipment will decrease the cost per order placed from $30 to $7.50, determine the economic order quantity, using the formula.

(continued)

(3) Assuming that both the new storage equipment and the microcomputer equipment are purchased, determine the economic order quantity, using the formula. As indicated in (1) and (2), the purchase of the storage equipment is expected to increase the storage cost per unit from $.15 to $.60, and the microcomputer equipment is expected to decrease the cost per order placed from $30 to $7.50.

(4) Based on the answers to Problem 26-25 and (1), (2), and (3) above, what generalizations can be made concerning how changes in the cost per order placed and the storage cost per unit affect the economic order quantity?

26–27. Schellenberg Company purchases Part V for use at both its Elgin and Pekin branches. Part V is available in limited quantities from two suppliers. The relevant data are as follows:

Units required:
Elgin Branch 60
Pekin Branch........................ 100

Supplier K:
Units available...................... 100
Unit cost delivered to:
Elgin Branch $25
Pekin Branch...................... $50

Supplier L:
Units available...................... 100
Unit cost delivered to:
Elgin Branch $30
Pekin Branch...................... $70

The new manager of the purchasing department of Schellenberg Company has prepared the following purchase plan for the Elgin and Pekin Branches:

	Purchases by Elgin Branch	Purchases by Pekin Branch
From Supplier K	60 units	40 units
From Supplier L	0	60

Instructions:

(1) Construct a linear programming graph for units to be purchased from Supplier K. Plot the units for the Elgin Branch along the horizontal axis.

(2) Identify the four corners at which an economical purchase plan might be identified on the linear programming graph. Label the corners A through D, as shown in the illustration on page 831.

(3) For each corner in (2), indicate purchases from Suppliers K and L for the Elgin and Pekin branches. Identify Plan 1 with Corner A, Plan 2 with Corner B, Plan 3 with Corner C, and Plan 4 with Corner D.

(4) Determine the most economical purchase plan by computing the total cost of purchases for each plan identified in (3).

(5) Was the purchasing department manager's plan the most economical? Explain.

26–28. The controller for Gillespie Company is preparing some preliminary cost projections for the 1987 budget and has accumulated the following cost and production data for 1986:

	Units Produced	Total Costs
January..............	20,000	$36,000
February.............	30,000	44,000
March	40,000	52,000
April................	25,000	40,000
May.................	35,000	50,000
June	42,000	54,000
July	50,000	65,000
August	60,000	70,000
September...........	64,000	72,000
October.............	70,000	75,000
November	74,000	76,500
December	68,000	72,000

Instructions:

(1) Estimate the variable cost per unit and the total fixed cost, using the high-low method of cost estimation.
(2) Construct a scattergraph, including the total cost line.
(3) Based on the scattergraph in (2), estimate the variable cost per unit and the total fixed cost at 50,000 units of production.
(4) Why are there differences between the estimates in (1) and (3)?

26–29. The controller of Vaugh Company recently decided to use quantitative techniques for cost estimation purposes. Cost estimates were prepared using the high-low, scattergraph, and least squares methods, with the following results:

	Variable Cost per Unit	Total Fixed Costs
High-low method..............	$1.00	$45,000
Scattergraph method..........	1.05	34,500
Least squares method........	1.03	38,197

The controller expressed concern with the differences in the estimates, especially the differences between the estimates resulting from the high-low method and the estimates resulting from the scattergraph and least squares methods. The cost and production data used in developing these estimates are as follows:

	Units Produced	Total Costs
January..............	135,000	$180,000
February.............	190,000	232,000
March	200,000	244,000
April................	185,000	228,000
May.................	206,000	248,000

	Units Produced	Total Costs
June	197,000	238,000
July	212,000	255,000
August	223,000	272,000
September...........	218,000	266,000
October.............	235,000	280,000

Instructions:

(1) Based on each of the preceding cost estimates for the high-low, scattergraph, and least squares methods, (a) compute the estimated total cost for 200,000 units of production, and (b) compute the differences between each of the total cost estimates in (a) and the actual cost of $244,000.

(2) Assuming that the January production and cost data are not typical of normal operations, recompute the variable cost per unit and the total fixed cost, using the high-low method.

(3) Based on (2), recompute the estimated total cost for 200,000 units of production, using the high-low method.

(4) Based on the total cost estimate computed in (3), what is the difference between this estimate and the actual cost of $244,000?

(5) Regardless of which cost estimation method is used, why should the estimated total cost be compared periodically with the actual cost?

26–30. Tidmore Company began operations in January, 1986, and has decided to use the least squares method for estimating variable costs per unit and fixed costs. The following production and cost data have been gathered from the accounting and production records for the past 10 months:

	Units Produced	Total Costs
March	80,000	$170,000
April................	90,000	190,000
May.................	100,000	200,000
June	110,000	220,000
July	120,000	224,000
August	115,000	218,000
September...........	110,000	210,000
October.............	100,000	205,000
November	110,000	215,000
December	120,000	220,000

January and February cost and production data have been excluded, since operations during these months were in a start-up stage and were not typical.

Instructions:

(1) Prepare a computational table for the estimation of the variable cost per unit, using the following form. Do not include thousands in the table.

Total Units Produced (P_i)	Total Costs (C_i)	P_i^2	P_iC_i

(2) Determine the estimated variable cost per unit, using the table in (1) and the least squares formula. Round to the nearest cent.
(3) Determine the estimated fixed cost, using (1) and (2) and the least squares formula.
(4) Estimate the total cost of 100,000 units of production, using the results of (2) and (3).

26–25A. Strauss Company has recently decided to implement a policy designed to control inventory better. Based on past experience, the following data have been gathered for materials, which are used at a uniform rate throughout the year:

Alternate Problems

Units required during the year	4,800
Ordering cost, per order placed	$40.00
Storage cost, per unit.....................	.60

Instructions:
(1) Complete the following table for "number of orders" of 1 through 8. Round to the nearest dollar.

Number of Orders	Number of Units per Order	Average Units in Inventory	Order and Storage Costs		
			Order Cost	Storage Cost	Combined Cost
1	4,800	2,400	$40	$1,440	$1,480

(2) Determine the economic order quantity, based on the table completed in (1).
(3) Determine the economic order quantity, using the formula.

26–27A. Hansen Company purchases Part M for use at both its Akron and Tifton branches. Part M is available in limited quantities from two suppliers. The relevant data are as follows:

Units required:	
Akron Branch.......................	200
Tifton Branch.......................	300
Supplier X:	
Units available.....................	300
Unit cost delivered to:	
Akron Branch....................	$60
Tifton Branch....................	$80
Supplier Y:	
Units available.....................	300
Unit cost delivered to:	
Akron Branch....................	$75
Tifton Branch....................	$70

The manager of the purchasing department has prepared the following purchase plan for the Akron and Tifton branches:

(1) Purchase all units for Akron Branch from Supplier X.
(2) Purchase remaining available units of Supplier X for the Tifton Branch.
(3) Purchase any additional units required by the Tifton Branch from Supplier Y.

Instructions:

(1) Construct a linear programming graph for units to be purchased from Supplier X. Plot the units for the Akron Branch along the horizontal axis.
(2) Identify the four corners at which an economical purchase plan might be identified on the linear programming graph. Label the corners A through D, as shown in the illustration on page 831.
(3) For each corner in (2), indicate purchases from Suppliers X and Y for the Akron and Tifton branches. Identify Plan 1 with Corner A, Plan 2 with Corner B, Plan 3 with Corner C, and Plan 4 with Corner D.
(4) Determine the most economical purchase plan by computing the total cost of purchases for each plan identified in (3).
(5) Was the purchasing department manager's plan the most economical? Explain.

26–28A. The controller for Barrentine Company is preparing some preliminary cost projections for the 1987 budget and has accumulated the following cost and production data for 1986:

	Units Produced	Total Costs
January..............	15,000	$40,000
February.............	20,000	41,500
March	26,000	46,000
April................	35,000	52,000
May.................	48,000	59,000
June	54,000	62,000
July	60,000	65,200
August	45,000	57,000
September...........	31,000	48,000
October.............	21,000	42,000
November	10,000	34,200
December	12,000	37,000

Instructions:

(1) Estimate the variable cost per unit and the total fixed cost, using the high-low method of cost estimation.
(2) Construct a scattergraph, including the total cost line.
(3) Based on the scattergraph in (2), estimate the variable cost per unit and the total fixed cost at 20,000 units of production.
(4) Why are there differences between the estimates in (1) and (3)?

26–30A. The management of Mathis Company has decided to use the least squares method for estimating variable costs per unit and fixed costs. The following production and cost data have been gathered from the accounting and production records.

	Units Produced	Total Costs
January..............	60,000	$160,000
February............	70,000	180,000
March	80,000	200,000
April................	90,000	220,000
May.................	100,000	238,000
June	95,000	226,000
July	110,000	260,000
August	120,000	282,000
September...........	105,000	249,000
October.............	85,000	212,000

Cost and production data for November and December have been excluded, since operations during these months were not typical.

Instructions:

(1) Prepare a computational table for the estimation of the variable cost per unit, using the following form. Do not include thousands in the table.

Total Units Produced (P_i)	Total Costs (C_i)	P_i^2	$P_i C_i$

(2) Determine the estimated variable cost per unit, using the table in (1) and the least squares formula. Round to the nearest cent.
(3) Determine the estimated fixed cost, using (1) and (2) and the least squares formula.
(4) Estimate the total cost of 80,000 units of production, using the results of (2) and (3).

Mini-Case

26–31. McDuffie Company has recently become concerned with the accuracy of its cost estimates because of large monthly differences between actual and estimated total costs. In the past, the senior cost accountant has used the high-low method to develop estimates of variable costs per unit and fixed costs. These cost estimates are as follows:

Variable cost per unit.............. $ 3
Fixed cost........................ 20,000

As a new junior cost accountant, the controller has asked you to determine whether the least squares method of cost estimation would provide more accurate estimates. The following twelve-month cost and production data have been gathered as a basis for developing the least squares cost estimates:

	Units Produced	Total Costs
January	80,000	$240,000
February	60,000	196,000
March.	70,000	220,000
April	50,000	175,000
May	48,000	165,000
June.	40,000	140,000
July.	55,000	180,000
August	68,000	212,000
September	62,000	200,000
October	75,000	230,000
November	82,000	245,000
December	90,000	290,000

Instructions:

(1) Prepare a least squares computational table for the estimation of variable cost per unit, using the following form. Do not include thousands in the table.

Total Units Produced (P_i)	Total Costs (C_i)	P_i^2	$P_i C_i$

(2) Determine the estimated variable cost per unit, using the table in (1) and the least squares formula. Round to the nearest cent.
(3) Determine the estimated fixed cost, using (1) and (2) and the least squares formula.
(4) Prepare a table comparing the monthly differences between actual and estimated total costs for the high-low and least squares methods. Use the following headings:

Month	Units Produced	Total Actual Costs	Total Estimated Costs — High-Low Method	Total Estimated Costs — Least Squares Method	Monthly Differences — High-Low Method	Monthly Differences — Least Squares Method

(5) Which method is more accurate in estimating total costs? Explain.
(6) Which cost estimation method would you recommend to the controller?

Answers to Self-Examination Questions

1. B Linear programming (answer B) is a quantitative technique that can be useful to management in solving problems in which the objective is to minimize cost or maximize profits, subject to several limiting factors. The economic order quantity (answer A) is useful to management in determining the optimum quantity of inventory to be ordered at one time. The least squares (answer C) and high-low (answer D) methods are useful to management in cost estimation.

2. D Storage cost per unit (answer A), annual units required (answer B), and cost per order (answer C) are all important in the determination of economic order quantity.

3. B The point at which the total cost line intersects the vertical axis of the scatter-graph indicates the estimated total fixed cost of production (answer B). The total variable cost (answer A) for any level of production is the difference between the estimated total cost indicated on the scattergraph and the estimated total fixed cost. The estimated variable cost per unit (answer C) can be computed by dividing the total variable cost by the total units of production for a given level of production.

4. C The least squares method (answer C) uses statistical formulas to estimate the total cost and the variable and fixed cost components. The high-low method (answer A) uses only data for the highest and lowest levels of production in estimating costs. The scattergraph method (answer D) uses a graph to estimate costs. The linear programming method (answer B) is not a cost estimation method.

5. A The high-low method (answer A) is normally considered the least accurate method of estimating costs because it uses data for only the highest and lowest levels of production. On the other hand, the scattergraph method (answer B) and the least squares method (answer C) both utilize data for all the observed levels of production. Linear programming (answer D) is not a cost estimation method.

CHAPTER 27

Quantitative Techniques: Decision Making Under Uncertainty

CHAPTER OBJECTIVES

Describe and illustrate the use of the expected value concept for decision making under uncertainty.

Describe and illustrate the use of the maximin and maximax concepts for decision making under uncertainty.

The preceding chapter described and illustrated the use of quantitative techniques by management, including methods used for inventory control and cost estimation. This chapter focuses on quantitative techniques useful to management in decision making under uncertainty, which is characteristic of the environment in which managers must make decisions. The managerial accountant can aid management in making decisions under uncertainty by providing data useful to management in assessing the chances that future events will occur and the impact of those events. One quantitative technique useful for this purpose is the expected value concept. Two alternative concepts that managers may find useful in special situations, the maximin and maximax concepts, are also discussed and illustrated.

Quantitative Techniques: Decision Making Under Uncertainty

MANAGERIAL USE OF THE EXPECTED VALUE CONCEPT

The concept of **expected value** involves identifying the possible outcomes from a decision and estimating the likelihood that each outcome will occur. By using the expected value concept, managers can better evaluate the uncertainty of the occurrence of predicted outcomes from decisions.

The likelihood that an outcome will occur from a decision is usually expressed in terms of a probability or chance of occurrence. For example, the probability or chance that, on the flip of a coin, a head will appear is .50 or 50%. Likewise, the probability or chance that the introduction of a new product will be successful might be expressed as .60 or 60%.

The expected value of a decision is the sum of the values that result when the dollar value of each outcome is multiplied by the probability or chance of its occurrence. Thus, expected value can be thought of as an average value. That is, each possible outcome is weighted by its chance of occurrence to obtain an average expected outcome. For example, assume that you are playing a game in which a coin is flipped. If a head appears, you win $10,000; if a tail appears, you lose $6,000. The expected value of this game is **$2,000**, computed as follows:

Expected Value = .50($10,000) + .50(−$6,000)
Expected Value = $5,000 − $3,000
Expected Value = $2,000

If you played the preceding game a large number of times, 50% of the time you would win $10,000, 50% of the time you would lose $6,000, and on the average you would win $2,000 per game. For example, if you played the game twice and won once and lost once, you would have won $10,000 and lost $6,000. Hence, you would have net winnings of $4,000($10,000 − $6,000). Since you played the game twice, your average winnings would be $2,000 per game ($4,000 ÷ 2). Consequently, the expected value of playing the game is $2,000.

To illustrate the expected value concept within a managerial context, assume that the management of Faxon Company is faced with deciding on a location for a new hotel. The search for the best site has been narrowed to two choices within a large metropolitan area. One site is in the center of the city. The accessibility to the city's business and entertainment district makes this site attractive for conventions. The other location is twenty miles from the center of the city at the intersection of two interstate highways. This site is attractive because of its proximity to the city's international airport. After the hotel is constructed, the management of Faxon Company plans to operate the hotel for one year and then sell the hotel for a profit. Over the past five years, Faxon has successfully constructed and sold four hotels in this fashion.

The estimated profit or loss at each site depends on whether the occupancy rate the first year is high or low. Based on marketing studies, the following profit and loss data have been estimated:

City Site	Profit or Loss	Chance of Occurrence
High occupancy	$1,500,000	70%
Low occupancy	(500,000)	30

Interstate site	Profit or Loss	Chance of Occurrence
High occupancy	$1,000,000	60%
Low occupancy	100,000	40

The expected value of each site is computed by weighting each outcome by its chance of occurrence, as follows:

City Site

Expected value = .7($1,500,000) + .3(−$500,000)
Expected value = $1,050,000 − $150,000
Expected value = $900,000

Interstate Site

Expected value = .6($1,000,000) + .4($100,000)
Expected value = $600,000 + $40,000
Expected value = $640,000

Based on the expected values, the city site is more attractive than the interstate site because the city site has a higher expected value. Thus, on the average, the city site is expected to yield a higher profit than the interstate site.

The expected values for the city site and the interstate site of $900,000 and $640,000, respectively, will not actually occur. These values are weighted averages of the estimated profit or loss for each site. For the city site, the estimated outcome will be either a profit of $1,500,000 or a loss of $500,000. Likewise, for the interstate site, the estimated outcome will be either a profit of $1,000,000 or a profit of $100,000.

In the face of uncertainty, expected value is one of the most important pieces of information available to the manager for making a decision. Because expected value is an average concept, however, the range of possible outcomes (the variability of the outcomes) may also be valuable information for management's assessment of the uncertainty surrounding a decision. Although the city site in the preceding illustration has a higher expected value than the interstate site, the city site also has a wider range of possible outcomes (a profit of $1,500,000 or a loss of $500,000) than does the interstate site (a profit of $1,000,000 or $100,000). Consequently, the management of Faxon Company might select the interstate site in order to minimize the variability of the possible outcomes from the site decision. As with many other decisions, management must exercise judgment after weighing all available data and analyses.

The use of the expected value concept by management can be facilitated through the use of payoff tables and decision trees. In addition, the expected value concept may be used by managers in assessing the value of collecting additional information before a decision is made. The remainder of this section describes and illustrates the use of payoff tables and decision trees and discusses the value of obtaining additional information.

Payoff Tables

A **payoff table** presents a summary of the possible outcomes of one or more decisions. A payoff table is especially useful in managerial decision making when a wide variety of possible outcomes exists. One such situation might involve a decision facing a store manager who must decide on the amount of merchandise to purchase for various levels of possible consumer demand. To illustrate, assume that the new manager of Grocery Wholesalers Inc. must decide how many pounds of a perishable product to purchase on Monday for sale during the week. The product is purchased in 100-pound units, and by the end of the week, any unsold product is spoiled and lost. In the past, the former manager had noted that the maximum weekly sales had been 900 pounds. Therefore, to be assured that all demand could be met, 1,000 pounds were purchased.

The variable cost of the product is $1.50 per pound, and the selling price is $1.80 per pound. Thus, for each pound sold, Grocery Wholesalers Inc. earns a contribution margin of $.30 ($1.80 selling price − $1.50 variable cost per pound) to cover fixed costs and earn a profit. For each pound unsold at the end of the week, the $1.50 variable cost per pound is lost.

Based on sales records, it was determined that sales during the past ten weeks were as follows:

Number of Weeks	Actual Demand (Sales)
2	700 lbs.
5	800
3	900

The new manager must determine whether to purchase 700, 800, or 900 pounds. If the past ten weeks of sales data are used as an indication of future customer demand, the new manager should not purchase 1,000 pounds, since the recent sales data indicate that the maximum demand (sales) has not exceeded 900 pounds.

The outcomes (payoffs) in terms of contribution margin for each of the possible purchase amounts and possible levels of customer demand are summarized in the following payoff table:

Possible Demand	Contribution Margin of Purchases		
	700 lbs.	800 lbs.	900 lbs.
700 lbs.	$210	$ 60	$ (90)
800	210	240	90
900	210	240	270

PAYOFF TABLE OF POSSIBLE OUTCOMES

The entries in the payoff table indicate that if 700 pounds are demanded and 700 pounds are purchased, for example, then 700 pounds will be sold and a total contribution margin of $210 (700 lbs. × $.30 per lb.) will result. If 700 pounds are demanded and 800 pounds are purchased, then 700 pounds will be sold and 100 pounds will spoil. In this case, the 700 pounds sold will generate a contribution margin of $210 (700 lbs. × $.30 per lb.), the 100 pounds that spoil will generate a loss of $150 (100 lbs. × $1.50 per lb.), and the net contribution margin will be $60 ($210 − $150). If 700 pounds are demanded and 900 pounds are purchased, then 700 pounds will be sold and 200 pounds will spoil. In this case, the 700 pounds sold will generate a contribution margin of $210 (700 lbs. × $.30 per lb.), the 200 pounds that spoil will generate a loss of $300 (200 lbs. × $1.50 per lb.), and the net contribution margin will be a loss of $90 ($210 − $300). If 800 pounds are demanded and 700 pounds are purchased, then 700 pounds will be sold and a total contribution margin of $210 (700 lbs. × $.30 per lb.) will result. The remaining entries in the payoff table are determined in a similar manner.

Based on the past ten weeks of sales data, the chances that the various levels of customer demand will occur can be estimated as follows:

Possible Demand	Number of Weeks	Chance of Occurrence
700 lbs.	2	20% (2/10)
800	5	50% (5/10)
900	3	30% (3/10)
	10	

A payoff table of expected values can now be constructed. Each entry in the payoff table of possible outcomes is multiplied by its chance of occurrence, as indicated above, to determine its expected value. The resulting amounts are entered in the following payoff table:

PAYOFF TABLE
OF EXPECTED
VALUE OF
POSSIBLE
OUTCOMES

Possible Demand	Expected Value of Contribution Margin of Purchases		
	700 lbs.	800 lbs.	900 lbs.
700 lbs.	$ 42	$ 12	$ (18)
800	105	120	45
900	63	72	81
Totals	$210	$204	$ 108

The expected value of the outcome that 700 pounds are demanded and 700 pounds are purchased is computed by multiplying the contribution margin of $210 by the 20% chance that 700 pounds will be demanded. The resulting expected value is $42 ($210 × 20%). Likewise, the expected value of the outcome that 700 pounds are demanded and 800 pounds are purchased is computed by multiplying the contribution margin of $60 by the 20% chance that 700 pounds will be demanded. The resulting expected value is

$12 ($60 × 20%). The expected value of the outcome that 700 pounds are demanded and 900 pounds are purchased is a loss of $18 (−$90 × 20%). Similarly, the expected value of the outcome that 800 pounds are demanded and 700 pounds are purchased is computed by multiplying the contribution margin of $210 by the 50% chance that 800 pounds will be demanded. The resulting expected value is $105 ($210 × 50%). The remaining entries in the payoff table are determined in a similar manner.

The total expected value of each possible purchase is determined by summing the individual expected values at each level of possible demand. In the above table, this total expected value is represented by the totals of each column. For example, the total expected value of a purchase of 700 pounds is equal to the sum of expected values of a purchase of 700 pounds and possible demand of 700 pounds ($42), a purchase of 700 pounds and possible demand of 800 pounds ($105), and a purchase of 700 pounds and possible demand of 900 pounds ($63). The resulting total expected value of purchasing 700 pounds is $210 (the total of the first column). Likewise, the total expected value of a purchase of 800 pounds is $204, and the total expected value of purchasing 900 pounds is $108.

Based solely on the above payoff table of expected values, the new manager should select that purchase with the highest total expected value. Thus, the best purchase decision, on the average, will be the purchase of 700 pounds, since its expected value of $210 is higher than any other purchase alternative. Even though this decision will result in lost sales in some weeks, on the average it will result in the largest possible profits.

Decision Trees

Decision trees are graphical representations of decisions, possible outcomes, and chances that outcomes will occur. Decision trees are especially useful to managers who are choosing among alternatives when possible outcomes are dependent on several decisions. For example, if management decides to produce a new product, it must consider whether to offer the product in all consumer markets or only in specific markets, whether to offer special introductory rebates, whether to offer special warranties, and whether and how much to advertise. In this case, the expected profit from producing the new product depends on many decisions, each of which has an effect on the profitability of the new product.

To illustrate the use of decision trees, assume that Lampe Company is considering disposing of unimproved land. If the unimproved land is to be sold as is, its sales price would be $80,000. If the land is improved, however, there is a 40% chance that it can be rezoned for commercial development and sold for $120,000 more than the cost incurred in making improvements. There is a 60% chance that the improved land would be rezoned for residential use, in which case the land could be sold to a real estate developer for $70,000 more than the cost of improvements.

The decision tree for the preceding example can be diagrammed as follows:

DECISION TREE—
PROFIT FROM
SALE OF
UNIMPROVED OR
IMPROVED LAND

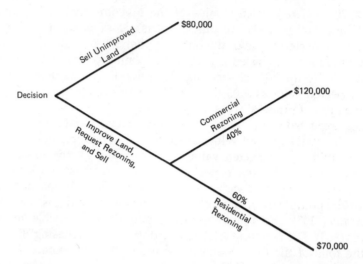

The expected values can be computed directly from the decision tree by tracing back through each branch of the decision tree and multiplying each of the possible outcomes by the chance of its occurrence. For example, the expected value of the land being rezoned for commercial use and sold for $120,000 is $48,000 ($120,000 × .4). The expected value of the residential rezoning is computed in a similar manner and is $42,000 ($70,000 × .6). Since there is no uncertainty concerning the selling of the unimproved land for $80,000, the expected value of selling the unimproved land is $80,000. These expected values are summarized in the following decision tree:

DECISION TREE
WITH EXPECTED
VALUES—PROFIT
FROM SALE OF
UNIMPROVED OR
IMPROVED LAND

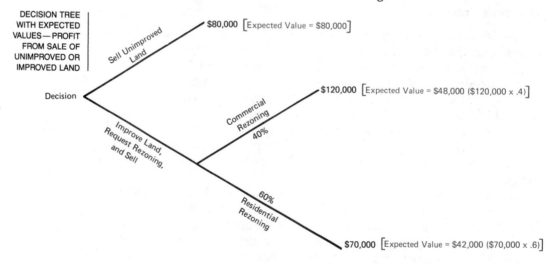

The total expected value of improving the land is equal to the sum of the expected values of the possible outcomes from the land improvement, or $90,000, computed as follows:

Commercial rezoning.	$48,000
Residential rezoning.	42,000
Total expected value of improving the land.	$90,000

The preceding analysis indicates that the land should be improved and sold, since the expected value of this course of action, $90,000, is higher than the expected value of selling the unimproved land, $80,000. Thus, on the average, a profit of $90,000 is expected from improving the land, with the worst possibility being a profit of $70,000 and the best possibility being a profit of $120,000.

Decision trees can be constructed to incorporate a large number of possible courses of action. The preceding illustration was intentionally brief in order to highlight the basic use of decision trees in aiding management's decision making under uncertainty.

Value of Information

In decision making, managers rarely have easy access to all the information they desire. In such cases, management must consider the information available and the value and the cost of seeking additional information relevant to the decision. If the expected value of acquiring additional information exceeds its expected cost, then additional information should be acquired.

To illustrate, assume that an investment in Proposal A is expected to have a 60% chance of earning net income of $10,000 and a 40% chance of suffering a net loss of $5,000. This situation is diagrammed in the following decision tree:

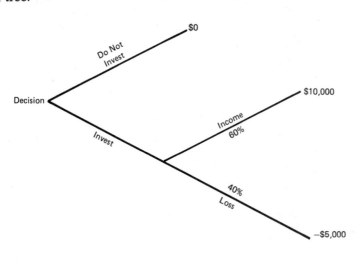

DECISION TREE—
PROPOSAL A

The expected value of investing in Proposal A is equal to the sum of the expected values of the possible outcomes, or $4,000, computed as follows:

Expected value of Proposal A = ($10,000 × .6) + (−$5,000 × .4)
Expected value of Proposal A = $6,000 − $2,000
Expected value of Proposal A = $4,000

Since the expected value of Proposal A is positive, the manager would normally invest in the proposal, even though there is a 40% chance of a loss of $5,000. Assume, however, that the manager could acquire additional information that would indicate with certainty whether Proposal A would earn the $10,000 income or suffer the loss of $5,000. How much would the manager be willing to pay for this additional (perfect) information?

The maximum amount (cost) that would be paid to obtain perfect information concerning a decision is termed the **value of perfect information.** It is the difference between (1) the expected value of a decision based on the perfect information and (2) the expected value of a decision based on existing information. To illustrate, the maximum amount that would be paid to obtain perfect information concerning Proposal A is determined by first computing the expected value of the proposal as if it is known beforehand whether the proposal would be successful or not. If the manager knows that the proposal will be successful, then a decision to invest would be made and income of $10,000 would be earned. If the manager knows that the proposal will be unsuccessful, then a decision not to invest would be made and no income or loss would result. For Proposal A, 60% of the time the perfect information will indicate that the proposal would be successful and therefore income of $10,000 would be earned. Also, 40% of the time the information will indicate that the proposal would be unsuccessful and therefore management would not invest. The expected value of perfect information is equal to the sum of the expected values of the possible outcomes, or **$6,000,** computed as follows:

Expected value of Proposal A,
  based on perfect information = ($10,000 × .6) + ($0 × .4)
Expected value of Proposal A,
  based on perfect information = $6,000

The value of perfect information concerning Proposal A is then determined by subtracting $4,000, the expected value of Proposal A, based on existing information, from the $6,000 computed above. Thus, as shown in the following computation, the manager would be willing to pay **$2,000** to obtain perfect information concerning Proposal A.

Expected value of Proposal A, based on perfect information	$6,000
Less expected value of Proposal A, based on existing information .	4,000
Value of perfect information concerning Proposal A..............	$2,000

VARIANCE ANALYSIS USING EXPECTED VALUE

When variances from standard costs occur, management must decide whether to investigate the causes and attempt corrective actions. To assist management in making this decision, the managerial accountant can use the expected value concept to focus on the expected costs relevant to the decision.

In prior illustrations, the use of the expected value concept focused on choosing among alternatives, so that the alternative with the highest expected value in terms of profit was chosen. Since management's primary focus in variance analysis is to minimize costs, however, the decision whether to investigate a variance is one of choosing that alternative with the lowest expected cost. In other words, in deciding whether to investigate a variance, management should compare the expected costs if an investigation is made with the expected costs if no investigation is made. It will then choose the alternative (investigate or not investigate) that provides the lowest expected costs.

To illustrate, assume that an unfavorable direct materials quantity variance of $1,000 has been reported for July and is expected to continue for one month if not corrected. Past experience indicates that 60% of the time the variance is caused by poor quality materials and can be eliminated (is controllable) by switching suppliers. On the other hand, 40% of the time the variance is caused by machine wear and tear and cannot be eliminated (is uncontrollable) without a major overhaul of the machinery. Due to sales commitments, production cannot be delayed for a machinery overhaul until the end of August, when regular maintenance is scheduled.

If the variance is not investigated, it will continue for August and the expected cost is the amount of the variance, $1,000. If the variance is investigated, using personnel who are available to conduct the investigation at no additional cost, the investigation may indicate that the variance is caused by poor quality materials and therefore is controllable. Management will then change suppliers and there will be no variance in August. If the investigation indicates that the variance is caused by machine wear and tear (and therefore is uncontrollable), the variance will continue for August at a cost of $1,000. However, the variance will be caused by machine wear and tear only 40% of the time, and thus the expected cost is $400 ($1,000 × 40%). These possible outcomes are diagrammed in the following decision tree:

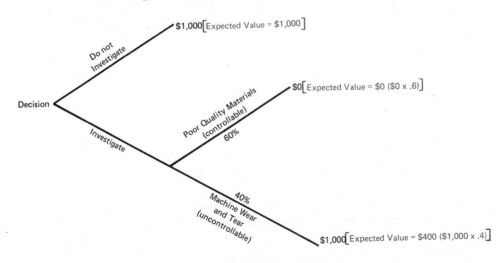

DECISION TREE—
VARIANCE INVES-
TIGATION WITH
EXPECTED COSTS

The total expected cost if the variance is investigated is the sum of the expected costs of the two possible outcomes, as shown in the following computation:

Expected cost if variance is caused by poor quality materials (controllable)...	$ 0
Plus expected cost if variance is caused by machine wear and tear (uncontrollable)	400
Total expected cost if variance is investigated.............................	$400

As indicated previously, management should select the alternative with the lowest expected cost. Since the total expected cost if the variance is investigated ($400) is less than the expected cost if no investigation is undertaken ($1,000), management should investigate the variance.

In this illustration, the cost of conducting the investigation was assumed to be zero. In practice, however, the cost may not be zero, and the important question therefore becomes: how much should management be willing to spend to investigate the variance? The answer for the direct materials variance illustration is $600, which is the difference between the total expected costs if (1) no investigation is undertaken and (2) an investigation is undertaken, as shown in the following computation:

Expected cost — no investigation...............	$1,000
Less expected cost — investigation.............	400
Value of conducting an investigation	$ 600

In the above illustration, $600 is the maximum amount that management would spend to conduct an investigation of the direct materials variance. In other words, the value of conducting an investigation and obtaining perfect information concerning the cause of the variance is $600. Thus, if it is estimated that the cost to conduct an investigation would be $700, no investigation should be undertaken. If, on the other hand, the estimated cost to conduct an investigation is $500, the investigation should be undertaken. In the latter case, the expected cost savings would be $100, as shown in the following computation:

Value of conducting an investigation.............	$600
Less cost of conducting the investigation	500
Expected cost savings from investigation	$100

MAXIMIN AND MAXIMAX CONCEPTS OF DECISION MAKING UNDER UNCERTAINTY

Alternate concepts to expected value are useful to management when it is extremely difficult to estimate the chances of occurrence of the various outcomes or when the potential loss or gain for a proposal is so great that management would ignore the expected value in making the decision. For example, management might be considering the possibility of introducing a revolutionary new product, which has a chance of earning extraordinarily large profits but which requires a total commitment of company resources. If the product is successful, the company will earn record profits; but if the product fails, the company may go bankrupt. In such a situation, the expected value concept may not be useful because management may not be willing to risk bankruptcy. The remainder of this chapter describes and illustrates two alternate concepts to expected value: (1) the maximin concept and (2) the maximax concept.

Maximin Concept

The use of the **maximin concept** leads management to decide in favor of the alternative with the maximum (largest), minimum profit. The maximin concept is applied as follows:

1. The minimum (smallest) profit for each decision alternative is listed.
2. The decision alternative with the maximum (largest) profit from the list in (1) is chosen.

To illustrate, assume that the management of Hayes Company is considering building a condominium development in one of three locations. Because of limited funds, only one of the locations can be selected. The success of each location depends on demand. The estimated profit and loss from two levels of demand (low and high) for the condominium units for each location are as follows:

	Low Demand	High Demand
Location 1	$(500,000)	$4,000,000
Location 2	100,000	1,200,000
Location 3	150,000	800,000

In applying the maximin concept, the maximum, minimum profit (or loss) from each alternative is selected. In this illustration, the minimum profit (loss) for each location appears in the low demand column. For Hayes Company, the maximin concept indicates that Location 3 should be chosen, since under conditions of low demand, Location 3 will earn more than either Locations 1 or 2. In this way, management is assured that in the worst possible case (that of low demand), a maximum profit of $150,000 will be earned. By using the maximin concept, management has avoided the possibility of losing $500,000 from the selection of Location 1 and earning only $100,000 profit from the selection of Location 2. At the same time, however, management has also forgone the possibility of earning a maximum profit of $4,000,000 from the selection of Location 1 under the most favorable (high demand) condition.

The maximin concept is used by managers when the primary concern is minimizing the risk of any loss. In such situations, managers can be said to be risk averse.

Maximax Concept

The use of the **maximax concept** leads management to decide in favor of the alternative with the maximum (largest) profit. The maximax is applied as follows:

1. The maximum (largest) profit for each decision alternative is listed.
2. The decision alternative with the maximum (largest) profit from the list in (1) is chosen.

To illustrate, assume the same facts as in the preceding illustration for Hayes Company. In applying the maximax concept, only the maximum (largest) profit for each location is considered. In this illustration, the maximum profit for each location appears in the high demand column on page 867. For Hayes Company, the maximax concept indicates that Location 1 should be selected, since under conditions of high demand, Location 1 will earn more than either Locations 2 or 3. In this way, management is assured that in the best possible case (that of high demand), the maximum profit of $4,000,000 will be earned. At the same time, however, management has also taken the risk of losing $500,000 from the selection of Location 1 under the worst (low demand) condition.

The maximax concept is used by managers when the primary concern is earning the largest possible profit, regardless of the risks. In such situations, managers can be said to be risk takers.

As illustrated by the Hayes Company, the maximin and maximax concepts depend on different philosophies of risk and thus lead to different decisions. The manager who uses the maximin concept is viewed as risk averse, while the manager who uses the maximax concept is viewed as a risk taker.

Self-Examination Questions

(Answers at end of chapter.)

1. The concept that involves identifying the possible outcomes from a decision and estimating the likelihood that each outcome will occur is the:
   A. maximin concept
   B. expected value concept
   C. maximax concept
   D. none of the above

2. Proposal R has a 60% chance of earning a profit of $80,000 and a 40% chance of incurring a loss of $60,000. What is the expected value of Proposal R?
   A. $24,000
   B. $48,000
   C. $72,000
   D. none of the above

3. Management's use of expected value can be facilitated through the use of payoff tables and:
A. the maximax concept
B. decision trees
C. the maximin concept
D. none of the above

4. The expected value of Proposal A, based on existing information, is $5,000, and the expected value of Proposal A, based on perfect information, is $8,000. What is the value of the perfect information concerning Proposal A?
A. $3,000
B. $5,000
C. $8,000
D. none of the above

5. The management of Freeman Co. is considering an investment in one of four real estate projects. The success of each project depends on whether demand is high or low. Based on the following data, which project would management select, using the maximin concept?

	Low Demand	High Demand
Project W	$120,000	$600,000
Project X	(40,000)	800,000
Project Y	110,000	500,000
Project Z	(60,000)	900,000

A. Project W
B. Project X
C. Project Y
D. Project Z

Discussion Questions

27-1. How can the managerial accountant aid management in making decisions under uncertainty?

27-2. What concept involves identifying possible outcomes from a decision and estimating the likelihood that each outcome will occur?

27-3. How is the expected value of a decision calculated?

27-4. Assume that you are playing a game in which a coin is flipped. If a head appears, you win $500, and if a tail appears, you lose $400. What is the expected value of playing this game?

27-5. Herrick Co. is considering an investment in a real estate project with the following outcomes and chances of occurrence. What is the expected value of the project?

Profit	Chance of Occurrence
$1,200,000	30%
400,000	70

27–6. What term is used to describe a table frequently used by managers to summarize the possible outcomes of one or more decisions?

27–7. The following data have been taken from the sales records of Kaufmann Co.:

Number of Weeks	Actual Demand (Sales)
4	1,000 units
10	1,500
3	2,000
2	2,500
1	3,000

Estimate the chance that each sales level will reoccur.

27–8. Based on the following payoff table of expected values, what should be the amount of monthly purchases?

	Expected Value of Contribution Margin of Purchases	
Possible Demand	5,000 units	10,000 units
5,000 units...........	$12,000	$ 3,000
10,000...............	8,000	16,000
Totals..............	$20,000	$19,000

27–9. What term is used to describe graphical representations of decisions, possible outcomes, and chances that outcomes will occur?

27–10. When are decision trees especially useful to managers in choosing among alternatives?

27–11. When should management acquire additional information before making a decision?

27–12. What term is used to describe the maximum amount that would be paid to obtain perfect information?

27–13. How is the value of perfect information computed?

27–14. Prete Co. is evaluating Proposal M as an investment. The expected value of Proposal M based on existing information is $10,000 and the expected value of Proposal M based on perfect information is $12,000. Prete Co. can obtain perfect information concerning Proposal M at a cost of $2,500. Should Prete Co. pay the $2,500 for the perfect information? Explain.

27–15. Using the expected value concept, how should management decide when to incur the costs necessary to investigate a variance?

27–16. What two alternate concepts to expected value can be used by management in making decisions under uncertainty?

27–17. When might the alternative concepts of maximax and maximin be more useful to management in decision making than the concept of expected value?

27-18. The president of Rosario Co. recently made the following statement concerning a proposed investment: "I don't care if the expected value is $1,500,000. I am not going to take the risk of losing $1,000,000 on Proposal Y. I'm selecting Proposal Z, with its expected value of $800,000, because its maximum possible loss is estimated to be $250,000." What decision-making concept was the president of Rosario Co. using?

27-19. Describe how the maximax concept of decision making is applied.

27-20. Would the use of the maximin and maximax concepts normally lead management to make the same decisions? Explain.

Exercises

27-21. While on vacation in Las Vegas, you are offered the opportunity to play one game of chance in which a die is thrown. The die is numbered one through six, and each number has an equal chance of appearing on any throw of the die. The winnings and losses established for each number on a throw of the die are as follows:

Number	Winnings (Losses)
1	$ 120
2	840
3	(480)
4	(240)
5	(540)
6	1,200

(a) Determine the expected value of playing the game. (b) If the cost of playing the game is $120, would you play? Explain.

27-22. Based on a rumor that a new shopping mall will locate near its office complex, McElroy Company is considering exercising an option to purchase twenty acres of land surrounding its offices. If the shopping mall is constructed, the land should increase substantially in value and be sold for a profit. The chance that the shopping mall will be built near the McElroy Company office complex and the potential profits that could result are as follows:

Outcome	Chance of Occurrence	Profit
Shopping mall locates near office complex	60%	$300,000
Shopping mall locates elsewhere	40	40,000

(a) Determine the expected value of exercising the option and purchasing the land. (b) Assuming that exercising the option is one of several investments being considered, briefly discuss how the expected values computed in (a) might be compared with the alternatives.

27-23. The new manager of Erickson Grocery must decide how many pounds of a perishable product to purchase on Monday for sale during the week. The outcomes for each of the possible purchases and the possible levels of customer demand are summarized in the following payoff table of possible outcomes.

Possible Demand	Contribution Margin of Purchases		
	100 lbs.	200 lbs.	300 lbs.
100 lbs..............	$200	$ 50	$(100)
200................	200	400	250
300................	200	400	600

The sales records for the past twenty weeks indicate the following levels of sales when 300 lbs. were purchased for sale each week:

Number of Weeks	Actual Demand (Sales)
8	100 lbs.
8	200
4	300

(a) Based on the sales data for the past twenty weeks, determine the chances that the various levels of customer demand (100 lbs., 200 lbs., 300 lbs.) will occur. (b) Constructed a payoff table of expected values of possible outcomes, using the format shown in the chapter. (c) What should be the amount of purchases for Erickson Grocery?

27-24. Sidwell Company is considering whether to offer a new product for sale in the South or in the West. Because of the uncertainty associated with introducing a new product, the decision will be made on the basis of expected annual income. The possible outcomes and chances of occurrence are summarized as follows:

Customer Demand	Southern Region		Western Region	
	Annual Income	Chance of Occurrence	Annual Income	Chance of Occurrence
High	$25,000,000	30%	$30,000,000	40%
Moderate	10,000,000	40	6,000,000	20
Low	2,000,000	30	2,000,000	40

(a) To aid management in deciding in which region to offer the new product, prepare a decision tree with expected values. (b) Which region should be selected for the introduction of the new product, based on the expected value concept?

27-25. The management of Newsome Company has the opportunity to invest in Proposal E, which is expected to have a 40% chance of earning income of $50,000 and a 60% chance of suffering a loss of $30,000. (a) What is the expected value of Proposal E, based on existing information? (b) What is the expected value of Proposal E, based on perfect information? (c) What is the value of perfect information concerning Proposal E? (d) If the management of Newsome Company could purchase perfect information concerning Proposal E for $10,000, should the perfect information be purchased?

27-26. The controller of Zeigler Company must decide whether to investigate an unfavorable direct labor quantity variance of $4,000 for September. The variance is expected to continue for October if no investigation is undertaken. Based on past experience, there is an 80% chance that the variance is controllable and can be eliminated for October if an investigation is conducted. There is a 20% chance that the variance is uncontrollable and cannot be eliminated for October. (a) Determine the expected cost if the variance is investigated, assuming that no additional cost will be incurred in conducting the investigation. (b) How much should management be willing to spend to investigate the variance?

27-27. Prepare a decision tree of expected values (costs) for (a) Exercise 27-25 and (b) Exercise 27-26.

27-28. Ling Company is considering an investment in one of three projects. The success of each project depends on whether customer demand is low or high. The possible profit or loss for each project is summarized as follows:

	Low Demand	High Demand
Project A...........	$100,000	$240,000
Project B...........	(40,000)	320,000
Project C...........	(60,000)	500,000

(a) Using the maximin concept, which project should management choose? (b) Using the maximax concept, which project should management choose? (c) Explain why the answers to (a) and (b) are not the same.

Problems

27-29. Hudson Science Corporation is considering purchasing the rights to one of two laser patents for purposes of research and development. Patent A has potential developmental applications in the areas of medicine, computer science, pharmacology, and military weaponry. Patent B has potential developmental applications in the areas of mining, automobile manufacturing, telecommunications, and energy. Whichever patent rights are purchased, it is likely that only one of the potential applications will yield research and development results promising enough to market commercially. The estimated profit for each patent application and the estimated chances of occurrence are as follows:

Patent A

Application	Estimated Profit	Chance of Occurrence
Medicine.....................	$ 5,000,000	20%
Computer science..............	6,500,000	40
Pharmacology	8,000,000	30
Military weaponry	12,000,000	10

Patent B

Application	Estimated Profit	Chance of Occurrence
Mining	$ 3,000,000	10%
Automobile manufacturing........	5,000,000	30
Telecommunications...........	9,000,000	40
Energy......................	15,000,000	20

Instructions:

(1) Determine the expected value of each patent.

(2) Based on the results of (1), which patent rights should be purchased?

27–30. Shiver News Distributors recently purchased a newsstand on the corner of 5th Avenue South and 2nd Street in downtown Clinton. The new manager of the newsstand must decide how many copies of the local newspaper to stock on a daily basis. The former manager had noted that the maximum daily sales, in the past, had been 175 papers, and to be assured that all demand could be met, 200 papers were purchased daily. The cost of the newspaper is $.20 per paper, and the paper is sold for $.30. Any papers remaining at the end of the day are worthless and are thrown away. The paper is published five days a week.

The records for the past month indicate the following sales:

Number of Days	Actual Demand (Sales)
2	100 papers
8	125
6	150
4	175

Instructions:

(1) Prepare a payoff table of possible outcomes in terms of contribution margin, using the format shown in the chapter.

(2) Based on the sales data for the past 20 days, estimate the chances of each level of possible demand for the newspaper.

(3) Prepare a payoff table of expected values of possible outcomes in terms of contribution margin, using the format shown in the chapter.

(4) Based on (3), how many newspapers should be purchased? Explain.

27–31. Tatum Mines Inc. is preparing to bid on the purchase of mining rights to one of two plats of federally owned land: Plat #1000 and Plat #1200. Both plats of land are known to contain deposits of uranium; however, the quality of the deposits will not be known until actual mining begins.

Preliminary estimates indicate that, for Plat #1000, there is a 60% chance that the deposit is of high quality and will yield total profits of $30,000,000. There is a 20% chance that the deposit is of moderate quality and will yield total profits of $16,000,000. Finally, there is a 20% chance that the deposit is of low quality and will yield total profits of $4,000,000.

Preliminary estimates indicate that, for Plat #1200, there is a 40% chance that the deposit is of high quality and will yield total profits of $50,000,000. There is a 40% chance that the deposit is of moderate quality and will yield total profits of $10,000,000.

Finally, there is a 20% chance that the deposit is of low quality and will yield total profits of $500,000.

Instructions:

(1) Prepare a decision tree with expected values to aid management in deciding on which plat rights to bid.

(2) On which plat rights should the management of Tatum Mines Inc. bid?

27-32. The controller of McFarland Company must decide whether to investigate an unfavorable direct labor time variance of $5,000 reported for March. The variance is expected to continue for April if not corrected. Past experience indicates that 70% of the time the variance is caused by lack of proper supervision and can be eliminated by reminding the supervisors of their responsibilities. On the other hand, 30% of the time the variance is caused by inexperienced personnel who lack proper training. Due to sales and production commitments, the appropriate training cannot be scheduled until the end of April.

Instructions:

(1) Assuming that no additional costs would be incurred in conducting an investigation, what is the expected cost of investigating the direct labor time variance?

(2) What is the value of conducting an investigation of the direct labor time variance?

(3) If the estimated cost to investigate the variance is $4,000, should the controller authorize an investigation? Explain.

(4) If the estimated cost to investigate the variance is $2,500, should the controller authorize an investigation? Explain.

27-33. The management of Investors Diversified Inc. is considering a speculative investment in one of three oil and gas ventures. The success or failure of each venture depends on the quantity of oil and gas discovered. The estimated profit or loss for each venture is as follows:

	Amount of Oil and Gas Discovered		
	None	**Moderate Quantities**	**Large Quantities**
Venture A...	$(3,000,000)	$24,000,000	$60,000,000
Venture B...	(2,000,000)	12,000,000	40,000,000
Venture C...	(5,000,000)	20,000,000	80,000,000

Instructions:

(1) If the management of Investors Diversified Inc. uses the maximin concept, which of the three ventures would be chosen?

(2) If the management of Investors Diversified Inc. uses the maximax concept, which of the three ventures would be chosen?

(3) Assuming that the Moderate Quantities column is the most likely estimate of profit from the oil and gas that will be discovered, what alternative decision concept can be used by Investors Diversified Inc.?

27-34. Vickery Company is considering building a condominium development in one of three locations: a city location, a country club location, and a lakefront location. The success of each location depends on buyer demand. Based on marketing studies, the following profits and losses have been estimated for each location, along with the chances of occurrence:

	High Buyer Demand		Low Buyer Demand	
	Profit (Loss)	Chance of Occurrence	Profit (Loss)	Chance of Occurrence
City.........	$25,000,000	75%	$(10,000,000)	25%
Country club..	15,000,000	60	(6,000,000)	40
Lakefront.....	30,000,000	70	(20,000,000)	30

Instructions:

(1) Determine the expected value of each location.
(2) Which location should be chosen, using the expected value concept?
(3) Which location should be chosen, using the maximin concept?
(4) Which location should be chosen, using the maximax concept?
(5) Which location should be chosen if management's primary objective is to choose that location with the smallest range of possible outcomes?
(6) Which location would be chosen if management uses the concept of selecting that location with the highest chance of profit?

Alternate Problems

27–29A. International Films Inc. is considering purchasing the rights to one of two autobiographies for the purposes of producing and marketing a motion picture. Each autobiography has the potential for development and sale as one of the following: (1) a cable TV movie, (2) a network (noncable) TV movie, (3) a weekly TV series, or (4) a commercial theater movie. The estimated profit for development and sale of each autobiography and the estimated chances of occurrence are as follows:

Autobiography E

	Estimated Profit	Chance of Occurrence
Cable TV movie............	$10,000,000	15%
Network TV movie..........	8,000,000	30
Weekly TV series	6,000,000	35
Theater movie	12,000,000	20

Autobiography F

	Estimated Profit	Chance of Occurrence
Cable TV movie............	$20,000,000	30%
Network TV movie..........	6,000,000	40
Weekly TV series	2,000,000	10
Theater movie	10,000,000	20

Instructions:

(1) Determine the expected value of each autobiography.
(2) Based on the results of (1), which autobiography rights should be purchased?

27–30A. Pfeiffer News Distributors recently purchased a newsstand on the corner of Elm Street and Hubbard Avenue in downtown Whitlock. The new manager of the newsstand must decide how many copies of a magazine to stock on a weekly basis. The magazine is published locally and features local civic and social events and has a large classified advertising section. The former manager had noted that the maximum weekly sales, in the past, had been 100 magazines, and to be assured that all demand could be met, 120 magazines were purchased. The cost of the magazine is $30 for quantities of 20 ($1.50 per magazine), and the magazine is sold for $3.50. Any magazines remaining at the end of the week are worthless and are thrown away.

The records for the past ten weeks indicate the following sales:

Number of Weeks	Actual Demand Sales
2	40 magazines
3	60
4	80
1	100

Instructions:

(1) Prepare a payoff table of possible outcomes in terms of contribution margin, using the format shown in the chapter.
(2) Based on the sales data for the past ten weeks, estimate the chances of each level of possible demand for the magazine.
(3) Prepare a payoff table of expected values of possible outcomes in terms of contribution margin, using the format shown in the chapter.
(4) Based on (3), how many magazines should be purchased? Explain.

27–31A. Davies Mines Inc. is preparing to bid on the purchase of mining rights to one of two plats of federally owned land: Plat #2400 and Plat #3100. Both plats of land are known to contain deposits of coal; however, the quality of the deposits will not be known until actual mining begins.

Preliminary estimates indicate that, for Plat #2400, there is a 60% chance that the deposit is of high quality and will yield total profits of $22,000,000. There is a 25% chance that the deposit is of moderate quality and will yield total profits of $5,000,000. Finally, there is a 15% chance that the deposit is of low quality and will yield total profits of $1,000,000.

Preliminary estimates indicate that, for Plat #3100, there is an 80% chance that the deposit is of high quality and will yield total profits of $16,000,000. There is a 15% chance that the deposit is of moderate quality and will yield total profits of $8,000,000. Finally, there is a 5% chance that the deposit is of low quality and will yield total profits of $2,000,000.

Instructions:

(1) Prepare a decision tree with expected values to aid management in deciding on which plat rights to bid.
(2) On which plat rights should the management of Davies Mines Inc. bid?

27–32A. The controller of Yung Company must decide whether to investigate an unfavorable direct labor rate variance of $10,000 reported for June. The variance is expected to continue for July if not corrected. Past experience indicates that 60% of the time the variance is caused by use of more experienced, higher paid employees in jobs budgeted for less experienced, lower paid employees. In this case, the variance can be eliminated by the rescheduling of job assignments. On the other hand, 40% of the time the variance is caused by overtime created by production commitments in excess of normal operations. If production demands continue, additional employees will be hired. However, because of training commitments, any new employees would not be available for assignment to normal operations until the end of July.

Instructions:

(1) Assuming that no additional costs would be incurred in conducting an investigation, what is the expected cost of investigating the direct labor rate variance?

(2) What is the value of conducting an investigation of the direct labor rate variance?

(3) If the estimated cost to investigate the variance is $4,500, should the controller authorize an investigation? Explain.

(4) If the estimated cost to investigate the variance is $6,500, should the controller authorize an investigation? Explain.

27–33A. The management of Inwood Realty Corporation is considering an investment in one of three real estate projects. The first project involves the construction of a medical office complex which will be sold to a group of practicing physicians.

The second project involves the construction of a professional office building in which space will be sold to nonmedical professional businesses, such as law firms and insurance agencies. The third project is the construction of a small shopping mall in which space will be sold to small businesses. The success of each project depends on whether demand for the constructed space is high, moderate, or low. The estimated profit or loss for each project is as follows:

Project	Demand for Space		
	High	Moderate	Low
Medical office complex	$5,000,000	$2,000,000	$(2,000,000)
Professional office complex ...	4,000,000	2,500,000	(1,000,000)
Shopping mall..............	3,000,000	1,500,000	(500,000)

Instructions:

(1) If the management of Inwood Realty Corporation uses the maximin concept, which of the three projects would be chosen?

(2) If the management of Inwood Realty Corporation uses the maximax concept, which of the three projects would be chosen?

(3) Assuming that the Moderate column is the most likely estimate of profit for each of the projects, what alternative decision concept can be used by Inwood Realty Corporation?

Mini-Case

27-35. Consolidated Oil Inc. must decide between two sites at which to drill for oil. At a desert site, there is a 75% chance that oil will be discovered, resulting in an estimated profit of $24,000,000. There is a 25% chance that no oil will be discovered at the desert site, resulting in an estimated loss of $4,000,000. At a mountain site, there is a 65% chance that oil will be discovered, resulting in an estimated profit of $30,000,000. There is a 35% chance that no oil will be discovered at the mountain site, resulting in an estimated loss of $10,000,000.

As a special summer intern serving in the capacity of assistant to the president, Deborah Keenan, you have been asked to analyze which site should be selected for drilling. In the past, Keenan has selected that site with the largest possible profit.

Instructions:

(1) What decision concept has Keenan used in the past?
(2) Using Keenan's concept identified in (1), which site should be selected?
(3) Prepare a decision tree with expected values to aid Keenan in the site selection decision.
(4) Based on the expected value concept, which site should be selected?
(5) Assuming that a new technology, using infrared photographs from satellites, can provide perfect information concerning the location of oil deposits, how much should Consolidated Oil Inc. be willing to pay for perfect information concerning (a) the desert site and (b) the mountain site?
(6) Assuming that the perfect information described in (5) costs $1,200,000 per site, should each site be analyzed at a cost of $1,200,000 per analysis to obtain perfect information?
(7) Assuming that Keenan agrees to use the expected value concept in the selection of a drilling site, prepare a final recommendation using the results of (3) through (6).

Answers
to Self-
Examination
Questions

1. **B** The expected value concept (answer B) involves identifying the possible outcomes from a decision and estimating the likelihood that each outcome will occur. The maximin concept (answer A) leads management to decide in favor of that alternative with the maximum (largest) minimum profit. The maximax concept (answer C) leads management to decide in favor of that alternative with the maximum (largest) profit.
2. **A** The expected value of Proposal R is $24,000 (answer A), computed as follows:

Expected Value = .60($80,000) + .40(−$60,000)
Expected Value = $48,000 − $24,000
Expected Value = $24,000

3. B Management's use of expected value can be facilitated through the use of payoff tables and decision trees (answer B). The maximax concept (answer A) and the maximin concept (answer C) do not use expected values.

4. A The value of perfect information concerning Proposal A is $3,000 (answer A), which is the difference between (1) the expected value of Proposal A based on perfect information, $8,000 (answer C), and (2) the expected value of a decision based on existing information, $5,000 (answer B).

5. A The maximin concept leads management to decide in favor of that alternative with the maximum, minimum profit. For Freeman Co., the minimum profit (loss) for each alternative appears in the low demand column. This column indicates that Project W (answer A) has the highest minimum profit ($120,000) of the four alternatives.

PART 10

Financial Analyses for Management Use

Perceptions of Financial Ratios

Financial statements serve as the primary financial reporting mechanism of an entity, both internally and externally. An analysis of the financial information communicated by these statements should include the computation and interpretation of financial ratios.

A survey of the views of financial executives on important issues relating to financial ratios indicated that financial ratios are an important tool in analyzing the financial results of a company and in managing a company. In addition, 93 of the 100 respondents to the survey indicated that their firms use financial ratios as part of their corporate objectives. The ratios most significant to the respondents are those that measure the ability of the firm to earn a profit.

SOURCE   Adapted from Charles H. Gibson, "How Industry Perceives Financial Ratios," *Management Accounting*, April, 1982, pp. 13-19.

Financial ratios are often more useful when they are compared with similar ratios of other companies or groups of companies. For this purpose, average ratios for many industries are compiled by various financial services and trade associations. In this process, however, it should be remembered that averages are just that—averages—and care should be taken in their use. The danger in interpreting averages was graphically illustrated by Eldon Grimm, a Wall Street analyst who said: "A statistician is an individual who has his head in the refrigerator, his feet in the oven and on the average feels comfortable."

SOURCE   Quotation from "Twenty-Five Years Ago in *Forbes*," *Forbes*, August 16, 1982, p. 107.

CHAPTER 28

Financial Statement Analysis and Price-Level Changes

CHAPTER OBJECTIVES

Describe the usefulness of financial statement analysis to management.

Describe basic financial statement analytical procedures.

Illustrate the application of financial statement analysis in assessing solvency and profitability.

Discuss financial reporting for price-level changes.

One of the primary objectives of accounting is to provide data to management for use in directing operations. In providing data to assist management, the accountant relies on a variety of concepts and techniques. Many of these concepts and techniques, such as budgeting, standard costs, differential analysis, break-even analysis, and variable costing, were discussed in preceding chapters. In this chapter, management's use of analyses of the data reported in the basic financial statements will be presented.

USEFULNESS OF FINANCIAL STATEMENT ANALYSIS

The financial condition and the results of operations, as reported in the basic financial statements, are of interest to many groups external to the reporting enterprise. Since the basic statements will be evaluated by outsiders, such as creditors and owners, management is concerned with the basic financial statements and how they are viewed by these external parties. Management is also interested in the basic financial statements for other reasons. For example, the basic financial statements are used to assess the effectiveness of management in planning and controlling operations. In addition, management recognizes that the evaluation of past operations, as revealed by the analysis of the basic statements, represents a good starting point in planning future operations. Management uses financial statement analysis, therefore, as an important means of assessing past performance and in forecasting and planning future performance.

TYPES OF FINANCIAL STATEMENT ANALYSIS

Most of the items in the basic statements are of limited significance when considered individually. Their usefulness can be enhanced through studying relationships and comparisons of items (1) within a single year's financial statements, (2) in a succession of financial statements, and (3) with other enterprises. The selection and the preparation of analytical aids are a part of the work of the accountant.

Certain aspects of financial condition or of operations are of greater importance to management than are other aspects. However, management is especially interested in the ability of a business to pay its debts as they come due and to earn a reasonable amount of income. These two aspects of the status of an enterprise are **solvency** and **profitability**. An enterprise that cannot meet its obligations to creditors on a timely basis is likely to experience difficulty in obtaining credit, and this may lead to a decline in profitability. Similarly, an enterprise whose earnings are less than those of its competitors is likely to be at a disadvantage in obtaining credit or new capital from stockholders. In this chapter, basic analytical procedures and various types of financial analysis useful in evaluating the solvency and profitability of an enterprise will be discussed.

BASIC ANALYTICAL PROCEDURES

The analytical measures obtained from financial statements are usually expressed as ratios or percentages. For example, the relationship of $150,000 to $100,000 ($150,000/$100,000 or $150,000 : $100,000) may be expressed as 1.5, 1.5 : 1, or 150%. This ease of computation and simplicity of form for expressing financial relationships are major reasons for the widespread use of ratios and percentages in financial analysis.

Analytical procedures may be used to compare the amount of specific items on a current statement with the corresponding amounts on earlier statements. For example, in comparing cash of $150,000 on the current balance sheet with cash of $100,000 on the balance sheet of a year earlier, the current amount may be expressed as 1.5 or 150% of the earlier amount. The relationship may also be expressed in terms of change, that is, the increase of $50,000 may be stated as a 50% increase.

Analytical procedures are also widely used to show the relationships of individual items to each other and of individual items to totals on a single statement. To illustrate, assume that included in the total of $1,000,000 of assets on a balance sheet are cash of $50,000 and inventories of $250,000. In relative terms, the cash balance is 5% of total assets and the inventories represent 25% of total assets. Individual items in the current asset group could also be related to total current assets. Assuming that the total of current assets in the example is $500,000, cash represents 10% of the total and inventories represent 50% of the total.

Increases or decreases in items may be expressed in percentage terms only when the base figure is positive. If the base figure is zero or a negative value, the amount of change cannot be expressed as a percentage. For example, if comparative balance sheets indicate no liability for notes payable on the first, or base, date and a liability of $10,000 on the later date, the increase of $10,000 cannot be stated as a percent of zero. Similarly, if a net loss of $10,000 in a particular year is followed by a net income of $5,000 in the next year, the increase of $15,000 cannot be stated as a percent of the loss of the base year.

In the following discussion and illustrations of analytical procedures, the basic significance of the various measures will be emphasized. The measures developed are not ends in themselves; they are only guides to the evaluation of financial and operating data. Many other factors, such as trends in the industry, changes in price levels, and general economic conditions and prospects may also need consideration in order to arrive at sound conclusions.

Horizontal Analysis

The percentage analysis of increases and decreases in corresponding items in comparative financial statements is called **horizontal analysis**. The amount of each item on the most recent statement is compared with the corresponding item on one or more earlier statements. The increase or decrease in the amount of the item is then listed, together with the percent of increase or decrease. When the comparison is made between two statements, the earlier statement is used as the base. If the analysis includes three or more statements, there are two alternatives in the selection of the base: the earliest date or period may be used as the basis for comparing all later dates or periods, or each statement may be compared with the immediately preceding statement. The two alternatives are illustrated as follows:

Base: Earliest Year

| | | | | Increase (Decrease*) | | | |
| | | | | 1986–87 | | 1986–88 | |
Item	1986	1987	1988	Amount	Percent	Amount	Percent
A	$100,000	$150,000	$200,000	$ 50,000	50%	$100,000	100%
B	100,000	200,000	150,000	100,000	100%	50,000	50%

Base: Preceding Year

| | | | | Increase (Decrease*) | | | |
| | | | | 1986–87 | | 1987–88 | |
Item	1986	1987	1988	Amount	Percent	Amount	Percent
A	$100,000	$150,000	$200,000	$ 50,000	50%	$ 50,000	33%
B	100,000	200,000	150,000	100,000	100%	50,000*	25%*

Comparison of the amounts in the last two columns of the first analysis with the amounts in the corresponding columns of the second analysis reveals the effect of the base year on the direction of change and the amount and percent of change.

A condensed comparative balance sheet for two years, with horizontal analysis, is illustrated as follows:

COMPARATIVE
BALANCE SHEET—
HORIZONTAL
ANALYSIS

Chung Company
Comparative Balance Sheet
December 31, 1987 and 1986

	1987	1986	Increase (Decrease*) Amount	Percent
Assets				
Current assets............	$ 550,000	$ 533,000	$ 17,000	3.2%
Long-term investments	95,000	177,500	82,500*	46.5%*
Plant assets (net)	444,500	470,000	25,500*	5.4%*
Intangible assets	50,000	50,000	——	
Total assets	$1,139,500	$1,230,500	$ 91,000*	7.4%*
Liabilities				
Current liabilities..........	$ 210,000	$ 243,000	$ 33,000*	13.6%*
Long-term liabilities	100,000	200,000	100,000*	50.0%*
Total liabilities	$ 310,000	$ 443,000	$133,000*	30.0%*
Stockholders' Equity				
Preferred 6% stock, $100 par...................	$ 150,000	$ 150,000	——	——
Common stock, $10 par ...	500,000	500,000	——	——
Retained earnings	179,500	137,500	$ 42,000	30.5%
Total stockholders' equity ..	$ 829,500	$ 787,500	$ 42,000	5.3%
Total liab. & stockholders' equity	$1,139,500	$1,230,500	$ 91,000*	7.4%*

The significance of the various increases and decreases in the items shown cannot be fully determined without additional information. Although total assets at the end of 1987 were $91,000 (7.4%) less than at the beginning of the year, liabilities were reduced by $133,000 (30%) and stockholders' equity increased $42,000 (5.3%). It would appear that the reduction of $100,000 in long-term liabilities was accomplished, for the most part, through the sale of long-term investments.

The foregoing balance sheet may be expanded to include the details of the various categories of assets and liabilities, or the details may be presented in separate schedules. Opinions differ as to which method presents the clearer picture. A supporting schedule with horizontal analysis is illustrated by the following comparative schedule of current assets:

COMPARATIVE
SCHEDULE OF
CURRENT
ASSETS—
HORIZONTAL
ANALYSIS

	1987	1986	Increase (Decrease*)	
			Amount	Percent
Chung Company Comparative Schedule of Current Assets December 31, 1987 and 1986				
Cash	$ 90,500	$ 64,700	$25,800	39.9%
Marketable securities......	75,000	60,000	15,000	25.0%
Accounts receivable (net) ..	115,000	120,000	5,000*	4.2%*
Inventory	264,000	283,000	19,000*	6.7%*
Prepaid expenses........	5,500	5,300	200	3.8%
Total current assets	$550,000	$533,000	$17,000	3.2%

The changes in the current assets would appear to be favorable, particularly in view of the 24.8% increase in net sales, shown in the following comparative income statement with horizontal analysis:

Chung Company
Comparative Income Statement
For Years Ended December 31, 1987 and 1986

	1987	1986	Increase (Decrease*)	
			Amount	Percent
Sales....................	$1,530,500	$1,234,000	$296,500	24.0%
Sales returns and allowances	32,500	34,000	1,500*	4.4%*
Net sales	$1,498,000	$1,200,000	$298,000	24.8%
Cost of goods sold	1,043,000	820,000	223,000	27.2%
Gross profit	$ 455,000	$ 380,000	$ 75,000	19.7%
Selling expenses	$ 191,000	$ 147,000	$ 44,000	29.9%
General expenses	104,000	97,400	6,600	6.8%
Total operating expenses ..	$ 295,000	$ 244,400	$ 50,600	20.7%
Operating income.........	$ 160,000	$ 135,600	$ 24,400	18.0%
Other income............	8,500	11,000	2,500*	22.7%*
	$ 168,500	$ 146,600	$ 21,900	14.9%
Other expense	6,000	12,000	6,000*	50.0%*
Income before income tax ..	$ 162,500	$ 134,600	$ 27,900	20.7%
Income tax................	71,500	58,100	13,400	23.1%
Net income	$ 91,000	$ 76,500	$ 14,500	19.0%

Financial Statement Analysis and Price-Level Changes

The reduction in accounts receivable may have come about through changes in credit terms or improved collection policies. Similarly, a reduction in the inventory during a period of increased sales probably indicates an improvement in the management of inventory.

An increase in net sales, considered alone, is not necessarily favorable. The increase in Chung Company's net sales was accompanied by a somewhat greater percentage increase in the cost of goods sold, which indicates a narrowing of the gross profit margin. Selling expenses increased markedly and general expenses increased slightly, making an overall increase in operating expenses of 20.7%, as contrasted with a 19.7% increase in gross profit.

Although the increase in operating income and in the final net income figure is favorable, it would be incorrect for management to conclude that its operations were at maximum efficiency. A study of the expenses and additional analysis and comparisons of individual expense accounts should be made.

The income statement illustrated is in condensed form. Such a condensed statement usually provides enough information for all interested groups except management. If desired, the statement may be expanded or supplemental schedules may be prepared to present details of the cost of goods sold, selling expenses, general expenses, other income, and other expenses.

A comparative retained earnings statement with horizontal analysis is illustrated as follows:

COMPARATIVE RETAINED EARNINGS STATEMENT— HORIZONTAL ANALYSIS

Chung Company Comparative Retained Earnings Statement For Years Ended December 31, 1987 and 1986			Increase (Decrease*)	
	1987	1986	Amount	Percent
Retained earnings, January 1	$137,500	$100,000	$37,500	37.5%
Net income for year	91,000	76,500	14,500	19.0%
Total	$228,500	$176,500	$52,000	29.5%
Dividends:				
On preferred stock	$ 9,000	$ 9,000	—	—
On common stock	40,000	30,000	$10,000	33.3%
Total	$ 49,000	$ 39,000	$10,000	25.6%
Retained earnings, December 31	$179,500	$137,500	$42,000	30.5%

Examination of the statement reveals an increase of 30.5% in retained earnings for the year. The increase was attributable to the retention of $42,000 of the net income for the year ($91,000 net income − $49,000 dividends paid).

Vertical Analysis

Percentage analysis may also be used to show the relationship of the component parts to the total in a single statement. This type of analysis is called vertical analysis. As in horizontal analysis, the statements may be prepared in either detailed or condensed form. In the latter case, additional details of the changes in the various categories may be presented in supporting schedules. If such schedules are prepared, the percentage analysis may be based on either the total of the schedule or the balance sheet total. Although vertical analysis is confined within each individual statement, the significance of both the amounts and the percents is increased by preparing comparative statements.

In vertical analysis of the balance sheet, each asset item is stated as a percent of total assets, and each liability and stockholders' equity item is stated as a percent of total liabilities and stockholders' equity. A condensed comparative balance sheet with vertical analysis is illustrated as follows:

COMPARATIVE
BALANCE
SHEET—
VERTICAL
ANALYSIS

Chung Company
Comparative Balance Sheet
December 31, 1987 and 1986

	1987		1986	
	Amount	Percent	Amount	Percent
Assets				
Current assets............	$ 550,000	48.3%	$ 533,000	43.3%
Long-term investments	95,000	8.3	177,500	14.4
Plant assets (net)	444,500	39.0	470,000	38.2
Intangible assets	50,000	4.4	50,000	4.1
Total assets	$1,139,500	100.0%	$1,230,500	100.0%
Liabilities				
Current liabilities..........	$ 210,000	18.4%	$ 243,000	19.7%
Long-term liabilities	100,000	8.8	200,000	16.3
Total liabilities	$ 310,000	27.2%	$ 443,000	36.0%
Stockholders' Equity				
Preferred 6% stock	$ 150,000	13.2%	$ 150,000	12.2%
Common stock	500,000	43.9	500,000	40.6
Retained earnings	179,500	15.7	137,500	11.2
Total stockholders' equity ..	$ 829,500	72.8%	$ 787,500	64.0%
Total liab. & stockholders' equity	$1,139,500	100.0%	$1,230,500	100.0%

The major relative changes in Chung Company's assets were in the current asset and long-term investment groups. In the lower half of the balance sheet, the greatest relative change was in long-term liabilities and retained earnings.

Stockholders' equity increased from 64% of total liabilities and stockholders' equity at the end of 1986 to 72.8% at the end of 1987, with a corresponding decrease in the claims of creditors.

In vertical analysis of the income statement, each item is stated as a percent of net sales. A condensed comparative income statement with vertical analysis is illustrated as follows:

Chung Company
Comparative Income Statement
For Years Ended December 31, 1987 and 1986

	1987		1986	
	Amount	Percent	Amount	Percent
Sales	$1,530,500	102.2%	$1,234,000	102.8%
Sales returns and allow- ances	32,500	2.2	34,000	2.8
Net sales	$1,498,000	100.0%	$1,200,000	100.0%
Cost of goods sold	1,043,000	69.6	820,000	68.3
Gross profit	$ 455,000	30.4%	$ 380,000	31.7%
Selling expenses	$ 191,000	12.8%	$ 147,000	12.3%
General expenses	104,000	6.9	97,400	8.1
Total operating expenses ..	$ 295,000	19.7%	$ 244,400	20.4%
Operating income.........	$ 160,000	10.7%	$ 135,600	11.3%
Other income............	8,500	.6	11,000	.9
	$ 168,500	11.3%	$ 146,600	12.2%
Other expense	6,000	.4	12,000	1.0
Income before income tax..	$ 162,500	10.9%	$ 134,600	11.2%
Income tax..............	71,500	4.8	58,100	4.8
Net income	$ 91,000	6.1%	$ 76,500	6.4%

Care must be used in judging the significance of differences between percentages for the two years. For example, the decline of the gross profit rate from 31.7% in 1986 to 30.4% in 1987 is only 1.3 percentage points. In terms of dollars of potential gross profit, however, it represents a decline of approximately $19,500 (1.3% × $1,498,000).

Common-Size Statements

Horizontal and vertical analyses with both dollar and percentage figures are helpful in disclosing relationships and trends in financial condition and operations of individual enterprises. Vertical analysis with both dollar and percentage figures is also useful in comparing one company with another or with industry averages. Such comparisons may be made easier by the use of common-size statements, in which all items are expressed only in relative terms.

Common-size statements may be prepared in order to compare percentages of a current period with past periods, to compare individual businesses, or to compare one business with industry percentages published by trade associations and financial information services. A comparative common-size income statement for two enterprises is illustrated as follows:

COMMON-SIZE
INCOME
STATEMENT

Chung Company and Ross Corporation Condensed Common-Size Income Statement For Year Ended December 31, 1987		
	Chung Company	Ross Corporation
Sales	102.2%	102.3%
Sales returns and allowances	2.2	2.3
Net sales	100.0%	100.0%
Cost of goods sold	69.6	70.0
Gross profit	30.4%	30.0%
Selling expenses	12.8%	11.5%
General expenses	6.9	4.1
Total operating expenses	19.7%	15.6%
Operating income	10.7%	14.4%
Other income	.6	.6
	11.3%	15.0%
Other expense	.4	.5
Income before income tax	10.9%	14.5%
Income tax	4.8	5.5
Net income	6.1%	9.0%

Examination of the statement reveals that although Chung Company has a slightly higher rate of gross profit than Ross Corporation, the advantage is more than offset by its higher percentage of both selling and general expenses. As a consequence, the operating income of Chung Company is 10.7% of net sales as compared with 14.4% for Ross Corporation, an unfavorable difference of 3.7 percentage points.

Other Analytical Measures

In addition to the percentage analyses discussed above, there are a number of other relationships that may be expressed in ratios and percentages. The items used in the measures are taken from the accounting statements of the current period and hence are a further development of vertical analysis. Comparison of the items with corresponding measures of earlier periods is an extension of horizontal analysis.

Some of the more important ratios useful in the evaluation of solvency and profitability are discussed in the sections that follow. The examples are based on the illustrative statements presented earlier. In a few instances, data from a company's statements of the preceding year and from other sources are also used.

SOLVENCY ANALYSIS

Solvency is the ability of a business to meet its financial obligations as they come due. Solvency analysis, therefore, focuses mainly on balance sheet relationships that indicate the ability to liquidate current and noncurrent liabilities. Major analyses used in assessing solvency include (1) current position analysis, (2) accounts receivable analysis, (3) inventory analysis, (4) the ratio of plant assets to long-term liabilities, and (5) the ratio of stockholders' equity to liabilities.

Current Position Analysis

To be useful, ratios relating to a firm's solvency must show the firm's ability to liquidate its liabilities. The use of ratios showing the ability to liquidate current liabilities is called current position analysis and is of particular interest to short-term creditors.

Working Capital

The excess of the current assets of an enterprise over its current liabilities at a certain moment of time is called working capital. The absolute amount of working capital and the flow of working capital during a period of time as reported by a statement of changes in financial position are often used in evaluating a company's ability to meet currently maturing obligations. Although useful for making intraperiod comparisons for a company, these absolute amounts are difficult to use in comparing companies of different sizes or in comparing such amounts with industry figures. For example, working capital of $250,000 may be very adequate for a small building contractor specializing in residential construction, but it may be completely inadequate for a large building contractor specializing in industrial and commercial construction.

Current Ratio

Another means of expressing the relationship between current assets and current liabilities is through the current ratio, sometimes referred to as the working capital ratio or bankers' ratio. The ratio is computed by dividing the total of current assets by the total of current liabilities. The determination of working capital and the current ratio for Chung Company is illustrated as follows:

	1987	1986
Current assets	$550,000	$533,000
Current liabilities	210,000	243,000
Working capital	$340,000	$290,000
Current ratio	2.6 : 1	2.2 : 1

The current ratio is a more dependable indication of solvency than is working capital. To illustrate, assume that as of December 31, 1987, the working capital of a competing corporation is much greater than $340,000, but its current ratio is only 1.3 : 1. Considering these factors alone, the Chung Company, with its current ratio of 2.6 : 1, is in a more favorable position to obtain short-term credit than the corporation with the greater amount of working capital.

Acid-Test Ratio

The amount of working capital and the current ratio are two solvency measures that indicate a company's ability to meet currently maturing obligations. However, these two measures do not take into account the composition of the current assets. To illustrate the significance of this additional factor, the following current position data for two companies are presented:

	Randall Corporation	Steward Company
Current assets:		
Cash	$ 200,000	$ 550,000
Marketable securities	100,000	100,000
Receivables (net)	200,000	200,000
Inventories	790,000	443,500
Prepaid expenses	10,000	6,500
Total current assets	$1,300,000	$1,300,000
Current liabilities	650,000	650,000
Working capital	$ 650,000	$ 650,000
Current ratio	2 : 1	2 : 1

Both companies have working capital of $650,000 and a current ratio of 2 to 1. But the ability of each company to meet its currently maturing debts is vastly different. Randall Corporation has a large part of its current assets in inventories, which must be sold and the receivables collected before the current liabilities can be paid in full. A considerable amount of time may be required to convert these inventories into cash. Declines in market prices and a reduction in demand could also impair the ability to pay current liabilities. Conversely, Steward Company has almost enough cash on hand to meet its current liabilities.

A ratio that measures the "instant" debt-paying ability of a company is called the acid-test ratio or **quick ratio.** It is the ratio of the sum of cash, receivables, and marketable securities, which are sometimes called quick assets, to current liabilities. The acid-test ratio data for Chung Company are as follows:

	1987	1986
Quick assets:		
Cash.....................................	$ 90,500	$ 64,700
Marketable securities	75,000	60,000
Receivables (net).............................	115,000	120,000
Total	$280,500	$244,700
Current liabilities	$210,000	$243,000
Acid-test ratio	1.3 : 1	1.0 : 1

A thorough analysis of a firm's current position would include the determination of the amount of working capital, the current ratio, and the acid-test ratio. These ratios are most useful when viewed together and when compared with similar ratios for previous periods and with those of other firms in the industry.

Accounts Receivable Analysis

The size and composition of accounts receivable change continually during business operations. The amount is increased by sales on account and reduced by collections. Firms that grant long credit terms tend to have relatively greater amounts tied up in accounts receivable than those granting short credit terms. Increases or decreases in the volume of sales also affect the amount of outstanding accounts receivable.

Accounts receivable yield no revenue, hence it is desirable to keep the amount invested in them at a minimum. The cash made available by prompt collection of receivables improves solvency and may be used to purchase merchandise in larger quantities at a lower price, to pay dividends to stockholders, or for other purposes. Prompt collection also lessens the risk of loss from uncollectible accounts.

Accounts Receivable Turnover

The relationship between credit sales and accounts receivable may be stated as the **accounts receivable turnover.** It is computed by dividing net sales on account by the average net accounts receivable. It is preferable to base the average on monthly balances, which gives effect to seasonal changes. When such data are not available, it is necessary to use the average of the balances at the beginning and the end of the year. If there are trade notes receivable as well as accounts, the two should be combined. The accounts receivable turnover data for Chung Company are as follows. All sales were made on account.

	1987	1986
Net sales on account	$1,498,000	$1,200,000
Accounts receivable (net):		
Beginning of year	$ 120,000	$ 140,000
End of year	115,000	120,000
Total	$ 235,000	$ 260,000
Average	$ 117,500	$ 130,000
Accounts receivable turnover	12.7	9.2

The increase in the accounts receivable turnover for 1987 indicates that there has been an acceleration in the collection of receivables, due perhaps to improvement in either the granting of credit or the collection practices used, or both.

Number of Days' Sales in Receivables

Another means of expressing the relationship between credit sales and accounts receivable is the **number of days' sales in receivables**. This measure is determined by dividing the net accounts receivable at the end of the year by the average daily sales on account (net sales on account divided by 365), illustrated as follows for Chung Company:

	1987	1986
Accounts receivable (net), end of year	$ 115,000	$ 120,000
Net sales on account	$1,498,000	$1,200,000
Average daily sales on account	$ 4,104	$ 3,288
Number of days' sales in receivables	28.0	36.5

The number of days' sales in receivables gives a rough measure of the length of time the accounts receivable have been outstanding. A comparison of this measure with the credit terms, with figures for comparable firms in the same industry, and with figures of Chung Company for prior years will help reveal the efficiency in collecting receivables and the trends in the management of credit.

Inventory Analysis

Although an enterprise must maintain sufficient inventory quantities to meet the demands of its operations, it is desirable to keep the amount invested in inventory to a minimum. Inventories in excess of the needs of business reduce solvency by tying up funds. Excess inventories may also cause increases in the amount of insurance, property taxes, storage, and other related expenses, further reducing funds that could be used to better advantage. There is also added risk of loss through price declines and deterioration or obsolescence of the inventory.

Inventory Turnover

The relationship between the volume of goods sold and inventory may be stated as the **inventory turnover.** It is computed by dividing the cost of goods sold by the average inventory. If monthly data are not available, it is necessary to use the average of the inventories at the beginning and the end of the year. The inventory turnover data for Chung Company are as follows:

	1987	1986
Cost of goods sold	$1,043,000	$820,000
Inventory:		
Beginning of year	$ 283,000	$311,000
End of year	264,000	283,000
Total	$ 547,000	$594,000
Average	$ 273,500	$297,000
Inventory turnover	3.8	2.8

The improvement in the turnover resulted from an increase in the cost of goods sold, combined with a decrease in average inventory. The variation in types of inventory is too great to permit any broad generalizations as to what is a satisfactory turnover. For example, a firm selling food should have a much higher turnover than one selling furniture or jewelry, and the perishable foods department of a supermarket should have a higher turnover than the soaps and cleansers department. However, for each business or each department within a business, there is a reasonable turnover rate. A turnover below this rate means that the company or the department is incurring extra expenses such as those for administration and storage, is increasing its risk of loss because of obsolescence and adverse price changes, is incurring interest charges in excess of those considered necessary, and is failing to free funds for other uses.

Number of Days' Sales in Inventory

Another means of expressing the relationship between the cost of goods sold and inventory is the **number of days' sales in inventory.** This measure is determined by dividing the inventory at the end of the year by the average daily cost of goods sold (cost of goods sold divided by 365), illustrated as follows for Chung Company:

	1987	1986
Inventory, end of year	$ 264,000	$283,000
Cost of goods sold	$1,043,000	$820,000
Average daily cost of goods sold	$ 2,858	$ 2,247
Number of days' sales in inventory	92.4	125.9

The number of days' sales in inventory gives a rough measure of the length of time it takes to acquire, sell, and then replace the average inventory. Although there was a substantial improvement in the second year, comparison of the measure with those of earlier years and of comparable firms is an essential element in judging the effectiveness of Chung Company's inventory control.

As with many attempts to analyze financial data, it is possible to determine more than one measure to express the relationship between the cost of goods sold and inventory. Both the inventory turnover and number of days' sales in inventory are useful for evaluating the efficiency in the management of inventory. Whether both measures are used or whether one measure is preferred over the other is a matter for the individual analyst to decide.

Ratio of Plant Assets to Long-Term Liabilities

Long-term notes and bonds are often secured by mortgages on plant assets. The **ratio of total plant assets to long-term liabilities** provides a solvency measure that shows the margin of safety of the noteholders or bondholders. It also gives an indication of the potential ability of the enterprise to borrow additional funds on a long-term basis. The ratio of plant assets to long-term liabilities of Chung Company is as follows:

	1987	1986
Plant assets (net)	$444,500	$470,000
Long-term liabilities	$100,000	$200,000
Ratio of plant assets to long-term liabilities	4.4 : 1	2.4 : 1

The marked increase in the ratio at the end of 1987 was mainly due to the liquidation of one half of Chung Company's long-term liabilities. If the company should need to borrow additional funds on a long-term basis, it is in a stronger position to do so.

Ratio of Stockholders' Equity to Liabilities

Claims against the total assets of an enterprise are divided into two basic groups, those of the creditors and those of the owners. The relationship between the total claims of the two groups provides a solvency measure that indicates the margin of safety for the creditors and the ability of the enterprise to withstand adverse business conditions. If the claims of the creditors are large in proportion to the equity of the stockholders, there are likely to be substantial charges for interest payments. If earnings decline to the point where the company is unable to meet its interest payments, control of the business may pass to the creditors.

The relationship between stockholder and creditor equity is shown in the vertical analysis of the balance sheet. For example, the balance sheet of Chung Company presented on page 888 indicates that on December 31, 1987, stockholders' equity represented 72.8% and liabilities represented 27.2% of the sum of the liabilities and stockholders' equity (100.0%). Instead of expressing each item as a percent of the total, the relationship may be expressed as a ratio of one to the other, as follows:

	1987	1986
Total stockholders' equity	$829,500	$787,500
Total liabilities	$310,000	$443,000
Ratio of stockholders' equity to liabilities	2.7 : 1	1.8 : 1

The balance sheet of Chung Company shows that the major factor affecting the change in the ratio was the $100,000 reduction in long-term liabilities during 1987. The ratio at both dates shows a large margin of safety for the creditors.

PROFITABILITY ANALYSIS

Profitability is the ability of an entity to earn income. It can be assessed by computing various relevant measures, including (1) the ratio of net sales to assets, (2) the rate earned on total assets, (3) the rate earned on stockholders' equity, (4) the rate earned on common stockholders' equity, (5) earnings per share on common stock, (6) the price-earnings ratio, and (7) dividend yield.

Ratio of Net Sales to Assets

The **ratio of net sales to assets** is a profitability measure that shows how effectively a firm utilizes its assets. Assume that two competing enterprises have equal amounts of assets, but the amount of the sales of one is double the amount of the sales of the other. Obviously, the former is making better use of its assets. In computing the ratio, any long-term investments should be excluded from total assets because they are wholly unrelated to sales of goods or services. Assets used in determining the ratio may be the total at the end of the year, the average at the beginning and the end of the year, or the average of the monthly totals. The basic data and the ratio of net sales to assets for Chung Company are as follows:

	1987	1986
Net sales	$1,498,000	$1,200,000
Total assets (excluding long-term investments):		
Beginning of year	$1,053,000	$1,010,000
End of year	1,044,500	1,053,000
Total	$2,097,500	$2,063,000
Average	$1,048,750	$1,031,500
Ratio of net sales to assets	1.4 : 1	1.2 : 1

The ratio improved to a minor degree in 1987, largely due to the increased sales volume. A comparison of the ratio with those of other enterprises in the same industry would be helpful in assessing Chung Company's effectiveness in the utilization of assets.

Rate Earned on Total Assets

The **rate earned on total assets** is a measure of the profitability of the assets, without regard to the equity of creditors and stockholders in the assets. The rate is therefore not affected by differences in methods of financing an enterprise.

The rate earned on total assets is derived by adding interest expense to net income and dividing this sum by total assets. By adding interest expense to net income, the profitability of the assets is determined without considering the means of financing the acquisition of the assets. The rate earned by Chung Company on total assets is determined as follows:

	1987	1986
Net income	$ 91,000	$ 76,500
Plus interest expense	6,000	12,000
Total	$ 97,000	$ 88,500
Total assets:		
Beginning of year	$1,230,500	$1,187,500
End of year	1,139,500	1,230,500
Total	$2,370,000	$2,418,000
Average	$1,185,000	$1,209,000
Rate earned on total assets	8.2%	7.3%

The rate earned on total assets of Chung Company for 1987 indicates an improvement over that for 1986. A comparison with other companies and with industry averages would also be useful in evaluating the effectiveness of management performance.

Rate Earned on Stockholders' Equity

Another relative measure of profitability is obtained by dividing net income by the total stockholders' equity. In contrast to the rate earned on total assets, the **rate earned on stockholders' equity** emphasizes the income yield in relationship to the amount invested by the stockholders.

The amount of the total stockholders' equity throughout the year varies for several reasons—the issuance of additional stock, the retirement of a class of stock, the payment of dividends, and the gradual accrual of net income. If monthly figures are not available, the average of the stockholders' equity at the beginning and the end of the year is used, as in the following illustration:

	1987	1986
Net income	$ 91,000	$ 76,500
Stockholders' equity:		
Beginning of year	$ 787,500	$ 750,000
End of year	829,500	787,500
Total	$1,617,000	$1,537,500
Average	$ 808,500	$ 768,750
Rate earned on stockholders' equity	11.3%	10.0%

The rate earned by a thriving enterprise on the equity of its stockholders is usually higher than the rate earned on total assets. The reason for the difference is that the amount earned on assets acquired through the use of funds provided by creditors is more than the interest charges paid to creditors. This tendency of the rate on stockholders' equity to vary disproportionately from the rate on total assets is sometimes called leverage. The Chung Company rate on stockholders' equity for 1987, 11.3%, compares favorably with the rate of 8.2% earned on total assets, as reported previously. The leverage factor of 3.1% (11.3% − 8.2%) for 1987 also compares favorably with the 2.7% (10.0% − 7.3%) differential for the preceding year.

Rate Earned on Common Stockholders' Equity

When a corporation has both preferred and common stock outstanding, the holders of the common stock have the residual claim on earnings. The rate earned on common stockholders' equity is the net income less preferred dividend requirements for the period, stated as a percent of the average equity of the common stockholders.

Chung Company has $150,000 of preferred 6% nonparticipating stock outstanding at both balance sheet dates, hence annual preferred dividends amount to $9,000. The common stockholders' equity is the total stockholders' equity, reduced by the par of the preferred stock ($150,000). The basic data and the rate earned on common stockholders' equity are as follows:

	1987	1986
Net income	$ 91,000	$ 76,500
Preferred dividends.............................	9,000	9,000
Remainder — identified with common stock........	$ 82,000	$ 67,500
Common stockholders' equity:		
Beginning of year.............................	$ 637,500	$ 600,000
End of year	679,500	637,500
Total	$1,317,000	$1,237,500
Average.....................................	$ 658,500	$ 618,750
Rate earned on common stockholders' equity......	12.5%	10.9%

The rate earned on common stockholders' equity differs from the rates earned by Chung Company on total assets and total stockholders' equity. This situation will occur if there are borrowed funds and also preferred stock outstanding, which rank ahead of the common shares in their claim on earnings. Thus the concept of leverage, as discussed in the preceding section, can be applied to the use of funds from the sale of preferred stock as well as from borrowing. Funds from both sources can be used in an attempt to increase the return on common stockholders' equity.

Earnings per Share on Common Stock

One of the profitability measures most commonly quoted in the financial press and included in the income statement in corporate annual reports is earnings per share on common stock. If a company has issued only one class of stock, the earnings per share are determined by dividing net income by the number of shares of stock outstanding. If there are both preferred and common stock outstanding, the net income must be reduced first by the amount necessary to meet the preferred dividend requirements.

Any changes in the number of shares outstanding during the year, such as would result from stock dividends or stock splits, should be disclosed in quoting earnings per share on common stock. Also if there are any nonrecurring (extraordinary, etc.) items in the income statement, the income per share, before such items, should be reported along with net income per share. In addition, if there are convertible bonds or preferred stock outstanding, the amount reported as net income per share should be stated without considering the conversion privilege, followed by net income per share, assuming conversion had occurred.

The data on the earnings per share of common stock for Chung Company are as follows:

	1987	1986
Net income	$91,000	$76,500
Preferred dividends	9,000	9,000
Remainder—identified with common stock	$82,000	$67,500
Shares of common stock outstanding	50,000	50,000
Earnings per share on common stock	$1.64	$1.35

Earnings per share data can be presented in conjunction with dividends per share data to indicate the relationship between earnings and dividends and the extent to which the corporation is retaining its earnings for use in the business. The following chart shows this relationship for Chung Company:

CHART OF
EARNINGS AND
DIVIDENDS ON
COMMON STOCK

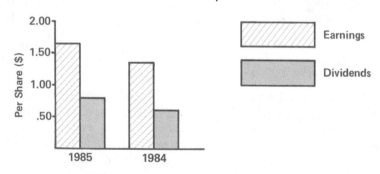

Price-Earnings Ratio

A profitability measure commonly quoted in the financial press is the price-earnings (P/E) ratio on common stock. It is computed by dividing the market price per share of common stock at a specific date by the annual earnings per share. Assuming market prices per common share of 20½ at the end of 1987 and 13½ at the end of 1986, the price-earnings ratio on common stock of Chung Company is as follows:

	1987	1986
Market price per share of common stock................	$20.50	$13.50
Earnings per share on common stock	$ 1.64	$ 1.35
Price-earnings ratio on common stock	12.5	10.0

The price-earnings ratio indicates that a share of common stock of Chung Company was selling for 12.5 and 10 times the amount of earnings per share at the end of 1987 and 1986 respectively.

Dividend Yield

The **dividend yield** on common stock is a profitability measure that shows the rate of return to common stockholders in terms of cash dividend distributions. The dividend yield is computed by dividing the annual dividends paid per share of common stock by the market price per share at a specific date. Assuming dividends of $.80 and $.60 per common share and market prices per common share of 20½ and 13½ at the end of 1987 and 1986 respectively, the dividend yield on common stock of Chung Company is as follows:

	1987	1986
Dividends per share on common stock	$ .80	$ .60
Market price per share of common stock...............	$20.50	$13.50
Dividend yield on common stock	3.9%	4.4%

SELECTION OF ANALYTICAL MEASURES

The analytical measures that have been discussed and illustrated are representative of many that can be developed for a medium-size business enterprise. Some of them might well be omitted in analyzing a specific firm, or additional measures could be developed. The type of business activity, the capital structure, and the size of the enterprise usually affect the measures used. For example, in analyzing railroads, public utilities, and other corporations with a high ratio of debt to stockholders' equity, it is customary to express the solvency measure that shows the relative risk of the bondholders in terms of the number of times the interest charges are earned during the year. The higher the ratio, the greater the assurance of continued interest payments in case of decreased earnings. The measure also provides an indication of general financial strength, which is of concern to stockholders and employees, as well as to creditors.

In the following data, the amount available to meet interest charges is not affected by taxes on income because interest is deductible in determining taxable income.

	1987	1986
Income before income tax	$ 900,000	$ 800,000
Add interest charges	300,000	250,000
Amount available to meet interest charges	$1,200,000	$1,050,000
Number of times interest charges earned	4	4.2

Analyses like the above can be applied to dividends on preferred stock. In such cases, net income would be divided by the amount of preferred dividends to yield the number of times preferred dividends were earned. This measure gives an indication of the relative assurance of continued dividend payments to preferred stockholders.

Percentage analyses, ratios, turnovers, and other measures of financial position and operating results are useful analytical devices. They are helpful in appraising the present performance of an enterprise and in forecasting its future. They are not, however, a substitute for sound judgment nor do they provide definitive guides to action. In selecting and interpreting analytical indexes, proper consideration should be given to any conditions peculiar to the particular enterprise or to the industry of which the enterprise is a part. The possible influence of the general economic and business environment should also be weighed.

To determine trends, the interrelationship of the measures used in appraising a certain enterprise should be carefully studied, as should comparable indexes of earlier fiscal periods. Data from competing enterprises may also be compared in order to determine the relative efficiency of the firm being analyzed. In making such comparisons, however, it is essential to consider the potential effects of any significant differences in the accounting methods used by the enterprises. The following presentation is a summary of the analytical measures discussed in this chapter:

	Method of Computation	Use
Solvency measures:		
Working capital	Current assets − current liabilities	To indicate the ability to meet currently maturing obligations
Current ratio	$\dfrac{\text{Current assets}}{\text{Current liabilities}}$	
Acid-test ratio	$\dfrac{\text{Quick assets}}{\text{Current liabilities}}$	To indicate instant debt-paying ability

	Method of Computation	Use
Solvency measures:		
Accounts receivable turnover	$$\frac{\text{Net sales on account}}{\text{Average accounts receivable}}$$	To assess the efficiency in collecting receivables and in the management of credit
Number of days' sales in receivables	$$\frac{\text{Accounts receivable, end of year}}{\text{Average daily sales on account}}$$	
Inventory turnover	$$\frac{\text{Cost of goods sold}}{\text{Average inventory}}$$	To assess the efficiency in the management of inventory
Number of days' sales in inventory	$$\frac{\text{Inventory, end of year}}{\text{Average daily cost of goods sold}}$$	
Ratio of plant assets to long-term liabilities	$$\frac{\text{Plant assets (net)}}{\text{Long-term liabilities}}$$	To indicate the margin of safety to long-term creditors
Ratio of stockholders' equity to liabilities	$$\frac{\text{Total stockholders' equity}}{\text{Total liabilities}}$$	To indicate the margin of safety to creditors
Profitability measures:		
Ratio of net sales to assets	$$\frac{\text{Net sales}}{\text{Average total assets (excluding long-term investments)}}$$	To assess the effectiveness in the use of assets
Rate earned on total assets	$$\frac{\text{Net income + interest expense}}{\text{Average total assets}}$$	To assess the profitability of the assets
Rate earned on stockholders' equity	$$\frac{\text{Net income}}{\text{Average stockholders' equity}}$$	To assess the profitability of the investment by stockholders
Rate earned on common stockholders' equity	$$\frac{\text{Net income} - \text{preferred dividends}}{\text{Average common stockholders' equity}}$$	To assess the profitability of the investment by common stockholders
Earnings per share on common stock	$$\frac{\text{Net income} - \text{preferred dividends}}{\text{Shares of common stock outstanding}}$$	
Dividends per share of common stock	$$\frac{\text{Dividends}}{\text{Shares of common stock outstanding}}$$	To indicate the extent to which earnings are being distributed to common stockholders
Price-earnings ratio	$$\frac{\text{Market price per share of common stock}}{\text{Earnings per share on common stock}}$$	To indicate the relationship between market value of common stock and earnings
Dividend yield	$$\frac{\text{Dividends per common share}}{\text{Market price per common share}}$$	To indicate the rate of return to common stockholders in terms of dividends
Number of times interest charges earned	$$\frac{\text{Income before income tax + interest expense}}{\text{Interest expense}}$$	To assess the risk to bondholders in terms of number of times interest charges were earned

FINANCIAL REPORTING FOR PRICE-LEVEL CHANGES

The analytical measures discussed in this chapter were illustrated using traditional financial statements. These statements are based on the recording of the effects of business transactions on the accounts of an enterprise in terms of money. As a means of measurement, however, money is subject to changes in value, and it therefore lacks the stability of the standards used in measuring time, distance, and the physical properties of matter. This instability of the purchasing power of money should be considered by management and other analysts of financial statements.

Because of its homogeneity and its use as a standard of value, money is the only practicable medium for recording and reporting financial data. Therefore, accountants are in general agreement that the changing value of money should not be given recognition in the accounts or in conventional financial statements. Conventional statements, because they report actual transactions based on historical costs arising from arms-length bargaining, can be independently verified and thus viewed as reliable. Also, since users are accustomed to the present statements, their understanding of changing prices may be enhanced by supplemental data indicating the effect of changing prices rather than by the alteration of conventional statements.

There are two widely discussed recommendations for supplementing conventional statements and thus resolving financial reporting problems created by increasing price levels: (1) supplemental financial data based on current costs, and (2) supplemental financial data based on constant dollars. The discussion in the following sections is confined to the basic concepts and problems of these recommendations.

Current Cost Data

Current cost is the amount of cash that would have to be paid currently to acquire assets of the same age and in the same condition as existing assets. When current costs are used as the basis for financial reporting, assets, liabilities, and owners' equity are stated at current values and expenses are stated at the current cost of doing business. The use of current costs permits the identification of gains and losses that result from holding assets during periods of changes in price levels. To illustrate, assume that a firm acquired land at the beginning of the fiscal year for $50,000 and that at the end of the year its current cost (value) is $60,000. The land could be reported at its current cost of $60,000, and the $10,000 increase in value could be reported as an unrealized gain from holding the land.

The major disadvantage in the use of current costs is the absence of established standards and procedures for determining such costs. However, many accountants believe that adequate standards and procedures will evolve through experimentation with actual applications.

Constant Dollar Data

Constant dollar data, also known as general price-level data, are historical costs that have been converted to constant dollars through the use of a price-level index. In this manner, financial statement elements are reported in dollars, each of which has the same (that is, constant) general purchasing power.

A **price-level index** is the ratio of the total cost of a group of commodities prevailing at a particular time to the total cost of the same group of commodities at an earlier base time. The total cost of the commodities at the base time is assigned a value of 100 and the price-level indexes for all later times are expressed as a ratio to 100. For example, assume that the cost of a selected group of commodities amounted to $12,000 at a particular time and $13,200 today. The price index for the earlier, or base, time becomes 100 and the current price index is 110 [(13,200 ÷ 12,000) × 100].

A general price-level index may be used to determine the effect of changes in price levels on certain financial statement items. To illustrate, assume a price index of 120 at the time of purchase of a plot of land for $10,000 and a current price index of 150. The **constant dollar equivalent** of the original cost of $10,000 may be computed as follows:

$$\frac{\text{Current Price Index}}{\text{Price Index at Date of Purchase}} \times \text{Original Cost} = \text{Constant Dollar Equivalent}$$

$$\frac{150}{120} \times \$10,000 = \$12,500$$

Current Annual Reporting Requirements for Price-Level Changes

In 1979, the Financial Accounting Standards Board undertook an experimental program for reporting the effects of changing prices by requiring approximately 1,300 large, publicly held enterprises to disclose certain current cost information and constant dollar information annually as supplemental data.[1] In 1984, after reviewing the experiences with these 1979 disclosure requirements, the Board concluded that current cost information was more useful than constant dollar information as a supplement to the basic financial statements. In addition, the Board concluded that requiring two different methods of reporting the effects of changing prices may detract from the usefulness of the information. As a result, the requirement to report constant dollar information was dropped for those companies that report current cost information.[2]

---

[1]*Statement of Financial Accounting Standards, No. 33,* "Financial Reporting and Changing Prices" (Stamford: Financial Accounting Standards Board, 1979.)

[2]*Statement of Financial Accounting Standards, No. 82,* "Financial Reporting and Changing Prices: Elimination of Certain Disclosures" (Stamford: Financial Accounting Standards Board, 1984).

Self-Examination Questions
(Answers at end of chapter.)

1. What type of analysis is indicated by the following?

	Amount	Percent
Current assets	$100,000	20%
Plant assets	400,000	80
Total assets	$500,000	100%

   A. Vertical analysis
   B. Horizontal analysis
   C. Differential analysis
   D. None of the above

2. Which of the following measures is useful as an indication of the ability of a firm to liquidate current liabilities?
   A. Working capital
   B. Current ratio
   C. Acid-test ratio
   D. All of the above

3. The ratio determined by dividing total current assets by total current liabilities is:
   A. current ratio
   B. working capital ratio
   C. bankers' ratio
   D. all of the above

4. The ratio of the "quick assets" to current liabilities, which indicates the "instant" debt-paying ability of a firm, is:
   A. current ratio
   B. working capital ratio
   C. acid-test ratio
   D. none of the above

5. A measure useful in evaluating the efficiency in the management of inventory is:
   A. inventory turnover
   B. number of days' sales in inventory
   C. both A and B
   D. none of the above

Discussion Questions

28–1. In the analysis of the financial status of an enterprise, what is meant by *solvency* and *profitability*?

28–2. Illustrate (a) horizontal analysis and (b) vertical analysis, using the following data taken from a comparative balance sheet:

	Current Year	Preceding Year
Cash.	$ 900,000	$ 600,000
Total current assets.	3,600,000	3,000,000

28–3. What is the advantage of using comparative statements for financial analysis rather than statements for a single date or period?

28–4. The current year's amount of net income (after income tax) is 15% larger than that of the preceding year. Does this indicate an improved operating performance? Discuss.

28–5. What are common-size financial statements?

28–6. (a) Name the major ratios useful in assessing solvency and profitability. (b) Why is it important not to rely on only one ratio or measure in assessing the solvency or profitability of an enterprise?

28–7. Identify the measure of current position analysis described by each of the following: (a) the excess of the current assets over current liabilities, (b) the ratio of current assets to current liabilities, (c) the ratio of quick assets to current liabilities.

28–8. The working capital for Robinson Company at the end of the current year is $60,000 greater than the working capital at the end of the preceding year, reported as follows. Does this mean that the current position has improved? Explain.

	Current Year	Preceding Year
Current assets:		
Cash, marketable securities, and receivables	$288,000	$240,000
Inventory	432,000	260,000
Total current assets	$720,000	$500,000
Current liabilities.	360,000	200,000
Working capital	$360,000	$300,000

28–9. A company that grants terms of n/30 on all sales has an accounts receivable turnover for the year, based on monthly averages, of 6. Is this a satisfactory turnover? Discuss.

28–10. What does an increase in the number of days' sales in receivables ordinarily indicate about the credit and collection policy of the firm?

28–11. (a) Why is it advantageous to have a high inventory turnover? (b) Is it possible for an inventory turnover to be too high? (c) Is it possible to have a high inventory turnover and a high number of days' sales in inventory? Discuss.

28–12. What does an increase in the ratio of stockholders' equity to liabilities indicate about the margin of safety for the firm's creditors and the ability of the firm to withstand adverse business conditions?

28–13. In computing the ratio of net sales to assets, why are long-term investments excluded in determining the amount of the total assets?

28–14. In determining the rate earned on total assets, why is interest expense added to net income before dividing by total assets?

28-15. (a) Why is the rate earned on stockholders' equity by a thriving enterprise ordinarily higher than the rate earned on total assets? (b) Should the rate earned on common stockholders' equity normally be higher or lower than the rate earned on total stockholders' equity? Explain.

28-16. The net income (after income tax) of Morgan Company was $10 per common share in the latest year and $15 per common share for the preceding year. At the beginning of the latest year, the number of shares outstanding was doubled by a stock split. There were no other changes in the amount of stock outstanding. What were the earnings per share in the preceding year, adjusted to place them on a comparable basis with the latest year?

28-17. The price earnings ratio for common stock of Mura Company was 15 at June 30, the end of the current fiscal year. What does the ratio indicate about the selling price of common stock in relation to current earnings?

28-18. Why would the dividend yield differ significantly from the rate earned on common stockholders' equity?

28-19. Favorable business conditions may bring about certain seemingly unfavorable ratios, and unfavorable business operations may result in apparently favorable ratios. For example, Almond Company increased its sales and net income substantially for the current year, yet the current ratio at the end of the year is lower than at the beginning of the year. Discuss some possible causes of the apparent weakening of the current position while sales and net income have increased substantially.

28-20. What is the current cost of an asset?

28-21. If land was purchased for $40,000 when the general price-level index was 220, and the general price-level index has risen to 242 in 1986, what is the constant dollar equivalent of the original cost of the land?

Exercises

28-22. Revenue and expense data for Eastern Company are as follows:

	1987	1986
Sales	$900,000	$800,000
Cost of goods sold	549,000	480,000
Selling expense	117,000	144,000
General expense	81,000	64,000
Income tax	63,000	48,000

(a) Prepare an income statement in comparative form, stating each item for both 1987 and 1986 as a percent of sales.

Financial Statement Analysis and Price-Level Changes

(b) Prepare a comparative income statement—horizontal analysis, using 1986 as the base year.
(c) Comment upon the significant changes disclosed by the comparative income statements.

28–23. The following data were abstracted from the balance sheet of Valenzuela Company:

	Current Year	Preceding Year
Cash	$116,000	$101,500
Marketable securities..........................	55,000	40,000
Accounts and notes receivable (net)	159,000	152,500
Inventory	229,800	160,000
Prepaid expenses..............................	10,200	8,000
Accounts and notes payable (short-term)	250,000	185,000
Accrued liabilities	50,000	25,000

(a) Determine for each year the (1) working capital, (2) current ratio, and (3) acid-test ratio. (Present figures used in your computations.)
(b) What conclusions can be drawn from these data as to the company's ability to meet its currently maturing debts?

28–24. The following data are taken from the financial statements for Lasorta Company:

	Current Year	Preceding Year
Accounts receivable, end of year	$ 563,200	$ 462,000
Monthly average accounts receivable (net)........	522,500	423,500
Net sales on account..........................	4,180,000	2,964,500

Terms of all sales are 1/10, n/60.
(a) Determine for each year (1) the accounts receivable turnover and (2) the number of days' sales in receivables.
(b) What conclusions can be drawn from these data concerning the composition of accounts receivable?

28–25. The following data were abstracted from the income statement of Cowans Corporation:

	Current Year	Preceding Year
Sales..	$4,680,000	$4,575,800
Beginning inventory	588,000	512,000
Purchases	2,424,000	2,496,000
Ending inventory..............................	612,000	588,000

(a) Determine for each year (1) the inventory turnover and (2) the number of days' sales in inventory.
(b) What conclusions can be drawn from these data concerning the composition of the inventory?

28–26. The following data were taken from the financial statements of John Concepcion and Co. for the current fiscal year:

Plant assets (net).......................................		$1,104,000
Liabilities:		
Current liabilities......................................		$ 360,000
Mortgage note payable, 10%, issued 1980, due 2000		480,000
Total liabilities		$ 840,000
Stockholders' equity:		
Preferred 9% stock, $100 par, cumulative, nonparticipating (no change during year)......................................		$ 180,000
Common stock, $10 par (no change during year)............		900,000
Retained earnings:		
Balance, beginning of year.................... $642,600		
Net income 198,000	$840,600	
Preferred dividends .... $ 16,200		
Common dividends 56,400	72,600	
Balance, end of year.......................		768,000
Total stockholders' equity		$1,848,000
Net sales		$3,295,200
Interest expense.......................................		48,000

Assuming that long-term investments totaled $180,000 throughout the year and that total assets were $2,322,600 at the beginning of the year, determine the following, presenting figures used in your computations: (a) ratio of plant assets to long-term liabilities, (b) ratio of stockholders' equity to liabilities, (c) ratio of net sales to assets, (d) rate earned on total assets, (e) rate earned on stockholders' equity, (f) rate earned on common stockholders' equity.

28–27. The net income reported on the income statement of A. B. Virgil Inc. was $2,200,000. There were 200,000 shares of $50 par common stock and 40,000 shares of $50 par 10% preferred stock outstanding throughout the current year. The income statement included two extraordinary items: a $900,000 gain from condemnation of property and a $700,000 loss arising from tornado damage, both after applicable income tax. Determine the per share figures for common stock for (a) income before extraordinary items and (b) net income.

28–28. The balance sheet for Henderson Corporation at the end of the current fiscal year indicated the following:

Bonds payable, 11% (issued in 1980, due in 2000)...........	$2,000,000
Preferred 9% stock, $100 par.............................	500,000
Common stock, $20 par	1,500,000

Income before income tax was $660,000 and income taxes were $300,000 for the current year. Cash dividends paid on common stock during the current year totaled $300,000. The common stock was selling for $42 per share at the end of the year.

Determine each of the following: (a) number of times bond interest charges were earned, (b) number of times preferred dividends were earned, (c) earnings per share on common stock, (d) price-earnings ratio, and (e) dividend yield.

28-29. Data pertaining to the current position of R. Staub Inc. are as follows: **Problems**

Cash.....................................	$125,000
Marketable securities........................	60,000
Accounts and notes receivable (net)	295,000
Inventory	487,000
Prepaid expenses	33,000
Accounts payable..........................	270,000
Notes payable (short-term)..................	110,000
Accrued liabilities..........................	20,000

Instructions:

(1) Compute (a) working capital (b) current ratio, and (c) acid-test ratio.

(2) List the following captions on a sheet of paper:

Transaction	Working Capital	Current Ratio	Acid-Test Ratio

Compute the working capital, current ratio, and acid-test ratio after each of the following transactions, and record the results in the appropriate columns. Consider each transaction separately and assume that only that transaction affects the data given above.

(a) Paid accounts payable, $150,000.

(b) Received cash on account, $100,000.

(c) Purchased goods on account, $70,000.

(d) Paid notes payable, $100,000.

(e) Declared a cash dividend, $50,000.

(f) Declared a common stock dividend on common stock, $100,000.

(g) Borrowed cash from bank on a long-term note, $200,000.

(h) Sold marketable securities, $60,000.

(i) Issued additional shares of stock for cash, $150,000.

(j) Paid cash for store supplies, $40,000.

28-30. Revenue and expense data for the current calendar year for Lopez Paper Company and for the paper industry are as follows. The Lopez Paper Company data are expressed in dollars; the paper industry averages are expressed in percentages.

	Lopez Paper Company	Paper Industry Average
Sales.................................	$7,070,000	100.5%
Sales returns and allowances	70,000	.5%
Cost of goods sold..........................	5,040,000	70.0%
Selling expenses............................	574,000	9.2%
General expenses	434,000	8.0%
Other income..............................	35,000	.6%
Other expense.............................	84,000	1.4%
Income tax................................	406,000	5.5%

Instructions:

(1) Prepare a common-size income statement comparing the results of operations for Lopez Paper Company with the industry average.

(2) As far as the data permit, comment on significant relationships revealed by the comparisons.

28–31. For 1987, Rose Company initiated an extensive sales promotion campaign that included the expenditure of an additional $40,000 for advertising. At the end of the year, Frank Rose, the president, is presented with the following condensed comparative income statement:

Rose Company
Comparative Income Statement
For Years Ended December 31, 1987 and 1986

	1987	1986
Sales..	$510,000	$303,000
Sales returns and allowances	10,000	3,000
Net sales	$500,000	$300,000
Cost of goods sold	310,000	180,000
Gross profit	$190,000	$120,000
Selling expenses................................	$ 90,000	$ 48,000
General expenses	20,000	13,500
Total operating expenses	$110,000	$ 61,500
Operating income...............................	$ 80,000	$ 58,500
Other income..................................	2,000	900
Income before income tax	$ 82,000	$ 59,400
Income tax....................................	20,000	15,000
Net income....................................	$ 62,000	$ 44,400

Instructions:

(1) Prepare a comparative income statement for the two-year period, presenting an analysis of each item in relationship to net sales for each of the years.

(2) To the extent the data permit, comment on the significant relationships revealed by the vertical analysis prepared in (1).

28–32. Prior to approving an application for a short-term loan, American National Bank required that Trillo Company provide evidence of working capital of at least $400,000, a current ratio of at least 1.5 : 1, and an acid-test ratio of at least 1.0 : 1. The chief accountant compiled the following data pertaining to the current position:

Financial Statement Analysis and Price-Level Changes

Trillo Company
Schedule of Current Assets and Current Liabilities
December 31, 1986

Current assets:
Cash...	$ 52,750
Accounts receivable......................................	262,250
Notes receivable...	200,000
Interest receivable	10,000
Marketable securities....................................	150,000
Inventory	205,000
Supplies...	20,000
Total	$900,000

Current liabilities:
Accounts payable..	$250,000
Notes payable...	200,000
Total	$450,000

Instructions:

(1) Compute (a) working capital, (b) current ratio, and (c) acid-test ratio.

(2) At the request of the bank, a firm of independent auditors was retained to examine data submitted with the loan application. This examination disclosed several errors. Prepare correcting entries for each of the following errors:

  (a) Accounts receivable of $42,250 are uncollectible and should be immediately written off. In addition, it was estimated that of the remaining receivables, 5% would eventually become uncollectible and an allowance should be made for these future uncollectible accounts.

  (b) Six months' interest had been accrued on the $200,000, 10%, six-month note receivable dated October 1, 1986.

  (c) The notes payable is a 12%, 90-day note dated October 17, 1986. No interest had been accrued on the note.

  (d) The marketable securities portfolio includes $100,000 of Porter Company stock that is held as a long-term investment.

  (e) A canceled check indicates that a bill for $25,000 for repairs on factory equipment had not been recorded in the accounts.

  (f) Accrued wages as of December 31, 1986, totaled $30,000.

  (g) Received a year's rent of $72,000 for warehouse space leased to Reese Inc., effective October 1, 1986. Upon receipt, rental income was credited for the full amount.

  (h) Supplies on hand at December 31, 1986, total $8,000.

(3) Consider each of the preceding errors separately and assume that only that error affects the current position of Trillo Company. Compute (a) working capital, (b) current ratio, and (c) acid-test ratio, giving effect to each of the preceding errors. Use the following column headings for recording your answers.

Error	Working Capital	Current Ratio	Acid-Test Ratio

(*continued*)

(4) Prepare a revised schedule of working capital as of December 31, 1986, and recompute the current ratio and acid-test ratio, giving effect to the corrections of all of the preceding errors.

(5) Discuss the action you would recommend the bank take regarding the pending loan application.

28–33. The comparative financial statements of T. Rice Inc. are as follows. On December 31, 1987 and 1986, the market price of T. Rice Inc. common stock was $107.50 and $154 respectively.

T. Rice Inc.
Comparative Income Statement
For Years Ended December 31, 1987 and 1986

	1987	1986
Sales	$8,585,000	$8,056,000
Sales returns and allowances	85,000	56,000
Net sales	$8,500,000	$8,000,000
Cost of goods sold	5,440,000	4,800,000
Gross profit	$3,060,000	$3,200,000
Selling expenses	$1,380,000	$1,250,000
General expenses	595,000	640,000
Total operating expenses	$1,975,000	$1,890,000
Operating income	$1,085,000	$1,310,000
Other income	119,500	120,000
	$1,204,500	$1,430,000
Other expense (interest)	204,500	180,000
Income before income tax	$1,000,000	$1,250,000
Income tax	490,000	610,000
Net income	$ 510,000	$ 640,000

T. Rice Inc.
Comparative Retained Earnings Statement
For Years Ended December 31, 1987 and 1986

	1987	1986
Retained earnings, January 1	$2,200,000	$1,800,000
Add net income for year	510,000	640,000
Total	$2,710,000	$2,440,000
Deduct dividends:		
On preferred stock	$ 80,000	$ 80,000
On common stock	175,000	160,000
Total	$ 255,000	$ 240,000
Retained earnings, December 31	$2,455,000	$2,200,000

Financial Statement Analysis and Price-Level Changes

T. Rice Inc.
Comparative Balance Sheet
December 31, 1987 and 1986

Assets	1987	1986
Current assets:		
Cash	$ 375,000	$ 330,000
Marketable securities	125,000	120,000
Accounts receivable (net)	500,000	450,000
Inventory	720,000	660,000
Prepaid expenses	80,000	40,000
Total current assets	$1,800,000	$1,600,000
Long-term investments	250,000	200,000
Plant assets	5,150,000	4,800,000
Total assets	$7,200,000	$6,600,000
Liabilities		
Current liabilities	$1,000,000	$ 900,000
Long-term liabilities:		
Mortgage note payable, 10%, due 1990	$ 245,000	——
Bonds payable, 12%, due 1999	1,500,000	$1,500,000
Total long-term liabilities	$1,745,000	$1,500,000
Total liabilities	$2,745,000	$2,400,000
Stockholders' Equity		
Preferred 8% stock, $100 par	$1,000,000	$1,000,000
Common stock, $25 par	1,000,000	1,000,000
Retained earnings	2,455,000	2,200,000
Total stockholders' equity	$4,455,000	$4,200,000
Total liabilities and stockholders' equity	$7,200,000	$6,600,000

Instructions:

Determine for 1987 the following ratios, turnovers, and other measures, presenting the figures used in your computations:
   (1) Working capital.
   (2) Current ratio.
   (3) Acid-test ratio.
   (4) Accounts receivable turnover.
   (5) Number of days' sales in receivables.
   (6) Inventory turnover.
   (7) Number of days' sales in inventory.
   (8) Ratio of plant assets to long-term liabilities.
   (9) Ratio of stockholders' equity to liabilities.
   (10) Ratio of net sales to assets.
   (11) Rate earned on total assets.
   (12) Rate earned on stockholders' equity.
   (13) Rate earned on common stockholders' equity.
   (14) Earnings per share on common stock.

(continued)

(15) Price-earnings ratio.
(16) Dividend yield.
(17) Number of times interest charges earned.
(18) Number of times preferred dividends earned.

28-34. The controller of T. Rice Inc. is evaluating the operating results for 1987 for presentation at the next meeting of the Board of Directors. The company's comparative financial statements for 1987 and 1986 were given in 28-33. To assist in the evaluation of the company, the controller secured the following additional data taken from the balance sheet at December 31, 1985.

Accounts receivable (net)	$ 400,000
Inventory	600,000
Long-term investments	50,000
Total assets	6,500,000
Total stockholders' equity (preferred and common stock outstanding same as in 1986)	4,000,000

Instructions:

Prepare a report for the controller, based on an analysis of the financial data presented. In preparing your report, include all ratios and other data that will be useful to the controller in preparing for the presentation at the Board meeting.

Alternate Problems

28-29A. Data pertaining to the current position of Carol Cavitt and Company are as follows:

Cash	$120,000
Marketable securities	50,000
Accounts and notes receivable (net)	130,000
Inventory	275,000
Prepaid expenses	25,000
Accounts payable	165,000
Notes payable (short-term)	100,000
Accrued liabilities	35,000

Instructions:

(1) Compute (a) working capital, (b) current ratio, and (c) acid-test ratio.
(2) List the following captions on a sheet of paper:

Transaction	Working Capital	Current Ratio	Acid-Test Ratio

Compute the working capital, current ratio, and acid-test ratio after each of the following transactions, and record the results in the appropriate columns. Consider each transaction separately and assume that only that transaction affects the data given above.

(a) Declared a cash dividend, $50,000.
(b) Issued additional shares of stock for cash, $100,000.
(c) Purchased goods on account, $40,000.
(d) Paid accounts payable, $60,000.
(e) Borrowed cash from bank on a long-term note, $50,000.
(f) Paid cash for office supplies, $25,000.
(g) Received cash on account, $75,000.
(h) Paid notes payable, $100,000.
(i) Declared a common stock dividend on common stock, $150,000.
(j) Sold marketable securities, $50,000.

28–31A. For 1987, Chapman Company initiated an extensive sales promotion campaign that included the expenditure of an additional $75,000 for advertising. At the end of the year, Susan Chapman, the president, is presented with the following condensed comparative income statement:

Chapman Company
Comparative Income Statement
For Years Ended December 31, 1987 and 1986

	1987	1986
Sales	$845,625	$689,520
Sales returns and allowances	20,625	9,520
Net sales	$825,000	$680,000
Cost of goods sold	528,000	442,000
Gross profit	$297,000	$238,000
Selling expenses	$198,000	$102,000
General expenses	36,300	40,800
Total operating expenses	$234,300	$142,800
Operating income	$ 62,700	$ 95,200
Other expense	3,300	3,400
Income before income tax	$ 59,400	$ 91,800
Income tax	14,025	23,800
Net income	$ 45,375	$ 68,000

Instructions:
(1) Prepare a comparative income statement for the two-year period, presenting an analysis of each item in relationship to net sales for each of the years.
(2) To the extent the data permit, comment on the significant relationships revealed by the vertical analysis prepared in (1).

28–33A. The comparative financial statements of R. C. Jain Company are as follows. On December 31, 1987 and 1986, the market price of R. C. Jain Company common stock was $60 and $47 respectively.

R. C. Jain Company
Comparative Income Statement
For Years Ended December 31, 1987 and 1986

	1987	1986
Sales	$4,590,000	$3,272,500
Sales returns and allowances	90,000	72,500
Net sales	$4,500,000	$3,200,000
Cost of goods sold	3,060,000	2,080,000
Gross profit	$1,440,000	$1,120,000
Selling expenses	$ 585,000	$ 464,000
General expenses	292,500	224,000
Total operating expenses	$ 877,500	$ 688,000
Operating income	$ 562,500	$ 432,000
Other income	22,500	19,200
	$ 585,000	$ 451,200
Other expense (interest)	129,200	110,000
Income before income tax	$ 455,800	$ 341,200
Income tax	210,800	150,200
Net income	$ 245,000	$ 191,000

R. C. Jain Company
Comparative Retained Earnings Statement
For Years Ended December 31, 1987 and 1986

	1987	1986
Retained earnings, January 1	$723,000	$602,000
Add net income for year	245,000	191,000
Total	$968,000	$793,000
Deduct dividends:		
On preferred stock	$ 40,000	$ 40,000
On common stock	45,000	30,000
Total	$ 85,000	$ 70,000
Retained earnings, December 31	$883,000	$723,000

Financial Statement Analysis and Price-Level Changes

R. C. Jain Company
Comparative Balance Sheet
December 31, 1987 and 1986

Assets	1987	1986
Current assets:		
Cash	$ 225,000	$ 175,000
Marketable securities............................	100,000	—
Accounts receivable (net)	425,000	325,000
Inventory	720,000	480,000
Prepaid expenses..............................	30,000	20,000
Total current assets	$1,500,000	$1,000,000
Long-term investments	250,000	225,000
Plant assets...................................	2,093,000	1,948,000
Total assets	$3,843,000	$3,173,000

Liabilities		
Current liabilities	$ 750,000	$ 650,000
Long-term liabilities:		
Mortgage note payable, 12%, due 1989...........	$ 410,000	—
Bonds payable, 10%, due 1995..................	800,000	$ 800,000
Total long-term liabilities	$1,210,000	$ 800,000
Total liabilities	$1,960,000	$1,450,000

Stockholders' Equity		
Preferred $4 stock, $50 par	$ 500,000	$ 500,000
Common stock, $20 par	500,000	500,000
Retained earnings..............................	883,000	723,000
Total stockholders' equity	$1,883,000	$1,723,000
Total liabilities and stockholders' equity	$3,843,000	$3,173,000

Instructions:

Determine for 1987 the following ratios, turnovers, and other measures, presenting the figures used in your computations:
(1) Working capital.
(2) Current ratio.
(3) Acid-test ratio.
(4) Accounts receivable turnover.
(5) Number of days' sales in receivables.
(6) Inventory turnover.
(7) Number of days' sales in inventory.
(8) Ratio of plant assets to long-term liabilities.
(9) Ratio of stockholders' equity to liabilities.
(10) Ratio of net sales to assets.
(11) Rate earned on total assets.
(12) Rate earned on stockholders' equity.

(continued)

(13) Rate earned on common stockholders' equity.
(14) Earnings per share on common stock.
(15) Price-earnings ratio.
(16) Dividend yield.
(17) Number of times interest charges earned.
(18) Number of times preferred dividends earned.

Mini-Case

28–35. You and your brother are both presidents of companies in the same industry, CMR Inc. and IMR Inc., respectively. Both companies were originally operated as a single-family business; but shortly after your father's death in 1965, the business was divided into two companies. Your brother took over IMR Inc., located in Indianapolis, while you took over CMR Inc., located in Cincinnati.

During a recent family reunion, your brother referred to the much larger rate of return to his stockholders than was the case in your company and suggested that you consider rearranging the method of financing your corporation. Since 1965, the growth in your brother's company has been financed largely through borrowing and yours largely through the issuance of additional common stock. Both companies have about the same volume of sales, gross profit, operating income, and total assets.

The income statements for both companies for the year ended December 31, 1987, and the balance sheets at December 31, 1987, are as follows:

	IMR Inc.	CMR Inc.
Sales	$2,066,800	$1,972,500
Sales returns and allowances	20,800	19,500
Net sales	$2,046,000	$1,953,000
Cost of goods sold	1,227,600	1,171,800
Gross profit	$ 818,400	$ 781,200
Selling expenses	$ 375,800	$ 340,400
General expenses	202,400	183,300
Total operating expenses	$ 578,200	$ 523,700
Operating income	$ 240,200	$ 257,500
Interest expense	35,200	7,500
Income before income tax	$ 205,000	$ 250,000
Income tax	82,000	100,400
Net income	$ 123,000	$ 149,600

Assets	IMR Inc.	CMR Inc.
Current assets	$ 42,000	$ 39,000
Plant assets (net)	880,000	906,000
Intangible assets	18,000	5,000
Total assets	$940,000	$950,000

Liabilities		
Current liabilities	$ 18,000	$ 18,500
Long-term liabilities	352,000	75,500
Total liabilities	$370,000	$ 94,000

Stockholders' Equity		
Common stock ($10 par)	$100,000	$500,000
Retained earnings	470,000	356,000
Total stockholders' equity	$570,000	$856,000
Total liabilities and stockholders' equity	$940,000	$950,000

In addition to the 1987 financial statements, the following data were taken from the balance sheets at December 31, 1986:

	IMR Inc.	CMR Inc.
Total assets	$920,000	$910,000
Total stockholders' equity	530,000	834,000

Instructions:
(1) Determine for 1987 the following ratios and other measures for both companies:
    (a) ratio of plant assets to long-term liabilities,
    (b) ratio of stockholders' equity to liabilities,
    (c) ratio of net sales to assets,
    (d) rate earned on total assets, and
    (e) rate earned on stockholders' equity.
(2) For both IMR Inc. and CMR Inc., the rate earned on stockholders' equity is greater than the rate earned on total assets. Explain why.
(3) Why is the rate of return on stockholders' equity for IMR Inc. more than 25% greater than for CMR Inc.?
(4) Comment on your brother's suggestion for rearranging the financing of CMR Inc.

Answers to Self-Examination Questions

1. A Percentage analysis indicating the relationship of the component parts to the total in a financial statement, such as the relationship of current assets to total assets (20% to 100%) in the question, is called vertical analysis (answer A). Percentage analysis of increases and decreases in corresponding items in comparative financial statements is called horizontal analysis (answer B). An example of horizontal analysis would be the presentation of the amount of current assets in the preceding balance sheet along with the amount of current assets for the current year, with the increase or decrease in current assets between the periods expressed as a percentage. Differential analysis (answer C), as discussed in Chapter 21, is the area of accounting concerned with the effect of alternative courses of action on revenue and expenses.

2. D Various solvency measures, categorized as current position analysis, indicate a firm's ability to meet currently maturing obligations. Each measure contributes in the analysis of a firm's current position and is most useful when viewed with other measures and when compared with similar measures for other periods and for other firms. Working capital (answer A) is the excess of current assets over current liabilities; the current ratio (answer B) is the ratio of current assets to current liabilities; and the acid-test ratio (answer C) is the ratio of the sum of cash, receivables, and marketable securities to current liabilities.

3. D The ratio of current assets to current liabilities is usually referred to as the current ratio (answer A) and is sometimes referred to as the working capital ratio (answer B) or bankers' ratio (answer C).

4. C The ratio of the sum of cash, receivables, and marketable securities (sometimes called "quick assets") to current liabilities is called the acid-test ratio (answer C) or quick ratio. The current ratio (answer A) and working capital ratio (answer B) are two terms that describe the ratio of current assets to current liabilities.

5. C As with many attempts at analyzing financial data, it is possible to determine more than one measure that is useful for evaluating the efficiency in the management of inventory. Both the inventory turnover (answer A), which is determined by dividing the cost of goods sold by the average inventory, and the number of days' sales in inventory (answer B), which is determined by dividing the inventory at the end of the year by the average daily cost of goods sold, express the relationship between the cost of goods sold and inventory.

PART 11

APPENDIXES

APPENDIX A

GLOSSARY

A

Absorption costing. The concept that considers the cost of manufactured products to be composed of direct materials, direct labor, and factory overhead.

Accelerated Cost Recovery System (ACRS). The system described in the Internal Revenue Code for determining depreciation (cost recovery) of plant asset acquisitions.

Accelerated depreciation method. A depreciation method that provides for a high depreciation charge in the first year of use of an asset and gradually declining periodic charges thereafter.

Account. The form used to record additions and deductions for each individual asset, liability, owner's equity, revenue, and expense.

Account form of balance sheet. A balance sheet with assets on the left-hand side and liabilities and owner's equity on the right-hand side.

Accounting. The process of identifying, measuring, and communicating economic information to permit informed judgments and decisions by users of the information.

Accounting cycle. The principal accounting procedures followed during a fiscal period.

Accounting equation. The expression of the relationship between assets, liabilities, and owner's equity; most commonly stated as Assets = Liabilities + Owner's Equity.

Accounting Principles Board. The AICPA board that provided most of the leadership in the development of accounting principles from 1959 to 1973.

Account payable. A liability created by a purchase made on credit.

Account receivable. A claim against a customer for sales made on credit.

Accounts payable ledger. The subsidiary ledger containing the individual accounts with suppliers (creditors).

Accounts receivable ledger. The subsidiary ledger containing the individual accounts with customers (debtors).

Accounts receivable turnover. The relationship between credit sales and accounts receivable, computed by dividing net sales on account by the average net accounts receivable.

Accrual. An expense or a revenue that gradually increases with the passage of time.

Accrual basis. Revenues are recognized in the period earned and expenses are recognized in the period incurred in the process of generating revenues.

Accrued expenses. Expenses accrued but unrecorded at the end of a fiscal period.

Accrued revenues. Revenues accrued but unrecorded at the end of a fiscal period.

Accumulated depreciation account. The contra asset account used to accumulate the depreciation recognized to date on plant assets.

Acid-test ratio. The ratio of the sum of cash, receivables, and marketable securities to current liabilities.

Adjusting entry. An entry required at the end of an accounting period to record an internal transaction and to bring the ledger up to date.

Affiliated companies. Two or more corporations closely related through stock ownership.

Aging the receivables. The process of analyzing the accounts receivable and classifying them according to various age groupings, with the due date being the base point for determining age.

Algorithm. Generalized arithmetic formula.

Allowance method. The method of accounting for uncollectible receivables, by which advance provision for the uncollectibles is made.

American Institute of CPAs (AICPA). The national professional organization of CPAs.

Amortization. The periodic expense attributed to the decline in usefulness of an intangible asset or the allocation of bond premium or discount over the life of a bond issue.

Annuity. A series of equal cash flows at fixed intervals.

Appropriation of retained earnings. The amount of a corporation's retained earnings that has been restricted and therefore is not available for distribution to shareholders as dividends.

Articles of partnership. The formal written contract creating a partnership.

Asset. Property owned by a business enterprise.

Average cost method. The method of inventory costing that is based on the assumption that costs should be charged against revenue in accordance with the weighted average unit costs of the commodities sold.

Average rate of return. A method of analysis of proposed capital expenditures that focuses on the anticipated profitability of the investment.

Bank reconciliation. The method of analysis that details the items that are responsible for the difference between the cash balance reported in the bank statement and the balance of the cash account in the ledger.

Bond. A form of interest-bearing note employed by corporations to borrow on a long-term basis.

Bond indenture. The contract between a corporation issuing bonds and the bondholders.

Book value of an asset. The cost of an asset less the balance of any related contra asset account.

Boot. The balance owed the supplier when old equipment is traded for new equipment.

Break-even point. The point in the operations of an enterprise at which revenues and expired costs are equal.

Budget. A formal written statement of management's plans for the future, expressed in financial terms.

Budget performance report. A report comparing actual results with budget figures.

Business entity concept. The concept that assumes that accounting applies to individual economic units and that each unit is separate and distinct from the persons who supply its assets.

Business transaction. The occurrence of an event or of a condition that must be recorded in the accounting records.

By-product. A product resulting from a manufacturing process and having little value in relation to the principal product or joint products.

B

Balance of an account. The amount of difference between the debits and the credits that have been entered into an account.

Balance sheet. A financial statement listing the assets, liabilities, and owner's equity of a business entity as of a specific date.

C

Capital. The rights (equity) of the owners in a business enterprise.

Capital account. The account used to record investments in a sole proprietorship.

Capital expenditure. A cost that adds to the utility of an asset for more than one accounting period.

Capital expenditures budget. The budget summarizing future plans for acquisition of plant facilities and equipment.

Capital gain or loss. A gain or loss resulting from the sale or exchange of a capital asset, as defined by the Internal Revenue Code and given special treatment for federal income tax purposes.

Capital investment analysis. The process by which management plans, evaluates, and controls long-term capital investments involving property, plant, and equipment.

Capital lease. A lease which includes one or more of four provisions that result in treating the leased asset as a purchased asset in the accounts.

Capital rationing. The process by which management allocates available investment funds among competing capital investment proposals.

Capital stock. Shares of ownership of a corporation.

Cash. Any medium of exchange that a bank will accept at face value.

Cash basis. Revenue is recognized in the period cash is received, and expenses are recognized in period cash is paid.

Cash discount. The deduction allowable if an invoice is paid by a specified date.

Cash dividend. A distribution of cash by a corporation to its shareholders.

Cash payback period. The expected period of time that will elapse between the date of a capital expenditure and the complete recovery in cash (or equivalent) of the amount invested.

Cash payments journal. The journal in which all cash payments are recorded.

Cash receipts journal. The journal in which all cash receipts are recorded.

Certified Management Accountant (CMA). An accountant who meets the requirements of the ICMA for professional status recognition.

Certified Public Accountant (CPA). An accountant who meets state licensing requirements for engaging in the practice of public accounting as a CPA.

Chart of accounts. A listing of all the accounts used by a business enterprise.

Check register. A modified form of the cash payments journal used to record all transactions paid by check.

Clock cards. The form on which the amount of time spent by an employee in the factory is recorded.

Closing entry. An entry necessary to eliminate the balance of the revenue, expense, and dividend accounts in preparation for the following accounting period.

Common-size statement. A financial statement in which all items are expressed only in relative terms.

Common stock. The basic ownership class of corporate capital stock.

Composite-rate depreciation method. A method of depreciation based on the use of a single rate that applies to entire groups of assets.

Compound journal entry. A journal entry composed of two or more debits or two or more credits.

Consistency. The concept that assumes that the same generally accepted accounting principles have been applied in the preparation of successive financial statements.

Consolidated statement. A financial statement resulting from combining parent and subsidiary company statements.

Consolidation. The creation of a new corporation by the transfer of assets and liabilities from two or more existing corporations.

Contingent liability. A potential obligation that will materialize only if certain events occur in the future.

Continuous budgeting. A method of budgeting that provides for maintenance of a twelve-month projection into the future.

Contra asset account. An account that is offset against an asset account.

Contract rate of interest. The interest rate specified on a bond.

Contribution margin. Sales less variable cost of goods sold and variable selling and general expenses.

Contribution margin ratio. The percentage of each sales dollar that is available to cover the fixed expenses and provide an operating income.

Control. The process of directing operations to achieve the organization's goals and plans.

Controller. The chief managerial accountant of an organization.

Controlling account. The account in the general ledger that summarizes the balance of a subsidiary ledger.

Corporation. A separate legal entity that is organized in accordance with state or federal statutes and in which ownership is divided into shares of stock.

Cost center. A decentralized unit in which the responsibility for control of costs incurred and the authority to make decisions that affect these costs is the responsibility of the unit's manager.

Cost ledger. A subsidiary ledger employed in a job order cost system and which contains an account for each job order.

Cost method. A method of accounting for an investment in stock, by which the investor recognizes as income the share of property dividends of the investee.

Cost of goods sold. The cost of the manufactured product sold.

Cost of merchandise sold. The cost of the merchandise purchased by a merchandise enterprise and sold.

Cost of production report. A report prepared periodically by a processing department, summarizing (1) the costs for which the department is accountable and the disposition of its units and (2) the costs charged to the department and the allocations of these costs.

Cost price approach. An approach to transfer pricing that uses cost as the basis for setting the transfer price.

Cost principle. The principle that assumes that the monetary record for properties and services purchased by a business should be maintained in terms of cost.

Cost-volume-profit analysis. The systematic examination of the interrelationships between selling prices, volume of sales and production, costs, expenses, and profits.

Cost-volume-profit chart. A chart used to assist management in understanding the relationships between costs, expenses, sales, and operating profit or loss.

Credit. (1) The right side of an account; (2) the amount entered on the right side of an account; (3) to enter an amount on the right side of an account.

Credit memorandum. The form issued by a seller to inform a debtor that a credit has been posted to the debtor's account receivable.

Cumulative preferred stock. Preferred stock that is entitled to current and past dividends before dividends may be paid on common stock.

Current asset. Cash or another asset that may reasonably be expected to be realized in cash or sold or consumed, usually within a year or less, through the normal operations of a business.

Current liability. A liability that will be due within a short time (usually one year or less) and that is to be paid out of current assets.

Currently attainable standards. Standards which represent levels of operation that can be attained with reasonable effort.

Current ratio. The ratio of current assets to current liabilities.

D

Data base. The entire amount of data needed by an enterprise.

Debit. (1) The left side of an account; (2) the amount entered on the left side of an account; (3) to enter an amount on the left side of an account.

Debit memorandum. The form issued by a purchaser to inform a creditor that a debit has been posted to the creditor's account payable.

Debt security. A bond or a note payable.

Decentralization. The separation of a business into more manageable units.

Decision tree. A graphical representation of decisions, possible outcomes, and chances that outcomes will occur.

Declining-balance depreciation method. A method of depreciation that provides declining periodic depreciation charges to expense over the estimated life of an asset.

Deferral. A postponement of the recognition of an expense already paid or a revenue already received.

Deficit. A debit balance in the retained earnings account.

Departmental margin. Departmental gross profit less direct departmental expenses.

Depletion. The cost of metal ores and other minerals removed from the earth.

Depreciation. The decrease in usefulness of all plant assets except land.

Differential analysis. The area of accounting concerned with the effect of alternative courses of action on revenues and costs.

Differential cost. The amount of increase or decrease in cost that is expected from a particular course of action compared with an alternative.

Differential revenue. The amount of increase or decrease in revenue expected from a particular course of action as compared with an alternative.

Direct expense. An expense directly traceable to or incurred for the sole benefit of a specific department and ordinarily subject to the control of the department manager.

Direct labor. Wages of factory workers who convert materials into a finished product.

Direct labor rate variance. The cost associated with the difference between the actual rate paid for direct labor used in producing a commodity and the standard rate for the commodity.

Direct labor time variance. The cost associated with the difference between the actual direct labor hours spent producing a commodity and the standard hours for the commodity.

Direct materials. The cost of materials that enter directly into the finished product.

Direct materials price variance. The cost associated with the difference between the actual price of direct materials used in producing a commodity and the standard price for the commodity.

Direct materials quantity variance. The cost associated with the difference between the actual quantity of direct materials used in producing a commodity and the standard quantity for the commodity.

Direct write-off method. A method of accounting for uncollectible receivables, whereby an expense is recognized only when specific accounts are judged to be uncollectible.

Discount. (a) The interest deducted from the maturity value of a non-interest-bearing note; (b) excess of par value of stock over its sales price; (c) excess of the face amount of bonds over their issue price.

Discounted cash flow method. A method of analysis of proposed capital investments that focuses on the present value of the cash flows expected from the investment.

Discounted internal rate of return method. A method of analysis of proposed capital investments that focuses on using present value concepts to compute the rate of return from the net cash flows expected from the investment.

Discount rate. The rate used in computing the interest to be deducted from the maturity value of a note.

Dishonored note receivable. A note which the maker fails to pay on the due date.

Dividends. The distribution of earnings of a corporation to its owners (stockholders).

Double-entry accounting. A system for recording transactions based on recording increases and decreases in accounts so that debits always equal credits.

Drawing account. The account used to record distributions to a sole proprietor.

E

Earnings per share (EPS) on common stock. The profitability ratio of net income available to common shareholders to the number of common shares outstanding.

Economic order quantity (EOQ). The optimum quantity of specified inventoriable materials to be ordered at one time.

Economies of scale. An economic concept that implies that, for a given amount of facilities, it is more efficient to produce and sell large quantities than small quantities.

Effective rate of interest. The market rate of interest at the time bonds are issued.

Employee's earnings record. A detailed record of each employee's earnings.

Equity. The right or claim to the properties of a business enterprise.

Equity method. A method of accounting for investments in common stock, by which the investment account is adjusted for the investor's share of periodic net income and property dividends of the investee.

Equity per share. The ratio of stockholders' equity to the related number of shares of stock outstanding.

Equity security. Preferred or common stock.

Equivalent units of production. The number of units that could have been manufactured from start to finish during a period.

Exchange rate. The rate at which one unit of a currency can be converted into another currency.

Expected value. A concept useful for managers in decision making which involves identifying the possible outcomes from a decision and estimating the likelihood that each outcome will occur.

Expense. The amount of assets consumed or services used in the process of earning revenue.

Extraordinary item. An event or transaction that is unusual and infrequent.

F

Factory overhead. All of the costs of operating the factory except for direct materials and direct labor.

Factory overhead controllable variance. The difference between the actual amount of factory overhead cost incurred and the amount of factory overhead budgeted for the level of operations achieved.

Factory overhead volume variance. The cost or benefit associated with operating at a level above or below 100% of normal productive capacity.

Federal unemployment compensation tax. A federal tax paid by employers and used to provide temporary relief to those who become unemployed.

FICA tax. Federal Insurance Contributions Act tax used to finance federal programs for old-age and disability benefits and health insurance for the aged.

Fifo (first-in, first-out). A method of inventory costing based on the assumption that the costs of merchandise sold should be charged against revenue in the order in which the costs were incurred.

Financial accounting. The branch of accounting that is concerned with the recording of transactions using generally accepted accounting principles (GAAP) for a business enterprise or other economic unit and with a periodic preparation of various statements from such records.

Financial Accounting Standards Board (FASB). The current authoritative body for the development of accounting principles.

Finished goods. Goods in the state in which they are to be sold.

Finished goods ledger. The subsidiary ledger that contains the individual accounts for each kind of commodity produced.

Fiscal year. The annual accounting period adopted by an enterprise.

Fixed expense (cost). An expense (cost) that tends to remain constant in amount regardless of variations in volume of activity.

Flexible budget. A series of budgets for varying rates of activity.

FOB destination. Terms of agreement between buyer and seller, requiring the seller to absorb the transportation costs.

FOB shipping point. Terms of agreement between buyer and seller, requiring the buyer to absorb the transportation costs.

Fund. A term with multiple meanings, including (1) segregations of cash for a special purpose, (2) working capital or cash as reported in the funds statement.

Funded. An appropriation of retained earnings accompanied by a segregation of cash or marketable securities.

Funds statement. The statement of changes in financial position.

G

General expense. Expense incurred in the general operation of a business.

General ledger. The principal ledger, when used in conjunction with subsidiary ledgers, that contains all of the balance sheet and income statement accounts.

Generally accepted accounting principles. Generally accepted guidelines for the preparation of financial statements.

Going concern concept. The concept that assumes that a business entity has a reasonable expectation of continuing in business at a profit for an indefinite period of time.

Goodwill. An intangible asset that attaches to a business as a result of such favorable factors as location, product superiority, reputation, and managerial skill.

Gross pay. The total earnings of an employee for a payroll period.

Gross profit. The excess of net revenue from sales over the cost of merchandise sold.

Gross profit analysis. The procedure used to develop information concerning the effect of changes in quantities and unit prices on sales and cost of goods sold.

Gross profit method. A means of estimating inventory on hand without the need for a physical count.

H

High-low method. A method used to estimate total cost as well as variable and fixed components by using the highest and lowest total costs revealed by past cost patterns.

Horizontal analysis. The percentage analysis of increases and decreases in corresponding items in comparative financial statements.

I

Income from operations. The excess of gross profit over total operating expenses.

Income statement. A summary of the revenues and expenses of a business entity for a specific period of time.

Income summary account. The account used in the closing process for summarizing the revenue and expense accounts.

Indirect expense. An expense that is incurred for an entire business enterprise as a unit and that is not subject to the control of individual department managers.

Installment method. The method of recognizing revenue, whereby each receipt of cash from installment sales is considered to be composed of partial payment of cost of merchandise sold and gross profit.

Intangible asset. A long-lived asset that is useful in the operations of an enterprise, is not held for sale, and is without physical qualities.

Interim statement. A financial statement issued for a period covering less than a fiscal year.

Internal accounting controls. Procedures and records that are mainly concerned with the reliability of financial records and reports and with the safeguarding of assets.

Internal administrative controls. Procedures and records that aid management in achieving business goals.

Internal controls. The detailed procedures adopted by an enterprise to control its operations.

Internal Revenue Code (IRC). The codification of current federal tax statutes.

Internal Revenue Service (IRS). The branch of the U.S. Treasury Department concerned with enforcement and collection of the income tax.

Inventory order point. The level to which inventory is allowed to fall before an order for additional inventory is placed.

Inventory turnover. The relationship between the volume of goods sold and inventory, computed by dividing the cost of goods sold by the average inventory.

Investment center. A decentralized unit in which the manager has the responsibility and authority to make decisions that affect not only cost and revenues, but also the plant assets available to the center.

Investment tax credit. An income tax credit allowed for the purchase of capital assets which reduces the amount of federal income tax payable.

Investment turnover. A component of the rate of return on investment, computed as the ratio of sales to invested assets.

Invoice. The bill provided by the seller (referred to as a sales invoice) to a purchaser (referred to as a purchase invoice) for items purchased.

J

Job cost sheet. An account in the cost ledger in which the costs charged to a particular job order are recorded.

Job order cost system. A type of cost system that provides for a separate record of the cost of each particular quantity of product that passes through the factory.

Joint cost. The cost common to the manufacture of two or more products (joint products).

Joint products. Two or more commodities of significant value produced from a single principal direct material.

Journal. The two-column form used to record journal entries.

Journal entry. The form of presentation of a transaction recorded in a journal.

Journalizing. The process of recording a transaction in the journal.

L

Lead time. The time, usually expressed in days, that it takes to receive an order for inventory.

Learning effect (learning curve). The effect on costs determined by how rapidly new employees learn their jobs or by how rapidly experienced employees learn new job assignments.

Least squares method. A method that uses statistics to estimate total cost and the fixed and variable cost components.

Lease. A contractual agreement conveying the right to use an asset for a stated period of time.

Ledger. The group of accounts used by an enterprise.

Leverage. The tendency of the rate earned on stockholders' equity to vary from the rate earned on total assets because the amount earned on assets acquired through the use of funds provided by creditors varies from the interest paid to these creditors.

Liability. A debt of a business enterprise.

Lifo (last-in, first-out). A method of inventory costing based on the assumption that the most recent costs incurred should be charged against revenue.

Linear programming. A quantitative method that can be used in providing data for solving a variety of business problems in which management's objective is to minimize cost or maximize profits, subject to several limiting factors.

Liquidating dividend. A distribution out of paid-in capital when a corporation permanently reduces its operations or winds up its affairs completely.

Liquidation. The winding-up process when a partnership goes out of business.

Long-term investment. An investment that is not intended to be a ready source of cash in the normal operations of a business and that is listed in the "investments" section of the balance sheet.

Long-term liability. A liability that is not due for a comparatively long time (usually more than one year).

Lower of cost or market. A method of costing inventory or valuing temporary investments that carries those assets at the lower of their cost or current market prices.

M

Management. Individuals who are charged with the responsibility of directing the operations of enterprises.

Managerial accounting. The branch of accounting that uses both historical and estimated data in providing information which management uses in conducting daily operations and in planning future operations.

Manufacturing margin. Sales less variable cost of goods sold.

Marginal cost. The increase in total cost of producing and selling an additional unit of product.

Marginal revenue. The increase (or decrease) in total revenue realized from the sale of an additional unit of product.

Marginal tax rate. The highest rate applied to the income of any particular taxpayer.

Margin of safety. The difference between current sales revenue and the sales at the break-even point.

Market price approach. An approach to transfer pricing that uses the price at which the product or service transferred could be sold to outside buyers as the transfer price.

Market (sales) value method. A method of allocating joint costs among products according to their relative sales values.

Marketable security. An investment in a security that can be readily sold when cash is needed.

Markup. An amount which is added to a "cost" amount to determine product price.

Master budget. The comprehensive budget plan encompassing all the individual budgets related to sales, cost of goods sold, operating expenses, capital expenditures, and cash.

Matching. The principle of accounting that all revenues should be matched with the expenses incurred in earning those revenues during a period of time.

Materiality. The concept that recognizes the practicality of ignoring small or insignificant deviations from generally accepted accounting principles.

Materials. Goods in the state in which they were acquired for use in manufacturing operations.

Materials ledger. The subsidiary ledger containing the individual accounts for each type of material.

Materials requisition. The form used by the appropriate manufacturing department to authorize the issuance of materials from the storeroom.

Maturity value. The amount due at the maturity or due date of a note.

Maximax concept. A concept useful for managerial decision making, which leads management to decide in favor of that alternative with the maximum (largest) profit.

Maximin concept. A concept useful for managerial decision making, which leads management to decide in favor of that alternative with the maximum (largest) minimum profit.

Merchandise inventory. Merchandise on hand and available for sale.

Merchandise inventory turnover. The relationship between the volume of merchandise sold and merchandise inventory, computed by dividing the cost of merchandise sold by the average inventory.

Merger. The fusion of two corporations by the acquisition of the properties of one corporation by another, with the dissolution of one of the corporations.

Minority interest. The portion of a subsidiary corporation's capital stock that is not owned by the parent corporation.

Mixed cost. A cost with both variable and fixed characteristics, sometimes referred to as semivariable or semifixed cost.

Mortgage. A form of security for a debt which gives the creditor a lien or claim to property owned by the debtor in the event the debtor defaults on an obligation.

Moving average. An averaging technique used when the average cost method of inventory costing is applied in a perpetual inventory system.

Multiple-step income statement. An income statement with numerous sections and subsections with several intermediate balances before net income.

N

National Association of Accountants (NAA). The national professional organization of managerial accountants.

Natural business year. A year that ends when a business's activities have reached the lowest point in its annual operating cycle.

Negotiated price approach. An approach to transfer pricing that allows the managers of decentralized units to agree (negotiate) among themselves as to the proper transfer price.

Net income. The final figure in the income statement when revenues exceed expenses.

Net loss. The final figure in the income statement when expenses exceed revenues.

Net pay. Gross pay less payroll deductions; the amount the employer is obligated to pay the employee.

Net worth. The owner's equity in a business.

Normal pension cost. The cost of pension benefits earned by employees during the current year of service.

Note payable. A written promise to pay, representing an amount owed by a business.

Note receivable. A written promise to pay, representing an amount to be received by a business.

Number of days' sales in inventory. The relationship between the volume of goods sold and inventory, computed by dividing the inventory at the end of the year by the average daily cost of goods sold.

Number of days' sales in receivables. The relationship between credit sales and accounts receivable, computed by dividing the net accounts receivable at the end of the year by the average daily sales on account.

O

Operating expense. An expense associated with operations.

Operating lease. A lease which does not meet the criteria for a capital lease, and thus which is accounted for as an operating expense, so that neither future lease obligations nor future rights to use the leased asset are recognized in the accounts.

Opportunity cost. The amount of income that would result from the best available alternative to a proposed use of cash or its equivalent.

Other expense. An expense that cannot be associated definitely with operations.

Other income. Revenue from sources other than the principal activity of a business.

Overapplied factory overhead. The amount of factory overhead applied in excess of the actual factory overhead costs incurred for production during a period.

Owner's equity. The rights of the owners in a business enterprise.

P-Q

Paid-in capital. The capital (owner's equity) acquired from stockholders.

Par. The arbitrary monetary figure printed on a stock certificate.

Parent company. The company owning all or a majority of the voting stock of another corporation.

Participating preferred stock. Preferred stock that could receive dividends in excess of the specified amount granted by its preferential rights.

Partnership. A business owned by two or more individuals.

Past service cost. The cost of pension benefits granted to employees for prior years of service.

Payables. Liabilities of various types.

Payoff table. A table that summarizes the possible outcomes of one or more decisions for management's use in decision making.

Payroll. The total amount paid to employees for a certain period.

Payroll register. A multi-column form used to assemble and summarize payroll data at the end of each payroll period.

Percentage-of-completion method. The method of recognizing revenue from long-term contracts over the entire life of the contract.

Periodic inventory system. A system of inventory accounting in which only the revenue from sales is recorded each time a sale is made; the cost of merchandise on hand at the end of a period is determined by a detailed listing (physical inventory) of the merchandise on hand.

Perpetual inventory system. A system of inventory accounting that employs records that continually disclose the amount of the inventory.

Petty cash fund. A special cash fund used to pay relatively small amounts.

Physical inventory. The detailed listing of merchandise on hand.

Planning. The process of setting goals for the use of an organization's resources and developing ways to achieve these goals.

Plant asset. A tangible asset of a relatively fixed or permanent nature owned by a business enterprise.

Pooling of interests method. A method of accounting for an affiliation of two corporations resulting from an exchange of voting stock of one corporation for substantially all of the voting stock of the other corporation.

Post-closing trial balance. A trial balance prepared after all of the temporary accounts have been closed.

Posting. The process of transferring debits and credits from a journal to the accounts.

Predetermined factory overhead rate. The rate used to apply factory overhead costs to the goods manufactured.

Preemptive right. The right of each shareholder to maintain the same fractional interest in the corporation by purchasing a proportionate number of shares of any additional issuances of stock.

Preferred stock. A class of stock with preferential rights over common stock.

Premium. (a) Excess of the sales price of stock over its par amount; (b) excess of the issue price of bonds over their face amount.

Prepaid expense. A purchased commodity or service that has not been consumed at the end of an accounting period.

Present value. The estimated present worth of an amount of cash to be received (or paid) in the future.

Present value index. An index computed by dividing the total present value of the net cash flow to be received from a proposed capital investment by the amount to be invested.

Present value of an annuity. The sum of the present values of a series of equal cash flows to be received at fixed intervals.

Price-earnings (P/E) ratio. The ratio of the market price per share of common stock, at a specific date, to the annual earnings per share.

Price graph. A graph used to determine the price-cost combination that maximizes the total profit of an enterprise by plotting the marginal revenues and marginal costs.

Price theory. A separate discipline in the area of microeconomics which studies the setting of product prices.

Prior period adjustment. Correction of a material error related to a prior period or periods, excluded from the determination of net income.

Private accounting. The profession whose members are accountants employed by a business firm or nonprofit organization.

Proceeds. The net amount available from discounting a note.

Process cost system. A type of cost system that accumulates costs for each of the various departments or processes within a factory.

Processing cost. The direct labor and factory overhead costs associated with the manufacture of a product.

Product cost concept. A concept used in applying the cost-plus approach to product pricing in which only the costs of manufacturing the product, termed the product cost, are included in the cost amount to which the markup is added.

Profitability. The ability of a firm to earn income.

Profit center. A decentralized unit in which the manager has the responsibility and the authority to make decisions that affect both cost and revenues (and thus profits).

Profit margin. A component of the rate of return on investment, computed as the ratio of operating income to sales.

Profit-volume chart. A chart used to assist management in understanding the relationship between profit and volume.

Promissory note. A written promise to pay a sum in money on demand or at a definite time.

Public accounting. The profession whose members provide accounting services on a fee basis.

Purchase method. The accounting method employed when a parent company acquires a controlling share of the voting stock of a subsidiary other than by the exchange of voting common stock.

Purchase order. The form issued by the purchasing department to suppliers, requesting the delivery of materials.

Purchase requisition. The form used to inform the purchasing department that items are needed by a business.

Purchases discount. An available discount taken by the purchaser for early payment of an invoice.

Purchases journal. The journal in which all items purchased on account are recorded.

Quick assets. The sum of cash, receivables, and marketable securities.

R

Rate earned on common stockholders' equity. A measure of profitability computed by dividing net income, reduced by preferred dividend requirements, by common stockholders' equity.

Rate earned on stockholders' equity. A measure of profitability computed by dividing net income by total stockholders' equity.

Rate earned on total assets. A measure of the profitability of assets, without regard to the equity of creditors and stockholders in the assets.

Rate of return on investment (ROI). A measure of managerial efficiency in the use of investments in assets.

Realization. The sale of assets when a partnership is being liquidated.

Realization principle. Sales are recorded when title to the merchandise passes to the buyer.

Receiving report. The form used by the receiving department to indicate that materials have been received and inspected.

Reciprocal accounts. Accounts that have equal but opposite balances in two different ledgers.

Report form of balance sheet. The form of balance sheet with the liability and owner's equity sections presented below the asset section.

Residual income. The excess of divisional operating income over a "minimum" amount of desired operating income.

Residual value. The estimated recoverable cost of a depreciable asset as of the time of its removal from service.

Responsibility accounting. The process of measuring and reporting operating data by areas of responsibility.

Retail inventory method. A method of inventory costing based on the relationship of the cost and retail price of merchandise.

Retained earnings. Net income retained in a corporation.

Retained earnings statement. A statement for a corporate enterprise, summarizing the changes in retained earnings during a specific period of time.

Revenue. The amount charged to customers for goods sold or services rendered.

Revenue expenditure. An expenditure that benefits only the current period.

Reversing entry. An entry that reverses a specific adjusting entry to facilitate the recording of routine transactions in the subsequent period.

S

Safety stock. The amount of inventory that serves as a reserve for unforeseen circumstances, and therefore is not normally used in regular operations.

Sales. Revenue from the sale of merchandise.

Sales discount. An available discount granted by the seller for early payment of an invoice.

Sales journal. The journal in which all sales of merchandise on account are recorded.

Sales mix. The relative distribution of sales among the various products available for sale.

Sales returns and allowances. Reductions in sales, resulting from merchandise returned by customers or from the seller's reduction in the original sales price.

Scattergraph method. A method that uses a graph to estimate total cost and the fixed and variable cost components.

Securities and Exchange Commission (SEC). The federal agency that exercises a dominant influence over the development of accounting principles for most companies whose securities are traded in interstate commerce.

Selling expense. An expense incurred directly and entirely in connection with the sale of merchandise.

Serial bonds. Bonds of an issue with maturities spread over several dates.

Service department. A factory department that does not process materials directly but renders services for the benefit of production departments.

Simplex method. A mathematical equation approach to linear programming, which is often used more practically with a computer.

Single-step income statement. An income statement with the total of all expenses deducted from the total of all revenues.

Sinking fund. Assets set aside in a special fund to be used for a specific purpose.

Slide. The erroneous movement of all digits in a number, one or more spaces to the right or the left, such as writing $542 as $5,420.

Sole proprietorship. A business owned by one individual.

Solvency. The ability of a firm to pay its debts as they come due.

Special journal. A journal designed to record a single type of transaction.

Standard account form. A form of account that includes balance columns.

Standard costs. Detailed estimates of what a product should cost.

Standard cost system. An accounting system that uses standards for each element of manufacturing costs entering into the finished product.

Stated value. An amount assigned by the board of directors to each share of no-par stock.

Statement of changes in financial position. A basic financial statement devoted exclusively to reporting changes in financial position for a specified period of time.

Statement of cost of goods manufactured. A separate statement for a manufacturer that reports the cost of goods manufactured during a period.

Statements of Financial Accounting Standards. Pronouncements issued by the Financial Accounting Standards Board which become part of generally accepted accounting principles.

State unemployment compensation tax. A state tax generally paid by employers and used to provide temporary relief to those who become unemployed.

Stock dividend. Distribution of a company's own stock to its shareholders.

Stockholders. The owners of a corporation.

Stockholders' equity. The equity of the shareholders in a corporation.

Stock options. Rights given by a corporation to its employees to purchase shares of the corporation's stock at a stated price.

Stock outstanding. The stock in the hands of the stockholders.

Stock split. A reduction in the par or stated value of a share of common stock and the issuance of a proportionate number of additional shares.

Straight-line depreciation method. A method of depreciation that provides for equal periodic charges to expense over the estimated life of an asset.

Strategic planning. The process of establishing long-term goals for an enterprise and developing ways to achieve these goals.

Subsidiary company. The corporation that is controlled by a parent company.

Subsidiary ledger. A ledger containing individual accounts with a common characteristic.

Sum-of-the-years-digits depreciation method. A method of depreciation that provides for declining periodic depreciation charges to expense over the estimated life of an asset.

Sunk cost. A cost that is not affected by subsequent decisions.

Systems analysis. The determination of the informational needs, the sources of such information, and the deficiencies in the current system.

T

T account. A form of account resembling the letter T.

Taxable income. The base on which the amount of income tax is determined.

Temporary investment. An investment in securities that can be readily sold when cash is needed.

Term bonds. Bonds of an issue, all of which mature at the same time.

Theoretical standards. Standards that represent levels of performance that can be achieved only under perfect operating conditions, such as no idle time, no machine breakdowns, and no materials spoilage.

Time tickets. The form on which the amount of time spent by each employee and the labor cost incurred for each individual job, or for factory overhead, are recorded.

Total cost concept. A concept used in applying the cost-plus approach to product pricing in which all costs of manufacturing a product plus selling and general expenses are included in the cost amount to which the markup is added.

Transfer price. The price charged one decentralized unit by another for the goods or services provided.

Transposition. The erroneous arrangement of digits in a number, such as writing $542 as $524.

Treasury stock. A corporation's own outstanding stock that has been reacquired.

Trial balance. A summary listing of the balances and the titles of the accounts.

U-V

Underapplied factory overhead. The amount of actual factory overhead in excess of the factory overhead applied to production during a period.

Unearned revenue. Revenue received in advance of its being earned.

Units-of-production depreciation method. A method of depreciation that provides for depreciation expense based on the expected productive capacity of an asset.

Value of perfect information. The maximum amount (cost) that will be paid to obtain perfect information concerning a decision.

Variable cost concept. A concept used in applying the cost-plus approach to product pricing in which only variable costs and expenses are included in the cost amount to which the markup is added.

Variable costing. The concept that considers the cost of products manufactured to be composed only of those manufacturing costs that increase or decrease as the volume of production rises or falls (direct materials, direct labor, and variable factory overhead).

Variable expense (cost). An expense (cost) that tends to fluctuate in amount in accordance with variations in volume of activity.

Variances from standard. Difference between standard cost and actual cost.

Vertical analysis. The percentage analysis of component parts in relation to the total of the parts in a single financial statement.

Voucher. A document that serves as evidence of authority to pay cash.

Voucher register. The journal in which all vouchers are recorded.

Voucher system. Records, methods, and procedures employed in verifying and recording liabilities and paying and recording cash payments.

W-Z

Working capital. The excess of total current assets over total current liabilities at some point in time.

Work in process. Goods in the process of manufacture.

Work sheet. A working paper used to assist in the preparation of financial statements.

Zero-base budgeting. A concept of budgeting that requires all levels of management to start from zero and estimate budget data as if there had been no previous activities in their unit.

APPENDIX B

Special Journals and Subsidiary Ledgers

A manual accounting system is used in the text because such a system enables the student to focus most easily on the basic principles of accounting. In practice, when the manual system is used, it is often modified somewhat in order to process accounting data more effectively. One such modification is discussed in this appendix.

In the text, all transactions were initially recorded in a two-column journal, then posted individually to the appropriate accounts in the ledger. Applying such detailed procedures to a large number of transactions that are often repeated is impractical. For example, if many credit sales are made, each of these transactions would require an entry debiting Accounts Receivable and crediting Sales. In addition, the accounts receivable account in the ledger would include receivables from a large number of customers. In such cases, special journals can be used to record like kinds of transactions, and subsidiary ledgers can be used for accounts with a common characteristic.

Special Journals

One of the simplest methods of reducing the processing time and expense of recording a large number of transactions is to expand the two-column journal to a **multicolumn journal**. Each money column added to the general purpose journal is restricted to the recording of transactions affecting a certain account. For example, a special column could be used only for recording debits to the cash account and another special column could be used only for recording credits to the cash account. The addition of the two special columns would eliminate the writing of "Cash" in the journal for every receipt and payment of cash. Furthermore, there would be no need to post each individual debit and credit to the cash account. Instead, the "Cash Dr." and "Cash Cr." columns could be totaled periodically and only the totals posted, yielding additional economies. In a similar manner, special columns could be added for recording credits to Sales, debits and credits to Accounts Receivable and Accounts Payable, and for other entries that are repeated. Although there is no exact number of columns that may be effectively used in a single journal, there is a maximum number beyond which the journal would become unmanageable. Also, the possibilities of errors in recording become greater as the number of columns and the width of the page increase.

An all-purpose multicolumn journal is usually satisfactory for a small business enterprise that needs the services of only one bookkeeper. If the number of transactions is enough to require two or more bookkeepers, the use of a single journal is usually not efficient. The next logical development in expanding the system is to replace an all-purpose journal with a number of **special journals,** each designed to record a single kind of transaction. Special journals would be needed only for the kinds of transactions that occur frequently. Since most enterprises have many transactions in which cash is received and many in which cash is paid out, it is common practice to use a special journal for recording cash receipts and another special journal for recording cash payments. An enterprise that sells services or merchandise to customers on account might use a special journal designed for recording only such transactions. On the other hand, a business that does not give credit would have no need for such a journal.

The transactions that occur most often in a medium-size merchandising firm and the special journals in which they are recorded are as follows:

Transaction:	*Recorded In:*
Purchase of merchandise or other items *on account*	→ Purchases journal
Payment of cash for *any* purpose	→ Cash payments journal
Sale of merchandise *on account*	→ Sales journal
Receipt of cash from *any* source	→ Cash receipts journal

Sometimes the business documents evidencing purchases and sales transactions are used as special journals. When there are a large number of such transactions on a credit basis, the use of this procedure may result in a substantial savings in bookkeeping expenses and a reduction of bookkeeping errors.

The two-column form illustrated in earlier chapters can be used for miscellaneous entries, such as adjusting and closing entries, that do not "fit" in any of the special journals. The two-column form is commonly called the **general journal** or simply the journal.

Subsidiary Ledgers

As the number of purchases and sales on account increase, the need for maintaining a separate account for each creditor and debtor is clear. If such accounts are numerous, their inclusion in the same ledger with all other accounts would cause the ledger to become unmanageable. The chance of posting errors would also be increased and the preparation of the trial balance and the financial statements would be delayed.

When there are a large number of individual accounts with a common characteristic, it is common to place them in a separate ledger called a **subsidiary ledger**. The principal ledger, which contains all of the balance sheet and income statement accounts, is then called the **general ledger**. Each subsidiary ledger is represented by a summarizing account in the general ledger called a **controlling account**. The sum of the balances of the accounts in a subsidiary ledger must agree with the balance of the related controlling account. Thus, a subsidiary ledger may be said to be *controlled* by its controlling account.

The individual accounts with creditors are arranged in alphabetical order in a subsidiary ledger called the **accounts payable ledger** or **creditors ledger**. The related controlling account in the general ledger is Accounts Payable.

A subsidiary ledger for credit customers is needed for most business enterprises. This ledger containing the individual accounts is called the **accounts receivable ledger** or **customers' ledger**. The controlling account in the general ledger that summarizes the debits and credits to the individual customers accounts is Accounts Receivable.

Purchases Journal

Property most frequently purchased on account by a merchandising concern is of the following types: (1) merchandise for resale to customers, (2) supplies for use in conducting the business, and (3) equipment and other plant assets. Because of the variety of items acquired on credit terms, the purchases journal should be designed to allow for the recording of everything purchased on account. The form of purchases journal used by Kimco Inc. is illustrated on pages 942-943.

For each transaction recorded in the purchases journal, the credit is entered in the Accounts Payable Cr. column. The next three columns are used for accumulating debits to the particular accounts most frequently affected. Invoice amounts for merchandise purchased for resale to customers are recorded in the Purchases Dr. column. The purpose of the Store Supplies Dr. and Office Supplies Dr. columns is readily apparent. If supplies of these two categories were purchased only once in a while, the two columns could be omitted from the journal.

The final set of columns, under the main heading Sundry Accounts Dr., is used to record acquisitions, on account, of items not provided for in the special debit columns, such as plant assets and equipment. The title of the account to be debited is entered in the Account column and the amount is entered in the Amount column.

PURCHASES
JOURNAL

PAGE 19   PURCHASES

	DATE	ACCOUNT CREDITED	POST. REF.	ACCOUNTS PAYABLE CR.
1	1986 Oct. 2	Video-Audio Co.	✔	5 7 2 4 00
2	3	Marsh Electronics Inc.	✔	7 4 0 6 00
3	9	Parker Supply Co.	✔	2 5 7 00
4	11	Marsh Electronics Inc.	✔	3 2 0 8 00
5	16	Dunlap Electric Corporation	✔	3 5 9 3 00
6	17	Acosta Electronics Supply	✔	1 5 0 0 00
7	20	Walton Manufacturing Co.	✔	15 1 2 5 00
8	23	Parker Supply Co.	✔	1 3 2 00
9	27	Dunlap Electric Corporation	✔	6 3 7 5 00
10	31			43 3 2 0 00
11				(2 1 1)

Posting the Purchases Journal

The special journals used in recording most of the transactions affecting creditors' accounts are designed to allow the posting of individual transactions to the accounts payable ledger and a single monthly total to Accounts Payable. The basic techniques of posting credits from a purchases journal to an accounts payable ledger and the controlling account are shown in the following flowchart.

FLOW OF CREDITS FROM PURCHASES JOURNAL TO LEDGERS

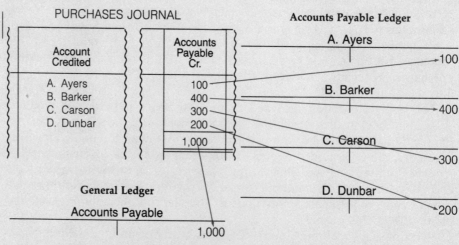

The individual credits of $100, $400, $300, and $200 to Ayers, Barker, Carson, and Dunbar respectively are posted to their accounts in the accounts payable ledger. The sum of the credits to the four individual accounts in the subsidiary ledger is posted as a single $1,000 credit to Accounts Payable, the controlling account in the general ledger.

JOURNAL   PAGE 19 | PURCHASES
                                                                           | JOURNAL

PURCHASES DR.	STORE SUPPLIES DR.	OFFICE SUPPLIES DR.	SUNDRY ACCOUNTS DR.			
			ACCOUNT	POST.	AMOUNT	
5 7 2 4 00						1
7 4 0 6 00						2
	1 3 1 00	1 2 6 00				3
3 2 0 8 00						4
3 5 9 3 00						5
1 5 0 0 00						6
			Store Equipment	121	15 1 2 5 00	7
	7 5 00	5 7 00				8
6 3 7 5 00						9
27 8 0 6 00	2 0 6 00	1 8 3 00			15 1 2 5 00	10
(511)	(115)	(116)			(✓)	11

The source of the entries posted to the subsidiary and general ledgers is indicated in the posting reference column of each account by inserting the letter "P" and the page number of the purchases journal. An account in the accounts payable ledger of Kimco Inc. is presented as an example.

NAME   Acosta Electronics Supply | AN ACCOUNT
ADDRESS   3800 Mission Street, San Francisco, California 94110-1732 | IN THE ACCOUNTS
                                                                           | PAYABLE LEDGER

DATE	ITEM	POST. REF.	DEBIT	CREDIT	BALANCE
1986 Oct. 17		P19		1 5 0 0 00	1 5 0 0 00

Since the balances in the creditors' accounts are usually credit balances, a three-column account form is used instead of the four-column account form illustrated earlier. When a creditor's account is overpaid and a debit balance occurs, such fact should be indicated by an asterisk or parentheses in the Balance column. When an account's balance is zero, a line may be drawn in the Balance column.

The creditors' accounts in the subsidiary ledger are not numbered because the order changes each time a new account is inserted alphabetically or an old account is removed. Thus, instead of a number, a check mark (✓) is inserted in the posting reference column of the purchases journal after a credit is posted.

The amounts in the Sundry Accounts Dr. column of the purchases journal are posted to the appropriate accounts in the general ledger and the posting reference ("P" and page number) are inserted in the accounts. As each amount is posted, the related general ledger account number is inserted in the posting reference column of the Sundry Accounts section.

At the end of each month, the purchases journal is totaled and ruled in the manner illustrated on pages 942 and 943. Before posting the totals to the general ledger, the sum of the totals of the four debit columns should be compared with the total of the credit column to prove their equality.

The totals of the four special columns are posted to the appropriate general ledger accounts in the usual manner, with the related account numbers inserted below the columnar totals. Because each amount in the Sundry Accounts Dr. was posted individually, a check mark is placed below the $15,125 total to show that no further action is needed.

Two of the general ledger accounts to which postings were made are presented as examples. The debit posting to Store Equipment was from the Sundry Accounts Dr. column; the credit posting to Accounts Payable was from the total of the Accounts Payable Cr. column.

GENERAL LEDGER
ACCOUNTS AFTER
POSTING FROM
PURCHASES JOURNAL

ACCOUNT Store Equipment — ACCOUNT NO. 121

DATE	ITEM	POST. REF.	DEBIT	CREDIT	BALANCE DEBIT	BALANCE CREDIT
1986 Oct. 1	Balance	✓			11 975 00	
20		P19	15 125 00		27 100 00	

ACCOUNT Accounts Payable — ACCOUNT NO. 211

DATE	ITEM	POST. REF.	DEBIT	CREDIT	BALANCE DEBIT	BALANCE CREDIT
1986 Oct. 1	Balance	✓				21 975 00
31		P19		43 320 00		65 295 00

The flow of data from the purchases journal of Kimco Inc. to its two related ledgers is presented graphically in the diagram at the top of page 945. Two procedures revealed by the flow diagram should be given special attention:

1. Postings are made from the purchases journal to both (a) accounts in the subsidiary ledger and (b) accounts in the general ledger.
2. The sum of the postings to individual accounts payable in the subsidiary ledger equals the columnar total posted to Accounts Payable (controlling account) in the general ledger.

Special Journals and Subsidiary Ledgers

PURCHASES JOURNAL

Account Credited	P. R.	Accts. Payable Cr.	Pur- chases Dr.	Store Sup. Dr.	Office Sup. Dr.	Sundry Accounts Debit		
						Account	P. R.	Amount
Video-Audio Co.	✔	5,724	5,724					
Marsh Electronics Inc.	✔	7,406	7,406					
Parker Supply Co.	✔	257		131	126			
Walton Mfg. Co.	✔	15,125				Store Equip.	121	15,125
Parker Supply Co.	✔	132		75	57			
Dunlap Electric Corp.	✔	6,375	6,375					
		43,320	27,806	206	183			15,125

Accounts Payable Ledger

Each individual entry is posted as a credit to an account in the accounts payable ledger, making a total of $43,320.

General Ledger

Accounts Payable   Store Supplies   Office Supplies
43,320   206   183

Purchases   Store Equipment
27,806   15,125

Purchase Returns and Allowances

When merchandise purchased is returned or a price adjustment is requested, an entry is made in the general journal according to the principles described in Chapter 2. To illustrate, assume that during October, Kimco Inc. issued a debit memorandum for a return of merchandise. The entry may be recorded in a two-column general journal, as follows:

JOURNAL   PAGE 18

	DATE		DESCRIPTION	POST. REF.	DEBIT	CREDIT	
17	Oct.	20	Accounts Payable—Dunlap Electric Corp.	211 ✔	9 7 50		17
18			Purchases	511		9 7 50	18
19			Debit Memo No. 20.				19

The debit portion of the entry is posted to the accounts payable account in the general ledger (No. 211) and also to the creditor's account in the subsidiary ledger (✔). The need for posting the debits to two different accounts is indicated, at the time these entries are journalized, by drawing a diagonal line in the posting reference column. The account number and check mark are inserted, in the usual manner, at the time the entry is posted.

After the entry has been recorded, the memorandum is attached to the related unpaid invoice. If the invoice had been paid before the return or allowance was granted, the settlement might be a cash refund.

If goods other than merchandise are returned or a price adjustment is granted, the account to which the goods were first debited should be credited. For example, if a purchase of office equipment is returned, the credit would be to Office Equipment rather than Purchases.

Cash Payments Journal

The standards for determining the special columns to be provided in the cash payments journal are the same as for the purchases journal, namely, the kind of transactions to be recorded and the frequency of their occurrence. It is necessary to have a Cash Cr. column. Payments to creditors on account happen often enough to require columns for Accounts Payable Dr. and Purchases Discount Cr. The cash payments journal illustrated as follows has these three columns and an additional column for Sundry Accounts Dr.

CASH PAYMENTS JOURNAL
AFTER POSTING

	DATE	CK. NO.	ACCOUNT DEBITED	POST. REF.	SUNDRY ACCOUNTS DR.	ACCOUNTS PAYABLE DR.	PURCHASES DISCOUNT CR.	CASH CR.	
1	1986 Oct. 2	312	Purchases	511	1 2 7 5 00			1 2 7 5 00	1
2	4	313	Store Equipment	121	3 5 0 00			3 5 0 00	2
3	12	314	Marsh Elec. Inc.	✔		7 4 0 6 00	7 4 06	7 3 3 1 94	3
4	12	315	Sales Salaries Exp.	611	2 5 6 0 00			2 5 6 0 00	4
5	12	316	Office Salaries Exp.	711	8 8 0 00			8 8 0 00	5
6	14	317	Misc. Gen. Exp.	715	5 6 40			5 6 40	6
7	16	318	Prepaid Insurance	117	9 8 4 00			9 8 4 00	7
8	20	319	Marsh Elec. Inc.	✔		3 2 0 8 00	3 2 08	3 1 7 5 92	8
9	20	320	M. B. Heath Co.	✔		4 8 5 0 00		4 8 5 0 00	9
10	21	321	Sales Ret. & Allow.	412	4 6 2 00			4 6 2 00	10
11	23	322	Acosta Elec. Supply	✔		1 5 0 0 00	3 0 00	1 4 7 0 00	11
12	23	323	Video — Audio Co.	✔		7 6 0 0 00		7 6 0 0 00	12
13	23	324	Heat. & Light. Exp.	712	7 8 9 20			7 8 9 20	13
14	24	325	Walton Mfg. Co.	✔		9 5 2 5 00		9 5 2 5 00	14
15	26	326	Sales Salaries Exp.	611	2 5 6 0 00			2 5 6 0 00	15
16	26	327	Office Salaries Exp.	711	8 8 0 00			8 8 0 00	16
17	26	328	Advertising Expense	613	7 8 6 00			7 8 6 00	17
18	27	329	Misc. Selling Exp.	617	4 1 50			4 1 50	18
19	28	330	Office Equipment	122	9 0 0 00			9 0 0 00	19
20	31				12 5 2 4 10	34 0 8 9 00	1 3 6 14	46 4 7 6 96	20
21					(✔)	(211)	(512)	(111)	21

CASH PAYMENTS JOURNAL   PAGE 16

All payments by Kimco Inc. are made by check. As each transaction is recorded in the cash payments journal, the related check number is entered in the column at the right of the Date column. The check numbers provide a convenient cross-reference, and their use also is helpful in controlling cash payments.

The Sundry Accounts Dr. column is used to record debits to any account for which there is no special column. For example, on October 2 Kimco Inc. paid $1,275 for a cash purchase of merchandise. The transaction was recorded by writing "Purchases" in the space provided and $1,275 in the Sundry Accounts Dr. and the Cash Cr. columns. The posting reference (511) was inserted later, at the time the debit was posted.

Debits to creditors accounts for invoices paid are recorded in the Accounts Payable Dr. column and credits for the amounts paid are recorded in the Cash Cr. column. If a discount is taken, the debit to the account payable will, of course, differ from the amount of the payment. Cash discounts taken on merchandise purchased for resale are recorded in the Purchases Discount Cr. column.

At frequent intervals during the month, the amounts entered in the Accounts Payable Dr. column are posted to the creditors accounts in the accounts payable ledger. After each posting, "CP" and the page number of the journal are inserted in the posting reference column of the account. Check marks are placed in the posting reference column of the cash payments journal to indicate that the amounts have been posted. The items in the Sundry Accounts Dr. column are also posted to the appropriate accounts in the general ledger at frequent intervals. The posting is indicated by writing the account numbers in the posting reference column of the cash payments journal. At the end of the month, each of the money columns in the cash payments journal is footed, the sum of the two debit totals is compared with the sum of the two credit totals to determine their equality, and the journal is ruled.

A check mark is placed below the total of the Sundry Accounts Dr. column to indicate that it is not posted. As each of the totals of the other three columns is posted to a general ledger account, the proper account numbers are inserted below the column totals.

Accounts Payable Control and Subsidiary Ledger

During October, the following postings were made to Accounts Payable in the general ledger of Kimco Inc.:

Credits to Accounts Payable

Oct. 31 Total purchases on account (purchases journal) $43,320.00

Debits to Accounts Payable

Oct. 20 A return of merchandise (general journal) 97.50
    31 Total cash payments on account (cash payments journal)........ 34,089.00

The accounts payable controlling account and the subsidiary accounts payable ledger of Kimco Inc. as of October 31 are presented on pages 948 and 949.

GENERAL LEDGER

ACCOUNT Accounts Payable   ACCOUNT NO. 211

DATE		ITEM	POST. REF.	DEBIT	CREDIT	BALANCE DEBIT	BALANCE CREDIT
1986 Oct.	1	Balance	✔				21 975 00
	20		J18	97 50			21 877 50
	31		P19		43 320 00		65 197 50
	31		CP16	34 089 00			31 108 50

ACCOUNTS PAYABLE LEDGER

NAME Acosta Electronics Supply

ADDRESS 3800 Mission Street, San Francisco, California 94110-1732

DATE		ITEM	POST. REF.	DEBIT	CREDIT	BALANCE
1986 Oct.	17		P19		1 500 00	1 500 00
	23		CP16	1 500 00		—

NAME Dunlap Electric Corporation

ADDRESS 521 Scottsdale Blvd., Phoenix, Arizona 85004-1100

DATE		ITEM	POST. REF.	DEBIT	CREDIT	BALANCE
1986 Oct.	16		P19		3 593 00	3 593 00
	20		J18	97 50		3 495 50
	27		P19		6 375 00	9 870 50

NAME M. B. Heath Co.

ADDRESS 9950 Ridge Ave., Los Angeles, California 90048-3694

DATE		ITEM	POST. REF.	DEBIT	CREDIT	BALANCE
1986 Sept.	21		P18		4 850 00	4 850 00
Oct.	20		CP16	4 850 00		—

NAME   March Electronics Inc.

ADDRESS   650 Wilson, Portland, Oregon 97209-1406

DATE		ITEM	POST. REF.	DEBIT	CREDIT	BALANCE
1986 Oct.	3		P19		7 4 0 6 00	7 4 0 6 00
	11		P19		3 2 0 8 00	10 6 1 4 00
	12		CP16	7 4 0 6 00		3 2 0 8 00
	20		CP16	3 2 0 8 00		

NAME   Parker Supply Co.

ADDRESS   142 West 8th, Los Angeles, California 90014-1225

DATE		ITEM	POST. REF.	DEBIT	CREDIT	BALANCE
1986 Oct.	9		P19		2 5 7 00	2 5 7 00
	23		P19		1 3 2 00	3 8 9 00

NAME   Video-Audio Co.

ADDRESS   1200 Capitol Ave., Sacramento, California 95814-1048

DATE		ITEM	POST. REF.	DEBIT	CREDIT	BALANCE
1986 Sept.	25		P18		7 6 0 0 00	7 6 0 0 00
Oct.	2		P19		5 7 2 4 00	13 3 2 4 00
	23		CP16	7 6 0 0 00		5 7 2 4 00

NAME   Walton Manufacturing Co.

ADDRESS   9554 W. Colorado Blvd., Pasadena, California 91107-1318

DATE		ITEM	POST. REF.	DEBIT	CREDIT	BALANCE
1986 Sept.	28		P18		9 5 2 5 00	9 5 2 5 00
Oct.	20		P19		15 1 2 5 00	24 6 5 0 00
	24		CP16	9 5 2 5 00		15 1 2 5 00

After all posting has been completed for the month, the sum of the balances in the accounts payable ledger should be compared with the balance of the accounts payable account in the general ledger. If the controlling account and the subsidiary ledger do not agree, the error or errors must be located and corrected. The balances of the individual creditors accounts may be summarized on an adding machine tape, or a schedule such as the following may be prepared. The total of the schedule, $31,108.50, agrees with the balance of the accounts payable account shown on page 948.

the accounts payable account shown on page 948.

SCHEDULE OF
ACCOUNTS PAYABLE

Kimco Inc. Schedule of Accounts Payable October 31, 1986	
Dunlap Electric Corporation............................	$ 9,870.50
Parker Supply Co.	389.00
Video-Audio Co.	5,724.00
Walton Manufacturing Co.	15,125.00
Total accounts payable............................	$31,108.50

Sales Journal

The **sales journal** is used only for recording *sales of merchandise on account,* sales of merchandise for cash are recorded in the cash receipts journal. Sales of assets not a part of the stock in trade are recorded in the cash receipts journal or the general journal, depending upon whether the sale was made for cash or on account. The sales journal of Kimco Inc. for October is as follows:

SALES JOURNAL
AFTER POSTING

	DATE		INVOICE NO.	ACCOUNT DEBITED	POST. REF.	ACCTS. REC. DR. SALES CR.	
1	1986 Oct.	2	615	R. A. Barnes Inc.	✔	9 3 5 0 00	1
2		3	616	Standard Supply Co.	✔	1 6 0 4 00	2
3		5	617	David T. Mattox	✔	15 3 0 5 00	3
4		9	618	R. A. Barnes Inc.	✔	1 3 9 6 00	4
5		10	619	Adler Company	✔	6 7 5 0 00	5
6		17	620	R. E. Hamilton Inc.	✔	7 8 6 5 00	6
7		23	621	Cooper & Co.	✔	1 5 0 2 00	7
8		26	622	Tracy & Lee Inc.	✔	3 2 6 0 00	8
9		27	623	Standard Supply Co.	✔	1 9 0 8 00	9
10		31				48 9 4 0 00	10
11						(113) (411)	11

SALES JOURNAL — PAGE 35

Details of the first sale recorded by Kimco Inc. in October are taken from invoice No. 615. The customer is R. A. Barnes Inc., and the invoice total is $9,350. Since the amount of the debit to Accounts Receivable is the same as the credit to Sales, a single amount column in the sales journal is sufficient. However, if sales are subject to a sales tax, a special column may be added to the sales journal for recording the credit to Sales Tax Payable.

Posting the Sales Journal

The procedures used in posting the sales journal are similar to those used in posting the purchases journal. The source of the entry being posted is shown in the posting reference column of an account by the letter "S" and the proper page number. A customer's account with a posting from the sales journal is as follows:

NAME	Adler Company												
ADDRESS	7608 Melton Ave., Los Angeles, California 90025-3942												

DATE	ITEM	POST. REF.	DEBIT	CREDIT	BALANCE
1986 Oct. 10		S35	6 7 5 0 00		6 7 5 0 00

AN ACCOUNT IN THE ACCOUNTS RECEIVABLE LEDGER

As each debit to a customer's account is posted, a check mark (✔) is inserted in the posting reference column of the sales journal. At the end of each month, the amount column of the sales journal is added, the journal is ruled, and the total is posted as a debit to Accounts Receivable and a credit to Sales. The respective account numbers are then inserted below the total to indicate that the posting is completed.

Sales Returns and Allowances

When merchandise sold is returned or a price adjustment is granted, an entry is made in the general journal according to the principles described in Chapter 2. During October, Kimco Inc. issued a credit memorandum and prepared the following entry in a two-column general journal:

		JOURNAL			PAGE 18		
	DATE	DESCRIPTION	POST. REF.	DEBIT	CREDIT	
1	1986 Oct. 13	Sales Returns and Allowances	412	2 2 5 00		1
2		Accounts Receivable — Adler Company	113 ✔		2 2 5 00	2
3		Credit Memo No. 32.				3

GENERAL JOURNAL ENTRY FOR SALES RETURNS AND ALLOWANCES

Note the diagonal line and double posting in the entry to record the credit memorandum. The diagonal line is placed in the posting reference column *at the time the entry is recorded in the general journal.*

If a cash refund is made because of merchandise returned or for an allowance, Sales Returns and Allowances is debited and Cash is credited. The entry would be recorded in the cash payments journal.

Cash Receipts Journal

All transactions that increase the amount of cash are recorded in a **cash receipts journal.** In a typical merchandising business, the most frequent sources of cash receipts are likely to be cash sales and collections from customers on account.

The cash receipts journal has a special column entitled Cash Dr. The frequency of the various kinds of transactions in which cash is received determines the titles of the other columns. The cash receipts journal of Kimco Inc. for October is as follows:

CASH RECEIPTS JOURNAL   PAGE 14

	DATE		ACCOUNT CREDITED	POST. REF.	SUNDRY ACCOUNTS CR.	SALES CR.	ACCOUNTS REC. CR.	SALES DISCOUNT DR.	CASH DR.	
1	1986 Oct.	2	Notes Receivable	112	2 4 0 0 00				2 5 4 4 00	1
2			Interest Income	811	1 4 4 00					2
3		5	R. A. Barnes Inc.	✓			5 8 0 0 00	1 1 6 00	5 6 8 4 00	3
4		6	Fogarty & Jacobs	✓			2 6 2 5 00	5 2 50	2 5 7 2 50	4
5		7	Sales	✓		3 7 0 0 00			3 7 0 0 00	5
6		10	David T. Mattox	✓			6 0 0 00	1 2 00	5 8 8 00	6
7		13	Standard Supply Co.	✓			1 6 0 4 00	3 2 08	1 5 7 1 92	7
8		14	Sales	✓		1 6 3 2 00			1 6 3 2 00	8
9		17	Adler Company	✓			6 5 2 5 00	1 3 0 50	6 3 9 4 50	9
10		19	R. E. Hamilton Inc.	✓			4 8 5 0 00		4 8 5 0 00	10
11		21	Sales	✓		1 9 2 0 30			1 9 2 0 30	11
12		23	Purchases	511	8 6 20				8 6 20	12
13		24	B. C. Wallace Corporation	✓			2 2 0 0 00		2 2 0 0 00	13
14		27	R. E. Hamilton Inc.	✓			7 8 6 5 00	1 5 7 30	7 7 0 7 70	14
15		28	Sales	✓		2 0 8 6 00			2 0 8 6 00	15
16		31	Sales	✓		2 4 2 3 40			2 4 2 3 40	16
17		31			2 6 3 0 20	11 7 6 1 70	32 0 6 9 00	5 0 0 38	45 9 6 0 52	17
18					(✓)	(411)	(113)	(413)	(111)	18

CASH RECEIPTS JOURNAL AFTER POSTING

The Sundry Accounts Cr. column is used for recording credits to any account for which there is no special column. For example, as of October 2, in the illustration, the receipt of $2,544 in payment of an interest-bearing note was recorded by a credit to Notes Receivable of $2,400 and a credit to Interest Income of $144. Both amounts were entered in the Sundry Accounts Cr. column. The posting references for the credits were inserted at the time the amounts were posted.

The Sales Cr. column is used for recording sales of merchandise for cash. Each individual sale is recorded on a cash register, and the totals thus accumulated are recorded in the cash receipts journal daily, weekly, or at other regular intervals. This is illustrated by the entry of October 7 recording weekly sales and cash receipts of $3,700. Since the total of the Sales Cr. column will be posted at the end of the month, a check mark is inserted in the posting reference column to show that the $3,700 item needs no further attention.

Credits to customers accounts for payments of invoices are recorded in the Accounts Receivable Cr. column. The amount of the cash discount granted, if any, is recorded in the Sales Discount Dr. column, and the amount of cash actually received is recorded in the Cash Dr. column. The entry on October 5 illustrates the use of these columns. Cash in the amount of $5,684 was received from R. A. Barnes Inc. in payment of its account of $5,800, the cash discount being 2% of $5,800, or $116.

Each amount in the Sundry Accounts Cr. column of the cash receipts journal is posted to the proper account in the general ledger at frequent intervals during the month. The posting is indicated by inserting the account number in the posting reference column. At regular intervals the amounts in the Accounts Receivable Cr. column are posted to the customers accounts in the subsidiary ledger and "CR" and the proper page number are inserted in the posting reference columns of the accounts. Check marks are placed in the posting reference column of the journal to show that the amounts have been posted. None of the individual amounts in the remaining three columns of the cash receipts journal are posted.

At the end of the month, all of the amount columns are footed, the equality of the debits and credits is proved, and the journal is ruled. Because each amount in the Sundry Accounts Cr. column has been posted individually to a general ledger account, a check mark is inserted below the column total to indicate that no further action is needed. The totals of the other four columns are posted to the proper accounts in the general ledger and their account numbers are inserted below the totals to show that the posting has been completed.

The flow of data from the cash receipts journal to the ledgers of Kimco Inc. is illustrated in the following diagram:

CASH RECEIPTS JOURNAL

Account Credited	P. R.	Sundry Accounts Cr.	Sales Cr.	Accounts Receivable Cr.	Sales Discount Dr.	Cash Dr.
Notes Receivable	112	2,400.00				2,544.00
Interest Income	811	144.00				
R. A. Barnes Inc.	✓			5,800.00	116.00	5,684.00
Fogarty & Jacobs	✓			2,625.00	52.50	2,572.50
Sales	✓		3,700.00			3,700.00
David T. Mattox	✓			600.00	12.00	588.00
Sales	✓		2,423.40			2,423.40
		2,630.20	11,761.70	32,069.00	500.38	45,960.52

FLOW OF DATA FROM CASH RECEIPTS JOURNAL TO LEDGERS

General Ledger

Accounts Receivable Ledger

Each individual entry is posted as a credit to an account in the accounts receivable ledger, making a total of $32,069.

Notes Receivable 2,400.00
Interest Income 144.00
Accounts Receivable 32,069.00
Sales 11,761.70
Sales Discount 500.38
Cash 45,960.52

Accounts Receivable Control and Subsidiary Ledger

During October, the following postings were made to Accounts Receivable in the general ledger of Kimco Inc.:

Debits

Oct. 31 Total sales on account (**sales journal**) $48,940.00

Credits

Oct. 13 A sales return (**general journal**) 225.00
Oct. 31 Total cash received on account (**cash receipts journal**) 32,069.00

The accounts receivable controlling account of Kimco Inc. as of October 31 is as follows:

GENERAL LEDGER

ACCOUNTS RECEIVABLE
ACCOUNT IN THE GENERAL
LEDGER AT THE END OF
THE MONTH

ACCOUNT Accounts Receivable					ACCOUNT NO. 113	
DATE	ITEM	POST. REF.	DEBIT	CREDIT	BALANCE DEBIT	BALANCE CREDIT
1986 Oct. 1	Balance	✔			17 260 00	
13		J18		2 25 00	17 035 00	
31		S35	48 940 00		65 975 00	
31		CR14		32 069 00	33 906 00	

The posting procedures and determination of the balances of the accounts in the accounts receivable ledger and the preparation of the schedule of accounts receivable are similar to those for accounts payable and are therefore not illustrated.

Problems

B–1. For the past few years, your uncle has operated a small jewelry store, Pride Jewelers. Its current annual revenues are approximately $500,000. Because the company's bookkeeper has been taking more and more time each month to record all transactions in a two-column journal and to prepare the financial statements, your uncle is considering improving the company's accounting system by adding special journals and subsidiary ledgers. Your uncle has asked you to help him with this project. He has compiled the following information:

(1)

Type of Transaction	Estimated Frequency per Month
Purchases of merchandise on account	250
Sales on account	160
Daily cash register summaries of cash sales	25
Purchases of merchandise for cash	20
Purchases of office supplies on account	5
Purchases of store supplies on account	5
Cash payments for utilities expenses	4
Cash purchases of office supplies	5
Cash purchases of store supplies	5
Cash receipts from customers on account	160

(2) For merchandise purchases of high dollar-value items, Pride Jewelers issues notes payable at current interest rates to vendors. These notes are issued because many of the high-value items may not sell immediately and the issuance of the notes reduces the need to maintain large balances of cash or assets that can be readily converted to cash. Notes are issued for approximately 10% of the purchases on account.

(3) All purchases discounts are taken when available.

(4) A sales discount of 2/10, n/30 is offered to all credit customers.

(5) A local sales tax of 6% is collected on all intrastate sales of merchandise.

(6) Monthly financial statements are prepared.

Instructions:

(1) Based upon the preceding description of Pride Jewelers, indicate which special journals you would recommend as part of Pride Jewelers' accounting system.

(2) Assume that your uncle has decided to use a sales journal and a purchases journal. Design the format for each journal, giving special consideration to the needs of Pride Jewelers.

(3) Which subsidiary ledgers would you recommend for Pride Jewelers?

B–2. Purchases on account and related returns and allowances completed by Robinson Stereo during June of the current year are as follows:

June 1. Purchased merchandise on account from Matzu Co., $7,652.50.

  4. Purchased merchandise on account from Vance Radio Corp., $4,150.75.

  6. Received a credit memorandum from Matzu Co. for merchandise returned, $112.50.

  8. Purchased store supplies on account from Baker Supply Co., $187.50.

  10. Purchased office equipment on account from Mann Equipment Co., $4,200.

  13. Purchased merchandise on account from Matzu Co., $3,250.10.

  17. Purchased merchandise on account from C. Wilson and Son, $875.40.

  19. Received a credit memorandum from Baker Supply Co. for store supplies returned, $37.50.

  20. Purchased merchandise on account from Klos Co., $1,010.

  24. Purchased office supplies on account from Baker Supply Co., $85.25.

  25. Received a credit memorandum from Vance Radio Corp. as an allowance for damaged merchandise, $100.

  27. Purchased merchandise on account from C. Wilson and Son, $475.15.

  30. Purchased store supplies on account from Baker Supply Co., $210.50.

Instructions:

    (1) Open the following accounts in the general ledger and enter the balances as of June 1:

114	Store Supplies	$ 442.75	211	Accounts Payable	$11,556.75
115	Office Supplies	210.10	511	Purchases..............	77,650.50
122	Office Equipment	22,400.00			

    (2) Open the following accounts in the accounts payable ledger and enter the balances in the balance columns as of June 1: Baker Supply Co.; Klos Co.; Mann Equipment Co.; Matzu Co., $4,155.10; Vance Radio Corp., $6,751.50; C. Wilson and Son, $650.15.

    (3) Record the transactions for June, posting to the creditors' accounts in the accounts payable ledger immediately after each entry. Use a purchases journal similar to the one illustrated on pages 942 and 943 and a two-column general journal.

    (4) Post the general journal and the purchases journal to the accounts in the general ledger.

    (5) (a) What is the sum of the balances in the subsidiary ledger at June 30?
        (b) What is the balance of the controlling account at June 30?

B–3. Britt Clothiers began operations on July 16 of the current year. Transactions related to purchases, returns and allowances, and cash payments during the remainder of the month are as follows:

July 16. Issued Check No. 1 in payment of rent for the remainder of July, $750.
     16. Purchased office equipment on account from Horner Supply Corp., $9,850.
     16. Purchased merchandise on account from Oester Clothing, $11,900.
     17. Issued Check No. 2 in payment of store supplies, $225, and office supplies, $190.
     17. Purchased merchandise on account from Cedeno Clothing Co., $8,715.
     19. Purchased merchandise on account from Boggs Co., $2,150.
     20. Received a credit memorandum from Cedeno Clothing Co. for returned merchandise, $715.
         Post the journals to the accounts payable ledger.
     23. Issued Check No. 3 to Horner Supply Corp. in payment of invoice of $9,850.
     23. Received a credit memorandum from Boggs Co. for defective merchandise, $465.
     24. Issued Check No. 4 to Oester Clothing, in payment of invoice of $11,900, less 1% discount.
     25. Issued Check No. 5 to a cash customer for merchandise returned, $165.
     26. Issued Check No. 6 to Cedeno Clothing Co. in payment of the balance owed, less 2% discount.
     26. Purchased merchandise on account from Boggs Co., $1,610.
         Post the journals to the accounts payable ledger.
     30. Purchased the following from Horner Supply Corp. on account: store supplies, $150; office supplies, $75; store equipment, $675.
     30. Issued Check No. 7 to Boggs Co. in payment of invoice of $2,150, less the credit of $465.
     30. Purchased merchandise on account from Oester Clothing, $3,900.

July 31. Issued Check No. 8 in payment of incoming transportation charges on merchandise delivered during July, $615.

31. Issued Check No. 9 in payment of sales salaries, $1,775.

31. Received a credit memorandum from Horner Supply Corp. for defect in office equipment, $75.
Post the journals to the accounts payable ledger.

Instructions:

(1) Open the following accounts in the general ledger, using the account numbers indicated.

111	Cash	412	Sales Returns and Allowances
116	Store Supplies	511	Purchases
117	Office Supplies	512	Purchases Discount
121	Store Equipment	611	Sales Salaries Expense
122	Office Equipment	712	Rent Expense
211	Accounts Payable		

(2) Open the following accounts in the accounts payable ledger: Boggs Co.; Cedeno Clothing Co.; Horner Supply Corp.; Oester Clothing.

(3) Record the transactions for July, using a purchases journal similar to the one illustrated on pages 942 and 943, a cash payments journal similar to the one illustrated on page 946, and a two-column general journal. Post to the accounts payable ledger at the points indicated in the narrative of transactions.

(4) Post the appropriate individual entries to the general ledger (Sundry Accounts columns of the purchases journal and the cash payments journal; both columns of the general journal).

(5) Add the columns of the purchases journal and the cash payments journal, and post the appropriate totals to the general ledger. (Because the problem does not include transactions related to cash receipts, the cash account in the ledger will have a credit balance.)

(6) Prepare a schedule of accounts payable.

B–4. C. G. Murphy Inc. was established in June of the current year. Its sales of merchandise on account and related returns and allowances during the remainder of the month are as follows. Terms of all sales were 2/10, n/30, FOB destination.

June 21. Sold merchandise on account to Rusk Inc., Invoice No. 1, $2,000.

22. Sold merchandise on account to Allen Co., Invoice No. 2, $850.

22. Sold merchandise on account to Lane Co., Invoice No. 3, $1,550.

24. Issued Credit Memorandum No. 1 for $50 to Rusk Inc. for merchandise returned.

25. Sold merchandise on account to D. W. Raines, Invoice No. 4, $2,500.

28. Sold merchandise on account to Unisac Inc., Invoice No. 5, $2,950.

29. Issued Credit Memorandum No. 2 for $150 to Allen Co. for merchandise returned.

30. Sold merchandise on account to Allen Co., Invoice No. 6, $3,100.

30. Issued Credit Memorandum No. 3 for $90 to D. W. Raines for damages to merchandise caused by faulty packing.

30. Sold merchandise on account to Lane Co., Invoice No. 7, $725.

Instructions:

(1) Open the following accounts in the general ledger, using the account numbers indicated: Accounts Receivable, 113; Sales, 411; Sales Returns and Allowances, 412.

(2) Open the following accounts in the accounts receivable ledger: Allen Co.; Lane Co.; D. W. Raines; Rusk Inc.; Unisac Inc.

(3) Record the transactions for June, posting to the customers' accounts in the accounts receivable ledger and inserting the balance immediately after recording each entry. Use a sales journal similar to the one illustrated on page 950 and a two-column general journal.

(4) Post the general journal and the sales journal to the three accounts opened in the general ledger, inserting the account balances only after the last postings.

(5) (a) What is the sum of the balances of the accounts in the subsidiary ledger at June 30?

(b) What is the balance of the controlling account at June 30?

If the work-
ing papers
correlating with
the textbook are
not used, omit
Problem B-5.

B-5. Three journals, the accounts receivable ledger, and portions of the general ledger of Wilcox Company are presented in the working papers. Sales invoices and credit memorandums were entered in the journals by an assistant. Terms of sales on account are 2/10, n/30, FOB shipping point. Transactions in which cash and notes receivable were received during May are as follows:

May   1. Received $5,586 cash from Nance Co. in payment of April 21 invoice, less discount.

4. Received $10,300 cash in payment of $10,000 note receivable and interest of $300.
   Post transactions of May 1, 2, and 6 to accounts receivable ledger.

7. Received $4,312 cash from C. E. Rea and Son in payment of April 27 invoice, less discount.

8. Received $1,250 cash from Downs & Franks in payment of April 9 invoice, no discount.
   Post transactions of May 7, 8, 10, 12, and 15 to accounts receivable ledger.

16. Cash sales for first half of May totaled $4,610.

19. Received $1,000 cash refund for return of defective equipment purchased for cash in April.

20. Received $1,470 cash from Nance Co. in payment of balance due on May 10 invoice, less discount.

21. Received $1,176 cash from Downs & Franks in payment of May 12 invoice, less discount.
    Post transactions of May 18, 20, 21, 22, and 25 to accounts receivable ledger.

27. Received $40 cash for sale of office supplies at cost.

31. Received $500 cash and a $2,500 note receivable from Howard Corp. in settlement of the balance due on the invoice of May 1, no discount. (Record receipt of note in the general journal.)

31. Cash sales for second half of May totaled $4,150.
    Post transactions of May 28, 30, and 31 to accounts receivable ledger.

Instructions:

(1) Record the cash receipts in the cash receipts journal and the note in the general journal. *Before recording a receipt of cash on account, determine the balance of the customer's account.* Post the entries from the three journals, in date sequence, to the accounts receivable ledger in accordance with the instructions in the narrative of transactions. Insert the new balance after each posting to an account.

(2) Post the appropriate individual entries from the cash receipts journal and the general journal to the general ledger.

(3) Add the columns of the sales journal and the cash receipts journal and post the appropriate totals to the general ledger. Insert the balance of each account after the last posting.

(4) Prepare a schedule of the accounts receivable as of May 31 and compare the total with the balance of the controlling account.

B–6. Transactions related to sales and cash receipts completed by R & R Company during the period July 16–31 of the current year are as follows. The terms of all sales on account are 2/10, n/30, FOB shipping point.

July 16. Issued Invoice No. 793 to Seaview Co., $4,425.
18. Received cash from Dumont Co. for the balance due on its account, less discount.
19. Issued Invoice No. 794 to R. W. Kane Co., $7,500.
20. Issued Invoice No. 795 to Frank Parker Co., $2,975.
Post all journals to the accounts receivable ledger.
23. Received cash from R. W. Kane Co. for the balance owed on July 16; no discount.
24. Issued Credit Memo No. 35 to Seaview Co., $275.
25. Issued Invoice No. 796 to R. W. Kane Co., $4,950.
25. Received $1,560 cash in payment of a $1,500 note receivable and interest of $60.
Post all journals to the accounts receivable ledger.
26. Received cash from Seaview Co. for the balance due on invoice of July 16, less discount.
28. Received cash from R. W. Kane Co. for invoice of July 19, less discount.
28. Issued Invoice No. 797 to Dumont Co., $2,100.
30. Issued Credit Memo No. 36 to Dumont Co., $250.
31. Recorded cash sales for the second half of the month, $8,155.
Post all journals to the accounts receivable ledger.

Instructions:

(1) Open the following accounts in the general ledger, inserting the balances indicated, as of July 1:

111 Cash	$12,125	412 Sales Returns and Allowances..	—
112 Notes Receivable	5,500	413 Sales Discount	—
113 Accounts Receivable	8,725	811 Interest Income	—
411 Sales	—		

(2) Open the following accounts in the accounts receivable ledger, inserting the balances indicated, as of July 16: Dumont Co., $2,500; R. W. Kane Co., $5,125; Frank Parker Co.; Seaview Co.

(3) The transactions are to be recorded in a sales journal similar to the one illustrated on page 950, a cash receipts journal similar to the one illustrated on page 952, and a 2-column general journal. Insert on the first line of the two special journals "July 16 Total(s) Forwarded ✔" and the following dollar figures in the amount columns:

Sales journal: 20,200
Cash receipts journal: 1,077; 6,950; 21,300; 255; 29,072.

(continued)

(4) Record the transactions for the remainder of July, posting to the accounts receivable ledger and inserting the balances at the points indicated in the narrative of transactions. *Determine the balance in the customer's account before recording a cash receipt.*

(5) Add the columns of the special journals and post the individual entries and totals to the general ledger. Insert account balances after the last posting.

(6) Determine that the subsidiary ledger agrees with the controlling account in the general ledger.

B–7. The transactions completed by Cannon Supply Co. during January, the first month of the current fiscal year, were as follows:

Jan. 2. Issued Check No. 610 for January rent, $1,400.

2. Purchased merchandise on account from Bidwell Co., $2,590.

3. Purchased equipment on account from Weber Equipment Co., $11,100.

5. Issued Invoice No. 940 to W. Cox, Inc., $1,700.

6. Received check for $2,772 from Powell Corp. in payment of $2,800 invoice, less discount.

6. Issued Check No. 611 for miscellaneous selling expense, $310.

9. Received credit memorandum from Bidwell Co. for merchandise returned to them, $290.

9. Issued Invoice No. 941 to Collins Corp., $8,500.

10. Issued Check No. 612 for $9,405 to Howell Inc. in payment of $9,500 invoice, less 1% discount.

10. Received check for $9,702 from Sax Manufacturing Co. in payment of $9,800 invoice, less discount.

10. Issued Check No. 613 to Bone Enterprises in payment of invoice of $2,120, no discount.

11. Issued Invoice No. 942 to Joy Corp., $3,120.

11. Issued Check No. 614 to Porter Corp. in payment of account, $705, no discount.

12. Received check for $1,683 from W. Cox Inc. in payment of $1,700 invoice, less discount.

13. Issued credit memorandum to Joy Corp. for damaged merchandise, $320.

13. Issued Check No. 615 for $2,254 to Bidwell Co. in payment of $2,300 balance, less 2% discount.

16. Issued Check No. 616 for $2,725 for cash purchase of merchandise.

16. Cash sales for January 2-15, $21,520.

17. Purchased merchandise on account from Bone Enterprises, $7,920.

18. Received check for return of merchandise that had been purchased for cash, $790.

18. Issued Check No. 617 for miscellaneous general expense, $238.

19. Purchased the following on account from Moore Supply Inc.: store supplies, $248; office supplies, $197.

20. Issued Check No. 618 in payment of advertising expense, $1,850.

23. Issued Invoice No. 943 to Sax Manufacturing Co., $8,172.

24. Purchased the following on account from Howell Inc.: merchandise, $5,127; store supplies, $292.

25. Issued Invoice No. 944 to Collins Corp., $4,650.

25. Received check for $2,800 from Powell Corp. in payment of $2,800 balance, no discount.

Jan. 26. Issued Check No. 619 to Weber Equipment Co. in payment of invoice of January 3, $11,100, no discount.

27. Issued Check No. 620 for dividends, $3,500.

30. Issued Check No. 621 for monthly salaries as follows: sales salaries, $9,100; office salaries, $3,800.

31. Cash sales for January 16–31, $18,150.

31. Issued Check No. 622 for transportation on commodities purchased during the month as follows: merchandise, $720; equipment, $210.

Instructions:

(1) Open the following accounts in the general ledger, entering the balances indicated as of January 1:

111	Cash	$ 9,100	411	Sales	—
113	Accounts Receivable	16,200	412	Sales Returns and Allow.	—
114	Merchandise Inventory	31,500	413	Sales Discount	—
115	Store Supplies	410	511	Purchases	—
116	Office Supplies	225	512	Purchases Discount	—
117	Prepaid Insurance	2,100	611	Sales Salaries Expense	—
121	Equipment	40,650	612	Advertising Expense	—
122	Accumulated Depr.	12,350	619	Miscellaneous Selling Expense	—
211	Accounts Payable	12,325	711	Office Salaries Expense	—
311	Capital Stock	50,000	712	Rent Expense	—
312	Retained Earnings	25,510	719	Miscellaneous General Expense	—
313	Dividends	—			

(2) Record the transactions for January, using a purchases journal (as on pages 942 and 943), a sales journal (as on page 950), a cash payments journal (as on page 946), a cash receipts journal (as on page 952), and a 2-column general journal. The terms of all sales on account are FOB shipping point, 1/10, n/30. Assume that an assistant makes daily postings to the individual accounts in the accounts payable and the accounts receivable ledgers.

(3) Post the appropriate individual entries to the general ledger.

(4) Add the columns of the special journals and post the appropriate totals to the general ledger; insert the account balances.

(5) Prepare a trial balance.

(6) Balances in the accounts in the subsidiary ledgers as of January 31 are listed below. Verify the agreement of the ledgers with their respective controlling accounts.

Accounts Receivable: Balances of $800; $8,500; $2,800; $8,172; $4,650.

Accounts Payable: Balances of $7,920; $5,419; $445.

APPENDIX C

Work Sheet for Statement of Changes in Financial Position

Some accountants prefer to use a work sheet to assist them in assembling data for the statement of changes in financial position (funds statement). Although a work sheet is not essential, it is especially useful when a large number of transactions must be analyzed. Also, whether or not a work sheet is used, the concepts of funds and the funds statement are not affected.

The following sections describe and illustrate the use of the work sheet. Attention is directed to its use in preparing the funds statement (1) based on working capital and (2) based on cash. The data that appear in Chapter 14 for T. R. Morgan Corporation are used for the illustrations.

WORK SHEET PROCEDURES FOR FUNDS STATEMENT BASED ON WORKING CAPITAL

The comparative balance sheet and additional data obtained from the accounts of T. R. Morgan Corporation are presented on page 963. The work sheet prepared from these data is presented on page 964.

The procedures to prepare the work sheet for the funds statement based on working capital are outlined as follows:

1. List the title of each noncurrent account in the Description column. For each account, enter that debit or credit representing the change (increase or decrease) in the account balance for the year in the Change During Year column.
2. Add the debits and credits in the Change During Year column and determine the subtotals. Enter the change (increase or decrease) in working capital during the year in the appropriate column to balance the totals of the debits and credits.
3. Provide space in the bottom portion of the work sheet for later use in identifying the various (1) sources of working capital and (2) applications of working capital.
4. Analyze the change during the year in each noncurrent account in order to determine the sources and/or applications of working capital related to the transactions recorded in each account. Record these sources and

applications in the bottom portion of the work sheet by means of entries in the Work Sheet Entries columns.

5. Complete the work sheet.

These procedures are explained in detail in the following paragraphs.

COMPARATIVE
BALANCE SHEET

T. R. Morgan Corporation
Comparative Balance Sheet
December 31, 1987 and 1986

	1987	1986	Increase Decrease*
Assets			
Cash	$ 49,000	$ 26,000	$ 23,000
Trade receivables (net)	74,000	65,000	9,000
Inventories	172,000	180,000	8,000*
Prepaid expenses	4,000	3,000	1,000
Investments (long-term)	—	45,000	45,000*
Land	90,000	40,000	50,000
Building	200,000	200,000	—
Accumulated depreciation—building	(36,000)	(30,000)	(6,000)
Equipment	180,000	142,000	38,000
Accumulated depreciation—equipment	(43,000)	(40,000)	(3,000)
Total assets	$690,000	$631,000	$ 59,000
Liabilities			
Accounts payable (merchandise creditors)	$ 50,000	$ 32,000	$ 18,000
Income tax payable	2,500	4,000	1,500*
Dividends payable	15,000	8,000	7,000
Bonds payable	120,000	245,000	125,000*
Total liabilities	$187,500	$289,000	$101,500*
Stockholders' Equity			
Common stock	$280,000	$230,000	$ 50,000
Retained earnings	222,500	112,000	110,500
Total stockholders' equity	$502,500	$342,000	$160,500
Total liabilities and stockholders' equity	$690,000	$631,000	$ 59,000

Additional data:

(1) Net income, $140,500.

(2) Cash dividends declared, $30,000.

(3) Common stock issued at par for land, $50,000.

(4) Bonds payable retired for cash, $125,000.

(5) Depreciation for year: equipment, $12,000; building, $6,000.

(6) Fully depreciated equipment discarded, $9,000.

(7) Equipment purchased for cash, $47,000.

(8) Book value of investments sold for $75,000 cash, $45,000.

T. R. Morgan Corporation
Work Sheet for Statement of Changes in Financial Position
For Year Ended December 31, 1987

Description	Change During Year		Work Sheet Entries	
	Debit	Credit	Debit	Credit
Investments		45,000	(j) 45,000	
Land	50,000			(i) 50,000
Building.	—	—		
Accumulated depreciation— building.		6,000	(h) 6,000	
Equipment	38,000		(f) 9,000	(g) 47,000
Accumulated depreciation— equipment		3,000	(e) 12,000	(f) 9,000
Bonds payable	125,000			(d) 125,000
Common stock		50,000	(c) 50,000	
Retained earnings		110,500	(a) 140,500	(b) 30,000
	213,000	214,500		
Increase in working capital	1,500			
Totals.	214,500	214,500		
Sources of working capital: Operations:				
Net income				(a) 140,500
Depreciation of equipment.				(e) 12,000
Depreciation of building				(h) 6,000
Issuance of common stock for land				(c) 50,000
Book value of investments sold.				(j) 45,000
Applications of working capital:				
Declaration of cash dividends.			(b) 30,000	
Retirement of bonds.			(d) 125,000	
Purchase of equipment.			(g) 47,000	
Purchase of land by issuance of common stock. . .			(i) 50,000	
Totals.			514,500	514,500

Noncurrent Accounts

Since the analysis of transactions recorded in the noncurrent accounts reveals the sources and applications of working capital, the work sheet focuses on the noncurrent accounts. For this purpose, the titles of the noncurrent accounts are entered in the Description column. Next, the debit or credit change for the year in each account balance is entered in the Change During Year column. For example, the beginning and ending balances of Investments were $45,000 and zero, respectively. Thus, the change for the year was a decrease, or credit, of $45,000. The beginning and ending balances of Land were $40,000 and $90,000, respectively. Thus, the change for the year was an increase , or debit, of $50,000. The changes in the other accounts are determined in a like manner.

Change in Working Capital

Since transactions that result in changes in working capital (the current accounts) also result in changes in the noncurrent accounts, the change in working capital for the period will equal the change in the noncurrent accounts for the period. Thus, if a subtotal of the debits and credits for the noncurrent accounts (as indicated in the Change During Year column) is determined, the increase or decrease in working capital for the period can be inserted in the appropriate column and the two columns will balance. In the illustration, the subtotal of the credit column ($214,500) exceeds the subtotal of the debit column ($213,000) by $1,500, which is identified as the increase in working capital. By entering the $1,500 as a debit in the Change During Year column, the debit and credit columns are balanced. This $1,500 increase in working capital will be reported on the funds statement as the difference between the total of the sources section and the total of the applications section. This change is supported by details of the change in each of the working capital components, as follows:

CHANGES IN
COMPONENTS
OF WORKING
CAPITAL

Changes in components of working capital:		
Increase (decrease) in current assets:		
Cash	$23,000	
Trade receivables (net)	9,000	
Inventories	(8,000)	
Prepaid expenses	1,000	$25,000
Increase (decrease) in current liabilities:		
Accounts payable	$18,000	
Income tax payable	(1,500)	
Dividends payable	7,000	23,500
Increase in working capital		$ 1,500

If the subtotals in the Change During Year columns indicate that the debits exceed the credits, the balancing figure would be identified as a decrease in working capital.

Sources and Applications Sections

After the debit and credit columns are totaled and ruled, "Sources of working capital" is written in the Description column. Several lines are skipped, so that at a later time the various sources of working capital can be entered, and "Applications of working capital" is written in the Description column. When the work sheet is completed, this bottom portion will contain the data necessary to prepare the sources section and the applications section of the funds statement.

Analysis of Noncurrent Accounts

As was discussed on pages 461–464, transactions that result in sources and applications of working capital can be classified in terms of their effect on the noncurrent accounts. Therefore, to determine the various sources and applications for the year, the changes in the noncurrent accounts are analyzed. As each account is analyzed, entries made in the work sheet relate specific sources or applications of working capital to the noncurrent account. It should be noted that the work sheet entries are not entered into the accounts. They are, as is the entire work sheet, strictly an aid in assembling the data for later use in preparing the funds statement.

The sequence in which the noncurrent accounts are analyzed is unimportant. However, because it is more convenient and efficient, and the chance for errors is reduced, the analysis illustrated will begin with the retained earnings account and proceed upward in the listing in sequential order.

Retained Earnings

The work sheet indicates that there was an increase of $110,500 in retained earnings for the year. The additional data, taken from an examination of the account, indicate that the increase was the result of two factors: (1) net income of $140,500 and (2) declaration of cash dividends of $30,000. To identify the sources and applications of working capital, two entries are made on the work sheet. These entries also serve to account for, or explain, the increase of $110,500.

Net income. In closing the accounts at the end of the year, the retained earnings account was credited for $140,500, representing the net income. The $140,500 is also reported on the funds statement as a source of working capital. An entry on the work sheet to debit retained earnings and to credit "Sources of working capital—operations: net income" accomplishes the following: (1) the credit portion of the closing entry (to retained earnings) is accounted for, or in effect canceled, and (2) the source of working capital is identified in the bottom portion of the work sheet. The entry on the work sheet is as follows:

```
(a)  Retained Earnings...............................  140,500
        Sources of Working Capital—Operations:
          Net Income...................................            140,500
```

Dividends. In closing the accounts at the end of the year, the retained earnings account was debited for $30,000, representing the cash dividends declared.

The $30,000 is also reported on the funds statement as an application of working capital. An entry on the work sheet to debit "Applications of working capital—declaration of cash dividends" and to credit retained earnings accomplishes the following: (1) the debit portion of the closing entry (to retained earnings) is accounted for, or in effect canceled, and (2) the application of working capital is identified in the bottom portion of the work sheet. The entry on the work sheet is as follows:

(b) Applications of Working Capital—Declaration		
of Cash Dividends	30,000	
Retained Earnings..............................		30,000

Common Stock

The next noncurrent item on the work sheet, common stock, increased by $50,000 during the year. The additional data, taken from an examination of the account, indicate that the stock was exchanged for land. The work sheet entry to account for this increase and to identify the source of working capital is as follows:

(c) Common Stock	50,000	
Sources of Working Capital—Issuance of		
Common Stock for Land		50,000

It should be noted that the effect of the exchange will also be analyzed when the land account is examined.

Bonds Payable

The decrease of $125,000 in the bonds payable account during the year resulted from the retirement of the bonds for cash. The work sheet entry to record the effect of this transaction on working capital is as follows:

(d) Applications of Working Capital—Retirement of		
Bonds Payable.................................	125,000	
Bonds Payable................................		125,000

Accumulated Depreciation—Equipment

The work sheet indicates that the accumulated depreciation—equipment account increased by $3,000 during the year. The additional data indicate that the increase resulted from (1) depreciation expense of $12,000 (credit) for the year and (2) discarding $9,000 (debit) of fully depreciated equipment. Since depreciation expense does not affect working capital but does decrease the amount of net income, it should be added to net income to determine the amount of working capital from operations. This effect is indicated on the work sheet by the following entry:

(e) Accumulated Depreciation—Equipment...........	12,000	
Sources of Working Capital—Operations:		
Depreciation of Equipment.....................		12,000

It should be noted that the notation in the Description column is placed so that the $12,000 can be added to "Sources of working capital—operations: net income."

Since the discarding of the fully depreciated equipment did not affect working capital, the following entry is made on the work sheet in order to fully account for the change of $3,000 in the accumulated depreciation—equipment account:

(f) Equipment	9,000	
Accumulated Depreciation—Equipment...........		9,000

It should be noted that this entry, like the transaction that was recorded in the accounts, does not affect working capital. It serves only to complete the accounting for all transactions that resulted in the change in the account during the year and thus helps assure that no transactions affecting working capital are overlooked in the analysis.

Equipment

The work sheet indicated that the equipment account increased by $38,000 during the year. The additional data, determined from an examination of the ledger account, indicated that the increase resulted from (1) discarding $9,000 of fully depreciated equipment and (2) purchasing $47,000 of equipment. The discarding of the equipment was included in, or accounted for, in (f) and needs no additional attention. The application of working capital to the purchase of equipment is recognized by the following entry on the work sheet:

(g) Applications of Working Capital—Purchase		
of Equipment	47,000	
Equipment		47,000

Accumulated Depreciation—Building

The $6,000 increase in the accumulated depreciation—building account during the year resulted from the entry to record depreciation expense. Since depreciation expense does not affect working capital but does decrease the amount of net income, it should be added to net income to determine the amount of working capital from operations. This effect is accomplished by the following entry on the work sheet:

(h) Accumulated Depreciation—Building	6,000	
Sources of Working Capital—Operations:		
Depreciation of Building		6,000

Building

There was no change in the beginning and ending balances of the building account and reference to the account confirms that no entries were made in it during the year. Hence, no entry is necessary on the work sheet.

Land

As indicated in the analysis of the common stock account, the $50,000 increase in land resulted from a purchase by issuance of common stock. The work sheet entry to indicate this application of working capital is as follows:

(i) Applications of Working Capital—Purchase of
    Land by Issuance of Common Stock   50,000
        Land   50,000

Investments

The work sheet indicates that investments decreased by $45,000. The examination of the ledger account indicates that investments were sold for $75,000. As was explained on page 466, the $30,000 gain on the sale is already included in net income and consequently has already been accounted for as a source of working capital. Only the $45,000 book value of the investments sold would be reported as a source of working capital. To indicate this source on the work sheet, the following entry is made:

(j) Investments   45,000
    Sources of Working Capital—Book Value of
        Investments Sold   45,000

Completing the Work Sheet

After all of the noncurrent accounts have been analyzed, all of the sources and applications are identified in the bottom portion of the work sheet. To assure the equality of the work sheet entries, the last step is to total the Work Sheet Entries columns.

Preparation of the Funds Statement

The data for the sources section and the applications section of the funds statement are obtained from the bottom portion of the work sheet. Some modifications are made to the work sheet data for presentation on the statement. For example, in presenting the working capital provided by operations, the additions to net income are labeled "Add deductions not decreasing working capital during the year." Another example is the reporting of the total depreciation expense ($18,000) instead of the two separate amounts ($12,000 and $6,000).

The increase (or decrease) in working capital that is reported on the statement is also identified on the work sheet. The funds statement prepared from the work sheet, including the details of the changes in each working capital component, is as follows:

T. R. Morgan Corporation
Statement of Changes in Financial Position
For Year Ended December 31, 1987

Sources of working capital:			
Operations during the year:			
Net income		$140,500	
Add deduction not decreasing working capital during the year:			
Depreciation		18,000	$158,500
Issuance of common stock at par for land			50,000
Book value of investments sold (excludes $30,000 gain reported in net income)			45,000	$253,500
Applications of working capital:			
Declaration of cash dividends		$ 30,000	
Retirement of bonds payable		125,000	
Purchase of equipment		47,000	
Purchase of land by issuance of common stock at par		50,000	252,000
Increase in working capital			$ 1,500
Changes in components of working capital:			
Increase (decrease) in current assets:			
Cash		$ 23,000	
Trade receivables (net)		9,000	
Inventories		(8,000)	
Prepaid expenses		1,000	$ 25,000
Increase (decrease) in current liabilities:			
Accounts payable		$ 18,000	
Income tax payable		(1,500)	
Dividends payable		7,000	23,500
Increase in working capital			$ 1,500

WORK SHEET PROCEDURES FOR FUNDS STATEMENT BASED ON CASH

The work sheet used to assemble the data for the funds statement based on working capital is also used to assemble data for the funds statement based on cash. The procedures differ in that the focus for the statement based on cash is on the analysis of the *noncash* accounts instead of the *noncurrent* accounts, as was the case when the statement was based on working capital. In other words, *in addition* to analyzing the changes in the noncurrent accounts, all of the current accounts *except cash* are analyzed in preparing the work sheet for the funds statement based on cash. To illustrate such a work sheet, the data for T. R. Morgan Corporation presented on page 963 are used. The work sheet prepared from these data is presented as follows:

T. R. Morgan Corporation
Work Sheet for Statement of Changes in Financial Position
For Year Ended December 31, 1987

Description	Change During Year Debit	Change During Year Credit	Work Sheet Entries Debit		Work Sheet Entries Credit	
Trade receivables	9,000				(p)	9,000
Inventories		8,000	(o)	8,000		
Prepaid expenses	1,000				(n)	1,000
Accounts payable		18,000	(m)	18,000		
Income tax payable	1,500				(l)	1,500
Dividends payable		7,000	(k)	7,000		
Investments		45,000	(j)	45,000		
Land	50,000				(i)	50,000
Building	—	—				
Accumulated depreciation—building		6,000	(h)	6,000		
Equipment	38,000		(f)	9,000	(g)	47,000
Accumulated depreciation— equipment		3,000	(e)	12,000	(f)	9,000
Bonds payable	125,000				(d)	125,000
Common stock		50,000	(c)	50,000		
Retained earnings		110,500	(a)	140,500	(b)	30,000
	224,500	247,500				
Increase in cash	23,000					
Totals	247,500	247,500				
Sources of cash:						
Operations:						
Net income					(a)	140,500
Depreciation of equipment					(e)	12,000
Depreciation of building					(h)	6,000
Decrease in income tax payable			(l)	1,500		
Increase in accounts payable					(m)	18,000
Increase in prepaid expenses			(n)	1,000		
Decrease in inventories					(o)	8,000
Increase in trade receivables			(p)	9,000		
Issuance of common stock for land					(c)	50,000
Book value of investments sold					(j)	45,000
Applications of cash:						
Declaration of cash dividends			(b)	30,000		
Increase in dividends payable					(k)	7,000
Retirement of bonds			(d)	125,000		
Purchase of equipment			(g)	47,000		
Purchase of land by issuance of common stock			(i)	50,000		
Totals				559,000		559,000

The procedures to prepare the work sheet for the funds statement based on cash are outlined as follows:

1. List the title of each *noncash* account in the Description column. For each account, enter the debit or credit representing the change (increase or decrease) in the account balance for the year in the Change During Year column.
2. Add the debits and credits in the Change During Year column and determine the subtotals. Enter the change (increase or decrease) in cash during the year in the appropriate column to balance the totals of the debits and credits.
3. Provide space in the bottom portion of the work sheet for later use in identifying the various (1) sources of cash and (2) applications of cash.
4. Analyze the change during the year in each noncash account to determine the sources and/or applications of cash related to the transactions recorded in each account. Record these sources and applications in the bottom portion of the work sheet by means of entries in the Work Sheet Entries columns.
5. Complete the work sheet.

These procedures are explained in detail in the following paragraphs.

Noncash Accounts

Since the analysis of transactions recorded in the noncash accounts reveals the sources and applications of cash, the work sheet focuses on noncash accounts. For this purpose, the titles of the noncash accounts are entered in the Description column. To facilitate reference in the illustration, noncash current accounts are listed first, followed by the noncurrent accounts. The order of the listing is not important.

The debit or credit change for the year in each account balance is entered in the Change During Year column. For example, the beginning and ending balances of Trade Receivables were $65,000 and $74,000, respectively. Thus, the change for the year was an increase, or debit, of $9,000. The changes in the other accounts are determined in a like manner.

Change in Cash

Since transactions that result in changes in cash also result in changes in the noncash accounts, the change in cash for the period will equal the change in the noncash accounts for the period. Thus, if a subtotal of the debits and credits for the noncash accounts (as indicated in the Change During Year column) is determined, the increase or decrease in cash for the period can be inserted in the appropriate column and the two columns will balance. In the illustration, the subtotal of the credit column ($247,500) exceeds the subtotal of the debit column ($224,500) by $23,000, which is identified as the increase in cash. By entering the $23,000 as a debit in the Change During Year column, the debit and credit columns are balanced. This $23,000 increase in cash will be reported on the funds statement as the difference between the total of the sources section and the total of the applications section.

If the subtotals in the Change During Year columns indicate that the debits exceed the credits, the balancing figure would be identified as a decrease in cash.

Sources and Applications of Cash

After the debit and credit columns are totaled and ruled, "Sources of cash" is written in the Description column. Several lines are skipped, so that at a later time the various sources of cash can be entered, and "Applications of cash" is written in the Description column. When the work sheet is completed, this bottom portion will contain the data necessary to prepare the sources section and the applications section of the funds statement.

To determine the various sources and applications of cash for the year, the changes in the noncash accounts are analyzed. As each account is analyzed, entries made in the work sheet relate specific sources or applications of cash to the noncash accounts. For purposes of discussion, the noncash accounts can be classified as (1) noncurrent accounts and (2) current accounts (except cash).

The analysis of the noncurrent accounts for T. R. Morgan Corporation, discussed on pages 462–464, revealed (as does the additional data presented on page 963) that the sale of investments yielded cash, that there were cash outlays for equipment and the retirement of bonds, and that land was acquired by the issuance of common stock. The effect of these transactions on both cash and working capital is therefore the same. For the statement based on cash, it is necessary to add the analysis of the current accounts (except cash).

Analysis of Noncurrent Accounts

The entries resulting from the analysis of the noncurrent accounts are summarized as follows (the letters refer to those used on the work sheet to identify the entries). These entries are identical to the entries shown on pages 966–969, except that they have been adjusted to reflect the cash concept.

(a) Retained Earnings............................ 140,500
    Sources of Cash — Operations: Net Income...... 140,500

(b) Applications of Cash — Declaration of Cash
    Dividends...................................... 30,000
        Retained Earnings.............................. 30,000

(c) Common Stock................................ 50,000
    Sources of Cash — Issuance of Common Stock
    for Land...................................... 50,000

(d) Applications of Cash — Retirement of Bonds
    Payable....................................... 125,000
        Bonds Payable................................. 125,000

(e) Accumulated Depreciation—Equipment........... 12,000
    Sources of Cash—Operations: Depreciation
    of Equipment................................. 12,000

(f) Equipment 9,000
    Accumulated Depreciation—Equipment......... 9,000

(g) Applications of Cash—Purchase of Equipment..... 47,000
    Equipment 47,000

(h) Accumulated Depreciation—Building 6,000
    Sources of Cash—Operations: Depreciation
    of Building 6,000

(i) Applications of Cash—Purchase of Land by
    Issuance of Common Stock 50,000
    Land... 50,000

(j) Investments 45,000
    Sources of Cash—Book Value of Investments
    Sold 45,000

Analysis of Current Accounts (Except Cash)

The amount of cash used to pay dividends may differ from the amount of cash dividends declared. Timing differences between the incurrence of an expense and the related cash outflow and the recognition of revenue and the receipt of cash must be considered in determining the amount of cash provided by operations. Therefore, the current accounts (other than cash) are analyzed to determine (1) cash applied to payment of dividends and (2) cash provided by operations.

Cash Applied to Payment of Dividends

The additional data indicate that $30,000 of dividends had been declared, which was identified as an application in entry (b). The $7,000 credit in the Change During Year column of the work sheet for Dividends Payable reveals a timing difference between the declaration and the payment. In other words, the $7,000 increase in Dividends Payable for the year indicates that dividends paid were $7,000 less than dividends declared. The work sheet entry to adjust the dividends declared of $30,000 to reflect the dividends paid of $23,000 is as follows:

(k) Dividends Payable 7,000
    Applications of Cash—Declaration of Cash
    Dividends: Increase in Dividends Payable.......... 7,000

When the $7,000, which represents the increase in dividends payable, is deducted from the $30,000 of "application of cash—declaration of cash dividends," $23,000 is subsequently reported on the funds statement as an application of cash.

Cash Provided by Operations

The starting point in the analysis of the effect of operations on cash is net income for the period. The effect of this amount, $140,500, is indicated by entry **(a)**. As in the earlier analysis, depreciation expense of $18,000 must be added [**(e) and (h)**] to the $140,500 because depreciation expense did not decrease the amount of cash. In addition, it is necessary to recognize the relationship of the accrual method of accounting to the movement of cash. Ordinarily, a portion of some of the other costs and expenses reported on the income statement, as well as a portion of the revenue earned, is not accompanied by cash outflow or inflow.

The effect of timing differences is indicated by the amount and the direction of change in the balances of the asset and liability accounts affected by operations. Decreases in such assets and increases in such liabilities during the period must be added to the amount reported as net income to determine the amount of cash provided by operations. Conversely, increases in such assets and decreases in such liabilities must be deducted from the amount reported as net income.

The noncash current accounts (except Dividends Payable) provide the following data that indicate the effect of timing differences on the amount of cash inflow and outflow from operations:

Accounts	Increase Decrease*
Trade receivables (net)	$ 9,000
Inventories	8,000*
Prepaid expenses	1,000
Accounts payable (merchandise creditors)	18,000
Income tax payable	1,500*

The sequence in which the noncash current accounts are analyzed is unimportant. However, to continue the sequence used in analyzing preceding accounts, the analysis illustrated will begin with the income tax payable account and proceed upward in the listing in sequential order.

Income tax payable decrease. The outlay of cash for income taxes exceeded by $1,500 the amount of income tax deducted as an expense during the period. Accordingly, $1,500 must be deducted from income to determine the amount of cash provided by operations. This procedure is indicated on the work sheet by the following entry:

(1) Sources of Cash—Operations: Decrease in Income		
Tax Payable	1,500	
Income Tax Payable		1,500

Accounts payable increase. The effect of the increase in the amount owed creditors for goods and services was to include in expired costs and expenses the sum of $18,000. Income was thereby reduced by $18,000, though there had been no cash outlay during the year. Hence, $18,000 must be added to income to determine the amount of cash provided by operations. The work sheet entry is as follows:

```
(m) Accounts Payable .............................    18,000
        Sources of Cash—Operations: Increase in
        Accounts Payable ...........................             18,000
```

Prepaid expenses increase. The outlay of cash for prepaid expenses exceeded by $1,000 the amount deducted as an expense during the year. Hence, $1,000 must be deducted from income to determine the amount of cash provided by operations. The work sheet entry is as follows:

```
(n) Sources of Cash—Operations: Increase in Prepaid
        Expenses........................................    1,000
        Prepaid Expenses ..............................             1,000
```

Inventories decrease. The $8,000 decrease in inventories indicates that the merchandise sold exceeded the cost of the merchandise purchased by $8,000. The amount reported on the income statement as a deduction from the revenue therefore included $8,000 that did not require cash outflow during the year. Accordingly, $8,000 must be added to income to determine the amount of cash provided by operations. The work sheet entry is as follows:

```
(o) Inventories........................................    8,000
        Sources of Cash—Operations: Decrease in
        Inventories......................................             8,000
```

Trade receivables (net) increase. The additions to trade receivables for sales on account during the year exceeded by $9,000 the deductions for amounts collected from customers on account. The amount reported on the income statement as sales therefore included $9,000 that did not yield cash inflow during the year. Accordingly, $9,000 must be deducted from income to determine the amount of cash provided by operations. The work sheet entry is as follows:

```
(p) Sources of Cash—Operations: Increase in Trade
        Receivables.....................................    9,000
        Trade Receivables..............................             9,000
```

Completing the Work Sheet

After all of the noncash accounts have been analyzed, all of the sources and applications are identified in the bottom portion of the work sheet. To assure the equality of the work sheet entries, the last step is to total the Work Sheet Entries columns.

Preparation of the Funds Statement

The data for the sources section and the applications section of the funds statement are obtained from the bottom portion of the work sheet. The increase (or decrease) in cash that is reported on the statement is also identified on the work sheet. The funds statement prepared from the work sheet, including the details of the changes in the cash account, is as follows:

T. R. Morgan Corporation
Statement of Changes in Financial Position
For Year Ended December 31, 1987

Sources of cash:
  Operations during the year:
    Net income............................ $140,500
    Add deductions not decreasing cash
    during the year:
      Depreciation $18,000
      Increase in accounts payable ... 18,000
      Decrease in inventories......... 8,000   44,000
                                      $184,5C0

    Deduct additions not increasing
    cash during the year:
      Decrease in income tax payable . $ 1,500
      Increase in prepaid expenses... 1,000
      Increase in trade receivables.... 9,000   11,500 $173,000
  Issuance of common stock at par for land.............   50,000
  Book value of investments sold (excludes $30,000 gain
    reported in net income)..........................   45,000 $268,000

Applications of cash:
  Payment of dividends:
    Cash dividends declared .... $ 30,000
    Deduct increase in dividends payable ..... 7,000 $ 23,000

  Retirement of bonds payable........................ 125,000
  Purchase of equipment............................. 47,000
  Purchase of land by issuance of common stock at par .. 50,000   245,000

Increase in cash...................................... $ 23,000

Change in cash balance:
  Cash balance, December 31, 1987 .... $ 49,000
  Cash balance, December 31, 1986 26,000

Increase in cash...................................... $ 23,000

STATEMENT OF CHANGES IN FINANCIAL POSITION—BASED ON CASH

APPENDIX D

General Accounting Systems for Manufacturing Operations

A general accounting system for manufacturing operations is essentially an extension of the periodic inventory procedures commonly used by merchandising enterprises. A general accounting system is fairly simple and may be used when only a single product or several similar products are manufactured and the manufacturing processes are neither complicated nor numerous. Such a situation will be assumed in the following discussion.

STATEMENT OF COST OF GOODS MANUFACTURED

Since manufacturing activities differ greatly from selling and general administration activities, it is customary to separate the two groups of accounts in the summarizing process at the end of an accounting period. In addition, the manufacturing group is usually reported in a separate **statement of cost of goods manufactured** in order to avoid a long, complicated income statement. An income statement and its supporting statement of cost of goods manufactured are illustrated on page 979.

In the statement of cost of goods manufactured, the amount listed for the work in process inventory at the beginning of the period is composed of the estimated cost of the direct materials, the direct labor, and the factory overhead applicable to the inventory of partially processed products at the end of the preceding period. The cost of the direct materials placed in production is determined by adding to the beginning inventory of materials the net cost of the direct materials purchased and deducting the ending inventory. The amount listed for direct labor is determined by referring to the direct labor account. The factory overhead costs, which are determined by referring to the

Cox Manufacturing Company
Income Statement
For Year Ended December 31, 1987

Sales		$821,400
Cost of goods sold:		
Finished goods inventory, January 1, 1987	$ 71,250	
Cost of goods manufactured	462,750	
Cost of finished goods available for sale	$534,000	
Less finished goods inventory, December 31, 1987	80,500	
Cost of goods sold		453,500

Cox Manufacturing Company
Statement of Cost of Goods Manufactured
For Year Ended December 31, 1987

Work in process inventory, January 1, 1987		$ 47,500
Direct materials:		
Inventory, January 1, 1987	$ 50,750	
Purchases	195,000	
Cost of materials available for use	$245,750	
Less inventory, December 31, 1987	48,250	
Cost of materials placed in production	$197,500	
Direct labor	145,500	
Factory overhead	116,400	
Total manufacturing costs		459,400
Total work in process during period		$506,900
Less work in process inventory, December 31, 1987		44,150
Cost of goods manufactured		$462,750

ledger, can be listed individually in the statement of cost of goods manufactured or reported in a separate schedule, as was assumed for the illustration. The sum of the costs of direct materials placed in production, the direct labor, and the factory overhead represents the total manufacturing costs incurred during the period. Addition of this amount to the beginning inventory of work in process yields the total cost of the work that has been in process during the period. The estimated cost of the ending inventory of work in process is then deducted to yield the cost of goods manufactured. The "cost of goods manufactured" reported in the statement of cost of goods manufactured and income statement is comparable to the "purchases" reported by a merchandising enterprise.

PERIODIC INVENTORY PROCEDURES

The process of adjusting the periodic inventory and other accounts of a manufacturing business is like that for a merchandising enterprise. Adjustments to the merchandise inventory account are replaced by adjusting entries for the three inventory accounts: Finished Goods, Work in Process, and Materials. The first account (Finished Goods) is adjusted through Income Summary, and the other two accounts (Work in Process and Materials) are adjusted through Manufacturing Summary.

At the end of the accounting period, the temporary accounts that appear in the statement of cost of goods manufactured are closed to Manufacturing Summary. This account's final balance, which represents the cost of goods manufactured during the period, is then closed to Income Summary. The remaining temporary accounts (Sales, Expenses, etc.) are then closed to Income Summary in the usual manner.

The relationship of the manufacturing summary account to the income summary account is illustrated as follows:

Manufacturing Summary

Dec. 31	Work in process inventory, Jan. 1	47,500	Dec. 31 Work in process inventory, Dec. 31	44,150
31	Direct materials inventory, Jan. 1	50,750	31 Direct materials inventory, Dec. 31	48,250
31	Direct materials purchases	195,000	31 To Income Summary	462,750
31	Direct labor	145,500		
31	Factory overhead	116,400		
		555,150		555,150

Income Summary

Dec. 31	Finished goods inventory, Jan. 1	71,250	Dec. 31 Finished goods inventory, Dec. 31	80,500
31	From Manufacturing Summary	462,750		

COST OF GOODS MANUFACTURED CLOSED TO INCOME SUMMARY

To simplify the illustration, the individual overhead accounts are presented as a total. Note that the balance transferred from the manufacturing summary account to the income summary account, $462,750, is the same as the final figure reported on the statement of cost of goods manufactured.

MANUFACTURING WORK SHEET

Many accountants use a work sheet to assist them in adjusting the inventory and other accounts and in the preparation of the financial statements. The work sheet used for manufacturing enterprises using periodic inventory procedures includes a column for account titles and ten money columns, arranged in five pairs of debit and credit columns. The principal headings of the five sets of money columns are as follows:

1. Trial Balance
2. Adjustments
3. Cost of Goods Manufactured
4. Income Statement
5. Balance Sheet

The following sections describe and illustrate the use of a work sheet for the manufacturing operations of Ming Manufacturing Company.

Trial Balance and Adjustments on the Work Sheet

The trial balance for Ming Manufacturing Company as of December 31, 1987, appears on the work sheet presented on pages 982-983. The data needed for year-end adjustments on December 31, 1987, are summarized as follows:

Wages payable on December 31, 1987:	
Direct labor...	$ 4,500
Indirect labor.......................................	950
Depreciation for the year:	
Factory equipment..................................	22,300
Factory buildings...................................	6,000
Inventories on December 31, 1987:	
Factory supplies....................................	1,800
Finished goods.....................................	91,000
Work in process....................................	65,800
Direct materials	58,725

Explanations of the adjusting entries in the work sheet are given in the paragraphs that follow.

Wages Payable

The liability for the wages earned by employees but not yet paid is recorded by a credit of $5,450 to Wages and Salaries Payable and debit to Direct Labor and Indirect Factory Labor of $4,500 and $950 respectively (entry (a) on the work sheet).

Depreciation

The adjustment for depreciation expense of factory equipment is recorded by a debit to Depreciation—Factory Equipment for $22,300 and a credit to Accumulated Depreciation—Factory Equipment for $22,300 (entry (b) on the work sheet). The adjustment for depreciation expense of factory buildings is recorded by a debit to Depreciation Factory Buildings for $6,000 and a credit to Accumulated Depreciation—Factory Buildings for $6,000 (entry (c) on the work sheet).

MING MANUFACTURING
Work
For Year Ended

ACCOUNT TITLE	TRIAL BALANCE		ADJUSTMENTS	
	DEBIT	CREDIT	DEBIT	CREDIT
Cash...	18,200			
Accounts Receivable............................	66,100			
Allowance for Doubtful Accounts		1,500		
Finished Goods	78,500		(f) 91,000	(e) 78,500
Work in Process.................................	55,000		(h) 65,800	(g) 55,000
Direct Materials.................................	62,000		(j) 58,725	(i) 62,000
Factory Supplies	4,700			(d) 2,900
Prepaid Insurance	1,250			
Land...	50,000			
Factory Buildings	240,000			
Accumulated Depreciation—Factory Buildings........		30,000		(c) 6,000
Factory Equipment..............................	446,000			
Accumulated Depreciation—Factory Equipment		111,500		(b) 22,300
Accounts Payable...............................		45,600		
Wages and Salaries Payable......................				(a) 5,450
Income Tax Payable		13,200		
Common Stock ($10 par)..........................		200,000		
Retained Earnings...............................		537,325		
Dividends......................................	40,000			
Income Summary................................			(e) 78,500	(f) 91,000
Manufacturing Summary..........................			(g) 55,000	(h) 65,800
			(i) 62,000	(j) 58,725
Sales..		915,800		
Direct Materials Purchases	220,800			
Direct Labor....................................	214,250		(a) 4,500	
Indirect Factory Labor............................	48,350		(a) 950	
Depreciation—Factory Equipment..................			(b) 22,300	
Factory Heat, Light, and Power	21,800			
Factory Property Taxes...........................	9,750			
Depreciation—Factory Buildings			(c) 6,000	
Insurance Expense—Factory	4,750			
Factory Supplies Expense			(d) 2,900	
Miscellaneous Factory Expense	2,050			
Selling Expenses	130,500			
General Expenses...............................	88,700			
Income Tax.....................................	52,225			
	1,854,925	1,854,925	447,675	447,675
Cost of Goods Manufactured......................				
Net Income				

Factory Supplies

The $4,700 balance of factory supplies in the trial balance is the cost of supplies on hand at the beginning of the year and the cost of supplies purchased during the year. The amount on hand at the end of the year (inventory) is $1,800. The excess of $2,900 over the inventory of $1,800 represents the supplies used, and the adjustment is a debit to Factory Supplies Expense and a credit to Factory Supplies for $2,900 (entry (d) on the work sheet).

General Accounting Systems for Manufacturing Operations

COMPANY
Sheet
December 31, 1987

STATEMENT OF COST OF GOODS MANUFACTURED		INCOME STATEMENT		BALANCE SHEET	
DEBIT	CREDIT	DEBIT	CREDIT	DEBIT	CREDIT
				18,200	
				66,100	1,500
				91,000	
				65,800	
				58,725	
				1,800	
				1,250	
				50,000	
				240,000	
					36,000
				446,000	
					133,800
					45,600
					5,450
					13,200
					200,000
					537,325
				40,000	
		78,500	91,000		
55,000	65,800				
62,000	58,725		915,800		
220,800					
218,750					
49,300					
22,300					
21,800					
9,750					
6,000					
4,750					
2,900					
2,050		130,500			
		88,700			
		52,225			
675,400	124,525				
	550,875	550,875			
675,400	675,400	900,800	1,006,800	1,078,875	972,875
		106,000			106,000
		1,006,800	1,006,800	1,078,875	1,078,875

Finished Goods Inventory

The finished goods inventory account is adjusted through the income summary account. The beginning finished goods inventory is transferred to the income summary account by crediting Finished Goods and debiting Income Summary for $78,500 (entry (e) on the work sheet). The ending finished goods inventory is recorded by debiting Finished Goods and crediting Income Summary for $91,000 (entry (f) on the work sheet).

Work in Process Inventory

As explained in a preceding section, the work in process inventory account is adjusted through Manufacturing Summary. The inventory of work in process at the beginning of the period is transferred to the manufacturing summary account by crediting Work in Process and debiting Manufacturing Summary for $55,000 (entry (g) on the work sheet). The ending work in process inventory is recorded by debiting Work in Process and crediting Manufacturing Summary for $65,800 (entry (h) on the work sheet).

Direct Materials Inventory

Like the work in process inventory, the direct materials inventory at the beginning of the fiscal period is transferred to the manufacturing summary account by crediting Direct Materials and debiting Manufacturing Summary for $62,000 (entry (i) on the work sheet). The direct materials inventory at the end of the period is recorded by debiting Direct Materials and crediting Manufacturing Summary for $58,725 (entry (j) on the work sheet).

Completing the Work Sheet

After all the adjustments have been entered on the work sheet, each account balance, as adjusted, is then extended to the proper financial statement columns. The temporary accounts that appear in the statement of cost of goods manufactured are extended to the statement of cost of goods manufactured columns. The other accounts are extended to the income statement and balance sheet columns as appropriate. Note that the beginning and ending inventory amounts appearing opposite Income Summary and Manufacturing Summary in the adjustments column are extended individually rather than as the net figure, since both amounts will be used in preparing the statements.

After all of the amounts have been extended to the appropriate columns, the work sheet is completed in the following manner:

(1) The statement of cost of goods manufactured columns are totaled. In the illustration, the total of the debit column is $675,400 and the total of the credit column is $124,525.

(2) The amount of the difference between the two statement of cost of goods manufactured columns is determined and entered in the statement of cost of goods manufactured credit column and the income statement debit column. This amount ($550,875 in the illustration) is the cost of goods manufactured for the period.

(3) The totals of the statement of cost of goods manufactured columns are then entered. The columns should now be in balance.

(4) The income statement columns and the balance sheet columns are totaled. The difference between the debits and credits in each of the two sets of columns is the amount of net income or loss for the period. This

amount (net income of $106,000 in the illustration) is then entered as a balancing figure on the work sheet. For Ming Manufacturing Company, the net income of $106,000 is entered in the income statement debit column and in the balance sheet credit column.

(5) The totals of the last four columns, which should now be in balance, are entered.

FINANCIAL STATEMENTS

The completed work sheet provides the information necessary for preparing the financial statements. For Ming Manufacturing Company, the income statement, statement of cost of goods manufactured, retained earnings statement, and balance sheet are shown below and on pages 986-987. It should be noted that the factory overhead items are listed separately in the statement of cost of goods manufactured. An alternative would be to report the items in a separate schedule and list only the total in the statement of cost of goods manufactured.

INCOME
STATEMENT

Ming Manufacturing Company
Income Statement
For Year Ended December 31, 1987

Sales		$915,800
Cost of goods sold:		
Finished goods inventory, January 1, 1987	$ 78,500	
Cost of goods manufactured	550,875	
Cost of finished goods available for sale	$629,375	
Less finished goods inventory, December 31, 1987	91,000	
Cost of goods sold		538,375
Gross profit		$377,425
Operating expenses:		
Selling expenses	$130,500	
General expenses	88,700	
Total operating expenses		219,200
Income before income tax		$158,225
Income tax		52,225
Net income (per share, $5.30)		$106,000

Ming Manufacturing Company
Statement of Cost of Goods Manufactured
For Year Ended December 31, 1987

Work in process inventory, January 1, 1987.....		$ 55,000
Direct materials:		
Inventory, January 1, 1987.................	$ 62,000	
Purchases................................	220,800	
Cost of materials available for use..........	$282,800	
Less inventory, December 31, 1987.........	58,725	
Cost of materials placed in production.....	$224,075	
Direct labor..............................	218,750	
Factory overhead:		
Indirect labor............................	$49,300	
Depreciation of factory equipment...........	22,300	
Heat, light, and power.....................	21,800	
Property taxes............................	9,750	
Depreciation on buildings..................	6,000	
Insurance expired.........................	4,750	
Factory supplies used......................	2,900	
Miscellaneous factory costs................	2,050	
Total factory overhead...................	118,850	
Total manufacturing costs....................		561,675
Total work in process during period............		$616,675
Less work in process inventory, December 31, 1987......................................		65,800
Cost of goods manufactured.................		$550,875

Ming Manufacturing Company
Retained Earnings Statement
For Year Ended December 31, 1987

Retained earnings, January 1, 1987...................		$537,325
Net income for year................................	$106,000	
Less dividends....................................	40,000	
Increase in retained earnings.......................		66,000
Retained earnings, December 31, 1987................		$603,325

Ming Manufacturing Company
Balance Sheet
December 31, 1987

Assets

Current assets:

Cash		$ 18,200
Accounts receivable	$ 66,100	
Less allowance for doubtful accounts	1,500	64,600

Inventories:

Finished goods	$ 91,000	
Work in process	65,800	
Direct materials	58,725	215,525
Factory supplies		1,800
Prepaid insurance		1,250
Total current assets		$301,375

Plant assets:

Land		$ 50,000
Buildings	$240,000	
Less accumulated depreciation	36,000	204,000
Factory equipment	$446,000	
Less accumulated depreciation	133,800	312,200
Total plant assets		566,200
Total assets		$867,575

Liabilities

Current liabilities:

Accounts payable	$ 45,600
Wages and salaries payable	5,450
Income tax payable	13,200
Total current liabilities	$ 64,250

Stockholders' Equity

Common stock, $10 par	$200,000
Retained earnings	603,325
Total stockholders' equity	803,325
Total liabilities and stockholders' equity	$867,575

ADJUSTING ENTRIES

At the end of the accounting period, the adjusting entries appearing in the work sheet are recorded in the journal and posted to the ledger, bringing the ledger into agreement with the data reported in the financial statements. The adjusting entries for Ming Manufacturing Company are as follows:

Adjusting Entries

(a) Direct Labor	4,500	
Indirect Factory Labor	950	
Wages and Salaries Payable		5,450
(b) Depreciation—Factory Equipment	22,300	
Accumulated Depreciation—Factory Equipment		22,300
(c) Depreciation—Factory Buildings	6,000	
Accumulated Depreciation—Factory Buildings		6,000
(d) Factory Supplies Expense	2,900	
Factory Supplies		2,900
(e) Income Summary	78,500	
Finished Goods		78,500
(f) Finished Goods	91,000	
Income Summary		91,000
(g) Manufacturing Summary	55,000	
Work in Process		55,000
(h) Work in Process	65,800	
Manufacturing Summary		65,800
(i) Manufacturing Summary	62,000	
Direct Materials		62,000
(j) Direct Materials	58,725	
Manufacturing Summary		58,725

CLOSING ENTRIES

The closing entries are recorded in the general journal immediately following the adjusting entries, illustrated as follows:

Closing Entries

Manufacturing Summary	558,400	
Direct Materials Purchases		220,800
Direct Labor		218,750
Indirect Factory Labor		49,300
Depreciation—Factory Equipment		22,300
Factory Heat, Light, and Power		21,800
Factory Property Taxes		9,750
Depreciation—Factory Buildings		6,000
Insurance Expense—Factory		4,750
Factory Supplies Expense		2,900
Miscellaneous Factory Expense		2,050
Sales	915,800	
Income Summary		915,800
Income Summary	822,300	
Selling Expenses		130,500
General Expenses		88,700
Income Tax		52,225
Manufacturing Summary		550,875
Income Summary	106,000	
Retained Earnings		106,000
Retained Earnings	40,000	
Dividends		40,000

The manufacturing accounts are closed to Manufacturing Summary. The revenue account, Sales, is closed to Income Summary. The expense accounts, including the balance in Manufacturing Summary ($550,875, which represents the cost of goods manufactured), are also closed to Income Summary. The final steps in the closing process are to close the balance in Income Summary (representing the net income) and Dividends to Retained Earnings.

D-1. The following accounts related to manufacturing operations were selected from the pre-closing trial balance of Thomas Co. at December 31, the end of the current fiscal year:

Problems

Depreciation of Factory Buildings.	$ 19,000
Depreciation of Factory Equipment	30,000
Direct Labor	210,600
Direct Materials Inventory	59,100
Direct Materials Purchases	290,500
Factory Supplies Expense	5,150
Finished Goods Inventory	87,750
Heat, Light, and Power Expense	29,750
Indirect Labor	47,250
Insurance Expense	9,000
Miscellaneous Factory Costs	4,850
Property Taxes Expense	12,500
Work in Process Inventory.	61,500

Inventories at December 31 were as follows:

Finished Goods	$ 90,000
Work in Process	72,000
Direct Materials	70,500

Instructions:

(1) Prepare a statement of cost of goods manufactured.
(2) Prepare journal entries to adjust the work in process and direct materials inventories.
(3) Prepare journal entries to close the appropriate accounts to Manufacturing Summary.
(4) Prepare the journal entry to close Manufacturing Summary.

D-2. The work sheet for Centennial Manufacturing Company, for the current year ended August 31, 1987, is presented in the working papers. Data concerning account titles, trial balance amounts, and selected adjustments have been entered on the work sheet.

Instructions:

(1) Enter the six adjustments required for the inventories on the work sheet. Additional adjustment data are:

Finished goods inventory at August 31	$109,200
Work in process inventory at August 31	78,960
Direct materials inventory at August 31	70,470

(If the working papers correlating with the textbook are not used, omit Problem D-2.)

continued

(2) Complete the work sheet.
(3) Prepare a statement of cost of goods manufactured.
(4) Prepare an income statement.
(5) Prepare a retained earnings statement.
(6) Prepare a balance sheet.

D-3. The chief accountant for Adams Co. prepared the following manufacturing work sheet for the current year:

ADAMS
Work
For Year Ended

ACCOUNT TITLE	TRIAL BALANCE		ADJUSTMENTS	
	DEBIT	CREDIT	DEBIT	CREDIT
Cash	20,450			
Accounts Receivable	75,500			
Allowance for Doubtful Accounts		1,800		
Finished Goods	88,500		(f) 99,000	(e) 88,500
Work in Process	75,000		(h) 65,800	(g) 75,000
Direct Materials	62,800		(j) 58,725	(i) 62,800
Prepaid Insurance	8,700			(k) 5,900
Factory Supplies	8,250			(d) 5,250
Land	75,000			
Factory Buildings	290,000			
Accumulated Depreciation—Factory Buildings		170,000		(c) 16,000
Factory Equipment	446,000			
Accumulated Depreciation—Factory Equipment		211,500		(b) 22,300
Accounts Payable		55,900		
Wages Payable				(a) 4,550
Income Tax Payable		8,200		
Common Stock ($20 par)		300,000		
Retained Earnings		331,025		
Dividends	60,000			
Income Summary			(e) 88,500	(f) 99,000
Manufacturing Summary			(g) 75,000	(h) 65,800
			(i) 62,800	(j) 58,725
Sales		785,500		
Direct Materials Purchases	184,800			
Direct Labor	174,250		(a) 3,800	
Indirect Factory Labor	47,250		(a) 750	
Depreciation—Factory Equipment			(b) 22,300	
Factory Heat, Light, Power	31,800			
Factory Property Taxes	12,750			
Depreciation—Factory Buildings			(c) 16,000	
Insurance Expense—Factory			(k) 5,900	
Factory Supplies Expense			(d) 5,250	
Miscellaneous Factory Expense	3,650			
Selling Expenses	100,500			
General Expenses	58,500			
Income Tax	40,225			
	1,863,925	1,863,925	503,825	503,825
Cost of Goods Manufactured				
Net Income				

Instructions:

(1) Prepare a statement of cost of goods manufactured.
(2) Prepare an income statement.
(3) Prepare a retained earnings statement.
(4) Prepare a balance sheet.

CO.
Sheet
December 31, 19--

STATEMENT OF COST OF GOODS MANUFACTURED		INCOME STATEMENT		BALANCE SHEET	
DEBIT	CREDIT	DEBIT	CREDIT	DEBIT	CREDIT
				20,450	
				75,500	
					1,800
				99,000	
				65,800	
				58,725	
				2,800	
				3,000	
				75,000	
				290,000	
					186,000
				446,000	
					233,800
					55,900
					4,550
					8,200
					300,000
					331,025
				60,000	
		88,500	99,000		
75,000	65,800				
62,800	58,725		785,500		
184,800					
178,050					
48,000					
22,300					
31,800					
12,750					
16,000					
5,900					
5,250					
3,650					
		100,500			
		58,500			
		40,225			
646,300	124,525				
	521,775	521,775			
646,300	646,300	809,500	884,500	1,196,275	1,121,275
		75,000			75,000
		884,500	884,500	1,196,275	1,196,275

D-4. The accounts in the ledger of Payne Manufacturing Inc., with unadjusted balances on December 31, the end of the current year, are as follows:

Cash	30,550
Accounts Receivable	47,450
Allowance for Doubtful Accounts	900
Finished Goods	53,150
Work in Process	36,500
Direct Materials	34,100
Prepaid Expenses (Controlling)	10,000
Land	50,000
Factory Buildings	260,000
Accumulated Depreciation—Factory Buildings	90,000
Factory Equipment	172,650
Accumulated Depreciation—Factory Equipment	97,950
Office Equipment	30,000
Accumulated Depreciation—Office Equipment	10,000
Accounts Payable	40,400
Income Tax Payable	—
Wages Payable	—
Common Stock ($25 par)	300,000
Retained Earnings	120,300
Dividends	20,000
Income Summary	—
Manufacturing Summary	—
Sales	668,500
Direct Materials Purchases	197,000
Direct Labor	178,900
Factory Overhead (Controlling)	65,150
Selling Expenses (Controlling)	70,275
General Expenses (Controlling)	45,825
Interest Expense	3,500
Income Tax	23,000

The data needed for the year-end adjustments on December 31 are as follows:

Doubtful accounts at December 31 from analysis of accounts receivable		$ 2,400
Prepaid insurance expired during year:		
Factory overhead	$ 4,800	
General expenses	1,100	5,900
Accrued wages at December 31:		
Direct labor	$ 2,900	
Indirect labor	500	3,400
Depreciation expense for year:		
Factory building	$ 8,000	
Factory equipment	16,700	
Office equipment	2,600	27,300

General Accounting Systems for Manufacturing Operations

Income tax owed at December 31..........................		$ 8,500
Inventories on December 31:		
Finished goods.......................................	$55,000	
Work in process......................................	38,500	
Direct materials	33,150	126,650

Instructions:

(1) Prepare a manufacturing work sheet. (Leave one extra line after Manufacturing Summary and two extra lines after Factory Overhead and General Expenses for use in recording the adjusting entries.)

(2) Prepare a statement of cost of goods manufactured.

(3) Prepare an income statement.

(4) Prepare a retained earnings statement.

(5) Prepare a balance sheet.

APPENDIX E

Annual Reports and Specimen Financial Statements

Corporations ordinarily issue to their stockholders and other interested parties annual reports summarizing activities of the past year and any significant plans for the future. Although there are many differences in the form and sequence of the major sections of annual reports, one section is always devoted to the financial statements, including the accompanying notes. In addition, annual reports usually include (a) selected data referred to as financial highlights, (b) a letter from the president of the corporation, which is sometimes also signed by the chairperson of the board of directors, (c) the independent auditor's report, (d) the management report, and (e) a five- or ten-year historical summary of financial data. A description of financial reporting for segments of a business, supplemental data on effects of price-level changes, and interim financial reports may also be included, either separately or as footnotes to the financial statements.

The following paragraphs describe the portions of annual reports commonly related to financial matters. This appendix concludes with specimen financial statements that illustrate the actual financial reporting practices of a small, privately held company (Carter Manufacturing Company) and a large, publicly held company (The Coca Cola Company). Because privately held companies are not required to release their financial statements to the public, the Carter Manufacturing Company statements were modified to protect the confidentiality of the company. We are grateful for the assistance of the public accounting firm of Deloitte Haskins & Sells and Mr. Mark Young in developing these statements.

FINANCIAL HIGHLIGHTS

This section, sometimes called *Results in Brief*, typically summarizes the major financial results for the last year or two. It is usually presented on the first one or two pages of the annual report. Such items as sales, income before income taxes, net income, net income per common share, cash dividends, cash dividends per common share, and the amount of capital expenditures are typically presented. An example of a financial highlights section from a corporation's annual report is as follows:

FINANCIAL HIGHLIGHTS SECTION

FINANCIAL HIGHLIGHTS

(Dollars in thousands except per share amounts)

For the Year	Current Year	Preceding Year
Sales.................................	$1,336,750	$ 876,400
Income before income tax.....................	149,550	90,770
Net income	105,120	66,190
Per common share	4.03	2.62
Dividends declared on common stock	34,990	33,150
Per common share	1.48	1.40
Capital expenditures and investments	265,120	157,050
At Year-End		
Working capital..............................	$ 415,410	$ 423,780
Total assets.................................	1,712,170	1,457,240
Long-term debt..............................	440,680	457,350
Stockholders' equity	840,350	692,950

There are many variations in format and content of the financial highlights section of the annual report. In addition to the selected income statement data, information about the financial position at year end, such as the amount of working capital (excess of current assets over current liabilities), total assets, long-term debt, and stockholders' equity, is often provided. Other year-end data often reported are the number of common and preferred shares outstanding, number of common and preferred stockholders, and number of employees.

PRESIDENT'S LETTER

A letter by the president to the stockholders, discussing such items as reasons for an increase or decrease in net income, changes in existing plant or purchase or construction of new plants, significant new financing commitments, attention given to social responsibility issues, and future prospects, is also found in most annual reports. A condensed version of a president's letter adapted from a corporation's annual report is as follows:

To the Stockholders:

FISCAL YEAR REVIEWED

The record net income in this fiscal year resulted from very strong product demand experienced for about two thirds of the fiscal year, more complete utilization of plants, and a continued improvement in sales mix. Income was strong both domestically and internationally during this period.

PLANT EXPANSION CONTINUES

Capital expenditures during the year were $14.5 million. Expansions were in progress or completed at all locations. Portions of the Company's major new expansion at one of its West Coast plants came on stream in March of this year and will provide much needed capacity in existing and new product areas. Capital expenditures will be somewhat less during next year.

ENVIRONMENTAL CONCERN

The Company recognizes its responsibility to provide a safe and healthy environment at each of its plants. The Company expects to spend approximately $1 million in the forthcoming year to help continue its position as a constructive corporate citizen.

OUTLOOK

During the past 10 years the Company's net income and sales have more than tripled. Net income increased from $3.1 million to $10.7 million, and sales from $45 million to $181 million.

The Company's employees are proud of this record and are determined to carry the momentum into the future. The current economic slowdown makes results for the new fiscal year difficult to predict. However, we are confident and enthusiastic about the Company's prospects for continued growth over the longer term.

Respectfully submitted,

Frances B. Davis

Frances B. Davis
President

March 24, 19--

During recent years, corporate enterprises have become increasingly active in accepting environmental and other social responsibilities. In addition to the brief discussion that may be contained in the president's letter, a more detailed analysis of the company's social concerns may be included elsewhere in the annual report. Knowledgeable investors recognize that the failure of a business enterprise to meet acceptable social norms can have long-run unfavorable implications. In the near future, an important function of accounting may be to assist management in developing a statement of social responsibilities of corporate enterprises and what management is doing about them.

INDEPENDENT AUDITORS' REPORT

Before issuing annual statements, all publicly held corporations, as well as many other corporations, engage independent public accountants, usually CPAs, to conduct an *examination* of the financial statements. Such an examination is for the purpose of adding credibility to the statements that have been prepared by management. Upon completion of the examination, which for large corporations may engage many accountants for several weeks or longer, an **independent auditors' report** is prepared. This report accompanies the financial statements. A typical report briefly describes, in two paragraphs, (1) the scope of the auditors' examination and (2) their opinion as to the fairness of the statements. The wording used in the following report conforms with general usage.[1]

INDEPENDENT
AUDITORS'
REPORT SECTION

To the Stockholders of X Corporation:

We have examined the balance sheet of X Corporation as of December 31, 19-- and the related statements of income and retained earnings and changes in financial position for the year then ended. Our examination was made in accordance with generally accepted auditing standards, and accordingly included such tests of the accounting records and such other auditing procedures as we considered necessary in the circumstances.

In our opinion, the aforementioned financial statements present fairly the financial position of X Corporation at December 31, 19--, and the results of its operations and the changes in its financial position for the year then ended, in conformity with generally accepted accounting principles applied on a basis consistent with that of the preceding year.

Cincinnati, Ohio   *Gordon and Staun*
January 28, 19--   Certified Public Accountants

In most instances, the auditors can render a report such as the one illustrated, which may be said to be "unqualified." However, it is possible that accounting methods used by a client do not conform with generally accepted accounting principles or that a client has not been consistent in the application of principles. In such cases, a "qualified" opinion must be rendered and the exception briefly described. If the effect of the departure from accepted principles is sufficiently material, an "adverse" or negative opinion must be issued and the exception described. In rare circumstances, the auditors may be unable to perform sufficient auditing procedures to enable them to reach a conclusion as to the fairness of the financial statements. In such circumstances, the auditors must issue a "disclaimer" and briefly describe the reasons for their failure to be able to reach a decision as to the fairness of the statements.

Professional accountants cannot disregard their responsibility in attesting to the fairness of financial statements without seriously jeopardizing their reputations. This responsibility is described as follows:

The report shall either contain an expression of opinion regarding the financial statements, taken as a whole, or an assertion to the effect that an opinion cannot be expressed. When an overall opinion cannot be expressed, the reasons therefor should be stated. In all cases where an auditor's name is

---

[1]*Codification of Statements on Auditing Standards* (New York: American Institute of Certified Public Accountants, 1985), par. 509.07.

associated with financial statements, the report should contain a clear-cut indication of the character of the auditor's examination, if any, and the degree of responsibility he is taking.[2]

MANAGEMENT REPORT

Responsibility for the accounting system and the resultant financial statements rests mainly with the principal officers of a corporation. In the **management report,** the chief financial officer or other representative of management (1) states that the financial statements are management's responsibility and that they have been prepared according to generally accepted accounting principles, (2) presents management's assessment of the company's internal accounting control system, and (3) comments on any other pertinent matters related to the accounting system, the financial statements, and the examination by the independent auditor.

Although the concept of a management report is relatively new, an increasing number of corporations are including such a report in the annual report. An example of such a report is as follows:

MANAGEMENT
REPORT SECTION

REPORT BY MANAGEMENT

Financial Statements

We prepared the accompanying balance sheet of X Corporation as of December 31, 19--, and the related statements of income, retained earnings, and changes in financial position for the year then ended. The statements have been prepared in conformity with generally accepted accounting principles appropriate in the circumstances, and necessarily include some amounts that are based on our best estimates and judgments.

Internal Accounting Controls

The company maintains an accounting system and related controls to provide reasonable assurance that assets are safeguarded against loss from unauthorized use or disposition and that the financial records are reliable for preparing financial statements and maintaining accountability for assets. The concept of reasonable assurance is based on the recognition that the cost of a system of internal control should not exceed the benefits derived and that the evaluation of those factors requires estimates and judgments by management.

Other Matters

The functioning of the accounting system and related controls is under the general oversight of the board of directors. The accounting system and related controls are reviewed by an extensive program of internal audits and by the company's independent auditors.

James O. Hiller

James O. Hiller
Chief Financial Officer

March 24, 19--

---

[2]*Ibid.,* par. 509.04.

HISTORICAL SUMMARY OF FINANCIAL DATA

This section, for which there are many variations in title, reports selected financial and operating data of past periods, usually for five or ten years. It is usually presented in close proximity to the financial statements for the current year, and the types of data reported are varied. An example of a portion of such a report is presented below.

HISTORICAL
SUMMARY SECTION

Five-Year Consolidated Financial and Statistical Summary
for Years Ended December 31
(Dollar amounts in millions except for per share data)

For the Year	1986	1985	1982
Net sales	$1,759.7	$1,550.1	$ 997.4
Gross profit	453.5	402.8	270.8
Percent to net sales	25.8%	26.0%	27.2%
Interest expense	33.9	21.3	15.0
Income before income tax	172.7	163.4	87.5
Income tax	82.8	77.8	40.2
Net income	89.9	85.6	47.3
Percent to net sales	5.1%	5.5%	4.7%
Per common share:			
Net income	5.19	4.84	2.54
Dividends	1.80	1.65	1.40
Return on stockholders' equity	15.9%	16.4%	11.2%
Common share market price:			
High	31	41½	40⅝
Low	18	22⅜	22¼
Depreciation and amortization	43.3	41.0	23.6
Capital expenditures	98.5	72.1	55.5
At Year End			
Working capital	$ 443.9	$ 434.8	$ 254.6
Plant assets—gross	704.7	620.3	453.7
Plant assets—net	420.0	362.7	263.4
Stockholders' equity	594.3	536.9	447.6
Stockholders' equity per common share	33.07	29.69	23.02
Number of holders of common shares	39,503	39,275	43,852
Number of employees	50,225	50,134	42,826

FINANCIAL REPORTING FOR SEGMENTS OF A BUSINESS

Conglomerates, or companies that diversify their operations, make up a large number of the total business enterprises in the United States. The individual segments of a diversified company ordinarily experience differing rates of profitability, degrees of risk, and opportunities for growth. For example, one prominent diversified company is involved in such diverse markets as telecommunications equipment, industrial products, automotive and consumer products, natural resources, defense and space programs, food processing, financial services, and insurance.

To help financial statement users in assessing the past performance and the future potential of an enterprise, financial reports should disclose such information as the enterprise's operations in different industries, its foreign markets, and its major customers. The required information for each significant reporting segment includes the following: revenue, income from operations, and identifiable assets associated with the segment.[3] This information may be included within the body of the statements or in accompanying notes. An example of a note disclosing segment information is as follows:

REPORTING FOR
SEGMENTS

NOTE 11 — SEGMENT REPORTING
The following industry and geographic segment data (dollars in millions) are reported in accordance with *Financial Accounting Standards Board Statement No. 14.*

	Airline Operations	Hotel Operations	Food Services	Total
Revenues:				
United States.................	$ 293.1	$129.7	$ 95.7	$ 518.5
Foreign	187.7	46.5	31.3	265.5
Total....................	$ 480.8	$176.2	$127.0	$ 784.0
Income from operations:				
United States.................	$ 4.7	$ 12.1	$ 3.9	$ 20.7
Foreign	8.1	5.1	1.0	14.2
Total....................	$ 12.8	$ 17.2	$ 4.9	$ 34.9
Assets:				
United States.................	$1,010.0	$391.5	$112.1	$1,513.6
Foreign	617.5	91.2	47.0	755.7
Total....................	$1,627.5	$482.7	$159.1	$2,269.3

[3]*Statement of Financial Accounting Standards, No. 14,* "Financial Reporting for Segments of a Business Enterprise" (Stamford: Financial Accounting Standards Board, 1976). Nonpublic corporations are exempted from this requirement by *Statement of Financial Accounting Standards, No. 21,* "Suspension of the Reporting of Earnings per Share and Segment Information by Nonpublic Enterprises" (Stamford: Financial Accounting Standards Board, 1978).

SUPPLEMENTAL DATA ON THE EFFECTS OF PRICE-LEVEL CHANGES

Financial statements are expressed in terms of money. Because money changes in value as prices change, changing price levels will affect financial reporting. Chapter 28 discusses two recommendations for supplementing conventional financial statements with supplemental data on the effects of price-level changes. The Financial Accounting Standards Board currently requires approximately 1,300 large, publicly held corporations to disclose supplemental data, using either current cost or constant dollar information.[4]

INTERIM FINANCIAL REPORTS

Corporate enterprises customarily issue interim financial reports to their stockholders. Corporations that are listed on a stock exchange or file reports with the Securities and Exchange Commission or other regulatory agencies are required to submit interim reports, usually on a quarterly basis. Such reports often have a significant influence on the valuation of a corporation's equity securities on stock exchanges.

Quarterly income statements, which are ordinarily included in interim financial reports, are usually quite brief and report comparative figures for the comparable period of the preceding year. When interim balance sheets or statements of changes in financial position are issued, they are also severely condensed and accompanied by comparative data. Interim reports of an enterprise should disclose such information as gross revenue, costs and expenses, provision for income taxes, extraordinary or infrequently occurring items, net income, earnings per share, contingent items, and significant changes in financial position.[5] The particular accounting principles used on an annual basis, such as depreciation methods and inventory cost flow assumptions, are usually followed in preparing interim statements. However, if changes in accounting principles occur before the end of a fiscal year, there are detailed guidelines for their disclosure.[6]

Much of the value of interim financial reports to the investing public is based on their timeliness. Lengthy delays between the end of a quarter and the issuance of reports would greatly reduce their value. This is one of the reasons that interim reports are usually not audited by independent CPAs. In some cases, the interim reports are subjected to a "limited review" by the CPA and a report on this limited review is issued.

---

[4]*Statement of Financial Accounting Standards, No. 33*, "Financial Reporting and Changing Prices" and *Statement of Financial Accounting Standards, No. 82*, "Financial Reporting and Changing Prices: Elimination of Certain Disclosures" (Stamford: Financial Accounting Standards Board, 1979 and 1984).

[5]*Opinions of the Accounting Principles Board, No. 28*, "Interim Financial Reporting" (New York: American Institute of Certified Public Accountants, 1973).

[6]*Statement of Financial Accounting Standards, No. 3*, "Reporting Accounting Changes in Interim Financial Statements" (Stamford: Financial Accounting Standards Board, 1974).

SPECIMEN FINANCIAL STATEMENTS

AUDITORS' OPINION

Carter Manufacturing Company:

We have examined the balance sheets of Carter Manufacturing Company as of December 31, 1985 and 1984, and the related statements of income and retained earnings and of changes in financial position for the years then ended. Our examinations were made in accordance with generally accepted auditing standards and, accordingly, included such tests of the accounting records and such other auditing procedures as we considered necessary in the circumstances.

In our opinion, the accompanying financial statements present fairly the financial position of Carter Manufacturing Company as of December 31, 1985 and 1984, and the results of its operations and the changes in its financial position for the years then ended, in conformity with generally accepted accounting principles consistently applied.

Masters & Young

February 22, 1986
Atlanta, Georgia

CARTER MANUFACTURING COMPANY

BALANCE SHEETS, DECEMBER 31, 1985 and 1984

ASSETS	NOTES	1985	1984
CURRENT ASSETS:			
Cash:			
Cash in bank.............................		$ 38,526	$ 88,443
Petty cash		7,650	12,300
Savings certificates		375,000	235,344
Marketable securities	2,5	332,238	361,842
Receivables:			
Customers—less allowance for doubtful accounts of $486,000 in 1985 and $45,000 in 1984	3	2,979,197	2,809,352
Dividends.............................		2,157	2,091
Interest................................		16,680	6,288
Other.................................		20,736	8,034
Inventories...............................	4	5,927,631	6,033,126
Prepaid insurance		38,604	45,234
Other prepayments		22,566	32,586
Total current assets.......................		9,760,985	9,634,640
PLANT AND EQUIPMENT:			
Machinery and equipment		2,901,148	2,788,225
Delivery equipment		745,893	771,873
Furniture and fixtures		214,119	214,437
Leasehold improvements		97,758	94,011
Total		3,958,918	3,868,546
Less accumulated depreciation and amortization.............................		2,172,171	2,085,417
Plant and equipment—net.................		1,786,747	1,783,129
TOTAL ASSETS...........................		$11,547,732	$11,417,769

See notes to financial statements.

LIABILITIES AND SHAREHOLDERS' EQUITY	NOTES	1985	1984
CURRENT LIABILITIES:			
Trade accounts payable		$ 1,804,807	$ 1,700,652
Due under line of credit	5	120,000	180,000
Current portion of long-term debt	6	266,676	236,709
Accrued salaries, wages and commissions		369,009	194,910
Accrued and withheld payroll taxes		69,267	144,111
Income taxes payable		48,081	37,287
Contributions to employee benefit plans	8	277,521	100,647
Accrued rent		67,500	270,000
Total current liabilities		3,022,861	2,864,316
LONG-TERM DEBT	6,7,9	1,028,682	1,295,358
DEFERRED INCOME TAXES		56,091	44,877
SHAREHOLDERS' EQUITY:			
Capital stock — authorized and outstanding, 172,000 shares of $3 par value		516,000	516,000
Additional paid-in capital		36,927	36,927
Retained earnings		6,887,171	6,660,291
Shareholders' equity		7,440,098	7,213,218
TOTAL LIABILITIES AND SHAREHOLDERS' EQUITY		$11,547,732	$11,417,769

CARTER MANUFACTURING COMPANY

STATEMENTS OF INCOME AND RETAINED EARNINGS FOR THE YEARS ENDED DECEMBER 31, 1985 AND 1984

	NOTE	1985	1984
SALES (Less returns of $237,782 in 1985 and $345,762 in 1984)		$23,555,271	$23,401,635
COST OF GOODS SOLD		17,130,648	17,767,857
GROSS PROFIT		6,424,623	5,633,778
SELLING AND GENERAL EXPENSES.		6,136,161	5,406,762
INCOME FROM OPERATIONS		288,462	227,016
OTHER INCOME (EXPENSES):			
Interest.		167,978	84,732
Dividends.		50,268	50,124
Sale of waste materials, etc.		183,526	91,365
Gain from sale of property and equipment		4,581	3,600
Unrealized loss on marketable securities	2	(28,824)	(80,388)
Interest expense.		(233,385)	(112,641)
Cash discount lost		(63,924)	(108,987)
Total		80,220	(72,195)
INCOME BEFORE INCOME TAXES.		368,682	154,821
INCOME TAX EXPENSE:			
Federal:			
Current.		112,336	31,410
Deferred.		9,303	18,036
Total federal		121,639	49,446
State:			
Current.		18,252	11,955
Deferred.		1,911	3,021
Total state		20,163	14,976
Total		141,802	64,422
NET INCOME.		226,880	90,399
RETAINED EARNINGS, BEGINNING OF YEAR		6,660,291	6,569,892
RETAINED EARNINGS, END OF YEAR		$ 6,887,171	$ 6,660,291

See notes to financial statements.

CARTER MANUFACTURING COMPANY

STATEMENTS OF CHANGES IN FINANCIAL POSITION FOR THE YEARS ENDED DECEMBER 31, 1985 AND 1984

	1985	1984
SOURCES OF WORKING CAPITAL:		
Net income	$ 226,880	$ 90,399
Add charges not requiring an outlay of working capital:		
Depreciation and amortization	173,145	181,638
Deferred income taxes	11,214	21,057
Total from operations	411,239	293,094
Proceeds from sale of plant and equipment—net of gains included in operations	11,019	1,800
Increase in long-term debt		1,295,358
Total	422,258	1,590,252
USES OF WORKING CAPITAL:		
Purchase of plant and equipment	187,782	1,322,398
Reduction of long-term debt	266,676	
Total	454,458	1,322,398
INCREASE (DECREASE) IN WORKING CAPITAL	$ (32,200)	$ 267,854
COMPONENTS OF CHANGE IN WORKING CAPITAL:		
Cash and savings certificates and account	$ 85,089	$ 325,572
Marketable securities	(29,604)	(80,388)
Receivables	193,005	290,889
Inventories	(105,495)	(3,918)
Prepaid expenses	(16,650)	77,820
Trade accounts payable	(104,155)	(1,177)
Due under line of credit	60,000	(60,000)
Current portion of long-term debt	(29,967)	(236,709)
Accrued salaries, wages and commissions	(174,099)	(28,560)
Accrued and withheld payroll taxes	74,844	(102,966)
Income taxes payable—net	(10,794)	(35,937)
Contributions to employee benefit plans	(176,874)	123,228
Accrued rent	202,500	
INCREASE (DECREASE) IN WORKING CAPITAL	$ (32,200)	$ 267,854

See notes to financial statements.

CARTER MANUFACTURING COMPANY

NOTES TO FINANCIAL STATEMENTS FOR
THE YEARS ENDED DECEMBER 31, 1985 AND 1984

1. SIGNIFICANT ACCOUNTING POLICIES

Nature of Business — The Company is principally engaged in the manufacture and sale of metal products.

Inventories

For the year ended December 31, 1983, the Company changed its method of accounting for inventories to a last-in, first-out (lifo) method. During a time of rapid price increases, the lifo method provides a better matching of revenue and expense than does the fifo method. The total effect of the change was included in the 1983 financial statements, and no restatement was made of amounts reported in prior years. The effect of this change was to reduce net income for 1983 by $298,944.

Plant and Equipment

Plant and equipment are stated at cost less accumulated depreciation and amortization. Depreciation on plant and equipment acquired after 1978 is computed using the straight-line method for financial reporting and accelerated methods for income tax purposes. Depreciation on previously acquired plant and equipment is computed using accelerated methods for financial reporting and income tax purposes, except that the straight-line method is used for tax purposes at such time as it results in a greater deduction than would result from continued use of an accelerated method. Rates are based upon the following estimated useful lives:

Classification	Useful Life
Machinery and equipment	7-10 Years
Delivery equipment	6-7 Years
Furniture and fixtures	8-10 Years
Leasehold improvements	5-6 Years

Revenue Recognition — Revenue from merchandise sales is recognized when the merchandise is shipped to the customer.

Deferred Income Taxes

Deferred income taxes are provided for timing differences between reported financial income before income taxes and taxable income. The timing differences arise from depreciation deductions for income tax purposes in excess of depreciation expense for financial reporting purposes.

2. MARKETABLE SECURITIES

The Company's marketable securities are stated at the lower of cost or market. At December 31, 1985 and 1984, the Company's investments had a cost of $582,876 and

$583,656 respectively. To reduce the carrying amount of this investment to market, which was lower than cost at Decmber 31, 1985 and 1984, valuation allowances of $250,638 and $221,814, respectively, were established. This resulted in a charge to earnings of $28,824 in 1985 and a charge to earnings of $80,388 in 1984.

3. RECEIVABLE DUE FROM A SINGLE CUSTOMER

At December 31, 1985, approximately $700,000 was due from a single distributor. Approximately $435,000 of the allowance for doubtful accounts at December 31, 1985, relates specifically to this receivable.

At December 31, 1984, approximately $350,000 was due from the distributor.

4. INVENTORIES

At December 31, 1985 and 1984, inventories (see Note 1) consisted of the following:

	1985	1984
Raw materials	$1,654,563	$1,491,876
Work in process	2,427,513	2,255,574
Finished goods	2,684,409	2,839,278
Total cost	6,766,485	6,586,728
Less lifo reserve	838,854	553,602
Total lifo	$5,927,631	$6,033,126

5. LINE OF CREDIT

The Company has an agreement with a bank for a line of credit, of which $180,000 was unused at December 31, 1985. Borrowings under the line are at an interest rate (14% at December 31, 1985) of 2% above the bank's prime lending rate. The Company's marketable securities are pledged as collateral for borrowings under the line.

6. LONG-TERM DEBT

At December 31, 1985 and 1984, the Company had three installment notes, payable to a bank as follows:

	1985	1984
Note dated February 2, 1984, due in $60,000 semi-annual installments, with interest payable monthly at 12.625%	$ 120,000	$ 240,000
Note dated March 2, 1984, due in $10,000 semiannual installments, with interest payable monthly at 14.125%	20,000	40,000
Note dated December 12, 1984, due in 120 monthly payments of increasing amounts with interest at 14.00%	1,155,358	1,252,067
Total	1,295,358	1,532,067
Less amount due within one year	266,676	236,709
Total	$1,028,682	$1,295,358

CARTER MANUFACTURING COMPANY

NOTES TO FINANCIAL STATEMENTS

7. LONG-TERM LIABILITIES

The long-term liabilities have the following aggregate minimum maturities during the next five years:

1986	$ 266,676
1987	131,122
1988	135,103
1989	140,503
1990	146,299
After 1991	475,655
Total	$1,295,358

8. EMPLOYEE BENEFIT PLANS

The Company has a profit-sharing plan for its salaried employees and a defined benefit retirement plan for its hourly paid employees. Both plans are noncontributory, are funded annually, and have been amended to comply with the Employee Retirement Income Security Act of 1974.

The contributions to the profit-sharing plan are made at the discretion of the Board of Directors and were $138,261 for 1985 and $57,750 for 1984.

Annual contributions to the retirement plan were $139,260 for 1985 and $42,897 for 1984. The plan is being funded based upon actuarial computations of costs which include consideration of normal cost, interest on the unfunded prior service cost, and amortization of the prior service cost over a forty-year period.

At January 1, 1985 and 1984, net assets available for retirement plan benefits were $824,214 and $622,518 respectively; the actuarial present values of vested plan benefits were $984,666 and $885,435, respectively; and nonvested accumulated plan benefits were $87,522 and $90,788, respectively. The assumed rate of return used in determining the actuarial present values of accumulated plan benefits was 5%.

9. OPERATING LEASE

The Company leases land and buildings under a 5-year noncancelable operating lease which expires on December 31, 1988. Future minimum lease payments are as follows:

1986	$ 300,000
1987	330,000
1988	360,000
Total	$ 990,000

Financial Highlights
(In millions except per share data)

The Coca-Cola Company and Consolidated Subsidiaries

Year Ended December 31,	1984	1983	% Change
Net operating revenues	$7,364.0	$6,829.0	7.8 %
Operating income	$1,057.5	$ 992.6	6.5 %
Income from continuing operations before income taxes	$1,068.0	$1,000.3	6.8 %
Income from continuing operations	$ 628.8	$ 558.3	12.6 %
Income per share from continuing operations	$ 4.76	$ 4.10	16.1 %
Dividends per share	$ 2.76	$ 2.68	3.0 %
Shareholders' equity at year-end	$2,778.1	$2,920.8	(4.9)%
Income from continuing operations to net operating revenues	8.5%	8.2%	
Income from continuing operations to average shareholders' equity	22.1%	19.6%	

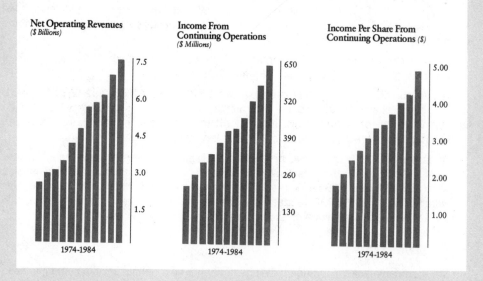

Net Operating Revenues
($ Billions)

1974-1984

Income From Continuing Operations
($ Millions)

1974-1984

Income Per Share From Continuing Operations *($)*

1974-1984

To Our Shareholders:

"We are committed to a culture of change...which will only serve to enhance the basic values of our business."

In the spring of 1981, the management of your Company set a clear-cut strategy—to increase the value of your investment in The Coca-Cola Company. With the strongest gain in earnings per share in eight years and a significant increase in return on average shareholders' equity to 22.1 percent, 1984 was a year of progress toward this primary corporate objective.

From April 1, 1981, through year-end 1984, the total return on your investment, stock price appreciation plus dividends, was 95 percent, compared with 42 percent for Standard and Poor's index of 500 stocks. This growth in value largely results from our efforts to further strengthen the Company by capitalizing on our considerable resources. These resources include the world's best-known trademarks, unparalleled distribution systems, marketing capabilities second to none, exceptional financial strength, and a dedicated management and employee team.

For details of the Company's 1984 performance, we direct your attention to the financial section of this report and to the pages that describe each business sector's operations. Highlights for the year included a 16.1-percent increase in income per share from continuing operations to $4.76, and a gain of 12.6 percent in income from continuing operations to $629 million. Operating income of over $1 billion in 1984 was the highest in the Company's history, up 6.5 percent from 1983.

Our increased earnings per share benefited from operating income gains from our business sectors, combined with fewer outstanding shares and a reduced effective tax rate. Our strong 1984 per-share achievement is particularly gratifying because it came in a year of significant marketing and capital investments for future growth.

In the soft drink business, our renewed competitive thrust increased our worldwide share to over 35 percent, more than twice that of our nearest competitor. We are introducing new products, supporting our products with bolder, more aggressive marketing, and revitalizing our bottler system. The success of diet Coke has given the Company and our bottler system the leading position, worldwide, in the burgeoning low-calorie market.

Our soft drink unit volume rose 6 percent worldwide in 1984, 10 percent in the North America Soft Drink Business Sector and 4 percent in the International Soft Drink Business Sector. Total soft drink operating income grew at a slower rate, up 2 percent, due to two factors—increased marketing investments in the United States and the translation of local currency results into dollars at rates well below 1983 levels. The currency translation effects limited results in Europe and Africa. However, operating income in the Pacific and Latin America increased more than 10 percent and 29 percent, respectively.

LETTER TO SHAREHOLDERS

> *"Our more aggressive financial policies enable us to take advantage of high-return opportunities within our existing lines of business."*

Diet Coke, a product only two years old, accounted for 8 percent of our 1984 worldwide soft drink volume. The number one low-calorie soft drink in the United States, diet Coke became this country's third largest-selling soft drink of any kind in 1984. It was introduced in 10 major markets last year, with a number of additional introductions planned for 1985. Diet Coke is capturing the developing low-calorie business in 41 markets, selling at more than 15 percent of Coca-Cola sales in many of those countries.

We demonstrated a more assertive marketing stance in 1984 with strong competitive advertising for Coke, Sprite and our caffeine-free colas. And the ability of our U.S. bottler system to implement marketing strategies swiftly was evidenced by the December rollout of diet Coke with 100-percent aspartame, which was available virtually nationwide within one month.

We invested more than $100 million last year in strategically important bottling operations to ensure that our bottling system is both committed and positioned to achieve growth goals consistent with ours. One of the year's largest transactions was the Company's purchase of bottling operations for southern England, including the important London market. In the United States, we acquired The Akron Coca-Cola Bottling Company and several other bottling operations contiguous to existing Company-owned territories. Since 1981, we have facilitated bottler ownership changes valued at about $3 billion.

Our Foods Business Sector continued its growth in 1984, posting a 14-percent increase in operating income to $138 million. It further leveraged its distribution systems with new products by expanding its frozen, chilled and aseptically packaged product lines during the year.

Minute Maid orange juice, the number one product of any type in the supermarket frozen foods section, posted another year of category leadership and record share of more than 25 percent. Minute Maid chilled orange juice successfully responded to intense competition with a share of about 18 percent.

Nine products were introduced in aseptic packaging last year, including a range of Minute Maid juices and flavors for Hi-C and Five Alive. Most of the sector's $40 million in 1984 capital investment was used to increase aseptic production capacity, reflecting the growth potential of this rapidly expanding packaging category.

The Entertainment Business Sector increased operating income 34 percent in 1984 to $121 million. Television, which contributed more than half the sector's earnings, continued its excellent trends with the syndication of "Hart to Hart" and "Benson." A successful program of film production and distribution, highlighted by the record-breaking "Ghostbusters," generated significant growth in film earnings.

To maximize its film distribution capacity, Columbia Pictures is increasing the number of films it produces annually. Central to this strategy are equity and licensing agreements that reduce the financial risk of film production. By involving investment partners and by pre-licensing films to ancillary markets, we have nearly doubled the number of films distributed without a dramatic increase in internal production expenditure risk.

Tri-Star Pictures released its first 17 films in 1984, earning Columbia significant distribution fees. Together, Columbia and Tri-Star released 30 films last year, up from 12 distributed by Columbia in 1983. Positive benefits from our strategy to increase film production should be realized in 1985 and 1986.

The Company's more aggressive financial policies were a significant factor in the year's increased return on equity and earnings per share. We completed the repurchase of six million shares of our common stock during the year, not only benefiting returns, but indicating strong confidence in our operations. The repurchase was completed at an average cost of about $55 per share.

We utilized more low-cost debt to fund our investment programs by going to the European financial markets three times with successful debt issues of $100 million each. We borrowed at lower rates than rates on U.S. Treasury obligations of like maturity, an indication that The Coca-Cola Company is regarded as one of the most attractive credits in the world.

At its February 21, 1985, meeting, the Board of Directors increased the quarterly dividend to 74 cents, equivalent to a full-year 1985 dividend of $2.96 per share and 7-percent higher than 1984's dividend. This is the 23rd consecutive year your Board of Directors has approved dividend increases. In 1984 we improved the Company's Automatic Dividend Reinvestment Plan by offering greater flexibility and cost savings in acquiring additional shares of Company stock through reinvested cash dividends and optional cash investments.

Last year Robert W. Woodruff, after completing an unparalleled 61 years as a full-time member of our Board of Directors, was elected the Company's first and only Director Emeritus. Mr. Woodruff's keen instinct and perceptive insight over six decades have guided this Company during the best of times and the worst of times, and today it stands as one of the strongest in world commerce.

C.H. Candler, Jr., also did not stand for re-election to the Board in 1984. We are grateful for his more than 25 years of dedicated service and for the Candler legacy associated with the Company.

We were deeply saddened by the death in July of Dr. E. Garland Herndon, Jr., who had served with distinction as a director since 1974. His wise counsel is missed.

LETTER TO SHAREHOLDERS

"By capitalizing on the strengths of our business, we are building the foundation for even greater success…we are stronger than ever."

In December the Board elected as a director Dr. James T. Laney, president of Atlanta's Emory University since 1977. We are fortunate to have his expertise and wisdom as we chart the future of this Company.

Our primary objective will continue to be the maximization of shareholder value. We will manage our businesses to generate earnings growth and improved returns. We plan to reinvest a greater portion of our resources in projects and investments that strategically augment and leverage our operations—investments where the long-term cash returns on invested capital exceed our overall cost of capital. In making such investments, we have no plans to venture outside our three lines of business, as there are significant growth opportunities in these businesses.

A paramount objective is to increase international per capita consumption of soft drinks to rates well above their present, relatively low levels. By investing in vending and fountain equipment, helping to restructure bottler systems, developing emerging categories like low-calorie, and achieving greater acceptability for soft drinks as all-occasion beverages, we expect to progressively raise per capita consumption.

In our Foods Business Sector, we are striving for greater utilization of our existing distribution system by adding new products in fast-growing frozen-food categories. In Entertainment, we will continue to increase our participation in growing ancillary markets through joint ventures and other arrangements. When the Company's resources exceed our investment requirements, we will again consider share repurchases.

While every year presents obstacles outside our control, such as the rising value of the U.S. dollar, the underlying health of our business has never been stronger. With the solid strategic positioning we have attained, we are optimistic about having another good year in 1985.

All our associates at The Coca-Cola Company join us at this time to thank you for your support and to express our pride of being employed in this great Company.

Roberto C. Goizueta
Chairman, Board of Directors,
and Chief Executive Officer

Donald R. Keough
President and
Chief Operating Officer

February 21, 1985

Selected Financial Data
(In millions except per share data)

Year Ended December 31,	1984	1983	1982(b)	1981
Summary of Operations (a)				
Net operating revenues	$7,364	$6,829	$6,021	$5,699
Cost of goods and services	3,993	3,773	3,311	3,188
Gross profit	3,371	3,056	2,710	2,511
Selling, administrative and general expenses	2,313	2,063	1,830	1,725
Operating income	1,058	993	880	786
Interest income	129	83	106	71
Interest expense	124	73	75	39
Other income (deductions)—net	5	(3)	7	(23)
Income from continuing operations before income taxes	1,068	1,000	918	795
Income taxes	439	442	415	355
Income from continuing operations	$ 629	$ 558	$ 503	$ 440
Net income	$ 629	$ 559	$ 512	$ 482
Per Share Data (c)				
Income from continuing operations	$ 4.76	$ 4.10	$ 3.88	$ 3.56
Net income	4.76	4.10	3.95	3.90
Dividends	2.76	2.68	2.48	2.32
Year-End Position				
Cash and marketable securities	$ 782	$ 611	$ 261	$ 340
Property, plant and equipment—net	1,623	1,561	1,539	1,409
Total assets	5,958	5,228	4,923	3,565
Long-term debt	740	513	462	137
Total debt	1,363	620	583	232
Shareholders' equity	2,778	2,921	2,779	2,271
Total capital (d)	4,141	3,541	3,362	2,503
Financial Ratios				
Income from continuing operations to net operating revenues	8.5%	8.2%	8.4%	7.7%
Income from continuing operations to average shareholders' equity	22.1%	19.6%	19.9%	20.2%
Long-term debt to total capital	17.9%	14.5%	13.7%	5.5%
Total debt to total capital	32.9%	17.5%	17.3%	9.3%
Dividend payout	58.0%	65.3%	62.8%	59.5%
Other Data				
Average shares outstanding (c)	132	136	130	124
Capital expenditures	$ 391	$ 384	$ 382	$ 330
Depreciation	166	154	144	133

Notes:

(a) In June 1982 the Company acquired Columbia Pictures Industries, Inc., in a purchase transaction.

(b) In 1982 the Company adopted Statement of Financial Accounting Standards No. 52, "Foreign Currency Translation." See Note 10 to the Consolidated Financial Statements.

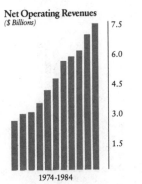

Net Operating Revenues
($ Billions)
1974-1984

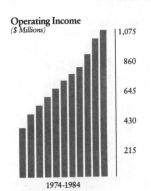

Operating Income
($ Millions)
1974-1984

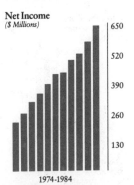

Net Income
($ Millions)
1974-1984

The Coca-Cola Company and Consolidated Subsidiaries

1980	1979	1978	1977	1976	1975	1974
$5,475	$4,588	$4,013	$3,328	$2,928	$2,773	$2,425
3,103	2,521	2,203	1,836	1,614	1,633	1,462
2,372	2,067	1,810	1,492	1,314	1,140	963
1,635	1,378	1,167	922	806	693	616
737	689	643	570	508	447	347
40	37	35	29	29	22	21
35	11	7	6	6	6	6
(9)	(3)	(14)	(9)	(4)	(8)	5
733	712	657	584	527	455	367
329	318	300	268	245	218	170
$ 404	$ 394	$ 357	$ 316	$ 282	$ 237	$ 197(e)
$ 422	$ 420	$ 375	$ 331	$ 294	$ 249	$ 204(e)
$ 3.27	$ 3.18	$ 2.89	$ 2.56	$ 2.29	$ 1.93	$ 1.60(e)
3.42	3.40	3.03	2.68	2.38	2.02	1.65(e)
2.16	1.96	1.74	1.54	1.325	1.15	1.04
$ 231	$ 149	$ 321	$ 350	$ 364	$ 389	$ 241
1,341	1,284	1,065	887	738	647	601
3,406	2,938	2,583	2,254	2,007	1,801	1,610
133	31	15	15	11	16	12
228	139	69	57	52	42	69
2,075	1,919	1,740	1,578	1,434	1,302	1,190
2,303	2,058	1,809	1,635	1,486	1,344	1,259
7.4%	8.6%	8.9%	9.5%	9.6%	8.5%	8.1%
20.2%	21.5%	21.6%	21.0%	20.6%	19.0%	17.1%
5.8%	1.5%	.8%	.9%	.7%	1.2%	1.0%
9.9%	6.8%	3.8%	3.5%	3.5%	3.1%	5.5%
63.2%	57.6%	57.4%	57.5%	55.7%	56.9%	63.0%
124	124	124	123	123	123	123
$ 293	$ 381	$ 306	$ 264	$ 191	$ 145	$ 154
127	106	88	77	67	64	57

(c) Adjusted for a two-for-one stock split in 1977.
(d) Includes shareholders' equity and total debt.
(e) In 1974 the Company adopted the last-in, first-out (LIFO) accounting method for certain major categories of inventories. This accounting change caused a reduction in net income of $31.2 million (25 cents per share) in 1974.

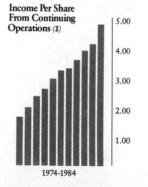

Income Per Share From Continuing Operations ($)
1974-1984

Return on Shareholders' Equity (%)
1974-1984

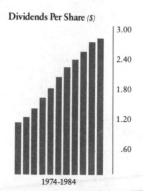

Dividends Per Share ($)
1974-1984

Consolidated Statements of Income

The Coca-Cola Company and Consolidated Subsidiaries

(In thousands except per share data)

Year Ended December 31,	1984	1983	1982
Net Operating Revenues	$7,363,993	$6,828,992	$6,021,135
Cost of goods and services	3,992,923	3,772,741	3,310,847
Gross Profit	3,371,070	3,056,251	2,710,288
Selling, administrative and general expenses	2,313,562	2,063,626	1,830,527
Operating Income	1,057,508	992,625	879,761
Interest income	128,837	82,912	106,172
Interest expense	123,750	72,677	74,560
Other income (deductions)—net	5,438	(2,528)	6,679
Income From Continuing Operations			
Before Income Taxes	1,068,033	1,000,332	918,052
Income taxes	439,215	442,072	415,076
Income From Continuing Operations	628,818	558,260	502,976
Income from discontinued operations			
(net of applicable income taxes of			
$414 in 1983 and $4,683 in 1982)	—	527	9,256
Net Income	$ 628,818	$ 558,787	$ 512,232
Per Share:			
Continuing operations	$ 4.76	$ 4.10	$ 3.88
Discontinued operations	—	—	.07
Net income	$ 4.76	$ 4.10	$ 3.95
Average Shares Outstanding	132,210	136,222	129,793

See Notes to Consolidated Financial Statements.

Consolidated Balance Sheets
(In thousands except share data)

The Coca-Cola Company and Consolidated Subsidiaries

Assets	December 31, 1984	December 31, 1983
Current		
Cash	$ 307,564	$ 319,385
Marketable securities, at cost (approximates market)	474,575	292,084
Trade accounts receivable, less allowances of $20,670 in 1984 and $20,160 in 1983	872,332	779,729
Inventories and unamortized film costs	740,063	744,107
Prepaid expenses and other assets	241,326	195,009
Total Current Assets	2,635,860	2,330,314
Investments, Film Costs and Other Assets		
Investments (principally investments in affiliates)	334,220	241,780
Unamortized film costs	341,662	252,612
Long-term receivables and other assets	408,324	240,880
	1,084,206	735,272
Property, Plant and Equipment		
Land	130,883	128,642
Buildings and improvements	645,150	618,586
Machinery and equipment	1,518,264	1,412,697
Containers	337,993	341,597
	2,632,290	2,501,522
Less allowances for depreciation	1,009,715	940,716
	1,622,575	1,560,806
Goodwill and Other Intangible Assets	615,428	601,430
	$5,958,069	$5,227,822

Liabilities and Shareholders' Equity	1984	1983
Current		
Loans and notes payable	$ 502,216	$ 85,913
Current maturities of long-term debt	120,300	20,783
Accounts payable and accrued expenses	1,020,807	910,951
Participations and other entertainment obligations	192,537	154,213
Accrued taxes—including income taxes	186,942	219,240
Total Current Liabilities	2,022,802	1,391,100
Participations and Other Entertainment Obligations	175,234	226,129
Long-Term Debt	740,001	513,202
Deferred Income Taxes	241,966	176,635
Shareholders' Equity		
Common stock, no par value— Authorized: 180,000,000 shares in 1984 and 1983; Issued: 137,263,936 shares in 1984 and 136,653,676 shares in 1983	69,009	68,704
Capital surplus	532,186	500,031
Reinvested earnings	2,758,895	2,494,215
Foreign currency translation adjustment	(234,811)	(130,640)
	3,125,279	2,932,310
Less treasury stock, at cost (6,438,873 shares in 1984; 300,588 shares in 1983)	347,213	11,554
	2,778,066	2,920,756
	$5,958,069	$5,227,822

See Notes to Consolidated Financial Statements.

Annual Reports and Specimen Financial Statements

Consolidated Statements of Shareholders' Equity

The Coca-Cola Company and Consolidated Subsidiaries

(In thousands except per share data)

Three Years Ended December 31, 1984	Number of Shares		Amount				
	Common Stock	Treasury Stock	Common Stock	Capital Surplus	Reinvested Earnings	Foreign Currency Translation	Treasury Stock
Balance January 1, 1982	124,025	401	$62,389	$114,194	$2,109,542	$ (11,657)	$ (15,353)
Sales to employees exercising stock options and appreciation rights	121	—	61	3,685	—	—	—
Tax benefit from sale of option shares by employees	—	—	—	814	—	—	—
Purchase of Columbia Pictures Industries, Inc.	11,954	—	5,977	359,579	—	—	—
Translation adjustments (net of income taxes of $11,188)	—	—	—	—	—	(42,829)	—
Treasury stock issued to officers	—	(42)	—	36	—	—	1,541
Net income	—	—	—	—	512,232	—	—
Dividends (per share—$2.48)	—	—	—	—	(321,557)	—	—
Balance December 31, 1982	136,100	359	68,427	478,308	2,300,217	(54,486)	(13,812)
Sales to employees exercising stock options and appreciation rights	387	—	194	13,327	—	—	—
Tax benefit from sale of option shares by employees	—	—	—	1,616	—	—	—
Translation adjustments (net of income taxes of $13,346)	—	—	—	—	—	(76,154)	—
Treasury stock issued in connection with an acquisition	—	(58)	—	(1,847)	—	—	2,258
Stock issued under Restricted Stock Award Plan	167	—	83	8,627	—	—	—
Net income	—	—	—	—	558,787	—	—
Dividends (per share—$2.68)	—	—	—	—	(364,789)	—	—
Balance December 31, 1983	136,654	301	68,704	500,031	2,494,215	(130,640)	(11,554)
Sales to employees exercising stock options and appreciation rights	316	—	158	10,931	—	—	—
Tax benefit from sale of option shares by employees	—	—	—	2,557	—	—	—
Translation adjustments (net of income taxes of $2,950)	—	—	—	—	—	(104,171)	—
Stock issued under Restricted Stock Award Plan	294	—	147	18,667	—	—	—
Treasury stock purchased	—	6,138	—	—	—	—	(335,659)
Net income	—	—	—	—	628,818	—	—
Dividends (per share—$2.76)	—	—	—	—	(364,138)	—	—
Balance December 31, 1984	137,264	6,439	$69,009	$532,186	$2,758,895	$(234,811)	$(347,213)

See Notes to Consolidated Financial Statements.

Consolidated Statements of Changes in Financial Position (In thousands)

The Coca-Cola Company and Consolidated Subsidiaries

Year Ended December 31,	1984	1983	1982
Operations			
Income from continuing operations	$ 628,818	$558,260	$502,976
Depreciation	166,104	153,655	143,549
Amortization:			
Goodwill	17,161	16,468	10,101
Noncurrent film costs	136,714	57,167	43,495
Deferred income taxes	84,931	12,220	48,702
Other	18,608	25,460	24,111
Discontinued operations (provisions for depreciation, amortization and deferred income taxes were $8,219 in 1983, and $7,504 in 1982)	—	8,746	16,760
Working capital provided by operations	1,052,336	831,976	789,694
Decrease (increase) in other current assets:			
Trade accounts receivable	(72,127)	(69,107)	(276,196)
Inventories and film costs	18,070	(57,776)	(90,973)
Prepaid expenses and other assets	(45,737)	55,663	(192,773)
Increase (decrease) in current liabilities:			
Accounts payable and accrued expenses	47,472	143,957	128,052
Participations and other entertainment obligations	38,324	(590)	154,803
Accrued taxes	(31,506)	(39,512)	19,434
Net additions to noncurrent film costs	(225,764)	(98,319)	(1,895)
Net cash provided by operations	781,068	766,292	530,146
Decrease (increase) in investments and other assets	(259,953)	(19,361)	21,836
Additions to property, plant and equipment	(338,929)	(376,197)	(325,016)
Disposals of property, plant and equipment	67,161	34,972	44,467
Increase (decrease) in noncurrent participations and other entertainment obligations	(50,895)	35,721	—
Other	(22,241)	(2,595)	(46,544)
Net cash invested in operations	(604,857)	(327,460)	(305,257)
Net cash available from operations	176,211	438,832	224,889
Financing Activities			
Common stock issued	32,460	22,000	370,152
Increase (decrease) in loans and notes payable and current portion of long-term debt	510,260	(15,220)	25,970
Increase in long-term debt	347,099	71,181	300,015
Decrease in long-term debt (includes reclassifications to short-term)	(120,300)	(20,783)	(50,623)
Repurchase of common stock	(335,659)	—	—
Net cash provided by financing activities	433,860	57,178	645,514
Acquisitions and Discontinued Operations			
Acquisitions of purchased companies:			
Net working capital	32,070	(1,847)	(1,081)
Property, plant and equipment—net	(51,829)	(7,439)	(56,739)
Other assets net of other liabilities	69	583	(89,693)
Goodwill	(55,573)	(7,480)	(516,115)
Discontinued operations:			
Net working capital	—	145,530	34,300
Net long-term assets (including property, plant and equipment)	—	89,990	1,851
Net cash provided by (used for) acquisitions and discontinued operations	(75,263)	219,337	(627,477)
Dividends	(364,138)	(364,789)	(321,557)
Increase (Decrease) in Cash and Marketable Securities	170,670	350,558	(78,631)
Cash and Marketable Securities at Beginning of Year	611,469	260,911	339,542
Cash and Marketable Securities at End of Year	$ 782,139	$611,469	$260,911

See Notes to Consolidated Financial Statements.

Notes to Consolidated Financial Statements

1. Accounting Policies. The major accounting policies and practices followed by the Company and its consolidated subsidiaries are as follows:

Consolidation: The consolidated financial statements include the accounts of the Company and its majority-owned subsidiaries except for Coca-Cola Financial Corporation (CCFC). All significant intercompany accounts and transactions are eliminated in consolidation. CCFC, a wholly owned finance subsidiary, initiated operations in 1984 and is accounted for under the equity method. CCFC's operations for 1984 were not significant to the consolidated financial statements.

Consolidated statements of changes in financial position for the years ended December 31, 1983 and 1982, have been restated to a cash basis format.

Inventories and Unamortized Film Costs: Inventories are valued at the lower of cost or market. The last-in, first-out (LIFO) method of inventory valuation generally is used for sugar and other sweeteners, except for aspartame, used in beverages in the United States, for certain major citrus concentrate products, for substantially all inventories of United States bottling subsidiaries and for certain other operations. All other inventories are valued on the basis of average cost or first-in, first-out (FIFO) methods. The excess of current costs over LIFO stated values amounted to approximately $54 million and $59 million at December 31, 1984 and 1983, respectively.

Unamortized film costs include film production, print, prerelease and other advertising costs expected to benefit future periods, accrued profit participations, and capitalized interest. The individual film forecast method is used to amortize these costs based on the revenues recognized in proportion to management's estimate of ultimate revenues to be received. Based on the Company's estimate of revenues as of December 31, 1984, approximately 90% of unamortized film costs are expected to be amortized over the next five years.

The costs of feature and television films are classified as current assets to the extent such costs are expected to be recovered through the respective primary markets. Other costs relating to film production are classified as noncurrent.

Revenues from theatrical exhibition of feature films are recognized on the dates of exhibition. Revenues from television licensing agreements are recognized when films are available for telecasting. Motion picture revenues are derived from the following markets: domestic and foreign theater, home video, pay television and network and independent broadcast television. The Company's average revenue recognition cycle for motion picture films is approximately seven years.

Property, Plant and Equipment: Property, plant and equipment is stated at cost, less allowance for depreciation, except that foreign subsidiaries carry bottles and shells in service at amounts (less than cost) which generally correspond with deposit prices obtained from customers. Approximately 92% of depreciation expense was determined by the straight-line method for the years ended December 31, 1984, 1983 and 1982. The annual rates of depreciation are 2% to 10% for buildings and improvements and 7% to 34% for machinery and equipment. Investment tax credits are accounted for by the flow-through method.

Capitalized Interest: Interest capitalized as part of the cost of acquisition, construction or production of major assets (including film costs) was $26 million, $18 million and $14 million in 1984, 1983 and 1982, respectively.

Goodwill and Other Intangible Assets: Goodwill and other intangible assets are stated on the basis of cost and, if acquired subsequent to October 31, 1970, are being amortized, principally on a straight-line basis, over the estimated future periods to be benefited (not exceeding 40 years). Accumulated amortization amounted to $57 million and $42 million at December 31, 1984 and 1983, respectively.

2. Inventories and Unamortized Film Costs are comprised of the following (in thousands):

	December 31,	
	1984	1983
Finished goods	$284,711	$217,329
Work in process	17,154	15,173
Raw materials and supplies	341,098	366,000
Unamortized film costs (includes in process costs of $31,043 in 1984 and $60,669 in 1983)	97,100	145,605
	$740,063	$744,107
Noncurrent—		
Unamortized film costs:		
Completed	$192,877	$147,697
In process	148,785	104,915
	$341,662	$252,612

3. Short-Term Borrowings and Credit Arrangements. Loans and notes payable include commercial paper and notes payable to banks and other financial institutions of $502 million and $86 million at December 31, 1984 and 1983, respectively.

Under line of credit arrangements for short-term debt with various financial institutions, the Company, including Coca-Cola Financial Corporation, may borrow up to $457 million. These lines of credit are subject to normal banking terms and conditions. At December 31, 1984, the unused portion of the credit lines was $353 million. Some of the financial arrangements require compensating balances which are not material.

The Coca-Cola Company and Consolidated Subsidiaries

4. Accounts Payable and Accrued Expenses are composed of the following amounts (in thousands):

	December 31,	
	1984	1983
Trade accounts payable	$ 878,564	$768,913
Deposits on bottles and shells	47,848	51,371
Other	94,395	90,667
	$1,020,807	$910,951

5. Accrued Taxes are composed of the following amounts (in thousands):

	December 31,	
	1984	1983
Income taxes	$128,372	$166,228
Sales, payroll and miscellaneous taxes	58,570	53,012
	$186,942	$219,240

6. Long-Term Debt consists of the following amounts (in thousands):

	December 31,	
	1984	1983
9⅞% notes due June 1, 1985	$ 99,988	$ 99,958
10⅜% notes due June 1, 1988	98,866	98,534
11⅜% notes due November 28, 1988	100,000	–
12¾% notes due August 1, 1989	99,771	–
11¾% notes due October 1, 1989 (redeemable after September 30, 1986)	98,279	97,916
11¾% notes due October 16, 1991 (redeemable after October 16, 1988)	99,757	–
9⅞% notes due August 1, 1992 (redeemable after July 31, 1989)	98,345	98,125
Other	165,295	139,452
	860,301	533,985
Less current portion	120,300	20,783
	$740,001	$513,202

The above notes, except for the 9⅞% notes due June 1, 1985, were issued outside the United States and are redeemable at the Company's option under certain limited conditions related to United States and foreign tax laws.

The 11⅜% notes were issued with detachable warrants which grant the holder the right to purchase additional notes bearing the same interest rate and maturing in 1991. The warrants expire November 28, 1988.

Other long-term debt consists of various mortgages and notes with maturity dates ranging from 1985 to 2010. Interest on a portion of this debt varies with the changes in the prime rate, and the weighted average interest rate applicable to the remainder is approximately 12.3%.

Maturities of long-term debt for the five years succeeding December 31, 1984, are as follows (in thousands):

1985	$120,300
1986	22,883
1987	17,941
1988	214,092
1989	210,847

The above notes include various restrictions, none of which are presently significant to the Company. The Company is contingently liable for guarantees of indebtedness owed by its independent bottling companies, Coca-Cola Financial Corporation, and others in the approximate amount of $213 million at December 31, 1984.

7. Pension Plans. The Company and its subsidiaries sponsor and/or contribute to various pension plans covering substantially all United States employees and certain employees in non-United States locations. Pension expense for continuing operations determined under various actuarial cost methods, principally the aggregate level cost method, amounted to approximately $36 million in 1984, $39 million in 1983 and $35 million in 1982. Pension costs are generally funded currently.

The actuarial present value of accumulated benefits, as estimated by consulting actuaries, and net assets available for benefits of Company and subsidiary-sponsored plans in the United States are presented below (in thousands):

	January 1,	
	1984	1983
Actuarial present value of accumulated plan benefits:		
Vested	$217,558	$193,122
Nonvested	17,527	15,940
	$235,085	$209,062
Net assets available for benefits	$334,357	$280,731

The weighted average assumed rates of return used in determining the actuarial present value of accumulated plan benefits were approximately 9% for 1984 and 9.5% for 1983. This change in the assumed rate of return increased the actuarial present value of accumulated plan benefits by approximately $9 million at January 1, 1984.

The Company has various pension plans in locations outside the United States. These locations are not required to report to United States governmental agencies and do not determine the actuarial present value of accumulated plan benefits or net assets available for benefits as calculated and disclosed above. For such plans, the value of the pension funds and balance sheet accruals exceeded the actuarially computed value of vested benefits as of January 1, 1984 and 1983, as estimated by consulting actuaries.

The Company also has a plan which provides post-retirement health care and life insurance benefits to virtually all employees who retire with a minimum of five years of service; the aggregate cost of these benefits is not significant.

Notes To Consolidated Financial Statements

8. Income Taxes. The components of income before income taxes for both continuing and discontinued operations consist of the following (in thousands):

	Year Ended December 31,		
	1984	1983	1982
United States	$ 457,260	$ 409,613	$357,063
Foreign	610,773	591,660	574,928
	$1,068,033	$1,001,273	$931,991

Income taxes for continuing and discontinued operations consist of the following amounts (in thousands):

Year Ended December 31,	United States	State & Local	Foreign	Total
1984				
Current	$ 45,411	$23,085	$285,788	$354,284
Deferred	67,891	3,403	13,637	84,931
1983				
Current	$114,195	$25,615	$287,846	$427,656
Deferred	4,493	1,068	9,269	14,830
1982				
Current	$ 79,605	$22,638	$266,709	$368,952
Deferred	33,281	1,363	16,163	50,807

A reconciliation of the statutory U.S. federal rate and effective rates is as follows:

	Year Ended December 31,		
	1984	1983	1982
Statutory rate	46.0%	46.0%	46.0%
State income taxes-net of federal benefit	1.3	1.4	1.4
Earnings in jurisdictions taxed at varying rates	(3.0)	(1.9)	(2.2)
Investment tax credits	(2.9)	(2.0)	(2.6)
Other-net	(.3)	.7	2.4
	41.1%	44.2%	45.0%

Investment tax credits were approximately $34 million in 1984, $20 million in 1983 and $24 million in 1982.

Deferred taxes are provided principally for depreciation, film costs and television and other licensing income which are recognized in different years for financial statement and income tax purposes.

In 1984 certain current tax amounts were reclassified to deferred. Also in 1984, the Company completed an organizational restructuring in the Entertainment Business Sector which resulted in an increase in the tax bases of certain assets.

9. Restricted Stock Award Plan and Stock Options. The amended 1983 Restricted Stock Award Plan provides that 1,000,000 shares of restricted common stock may be granted to certain officers and key employees of the Company. The shares are subject to forfeiture if the employee leaves the Company for reasons other than death, disability or retirement and may not be transferred by the employee prior to death, disability or retirement. The employee receives dividends on the shares and may vote the shares. The market value of the shares at the date of grant is charged to operations over those periods. Shares granted were 294,500 shares and 166,500 shares in 1984 and 1983, respectively. At December 31, 1984, 539,000 shares were available to be granted under this Plan.

The Company's 1983 Stock Option Plan covers 2,000,000 shares of the Company's common stock. The Plan provides for the granting of stock appreciation rights and stock options to certain officers and employees. Stock appreciation rights permit the holder, upon surrendering all or part of the related stock option, to receive cash, common stock, or a combination thereof, in an amount up to 100% of the difference between the market price and the option price. Included in options outstanding at December 31, 1984, were various options granted under previous plans and other options granted not as a part of an option plan.

Further information relating to options is as follows:

	December 31,		
	1984	1983	1982
Options outstanding at January 1	1,713,222	1,507,162	1,406,360
Options granted in the year	454,650	487,900	288,300
Options exercised in the year	(264,845)	(203,361)	(120,791)
Options cancelled in the year	(36,582)	(78,479)	(66,707)
Options outstanding at December 31	1,866,445	1,713,222	1,507,162
Options exercisable at December 31	868,596	750,026	781,906
Shares available at December 31 for options which may be granted	1,131,950	1,577,858	25,261
Option prices per share			
Exercised in the year	$25-$52	$25-$50	$22-$44
Unexercised at year-end	$31-$64	$25-$52	$25-$68

The Coca-Cola Company and Consolidated Subsidiaries

Not reflected above are options assumed in connection with the acquisition of Columbia Pictures Industries, Inc., covering 27,400 shares of the Company's common stock at December 31, 1984. The average option price for these options is $37. During 1984 options for 50,680 such shares were exercised, and options for 16,001 shares were cancelled.

10. Foreign Operations Currency Translation. In 1982 the Company adopted Statement of Financial Accounting Standards No. 52, "Foreign Currency Translation" (SFAS 52) for translating the financial statements of its foreign operations. An equity adjustment ($11.7 million) was recorded as of January 1, 1982, for the cumulative effect of SFAS 52 on prior years. Net exchange gains (losses) included in income, i.e., gains and losses on foreign currency transactions and translation of balance sheet accounts of operations in hyperinflationary economies, were $(18) million for 1984, $9 million for 1983 and $27 million for 1982.

Appropriate United States and foreign income taxes have been provided for earnings of subsidiary companies which are expected to be remitted to the parent company in the near future. Accumulated unremitted earnings of foreign subsidiaries which are expected to be required for use in the foreign operations were approximately $62 million at December 31, 1984, exclusive of amounts which if remitted would result in little or no tax.

11. Acquisitions. In 1984, 1983 and 1982 the Company purchased various bottling companies to operate. The operating results for these companies have been included in the consolidated statement of income from the dates of acquisition and do not have a significant effect on operating results for those respective years.

In addition, in 1984 the Company purchased a substantial equity interest in The Mid-Atlantic Coca-Cola Bottling Company, Inc., at a cost of more than $60 million. This operation was purchased with the intent of selling it to other purchasers as part of the bottler restructuring efforts. Accordingly, the acquisition has been accounted for as a temporary investment under the cost method of accounting.

Included in current marketable securities at December 31, 1984, is $148.8 million on deposit with an escrow agent. Such amount will be used to acquire Louisiana Coca-Cola Bottling Co. ("Louisiana") or released to the Company, depending upon resolution of current differences between the Company and principal owners of Louisiana.

In June 1982 the Company acquired all of the outstanding capital stock of Columbia Pictures Industries, Inc., ("Columbia") in a purchase transaction. The purchase price, consisting of cash and common stock of the Company, was valued at approximately $692 million. The values assigned to assets acquired and liabilities assumed are based on studies conducted to determine their fair values. The excess cost over net fair value is being amortized over 40 years using the straight-line method.

The pro forma consolidated results of continuing operations of the Company, as if Columbia had been acquired as of January 1, 1982, are as follows for the year ended December 31, 1982 (in millions except per share data):

Net operating revenues	$6,374
Income from continuing operations	489
Income from continuing operations per share	3.60

The pro forma results include adjustments to reflect interest expense on $333 million of the purchase price assumed to be financed with debt bearing interest at an annual rate of 11%, the amortization of the unallocated excess cost over net assets of Columbia, the income tax effects of pro forma adjustments and the issuance of 12.2 million shares of the Company's common stock.

12. Divestitures and Discontinued Operations. In 1984 the Company sold Ronco Enterprises, Inc., a manufacturer and distributor of pasta products, for cash. This transaction had no significant effect on consolidated operating results.

In conjunction with its continuing bottler restructuring efforts, the Company sold bottling interests in Australia and Japan and provided for possible losses in Guatemala, where an independent bottler ceased operations. Such efforts resulted in net pretax gains of approximately $18 million.

In November 1983 the Company sold its wine business for book value plus advances, amounting to approximately $230 million. In February 1982 the Company sold its Tenco Division, which manufactured and distributed private label instant coffees and teas, for approximately book value. Net revenues of discontinued operations were $162 million and $229 million in 1983 and 1982, respectively.

NOTES TO CONSOLIDATED FINANCIAL STATEMENTS

13. Lines of Business. The Company operates principally in the soft drink industry. Citrus, Hi-C fruit drinks, coffee and other products are included in the Foods Business Sector. Plastic products are not material and are also included in the Foods Business Sector. In June 1982 the Company acquired Columbia Pictures Industries, Inc., which operates in the entertainment industry. Intercompany transfers between sectors are not material. Information concerning operations in different lines of business is as follows (in millions):

Year Ended December 31,	1984	1983	1982
Net operating revenues:			
Soft drinks	$5,014.9	$4,694.6	$4,413.8
Foods	1,464.4	1,284.9	1,150.0
Entertainment	884.7	849.5	457.3
Consolidated net operating revenues	$7,364.0	$6,829.0	$6,021.1
Operating income:			
Soft drinks	$ 879.6	$ 858.6	$ 800.0
Foods	137.7	121.3	117.9
Entertainment	121.1	90.6	35.8
General expenses	(80.9)	(77.9)	(73.9)
Consolidated operating income	$1,057.5	$ 992.6	$ 879.8
Identifiable assets at year-end:			
Soft drinks	$3,009.6	$2,670.6	$2,521.4
Foods	460.0	431.9	380.4
Entertainment	1,615.4	1,394.0	1,309.8
Corporate assets (principally marketable securities, investments and fixed assets)	873.1	731.3	476.2
Discontinued operations	—	—	235.5
Consolidated assets	$5,958.1	$5,227.8	$4,923.3
Capital expenditures (including fixed assets of purchased companies):			
Soft drinks	$ 294.6	$ 237.6	$ 249.5
Foods	39.9	45.1	53.7
Entertainment	31.2	72.9	53.9
Corporate	25.1	28.0	24.6
Consolidated capital expenditures	$ 390.8	$ 383.6	$ 381.7
Depreciation and amortization of goodwill:			
Soft drinks	$ 127.0	$ 120.4	$ 117.6
Foods	27.4	25.2	20.8
Entertainment	17.6	15.7	7.6
Corporate	11.3	8.8	7.6
Consolidated depreciation and amortization of goodwill	$ 183.3	$ 170.1	$ 153.6

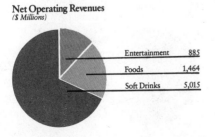

Net Operating Revenues
($ Millions)

Entertainment	885
Foods	1,464
Soft Drinks	5,015

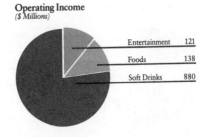

Operating Income
($ Millions)

Entertainment	121
Foods	138
Soft Drinks	880

The Coca-Cola Company and Consolidated Subsidiaries

14. Operations in Geographic Areas. Information about the Company's operations in different geographic areas is presented below (in millions). Intercompany transfers between geographic areas are not material.

Year Ended December 31,	1984	1983	1982
Net operating revenues:			
United States	$4,566.4	$4,071.4	$3,351.5
Latin America	429.6	401.3	516.3
Europe and Africa	1,183.8	1,225.6	1,155.6
Pacific and Canada	1,184.2	1,130.7	997.7
Consolidated net operating revenues	$7,364.0	$6,829.0	$6,021.1
Operating income:			
United States	$ 550.2	$ 498.7	$ 403.2
Latin America	89.6	69.4	123.2
Europe and Africa	272.5	295.4	249.5
Pacific and Canada	226.1	207.0	177.8
General expenses	(80.9)	(77.9)	(73.9)
Consolidated operating income	$1,057.5	$ 992.6	$ 879.8
Identifiable assets at year-end:			
United States	$3,575.5	$2,996.5	$2,773.2
Latin America	409.8	420.9	435.9
Europe and Africa	636.4	606.5	582.0
Pacific and Canada	463.3	472.6	420.5
Corporate assets (principally marketable securities, investments and fixed assets)	873.1	731.3	476.2
Discontinued operations	—	—	235.5
Consolidated assets	$5,958.1	$5,227.8	$4,923.3
Identifiable liabilities of operations outside the United States	$ 714.5	$ 652.0	$ 627.0

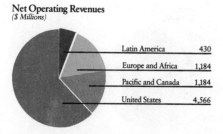

Net Operating Revenues
($ Millions)

Latin America	430
Europe and Africa	1,184
Pacific and Canada	1,184
United States	4,566

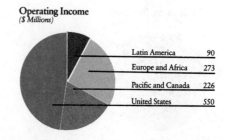

Operating Income
($ Millions)

Latin America	90
Europe and Africa	273
Pacific and Canada	226
United States	550

Report of Independent Accountants

The Coca-Cola Company and
Consolidated Subsidiaries

Board of Directors and Shareholders
The Coca-Cola Company
Atlanta, Georgia

We have examined the consolidated balance sheets of The Coca-Cola Company and consolidated subsidiaries as of December 31, 1984 and 1983, and the related consolidated statements of income, shareholders' equity and changes in financial position for each of the three years in the period ended December 31, 1984. Our examinations were made in accordance with generally accepted auditing standards and, accordingly, included such tests of the accounting records and such other auditing procedures as we considered necessary in the circumstances.

In our opinion, the financial statements referred to above present fairly the consolidated financial position of The Coca-Cola Company and consolidated subsidiaries at December 31, 1984 and 1983, and the consolidated results of their operations and changes in their financial position for each of the three years in the period ended December 31, 1984, in conformity with generally accepted accounting principles applied on a consistent basis.

Ernst & Whinney

Atlanta, Georgia
February 1, 1985

Report of Management

The Coca-Cola Company and
Consolidated Subsidiaries

Management is responsible for the preparation and integrity of the consolidated financial statements appearing in this Annual Report. The financial statements were prepared in conformity with generally accepted accounting principles appropriate in the circumstances and, accordingly, include some amounts based on management's best judgments and estimates. Financial information in this Annual Report is consistent with that in the financial statements.

Management is responsible for maintaining a system of internal accounting controls and procedures to provide reasonable assurance, at an appropriate cost/benefit relationship, that assets are safeguarded and that transactions are authorized, recorded and reported properly. The internal accounting control system is augmented by a program of internal audits and appropriate reviews by management, written policies and guidelines, careful selection and training of qualified personnel and a written Code of Business Conduct adopted by the Board of Directors, applicable to all employees of the Company and its subsidiaries. Management believes that the Company's internal accounting controls provide reasonable assurance that assets are safeguarded against material loss from unauthorized use or disposition and that the financial records are reliable for preparing financial statements and other data and maintaining accountability for assets.

The Audit Committee of the Board of Directors, composed solely of Directors who are not officers of the Company, meets with the independent accountants, management and internal auditors periodically to discuss internal accounting controls, auditing and financial reporting matters. The Committee reviews with the independent accountants the scope and results of the audit effort. The Committee also meets with the independent accountants without management present to ensure that the independent accountants have free access to the Committee.

The independent accountants, Ernst & Whinney, are recommended by the Audit Committee of the Board of Directors, selected by the Board of Directors and ratified by the shareholders. Ernst & Whinney is engaged to examine the consolidated financial statements of The Coca-Cola Company and consolidated subsidiaries and conduct such tests and related procedures as they deem necessary in conformity with generally accepted auditing standards. The opinion of the independent accountants, based upon their examination of the consolidated financial statements, is contained in this Annual Report.

Roberto C. Goizueta
Chairman, Board of Directors,
and Chief Executive Officer

M. Douglas Ivester
Senior Vice President
and Chief Financial Officer

February 1, 1985

Supplemental Information on the Effects of Changing Prices (Unaudited)

General. The following unaudited disclosures were prepared in accordance with standards issued by the Financial Accounting Standards Board and are intended to quantify the impact of inflation on earnings and production facilities. The inflation-adjusted data is presented under the specific price changes method (current cost). Only those items most affected by inflation have been adjusted; i.e., inventories, property, plant and equipment, the related costs of goods and services sold and depreciation and amortization expense. Although the resulting measurements cannot be used as precise indicators of the effects of inflation, they do provide an indication of the effect of increases in specific prices of the Company's inventories and properties.

The adjustments for specific price changes involve a substantial number of judgments as well as the use of various estimating techniques employed to control the cost of accumulating the data. The data reported should not be thought of as precise measurements of the assets and expenses involved, or of the amount at which the assets could be sold. Rather, they represent reasonable approximations of the price changes that have occurred in the business environment in which the Company operates.

A brief explanation of the current cost method is presented below.

The current cost method attempts to measure the effect of increases in the specific prices of the Company's inventories and properties. It is intended to estimate what it would cost in 1984 dollars to replace the Company's inventories and existing properties.

Under this method, cost of goods sold valued on the average method is adjusted to reflect the current cost of inventories at the date of sale. That portion of cost of goods sold valued on the LIFO method approximates the current cost of inventory at the date of sale and generally remains unchanged from the amounts presented in the primary financial statements.

Current cost depreciation expense is based on the average current cost of properties in the year. The depreciation methods, salvage values and useful lives are the same as those used in the primary statements.

The current cost of finished products inventory was approximated by adjusting historical amounts to reflect current costs for material, labor and overhead expenses as well as current cost depreciation, where applicable. The current cost

Statement of Income Adjusted for Changing Prices (In millions except per share data) Year Ended December 31, 1984	As Reported in the Primary Statements	Adjusted for Changes in Specific Prices (Current Costs)
Net operating revenues	$7,364.0	$7,364.0
Cost of goods and services (excluding depreciation)	3,924.4	3,938.9
Depreciation and amortization	169.5	227.4
Other operating expenses	2,214.2	2,214.2
Net of other (income) and deductions	(12.1)	(3.6)
Income from continuing operations before income taxes	1,068.0	987.1
Income taxes	439.2	439.2
Income from continuing operations	$ 628.8	$ 547.9
Income per share from continuing operations	$ 4.76	$ 4.15
Effective income tax rate	41.1%	44.5%
Purchasing power gain from holding net monetary liabilities in the year		$ 26.1
Increase in specific prices of inventories and property, plant and equipment held in the year Less effect of increase in general price level		$ 44.7 184.5
Increase in specific prices over increase in the general price level		$ (139.8)
Estimated translation adjustment		$ (110.0)
Inventory and film costs	$1,081.7	$1,127.0
Property, plant and equipment—net	$1,622.6	$2,215.2

A significant part of the Company's operations is measured in functional currencies other than the United States dollar. Adjustments to reflect the effects of general inflation were determined on the translate-restate method using the U.S. CPI(U).

The Coca-Cola Company and Consolidated Subsidiaries

for inventories other than finished products was determined on the basis of price lists or appropriate supplier quotations and by other managerial estimates consistent with established purchasing and production procedures.

Since motion picture films are the result of a unique blending of the artistic talents of many individuals and are produced under widely varying circumstances, it is not feasible to develop the current cost of film inventories, particularly since the Company would rarely, if ever, attempt to duplicate an existing film property. In view of these considerations and as permitted by Statement of Financial Accounting Standards No. 46, film inventories have been valued on the basis of constant dollar equivalents. Direct supplier quotations, published price lists, engineering estimates, construction quotations, appraisals and published and internally developed indexes were the methods used to determine the current cost of property, plant and equipment.

Under current cost accounting, increases in specific prices (current cost) of inventories and properties held during the year are not included in income from continuing operations.

Income Taxes. Taxes on income included in the supplementary statement of income are the same as reported in the primary financial statements. In most countries present tax laws do not allow deductions for the effects of inflation.

Purchasing Power Gain. During periods of inflation, monetary assets, such as cash, marketable securities and accounts receivable, lose purchasing power since they will buy fewer goods when the general price level increases. The holding of monetary liabilities, such as accounts payable, accruals and debt, results in a gain of purchasing power because cheaper dollars will be used to repay the obligations. The Company has benefited from a net monetary liability position in recent years, resulting in a net gain in purchasing power. This gain does not represent an increase in funds available for distribution to shareholders and does not necessarily imply that incurring more debt would be beneficial to the Company.

Increase in Specific Prices. Shown separately are the total changes in current costs for inventories and properties, that component of the total change due to general inflation and that component of the change attributable to fluctuations in exchange rates.

Five-Year Comparison of Selected Supplemental Financial Data Adjusted for Effects of Changing Prices (In Average 1984 Dollars)
(In millions except per share data)

Year Ended December 31,	1984	1983	1982	1981	1980
Net operating revenues	$7,364.0	$7,119.6	$6,479.2	$6,508.6	$6,901.4
Current cost information:					
Income from continuing operations	547.9	505.9	426.4	392.3	331.2
Income per share from continuing operations	4.15	3.72	3.28	3.16	2.67
Increase in specific prices over (under) increase in the general price level, including translation adjustments	(249.8)	(240.0)	(199.1)	(236.3)	27.8
Net assets at year-end	3,424.3	3,757.3	3,891.8	3,581.7	4,010.4
Purchasing power gain on net monetary items	26.1	29.0	19.0	27.9	54.3
Cash dividends declared per share:					
As reported	2.76	2.68	2.48	2.32	2.16
Adjusted for general inflation	2.76	2.79	2.67	2.65	2.72
Market price per common share at year-end:					
Historical amount	62.375	53.50	52.00	34.75	33.375
Adjusted for general inflation	62.375	55.78	55.96	39.69	42.07
Average Consumer Price Index—Urban CPI(U) (1967 = 100)	311.1	298.4	289.1	272.4	246.8

Unaudited Quarterly Data
(For the years ended December 31, 1984 and 1983)

The Coca-Cola Company and Consolidated Subsidiaries

Quarterly Results of Operations
(In millions except per share data)

	Net Operating Revenues		Gross Profit	
	1984	1983	1984	1983
First quarter	$1,579.9	$1,483.5	$ 720.6	$ 664.2
Second quarter	1,926.3	1,780.0	906.9	808.4
Third quarter	2,074.1	1,832.6	937.4	827.4
Fourth quarter	1,783.7	1,732.9	806.2	756.3
	$7,364.0	$6,829.0	$3,371.1	$3,056.3

	Income From Continuing Operations		Net Income	
	1984	1983	1984	1983
First quarter	$ 138.0	$ 123.5	$ 138.0	$ 122.1
Second quarter	185.0	162.1	185.0	160.5
Third quarter	175.3	152.3	175.3	151.6
Fourth quarter	130.5	120.4	130.5	124.6
	$ 628.8	$ 558.3	$ 628.8	$ 558.8

	Income Per Share From Continuing Operations		Net Income Per Share	
	1984	1983	1984	1983
First quarter	$ 1.02	$ .91	$ 1.02	$ .90
Second quarter	1.40	1.19	1.40	1.18
Third quarter	1.34	1.12	1.34	1.11
Fourth quarter	1.00	.88	1.00	.91
	$ 4.76	$ 4.10	$ 4.76	$ 4.10

INDEX

CHECK FIGURES FOR SELECTED PROBLEMS

Agreement between the following "check" figures and those obtained in solving the problems is an indication that a significant portion of the solution is basically correct, aside from matters of form and procedure.

Problem 1–31	Trial balance totals, $99,400		Problem 5–36	Adjusted balance, $15,150.10
1–32	Net income, $62,960		5–37	Adjusted balance, $12,730.98
1–33	Trial balance totals, $37,900		5–40	Adjusted balance, $13,237.80
1–34	Trial balance totals, $140,525		5–36A	Adjusted balance, $9,481.85
1–35	Trial balance totals, $392,666		5–37A	Adjusted balance, $12,657.67
1–36	Trial balance totals, $109,555		5–40A	Adjusted balance, $7,129.70
1–32A	Net income, $15,640			
1–33A	Trial balance totals, $29,490		Problem 6–31	Interest Income, Feb. 14, $360
1–34A	Trial balance totals, $158,794		6–32	Allowance for Doubtful Accounts, Dec. 31, $14,700
			6–33	Allowance for Doubtful Accounts, end 4th year, $4,500
Problem 2–33	Trial balance totals, $125,945			
2–34	Trial balance totals, $44,338.10		6–34	Income from operations, third year, $47,845
2–35	Trial balance totals, $84,912			
2–34A	Trial balance totals, $33,338.10		6–31A	Interest Income, Feb. 29, $520
2–35A	Trial balance totals, $79,770		6–32A	Allowance for Doubtful Accounts, Dec. 31, $22,700
			6–34A	Income from operations, third year, $46,500
Problem 3–29	Insurance Expense, $1,063			
3–30	Prepaid Advertising, $250		Problem 7–32	Inventory (3), $9,511
3–32	Asset (3), $1,800		7–33	Inventory June 30, $1,480
3–29A	Insurance Expense, $808		7–34	Total inventory, lower of C or M, $34,813
3–30A	Prepaid Advertising, $2,250			
			7–35	Inventory, (1) $269,920; (2) $446,350
Problem 4–29	Total assets, $512,200			
4–30	Net income, $93,555		7–36	Net income, $80,800
4–31	Net income, $60,425		7–37	Net income, $56,600
4–32	Retained earnings, June 30, $104,650		7–32A	Inventory (3), $6,003
			7–33A	Inventory, August 30, $292,500
4–33	Net income for Sept., $4,642			
4–34	Total assets, March 31, $369,840		7–34A	Total inventory, lower of C or M, $34,903
4–29A	Total assets, $579,650		7–35A	Inventory, (1) $208,250; (2) $607,550
4–30A	Net income, $32,500			
4–32A	Retained earnings, May 31, $74,950			
4–34A	Total assets, March 31, $368,440			

Problem 8–41	Accumulated Depreciation, Oct. 2, 1985, $170,300	Problem 13–32	Total assets, $995,850
8–42	Accumulated Depreciation, June 30, 1987, $1,500	13–33	Total assets, $2,088,360
8–44	Net income, $101,820	13–34	Total assets, $997,200
8–41A	Accumulated Depreciation, March 30, 1985, $165,300	13–35	Total assets, (1) $1,790,000; (2) $1,730,000; (3) $1,730,000
8–42A	Accumulated Depreciation, Dec. 31, 1986, $1,350	13–36	Total assets, $1,675,000; net income, $250,000
		13–38	Net income, $89,608
Problem 9–32	Total payroll taxes expense (2), $16,475	13–32A	Total assets, $999,050
9–32A	Total payroll taxes expense (2), $14,776.80	13–33A	Total assets, $2,140,050
		13–36A	Total assets, $1,928,575; net income, $302,800
Problem 10–31	Total stockholders' equity, $397,830	Problem 14–29	Increase in working capital, $1,250
10–32	Total common dividends per share, $16.10	14–30	Increase in working capital, $14,700
10–34	Total stockholders' equity, $1,754,000	14–31	Cash provided by operations, $95,350
10–32A	Total common dividends per share, $9	14–32	Working capital provided by operations, $45,850
		14–33	Cash provided by operations, $11,800
Problem 11–29	Deferred Income Tax Payable, end 4th year, $63,900	14–34	Working capital provided by operations (1), $120,000; Cash provided by operations (2), $79,700
11–31	Total retained earnings, $1,464,000	14–29A	Decrease in working capital, $27,500
11–32	Net income, $60,200	14–30A	Increase in working capital, $48,450
11–33	Total stockholders' equity, $2,113,534	14–31A	Cash provided by operations, $97,600
11–34	Total stockholders' equity, $1,585,000	14–32A	Working capital provided by operations, $184,775
11–35	Net income, $93,500	14–33A	Cash provided by operations, $138,500
11–29A	Deferred Income Tax Payable, end 4th year, $22,500		
11–31A	Total retained earnings, $1,445,000	Problem 15–33	Finished goods, $14,674
11–32A	Net income, $124,000	15–35	Total assets, $429,435
11–33A	Total stockholders' equity, $1,694,000	15–36	Trial balance totals, $2,254,550
		15–33A	Finished goods, $13,356
		15–36A	Trial balance totals, $935,650
Problem 12–27	Carrying value of bonds, Dec. 31, 1985, $3,786,597	Problem 16–24	Work in process, May 31, $32,160
12–29	Premium on Bonds, end 1987, $72,695	16–25	Equivalent units of production, 7,850 units
12–27A	Carrying value of bonds, Dec. 31, 1985, $5,574,147	16–26	Total assets, $1,167,330
12–29A	Discount on Bonds, end 1987, $192,640	16–27	Work in process, Oct. 31, $124,200

16–29   Work in process, May 31, $8,625

16–24A   Work in process, March 31, $51,730

16–27A   Work in process, March 31, $44,160

16–29A   Work in process, Sept. 30, $15,125

Problem 17–25   Total production, Product P2, 40,400 units

17–26   Total revenue from sales, $2,985,975

17–27   Deficiency, Sept., $30,500

17–28   Net income, $84,000; cash, $37,800

17–26A   Total revenue from sales, $2,694,000

17–27A   Deficiency, June, $13,500

Problem 18–22   Total factory overhead cost variance—unfavorable, $3,000

18–23   Total factory overhead cost variance—unfavorable, $7,025

18–24   Total factory overhead cost variance—unfavorable, $8,520

18–25   Income from operations, $39,375

18–26   Work in Process (debit), $2,225

18–22A   Total factory overhead cost variance—unfavorable, $2,900

18–24A   Total factory overhead cost variance—unfavorable, $3,920

18–26A   Work in Process (debit), $2,570

Problem 19–21   Decrease in gross profit, $45,000

19–22   Income from operations, variable costing, $60,000

19–23   Operating loss, $49,000

19–24   Contribution to company profit, F, $72,700

19–25   Total contribution margin, (1) $308,000; (3) $332,780

19–21A   Decrease in gross profit, $25,000

19–22A   Income from operations, variable costing, $50,000

19–23A   Operating loss, $53,600

Problem 20–28   Break-even point, $600,000

20–29   Maximum operating profit: (2), $1,000,000; (4) $750,000

20–30   Maximum operating profit: (2), $200,000; (4) $150,000

20–31   Break-even point, $900,000

20–32   Break-even point, $1,650,000

20–33   Present break-even point, $1,800,000

20–28A   Break-even point, $400,000

20–29A   Maximum operating profit: (2), $1,000,000; (4) $800,000

20–30A   Maximum operating profit: (2), $300,000; (4) $250,000

20–32A   Break-even point, $1,440,000

Problem 21–31   Gain from operating warehouse, $202,500

21–32   Net cost reduction, $165,000

21–33   Gain from promotion campaign, Product A, $348,000

21–34   Net disadvantage, $(200)

21–35   Net advantage, $3,136

21–36   Selling price, $15.60

21–31A   Gain from operating warehouse, $250,000

21–32A   Net cost reduction, $164,000

21–35A   Net advantage, $6,590

21–36A   Selling price, $14.40

Problem 22–25   Excess of present value over amount to be invested, Project A, $9,992

22–26   Excess of present value over amount to be invested, Project P, $3,600

22–27   Present value index, Proposal Y, 1.06

22–28   Discounted rate of return, Proposal II, 15%

22–29   Excess of present value over amount to be invested, $17,058

22–30   Excess of present value over amount to be invested, (2) Project Z, $20,000

22–25A   Excess of present value over amount to be invested, Project B, $11,260

22–26A   Excess of present value over amount to be invested, Project Y, $14,750

22–27A   Present value index, Project A, 1.12

22–28A   Discounted rate of return, Project B, 12%

Problem 23–28   Corporation form less, A, (3), $1,377

23–29   Net income, cash method, $33,100

23–30   Net income, lifo, $35,200

23–31   Income, percentage-of-completion method, 1986, $974,500

23–32   Earnings per share on common stock, Plan 1, $2.90

23–30A   Net income, fifo, $24,225

23–31A   Income, percentage-of-completion method, 1987, $540,000

23–32A   Earnings per share on common stock, Plan 2, $2.73

Problem 24–23   Net income, $22,340

24–24   Departmental margin, Department 8, $5,400

24–25   Total departmental margin, $219,610

24–26   Total departmental margin, $162,800

24–23A   Net income, $64,954

24–24A   Departmental margin, Department L, $4,000

24–25A   Total departmental margin, $153,956

Problem 25–31   Rate of return on investment, Division F, 13.2%

25–32   Rate of return on investment, Proposal 3, 17.4%

25–33   Division X is most profitable

25–34   Rate of return on investment, Division J, 18%

25–35   Total operating income, $1,360,000

25–31A   Rate of return on investment, Division R, 16%

25–33A   Division Q is most profitable

25–34A   Rate of return on investment, Division M, 17%

25–35A   Total operating income, $2,500,000

Problem 26–25   Economic order quantity, 1,200 units

26–26   Economic order quantity (2), 600 units

26–27   Most economical purchase, 100 units from Supplier K for Pekin Branch; 60 units from Supplier L for Elgin Branch

26–28   Variable cost per unit (1), $.75

26–29   Variable cost per unit (2), $1.04

26–30   Variable cost per unit (2), $1.25

26–25A   Economic order quantity, 800 units

26–27A   Most economical purchase, 200 units from Supplier X for Akron Branch; 300 units from Supplier Y for Tifton Branch

26–28A   Variable cost per unit (1), $.62

26–30A   Variable cost per unit (2), $2.00

Problem 27–29   Expected value, Patent B, $8,400,000

27–30   Total expected value of purchase of 125 papers, $11.75

27–31   Total expected value of Plat #1200, $24,100,000

27–32   Value of conducting an investigation, $3,500

27–34   Expected value, lake front location, $15,000,000

27–29A   Expected value, Autobiography F, $10,600,000

27–30A Total expected value of purchase of 60 magazines, $106

27–31A Total expected value of Plat #2400, $14,600,000

27–32A Value of conducting an investigation, $6,000

Problem 28–32 Working capital, Dec. 31, 1986 (4), $165,750

Problem B–2 Accounts Payable, $33,403.90

B–3 Accounts Payable, $6,335

B–4 Accounts Receivable, $13,385

B–5 Accounts Receivable, $4,635

B–6 Accounts Receivable, $9,775

B–7 Trial balance totals, $167,597

Problem D–1 Cost of goods manufactured, $636,700

D–2 Cost of goods manufactured, $661,050

D–3 Cost of goods manufactured, $521,775

D–4 Cost of goods manufactured, $472,900